East Central Europe

East Central Europe

A GUIDE TO BASIC PUBLICATIONS

paul l. horecky
EDITOR

THE UNIVERSITY OF CHICAGO PRESS
CHICAGO & LONDON

The research reported herein was performed pursuant to a contract No. OEC-1-6-062251 between the American Council of Learned Societies and the United States Department of Health, Education, and Welfare, Office of Education (under provisions of Section 602, Title VI, P.L. 85-864).

Library of Congress Catalog Card Number: 70-79472
The University of Chicago Press, Chicago 60637
The University of Chicago Press, Ltd., London

Published 1969. Printed in the United States of America

contents

PART FIVE POLAND

PART SIX SORBIANS (LUSATIANS) AND POLABIANS

PREFACE

CONCEPT AND PURPOSE

In the summer of 1966 the Subcommittee on East Central and Southeast European Studies (American Council of Learned Societies and the Social Science Research Council) initiated a two-pronged survey of language and area studies and of the corresponding bibliographic resources in the field. Earlier this year the first stage of this investigation came to a conclusion with the publication of *Area and Language Studies: East Central and Southeastern Europe*, under the editorship of Charles Jelavich. The second stage was entrusted to me, with a mandate for the compilation of two separate books containing a highly selective and judiciously evaluated inventory of the most important publications relating to these two areas. The present guide on East Central Europe and its companion volume on Southeastern Europe bring the entire survey to fruition.

East Central Europe is viewed here as a congeries of four countries which are inhabited by a population of varying ethnic backgrounds, tongues, and religions. East Germany holds a place sui generis as a product of recent political developments. The peoples of Czechoslovakia, Hungary, and Poland, living in a territory sometimes referred to as the borderlands of Western civilization, can pride themselves on memorable cultural traditions spanning well over a millennium of recorded history. Yet much of their existence has been passed under foreign influence or rule and even at times of relative normalcy their sovereignty has often been imperiled by external pressures and encroachments. Throughout the ages they have stubbornly preserved their national identity and, firmly rooted in Western tradition, have inscribed numerous illustrious pages in the world's intellectual history, from Hus, Comenius, and Copernicus to Chopin, Dvořák, and Liszt. Since the seventeenth century, emigrants from those lands have come to America's shores in ever increasing numbers, finding a new home and freedom from oppression and want, and making notable contributions to American life, both in peacetime and in wartime.

Aside from some similarities among these nations with respect to their historical experience and cultural heritage, mutual geographic proximity, and present inclusion in the Soviet domain, the area per se reveals few homogeneous and unifying characteristics in terms of well-defined geographic borders, close linguistic affinity, or a feeling of belonging together on the part of its components. The collective term East Central Europe therefore lacks precision and is susceptible to differing interpretations. Nevertheless, it is in frequent usage by geographers and area specialists and serves as a common denominator for area study programs organized within academic institutions. Thus, we too have chosen to adopt the concept East Central Europe in the title for this publication.

The complexities and obvious limitations of an undertaking such as ours — which requires sifting the most essential writings on the present and past of a multinational and multilingual conglomerate — can be graphically illustrated by a few rough statistics. The aggregate book output foı the past fifty years in and about the area under scrutiny exceeded in all probability 600,000 titles. Supposing that a mere 20 percent of this total is of continuing research value, the agonizing problem still persists of selecting for this current guide some 5,000 out of a potential reservoir of at least 120,000 publications. Along similar lines, one might mention the plethora of literature published just on very narrowly circumscribed facets of the total picture. For example, self-contained and book-length bibliographies of a mass of writings exist on personalities such as Comenius, Mickiewicz, Morisz, Masaryk, and many others. A recent bibliography of Polish dictionaries fills 286 pages, and a listing of Slavic works of literature in English translation was published in two massive volumes.

Inexorable limitations of time, manpower, and funds dictated that the essential record of knowledge of such enormous proportions be telescoped into one single volume. High selectivity was the obvious modus operandi toward that end. In facing the prospect, I found solace in an idea of the Spanish philosopher Ortega y Gasset, who some thirty years ago envisioned the role of the future librarian as that of a sensitive filter standing between man and the unending flood of print. When espousing such an assignment, the bibliographer must assume cheerfully — so to say as an occupational hazard — the task of navigating the perilous channel between the Scylla of too much and the Charybdis of too little — especially since such a voyage makes no provision for travel insurance against the slings and barbs of the critic who may doubt the wisdom of the course charted.

We profess candidly that we have not been able to conjure up either a magic formula for miniaturizing knowledge or a technique for a foolproof selection process. But, despite these reservations, we venture to hope that we did manage to come up with a relatively concentrated distillate of information which can be reconstituted into a panoramic and synoptic view of the area. This guide traces general contours, as would a large-scale map, the further exploitation of which is best served by reference to more detailed small-scale maps. To translate this thought into the present context, it would be very desirable if in the future the data of this bibliography could be expanded through a whole series of specialized subject bibliographies.

Keeping in mind the need of maximizing the informational potentiality of our guide, we have given generous coverage to bibliographic material both in separate chapters and in the context of specific subjects. Such bibliographic sources should be regarded as a sort of master key to a wealth of other literature which could not be explicitly included here. Thus, with proper exploration, only very few targets of bibliographic search should, in the final analysis, remain terra incognita.

In a situation marked by an unprecedented proliferation of printed information and by the evolvement of the study of the area from a single discipline to a constantly widening complex of subspecialties, a far-reaching degree of multidisciplinary teamwork was the obvious answer to the problem posed by a selective approach. Thus, this work embodies the collective subject and area expertise of many specialists from this country and abroad. It was our common aim to base the selection of publications on scholarly and informational merits only and to reflect the character of the individual entries in thoughtful and restrained comment. The design and structure of the guide, including allocation of space by language and subject, as well as the overall direction of the project, were my responsibilities. Our editorial policy endeavored to preserve as much as possible the authentic style and format of the contributors' presentation, subject to the needs of bibliographic consistency. When major alterations, expansions, or contractions appeared indicated for reasons of balanced coverage or topical coherence, I strove, circumstances permitting, to resolve such questions with the advice and consent of the contributor concerned.

This guide addresses itself to a multiple audience — the educated general reader, the researcher, the student, the teacher, and the librarian. It is our hope that it may serve several useful functions: as a study aid to those who wish to work on one or more aspects of the area; as a classroom tool for the more advanced investigation of the area; as a medium for the development of concentrated library collections at the growing number of educational institutions which are extending their programs in the field; and, finally, as a basis for determining important out-of-print material and identifying hitherto neglected domains of published research.

SCOPE AND ORGANIZATION

Scope. This volume records basic books, periodicals, and, occasionally, articles of special pertinence, on the lands and peoples of Czechoslovakia, East Germany (including, in a separate section, the Lusatians and Polabians), Hungary, and Poland. The subject coverage focuses on the political, socioeconomic, and intellectual life — along with the organization of scientific research activities — in the respective areas of Europe. Science and technology per se are outside the ken of this conspectus. The bibliography lists writings in languages indigenous to the countries concerned, as well as in other languages in which significant contributions to the knowledge of the area have been made. Among the latter, the emphasis is on English-language publications. In determining the relative language representation we were guided both by the relevance of the material and by the presumed linguistic capabilities of the book's potential reading public. In keeping with the intended function of this biliography as an area research aid, its temporal reach spans primarily the more recent period of statehood of the various countries, although the background and general historical development leading up to the present are given consideration. As a rule, the latest imprints included are those which were available for physical inspection in the early part of 1968.

Methodological Approach. For each country the material is structured under eight or nine major sectors of knowledge, which are subdivided into more specialized categories as suggested by the particularities of the respective country. The availability of a substantial body of information offering a total view of the area or segments thereof counseled the inclusion of an introductory overview.

The intertwined and stratified character of knowledge, particularly in its application to the study of an area, renders the strict delineation of a discipline an arduous task. Where is the Great Divide between history and politics and government? How can a precise boundary be drawn between the societal and political systems of a country? Is there a readily identifiable demarcation line between the national characteristics of a people and the makeup of its society? In the face of such uncertainties the reader will be well advised not to limit his bibliographic investigation to the seemingly indicated chapter or section heading but to refer in case of need to kindred and contiguous topical sections.

To improve subject control we have followed the practice — notwithstanding a very acute shortage of space in this volume — of including in two or more subject contexts such identical titles as deal significantly with several subjects. Such multiple listings by different contributors sometimes bear divergent assessments — a fact which underscores the inherently subjective and personal nature of book evaluation, as well as the versatility of coverage by some publications. The prefatory table of contents, detailed statements of content at the beginning of major chapters, and an extensive author-title-subject index should guide the reader and enhance reference use.

Entries. We have endeavored to keep the form of entry as succinct and nontechnical as is consistent with the need for clear bibliographic identification of a title. Basically, the Library of Congress bibliographic style was followed because it permits ready referrals to, and collation with, the widely used Library of Congress printed cards and catalogs. Occasional departures from this procedure were thought advisable in the interests of economy of space and simplified presentation. English translations are given for titles cited in the Slavic languages and in Hungarian. Alternate versions of authors' names are indicated parenthetically. The consecutively numbered lead entries are followed by annotative comments, often accompanied by additional citations of collateral writings. Within subject groups, entries usually are in alphabetic order. Divergent methods, such as arrangement by chronology or topical affinity, are explained in footnotes wherever they are employed.

The Cyrillic alphabet is transliterated according to Library of Congress practices, as a rule, but ligatures have been omitted.

ACKNOWLEDGMENTS

My foremost thanks go to the team of distinguished contributors and consultants on foreign-language publications who, notwithstanding many pressing professional commitments, spiritedly responded to my call and joined forces in our venture. Their names are mentioned individually in the roster of participants which appears elsewhere in this book. I was most fortunate to benefit again in this current enterprise from the invaluable help of my colleagues Robert V. Allen and Robert G. Carlton, who served as Assistant Editors. They stood at my side in almost every phase of the project. Their rare combination of talent as bookmen and area specialists was an incalculable asset in melding a mass of raw material into a homogeneous entity. Additionally, Mr. Carlton undertoook the task of preparing the very detailed index. Barbara A. Burkey, Constance Carter, and Ruth M. Miller helped with the preparation of prefatory matter. The aforementioned assistants are on the staff of the Library of Congress.

In various phases of our undertaking the need arose to seek ad hoc advice on specific questions from specialists here and abroad. Among those who gave generously of their thought and time were Andrew Gyorgy (George Washington University) and Albert Tezla (University of Minnesota, Duluth). I am much indebted to Werner Philipp (Freie Universität, Berlin) and Mathias W. Bernath (Südost-Institut, Munich) for arranging the participation of their staffs in recommending pertinent German-language materials for final selection by the subject compilers.

A veritable key aide on the team, to whom I am greatly obliged, is Martha L. Rose who, undaunted by a spate of drafts in a Babel of languages and a profusion of diacritical marks, exhibited both initiative and dispatch in preparing the final manuscript for the printers. Basil Nadraga and Gerald F. Stowell checked many an item in this volume against the pertinent catalogs and bibliographic sources. And finally, my wife, Emily I. Horecky, has once again—as perennially—borne with my involvement in such an undertaking. Beyond this, she was of truly indispensable assistance in taking a most active hand in a vast variety of editorial and administrative endeavors.

The present volume was sponsored by the Subcommittee on East Central and Southeast European Studies under the dynamic chairmanship of Charles Jelavich (Indiana University), who was the moving spirit in activating the overall project. Gordon B. Turner, Vice President of the American Council of Learned Societies, guided the operational aspects of this project, and I am profoundly grateful to him for his unflagging support and generous understanding of our needs and problems. Finally, I should like to add my own very great appreciation to the sponsoring bodies for according me complete freedom of action in planning and executing this undertaking.

Alexandria, Virginia
November 1968

PAUL L. HORECKY

participants

CONTRIBUTORS

JOSEF ANDERLE (Czechoslovakia: History) studied at the universities of Prague, Munich, and Chicago, where he received his doctorate in history. He is now Associate Professor of Russian and East European History at the University of North Carolina at Chapel Hill. Dr. Anderle is coauthor of *Latvia: An Area Study* (New Haven, Human Relations Area Files, 1956, 2 v.) and he has published a number of chapters and articles in scholarly books and journals on Czechoslovak history.

VOJTECH E. ANDIC (Czechoslovakia: Education) is Associate Professor of Economics at Union University, Albany, New York. He has been a contributor to numerous professional publications, including the *Slavic and East European Review*, the *Journal of Central European Affairs*, and the *Slavonic Encyclopedia* (Philosophical Library, 1949). Active in professional societies, Dr. Andic was elected General Secretary of the Czechoslovak Society of Arts and Sciences in America in 1966 and was reelected in 1967.

ELEMER BAKO (Hungary: General Reference Aids and Bibliographies; The People) is Finno-Ugrian Area Specialist, Slavic and Central European Division, Library of Congress. He is editor of the *Hungarian Library Journal of America*, issued by the Organization Committee of the Hungarian Library Association of America. Dr. Bako's writings have focused on Hungarian and Finno-Ugrian librarianship and linguistics.

GEORGE Z. F. BEREDAY (Poland: Education) is Professor of Comparative Education at Teachers College, Columbia University. An Associate of the University's Russian Institute and a member of the Faculty of International Affairs, Dr. Bereday is Director of the Center for Education in Industrial Nations. He is the author of *Comparative Method in Education* (Holt, Rinehart and Winston, 1964) and coeditor of *The Changing Soviet School* (Houghton Mifflin, 1960) and *The Politics of Soviet Education* (Praeger, 1960).

ELIZABETH BEYERLY (Overview: General Reference Aids and Bibliographies; Bibliographies of Slavic Literature) is completing her doctorate in international relations at the Institut Universitaire de Hautes Études Internationales,

Geneva. With Master's degrees from Columbia University in Russian language and literature and in library science, she has served, mainly as a Slavic specialist, in government and university libraries and at the World Health Organization. She has contributed articles to professional journals concerned with Russian and East European librarianship and documentation.

IMRE BOBA (Poland: Anthropology and Archaeology; Ethnography; Nationalities; Society) is Associate Professor of History and Bibliographic Consultant at the University of Washington. Author of the forthcoming *Nomads, Northmen and Slavs* (Mouton) and coauthor of *Master Nicholas of Dresden* (American Philosophical Society, 1965), Dr. Boba was a contributing editor to the *Dictionary of Political Sciences* (Philosophical Library, 1964). He is a frequent contributor to professional and scholarly journals.

ADAM BROMKE (Poland: Government and Politics; Diplomacy and Foreign Relations) is Professor of Political Science at Carleton University. He was Chairman of the Soviet and East European Studies Program there from 1963 to 1966. He is the author of *Poland's Politics: Idealism vs. Realism* (Harvard University Press, 1967) as well as of numerous articles on contemporary Polish affairs in professional journals.

JOSEF BROZEK (all sections on Psychology in this volume) is Research Professor at Lehigh University, Department of Psychology, of which he was Chairman from 1959 to 1963. His current interest, on which he has written copiously, is the history of psychology, with special reference to the Slavic countries and the USSR. He has served in editorial capacities for professional journals.

MELVIN CROAN (East Germany: The State; The Society) is Associate Professor of Political Science at the University of Wisconsin (Madison). Dr. Croan previously taught at Harvard University, where he also served as Director of the Regional Studies Program (Soviet Union). He has published numerous scholarly articles on communist politics in various professional journals and has contributed chapters to several books, including *The Communist States at the Crossroads* (Praeger, 1965) and *The Soviet System and Democratic Society* (Freiburg, Herderverlag, 1968–).

ISTVÁN CSICSERY-RÓNAY (Hungary: Education; Religion) is Associate Librarian of the University of Maryland Library. He is the author of *First Book of Hungary* (F. Watts, 1967) and *Russian Cultural Penetration* (3d rev. ed., New York, 1952) and contributor to *Collier's Encyclopedia*, *The Encyclopedia of Poetry and Poetics*, and *Books Abroad*. From 1957 to 1964, he was editor of the bibliographic quarterly *Bibliografia* (Washington, D.C.).

MOJMIR DRVOTA (Czechoslovakia: Theater and Cinema) is Assistant Professor of Dramatic Arts, Columbia University. A former screenplay writer for Czechoslovak State Films and stage director of State Theaters in Prague, Olomouc and Plzeň, Dr. Drvota was coauthor of *Laterna Magika*, the winning program at the Brussels World Fair, 1958.

M. KAMIL DZIEWANOWSKI (Poland: Military Affairs; Mass Media and Public Opinion; Christian Religions) is Professor of History at Boston University. A contributor to numerous scholarly journals, Dr. Dziewanowski is the author of *A European Federalist* (Stanford University Press, 1968) and *The Communist Party of Poland: An Outline of History* (Harvard University Press, 1959). Among the works to which he has contributed are the *Bibliography of*

Soviet Foreign Relations (Princeton University Press, 1965), *The Communist States at the Crossroads* (Praeger, 1965), and *Russian Thought and Politics* (Harvard University Press, 1957).

ANDREW ELIAS (Czechoslovakia and Poland: Demography) is a Senior Statistician with the Foreign Demographic Analysis Division, U.S. Bureau of the Census. His writings include the following publications of the Bureau of the Census: *The Labor Force of Yugoslavia* (1965), *The Labor Force of Czechoslovakia: Scope and Concepts* (1963) and *The Magnitude and Distribution of Civilian Employment in the USSR, 1928-1959* (1961), which he coauthored with M. S. Weitzman.

MOJMIR S. FRINTA (Czechoslovakia: The Fine Arts) is Professor of Art History at the State University of New York, Albany. A former staff member of the Metropolitan Museum of Art, Mr. Frinta is interested primarily in late medieval painting and sculpture. He is the author of *The Genius of Robert Campin* (Mouton, 1966) and of numerous articles on medieval painting and sculpture.

KAZIMIERZ GRZYBOWSKI (Overview: COMECON) is a professor at Duke University. Formerly he was Editor, European Law Division, Library of Congress, and an Associate Professor of Law in Poland. He is coeditor of *Government, Law and Courts in the Soviet Union and Eastern Europe* (Praeger, 1959) and author of *Soviet Private International Law* (Leyden, Sijthoff, 1965), *The Socialist Commonwealth of Nations* (Yale University Press, 1964), *Soviet Legal Institutions* (Michigan University Press, 1962), and other publications.

ANDREW GYORGY (Overview: Government and Politics; Foreign Relations and Diplomacy) is Professor of International Affairs at the Institute for Sino-Soviet Studies, George Washington University. His numerous publications on world affairs, communism and East Europe include, most recently: as author, *Ideologies in World Affairs* (Blaisdell, 1967) and *Issues of World Communism* (Van Nostrand, 1966); and as editor/contributor, *Basic Issues in International Relations* (Allyn and Bacon, 1967) and *Eastern European Government and Politics* (Harper and Row, 1966). He has also written widely for scholarly journals.

JAN HAJDA (Czechoslovakia: Society Sections A-F) is Associate Professor of Sociology, Portland State College. He has taught sociology at several universities, is the author of *A Study of Contemporary Czechoslovakia* (University of Chicago, 1955), and was the recipient of a Fulbright Fellowship for the year 1966/67.

WILLIAM E. HARKINS (Overview: Slavic Literatures) is Professor of Slavic Languages and Chairman of the Department of Slavic Languages at Columbia University. His publications include *Karel Čapek* (Columbia University Press, 1962), *A Dictionary of Russian Literature* (Philosophical Library, 1956), and *The Russian Folk Epos in Czech Literature* (King's Crown Press, 1953).

CHAUNCY D. HARRIS (East Germany: The Land) is Professor of Geography at the University of Chicago and Director of the University's Center for International Studies. He has published extensively in the field of geography, particularly geographic bibliography, of various world areas. Dr. Harris has served as Visiting Professor at the Johann Wolfgang Goethe Universität, Frankfurt am Main. His writings on Germany include articles on the Ruhr coal mining district and on the refugee problem.

GEORGE W. HOFFMAN (Hungary: The Land; Overview: Geographic Aspects) is Professor of Geography at the University of Texas. Author of *The Balkans in Transition* (Van Nostrand, 1963), coauthor of *Yugoslavia and the New Communism* (Twentieth Century Fund, 1962), and editor of *A Geography of Europe* (2d ed., Ronald Press, 1961), Dr. Hoffman has contributed numerous articles to professional journals both here and abroad. He has been a recipient of several academic awards.

PAUL L. HORECKY, Chief Editor of this book and contributor of Sections C-E of Czechoslovakia: General Reference Aids and Bibliographies, is Assistant Chief, Slavic and Central European Division, Library of Congress. His publications include *Russia and the Soviet Union* (University of Chicago Press, 1965); *Basic Russian Publications* (University of Chicago Press, 1962); *Libraries and Bibliographic Centers in the Soviet Union* (Indiana University Publications, 1959); and other monographs and articles on cultural affairs of the USSR and Eastern Europe.

JANINA W. HOSKINS (Poland: General Reference Aids and Bibliographies) is Area Specialist (Poland), Slavic and Central European Division, Library of Congress. She has written on bibliographic, historical, and cultural affairs of Poland for professional publications.

ALEXANDER JANTA (Poland: Music) is a bookman and writer. Prior to World War II he published several travel books recounting his impressions as a foreign correspondent for the press in his native Poland. His experience in and escape from a German POW camp in the Second World War are the subject of *I Lied to Live* (New York, 1944) and *Psalms of Captivity* (New York, 1947). More recently he has authored several volumes of poetry and published in the *Polish Review* an annotated bibliography of "Early XIX Century American-Polish Music."

ESTHER JERABEK (Czechoslovakia: Czechs and Slovaks Abroad) recently retired as librarian of the Minnesota Historical Society, a position she held for thirty-three years. Compiler of *Check List of Minnesota Public Documents, 1941-1950* (Minnesota Historical Society, 1952) and *A Bibliography of Minnesota Territorial Documents* (Minnesota Historical Society, 1936), Miss Jerabek has been a frequent contributor to a number of professional journals.

HEINRICH JILEK (Czechoslovakia: Germans in Czechoslovakia) is Director of the Library and a member of the research staff of the J. G. Herder Institute in Marburg/Lahn. Specializing in the bibliography of the Sudeten area, Dr. Jilek is author of *Sudetendeutsche Bibliographie, 1954-57* (Marburg, ad.. Lahn, 1965) and coauthor of *Bücherkunde Ostdeutschlands und des Deutschtums in Osmitteleuropa* (Cologne, 1963). He has also written numerous articles on Russian and Czech publications.

KAREL J. KANSKY (Czechoslovakia: The Land) received his doctorate from the University of Chicago. An Associate Professor at the University of Pittsburgh, he specializes in transportation and economic and urban geography, and the application of these subjects to Eastern Europe. His publications include *Structure of Transportation Networks* (The University of Chicago, Department of Geography Research Paper, No. 84, 1963) and articles in professional journals.

JOHN KOSA (Hungary: The Society) is presently associated with Harvard Medical School. He received a Ph.D from the University of Budapest in 1937 and has taught at the universities of Budapest and Szeged, and, more recently, at Cornell University and the University of North Carolina. Among his writings are studies on medical sociology and on Hungarian social problems. His books on the latter subject are *Land of Choice* (Toronto, 1957), *Two Generations of Soviet Man* (Chapel Hill, 1962), and *The Home of the Learned Man* (New Haven, 1968).

BARBARA KRADER (Czechoslovakia: Folklore; Music) was a student of musicology and folklore in Prague in 1948/49. She received her doctorate from Radcliffe College, has served as editor for musicological journals, and has published articles on folklore, music, and East European cultural affairs. During 1965 and 1966, she was Executive Secretary of the International Folk Music Council.

GEORGE KRZYWICKI-HERBURT (Poland: History of Thought, Culture and Scholarship) is Associate Professor of Philosophy at Queen's College, New York City University. A member of the Mind Association and of the Philosophy of Science Association, Mr. Krzywicki serves on the Board of Directors of the Polish Institute of Arts and Sciences in America. He is the author of *Filozofia Amerykańska* (Boston University Press, 1958), as well as of numerous articles in scholarly publications.

RADO L. LENCEK (Overview: Slavic Languages; Slavic Civilization) is Assistant Professor of South Slavic Languages at Columbia University. He prepared *A Bibliographical Guide to the Literature on Slavic Civilizations* (Department of Slavic Languages, Columbia University, 1966) and has contributed articles to professional journals.

LYMAN H. LEGTERS (East Germany: History; History of Thought, Culture, and Scholarship; Education) is Professor of Russian Studies at the University of Washington. He serves currently as Assistant Director of the University's Far Eastern and Russian Institute, Head of the Russian and East European program, and Director of the National Defense Education Act Center. Dr. Legters has written on Russian and East European affairs.

KAETHE LEWY (Overview: Co-compiler, The Jews in Eastern Europe [excluding Poland]) is Head of Bibliographic Services and Serials Catalogue, Jewish National and University Library, Jerusalem, and is a Lecturer in General Bibliography, Graduate Library School, Hebrew University, Jerusalem. She is editor of *Union List of Serials in Israel Libraries* (Jerusalem, 1964-1967) and author of *Guide to General Bibliographies and Reference Books* (Hebrew University, Graduate Library School, 1967). She is a contributor to the professional library journal of Israel.

B. PHILIP LOZINSKI (Poland: The Fine Arts) is Associate Professor of Art History at the Southeastern Massachusetts Technological Institute, North Dartmouth, Massachusetts. He is author of *The Original Homeland of the Parthians* (Mouton, 1959) and the forthcoming *Early Slavonic Art as Historical Evidence*. Dr. Lozinski's special interests include the archaeology of the First

Millennium, A.D., and medieval, Iranian, and Slavic art. He has contributed articles to professional and scholarly journals.

LAWRENCE MARWICK (Overview: Jews in Poland) is Head of the Hebraic Section, Library of Congress. Author of *Handbook of Diplomatic Hebrew* (Davelle, 1957) and of numerous articles in scholarly journals, Dr. Marwick is currently Adjunct Professor of Arabic and Islamic Studies at Dropsie College in Philadelphia.

LADISLAV MATEJKA (Czechoslovakia: Languages and Literatures) is Professor of Slavic Languages and Literatures at the University of Michigan. A former editor of the cultural section of the Czech newspaper, *Lidové Noviny*, Dr. Matejka currently edits *Michigan Slavic Materials* and *Michigan Slavic Contributions*. Recipient of a Fulbright fellowship in 1965/66, he is a contributor to scholarly and professional publications.

CZESŁAW MIŁOSZ (Poland: Literature; Folklore) is Professor of Slavic Languages and Literatures at the University of California, Berkeley. He is the author of several books of poetry and of essays in Polish. When living in Paris as a freelance writer, he was awarded a Prix Littéraire Européen in 1953. His publications in English include: *Native Realm* (Doubleday, 1968); Zbigniew Herbert's *Selected Poems* (Co-translator; Penguin Books, 1968); *Postwar Polish Poetry* (Doubleday, 1965); and *The Captive Mind* (A. Knopf, 1953).

JOHN M. MONTIAS (Overview: The Economy) is Professor of Economics at Yale University. His academic honors include both Ford and Guggenheim Fellowships. Dr. Montias has written *Central Planning in Poland* (Yale University Press, 1962) and *Economic Development in Communist Rumania* (Massachusetts Institute of Technology Press, 1967). His articles have appeared in *Foreign Affairs*, *Journal of Political Economy*, *American Economic Review*, and numerous and other scholarly journals.

STANLEY Z. PECH (Overview: History) is Associate Professor of History at the University of British Columbia. He is a past President of the Canadian Association of Slavists. Dr. Pech's articles have appeared in *Canadian Slavic Paper*, *Journal of Central European Affairs*, *East European Quarterly*, and numerous other scholarly journals, and his book entitled *The Czech Revolution of 1848* is scheduled for publication in 1969 by the University of North Carolina Press.

JAROSLAV PELIKAN (Czechoslovakia: Christian Religions) is Titus Street Professor of Ecclesiastical History, Yale University. Editor, translator, and contributor to numerous learned journals, Dr. Pelikan has published several works, including most recently *The Preaching of Chrysostom* (Fortress Press, 1967), *The Finality of Jesus Christ in an Age of Universal History* (John Knox Press, 1966), and *The Christian Intellectual* (Harper and Row, 1965). Active in a number of professional organizations, Dr. Pelikan is a past President of the American Society of Church History. He has been the recipient of many academic honors.

ARNOLD H. PRICE (East Germany: General Reference Aids and Bibliographies; The People) has observed East German developments since 1945, first in the Department of State, and since 1960 in the Library of Congress. He wrote *The Evolution of the Zollverein* (University of Michigan Press, 1959) and compiled *East Germany: A Selected Bibliography* (U.S. Library of Congress, 1967). He is a Lecturer at American University and is a Section Editor of the *American Historical Review*.

MILOSLAV RECHCÍGL, Jr. (Czechoslovakia: History of Thought, Culture and Scholarship) is Grants Associate, Division of Research Grants, National Institutes of Health, Bethesda. An ardent student of Czechoslovak cultural affairs, Dr. Rechcígl is author of *Czechoslovakia and Its Arts and Sciences: A Selective Bibliography in the Western European Languages* (1964), and is editor of *Czechoslovakia Past and Present* (2 v., 1967) and *The Czechoslovak Contribution to World Culture* (Mouton, 1964).

ZDENĚK SALZMANN (Czechoslovakia: Anthropology and Ethnology) is Associate Professor of Anthropology at the University of Massachusetts. Primarily interested in the field of linguistic anthropology, Dr. Salzmann has published articles in the *International Journal of American Linguistics, Word* and other scholarly journals. Harcourt, Brace and World is the publisher of his textbook of general anthropology, the first written especially for secondary school students. He is the author of *Czech Literature before Hus* (Sedona, Arizona, 1961).

JAMES A. SEHNERT (Sorbians and Polabians) is Assistant Professor in the Department of Slavic Languages and Literatures, Indiana University. He is the author of *The Morphology of German Loanwords in Upper Lusatian* (Indiana University, 1966) and coauthor of the *Polabian-English Dictionary* (Mouton, 1967.)

VLADIMIR SLAMECKA (Overview: Research and Organization of Science) is Professor and Director of the Graduate School of Information Science, Georgia Institute of Technology. His publications include *Science in East Germany* (Columbia University Press, 1963) and *Science in Czechoslovakia* (Columbia University Press, 1963). Dr. Slamecka has contributed numerous articles to professional journals and holds a number of patents in the fields of chemistry and engineering.

ROBERT M. SLUSSER (East Germany: Intellectual and Cultural Life) is Associate Professor of History at Johns Hopkins University. He is coauthor of *Soviet Foreign Policy, 1928-1934* (Pennsylvania State University Press, 1967), *The Theory, Law and Policy of Soviet Treaties* (Stanford University Press, 1962), *A Calendar of Soviet Treaties, 1917-1957* (Stanford University Press, 1959), and *The Soviet Secret Police* (Praeger, 1957). Dr. Slusser's work in recent years has focused on Soviet foreign and domestic policy, with particular regard to Soviet-American relations.

GEORGE J. STALLER (Czechoslovakia: The Economy) is Associate Professor in the Department of Economics at Cornell University. He has written frequently on Czechoslovak and East European economic developments for professional journals, most recently contributing a study on "Czechoslovakia: The New Model of Planning and Management," *American Economic Review, Proceedings*, May 1968.

EDWARD STANKIEWICZ (Poland: Language) received his Ph.D. from Harvard University. He is Professor of Slavic Languages at the University of Chicago. His writings include *A Selected Bibliography of Slavic Linguistics*, prepared with Dean S. Worth (v. 1: Mouton, 1966; v. 2 to appear shortly);

Declension and Gradation of Russian Substantives (The Hague, 1968); and a number of contributions to professional publications.

HALSEY STEVENS (Hungary: Music) is Professor of Music, University of Southern California. His academic honors include Litt. D. (Syracuse University) and a Guggenheim Fellowship. Dr. Stevens is a composer of orchestral, chamber, and vocal music. He is the author of *The Life and Music of Bela Bartok* (Rev. ed., Oxford University Press, 1964) and of many articles in professional journals. He has lectured extensively in the United States and abroad.

RUDOLF STURM (Czechoslovakia: Co-contributor, General Reference Aids and Bibliographies) is Professor of Italian and Slavic Literatures at Skidmore College. He is the author of a number of studies dealing with Czech and Slovak matters and appearing in the *Slavonic Encyclopedia, Harvard Slavic Studies,* and *Books Abroad.* An Associate Bibliographer of the Modern Language Association, Dr. Sturm recently published *Czechoslovakia: A Bibliographic Guide* (U.S. Library of Congress, 1967).

KONSTANTIN SYMMONS-SYMONOLEWICZ (Poland: Poles Abroad) received his doctorate in sociology and anthropology from Columbia University. His articles and book reviews have appeared in numerous periodicals, including *Sprawy Narodowościowe, Polish Review, Slavic Review, American Historical Review, Sociological Quarterly,* and *Annals of the American Academy.*

EDWARD TABORSKY (Czechoslovakia: The State; Mass Media and Public Opinion) is presently Professor of Government at the University of Texas. A former member of Czechoslovakia's diplomatic service, Dr. Taborsky served successively as Secretary to the Czechoslovak Foreign Minister, Personal Aide to President Edward Beneš, and Envoy to Sweden. He is the author of six books and of numerous articles in scholarly journals.

TYMON TERLECKI (Poland: Theater and Cinema) is Professor of Polish Literature at the University of Chicago. A former Professor of World Drama at the State Institute of Dramatic Art in Warsaw and onetime editor of several Polish theater journals, including *Scena Polska* and *Teatr,* Dr. Terlecki has authored numerous books and essays on a variety of cultural subjects and has served as editor of collaborative works. Among his more recent publications are *Literatura polska na obczyżnie, 1940-1960* (London, B. Swiderski, 1964-1965), *Pani Helena* (London, Veritas, 1962) and *Ludzie, książki i kulisy* (London, B. Świderski, 1960).

ALBERT TEZLA (Hungary: Language; Literature; Folklore; Theater, Drama, Dance, and Cinema) is Professor of English at the University of Minnesota, Duluth. He is advisor to candidates preparing doctoral dissertations in Hungarian Literature at Columbia University, where he was Visiting Professor of Hungarian Literature in 1966. Dr. Tezla is the author of *An Introductory Bibliography to the Study of Hungarian Literature* (Harvard University Press, 1964). His *Hungarian Authors: A Bibliographical Handbook* will be published by Harvard University Press in 1969.

HANS-JOACHIM TORKE (East Germany: The Economy) is Assistant Professor, Seminar für osteuropäische Geschichte der Freien Universität Berlin. His latest publication is *Das russische Beamtentum in der ersten Hälfte des 19. Jahrhunderts* (Berlin, 1967).

RUTH TRONIK (Overview: Co-compiler, The Jews in Eastern Europe [excluding Poland]) is Assistant Head of the Bibliographic Services and Serials Catalogue, Jewish National and University Library, Jerusalem. She is editor of *Bibliographie d'ouvrages hébraiques traduits en français* (Jerusalem, Ministère des affaires étrangères, 1966) and other bibliographies published in the professional library journal of Israel.

ALEXANDER USCHAKOW (Poland: Law) is Executive Secretary of the Institute for East European Law at the Universität zu Köln, where he also serves as a research associate specializing in the Soviet Union, Poland, and the integration of East Europe. He is editor of the journal *Osteuropa-Recht*, author of *Das sowjetische internationale privatrecht 1917-1962* (Köln, 1964) and *Der Rat für gegenseitige Wirtschaftshilfe (COMECON)* (Köln, 1962), and he is coauthor of *Die Integration Osteuropas 1961-1965* (Köln, 1966).

FERENC A. VALI (Hungary: The State; Mass Media and Public Opinion) is Professor of Government at the University of Massachusetts. A specialist in the fields of international law and government, Dr. Vali has most recently published *The Quest for a United Germany* (Johns Hopkins Press, 1967). He is the author of several other publications, including *Rift and Revolution in Hungary: Nationalism Versus Communism* (Harvard University Press, 1961) and *Servitudes of International Law: A Study of Rights in Foreign Territory* (2d rev. ed., Praeger, 1958).

FRANCIS S. WAGNER (Overview: The Nationality Question, and Hungary: History; History of Thought, Culture and Scholarship; The Fine Arts) serves on the staff of the Library of Congress. His writings include *The Hungarian Revolution in Perspective* (F. F. Memorial Foundation, Washington, D.C., 1967), *A szlovák nacionalizmus elsö korszaka* (Budapest, 1940) and numerous contributions to scholarly monographs and journals. His current interest focuses on nationality problems, dialectical materialism, and the U.S. image abroad.

PIOTR S. WANDYCZ (Poland: History) is Professor of History at Yale University and a member of the Council on Russian and East European Studies. He is author of *Czechoslovak-Polish Confederation and the Great Powers 1940-1943* (Indiana University Press, 1956), *France and Her Eastern Allies 1919-1925* (University of Minnesota Press, 1962), and *Soviet-Polish Relations* (Harvard University Press, 1969), and has contributed numerous articles to learned journals.

BOGDAN ZABORSKI (Poland: The Land) was until his recent partial retirement Professor of Geography at the University of Ottawa and is now visiting Professor at Sir George Williams University at Montreal. During his teaching career, which also comprised posts at the Polish University College in London, England, McGill University, and the Universities of Cracow and Warsaw, he has conducted research on settlements, ethnic differentiation, and landscapes. He is coauthor of a Polish-language university textbook of human geography.

ALFRED ZAUBERMAN (Poland: The Economy) obtained his doctorate at Cracow University with a thesis on Soviet monetary policy. He is the author of *Industrial Progress in Poland, Czechoslovakia and East Germany 1937-62* (Oxford University Press, 1964), published under the auspices of the Royal Institute of International Affairs. A reader in the London School of Economics,

University of London, Dr. Zauberman is particularly interested in techniques of planning.

LASLOZ ZSOLDOS (Hungary: The Economy) is Associate Professor of Economics and Chairman of the Department of Economics at the University of Delaware. He is the author of the book *The Economic Integration of Hungary into the Soviet Bloc* (Columbus, Ohio: Bureau of Business Research, The Ohio State University, 1963) and coauthor of *International Finance* (D. C. Heath, 1967).

CONSULTANTS FOR GERMAN-LANGUAGE PUBLICATIONS

JOHANNES GERTLER (for Czechoslovakia) is Instructor in Political Science at the Stabsakademie der Bundeswehr in Hamburg. He is the author of *Die deutsche Russlandpublizistik der Jahre 1853 bis 1870* (Berlin, 1959).

GERTRUD KRALLERT-SATTLER (for Hungary), a historian who received her doctor's degree from the Universität Wien, is a research librarian at the Südost-Institut München. Dr. Krallert-Sattler is the editor of *Südosteuropa-Bibliographie* (München, Oldenbourg, 1956–).

WILHELM SCHULZ (for Overview; Poland) is Assistant Professor, Seminar für osteuropäische Geschichte der Freien Universität Berlin. He is the author of *Die Immunität im nordöstlichen Russland des 14. und 15. Jahrhunderts* (Berlin, 1962).

HANS-JOACHIM TORKE (East Germany) is Assistant Professor, Seminar für osteuropäische Geschichte der Freien Universität Berlin. His latest publication is *Das russische Beamtentum in der ersten Hälfte des 19. Jahrhunderts* (Berlin, 1967).

ASSISTANT EDITORS

ROBERT V. ALLEN is Russian Area Specialist, Slavic and Central European Division, Library of Congress. He was a contributor to *Russia and the Soviet Union: A Bibliographic Guide to Western-Language Publications* (The University of Chicago Press, 1965) and an editor and translator of and contributor to other bibliographic publications in the Slavic field. He has also contributed numerous articles and reviews to professional journals.

ROBERT G. CARLTON is an Area Specialist with the Slavic and Central European Division of the Library of Congress. Co-compiler of *The USSR and Eastern Europe; Periodicals in Western Languages* (Library of Congress, 1967), he has also edited *Newspapers of East Central and Southeastern Europe in the Library of Congress* (Washington, D.C., 1965), *Latin America in Soviet Writings; a Bibliography* (Baltimore, Johns Hopkins Press, 1966), and the forthcoming *Soviet View of Contemporary Latin America, 1960-1968* (Austin, University of Texas Press).

RUTH S. FREITAG, Head, Bibliography and Reference Correspondence Section, General Reference and Bibliography Division, Library of Congress, has specialized in bibliographical and reference work over a wide range of subjects. She is the compiler of *Agricultural Development Schemes in Sub-Saharan Africa, a Bibliography* (1963) and of *Union Lists of Serials, a Bibliography* (1964), both published by the Library of Congress. From 1963 to 1967 she was assistant editor, *D.C. Libraries*.

part one

OVERVIEW of the East Central European Area

This part deals with publications which pertain either to two or more countries of the area or to subjects for which a consolidated rather than a separate presentation by countries seemed indicated.

1

General Reference Aids and Bibliographies*

by Elizabeth Beyerly

A. BIBLIOGRAPHIC AIDS

1. Bibliography of Bibliographies

1. Borov, Todor, *and others*. Die Bibliographie in den europäischen Ländern der Volksdemokratie; Entwicklung und gegenwärtiger Stand. Leipzig, Verlag für Buch- und Bibliothekswesen, 1960. 165 p. (Bibliothekswissenschaftliche Arbeiten aus der Sowjetunion und den Ländern der Volksdemokratie in deutscher Übersetzung, Reihe B, 3)

   An East German translation of a Bulgarian original. Analysis by country of bibliographical work from 1918 to the late 1950s. Contains a list of useful current reference works including selected subject bibliographies and indexing journals. An appendix lists bibliographies published in East Germany since 1945.

   For a detailed discussion of the historical evolution of national bibliographies in Eastern Europe, *see:*

   Simon, Konstantin R. Istoriia inostrannoi bibliografii (History of foreign bibliography). Moskva, Izdatel'stvo Vsesoiuznoi knizhnoi palaty, 1963. p. 450-482.

* The arrangement in this chapter is by language and by chronological and topical affinity of the publications listed.

2. Akademiia nauk SSSR. *Biblioteka.* Bibliografiia cheshkikh i slovatskikh bibliografii o Chekho-Slovakii; literatura, opublikovanaia v 1945-1960 gg. (Bibliography of Czech and Slovak bibliographies about Czechoslovakia; literature published 1945-1960). Moskva, 1962. 38 p.

———. . . . pol'skikh bibliografii o Pol'she; . . . (. . . of Polish bibliographies about Poland; . . .). Moskva, 1962. 52 p.

———. . . . vengerskikh bibliografii o Vengrii; . . . (. . . of Hungarian bibliographies about Hungary; . . .). Moskva, 1962. 27 p.

Bibliographies of bibliographies relating to Czechoslovakia, Hungary, and Poland, issued jointly by the Library of the Academy of Sciences of the USSR and the Fundamental Library of Social Sciences. Each individual volume lists from 100 to 400 references to bibliographies published in these countries during 1945-1960.

3. New York. Public Library. *Slavonic Division.* A Bibliography of Slavonic Bibliography in English. New York, New York Public Library, 1947. 11 pp.

Contains 14 general Slavic, 15 Czech, 16 Polish (as well as Russian) bibliographies of English-language references.

2. Area Bibliographies

4. Novaia literatura po evropeiskim stranam narodnoi demokratii (Recent literature concerning the European peoples' democracies). v. 1-12; 1948-1959. Moskva, Akademiia nauk SSSR. Monthly.

International coverage of monographs and journal articles concerning socioeconomic, political, and cultural problems, emphasizing works published in Eastern Europe. Since 1960 this has been superseded by separate series for each of the East European countries, viz.:

Novaia literatura po Chekhoslovakii (. . . Czechoslovakia). 1960– Moskva. Monthly.

Novaia literatura po Germanskoi Demokraticheskoi Respublike (. . . German Democratic Republic). 1962– Moskva. Monthly.

Novaia literatura po Pol'she (. . . Poland). 1960– Moskva.

Novaia literatura po Vengrii (. . . Hungary). 1960– Moskva.

See also, for publications of more general content:

Novaia literatura po obshchim problemam evropeiskikh sotsialisticheskikh stran (New literature on the common problems of the European socialist countries). 1964– Moskva. Monthly.

Novaia literatura po obshchim problemam slavianovedeniia (New literature on general problems of Slavic studies). 1966– Moskva. Quarterly.

5. Novinky literatury. Společenské vědy (New writings. Social sciences). 1966– Praha, Státní knihovna. 10-12 times a year.

This publication appears in the following 10 series: *Filosofické vědy* (Philosophy), I. řada; *Bibliografie ekonomické literatury* (Bibliography of economic literature), II. řada; *Stát a právo* (State and law),

III. řada; *Historie* (History), IV. řada; *Politika* (Politics), V. řada; *Jaszykověda-Literární věda* (Linguistics-literature), VI. řada; *Umění* (Arts), VII. řada; *Přehled pedagogické literatury* (Survey of writings in education), VIII. řada; Psychologie (Psychology), IX. řada; *Sociologie* (Sociology), X. řada.

This series of continuing subject bibliographies of current books and articles is general in scope, but covers extensively writings on Czechoslovakia, East Germany, Hungary, and Poland.

6. American Bibliography of Russian and East European Studies. 1– 1956– Bloomington, Indiana University Press. Annual.

Title varies: 1956-1959, *American Bibliography of Slavic and East European Studies.* Lists titles of monographs and journal articles concerning the humanities and, since 1957, the social sciences in the USSR and Eastern Europe in English (1956-1960, published in the United States and Canada only, 1961– in English and published outside Eastern Europe). Each volume appears approximately two years after the date to which it refers. Entries are grouped by broad subject arrangement. Author index.

Continues on a current basis the work by Robert F. Byrnes (*see* entry no. 13). A more restricted, specialized bibliography is:

U.S. *Department of State. Office of Intelligence Research and Analysis.* External Research: Eastern Europe. 1– 1952-68. Washington, D.C. Semiannual. The April issue lists research in progress; and the October one, completed research. Publications principally in the field of international affairs, reporting results of research undertaken by private American scholars.

7. L'URSS et les pays de l'Est; revue des revues. 1– 1960– Paris, Centre Nationale de la Recherche Scientifique. Quarterly.

Appears in two parts. The first (Bulletin analytique) contains summaries of major articles published in Soviet and East European journals on legal, economic, and social problems. The second (Répertoire systematique) is an index to the contents of about 20 Soviet and 20 East European periodicals. Sponsored by the Centre de Recherche sur l'URSS et les pays d l'Est of the Université de Strasbourg. May be compared with *Notes et études documentaires* issued since 1945 by the Direction de Documentation in Paris, certain numbers of which are devoted to Eastern Europe.

8. Wissenshaftlicher Dienst Südosteuropa. 1– 1952– München, Südost-Institut. Monthly.

German summaries and partial translations, mainly of articles published in Southeastern Europe (including Hungary), concerning current economic and political developments. A similar service, but primarily concerning itself with current events in Czechoslovakia and Poland, is:

Wissenschaftlicher Dienst für Ost-Mitteleuropa. 1– 1951– Marburg/Lahn, Johann Gottfried Herder-Institut. Monthly.

Both services include bibliographical references.

9. To supplement information in current bibliographies consult the extensive bibliographic sections and book reviews in the following journals:

   Canadian Slavic Studies. Revue canadienne d'études slaves. 1– 1967– Montreal, Loyola College. Quarterly.

   Revue des études slaves. 1921– Paris. Annual. This contains a "Chronique bibliographique" which lists monographs and journal articles published in Eastern Europe and elsewhere, emphasizing language, literature, and historical topics.

   Slavic Review. 1940– Seattle, Washington. Quarterly. A subject, author, and book review index for the period 1941-1964 has been compiled by L. Charbonneau.

   Slavonic and East European Review. 1922– London. Semiannual. Contains many bibliographical references and extensive book reviews, largely of publications issued outside East Europe.

   Berlin. Freie Universität. *Osteuropa Institut.* Bibliographische Mitteilungen. 1952– Irregular. Bibliographies on special subjects, including sciences and the humanities.

   Zeitschrift für Ostforschung. 1952– Marburg/Lahn, Johann Gottfried Herder-Institut. Quarterly.

   Osteuropa. 1951– Stuttgart, Deutsche Gesellschaft für Osteuropakunde. Monthly. This and the preceding publication contain numerous bibliographical references, chiefly to works in the German language.

10. Moscow. Publichnaia biblioteka. Strany Evropy. Chast' 1: Sotsialisticheskie strany; rekomendatel'nyi ukazatel' literatury (The countries of Europe. Part 1: The socialist countries; suggested reading list). Moskva, Kniga, 1965. 92 p.

    Contains 324 annotated references to monographs and journal articles published in the USSR and also in Eastern Europe in the period 1956 to 1964. Two-thirds of the references concern the humanities, and materials on social sciences are included only for the years 1962-1964. An earlier edition, covering material published during 1945-1955, appeared as *Evropeiskie strany narodnoi demokratii na puti k sotsializmu; rekomendatel'nyi ukazatel' literatury* (The European peoples' democracies on the road to socialism; suggested reading list) (Moskva, 1956, 112 p.).

11. Munich. Südost-Institut. Südosteuropa-Bibliographie. München, R. Oldenbourg, 1956.

    Each volume provides a five-year bibliographic survey of monographs and journals published in or relating to Eastern Europe. Volume one covered the period from 1945 to 1950; volume two, 1951-1955; and volume three, 1956-1960. Each volume consists of two parts, one listing materials on Slovakia, Romania, and Bulgaria, and the other on Yugoslavia, Hungary, Albania, and Southeast Europe as a whole.

From 3,000 to 4,500 entries are contained in each volume, principally in the social sciences. Author indexes. *See also*:

Munich. Osteuropa Institut. Ost- und Südosteuropa im westlichen Schrifttum der Nachkriegzeit; ein bibliographischer Leitfaden für Dozenten und Hörer an Volkshochschulen. München, Im Auftrage des Deutschen Volkshochschulverbandes und der Deutschen Gesellschaft für Osteuropakunde, 1956. 113 p. Annotated bibliography of materials on Eastern Europe published outside that area and intended for students and teachers of adult education. References are principally to German and English language materials.

12. East European Accessions Index. v.1-11; 1951-1961. Washington, D.C., U.S. Govt. Print. Off. Bimonthly 1951; monthly 1952-1961.

While primarily an accessions index of monographs (1944–) and journals (1950–) published in Eastern Europe and received by the U. S. Library of Congress and some 100 major American libraries, the index listed an annual average of 100,000 titles (in English translation) of monographs and of articles in journals published in the Baltic and East European countries. Arranged by country of publication, with subdivision by broad subject categories. Author indexes.

13. Byrnes, Robert F. Bibliography of American Publications on East Central Europe, 1945-1957. Bloomington, Indiana, 1958. 213 p. (Indiana University Publications, Slavic and East European Series, 12)

Contains titles of about 2,800 monographs and journal articles published mainly in the United States, but with a few Canadian imprints, concerning East European humanities and to a lesser extent the social sciences. Arranged by country, with broad subject subdivisions. Author index. Continued by *American Bibliography of Russian and East European Studies* (*see* entry no. 6). Byrnes has also contributed a selective listing of about 350 English language monographs on Eastern Europe considered important for American colleges and universities in:

East Central Europe. *In*: American Universities Field Staff. A Select Bibliography: Asia, Africa, Eastern Europe, Latin America. New York, 1960. p. 325-353. Additional entries on Eastern Europe are included in supplements which appeared in 1961, 1963, and 1965.

Other English language materials from the late 1950s to mid-1960s may be found in the bibliographic section of *Focus on Eastern Europe* (*see* entry no. 40).

14. Spector, Sherman D., *and* Lyman Legters. Checklist of Paperbound Books on Russia and East Europe. Albany, University of the State of New York, 1966. 79 p.

Pages 53-72 list publications relating to Eastern Europe.

15. Halpern, Joel M., John A. McKinstry, *and* Dalip Saund. Bibliography of Anthropological and Sociological Publications on Eastern Europe and the USSR (English Language Sources). Los Angeles, Russian and East European Studies Center, University of California, 1961. 142 p. (Russian and East European Studies Center Series, v. 1, no. 2).

About one-third of the monographs and journal articles listed refer to the ecology, archaeology, linguistics, and social change of the Slavs and the peoples of the Balkans. Materials are mostly from the late 1940s through the 1950s. For a bibliography on Slavic civilization containing references in German, Russian, and other Slavic languages, *see*:

Adamczyk, A. Literaturübersicht. *In*: Diels, Paul. Die slavischen Völker. Wiesbaden, O. Harrassowitz, 1963. p. 311-357. A similar bibliographic survey is:

Lencek, Rado L. A Bibliographical Guide to the Literature on Slavic Civilizations. New York, Columbia University, Department of Slavic Languages, 1966. 52 p.

16. Sztachova, Jirina. Mid-Europe; a Selective Bibliography. New York, Mid-European Studies Center, 1953. 197 p.

Contains mainly titles of monographs published in West European languages in the period from 1930 to the 1950s concerning the political, historical, and, to a lesser degree, economic development of Eastern Europe. Arranged by broad subjects, with subdivision by countries. Author index. For a bibliography of unpublished works sponsored by the Mid-European Studies Center, *see*:

Free Europe Committee. Index to Unpublished Studies Prepared for Free Europe Committee, Inc.; Studies 1-378. New York, 1958. 21 p. The index is also included as part of the February 1953 issue of the *East European Accessions Index* (*see* entry no. 12). Arranged numerically, by author and subject of reports. May also be compared with the *External Research: Eastern Europe*, issued by the State Department.

17. Breslau. Osteuropa-Institut. Osteuropäische Bibliographie. Breslau, Pribratsch's Buchhandlung, 1921-1928. 4 v.

Lists titles of monographs and journal articles in Russian and the languages of Western and Eastern Europe published in 1920-1923. Author indexes.

18. Kerner, Robert J. Slavic Europe; a Selected Bibliography in the Western European Languages, Comprising History, Languages and Literatures. Cambridge, Harvard University Press, 1918. 402 p.

See also entry no. 77.

Of the 4,500 entries, mostly for monographs published before 1914, approximately 2,800 refer to Slavic (other than Russian) languages, literature, and history. Arranged by ethnic group, with subject subdivisions. Author index.

3. Dictionaries

19. Bibliographie der Wörterbücher erschienen in der Deutschen Demokratischen Republik, Rumänischen Volksrepublik, Tschechoslowakischen Sozialistischen Republik, Ungarischen Volksrepublik, Union der Sozialistischen Sowjetrepubliken, Volksrepublik Bulgarien, Volksre-

publik China, Volksrepublik Polen, 1945-1961. Edited by D. Rymsza-Zalewska and I. Siedlecka. Warszawa, Wydawnictwo Nauko-Techniczne, 1965. 248 p.

In two sections, the first of which lists monolingual, and the second, bilingual dictionaries. Entries are arranged by Dewey Decimal classification. Language, author, subject, and title indexes. Editorial material in Russian and German. *Supplement*:

Bibliographie der Wörterbücher . . . , 1962-1964 (Warszawa, Wydawnictwa Naukowo-Techniczne, 1968, 166 p.)

20. Lewanski, Richard C. A Bibliography of Slavic Dictionaries. New York, New York Public Library, 1959-1963. 3 v.

Contents: v. 1: Polish; v. 2: Belorussian, Bulgarian, Czech, Kashubian, Lusatian, Old Church Slavic, Macedonian, Polabian, Serbocroatian, Slovak, Slovenian, Ukrainian; v. 3: Russian.

Each volume lists monolingual and multilingual dictionaries, as well as dictionaries of abbreviations, pseudonyms, slang, and dialects. Author and subject indexes. *See also*:

Kiss, L. Die erklärenden Wörterbücher der slawischen Sprachen. Studia Slavica (Budapest), v. 9, 1963: 74-122. Analysis of outstanding monolingual dictionaries published by national academies in the Slavic countries.

4. Bibliographies of Serials

21. U.S. *Bureau of the Census.* Bibliography of Social Science Periodicals and Monograph Series: Czechoslovakia, 1948-1963. Washington, D.C., 1964. 129 p. (Foreign Social Science Bibliographies. Series P-92, no. 19)

See also entry no. 566.

———. Bibliography of Social Science Periodicals and Monograph Series: Hungary, 1947-1962. Washington, D.C., 1964. 137 p. (Foreign Social Science Bibliographies. Series P-92, no. 13)

———. Bibliography of Social Science Periodicals and Monograph Series: Poland, 1945-1962. Washington, D.C., 1964. 312 p. (Foreign Social Science Bibliographies. Series P-92, no. 16)

See also entry no. 2433.

In each volume, titles of periodicals published in the countries and languages of Eastern Europe after the Second World War are arranged under broad subject headings in the social sciences; subject, title, author, and issuing-agency indexes.

22. U.S. *Library of Congress. Slavic and Central European Division.* The USSR and Eastern Europe: Periodicals in Western Languages. Compiled by Paul L. Horecky and Robert G. Carlton. 3d ed. Washington, D.C., 1967. 89 p.

Entries are grouped by country and include English and other West European language periodicals issued in the East European countries as well as those appearing elsewhere which refer to these countries. All subjects, with the exclusion of those in the natural or technical sciences, are included. Library of Congress call numbers are given, as are addresses of publishers.

For a short-title list of periodicals published in Eastern Europe and of western periodicals concerning Eastern Europe which are available in British libraries, *see*:

Fyfe, J., *comp.* List of Current Acquisitions of Periodicals and Newspapers Dealing with the Soviet Union and the East European Countries. Economics of Planning (Oslo), v. 4, 1964: 185-199.

23. U.S. *Library of Congress. Slavic and Central European Division.* Newspapers of East Central and Southeastern Europe in the Library of Congress. Edited by Robert G. Carlton. Washington, D.C., 1965. 204 p.

Entries are arranged by country and include about 800 newspaper titles published in Eastern Europe and available in the Library of Congress. Place, language, and title indexes.

A shorter list of holdings is:

Periodicals and Newspapers Concerning East-Central and East Europe in the Library of the Hoover Institution on War, Revolution and Peace, 1958; a Checklist. Stanford University, California, 1958. 22 p.

This mimeographed list includes brief titles of 314 journals and newspapers, many published outside East Europe, largely by émigré groups.

24. Paris. Bibliothèque nationale. *Département des périodiques.* Périodiques slaves en caractères cyrilliques; état des collections en 1950. Edited and compiled by E. Belin de Ballu. Paris, 1956. 2 v. Supplément, 1951-1960: Paris, 1963. 497 p. Addendum et errata: Paris, 1965. 223 p.

The list, predominantly of Russian language periodicals, also includes titles of Bulgarian and Serbian periodicals available in Paris libraries. A partial continuation of:

Unbegaun, Boris O. Catalogue des périodiques slaves et relatifs aux études slaves des bibliothèques de Paris. Paris, Champion, 1929. 221 p.

25. Current periodicals concerning Eastern Europe include:

East European Quarterly. 1– 1967– Boulder, Colorado, University of Colorado. Quarterly.

Österreichische Ost-Hefte. Sept. 1959– Wien. Bimonthly. Intended for intellectuals, businessmen, and politicians, it provides critical information on facts and trends in Eastern European life.

Ost-Probleme. 1949– Bonn. Biweekly (weekly until 1956). A bulletin which selects and republishes in German translation current materials from East European and Asian Communist countries; includes analysis of current events and book reviews.

5. Dissertations

26. Dossick, Jesse J. Doctoral Dissertations on Russia, the Soviet Union and Eastern Europe Accepted by American, Canadian and British Universities. Slavic Review, v. 24, 1965: 752-761; v. 25, 1966: 710-717; v. 26, 1967: 705-712; v. 27, 1968: 694-704.

Lists about 100 theses concerning the humanities and social sciences in Eastern Europe. No such coverage available before 1965, but compare with:

Aronson, H. I. American Doctoral Dissertations in the Fields of Slavic and East European Languages. Slavic Review, v. 22, 1963: 1-8, 449-450. Lists 139 theses presented in the United States from 1921 to 1961.

In general, dissertations in the field of Slavic languages and literatures and in the fields of East European history should be approached through the relevant subject bibliographies.

27. Hanusch, G. Osteuropa Dissertationen. Jahrbücher für Geschichte Osteuropas, Neue Folge. v. 1, 1953, no. 4, supplement: 1-44; v. 2, 1954, no. 2, supplement: 45-72; v. 3, 1955, no. 1, supplement: 74-114; v. 4, 1956, no. 3, supplement: 115-152; v. 6, 1958, no. 4, supplement: 153-194; v. 8, 1960, no. 2, supplement: 195-239.

Theses in all fields of the humanities and social sciences submitted to German speaking universities in Western Europe and to universities in Northern Europe and the United States during the period 1945-1960.

6. Library Catalogs, Services, and Accession Records

28. Cyrillic Union Catalog in Microprint. New York, Readex Microprint Corp., 1962.

A microprint reproduction of the Cyrillic Union Catalog of the Library of Congress, listing monographs in Russian, Ukrainian, Belorussian, Bulgarian, and Serbian reported as of 1956 by 186 cooperating libraries in the United States and Canada. Entries arranged separately by author, subject, and title.

29. New York. Public Library. *Slavonic Division.* Dictionary Catalog of the Slavonic Collection of the New York Public Library. Boston, G. K. Hall, 1959. 26 v.

A photographic reproduction of the original catalog entries, 60 per cent of which are in the Cyrillic alphabet, mainly in the fields of Slavic languages and literature. Included are many translations from Slavic languages and original works in Western languages, as well as references to journal articles not indexed elsewhere. Alphabetic arrangement by author, title, and subject. *See also*:

Rosenthal, H. A List of Russian, Other Slavonic and Baltic Periodicals in the New York Public Library. *In*: New York. Public Library. Bulletin, v. 20, 1916: 339-372.

30. Jena. Universität. *Bibliothek.* Slavica-Auswahl-Katalog der Universitätsbibliothek Jena; ein Hilfsbuch für Slawisten und Germanoslavica-Forscher. Edited by O. Feyl. Weimar, H. Böhlaus Nachfolger, 1956-1959. 2 v. in 3. (Claves Jenenses, 4-6)

A similar East German catalog of Slavic holdings is:

Gotha (City) Landesbibliothek. Slavica Auswahl-Katalog der Landesbibliothek Gotha. Edited by Helmut Claus. Berlin, Akademie Verlag, 1961. 531 p. (Quellen und Studien zur Geschichte Osteuropas, Bd. 10)

In West Germany there is:

Johann Gottfried Herder-Institut, *Marburg. Bibliothek.* Bibliothek des Johann Gottfried Herder-Instituts; alphabetischer Katalog. Boston, G. K. Hall, 1964. 5 v.

A photographic reproduction of a catalog which includes numerous East European, particularly Slavic, monographs and journals, reflecting in part the holdings of the former Preussische Staatsbibliothek in Berlin.

31. Accession Records: Supplementing the regular Slavica catalogs of the various libraries are the accession lists reporting new additions both of monographs and journals published in the countries of Eastern Europe. Such lists include:

East European Accessions Index. Washington, 1951-1961. Monthly. (*See* entry no. 12).

British Museum. *Department of Printed Books.* Catalogue of Printed Books. Accessions: Slavonic, Hungarian, etc. London, 1931-1947.

Munich. Bayerische Staatsbibliothek. Slavica Neuerwerbungen. 1– 1950– Annual.

Berliner Titeldrucke. Neue Folge. 1954-1959. Zugänge aus der Sowjetunion und den europäischen Ländern der Volksdemokratie. Berlin, Deutsche Staatsbibliothek. 6 v. in 5.

32. Library Service: Moscow. Publichnaia biblioteka. Bibliotekovedenie i bibliografiia za rubezhom (Library service and bibliography abroad). vyp. 1– 1958– Irregular.

Numbers 1-2, 5-6, 8, 10, and 20 concern library service in various countries of Eastern Europe and describe cooperation of these countries with the USSR in library matters. *See also*:

Moscow. Vsesoiuznaia gosudarstvennaia biblioteka inostrannoi literatury. Inostrannye periodicheskie izdaniia po bibliografii i bibliotekovedeniiu, imeiushchiesia bibliotekakh Moskvy i Leningrada (Foreign bibliography and library service journals available in the libraries of Moscow and Leningrad). Moscow, Vsesoiuznaia knizhnaia palata, 1959. 169 p. Includes many East European publications in the field. Arranged alphabetically. Country and subject indexes.

33. Buist, Eleanor, *and* Robert F. Byrnes. Area Programs for the Soviet Union and East Europe; Some Current Concerns of the Libraries. *In*: Chien, Ts'un-hsün, *and* H. W. Winger, *eds.* Area Studies and

the Library. Proceedings of the 30th Annual Conference of the University of Chicago Graduate Library School, May 20-22, 1965. Chicago, University of Chicago Press, 1966. p. 108-127.

Cooperation among the libraries of the countries of Eastern Europe is discussed in:

Lavrova, M. A. Mezhdunarodnaia bibliograficheskaia konferentsiia v Varshave (The international bibliographic conference in Warsaw). Sovetskaia bibliografiia, vyp. 49, 1958: 84-89.

34. Kjellberg, Lennert. Slavistik för bibliotekarier. Lund, Distribution Bibliotekstjänst, 1963. 76 p. (Svenska bibliotekariesamfundet. Skriftserie, 5).

Useful information for librarians on Cyrillic script and on title description of Slavic imprints and series. Includes a brief comparative morphology of Slavic languages. G. G. Firsov's article "Tsentralizovannaia katalogizatsiia v sotsialisticheskikh stranakh" (Centralized cataloging in the Socialist countries), *Sovetskaia bibliografiia*, vyp. 45, 1957: 91-101, discusses cataloging rules and printed catalogs in Eastern Europe.

B. THE STATE OF AREA RESEARCH

1. Bibliographies

35. Akademiia nauk SSSR. *Fundamental'naia biblioteka obshchestvennykh nauk.* Sovetskoe slavianovedenie; literatura o zarubezhnykh stranakh na russkom iazyke, 1918-1960 (Soviet Slavic research; literature about other Slavic countries in Russian, 1918-1960). Compiled by I. A. Kaloeva. Moskva, Izd-vo Akademii nauk SSSR, 1963. 401 p. *See also* entry no. 71.

Covers the literature published from 1918 to 1960, with a supplement for the years 1961-1962. More than 10,000 entries referring to scholarly works on area study, including the Soviet approach to world socialism and international scholarly cooperation, as well as many references to political, economic, and cultural affairs in the individual Slavic countries. Includes a section on reference works and bibliographies. Author index. *See also*:

Cronia, Arturo. La conoscenza del mondo Slavo in Italia; bilancia storico-bibliografica di un millennio. Padova, Officine grafiche Stediv, 1958. 792 p. Bibliography of Italian works on Slavic research and area study.

2. Analyses, Guides, and Surveys of Library Collections

36. Ornstein, Jacob. Slavic and East European Studies; Their Development and Status in the Western Hemisphere. Washington, Department of State, External Research Staff, Office of Intelligence Research, 1957. 65 p. Bibliography: p. 61-65. (External Research Paper, no. 129)

Contains analysis mainly of the state of Slavic language study, largely in the United States. Additional relevant information is contained in:

Manning, Clarence A. A History of Slavic Studies in the United States. Milwaukee, Marquette University Press, 1957. 117 p. Bibliography: p. 109-113. (Marquette Slavic Studies, 3) Deals with the evolution of area study in the United States, primarily in the period before the Second World War.

Horna, Dagmar, *ed.* Current Research on Central and Eastern Europe. New York, Mid-European Studies Center, Free Europe Committee, 1956. 251 p. (Mid-European Studies Center Publication, no. 28) Survey of the nature and extent of area study between the end of the Second World War and 1955, emphasizing work conducted by the Mid-European Studies Center. Lists 1,400 topics, mostly in history and politics.

37. Soviet Union and Eastern Europe. *In*: U.S. *Department of State. External Research Staff.* Language and Area Study Programs in American Universities. Washington, D.C., 1964. p. 99-124.

A summary of the area study programs at the graduate level which are offered by American universities. *See also*:

Free Europe Committee. *Mid-European Studies Center.* Area Study Programs: The Soviet Union and Eastern Europe. Edited by Royden Dangerfield. Champaign, Institute of Government and Public Affairs, University of Illinois, 1955. 87 1. Bibliography: leaves 79-84. Papers read at the Conference on the Soviet Union and Eastern Europe, University of Illinois, January 9-10, 1954.

38. For guides to and surveys of area studies in a number of countries of Europe, *see*:

Great Britain: Jopson, N. B., *and others.* The School of Slavonic and East European Studies; the First Forty Years, 1922-1962. Slavonic and East European Review, 1966, no. 102: 1-30.

Germany (West): Berlin. Freie Universität. *Osteuropa Institut.* Tätigkeitsbericht, 1951-1966. Berlin, 1967. 59 p. A description of the work of this institute, together with lists of its publications and of the activities of its staff members. The institute's publications are also described in its *Veröffentlichungen*, 1952-1967 (Berlin, 1967, 26 p.).

Deutsche Gesellschaft für Osteuropakunde. Fünfzig Jahre Osteuropa-Studien; zur Geschichte der Deutschen Gesellschaft zum Studium Osteuropas und der Deutschen Gesselschaft für Osteuropakunde. Stuttgart, 1963. 48 p. The evolution of the society's research from 1913 to 1945 and from its reconstitution under a somewhat different name in 1949 to 1963. Contains a list of the society's publications and of its annual conferences. *See also*:

Hacker, Jens. Osteuropa-Forschung in der Bundesrepublik. Das Parlament. Beilage "Aus Politik und Zeitgeschichte," September 14, 1960: 591-622.

Osteuropa-Institut München, 1952-1967. München, 1968. 20 p.

Switzerland: La Suisse, l'URSS et l'Europe Orientale. Revue économique et sociale (Lausanne). Special issue, April, 1963. 164 p.

39. For descriptions of the collections and facilities in various libraries with Slavic and East European specialization *see* particularly:

Horecky, Paul L. The Slavic and East European Resources and Facilities in the Library of Congress. Slavic Review, v. 23, 1964: 309-327.

Lewanski, Richard C. European Library Directory. Florence, Leo S. Olschki, 1967. 774 p. The arrangement is geographical, by country and then by city. Contains detailed coverage of East Central European countries.

Pulaska, Jadwiga. The Slavonic Division of the New York Public Library. New York, 1953. 52 p.

Mach, Otto. Die Osteuropasammlung der bayerischen Staatsbibliothek und ihre Entwicklung in den letzten Jahren. Österreichische Osthefte (Wien), January 1963: 71-73.

40. Focus on Eastern Europe. Intercom, v. 7, 1965, no. 4. 64 p.

Concise guide to recent U. S. ideas, programs, public opinion, teaching aids, services in the field of Eastern Europe. Includes bibliography.

41. Ruggles, Melville, *and* Vaclav Mostecky. Russian and East European Publications in the Libraries of the United States. New York, Columbia University Press, 1960. 396 p. (Columbia University Studies in Library Service, 11)

Quantitative analysis of American library resources, including suggestions for possible improvement of existing service. *See also*:

Ash, Lee. Subject Collections. New York, Bowker, 1961. 203 p. A survey of East European materials in American libraries.

C. REFERENCE AIDS FOR AREA STUDIES

1. General Surveys and Handbooks

42. Byrnes, Robert F., *ed.* The United States and Eastern Europe. Englewood Cliffs, N.J., Prentice-Hall, 1967. 176 p. Maps.

See also entry no. 227.

A panoramic view of the major aspects of domestic and foreign affairs, present and past, of the eight European countries with communist-type governments. This collection of eight essays, authored by distinguished experts in the respective fields, was prepared as a background for American Assembly meetings on this subject throughout the United States.

43. Fischer-Galati, Stephen A., *ed.* Eastern Europe in the Sixties. New York, Praeger, 1963. 239 p. Illus. (Praeger Publications in Russian History and World Communism, no. 137)

See also entry no. 156.

Essays by ten specialists on social, economic, domestic and international political problems. For similar information published in Great Britain and France, *see*:

Singleton, Frederick B. Background to Eastern Europe. Oxford, New York, Pergamon Press, 1965. 226 p.

Paraf, P. Les démocraties populaires: Albanie, Bulgarie, Hongrie, Pologne, Roumanie, Tchechoslovaquie, Yougoslavie, République Démocratique Allemande. Paris, Payot, 1962. 229 p.

44. Strakhovsky, Leonid I., *ed.* A Handbook of Slavic Studies. Cambridge, Harvard University Press, 1949. 753 p.
See also entry no. 150.

Chapters written by specialists, chiefly on the history and literature of the Slavs. Intended for the reader not familiar with the Slavic languages. Includes bibliographies of materials in Western European languages and a comparative historical chronology. *See also*:

Roucek, Joseph S. Slavonic Encyclopedia. New York, Philosophical Library, 1949. 1445 p. Alphabetically arranged, unsigned articles, mainly of historical and biographical value. No bibliographies. Based, as is Strakhovsky, on data through the mid-1940s. For English-language data of the mid- and late 1930s, *see*:

Handbook of Central and East Europe, 1932-1938(?). Zürich, Central European Times Publishing Co., 1932-1938(?). For data of the 1920s, *see*:

Great Britain. *Foreign Office. Historical Section.* Handbooks. Prepared under the Direction of the Historical Section of the Foreign Office . . . London, His Majesty's Stationery Office, 1920. Numbers 2, 3, 5-8, 11-14, 17-23, 43-46 and 51 of this series, which are often known as the "Peace Handbooks," are devoted to the countries and areas of Eastern Europe.

45. Markert, Werner, *ed.* Osteuropa Handbuch; namens der Arbeitsgemeinschaft für Osteuropaforschung. Köln, Böhlau, 1954-1965. 3 v. (v. 1: Jugoslawien; v. 2: Polen; v. 3: Sowjetunion)
See also entries no. 2443 *and* 3137.

Each volume of this handbook provides an extensive geographical, economic, historical, and social survey of a country, principally in the period after the Second World War, based on literature from Eastern and Western Europe and the United States. Each volume contains a bibliography. *See also*:

Südosteuropa-Jahrbuch. v. 1– München, R. Oldenbourg, 1957– Annual contributions by experts, primarily relating to cultural, historical and socioeconomic problems. Reflect reports presented to the Internationale Hochschulwoche sponsored by the Südosteuropa Gesellschaft.

Matl, Josef. Südslawische Studien. München, R. Oldenbourg, 1965. 598 p. (Südosteuropäische Arbeiten, 63)

Britz, N., *ed.* Wiener Südostbuch. 1959– Wien, Wiener Forschungsstelle der Österreicher aus dem Donau-, Sudeten- und Karpatenraum. Annual. Relates principally to cultural and historical ties between Austria-Hungary and the Slavs of Eastern Europe.

Die Deutschen und ihre östlichen Nachbarn. Ein Handbuch. Edited by Viktor Aschenbrenner and others. Frankfurt a. M., Diesterweg, 1967. 634 p. Illus., maps. A handbook focusing on German relations with Eastern Europe. Rather interpretive in approach, but useful for factual and bibliographic data on the area.

2. Guidebooks and Gazetteers

46. Germany (*Federal Republic, 1949–*) *Bundesanstalt für Landeskunde* Amtliches Gemeinde- und Ortsnamenverzeichnis der deutschen Gebiete unter fremder Verwaltung nach dem Gebietsstand am 1. 9. 1939. Remagen, 1953-1955. 3 v.

A comprehensive list of place names in all the eastern German provinces belonging to Germany on the first of September 1939. Divided into two sections: one, German–foreign-language names; the other, foreign-language–German names. This work contains all the changing names of any place in those territories in modern history as well as data on administrative organization and the number of the German topographic map on scale 1:25,000 on which the place can be found. In addition, there is a list of new Polish towns in these regions.

47. U.S. *Office of Geography.* Germany–Soviet Zone and East Berlin; Official Standard Names Approved by the United States Board on Geographic Names. Washington, D.C., U.S. Govt. Print. Off., 1959. 487 p. (U.S. Board on Geographic Names. Gazetteer no. 43)

———. Hungary; Official Standard Names Approved by the United States Board on Geographic Names. Washington, D.C., U.S. Govt. Print. Off., 1961. 301 p. (U.S. Board on Geographic Names. Gazetteer no. 52)

These gazetteers show the geographical names of places in Eastern Europe employed by agencies of the United States Government.

48. Kane, Robert S. Eastern Europe, A to Z; Bulgaria, Czechoslovakia, East Germany, Hungary, Poland, Romania, Yugoslavia, and the Soviet Union. Garden City, N.Y., Doubleday, 1968. 348 p. Maps.

An up-to-date travel guide written in somewhat breezy style and aimed primarily at the American tourist with little or no knowledge of the area.

49. Das Ferien- und Bäderbuch; von der Ostsee bis zum Schwarzen Meer. Berlin, Verlag Tribüne, 1963. 624 p. Illus.

Illustrated tourist guide, chiefly to places in East Germany. Pages 514-617 contain information on Poland, Hungary, Bulgaria, Czechoslovakia, Romania, and the USSR. For good illustrations, accompanied by a newspaperman's reportages, *see*:

Blunden, Godfrey. Eastern Europe: Czechoslovakia, Hungary and Poland. New York, Time, Inc., 1965. 176 p. Illus., maps.

3. Reproductions and Translations

50. Ouvrages cyrilliques concernant les sciences sociales et humaines; liste

des reproductions disponibles. Paris, Mouton, 1964-1965. 2 v. (Cahiers du monde russe et soviétique. Supplément, 1-2)

Although predominantly devoted to material in the Russian language, Supplement no. 2 also lists publications in Bulgarian and Serbian, copies of which are available in photographic reproduction or in microforms.

51. Materials published in Eastern Europe are made available in other languages through a number of translation services. No such service in the United States deals exclusively with East European sources. However, extensive translations may be found in:

U.S. *Joint Publications Research Service.* Selected Translations from East European Political Journals and Newspapers. 1958– 1– Irregular.

———. Political translations on Eastern Europe. 1962– Irregular. Emphasis on political and military problems, industrial development, and economics. Distribution of these reports in the United States is the subject of:

Lucas, R., *and* G. Caldwell. JPRS Translations. College and Research Libraries, v. 25, 1964: 103-110. For guides to the contents of JPRS publications, *see*:

East Europe; a Bibliography-Index. 1962– New York, Research and Microfilm Publications. Monthly. Formerly issued in Annapolis, Md., by T. E. Kyriak, this is "a complete bibliographic listing of the most recent JPRS translations relevant to . . . Albania, Bulgaria, Czechoslovakia, East Germany, Hungary, Poland, Romania and Yugoslavia."

A numerical index to the microprinted JPRS reports is provided by M. E. Poole's *Index to Readex Microprint Edition of JPRS Reports* (New York, Readex Microprint Corporation, 1964, 137 p.).

52. Material from Eastern Europe relating to the social sciences is also made available by the International Arts and Sciences Press of White Plains, New York. Journals and monographs published by this firm are listed in its catalog, *Translations in the Social Sciences* (White Plains, New York, 1967, 24 p.). For English-language summaries from the East-Central European press, *see*:

Great Britain. *Embassy. Czechoslovak Republic.* Press Review. Prague. Daily.

U.S. *Joint Publications Research Service.* Summary of the Czechoslovak Provincial Press. 1958– Washington, D.C. Irregular.

Hungarian Press Summary. Budapest, British Legation. Daily.

U.S. *Joint Publications Research Service.* Summary of the Hungarian Provincial Press. 1957– Washington, D.C. Weekly.

Polish News Bulletin. 1950– Warsaw, British and American Embassies. Daily.

U.S. *Joint Publications Research Service.* Summary of the Polish Provincial Press. 1958– Washington, D.C. Weekly.

53. Wiener Quellenheft zur Ostkunde. Reihe: 1., Kultur; 2., Landeskunde; 3., Recht; 4., Technik; 5., Wirtschaft. 1– 1958– Wien, Arbeitsgemeinschaft Ost. Quarterly.

German translations, chiefly from journal articles published in the USSR and Eastern Europe. Extensive bibliographical citations from the original sources.

For journals devoted primarily to abstracts and summaries of Eastern European publications, *see* entries 7 and 8.

4. Publishing and Copyright

54. Böhmer, Alois. Copyright in the USSR and Other European Countries under Communist Governments; Selective Bibliography with Digest and Preface. South Hackensack, New Jersey. Published for the Copyright Society of the USA by F. B. Rothman, 1960. 62 p.

Contains 91 brief annotations on copyright in East European countries other than the Soviet Union together with a selected bibliography of literature on the subject published outside of Eastern Europe. *See also*:

Kase, Francis Joseph. Copyright in Czechoslovakia; the New Copyright Statute of 1965. New York, New York University Law Center, 1966. p. 28-65.

55. For publishing activity in East Central Europe, reference may be made to the following:

Czechoslovakia: Publishing statistics of Czechoslovakia are given annually in the last December issue of the Czechoslovak national bibliography *České knihy*.

Hungary: Hungary. *Központi Statisztikai Hivatal.* Könyvkiadas (Book publishing). Budapest. A statistical survey.

Poland: Bromberg, Adam. Książki i wydawcy; ruch wydawniczy w Polsce Ludowej w latach 1944-1957 (Books and publishing; publishing activities in People's Poland in the years 1944-1957). Warszawa, Państwowy Instytut Wydawniczy, 1958. 273 p. Tables.

Warszawa. Biblioteka Narodowa. *Instytut Bibliograficzny.* Ruch wydawniczy w liczbach (Publishing activities in figures). 1955– Warszawa. Annual.

5. Monographic Series

56. The following series should be noted as periodically contributing handbooks or survey studies of Eastern Europe:

Praeger Series on East Central Europe under Communism. Begun in New York in the mid-1950s under the general guidance of Robert F. Byrnes and later of Stephen Fischer-Galati and in cooperation with Radio Free Europe. The series contains handbooks mainly on geographical, demographic, economic and political problems of the individual countries of Eastern Europe in the period after the Second World War. Each volume includes bibliographies.

Other series published in the United States are chiefly devoted to linguistic and historical research on Slavic Eastern Europe. Note especially the following:

Russian and East European Studies. 1– 1960– Los Angeles, University of California.

California Slavic Studies. 1– 1960– Berkeley, University of California Press.

Harvard Slavic Studies. 1953-1957. Cambridge, Harvard University Press. 4 v.

Indiana Slavic Studies. 1– 1956– Bloomington, Indiana University Press.

Florida State University Slavic Papers. 1– 1966– Tallahassee, Florida State University, Center for Slavic and East European Studies.

In Switzerland the Schweizerisches Ost Institut since 1958 has issued its *Schriftenreihe* (now *Materialien*), which comprise mainly bibliographic surveys, with much attention to Hungary in the period after the Second World War.

6. Directories and Biographic Information

57. Little, Arthur D., Inc. Directory of Selected Research Institutes in Eastern Europe. Prepared for the National Science Foundation. New York, Columbia University Press, 1967. 445 p.

See also entry no. 301.

A descriptive guide to the location and type of research institutes, academies, and universities in Bulgaria, Czechoslovakia, Hungary, Poland, Romania and Yugoslavia. The emphasis is on biological and physical science institutes. The address, name of director, and titles of selected institute publications are given. Name and subject index. *See also*:

Leska, M. Instytucje naukowo badawcze w państwach demokracji ludowych (Scientific research institutes in the peoples' democracies). Warszawa, Centralny Instytut Informacji Naukowo-Technicznej i Ekonomicznej, 1961. 106 p.

58. National Science Foundation. The Eastern European Academies of Sciences; a Directory. Washington, D.C., National Academy of Sciences-National Research Council, 1963. 148 p.

Names of social scientists and academicians are included. Brief biographical information provided. Supplementary information on university studies in general and Eastern Europe in particular can be located in:

Moscow. Universitet. *Biblioteka.* Universitetskoe obrazovanie v SSSR i za rubezhom; bibliograficheskii ukazatel' russkoi i inostrannoi literatury za 1950-1960 gg. (University education in the USSR and abroad. Bibliography of Russian and foreign literature for 1950-1960). Edited by G. G. Krichevskii and E. A. Nersesova. Moskva, Izdatel'stvo Moskovskogo universiteta, 1966. 645 p. Author and subject indexes.

59. Who's Who in Eastern Europe. n.p., 1962. 2 v. (loose leaf). Ports.

May be supplemented by: International Who's Who. London, International Who's Who Publishing Company, 1910– For the period prior to the Second World War, *see*:

Who's Who in Central and Eastern Europe. Edited by Stephen Taylor. Zurich, Central European Times Publishing Co., 1933-34, 1935-36. 2 v.

Wurzbach, Constantin. Biographisches Lexikon des Kaiserthums Österreichs, enthaltend die Lebensskizzen der denkwürdigen Personen, welche seit 1750 in den österreichischen Kron-Ländern geboren wurden oder darin gelebt und gewiirkt haben. Wien, Kaiserlich-Königlich Hof- und Staatsdruckerei, 1856-1891. 60 v. Fold. geneal. tables. A classic containing over 24,000 biographies for the period from 1750 to the 1850s, including Austria's East European crown lands.

60. Kleine slavische Biographie. Edited by A. Schmaus. Wiesbaden, O. Harrassowitz, 1958. 832 p.

Contains 3,500 short biographies of outstanding personalities and titles of their principal works. Emphasis is on representatives of the cultural life. For mainly political biographical data, *see*:

Brown, James F. The New Eastern Europe; the Khrushchev Era and After. New York, Praeger, 1966. Appendix one provides data on state and party officials, and appendix two, on other East European personalities.

2

Geographic aspects of the area

by George W. Hoffman

61. American Geographic Society of New York. Research Catalogue. Boston, G. K. Hall, 1962. 15 v.

    A major research bibliography including books, periodicals, monographs, and documents in all languages, mainly since 1923. Czechoslovakia, Hungary, and Poland are covered in v. 10, and East Germany in v. 9. For other basic reference works in the field, *see*:

    Bibliographie géographique internationale. v. 1– 1891– Paris, Association de géographes français. Each annual volume of this bibliography includes coverage of East Central Europe.

    Harris, Chauncy D., *and* Jerome D. Fellmann. International List of Geographical Serials. Chicago, 1960. 189 p. (University of Chicago, Department of Geography. Research Paper no. 63). Includes lists of all known geographic periodicals and non-periodical serials. Czechoslovakia, p. 27-28; East Germany (listed under Germany), p. 42-67; Hungary, p. 69-71; Poland, p. 91-94.

62. Blanc, André. Les Républiques socialistes d'Europe centrale. Paris, Presses universitaires de France, 1967. 300 p. Illus., plates. Bibliography: p. 281-295. (Magellan; la géographie et ses problèmes, 15)

    Basic regional geography of Czechoslovakia, Poland, the German Democratic Republic, Hungary, and Romania.

63. Enyedi, György. The Changing Face of Agriculture in Eastern Europe. The Geographical Review (New York), v. 57, July 1967: 358-372.

    Historical geographic discussion of the changing role of agriculture in the national economies.

64. Hoffman, George W. Eastern Europe. *In his* Geography of Europe, Including Asiatic U.S.S.R. 3d ed. New York, The Ronald Press Co., 1969. p. 431-524.

Detailed regional survey of the countries of East-Central and Southeast Europe (except Greece). *See also*:

———. Eastern Europe: a Study in Political Geography. The Texas Quarterly (Austin), v. 2, Autumn 1959: 57-88. Political geographic study of the countries of Eastern Europe.

65. Kraus, Theodor, *and* others, *eds.* Atlas Östliches Mitteleuropa. Bielefeld, Velhagen und Klasing, 1959. 289, 19 p. Illus., maps (part fold.). *See also* entries no. 145 *and* 2516.

Detailed atlas on the physical and cultural geography of East Central Europe. Each map is documented by sources and secondary literature. For a basic reference work on various geographic subjects which is of continued usefulness, *see*:

Vosseler, Paul, *and others.* Mitteleuropa ausser Deutsches Reich; Osteuropa in Natur, Kultur und Wirtschaft. Potsdam, Akademische Verlagsgesellschaft Atheneion, 1933. 498 p. Illus., maps. Contains contributions by Fritz Machatschek on Czechoslovakia, and by Max Friedrichsen on Poland as well as on the then independent Baltic states and on European Russia. Includes indexes.

66. Kostrowicki, Jerzy, *ed.* Land Utilization in East-Central Europe; Case Studies. Geographia Polonia (Warszawa), v. 5, 1965: 7-498.

An attempt to determine the relationship between geography and agriculture in East Central Europe on the basis of case studies on land utilization in Poland, Hungary, Yugoslavia, and Bulgaria. Includes a final evaluation by the editor. The subject is also covered in:

Sárfalvi, Béla, *ed.* Land Utilization in Eastern Europe. Budapest, Akadémiai Kiadó, 1967. 160 p. (Magyar Tudományos Akadémia. Földrajztudományi Kutatócsoport. Studies in Geography, 4) Ten papers presented at a conference in Budapest in 1964 and discussing the varied forms and ways of land utilization in East European countries.

67. Marinov, Khristo. Sotsialisticheski mezhdunarodni kompleksi i raioni (Socialist international complexes and regions). Varna, Durzhavno izdatelstvo, 1965, 173 p. Fold. maps. Bibliography: p. 167-171.

Economic geographic development among Comecon countries, considering such topics as integration of individual economies and regrouping of productive forces.

68. Osborne, Richard H. East-Central Europe; an Introductory Geography. New York, Praeger, 1967. 384 p. Maps.

Survey of various geographical topics in East Central and Southeast Europe (except East Germany and Greece). Published in London by Chatto and Windus, 1967, under the title *East-Central Europe: a Geographical Introduction to Seven Socialist States.* See also:

Hall, Elvajean, *and* Calvin L. Criner. Picture Map Geography of Eastern Europe. Illustrated by Thomas R. Funderburk. Philadelphia, Lippincott, 1968. 155 p. Illus.

69. Pounds, Norman, J. G., *ed.* Geographical Essays on Eastern Europe.

Bloomington, Indiana University, 1961. 159 p. Illus. (Indiana University Publications. Russian and East European Series, v. 24)

Series of essays by American and European geographers on the region as a whole ("The Concept and Political Status of the Shatter Zone") and individual topics.

70. Pounds, Norman J. G., *and* Robert C. Kingsbury. An Atlas of European Affairs. New York, Praeger, 1964. 135 p. Maps.

The maps also cover the East Central European area. A useful, small, black-and-white atlas, with text is:

Adams, Arthur E., Ian M. Matley, *and* William O. McCagg. An Atlas of Russian and East European History. New York. Praeger, 1967. 204 p. Maps. Useful reference tools for cartographic materials are:

American Geographical Society of New York. *Map Department*. Index to Maps in Books and Periodicals. Boston, G. K. Hall, 1968. 10 v.

Bibliographie cartographique internationale. 1937– Paris, Comité national français de géographie. Annual.

3

history*

by Stanley Z. Pech

A. BIBLIOGRAPHIES AND ABSTRACTS

71. Akademiia nauk SSSR. *Fundamental'naia biblioteka obshchestvennykh nauk.* Sovetskoe slavianovedenie; literatura o zarubezhnykh slavianskikh stranakh na russkom iazyke 1918-1960 (Soviet Slavic studies; literature concerning non-Soviet Slavic countries in the Russian language 1918-1960). Compiled by I. A. Kaloeva. Moskva, Izd-vo Akademiia nauk SSSR, 1963. 401 p.
   See also entry no. 35.

   Covers Czechoslovakia, Poland, Yugoslavia, Bulgaria, Lusatian Sorbs, and Pomeranian and Elbean Slavs, with history, literature, art, economics, law, etc. included; history comprises about half of the titles. An important bibliography, listing virtually the entire relevant Soviet output of books, and also of articles distilled from seven hundred serials. Its value is enhanced by an author and title index. This is a welcome tool and shortcut for locating bibliographical information which even the best Western libraries might not yield.

72. American Historical Association. Guide to Historical Literature. New York, Macmillan, 1961. 962 p.

   Contains a section on "East Europe" (p. 567-620), prepared by S. Harrison Thomson, in cooperation with other specialists, and comprising 1,375 titles arranged by country and, within country, by

* Not being familiar with the Hungarian language, the author had to be guided in his Hungarian selections by expert advice and bibliographic references in West European sources.

subject or period. Most titles are briefly annotated. For each country, there is usually a list of the leading periodicals and a valuable list of source collections and academy publications. The selection process has been rigorous, the end product adding up to an inventory of the best and most significant works on the history of Eastern Europe that had appeared up to the time of publication.

73. Historical Abstracts, 1775-1945. 1955– Santa Barbara, Calif. Quarterly.

Contains classified lists of English-language abstracts of articles selected from a vast range of serials appearing in all relevant languages; encompasses all continents except (from 1964) North America. Articles in various series of "Proceedings," and in occasional publications, such as festschriften, are likewise abstracted. Coverage restricted to materials dealing with the period 1775-1945. A system of "cues" radically simplifies a search for the topic in which the user is interested. Annual indexes; in addition, two five-year cumulative indexes produced thus far, for 1955-1959, and 1960-1964. East and Southeast Europe is covered excellently throughout; issue 2/3 of each year, which is published as a single fascicle, contains a special section on East and Southeast Europe, with each country — also the Habsburg Empire (combined with Austria) — having its own separate listing. Abstracts of articles on conferences, archives and libraries enhance the value of this bibliography as a means of keeping abreast of the latest developments in historical research. This is the most indispensable single reference instrument for anyone plying the historian's craft who is interested in the nineteenth and twentieth centuries.

74. International Bibliography of Historical Sciences. 1926– Paris, 1930– Annual.

Each volume represents the essence of world historiographical output in a given year, and consists of classified lists of books, articles, and major book reviews, for all periods and all standard fields, as determined by the Commission on Bibliography of the International Committee of Historical Sciences. Rigorously selective, it includes only works of acceptable quality transcending local significance. Not annotated, except for occasional brief descriptive comments. Cooperation of specialists from Eastern Europe (including East Germany and the USSR) ensures authenticity of bibliographic information concerning this region. Because this bibliography is highly selective, for more detailed information it is necessary to consult specialized current bibliographies relating to Eastern Europe. Chief among them are: the annual *American Bibliography of Russian and East European Studies* (Bloomington, Ind., 1956–); the lists appearing in the bimonthly *Sovetskoe slavianovedenie* (Moscow, 1965–); the surveys appearing in the annual *Revue des études slaves* (Paris, 1921–); the "Ostdeutsche Bibliographie" published in the annual *Jahrbuch der Albertus-Universität zu Königsberg* (Freiburg i. Br., 1951–), which is overburdened with trivia; and the periodic lists in *Zeitschrift für Ostforschung* (Marburg/Lahn, 1952–).

75. Jilek, Heinrich, Herbert Rister, *and* Helmuth Weiss. Bücherkunde Ostdeutschlands und des Deutschtums in Ostmitteleuropa. Köln, Böhlau, 1963. 560 p. (Ostmitteleuropa in Vergangenheit und Gegenwart, 8)

See also entry no. 641.

A bibliography of essential works on all aspects of the past and present role of Germans in Poland, Czechoslovakia, and the former Baltic States. History is the main concern. Lists, besides German titles, the important works in Polish, Czech, etc., including such items as the principal collections of historical sources. This makes the volume the only comprehensive retrospective bibliography of the history of East Central Europe. "East Germany" in the title does not refer to the German Democratic Republic but to Western Polish territories. The period before 1939 and the fate of Germans after 1945 are amply covered, but the coverage for the German role in German-occupied regions in 1939-1945 is slight.

76. Keep, J. L. H. Verzeichnis des englischsprachigen Schrifttums (ausser USA) 1939-1952 zur Geschichte Osteuropas und Südosteuropas. Forschungen zur osteuropäischen Geschichte (Berlin), v. 5, 1957: 119-162.

The Second World War interrupted the regular flow of bibliographies in Europe, leaving serious gaps; this list closes the gap for English-language publications (outside USA) relating to the history of Eastern and Southeast Europe. For articles in the *Forschungen zur Geschichte Osteuropas* relating to pertinent literature published in other countries, *see*:

Keep, J. L. H. Verzeichnis des Amerikanischen Schrifttums 1939-1952 zur Geschichte Osteuropas und Südosteuropas. v. 7, 1959: 397-446.

Portal, R., *and others.* Verzeichnis des französischsprachigen Schrifttums 1939-1952. v. 4, 1956: 219-239.

Tamborra, A. Verzeichnis des italienischsprachigen Schrifttums 1939-1952. v. 4, 1956: 240-259.

Philipp, W. Verzeichnis des deutschsprachigen Schrifttums 1939-1952. v. 1, 1954: 251-316.

Smolitsch, I., *and* M. Bernath. Verzeichnis des sovetrussischen Schrifttums 1939-1952. v. 3, 1956: 99-281.

The Osteuropa-Institut in Berlin has recently lengthened its catalogue of exhaustive bibliographies by Klaus Meyer's *Bibliographie der Arbeiten zur osteuropäischen Geschichte aus den deutschsprachigen Fachzeitschriften 1858-1964* (Berlin, Freie Universität, Osteuropa-Institut, 1966, 314 p. Bibliographische Mitteilungen, 9). This is a bibliography of German periodical articles produced in over one hundred years of German concern with Eastern Europe. Excludes Bohemia, includes Slovakia.

For a critical bibliography of books and pamphlets published in the United Kingdom between 1818 and 1967, *see*:

Bridge, F. R. , The Habsburg Monarchy, 1804-1918. London, University of London, School of Slavonic and East European Studies, 1967. 82 p.

77. Kerner, Robert J. Slavic Europe; a Selected Bibliography in the Western European Languages, Comprising History, Languages, and Literatures. Cambridge, Harvard University Press, 1918. 402 p.

See also entry no. 18.

A milestone in Slavonic bibliography in the West, by a historian who belonged to the first handful of ardent Slavists in the English-speaking world. Chapters correspond to six major Slavic ethnic groups, with each chapter further subdivided into history, language, and literature. Compiled with meticulous care; the only Slavic-language titles included are bibliographies and source collections containing documents in Western languages. More than half of the titles relate to non-Russian Slavs and to Slavic questions in general. Kerner's work is now dated. The most complete and up-to-date Slavic bibliography available today is the list prepared by A. Adamczyk, in Paul Diels' *Die slavischen Völker* (Wiesbaden, Harrassowitz, 1963), p. 313-358). Like Kerner, he embraces the whole Slavic world, but unlike him, lists works in all pertinent Slavic and non-Slavic languages, not excepting such languages of limited currency as Sorbian. The bibliography conforms broadly to the chapter arrangement of the text to which it is appended (as described elsewhere in this section); in addition, there is a helpful list of encyclopedias, handbooks, biographical collections, and periodicals.

78. Kramm, Heinrich, *comp*. Bibliographie historischer Zeitschriften 1939-1951. 3. Lieferung: Norwegen, Schweden, Dänemark, Finnland, Tschechoslowakei, Ungarn, Jugoslawien, Rumänien, Bulgarien, Griechenland, Polen, Baltische Länder, Sowjetunion. Marburg, O. Rasch, 1954. 366 p.

The compiler attempts to follow the course of historical periodicals during the period when many periodicals suspended publication or died altogether, and for which library records and holdings are woefully incomplete. With the best of intention, the question mark often takes the place of pertinent information. His conscientious search takes him through bewildering changes of titles and format often back into the nineteenth century, making this in effect a full-fledged bibliography of East European historical periodicals. For current periodicals, with authoritative listings for Eastern Europe, *see*: Eric H. Boehm, *Historical Periodicals; an Annotated World List of Historical and Related Serial Publications* (Santa Barbara, Calif., Clio Press, 1961, 618 p.).

79. Niederhauser, E. Beiträge zur Bibliographie der Geschichte der slawischen Völker in der ungarischen bürgerlichen Geschichtsschreibung. Studia Slavica (Budapest), v. 6, 1961: 457-473.

Hungarian historians have written a great deal about the history of Eastern Europe, yet their works, due to the language barrier, have remained largely unknown abroad. This welcome survey should go far toward reducing that ignorance; it reviews the whole of the Hungarian historiography relating to Eastern Europe from the latter part of the nineteenth century to 1945, listing both books and articles produced by the country's historians in Hungarian and other languages. The author's stated purpose is to describe briefly the works in question, not evaluate them. Such comments as he adds are on the whole moderate in tone. All Hungarian titles are translated into German.

Hungarian historiography about Eastern Europe since 1945 is surveyed in one section of Endre Arató's "Die ungarische Geschichtsschreibung nach 1945 und ihre Aufgaben," *Jahrbuch für Geschichte der UdSSR und der volksdemokratischen Länder Europas* (Berlin), v. 8, 1964: 409-419. Each work is briefly characterized but the Hungarian-language titles are not translated.

80. Novaia literatura po obshchim problemam slavianovedeniia (New literature on general problems of Slavic studies). 1966– Moskva. Quarterly.

See also entry no. 437.

Issued under the auspices of the Fundamental Library of Social Sciences of the USSR Academy of Sciences, this bibliographic serial includes entries referring to publications in both the Slavic and West European languages.

81. Spiru, Basil. Forschungen zur Geschichte der europäischen Volksdemokratien. Historische Forschungen in der DDR; Analysen und Berichte. Zeitschrift für Geschichtswissenschaft (Berlin), v. 8, 1960, Sonderheft: 474-507.

A survey of East German research, from 1945-1960, on the history of the "People's Democracies," divided into sections on Poland, Czechoslovakia, and Southeast Europe; it is part of a volume prepared for the Eleventh International Congress of Historical Sciences in Stockholm in 1960. Strident and aggressive in tone, it is useful for the record of the many publications on relations between Germany and her Eastern neighbors which East German historians have produced.

B. JOURNALS AND INSTITUTES*

1. West European Languages

82. East European Quarterly. 1967– Boulder, Colo. Quarterly.

The first and only journal in the West specifically devoted to Eastern Europe being issued under genuine international auspices, its editorial board consisting of scholars from both the West and the socialist bloc; United States, Canada, Britain, France, Czechoslovakia, Yugoslavia, and Poland are among the countries represented. Within its compass are the peoples of East Central Europe and the Balkans, with Russia, Germany, and Turkey included where relevant to the above. Ranges over the whole field of social sciences, the stress being on history. Deals with all historical periods and draws contributors from the international community, with articles published in English, French, and

* Only institutes publishing journals are listed.

German. Its predecessor, the *Journal of Central European Affairs* (Boulder, Colo., 1941-1964, 23 v.), founded and edited by S. Harrison Thomson, was the first learned journal in the West to focus attention on East Central Europe; it served as a publishing medium for a whole generation of North Americans interested in this terra incognita.

83. Eastern European Studies in History. 1967– New York, International Arts and Sciences Press. Quarterly.

Translations of articles from the historical journals of Albania, Bulgaria, Czechoslovakia, East Germany, Hungary, Poland, Romania, and Yugoslavia. The value of such a publication, designed to complement a similar one existing for the USSR, is obvious although only a fraction of the total scholarly output can be telescoped into the limited space available.

84. Jahrbuch für Geschichte der UdSSR und der volksdemokratischen Länder Europas. Bd. 1– 1956– Berlin, Rütten und Loening. Annual.

Published in Berlin and edited, beginning with volume 8 (1964), under the auspices of the Institut für Geschichte der europäischen Volksdemokratien, Karl-Marx-Universität, Leipzig. Marked by a rigid Marxist orthodoxy of the kind no longer upheld in most other East European countries. The only historical journal in the socialist bloc appearing in a Western language and concerned with the whole area. Its extensive historiographical reviews make it possible to follow the highlights of historical research throughout Eastern Europe without the knowledge of East European languages. Focuses on relations between Germany and her Eastern neighbors, including cultural contacts.

Volumes 1 and 2 issued as *Jahrbuch für Geschichte der deutsch-slawischen Beziehungen.*

85. Jahrbücher für Geschichte Osteuropas; neue Folge. Jahrg. 1– 1953– München, Osteuropa-Institut. Quarterly.

Supersedes *Jahrbücher für Kultur und Geschichte der Slaven,* (Breslau, Prietbatsch, 1924-1935, semiannual), and *Jahrbücher für Geschichte Osteuropas* (Breslau, Priebatsch, 1936-1941, quarterly).

Associated during the interwar period with the Osteuropa-Institut in Breslau (founded in 1918), then the most active German research center for Eastern Europe, this journal, with its supporting institute now established in Munich (founded in 1952), is heir to a long tradition of German Ostforschung. Today, frequent contributions in English, by English-speaking historians, lend it cosmopolitan flavor. Concentrates on Russia, Poland, the Baltic, and the problems common to the East European world; publishes valuable review articles on research. Much the same field is covered by:

Berlin. Freie Universität. *Osteuropa-Institut.* Forschungen zur osteuropäischen Geschichte. 1954– Irregular.

86. Kirche im Osten. Bd. 1– 1958– Stuttgart, Evangelisches Verlagswerk. Annual.

Articles on the history of the churches in Eastern Europe, Orthodox, Protestant and others. *See also*:

Kyrios; Vierteljahrsschrift für Kirchen- und Geistesgeschichte Osteuropas. 1.-6. Bd., Heft 1/2; 1936-1942/43; N.F., Bd. 1– 1960/61– Berlin, Lutherisches Verlagshaus H. Renner. Quarterly.

The above journals are Protestant. For the leading Roman Catholic journals, *see*:

Ostkirchliche Studien. 1952– Würzburg, Augustinus-Verlag. Quarterly. Articles in German, French, and English.

Orientalia christiana periodica; commentarii de re orientali aetatis christianae sacra et profana. v. 1– 1935– Rome, Pontificum institutum orientalium studium. Quarterly. Eastern Church, Byzantine history, Balkans; articles in English, French, German, Italian, Latin and Spanish.

Orientalia Christiana analecta. No. 1– 1923– Rome, Pontificum institutum orientalium studiorum. Irregular. Archaeology and history.

87. Österreichische Ost-Hefte. 1.– Jahrg.; September 1959– Wien, Österreichisches Ost- und Südosteuropa-Institut. Bimonthly.

A newcomer to the field, this journal has been rapidly transformed from an "upstart" into a vigorous and alert challenger in quest of new perspectives on old problems. Its interest runs the gamut of social sciences and the humanities, with the history of the Danubian region being among its primary concerns. Publishes shorter articles whose aim is to stimulate rather than purvey weighty scholarship. It seeks to overcome the legacy of division between the German-speaking peoples and the East Europeans, and pursues a specifically Austrian orientation. Has a lively section reporting on the progress of East European Studies, ranging from the work of top-notch research institutes to programs designed for the broadest audiences. Its pages now play host to articles penned by East European Marxist historians.

88. Revue d'histoire comparée; nouvelle série. Budapest, Paris, Institut Paul Teleki, 1943-1948. 7 v.

The Hungarians being less fortunate than the Slavs in finding champions abroad, their quandary compounded by the forbidding language, their historians find it difficult to plead their cause in the international arena; this journal specialized in comparative history of Danubian Europe, as viewed from Budapest, in the form of articles and reviews in French. Established by a group of young Hungarian historians in search of an understanding with Danube's non-Hungarian nationalities, its viewpoint is tempered by a sympathetic consideration shown to these nationalities. The promising experiment was cut short by political upheavals, and its supporting institute eventually absorbed (1951) by the reorganized Hungarian Academy of Sciences. A more assertive Hungarian viewpoint may be gleaned from the pages of *Archivum Europae Centro-Orientalis* (Budapest, 1935-1944, 10 v.), sponsored by the "Institut d'histoire de l'Europe orientale, à l'Université Pierre Pázmány, Budapest," and containing articles, bibliographies, and reviews in French and German, primarily on history, and to a lesser extent, on culture, literature, and languages of the peoples of East Central Europe.

89. Zeitschrift für Ostforschung. 1952– Marburg/Lahn, Johann Gottfried Herder Institut. Quarterly.

Specializes in the history of Czechoslovakia, Poland, and the former Baltic states, with emphasis on the role of the Germans. Publishes regular bibliographies. Views Poland's Oder-Neisse territories as a German possession temporarily under Polish administration. The institute also issues *Wissenschaftlicher Dienst für Ost-Mitteleuropa* (1951– monthly), consisting of translations and summaries of articles from the Czechoslovak, Polish, and Baltic press, highlighting significant developments in the humanities, social sciences, and the organization of science in general; also reports on émigré scholarly activity.

A journal specifically devoted to the past role of Germans in East and Southeast Europe is *Ostdeutsche Wissenschaft* (Bd. 1– 1954– München, R. Oldenbourg, annual). For shorter studies addressed to a wider audience, see *Der Donauraum* (1.– Jahrg.; 1956–, Salzburg, Forschungsinstitut für den Donauraum, quarterly), a mixed fare of history, economics, and current affairs of the Danubian region.

2. Other Languages

90. Roczniki dziejów społecznych i gospodarczych. Annales d'histoire sociale et économique. 1931– Poznań, Poznańskie Towarzystwo Przyjaciół Nauk. Annual.

Until the First World War, European economic and social history had been the exclusive domain of West European historians. One of the objectives of this journal (published originally in Lwów) was to redress this imbalance; in addition to providing a forum for Polish research, it undertook to publish reviews of the pertinent literature of Russia, Czechoslovakia, Hungary, Yugoslavia, and Bulgaria, in the hope that this would focus attention on Eastern Europe and that the results of this research would be integrated into the mainstream of European scholarship. For a journal dealing entirely with the agrarian history of Eastern Europe, *see*:

Ezhegodnik po agrarnoi istorii Vostochnoi Evropy (Yearbook of the agrarian history of Eastern Europe). 1958– Tallin. Annual. Each issue consists of papers presented at a symposium of this subject, held annually in different cities in the Soviet Union; published always in the city in which the symposium in question is held. Important contributions to the socioeconomic history of Eastern Europe often appear in the following Western journals:

International Review of Social History. v. 1– 1956– Assen Royal Van Gorcum. Three times yearly.

Annales; économies, société, civilisations. 1.– année; 1946– Paris, A. Colin. Quarterly.

Archiv für Sozialgeschichte. 1.– Bd.; 1961– Hannover, Verlag für Literatur und Zeitgeschehen. Annual.

91. Slovanský přehled (Slavic review). Roč. 1-31, 1899-1939; roč. 32–
The establishment in 1962 of this department, like the later comparable

1946– Praha, Československá akademie věd, Ústav dějin evropských socialistických zemí. Bimonthly.

The oldest Slavic review now in existence, it exercised considerable influence before the First World War in furthering mutual understanding among the Slavs. Later its quality fluctuated; in 1964 it was taken over by the Czechoslovak Academy's Institute for the History of the European Socialist Countries (founded in the same year), and constitutes its "official" organ. Includes shorter articles of popular-scientific character; in spite of the title, non-Slavic countries of the Bloc are within its purview. The foundation of the institute and the revitalization of the journal reflect the desire of Marxist historians to broaden their sights and to overcome the "ethnocentrism" of the period of the "cult of personality." The new institute assumed responsibility for two other established serials: *Byzantinoslavica* (année 1–; 1929–, Praha, Nakl. ČSAV., semiannual); *Slovanské historické studie* (Slavic historical studies) (1–, Praha, Nakl. Československé akademie věd, 1955–, irregular). Both are journals of high caliber, the former containing articles in Western languages, the latter foreign-language summaries.

The Slovak counterpart of the Czechoslovak institution is: Slovenská académia vied. Ústav dejín evrópskych socialistických krajín, in Bratislava, also founded in 1964. It has assumed publication of the annual *Slovanské štúdie* (Slavic studies), which first appeared in 1957.

92. Sovetskoe slavianovedenie (Soviet Slavic studies). 1965– Moskva, Akademiia nauk SSSR, Institut slavianovedeniia. Bimonthly.

The most comprehensive Slavic review now appearing in Eastern Europe, and the chief vehicle of Slavic scholarship in the Soviet Union. Concerned with the history and culture of the Slavs outside the USSR and their relations with the USSR. Reports on work of academies and universities throughout the socialist bloc, and on research plans. The product of the seven-year plan of the Institute (1959-1965), it was started in part as an answer to a successful development of Slavic studies in the West. The Institute has also sponsored two other series, *Kratkie soobshcheniia* (Short communications; 1951-1964) and *Uchenye zapiski* (Learned reports; 1949–). It is this institute founded in 1946, rather than the Academy's Institute of History, that constitutes the chief center of historical research relating to non-Soviet Slavs; it is under its auspices that the multivolume Russian histories of Czechoslovakia, Poland, Yugoslavia, and Bulgaria have been produced. Research in the history of Hungary and other non-Slavic countries is the task of the Academy's Institute of History (founded in 1936).

93. Studia z dziejów ZSSR i Europy Środkowej (Studies on the history of the USSR and Central Europe). t. 1– 1965– Wrocław, Zakład Narodowy im. Ossolińskich. Annual.

Issued under the sponsorship of the Zakład Historii ZSSR i Europy Środkowej (Department of the History of the USSR and Central Europe) of the Institute of History of the Polish Academy of Sciences.

institution in Czechoslovakia (*see* entry 97), was motivated by a desire to broaden the scope of historical investigation. This publication encompasses the history of the Balkans (with the exception of modern Greece), Austria, Hungary, Czechoslovakia, and the USSR, from 1848 to the mid-twentieth century. Special attention is paid to national and social movements as well as to the binding forces in the Bloc. The history of Poland and Germany is excluded except insofar as it involves contact with the other countries of the region. Contributors are from various socialist bloc countries; articles are provided with Western-language summaries. Book reviews.

C. HISTORIES OF THE SLAVS AND OF THE AREA; HISTORIOGRAPHY

94. Diels, Paul. Die slavischen Völker. Mit einer Literaturübersicht von Alexander Adamczyk. Wiesbaden, Harrassowitz, 1963. 381 p. Maps. Bibliography: p. 311-357. (Veröffentlichungen des Osteuropa-Institutes, München, Bd. 11)

See also entry no. 318.

This survey, by the late dean of German Slavists, is a valuable compendium of Slavic history and culture; comes close to being a one-volume encyclopedia, with separate chapters devoted to the history of each Slavic nation, to Slavic languages, literatures, law, music, religion, etc. The account is brought down to circa 1945. Includes a comprehensive bibliography by Alexander Adamczyk. *See also*:

Kohn, Hans, *ed.* Die Welt der Slawen, Bd. 1: Die West- und Südslawen; Bd. 2: Russen, Weissrussen, Ukrainer. Frankfurt am Main, Fischer Bücherei, 1960-1962. 2 v.

95. Dvornik, Francis. The Slavs in European History and Civilization. New Brunswick, N.J., Rutgers University Press, 1962. 688 p. Maps. Bibliography: p. 565-635.

See also entry no. 320.

The only major history of the Slavs in English. Covers the period from the early Middle Ages to 1848 (inclusive); the author's command of numerous languages — Slavic, non-Slavic and classical — lends an authentic flavor to his account, the greater part of which is concerned with Western and Southern Slavs. Though attempting to deal with social and economic history, the book's strength lies in cultural and political history. Like the author's other writings, this one too is marked by overtones of "Slavic nationalism." A Roman Catholic theologian, he strives to come to terms with Slav "heretics" (Jan Hus). An ecclesiastical historian by training, Dvornik has come to be recognized as a leading specialist on Slavdom in the English-speaking world. The above work may be viewed as a sequel to his *The Slavs; Their Early History and Civilization* (Boston, American Academy of Arts and Sciences, 1956, 394 p.), this being the only comprehensive account in English of the dawn of Slavic history. Dvornik's *The Making of Central and Eastern Europe* (London, The Polish Research Centre,

1949, 350 p.), examines the relations between Germany and its eastern neighbors during the period of the formation of national states (tenth and eleventh centuries); it is marred by many misprints of Slavic names. His first major work, *Les Slaves, Byzance et Rome au IX siècle* (Paris, Champion, 1926, 360 p.), and his *Les légendes de Constantin et de Méthode vues de Byzance* (Prague, Orbis, 1933, 433 p.), constitute an enduring contribution to the Cyrillo-Methodian question and are still a *conditio sine qua non* for anyone concerned with it.

96. Halecki, Oskar. Borderlands of Western Civilization; a History of East Central Europe. New York, Ronald Press Co., 1952. 503 p. Illus.

A pioneer work in English-language historiography; the first history of the entire region between the Baltic and the Adriatic presented in one sweep, by a Polish émigré historian. The supporting conception of history is Christian (Roman Catholic). Severe in judging the sins of the great powers (Germany and Russia), correspondingly indulgent in its judgment of the nations situated in between. The author had earlier made a plea for the recognition of East Central Europe, in spite of its differences, as a distinct complex, in his stimulating, methodologically-oriented volume, *The Limits and Divisions of European History* (New York, Sheed and Ward, 1950, 242 p.). Other works include:

Stadtmüller, Georg. Grundfragen der europäischen Geschichte. München, Oldenbourg, 1965. 281 p.

———. Geschichtliche Ostkunde. 2d ed. München, Bogen-Verlag, 1963. 2 v.

Roucek, J. S., *ed.* Central-Eastern Europe; Crucible of World Wars. New York, Prentice-Hall, 1946. 683 p.

Burks, Richard V. Some Elements of East European History. Washington, D.C., 1961. 26 p. (Service Center for Teachers of History, No. 38)

Arató, Endre. Kelet-Europá története a 19. században, I (History of Eastern Europe during the 19th century, I). Budapest, Tankönyvkiadó, 1968. 398 p.

97. McNeill, William H. Europe's Steppe Frontier, 1500-1800. Chicago, University of Chicago Press, 1964. 252 p. Maps. Bibliographical Essay: p. 223-235.

Views the history of the countries of Danubian and Pontic Europe as being determined by the common legacy of the steppe; challenges the traditional emphasis on the shaping role of nationalism. Based exclusively on Western-language sources.

98. Macůrek, Josef. Dějepisectví evropského východu (Historiography of the European East). Praha, Nákladem Historického klubu, 1946. 349 p.

The author, noted for his gift of synthesis, achieves the seemingly unachievable: a readable account, produced single-handedly, of the historiography of the polyglot region from the Baltic to the Adriatic, from the sixth to the twentieth century. Excludes Czech and Slovak, includes Byzantine and Turkish historians. In the first part of his work, he wrestles with the perennial difficulty of defining Eastern Europe.

A recent Marxist view of the dominant features of East European history is presented by J. Perényi's "L'est européen dans une synthèse d'histoire universelle," in *Nouvelles études historiques . . .* (v. 2, Budapest, Académie des sciences de Hongrie, 1965: 379-405). Also to be noted is Peter Hanák's "Problems of East European History in Recent Hungarian Historiography," *East European Quarterly*, v. 1 (1967): 123-142, which, in spite of its title, is a review of not merely Hungarian but of East European historiography.

99. Portal, Roger. Les Slaves, peuples et nations. Paris, A. Colin, 1965. 518 p. Illus., facsims., maps, ports. Bibliography: p. 437-442.

A semipopular survey of Slavic history and culture from the eighth century to the present. The treatment is chronological by periods and within each period by country or region. One-third of the volume deals with Western and Southern Slavs. Its value is enhanced by the attention the author pays to social and economic history, a feature which sets it apart from most other works of this nature.

A penetrating, if short, synthesis in English is provided by the late Harvard scholar S. H. Cross in his *Slavic Civilization Through the Ages*, edited by L. I. Strakhovsky (Cambridge, Harvard University Press, 1948, 195 p. Reprint: New York, Russell, 1963, 195 p.). *See also*:

Droz, Jacques. L'Europe, centrale; évolution historique de l'idée de "Mitteleuropa." Paris, Payot, 1960. 283 p. Traces the evolution of the concept of a supranational state in Central and East Central Europe, from Metternich to the present. The author appears to favor such a polity; restricted to the use of Western-language sources. Similar thoughts are expressed in Henry C. Meyer's *Mitteleuropa in German Thought and Action, 1815-1945* (The Hague, Nijhoff, 1955, 378 p.

100. Slované; kulturní obraz slovanského světa (Slavs; a cultural picture of the Slavic world). Praha, Vesmír, 1927-1929. 3 v.

Contents: díl 1: J. Bidlo. Dějiny Slovanstva (History of the Slavs); díl 2: F. Wollman. Slovesnost Slovanů (Literature of the Slavs); díl 3: F. Štůla and others: Zeměpisný obraz, statistika, ústavní zřízení a filosofie Slovanstva (Geographical picture, statistics, constitutional system and philosophy of the Slavs).

Written in the spirit of scientific popularization, this work seeks to identify the principal lines of development of the Slavic world, while treating the Slavs as an integral part of the European community. A Marxist treatment will be found in *Istoriia iuzhnykh i zapadnykh Slavian* (History of Southern and Western Slavs), edited by S. A. Nikitin and others (Moskva, Izdatel'stvo Moskovskogo universiteta, 1957, 573 p.). Though written originally as a university textbook, this is in fact a major survey, its importance underscored by the fact that it is the joint product of the labor of 15 Soviet specialists. New edition in preparation. A more recent Soviet treatment is *Istoriia pivdennikh i zakhidnikh Slovian* (History of Southern and Western Slavs), ed. by

V. A. Zhebokritskij and others (Kiev, Vid-vo Kiivskogo universitetu, 1966, 423 p.).

D. SPECIAL WORKS

1. Slavic Antiquities

101. Labuda, Gerard, *ed.* Słowiańszczyzna pierwotna; wybór tekstów (Early Slavs; selected readings). Warszawa, Państwowe Wydawnictwo Naukowe, 1954. 359 p. (Materiały Zrodłowe do Historii Polski Epoki Feudalnej, t. 1)

Selections, in Polish translation, from Greek, Roman, Byzantine, Arabic, Slavic and other sources, illustrating the origin and expansion of the ancient Slavs, the formation of the first Slavic states, conversion to Christianity, art of war, and social life. Ends with the year 1200 A.D.

Polish historians have performed the invaluable service of publishing systematic editions of original non-Slavic sources relating to early Slavs. The following volumes have appeared thus far:

Kupfer, Efraim F., *ed.* Źródła hebrajskie do dziejów Słowian i niektórych innych ludow Środkowej i Wschodniej Europy (Hebrew sources for the history of Slavs and certain other peoples of Central and Eastern Europe). Wróclaw, Zakład im. Ossolińskich, 1956. 321 p.

Lewicki, Tadeusz, *ed.* Źródła arabskie do dziejów Słowiańszczyzny (Arab sources for the history of the Slavs). Wrócław, Zakład im. Ossolińskich, 1956– (Źródła objaśniające początki Państwa Polskiego: Źródła orientalne, t. 1–)

Labuda, Gerard, *ed.* Źródła skandynawskie i anglosaskie do dziejów Słowiańszczyzny (Scandinavian and Anglo-Saxon sources for the history of the Slavs). Warszawa, Państwowe Wydawn. Naukowe, 1961. 261 p. Illus., fold. map. (Źródła objasniające początki Państwa Polskiego: Źródła nordyckie, t. 1)

Plezia, Marian, *ed and tr.* Greckie i łacińskie źródła do najstarszych dziejów Słowian (Greek and Latin sources for the earliest history of the Slavs). Poznań, Nakł. Polskiego Tow. Ludoznawczego, 1952. 201 p. (Prace etnologiczne, t. 3)

All volumes are provided with extensive commentaries; the original text is accompanied by a translation into Polish; for some documents a Latin translation is supplied, in addition to the Polish one, for the benefit of non-Polish scholars. To this may be added:

Tveretinova, Anna S., *ed.* Vostochnye istochniki po istorii narodov Iugo-Vostochnoi i Tsentral'noi Evropy (Eastern sources for the history of the peoples of Southeast and Central Europe). Moskva, "Nauka," 1964. 301 p. Documents and essays on the Oriental (Arabic, Turkish and Armenian) sources, by specialists from several East European countries; with foreign-language summaries or translations.

102. Lehr-Spławiński, Tadeusz. O pochodzeniu i praojczyźnie Słowian (On the origin and ancestral home of the Slavs). Poznań, Wydawn. Instytutu Zachodniego, 1946. 237 p. Maps. (Prace Instytutu Zachodniego, nr. 2)

See also entry no. 322.

The most significant work on the ethnogenesis of the Slavs since Šafárik and Niederle. More than any other volume since the Second World War, it stimulated a lively international dialogue; the author (d. 1965) was a prominent Polish specialist in Slavic linguistics, and a persuasive and erudite exponent of the "Vistula-Oder" hypothesis, which seeks the Slavic homeland in the basins of the Vistula and Oder rivers. Though a linguist, he marshalled a vast array of supporting evidence from other disciplines, not excluding the history of law. A shorter English version of this work is incorporated, under the same title, as a chapter in Zygmunt Wojciechowski's *Poland's Place in Europe* (Poznań, Instytut Zachodni, 1947, p. 63-83).

The main work by a Soviet linguist is Nikolai S. Derzhavin's *Slaviane v drevnosti* (The Slavs in antiquity) (Moskva, Izd-vo Akademii nauk SSSR, 1946, 215 p.), which is also available in German as *Die Slaven im Altertum; eine kulturhistorische Abhandlung* (Weimar, H. Böhlau, 1948, 286 p., maps, geneal. tables. Leipzig, Universität. Slavisches Institut. Arbeiten aus dem Gebiet der Slavistik in Übersetzung, Heft 1). It shows the influence of the theories of the Soviet linguist N. Ia. Marr, since discredited.

The main contributions since Niederle to Slavic origins and early culture by scholars of other disciplines:

Archaeology: Hensel, Witold. Słowiańszczyzna wczesnośredniowieczna; zarys kultury materialnej (The Slavs in the early Middle Ages; outline of material culture). 3d enl. ed. Warszawa, Państwowe Wydawnictwo Naukowe, 1965. 678 p. Illus., maps, col. plates, plans, bibliographical footnotes.

The second edition (1956) was translated into German as *Die Slawen im frühen Mittelalter; ihre materielle Kultur* (Berlin, Akademie-Verlag, 1965, 508 p.). The best one-volume account of the life of the ancient Slavs. Separate chapters deal with fishing, hunting, animal breeding, etc., and with over 20 different handicrafts. Special sections devoted to the Slavic house, dress, and hygiene and to transport and communications. Spans the period to the thirteenth century A.D. Based largely on archaeology.

Kostrzewski, Józef. Les origines de la civilisation polonaise; préhistoire-protohistoire. Translated by Bernard Hamel. Paris, Presses Universitaires, 1949. 671 p. Illus. (Publications de l'Institut occidental, no. 1) The Polish original is *Kultura prapolska* (Ancient Polish culture), 3d ed. (Warszawa, Państwowe Wydawnictwo Naukowe, 1962, 499 p.). In spite of its title, this work by a noted Polish archaeologist has implications transcending the Polish scene. Kostrzewski (b. 1885) trained several generations of Polish archaeologists and was the founder of the "neo-autochthonic" school which identified the much-disputed Lusatian Culture with Slavs and supported the "Vistula-Oder" hypothesis.

Korošec, Josip. Uvod v materialno kulturo Slovanov zgodnjega srednjega veka (Introduction to the material culture of early medieval Slavs). Ljubljana, Državna založba Slovenije, 1952. 403 p. Illus. The chief Yugoslav archeological contribution.

Tret'iakov, Petr N. Vostochnoslavianskie plemena (East Slavic tribes). 2d rev. and enl. ed. Moskva, Izd-vo Akademii nauk SSSR, 1953. 310 p. Illus. The chief Soviet archaeological contribution.

Anthropology: Czekanowski, Jan. Wstęp do historii Słowian; perspektywy antropologiczne, etnograficzne, archeologiczne i językowe (Introduction to the history of the Slavs; anthropological, ethnographical, archaeological and linguistic perspectives). 2d rev. and enl. ed. Poznań, Instytut Zachodni, 1957. 514 p. Illus., tables, maps. (Prace Instytutu Zachodniego, nr. 21) Here the Nestor of Polish anthropologists (d. 1965) applies the tools of his craft in order to contribute to the discussion. First published in 1927 in Lwów, the work opened new vistas in research regarding the question of the ethnogenesis of the Slavs.

Ethnography: Moszyński, Kazimierz. Kultura ludowa Słowian (Popular culture of the Slavs). Kraków, Polska Akademja Umiejętności, 1929-1939. 3 v. (2352 p.). Illus., maps, music. Uses ethnographical material as a basis for the study of ancient Slavic culture.

103. Niederle, Lubor. Slovanské starožitnosti (Slavic antiquities). Praha, Bursík a Kohout, 1902-1934. 7 v. in 12. Illus., plates, maps. (Biblioteka historická, čís. 4-15)

See also entry no. 326.

Contents: Oddíl historický (Historical section), 1902-1924, 4 v. in 6; Oddíl kulturní; život starých Slovanů (Cultural section; life of the ancient Slavs), 1911-1934, 3 v. in 6 (v. 2, pt. 2 by Th. Saturník, Praha, 1934). A classic in its field, by a Czech scholar who was the last to master the whole range of Slavic antiquities and whose achievement today could only be matched by a task force of archaeologists, linguists, ethnographers, and historians. Niederle brought a number of disciplines to bear on his subject, producing a synthesis the main outlines of which have been reinforced rather than refuted by recent research. The findings of this work must be supplemented by the archaeological discoveries of the last 15 years. Its present value lies, among other things, in the thorough exposition of written sources. Published in the following abridged versions: *Manuel de l'antiquité slave* (Paris, Champion, 1923-1926, 2 v.); *Rukověť slovanských starožitností* (A manual of Slavic antiquities) (Praha, Československá akademie věd, 1953, 513 p.); *Slavianskie drevnosti* (Slavic antiquities) (Moskva, Izdatel'stvo inostrannoi literatury, 1956, 449 p.).

Niederle's work is being periodically reviewed and revised in *Vznik a počátky Slovanů* (Origins and beginnings of the Slavs) (Praha, Nakl. Československé akademie věd, 1956–, irregular). Beginning with volume six (1966), it publishes contributions in Western languages only and bears the title *Origine et débuts des Slaves.*

A complete updating of Niederle's work is offered by Jan Eisner's Rukověť slovanské archeologie: počátky Slovanů a jejich kultury (Manual of Slavic archaeology; the origins of the Slavs and their culture) (Praha, Academia, 1966–). To be completed in three volumes, it presents a survey of archaeological research between the years 1930 and 1963.

A valuable statistical survey of Slavdom, extracted by Aleš Hrdlička from Niederle's *Slovanský svět; Zeměpisný a statistický obraz současného slovanstva* (The Slavic world; a geographical and statistical picture of contemporary Slavdom) (Praha, Nákladem J. Laichtera, 1909, 197 p.), was published as "Geographical and Statistical Views of the Contemporary Slav Peoples" in the Smithsonian Institution's *Annual Report for 1910* (Washington, U.S. Govt. Print. Off., 1911, p. 599-612). *See also*:

Niederle, Lubor. La race slave; statistique, démographie, anthropologie. Paris, F. Alcan, 1911. 231 p. Fold. map. Bibliography: p. 219-231.

104. Polska Akademia Nauk. *Komitet Słowianoznawstwa. Słownik starożytności słowiańskich* (A dictionary of Slavic antiquities). Edited by Władysław Kowalenko and others. Wrocław, Zakład Narodowy im. Ossolińskich, 1961– Illus., maps.

See also entries no. 327 *and* 2527.

A monumental project, sponsored by the Committee on Slavic Studies of the Polish Academy of Sciences and undertaken with the cooperation of the leading scholars from various Slavic countries on the occasion of the Polish millennium. Constitutes a fourth attempt to produce a reference work of this kind, the three previous ones (Russian, German, Polish) having failed. Spans the period from the earliest times to 1200 A.D. Appears in fascicles, the total to include five or six volumes. Illustrations, genealogical tables for earliest Slavic dynasties, plans of buildings, maps. An engrossing panorama offering facts on topics ranging from "Slavs in Africa" to "debtors" among early Slavs. Both archaeological and written sources (23 separate entries for medieval German annals bearing on Slavic problems) are within this dictionary's scope.

See also Konrad Jażdżewski's *Atlas to the Prehistory of the Slavs* (Łódź, 1948-1949, 2 pts. Acta Praehistorica Universitatis Lodziensis, 1, 2). Contains 20 colored maps. It appeared in Polish as *Atlas do pradziejów Słowian* (Łódź, 1948-1949, 2 pts.). The only monograph on the first Slavic state is Gerard Labuda's *Pierwsze państwo Słowiańskie, państwo Samona* (The first Slavic state of Samo) (Poznań, Księgarnia akademicka, 1949, 357 p., illus., fold. maps).

105. Preidel, H. Slawische Altertumskunde des östlichen Mitteleuropas im 9. und 10. Jahrhundert. Gräfelfing bei München, E. Gans, 1961-1964. 2 v. Illus. (Adalbert-Stifter-Verein, München. Veröffentlichungen der Wissenschaftlichen Abteilung, 6, 9)

The only recent Western contribution of substance to Slavic antiquities. The author, an archaeologist of Sudeten German origin, criticizes many conclusions drawn by Slavic scholars from recent discoveries; occasionally lapses into a sharp, polemical tone. *See also*: Reinhold Trautmann's *Die slavischen Völker und Sprachen; eine Einführung in die Slavistik* (Göttingen, Vandenhoeck und Ruprecht, 1947, 173 p.), and the short study by Karl Treimer, *Ethnogenese der Slawen* (Wien, Gerold, 1954, 115 p.).

106. Šafárik, Pavel J. Slovanské starožitnosti (Slavic antiquities). 2d ed. Praha, B. Tempský, 1862-1863. 2 v. (*His* Sebrané spisy, díl 1-2).

The founding work of Slavic antiquities by a scholar of Slovak origin, it was first published in fascicle form in 1836-1837. By a most diligent examination of sources, Šafárik proved — as was his intention — that the Slavs were ancient members of the Indo-European family, with a claim to a past as legitimate as their claim to a future. The work became a success and, through translations, gained the author international recognition. Though Šafárik was a cautious scholar, the work inevitably bears the character of an apologia — albeit a learned one. Along with Kollár's *Daughter of Sláva*, it became a Slavic "best seller," paving the way for the Slavic emancipation movement of 1848. Subsequent research has invalidated many of Šafárik's theses, but the measure of his accomplishment is indicated by the fact that what he proved will never need to be proved again. Translations include: *Slavianskie drevnosti* (Moscow, v. universitetskoi tip., 1848, 2 v.); *Slawische Alterthümer* (Leipzig, W. Engelmann, 1843-1844, 2 v.); *Starożytności słowianskie* (Poznań, W. Stefański, 1844, 2 v.). The companion volume is:

Šafárik, Pavel J. Slovanský národopis (Ethnography of the Slavs). 4th ed. Edited by Hana Hlynková and others. Praha, Československá Akademie věd, 1955. 288 p. Port., fold. maps, diagrs. (Československá akademie věd. Ústav pro ethnografii a folkloristiku. Klasikové vědy. Sekce filosofie a historie, sv. 2) This is the latest edition of a work first published in Prague in 1842.

2. Cyril and Methodius*

107. Georgiev, Emil I. Kiril i Metodii, osnovopoloznitsi na slavianskite literaturi (Cyril and Methodius, founders of Slavic literature). Sofiia, Bulgarska akademii na naukite, 1956. 293 p. Bibliographical footnotes.

The chief recent Bulgarian contribution by that country's specialist in Slavic and Church-Slavic literature. Almost alone among Slavists, the author still holds that the Cyrillic script preceded the Glagolitic.

108. Grivec, Franc. Konstantin und Method, Lehrer der Slaven. Wiesbaden, O. Harrassowitz, 1960. 270 p. Bibliography: p. 11-16.

With this volume — which may be regarded as a testament — the late (d. 1963) Slovene Catholic theologian and historian capped a lifetime devoted to the Cyrillo-Methodian question. The most authoritative survey in a Western language of the life and significance of the "Apostles of the Slavs," it treats its theme entirely at the religious and cultural level, with the political forces given little consideration. The author's view of the apostles as conscious advocates of the unity of Latin and Orthodox Christendom is influenced by his own lifelong dedication to this goal. The appendix includes a valuable history of *Quellenforschung* and a survey of manuscript sources. The Slovene edition, somewhat more popular, was published as: *Slovanska blagovestnika sv. Ciril in Metod 863-1963* (The Slav apostles SS. Cyril and

* *See also* the preceding section and the chapter on Czechoslovakia's history.

Methodius) (Celje, Mohorjeva družba, 1963, 241 p., illus., maps. Bibliography: p. 239-241). The companion volume is:

Grivec, Franc, *and* F. Tomšič, *eds.*, Constantinus et Methodius Thessalonicenses. Fontes. Zagreb, 1960. 274 p. (Zagreb. Staroslavenski institut. Radovi, knjiga 4) Contains new critical editions of the Church Slavonic *Vita Constantini* and *Vita Methodii*, with a Latin translation and commentaries. Also a text of the principal Latin sources, based on existing editions.

A few important sources (largely hagiographical) for Constantine and Methodius in German translation are collected in Josef Bujnoch's *Zwischen Rom und Byzanz; Leben und Wirken der Slavenapostel Kyrillos und Methodios . . .* (Graz, Verlag Styria, 1958, 197 p., Slavische Geschichtsschreiber, Bd. 1). This supplies a commentary, but not without inaccuracies in rendering the originals. No comparable source book exists in English or any other Western language.

109. Hellmann, Manfred, *ed.* Cyrillo-Methodiana; zur Frühgeschichte des Christentums bei den Slaven 863-1963. Köln, Böhlau, 1964. 505 p. Illus., maps, plans, bibliographical footnotes. (Slavistische Forschungen, Bd. 6)

A collection of 26 studies, published on the occasion of the 1,100th anniversary of the arrival of Cyril and Methodius in Moravia, and contributed to by scholars from both Western and Eastern Europe and the United States. History, philology, and archaeology are all represented. Another worthy product of labors stimulated by the anniversary is P. Duthilleul's *L'Evangélisation des Slaves; Cyrille et Méthode* (Tournai, Desclée, 1963, 201 p., Bibliothèque de la théologie, Ser. 4. Histoire de la théologie, t. 5).

110. Lacko, Michael. Saints Cyril and Methodius. Rome, Slovak Editions "Sts. Cyril and Methodius," 1963. 235 p. Illus., maps.

A short work, without an *apparatus criticus*, intended for a wider audience; the only account in English specifically devoted to this subject. Has illustrations and photographs of the landmarks. Available in Slovak as: *Sv. Cyril a Metod* (Rím, Slovenské vydavatel'stvo Sv. Cyrila a Metoda, 1963, 222 p.). *See also* the symposium on Cyril and Methodius by Francis Dvornik, Ihor Ševčenko, and H. Lunt, in *Slavic Review* (Seattle), v. 23, 1964: 195-236.

111. Das östliche Mitteleuropa in Geschichte und Gegenwart. Acta Congressus historiae Slavicae Salisburgensis in memoriam SS. Cyrilli et Methodii anno 1963 celebrati. Wiesbaden, Harrassowitz, 1966. 252 p. (Annales Instituti slavici, Bd. 1/2)

3. Spring of the Nations: 1848; National Movements

112. Kohn, Hans. Pan-Slavism; Its History and Ideology. Notre Dame, Ind., University of Notre Dame Press, 1953. 356 p. Bibliography: p. 339-348.

See also entries no. 182, 358, *and* 447.

Lucidly written and highly informed, by a lifelong student of the Slavs. A second, revised edition appeared in 1960 (New York, Vintage Books, 468 p.).

Kohn's pioneer work on nationalism in general, with extensive sections on East Central Europe and the Slavs, is *The Idea of Nationalism* (New York, Macmillan, 1944, 735 p. Reprinted: New York, Macmillan, 1961). Translated into German as *Die Idee des Nationalismus* (Heidelberg, L. Schneider, 1950, 971 p.). A concise version was published as *Nationalism; Its Meaning and History* (Princeton, N. J., Van Nostrand, 1965, 192 p.).

A strongly pro-Slavic point of view is Edvard Beněs' *Où vont les Slaves? Úvahy o slovanství (Essais sur le slavisme)* (Paris, Editions de Notre Temps, 1948, 317 p.). Czech original: *Úvahy o slovanství* (Reflections on Slavism) (2d ed., Praha, Čin, 1947, 366 p. 1st ed., London, 1944). A history of the movement of Slavic reciprocity, with concluding reflections strongly shaped by the sentiments generated by the Second World War; important as an authoritative Slavic voice of the former president of Czechoslovakia.

A pro-German viewpoint, also influenced by a world war — the first — is Alfred Fischel's *Der Panslawismus bis zum Weltkrieg* (Stuttgart, Berlin, Cotta, 1919, 590 p.). The first major history of Pan-Slavism; may be still consulted with profit. See also *Geschichtsbewusstsein in Ost-Mitteleuropa*, edited by Ernst Birke (Marburg/Lahn, N. G. Elwert-Verlag, 1961, 149 p.).

113. Namier, Lewis B. 1848; the Revolution of the Intellectuals. London, G. Cumberlege, 1944. 124 p.

A trenchant and at times refreshingly irreverent view of an irreverent year in Central and East Central Europe, based on sources in a wide range of languages. No partisan will derive comfort, but everybody will benefit from the perusal of this short work, originally prepared as a Raleigh Lecture on History and delivered in 1944. First published in the *Proceedings of the British Academy* (London), 1944: 161-282. Paperback reprint: Garden City, N. Y., Anchor Books, 1964, 153 p.

The centenary of the revolution in 1948 produced a number of works in 1848. The *Slavonic and East European Review* (London) devoted special sections to that subject in volumes 26 (1947-1948) and 27 (1948-1949). For East Central Europe *see also*:

Fejtö, François, *ed.* The Opening of an Era; an Historical Symposium. London, A. Wingate, 1948. 443 p.

Akademiia nauk SSSR. *Institut istorii.* Revoliutsii 1848-1849 (The Revolutions of 1848-1849). Edited by F. V. Potemkin and A. I. Moloka. Moskva, Izd-vo Akademii nauk SSSR, 1952. 2 v. Illus., ports., maps, facsims. Bibliography: v. 2, p. 487-559.

W stulecie wiosny ludów, 1848-1948; wydawnictwo zbiorowe. Edited by Natalia Gąsiorowska. Warszawa, Państwowy Instytut Wydawniczy, 1948-1953. 5 v. The French original is: *Le printemps des peuples, 1848 dans le monde* (Paris, Editions de minuit, 1948, 2 v.).

114. Sjezd slovanský. *1st, Prague, 1848.* Slovanský sjezd v Praze roku 1848; sbírka dokumentů (The Slavic Congress in Prague in the year

1848; a collection of documents). Edited by Václav Žáček and Zdeněk Tobolka. Praha, Nakl. Československé akademie věd, 1958. 614 p. Illus., ports.

The Congress was the first open manifestation of Slavic awakening. This collection includes protocols of meetings, letters, newspaper accounts, and police reports. Documents — some being published for the first time — are reproduced in the original languages, untranslated, except for Hungarian-language documents which are reproduced in the original and in Czech translation. The Congress still awaits its historian; the only history is the short work by Zdeněk Tobolka, *Slovanský sjezd v Praze roku 1848* (The Slavic Congress in Prague in 1848) (Praha, F. Šimáček, 1901, 240 p.). For the pre-1848 background, *see*:

Prelog, Milan. Slavenska renesansa, 1780-1848 (Slavic renaissance, 1780-1848). Zagreb, Nakl. Jugoslovenske štampe, 1924. 484 p. (Istorijska biblioteka, knjiga 1) Bibliography: p. 458-466. This is the first history of the national awakening encompassing all Slavic peoples; still valuable.

Wollman, Frank. Slovanství v jazykově literárním obrození u Slovanů (Slavism in the linguistic-literary renaissance of the Slavs). Praha, Státní pedagogické nakl., 1958. 230 p. Bibliography: p. 211-231. (Spisy University v Brně, Filosofická fakulta, 52) An unusually provocative treatment, offering new perspectives.

Kolejka, Iosef. Slavianskie programmy i ideia slavianskoi solidarnosti v XIX vekakh (Slavic programs and the idea of Slavic solidarity in the 19th and 20th centuries). Praga, Státní pedagogické nakl., 1964. 261 p. (Spisy University v Brně, Filosofická fakulta, 98)

115. Žaček, Václav. Čechové a Poláci roku 1848; studie k novodobým politickým stykům česko-polským (Czechs and Poles in 1848; a study on more recent Czech-Polish political relations). Praha, Nákladem Slovanského ústavu a Slovanského výboru Československa, 1947-1948. 2 v. (Slovanský ústav v Praze. Práce, sv. 22-23)

Volume 1 covers the years from circa 1830 to 1847, volume 2, the year 1848 proper. Based on a thorough research of archival sources, explores in great detail the Czech-Polish relationship during the period covered. Much attention is given to the collaboration between the radicals of the two nationalities. Not likely to be superseded in the foreseeable future. Has French summary. The Hungarian-Polish relationship is the subject of:

Russjan, Lucjan. Polacy i sprawa polska na Węgrzech w roku 1848-1849 (Poles and the Polish question in Hungary in the years 1848-1849). Warszawa, Towarzystwo Naukowe Warszawskie, 1934. 302 p. Bibliography: p. 1-11. Résumé in French. (Towarzystwo Naukowe Warszawskie. Rozprawy historyczne, tom 13, zeszyt 2).

4. The Habsburg Monarchy

116. Kann, Robert A. The Multinational Empire; Nationalism and National Reform in the Habsburg Monarchy, 1848-1918. New York,

Columbia University Press, 1950. 2 v. Reprint: New York, Octagon Books, 1964. 2 v. Bibliography: v. 2, p. 375-380.

An encyclopedic work, by far the most comprehensive on the subject in English by a single author; each nationality is given a just treatment, in a separate chapter. Based on Western-language sources, but Slavic, Hungarian, and other works are listed in the bibliography, which is brought completely up to date in the second revised edition, available only in German: *Das Nationalitätenproblem der Habsburgermonarchie* (Graz, Böhlau, 1964, 2 v.). *See also* the sociologically-oriented short volume by the same author: *The Habsburg Empire; a Study in Integration and Disintegration* (New York, Praeger, 1957, 227 p.). The same problem is treated by several authors in "The Nationality Problem in the Habsburg Monarchy in the Nineteenth Century: A Critical Appraisal," *Austrian History Yearbook* (Houston), v. 3, 1967. Consists of papers and comments presented at an international conference held at Indiana University in April 1966. The contributors are from both the West and the socialist bloc, and the papers represent the principal currents of research and thought on the subject today. All contributions, as printed, are in English. Shorter surveys:

Taylor, A. J. P. The Habsburg Monarchy, 1809-1918. 2d ed. London, Hamish Hamilton, 1948. 279 p.; London, Penguin Books, 1964. More stimulating than reliable.

Kohn, Hans. The Habsburg Empire, 1804-1918. Princeton, N.J., Van Nostrand, 1961. 87 p.

Jelavich, Charles, *ed.* The Habsburg Monarchy; Toward a Multinational Empire or National States? New York, Rinehart, 1959. 57 p. A few of the important sources, in English translation, are most conveniently brought together and introduced in this booklet.

To keep abreast of research, the historian should follow the *Austrian History Yearbook* (1965– Houston, Rice University, annual). Gives generous coverage to non-German nationalities; within its purview are the Habsburg Monarchy to 1918 and Austria and Hungary after that year.

117. Uhlirz, Mathilde, *and* Karl Uhlirz. Handbuch der Geschichte Österreichs und seiner Nachbarländer Böhmen und Ungarn. Graz, Leuschner & Lubensky, 1927-1944. 4 v. in 5.

Important for its vast bibliographical apparatus and for its detailed indexes (in volume 4), especially the 125-page author index. The last volumes influenced by National Socialist and anti-Semitic ideology. As a bibliographical guide, will retain its value for years to come. A revised edition is under way as:

Uhlirz, Karl. Handbuch der Geschichte Österreich-Ungarns. 2d ed., rev. and enl. by Mathilde Uhlirz. Graz, H. Böhlaus Nachf., 1963. Bd. 1: -1526. 487 p.

Redlich, Joseph. Das Österreichische Staats- und Reichsproblem; geschichtliche Darstellung der inneren Politik der Habsburgischen Monarchie von 1848 bis zum Untergang des Reiches. Leipzig, P. Reinhold, 1920-1926. 2 v. The magnum opus in German on the constitutional and nationalist conflicts of the monarchy from 1848 to 1918. *See* also:

Eisenmann, Louis. Le compromis austro-hongrois de 1867 — étude sur le dualisme. Paris, Société nouvelle de librairie et d'édition (G. Bellais), 1904. 695 p. Bibliography: p. xiii-xx. The title does not do justice to this masterful study which treats the whole period before 1867. Uses Hungarian-language sources, in addition to Slavic and Western ones.

118. Zeman, Z. A. B. The Break-up of the Habsburg Empire, 1914-1918; a Study in National and Social Revolution. London, New York, Oxford University Press, 1961. 274 p. Maps. Bibliography: p. 257-265. *See also* entry no. 191.

A volume modest of size, but affording new insights into the revolutionary forces that precipitated the collapse of the Habsburg Empire. Based in part on research in Vienna archives; the author uses both Western and Slavic languages. The same subject is explored in:

May, Arthur J. The Passing of the Hapsburg Monarchy, 1914-1918. Philadelphia, University of Pennsylvania Press, 1966. 2 v. Bibliography: v. 2, p. 827-848. Fortified by archival research and based on Western-language sources. A sequel to the author's *The Hapsburg Monarchy, 1867-1914* (Cambridge, Mass., Harvard University Press, 1951, 532 p. Bibliography: p. 513-522). Reprinted in 1965. *See also*:

Jászi, Oscar. The Dissolution of the Habsburg Monarchy. Chicago, University of Chicago Press, 1929. 482 p. Reprinted, 1961. (Phoenix Books, P70). The first study in English to probe thoroughly the social and economic background of the monarchy's disintegration.

119. Zwitter, Fran. Les Problèmes nationaux dans la monarchie des Habsbourg. Beograd, Comité National Yougoslave des Sciences Historiques, 1960. 148 p.

A concise but skillfully presented survey of the main national issues and conflicts in the Habsburg monarchy, by Yugoslavia's leading specialists. Written from a moderate Marxist viewpoint. Available in Slovene as: *Nacionalni problemi v habsburški monarhiji* (Ljubljana, Slovenska Matica, 1962, 230 p., maps). The main Polish Marxist contribution, likewise moderate, is Henryk Batowski's *Rozpad Austro-Węgier, 1914-1918; sprawy narodowościowe i działania dyplomatyczne* (The collapse of Austria-Hungary, 1914-1918; national questions and diplomatic developments) (Wrocław, Zakład Narodowy im. Ossolińskich, 1965, 270 p., ports.). The chief Soviet study is:

Rubinshtein, Evengiia I. Krushenie Avstro-Vengerskoi Monarkhii (The collapse of the Austro-Hungarian monarchy). Moskva, Izd-vo Akademii nauk SSSR, 1963. 427 p. Bibliography: p. 396-415. The authoress' merit lies in drawing attention to social discontent within the monarchy and to the influence of the Russian Revolutions of 1917, as factors involved in the monarchy's collapse. Apart from this, hers is the customary dogmatic Marxist tale in which the workers can do no wrong and the "bourgeoisie" no right, no matter how hard they try. The bibliographical appendix contains 77 separately listed titles by Lenin, and three by Khrushchev. *See also*:

Akademiia nauk SSSR. *Institut slavianovedeniia.* Avstro-Vengriia i slaviano-germanskie otnosheniia (Austria-Hungary and Slav-German relations). Edited by V. D. Koroliuk. Moskva, Nauka, 1965. 282 p.

5. Relations between States

120. Akademiia nauk SSSR. *Institut slavianovedeniia.* Mezhdunarodnye otnosheniia v Tsentral'noi i Vostochnoi Evrope i ikh istoriografiia (International relations in Central and Eastern Europe and their historiography). Moskva, Nauka, 1966. 281 p.

Collection of studies on international relations among Slavic countries, from the 16th century to the present, with some special attention paid to revolutionary movements. For an earlier period *see*:

Grekov, I. B. Ocherki po istorii mezhdunarodnykh otnoshenii vostochnoi Evropy XIV-XVI vv. (Essays on the history of the international relations of Eastern Europe during the 14th to 16th centuries). Moskva, Izdatel'stvo vostochnoi literatury, 1963. 373 p. *See also*:

Akademiia nauk SSSR. *Institut slavianovedeniia.* Oktiabr'skaia revoliutsiia i zarubezhnye slavianskie narody; sbornik statei (The October Revolution and the non-Soviet Slavic nations; a collection of studies). Edited by A. Ia. Manusevich. Moskva, Gospolitizdat, 1957. 385 p. Emphasizes, and exaggerates, the significance of the October Revolution as a factor responsible for the formation of new Slavic national states in 1918.

121. Birke, Ernst. Frankreich und Ostmitteleuropa im 19. Jahrhundert; Beiträge zur Politik und Geschichte. Köln, Böhlau, 1960. 527 p. Fold. maps, facsim. Bibliography: p. 493-517. (Ostmitteleuropa in Vergangenheit und Gegenwart, 6)

The author dwells on official and intellectual rather than popular contacts, and fills a gap in historiography by this account of French policy toward Poland, Bohemia, Hungary, and Romania, from the French Revolution to the end of the 19th century. The book has helpful sections on the influential French historians Leger and Denis who represent the founding generation of Slavic studies in France.

For more recent French policy, *see* Piotr S. Wandycz's *France and Her Eastern Allies, 1919-1925; French-Czechoslovak-Polish Relations from the Paris Peace Conference to Locarno* (Minneapolis, University of Minnesota Press, 1962, 454 p., maps. Bibliographical essay: p. 407-425). For U.S. policy, *see* Victor S. Mamatey's *The United States and East Central Europe, 1914-1918; A Study in Wilsonian Diplomacy and Propaganda* (Princeton, N. J., Princeton University Press, 1957, 431 p. Bibliography: p. 385-401.

122. Československá akademie věd. *Ústav dějin evropských socialistických zemí. Češi a Poláci v minulosti* (Czechs and Poles in the past). Praha, Nakl. Československé akademie věd, 1964-1967. 2 v. Illus., facsims., maps, bibliographies.

See also entry no. 731.

A history of political, economic, and cultural relations between Czechs and Poles. Unlike most works of this kind, this one is not only based on secondary literature, but also incorporates new research. Though the product of many hands, it is not merely a series of contributions, but a systematic and exhaustive treatment of the subject, unmatched by any other work. Volume 1 edited by Josef Macůrek; volume 2 edited by Václav Žáček. A more modest contribution to the subject is:

Wojciechowski, Zygmunt, *ed.* Polska-Czechy, dziesięc wieków sąsiedztwa (Poland-Bohemia, neighbors of a thousand years). Katowice, 1947. 315 p. (Pamietnik Instytutu Sląskiego, Seria II, 7) Bibliography: p. 307-315). Political and cultural relations from the tenth century to 1945. For relations between Poles and Slovaks, *see*:

Poliaci a my. K tisícročnej tradícii slovensko-pol'ských vzt'ahoch (Poles and we; a thousand year tradition of Slovak-Polish relations). Bratislava, Osveta, 1964. 199 p. Illus., facsims., ports. Addressed to a wider audience, this volume is noteworthy as the first attempt at a synthesis of Slovak-Polish relations from the early Middle Ages to the present.

Heymann, Frederick G. Poland and Czechoslovakia. Englewood Cliffs, N. J., Prentice-Hall, 1966. 181 p. Bibliography: p. 163-171. This is an introduction to the history of Western Slavs rather than a history of Polish-Czechoslovak relations.

123. Československá akademie věd. Československo-bulharské vztahy v zrcadle staletí; sborník vědeckých prací (Czechoslovak-Bulgarian relations in the mirror of the centuries; a collection of scholarly studies). Edited by Bohuslav Havránek. Praha, 1963. 439 p.

Issued by the Czechoslovak Academy of Sciences, but a joint product of the Bulgarian and Czechoslovak Academies of Sciences. Contributions by both Czechoslovak and Bulgarian scholars; half of the volume is devoted to history, the balance to literature and linguistics. Résumés in French and Russian.

Yugoslavia's relations with the countries of East Central Europe are conveniently presented, with bibliographies, in survey articles in the *Enciklopedija Jugoslavije* (Yugoslav encyclopedia) (Zagreb, Leksikografski zavod SFRJ, 1955–). *See* "Češkoslovačko-južnoslavenski odnosi" (Czechoslovak-Yugoslav relations), v. 2, 1956: 557-572; "Madarsko-jugoslavenski kulturni odnosi" (Hungarian-Yugoslav relations), v. 5, 1962: 583-594; "Poljsko-jugoslavenski odnosi" (Polish-Yugoslav relations), v. 6, 1965: 534-549. The outstanding features of the above articles are the exhaustive lists of translations of Yugoslav literary works into the respective foreign languages, and of the respective foreign works into the Yugoslav languages.

124. Huszár, Károly, *ed.* Magyarország és Lengyelország. Magyar-lengyel kapcsolatok a történelemben, a kultúrában és gazdasági téren (Hungary and Poland. Hungarian-Polish relations in history, culture, and economics. Budapest, Forbát, 1936. 400 p.

Favored by an absence of common frontiers and an historical presence of common foes, Poles and Magyars have established a record of perhaps the friendliest relations of any two nationalities in Eastern

Europe. This volume, a joint Polish-Hungarian undertaking, is a tribute to that record. The Polish edition is *Polska i Węgry; stosunki polsko-węgierskie w historji, kulturze i gospodarstwie* (Budapeszt, 1936, 462 p., illus., ports., map). A more recent testimonial to this fact is:

Academiae Cracoviensi 600 annis ante fundatae. Slavica; Annales Instituti Philologiae Slavicae Universitatis Debreceniensis de Ludvigo Kossuth nominatae (Debrecen, Hungary), v. 4, 1964. 163 p. The entire issue of this serial is devoted to the history of Polish-Hungarian relations, on the occasion of the 600th anniversary of the foundation of the University of Kraków; all contributions are in languages other than Hungarian.

125. Kovács, Endre, *and* Jan Novotny. Mad'aři a my; z dějin mad'arsko-československých vztahů (The Hungarians and we; the history of Hungarian-Czechoslovak relations). Praha, Státní nakladatelství politické literatury, 1959. 313 p. Illus.

See also entry no. 891.

The Hungarian original, *Magyar-cseh történelmi kapcsolatok* (Budapest, Közoktatasügyi Kiadovallalat, 1952, 375 p.), is not without serious defects; the Czech text represents not merely a translation, but a revised and improved version, prepared with the collaboration of the Czechoslovak historian Jan Novotný.

126. Matl, J. Europa und die Slaven. Wiesbaden, O. Harrassowitz, 1964. 357 p.

Essays by Austria's historian-Slavist telling the story of cultural contacts between Slavs (chiefly Western and Southern Slavs) and Western Europe. Written with objectivity; by concentrating on peaceful and friendly contacts, the work serves as a healthy antidote to the oft-told drama of German-Slav conflict. *See also*:

Ost und West in der Geschichte des Denkens und der kulturellen Beziehungen. Festschrift für Eduard Winter zum 70. Geburtstag. Introduction by A. P. Juskevic. Edited by W. Steinitz. Berlin, Akademie-Verlag, 1966. 816 p. (Quellen und Studien zur Geschichte Osteuropas, Bd. 15). Chronologische Bibliographie der Veröffentlichungen von Eduard Winter von 1924 bis 1965, prepared by C. Grau und I. Flentje: p. 5-27.

6. German Eastward Movement and Relations between Germany and Eastern Europe

127. Akademiia nauk SSSR. *Institut slavianovedeniia.* Slaviano-germanskie issledovaniia (Slav-German studies). Moskva, Izd-vo Akademii nauk SSSR, 1963. 442 p.

The first product of a "work group" on Slav-German relations, formed at the Institute of Slavic Studies of the Academy of Sciences of the USSR, for the purpose of conducting research and publication on relations between Germany and non-Soviet Slavs. Contributions by Soviet, East German, Bulgarian, and Czechoslovak scholars. Highly polemical, emphasizes the modern period. The "work group" has since been publishing studies at the rate of one volume yearly.

128. Fischer, Fritz. Germany's Aims in the First World War. Translated from the German, with an introduction by James Joll. London, Chatto and Windus, 1967. 652 p. Illus., maps, ports. Bibliography: p. 639-644.

The most significant — and most controversial — product of German historiography since the Second World War. On the basis of hitherto unknown archival documents, the author constructs a powerful indictment of German civilian and military leadership during the First World War, charging it with expansionist goals, in particular vis-à-vis Germany's neighbors in Eastern Europe. The work, the first edition of which appeared in 1961 (*Griff nach der Weltmacht*), provoked a veritable avalanche of literature, both favorable and critical. Among the most articulate critics was the late dean of German historians, Gerhard Ritter, especially his "Weltpolitik, Weltmachtstreben und deutsche Kriegsziele," *Historische Zeitschrift* (München), v. 199, 1964: 265-346. *See* the paperback volume of essays, stimulated by Fischer's book:

Lynar, Ernst W., *Graf*, *ed.* Deutsche Kriegsziele 1914-1918. Frankfurt/Main, Verlag Ullstein, 1964. 194 p. For an objective review of recent literature, *see*:

Epstein, Fritz T. "Neue Literatur zur Geschichte der Ostpolitik im Ersten Weltkrieg." Jahrbücher für Geschichte Osteuropas (München), v. 14, 1966: 63-94.

129. Kaczmarczyk, Zdisław. Kolonizacja niemiecka na wschód od Odry (German colonization east of the Oder). Poznan, Wydawn. Instytutu Zachodniego, 1945. 267 p. Maps. Bibliography: p. 260-264. (Prace Instytutu Zachodniego, nr. 4)

Though it deals only with German colonization in Poland, this is in fact the sole systematic account of the German "Ostbewegung" from a Slavic viewpoint, and at the same time a critique of German historiography of this question. It stresses the role of internal rather than external (*i.e.*, German) forces in Polish development, and views the "Ostbewegung" as part of continentwide European trends. A more recent appraisal will be found in *Wschodnia ekspansia Niemiec w Europe środkowej; zbiór studiów nad tzw. niemieckim "Drang nach Osten"* (German Eastern expansion in Central Europe; a collection of studies on the so-called German "Drang nach Osten"), edited by Gerard Labuda (Poznań, Instytut Zachodni, 1963, 321 p.), which contains papers originally presented at a joint Polish-Czechoslovak conference in Bratislava.

See also the special issue of *Przegląd zachodni* (Poznań), volume 20, 1964, containing the text of papers collectively entitled "Węzłowe problemy stosunków słowiańsko-niemieckich w XIX i XX wieku" (Crucial problems of Slav-German relations in the 19th and 20th centuries), originally presented at a conference in Poznań in 1964 with highly polemical contributions by Polish, East German, and

Soviet historians. The leading Slavic institute concerned with the German "Ostbewegung" is the Polish Instytut Zachodni in Poznań, founded in 1945, which publishes three journals: *Przegląd zachodni*, 1945–; *Polish Western Affairs*, 1960–; *La Pologne et les affaires occidentales*, 1965–. The articles in the last two mentioned journals are usually identical.

130. Kuhn, Walter. Geschichte der deutschen Ostsiedlung in der Neuzeit. 1. Band: Das 15. bis 17. Jahrhundert (Allgemeiner Teil). 2. Band: Das 15. bis 17. Jahrhundert (Landschaftlicher Teil). Köln, Böhlau, 1955-1957. 2 v. Maps. Bibliography: v. 1, p. 1-31.

A monograph displaying great erudition, based on German and Slavic (mostly Polish) sources. Reflects a German viewpoint; written with restraint and a desire to maintain objectivity in an undertaking in which objectivity could be considered unpatriotic. The best book on the German "Ostbewegung" produced thus far, it encompasses, for the period covered, all areas of German colonization, among them present-day Poland, Czechoslovakia, Hungary, Yugoslavia, and Romania. The first attempt of this kind was:

Kaindl, Raimund F. Geschichte der Deutschen in den Karpatenländern. Gotha, F. A. Perthes, 1907-1911. 3 v. Deals with Galicia, Hungary and Transylvania, Romania, and Bukovina, from the earliest times to 1800, and is still indispensable.

The only survey to cover the entire German eastward movement across the past thousand years, into the present century, is the concise work by Rudolf Kötzschke and Wolfgang Ebert, *Geschichte der ostdeutschen Kolonisation* (Leipzig, Bibliographisches Institut AG, 1937, 251 p., illus., maps. "Schrifttum:" p. 239-251).

A fresh interpretation of the controversial "Ostbewegung" which seeks to replace rhetoric by reflection is W. Schlesinger's "Die geschichtliche Stellung der mittelalterlichen deutschen Ostbewegung," *Historische Zeitschrift* (München), v. 183, 1957: 517-542. It rejects some of the excessive claims made for the "Ostbewegung" by German historians in the past.

The leading West German institute concerned with the "Ostbewegung" is the Johann-Gottfried-Herder Institut of Marburg/Lahn, founded in 1950, with its *Zeitschrift für Ostforschung*, 1952–. *See also* the two journals issued in West Germany by Der Göttinger Arbeitskreis, founded in 1946, in Göttingen: *Jahrbuch der Albertus-Universität zu Königsberg/Pr.*, 1951–, and *Jahrbuch der Schlesischen Friedrich-Wilhelms-Universität zu Breslau*, 1955–. The titles of these journals, both named after universities which at one time existed in cities now situated, respectively, on Soviet and Polish territory, suggest a political purpose.

See also the journal: *Germanoslavica; Vierteljahrsschrift für die Erforschung der germanisch-slavischen Kulturbeziehungen* (Brünn, R. M. Rohrer, 1931/32-1937).

131. Schreiber, Hermann. Teuton and Slav; the Struggle for Central Europe. Translated from the German by James Cleugh. New York, Knopf, 1965. 392 p. Illus., maps, ports. Bibliography: p. 373-375.

Addressed to nonspecialists, this account by a German exile from beyond the Oder-Neisse reviews the history of relations between Germans and their immediate Slavic neighbors, in a vein sympathetic to the latter, and counsels moderation to fellow Germans in advancing territorial claims. Translation based on *Land im Osten; Verheissung und Verhängnis der Deutschen* (3d ed., Stuttgart, Deutscher Bücherbund, 1963, 416 p.).

A strongly pro-Slavic viewpoint will be found in the short work by Jacques Ancel, *Slaves et Germains* (Paris, A. Colin, 1947, 224 p., illus., maps), which deals largely with Western and Southern Slavs.

See also Viktor Aschenbrenner and others, *Die Deutschen und ihre östlichen Nachbarn; ein Handbuch* (Frankfurt am Main, Verlag Moritz Diesterweg, 1967, 634 p., illus., maps), and the excellent short synthesis by Günther Stökl, *Osteuropa und die Deutschen; Geschichte und Gegenwart ihrer spannungsreichen Nachbarschaft* (Oldenburg, Stalling, 1967, 240 p.).

132. Wiskemann, Elizabeth. Germany's Eastern Neighbours; Problems Relating to the Oder-Neisse Line and the Czech Frontier Regions. London, New York, Oxford University Press, 1956. 309 p. Maps, tables. Bibliography: p. 297-300.

See also entries no. 903 *and* 2793.

The story of the transfer of the Germans from East Central Europe, told against the background of previous tensions and experiences of the Second World War. Argues in favor of the present borders.

German rule in wartime is the subject of Ihor Kamenetsky's *Secret Nazi Plans for Eastern Europe; a Study of Lebensraum Policies* (New York, Bookman Associates, 1961, 263 p.; New Haven, Conn., College and University Press Services, 1964).

A German view of the transfer is developed in great detail in *Eastern Germany; a Handbook*, released under the auspices of the Göttinger Arbeitskreis (Würzburg, Holzner-Verlag, 1960-1963, 3 v.). German original issued in one volume as: *Das östliche Deutschland; ein Handbuch* (Würzburg, Holzner-Verlag, 1959, 1013 p.). A massive critique of the transfer and of the resulting territorial changes, with extensive historical sections.

7. Cultural and Legal History

133. Irmscher, Johannes, *ed.* Renaissance und Humanismus in Mittel- und Osteuropa; eine Sammlung von Materialen. Berlin, Akademie-Verlag, 1962. 2 v. Illus. (Deutsche Akademie der Wissenschaften zu Berlin. Schriften der Sektion für Altertumswissenschaft, 32)

Consists of papers originally read at a conference in Wittenberg, 1959. Contributions in German and French. The second volume deals with Hungary, Poland, and Czechoslovakia. Most contributions stress, in the Marxist spirit, the socioeconomic basis of the Renaissance and humanism; a few rise above their framework. Somewhat similar ground is covered in:

La Renaissance et al Réformation en Pologne et en Hongrie. Edited by Gy. Székely and E. Fügedi. Budapest, Akadémiai Kiadó, 1963. 562 p. Papers presented at a conference in Budapest and Eger (Erlau) in 1961.

134. Kadlec, Karel. Introduction à l'étude comparative de l'histoire du droit public des peuples slaves. Paris, H. Champion, 1933. 328 p. Bibliography: p. 317-322. (Collection des manuels publiée par l'Institut d'études slaves, 3)

See also entry no. 349.

The author intended to deal with public law, private law, and judicial procedure, but death prevented him from completing the task. What remains is the comparative history of Slavic public law, notably constitutional law; there are also references to legal sources and the literature. Still the most authoritative compendium of the history of Slavic law in any language.

See also, by the same author, the university textbook *Dějiny veřejného práva ve střední Evropě* (History of public law in Central Europe) (3rd rev. and enl. ed., Praha, Nákl. vlastním, 1923, 514 p. Bibliography: p. 458-475). Rich with dates and data, this is in effect a constitutional history of the Czech Lands, Hungary, Croatia, Poland, the Habsburg Monarchy, and Germany. A more recent account is Vladislav Aleksiev-Miladinov's *Osnovi na istoriia na slaviansko pravo* (Principles of the history of Slavic law) (2d ed., Sofiia, Univ. pechatnitsa, 1946, 475 p. Bibliography: p. 445-450).

The only account in English is the short work by Fedor F. Zigel', *Lectures on Slavonic Law, Being the Ilchester Lectures for the Year 1900* (London, H. Frowde, 1902, 152 p.).

After years of neglect during the period of the "cult of personality," the study of the history of Slavic law is reviving, especially after the impetus supplied by the Fifth International Congress of Slavists held in Sofia in 1963. For a program of future research, *see* V. Procházka's "The Problem of Slavonic Law," *Origine et débuts des Slaves* (Prague), v. 6, 1966: 53-86. In departure from earlier practice, the author does not propose to concentrate on the law of the ancient Slavic period, but sees Slavic law as a tool for the study of questions extending chronologically from the earliest times to the 19th century.

135. Meyendorff, Jean. The Orthodox Church; Its Past and Its Role in the World Today. Translated from the French by John Chapin. New York, Pantheon Books, 1962. 244 p.

The best short account of the history and present situation of the Orthodox Church, with the added feature of presenting a survey of 17 national (or regional) Orthodox communities, among them those of Czechoslovakia, Poland, etc. Obliges the reader with such hard-to-get information as names of ecclesiastical heads, administrative divisions, statistics on the number of believers, and training facilities for the clergy. The French original is *L'Église orthodoxe: hier et aujourd'hui* (Paris, Éditions du Seuil, 1960, 224 p.). German translation: *Die Orthodoxe Kirche gestern und heute (in der Sicht eines orthodoxen Theologen)* (Salzburg, Otto Müller, 1963, 284 p.).

There is no history of Protestantism in East Central Europe as a whole, although such surveys exist for individual countries. For a brief outline, *see* H. Koch's "Der Protestantismus bei den Slaven," *Ostdeutsche Wissenschaft* (München), v. 2, 1955: 82-115, which discusses Protestantism from the Reformation to the present, with facts and figures.

Sources in: Ostkirchenausschuss. *Ausgewählte Quellen zur Kirchengeschichte Ostmitteleuropas* (Ulm-Donau, Verlag "Unser Weg," 1949, 130 p., plates). Current sources periodically reprinted in: *Religion in Communist Dominated Areas, 1962–* (New York, International Affairs Commission of the National Council of Churches).

For the Jews, *see* Lucy S. Dawidowicz's *The Golden Tradition; Jewish Life and Thought in Eastern Europe* (New York, Holt, 1967, 502 p.). Illustrates, through the memoirs of about 60 figures, Jewish culture in Eastern Europe from the First Partition of Poland (1772) to the eve of the Second World War.

The best single source for the history of East European Jewry before the Second World War is *Universal Jewish Encyclopedia* (New York, The Universal Jewish Encyclopedia, Inc., 1939-1943, 10 v.; reading guide and index: 1944). Current conditions may be conveniently followed in *Jews in Eastern Europe* (1959-, London, irregular).

8. Social and Economic History

136. Ludat, Herbert, *ed.* Agrar-, Wirtschafts- und Sozialprobleme Mittel- und Osteuropas in Geschichte und Gegenwart. Wiesban, O. Harrassowitz, 1965. 503 p. (Osteuropastudien der Hochschulen des Landes Hessen. Reihe I: Giessener Abhandlungen zur Agrar- und Wirtschaftsforschung des europäischen Ostens, Bd. 32)

Ranges from geological questions to agrarian history and policy. The *Giessener Abhandlungen* are published under the auspices of the Institut für kontinentale Agrar- und Wirtschaftsforschung of the University of Giessen in West Germany. The Institute, founded in 1955, is the only one in the Western world specializing in the economic and social history of Eastern Europe. The thirty-odd volumes of *Giessener Abhandlungen* issued thus far (volume 1 in 1957) have dealt predominantly with East European agriculture, concentrating on the most recent period.

There is no social and economic history of East Central Europe as a whole in any language. Insofar as such topics have been treated, the treatment has been restricted to one country. Only limited help is to be derived from the *Cambridge Economic History of Europe . . .* (Cambridge, England, Cambridge University Press, 1941–), which is still in progress. *See also*:

Obermann, Karl, *ed.* Probleme der Ökonomie und Politik in den Beziehungen zwischen Ost- und Westeuropa vom 17. Jahrhundert bis zur Gegenwart. Berlin, Rütten und Loening, 1960. 304 p. (Schriftenreihe der Kommission der Historiker der DDR und CSR, Bd. 3) A Marxist assessment.

137. Mommsen, Hans. Die Sozialdemokratie und die Nationalitätenfrage im habsburgischen Vielvölkerstaat. v. 1: Das Ringen um die supranationale Integration der zisleithanischen Arbeiterbewegung, 1867-1907. Wien, Europa-Verlag, 1963. 467 p. Bibliography: p. 451-462.

The credentials are of the best. The son of the Bismarckian scholar Wilhelm Mommsen and grandson of the famed historian of Rome, Theodor Mommsen, the author has a tradition to live up to, and he does it well. He knows no favorites save the integrity of his craft, and brings a discerning approach to the delicate question of the impact of national sentiment on the socialist movement in the Habsburg Monarchy. Based on a wealth of sources, published and archival, minutes of party meetings, unpublished correspondence of socialist leaders, etc. A truly impressive achievement.

See also *Viehzucht und Hirtenleben in Ostmitteleuropa; ethnographische Studien*, edited by László Földers (Budapest, Verlag der Ungarischen Akademie der Wissenschaften, 1961, 699 p., illus., maps), which is an unusual collection of studies on the shepherd, a phenomenon typical of Carpathian Europe. Deals with the shepherd, animal breeding, and implements in the mountain regions of Czechoslovakia, Hungary, Poland, Yugoslavia, Romania, and Bulgaria. Covers almost entirely the period before 1918 and goes back into the Middle Ages; articles contributed by historians from the countries concerned.

138. Neiderhauser, Emil. A jobbágy-felszabadítás Kelet-Európában (The emancipation of the peasantry from serfdom in Eastern Europe). Budapest, Akadémiai Kiadó, 1962. 353 p.

The first monograph in any language to employ a comparative approach to a problem common to several East European countries. Discusses and compares the abolition of serfdom in Prussia, the Czech Lands, Galicia, Hungary, Transylvania, Romania, Croatia, Slovakia, the Baltic States, Poland, Bessarabia, and Russia. Seeks to establish both the differences and the similarities in the process of the dissolution of serfdom. The Balkans are purposely omitted, as a region with its own special characteristics. *See* the Russian- language review in *Acta Historica* (Budapest), v. 10, 1963: 403-407. The earlier period is treated, also on a comparative basis, in Zsigmond P. Pach's *Nyugat-európai és magyarországi agrárfejlődés a XV-XVII. században* (Agrarian development in Eastern Europe and in Hungary in the 15th to 17th centuries) (Budapest, Kossuth könyvkiadó, 1963, 359 p.).

There is no general history of the peasantry in East Central Europe. The main outlines of the development may be glimpsed from the pamphlet by Jerome Blum, *The European Peasantry From the Fifteenth to the Nineteenth Century* (Washington, D.C., American Historical Association, 1960, 30 p., Service Center for Teachers of History, No. 33). The author is a specialist in the history of East European peasantry. *See also* his article "The Rise of Serfdom in Eastern Europe," *American Historical Review* (Washington, D.C.), v. 62, 1956-57: 807-836. For a valuable comparison between Western and Eastern Europe, *see* K. Tymieniecki's "Quelques parallèles d'histoire agraire du Moyen Age," *Acta Poloniae Historica* (Warszawa),

v. 1, 1958: 9-32. An annual bibliography is contained in *Bibliographia Historiae Rerum Rusticarum Internationalis*, 1960/61– (Budapest, Mezögazdasági Múzeum, 1964–). Also to be noted is Laszlo Revesz, *Der osteuropäische Bauer; seine Rechtslage im 17. und 18. Jahrhundert unter besonderer Berücksichtigung Ungarns* (Bern, Schweizerisches Ost-Institut Bern, 1964, 311 p.), which includes much comparative material relating to Poland, Bohemia, and Russia.

9. Since 1918

139. Mitrany, David. Marx against the Peasant; a Study in Social Dogmatism. New York, Collier Books, 1961. 320 p. Bibliography: p. 290-310.

An informed study of East European (including Russian) agrarian movements and reform, from the latter part of the 19th century to the post-World War II era, with the bulk of the study devoted to the years since 1918. First published in clothbound edition by the University of North Carolina Press in 1951.

Another socioeconomic aspect of the 20th century is explored in V. N. Bandera's *Foreign Capital as an Instrument of National Economic Policy; a Study Based on the Experience of East European Countries Between the World Wars* (The Hague, M. Nijhoff, 1964, 155 p. Bibliography: p. 145-150). In a realm laden with slogans and clichés, this volume seeks to approach the sensitive subject *sine ira et studio.*

140. Seton-Watson, Hugh. The East European Revolution. 3d ed. New York, Praeger, 1956. 435 p. Illus., bibliography.

See also entry no. 163.

The standard and reliable history of the Communist seizure of power after 1945 in Poland, Czechoslovakia, Hungary, Romania, Bulgaria, Yugoslavia, and Albania, and of an attempted seizure in Greece. Takes due cognizance of prewar conditions and wartime circumstances, with well over one-third of the volume being devoted to this background.

See also Hubert Ripka's *Eastern Europe in the Post-War World*, with an introduction by Hugh Seton-Watson (New York, Praeger, 1961, 266 p.), presenting a plea by Czechoslovakia's late democratic exile for a new East Central Europe, independent of Soviet influence and having its own social forms, democratic, but different from those of the West. The revolutionary year of 1956 is one of the focal points. *See also*:

De Battaglia, Otto Forst. Zwischeneuropa. Von der Ostsee bis zur Adria. V. I. Polen, Tschechoslowakei, Ungarn. Frankfurt am Main, Verlag der Frankfurter Hefte, 1954. 438 p. The story of the establishment of Communist regimes in Poland, Czechoslovakia, and Hungary.

Birke, Ernst, *ed.* Die Sowjetisierung Ost-Mitteleuropas; Untersuchungen zu ihrem Ablauf in den einzelnen Ländern. Frankfurt, A. Metzner, 1959. 398 p. Covers the Baltic States, Poland, Czechoslovakia, Danubian and Balkan states, East Germany. The helpful features of this work are the special sections for each country or region devoted to the press, schools, church, army, sports, science, etc.

141. Seton-Watson, Hugh. Eastern Europe Between the Wars, 1918-1941. 3d ed. Hamden, Conn., Archon Books, 1962. 425 p.

See also entry no. 236.

First edition in London, 1945; second edition, slightly revised, in 1946; the present third edition is an unchanged reprint of the second, with a new preface added and the last chapter ("Eastern Europe and the Great Powers") omitted. A most penetrating survey — the first of its kind — of East Central Europe during the interwar years, highly critical — at times too harshly so — of the governments of the countries in question. Covers Poland, Czechoslovakia, Hungary, Romania, Yugoslavia, and Bulgaria. Into its pages are telescoped the main conflicts and crises that kept East Central Europe in a state of turmoil: the nationality question, the agrarian question, the conflicts between social classes, the political strife. The lapse of years has hardly diminished its value.

Another informed account is C. A. Macartney's *Hungary and Her Successors; the Treaty of Trianon and its Consequences, 1919-1937* (London, New York, Oxford University Press, 1937, 504 p., maps. Reprint: 1965). This volume is, in effect, an account of Danubian Europe during the '20s and '30s, with emphasis on the nationality problems. Has a wealth of useful data. Almost alone among English-speaking specialists on East Central Europe of his generation, the author is able to resist the Slavic spell, and casts an appraising rather than admiring eye on the Slavs. Reinforced by the rare combination of the knowledge of Hungarian and Slavic languages, his account is objective, giving due weight to seldom-heard grievances (Hungarian, Slovak).

The latest account of East Central Europe during this period is C. A. Macartney and Alan W. Palmer's *Independent Eastern Europe; a History* (New York, St. Martin's Press, 1962, 499 p., illus.), a conventional treatment. The "definitive" work on the interwar period remains yet to be written. *See also*:

Volkmann, Hans-Erich, *ed.* Die Krise des Parlamentarismus in Ostmitteleuropa zwischen den beiden Weltkriegen. Marburg/Lahn, J. G. Herder-Institut, 1967. 184 p.

E. REFERENCE WORKS

1. Historical Atlases

142. Adams, Arthur E., Ian M. Matley, *and* William O. McCagg. An Atlas of Russian and East European History. New York, Praeger, 1967. 204 p.

Contains 101 maps and concise text, depicting a thousand years of ethnic, political, social, and economic history, including Tartar and Turkish invasions, changing patterns of industry and trade, and territorial revisions. Maps in black and white only, small format.

143. Czechoslovak Republic. *Ministerstvo národní obrany.* Československý vojenský atlas (Czechoslovak military atlas). Edited by Jan Klíma. Praha, Naše vojsko-MNO, 1965. 376 p.

One of the achievements that have brought international recognition to Czechoslovak cartography in recent years. 142 of its 376 pages are devoted to military history, with East Central Europe prominently represented. Valuable for detailed maps illustrating wars, battlefields, the art of war, and revolutions which are not found in any standard historical atlas. As befits a publication bearing the imprimatur of the Ministry of National Defense, it is dominated by an aggressive anti-Western bias. For a Soviet contribution, *see*:

Russia (*1923– U.S.S.R.*) *Glavnoe upravlenie geodezii i kartografii.* Atlas istorii srednikh vekov (Atlas of the history of the Middle Ages). 2d ed. Edited by E. A. Kosminskii and A. P. Levandovskii. Moskva, 1959. 59 p. Col. maps. In accordance with the Soviet definition of the Middle Ages, brings the record down to the mid-seventeenth century. Excludes Russia, but has many maps of East Central Europe. The late historian Kosminskii, the chief editor of this atlas, was a noted Soviet medievalist.

144. Kovalevsky, Pierre. Bildatlas der Kultur und Geschichte der slawischen Welt. Preface by Alois Schmaus. München, Basel, Wien, BVL Verlagsgesellschaft, 1964. 215 p.

The French title of the original edition, *Atlas historique et culturel de la Russie et du monde slave* (Bruxelles, Paris, Elsevier, 1961, 228 p.), expresses more accurately the character of this work, which accords much less space to Western and Southern than to Eastern Slavs. The handsomely produced volume contains 15 maps and over 600 illustrations, accompanied by some 50 pages of outline of Slavic history and culture. Its value lies in the illustrations depicting subjects ranging from archaeological finds to 20th-century personalities. The gallery of personages accommodates figures of such varied hue as Masaryk, Mihailović, and Tito. There are pictures of manuscripts, works of art, battlefields, and a variety of cultural monuments. In a separate section, each picture is most carefully described and explained.

145. Kraus, Theodor, *and others, eds.* Atlas östliches Mitteleuropa. Bielefeld, Velhagen und Klasing, 1959. 289, 19 p. Illus., maps (part fold). *See also* entries no. 65 *and* 2516.

Volume 1 contains 68 colored maps of large format, volume 2, English and French legends. Combines the features of an historical and geographic atlas; it is focused largely on Poland and Czechoslovakia. Contains maps illustrating, in painstaking detail, ethnic patterns, administrative boundaries, ecclesiastical provinces, demographic development, flow of commerce, and industrial and agricultural production, in both the remote and the recent past. The stress is on the German role in East Central Europe, with maps showing the progress of German colonization in the Middle Ages, the spread of German law, etc. Technically of high quality. Polish Western territories are treated throughout as part of Germany. Suffers from a strong bias:

though it deals with the German rôle in East Central Europe, and includes detailed maps of the transfer of Germans after 1945, there is no map bearing on any aspect of the German role during the 1939-1945 period.

A small atlas, devoted exclusively to the German "Ostbewegung" throughout all of Eastern Europe, is Wilfried Krallert's *Atlas zur Geschichte der deutschen Ostsiedlung* (2d ed., Bielefeld, Velhagen und Klasing, 1958, 24, 32 p., 24 col. maps).

2. Other Works

146. Batowski, Henryk. Słownik nazw miejscowych Europy Środkowej i Wschodniej XIX i XX wieku (Dictionary of place names in Central and Eastern Europe in the 19th and 20th centuries). Warszawa, Państwowe Wydawn. Naukowe, 1964. 85 p.

A brave attempt to provide a guide through the changes of place names occasioned by wars and political upheavals. Records names in over 20 languages (including English, for Cyprus). The author supplies a useful historical introduction to the principal changes.

147. Die Österreichisch-Ungarische Monarchie in Wort und Bild. Wien, K. K. Hof- und Staatsdruckerei, 1886-1902. 24 v. Illus., facsims.

The Habsburg Monarchy was a house of nationalities and the largest polity in Eastern Europe; this circumstance lends special value to this geographic-historical encyclopedia, the publication of which was initiated by Crown Prince Rudolf. Each volume (or series of volumes) deals with one province and contains articles on geography, music, theater, costumes, economic life, currency, dialects, art, and other subjects, with particular attention paid to ethnic groups. Richly illustrated.

148. Radisics, Elemér, *ed.* A Dunatáj, történelmi, gazdasági, és földrajzi adatok a Dunatáj államainak életebol (The Danube region; historical, economic, and geographic data on the states of the Danube region). Budapest, Gergely R. r.-t., 1946-1947. 3 v. Maps, diagrs.

Austria, Bulgaria, Czechoslovakia, Hungary, Poland, Romania, Yugoslavia. Includes bibliographies, chronologies, and indexes. A geographer's view of East Central Europe is presented in Harriet G. Wanklyn's *The Eastern Marchlands of Europe* (London, Philip, 1941, 356 p.), including the Baltic States, Poland, Czechoslovakia, Hungary, and Yugoslavia.

149. Sovetskaia istoricheskaia entsiklopediia (Soviet historical encyclopedia). Editor-in-chief: E. M. Zhukov. Moskva, Izdatel'stvo "Sovetskaia entsiklopediia," 1961– Illus., ports, maps.

Planned to be complete in twelve volumes and appearing at the rate of two or three a year, this is the only monumental encyclopedia of history with worldwide coverage. Alphabetically arranged; will contain circa 25,000 entries. Kindred fields, notably archaeology and ethnology, amply covered. Intensely didactic (e.g., the lengthy aside on "Wars, Just and Unjust," volume 3, columns 625-627) and overburdened with archaic irrelevancies (two columns on "Intra-party Democracy" and nine on "Dictatorship of the Proletariat," in volume 5, columns 109-111, 201-211). The bibliographical apparatus of many articles is encumbered by the dutiful Marx-Engels-Lenin sequence, regardless of the value and pertinence of the Marxist works listed. Its unbendingly ideological approach is now out of date in most other countries of the socialist bloc. Three-fourths of the material deals with countries other than the USSR. Having endured the ideological tedium, a patient reader will be rewarded by a wealth of information on Eastern Europe which is not available in any single reference work in any language, with separate articles (usually provided with bibliographies) on individual countries and provinces, statesmen, historians, revolutions, political parties, and peasant and working class movements. The treatment of "bourgeois" national leaders and movements of the East European countries is negative to a degree which the present Marxist historians of these countries would not uphold.

150. Strakhovsky, Leonid I., *ed.* A Handbook of Slavic Studies. Cambridge, Harvard University Press, 1949. 753 p.
See also entry no. 44.

Cooperative work, with different authors contributing chapters on the history and literature of each Slavic nationality. Bibliographies limited to Western languages; Slavic-language titles in the footnotes. Most contributors are top-notch specialists in their disciplines. The work was basically completed in 1944 and parts of it are now dated.

4

Government and politics

by Andrew Gyorgy

151. Beneš, Václav, Andrew Gyorgy, *and* George Stambuk. Eastern European Government and Politics. New York, Harper and Row, 1966. 247 p. Map.

Deals with entire Eastern European area on a country-by-country basis. For a survey of the East-Central European "Northern Tier," *see* chapters 2-5.

152. Brown, James F. The New Eastern Europe; the Khrushchev Era and After. New York, Praeger, 1966. 306 p. (Praeger Publications in Russian History and World Communism, no. 169)

Deals with the area on a topical and functional basis rather than in the standard country-by-country manner. Stresses political and cultural developments as well as the growth of nationalism.

153. Brzezinski, Zbigniew K. The Soviet Bloc: Unity and Conflict. Rev. and enl. ed. Cambridge, Harvard University Press, 1967. 599 p. (Russian Research Center Studies, 37)

See also entry no. 2725.

A standard work in this field, emphasizing party-government, intraparty, and intrabloc relationships. It cuts across government-politics lines and contains much valuable material in the field of Eastern European diplomacy and foreign relations.

154. Fejtő, François. Histoire des Democraties Populaires. Paris, Seuil, 1952. 446 p.

This ably written work is one of the first studies of the postwar development of the "People's Democracies" of Eastern Europe. It is particularly useful in its sections on Hungary and Czechoslovakia.

155. Frenzke, Dietrich, *and* Alexander Uschakow. Macht und Recht im

kommunistischen Herrschaftssystem. Köln, Verlag Wissenschaft und Politik, 1965. 335 p. Map.

Relating to East Central Europe, the sections dealing with administrative law in Hungary, the court system in Poland, the economic development of Poland, and the methodological issues in "East-bloc" legal research are the most significant.

156. Fischer-Galati, Stephen, *ed.* Eastern Europe in the Sixties. New York, Praeger, 1963. 239 p. Illus. (Praeger Publications in Russian History and World Communism, no. 137)

See also entry no. 43.

For purposes of this bibliography, chapters 1, 2, 5, and 6 are the most useful. A broad and well-documented survey.

157. Graham, Malbone W. New Governments of Eastern Europe. New York, Holt, 1927. 826 p.

Of potential interest for the study of the structure of governments prior to the Second World War. Its counterpart for the post-World War II period is Gordon Skilling's *The Governments of Communist East Europe* (*see* entry no. 164).

158. Griffith, William E., *ed.* Communism in Europe; Continuity, Change, and the Sino-Soviet Dispute. Cambridge, M.I.T. Press, 1964-1966. 2 v.

Relevant for East Central Europe are chapters 3 and 4 in volume 1 and parts 1 and 2 in volume 2. The former deal with Polish and Hungarian communism; the latter, with the East German and Czechoslovak brands. The best single section is Carola Stern's analysis of East Germany.

159. Ionescu, Ghita. The Politics of the European Communist States. New York, Praeger, 1967. 303 p.

Part 3 ("The Manifestation of Dissent") is probably the most useful section of this broadly conceived study.

160. Korab, Alexander. Die Entwicklung der kommunistischen Parteien in Ost-Mitteleuropa. v. 1. Hamburg, Terrapress, 1962. 204 p.

This first volume of a series contains a comprehensive outline of the history of the communist parties of Poland, Hungary, and Czechoslovakia from an objective and noncommunist point of view.

161. Kotok, V. F., *ed.* Gosudarstvennoe pravo stran narodnoi demokratii (State law of the People's Democracies). Moskva, Gosiurizdat, 1961. 571 p.

A presentation of the legal and constitutional characteristics of the "People's Democracies."

162. Meissner, Boris, *comp.* Das Ostpakt-System. Frankfurt, Berlin, Metzner, 1955. 208 p. (Dokumente Hrsg. von der Forschungsstelle für Völkerrecht und ausländisches öffentliches Recht der Universität Hamburg, Heft 18)

———, *ed.* Der Warschauer Pakt; Dokumentensammlung. Köln, Verlag Wissenschaft und Politik, 1962. 203 p. (Dokumente zum Ostrecht, Bd. 1)

Two related and significant series of documents dealing with the impact of Soviet-East Central European treaties on the governmental and political structures of the various "Northern Tier" countries. The first focuses on the Sovietization process of the 1944-1955 period, while the second analyzes the Warsaw Treaty Organization from the point of view of contemporary international law.

163. Seton-Watson, Hugh. The East European Revolution. 3d ed. New York, Praeger, 1956. 435 p. Illus., bibliography.

See also entry no. 140.

A classic in this field. This work offers a panoramic survey of the long drawn out "takeover" periods in the lives of Eastern Europe's postwar governments.

164. Skilling, H. Gordon. The Governments of Communist East Europe. New York, Crowell, 1966. 256 p. Maps.

The advantage of this work is its functional approach, cutting across the boundaries of individual Eastern European governments. Particularly useful are parts 3 ("The Holders of Power") and 6 ("Totalitarianism in Transition").

The constitutions of the four countries covered in the present bibliographic guide are contained in Jan F. Triska's *Constitutions of the Communist-Party States* (Stanford, Hoover Institution, 1968, 541 p.).

165. Staar, Richard F. The Communist Regimes of Eastern Europe. Stanford, The Hoover Institution on War, Revolution, and Peace, 1967. 406 p.

An excellent study based on a geographic and topical approach and dealing with the post-1945 history as well as the current situation of each of the new Eastern European communist states. Focuses on the origin of communism, governmental structure, and domestic and foreign policies in each country.

166. Ulam, Adam B. Titoism and the Cominform. Cambridge, Harvard University Press, 1952. 243 p. Bibliographical note: p. 235-236. (Russian Research Center Studies, 5)

See also entry no. 2750.

A brilliant theoretical survey of the origins of the Stalin-Tito dispute and of the ideological foundations of Titoism as a prototype of "national communism."

5

the nationality question*

by Francis S. Wagner

A. REFERENCE MATERIALS, SOURCES, AND PERIODICALS

167. Kisebbségi Körlevél (Minority circular). 1937-1944. Pécs. Bimonthly.
Issued by the Research Institute of Minorities at the University of Pécs. Devoted to the problems of national minorities in the Danubian Basin, with emphasis on East Central Europe. Includes book reviews, maps, statistics, surveys, laws, decrees, statutory provisions, and published texts. The following periodicals also contain much material relative to the whole area:
Magyar Kisebbség; nemzetpolitikai szemle (Magyar minorities; a nationality review). v. 1-17; 1922-1938. Lugos, Husvéth és Hoffer Könyvnyomdája. Semimonthly.
Láthatár (Horizon). 1933– Budapest. Biweekly.

168. Kulturwehr; Zeitschrift für Volkstumsfragen. v. 1-14, no. 4; 1925-1938. Berlin, Verband der nationalen Minderheiten im Deutschen Reich. Monthly. *See also*:
Voix des peuples; revue de politique internationale. v. 1-12; 1934-1945. Genève, Bureau central des minorités. 10 times yearly.
Minorité; informations concernant les minorités et l'évolution du droit minoritaire. Jan. 1934– Genève. Monthly.

* The entries in this section represent published materials, but the student should also note the significant holdings of unpublished documents in such institutions as the Haus-, Hof- und Staatsarchiv, the Allgemeines Verwaltungsarchiv, and the Österreichische Nationalbibliothek, all in Vienna; the Magyar Országos Levéltár (Hungarian National Archives) and the Országos Széchényi Könyvtár (National Széchényi Library), in Budapest; and the Archiwum Czartoryskich in Kraków. Published guides or inventories are available for some of these collections.

Danubian Review (Danubian News); a Review devoted to Research into Problems of the Danubian Basin. 1934-1943. Budapest, Hungarian Frontier Readjustment League. Monthly.

Prosveshchenie natsional'nostei; obshchestvenno-politicheskii i nauchno-pedagogicheskii zhurnal (Education of the nationalities; a socio-political and scholarly-pedagogical journal). 1929-1935, no. 4. Moscow. Monthly.

169. Magyar Tudományos Akadémia, *Budapest. Történettudományi Intézet.* Magyar történeti bibliográfia 1825-1867 (Hungarian historical bibliography, 1825-1867). Budapest, Akadémiai Kiadó, 1950-1959. 4 v.

See also entry no. 1830.

The fourth volume of this work bears the subtitle "Nemmagyar népek — Nemzetiségek" (Non-Hungarian peoples — nationalities) and is, with over 29,000 entries, the largest bibliography ever compiled on the topic of ethnic minorities. References are to monographs and periodical articles in Hungarian, Slavic, and West European languages. Subjects cover more than historic Hungary, including all minorities of the Danube Valley and emphasizing history, cultural, social, and legal relationships. Table of contents in English, French, German, and Russian.

170. Národnostní obzor; časopis Čsl. společnosti pro studium menšinových (národnostních) otázek (Nationality review; publication of the Czechoslovak Society for the Study of Minority [Nationality] Questions). 1930-1938. Praha. Quarterly.

Contains documented articles by Czech, Slovak, and foreign authors, with surveys of legal, political, cultural, and other aspects of events. Emphasis on Czechoslovakia, Hungary, and Poland. Book and periodical reviews. Table of contents in Czech, French, and German.

171. Schwartner, Martin. Statistik des Königreichs Ungern. Pest, gedruckt bey Matthias Trattner, 1798. 606 p.

Historical background and basic figures concerning Hungarians, Slavs, Germans, Romanians, etc. living in the Danubian area. Nations are grouped into two categories: Hauptnationen (Hungarians, Slavs, Germans, Romanians) and Nebenvölker (Gypsies, Armenians, etc.). It is one of the earliest systematic descriptions of ethnic minorities of the area. For further historical statistics, *see*:

Kovacsics, József, *ed.* A történeti statisztika forrásai (Sources of historical statistics). Budapest, Közgazdasági és Jogi Könyvkiadó, 1957. 460 p. Contains studies, bibliographies, unpublished sources relating to the nationality statistics of the Danubian area, with heavy concentration on historical Hungary.

Kovacsics, József, *ed.* Magyarország történeti demográfiája; Magyarország népessége a honfoglalástól 1949-ig (Historical demography of Hungary; population of Hungary from the conquest up to 1949). Budapest, Közgazdasági és Jogi Könyvkiadó, 1963. 441 p. Bibliography: p. 389-405. A continuation of the previous volume. Useful in connection with Hungary, Czechoslovakia, Ruthenia, Transylvania, and Yugoslavia.

Studies for a New Central Europe. 1963– Quarterly. New York, Mid-European Research Institute. Devoted entirely to the search for nationality solutions.

172. Südostdeutsche Historische Kommission. Buchreihe. 1– München, 1958–

A monographic series largely devoted to the countries of the Habsburg Empire and primarily interested in intergroup (German–non-German) relations. In the years 1936-1943 there appeared under the auspices of the Institute of Minorities of the Royal Erszébet University of Pécs, Hungary, a monographic series, the issues of which may be found listed in *Kisebbségi Körlevél*, v. 8, no. 3-4, May-July 1944: 4th cover.

173. Teleki, Pál, *and* András Rónai. Memorandum on the Different Types of Ethnic Mixture of Population. Submitted to the Conference by the Hungarian Coordinating Committee for International Studies. Budapest, 1937. 30 p. Col. maps. (International Studies Conference. 10th session, Paris, 1937. General Study Conference on Peaceful Change. Hungarian Memorandum, no. 5)

Focused primarily on East Central Europe, Eastern Europe, and the Balkan Peninsula. Maps show historical development of the nationality problem by area. *See also*:

Rónai, András. Atlas of Central Europe. Budapest, 1945. 366 p. Maps (part col.).

———. Bibliographie des frontières politiques du centre-est européen; étude politico-géographique consacrée à l'histoire des frontières. Budapest, Édition de l'Institut des sciences politiques de la Société hongroise de statistique, 1936. 140 p. Illus., maps, diagrs.

B. GENERAL WORKS

174. Gumplowicz, Ludwig. Das Recht der Nationalitäten und Sprachen in Österreich-Ungarn. Innsbruck, Verlag der Wagner'schen Universitäts-Buchhandlung, 1879. 329 p.

Describes development of nationality thought since the mid-eighteenth century. Emphasis is given to the revolutionary years of 1848-1849 and to the Austro-Hungarian Compromise of 1867. Deals extensively with the legal situation of the ethnic minorities including the analysis of Law No. 44 of 1868, and reviews theories regarding the existence and role of minorities. For decades it was regarded as a handbook of views on the nationality question.

175. Johannet, René. Le principe des nationalités. Rev. and enl. ed. Paris, Nouvelle Librairie Nationale, 1923. 454 p.

Includes much material on the theory and workings of nationalism and deals also quite extensively with the de jure and de facto situation of ethnic minorities in Austro-Hungary, Poland, Czechoslovakia, Romania, etc. Based on select published writings. Many references to East Central Europe are also found in:

Burian, Peter. Die Nationalitäten in "Cisleithanien" und das Wahlrecht der Märzrevolution in 1848/49; zur Problematik des Parlamentarismus im alten Österreich. Graz, Köln, Verlag Herman Böhlaus Nachf., 1962. 239 p. (Veröffentlichungen der Arbeitsgemeinschaft Ost, Band II)

Arató, Endre. A nemzetségi kérdés töténete Magyarországon (History of the nationality question in Hungary). Budapest, Akadémiai Kiadó, 1960. 2 v. A Marxist-Leninist-Stalinist treatise which covers the period 1790-1848 and is based in part on archival sources.

176. Krofta, Kamil. Stará a nová střední Evropa (The old and the new Central Europe). Praha, Politický klub Československé národní demokracie, 1929. 129 p.

The nationality question in historical perspective, giving the percent distribution of national minorities of East Central Europe up to the census of 1910, and discussing the dissolution of the Habsburg Empire as a result of the failure of nationality policies. Minority situations in the succession states also dealt with. The same topics are reviewed from a Marxist-Leninist-Stalinist point of view by:

Trainin, Il'ia P. Natsional'nye protivorechiia v Avstro-Vengrii i ee raspad (Nationality conflicts in Austro-Hungary and her downfall). Moskva, Izdatel'stvo Akademii nauk SSSR, 1947. 304 p.

Macartney, C. A. The Habsburg Empire, 1790-1918. London, Weidenfeld & Nicolson, 1968. 886 p. Maps. Bibliography: p. 838-863. Much space is devoted to an account of the nationalities conflicts, based on Hungarian, German, and other Western publications.

177. Steinmetz, Sebald Rudolf. Die Nationalitäten in Europa. Berlin, Gesellschaft für Erdkunde, 1927. 67 p. Bibliography. p. 62-67. (Zeitschrift der Gesellschaft für Erdkunde. Ergänzungsheft, II).

Chapter 2 (p. 19-53) provides statistical data and historical background concerning European nationalities at the beginning of the twentieth century. The following publications also supply much information on the general state of minorities in Europe, with special regard to the Danube Valley:

Kastelianskii, A. I., *ed.* Formy natsional'nago dvizheniia v sovremennykh gosudarstvakh: Avstro-Vengriia, Rossiia, Germaniia (Forms of the national movement in contemporary states: Austria-Hungary, Russia, Germany). Sanktpeterburg, Izd. T-va "Obshchestvennaia pol'za," 1910. 821 p.

Petroff, Thomas. Les minorités nationales en Europe centrale et orientale. Paris, Domat-Montchrestien, 1935. 224 p.

Chmelar, Josef. National Minorities in Central Europe. Prague, "Orbis" Printing and Publishing Co., 1937. 104 p. Map.

Zwitter, Fran. Nacionalni problemi v habsburški monarhiji. Ljubljana, Slovenska matica, 1962. 230 p. Maps. This is a revised and enlarged edition of the author's *Les problèmes nationaux dans la monarchie des Habsbourg* (Belgrade, 1960, 148 p.).

178. Széchenyi, István. Akademischer Vortrag gehalten vom Grafen Stephan Széchenyi, Vice-Präsidenten der ungarischen Gelehrten-Gesellschaft. Pressburg, 1843. 72 p.

Analyzes political aspects of the language question in the Habsburg Empire. This address, delivered on November 24, 1842, was considered by contemporaries, chiefly non-Hungarians, as the most significant contribution to the idea of peaceful coexistence and against forced assimilation. *See also* Francis S. Wagner's discussion of the Academic Address in his article "Széchenyi and the Nationality Problem in the Habsburg Empire," *Journal of Central European Affairs*, v. 20, no. 3, Oct. 1960: 290-311. Furthermore there is Otto Folberth's "Schicksale des Pestalozzismus in dem ungarischen Raum," in *Gedenkschrift für Harold Steinacker, 1875-1965* (München, Verlag R. Oldenbourg, 1966, p. 195-197), and Wacław Felczak, *Węgierska polityka narodowościa przed wybuchem powstania 1848 roku* (Hungarian nationality policy before the outbreak of the insurrection of 1848) (Wrocław, Zakład Narodowy im. Ossolińskich, 1964, 168 p. Polska Akademia Nauk. Oddział w Krakowie. Prace Komisji Nauk Historycznych, nr. 9) For further relevant sources on the language question, which was prominent in the area for decades, *see*:

Fischel, Alfred, *ed.* Materialien zur Sprachenfrage in Österreich. Brünn, F. Irrgang, 1902. 344 p.

Auerhan, Jan. Die sprachlichen Minderheiten in Europa. Berlin, Hensel, 1926. 155 p. Bibliography: p. 153-155. A summary treatment, enlarged from the original Czech edition, *Jazykové menšiny v Evropě* (Praha, Nové Čechy, 1924, 187 p.).

Wagner, Francis S. A szlovák nacionalizmus első korszaka (first period of Slovak nationalism). Budapest, 1940. 59 p. Bibliographical footnotes. (A. M. Kir. Ferenc József Tudományegyetem Magyar Tőrténelmi Intézetének dolgozatai, 1. sz.)

C. MINORITY RIGHTS

179. Azcarate y Flórez, Pablo de. League of Nations and National Minorities; an Experiment. Washington, Carnegie Endowment for International Peace, 1945. 216 p. (Carnegie Endowment for International Peace. Division of International Law. Studies in the Administration of International Law and Organization, no. 5)

By the former Director of the Minorities Questions Section of the League of Nations. Discusses the situation of national minorities in Europe with emphasis on Central and Eastern Europe, the rights and duties of minorities, as well as the actions of the League of Nations in the interest of minorities. An appendix contains the official "Report of Work of the League of Nations in Relation to Protection of Minorities." Name and subject index. *See also*:

Viefhaus, Erwin. Die Minderheitenfrage und die Entstehung der Minderheitenschutzverträge auf der Pariser Friedenskonferenz 1919;

eine Studie zur Geschichte des Nationalitätenproblems im 19. und 20. Jahrhundert. Würzburg, Holzner, 1960. 244 p. (Marburger Ostforschungen, Bd. 11)

Buza, László. A kisebbségek jogi helyzete a békeszerződések és más nemzetközi egyezmények értelmében (Legal position of minorities in the light of peace treaties and other international agreements). Budapest, Magyar Tudományos Akadémia, 1930. 432 p. Bibliography: p. v-xiv. Deals with international pacts concluded between governments of East Central Europe to protect minorities.

180. Congress of European Nationalities. Sitzungsbericht des Kongresses der organisierten nationalen Gruppen in den Staaten Europas. Wien, Leipzig, In Kommission bei Wilhelm Braumüller Universitäts-Verlagsbuchhandlung, 1926-1938. 13 v.

Thirteen congresses were held annually between 1925 and 1937, usually in Geneva. Representatives of the ethnic minorities — chiefly from Poland, Czechoslovakia, Hungary, and Romania — made situation reports reflecting the problems of nationalities in those states as well as the degree of implementation of minority rights and the possibilities of peaceful solutions. Includes addresses, statistical materials, reports on group and individual cases, and resolutions presented to the congresses.

181. Flachbarth, Ernst. System des internationalen Minderheitenrechtes; Geschichte des internationalen Minderheitenschutzes. Positives materielles Minderheitenrecht. Introduction by Graf Stephan Bethlen. Budapest, R. Gergely Verlag, 1937. 475 p. Bibliography: p. xxi-xviii.

A global treatment, concentrating on East Central Europe. Includes interstate agreements on protection of minorities and reviews the role of the League of Nations. Contains relevant documents in their original languages. For more details concerning the area, *see*:

Erler, Georg H. J. Das Recht der nationalen Minderheiten. Münster in Westfalen, Aschendorffsche Verlagsbuchhandlung, 1931. 530 p. (Deutschtum und Ausland. Studien zur Auslandkultur, Heft 37/39) Bibliography: p. xvii-xxvii. Extensive review of nationality statistics, historical background, education, protection of minorites, politics, etc., in Czechoslovakia, Hungary and Poland.

Hugelmann, Karl Gottfried, *ed.* Das Nationalitätenrecht des alten Österreich. Wien, Leipzig, W. Braumüller, 1934. 814 p. Maps.

Systematic review of nationality laws and decrees of the Habsburg Empire.

D. PANSLAVISM — PANGERMANISM

182. The effect of these movements on the political and cultural efforts of minorities has not yet been dealt with systematically. The following monographs, which are listed chronologically in order of publication, more or less elucidate the role of the movements in intergroup relations.

Krasiński, Walerjan Skorobohaty. Panslavism and Germanism. London, T. C. Newby, 1848. 338 p. Front., fold. map.

Fischel, Alfred. Der Panslavismus bis zum Weltkrieg; ein geschichtlicher Überblick. Stuttgart, Berlin, Cotta, 1919. 590 p.

Pajewski, Janusz. "Mitteleuropa"; studia z dziejów imperializmu niemieckiego w dobie pierwszej wojny światowej ("Mitteleuropa"; studies in the history of German imperialism during the First World War). Poznań, Instytut Zachodni, 1939. 444 p. Bibliography. (Prace Instytutu Zachodniego, nr. 27)

Gogolák, Lajos. Pánszlávizmus (Panslavism). Budapest, Cserépfalvi, 1940. 135 p. (Kék könyvek, 3)

Kruck, Alfred. Geschichte des Alldeutschen Verbandes, 1890-1939. Wiesbaden, F. Steiner, 1954. 258 p. Bibliography. (Veröffentlichungen des Instituts für Europäische Geschichte, Mainz, Bd. 3)

Kohn, Hans. Pan-Slavism; Its History and Ideology. 2d rev. ed. New York, Vintage Books, 1960. 468 p.

Tokody, Gyula. Ausztria-Magyarország a Pángermán Szövetség (Alldeutscher Verband) világuralmi terveiben (Austria-Hungary in the world-conquering plans of the Alldeutscher Verband). Budapest, Akadémiai Kiadó, 1963. 283 p. Bibliographic references in "Jegyzetek" (Notes): p. 241-282.

E. THE SEARCH FOR NATIONALITY SOLUTIONS

183. Glaise von Horstenau, Edmund. The Collapse of the Austro-Hungarian Empire. London, Toronto, J. M. Dent, New York, E. P. Dutton, 1930. 347 p. Bibliography: p. 339-344.

Two of its chapters are especially worth mentioning: 6, "The Response from the Nationalities," (p. 149-188) and 7, "Woodrow Wilson's Pronouncement," (p. 188-234). Originally published in German as *Die Katastrophe; die Zertrümmerung Österreich-Ungarns und das Werden der Nachfolgestaaten* (Zürich, Amalthea-Verlag, 1929, 525 p., map).

184. Hantsch, Hugo. Die Nationalitätenfragen im alten Österreich; das Problem der konstruktiven Reichsgestaltung. Wien, Verlag Herold, 1953. 124 p. (Wiener Historische Studien, Band I)

The first chapter is a geopolitical treatise. After analyzing the ethnic structure of the empire, the book deals extensively with the national problem of 1848 and the years of Dualism (1867-1918). Social Democratic as well as Christian Democratic approaches to solving the minority problem are reviewed. The seventh chapter describes federalistic elements in the platform of Greater Austria.

185. Hodža, Milan. Federation in Central Europe; Reflections and Reminiscences. London, Jarrolds Publishers, 1942. 236 p. Illus., bibliographical footnotes.

Describes the nature of the nationality structure and policies of the multilingual Habsburg Empire up to its collapse in 1918. Attempts to rebuild the monarchy on a federative basis between 1905 and 1914 in collaboration with Archduke Franz Ferdinand are related partly on the grounds of the author's personal experience. Non-Hungarian suggestions for modernizing the empire are related at length. Name and subject index. For some historically based new aspects, *see*:

Habsburg, Otto von. Entscheidung um Europa. Innsbruck, Tyrolia-Verlag, 1953. 192 p. The chapter "Neuordnung im Donauraum. Die europäische Bedeutung des Donauraumes," (p. 64-101) is of special interest.

Madariaga, Salvador de. Portrait of Europe. London, Hollis and Carter, 1952. 204 p.

There are several bibliographies on the topic, including:

Association of Institutes for European Studies. Bibliographie européenne. 2d ed. Genève, 1954. 32 p.

Beljaars, G. A. C. Bibliographie historique et culturelle de l'intégration européenne. Bruxelles, Commission Belge de Bibliographie, 1957. 142 p. (Bibliographica Belgica, 30)

Paklons, L. L. Bibliographie européenne. European Bibliography. Bruges, De Tempel, Tempelhof, 1964. 217 p.

Bildungswerk Europäische Politik. Bibliographie zur europäischen Integration. 2d rev. and enl. ed. Compiled and with commentary by Gerda Zellentin with the assistance of Elisabeth Y. de Koster. Köln, Europa-Union Verlag, 1965. 209 p.

186. Kampelík, František Cyrill. Stav Rakouska a jeho budoucnost. Na dějinách a rovnoprávnosti založené rozoumovánie rakouského občana, povinnou uctou a upřímností ku slavné vládě projevené (The present state of Austria and its future. Argumentation of an Austrian citizen based on history and equal rights with due respect and sincerity toward the glorious government). Hradec Králové, Nákladem spisovatelovým, Tisk Ladislava Pospíšila, 1860. 268 p.

Illustrates how positively Austroslavism thought of the Habsburg empire by describing contemporary (German, Slav, Hungarian, Romanian) nationality movements. The empire should be reorganized on the principle of equal justice and rights for all nations and languages. Pro-Austrian, anti-Hungarian.

187. Kann, Robert A. The Habsburg Empire; a Study in Integration and Disintegration. New York, Praeger, 1957. 227 p. Bibliography: p. 198-207.

Reviews some basic problems and concepts, among them nationalism and its setting and the process of integration and disintegration between 1867 and 1918. *See also*:

Jászi, Oszkar. The Dissolution of the Habsburg Monarchy. Chicago, University of Chicago Press, 1929. 488 p. Discusses situation and aspirations of national minorities, especially in chapters 1-4.

Kann, Robert A. The Multinational Empire; Nationalism and National Reform in the Habsburg Monarchy, 1848-1918. New York, Octagon Books, 1964. 2 v. Maps. Bibliography: v. 2, p. 375-380.

188. Popovici, Aurel C. Die Vereinigten Staaten von Gross-Österreich;

politische Studien zur Lösung der nationalen Fragen und staatsrechtlichen Krisen in Österreich-Ungarn. 2d ed. Leipzig, Verlag von B. Elischer Nachfolger, 1906. 424 p. Map.

Summary treatment of various nationality trends and relevant government policies since 1867 scrutinized from the standpoint of federalism. On the grounds of experience, basic principles of a proposed Austrian federation of nations are discussed as a means of achieving peaceful coexistence in the multinational empire.The last attempt to federalize the empire was made by Emperor Karl. *See*:

Rumpler, Helmut. Das Völkermanifest Kaiser Karls vom 16. Oktober 1918; letzter Versuch zur Rettung des Habsburgerreiches. Wien, Verl. für Geschichte und Politik, 1966. 96 p.

189. Renner, Karl. Das Selbstbestimmungsrecht der Nationen in besonderer Anwendung auf Österreich. Leipzig, Wien, Franz Deuticke, 1918. 293 p.

Reviews the problem of ethnic minorities within the framework of the political structure of the Danubian monarchy and makes suggestions for its reorganization in line with the principle of self-determination. Language question and local administrative reforms are also discussed, as well as socioeconomic aspects of the nationality questions in East Central Europe. A revised version of the author's *Der Kampf der österreichischen Nationen um den Staat* (Leipzig, Wien, F. Deuticke, 1902, 252 p.). For a more Social Democratic standpoint, *see*:

Bauer, Otto. Die Nationalitätenfrage und die Sozialdemokratie. Wien, Verlag der Wiener Volksbuchhandlung, 1924. 576 p. (Marx-Studien. Blätter zur Theorie und Politik des wissenschaftlichen Sozialismus, 2. Band) Publishes the official party platform relating to the multinational Habsburg Empire.

Mommsen, Hans. Die Sozialdemokratie und die Nationalitätenfrage im habsburgischen Vielvölkerstaat. v. 1: Das Ringen um die supranationale Integration der zisleithanischen Arbeiterbewegung, 1867-1907. Wien, Europa-Verlag, 1963. 467 p. (Veröffentlichungen der Arbeitsgemeinschaft für Geschichte der Arbeiterbewegung in Österreich, 1) Bibliography: p. 451-462. For a Leninist-Stalinist criticism of Social Democratic (Austromarxist) and bourgeois views, *see*:

Foustka, Radim. Národnostní otázka (The nationality question). Praha, Státní pedagogické nakladatelství, 1952. 74 p.

190. Seipel, Ignaz. Nation und Staat. Wien, Leipzig, Wilhelm Braumüller K. K. Universitäts-Verlagsbuchhandlung, 1916. 195 p. Bibliography: p. viii-xx.

Examines the development of nationalism and the nationality question in nineteenth and twentieth century Europe. Then focuses on the Danube Valley, including all of its nations and nationalities. Panslavism, Austroslavism, and other history-making forces are reviewed, as well as such concepts as "Mitteleuropa und überstaatliche Organisation." The author's views are regarded as representing the Catholic standpoint. Bibliography lists material predominantly in German. Extensive notes and subject and name index.

191. Zeman, Z. A. B. The Break-up of the Habsburg Empire, 1914-1918; a Study in National and Social Revolution. London, New York, Oxford University Press, 1961. 274 p. Maps. Bibliography: p. 257-265. *See also* entry no. 118.

Examines nationality struggles, especially Slavic movements and Russophilism. Verdict is that the collapse was due to nationality aspirations. Prepared chiefly on the basis of published materials, largely of Czech origin. For further details and ethnic maps, *see*:

Jelavich, Charles. The Habsburg Monarchy; Toward a Multinational Empire or National States? New York, Rinehart, 1959. 57 p. Illus.

May, Arthur J. The Passing of the Hapsburg Monarchy, 1914-1918. Philadelphia, University of Pennsylvania Press, 1966. 2 v. Maps. Bibliography: v. 2, p. 827-848.

6

Jews in East Central Europe

by Kaethe Lewy and Ruth Tronik
(except for the section on Poland)

A. GENERAL PUBLICATIONS

192. The American Jewish Yearbook. 1899– Philadelphia, New York, American Jewish Committee and Jewish Publication Society of America.

An authoritative compendium of demographic, civic, political, religious, and cultural data concerning Jews in the United States and around the world. Each yearbook presents reviews on countries that have Jewish communities. Each survey begins with a description of the general situation in a particular country and then details the situation of the Jewish community. Most issues also include special articles of an historic nature.

193. Dawidowicz, Lucy S., *ed.* The Golden Tradition; Jewish Life and Thought in Eastern Europe. New York, Holt, Rinehart and Winston, 1967. 502 p. Maps. Bibliography: p. 493-495.

Anthology of memoirs and biographical sketches of Jewish writers, politicians, revolutionaries, and scholars from Eastern Europe. Taken all together the effect is a picture of the spiritual atmosphere and cross currents of East European Jewry from the beginning of the eighteenth century up to the Second World War. A scholarly introduction traces the history of spiritual and political movements of the period.

194. Meyer, Peter, *and others.* The Jews in the Soviet Satellites. Syracuse, N.Y., Syracuse University Press, 1953. 637 p.

A collection of surveys on the situation of the Jews in five Soviet bloc countries up to spring of 1953. Each survey begins with a review of the situation of the Jews before the Second World War and during the Nazi occupation, but mainly deals with the communist attitude toward Jewish problems and the effect of the Soviet system on Jewish life. Based on communist sponsored Jewish publications, official documents, and Jewish press from the West. Excellent extensive bibliographical notes. "Czechoslovakia" by Peter Meyer, p. 49-204; "Hungary" by Eugene Duchinsky, p. 373-489; "Poland" and "Polish Jews under Soviet Rule," by Bernard D. Weinryb, p. 207-369.

Material through 1957 can be found in *The Position of the Jewish Communities in Eastern Europe on the Eve of 1958* (New York, Institute of Jewish Affairs, World Jewish Congress, 1957, 30 p.): Hungary, p. 13-16; Czechoslovakia, p. 25-28; Poland, p. 17-24.

195. Schmelz, Uziel O., *comp.* Jewish Demography and Statistics; Bibliography for 1920-1960 + Addenda. Jerusalem, Hebrew University, Institute for Contemporary Jewry, 1961. 2 v.

A very useful extensive bibliography listing approximately 5,000 items relating to Jewish communities throughout the world. Includes books and articles in many languages, adding English translations of titles in lesser known languages. Demography is used here in a wide sense to include health, economy, education, social matters, and community organization. Author index in addenda. The editor calls this publication a "first draft; not for publication or circulation," and a definitive edition is planned. A third volume with new material up to 1966 and an addendum for 1920-1960 is to be published in 1968. For material on Eastern Europe in general *see* under Europe; other pertinent listings are Czechoslovakia, Hungary, and Poland.

Another bibliography, narrower in scope, is *Jews in the Communist World; a Bibliography, 1945-1962* (New York, Pro Arte, 1963, 125 p.), by Randolph L. Braham and Mordecai M. Hauer. This selected bibliography of books and articles lists 845 entries. Part A lists references to non-English literature, with titles in lesser known languages translated into English. Part B supplements an earlier compilation by Braham entitled *Jews in the Communist World; a Bibliography, 1945-1960* (New York, Twayne Publishers, 1961, 64 p.), which listed materials in English only.

196. Seraphim, Peter H. Das Judentum im osteuropäischen Raum. Essen, Essener Verlagsanstalt, 1938. 736 p. Illus., maps, ports. Bibliography: p. 675-705.

History of the Jews in Eastern Europe from their first settlement there until the Second World War. Prepared in cooperation with the Institut für osteuropäische Wirtschaft of Königsberg University. Presents more details on the economic aspect of Jewish life and the participation of Jews in the economy of the various countries than on the cultural and religious life of the Jews. Special chapter devoted to demography and statistics. Anti-Semitic, but the only general history of East European Jewry in a Western language.

197. Stillschweig, Kurt. Die Juden Osteuropas in den Minderheitenverträgen. Berlin, J. Jastrow, 1936. 207 p.

The Minority Treaties between the Allied Powers of the First World War and new states, and the provisions in peace treaties with defeated nations, guaranteed the religious, linguistic, and educational rights of Jews in Eastern Europe. This book discusses these rights and the factors involved in their adoption.

On the struggle for Jewish autonomy and minority rights in Europe and the United States, *see also* the excellent, well-documented study by Oscar I. Janowsky, *The Jews and Minority Rights (1898-1919)* (New York, Columbia University Press, 1933, 419 p.).

B. CZECHOSLOVAKIA

198. Adler, Hans G. Theresienstadt, 1941-1945; das Antlitz einer Zwangsgemeinschaft, Geschichte, Soziologie, Psychologie. 2d rev. ed. Tübingen, J. C. B. Mohr, 1960. 892 p. Plan. Bibliography: p. 703-855.

The most important study of Czech Jewry during the holocaust. Introduction on the "Protectorate" period of 1939 to 1941. Extensive bibliography on all aspects of the holocaust. As no general work on the holocaust in Czechoslovakia has yet been published, this work may be supplemented by the detailed study on Slovakia by Livia Rotkirchen, *The Destruction of Slovak Jewry; a Documentary History* (Jerusalem, Yad Washem Martyrs' and Heroes' Memorial Authority, 1961, lxxv, 257 p., facsims. From the Yad Washem Archives, v. 3). Text in Hebrew with a 75-page English introduction, table of documents, and indexes of persons and places.

199. Gesellschaft für Geschichte der Juden in der Čechoslovakischen Republik. Jahrbuch. 1929-1938. Prag.

Scholarly articles based on source material. Edited by Samuel Steinherz. May be supplemented by *Zeitschrift für die Geschichte der Juden in der Tschechoslovakei* (1930-1938, Brünn, quarterly), edited by Hugo Gold.

See also *Judaica Bohemiae*, a semiannual publication in French and German of the Jewish State Museum in Prague. It began in 1965 and is intended as the successor to the *Jahrbuch*.

200. Gold, Hugo, *ed.* Die Juden und Judengemeinden Mährens in Vergangenheit und Gegenwart. Brünn, Jüdischer Buch- und Kunstverlag, 1929. 623 p. Illus., ports., map.

This very important source of information on Moravian Jewry was prepared by a panel of historians. Each community is treated separately. Includes much biographical material, a chapter of statistics, and a list of Regesta. Detailed index of persons and places.

A similar book also edited by H. Gold is *Die Juden und Judengemeinden Böhmens in Vergangenheit und Gegenwart*, v. 1 (Brünn, Jüdischer Buch- und Kunstverlag, 1934, 735 p., illus., ports.). This work deals with 342 Bohemian Jewish communities excluding Prague, which was intended to be the subject of a second volume that was never published. Lacks indexes.

The history of Czechoslovakian Jewry is supplemented by an additional volume edited by H. Gold: *Die Juden und die Judengemeinde Bratislava in Vergangenheit und Gegenwart* (Brünn, Jüdischer Buchverlag, 1932, 192 p., illus., ports.). This many-faceted work is devoted to Bratislava, the most important Jewish community in Slovakia.

201. The Jews of Czechoslovakia. New York, Society for the History of Czechoslovak Jews, in cooperation with the Jewish Publication Society of America, 1968. 576 p.

A collection of essays describing the story of Jewish participation in every aspect of Czechoslovak life between the two World Wars.

202. Muneles, Otto. Bibliographical Survey of Jewish Prague. Prague, Orbis, 1952. 562 p. Illus. (Jewish Monuments in Bohemia and Moravia, v. 1, pt. 1)

As no comprehensive history of the Jewish community of Prague has been written, this bibliography was published in an attempt to provide the groundwork for such a history. Lists chronologically 2,256 items—Judaica printed in Prague and books and articles in various languages relating in any way to the Jews of Prague. This is a publication of the Jewish State Museum of Prague. Published also in Czech edition entitled: *Bibliografický přehled židovské Prahy.*

203. Rat der jüdischen Gemeinden in Böhmen und Mähren, *and* Zentralverband der jüdischen Gemeinden in der Slowakei. Die aussäen unter Tränen mit Jubel werden sie ernten (Psalm 126). Die jüdischen Gemeinden in der Tschechoslowakischen Republik nach dem zweiten Weltkrieg. Prag, Zentral-Kirchenverlag, 1959. 215 p. Illus.

Surveys on the situation of the Jewish communities in the cities of Czechoslovakia after the Second World War. Many illustrations of synagogues, ritual objects, gravestones, etc. accompany the text.

204. Rat der jüdischen Gemeinden in Böhmen und Mähren, *and* Zentralverband der jüdischen Gemeinden in der Slowakei. Informationsbulletin. 1956– Prag. Quarterly.

Organ of the federations of Jewish communities in Czechoslovakia. News on events in the Jewish communities. Intended for circulation abroad. For home use a monthly bulletin is published in Czech with the title: *Věstník židovských náboženských obcí v Československu* (Herald of the Jewish communities in Czechoslovakia).

205. Stein, Adolf. Die Geschichte der Juden in Böhmen. Brünn, Jüdischer Buch- und Kunstverlag, 1904. 172 p.

A popular outline of the history of the Jews of Bohemia through the 19th century. Sketches of outstanding personalities.

As background supplementary reading, the following collection of documents (in Latin, Czech, and German) is recommended: *Zur Geschichte der Juden in Böhmen, Mähren und Schlesien von 906 bis 1620*, edited by Gottlieb Bondy (Prag, G. Bondy, 1906, 2 v.).

C. EAST GERMANY

206. Nachrichtenblatt der jüdischen Gemeinde von Gross-Berlin und des Verbandes der jüdischen Gemeinden in der Deutschen Demokratischen Republik. 1961– Berlin. Quarterly.

This is the only publication of the Jewish communities of East Germany. Gives brief notices on current events. Postwar material is also to be found in Greta Beigel's *Recent Events in Eastern Germany* (New York, Institute of Jewish Affairs, World Jewish Congress, 1953, 19 p.). Based on information from Western newspapers, it describes the sovietization of East Germany and its impact on Jewish life.

D. HUNGARY

207. Braham, Randolph L. The Hungarian Jewish Catastrophe; a Selected and Annotated Bibliography. New York, 1962. 86 p. (Yad Washem Martyrs' and Heroes' Memorial Authority, Jerusalem, *and* YIVO Institute for Jewish Research, New York. Joint Documentary Projects. Bibliographical Series no. 4)

Lists 732 items — pamphlets, books, articles — in various languages. Material on the holocaust, its background, and aftermath.

May be supplemented by the author's *The Destruction of Hungarian Jewry* (New York, Pro Arte for the World Federation of Hungarian Jews, 1963, 2 v.), a well-presented collection of documents mainly from the German Foreign Office Archives. Historical background is given in the introduction. An analytical list of documents provides a short English summary of each document.

208. Braham, Randolph L., *ed.* Hungarian-Jewish Studies. New York, World Federation of Hungarian Jews, 1966. 346 p. Includes bibliographies.

A collection of studies by experts on Hungary dealing with the history of the Jews in Hungary, their extermination during the last years of the Second World War, and the present situation of the survivors.

209. Kohn, Sámuel. A zsidók története Magyárországon (The history of the Jews in Hungary). Budapest, Athenaeum, 1884. 489 p.

The important basic book on the history of the Jews in Hungary from their first settlement there until 1526. Sources and documents appended (p. 403-480).

May be supplemented by a more popular work by Joseph Bergl,

which, however, carries the history of Hungarian Jewry down to 1877: *Geschichte der ungarischen Juden* (Kaposvár, Druck von H. Jeiteles, 1879, 158 p.).

A further useful account is Robert A. Kann's "Hungarian Jewry during Austria-Hungary's Constitutional Period (1867-1918)," in *Jewish Social Studies* (New York), v. 7, Oct. 1945: 357-386.

210. Institute of Jewish Affairs, *New York*. The Jews of Hungary; Survery of Their History and Postwar Situation. New York, Institute of Jewish Affairs, World Jewish Congress, 1952. 22 p.

A brief outline on the situation of the Jews in Hungary during the periods of liberation (1945-1948) and of consolidation of the communist regime (1948-1952). Deals with the effect of political changes on Jewish life. Based on information from the Hungarian Jewish periodical *Uj élet* (New life) and from Western periodicals.

211. Magyar zsidó lexikon (Hungarian Jewish lexicon). Edited by Peter Ujvár. Budapest, Magyar zsidó lexikon, 1929. 1028 p.

An encyclopedia of Jewish communities and personalities. Covers Hungary in its pre-1918 borders.

212. Monumenta Hungariae-Judaica. Budapestini, 1903–

An important collection of documents from public and private archives illustrating the history of the Jews in Hungary — their legal status, relation with non-Jewish population and authorities, economic activities, etc. Nine volumes, covering the period 1092 to 1760, appeared until 1966.

Between 1903 and 1938, published by the Hungarian Jewish Literary Society (Izraelita magyár irodalmi társulat), and from 1959 by the Central Board of the Jewish Communities in Hungary (Magyár izraeliták országos képviseleté) under the editorship of Alexander Scheiber. Hungarian title: *Magyár-zsidó oklevéltár.*

213. Uj élet; a magyár izraeliták lapja (New life; the journal of Hungarian Jewry). 1945– Budapest. Fortnightly.

Organ of the Central Board of Jewish Communities, and the only Jewish periodical published in postwar Hungary.

E. POLAND

by Lawrence Marwick

214. Balaban, Majer. Bibliografia historii Żydow w Polsce i w krajach ościęnnych za lata 1900-1930 (A bibliography of the history of the Jews in Poland and in neighboring countries in the years 1900-1930). Warszawa, Nakł. Tow. Szerzenia Wiedzy Judaistycznej w Polsce, 1939. 1 v.

An exhaustive bibliography devoted to all aspects of Jewish life and activities in Poland and the neighboring countries for the years 1900-1930 by the foremost historian of Polish Jewry. Unfortunately only the first fascicle of this work, which required several decades of assiduous and dedicated effort to plan and complete, managed to reach the public in printed form.

215. Bornstein, I. Rzemiosło żydowskie w Polsce (Jewish handicrafts in Poland). Warszawa, Nakł. Inst. Badán Spraw Narodowsciowych, 1936. 189 p. Bibliography.

A work devoted to Jewish artisans and their contributions to Polish economic life.

216. Bronsztein, Szyja. Ludnošć żydowska w Polsce w okresie międzywojennym; studium statystyczne (The Jewish population in Poland in the interwar period; a statistical study). Wrocław, Zakład Narodowy im. Ossolińskich, 1963. 295 p.

A most useful statistical study and account, based on many hitherto inaccessible sources in various depositories, of the Jewish population of Poland in the years from 1914 to 1939. Contains an English summary and bibliographical footnotes.

217. Dubnov, Semen Markovich. History of the Jews in Russia and Poland, from the Earliest Times until the Present Day. Translated from the Russian by I. Friedlaender. Philadelphia, The Jewish Publication Society of America, 1916-1920. 3 v. Bibliography: v. 3, p. 171-203.

"The translation is based upon a work in Russian which was especially prepared by Mr. Dubnov for the Jewish Publication Society of America." The distinguished historian also treated the history of the Jews of Poland in his 10-volume general history of the Jewish people, now available in German, Hebrew, and Yiddish translations. An English translation of the latest edition of the Russian original, including revisions and additions, will soon be made available by the publishing firm of Thomas Yoseloff.

218. Lestschinsky, Jacob. Economic Aspects of Jewish Community Organization in Independent Poland. Jewish Social Studies (New York), v. 9, 1945: 319-362.

An authoritative and informed summary by a leading expert on East European Jewish affairs. His extensive writings in the fields of Jewish sociology and economics over half a century are universally recognized and appreciated.

219. Mark, Bernard. Męczeństwo i walka żydów w latach okupacij; poradnik bibliograficzny (The martyrdom and struggle of the Jews during the years of occupation; a bibliographic guide). Warszawa, 1963. 44 p.

A fully annotated short bibliography, consisting of 114 items in Polish, with author and subject indexes, by the leading Jewish historian of communist Poland.

220. Segal, Simon. The New Poland and the Jews. New York, L. Furman, Inc., 1938. 223 p. Bibliography: p. 217-219.

Another brief, well-written and authoritative account, presenting a rounded picture of all facets of Jewish life and activities, accompanied by selective bibliographies, is Harry M. Rabinowicz, *The Legacy of Polish Jewry; a History of Polish Jews in the Inter-war Years, 1919-1939* (New York, Thomas Yoseloff, 1965, 256 p.). Both works are indispensable introductions to the subject.

221. Schiper, Ignacy. Dzieje handlu żydowskiego na ziemiach polskich (A history of Jewish commerce in the Polish lands). Warszawa, Nakł. Centrali Związku Kupców, 1937. 791 p. Ports. Bibliography: p. 777-790.

222. Schiper, Ignacy, *ed.* Żydzi w Polsce odrodzonej; działalność społeczna, óswiatowa i kulturalna (The Jews in the reborn Poland; social, educational, and cultural activity). Warszawa, Nakł. Wydawn. "Żydzi w Polsce odrodzonej," 1932-1933. 2 v. Bibliographies.

The intrinsic value of this scholarly work, ably planned and edited, lies in its exhaustive treatment of the social, educational, and cultural activities of the Jews during the first decade of Poland's independence after the First World War.

7

Diplomacy and Foreign Relations

by Andrew Gyorgy

223. Braunthal, Julius. History of the International. v. 1, 1864-1914. Translated from the German by M. Collins and K. Mitchell. New York, Praeger, 1967. 393 p.

    Background reading. Essential for an understanding of the origins of the workers' movements in the countries of East Central Europe and their first more or less systematic international organizational framework.

224. Bromke, Adam, *ed.* The Communist States at the Crossroads between Moscow and Peking. New York, Praeger, 1965. 270 p. (Praeger Publications in Russian History and World Communism, no. 154)

    A useful and well-edited book. Relevant for this bibliography are Professor Philip Mosely's introduction and chapters 3, 4, and 5, on Poland, Hungary, and Czechoslovakia, respectively.

225. Brzezinski, Zbigniew K. Alternative to Partition; for a Broader Conception of America's Role in Europe. New York, McGraw-Hill, 1965. 208 p. Illus.

    Places the German problem within the broader context of the present state of "disarray" in Eastern Europe. Proposes an increase of social, cultural, and economic ties with the Soviet-bloc states.

226. Burks, Richard V. The Dynamics of Communism in Eastern Europe. Princeton, Princeton University Press, 1961. 244 p. Maps, tables.

    Using behavioral techniques and quantitative statistical data, this book surveys the social structures and leadership elites of various Eastern European regimes.

227. Byrnes, Robert F., *ed.* The United States and Eastern Europe. Englewood Cliffs, N.J., Prentice-Hall, 1967. 176 p. Maps.

    See also entry no. 42.

A comprehensive survey of some current facets of the East Central European political landscape. Most relevant are the sections dealing with "Politics and Political Change," "Social Forces and Cultural Change," and Kurt L. London's well written essay on "Eastern Europe in the Communist World."

228. Čelovský, Boris. Das Münchener Abkommen von 1938. Stuttgart, Deutsche Verlags-Anstalt, 1958. 518 p. Maps. Bibliography: p. 487-504.

See also entry no. 885.

A detailed discussion of the Munich Conference, the resultant agreements, and their impact on the diplomacy of East Central Europe prior to the Second World War.

229. Domes, Alfred, *ed.* Die Politik des Westens und Osteuropa. Köln, Verlag Wissenschaft und Politik, 1966. 238 p.

Well-edited essays analyzing the various economic, social, and political facets of East-West relations within the confines of the European continent.

230. Horváth, Zoltán. Die Jahrhundertwende in Ungarn; Geschichte der zweiten Reformgeneration, 1896-1914. Neuwied am Rhein, Luchter-Rand, 1966. 547 p.

See also entry no. 2287.

Essential background study for an understanding of the various early socialist and Marxist intellectual movements in a crucial period of Hungarian history. The Hungarian title is *Magyar századforduló.*

231. London, Kurt L., *ed.* Eastern Europe in Transition. Baltimore, The Johns Hopkins Press, 1966. 364 p.

Based on selected papers from the Fifth International Conference on World Politics held in Holland in 1965, this superbly edited work has a number of important essays relevant to the diplomacy and foreign relations of East Central Europe. Contributions by London, Kraus, Wolfe, Meissner, and Hassner are particularly notable.

The Hoover Institution at Stanford University has initiated under the editorship of Jan F. Triska a monographic series, *Integration and Community Building in Eastern Europe*, with the focus on the relations of communist-governed countries of East and Southeast Europe with each other and with other communist-type states. Two monographs on *The German Democratic Republic* and *The Polish People's Republic* appeared in 1968, and two additional volumes on Czechoslovakia and Hungary are scheduled for 1969.

232. Lukács, John A. The Great Powers and Eastern Europe. New York, American Book Company, 1953. 878 p. Maps.

Interestingly and provocatively organized, this comprehensive work contains a great deal of information, particularly in part 3 (October 1938-June 1941), entitled "Between German Hammer and Russian

Anvil," and part 5 (January 1944-July 1945), "The Russian Era Begins."

233. Macartney, C. A., *and* Alan Warwick Palmer. Independent Eastern Europe: A History. New York, St. Martin's Press, 1962. 499 p. Illus.

An encyclopedic, factual, and carefully conceived history of the region.

234. Macartney, C. A. Hungary and Her Successors; the Treaty of Trianon and Its Consequences, 1919-1937. London, New York, Oxford University Press, 1965. 504 p. Maps. Bibliographical note: p. xii-xxi.
See also entry no. 1909.

A broadly based analysis by an eminent historian of the impact of the First World War not only on Hungary but also on the "successor states" of the Austro-Hungarian monarchy. First published in 1937.

235. Rozek, Edward J. Allied Wartime Diplomacy: A Pattern in Poland. New York, John Wiley and Sons, 1958. 481 p. Maps.

This valuable book is not only a documented study of Soviet foreign policy but also a scholarly portrayal of the aspects of the perennial "Polish Question" surviving the Second World War.

236. Seton-Watson, Hugh. Eastern Europe Between the Wars, 1918-1941. Cambridge, Cambridge University Press; New York, Macmillan, 1945. 442 p. Illus., maps, tables.
See also entry no. 141.

Standard and basic reference work including not only the countries of Eastern Europe specifically, but also adjacent nations like Austria, Finland, Greece, and Turkey. Reprint: Hamden, Conn., Archon Books, 1962, 425 p.

237. Wheeler-Bennett, John W. Munich: Prologue to Tragedy. New York, Duell, Sloan, and Pearce, 1963. 507 p. Illus., maps. Bibliography: p. 489-493.
See also entry no. 897.

A British historian's careful reconstruction of the climactic events related to the Munich Conference of 1938. First published in 1948.

8

the economy

by John M. Montias

Books and Articles 238-270
Serials 271-274

A. BOOKS AND ARTICLES

238. Basch, Antonín. The Danube Basin and the German Economic Sphere. New York, Columbia University Press, 1943. 275 p. Tables. Bibliography: p. 261-265.

   An informative and competent account of the breakdown of East European trade relations during the early 1930s and the subsequent economic penetration of Hungary and the Balkans by Nazi Germany. More detailed information on Germany's trade with Hungary and the Balkans may be found in N. Montchiloff's *Ten Years of Controlled Trade in South-Eastern Europe* (Cambridge, University Press, 1944, 89 p.)

239. Bodnar, Artur. Gospodarka europejskich krajów socjalistycznych; zarys rozwoju w latach 1950-1975 (The economy of the European socialist states; an outline of development in the years 1950-1975). Warszawa, Książka i wiedza, 1962. 390 p. Illus., bibliography.

   The most informative survey of the Eastern European economies to have come out of the region itself. The abundant data are collated from a wide variety of published sources, not all easily accessible in the West. The analysis is fairly superficial but, within limits, objective.

240. Economic Development for Eastern Europe. Edited by M. C. Kaser. London. Macmillan; New York, St. Martin's Press, 1968. 329 p.

   A collection of papers on a variety of economic topics presented at a conference of the International Economic Association held in 1964 at Plovdiv, Bulgaria, with the participation of economists from Eastern European and other countries. Summaries of the discussion are also contained. For other recent collective works, *see*:

Thalheim, Karl C., *ed.* Wirtschaftsreformen in Osteuropa. Köln, Verlag Wissenschaft und Politik, 1968. 309 p.

Probleme zentraler Wirtschaftsplanung. Nationalökonomen Osteuropas über Theorie und Praxis der Wirtschaftspolitik. Edited by Kurt Wessely. München, Oldenbourg, 1967. 200 p. Illus. (Schriftenreihe des Österreichischen Ost und Südosteuropainstituts, Bd. 2)

241. Economic Development in S.E. Europe, including Poland, Czechoslovakia, Austria, Hungary, Roumania, Yugoslavia, Bulgaria, and Greece. With an introduction by Professor David Mitrany. London, PEP, distributed by Oxford University Press, 1945. 165 p.

A highly condensed, well-documented survey of economic conditions in Eastern Europe in the 1930s. Also contains sketches of possible future plans for the postwar period.

242. Ernst, Maurice. Postwar Economic Growth in Eastern Europe (A Comparison with Western Europe). Washington, U. S. Government Printing Office, 1966. 220 p. Illus., maps. (New Directions in the Soviet Economy; Studies Prepared for the Subcommittee on Foreign Economic Policy of the Joint Economic Committee, Congress of the United States, Part 4)

A summary of extensive research on postwar economic growth in Eastern and Western Europe. Ernst's indexes are recomputed from basic physical series which generally show substantially less rapid growth than comparable official series.

243. Fox, Ursula. Das Bankwesen der europäischen Volksdemokratien. Wiesbaden, Betriebswirtschaftlicher Verlag Gabler, 1967. 209 p.

An up-to-date survey of banking in Eastern Europe.

244. Grossman, Gregory, *ed.* Value and Plan; Economic Calculation and Organization in Eastern Europe. Berkeley, University of California Press, 1960. 370 p. Tables. Includes bibliographical references.

A collection of essays, including, in addition to the papers on the Soviet economy that represent the bulk of the book, contributions on Poland's price-setting problems and Yugoslavia's institutional reforms. The papers by L. Hurwicz and B. Ward explore theoretical problems common to all Soviet-type economies. *See also*:

Grossman, Gregory, *ed.* Money and Plan; Financial Aspects of East European Economic Reforms. Berkeley, University of California Press, 1968. 188 p.

Grossman, Gregory. Economic Reform: The Interplay of Economics and Politics. *In* Burks, R. V., *ed.* The Future of Communism in Europe. Detroit, Wayne State University Press, 1968. p. 103-140.

245. Hertz, Friedrich Otto. The Economic Problem of the Danubian States. London, V. Gollancz, 1947. 223 p.

Devoted mainly to the problems of Austria and Hungary after the breakdown of the Dual Monarchy. The Balkan economies receive only superficial treatment.

On trade restrictions in the 1920's, *see* the classic study *Economic Nationalism of the Danubian States* by L. Pasvolsky (New York, Macmillan, 1928, 609 p., maps).

246. Holešovský, Václav. Personal Consumption in Czechoslovakia, Hungary and Poland, 1950-1960: a Comparison. Slavic Review, v. 24, Dec. 1965: 622-635.

Summarizes the results of a meticulously prepared statistical study of consumption in three countries of Eastern Europe. Comparisons are made with the rates of growth and absolute levels of consumption in Western Europe, Canada, and the United States.

247. Jahn, Georg M. *and* W. M. v. Bissing, *eds.* Die Wirtschaftssysteme der Staaten Osteuropas und der Volksrepublik China; Untersuchungen der Entstehung, Entfaltung und Wandlung sozialistischer Wirtschaftssysteme. Berlin, Duncker und Humblot, 1961-1962. 2 v. Illus. Includes bibliographies. (Schriften des Vereins für Sozialpolitik, n. F., Bd. 23)

Contains lengthy and detailed essays on the economies of Czechoslovakia, East Germany ("Mitteldeutschland"), Hungary, Romania, Bulgaria, Albania, and Yugoslavia (as well as China and the USSR). The essays, on the whole, are more descriptive than analytical, but the material is well presented and carefully compiled.

248. Karcz, Jerzy F., *ed.* Soviet and East European Agriculture. Berkeley, University of California Press, 1967. 445 p.

Only the last three papers in this conference volume deal with Eastern Europe: Joel Halpern's demographic and sociological study of the Yugoslav peasantry, Gregor Lazarčík's statistical analysis of Czechoslovak agriculture, and Andrzej Korbonski's essay on socialized and private agriculture in Poland. Together with the shorter comments of their discussants, these papers represent one of the more significant contributions to the scant literature on the postwar agricultural problems of Eastern Europe.

249. Lipťak, Julius. Pol'nohospodárstvo v socialistických krajinach (Agriculture in the socialist countries). Bratislava, Vydavatel'stvo politickej literatury, 1963. 405 p.

This survey of agricultural trends in Eastern Europe by an economist of the region delves into some of the technical problems of agriculture but is short on economic analysis. *See also* the same author's *Mezinárodní dělba práce v zemědělství zemí RVHP* (The international division of labor in agriculture in the countries of CEMA) (Praha, Nakladatelství politické literatury, 1965, 319 p.; bibliography: p. 316-320). This more recent book, while it is nominally devoted to intra-CEMA specialization in farm products, also contains a good deal of information on the output and consumption of foodstuffs and other agricultural products in individual East European countries.

250. Mandelbaum, Karl. The Industrialization of Backward Areas. Ox-

ford, B. Blackwell, 1945. 111 p. Tables, diagrs. (Oxford University Institute of Statistics, Monograph No. 2)

Prepared with the assistance of J. R. L. Schneider. Following a short description of the development problems of Eastern Europe, focused on the surplus-labor hypothesis, the author formulates an aggregative plan for the industrialization of the region, relying on projections and on sectoral allocations of investment resources in line with derived demand. Mandelbaum's methodology thus diverges essentially from the teleological principles underlying Soviet-style long-term planning in the early 1950's. Second edition published in 1955.

251. Marczewski, Jan. Planification et croissance économique des démocraties populaires. Paris, Presses Universitaires de France, 1956. 2 v. Bibliography: v. 2, p. 551-560.

See also entry no. 2820.

Broad panorama of the East European economic scene. The volume on growth is limited essentially to the targets and achievements under the first long-term plans (four to six years) in the People's Democracies. The volume on planning draws mainly from pre-1956 accounts of the Polish experience.

252. Miller, Margaret S., *ed.* Communist Economy under Change; Studies in the Theory and Practice of Markets in Competition in Russia, Poland and Yugoslavia. London, Published for the Institute of Economic Affairs by A. Deutsch, 1963. 272 p. Bibliographies: p. 254-266.

A study of economic reforms in the USSR, Poland, and Yugoslavia. The authors concentrate on the malfunctions of centralized schemes and on the potential benefits of market-type decentralization.

253. Montias, John M. Economic Nationalism in Eastern Europe: Forty Years of Continuity and Change. Journal of International Affairs, v. 20, Jan. 1966: 45-71.

An attempt to link East European trade trends before and after the Second World War, with special emphasis on exchanges by broad commodity groups. Compares the character of economic nationalism under prewar capitalism and under communist conditions.

254. Montias, John M. Inflation and Growth: The Experience of Eastern Europe. *In* Baer, W., *and* I. Kerstenetsky, *eds.* Inflation and Growth in Latin America. Chicago, Irwin, 1964. p. 216-249.

Describes monetary planning via the synthetic balances and surveys the monetary experiences of the East European countries. Special emphasis is placed on the inflationary pressures released by the political and economic disturbances of 1956 in Poland and Hungary. For further information on monetary reforms after the Second World War, *see* Henri Wronski's *Le Rôle économique et social de la monnaie dans les Démocraties Populaires: La Réforme monétaire polonaise 1950-1953* (Paris, M. Rivière, 1954, 181 p.). For a Soviet survey of monetary institutions in various Eastern European countries, throughout which financial statistics are thinly scattered, see also *Banki i kredit v stranakh narodnoi demokratsii* (Banks and credit in the people's democratic countries) by V. Bochkova and others (Moskva, Gosfinizdat, 1961, 323 p., illus., bibliography).

255. Novozámsky, Jiří. Vyrovnávání ekonomické úrovně zemí RVHP (The leveling of economic levels among the countries of CEMA). Praha, Nakladatelství politické literatury, 1964. 172 p. Bibliographical footnotes.

A short but important book dealing with the levels of development, rates of growth, and foreign-trade policies of CEMA members. The author argues that disparities in development will be gradually reduced as the less developed countries surpass the more developed in their rates of growth of national income per head, but warns against the sanguine view that all members will attain communism at exactly the same time.

256. Pryor, Frederic L. The Communist Foreign Trade System. Cambridge, M.I.T. Press, 1963. 296 p. Bibliography: p. 289-293.

The only available treatment *in extenso* of the relation between central planning and foreign-trade decisions in Soviet-type economies. The author's evidence for the description of foreign-trade planning methods is drawn mainly from East Germany. Contains very useful statistical information on East European trade. For institutional details on the organization of foreign trade in Eastern Europe, *see also*:

Hermes, Theodor. Der Aussenhandel den Ostblockstaaten. Hamburg, Cram, de Gruyter, 1958. 177 p.

257. Pryor, Frederic L., *and* George J. Staller. The Dollar Values of the Gross National Product in Eastern Europe. Economics of Planning, v. 6, 1966, no. 1: 1-26.

Independent calculations, based upon sectoral estimates, of the national incomes of East European countries in 1955.

258. Rosenstein-Rodan, P. N. Problems of Industrialization of Eastern and South-Eastern Europe. The Economic Journal, v. 53, June 1943: 202-211.

This influential article by a well-known specialist on economic development contains a plea for the rapid industrialization of Eastern Europe, which the author considers to be the best, if not the only, means for absorbing the surplus labor of the region.

259. Sanders, Irwin T., *ed.* Collectivization of Agriculture in Eastern Europe. Lexington, University of Kentucky Press, 1958. 214 p. Maps, tables. Includes bibliographical references.

See also entry no. 2031.

Completed before the onset of full-scale collectivization in Eastern Europe. Generally obsolete, but still the only multicountry survey in English of the first stages of collectivization in the region.

260. Spulber, Nicolas. The Economics of Communist Eastern Europe. Cambridge, Technology Press of M.I.T., 1957. 525 p. Illus.

Ten years after its publication, this was still the only comprehensive English-language survey of the economies of Eastern Europe, even though it appeared before most of the official statistical yearbooks of the East European countries were issued on a regular basis (after an interruption of nearly a decade). Still authoritative on the nationalization of industry and trade, on reparation payments, and on other yearly postwar events.

261. Spulber, Nicolas. The State and Economic Development in Eastern Europe. New York, Random House, 1966. 179 p. "Bibliographical essay": p. 153-173.

Three essays on the economic history of Eastern Europe, chiefly devoted to the development of the region prior to the onset of communist rule. Basic themes treated in the essays include the role of the state in industrial progress, the expanding web of credit relations, and the generation of an entrepreneurial class in Eastern Europe. A good selection of growth statistics and an annotated bibliography add to the value of the book.

262. Suranyi-Unger, Theo. Studien zum Wirtschaftswachstum Südosteuropas. Stuttgart, Gustav Fischer Verlag, 1964. 216 p. Bibliographical footnotes.

A valuable analysis of economic growth in Hungary, Romania, Bulgaria, and Albania, stressing the synthetic, and especially the financial, aspects of development (budget policy, sectoral allocation of investments, distribution of national income, etc.).

263. Svennilson, Ingvar. Growth and Stagnation in the European Economy. Geneva, United Nations, Economic Commission for Europe, 1954. 342 p. Diagrs., tables.

A synthesis of the quantitative aspects of European economic development in the interwar period, corroborating the pessimistic appraisal of P. N. Rosenstein-Rodan, K. Mandelbaum, and others on the performance of the East European economies during this period.

264. *United Nations. Economic Commission for Europe.* Economic Survey of Europe in 1961. Part 2. Some Factors in Economic Growth in Europe During the 1950's. Geneva. 283 p.

A simple econometric analysis of the contribution of labor, capital, and technical progress to growth in Eastern and Western Europe during the 1950s. The study is marred, in the case of Eastern Europe, by the undiscriminating use of official statistics of national income and industry. The same criticism applies to the otherwise highly informative and useful annual surveys of economic development in the Eastern European countries prepared by the Secretariat of the Economic Commission for Europe contained in the annual series *Economic Survey of Europe.*

265. Warriner, Doreen. Economics of Peasant Farming. 2d ed. New York, Barnes & Noble, 1965. 208 p. Illus., maps.

First published in 1939. Essays by a well-known specialist on peasant problems, overpopulation, rural standards of living, efficiency of farming operations, and labor conditions in Eastern Europe. Numerous maps and photographs.

266. Warriner, Doreen, *ed.* Contrasts in Emerging Societies; Readings in the Social and Economic History of South-Eastern Europe in the Nineteenth Century. Bloomington, Indiana University Press, 1965. 402 p. Maps. Bibliographical footnotes.

A judicious selection of annotated readings on Hungary, Romania, Bulgaria, and the regions now making up Yugoslavia, chiefly based upon 19th-century writings but also containing a few extracts from documents of the 18th century.

267. Wellisz, Stanisław. The Economies of the Soviet Bloc; a Study of Decision Making and Resource Allocation. New York, McGraw-Hill, 1964. 245 p. Bibliographical footnotes.

See also entry no. 2826.

A systematic analysis of the sources of static inefficiency in central planning. The author particularly deplores the absence of rational prices. Based almost entirely on Polish sources.

268. Zagoroff, Slavcho D., Jenö Végh, *and* Alexander D. Bilimovich. The Agricultural Economy of the Danubian Countries, 1935-1945. Stanford, Calif., Stanford University Press, 1955. 478 p. Illus., maps.

Technical and competent essays on agricultural conditions in Bulgaria, Hungary, Romania, and Yugoslavia before and during the Second World War. Also contains a general survey of agriculture in the Balkans, together with an economic and statistical analysis of land reforms after the First World War.

269. Zaleski, Eugène. Les courants commerciaux de l'Europe Danubienne au cours de la première moitié du vingtième siècle. Paris, Librairie Générale de Droit et de Jurisprudence, 1952. 564 p. Diagrs. Bibliography: p. 553-561.

A sound analysis of trade trends among the Danubian states in the first half of the twentieth century. The discussion of multilateral European exchanges is particularly enlightening.

270. Zauberman, Alfred. Industrial Progress in Poland, Czechoslovakia, and East Germany, 1937-1962. London, New York, Oxford University Press, 1964. 338 p. Bibliography.

See also entries no. 602, 943, 1520, *and* 2829.

A scholarly analysis of the expansion of industry in the northern tier of the CEMA countries. Partly based on the author's independently computed indexes of production. The focus is on the heavy industrial complex, including metals, chemicals, and power.

B. SERIALS

271. The American Review of Soviet and Eastern European Foreign Trade. 1965– White Plains, N.Y. Bimonthly.

This journal, published by the International Arts and Sciences Press, contains translations of articles from Soviet and East European journals on specialization in Comecon, the effects of economic reforms on the conduct and practice of foreign trade, and numerous other economic problems arising from the external economic relations of the communist countries.

272. Eastern European Economics. 1962– White Plains, N.Y. Quarterly.

This periodical, published by the International Arts and Sciences Press, contains translated articles from East European economic journals, selected by American scholars. From time to time an entire issue is taken up with a single source, such as J. Timár's "Planning the Labor Force in Hungary" (v. 4, 1966, no. 3, 145 p.), prepared and translated by the National Planning Office in Budapest with an introduction by Lynn Turgeon. Articles on economic growth and on institutional reforms are featured.

273. Osteuropa-Wirtschaft. 1956– Stuttgart. Quarterly.

Economic developments in the USSR and East Central Europe.

274. Quarterly Economic Review. Eastern Europe, North. 1956– London, Economist Intelligence Unit. Quarterly.

Surveys economic developments in Czechoslovakia, East Germany, and Poland. Its counterpart for Albania, Bulgaria, Hungary, and Romania is provided by *Quarterly Economic Review. Eastern Europe, South* (same publisher and frequency as above).

9

Council for Economic Mutual Assistance (Comecon)

by Kazimierz Grzybowski

275. Akademiia nauk SSSR. *Fundamental'naia biblioteka obshchestvennykh nauk.* Razvitie mirovoi sotsialisticheskoi sistemy khoziaistva i ekonomicheskoe sotrudnichestvo evropeiskikh stran-uchastnits SEV; bibliografiia, knigi i stat'i 1957-1962 (The development of the world socialist economic system and the economic cooperation of the European countries participating in the Council for Economic Mutual Assistance; bibliography, books and articles, 1957-1962). Edited by E. M. Kan. Moskva, 1964. 167 p.

   Includes works which have appeared in the socialist countries in Eastern Europe.

276. Ágoston, István. Le marché commun communiste; principes et pratique du COMECON. Genève, Droz, 1964. 353 p. Illus., maps. Bibliography: p. 335-347.

   A highly useful analysis of the Council for Economic Mutual Assistance, primarily from the economic and political point of view.

277. Akademiia nauk SSSR. *Institut mirovoi ekonomiki i mezhdunarodnykh otnoshenii.* Mezhdunarodnye ekonomicheskie organizatsii; spravochnik (International economic organizations; a handbook). Edited by V. G. Solodovnikov. Moskva, Izd-vo Akademii nauk SSSR, 1962. 1,108 p. Diagrs.

   An important encyclopedia of international economic organizations, both capitalist and socialist, including a number of those connected with Comecon.

278. Baikov, Vladimir S. Razvitie ekonomiki stran-uchastnits SEV v 1963-1964; tsifry i fakty (The development of the economy of the countries participating in the Council for Economic Mutual Assistance in 1963-1964; facts and figures). Moskva, Znanie, 1965. 63 p.

Important for statistical data illustrating the work of the Council for Economic Mutual Assistance.

279. Fadeev, Nikolai V. Sovet ekonomicheskoi vzaimopomoshchi (The Council for Economic Mutual Assistance). Moskva, Ekonomika, 1964. 166 p.

A thorough and systematic description of Comecon, including the most recent changes. A German translation appeared as *Der Rat für gegenseitige Wirtschaftshilfe* (Berlin, Staatsverlag der DDR, 1965. 176 p.).

280. Grzybowski, Kazimierz. The Socialist Commonwealth of Nations; Organizations and Institutions. New Haven, Yale University Press, 1964. 300 p. Bibliography: p. 273-278.

The Council for Economic Mutual Assistance is described as an important part of the socialist system, including all ancillary economic organizations and various techniques of economic cooperation.

281. Hacker, Jens, *and* Alexander Uschakow. Die Integration Osteuropas 1961 bis 1965. Köln, Verlag Wissenschaft und Politik, 1966. 323 p. Bibliography: p. 149-155. (Dokumente zum Ostrecht, Bd. 6).

The book consists of two parts, one on the Warsaw Treaty Organization and one on the Comecon. Each part is divided into a systematic monographic study and a collection of the more important documents in the German version or in German translation. For agricultural cooperation within Comecon, *see*:

Jaehne, Günter. Landwirtschaft und Landwirtschaftliche Zusammenarbeit im Rat für Gegenseitige Wirtschaftshilfe (COMECON) Wiesbaden, Harrassowitz, 1968. 327 p.

282. Hoffmann, Emil. COMECON; der gemeinsame Markt in Ost-Europa. Opladen, C. W. Leske, 1961. 174 p. (Die grossen Märkte der Welt, 3)

A description of the organization and functions of the Council for Economic Mutual Assistance.

283. Kaser, Michael. Comecon; Integration Problems of the Planned Economies. London, Oxford University Press, 1965. 215 p. Tables, diagrs.

The author has focused his attention on the process of integration of the Eastern European countries, including the Soviet Union, into a supranational economic system.

284. Korbonski, Andrzej. Comecon. New York, Carnegie Endowment for International Peace, 1964. 62 p. Bibliographical footnotes. (International Conciliation, no. 549)

A useful description of the organization and functions of the Council for Economic Mutual Assistance.

285. Košnár, Jozef. Rada Vzajomnej hospodarskej pomoci; výsledky a problémy (The Council for Economic Mutual Assistance; results and problems). Bratislava, Vydavatel'stvo politickej literatury, 1964. 307 p.

A very useful and up-to-date discussion of the Comecon organization and problems in Slovak.

286. Kunz, Willi. Grundfragen der internationalen Wirtschaftszusammenarbeit der Länder des Rates für gegenseitige Wirtschaftshilfe (RgW). Berlin, Akademie-Verlag, 1964. 125 p. (Deutsche Akademie der Wissenschaften zu Berlin. Schriften des Instituts für Wirtschaftswissenschaften, Nr. 18)

An outline of the aims and working principles of Comecon from the communist point of view. Appendixes with tables containing statistical information on the period 1950-1960.

287. Morozov, Vasilii I. Sovet ekonomicheskoi vzaimopomoshchi — soiuz ravnykh (The Council for Economic Mutual Assistance — a union of equals). Moskva, 1964. 127 p. Bibliographical footnotes.

A detailed description of the organization and operation of Comecon as an association of sovereign countries. A highly propagandistic approach.

288. Novaia literatura po obshchim problemam evropeiskikh sotsialisticheskikh stran (New literature on the common problems of the European socialist countries). 1964– Moskva. Monthly. (Akademiia nauk SSSR. Fundamental'naia biblioteka obshchestvennykh nauk)

A bibliography of books and articles in Russian and in both Western and Eastern languages, with many references to Comecon and its operations.

289. Philipson, Stanley. Die dritte Macht; E. W. G. und COMECON zwischen Amerika und Sowjet-Russland. Jerusalem, Massadeh, 1965. 97 p.

The author considers that Comecon and the Common Market represent organizations with possibilities for the economic organization of Western and Central Europe to counterbalance the United States and the Soviet Union in terms of economic potential.

290. Schenk, Karl-Ernst. Arbeitsteilung im Rat für gegenseitige Wirtschaftshilfe. Berlin, Duncker und Humblot, 1964. 158 p. (Osteuropa-Institut an der Freien Universität Berlin. Wirtschaftswissenschaftliche Veröffentlichungen, Bd. 21) Bibliography: p. 145-154.

The monograph deals with the functional relationship of the organs of the Comecon and the possibilities and limitations of the integration in a planned economy. It may be regarded as a continuation and supplement to E. Klinkmüller and E. Ruban's *Die wirtschaftliche Zusam-*

menarbeit der Ostblockstaaten (Berlin, Duncker und Humblot, 1960, 310 p., Osteuropa-Institut an der Freien Universität Berlin. Wirtschaftwissenschaftliche Veröffentlichungen, Bd. 12), which was published in the same series.

291. Shurshalov, Vladimir M. Mezhdunarodno-pravovye formy sotrudnichestva sotsialisticheskikh gosudarstv (Juridical forms of international cooperation of socialist states). Moskva, Izd-vo Akademii nauk SSSR, 1962. 466 p. Bibliography.

A work of one of the leading Soviet specialists in the field of international law, dealing with legal aspects of international organizations of socialist states and focusing on the Council for Economic Mutual Assistance as the center of the socialist system in Eastern Europe.

292. Teich, Gerhard. Der Rat für gegenseitige Wirtschaftshilfe, 1949-1963; fünfzehn Jahre wirtschaftliche Integration in Ostblock. Kiel, Institut für Weltwirtschaft, Bibliothek, 1966. 445 p. (Kieler Schrifttumskunden zu Wirtschaft und Gesellschaft, 14)

An exhaustive bibliography of books and articles, both Western and Eastern, on Comecon, covering the entire period from its establishment in 1949 to 1963.

293. Uschakow, Alexander. Der Rat für gegenseitige Wirtschaftshilfe (Comecon). Köln, Verlag Wissenschaft und Politik, 1962. 199 p. (Dokumente zum Ostrecht, Bd. 2) Bibliography: p. 63-68.

10

RESEARCH AND ORGANIZATION OF SCIENCE

by Vladimir Slamecka

A. SERIALS

294. Minerva. 1962– London. Quarterly.

A review of science learning and science policy, containing papers on general problems and on national science policies, including those of Eastern Europe and the Balkans. Published by the Committee on Science and Freedom.

295. Osteuropa-Naturwissenschaft. 1957– Stuttgart. Semiannual.

A review of the status of science in the Soviet Union and Eastern Europe. Published by the Deutsche Gesellschaft für Osteuropakunde.

296. Předpoklady rozvoje vědy a techniky (Prerequisites for the development of science and technology). 1963– Praha. Monthly.

A review of non-Czech literature on the organization, management, and financing of science and technology and on education in these fields. Eastern Europe and the Balkans are included. Published by the Institute for Scientific, Technical, and Economic Information (UVTEI).

297. Science Policy Information. 1967– Paris. Quarterly.

Reviews of science policy and organization on both national and international levels. A bibliography section is included in each issue.

Published by the Organization for Economic Cooperation and Development.

298. Tudományszervezési tájékoztató (Bulletin of science organization). 1961– Budapest. Bimonthly.

Information on science organization, planning, and management is given in three sections: original survey articles, with summaries in English and Russian; long reviews of significant papers; and annotated special bibliographies of foreign literature and unannotated bibliographies of recent Hungarian literature. Published by the Hungarian Academy of Sciences.

299. Zagadnienia naukoznawstwa; studia i materiały (Problems of scientific research; studies and materials). 1965– Warszawa. Irregular.

A journal devoted to problems of the dynamics of scientific research, including methods, information, personnel, and planning. Published by the Polish Academy of Sciences.

B. DIRECTORIES AND SURVEYS

300. Geyer, Dietrich. Wissenschaft in kommunistischen Ländern. Tübingen, Rainer Wunderlich Verlag, Hermann Leins, 1967. 309 p.

A collection of papers, originally read at the University of Tübingen, on numerous aspects of study and research in the humanities and social sciences.

301. Little, Arthur D., *Inc.* Directory of Selected Research Institutes in Eastern Europe. Prepared for the National Science Foundation. New York, Columbia University Press, 1967. 445 p.

See also entry no. 57.

A directory of 861 research institutes in Bulgaria, Czechoslovakia, Hungary, Poland, Romania, and Yugoslavia, primarily in science and engineering, but including some in agriculture and economics. Each entry contains the title of the institute in the original language and in English translation, the address, the names of the director and deputy director, the program and scope of the institute, and a list of its publications. Indexes of directors and deputy directors, institutes, and subjects are included. The introductions to the sections for each country describe the particular structure and organization of scientific research in that country.

302. United Nations Educational, Scientific, and Cultural Organization. World Directory of National Science Policy-Making Bodies. v. 1. Europe and North America. Paris, UNESCO, Guernsey, Hodgson, 1966. 356 p.

A directory of national policy-making bodies for the planning, organization, and coordination of scientific and technological research in one or more disciplines. Twenty-nine countries of Europe are treated, including Bulgaria, Czechoslovakia, Greece, Hungary, Poland, Romania, and Yugoslavia. The title of each organization is given in the original and in French and English translations. The address, telephone number, and name of the director are listed. The scope of activities, jurisdiction, governmental status, administrative and financial structure, publication activity, international relations, history, and current status of each organization are summarized. An index of organizations is provided in English and French.

303. Zsolnay, Vilmos von. Die Wissenschaft in Osteuropa. Mainz, v. Hase und Koehler Verlag, 1967. 230 p.

An up-to-date survey of the state of science and research in the Soviet Union, Poland, Hungary, Czechoslovakia, and Romania. The social and natural sciences are covered.

C. CZECHOSLOVAKIA

304. Dobruská, Naděžda, *comp.* Řízení a organizace vědeckého výzkumu e efektivnost výzkumné a vývojové práce. Výběrová bibliografie knižní a časopisecké literatury (Administration and organization of scientific research and the effectiveness of research and development work; a selected bibliography of books and periodical literature). Praha, UVTEI, 1966. 86 p.

This bibliography covers 17 categories of the administration and organization of science, including the following: Czechoslovakia, the socialist countries, international cooperation, efficiency of research and development, planning, financing, economics of research, management, incentives, and institutions. Special sections are devoted to the literature of symposiums, seminars, and conferences. An author index is included.

305. Nováček, M., J. Slapánek, *and* J. Mráz, *comps.* Výzkumná a vývojová základna. Struktura a zaměření (Research and development base; structure and trends). Praha, UTEIN, 1966. 203 p.

A listing of 481 research and development institutions in Czechoslovakia, comprising those of the Czechoslovak Academy of Science, universities, and industry. The publication reflects the status of the institutions listed as of October 1965 (including changes effective January 1966) and gives the name of each institution, its address, the name of the director, and a brief definition of the scope of its interest and activities.

306. Richter, Miloslav, *and* Vratislav Doležel. Research and Development Network in the Czechoslovak Socialist Republic. Translated from the Czech by Adolf Hermann. Prague, Institute for Technical and Economic Information, 1965. 82 p.

An outline of the development, current status (as of the end of 1964), scope, and extent of the Czechoslovak research and development network, with data on its current structure and the various categories of workers engaged in it. Information is given on the qualifications and training of scientists and technicians and on the equipment and financing of laboratories and research institutes. The information pertains to the period before the adoption of the new program for management of the national economy, but remains valid in the main. A list of Czechoslovak research institutes (with their addresses) is given in English and in Czech, according to their affiliation (academies of science, ministries, administrations).

307. Richter, Miloslav, *and* Vratislav Doležel. Výzkumná a vývojová základna v ČSSR. Organizace, řízení a plánování (Research and development base in the Czechoslovak Socialist Republic; organization, management, and planning). Praha, UTVEI, 1966. 161 p.

A basic survey of the organization and structure of research and development in Czechoslovakia, including the forms of management and planning. Describing the evolution of research and development during the recent years, the publication gives data on the number of scientists, wage trends, research and development, expenditures and investments, trends, and manpower analysis. The system of science education in Czechoslovakia and its accomplishments since 1956 are also discussed. Eight supplements give partial citations of pertinent laws and policies.

308. Slamecka, Vladimir. Science in Czechoslovakia. New York, Columbia University Press, 1963. 175 p. Map. Bibliography: p. 173-175.

A description of the organization and substantive content of science and engineering research in the academies of science, professional societies, universities, and industry in Czechoslovakia as of early 1963. Scientific manpower and training are discussed, and a comprehensive account of the scientific documentation and information system is given. Appendixes contain listings of research organizations, institutes, faculties, and industrial and government agencies engaged in research. Serial publications in the physical, engineering, and life sciences are listed with descriptive annotations by subject and field.

309. United Nations Educational, Scientific, and Cultural Organization. Science Policy and Organization of Scientific Research in the Czechoslovak Socialist Republic. Paris, UNESCO, 1965. 88 p. Illus. Bibliography: p. 87-88. (*Its* Science Policy Studies and Documents, no. 2)

The historical development of science in Czechoslovakia is described briefly, and the status of science policy, organization, and research as of 1963 is summarized. The financing of research and scientific manpower problems are discussed. The dynamic aspects of planning and coordination of research are considered, and the main trends of research in the third five-year plan (1961-1965) are stated. Extensive economic and social sciences data are presented in the appendixes.

D. EAST GERMANY

310. Slamecka, Vladimir. Science in East Germany. New York, Columbia University Press, 1963. 124 p. Map. Bibliography: p. 121-124.

A description of the organization of scientific and professional societies, universities, and industry in East Germany as of early 1963. Scientific manpower and training are discussed, and a comprehensive account is given of scientific documentation and information systems, including monographic publications, periodicals, technical reports, and patents. The appendixes contain reasonably complete listings of research organizations, institutes, faculties, and industrial and government agencies engaged in research in the physical, engineering, and life sciences. Serial publications in these fields are listed by subject with descriptive annotations.

E. HUNGARY

311. Aba, Iván. Műszaki-tudományos kutatás Magyarországon (Scientific and technical research in Hungary). Budapest, Műzaki Könyvkiadó, 1965. 434 p. Bibliography, illus.

A comprehensive survey of the programs of 42 major industrial and technical research institutes, including a brief sketch of the development of each institute. The persons responsible for specific projects are named, and the projects are reported in detail, including results and products. The research institutes treated are attached to the Hungarian Academy of Sciences (6), the Ministry of Heavy Industries (9), the Ministry of the Metallurgy and the Machine Industries (8), the Ministry of Light Industries (5), the Ministry of Food Supply (7), the Ministry of Construction (2), the Ministry of Traffic and Post (4), and the National Trade Union Council (1).

312. Erdey-Grúz, Tibor, *and* Imre Trencsényi-Waldapfel, *eds.* Science in Hungary. Budapest, Corvina Press, 1965. 316 p. Bibliography, illus.

The principal features of the organization of scientific research in Hungary are surveyed, and an account is given of 19 specific areas of the physical and social sciences. Each chapter is written by an outstanding Hungarian in the field and includes a brief report on the organization and present status of the discipline, the history of its development in Hungary, and the persons and organizations who have contributed and are contributing to that development. The areas treated are physics, chemistry, earth sciences, biology and medicine, veterinary science, agronomy, mathematics, economics, political science and law, history, linguistics, ethnography and folklore, literature, history of art, music, study of antiquity, archaeology, Orientology, and philosophy.

F. POLAND

313. Polish Research Guide; 1964. Compiled by Jerzy Kozłowski. Published for the National Science Foundation, Washington, D.C. Warszawa, Państwowe Wydaw. Naukowe, 1963. 419 p.

A complete guide to Polish scientific organizations, including the Polish Academy of Sciences, institutions of higher learning, museums, archives, and societies as of March 1963. The address, name of the director, scope of operations, facilities, and professional staff of each organization are stated. An index of institution names, with addresses, and an index of personal names, with addresses, are provided. General information on the organization of science and scientific institutions is given in the introduction. This guide has been published annually in Polish since 1958 as *Informator nauki polskiej.*

314. Rozwój techniki w PRL (Development of technology in the Polish People's Republic). Warszawa, Wydawnictwa Naukowo-Techniczne, 1965. 748 p. Illus., maps. Bibliography: p. 720-721.

This broad analysis of the attainments of Polish technology from 1945 to 1965 is divided into 15 sections by individual authors covering the history, current status, prospects, and plans for further development of the following areas of technology: geology; electrification and power; coal and gas; ferrous metallurgy; chemistry; clothing, leather, wood, paper, and food; construction and construction materials; transportation and communication; machinery and electrical engineering; new technologies (semiconductors, computers, isotopes); scientific and technical research; scientific and technical cooperation with other countries; promotion of new technology; technical publications and scientific and technical information in Poland; and standardization. The roles of the government, the party, and the national planning organizations are included in the treatment.

315. Suchodolski, Bogdan, *and* Eugeniusz Olszewski. The Development of Polish Science, 1945-1955. Warsaw, Polonia Publishing House, 1956. 90 p.

A summary of the social, economic, and educational situation in Poland following the Second World War provides the background for a survey of the reorganization of science in the decade following the war. Problems of science planning, and Polish achievements in the natural, applied, and social sciences are reviewed. Brief statements are made on the participation of Polish science in world science and the prospects for scientific development in Poland.

11

slavic civilization

by Rado L. Lencek

A. BIBLIOGRAPHIES AND GENERAL SURVEYS

316. Cross, Samuel H. Slavic Civilization Through the Ages. Cambridge, Harvard University Press, 1948. 195 p.

Eight lectures on the history and civilization of Slavs up to the time of their emergence as modern nationalities. An objective interpretation of the problems of influences and differentiation of Slavic cultures.

317. Derzhavin, N. S. Slaviane v drevnosti; kul'turno-istoricheskii ocherk (The Slavs in antiquity; a cultural-historical essay). Moskva, Akademiia nauk SSSR, 1946. 215 p.

To be used with caution, particularly wherever the author operates with Marr's pseudo-linguistic argumentation and applies aprioristic economic and social theories to Slavic prehistory. Available also in German translation: *Die Slaven im Altertum; eine kulturhistorische Abhandlung* (Weimar, Hermann Böhlau, 1948, 286 p., maps).

318. Diels, Paul. Die slavischen Völker. Mit einer Literaturübersicht von Alexander Adamczyk. Wiesbaden, Harrassowitz, 1963. 381 p. Maps. Bibliography: p. 311-357. (Veröffentlichungen des Osteuropa-Institutes, München, Bd. 11)

See also entry no. 94.

A good survey of Slavic peoples and their cultures by an authority in Slavic studies, written after the Second World War. Content: a chapter on the geography and history for each individual Slavic people; chapters on: Slavic Reciprocities and Panslavism, Slavic languages, dialects, literary languages, writing systems, Slavic religions, Church politics, oral poetry, literature, education, science, plastic and graphic arts, music, and law.

319. Dvornik, Francis. The Slavs: Their Early History and Civilization. Boston, American Academy of Arts and Sciences, 1956. 394 p. Maps. Bibliography: p. 341-371. (Survey of Slavic Civilization, v. 2)

A good attempt at a synoptic presentation of the early history and civilization of Slavs treating them as a whole. The bibliography is limited to works in non-Slavic languages; unfortunately it contains a few errors. For a criticism *see* M. Hellmann's "Zur Problematik der slavischen Frühzeit," *Jahrbücher für Geschichte Osteuropas* (München), v. 7, 1959: 196-203.

320. Dvornik, Francis. The Slavs in European History and Civilization. New Brunswick, N.J., Rutgers University Press, 1962. 688 p. Maps. Bibliography: p. 565-635.

See also entry no. 95.

An attempt to treat the history and culture of the Slavic peoples (thirteenth to eighteenth century) as a unity within the framework of European history and civilization.

321. Harkins, William E. Bibliography of Slavic Folk Literature. New York, King's Crown Press, 1953. 28 p.

A good bibliographic guide to the subject.

322. Lehr-Spławiński, Tadeusz. O pochodzeniu i praojczyźnie Słowian (On the origin and ancestral home of the Slavs). Poznań, Wydawn. Instytutu Zachodniego, 1946. 237 p. Maps. (Prace Instytutu Zachodniego, nr. 2)

Presents Lehr-Spławiński's version of the Polish hypothesis on Slavic ethnogenesis on the territory of the prehistoric Lusatian culture.

For an English summary of the author's views *see* "The Origin and Ancestral Home of the Slavs," in *Poland's Place in Europe*, edited by Zygmunt Wojciechowski (Poznań, Wydawnictwo Instytutu Zachodniego, 1947), p. 61-83.

For a criticism of the author's views *see* V. Felkenhahn's "Entstehung, Entwicklung und Ende der urslavischen Sprachgemeinschaft in polnischen Veröffentlichungen von T. Lehr-Spławinski," in *Zeitschrift für Slawistik* (Berlin), v. 1, 1956: 49-88.

323. Lencek, Rado L. A Bibliographical Guide to the Literature on Slavic Civilizations. New York, Columbia University, Department of Slavic Languages, 1966. 52 p.

A selected bibliography of 500 entries relevant to the study of Slavic civilizations in its broadest sense.

324. Niederle, Lubor. Manuel de l'antiquité slave. Paris, H. Champion,

1923-1926. 2 v. Illus., maps, diagr. (Collection de manuels publiée par l'Institut d'études slaves, 1)

A concise and documented presentation of the ethnogenesis of Slavic peoples, their early history, and civilization approximately up to 1000 A.D. In essence a short version of the monumental *Slovanské starožitnosti* (Slavic antiquities) of the same author (Praha, 1902-1934, 3 v. in 6), written for a French edition. Two recent translations of this work, into Czech (1953) and Russian (1956), argue for its continuing scholarly value.

325. Niederle, Lubor. Obozrienie sovremennago slavianstva (A survey of the contemporary Slavic world). Sanktpeterburg, Izdanie Otdieleniia russkago iazyka i slovesnosti Imperatorskoi Akademii nauk, 1909. 160 p. Map. (Entsiklopediia slavianskoi filologii, 2)

A basic geographic-statistical, historical, and ethnographic characterization of Slavic peoples before the First World War. Rich bibliographical sections attached to each chapter.

326. Niederle, Lubor. Slovanské starožitnosti (Slavic antiquities). Praha, Bursík a Kohout, 1902-1934. 7 v. in 12. Illus., maps, plates. (Biblioteka historická, čís. 4-15)

See also entry no. 103.

I. Oddíl historický (Historical section), 4 parts: Part 1. Původ a počátky národa slovanského (The origin and the beginnings of Slavic peoples), 2 v., 1902-1904, 528 p.; Part 2. Původ a počátky Slovanů jižních (The origin and the beginnings of Southern Slavs), 2 v., 1906-1910, 548 p.; Part 3. Původ a počátky Slovanů západních (The origin and the beginnings of Western Slavs), 1919, 258 p.; Part 4. Původ a počátky Slovanů východních (The origin and the beginnings of Eastern Slavs), 1924, 286 p.

II. Oddíl kulturní (Cultural section), 3 parts: Život starých Slovanů. Základy kulturních starožitností slovanských (Life of the Ancient Slavs. Foundations of Slavic cultural antiquities). Part 1: 2 v., 1911-1913, 897 p.; Part 2, v. 1, 1910, 299 p.; Part 2, v. 2, 1934, 211 p.; Part 3, 2 v., 1921-1925, 789 p.

The most authoritative comprehensive survey of Slavic antiquities covering the problems of the ethnogenesis and early history of Slavic peoples, and their oldest material, social, and spiritual culture up to the beginning of Christianization. Niederle's work represents lifelong research and a synthesis of most of the available information about the Slavs accumulated before the First World War. Thoroughly documented, it is objective and dependable. The six volumes of the second section (also published separately under the title *Život starých Slovanů*) offer an encyclopedic description of the primitive Slavic civilization. The chapter on primitive Slavic law (Part 2, v. 2) was written by Th. Saturník. The entire work is richly illustrated, with a number of maps.

327. Polska Akademia Nauk. *Komitet Słowianoznawstwa.* Słownik starożytności słowiańskich (A dictionary of Slavic antiquities). Edited by

Władysław Kowalenko and others. Wrocław, Zakład Narodowy im. Ossolińskich, 1961– Illus., maps.

See also entries no. 104 *and* 2527.

This encyclopedia of Slavic antiquities, thus far incomplete, covers the period up to 1200 A.D. So far volumes for the letters A to M have been published.

328. Šafárik, Pavel J. Slowanské starožitnosti (Slavic antiquities). Praha, Spurný, 1837. 1005 p. 2d ed.: Praha, B. Tempsky, 1862-1863. 2 v. (*His* Sebrané spisy, dil 1-2)

A pioneering work on the earliest history of Slavic peoples, written to prove their autochthonism. Available in Polish, Russian, German, and French translations.

Šafárik is credited as well with a pioneer attempt at an ethnographic description of Slavic peoples. *See* his *Slowanský národopis* (Slavic ethnography) (2d ed., Praha, 1842, 189 p.; 4th ed., Praha, Československá akademie věd, 1955, 288 p. Československá Akademie věd, Ústav pro ethnografii a folkloristiku. Klasikově vědy. Sekce filosofii a historie, sv. 2).

329. Slavia antiqua; czasopismo poświęcone starożytnósciom słowiańskim Slavia antiqua; a journal of Slavic antiquities). 1948– Poznań, Wrocław, Organ Katedry Archeologii Polski Uniwersytetu im. Adama Mickiewicza w Poznaniu i Katedry Archeologii Słowiańskiej Uniwersytetu Warszawskiego. Irregular. Illus., ports., maps.

Contains bibliographical review articles on Slavic antiquities. Some articles with English, French, or Russian summaries.

330. Vznik a počátky Slovanů. Sborník pro studium slovanských starožitností (The origins and the beginnings of the Slavs. Miscellany for the study of Slavic antiquities). 1– Praha, Ntkl. Československé akademie věd, 1956– Irregular.

Edited by Jan Eisner, this constitutes a periodic review and revision of Niederle's work. Each volume contains contributions to the study of the prehistory, early history of Slavic peoples. From volume 6, articles are in English, French, or German.

A classified and annotated bibliography of writings on Slavic antiquities and ethnography for the years 1955-1961 appeared in v. 3, p. 317-480; v. 4, p. 357-478; v. 5, p. 251-377.

B. SLAVIC ETHNOGENESIS

331. Czekanowski, Jan. Wstęp do historii Słowian; perspektywy antropologiczne, etnograficzne, archeologiczne i językowe (Introduction to the history of the Slavs; anthropologic, ethnographic, archaeologic and linguistic perspectives). 2d rev. and enl. ed. Poznań, Instytut Zachodni, 1957. 514 p. Illus., tables, maps. Bibliography: p. 454-470. (Prace Instytutu Zachodniego, nr. 21)

The most detailed presentation of the hypothesis of the modern

Polish school of archaeologists (J. Czekanowski, L. Kozłowski, J. Kostrzewski, T. Sulimirski) about the proto-home of Slavs in the eastern part of Central Europe. Based primarily on a mathematical-statistical analysis of anthropological, linguistic, and archaeological data.

For an English summary of author's views *see* "The Ancient Home of Slavs," *The Slavonic and East European Review* (London), v. 25, 1947: 356-372.

332. International Congress of Slavists, *4th, Moscow, 1958. Sovetskii komitet.* Sbornik otvetov na voprosy po iazykoznaniiu (k IV Mezhdunarodnomu s"ezdu slavistov) (A collection of answers to questions on linguistics for the Fourth International Congress of Slavists). Moskva, Izdatel'stvo Akademii nauk SSSR, 1958. 294 p.

Contains on pages 152-197 the most recent discussion of the problems of Slavic ethnogenesis and early Balto-Slavic linguistic relations by such authorities as J. Czekanowski, T. Lehr-Spławinski, P. N. Tret'iakov, M. Vasmer. The discussion is presented around the following questions: (No. 20) Did the Balto-Slavic ethnic and linguistic unity exist and how is it to be understood? (No. 21) How to represent the territory of the home of the ancient Slavs? (No. 22) When did the division of Slavs into main branches occur? For a résumé of the papers delivered at the Moscow Congress and for further biographical data, *see*:

International Congress of Slavists, *4th, Moscow, 1958.* Materialy diskussii. Tom vtoroi: Problemy slavianskogo iazykoznaniia (Materials for discussion. Volume 2: Problems of Slavic linguistics). Moskva, Izdatel'stvo Akademii nauk SSSR, 1962. p. 419-455.

333. Jażdżewski, Konrad. Atlas to the Prehistory of the Slavs. Łódź, 1948-1949. 2 v. (20 col. maps, 143 p. text). Bibliography: v. 2, p. 19-25. (Acta praehistorica Universitatis Lodziensis, 1, 2)

See also entry no. 2515.

A cartographic presentation of the stages in the ethnogenesis and expansion of Slavs from 1300 B.C to A.D. 1025, based on the hypothesis postulating the presence of Slavs in the territories of the Bronze Age Lusatian culture.

Jażdżewski's work was published by the same publisher and in the same format also in a Polish edition: *Atlas do pradziejów Słowian* (Łódź, 1948-1949).

334. Vasmer, Max. Die alten Bevölkerungsverhältnisse Russlands im Lichte der Sprachforschung. Berlin, Walter De Gruyter & Co., 1941. 35 p. Maps. (Preussische Akademie der Wissenschaften; Vorträge und Schriften, 5)

A linguist's projection of the ethnical structure of Eastern Europe before the ninth century A.D., based exclusively on the analysis of loanwords and geographical names and their patterns in Baltic, Iranian, Germanic, Finno-Ugrian, and Slavic-language material. An attempt at defining the proto-home of Slavs in the last centuries B.C. in the area between the upper Dniester, Pripet, the upper Don River, and the direction of the expansion of Eastern Slavs in subsequent centuries.

For Vasmer's earlier treatment of the same subject *see* his *Untersuchungen über die ältesten Wohnsitze der Slaven. I Die Iranier in Südrussland* (Leipzig, Markert & Petters, 1923; Veröffentlichungen des Balt. u. Slav. Instituts d. Universität Leipzig, 3). *See also* Vasmer's "Die Urheimat der Slaven," in *Der ostdeutsche Volksboden: Aufsätze zu den Fragen des Ostens*, edited by W. Volz (Breslau, 1926), p. 118-143.

C. ARCHAEOLOGY AND MATERIAL CULTURE

335. Borkovský, Ivan. Staroslovanská keramika ve střední Evropě; studie k počátkům slovanské kultury (Old Slavic ceramics in Central Europe; a contribution to the beginnings of Slavic culture). Praha, Nákladem vlastním, 1940. 113 p. Illus.

A monographic treatment of the early Slavic "hradiště" ceramics of the Prague type pottery of the fifth and sixth centuries.

336. Eisner, Jan, *ed.* Rukovět slovanské archeologie; počátky Slovanů a jejich kultury (A handbook of Slavic archeology; the beginnings of the Slavs and their culture). v. 1– Praha, Academia, 1966– Illus., maps.

The first part of a three-volume handbook designed to update Niederle's older *Manuel de l'antiquité slave* (Paris, H. Champion, 1923-1926, 2 v.). This volume deals with the problems of the origin and the beginnings of Slavs, their historical expansion, Slavic pottery, burial rituals, cults, and magic — as reflected by the archaeological discoveries made between 1930 and 1963. An excellent vademecum into the problems of Slavic antiquities, it summarizes a mass of reports of new discoveries and studies from all Slavic areas.

For a French summary of author's views on the problems of Slavic ethnogenesis *see* "Les origines des Slaves d'après les préhistoriens tchèques," *Revue des études slaves* (Paris), v. 24, 1948: 129-142.

337. Gimbutas, Marija. Bronze Age Cultures in Central and Eastern Europe. The Hague, Mouton, 1965. 681 p. Illus., maps, tables, bibliography.

A solid archaeological study of the European Bronze Age. The chapters on the cultures in Eastern Central Europe, in particular on the branch of the Corded Pottery Culture of the first half of the second millennium B.C. between the upper Vistula basin and the middle Dnieper River (the North Carpathian Culture), offer new archaeological documentation for the location of the earliest Slavic area in southeast Poland, former Galicia, Volynia, and Podolia.

For a summary of the author's thesis *see* "From the Neolithic to the Iron Age in the Region Between the Upper Vistula and Middle Dnieper Rivers; a Survey; Archaeology Contributes to the Question of Slavic Origins," *International Journal of Slavic Linguistics and Poetics* (The Hague), v. 3, 1960: 1-12.

338. Hensel, Witold. Archeologia o początkach miast słowiańskich (Archaeology of the beginnings of Slavic towns). Wrocław, Zakład Narodowy im. Ossolińskich, 1963. 187 p. Illus., maps, bibliographical footnotes.

An outline of the basic problems in archaeological investigation of earlier Slavic towns.

339. Hensel, Witold. Słowiańszczyzna wczesnośredniowieczna; zarys kultury materialnej (The Slavic peoples in the Middle Ages; an outline of the material culture). 3d rev. and enl. ed. Warszawa, Państwowe Wydawn. Naukowe, 1965. 678 p. Illus., maps, col. plates, plans, bibliographical footnotes.

Though not final, an excellent comprehensive survey of the material culture of Slavs between the fifth and thirteenth centuries. Following in the main Niederle's and Moszyński's studies (*see* entries 326, 341, 353), it primarily exploits an extensive postwar literature, mostly Polish, Czech, and Russian. Documentation is limited to the bibliographical notes under the text. Available also in German translation: *Die Slawen im frühen Mittelalter; ihre materielle Kultur* (Berlin, Akademie-Verlag, 508 p., illus., maps. Bibliography: p. 461-477).

340. Hołubowicz, Włodzimierz. Garncarstwo wczesnośredniowieczne Słowian (Medieval Slavic pottery). Wrocław, 1965. 196 p. Illus., bibliographical references. (Acta Universitatis Wratislaviensis, no. 31)

A good account of early Slavic traditions in ceramics throughout the Middle Ages.

341. Niederle, Lubor. Rukovět slovanské archeologie (A handbook of Slavic archaeology). Praha, Slovanský ústav, 1931. 292 p. Illus., maps. (Rukověti Slovanského ústavu, sč. 1)

The first compendium of an archaeology of Slavic peoples. From the point of view of new discoveries since 1930 it is dated, yet still valid in its analyses and conclusions.

342. Obrysy Slovanstva. Sborník přednášek Slovanského ústavu v Praze (A profile of Slavdom: a collection of papers of the Slavic Institute in Prague). Edited by A. Boháč and others. Praha, Orbis, 1948. 230 p.

Six papers by leading Czechoslovak authorities on some problems of Slavic civilization in anthropology (J. Malý), prehistory (J. Eisner, J. Filip), historiography (J. Macůrek), and literature (F. Wollman).

D. THE ROLE OF LANGUAGE

343. Budilovich, Anton Semenovich. Pervobytnye slaviane v ikh iazyke, bytie i poniatiakh po dannym leksikal'nym; izsliedovaniia v oblasti lingvisticheskoi paleontogii slavian (The primitive Slavs in their language, way of life, and concepts according to lexical data; investigations in the linguistic paleontology of the Slavs). Kiev, 1878. 2 v. in 1.

An early investigation of the lexical heritage of the Slavic languages seeking to discover the fundamental features of the oldest common Slavic civilization. Although obsolete in its conclusions, the book is still valuable in the organization of its material. For a modern treatment of the same problem *see* Louise Wanstrat's *Beiträge zur Charakteristik des russischen Wortschatzes* (Leipzig, Markert und Petters, 1933, 114 p., Veröffentlichungen des Slavischen Instituts an der Friedrich-Wilhelms-Universität Berlin, 7).

344. Filin, F. P. Obrazovanie iazyka vostochnykh slavian (The formation of the language of the Eastern Slavs). Leningrad, Izd-vo Akademii nauk SSSR, 1962. 293 p.

The first part of the book deals comprehensively and critically with the problems of the origin of the Slavs as well as the origin and the evolution of a common Slavic language. The second part is exclusively concerned with the history of Eastern Slavic languages.

345. Moszyński, Kazimierz. Pierwotny zasiąg języka prasłowiańskiego (The original extent of the proto-Slavic language). Wrocław, Zakład Narodowy im. Ossolińskich, 1957. 332 p. Illus. (Polska Akademia Nauk. Komitet Językoznawczy. Prace językoznawcze, no. 16)

Presents Moszyński's proposition for localization of the proto-Slavic linguistic territory in the area between the Vistula River, the Upper Dnestr, and the Dnepr Basins. Moszyński's arguments are based on a linguistic analysis of botanic, river, and place names.

346. Reiter, Norbert. Mythologie der alten Slaven. *In* Wörterbuch der Mythologie. Stuttgart, Klett, 1964. p. 165-208.

A good survey of the subject, alphabetically arranged according to subject entries, with the latest results of historical and linguistic research.

E. RELIGION AND LAW

347. Gasparini, Evel. (I) Le città sacre del Baltico; (II) L'ergologia degli Slavi. Venezia, Istituto Universitario Cà Foscari, 1950. 240 p. Illus. Bibliography: p. 219-237.

An interesting attempt at a cultural-historical interpretation of the primitive culture of early Slavs in the light of the ethnographic and ethnologic comparative data of Slavic and non-Slavic peoples. Author's thesis: the primary stratum of Slavic culture reflects the mentality of a matriarchic society; the subsequent Indo-Europeanization of the Slavs left this stratum virtually intact.

348. Jakobson, Roman. Slavic Mythology. *In* Funk & Wagnalls Standard Dictionary of Folklore, Myth, and Legend. v. 2. New York, Funk & Wagnalls, 1950. p. 1025-1028. Bibliography: p. 1027-1028.

A concise outline of Slavic pre-Christian beliefs with particular stress on the linguistic interpretation of the common Slavic religious terminology and of the recorded names of Slavic deities and demons.

349. Kadlec, Karel. Introduction à l'étude comparative de l'histoire du droit public des peuples slaves. Paris, H. Champion, 1933. 328 p. Bibliography: p. 317-322. (Collection de manuels publiée par l'Institut d'études slaves, 3)

See also entry no. 134.

An attempt at a synthesis of the history of Slavic law, conceived to give a comprehensive view of the legal traditions of the Slavic peoples. The published volume covers only the earliest forms of the constitutional law of Slavic societies up to the tenth century. A sequel which would have treated the civil and penal law was never written. As a whole, a good survey of the subject; some chapters would need updating.

350. Máchal, Jan. Slavic Mythology. *In* Gray, Louis H., *ed.* The Mythology of All Races. v. 3. Boston, Marshall Jones Co., 1918. p. 215-314, 351-361. Illus. Bibliography: p. 387-398.

A most comprehensive survey of Slavic mythology. With notes and bibliography.

351. Unbegaun, Boris. La réligion des anciens slaves. *In* Mana; introduction à l'histoire des réligions. v. 2, Les réligions de l'Europe ancienne, pt. 3. Paris, Presses universitaires de France, 1948. p. 387-445.

An excellent survey of the religious beliefs and practices of ancient Slavs.

F. ART, ETHNOGRAPHY, AND FOLKLORE

352. Anfänge der slavischen Musik. Edited by Ladislav Mokrý. Bratislava, Slowakische Akademie der Wissenschaften, 1966. 178 p. Facsims., music. (Slowakische Akademie der Wissenschaften. Institut für Musikwissenschaft. Symposia, 1).

A collection of papers presented at the first Symposium on early Slavic music (Bratislava, 1964), concerned predominantly with the problems of Church Slavonic music.

353. Moszyński, Kazimierz. Kultura ludowa Słowian (Slavic folk culture). Kraków, Polska Akademja Umiejętności, 1929-1939. 3 v. (2352 p.) Illus., maps, music.

A successful attempt at a synthetical ethnographic description of the Slavic peasant societies' culture. Part 1 deals with the material culture: economics, gathering and production of food and goods, primitive technology, transportation, and communication; part 2 treats different aspects of the "spiritual" culture: "scientific" knowledge, primitive religion, beliefs, magic, arts. A strong emphasis is on this last aspect of spiritual culture; excellent are the syntheses on plastic art, drama, dance, music, and oral literature. The work, compiled with the help of a number of authorities in West and South Slavic ethnography, draws from the author's own unpublished collections and from an extensive literature; unfortunately little or no documentation is given.

354. Pírkova-Jakobson, Svatava. Slavic Folklore. *In* Funk & Wagnalls Standard Dictionary of Folklore, Myth, and Legend. v. 2. New York, Funk & Wagnalls, 1950. p. 1019-1025.

A short characterization of Slavic folklore and its classification according to genres.

355. Rybakov, Boris A. Iskusstvo drevnikh slavian (the art of the ancient Slavs). *In* Grabar', Igor E., V. N. Lazarev, *and* V. S. Kemenov, *eds.* Istoriia russkogo iskusstva (The history of Russian art). v. 1. Moskva, Izdatel'stvo Akademii nauk SSSR, 1953. p. 39-92. Illus.

A competent survey of the art of the ancient Slavs. Available also in German, "Die Kunst der alten Slawen," *in* Grabar', I. E., V. N. Lazarev, *and* V. S. Kemenov, eds., *Geschichte der russische Kunst*, v. 1 (Dresden, Verlag der Kunst, 1957, p. 23-58).

G. PAN-SLAVISM AND SLAVIC RELATIONS

356. Brtáň, Rudo. Barokový slavizmus; porovnávacia štúdia z dejín slovanskej slovesnosti (Baroque Slavism; comparative studies in the history of Slavic literature). Lipt. Sv. Mikuláš, Nákl. Spolku Tranoscius, 1939. 293 p.

An analysis of the themes and motifs in Slavic literary creation during the period of "baroque Slavism" (16th to 17th centuries).

357. Horák, Jiří, *ed.* Slovanská vzájemnost, 1836-1936; sborník prací k 100. výročí vydání rozpravy Jana Kollára o slovanské vzájemnosti (Slavic reciprocity, 1836-1936; collected papers on the occasion of the 100th anniversary of Jan Kollár's essay on Slavic reciprocity). Praha, Nákl. České akademie věd a umění, v komisi Orbis, 1938. 428 p. Ports.. facsims., bibliographical footnotes.

Papers discussing the origin of J. Kollár's *Über die literarische Wechselseitigkeit zwischen den . . .* and its influence on different Slavic peoples.

For the same occasion, a complete edition of Kollár's versions of the essay on "Slavic reciprocity" with an introductory study by M. Weingart was published in: *Jan Kollár, Rozpravy o slovanské vzájemnosti* (Jan Kollár, essays on Slavic reciprocity) (Praha, Nakl. Slovanského ústavu v komisi Orbis, 1929, 242 p., port., Knihovna Slovanského ústavu v Praze, sv. 1).

358. Kohn, Hans. Pan-Slavism; Its History and Ideology. Notre Dame, Ind., University of Notre Dame Press, 1953. 356 p. Bibliography: p. 339-348.

See also entries no. 112, 182, *and* 447.

A comprehensive survey and analysis of the history and ideology of Pan-Slavism from its beginnings after the Napoleonic Wars to the period following the Second World War.

359. Perwolf, Josef. Slaviane, ikh vzaimnyia otnosheniia i sviazi (The

Slavs, their mutual relations and ties). Varshava, Tip. K. Kovalevskago, 1886-1893. 3 v. in 4.

A dated discussion of Slavic cultural interrelations. The framework is Pan-Slavic, the problems are presented from the Russian point of view.

360. Pypin, Aleksandr N. Panslavizm v proshlom i nastoiashchem (1878) (Pan-Slavism in the past and present [1878]). Foreword and notes by V. V. Vodovzov. Sanktpeterburg, "Kolos," 1913. 189 p.

A sound historical interpretation of Pan-Slavism from the point of view of a Russian scholar. Originally written immediately after the Congress of Berlin (1878), and reprinted from *Vestnik Evropy*, 1878, no. 9-12, it is in many respects dated, though still of some relevance.

361. Weingart, Miloš. Slovanská vzájemnost; úvahy o jejích základech a osudech (Slavic reciprocity; a dissertation on its beginnings and fate). Bratislava, Nákl. "Akademie," 1926. 255 p. Bibliography: p. 231-240. (Sbírka přednášek a rozprav Extense University Komenského v Bratislavě, sv. 2)

An attempt at a characterization of the idea and movement of Slavic reciprocity during the 19th century.

362. Wollman, Frank. Slovanství v jazykově literárním obrození u Slovanů (Slavdom in the linguistic and literary revival of the Slavs). Praha, Státní pedagogické nakl., 1958. 230 p. Bibliography: p. 211-231. (Spisy University v Brně, Filosofická fakulta, 52)

A good analysis of the ideological current which prepared and led to the revival of Slavic peoples. It focuses on the processes of the proliferation of Slavic literary languages in the beginning of the 19th century.

12

SLAVIC LANGUAGES

by Rado L. Lencek
(except for the section on bibliographies)

A. BIBLIOGRAPHIES

by Elizabeth Beyerly

363. Akademiia nauk SSSR. *Institut russkogo iazyka.* Slavianskoe iazykoznanie; bibliograficheskii ukazatel' literatury izdannoi v SSSR s 1918 po 1960 gg. (Slavic linguistics; a bibliographic guide to literature published in the USSR, 1918-1960). Compiled by S. B. Bernshtein, D. E. Mikhal'chi, and V. I. Shunkov. Moskva, Izdatel'stvo Akademii nauk SSSR, 1963. 2 v.

V. 1: 1918-1955; v. 2: 1956-1960. Lists material in Russian, Ukrainian, and Belorussian concerning the history, dialects, morphology, and lexicology of the Slavic languages. *See also*:

Berkov, Pavel N. Mezhdunarodnoe sotrudnichestvo slavistov i voprosy organizatsii slavianovedcheskikh bibliografii (International cooperation of Slavists and organizational aspects of Slavistic bibliographies). Moskva, Izdatel'stvo Akademii nauk SSSR, 1958. 31 p. Bibliographical footnotes. (IV Mezhdunarodnyi s"ezd slavistov. Soobshcheniia)

364. Anzeiger für slavische Philologie. Bd. 1– 1966– Wiesbaden, Harrassowitz. Irregular.

365. Dissertationen auf dem Gebiete der Slawistik und osteuropäische Geschichte angenommen an den Universitäten der DDR bis zum Jahre 1955. Zeitschrift für Slawistik, v. 1, 1956: 158-160.

A list of 33 titles, mainly in the field of linguistics. Dissertations in the university in Vienna are listed in the *Wiener slavistisches Jahrbuch*, v. 10, 1963: 195-205; v. 11, 1964: 216-218.

366. Hille, Annemarie. Bibliographische Einführung in das Studium der slawischen Philologie. Halle (Saale), M. Niemeyer, 1959. 149 p.

Intended for the student of Slavic languages, it also includes general linguistic reference works and lists for the individual Slavic languages, descriptive grammars, phonetic and dialect studies, dictionaries, and chrestomathies appearing between 1900 and the late 1950's.

367. Mahnken, Irmgard. Materialen zu einer slawistischen Bibliographie; Arbeiten der in Österreich, der Schweiz and der Bundesrepublik Deutschland tätigen Slawisten, 1945-1963. München, O. Sagner, 1963. 257 p.

Contains 2,561 titles of monographs and selected journal articles published by Slavists in West Germany, Switzerland, and Austria. Includes Festschriften for and book reviews by Slavic scholars in German-speaking countries. Author and subject index. For an analogous East German publication, *see*:

Rappich, Heinz. Slawistische Publikationen der DDR bis 1962; Bibliographie . . . Berlin, Akademie-Verlag, 1963. 152 p.

368. Modern Language Association of America. MLA International Bibliography of Books and Articles on the Modern Languages and Literatures. 1921-1962. New York, Kraus Reprint Co., 1964. 15 v.; 1963– New York, New York University Press, 1964–

Reprints of the annual bibliography contained in the *Publications of the Modern Language Association*. Beginning in 1950, each issue has contained a section on "East European Languages and Literatures."

Also to be consulted are:

Permanent International Committee of Linguists. Bibliographie linguistique. 1939-1947. Utrecht, Spectrum.

The Year's Work in Modern Language Studies. v. 1– 1929/30– London, Oxford University Press, 1931–

369. Moscow. Publichnaia bibloteka. *Otdel spravochno-bibliograficheskoi i informatsionnoi raboty*. Bibliografiia bibliografii po iazykoznaniiu; annotirovannyi sistematicheskii ukazatel' otechestvennykh izdanii (Bibliography of bibliographies on linguistics; annotated, systematic index to Russian and Soviet publications). Compiled by E. I. Kukushkina and A. G. Stepanova. Moskva, 1963. 411 p.

370. Novaia inostrannaia literatura po iazykoznaniiu (New foreign literature on linguistics). 1– 1960– Moskva, Fundamental'naia biblioteka obshchestvennykh nauk. Monthly.

Novaia sovetskaia literatura po iazykoznaniiu (New Soviet literature on linguistics). 1– 1960– Moskva, Fundamental'naia biblioteka obshchestvennykh nauk. Monthly.

These bibliographic serials, which are issued only in a restricted edition, provide a current guide to linguistic publications recorded by major libraries in Moscow, including many references to the Slavic languages. A similar publication is *Novaia literatura po obshchim problemam slavianovedeniia* (New literature on common problems of Slavic studies) (1–, 1966–, Moskva, Fundamental'naia biblioteka obshchestvennykh nauk, quarterly), largely devoted to Slavic studies in general, but offering material relevant to the study of languages. For an earlier effort at a current bibliography of Slavic linguistics, *see*:

Mach, Otto. Auswahl der wichtigsten Literatur zur Slavistik. Welt der Slaven, v. 1, 1956: 93-136, 232-264, 358-392, 450-507; v. 2, 1957: 90-128, 222-255, 343-375, 426-488; v. 3, 1958: 56-96, 187-224, 329-368, 441-503; v. 4, 1959: 98-128, 457-484. Intended as a current bibliography on Slavistic matters, compilation ceased when Dr. Mach took on other duties. The entries in volume four list materials relating to the Fourth International Congress of Slavists, held in 1958.

371. Seemann, Klaus-Dieter, *and* Frank Siegmann. Bibliographie der slavistischen Arbeiten aus den deutschsprachigen Fachzeitschriften, 1876-1963. Wiesbaden, Harrassowitz, 1965. 422 p. (Bibliographische Mitteilungen des Osteuropa Instituts an der Freien Universität Berlin, Heft 8)

See also entry no. 439.

This work is primarily an index to articles published from 1876 to 1963 in *Archiv für slawische Philologie, Zeitschrift für slavische Philologie, Wiener slavistisches Jahrbuch, Die Welt der Slaven*, and *Zeitschrift für Slawistik*. In addition, articles from 25 other German journals concerned with Slavic literature, culture, and history are listed. Entries arranged by language with subject subdivision. Author index.

372. Stankiewicz, Edward, *and* Dean S. Worth. A Selected Bibliography of Slavic Linguistics. v. 1. The Hague, Mouton, 1966. 315 p. (Slavistic Printings and Reprintings, 49)

See also entry no. 2941.

This is the first volume of a projected bibliographical survey of selected literature on Slavic languages; it is not annotated. Volume 1, devoted to the South Slavic languages, comprises as well chapters on general all-Slavic topics, such as Balto-Slavic, Slavic accentology, Common Slavic, and Comparative Slavic.

For an annotated survey of the most important all-Slavic linguistical topics, see *A Bibliographical Guide to the Russian Language* by Boris O. Unbegaun with the collaboration of J. S. G. Simmons (Oxford, Clarendon Press, 1953, 174 p.). *See also*:

Birkenmayer, Sigmund S. A Selective Bibliography of Works Related to the Teaching of Slavic Languages and Literatures in the United States and Canada, 1942-1967. New York, American Council on the Teaching of Foreign Languages, 1968. 40 p. *See also* Miroslav Laiske's *Slavistické bibliografie vydané v českých zemích 1945-1967.* (Praha, Ústav pro čes. literaturu, ČSAV, 1968, 273 p.).

B. MONOGRAPHIC STUDIES

1. Surveys and Histories of Slavic Languages

373. De Bray, Reginald G. A. Guide to the Slavonic Languages. London, J. M. Dent & Sons, 1951. 797 p. Bibliography: p. 791-797.

A competent though not technically complicated presentation of the grammars of the 11 Slavic standard languages (including Old Church Slavonic). De Bray's *Guide* gives basic information about the history and evolution of each language, its orthography, main dialects; it presents a concise summary of the grammar and a few texts of each language. The book might serve as an excellent introduction to the comparative study of the modern Slavic languages.

374. Lehr-Spławiński, Tadeusz, W. Kuraszkiewicz, *and* F. Sławski. Przegląd i charakterystyka języków słowiańskich (A survey and characterization of Slavic languages). Warszawa, Państwowe Wydawn. Naukowe, 1954. 166 p. Maps. Bibliographical notes: p. 41-42, 75-76, 121-122, 165-166.

A short comprehensive description of Slavic languages with a general section on Common Slavic linguistic unity and chapters on individual Slavic languages, their linguistic characterization, description of their dialects, a short history of their literary standards and literatures. The description of each language also contains a selection of texts illustrating the contemporary Slavic standards.

375. Stieber, Zdzisław. Zarys dialektologii języków zachodniosłowiańskich z wyborem tekstów gwarowych (An outline of the dialectology of the West-Slavic languages with a selection of dialectal texts). Warszawa, Państwowe Wydawnictwo Naukowe, 1956. 132 p. Maps. Bibliography: p. 131-132.

See also entry no. 2949.

Sławski, Franciszek. Zarys dialektologii południowosłowiańskiej z wyborem tekstów gwarowych (An outline of South-Slavic dialectology with a selection of dialectal texts). Warszawa, Państwowe Wydawn. Naukowe, 1962. 252 p. Maps.

Kuraszkiewicz, Władysław. Zarys dialektologii wschodniosłowiańskiej z wyborem tekstów gwarowych (An outline of East-Slavic dialectology with a selection of dialectal texts). 2d rev. and enl. ed. Warszawa, Państwowe Wydawn. Naukowe, 1963. 166 p. Maps.

Three handbooks on Slavic dialectology. Each contains a general characterization of one of the three language groups — West, South, and East Slavic — and of their literary standards, and gives a concise description of their dialects. The main individual dialects are illustrated by a representative selection of specimens.

376. Weingart, Miloš, *ed.* Slovanské spisovné jazyky v době přítomné (Slavic literary languages in our time). Written by J. Frček, J. Haller,

J. Heidenreich, K. Krejčí, J. Páta, J. Stanislav, F. Tichý. Praha, Melantrich, 1937. 314 p. (Dobrovského Knižnice duchovědná, 1)

A synoptic survey, written by numerous authors, of the history of Slavic literary languages, their main problems, and such evolutionary tendencies as appeared in the late thirties. The description of each language is followed by a selected bibliography.

2. General Comparative Studies

377. Bernshtein, Samuil B. Ocherk sravnitel'noi grammatiki slavianskikh iazykov (An outline of the comparative grammar of Slavic languages). Moskva, Akademiia nauk SSSR, Institut slavianovedeniia, 1961. 350 p. Bibliography: p. 309-315.

A compendium of the comparative phonology of the Slavic languages aiming at a modern structural description of the evolution of the common Slavic phonemic system. Essentially eclectic, Bernshtein's work gives the impression of a rather heterogeneous treatment. In its introductory chapter (p. 8-118) there is an excellent résumé of various aspects of the external linguistics of Slavic languages.

378. Horálek, Karel. Úvod do studia slovanských jazyků (An introduction to the study of Slavic languages). 2d ed. Praha, Nakl. Československé akademie věd, 1962. 535 p. Bibliography: p. 458-527. (Práce Československé akademie věd, 4)

A most comprehensive presentation of the problems of synchrony and diachrony of the Slavic languages. It discusses the questions of the oldest relations of Slavic with the Indo-European and Baltic languages; the phonology, morphology, syntax, and lexicology of Slavic languages; the history of Slavic literary languages; their graphic systems; the individual natural Slavic languages; and the history of comparative Slavic linguistics. It gives as well an extensive bibliography classified by subject.

The second edition of Horálek's work represents an updated revision of the first (Praha, Nakl. Československé akademie věd, 1955, 487 p.; bibliography: p. 436-482).

379. Jakobson, Roman. Slavic Languages; a Condensed Survey. 2d ed. New York, King's Crown Press, 1955. 36 p. Selected bibliography: p. 22-36.

A short presentation of the Slavic languages and of the history of their literary standards; a condensed structural statement on their comparative phonology and comparative grammar.

380. Kořínek, J. M. Od indoeuropského prajazyka k praslovančine (From the primitive Indo-European to the Common Slavic). Bratislava, Slovenská Akadémia vied a umení, 1948. 126 p. (3 sv. Náučnej knižnice Slovenskej Akadémie vied a umení)

A synthesis of the neogrammarian treatment of the problem of the Primitive Indo-European and the oldest phase of the Primitive Slavic. It contains a general introduction into the methods used in linguistic prehistory, a structural outline of phonology, and a chapter on morphology with a complete discussion of substantives.

381. Meillet, Antoine. Le slave commun. 2d ed., revised and enlarged with the assistance of A. Vaillant. Paris, H. Champion, 1934. 538 p. Bibliography: p. xiii-xiv. (Collection de manuels publiée par l'Institut d'études slaves, 2; Collection linguistique, XV)

A model structural description of Common Slavic in its evolution from the Indo-European to the dissolution of its unity through the eighth century. Two central sections deal with the phonetics and morphology of Common Slavic; two additional chapters treat some problems of Common Slavic phrase and vocabulary.

The first edition appeared in 1924. The latest printing of the second edition was in 1965. The second edition in Russian translation is annotated by P. S. Kuznetsov, *Obshcheslavianskii iazyk* (Common Slavic) Moskva, Izdatel'stvo inostrannoi literatury, 1951, 491 p.; bibliography: p. 413-416).

382. Mikkola, Julius J. Urslavische Grammatik; Einführung in das vergleichende Studium der slavischen Sprachen. Heidelberg, Carl Winter, 1913-1950. 3 v. Bibliography: v. 3, p. 104-106.

Contents: v. 1, Lautlehre, Vokalismus, Betonung, 1913, 146 p.; v. 2, Konsonantismus, 1942, 56 p.; v. 3, Formenlehre, 1950, 108 p. A neogrammarian outline of the grammar of Common Slavic, completely detached from the historical Slavic languages.

383. Miklosich, Franz, *Ritter von.* Vergleichende Grammatik der slavischen Sprachen, 2d ed. Wien, Wilhelm Braumüller, 1875-1883. 4 v.

This is a pioneering work in Slavic linguistics which in applying the comparative method to Slavic languages did not go beyond the mere juxtaposing of linguistic data. The fourth volume of Miklosich's work still represents the best comprehensive documentation of the syntax of Slavic languages.

384. Nahtigal, Rajko. Slovanski jeziki (The Slavic languages). 2d rev. and enl. ed. Ljubljana, Državna založba Slovenije, 1952. 335 p. Bibliography: p. 291-327.

An elegant, though not structural, comparative survey of the evolution of the phonetics and morphology of Slavic languages. The first part deals with Common Slavic, the second part with the historical Slavic languages.

The first edition appeared in 1938, and there is a German translation, *Die slavischen Sprachen; Abriss der vergleichenden Grammatik* (Wiesbaden, O. Harrassowitz, 1961, 270 p.), as well as a Russian translation, *Slavianskie iazyki* (The Slavic languages) (Moskva, Izdatel'stvo inostrannoi literatury, 1963, 341 p.).

385. Selishchev, Afanasii M. Slavianskoe iazykoznanie. Tom I. Zapadnoslavianskie iazyki (Slavic linguistics. v. 1, West-Slavic languages). Moskva, Gosudarstvennoe Uchebno-pedagogicheskoe izdatel'stvo Narkomprosa RSFSR, 1941. 463 p. Illus.

A good introduction to the Western-Slavic languages with extensive chapters on linguistic geography, dialects, literary monuments, evolution of literary standards, basic features of the individual languages, texts, and differential vocabularies of the Czech, Slovak, Lusatian, Polish with Kashubian, and Polabian.

Volumes 2 and 3, planned to cover the Southern and Eastern Slavic languages, never appeared.

386. Vaillant, André. Grammaire comparée des langues slaves. Lyon, IAC, Paris, Klincksieck, 1950-1966. 3 v.

A solid up-to-date comparative grammar of Slavic languages. It presents the modern Slavic languages in their parallel and divergent evolution from the Indo-European, Balto-Slavic, and Common Slavic unity. Contents: v. 1, Phonétique; v. 2, Morphologie (Part 1: Flexion nominale, Part 2: Flexion pronominale); v. 3, Le Verbe, 1-2.

387. Vondrák, Václav. Vergleichende slavische Grammatik. 2d rev. ed. Göttingen, Vandenhoeck & Ruprecht, 1924-1928. 2 v.

Contents: I. Band: Lautlehre und Stammbildungslehre; II. Band: Formenlehre und Syntax. The first comparative grammar of Slavic languages after Miklosich, juxtaposing for the first time synchronic data with the neogrammarian comparative method. A first edition appeared in 1906-1908.

388. Wijk, Nicolaas van. Les langues slaves: de l'unité à la pluralité; Série de leçons faites à la Sorbonne. 2d ed. The Hague, Mouton & Co., 1956. 118 p. (Janua linguarum; studia memoriae Nicolai van Wijk dedicata, nr. 2)

A short and most elegant exposition of the main problems of the evolution of Slavic languages through parallel and divergent tendencies from the time of their unity. Written as a series of lectures, van Wijk's essays are not annotated. Their first publication was in *Le Monde slave* in 1937 and the first edition is a reprint from *Le Monde slave.*

3. Phonology and Accentuation

389. Bräuer, Herbert. Slavische Sprachwissenschaft. I. Einleitung, Lautlehre. Berlin, Walter de Gruyter, 1961. 221 p.

A concise survey of Slavic comparative phonology with a broad introductory historical characterization of the Slavic languages. It contains a good selected bibliography.

390. Broch, Olaf. Slavische Phonetik. Heidelberg, Carl Winter, 1911. 347 p. "Literatur": p. viii-x.

A most comprehensive survey of the phonetics of all Slavic languages. Originally published in Russian as:

Ocherk fiziologii slavianskoi rechi. Sanktpeterburg, Tip. Imperatorskoi Akademii nauk, 1910. 262 p. (Entsiklopediia slavianskoi filologii, Vyp. 5/2) Bibliography: p. 255-257.

391. Jakobson, Roman. Remarques sur l'évolution phonologique du russe

comparée à celle des autres langues slaves. Prague, Jednota československých matematiků a fyziků, 1929. 118 p. (Travaux du Cercle linguistique de Prague, 2)

The first structural description of the evolution of the Russian phonological system in relation to Common Slavic and to other Slavic languages, which remains the fountainhead of the structural postulates of Slavic structural linguistics.

392. Kuryłowicz, Jerzy. L'accentuation des langues indo-européennes. 2d ed. Wrocław, Zakład Narodowy im Ossolińskich, 1958. 433 p. (Polska Akademia Nauk. Komitet Językoznawczy. Prace Językoznawcze, 17)

A comparative structural analysis of the role of the prosodic features of stress, pitch, and duration in the morphological patterning of the Indo-European languages. Chapter 3 (p. 162-356) deals with the origin of the Balto-Slavic intonations, their later internal transformations in Common Slavic, and their influence on the Balto-Slavic morphology and derivation. The second edition of Kuryłowicz's study contains a number of corrections and changes suggested by the critics of its first edition (Kraków, Nakł. Polskiej Akademii Umiejętności, 1952, 526 p. Polska Akademia Umiejętności. Prace Komisji Językowej, nr. 37).

393. Shevelov, George Y. A Prehistory of Slavic; The Historical Phonology of Common Slavic. Heidelberg, Carl Winter, 1964; New York, Columbia University Press, 1965. 662 p.

An extensive and detailed treatment of common Slavic phonology with a wealth of examples and a rich selected bibliography on every phase of phonological evolution.

394. Stang, S. Christian. Slavonic Accentuation. Oslo, 1957. 192 p. (Norske Videnskaps- Akademi i Oslo, Historisk-filosofisk klasse. Skrifter. 1957, no. 3)

An attempt at a reconstruction of the later Common Slavic system of prosodic features of stress, pitch, and duration with an interpretation of the systems of accentuations in individual Slavic languages.

4. Grammar

395. Havránek, Bohuslav. Genera verbi v slovanských jazycích (Genera Verbi in Slavic languages). Praha, 1928-1937. 2 v. 184, 205 p. (Rozpravy Král. české společnosti nauk, třída fil.-hist.-jezykozpyt, Nová řada VIII, čís. 2, 4)

A most comprehensive treatment of the grammatical category of voice in Slavic languages. For a thorough discussion of Slavic reflexive verbs, *see*:

Marguliés, Alfons. Die Verba Reflexiva in den slavischen Sprachen. Heidelberg, Carl Winter, 1924. 283 p.

396. Hujer, O. Slovanská deklinace jmenná (The Slavic declension of

nouns). Praha, 1910. 173 p. (Rozpravy Čes. Akademie Čisaře Františka Josefa pro vědy, slovesnost a umění. Třída III, čis. 33)

The best available description of the Slavic nominal inflectional system.

397. Regnéll, Carl Göran. Über den Ursprung des slavischen Verbalaspektes. Lund, Häkan Ohlssons Boktryckeri, 1944. 110 p. Bibliography: p. 100-110.

A concise analysis of the verbal aspectual system in Slavic languages with a classification of its basic correlations, and an attempt at an explanation of their genesis. For a comprehensive survey of the treatment of Slavic aspect, *see*:

Maslov, Iu. S., *ed.* Voprosy glagol'nogo vida; sbornik (Problems of verbal aspect; a collection of articles). Moskva, Izdatel'stvo inostrannoi literatury, 1962. 437 p.

398. Stang, S. Christian. Das slavische und baltische Verbum. Oslo, I Kommisjon hos J. Dybwad, 1942. 280 p. (Skrifter utgitt av Det Norske Videnskaps-Akademi i Oslo II. Hist.-filos. klasse. 1942, no. 1)

A fundamental historical-comparative treatment of the prehistory of the Slavic verbal categories and forms in relation to the Baltic and Indo-European verbal systems.

5. Etymological Dictionaries

399. Berneker, Erich. Slavisches etymologisches Wörterbuch. 2d ed. Heidelberg, Carl Winter, 1924. 2 v. Bibliography: v. 1, p. 8-18.

Berneker's dictionary is to date the only existing etymological dictionary of Slavic languages. It is unfinished; volume 2 includes items up to *morě*. First edition, 1908-1913. For an earlier work, *see*:

Miklosich, Franz, *Ritter von.* Etymologisches Wörterbuch der slavischen Sprachen. Wien, Wilhelm Braumüller, 1886. 547 p. This was a first attempt at a Slavic etymological dictionary, which simply juxtaposed cognates of different Slavic languages. The work retains only historical value. The common Balto-Slavic lexical heritage is covered by:

Trautmann, Reinhold. Baltisch-Slavisches Wörterbuch. Göttingen, Vandenhoeck & Ruprecht, 1923. 382 p. Bibliography: p. 376-382. For an up-to-date review of the etymological dictionaries of individual Slavic languages *see*:

Scholz, Friedrich. Slavische Etymologie. Eine Anleitung zur Benutzung etymologischer Wörterbücher. Wiesbaden, Otto Harrassowitz, 1966. 126 p.

6. Slavic Philology

400. Jagič, Vatroslav. Istoriia slavianskoi filologii (The history of Slavic philology). Sanktpeterburg, Tip. Imperatorskoi Akademii nauk, 1910. 961 p. (Entsiklopediia slavianskoi filologii. Vypusk 1)

A monumental chronological account of Slavic scholarship in the areas traditionally classified as Slavic philology—from the time of the first medieval chroniclers till the beginning of the twentieth century.

401. Nahtigal, Rajko. Uvod v slovansko filologijo (An introduction to Slavic philology). Ljubljana, Državna založba Slovenije, 1949. 119 p.

One of the best concise treatments of the concept and scope of Slavic philology. A good Western counterpart is to be found in Arturo Cronia's *Introduzione allo Studio della Filologia slava* Padova, Editoria Liviana, 1949, 106 p.). A stress on bibliography can be found in Annemarie Hille's *Bibliographische Einführung in das Studium der slawischen Philologie* (Halle, M. Niemeyer, 1959, 149 p.), and in William E. Harkins' *Bibliography of Slavic Philology* (New York, King's Crown Press, 1951, 32 p.).

402. Trautmann, Reinhold. Die slavischen Völker und Sprachen; eine Einführung in die Slavistik. Göttingen, Vandenhoeck & Ruprecht, 1947. 173 p.

A short introduction into the study of Slavic linguistics. It contains a tangential survey of Slavic languages.

C. SERIALS

403. Akademiia nauk SSSR. Izvestiia. Seriia literatury i iazyka (Proceedings. Literary and linguistic series). t. 1– 1940– Moskva. 6 numbers yearly.

404. Akademiia nauk SSSR. *Otdelenie russkogo iazyka i slovesnosti.* Izvestiia (Proceedings). 1 seriia: t. 1-10, 1852-1863; 2 seriia, t. 1-32, 1896-1927. Leningrad (Sanktpeterburg, Petrograd). Illus., plates, ports., maps. Irregular.

Index: Ukazatel' avtorov i ikh statei, napechatannykh v Izvestiiakh Otdeleniia russkogo iazyka i slovestnosti za vse vremia sushchestvovaniia etogo izdaniia s 1896 g. po 1927 g., tt. I-XXXII. Leningrad, 1928. 55 p.

For the journals which after 1927 continued the tradition of the *Izvestiia . . . , see* items 43-46 in B. O. Unbegaun's *Bibliographical Guide to the Russian Language* (Oxford, Clarendon Press, 1953, 174 p.).

405. Akademiia nauk URSR, *Kiev. Istorychno-filologichnyi viddil.* Zapiski. Bulletin. Kn. 1-26; 1919-1931. Kyiv. Illus., ports., maps.

406. Archiv für slavische Philologie. 1.-42. Bd.; 1875-1929. Berlin, Weidmann, 1876-1929. 42 v. Illus., plates, ports., facsims.

An index to volumes 1-13 is contained in:

Bibliographische Übersicht über die slavische Philologie, 1876-1891. Prepared by Dr. Fr. Pastrnek. Zugleich general Register zu Archiv für slavische Philologie, Band 1-13. Berlin, Wiedmann, 1892. 415 p. *See also*:

Archiv für slavische Philologie; Gesamtinhaltsverzeichnis. Berlin, Akademie-Verlag, 1962. 88 p.

407. International Journal of Slavic Linguistics and Poetics. 1959– The Hague, Mouton. Irregular.

408. Jugoslavenska akademija znanosti i umjetnosti, *Zagreb*. Rad Jugoslavenske Akademije znanosti i umjetnosti (Proceedings of the Yugoslav Academy of Sciences and Arts). Knjiga 1– Zagreb, 1867–

409. Južnoslovenski filolog (The South Slavic philologist). Kn. 1– Beograd, 1913– Illus., plates, ports., map. Quarterly.

Published by the Institut za srpski jezik of the Srpska akademija nauka. Suspended during 1914-1920 and 1941-1948. From 1930 (v. 9) it carries a complete bibliography of all Yugoslav publications.

410. Matica Srpska, *Novi Sad. Lingvisticka sekcija*. Zbornik za filologiju i lingvistiku (Philological and linguistic melanges). 1– 1957– Novi Sad. Annual.

411. Oxford Slavonic Papers. v. 1– 1950– Oxford, Clarendon Press. Annual.

412. Polskie Towarzystwo Językoznawcze. Biuletyn (Bulletin). 1– 1927– Wrocław.

See also entry no. 2943.

413. Prace Filologiczne (Philological transactions). t. 1– Warszawa, Skł. gł w. Kasie im. Mianowskiego, 1884– Irregular.

Suspended from 1937 to 1963.

414. Pražský linguistický kroužek. Travaux du Cercle linguistique de Prague. Číslo 1-8; 1929-1939. Prague, 1929-1939.

415. Revue des études slaves. t. 1– 1921– Paris, Imprimerie nationale. Annual.

See also entries no. 9 *and* 455.

Suspended in 1940-1941, 1943. Volume 27 is *Mélanges André Mazon*, volume 28 is *Mélanges Pierre Pascal*. Each volume contains a bibliographical survey which covers the more important publications on the problems of Slavic philology. Index:

Bakounine, T. Revue des études slaves. Indexe des tomes I-XXI (1921-1944). Paris, 1949. 145 p.

416. Ricerche slavistiche. v. 1– 1952– Rome, G. Casini. Annual.

See also entry no. 455.

417. Rocznik Sławistyczny. Revue slavistique. t. 1– 1908– Kraków, Nakł. Studium Słowiańskiego Uniw. Jagiell. Annual.

See also entry no. 2943.

Not published during 1923-1930, and 1940-1947. Volumes 1-8 and 10-26 contain bibliographical surveys for 1907-1915/17 and 1929-1961, respectively.

418. Romanoslavica. 1– 1958– Bucureşti. Annual.

419. Russkii filologicheskii viestnik (Russian philological herald). g. 1-39; 1879-1917. Varshava. Quarterly.

420. Scando-Slavica. t. 1– 1954– Copenhagen, Munskaard. Annual.
See also entry no. 455.

421. Slavia; časopis pro slovanskou filologii (Slavia; journal for Slavic philology). ročník 1– 1922– Praha. Illus., ports. Quarterly.
See also entry no. 455.
Not published during 1941-1946. Volume 33 contains an index for volumes 1-30.

422. Slavica. 1– 1961– Debrecen. Illus., maps, facsims. Annual. (Annales Instituti Philologiae Slavicae Universitatis Debreciensis de Ludvigo Kossuth nominatae)

423. Slavica Pragensia. 1– 1959– Praha, Universita Karlova. Illus., ports. Annual.

424. Slavistična revija; časopis za literarno zgodovino in jezik (Slavistic review; journal of literary history and of language). letnik 1– 1948– Ljubljana. Irregular.
Issued by the Slavistično društvo in Ljubljana, and by the Institut za slovenski jezik and the Institut za literature of the Slovenska akademija znanosti in umetnosti.

425. The Slavonic and East European Review. v. 1– 1922– London. Semiannual.
See also entries no. 9 *and* 455.

426. Studia Slavica. t. 1– 1955– Budapest, Magyar Tudományos Akadémia. Quarterly.

427. Studia z filologii polskiej i słowiańskiej (Studies in Polish and Slavic philology). 1– 1955– Warszawa, Państwowe Wydawn. Naukowe.

428. Travaux linguistiques de Prague. 1– 1964– Prague, Éditions de l'Académie tchécoslovaque des sciences. Annual.
See also entry no. 1049.

429. Voprosy iazykoznaniia (Problems of linguistics). 1952– Moskva, Izd-vo Akademii nauk SSSR. Bimonthly.
Issued by the Institut iazykoznaniia of the Akademiia nauk SSSR.

430. Voprosy slavianskogo iazykoznaniia (Problems of Slavic linguistics). Vyp. 1– 1954– Moskva. Illus., maps. Irregular.

Issued by the Institut slavianovedeniia of the Akademiia nauk SSSR.

431. Die Welt der Slaven; Vierteljahrsschrift für Slavistik. Jahrg. 1– 1956– Wiesbaden, O. Harrassowitz. Illus., ports., facsims. Quarterly.
See also entry no. 455.

432. Wiener slavistisches Jahrbuch. 1– 1950– Wien, A. Sexl. Annual.

433. Word. v. 1– Apr. 1945– New York.

Journal of the Linguistic Circle of New York. Special issues devoted to Slavic languages and their problems have appeared since 1952 as a supplement, *Slavic Word.*

434. Zeitschrift für slavische Philologie. 1– 1925– Heidelberg. Semi-annual.
See also entry no. 455.

Published in Leipzig, 1925-1944. Publication suspended, 1944-1947.

435. Zeitschrift für Slawistik. 1956– Berlin, Akademie-Verlag. Quarterly.
See also entry no. 455.

13

Slavic Literatures

by William E. Harkins

There are a number of reasonably good synthetic surveys of the histories of the Slavic literatures, though few of these date from the most recent period. All of these works suffer to some extent from the effort to include a material too broad for even the scholar's grasp, and errors are fairly numerous, though perhaps less than one might expect in the circumstances. Although such synthetic surveys were compiled in almost all cases by scholars with a comparatist literary ideology and training, few of them are comparative in any real sense. Beginning with the work of Jan Máchal, however, they do attempt to set the Slavic literatures against a European literary and ideological background, and with the work of Wollman and, in particular, Čiževsky, they become truly comparatist in the modern sense of the word.

A. HANDBOOKS AND BIBLIOGRAPHICAL AIDS

436. Lewanski, Richard C. The Slavic Literatures. New York, New York Public Library and Frederick Ungar Publishing Co., 1967. 630 p. (Literatures of the World in English Translation; a Bibliography, v. 2)

Entries arranged by language of the original, subdivided into individual authors or works, and anthologies. Lists also translations of publications in serials. Indexes of authors and individual titles and of anthologies and compilers.

437. Novaia literatura po obshchim problemam slavianovedeniia (New literature on the general problems of Slavic studies). 1966– Moskva, Fundamental'naia biblioteka obshchestvennykh nauk. Quarterly.

See also entry no. 80.

One section of this bibliographic bulletin lists publications on Slavic literature and culture. Other pertinent materials may be found entered in:

Novaia inostrannaia literatura po literaturovedeniiu (New foreign literature on literary studies). 1960– Moskva, Fundamental'naia biblioteka obshchestvennykh nauk. Monthly.

Novaia sovetskaia literatura po literaturovedeniiu (New Soviet literature on literary studies). 1960– Moskva, Fundamental'naia bibblioteka obshchestvennykh nauk. Monthly.

These bibliographical bulletins are issued in mimeographed form and in very limited editions, but provide broad coverage of monographic and serial literature throughout the world. Another bibliographic guide which is issued in printed form but which is largely concerned with modern literature, listing translations and critical material about specific authors, is:

Literatura i iskusstvo narodov SSSR i zarubezhnykh stran (Literature and art of the peoples of the USSR and of foreign countries). 1957– Moskva, Vsesoiuznaia knizhnaia palata. Six times yearly. Compiled with the cooperation of the All-Union State Library of Foreign Literature in Moscow.

438. Preminger, Alex., *ed.* Encyclopedia of Poetry and Poetics. Princeton, Princeton University Press, 1965. 906 p.

Contains an excellent article on Slavic prosody, as well as mostly good articles on the individual Slavic poetries, particularly on Russian and Polish. Among other reference books in English to be recommended is:

Smith, Horatio, *ed.* Columbia Dictionary of Modern European Literature. New York, Columbia University Press, 1947. 899 p. Contains many articles on Slavic writers from the period 1870-1947. Also usable is:

Kunitz, Stanley J., *and* Vineta Colby, *eds.* European Authors, 1000-1900. New York, H. W. Wilson, 1967. 1016 p.

A forthcoming work edited by John Gassner and Edward G. Quinn is *Reader's Encyclopedia of World Drama*, to be issued by Yale University Press, which will treat the dramatic literatures of most of the Slavic peoples.

439. Seemann, Klaus-Dieter, *and* Frank Siegmann. Bibliographie der slavistischen Arbeiten aus den deutschsprachigen Fachzeitschriften, 1876-1963. Berlin, Wiesbaden, Harrassowitz, 1965. 422 p. (Bibliographische Mitteilungen des Osteuropa-Instituts an der Freien Universität Berlin, Heft 8)

See also entry no. 371.

A general index of five journals for Slavic studies in the German language (*Archiv für slavische Philologie*, 1876-1929; *Zeitschrift für slavische Philologie*, 1925-1963; *Wiener slavistisches Jahrbuch*, 1950-1963; *Die Welt der Slaven*, 1956-1963; and *Zeitschrift für Slawistik*, 1956-1963), including relevant contributions from East European historical journals. It is classified according to languages and subjects such as linguistics, mythology, literature, art, culture, and history.

B. MONOGRAPHS AND ANALYTICAL SURVEYS

440. Angyal, Andreas. Die slawische Barockwelt. Leipzig, E. A. Seemann, 1961. 321 p. Illus.

A study in intellectual history, with considerable use of literary materials and a useful bibliography. Angyal's book concentrates more on higher cultural strata, while another book, Rudo Brtáň's *Barokový slavizmus, porovnávacia štúdia z dejín slovanskej slovesnosti* (Baroque Slavism, a comparative study from the history of Slavic literature) (Lipt. Sv. Mikuláš, Nakl. Spolku Tranoscius, 1939, 293 p.), emphasizes popular and folk culture for the same period.

441. Bezzenberger, Adalbert, *and others*. Die osteuropäischen Literaturen und die slawischen Sprachen. Berlin und Leipzig, B. G. Teubner, 1908. 396 p. (Die Kultur der Gegenwart, herausgegeben von Paul Hinneberg, Teil 1, Abteilung 9)

Includes chapters on Russian literature (A. Wesselovsky), Polish (A. Brückner), Czech (Jan Máchal), and South Slavic (M. Murko), as well as Modern Greek, Hungarian, Finnish, Estonian, Lithuanian, and Latvian literatures. The surveys are brief and of varying quality.

442. Brückner, Alexander, *and* Tadeusz Lehr-Spławiński. Zarys dziejów literatur i języków literackich słowiańskich (Outline of the history of the literatures and literary languages of the Slavs). Lwów, nakład i własność K. S. Jakubowskiego, 1929. 206 p. (Lwowska biblioteka sławistyczna, t. 9)

Contains short surveys by Brückner of all the Slavic literatures, including Lusatian, but almost without comparative treatment.

443. Česko-polský sborník vědeckých prací (Czech-Polish collection of scholarly studies). Edited by Milan Kudělka. Praha, Státní pedagogické nakladatelství, 1955. 2 v. Illus., ports., facsims. (Publikace Sleszkého studijního ústavu v Opavě, sv. 11-12)

Volume 1 contains articles on Czech-Polish historical relations; volume 2, on literary and linguistic relations. With summaries in Polish (or Czech when the original article is in Polish), French, and Russian. A number of other volumes of comparative literary and historical studies have been published since the Second World War. These include the following:

O vzájomných vzťahoch Čechov a Slovákov; sborník materialov z konferencie Historického ústavu S.A.V. (On Czech and Slovak mutual ties; a collection of materials from the conference of the Historical Commission of the Slovak Academy of Sciences). Bratislava, Vydavateľstvo Slovenskej akademie vied, 1956. 450 p.

Slovenská akadémia vied. *Sekcia spoločenskych vied.* Z dejín československo-slovanských vzťahov (On the history of Czecho-Slovak and Slovak ties). Bratislava, Vydavateľstvo Slovenskej akademie vied, 1959. 490 p. Summaries in Russian. (Slovanské štúdie, sv. 2)

Slovenská akadémie vied. *Sekcia spoločenských vied.* Prispevky k medzislovanským vzťahom v československých dejinách (Contributions on inter-Slavic ties in Czech and Slovak history). Bratislava, Vydavatel'stvo Slovenskej akadémie vied, 1960. 562 p. Summaries in Russian. (Slovanské štúdie, sv. 3)

Československá akademie věd. Československo-bulharské vztahy v zrcadle staletí; sborník vědeckých prací (Czecho-Slovak and Bulgarian ties in the mirror of the centuries; a collection of scholarly studies). Edited by Bohuslav Havránek. Praha, 1963. 439 p. Summaries in Russian and French.

Urban, Zdeněk, *ed.* Z dějin česko-bulharských kulturních styků (From the history of Czech and Bulgarian cultural contacts). Praha, Nakladatelství Československé akademie věd, 1957. 177 p. Summaries in Russian.

444. Chyzhevs'kyi, Dmytro (Dmitry Čiževsky). Outline of Comparative Slavic Literatures. Boston, American Academy of Arts and Sciences, 1952. 143 p. (Survey of Slavic Civilization, v. 1)

See also entry no. 1097.

The only synthetic study in English, and the most truly comparative of all the synthetic histories of the Slavic literatures. Chyzhevs'kyi regards style, conditioned by period, as the basic study of literary history; a given period (e.g., Baroque) gives rise to similar styles among the various Slavic peoples. The treatment is far too brief and often simplified, but still the work is of great value.

445. Golenishchev-Kutuzov, Il'ia N. Ital'ianskoe vozrozhdenie i slavianskie literatury XV-XVI vekov (The Italian Renaissance and the Slavic literatures of the 15th and 16th centuries). Moskva, Izdatel'stvo Akademii nauk SSSR, 1963. 414 p. Illus., ports., facsims. Bibliography: p. 340-379.

A comprehensive, detailed, and superbly documented study of the influence of the Renaissance on the West and South Slavic lands.

446. Jakobson, Roman. The Kernel of Comparative Slavic Literature. Harvard Slavic Studies, v. 1, 1953: 1-71.

See also entry no. 1103.

The strongest defense for the comparative study of the Slavic literatures, one rooted in common features of the languages used expressively in literature, as well as in the community of the Church Slavonic ideological and literary tradition.

447. Kohn, Hans. Pan-Slavism; Its History and Ideology. Notre Dame, Ind., University of Notre Dame Press, 1953. 356 p. Bibliography: p. 339-348.

See also entries no. 112, 182, *and* 358.

A standard historical account with many though sporadic references to literary developments; omits all discussions of Pan-Slavism prior to the 19th century.

Frank Wollman's *Slovanství v jazykově literárním obrození u Slovanů* (The Slavic idea in the linguistic and literary renaissance of the Slavs) (Praha, Vesmír, 1928, 230 p.; Kulturní obraz slovanského světa, sv. 2), is a series of essays on various phases of the idea of Slavic unity which does treat the earlier period, but it is not a continuous survey of the Pan-Slavic movement.

448. Máchal, Jan. Slovanské literatury (The Slavic literatures). Praha, Matice česká, 1922-1929. 3 v. (Novočeská bibliotéka, čis. 36)

The most comprehensive and ambitious in scope of the synthetic treatments of Slavic literatures, though it makes almost no real comparison. Still it does attempt to set the Slavic literatures within a European framework, particularly during the 19th century. Treats all the Slavic peoples, including the Lusatians. Includes a survey of folk epos (on which its author was a specialist), but not other folklore. Divided by literary periods, then by national literatures.

449. Murko, Matthias. Geschichte der älteren südslawischen Literaturen. Leipzig, C. F. Amelang, 1908. 248 p.

Despite its age, it is still a classic in the field; treats comparatively the medieval literatures of all the South Slavic peoples.

Murko's study, "Die Bedeutung der Reformation und Gegenreformation für das geistige Leben der Südslaven," *Slavia*, v. 4, 1925-1926: 499-522, 694-719; v. 4, 1926-1927: 65-99, 277-302, 500-534, 718-744, is an excellent monograph from the field of intellectual history, with extensive reference to literature as such.

450. Pypin, Aleksandr N., *and* Vladimir D. Spasovich (Włodzimierz D. Spasowicz). Istoriia slaviansikh literatur (History of the Slavic literatures). 2d rev. ed. S.-Peterburg, Tipografiia M. M. Stasiulevicha, 1879-1881. 2 v.

German translation by Traugott Pech, *Geschichte der slavischen Literaturen* (Leipzig, F. A. Brockhaus, 1880-1884, 2 v.). French translation by Ernest Denis as *Histoire des littératures slaves* (Paris, Leroux, 1881, 627 p.). Czech translation by Antonín Kotík as *Historie literatur slovanských* (Praha, 1880-1882, 2 v.). Treats the principal Slavic literatures, including Lusatian, but without Russian. Contains a good deal of information on cultural history as well as literature. Treats folklore.

451. Šafárik, Pavel J. Geschichte der slawischen Sprache und Literatur nach allen Mundarten. Ofen, Kön. ung. Universitätsschriften, 1826. 524 p.

The first synthetic survey of the histories of the Slavic literatures, it had a strong influence on the first such work in English: Talvj (Therese Albertine Louise von Jacob), *Historical View of the Languages and Literatures of the Slavic Nations, with a Sketch of Their Popular Poetry* (New York, Putnam, 1850, 412 p.). Another early survey in English is W. R. Morfill's *Slavonic Literature* (London, Society for Promoting Christian Knowledge; New York, E. & J. B. Young, 1883, 264 p.), which, however, displays more real interest in antiquities than in literature as such. All of these works are long since outdated and have a purely historical interest today.

452. Šafárik, Pavel J. Geschichte der südslawischen Literatur. Edited by J. Jireček. Prague, Friedrich von Tempsky, 1864-1865. 3 v. in 4.

More detailed and accurate than Šafárik's general history of the Slavic literatures, but also of largely historical interest.

453. Szyjkowski, Marjan. Polská účast v českém národím obrození (The Polish role in the Czech national revival). Praha, Nákladem Slovanského ústavu, 1931-1946. 3 v. (Práce Slovanského ústavu v Praze, sv. 3, 15, 19)

The first three volumes (of a projected six) of a classic study on Polish-Czech literary relations. Each volume has a résumé in French. A shorter Polish version of the entire completed work is the author's *Polski romantyzm w czeskim życiu duchowyn* (Polish romanticism in Czech spiritual life) (Poznań, Instytut zachodni, 1947, 429 p.; Biblioteka czeska, tom 1). Other important studies of Czech-Polish relations include:

Magnuszewski, Józef. Stosunki literackie polsko-czeskie w końcu XIX i na początku XX wieku (Polish-Czech literary relations at the end of the 19th and beginning of the 20th century). Wrocław, Wydawn. Zakładu narodowego im. Ossolińskich, 1951. 199 p.

Wojciechowski, Zygmunt, *ed.* Polska-Czechy. Dziesięć wieków sąsiedztwa (Poland and Bohemia: ten centuries of contact). Katowice, 1947. 315 p. Bibliography: p. 307-315. (Pamiętnik Insttytutu śląskiego, seria II, 7)

454. Wollman, Frank. Slovesnost Slovanů (The literature of the Slavs). Praha, Vesmír, 1928. 259 p. (Slované; kulturní obraz slovanského světa, díl 2)

The first truly comparative history of Slavic literature. Denies the importance of Eastern influence for the Slavs, and places their literature firmly within a Western setting. For Wollman the Slavic literatures constitute a whole not by virtue of any cultural or social unity, but because of community of genres, materials, and forms, evolving in parallel fashion. The work is divided according to literary periods, then according to national literatures.

Also worthy of note is Wollman's *Dramatika slovanského jihu* (Drama of the Slavic south) (Praha, 1930, 248 p.; Práce Slovanského ústavu v Praze, sv. 2), a comparative study of the drama of the Slovenes, Croats, Serbs and Bulgars.

The same author's *K methodologii srovnávací slovesnosti slovanské* (On the methodology of Slavic comparative literature) (Brno, 1936, 1954 p.; Spisy Filosofické fakulty Masarykovy university v Brně, sv. 43, 1936) provides a strong argument for comparative study of the Slavic literatures, against such skeptics as Bittner and Lednicki; a detailed French summary is given.

C. SERIALS

455. Among the serials containing significant material on the Slavic literatures are:

Archiv für slavische Philologie. 1.-42. Bd.; 1875-1929. Berlin, Wiedman. Quarterly.

Canadian Slavic Studies; Revue canadienne d'études slaves. 1967– Montreal, Loyola College. Quarterly.

Canadian Slavonic Papers. 1956– Toronto. Annual.

East European Quarterly. 1967– Boulder, Col. Quarterly.

International Journal of Slavic Linguistics and Poetics. 1959– The Hague. Mouton. Irregular.

Oxford Slavonic Papers. 1950– Oxford, Clarendon Press. Annual.

Pamiętnik literacki; czasopismo kwartalne poświecone historii i krytyce literatury polskiej, wydawane przez Instytut badań literackich i Towarzystwo literackie im. Adama Mickiewicza (Literary memoirs; a quarterly journal dedicated to the history and criticism of Polish literature, issued by the Institute for Literary Research and the Adam Mickiewicz Literary Society). Warszawa, 1902– Annual.

Prilozi za književnost, jezik, istoriju i folklor (Supplements for literature, language, history, and folklore). 1921– Beograd. Semiannual.

Przegląd humanisticzyny (Humanistic review). Warszawa, Państwowe Wydawn. Naukowe. 1957– Illus. Bimonthly.

Przeglad zachodni (Western review). 1945– Poznań. Monthly.

Revue des études slaves. 1921– Paris, Imprimerie Nationale. Annual.
See also entries no. 9 *and* 455.

Ricerche slavistiche. 1952– Roma, G. Carsini. Annual.
See also entry no. 416.

Scando-Slavica. Copenhagen, Munksgard. 1954– Annual.
See also entry no. 420.

Slavia; časopis pro slovanskou filologii (Slavia; journal for Slavic philology). Ročník 1– 1922– Praha. Česká Grafická Unie A. S. Illus., ports. Quarterly.
See also entry no. 421.

Slavic and East European Journal. 1943– Madison, Wis. Quarterly.

Slavic Review. 1940– New York. Quarterly.

Slavische Rundschau; berichtende und kritische Zeitschrift für das geistige Leben der slavischen Völker. 1929-1937. Prag, Slavisches Institut. Bimonthly.

Slavonic and East European Review; a Survey of the Peoples of Eastern Europe, Their History, Economics, Philology and Literature. v. 1– 1922– London. Semiannual. *See also* entry no. 425.

Die Welt der Slaven. 1956– Wiesbaden, O. Harrassowitz. Illus., ports., facsims. Quarterly.
See also entry no. 431.

Zagreb. Staroslavenski institut. Radovi (Studies). Knjiga 1– Zagreb. 1952– Annual.

Zeitschrift für slavische Philologie. 1925– Heidelberg. Semiannual. *See also* entry no. 434.

Zeitschrift für Slawistik. 1956– Berlin, Akademie-Verlag. Quarterly. *See also* entry no. 435.

part two

CZECHOSLOVAKIA

14

General Reference Aids and Bibliographies

by Rudolf Sturm (Sections A and B) and Paul L. Horecky (Sections C-F)

A. BIBLIOGRAPHIES*

1. Of Bibliographies

456. Malec, Karel. Soupis bibliografií novin a časopisů vydávaných na území Československé republiky (Register of bibliographies of newspapers and periodicals published on the territory of the Czechoslovak Republic). Praha, Orbis, 1959. 216 p.

Contains 965 entries for bibliographies published from 1803 through 1958. An invaluable guide, comprehensive and accurate, covering all fields and all languages. A supplement, pages 185-193, cites bibliographies of Czech and Slovak serials published abroad. Has indexes.

457. Palivec, Viktor. České regionální bibliografie; přehled publikací a

* Entries are listed in chronological order by period treated.

článků z let 1945-1965 (Czech regional bibliographies; a survey of publications and articles, 1945-1965). Praha, Státní knihovna ČSSR, 1966. 56 p.

A list of biliographies pertaining to various regions, cities, and towns in Bohemia and Moravia. Some entries are annotated. Contains indexes of personal names and places.

458. Soupis českých bibliografií za roky 1951-1955 (Register of Czech bibliographies for 1951-1955). Praha, Státní knihovna ČSSR, 1964. (České knihy 1964. Zvláštní sešit 8)

Contains 3,000 entries, briefly annotated. Continued by *Soupis českých bibliografií* (Register of Czech bibliographies) (v. 1–, 1956–, Praha, Národní knihovna ČSSR, annual). Its last volume, covering the year 1965, lists 1,900 entries.

459. Česká bibliografie; přehled a plánovaných bibliografických publikací (Czech bibliography; a survey of planned bibliographic publications). 1956– Praha, Národní knihovna. Annual.

An official register of planned bibliographies. Not all of the planned works are subsequently issued, however. Activities of Czech bibliographers and their thinking are reflected also in the annual *Česká bibliografie; sborník statí a materiálů* (Czech bibliography; a collection of articles and materials) (1959–, Praha, Státní pedagogické nakl.)

460. Evidenčný súpis plánovaných bibliografických prác na Slovensku (Register of planned bibliographic works in Slovakia). 1956– Martin, Matica slovenská. Annual.

A Slovak counterpart of the Czech publication (*see* entry 459). An analogous publication for all of Czechoslovakia appeared under the title *Evidenční soupis plánovaných bibliografických prací v ČSSR v roce 1967.* (Register of planned bibliographic work in Czechoslovakia for 1967) (Praha, Státní knihovna, 1967, 63 p.). For additional Slovak bibliographic activities, one can consult the annual *Bibliografický sborník* (Bibliographic collection) (1957–, Martin, Matica slovenská).

461. Bibliografia slovenských bibliografií (Bibliography of Slovak bibliographies). 1961/1962– Martin, Matica slovenská.

A list of Slovak bibliographies that were published in a particular year. Includes a small number of Czech bibliographies dealing with Slovak subjects. All entries are briefly annotated. The last volume published is for 1966 and contains 3,000 entries.

2. Of Monographs

462. Rizner, L'udovít V. Bibliografia písomníctva slovenského na spôsob slovníka od najstarších čias do konca r. 1900. S pripojenou bibliografiou archeologickou, historickou, miestopisnou a prírodovedeckou (Bibliography of Slovak literature in the form of a dictionary from the oldest time to the end of 1900. With a bibliography of archaeology,

history, geography, and natural sciences). Turčianský sv. Martin, Matica slovenská, 1929-1934. 6 v.

Provides an almost complete and on the whole reliable record of Slovak literary production. Its supplement is Ján Mišianik's *Bibliografia slovenského pisomníctva do konca XIX. storočia; doplnky k Riznerovej bibliografii* (Bibliography of Slovak literature to the end of the 19th century; supplement to Rizner's bibliography) (Bratislava, Slovenská akadémia vied a umení, 1946, 300 p., facsims.; bibliography: p. 7-8). These two works jointly cover the period up to 1900 very well.

463. Knihopis československých tisků od doby nejstarší až do konce XVIII. století (Bibliography of Czechoslovak imprints from earliest times to the end of the 18th century). Praha, V komisi knihkupectví F. Topiče, 1925- Facsims.

See also entry no. 1093.

Work of basic importance, comprehensive and accurate. Lists both incunabula (to 1500) and printing from 1501 through 1800. Includes belles-lettres, nonfiction, official publications, pamphlets, etc., with all entries annotated in detail. Indicates location of titles in Czechoslovak and foreign libraries. Now nearing its completion. For works published prior to the fifteenth century, one can consult Josef Jireček's *Rukovět k dějinám literatury české do konce XVIII. věku, ve spůsobě slovníka životopisného a knihoslovného* (Manual of the history of Czech literature to the end of the 18th century in the form of a biographical and bibliographic dictionary) (Praha, Tempský, 1875-1876, 2 v.).

464. Kuzmík, Jozef. Bibliografia kníh v západných rečiach týkajúcich sa slovenských vecí vydaných od XVI. stor. do r. 1955 (Bibliography of books in western languages on Slovak matters published from the 16th century to 1955). Martin, Matica slovenská, 1959. 420 p.

See also entry no. 1071.

An accurate and nearly complete register of books on Slovakia written in English, German, and other Germanic languages, the Romance languages, and classical Greek and Latin. Its continuation is *Bibliografia publikácií v európských rečiach týkajúcich sa slovenských vecí; doplnky do r. 1955, pokračovanie za r. 1956-1959 a súpis máp* (Bibliography of publications in European languages on Slovak matters; supplements to the year 1955, continuation for 1956-1959, and a register of maps) (Martin, Matica slovenská, 1960, 462 p.). It includes monographs in Slavic, Baltic, Romance, and Anglo-Saxon (Germanic) languages. Both these books are unique ventures, unsurpassed in scope, compiled with professional competence.

465. Kuzmík, Jozef. Bibliografia slovanských kníh týkajúcich sa slovenských vecí vydaných od XVI. stor. do r. 1955 (Bibliography of Slavic books on Slovak matters published from the 16th century to 1955). Martin, Matica slovenská, 1959. 456 p.

The largest part of this compendium is devoted to Czech books dealing with Slovakia, but publications in all the other Slavic languages are listed as well. For books written in Hungarian, Estonian, Finnish, Chinese, Japanese, Hindu, and other Asiatic languages *see* Kuzmík's *Bibliografia kníh vo východných rečiach týkajúcich sa slovenských vecí, vydaných do r. 1955* (Bibliography of books in eastern languages on Slovak matters published up to 1955) (Martin, Matica slovenská, 1960, 445 p.). Both are indispensable tools for further research in this field.

466. Urbánek, František A., *comp.* Biografický a bibliografický slovník českých spisovatelů (Biographical and bibliographical dictionary of Czech writers). Telč, 1909. 2 v. Contents — v. 1, Básníci a beletristé, 1800-1900; v. 2, Spisovatelé vědečtí, 1800-1900.

The first volume of this massive bibliography covers Czech poetry and prose fiction of the 19th century; the second volume deals with scholarly works. It is a selective listing, but all the important authors and books are included. For the first quarter of the 20th century see *Soupis československé literatury za léta 1901-1925* (Register of Czechoslovak literature for 1901-1925) (Praha, Nakl. Svazu knihkupců a nakladatelů Československé republiky, 1931-1938, 2 v. in 3), which provides accurate and comprehensive coverage for both Czech and Slovak materials.

467. Čapek, Thomas, *and* Anna V. Čapek. Bohemian (Čech) Bibliography; a Finding List of Writings in English Relating to Bohemia and the Čechs. New York, F. H. Revell, 1918. 256 p. Front., facsims., plates, ports. Bibliography: p. 64-65.

See also entry no. 1089.

In spite of its early date, this bibliography still has its value, especially for the 19th century and earlier imprints in the United States and England. With over 1,000 entries it covers all areas of human endeavor.

468. Halík, Miroslav, *and* Hana Teigeová, *comps.* Československá kniha v cizině; katalog výstavy (The Czechoslovak book abroad; catalog of an exposition). Praha, Nákladem obce pražské, 1938. 190 p. (Prague. Městká knihovna. Spisy, 28)

See also entry no. 1091.

A bibliography of Czech and Slovak books, both fiction and nonfiction, brought out in foreign translations abroad from the beginning of the 19th century through 1938. Includes a list of writings published in Esperanto. Well organized, comprehensive, indispensable for research in the field.

469. Rechcígl, Miloslav Jr. Czechoslovakia and Its Arts and Sciences; a Selective Bibliography in the Western European Languages. *In* Rechcigl, Miloslav Jr., *ed.* The Czechoslovak Contribution to World Culture. The Hague, Mouton, 1964. p. 556-634.

See also entries no. 565 *and* 1166.

In 1,318 entries the work covers the social sciences, humanities, and technical disciplines. One of the best tools in the field. Can be used in conjunction with Oldrich Cerny's *Czechoslovakia; a Selected Bibliography with a Brief Historical Survey* (Washington, 1959, 119 l., map. Thesis [M.S.] — Catholic University of America).

470. Sturm, Rudolf. Czechoslovakia; a Bibliographic Guide. Washington, D.C., U.S. Library of Congress, 1968. 157 p.

Part 1, "Bibliographic Survey," is "a discussion of books and periodicals covering in 13 categories the various fields of human endeavor, except for the natural sciences and technical disciplines. Part 2, 'Bibliographical Listing,' is an alphabetical listing of all sources discussed in Part I." Contains 1,513 entries, most of them in English, German, French, Italian, and Spanish, in this order. Basic Czech and Slovak publications are also listed. Holdings of the Library of Congress and other major American or Canadian libraries are indicated with each entry.

471. Buchhändler-Correspondenz. v. 1-62; Feb. 1860-1921. Wien. Illus. (part col.), ports. Frequency, title, and name of issuing body vary.

A professionally compiled weekly register of the publishing and bookselling trade of Austria-Hungary, listing Czech and Slovak books, pamphlets, newspapers, and periodicals from 1860 through 1918 with considerable accuracy and completeness. Includes yearly indexes. Another source of pre-1918 publishing is *Bibliographia Hungariae; Verzeichniss der 1861-1921 erschienenen, Ungarn betreffenden Schriften in nicht ungarischer Sprache* (Berlin, Leipzig, W. De Gruyter, 1923-1929, 4 v. in 1), which lists Slovak books and serials for that period.

472. Jaksch, Friedrich, *comp.* Lexikon sudetendeutscher Schriftsteller und ihrer Werke für die Jahre 1900-1929; mit zwei Anhängen: 1. Die sudetendeutschen Zeitungen. 2. Die sudetendeutschen Zeitschriften. Reichenberg, Verlag Gebrüder Stiepel, 1929. 358 p.

A basic bibliography for Sudeten German books, newspapers, and periodicals up to the late twenties. It can be supplemented for the thirties by Heinrich Jilek's selective bibliography *Reichsgau Sudetenland. Reichsprotektorat Böhmen-Mähren. Eine Bibliographie mit besonderer Berücksichtigung von Politik und Wirtschaft* (Leipzig, F. Prinzhorn, 1940-1942, 2 v.).

473. Fedor, Michal, *comp.* Bibliografia slovenských kníh 1901-1918 (Bibliography of Slovak books 1901-1918). Martin, Matica slovenská, 1964. 728 p.

Provides a complete and accurate coverage for the Slovak literary production of the period. For the interwar years, one can consult *Bibliografia slovenských kníh 1919-1938; provisórne vydanie* (Bibliography of Slovak books 1919-1938; a tentative edition) (Martin, Matica slovenská, 166), listing 13,000 entries.

474 Bestaux, Eugène. Bibliographie tchèque, contenant un certain nombre d'ouvrages sur la Tchécoslovaquie, en langues diverses (à l'exclusion des langues slaves). Prague, Imp. A. Reis, 1920. 105 p.

A useful tool, dealing mostly with Bohemia and the Czechs. Can be used in conjunction with two Orbis publications, *Katalog číslo 1* (1926, 79 p.) and *Katalog číslo 2* (1928, 144 p.) of *Publikace o Československu v cizích jazycích* (Publications on Czechoslovakia in foreign languages), that list books and articles in many languages with the exception of Russian.

475. Bibliografia slovenskej knižnej tvorby (Bibliography of Slovak book production). 1939/1941– Bratislava, Bibliografický ústav, Knižnica Slovenskej university. Irregular.

The last volume in this series covers the years 1945-1955; it contains 14,553 entries. The first volume can be complemented by Ján Sedlák and Ján Měst'ančik's *Slovenská kniha, 1939-1941* (Slovak books, 1939-1941) (Bratislava, Osvetové ústredie pri Ministerstve školstva a národnej osvety, 1942, 279 p.), which contains not only bibliographic references, but also literary history and criticism of the period.

476. Dvacet let ČSSR; výběrový seznam původních českých a slovenských knih a ruských knih a článků o ČSSR (Twenty years of the Czechoslovak Socialist Republic; a selective bibliography of original Czech and Slovak books and Russian books and articles about ČSSR). Praha, Státní knihovna ČSSR, 1965. 375 p. (Bibliografický katalog ČSSR-České knihy. 1965. Zvláštní sešit 2-září 1965)

The Czech part contains 3,584 entries on Czech and Slovak Communist books, divided into 31 topical groups. The Russian part lists 2,067 Soviet books and articles. This is the largest listing of literature for the period 1945-1965, covering all fields of human endeavor except belles-lettres.

477. Šprinc, Nicholas, *and* Michael Lacko, *comps.* Slovak Studies VI; Slovak Bibliography Abroad 1945-1965. Cleveland, Rome, Slovak Institute. Forthcoming.

An exhaustive listing of works which Slovak authors have written and published outside the Soviet orbit, as well as writings by non-Slovak authors dealing with Slovak matters. Lists books and major articles in the social sciences, the humanities, and technical disciplines. Entries are briefly annotated.

478. P.E.N. Club. Czechoslovak Republic. American Literature in Czechoslovakia 1945-1965. Prague, 1966. 79 p.

A nearly complete register of Czech and Slovak translations of U.S. writings published in book form. Similar compendia have been issued by the Czechoslovak P.E.N. Club for translations from Danish, Icelandic, Norwegian, and Swedish under the title *Scandinavian Literatures in Czechoslovakia from 1945 to May 1964* (1964, 47 p.). From French: Zdeňka Boukalová's *La littérature française en Tchécoslovaquie de 1945 à Janvier 1964* (1964, 107 p.). From German: *Deutsche Literatur in der Tschechoslowakei von 1945 bis Mai 1959* (1959, 61 p.). From Spanish and Portuguese: *Literatura brasileira e portuguêsa, literatura espanhola e latino americana na Tchecoslováquia desde 1945 até maio de 1960* (1960, 49 p.). All these bibliographies list fiction as well as nonfiction. Entries are not annotated. For the reverse side of the picture, *see*:

Seznam knih českých a slovenských autorů vydaných v zahraničí v letech 1961-65 (List of books by Czech and Slovak authors published abroad in the years 1961-1965) (Praha, Dilia, 1968?). Records 1687 translations into 48 languages.

479. České knihy (Czech books). 1951– Praha, Národní knihovna. Weekly.

Title varies: 1951-1954, *Česká kniha.* Supersedes *Bibliografický katalog, pt. A. Knihy české.*

Bibliografický katalog, after 1960 called *Bibliografický katalog ČSSR*, is the national bibliography of Czechoslovakia; it began publication in 1922. Since its major reorganization in 1951, its main components have been *České knihy* and *Slovenské knihy* (Slovak books), the latter being issued monthly in Martin by Matica slovenská. They contain comprehensive and accurate listings of all Czech and Slovak materials, respectively, including fiction, scientific books, and other monographs in all fields, with detailed annotations. Other components of the national bibliography are *České hudebniny* (Czech musical materials) (1955–, Praha, Národní knihovna) and *Slovenské hudobniny* (Slovak musical materials) (1955–, Martin, Matica slovenská).

480. Zahraniční bohemika a slovenika v roce . . . (Foreign Bohemica and Slovaca in . . .). 1956– Praha, Národní knihovna, 1957– Annual.

See also entry no. 567.

Title varies: 1957-1962, *Zahraniční bohemika.* A listing of Czech and Slovak works translated into foreign languages and works of foreign authors dealing with Czech and Slovak matters. A professionally compiled, systematic register.

481. Lettrich, Irena. Slovakia; a Selected List of References with a Brief Historical Survey. Washington, D.C., 1961. 76 1. Thesis (M.S.)—Catholic University of America.

A solid and reliable general bibliography covering many fields. The materials listed here deal primarily with the situation since the First World War.

3. Of Periodicals and Newspapers

482. Laiske, Miroslav. Časopisectví v Čechách, 1650-1847; příspěvek k soupisu periodického tisku, zejména novin a časopisů (Periodicals in Bohemia, 1650-1847; a contribution to the register of the periodical press, especially newspapers and magazines). Praha, Národní knihovna, 1959. 179 p. Facsims. (Bibliografický katalog ČSR. České knihy, 1959. Zvláštní seš., 6)

An accurate survey of serials in Bohemia, regardless of language, from the beginning of periodical publishing to 1847. For subsequent periods, one can consult two bibliographies by František Roubík, *Časopisectvo v Čechách v letech 1848-1862* (Periodicals in Bohemia, 1848-1862) (Praha, Duch novin, 1930, 207 p., facsims., pl.) and *Bibliografie časopisectva v Čechách z let 1863-1895* (Bibliography of serials in Bohemia in the years 1863-1895) (Praha, Nakl. České akademie věd a umění, 1936, 319 p.). Serials published in Moravia are discussed and recorded by Milada Wurmová in her *Soupis moravských novin a časopisů z let 1848-1918* (Register of Moravian newspapers and periodicals in the years 1848-1918) (Brno, Krajské nakl., 1955, 94 p.). For still later years, the researcher can turn to *Bibliografie novin a časopisů v českých krajích za léta 1895-1945* (Praha, Novinářský studijní ústav, 1956). A systematic register of current Czech periodicals has been provided since 1953 in the annual *Noviny a časopisy v českých krajích* (Newspapers and periodicals in Czech regions) (Praha, Národní knihovna).

483. Potemra, Michal, *comp.* Bibliografia slovenských novín a časopisov do roku 1918 (Bibliography of Slovak newspapers and periodicals to 1918). Martin, Matica slovenská, 1958. 145 p. (Slovenská národná bibliografia. Séria B. Periodiká, zväzok la)

See also entry no. 1124.

An excellent retrospective bibliography devoted to Slovak serials. Its continuation is Magda Horsáková's *Provizórny pomocný súpis novín a časopisov za roky 1919-1938* (Temporary auxiliary register of newspapers and periodicals for 1919-1938) (Bratislava, Universitná knižnica, 1957, 221 p.) and *Bibliografia slovenských a inorečových novín a časopisov z rokov 1919-1938* (Bibliography of Slovak and foreign-language newspapers and periodicals, 1919-1938), compiled by Mária Kipsová (Martin, Matica Slovenská, 1968, 1074 p.). The post-World War II production is recorded in *Súpis novín a časopisov na Slovensku* (Martin, Matica slovenská). The last volume available covers the years 1961-1965, encompassing in 2,000 entries possibly all serials issued in Slovakia in any language. In Andrej Halaša's *Bibliografia časopisov a novín vychádzajúcich na Slovensku v roku 1966* (Bibliography of periodicals and newspapers issued in Slovakia in 1966) (Martin, Matica slovenská, 1966, 101 p.) we have the most recent publication on the topic, and as complete as can be expected from any bibliographic aid.

484. Potemra, Michal, *comp.* Bibliografia inorečových novín a časopisov na Slovensku do roku 1918 (Bibliography of foreign-language newspapers and periodicals in Slovakia to 1918). Martin, Matica slovenská, 1963. 818 p. Maps. (Slovenská národná bibliografia. Séria B. Periodiká, zv. 1b)

A first-class tool, covering the field completely and accurately. More specialized lists, compiled also by Potemra, are *Pomocný súpis novín a časopisov v reči nemeckej, latinskej, poľskej a hebrejskej na Slovensku do roku 1918* (Auxiliary register of newspapers and periodicals published in Slovakia in German, Latin, Polish, and Hebrew to

1918) (Košice, Štátna vedecká knižnica, 1954, 43 p.) and *Pomocný súpis novín a časopisov v reši maďarskej na Slovensku do r. 1914* (Auxiliary register of newspapers and periodicals published in Slovakia in Hungarian to 1914) (Košice, Štátna vedecká knižnica, 1954, 93, 26 p.). For periodicals in Russian and Ukrainian, we can turn to A. H.'s (i.e., Antonín Hartl's) article "Rusínské časopisectvo na východním Slovensku" (Ruthenian periodicals in eastern Slovakia) in *Duch novin*, v. 3, 1930, p. 99-100, covering the years 1921-1930.

485. Vološin, Augustin. Vývoj časopisectva na Podkarpatské Rusi (Development of the periodical press in Ruthenia). Duch novin, v. 1, 1928: 52-55, 79-82, 111-114.

An historical survey from 1870 to 1923. For later years, *see* Iosif V. Kaminskii's "Karpatorusskaia zhurnalistika posle 1919 goda" (Sub-Carpathian journalism after 1919) in *Russkii narodnyi golos*, 1936, p. 137-139, which describes newspapers and periodicals for the years 1919-1936.

486. Nosovský, Karel, *comp.* Soupis českých a slovenských současně vycházejících časopisů v zemích koruny české, Vídni, Německu, Rusku a v Americe (Register of Czech and Slovak periodicals issued at present in the lands of the Czech crown, Vienna, Germany, Russia, and America). Praha, 1909. 151 p.

A nearly complete catalog of Czech and Slovak serials current in 1908. *Liste bibliographique des journaux paraissant dans la République tchécoslovaque pour l'année 1920* (Praha, Československý ústav bibliografický, 1921, 243 p.) is a register of Czech, Slovak, German, Hungarian, and Ukrainian newspapers and periodicals for that year. For the post-World War II period, one can consult the annual *Adresář československého tisku* (Register of the Czechoslovak press) (1948–, Praha, Orbis), the first volume covering 1945-May 1948. An accurate and well-organized survey is Karel A. Kase's master's thesis (Catholic University of America), called *Czechoslovak Periodicals in 1959-1960; an Annotated Bibliography* (Washington, 1964, 186 1.). Lists of periodicals available abroad for subscription are issued yearly by Artia under the title *Periodicals from the Czechoslovak Socialist Republic* (Praha, 1961–). Periodical publications in Esperanto issued in 1887-1934 on the territory of today's Czechoslovakia can be found in Josef Takács' *Katalogo de la esperanto-gazetaro* (Jablonné, Ant. Pražák, 1934, 168 p.). For a current Slovak bibliography of serials *see Bibliografia časopisov a novín vychádzajúcich na Slovensku v roku . . .* (Bibliography of periodicals and newspapers, published in Slovakia in . . .) (Martin, Matica Slovenská, 1966–, annual).

487. Časopisecký katalog ČSR (Catalog of periodicals of Czechoslovakia). Praha, R. Mosse, 1926-1939. 14 v.

The first part of each of these yearly catalogs lists the political press; the second part, specialized periodicals. Materials are divided by lands (Bohemia, Moravia-Silesia, Slovakia, Ruthenia) and by places of publication. All the volumes, except the last one, carry Czech and German texts and title, *Zeitungskatalog Čechoslovakei.* Has indexes.

4. Of Dissertations, Indexes, and Library Holdings

488. Matica slovenská. *Knižnica.* Katalóg slovákumových kníh Knižnice Matice slovenskej do roku 1918 (Register of books in the Library of Matica slovenská dealing with Slovak matters to 1918). Compiled by Božena Baricová and others. Chief editor: Štefan Valentovič. Martin, Matica slovenská, 1964. 3 v.

A well-organized catalog of what is probably the largest collection of books with Slovak subjects, regardless of language.

489. Soupis časopisectva (Register of periodicals). 1951– Praha, Národní knihovna. Annual.

A massive catalog of newspaper and periodical holdings of the Prague National Museum, undoubtedly the largest depository of Czech and Slovak serials in the world. Issued by Knihovna Národního musea (odd. časopisů).

490. Články v českých časopisech (Articles in Czech periodicals). 1953– Praha, Národní knihovna. Monthly.

Supersedes *České časopisy.* Constitutes part of *Bibliografický katalog ČSR.* A thoroughgoing index of major articles in all fields. Its Slovak counterpart is *Články v slovenských časopisoch* (Articles in Slovak periodicals) (1955–, Martin, Matica slovenská, monthly). Both cover, in addition to Czech and Slovak publications, periodicals in German, Hungarian, and Ukrainian.

491. Československé disertace (Czechoslovak dissertations). 1965– Praha, Státní knihovna. (Bibliografický katalog ČSSR. České knihy. Zvl. sešity)

This is probably a complete record of dissertations currently presented at the schools of higher learning in Czechoslovakia. The first volume, covering the year 1964, contains 1,414 entries encompassing all fields. A professional work, well organized and accurate.

See also *Disertace Pražské university* (Dissertations of Prague University) (Praha, Universita Karlova, 1965, 2 v. Sbírka pramenů a příruček k dějinám University Karlovy, 2, 3). Volume 1 covers Charles University, 1882-1953, volume 2 the German University, 1882-1945.

492. Dissertationen zur Problematik des böhmisch-mährischen Raumes. München, Sekretariat des Sudetendeutschen Archivs, 1955-1956. 2 v. (Schriftenreihe des Sudetendeutschen Archivs, Heft 1-2)

The volumes of this series record doctoral dissertations dealing with Bohemia and Moravia. All fields are represented. An important source of scholarly materials.

B. GENERAL AND DESCRIPTIVE WORKS*

1. Encyclopedias

493. Ottův slovník naučný; illustrovaná encyklopaedie obecných vědomostí (Otto's encyclopedic dictionary; an illustrated encyclopedia of general knowledge). Praha, J. Otto, 1888-1909. 28 v. Illus., plates, maps, plans.

A basic encyclopedia for information on Czech and Slovak matters prior to the First World War. The corresponding source for the interwar period is *Ottův slovník naučný nové doby; dodatky k velikému Ottovu slovníku naučnému* (Otto's new encyclopedic dictionary; supplements to the large Otto's encyclopedic dictionary) Praha, J. Otto, 1930-1943, 6 v.).

494. Masarykův slovník naučný; lidová encyklopedie všeobecných vědomostí (Masaryk's encyclopedic dictionary; a popular encyclopedia of universal knowledge). Praha, Československý kompas, 1925-1933. 7 v. Front., illus., plates (part col.), ports., maps (part fold.)

An authoritative source of information. May be supplemented by the more detailed but at times less reliable *Nový velký ilustrovaný slovník naučný* (A new, large, illustrated encyclopedic dictionary) (Praha, Gutenberg, 1929-1934, 20 v.; Praha, Nebeský a Beznoska, 1933-1934).

495. Československá vlastivěda (Book of knowledge on Czechoslovakia). Praha, Sfinx, 1929-36. 10 v. in 12. Illus., ports., maps, facsims. Includes bibliographies.

See also entries no. 614, 770, *and* 840.

A work of primary importance, dealing in great detail with all aspects of human endeavor. It is divided as follows: I. Nature; II. Man; III. Languages; IV. History; V. The State; VI. Labor; VII. Literature; VIII. The Arts; IX. Technology; X. Learning. The individual volumes were prepared by the most distinguished scholars in Czechoslovakia during the interwar period, under the general editorship of Professor Václav Dědina.

496. Slovenský náučný slovník. Príručná encyklopedia vedomostí v 3 dieloch (Slovak encyclopedic dictionary. A reference encyclopedia of knowledge in 3 volumes). Edited by Pavel Bujnák. Bratislava, "Litevna," 1932. 3 v. Diagrs., maps, tables.

A solid work, with particularly good coverage of the humanities and social sciences in Slovakia.

497. Slovenská vlastiveda (Book of knowledge on Slovakia). Bratislava, Slovenská akadémia vied a umení, 1943-1948. 5 v. Illus., ports., maps. Includes bibliographies.

See also entry no. 620.

A scholarly work comprising the following volumes: I. Geology,

* Entries in this section are listed in chronological order.

geography, flora, and fauna; II. Folklore, national characteristics, and anthropology; III. Sociology; IV. The history of Slovakia and the Slovaks; V. Literature and language. The principal studies were written by such prominent Slovak scholars as František Bokes, Andrej Mráz, Eugen Pauliny, and Anton Štefánek.

498. Příruční slovník naučný (An encyclopedic reference dictionary). Edited by Vladimír Procházka. Praha, Nakl. ČSAV, 1962-1967. 4 v. Illus., plates, ports., maps.

In addition to its coverage of Czech and Slovak subjects, includes extensive material on the USSR and other Communist countries. Much of the content reflects the Marxist point of view. Prepared by the Academy's Encyclopedický institut.

499. Československá vlastivěda (Book of knowledge on Cezchoslovakia). Praha, Orbis, 1963– Illus., plates, ports., facsims., maps. Includes bibliographies.

See also entry no. 615.

Published by the Czechoslovak Society for the Propagation of Political and Scientific Knowledge, in conjunction with the Academy of Sciences. Academician Josef Macek is Chairman of the Editorial Board. Intended to present, in 15 volumes, "a detailed picture of the present and the past" of the country. Solid and scholarly coverage of the humanities, social sciences, and technical disciplines, only occasionally tinged by communist ideology.

2. Surveys

500. Hassinger, Hugo. Die Tschechoslowakei; ein geographisches, politisches und wirtschaftliches Handbuch. Wien, Rikola Verlag, 1925. 618 p. Fold. maps. Bibliography: p. 602-618.

See also entry no. 775.

Reliable survey of geography, politics, and economics, offering a wealth of information for the first seven years of independent Czechoslovakia. For data on the post-World War II developments, one can consult Jiří Hronek's *Czechoslovakia; a Handbook of Facts and Figures* (2d rev. ed., Praha, Orbis, 1964, 188 p.), presenting officially released material.

501. Deset let Československé republiky (Ten years of the Czechoslovak Republic). Praha, 1928. 3 v. Illus., ports., maps.

A massive, official account of the progress achieved in the principal domains of governmental concerns during the first decade of independent Czechoslovakia. A well-organized work of great informational value.

502. Seton-Watson, Robert W., *ed.* Slovakia Then and Now; a Political Survey. London, Allen and Unwin; Prague, Orbis, 1931. 356 p. Col. front., plates, ports., fold. map.

See also entry no. 782.

Coverage includes nearly all aspects of national life. Contributors include such outstanding Slovaks as Vavro Šrobár, Anton Štefánek, Andrej Hlinka, Vladimír Fajnor, Ivan Dérer, and Štefan Osuský.

503. At the Cross-Roads of Europe; a Historical Outline of the Democratic Idea in Czechoslovakia. Prague, Pen Club, 1938. 275 p. Front., ports.

Written by such prominent authors as Karel Čapek, J. L. Hromádka, Ferdinand Peroutka, and Albert Pražák, the book discusses the country and its peoples in historical and geographical perspective. Emphasis is on history, literature, and religion. A first-rate work of rare lucidity and cogency.

504. Co daly naše země Evropě a lidstvu; od slovanských věrozvěstů k národnímu obrození (What our country has given Europe and mankind; from the time of Cyril and Methodius to the national awakening). Chief editor: Vilém Mathesius. Praha, Evropský literární klub, 1939. 230 p. Plates.

See also entry no. 1163.

A collection of scholarly essays written by prominent experts.

505. Kerner, Robert J., *ed.* Czechoslovakia, Twenty Years of Independence. Berkeley and Los Angeles, University of California Press, 1940. 504 p. Illus., maps.

See also entries no. 776 *and* 873.

A collection of fact-filled articles by such competent authorities as Aleš Hrdlička, S. Harrison Thomson, Hans Kohn, Joseph S. Roucek, Matthew Spinka, Henry Wickham Steed, James T. Shotwell, and Professor Kerner himself. Includes a chapter on Podkarpatská Rus by Oszkár Jászi. Most chapters include bibliographies. "An honest, unprejudiced, and frank appraisal" of developments during the interwar period.

506. Wanklyn, Harriet G. Czechoslovakia. New York, Praeger, 1954. 445 p. Illus., maps, bibliography.

See also entry no. 583.

Objective coverage of the geography, history, and economics through the early fifties. Includes an important chapter on Podkarpatská Rus.

507. Rowe, David N., *and* Willmore Kendall, *eds.* Czechoslovakia; an Area Manual. Chevy Chase, Md., Operations Research Office, Johns Hopkins University, 1955. 2 v. Tables, diagrs., maps.

Volume 1 is a survey of geographic, historical, and economic factors. Volume 2 describes and analyzes political, cultural, and sociological developments. A sophisticated, well-documented presentation, the greater part written by Ivo Duchacek, Andrew Gyorgy, and Rudolf Sturm.

508. Chicago. University. *Division of the Social Sciences.* A Study of Contemporary Czechoslovakia. Edited by Jan Hajda. Chicago, Uni-

versity of Chicago for the Human Relations Area Files, 1955. 637 p. Maps, tables.

See also entry no. 960.

Prepared by a group of researchers at the University of Chicago for the Human Relations Area Files, an organization affiliated with Yale University. Scholars from 20 other American colleges also contributed. A careful survey of the various social fields as of the mid-'50s, with only a slight pro-Western slant. Includes an 11-page bibliography.

509. Bušek, Vratislav, *and* Nicolas Spulber, *eds.* Czechoslovakia. New York, Praeger, 1957. 520 p. Maps, tables. Bibliography: p. 484-499. (Praeger Publications in Russian History and World Communism, no. 19)

A lucid and informative presentation by a variety of scholars, including Czech and Slovak exiles as well as native American specialists in the area. Covers a wide range of topics, from agriculture to belles-lettres to topology. Some of the studies have a pro-Western orientation.

510. Chekhoslovakiia sotsialisticheskaia, 1945-1965 (Socialist Czechoslovakia, 1945-1965). Moskva, Pravda, 1965. 301 p. Illus., maps.

A group of editors from *Pravda* (Moscow) and *Rudé právo* (Prague) describe and analyze "the road of the Czechoslovak people toward socialism." Economic, social, and political fields are covered. The companion volume for the first 10 years (1945-1955) is *Desiat' let narodno-demokraticheskoi Chekhoslovakii* (Ten years of Czechoslovakia under people's democracy) (Moskva, Izd-vo inostrannoi literatury, 1956, 202 p.). The books present an informative and well-written analysis from the communist point of view.

511. Rechcígl, Miloslav Jr., *ed.* The Czechoslovak Contribution to World Culture. The Hague, Mouton, 1964. 682 p. Illus. Bibliography: p. 555-634.

See also entries no. 681, 1108, *and* 1165.

A collection of scholarly papers, most of which were read at the First Congress of the Czechoslovak Society of Arts and Sciences in America, held April 20-22, 1962, in Washington, D.C. Covers the humanities, social sciences, and technology. Includes an extensive bibliography. Necessary reading for students of Czechoslovak culture.

512. Kuhn, Heinrich, Handbuch der Tschechoslowakei. München, Robert Lerche, 1967. 1021 p.

See also entry no. 818.

Offers, with a minimum of interpretation and comment, a wealth of factual data on land and people, government, administration, political parties, and cultural organizations. The emphasis is on the organizational structure and personnel in the governmental and political apparatus. For a similar reference work recently published in Czechoslovakia, *see*:

Brož, Václav, *ed.* Hospodářskopolitická rukověť (Economic-political handbook). Praha, Československá tisková kancelář, 1968. 2 v. Volume 1 deals with the organs of central administration and production; volume 2 contains substantive and personal data on producers' and consumers' cooperatives; political and social organizations; regional administrative organs; the press, publishing houses and the book trade; and higher educational, cultural, and other establishments. Václav Brož also edited *Organizace Československé socialistické republiky* (Organization of the Czechoslovak Socialist Republic) (Praha, Československá tisková kancelář, 1965, 1 v., looseleaf).

3. General Periodicals*

513. Prague News Letter. 1945– Prague, Nakladatelství Orbis. Biweekly.

Designed for the foreign dissemination of officially endorsed data and views, this illustrated survey covers "political, economic, and cultural life in Czechoslovakia." A weekly companion publication, also for readers abroad, is *Czechoslovak Digest; Background Information* (Prague, Pragopress, 1965–), which is based on selected articles from the Czech and Slovak press.

514. U.S. *Foreign Broadcast Information Service.* Daily Report, Foreign Radio Broadcasts. February 24, 1947– Washington, D.C.

The European section includes summaries of transmissions from most Czech and Slovak stations, dealing with all facets of life. A similar publication is *Monitoring Service*, issued daily by the British Broadcasting Corporation. These are excellent sources of information on current developments in Czechoslovakia.

515. Czechoslovak Republic. Československá tisková kancelář, Prague. Information Bulletin. 1956– Prague. Semiweekly.

A press survey published by the official Czechoslovak News Agency. Russian supplements accompany some issues. To balance the picture, the reader may wish to refer to the *Press Review* (Praha, 1945–), released daily except Monday by the British Embassy in Prague.

516. U.S. *Joint Publications Research Service.* Political Translations on Eastern Europe. 1962– Washington, D.C. Irregular.

See also entry no. 51.

Published by the Clearinghouse for Federal Scientific and Technical Information. An excellent source of information in English on various matters reflected in the Czech and Slovak press. Another useful publication of this agency is *Summary of the Czechoslovak Provincial Press* (New York, Dec. 15, 1958–), which includes both summaries and full or partial translations of articles from various fields.

* A detailed listing of periodicals in Horecky's West European languages on Czechoslovakia is given in *The USSR and Eastern Europe; Periodicals in Western Languages.* For Czech and Slovak periodicals see the preceding chapter.

4. Guides, Pictorial Publications, Travel Descriptions

517. Československé ústředí cizineckého ruchu, *Prague.* Příručka Československé republiky (Handbook of the Czechoslovak Republic). Praha, A. Koníček, 1937. 1060 p. Illus., ports., maps.

The largest and most accurate guide to prewar Czechoslovakia. Issued by the Central Bureau for Tourism, this handbook contains a wealth of information. In Czech, English, French, and German.

518. Czechoslovak Life. 1946– Prague. Monthly.

Also published in French, Italian, and Swedish, this illustrated magazine is designed for foreign circulation only. Other picture publications for readers abroad include *The Czechoslovak Weekly*, and the monthlies *Czechoslovakia* and *Czechoslovakia in Pictures.* All are sponsored by the Ministry of Information and Culture or its subsidiaries.

519. Kubíček, Alois. The Palaces of Prague. Translated by Norah Robinson-Hronková. Prague, V. Poláček, 1946. 231 p. Illus.

Features 108 pictures of the Prague palaces. The text discusses their artistic, historical, and political significance in the life of the Bohemian State. Also published in French as *Les palais de Prague* (Praha, V. Poláček, 1947, 229 p.).

520. Plicka, Karel. Slovensko ve fotografii (Slovakia in pictures). 2d ed. Turč sv. Martin, Matica slovenská, 1949. 12 p. of text, 224 p. of illus.

Masterpieces of the foremost Czech photographer. Introduction by the Slovak poet Laco Novomeský. Fourth edition: Martin, Osveta, 1953. In Slovak, Russian, English, and French. May be supplemented by V. A. Firsoff's *The Tatra Mountains* (London, L. Drummond, 1942, 128 p.).

521. Pargeter, Edith. The Coast of Bohemia. London, Heinemann, 1950. 324 p. Illus., group port.

Skillfully prepared and very informative, this travel book, with a title borrowed from Shakespeare, is rather sympathetic toward the communist regime. For other travel literature of communist vintage, *see* V. Druzhinin's *Puteshestviia po Chekhoslovakii* (Travels in Czechoslovakia) (Leningrad, Sovetskii pisatel', 1956, 285 p.) and *Die Slowakei* by František Bokes (Praha, Artia, 1954, 215 p.), the latter with an *excursus* into the history of Slovakia.

522. Plicka, Karel. Prague en images. Prague in Photographs. Introduction by Z. Wirth. Prague, Orbis, 1950. 208 p. Illus.

A classic among the many pictorial albums, with text in Czech, Russian, French, and English. May be supplemented by Plicka's *Pražský hrad* (The Prague castle) (Praha, Orbis, 1965, 52 p. of text, 178 p. of illus.), with summaries and captions in Russian, German, English, and French.

523. Čarek, Jiří. Ulicemi města Prahy od 14. století do dneška; názvy mostů, nábřeží, náměstí, ostrovů, sadů a ulic hlavního města Prahy,

jejich změny a výklad (A tour through the streets of Prague from the 14th century till today . . .). Praha, Orbis, 1958. 535 p. Illus.

Conceived as a guide to Prague from the 14th century to the late 1950s, the book records the names of streets, bridges, islands, and parks, and explains their changes through history.

524. Lion, Jindřich. The Prague Ghetto. The Story and Legend of the Jewish Quarter in Prague through Its One Thousand Year History. Photos by Jan Lukas. London, Spring Books, 1959. 96 p. 36 plates.

This handsome volume describes with great artistry, both verbal and pictorial, one of the oldest Jewish ghettos of Europe, reviving its history from the legendary Rabbi Loew and his *Golem* to the real Franz Kafka. Also published in German as *Das Prager Ghetto* (Praha, Artia, 1959, 102, 35 p.).

525. Vahala, Miroslav, *and others.* Brno; Guidebook. English version by Roberta Finlayson-Samsour. Praha, Sportovní a turistické nakl., 1961. 100 p. Illus.

The second largest city in Czechoslovakia and the capital of Moravia is described in this well-written volume. A German text, *Brno; Fremdenführer* (Praha, Sportovní a turistické nakl., 1958, 113 p.), is also available.

526. Chyský, Jiří, M. Skalník, *and* V. Adamec. Guide to Czechoslovakia. Translated by K. Kornell, O. Kuthanová, and M. Beranová. Praha, Artia, 1965. 413 p., Illus., maps, plates.

One of the more recent guides for foreign tourists, comprehensive, well written, and beautifully illustrated. It describes every corner of the country, indicating the available means of transportation. Those traveling by car may use *The automobile guide of the ČSSR*, by Josef Mašíček and others (Praha, Nakl. dopravy a spojů, 1964, 115 p.), available also as *Autoführer durch die ČSSR*, which includes information on travel documents, roads, hotels, and other facilities.

527. Svoboda, Alois. Prague; an Intimate Guide to Czechoslovakia's Thousand-Year-Old Capital, Its Beauties, Its Art-Historical Monuments, Its Sights, Ancient and Modern, Its Romantic Nooks and Corners, With Their Historical and Literary Associations. Prague, Sportovní a turistické nakl., 1965. 299 p. Illus., col. maps (1 fold. in pocket).

Probably the most imaginative and instructive of the recent guidebooks. A German translation, *Prag; das tausendjährige hunderttürmige Prag in Stadtwanderungen, ein intimer Führer . . .*, is also available.

528. Krejčí, Milan. Praha osmi století (Eight hundred years of Prague). Praha, Orbis, 1965. 175 p. Illus., col. map, plans.

Conveys the atmosphere of the past eight centuries in the life of the city. Includes 96 pages of photographs. Text in Czech, English, French, German, and Russian.

529. Lazištan, Eugen, *ed.* Bratislava. Introduction by Alžbeta Güntherová-Mayerová. 4th rev. ed. Bratislava, Osveta, 1965. 10 p. of text, 196 p. of illus.

The capital of Slovakia is described here with taste and accuracy. The summaries and lists of illustrations are in Russian, German, Hungarian, French, and English. Another reliable guide is V. Málek and D. Orlovský's *Potulky po Bratislave* (Wandering in Bratislava) (Bratislava, Obzor, 1965, 207 p.), which also encompasses the environs of the city, lists useful addresses, and includes a very good bibliography.

530. Linehan, Edward J. Czechoslovakia. The Dream and the Reality. National Geographic, February 1968: 151-192.

A perceptive, up-to-date, and profusely illustrated travel account.

C. BIOGRAPHIES

531. České biografie (Czech biographies). Serie 1-30; May 9, 1936-March 31, 1941. Praha, Tiskový odbor Presidia ministerské rady (Tiskárna Protektorátu Čechy a Morava . . .) 3 v.

Title varies: May 9, 1936-October 10, 1938: *Československo*. A looseleaf compilation with biographic sketches of men prominent in the public life of pre-World War II Czechoslovakia and the "Protektorat." For additional biographic sources on diverse strata of the society of the Czechoslovak Republic and its predecessor lands, *see*:

Kulturní adresář ČSR (Cultural directory of the Czechoslovak Republic). 2d rev. and enl. ed. Praha, J. Zeibrdlich, 1936. 670 p. Illus., col. plates.

Sekanina, František, *ed.* Album representantů všech oborů veřejného života československého (Album of representatives of all segments of Czechoslovak public life). Praha, J. Zeidbrdlich, 1927. 1202 p. Ports.

Navrátil, Michal. Almanach československých právníků . . . (Almanac of Czechoslovak jurists . . .). Praha, Tiskem knihtisk. J. Slováka v Kroměříži, 1930. 560 p. A biographic dictionary of Czechoslovak jurists who were active in the fields of the arts, sciences, belles-lettres, and politics for some 600 years from the time of Charles IV.

Heller, Hermann. Mährens Frauen der Gegenwart; biographisches Lexicon. Bruenn, 1901. 1 v.

———. Mährens Männer der Gegenwart; biographisches Lexicon. Bruenn, C. Winkler, 1885-1892. 3 v.

552. Československá akademie věd. *Ústav pro českou literaturu.* Slovník českých spisovatelů (Dictionary of Czech writers). Edited by Rudolf Havel and Jiří Opelík. Praha, Československý spisovatel, 1965. 625 p. Ports.

See also entry no. 1092.

A compendium of solid scholarship on writers from the beginning of Czech literature to the present, though with emphasis on the 20th century. The entries, in the form of succinct essays from the pens of numerous literary experts of the Academy's Institute of Czech Literature, offer profiles of the writer and his creative work, a bibliography of his works, and a summary of the essential literature about him. It is planned to enlarge this dictionary into a multivolume work. For cognate biographic data, the following materials can be consulted:

Kunc, Jaroslav. Slovník soudobých českých spisovatelů. Krásné písemnictví v letech 1918-1945 (Dictionary of contemporary Czech writers. Belles-lettres in the years 1918-1945). Praha, Orbis, 1945-1946. 2 v. A thoughtfully conceived and executed work covering in alphabetical order biographic data and characteristics of creative accomplishments of 780 poets, novelists, and playwrights. The author is director of the University Library in Prague and a leading Czech bibliographer. A sequel — at times devoid of the balance and objectivity of its predecessor volume — is his *Slovník českých spisovatelů beletristů, 1945-1956* (Dictionary of Czech literary authors, 1945-1956) (Praha, Státní pedagogické nakl., 1957, 483 p.). *Kdy zemřeli* (When did they die?) (2d enl. ed., Praha, Státní knihovna ČSSR, 1962, 337 p. Bibliografický katalog ČSSR, České knihy, 1962, zvláštní sešit 7), though based on obituaries, is not nearly so funereal as its title would seem to indicate, also giving data on the lives of 3,225 Czech literary authors, translators, illustrators, and publishers who died between 1937 and the end of 1962. A supplement, under the identical title and by the same author, appeared in 1966 (Bibliografický katalog ČSSR, České knihy, zvláštní sešit 6).

Urbánek, František A., *comp.* Biografický a bibliografický slovník českých spisovatelů (Biographic and bibliographic dictionary of Czech writers). Telč, 1909. 2 v. This is a convenient aid for biographic research on the 19th century. Volume 1 deals with authors in literature; volume 2, with authors in other fields.

Členové Československé akademie věd a členové českých národních vědeckých institucí na něž ČSAV navazuje ve své činnosti. (Members of the Czechoslovak Academy of Sciences and members of the learned institutions connected with the Academy's activities). Praha, ČSAV, 1968. 178 p.

553. Československý hudební slovník osob a institucí (Czechoslovak music dictionary of persons and institutions). Edited by Gracian Černušák, Bohumír Štědroň, and Zdenko Nováček. Praha, Státní hudební nakladatelství, 1963-1965. 2 v. Illus., facsims., ports., bibliographies.

See also entry no. 1285.

Some 9,500 pertinent entries. Volume 1: A-L; volume 2: M-Ž. Produced by distinguished musicologists.

534. Dolenský, Antonín, *comp.* Slovník pseudonymů a kryptonymů v československé literatuře (Dictionary of pseudonyms and cryptonyms in Czechoslovak literature). 4th ed. Praha, Nákladem vlastním, 1934. 155 p.

The standard source on literary pen names, supplemented and updated by Jaroslav Kunc in his *Vlastním jménem; slovníček pseudo-*

nymů novodobých českých spisovatelů (Their real names; a small dictionary of pseudonyms of Czech writers of recent times) (Praha, Národní knihovna, 1958, 67 p. Bibliografický katalog ČSSR, České knihy, 1958, zvláštní sešit, 5).

535. Gierach, Erich, *ed.* Sudetendeutsche Lebensbilder. Reichenberg, Verlag Gebrüder Stiepel, 1926-1934. 3 v. Fronts., illus., plates, ports., bibliographies.

See also entry no. 640.

The standard work of historical biography of prominent Germans on the territory of the Czechoslovak Republic. The work is organized by broad categories of human endeavor. For a biographic lexicon of Sudeten-German writers, *see*:

Jaksch, Friedrich. Lexikon sudetendeutscher Schriftsteller und ihrer Werke für die Jahre 1900-1929. Reichenberg, Gebrüder Stiepel, 1929. 358 p.

536. Gintl, Zdeněk, *comp.* Postavy a osobnosti. Seznam životopisů a osobních monografií (Figures and personalities. A list of biographies and personal monographs). Praha, Melantrich, 1936. 836 p. (Spisy Knihovny Hl. města Prahy, č. 20)

Part 1 offers a list of books and articles written about prominent personalities; part 2 lists biographic studies by writers about others. The arrangement of entries in both parts is alphabetical. While general in scope, this work gives generous coverage to Czechoslovak personalities.

537. Hrdinové a věštci českého národa. (Heroes and prophets of the Czech nation). Přerov, Společenské podniky, 1948. 484 p. Illus., ports., bibliographies.

A collection of profiles of notable personalities of the Czech past, from Cyril and Methodius to Edvard Beneš. Similar selective historical biographies are:

Hrbek, Josef, *and others.* Český kulturní Slavín duchovní, terórní hudební a výtvarnický (The Czech cultural pantheon in the intellectual, literary, musical, and artistic fields). Praha, Šolc a Šimáček, 1948. 627 p. Illus.

Stloukal, Karel, *ed.* Královny, kněžny a velké ženy české (Queens, princesses, and other notable Czech women). Praha, J. R. Vilímek, 1940. 591 p. Illus.

538. Kolář, Martin. Českomoravská heraldika (Czech and Moravian heraldy). Praha, Česká akademie věd a umění, 1902-1925. 2 v.

An important armorial for genealogical research on the area.

539. Kuhn, Heinrich, *and* Otto Böss. Biographisches Handbuch der Tschechoslowakei. München, R. Lerche, 1961. 640 p.

The only Who's Who-type handbook for contemporary Czechoslovakia. The first part gives the organizational breakdown, along with corresponding office holders, of the top echelons of the party, government, public bodies as well as cultural, educational, and religious institutions. This section is now superseded by the up-to-date version contained in the fourth, almost 500-page, chapter of *Handbuch der Tschechoslowakei* by the same author (*see entry* no. 512). The second part is a biographical dictionary of leading personalities in Czechoslovakia's public life. For later coverage *see* Marie Riedlová's *Česká životopisná literatura vydaná v letech 1963-1967* (Czech biographic literature, 1963-1967) (Olomouc, Státní vědecká knihovna, 1968, 201 p.).

540. Matoušek, Miloslav. Malý biografický slovník československých lékařů (A small biographic dictionary of Czechoslovak physicians). Praha, Státní pedogogické nakl., 1964. 198 p. Bibliography: p. 197-198.

Sponsored by the Medical Faculty of the Palacký University in Olomouc.

541. Ormis, Ján V. Slovník slovenských pseudonymov (Dictionary of Slovak pseudonyms). Turčianský sv. Martin, Slovenská národná knižnica, 1944. 366 p. Bibliography: p. 78-85.

A pioneer Slovak work on the subject. Should be used together with the following later work, which supplements it:

Matica slovenská. Slovník pseudonymov slovenských spisovatel'ov (Dictionary of pseudonyms of Slovak writers). Prepared by Štefan Hanakovič and others. Martin, 1961. 334 p.

542. Radványi, Čelo. Slovenská krv (Of Slovak blood). Bratislava, Slovenská krv, 1942. 568 p.

This book — with a title reminiscent of the spirit prevailing at the time of its publication — assembles biographic information on people then considered prominent representatives of Slovak society. The following two biographic compilations on a strife-torn period in recent Slovak history are expressive of the political thinking in present-day Slovakia. The portrayals drawn in them must be viewed in the light of the polarized political struggle of recent memory.

Chreňo, Josef. Malý slovník slovenského, štátu, 1938-1945 (Small dictionary of the Slovak State, 1938-1945). Bratislava, Slovenská archivná správa, 1965. 297 p. Contains biographic data on representatives of the establishment in the Slovak State and on foreign nationals connected with Slovak affairs in an official capacity. A chronology of events during this period and two indexes of organizations and subjects are appended.

Kropilák, Miroslav, *and* J. Jablonický. Malý slovník národného povstania (Small dictionary of the National Uprising). Bratislava, Vydavatel'stvo politickej literatúry, 1964. 311 p. Deals with persons and localities involved in the Slovak National Uprising in the final phase of the Second World War.

543. Toman, Prokop. Nový slovník československých výtvarných umělců (New dictionary of Czechoslovak creative artists). 3d enl. ed. Praha,

R. Ryšavý, 1947-1950. 2 v. Ports. Bibliography: v. 1, p. 3-4. *See also* entry no. 1245.

———. Dodatky ke Slovníku československých výtvarných umělců (Supplements to the dictionary of Czechoslovak creative artists). Prepared by Prokop Toman and Prokop H. Toman. Praha, Státní nakl. krásné literatury, hudby a umění, 1955. 224 p. Port.

This massive biographic work on Czech and Slovak representational artists in past and present is the impressive product of the labors of three generations of the Toman family. The pioneer work in this field for the period of the Austro-Hungarian monarchy is:

Dlabač, Jan B. (Johann G. Dlabacz), *comp. and ed.* Allgemeines historisches Künstler-lexikon für Böhmen and zum Theil auch für Mähren und Schlesien. Prag, G. Haase, 1815. 3 v. Supplement:

Sternberg-Manderscheidt, Franz Joseph. Beiträge u. Berichtigungen zum Dlabačž Lexikon böhmischer Künstler. Prag, K. André'sche Buchhandlung M. Berwald, 1913. 63 p.

D. MULTILINGUAL DICTIONARIES

544. The following list includes bilingual and multilingual dictionaries only. For monolingual dictionaries the reader should consult chapter 21, section A.

Bibliography: Československá akademie věd. *Základní knihovna.* Bibliografie odborných překladových slovníků; dvojjazčné a vícejazyčné slovníky, v nichž se kombinuje čeština s angličtinou, francouzštinou, němčinou a ruštinou (Bibliography of specialized translators' dictionaries; bilingual and multilingual glossaries in which Czech is combined with English, French, German, and Russian). Praha, Základní knihovna ČSAV, 1962. 36 p.

English: Anglicko-český slovník (English-Czech dictionary). Compiled by Jan Caha and Jiří Krámský. 3d rev. ed. Praha, Státní pedagogické nakl., 1968. 877 p.

Česko-anglický slovník středního rozsahu (Czech-English medium-sized dictionary). Compiled by Ivan Poldauf. 3d ed. Praha, Státní pedagogické nakl., 1968. 1236 p.

Anglicko-slovenský a slovensko-anglický vreckový slovník (English-Slovak and Slovak-English pocket dictionary). Bratislava, Slovenské pedagogické nakl., 1968. 2d ed. 795 p.

Anglicko-slovenský slovník (English-Slovak dictionary). Compiled by Ján Šimko. Bratislava, Slovenské pedagogické nakl., 1968. 1443 p.

French: Buben, Vladimir. Francouzsko-český, česko-francouzský slovník (French-Czech, Czech-French dictionary). 4th rev. ed. Compiled by Milada Bubnová and Vladimír Hořejsí. Praha, Státní pedagogické nakl., 1967. 1243 p.

Šedivý, Vladimír. Francúzsko-slovenský slovník (French-Slovak dictionary). Bratislava, Slovenské pedagogické nakl., 1967. 1000 p.

Dictionnaire portatif slovaque-français. Bratislava, Slovenské pedagogické nakl., 1963. 453 p.

German: Německo-český slovník (German-Czech dictionary). Compiled by Jan Volný. 3d ed. Praha, Státní pedagogické nakl., 1966. 1412 p.

Česko-německý slovník (Czech-German dictionary). Compiled by Hugo Siebenschein. Praha, Státní pedagogické nakl., 1968. 2 v.

Nemecko-slovenský slovník (German-Slovak dictionary). 3d ed. Bratislava, Slovenské pedagogické nakl., 1966. 689 p.

Dratva, Tomáš. Slovensko-nemecký slovník (Slovak-German dictionary). Bratislava, Slovenské pedagogické nakl., 1967. 893 p.

Italian: Italsko-český slovník (Italian-Czech dictionary). Compiled by Jaroslav Rosendorfský. 2d enl. ed. Praha, Státní pedagogické nakl., 1964. 716 p.

Česko-italský slovník (Czech-Italian dictionary). Compiled by Jaroslav Rosendorfský. 2d enl. ed. Praha, Státní pedagogické nakl., 1964. 820 p.

Russian: Velký rusko-český slovník (Large Russian-Czech dictionary). Chief editors: L. Kopecký and others. Praha, Nakl. Československo-sovětského institutu, 1952-1964. 6 v.

Česko-ruský slovník (Czech-Russian dictionary). Chief editors: K. Horálek and others. Praha, Státní pedagogické nakl., 1958. 1302 p.

Velký rusko-slovenský slovník (Large Russian-Slovak dictionary). Vydavatel'stvo Slovenskej akadémie vied, 1960-1965. 3 v.

Slovensko-ruský prekladový slovník (Slovak-Russian translation dictionary). Compiled by Alexander V. Isačenko. Bratislava, Slovenská akadémia vied a umení, 1950-1957. 2 v.

Slovak: Slovensko-český, česko-slovenský slovník rozdílných výrazů (Slovak-Czech, Czech-Slovak dictionary of lexical differences). Praha, Státní pedagogické nakl., 1964. 512 p.

Slovensko-český slovník (Slovak-Czech dictionary). Compiled by Želmira Gašparíková and Adolf Kamiš. Praha, Státní pedagogické nakl., 1967. 812 p.

Spanish: Španělsko-český slovník (Spanish-Czech dictionary). 2d ed. Compiled by Josef Dubský. Praha, Státní pedagogické nakl., 1963. 778 p.

Česko-španělský slovník. Compiled by Josef Dubský. Praha, Státní pedagogické nakl., 1964. 907 p.

E. ARCHIVES, MUSEUMS, LIBRARIES, PRINTING AND PUBLISHING

1. Archives, Museums

545. Czechoslovak Republic. *Ministerstvo vnitra. Archivní správa.* Soupis archivní literatury v českých zemích, 1895-1956 (List of archival literature in the Czech lands, 1895-1965). Compiled by Otakar Bauer and Ludmila Mrázková, with the cooperation of Rostislav Nový. Praha, 1959. 226 p.

See also entry no. 699.

An important research aid on the major aspects of archival organization, administration, and repositories. Since 1956 the Czechoslovak Archival Administration has been issuing numerous guides to central and regional archival collections in the series *Průvodce po státních archivech* (Guide to state archives) (Praha, Archivní správa Ministerstva vnitra). Under the same sponsorship the semiannual *Sborník archivních prací* (Collection of papers on archives) has been published since 1950, reporting on domestic and foreign archival developments. Access to the substantial archival materials of the Czechoslovak Academy of Sciences is provided by the following publication:

Československá akademie věd. *Archiv.* Archiv Československé akademie věd; průvodce po archivních fondech (The archives of the Czechoslovak Academy of Sciences; a guide to the archival collections). Chief editor: Jiří Beran. Praha, Nakl. Československé akademie věd, 1962. 125 p. Illus., facsims., port.

546. Kučera, Karel, *and* Miroslav Truc. Archiv University Karlovy (The archive of Charles University). Praha, Universita Karlova, 1961. 182 p. (Sbírka pramenů a příruček k dějinám University Karlovy, 1)

547. Lamoš, Teodor. Bibliografia k archívom na Slovensku (Bibliography of Slovakia's archives). Bratislava, Slovenský ústredný archív, 1953. 183 p. Map.

A bibliographic inventory with summaries in German and Russian. A recently inaugurated specialized journal on archives in Slovakia, *Slovenská archivistika* (v. 1– 1966–, Bratislava, Slovenská archívna správa) offers a wealth of data on all aspects of the subject. Its first issue features, on pages 170-175, a directory of Slovakia's archival repositories. The Slovak State Central Archives (Štátny slovenský ústredný archiv) has been issuing a useful series of archival guides, *Sprievodca po archívnych fondoch.* An up-to-date and detailed survey article on contemporary Slovak archives, "Archive in der Slowakei und ihre Bestände" by Michal Kušík can be found in *Studia historica slovaca,* v. 3, 1965: 215-262.

548. Rybecký, M., *and others.* Sprievodca po múzeách na Slovensku (Museum guide for Slovakia). Bratislava, Vydavatel'stvo politickej literatúry, 1964. 119 p. Illus.

For art collections in Prague *see*:

Laufer, Josef. Musées et galeries de Prague. Praha, Olympia, 1967. 155 p.

2. Libraries

549. Bratislava. Univerzita. *Knižnica.* Univerzitna knižnica v. Bratislave, 1914-1919-1959 (The Bratislava University Library, 1914-1919-1959). Martin, Matica slovenská, 1959. 200 p.

A detailed description of the Library's history, collections, and activities. For a guide to the Slovak Academy's library system *see* Jozef Boldiš's *Vedecké knižnice Slovenskej akadémie vied* (The research libraries of the Slovak Academy of Sciences) (Bratislava, Vydavatel'stvo Slovenskej akadémie vied, 1963, 158 p.).

550. Cejpek, Jiří. Československé knihovnictví; poslání a organizace (Czechoslovak libraries and librarianship; tasks and organization). Praha, Státní pedagogické nakl., 1965. 171 p. Bibliography: p. 157-164.

A recent textbook for the study of librarianship on the university level, reviewing all major facets of the topic. See also *Stručný přehled dějin českého knihovnictví* (Brief survey of Czech librarianship) (2d rev. and enl. ed., Praha, Státní pedagogické nakl., 1967, 184 p.) by the same author; and *Das Bibliothekswesen der Tschechoslowakei*, prepared by librarians from Czechoslovakia (Wien, Österreichische Nationalbibliothek, 1966, 57 p.).

An excellent source for pre-World War II developments in Czechoslovak librarianship is *Časopis československých knihovníků* (Journal of Czechoslovak librarians) (v. 1-19, 1922-1940, Praha, bimonthly). This journal featured from time to time an informative bibliography of library science. For post-World War II bibliographies of library science *see* particularly:

Kunc, Jaroslav, *and others.* Patnáct let české knihovnické literatury, 1945-1960 (Fifteen years of Czech library literature, 1945-1960). Praha, Orbis, 1960. 47 p.

Bibliografie československého knihovnictví (Bibliography of Czechoslovak librarianship). 1960/61– Praha. (Bibliografický katalog ČSSR. České knihy. Zvláštní sešit) This bibliography usually appears annually as a special issue of the national bibliography of Czech books (České knihy).

Súpis slovenskej knihovníckej literatury zo rok . . . (Register of Slovak library literature for the year . . . 1961–) 1966– Martin, Matica slovenská. Annual.

The Státní knihovna ČSSR in Prague, through its Ústřední vědeckometodický kabinet knihovnictví released in 1967 several statistical surveys such as: *Lidové knihovny ČSSR; statistický přehled o činnosti v roce 1966* (People's libraries in Czechoslovakia; a statistical survey for 1966), prepared by Jiří Pekař; *Státní vědecké knihovny v roce 1966* (State research libraries in 1966); and *Knihovny vysokých škol v roce 1966* (University libraries in 1966).

551. Matica slovenská. Matica slovenská ako národná knižnica a knihovedný ústav (The Matica slovenská as national library and institute of book research). Martin, 1964. 246 p.

A thorough work on collections, services, and publishing activities of this notable cultural institution, which has been intimately linked with the national renaissance of the Slovak nation and serves nowadays as its national library and center of bibliographic registration. For a record of the prolific publishing activities of the Matica during the past century and at present, the following publications can be consulted:

Liba, Peter. Vydavatel'ské dielo Matice slovenskej. Bibliografia s prehl'adom, 1863-1953 (Publications of the Matica slovenská. A bibliography and survey, 1863-1953). Martin, Matica slovenská, 557 p. Illus., summaries in English, German, and Russian.

Vagaský, Andrej. Vydavatel'ská činnost' Matice slovenskej, 1954-1963 (Publications of the Matica slovenská, 1954-1963). Martin, Matica slovenská, 1964. 339 p.

Matica slovenská. Zoznam knižných vydaní Matice slovenskej (List of book editions of the Matica slovenská). Martin, Edičné oddelenie Matice slovenskej, 1964. 91 p. A printed catalog of the strong pre-1918 Slovaca collections in the Matica slovenská is now available through the following publication:

Matica slovenská. *Knižnica.* Katalóg slovákumových kníh Knižnice Matice slovenskej do roku 1918 (Catalog of Slovakiana of the library of the Matica slovenská through 1918). Chief editor: Štefan Valentovič. Martin, 1964. 3 v. For a survey article in English reviewing this institution and its programs *see*:

Horecky, Paul L.. Centenary of the Matica Slovenská. The Quarterly Journal of the Library of Congress, v. 21, July 1964: 203-206.

552. Olomouc. Palackého universita. *Knihovna.* Slovník knihovnických termínů v šesti jazycích (Dictionary of library terms in six languages). Praha, Státní pedagogické nakl., 1958. 632 p.

Consists of five separate sections for English, French, German, Polish, and Russian terms with their Czech equivalents, and of one cumulative section from Czech into these languages. Other auxiliary aids in this discipline are:

Smejkal, Bohuslav. Státní vědecká knihovna v Olomouci, 1945-1965 (State Research Library in Olomouc, 1945-1965). Olomouc, Státní vědecká knihovna, 1965. 101 p.

Hanakovič, Štefan, *and* Jozef Špetko. Slovník knihovníckých skratiek (Dictionary of library abbreviations). Martin, Matica slovenská, 1963. 185 p.

Vodičková, Hana, *and* Jiří Cejpek. Terminologický slovník knihovnický a bibliografický (Terminological dictionary of library science and bibliography). Praha, Státní pedagogické nakl., 1965. 119 p.

553. Prague. Národní museum. Knihovna Národního musea (The library of the National Museum). Praha, 1959. 235 p. Illus.

A guide — with résumés in English, French, German, and Russian — to the outstanding collections of Bohemica in this august institution and in "castle libraries" affiliated with it. One of the latter houses the Museum of the Book, which traces the progress of the book, scripts, and communication symbols from ancient times to the early 19th century, with emphasis on the Czech scene. An illustrated catalog to this permanent exhibit appeared as follows:

Museum knihy ve státním zámku a klášteře Žd'ář nad Sázavou. Katalog (The Museum of the Book in the state castle and monastery Žd'ář on the Sázava. Catalog). Praha, Národní museum, 1958. 207 p. Illus. For a history of the National Museum Library during a crucial period of its development, *see*:

Vrchotka, Jaroslav. Dějiny Knihovny Národního muzea v Praze, 1818-1892 (History of the National Museum Library in Prague, 1818-1892). Praha, Státní politické nakladatelství, 1967. 200 pp. Illus.

A survey of library resources in Brno is presented in *Průvodce po Brněnských knihovnách* (Guide to libraries in Brno), prepared by Miloš Papírník and others (Brno, Státní vědecká knihovna, 1968, 59 p.).

554. 1. (První) československá bibliografická konference 1966. Sborník materiálů (First Czechoslovak conference on bibliography, 1966. A collection of materials). Compiled by Vladimír Černý under the chief editorship of Josef Vinárek. Praha, Státní knihovna ČSSR, 1967. 560 p.

An extensive collection of reports by leading Czech and Slovak librarians dealing with a variety of contemporary developments and activities in Czechoslovak bibliography.

3. Printing and Publishing

555. Knižní kultura doby staré i nové. Příručka pro výstavy mezinárodního sjezdu knihovníků a přátel knihy (The book in old and modern times. A reference book for the exhibits of the International Congress of Librarians and Friends of the Book). Chief editor: Antonín Dolenský. Praha, 1926. 368 p. Illus.

A collection of essays written by leading experts on a variety of phases of producing, illustrating, and disseminating books in Czechoslovakia. Libraries and bibliographic activities are also covered. Résumés in French or German are given for some of the articles.

556. Málek, Rudolf, *and* Miroslav Petrtýl. Knihy a Pražané (Books and the people of Prague). Praha, Orbis, 1964. 389 p. Illus.

An original little lexicon abounding with data on the past and present of the Czech book as it relates to the capital, telling many interesting things about those who have been engaged in printing, selling, promoting, and servicing books. An introductory essay gives a synoptic view of 500 years of book-related activities in Prague. Directories of libraries, bibliographic centers, book distributors, antiquarians, archives, museums, etc. are also provided.

557. Zíbrt, Čeněk. Z dějin českého knihtiskařství (From the history of Czech bookprinting). 3d enl. ed. Edited by Antonín Dolenský. Mladá Boleslav, Hejda and Zbrej, 1939. 140 p. Illus.

A fundamental work by a leading expert in the field. For other authoritative treatments of this and other kindred subjects, the following works can be used with benefit:

Horák, František. Česká kniha v minulosti a její význam (The Czech book in the past and its significance). Praha, F. Novák, 1948. 253 p. Facsims. Bibliography: p. 230-232. (Naše poklady, sv. 4)

Horák, František. Five Hundred Years of Czech Printing. Prague, Odeon, 1968. 156, 94 p. Illus.

Tobolka, Zdeněk V. Dějiny československého knihtisku v době nejstarší (History of early Czechoslovak book printing). Praha, Československá společnost knihovědná, 1930. 106 p. Illus. (Rozpravy Československé společnosti knihovědné, I)

Volf, Josef. Geschichte des Buchdrucks in Böhmen und Mähren bis 1848. Weimar, Straubing und Müller, 1928. 262 p., Illus., facsims. Bibliography: p. 215-250.

F. MISCELLANEOUS REFERENCE AIDS

558. Československá akademie věd. *Základní knihovna.* Seznam encyklopedií, biografií a bibliografií (List of encyclopedias, biographies, and bibliographies). 2d ed. Compiled by Milada Jedličková. Praha, 1965. 303 p.

Though general in scope, this list covers Czechoslovak materials extensively.

559. Czechoslovak Republic. *Ústřední komise lidové kontroly a statistiky.* Statistický lexikon obcí ČSSR, 1965. Podle správního rozdělení 1. ledna 1965, sčítání lidu, domů a bytů 1. března 1961 (Statistical lexicon of localities of the Czechoslovak Socialist Republic in 1965. According to the administrative division as of January 1, 1965 and the census of people, houses, and dwellings as of March 1, 1961). Praha, Statistické a evidenční vydavatelství tiskopisů, 1966. 668 p.

Lists localities, both by their place in the administrative structure (*kraj* and *okres*) and in alphabetical order. Changes in names that occurred since July 1, 1960 are indicated. A spate of statistical data pertaining to individual localities and their inhabitants is given. A number of similar compilations were published in the 1920s and 1930s by the Státní úřad statistický (State Statistical Office) under titles such as *Statistický lexikon obcí v Republice československé and Administrativní lexikon obcí v Republice československé,* and also in German as *Statistisches Gemeindelexikon der Čechoslovakischen Republik.*

560. Czechoslovak Republic. *Ústřední komise lidové kontroly a statistiky.* Vývoj společnosti ČSSR v číslech (The development of the society of the Czechoslovak Socialist Republic in figures). Prepared by F. Herbst and others. Praha, SEVT, 1965. 513 p. Illus., maps.

See also entry no. 636.

See also the important survey study *Hospodářský a společenský vývoj Československa 1918-1968* (Czechoslovakia's economic and social development, 1918-1968) (Praha, SEVT, 1968, 231 p.).

561. Malá, Anna. Statistika rozvoje kultury v ČSSR, 1945-1965 (Statistics of the development of culture in the Czechoslovak Socialist Republic). Praha, Scénografický ústav, 1966. 168 p. Graphs, bibliographies.

562. Profous, Antonín. Místní jména v Čechách. Jejich vznik, původní význam a změny (Names of localities in Bohemia. Their origin, original meaning, and changes). Praha, Nakladatelství Československé akademie věd, 1947-1960. 5 v.

This remarkable historical dictionary of toponymics is of great value for historical, cultural, geographic, and etymological research. The fifth volume, compiled by a team headed by Jan Svoboda and Vladimír Šmilauer, is a supplement to the preceding ones.

563. Statistická ročenka Československé socialistické republiky (Statistical yearbook of the Czechoslovak Socialist Republic). 1934– Praha, Státní nakladatelství technické literatury. Annual.

See also entries no. 574 *and* 932.

An elaborate statistical record of Czechoslovakia's land and climate, population, economy, administration, and culture. The statistical tables cover the entire territory as well as administrative subdivisions (*kraj*). A condensed version has been issued annually since 1961 by the same sponsor and publisher under the title *Čísla pro každého* (Figures for everyone). The researcher can avail himself of an abundant body of materials on a vast range of statistical aspects of the Czechoslovak Republic up to 1939, and also for Slovakia and the Protektorat Böhmen und Mähren during the Second World War. Some of these publications were issued in German or French. Those in need of more detailed bibliographic guidance are referred to the annotated bibliography *Statistical Yearbooks* (Washington, U.S. Library of Congress, 1953, p. 82-83); *Foreign Statistical Documents* (Stanford, Calif., The Hoover Institution on War, Revolution and Peace, 1967, p. 34-37); and *Czechoslovakia; a Bibliographic Guide*, prepared by Rudolf Sturm (Washington, Library of Congress, 1968, p. 15-16).

564. U.S. *Library of Congress. Slavic and Central European Division.* Czech and Slovak Abbreviations, a Selective List. Edited by Paul L. Horecky. Washington, 1956. 164 p.

An aid for identifying abbreviations, listing their expansions and English translations. To be supplemented by Viktor Palivec's *Bibliografické zkratky. Slovníček používaných zkratek a značek pro kulturní pracovníky a čtenaře* (Bibliographic abbreviations. A small dictionary of abbreviations and symbols for cultural workers and readers) (Praha, Státní pedagogické nakl., 1958, 120 p.).

15

the land

by Karel J. Kansky

A. REFERENCE AIDS

1. Bibliographies

565. Rechcígl, Miloslav Jr. Czechoslovakia and Its Arts and Sciences; a Selective Bibliography in the Western European Languages. *In*: Rechcígl, Miloslav Jr., *ed.* The Czechoslovak Contribution to World Culture. The Hague, Mouton, 1964. p. 555-634.
See also entries no. 469 *and* 1166.

This important source of information lists 1,318 books and a few articles published in English, French, and German. Entries are arranged in nine sections, with works on Czechoslovak geography being covered in the sections on social and natural sciences. An index of names is attached.

566. U.S. *Bureau of the Census.* Bibliography of Social Science Periodicals and Monograph Series: Czechoslovakia, 1948-1963. Washington, D.C. U.S. Govt. Print. Off., 1964. (*Its* Foreign Social Science Bibliographies. Series P-92, no. 19)
See also entry no. 21.

Based on Library of Congress holdings of periodicals. The entries are grouped into 15 sections, with those on economics, human geography, cultural anthropology, and statistics listing periodicals and monographs on Czechoslovak geography. Four indexes are attached.

567. Zahraniční bohemika a slovenika v roce . . . (Foreign Bohemica and Slovaca in . . .). 1956– Praha, Národní knihovna, 1957– Annual.
See also entry no. 480.

A bibliography of works of Czech authors translated into foreign languages and of foreign works about Czechoslovakia received by Národní knihovna, the Czech national library in Prague. Most of the entries relating to geography are in the section "Geographico-geological sciences."

2. Atlases

568. Česká akademie věd a umění, *Prague.* Atlas Republiky československé (Atlas of the Czechoslovak Republic). Praha, Orbis, 1935. 90 p. Maps.

Although published in 1935, the work offers a great amount of valid basic information on the geography of Czechoslovakia. It is divided into 55 sections, each containing several maps or cartograms. The legends, written in Czech and in French, are clear, and the maps are complemented by short discussions of the main topics in both Czech and English.

569. Czechoslovak Republic. *Ústřední správa geodezie a kartografie.* Atlas Československé socialistické republiky (Atlas of the Czechoslovak Socialist Republic). Praha, 1967. 58 sheets with 433 maps, diagrs., tables.

See also entry no. 911.

Divided into seven topical sections: geographic situation, natural environment, population, industry, agriculture, transport, and living standards of the population. The maps and cartograms are of a high quality. Methods of compilation and cartographic techniques employed in constructing the maps are described in detail. A text complementing the geographic distributions presented is attached to each map sheet together with a brief English and Russian summary of the display. The atlas is designed as an aid to education and research and as a source of information for the general public.

570. Czechoslovak Republic. *Ústřední správa geodezie a kartografie.* Atlas československých dějin (Atlas of Czechoslovak history). Praha, 1965. 17, 39 p. 45 fold. col. maps.

The atlas is divided into 45 topical sections, each with 5 to 16 maps and cartograms. The maps offer a great amount of detailed historico-geographic information on settlement patterns (from the paleolithic period to 1960) and on socio-demographic and politico-economic developments of the country. Eight final sections deal with the historical geography of the period after 1945. All maps are accompanied by a legend which often can be read without a knowledge of the Czech language. General literary sources and references are noted in the introduction. Each section is accompanied by a list of specific references, and each map is described briefly. A detailed historico-geographic index of names is included. The introductory text, the map descriptions, and the organization of the atlas reflect a Marxist point of view.

571. Czechoslovak Republic. *Ústřední správa geodezie a kartografie.* Atlas podnebí Československé republiky (Climatic atlas of the Czechoslovak Republic). Praha, 1958. 1 v.

An impressive collection of maps compiled by the staff of the Hydrometeorological Institute in Prague and Bratislava. It contains a number of general maps, specialized climatic and phenological maps, and diagrams of soil temperatures, with all maps being on the scale of 1:1,000,000. The methods of compiling maps, descriptions, and an introduction are also in Russian, English, and French.

A supplement, *Podnebí Československé socialistické republiky. Tabulky* (Climate of the Czechoslovak Socialist Republic. Tables) was published in 1961. It consists of 66 tables, on the basis of which the maps in the atlas were constructed.

572. Czechoslovak Republic. *Ústřední ústav geologický.* Geologický atlas ČSSR (Geological atlas of the Czechoslovak Socialist Republic). Praha, 1966.

This is a set of seven maps (scale 1:1,000,000): geological, tectonical, quaternary deposits, mineral deposits, metalogenetical, hydrogeological, and aeromagnetical. The maps are accompanied by textual explanations in Czech.

573. Kuchař, Karel. Early Maps of Bohemia, Moravia and Silesia. Translated by Zd. Šafařík. Praha, Ústřední správa geodezie a kartografie, 1961. 74 p. Illus., maps. Bibliographical footnotes.

This collection, an important source of information on the historical geography of the western portion of Czechoslovakia, is accompanied by expert descriptions. The maps are excellent reproductions of the originals. A bibliography, an index of names, and French and German summaries are included.

3. Statistical Handbooks

574. Statistiská ročenka Československé socialistické republiky (Statistical yearbook of the Czechoslovak Socialist Republic). 1934– Praha, Annual.

See also entries no. 563 *and* 932.

This yearbook, publication of which was suspended from 1939 to 1956, is the official handbook giving the most detailed information made public on the Czechoslovak Republic. Each section is introduced by a brief commentary. Some sections, such as topography and climate, population, employment, etc., give valuable information on Czechoslovak geography.

An abridged version in English appeared as *Statistical Abstracts* (Prague, Orbis, 1963, 167 p.) and the volume for 1958 was translated in full, *Translation and Glossary of Czechoslovak Statistical Yearbook* (New York, U.S. Joint Publications Research Service, 1959, 667 p.).

4. Serials

575. Československá společnost zeměpisná. Sborník (Journal). 1894– Praha. Quarterly.

The official journal of the Czechoslovak Geographical Society, containing professional articles in Czech, mostly dealing with topics of physical geography. Subjects in economic geography, settlement and transportation geography, cartography, regional studies, and the teaching of geography are also included. Some recently published articles are summarized in English, German, Russian, or French. Each issue reviews Czech and foreign books with frequent notes on professional activities in Czechoslovakia and in other countries.

576. Geodetický a kartografický sborník (Geodetic and cartographic collections). Praha, Statní nakl. technické literatury, 1961–

The official organ of the Geodetic and Cartographic Section of the Czechoslovak Academy of Sciences. Tables of contents and summaries occasionally given in English and Russian.

577. Geografický časopis (Geographical journal). 1949– Bratislava. Quarterly.

The official publication of the Geografický Ústav of the Slovenská akadémia vied (Geographical Institute, Slovak Academy of Sciences). Most articles, some of which are in the Slovak language, discuss topics of physical geography, but others relate to economic geography, settlement and transportation geography, and cartography. Regular reviews of books and of professional activities.

578. Meteorologické zprávy—Bulletin météorologique. 1947– Praha. Bimonthly.

A leading periodical in the field, with a well-established reputation.

579. Prague. Ústřední ústav geologický. Věstník (Bulletin). 1925– Praha, Nakl. Československé akademie věd. Bimonthly.

The oldest geological journal, recently serving as the official journal of the Geological Section of the Czechoslovak Academy of Sciences.

580. Statistika; ekonomicko-statistický časopis (Statistics; economico-statistical journal). 1964– Praha, Ústřední komise lidové kontroly a statistiky. Monthly.

Articles dealing with agriculture, transport, and manufacturing offer material of a geographic nature. This journal supersedes *Statistika a kontrola* (Statistics and control) which appeared in 1962-1963, and incorporates as a quarterly supplement *Statistické zprávy* (Statistical reports) which was issued separately in 1956-1963 and which supplies much statistical information relating to geographic matters.

B. GENERAL STUDIES

581. Bušek, Vratislav, *and* Nicolas Spulber, *eds.* Czechoslovakia. New York, Praeger, 1957. 520 p. Maps, tables. Bibliography: p. 484-499. *See also* entries no. 509, 804, *and* 909.

The study consists of articles mostly written by specialists in their fields. Some, however, are superficial, having been prepared by nonspecialists. Seven papers are descriptive geographic essays, giving information on the general geography of Czechoslovakia.

582. Häufler, Vlastislav. Zeměpis Československa (Geography of Czechoslovakia). Praha, Nakl. Československé akademie věd, 1960. 667 p. Illus., maps, bibliography.

This is the most extensive study available of the geography of Czechoslovakia. It is designed as a text for university students. The first part, written by V. Král, deals with physical geography and is considered the best introductory essay by a Czech geographer. The second part is less successful because of the lack of data and because of several Marxist interpretations of a questionable nature. The third part is an economic geographical survey of the 19 districts of Czechoslovakia and is valuable for its concise presentation of the basic geographic facts. A revised edition is in preparation. A collective work prepared by Josef Dostál and other specialists in physical geography is *Přirodní poměry Československa; vybrané kapitoly z fysického zeměpisu* (Natural conditions in Czechoslovakia; selected chapters on physical geography) (Praha, Státní pedagogické nakladatelství, 1960. 170 p., illus.).

583. Wanklyn, Harriet G. Czechoslovakia. New York, Praeger, 1954. 445 p. Illus., maps, bibliography.

See also entry no. 506.

A descriptive study of the historical geography of Czechoslovakia. It is based on sources published mostly before 1945, and on short field work in 1947. Historically valuable information is given on Czechoslovak geography before the Second World War. A short list of references is attached to the individual chapters of the study.

584. Wrzosek, Antoni. Czechoslowacja; zarys ogólnej geografii kraju (Czechoslovakia; general outline of the country's geography). Warszawa, Państwowe Wydawn. Naukowe, 1960. 226 p. Illus., maps.

A well-written essay on the general geography of Czechoslovakia by a Polish geographer.

C. THE PHYSICAL LANDSCAPE

585. Bouček, Bedřich. Geologie regionalní (Regional geology). 3d ed. Praha, Státní pedagogické nakl., 1958. 123 p.

A detailed description and inventory of the geological regions of Czechoslovakia.

586. Czechoslovak Republic. *Ministerstvo zemědělství.* Forests of Czechoslovakia. Prague, State Agricultural Publishing House, 1960. 222 p. Illus., maps, diagrs.

This publication, which was designed for the participants in the Fifth World Forestry Congress, is a basic source of information on the distribution of forests, their management and research. It consists of 18 short chapters on topics such as natural conditions in the

Czechoslovak Republic, forest statistics, and the organization and administration of Czech forests.

587\. Czechoslovak Republic. *Ministerstvo zemědělství a lesního a vodního hospodářství.* Referáty k VIII kongresu MPS, Bukurešt 1964 (Papers for the Eighth Congress of the International Soil Science Society, Bucharest, 1964). Rostlinná výroba, v. 10, no. 5/6, May/June 1964.

This collection of short papers by Czechoslovak authors reflects recent emphases in soil research in Czechoslovakia, with most offering information on the geography of soils. Papers are in German or English with summaries in Czech and Russian, and each is accompanied by a list of references.

588\. Demek, Jaromír, *and others.* Geomorfologie českých zemí (Geomorphology of the Czech lands). Praha, Nakl. Československé akademie věd, 1965. 335 p. Illus.

A detailed survey of the geomorphology of the western part of Czechoslovakia.

589\. Hynie, Ota. Hydrogeologie ČSSR (Hydrogeology of the Czechoslovak Socialist Republic). Praha, Nakl. Československé akademie věd, 1961. 2 v. Bibliography.

The first volume, *Obecné vody* (Common waters) offers in its second part (p. 293-517) information of a geographic nature, with emphasis on the distribution and circulation of underground water. The second part of the second volume, *Minerální vody* (Mineral waters) is devoted to the distribution and explanation of the origin of the springs, stressing their structure and their hydro-geographic relations. Indexes of names are supplied for both volumes.

590\. Kettner, Radim. Všeobecná geologie (General geology). Praha, Nakl. Československé akademie věd, 1956-1960. 4 v. Illus., maps, bibliographies.

This general geological study deals with the composition of the earth's crust, origin of minerals, and the outer geological forces, e.g., the earth's crust and the activity of water, ice, wind, gravity, organisms, and people. The exposition focuses on the regional geology of Czechoslovakia and offers a great amount of geographically valuable information. A German edition is *Allgemeine Geologie*, translated by Anton Wagner (Berlin, Deutscher Verlag der Wissenschaften, 1958-1960, 4 v., illus.).

591\. Prague. Ústřední ústav geologický. Regional Geology of Czechoslovakia. Prepared by Josef Svoboda and others. Prague, Geological Survey of Czechoslovakia, Publishing House of the Czechoslovak Academy of Sciences, 1966–

This is the first part of a series of studies on the regional geology of Czechoslovakia. Only the Bohemian Massif is considered. A detailed bibliography is attached. The study is a translation by Helena Zárubová of *Regionální geologie ČSSR* and was edited by Vojen Lozek and Jan Petránek. The scientific editor of the series is Vladimír Zoubek.

592. Prague. Ústřední ústav geologický. Tektonický vývoj Československa; sborník prací a tektonická mapa 1:1,000,000 (The tectonic development of Czechoslovakia; a collection of articles and a 1:1,000,000 tectonic map). Prepared by T. Buday and others. Edited by Alois Matějka. Praha, Nakl. Československé akademie věd, 1961. 254 p. Illus., fold. col. map. Bibliography: p. 232-249.

This symposium appeared originally in 1960, under the title *Tectonic Development of Czechoslovakia*, as an outgrowth of a program sponsored by the International Geological Congress in Mexico.

D. THE CULTURAL LANDSCAPE

593. Blažek, Miroslav. Hospodářský zeměpis Československa (Economic geography of Czechoslovakia). Praha, Orbis, 1958. 406 p. Illus., maps, bibliography.

A detailed study of economic geography, emphasizing industry, agriculture and forestry, and transportation. Brief consideration is given to foreign trade relations and to economic-geographic regionalization. The introductory part surveys general aspects of physical geography and demography. An appendix discusses each of the 19 economic areas of the country.

A German translation is *Ökonomische Geographie der Tschechoslowakischen Republik* (Berlin, Verlag Die Wirtschaft, 1959, 254 p., illus., maps, bibliography: p. 248-254), and a Russian one, *Ekonomicheskaia geografiia Chekhoslovakii* (Moskva, Izdatel'-stvo inostrannoi literatury, 1960, 476 p.). A Slovak edition, *Ekonomická geografia ČSSR* (Bratislava, Osveta, 1964, 296 p., maps), contains some revisions. An earlier work by this author is *Hospodářska geografie Československa* (Praha, Státní pedagogické nakladatelství, 1954, 381 p.), which appeared in German as *Wirstschafts-Geographie der Tschechoslowakei* (Marburg/Lahn, 1959. 204 p. Wissenschaftliche Übersetzungen, Nr. 37).

594. Czechoslovak Republic. *Ústřední komise lidové kontroly a statistiky.* Středočeský kraj v číslech (The district of Central Bohemia in figures). Compiled by K. Dolejší and others. Praha, SEVT, 1964. 397 p. Illus., maps, diagrs.

This publication is a detailed census of geographico-economic, mainly demographic, characteristics of the district, with 52 tables on population, employment patterns, households, localities, etc.

595. Häufler, Vlastislav. Changes in the Geographical Distribution of Population in Czechoslovakia. Prague, Academia, 1966. 130 p. Maps, diagrs. Bibliography: p. 123-127. (Československá akademie věd. Rozpravy. Řada MPV. Ročník 76, sešit 8)

An informative description and analysis of the changing population distribution.

596. Horbaly, William. Agricultural Conditions in Czechoslovakia; 1950. Chicago, 1951. 104 p. Illus., maps, bibliography. (University of Chicago. Department of Geography Research Paper No. 18)

An analysis of Czechoslovak agriculture in 1948-1949 based on extensive field work. The author subdivides the country into five agricultural regions and analyzes the agricultural conditions within each region. The study offers important information on animal husbandry and cultivation practices in a collectivized system of agriculture. The author emphasizes the similarity of the Czechoslovak agriculture with that of the Soviet Union.

597. Lazarčík, Gregor. The Performance of Socialist Agriculture; a Case Study of Production and Productivity in Czechoslovakia 1934-1938 and 1946-1961. New York, L. W. International Financial Research, 1963. 121 p. Tables, bibliography.

See also entry no. 938.

In this report the author discusses and quantifies the patterns of agricultural production and agricultural productivity of Czechoslovakia, comparing the performance of a "socialist" agricultural system with the prewar "private" agricultural system of Czechoslovakia and Western European countries. The statistical comparison is very general since only aggregated data are employed.

598. Macka, Miroslav, *ed.* Některé problémy ekonomické geografie ČSSR (Some problems of the economic geography of the Czechoslovak Socialist Republic). Brno, Geografický ústav ČSAV, 1967. 112 p. Maps, bibliographical footnotes. (Zprávy o vědecké činnosti, 6)

A set of eight brief studies discussing urban migration, classification of settlements and home-to-work commuting patterns in selected areas of Czechoslovakia. Abstracts in French or English are attached.

599. Maergoiz, Isaak. Chekhoslovatskaia sotsialisticheskaia respublika; ekonomicheskaia geografiia (The Czechoslovak Socialist Republic; economic geography). Moskva, Mysl', 1964. 731 p. Illus., maps. Bibliography: p. 708-716.

A detailed study of Czechoslovak economic geography. The subject is approached from a Marxist point of view and a strong emphasis is given to economic conditions after 1945. It is based entirely on sources published in Czechoslovakia and in the USSR. An index of names is included.

600. National Productivity Council, India. Oil Industry in the USSR, Czechoslovakia, and Rumania. New Delhi, 1961. (NPC Report No. 18)

———. Textile Industry in the USSR and Czechoslovakia. New Delhi, 1962. 104 p. Illus. (NPC Report No. 19)

———. Iron and Steel Industry in the USSR and Czechoslovakia. New Delhi, 1963. 283 p. Illus., maps. (NPC Report No. 20)

These reports were prepared by the "Indian Productivity Teams" who visited the respective countries during 1960-1962. Most of the information given on Czechoslovakia was collected directly from the manufacturing organization visited. The introductory chapters give important geographic facts; the remaining chapters of the reports are of a technical character and describe the plants visited.

601. Votrubec, Ctibor. K problému hospodářsko-geografických středisek; střediska středních a severních Čech (On the problem of economico-geographic centers; centers in Central and Northern Bohemia). Praha, Nakl. Československé akademie věd, 1963. 91 p. Maps, diagrs. Bibliography: p. 80-83. (Československé akademie věd. Rozpravy. Řada SV. Ročník 73, sešit 3)

A critical evaluation of some aspects of Christaller's Central Place Theory and the theories of the location of economic activities, leading to the formulation of a classificatory scheme of settlement centers and the designing of a hierarchy of centers in Central and Northern Bohemia.

602. Zauberman, Alfred. Industrial Progress in Poland, Czechoslovakia, and East Germany 1937-1962. London, New York, Oxford University Press, 1964. 338 p. Bibliography.

See also entries no. 270, 943, 1520, *and* 2829.

The author describes the general developmental changes both verbally and in terms of quantified indices, and attempts to compare the industrial growth of the individual countries in relation to the past and to other European countries. Although the book is a general study, based only on summarized data, it contains some geographically important information on Czechoslovakia's manufacturing.

16

the people

A. ANTHROPOLOGY AND ETHNOLOGY

by Zdeněk Salzmann

1. Bibliographies, Encyclopedia Articles, and Journals

603. Bratislava. Univerzita. *Prírodovědecká fakulta.* Acta. t. 1– 1956– Bratislava, Slovenské pedagogické nakl. Illus., ports., maps. Monthly (except July and August).

Issues in the subseries "Anthropologia," the first of which was published in 1959, are primarily devoted to the physical anthropology of Czechoslovakia; contributions are in all of the principal Western languages.

604. Anthropologie. v. 1– 1923– 1938(?); 1962– Prague. Illus., maps. Quarterly.

Devoted primarily to physical anthropology, and includes articles in all of the principal Western languages.

605. Archeologické rozhledy. Nouvelles archéologiques. v. 1– 1949– Praha. Illus., ports., maps. Bimonthly.

Offers information concerning the latest archaeological research in Czechoslovakia. Articles provided with a summary in one of the principal Western languages.

606. Český lid (The Czech people). v. 1– 1892– Praha. Illus., ports., music. Bimonthly.

Publication suspended 1915-1922, 1933-1945. Since 1946, the official journal of the Institute of Ethnography and Folklore Studies of the Czechoslovak Academy of Sciences; it deals with the folklore, ethnography, and ethnohistory of Bohemia and Moravia. A cumulative index to volumes 1-32, arranged by author and subject, was compiled by Ludvík Kunz and published in 1960: *Soupis prací Zíbrtova Českého lidu* (Index of articles in Zíbrt's *Český lid*) (Praha, Vydala Společnost čsl. národopisců při ČSAV, 229 p.). A subsequent cumulation is to be issued in 1971. Last issue of each year contains an annual index and also a classified and annotated bibliography for the preceding year of works concerning Czech ethnography and folklore, and of works by Czech scholars on the ethnography and folklore of other peoples and related fields. See also *Československá et(h)nografie* (v. 1-10; 1953-1962, Praha, Československá akademie věd), dealing primarily with the ethnography of the Czechs and Slovaks, which merged with *Český lid* as of 1963.

607. Dokládal, Milan, *comp.* Československá antropologická bibliografie 1945-1954 (Czechoslovak anthropological bibliography, 1945-1954). Brno, Antropologická společnost, 1955. 39 p.

A continuation by the same author, to cover the years 1955-1965, is forthcoming.

608. Jeřábková, Alena, *comp.* Soupis bibliografií české a slovenské etnografie a folkloristiky vydaných v letech 1945-1963 (A list of bibliographies of publications on Czech and Slovak ethnography and folklore published during the years 1945-1963). Brno, Universita J. E. Purkyně, 1965. 69 p. (Materiály k retrospektivní bibliografii české etnografie a folkloristiky, 1)

A bibliography of bibliographies containing 266 briefly annotated entries.

609. Repčák, Jozef, *and* Michal Potemra, *comps.* Bibliografia východného Slovenska 1945-1964, história a národopis (Bibliography of Eastern Slovakia for the years 1945-1964, history and ethnography). Košice, 1964. 355 p.

Part 1 (p. 1-84) is a bibliography of the archaeology of eastern Slovakia. Part 2 (p. 85-355) is a bibliography of the history and ethnography of eastern Slovakia.

610. Slovenský národopis (Slovak ethnography). v. 1– 1953– Bratislava. Illus., ports., maps, music. Annual, 1953; quarterly, 1954-55; bimonthly, 1956-58; quarterly since 1959.

See also entry no. 1145.

The official journal of the Slovak Academy of Sciences dealing primarily with the folklore, ethnography, and ethnohistory of the Slovaks and of Slovakia. An annual index appears in the last issue of each year. A cumulative index to v. 1-10, *Vecný a menný register Slovenského národopisu*, 1-10 (1953-1962), arranged by author and subject, was published in 1963. Occasionally featured are annual bibliographies of Slovak ethnography and folklore. *See also* Rudolf Žatko's article, "Výberová bibliografia ľudovej kultúry karpatskej na Slovensku" (A selective bibliography of Carpathian folk culture in Slovakia), published in *Bibliografická příloha Zpráv Společnosti československých národopisců a Slovenskej národopisnej spoločnosti,* no. 5, 1962, p. 1-60.

611. Stano, Pavol. Bibliografia slovenského l'udového výtvarného umenia so zretel'om na hmotnú kultúru od vzniku záujmu o l'udové výtvarné umenie do konca roku 1957 (Bibliography of Slovak folk art). Martin, Matica slovenská, 1959. 326 p. 33 illus.

Particularly concerned with material folk art and extends its coverage until 1957. English summary (p. 325-326).

2. Works Concerning the Czechs, Slovaks, and Minorities

612. Bednárik, Rudolf. Slowakische Volkskultur. Bratislava-Pressburg, Verlag "Die Slavische Rundschau," 1943. 243 p. Illus., plates.

An account of Slovak family customs and material culture.

613. Bohmann, Alfred. Das Sudetendeutschtum in Zahlen. Handbuch über den Bestand und die Entwicklung der sudetendeutschen Volksgruppe in den Jahren von 1910 bis 1950. München, Sudetendeutscher Rat, 1959. 283 p. Bibliography: p. 273-275.

See also entry no. 643.

614. Československá vlastivěda (Book of knowledge on Czechoslovakia). Praha, Sfinx, 1929-1936. 10 v. in 12. Illus., ports., maps, facsims. Includes bibliographies.

See also entries no. 495, 770, *and* 840.

A basic encyclopedia for information about Czechoslovakia before the Second World War. Somewhat difficult to use because of a topical rather than an alphabetical or chronological arrangement. Two volumes in particular deal with the peoples of Czechoslovakia from an anthropological point of view:

Člověk (Man) (Praha, 1933, 623 p.), edited by Jiří Horák, Jindřich Matiegka, and Karel Weigner. The three editors and several other specialists cover the following topics: Czechoslovak prehistory, p. 7-114; physical anthropology of the Czechoslovak population, p. 115-254; the people of Carpathian Ruthenia, p. 255-259; Czechoslovaks abroad, particularly in North America, p. 260-269; Germans in Czechoslovakia, p. 270-276; Magyars in Czechoslovakia, p. 277-278; Jews in Czechoslovakia, p. 279-286; Gypsies in Czechoslovakia, p. 287-293; the nature and significance of Czechoslovak culture, p. 294-304; a survey of Czechoslovak ethnography, p. 305-472; and health, hygiene, and medical services in Czechoslovakia, p. 473-606.

Národopis (Ethnography) (Praha, 1936, 391 p.), edited by Jiří Horák, Karel Chotek, and Jindřich Matiegka. The three editors and several other specialists cover the following topics: Czechoslovak population, p. 1-96; demography of Czechs and Slovaks living abroad, p. 97-139; material folk culture of the Czechoslovak people (settlement and housing, subsistence, occupations, folk art, social organization, folk costumes, family customs, annual and occasional customs, agricultural customs, and folk medicine), p. 143-340; ethnography of Germans in Czechoslovakia, p. 341-378.

615. Československá vlastivěda (Book of knowledge on Czechoslovakia). Praha, Orbis, 1963– Illus., plates, ports., facsims., maps. Includes bibliographies.
See also entry no. 499.

A basic encyclopedia for information on contemporary Czechoslovakia. Of relevance:

Volume 3, Lidová kultura (Folk culture) (Praha, 1968, 783 p., Andrej Melicherčík, chief ed.). Specialists from the Institute for Ethnography and Folklore of the Czechoslovak Academy of Sciences and from the Ethnographic Institute of the Slovak Academy of Sciences deal with the following topics: the study of folk culture, Czech folk culture (occupations and production, material culture, social and family life, customs, and folklore), Slovak folk culture (same outline as above), and folk art.

See also the forthcoming article "Czech Ethnography since World War II" by Zdenęk Salzmann (*East European Quarterly*, 1969).

616. Horváthová, Emília. Cigáni na Slovensku; historicko-etnografický náčrt (Gypsies in Slovakia; an ethnohistorical sketch). Bratislava, Vydavatel'stvo Slovenskej akadémie vied, 1964. 399 p. Illus., plates. (Práce Národopisného ústavu Slovenskej akadémie vied, 14)

An excellent study of the Gypsy minority group: history (p. 9-173), ethnography (p. 175-354), and the Gypsy problem at present (p. 355-372). English summary (p. 380-386).

617. Jelínek, Jan. Die Rassengeschichte der Tschechoslovakei.

A comprehensive overview of paleoanthropology and prehistoric anthropology of Czechoslovakia. Scheduled to appear in 1969.

618. Neustupný, Evžen, *and* Jiří Neustupný. Czechoslovakia before the Slavs. New York, Frederick A. Praeger, 1961. 255 p. Illus., plates, maps, charts. (Ancient Peoples and Places, v. 22)

Prehistory of the territory of today's Czechoslovakia up to the beginning of the settlement of the area by the Slavs in the sixth century A.D.

619. Niederle, Lubor, *ed.* Moravské Slovensko (Moravian Slovakia). Praha, Nakl. Národopisné společnosti československé. Illus., maps. Includes bibliographies. (Národopis lidu československého, díl 1)

Volume 1, fascicle 1, 2d ed. (Praha, 1923, 400 p.) contains the contributions of several ethnographers dealing with the geographical setting, settlement, dwelling types, costumes, and occupations of the people of Moravian Slovakia. Volume 1, fascicle 2 (Praha, 1922, p. 401-887) deals with the physical type, dialect, folk art and music, and customs of the people of Moravian Slovakia.

620. Slovenská vlastiveda (Book of knowledge on Slovakia). Bratislava,

Slovenská akadémia vied a umení, 1943-1948. 5 v. Illus., ports., maps. Includes bibliographies.

See also entry no. 497.

A basic encyclopedia of information about Slovakia and the Slovaks up to the mid-'40s, arranged topically rather than alphabetically or chronologically. Two volumes in particular deal with the Slovak people from an anthropological point of view: Volume 2, Národopis (Ethnography) (Bratislava, 1943, 464 p.). Rudolf Bednárik, L'udovít Franěk, Anton Jurovský, and Andrej Melicherčík deal with the following topics: spiritual culture, p. 5-121; material culture, p. 123-256; folklore, p. 257-331; national character, p. 333-398; and physical anthropology, p. 399-462. Volume 3, Základy sociografie Slovenska (Foundations of sociography of Slovakia) (Bratislava, 1944, 446 p.), by Anton Štefánek. The following topics are dealt with: theoretical foundations of sociology, principles and nature of sociological description and analysis, demography, material and nonmaterial culture, Czechs and other ethnic minorities in Slovakia, and sociology of the working class.

621. Vávra, Zdeněk. Tendence v dlouhodobém vývoji reprodukce obyvatelstva Českých zemí, léta 1870-1944 (Long-term trends of reproduction rates of population in Bohemia and Moravia during the years 1870-1944). Praha, Československá akademie věd, 1962. 150 p. Tables. (Rozpravy Československé akademie věd, Řada společenských věd, roč. 72, seš. 9)

Surveys changes in birthrates, trends in deathrates, and overall trends in the population development of Bohemia and Moravia during 1870-1944. English summary (p. 143-145).

622. Wynne, Waller. The Population of Czechoslovakia. Washington, D.C., U.S. Govt. Print. Off., 1953. 72 p. Illus, maps. (U.S. Dept. of Commerce. Bureau of the Census. International Population Statistics Reports, Series P-90, no. 3)

Surveys the population development of Czechoslovakia between 1921 and 1950 with special reference to the distribution of the population and its demographic and social characteristics. Information is given concerning the economically active population and the prospects for population growth.

B. DEMOGRAPHY

by Andrew Elias

1. Population Theory

623. Demografie (Demography). 1959– Praha. Quarterly.

A theoretical journal treating the research of population growth. Scholarly articles on population and labor force relate primarily to the present period.

624. Egermayer, František, *ed.* Statistika a demografie (Statistics and demography). Praha, Československá akademie věd, 1959. 441 p.

A collection of scholarly studies dealing with various aspects of Czechoslovak and other statistics. Includes three contributions on mortality trends in Slovakia and in the Czech Lands and on the population growth in Bohemia and Moravia in the 19th century. Later volumes under the same title also contain excellent studies in the field of demography.

625. Korčak, Jaromír. Úvod do všeobecné geografie obyvatelstva (Introduction to the general geography of the population). 2d ed. Praha, Státní pedagogické nakladatelství, 1964. 152 p.

A basic, though brief, college textbook on the geography of the population. Deals with demographic statistics and concepts from a primarily geographic point of view.

626. Roubíček, Vladimír. Demografická statistika (Demographic statistics). Praha, Státní pedagogické nakladatelství, 1958. 293 p. Illus., bibliography.

A college textbook dealing with the basic problems and methods of demographic statistics. Rich in definitions of demographic and related terms.

627. Srb, Vladimír, *ed.* Demografický sborník 1961 (Demographic symposium, 1961). Praha, Ústřední úřad státní kontroly a statistiky, 1962. 219 p.

The second publication under this title (the first one was published in 1959), it contains a collection of valuable contributions by the foremost Czechoslovak demographers pertaining to various aspects of the settlement and growth of the Czechoslovak population.

628. Srb, Vladimír. Úvod do demografie (Introduction to demography). Praha, Nakladatelství politické literatury, 1965. 228 p. Illus. Bibliography: p. 215-220.

A rather short, but very readable, Marxist presentation of demography as a scientific discipline, by one of the most prolific Czechoslovak demographers. The theoretical discussion is amply illustrated with examples based on actual statistics.

2. Size, Composition, and Distribution of the Population

629. Böker, H., *and* F. W. Bülow. The Rural Exodus in Czechoslovakia. Geneva, P. S. King & Son, 1935. 170 p. (Studies and Reports of the I.L.O., Series K, no. 13)

An analytical survey of the causes and magnitude of the internal migration in Czechoslovakia, primarily during the first 14 years of its independence. Some data relate to external migration and go as far back as the 1860s.

630. Placht, Otto. Lidnatost a společenská skladba českého státu v 16.-18.

století (Population density and social structure of the Czech state in the 16th-18th centuries). Praha, Nakl. Československé akademie věd, 1957. 366 p. Illus., maps. Bibliography: p. 330-343. (Československá akademie věd. Sekce filosofie a historie. Studie a prameny, cv. 14)

See also entry no. 965.

An analytical survey of the magnitude and social structure of the population of the Czech Lands, prior to the first population census in Austria in 1754. The volume is richly footnoted and draws heavily from old documents in the state and city archives, many of which have been used for the first time in such a study.

631. Srb, Vladimír. Demografická příručka 1966 (Demographic handbook 1966). Prague, Nakladatelství Svoboda, 1967. 286 p.

This is the third edition under this title, which is much more comprehensive than the first and second ones, published in 1958 and 1959, respectively. It covers population growth and structure, housing and households, migration, employment, and standard of living. It has also a section on international comparisons and a brief summary of the results of all major demographic surveys taken in Czechoslovakia since the Second World War.

632. Srb, Vladimír, *and* Milan Kučera. Výzkum o rodičovství 1956 (Research on parenthood, 1956). Praha, Státní úřad statistický, 1959. 152 p. Bibliography.

Published results of the first sample taken in this field for all of Czechoslovakia, based on 11,073 questionnaires. Compares planned with actual family sizes and shows the importance of factors by which they are influenced, such as age, income, nature, and size of living quarters, participation in economic activity, and knowledge of contraceptive methods.

633. Světoň, Ján. Obyvatel'stvo Slovenska za kapitalizmu (The population of Slovakia under capitalism). Bratislava, Slovenské vydavatel'stvo politickej literatúry, 1958. 368 p. Illus., bibliography.

Though Marxist in its tenor, it is a good historical presentation of the demographic and socioeconomic changes that took place in Slovakia from the middle of the last century to the middle of this century. It also covers the changes in the class and family structure and external migration.

3. Sources of Population Data

634. Czechoslovak Republic. *Státní úřad statistický.* Města nad 100,000 obyvatelů v Československu (Cities with a population of more than 100,000 in Czechoslovakia). Praha, 1957. 130 p.

A detailed summary of the demographic, social, economic, and educational structure of the five largest cities in Czechoslovakia. Contains a valuable section on definitions of statistical terms.

635. Czechoslovak Republic. *Ústřední komise lidové kontroly a statistiky.*

Severočeský kraj v číslech (The North Bohemian region in figures). Compiled by J. Zahalka and others. Praha, SEVT, 1963. 320 p. Bibliography: p. 312.

The first of the volumes published for each region and for the capital city of Prague, based primarily on the 1961 census. All volumes have sections with detailed population breakdown and population projections up to 1980.

636. Czechoslovak Republic. *Ústřední komise lidové kontroly a statistiky.* Vývoj společnosti ČSSR v číslech (The development of the society of the Czechoslovak Socialist Republic in figures). Prepared by F. Herbst and others. Praha, SEVT, 1965. 513 p. Illus., maps.
See also entry no. 560.

An extensive analytical summary of the results of the 1961 population census in Czechoslovakia.

637. Czechoslovak Republic. *Ústřední správa geodézie a kartografie.* Atlas obyvatelstva ČSSR (Population atlas of the Czechoslovak Socialist Republic). Edited by Milan Kučera and Vladimír Srb. Praha, 1962. 91 p. Maps.

In spite of its small size, this book represents one of the best sources of Czechoslovak population statistics. The data are arranged by age, sex, and territorial subdivisions, and they range from 1840 to (projections for) 1975.

638. Kárniková, Ludmila. Vývoj obyvatelstva v českých zemích 1754-1914 (The development of the population in Czech lands from 1754 to 1914). Praha, Nakladatelství Československé akademie věd, 1965. 404 p. Illus., maps. Bibliography: p. 368-373.
See also entry no. 752.

A comparative study of the population growth in Bohemia, Moravia, and Silesia by economic regions, from the first Austrian census to the outbreak of the First World War. A brief outline of the statistical coverage of each census taken during the period is presented in an appendix. Actual data for this period can be found in *Tafeln zur Statistik der österreichischen Monarchie*, published from 1825 to 1865; *Statistisches Jahrbuch der österreichischen Monarchie*, published from 1861 to 1881; and *Österreichische Statistik*, published from 1881 to 1913. In the Hungarian part of the former Dual Monarchy, the official statistics are available in *Magyar statisztikai évkönyv* (Hungarian statistical yearbook), published from 1870 to 1918; and in *Magyar statisztikai közlemények* (Hungarian statistical bulletin), published from 1893 to 1918.

639. Svetoň, Ján, *and* Zdeněk Vávra. Reprodukcia obyvatel'stva v Československu po druhej svetovej vojne (Reproduction of the population of Czechoslovakia after the Second World War). Bratislava, Vydavatel'stvo Slovenskej akadémie vied, 1965. 288 p. Illus.

A detailed analysis of natality, nuptiality, fertility, and mortality, broken down by the Czech and Slovak regions, from 1947 to 1959, with frequent comparisons with earlier periods. Demographic data pertaining to the period since the First World War can be found in *Československá statistika* (Czechoslovak statistics), series 4 and 14, published since 1922; *Zprávy Státního úřadu statistického RČS* (News of the state statistical office of the Czechoslovak Republic), series D, published from 1921 to 1950; *Statistická ročenka Republiky československé* (Statistical yearbook of the Czechoslovak Republic), published from 1934 to 1938 and since 1957. Starting with 1960, the title of the last source has been changed to *Statistická ročenka Československé socialistické republiky* (Statistical yearbook of the Czechoslovak Socialist Republic).

C. GERMANS IN CZECHOSLOVAKIA

by Heinrich Jilek

1. Bibliographies, Biographies, and Periodicals

640. Gierach, Erich, *ed.* Sudetendeutsche Lebensbilder. Reichenberg, Verlag Gebrüder Stiepel, 1926-1934. 3 v. Fronts., illus., plates, ports., bibliographies.

See also entry no. 535.

Contains about 250 biographies of persons who either lived in the German-speaking areas of present-day Czechoslovakia or who exercised a decisive influence on these regions. Those living at the time of the compilation are excluded. The biographies contain a review of the individuals' works and include bibliographical references.

641. Jilek, Heinrich, Herbert Rister, *and* Helmuth Weiss. Bücherkunde Ostdeutschlands und des Deutschtums in Ostmitteleuropa. Köln, Böhlau Verlag, 1963. 560 p. (Ostmitteleuropa in Vergangenheit und Gegenwart, 8)

See also entry no. 75.

Pages 218 to 314 comprise two sections, titled "Die Deutschen in den Sudetenländern" and "Die Deutschen in der Slowakei." These sections contain a list of 1,627 references to the most important monographs, periodicals, and articles on the background and situation of the German element in Czechoslovakia. Although only items of current interest were selected, titles of other pertinent bibliographies were cited.

Postwar publications on the Sudeten Germans are listed in Josef Hemmerle's *Sudetendeutsche Bibliographie 1949-53* (Marburg, Herder-Institut, 1959, 323 p.). A continuation of this work for the years 1954-1957 was prepared by Heinrich Jilek and published by the Institute in 1965 (532 p.).

642. Mitteilungen des Vereins für Geschichte der Deutschen in Böhmen. v. 1-82; 1862-1944. Prag. Quarterly.

Title changed to *Mitteilungen des Vereins für Geschichte der*

Deutschen in den Sudetenländern with volume 77. An index to volumes 1-60 was prepared by A. Schmidt (Prag, 1927) Contains many important contributions on all aspects of the history of the Germans in Bohemia, later volumes also covering those in Moravia and Austrian Silesia. It was in part and on a larger scale superseded by *Zeitschrift für sudetendeutsche Geschichte* (v. 1-6, 1937-1943, Brünn). See also the quarterly *Karpathenland* (v. 1-12, 1928-1942, Reichenberg), which was devoted to the history and culture of the Germans in Slovakia.

Currently, *Bohemia, Jahrbuch des Collegium Carolinum* (1962–, München) is dealing with all phases of the history of Bohemia, Moravia, and related areas, although placing special emphasis on Sudeten German problems. English summaries of its articles are provided. The *Stifter-Jahrbuch* (1949–, Gräfelfing bei München) is interested primarily in the intellectual and cultural history of the Sudeten Germans.

2. Land and People

643. Bohmann, Alfred. Das Sudetendeutschtum in Zahlen. Handbuch über den Bestand und die Entwicklung der sudetendeutschen Volksgruppe in den Jahren von 1910 bis 1950. München, Sudetendeutscher Rat, 1959. 283 p. Bibliography: p. 273-275.

See also entry no. 613.

Provides on the basis of official censuses and other surveys a detailed statistical account of the cultural, social, and economic conditions and development of the Sudeten German minority between 1918-1919 and 1938. Demographic data on the German element in Bohemia up to 1947 and its relative strength vis-à-vis the Czech population can be found in another work by the same author, titled *Bevölkerungsbewegungen in Böhmen 1847-1947 mit besonderer Berücksichtigung der Entwicklung der nationalen Verhältnisse* (München, Collegium Carolinum, 1958, 320 p.). The German minority problem and the various attempts to arrive at a different territorial settlement after 1918 are discussed on pages 214 to 257.

644. Kurth, Karl O., *ed.* Sudetenland. Ein Hand- und Nachschlagebuch über alle Siedlungsgebiete der Sudetendeutschen in Böhmen und Mähren-Schlesien. Kitzingen, Holzner-Verlag, 1954. 207 p. (Der Göttinger Arbeitskreis. Veröffentlichung, 98)

A brief survey of the Sudeten German area and population, including its history, culture, and economy. For a similar work on the German element in Slovakia and Carpathian Ruthenia, *see* the symposium edited by Eduard Winter, titled *Die Deutschen in der Slowakei und in Karpathorussland* (Münster, Aschendorff, 1926, 98 p.).

645. Meynen, Emil, *and others, eds.* Sudetendeutscher Atlas. München, Arbeitsgemeinschaft zur Wahrung sudetendeutscher Interessen, 1954. 56 p. Maps.

This atlas tries to indicate visually the economic and cultural foundations of the Sudeten German element, especially its minority problems, demography, trade and industry, schools, and other educational institutions. French and English translations of the explanations of the maps are supplied.

646. Rauchberg, Heinrich. Der nationale Besitzstand in Böhmen. Leipzig, Duncker und Humblot, 1905. 3 v.

This work, which is based on the 1900 Austrian census, provides extensive data on the important aspects of the interrelationship of Czech and German elements in Bohemia in regard to their ethnic and property distribution patterns. Shifts in the latter relationship during the last two decades of the 19th century are quantitatively noted by comparing the results of the 1880 and 1890 censuses. The most important part of this work is the volume with tables, which are explained in a text volume and graphically presented in the third volume.

647. Schwarz, Ernst. Sudetendeutsche Sprachräume. 2d rev. ed. München, Verlag R. Lerche, 1962. 386 p. Map. (Handbuch der sudetendeutschen Kulturgeschichte, 2)

First published in 1953, this work identifies and describes the various German dialect regions in Bohemia, Moravia, Austrian Silesia, and Slovakia. It reflects well-founded philological expertise. For an important source on Sudeten German dialects *see also* his *Sudetendeutscher Wortatlas* (München, Verlag R. Lerche, 1954-1958, 3 v.), containing 104 maps which show word usage and provide philological analysis.

648. Šimák, Josef V. Středověká kolonisace v zemích českých. Pronikání Němců do Čech v 13. a 14. století (The medieval colonization of the Bohemian lands. The penetration of Bohemia by the Germans in the 13th and 14th centuries). Praha, Laichter, 1938. [500]-1310 p. (České dějiny, no. 1, 5)

This fundamental work on the immigration and settlement of German colonists during the Middle Ages is based primarily on extant medieval sources. An introduction to the causes, execution, and legal aspects of the colonization is followed by an account of the historical development of the settlement patterns of individual Bohemian regions, cities, and villages.

3. History and Politics

649. Brügel, Johann W. Tschechen und Deutsche 1918-1938. München, Nymphenburger Verlagshandlung, 1967. 662 p. Bibliography: p. 637-654.

See also entry no. 789.

This work, dedicated to German-Czech relations in interwar Czechoslovakia, was prepared by the former secretary of Dr. Czech, the German Social Democratic Minister in the Czechoslovak cabinet. It supports the thesis that cooperation between these two groups would have been feasible and opposes strongly the policies of the German nationalistic parties, particularly the Henlein Party. It is the first study to utilize fully the German diplomatic documents pertaining to Czechoslovakia.

650. César, Jaroslav, *and* Bohumil Černý. Politika německých buržoazních stran v Československu v letech 1918-1938 (The policies of the German bourgeois parties in Czechoslovakia between 1918 and 1938). Praha, Nakl. Československé akademie věd, 1962. 2 v.

See also entry no. 769.

This detailed account is prepared from a Marxist point of view and on the basis of contemporary sources, particularly the daily press. Volume 1 covers the period to 1929; volume 2, the period up to the Munich Agreement. Each volume has a summary in German. *See also* the briefer account by the same author which was published in English with the title "The Nazi Fifth Column in Czechoslovakia," in *Historica* (Praha), v. 4, 1962: 191-255.

651. Jaksch, Wenzel. Europas Weg nach Potsdam. 2d ed. Stuttgart, Deutsche Verlags-Anstalt, 1967. 520 p.

This work, which first appeared in 1957, deals primarily with European political development up to the Potsdam Conference as it affected Central Europe and Czechoslovakia. Special attention is paid to the political situation in German-speaking areas, particularly for the period from 1918 on, as well as to the negotiations of the Sudeten German parties with the Czechoslovak government. Jaksch, who was chairman of the German Social Democratic Labor Party of Czechoslovakia, reports on the events in the 1930s on the basis of his own recollections.

652. Král, Václav, *ed.* Die Deutschen in der Tschechoslowakei 1933-1947. Dokumentensammlung. Praha, Nakl. Československé akademie věd, 1964. 663 p.

This collection of 494 documents from Czechoslovak archives, most of which were previously unpublished, deals with the origin and development of the Henlein Party and its negotiations with other parties, the government, and foreign agencies. Documents concerning the genesis of the Munich Agreement, the occupation of the remainder of Czechoslovakia in 1939, and the resettlement of the Sudeten Germans are also included. The introduction reflects the communist point of view of the editor.

653. Krofta, Kamil. Das Deutschtum in der tschechoslowakischen Geschichte. Prag, Orbis, 1934. 142 p.

See also entry no. 729.

These two lectures by a Czech historian, who served as minister for foreign affairs, provide a readable survey of the history of the German element from the beginning to the 19th century, especially in regard to its cultural achievements and relationship with the Czech population. The presentation is objective and based on a thorough knowledge of the facts. For an exposition of the official view of the Czechoslovak government *see* Josef Chmelar's pamphlet *The German Problem in Czechoslovakia* (Prague, Orbis, 1936, 92 p.).

654. Laffan, Robert G. D. The Crisis over Czechoslovakia, January to September 1938. Revised by V. M. Toynbee and P. E. Baker. London, Oxford University Press, 1951. 475 p. Maps. (Survey of International Affairs, v. 2, 1938)

This work surveys the diplomacy of the European powers during the Munich crisis. It also discusses in detail the decisions of the Czechoslovak government on the Sudeten German problem, its negotiations with the Sudeten German parties (particularly the Henlein Party), the situation in the German-speaking areas, and Lord Runciman's mission.

655. Luža, Radomír. The Transfer of the Sudeten Germans; a Study of Czech-German Relations 1933-1962. New York, New York University Press, 1964. 365 p. Illus., maps. Bibliography: p. 329-356.
See also entry no. 900.

The body of this work deals with German-Czech relations in the 1930s, the Munich Agreement and its consequences, the German occupation, and the expulsion of the Sudeten Germans. The introductory chapters describe the development of the three preceding decades. The author's views correspond roughly to the official position of the Czechoslovak government and that of its president, Edvard Beneš. The value of this work is enhanced by its numerous references to sources.

656. Pirchan, Gustav, Wilhelm Weizsäcker, *and* Heinz Zatschek, *eds.* Das Sudetendeutschtum. Sein Wesen und Werden im Wandel der Jahrhunderte. 2d ed. Brünn, Verlag R. M. Rohrer, 1939. 667 p. Illus., maps.

This symposium, first published in 1937, tries to develop as a theme the special role the Sudeten Germans have played in history and their various cultural achievements. The often extensive contributions, which are documented and scholarly in approach, were prepared by the best known Sudeten German experts. The articles deal in part with the general history of this area; however, special treatment is also given to the prehistoric period, medieval and modern history, German settlement, law, economic development, intellectual life, art, etc.

657. Preidel, Helmut, *ed.* Die Deutschen in Böhmen und Mähren. Ein historischer Rückblick. 2d rev. and enl. ed. Gräfelfing bei München, E. Gans Verlag, 1952. 392 p. Maps.

This symposium tried to refute the view that the history of Bohemia is a continuous struggle between Czechs and Germans — a concept followed by many Czech historians. It develops its own approach to the history of the Sudeten Germans by placing it in the framework of European history. It also attempts to provide a well-organized account of the cultural contributions made by the Sudeten Germans and a panoramic view of their history. Special topics treated are: the prehistoric settlement of Bohemia and Moravia, history of the German settlement, legal history, Sudeten German literature, economic history, the German contribution to the revival of Czech culture, and Sudeten German politics during the interwar period.

658. Rönnefarth, Helmuth K. Die Sudetenkrise in der internationalen Politik. Entstehung, Verlauf, Auswirkung. Wiesbaden, F. Steiner, 1961. 2 v. 3 fold. maps, ports. Bibliography: v. 2, p. 1-15. (Veröffentlichungen des Instituts für europäische Geschichte, 21)

See also entry no. 894.

The author first traces the causes of the Sudeten German problem from 1918 on, analyzes the role of the German parties and their relations with the government, and finally turns his special attention to the Henlein Party and its gradual transformation. The bulk of the work deals with the crisis of 1938. This discussion is based on an extensive use of primary sources from the Munich Agreement until the occupation of the whole country in 1939. Volume 2 contains a bibliography, notes, and excerpts from the sources. On the Sudeten German question *see also* the symposium prepared by German and émigré Czechoslovak scholars titled *Die Sudetenfrage in europäischer Sicht* (München, Lerche, 1962, 281 p.).

659. Wiskemann, Elizabeth. Czechs and Germans. A Study of the Struggle in the Historic Provinces of Bohemia and Moravia. 2d ed. London, Macmillan, 1967. 299 p. Maps.

See also entry no. 880.

This lively and penetrating study is essentially a history of the centuries-old German-Czech conflict. It traces this struggle through its various and changing manifestations, uncovering the underlying causes, whether political, economic, psychological, or sociological. Although publications which have appeared since the first edition of this book in 1938 have not been used, the conclusions reached in this study are still valid. It is particularly useful as an introduction to the essence of the German-Czech problem.

4. Economics and Law

660. Hübl, Karl, *ed.* Bauerntum und Landbau der Sudetendeutschen. München, Sudetendeutsches Landvolk in der Ackermann-Gemeinde, 1963. 656 p. Illus., maps.

The significance of this symposium, containing many popular articles of varying value, lies in the information it contains on German peasant life between 1919 and 1938 in Czechoslovakia. The various contributors often provide firsthand accounts of the daily life and the working conditions of these peasants, as well as their political representation, press, associations, cooperatives, and schools.

661. Raschhofer, Hermann. Die Sudetenfrage. Ihre völkerrechtliche Entwicklung vom Ersten Weltkrieg bis zur Gegenwart. München, Isar Verlag, 1953. 310 p.

See also entry no. 847.

The author attempts to identify the time when the Sudeten areas and their German inhabitants became subject to international law and regulation. It is his belief that any given situation after that time should be examined from the point of view of international law. The various sections of the book deal with the status of Sudeten areas up to 1919, the problem of the Sudeten Germans under the newly formed Czechoslovak Republic, and the Munich Agreement and its legal consequences.

662. Das Sudetenland im deutschen Wirtschaftsraum. Berlin, Deutsche Bank, 1938. 111 p.

This survey of the Sudeten German economy in 1938 was prepared by the Economic Section of the Deutsche Bank. It includes information on mineral resources, agriculture, forestry, industry, electric power, transportation, and credit structure. A list of Sudeten German industrial centers and enterprises is also furnished. *See also* the studies on the Sudeten German economy in *Deutsches Wirtschaftsjahrbuch für die Tschechoslowakei* (1932–, Prag). The volume for 1932 has a list of German economic organizations in Czechoslovakia.

5. Culture

663. Bittner, Konrad. Deutsche und Tschechen. Zur Geistesgeschichte des böhmischen Raumes. v. 1. Brünn, Verlag R. M. Rohrer, 1936. 239 p.

Bittner traces in the first and only volume of his work the cultural and literary relationships between Czechs and Germans up to the Hussite movement. His basic thesis is that the Czech and German cultures developed in opposing directions so that the cultural zenith of one group corresponded to the nadir of the other. The facts do not always uphold this theory.

664. Keil, Theo, *ed.* Die deutsche Schule in den Sudetenländern. Form und Inhalt des Bildungswesens. München, Lerche, 1967. 632 p. Illus., maps.

A comprehensive symposium on the history and nature of the German educational institutions in Bohemia, Moravia, and Austrian Silesia. It contains lengthy, annotated contributions on various types of schools, the German university, and facilities for education outside the school system. Statistical tables are appended.

665. Kletzl, Otto. Die deutsche Kunst in Böhmen und Mähren. Berlin, Deutscher Kunstverlag, 1941. 264 p.

The author tries to clarify the extent to which German artists participated in the architectural and sculptural achievements of Bohemia, Moravia, and Austrian Silesia during the early modern period and the 18th century. For a detailed account of the German influence on the arts and related crafts in the same regions *see* Josef Neuwirth's *Geschichte der deutschen Kunst und des deutschen Kunstgewerbes bis zum Ausgang des 19. Jahrhunderts* (Aussig, Stauda, 1926, 236 p., illus.).

666. Lehmann, Emil, *ed.* Handbuch der sudetendeutschen Volksbildung. Reichenberg, Sudetendeutscher Verlag F. Kraus, 1931. 592 p.

This work provides from information furnished by the various organizations a survey of the Sudeten German institutions in the field of scholarship, art, and general education. Among the topics discussed are adult education, libraries, museums, archives, educational associations, theaters, research, art, and institutions maintained by trade and industry.

667. Quoika, Rudolf. Die Musik der Deutschen in Böhmen und Mähren. Berlin, Verlag Merseburger, 1956. 161 p.

The first comprehensive account of Sudeten German musical life from its beginning to 1945. Designed as a handbook, it provides a wealth of general information as well as a discussion of local and regional developments.

668. Winter, Eduard. Tausend Jahre Geisteskampf im Sudetenraum. Das religiöse Ringen zweier Völker. 2d ed. München, Aufstieg-Verlag, 1955. 442 p.

This work describes the religious and ecclesiastical development of Bohemia, Moravia, and Austrian Silesia from the beginning to 1938, the date of the first edition. Its underlying theme is that the religious and intellectual condition of the Sudeten area has resulted from the collaboration between the Germans and Czechs living there. It stresses the religious and ecclesiastical circumstances of the Sudeten German minority. The European intellectual or religious movements brought to Bohemia from Germany or by persons of German origin are also emphasized.

669. Wolkan, Rudolf. Geschichte der deutschen Literatur in Böhmen und in den Sudetenländern. Aussig, J. Stauda Verlag, 1925. 184 p.

Attempts to provide as completely as possible a history of German literature in Bohemia, Moravia, and Austrian Silesia from its beginning to about 1920. Offering a wealth of material, it is an indispensable handbook in this field.

670. Wünsch, Franz J. Deutsche Archive und deutsche Archivpflege in den Sudetenländern. München, Historische Kommission der Sudetenländer, 1958. 307 p. (Wissenschaftliche Materialien zur Landeskunde der Böhmischen Länder, 2)

Lists alphabetically by place archives which were formerly in Sudeten German cities and settlements. Included are municipal archives, archives of castles, churches, monasteries, industrial enterprizes, manors, government agencies, and other organizations. For each archive, the holdings are described, and notes are added about its origin, history, archivists, and ultimate transfer to Czechoslovak authorities in 1945.

D. CZECHS AND SLOVAKS ABROAD

by Esther Jerabek

1. Czechs and Slovaks in the United States and Canada

a. Bibliographies

671. Čapek, Thomas. Padesát let českého tisku v Americe od vydání "Slowana amerikanského" v Racine, dne 1. ledna 1860 do 1. ledna 1910 (Fifty years of the Czech press in America from the publication of "Slowan amerikanský" in Racine, Jan. 1, 1860 to Jan. 1, 1910). New York, "Bank of Europe," 1911. 273 p. Illus., facsims.

The best source of information on the first 50 years of the Czech press in America. Supplemented in part by František Štědronský's *Zahraniční krajanské noviny, časopisy a kalendáře do roku 1938* (Newspapers, periodicals and almanacs, of our countrymen abroad to the year 1938) (Praha, Národní knihovna, 1958, 166 p.).

672. Nevlud, Vojtěch (V. N. Duben, *pseud.*). Czech and Slovak Periodical Press outside Czechoslovakia; the History and Status as of January 1962. Washington, Czechoslovak Society of Arts and Sciences in America, 1962. 99 p.

The largest part deals with the Czechoslovak press in America. It supplements Čapek's *Padesát let českého tisku v Americe* (*see* entry 671), but chiefly describes current publications. Nevlud has issued several continuations, the latest being *Czech and Slovak Periodicals Outside Czechoslovakia as of September, 1968* (Washington, D.C., 1968, 28 p.). For Czech books issued abroad, see *Zahraniční bohemika* (Foreign Bohemica), published periodically as part of the Czechoslovak national bibliography *České knihy*. See also entry no. 480.

673. Rechcígl, Miloslav, Jr. Stav a úkoly čs. zahraniční a krajanské bibliografie (The state and tasks of bibliography of Czechoslovak writings abroad and of publications relating to Czechoslovakia). Proměny, v. 4, Jan. 1967: 46-53.

A detailed bibliographic survey of writings authored by Czechs and Slovaks abroad and of publications concerning Czechoslovakia, irrespective of the author's nationality.

b. General Studies

674. Balch, Emily G. Our Slavic Fellow Citizens. New York, Charities Publication Committee, 1910. 536 p. Illus., maps. Bibliography: p. 481-512.

According to the preface, "the matter for this book was originally prepared as a series of magazine articles, which appeared in *Charities and the Commons* during 1906 and 1907." One of the first authoritative studies of the Slavs in the United States, it is still of value for an overall view. Coverage includes Czechs and Slovaks.

675. Beneš, Vojta. Československá Amerika v odboji (Czechoslovak America in the revolution). v. 1. Praha, Nakl. Pokrok, 1931. 424 p. No more published.

A record of the part played by American Czechs and Slovaks during the First World War in helping to establish a free Czechoslovakia, written by an organizer and publicist who later served in the Czechoslovak government. A similar publication for the Second World War is Stanislav Budin's *Věrni zůstali; druhý odboj amerických Čechů ve východních státech Unie, 1939-1945* (They remained faithful; the second struggle of American Czechs in the eastern states of the Union, 1939-1945) (New York, Nakl. Krajského výboru Českého národního sdružení, 1947, 303 p., illus.).

676. Buzek, Karel, *comp.* Památník československé Kanady (A memorial of Czechoslovak Canada). Toronto, Československé národní sdružení v Kanadě, 1944. 207 p. Map.

Commemorates the twenty-fifth anniversary of the Czechoslovak National Alliance in Canada and provides an overall sketch of Czechs and Slovaks in Canada during the Second World War. For a recent English-language history of the Czechs and Slovaks, their settlement and cultural organization in Canada, *see*:

Gellner, John, *and* John Smerek. The Czechs and Slovaks in Canada. Toronto, University of Toronto Press, 1968. 172 p.

For a recent survey of Canadian Slovaks *see*:

Kirschbaum, Joseph M. Slovaks in Canada. Toronto, Canadian Ethnic Press Association of Ontario, 1967. 468 p. Illus., maps, ports. Bibliography: p. 441-455.

677. Čapek, Thomas. The Čechs (Bohemians) in America; A Study of their National, Cultural, Political, Social, Economic and Religious life. Boston, New York, Houghton Mifflin, 1920. 293 p. Illus., maps, ports. Bibliography: p. 281-284.

Written by an immigrant businessman who spent many years of his life studying the Czechs in the United States. Better on urban than on rural settlements, but still the best source available on its subject. Čapek published a Czech version with numerous changes under the title *Naše Amerika* (Our America) (Praha, Nakl. Národní rady československé v. Praze, 1926, 684 p.) besides numerous other studies of lesser scope. A well-documented and illustrated history of American Jews from Czechoslovakia is the subject of Guido Kisch's *In Search of Freedom* (London, E. Goldstone, 1949, 373 p.).

678. Čulen, Konštantín. Dejiny Slovákov v Amerike (History of the

Slovaks in America). Bratislava, Nákl. Slovenskej ligy, 1942. 2 v. Illus., map. Bibliography: v. 2, p. 211-227.

The most complete treatment of the history of the Slovaks in America. Čulen also published a lesser work, *Slováci v Amerike; črty z kultúrnych dejín* (The Slovaks in America; sketches from cultural history) (Turčiansky Sv. Martin, Matica slovenská, 1938, 519 p.), as well as many other studies.

679. Habenicht, Jan. Dějiny Čechův amerikých (History of American Czechs). St. Louis, Tiskem a nakl. časopisu "Hlas," 1904. 777 p. Illus., map.

Although not entirely reliable, it is based on material gathered during 25 years of travel and correspondence with American Czechs. Arrangement is by States. Superseded in part by Capek's work (*see* entry 677).

680. Naše hlasy (Our voices). Centennial Issue, 1867-1967 (v. 13, no. 21/22 [515/516] May 27, 1967). Toronto, 1967. 98 p.

So far the best source of information on Czechs and Slovaks in Canada. Features articles on their contributions as well as their organizations and publications.

681. Rechcígl, Miloslav Jr., *ed.* The Czechoslovak Contribution to World Culture. The Hague, Mouton, 1964. 682 p. Illus. Bibliography of Czechs and Slovaks abroad: p. 620-625.

See also entries no. 511, 1108, *and* 1165.

Papers presented at the 1963 congress of the Czechoslovak Society of Arts and Sciences in America. Other publications of the society include monographs, its monthly *Zprávy* (News) and a literary quarterly, *Proměny* (Changes).

c. Local Studies

682. Rosicky, Rose. A History of the Czechs (Bohemians) in Nebraska. Omaha, Czech Historical Society of Nebraska, 1929. 492 p. Illus., maps.

A Czech edition appeared as *Dějiny Čechů v Nebrasce* (Omaha, Nákl. Českého historického klubu v Nebrasce, 1928. 471 p.). The author was a journalist who knew her people well. *Czechs and Nebraska,* commemorating the centennial of the declaration of Nebraska as a state of the Union, was recently published under the editorship of Vladimir Kucera and Alfred Novacek (Ord, Neb., Quiz Graphic Arts, 1967, 424 p., illus.). Another state history is *Czech Pioneers of the Southwest* (Dallas,, Southwest Press, 1934. 418 p.), by Estelle Hudson, assisted by Henry R. Maresh. Limited to Czechs in Texas, it is poorly organized and not entirely reliable. There is also *Dějiny Čechův ve státu South Dakota* (A history of the Czechs in South Dakota), edited by Josef A. Dvořák (Tabor, S.D., 1920, 109 p., illus.).

683. For cities with large Czech populations the following have appeared:

Česká osada a její spolkový život v Cleveland, O. (The Czech community and its social activity in Cleveland, O.). Cleveland, Volnost, 1895. 192 p.

Bubeníček, Rudolf, *comp.* *Dějiny Čechů v Chicagu* (A history of the Czechs in Chicago). Chicago, Nákl. vlastním, 1939. 568 p.

Belohlávek, Karol, *ed.* Dějiny detroitských a amerických Slovákov, 1921-1948 (History of Slovaks in Detroit and America, 1921-1948). Detroit, Společnost slovenského domu, 1948. 216 p. Illus.

Kutak, Robert I. The Story of a Bohemian-American Village (Louisville, Kentucky, Standard Printing Co., 1933, 156 p.). A Ph.D. thesis, this is a sociological study of Milligan, Nebraska, a rural community with a large Czech population.

d. Biography

684. Prantner, Emil F. These Help Build America. Chicago, Czechoslovak Review, 1922. 112 p. ports.

Biographies of sixteen prominent American Czechs. Another collection of biographies is *Czech and Slovak Leaders in Metropolitan Chicago*, edited by Daniel D. Droba (Chicago, Slavonic Club of the University of Chicago, 1934; 307 p., illus. Bibliography: p. 298-299), which includes brief sketches of 300 men and women. Biographic data on the members of the Czechoslovak Society of Arts and Sciences (381 Park Avenue South, Room 914, New York, New York 10016) are given in a *Directory* (New York, 1966, 80 p.), prepared by Eva Rechcigl.

Among biographies of individuals are the following: H. K. Barnard's *Anton, the Martyr* (Chicago, Marion Publishing Co., 1933, 93 p.), a sketch of Mayor Cermak of Chicago; Thomas Čapek's *Moje Amerika; vzpomínky a úvahy* (My America; reminiscences and reflections) (Praha, F. Borovký, 1935, 271 p., illus., bibliography); Peter V. Rovnianek's *Zápisky za živa pochovaného* (Notes of one buried alive) (Pittsburgh, Nicholson Printing Co., 1924, 336 p., illus., facsims.); and Frank J. Vlchek's *Povídka mého života* (Story of my life) (Praha, Družstevní práce, 1929, 365 p., plates, ports.).

e. Associations

685. Martínek, Josef. Století Jednoty Č.S.A.; dějiny Jednoty československých spolků v Americe (One hundred years of the Czechoslovak Society of America). Cicero, Illinois, Č.S.A., 1955. 443 p.

Detailed history of a large Czech-American fraternal organization specializing in insurance. It has published a fortnightly organ, *ČSA*, since 1891. Another kind of association is commemorated in J. J. Jelinek's *The Semi-centennial Jubilee of the Bohemian National Cemetery Association of Chicago, Illinois* (Chicago, The Bohemian National Cemetery Association, 1927, 134 p.) and *Sedmdesátipětileté jubileum Českého národního hřbitova v Chicagu, Ill.* (The seventy-fifth year jubilee of the Bohemian National Cemetery in Chicago,

Ill.) compiled by Rudolf Janda (Chicago, R. Mejdrich and Co., 1952, 571 p., illus.).

686. Neodvislý národny slovensky spolok. Pamätnica k zlatému jubileu Neodvislého nár. spolku všetkých Slovákov v Spojených Štatov (Memorial for the golden jubilee of the independent national associations of all Slovaks in the United States). Compiled by Vojtěch E. Andic. New York, Nemec Press, 1945. 204 p.

A study of Slovak associations in the United States. May be supplemented by Karol Bima's *Slovenské sokolstvo v Amerike* (Slovak Sokols in America) (Praha, Čsl. obec sokolská, 1926, 29 p.). Many of the individual Sokol gymnastic societies have issued histories of their own organizations.

687. Paučo, Jozef. 75 (Sedemdesiatpät) rokov Prvej katolíckej slovenskej jednoty (Seventy-five years of the First Catholic Slovak Union). Cleveland, Ohio, Prvá katolícka slovenská jednota, 1965. 560 p. Illus., bibliography.

History of a large Slovak society, based on its newspaper, *Jednota*, and official records. It gives a complete history of Slovak Catholics in America and much on politics and the Slovak separatist movement.

f. Education

688. Manning, Clarence A. A History of Slavic Studies in the United States. Milwaukee, Marquette University Press, 1957. 117 p. Bibliography: p. 109-113. (Marquette Slavic Studies, 3)

Includes Czech and Slovak studies in American colleges and universities and has a brief history of Slav immigration to the United States. Among histories of Czech and Slovak language schools is Anton Beneš' *Dějiny české svobodomyslné školy v Detroit, Michigan, 1881-1941* (History of the Czech Freethinking School in Detroit, Michigan, 1881-1941) (Detroit, 1942, 40 p.). A bimonthly, *Svobodná škola*, has been published by the Bohemian Freethinking School Society of Chicago since 1897.

2. Czechs and Slovaks in Other Countries

689. Auerhan, Jan. Československá větev v Jugoslavii (Czechoslovaks in Yugoslavia). Praha, Nákl. "Orbis," 1930. 403 p. Bibliographical footnotes. (Československý ústav zahraniční. Knihovna, sv. 1)

The Slovaks in Yugoslavia are treated in Rudolf Bednárik's *Slováci v Juhoslavii; materiály k ich hmotnej a duchovnej kultúre* (Slovaks in Yugoslavia; materials about their material and spiritual culture) (Bratislava, Vydavatel'stvo Slovenskej akadémie vied, 1964, 272 p.). For other Slavic lands there is Ján Michalko's *Naši v Bulharsku; pädesat rokov ich života, práce, piesne a žvykov* (Our people in Bulgaria; fifty years of their life, work, songs and customs) (Myjava, D. Pažickey, 1936, 386 p.); and Samo Fal'tan's *Slováci v partizánskych bojoch v Sovietskom Sväze* (Slovaks in the partisan battles in the

Soviet Union) (Bratislava, Slovenské vydavatel'stvo politickej literatúry, 1957, 208 p.).

690. Klíma, Stanislav. Čechové a Slováci za hranicemi (Czechs and Slovaks abroad). Praha, J. Otto, 1925. 303 p. Illus. Bibliography: p. 262-276.

Brief overall sketch of Czechoslovak émigrés everywhere, with special emphasis on Europe and the United States. Another general treatment is Jan Auerhan's *Československé jazykové menšiny v evropském zahraničí; národnostní poměry, v nichž žijí, a vztahy které je poutají k staré vlasti* (Czechoslovak linguistic minorities abroad in Europe; the political conditions under which they live, and the relations which draw them to their homeland) (Praha, Orbis, 1935, 105 p., Národnostní otázky, sv. 5).

For a detailed and thorough bibliography of publications issued from 1946 to 1966 in Czechoslovakia and elsewhere on the history and life of Slovaks in numerous countries of the world, *see* Elena Jakešová's *Krajania, Slováci v zahraničí* (Fellow Slovaks abroad). (Bratislava, Universitní knižnica, 1967).

691. Winter, Eduard. Die tschechische und slowakische Emigration in Deutschland im 17. und 18. Jahrhundert; Beiträge zur Geschichte der hussitischen Tradition. Berlin, Akademie-Verlag, 1955. 568 p. (Deutsche Akademie der Wissenschaften zu Berlin. Veröffentlichungen des Instituts für Slawistik, Nr. 7)

Emphasis is on migration to Germany for religious reasons. "A chronicle of the suffering of the Czech people after the battle on the White Mountain" is presented by Ernest Sommer in *Into Exile. The History of the Counter-Reformation in Bohemia (1620-1650)* (London, The New Europe Publishing Co., 1943, 154 p.) A book about Czechs and Slovaks in Austria is Antonín Machát's *Naši ve Vídni* (Our people in Vienna) (Praha, Práce, 1946, 417 p.).

692. Štěrba, Francisco Carlos. Češi a Slováci v Latinské Americe; přehled jejích kulturního přínosu (Czechs and Slovaks in Latin America; a review of their cultural contribution). Washington, Společnost pro vědy a umění, 1962. 60 l. Bibliography: leaf 60.

Contains brief biographical sketches of well-known Czechs and Slovaks in Latin America, living and dead. There is also a list of Czech and Slovak periodicals published in South America. For still another continent there is Charles J. Sousek's *Czechs in South Africa* (Johannesburg, 1942, 17 p.).

17

history*

by Josef Anderle

A. BIBLIOGRAPHY

693. Zíbrt, Čeněk. Bibliografie české historie (Bibliography of Czech history). Praha, Česká akademie Císaře Františka Josefa pro vědy, slovesnost a umění, 1900-1912. 5 v.

A comprehensive bibliography of all materials relevant to history, in the broadest sense of this word, of the Czech lands from prehistoric times to 1679. Unfortunately, inclusion of a vast number of trivial items, awkward organization, and lack of a good index make the use of this monumental work a trying experience.

694. Bibliografie české historie (Bibliography of Czech history). 1904-1941. Praha, Historický klub.

* The arrangement is generally by topics or periods. Within these subdivisions the presentation usually proceeds from the more general to the more specific. In some cases a chronological order was accepted. When geographical arrangement was chosen, titles relating to Bohemia precede those relating to Moravia, Silesia, Slovakia, and Podkarpatská Rus.

A periodical registering current literature relevant to Czech and Slovak history produced in 1904-1941. Originally published in yearly volumes as a supplement to *Český časopis historický*. In a way it is a continuation of Zíbrt's *Bibliografie české historie*, but it is better organized, although it too is overburdened with materials of marginal value. The gap between the two can be covered by consulting bibliographies of a more general nature or indexes to historical and other journals listed elsewhere in this book.

695. Bibliografia slovenskej histórie za roky 1939-1941 (Bibliography of Slovak history for the years 1939-1941). Edited by František Bokes, Vendelín Jankovič, and B. Polla. Turčiansky Svätý Martin, Matica slovenská, 1944. 56 p.

A valuable supplement to the last volume of *Bibliografie české historie* that covers the years 1937-1941, but does not treat Slovak history after 1939 sufficiently. Originally published in:

Matica Slovenská, *Turčiansky sv. Martin. Historický odbor*. Historický sborník Matice slovenskej (Historical miscellany of the Matica Slovenska), v. 1, 1943: 193-244.

Continued by Vendelín Jankovič's *Bibliografia slovenskej histórie 1942-1944; s doplnkami za roky 1939-1941* (Bibliography of Slovak history 1942-1944; with supplements for the years 1939-1941) (Turčiansky Svätý Martin, Matica slovenská, 1948, 122 p.).

Researchers in Slovak history will be served still better by the two following bibliographies:

Kuzmík, Jozef, *ed.* Bibliografia publikácií k miestnym a všeobecným dejinám Slovenska (Bibliography of publications on local and general history of Slovakia). Martin, Matica slovenská, 1962. 728 p. Map.

Bibliografia príspevkov k slovenským dejinám uverejnených v rokoch 1918-1939 (Bibliography of contributions to Slovak history published in the years 1918-1939). Martin, Matica, slovenská, 1963. 732 p.

Both of these are comprehensive, not selective, bibliographies, which even register articles from the daily press.

696. Bibliografie československé historie (Bibliography of Czechoslovak history). 1955– Praha, Československá akademie věd.

A continuation of *Bibliografie české historie* of equal nature and importance. It is planned to fill the gap between 1941 and 1955 with several volumes in the near future. Foreign publications strongly critical of communism are ignored.

697. Revue historique. Posledních padesát let české práce dějepisné; soubor zpráv Jaroslava Golla o české literatuře historické, vydaných v "Revue historique" v letech 1878-1906, a souhrnná zpráva Josefa Šusty za léta 1905-1924 (The last fifty years of Czech historical work; a collection of reports of Jaroslav Goll on Czech historical literature, published in "Revue historique" in the years 1878-1906, and a sum-

mary report of Josef Šusta for the years 1905-1924). Praha, Historický klub, 1926. 212 p.

A discriminating selection of, and commentary on, the most important works on Czech and Slovak history published between 1878 and 1924. Continued directly by a separate volume of Josef Šusta, *Posledních deset let československé práce dějepisné; soubor zpráv Josefa Šusty o československé literatuře historické, vydaných v "Revue historique" za léta 1925-1935* (The last ten years of Czechoslovak historical work; a collection of reports of Josef Šusta on Czechoslovak historical literature published in "Revue historique" for the years 1925-1935) (Praha, Historický klub, 1937, 238 p.).

Similar, though less successful service was provided for German readers by a number of Czech and German historians in *Jahresberichte der Geschichtswissenschaft* between 1880 and 1910; *Mitteilungen des Instituts für österreichische Geschichtsforschung* between 1881 and 1907; and *Jahresberichte für Deutsche Geschichte* between 1925 and 1939.

More successful was the effort of Václav Novotný to produce a pendant to Goll's and Šusta's books in a book of his own, covering Czechoslovak historical literature published in the first ten years of the Czechoslovak Republic, 1918-1928, *České dějepisectví v prvém desetiletí republiky* (Czech historiography in the first decade of the republic) (Praha, Historický spolek, 1929, 161 p.).

698. Československá akademie věd. *Sekce historická.* 25 [i.e. Vingt-cinq] ans d'historiographie tchécoslovaque, 1936-1960. Edited by Josef Macek. Praha, Nakladatelství Československé akademie věd, 1960. 494 p.

A continuation of Šusta's *Posledních deset let československé práce dějepisné,* prepared by a number of Czech and Slovak historians in French for the Ninth International Congress of Historical Sciences held in Stockholm, Sweden, in 1960. Emphasizes Marxist evaluations and works by Marxist authors at the expense of "bourgeois" historians.

For more general purposes, more useful than these works of Macek, Šusta, Novotný, and Goll, are the quite extensive, but easy to survey, lists of the most essential sources and works dating since the Middle Ages that can be found in the two largest surveys of Czechoslovak history, Kamil Krofta's *Dějiny československé* and *Přehled československých dějin.*

B. GUIDES TO ARCHIVES AND LIBRARIES

699. Czechoslovak Republic. *Ministerstvo vnitra. Archivní správa.* Soupis archivní literatury v českých zemích, 1895-1956 (Inventory of archival literature in Czech lands, 1895-1956). Compiled by Otakar Bauer and Ludmila Mrázková with the cooperation of Rostislav Nový. Praha, Archivní správa Ministerstva vnitra, 1959. 226 p.

See also entry no. 545.

An indispensable bibliography of Czech literature in the field of archival sciences, including guides to archival collections.

A list of archival collections in Slovakia was published by Teodor Lamoš in his *Bibliografia k archívom na Slovensku* (Bibliography on the archives in Slovakia) (Bratislava, Slovenský ústredný archív, 1953, 185 p.). A list of more recent archival aids can be found in:

Holl, Ivo, Michal Kušík, *and* Josef Nuklíček. Výsledky zpřístupňování archivního materiálu v československých státních archivech za léta 1956-1960 (The results of the efforts to make accessible archival materials in Czechoslovak state archives in the years 1956-1960). Sborník archivních prací (Praha), v. 11, 1961, no. 2: 189-298.

Continued by Ivo Holl for the years 1961-1965, but only for state archives in the Czech provinces, in *Sborník archivních prací* (Praha), v. 6, 1966, no. 2: 539-632.

For Slovak archives a similar list was published by Štefan Rudohradský in his "Archívne pomôcky štátnych a okresných archívov na Slovensku za desat'ročie 1956-1965" (Archival aids of the state and district archives in Slovakia for the decade 1956-1965), *Slovenská archivistika* (Bratislava), v. 1, 1956: 296-353.

Information on current archival aids can be followed, in addition to these two journals, in *Archivní časopis* (Praha), Archivní správa ministerstva vnitra, 1951–).

700. Czechoslovak Republic. *Ministerstvo vnitra. Archivní správa.* Inventáře a katalogy (Inventories and catalogs). Praha, 1956–

Appeared also under the title *Inventáře a katalogy Státního ústředního archivu v Praze* (Inventories and catalogs of the State Central Archives in Prague). A series in which archival aids to the collections of the State Central Archives in Prague are published. Such collections include materials that are of more than regional interest.

Aids to regional state archives in the Czech lands appear in the series *Průvodce po státních archivech* (Guides to state archives) (Praha, Archivní správa Ministerstva vnitra, 1956–). Volumes 1-6 appeared under the title *Průvodce po archivních fondech* (Guides to archival collections).

In Slovakia such guides appear in the series *Edícia sprievodcov po štátnych archívoch na Slovensku* (A series of guides to State Archives in Slovakia) (Bratislava, Slovenská archívna správa, 1959–).

Individual volumes of these series may be cataloged in some U.S. libraries under the name of their compilers, the issuing office (Ministerstvo vnitra. *Archivní správa*; Státní ústřední archiv; Archiv bývalé země české; etc.), or places of their location (Praha, Plzeň, Jablonec, Litomeřice, Třeboň, Zámrsk, Brno, Opava, Janovice u Rýmařova, Bratislava, Bytča, Baňská Bystrica, Košice, Prešov, etc.). Other archival aids which were published outside these series are cataloged in this way.

701. Brno. *Universita. Knihovna.* Soupisy rukopisných fondů (Inventories of manuscript collections). Brno, Universitní knihovna, 1957–

A series in which catalogs to manuscript collections owned or administered by the University of Brno appear. Most of them were compiled by V. Dokoupil. Similar catalogs have been published by other libraries of Czechoslovakia as well. Individual volumes may be catalogued in U.S. libraries separately under the names of their compilers, their issuing office, or the place of their location. This is the case with many catalogs that were published outside such series. Among the most valuable are those compiled by J. Truhlář and E. Urbánková for the Public and University Library of Prague, Jaromír Čelakovský for the Municipal Archives of Prague, Antonín Podlaha and Adolf Patera for the library and archives of the Metropolitan Chapter of Prague, F. M. Bartoš for the National Museum in Prague, E. Petrů for the University library in Olomouc, M. Boháček and F. Čáda for the Silesian Research Library in Opava, etc. Similar catalogs were published also for collections of incunabula in these and other libraries that are also important for the historian.

C. SOURCE COLLECTIONS

702. Fontes rerum Bohemicarum; Prameny dějin českých. v. 1-6, 8; 1873-1932. Praha, Museum království českého.

A collection of chronicles and other historical records relating to medieval and early modern history of Bohemia. Edited mostly by Josef Emler. A continuation, in a way, of this collection can be found in an older set founded by Antonín Gindely, *Monumenta historiae Bohemiae; Staré paměti dějin českých* (Praha, I. L. Kober, 1865-1874). It included documents, memoirs, and histories produced from the 15th to the 17th century. It should not be confused with a still older set published by Gelasius Dobner, *Monumenta historiae Bohemiae numquam antehac edita* (Praha, 1764-1785, 6 v.). That was the first attempt at a critical edition of a group of medieval chronicles and similar sources. Similar to it in age and nature was the set *Scriptores rerum Bohemicarum e bibliotheca ecclesiae metropolitanae Pragensis* (Pragae, 1783-1829, 3 v.). It was published by František Martin Pelcl, Josef Dobrovský, and František Palacký.

703. Archiv český; čili Staré písemné památky české i moravské, sebrané z archivů domácích i cizích (Czech archives; or Old written Bohemian and Moravian documents collected in domestic and foreign archives). Praha, Nákl. Domestikálního fondu českého, v komisi Bursík a Kohout, 1840-1941. 37 v.

A collection of documents relating to the medieval and early modern history of Bohemia and Moravia. Founded by F. Palacký.

A similar collection serving like purposes was published by the Czech Academy of Arts and Sciences in Prague:

Česká akademie věd a umění, *Prague. Třída I.* Historický archiv (Historical archives). v. 1-52, 1893-1949.

704. Codex diplomaticus et epistolaris Moraviae. Olomucii, ex typographia Aloysii Skarnitzl, 1836-1903. 15 v.

A collection of charters and letters relating to Moravia from the fourth century to 1411, unfortunately damaged in its first volumes by the uncritical methods of its founder Antonín Boček.

A collection of similar documents relating to both Bohemia and Moravia is *Regesta diplomatica nec non epistolaria Bohemiae et Moraviae* (Pragae, 1855–). Founded by Karel Jaromír Erben, the publication was recently resumed. Published volumes cover the years 600-1363.

A Bohemian pendant to the Moravian Codex is *Codex diplomaticus et epistolaris regni Bohemiae* (Pragae, Sumptibus Academiae Scientiarum Bohemoslovenicae, 1904-1942, 3 v.), a critical edition of early charters and letters relating to the history of Bohemia to 1238 that was undertaken by Gustav Friedrich to replace the unsatisfactory volumes of the *Regesta.*

Similar documents collected in the Vatican archives were published under the title *Monumenta Vaticana res gestas Bohemicas illustrantia* (Pragae, typis Gregerianis, 1903-1955, 5 v. in 8). Edited by various authors, the collection covers the period from 1342 to 1404.

705. Codex juris. Bohemici. Praha, 1867-1890. 5 v. in 12.

A collection of laws and other sources of legal nature reflecting history of Bohemia to 1628. Edited by Hermenegild Jireček. A modern pendant to it is the collection of Bohemian laws:

Bohemia. *Laws, Statutes, etc.* Provinzial-Gesetzsammlung des Königreichs Böhmen. Prag, 1820-1849. 30 v., 2 supp.

It was continued by another collection that is catalogued under the same heading, but with the title *Zákonník zemský království českého. Landes-Gesetz-Blatt für das Königreich Böhmen* (Ročník 1848/49-1918; Prag, G. Haase Söhne, 1850-1919, 70 v.). And finally by the collection of laws:

Czechoslovak Republic. *Laws, Statutes, etc.* Sbírka zákonů a nařízení Republiky Československé (Collection of laws and ordinances of the Czechoslovak Republic). Praha, 1918– Title varies. Also in Slovak and, between 1918 and 1945, German.

Similar codes of laws were published after 1819 for Moravia and Silesia. Hungarian legal sources listed elsewhere in this book are equally important for Slovak history.

706. Bohemia. *Zemský sněm.* Sněmy české od léta 1526 až po naši dobu (Bohemian Diets from 1526 until our time). Praha, 1877–

Records of, and documents relating to, the activities of the Bohemian Diet since 1526. Also in German. Founded by Antonín Gindely and continued by various editors, the publication has been resumed recently. The published volumes so far cover the period 1526-1611 with a gap between 1608-1610.

A modern pendant to this are the stenographic records and other related documents of the Bohemian Diet published under several titles between 1861 and 1911 and catalogued in U.S. libraries under the heading: "Bohemia. Sněm." Similar publication was undertaken for the Moravian and Silesian Diet. They all were superseded in part by the stenographic records and other documents of the Czechoslovak National Assembly published since 1918 in several series and catalogued in the U.S. under the heading "Czechoslovak Republic. Národní shromáždění." Also in German.

In addition to these legislative records, numerous publications of various administrative and judicial agencies are available in print since about the middle of the 19th century, too numerous to be listed here. Very relevant to Czechoslovak history also are similar records of Austria and Hungary. A good, though outdated, list of all such publications can be found in *List of Serial Publications of Foreign Governments, 1815-1931*, edited by Winifred Gregory (New York, H. W. Wilson, 1932, 720 p.).

707. Doskočil, Karel, *ed.* Listy a listiny z dějin československých, 869-1938 (Letters and charters from Czechoslovak history, 869-1938). Praha, Státní nakladatelství, 1938. 148 p.

A selection of the most important documents to Czechoslovak history. A similar collection, selected from the Marxist point of view, is *Naše národní minulost v dokumentech; Chrestomatie k dějinám Československa* (Our national past in documents; a chrestomathy to the history of Czechoslovakia), edited by Václav Husa (Praha, Nakladatelství Československé akademie věd, 1954–). The first two volumes published so far cover the period to 1848. A Slovak pendant to this was published by the Historical Institute of the Slovak Academy of Sciences.

Slovenská akadémia vied. *Historický ústav.* Dokumenty k protifeudálnym bojom slovenského l'udu, 1113-1848 (Documents on the antifeudal struggles of the Slovak people, 1113-1848). Edited by Alžbeta Gácsová. Bratislava, Vydavatel'stvo Slovenskej akadémie vied, 1955. 354 p. Illus. (Populárnovedná edícia Odkazy našej minulosti, zväzok 11)

Larger collections of documents to Slovak history comparable to the sets and series relating to Czech history do not exist. For that purpose it is necessary to use various Hungarian historical materials listed elsewhere in this book.

D. PERIODICALS

708. Český časopis historický (Czech historical journal). v. 1-50, 1895-1949. Praha, Historický klub.

The leading historical journal published in these years. Important also for its extensive coverage of all major contributions to Czechoslovak history, monographic and periodical. Its annual index is, therefore, a major bibliographical tool. A cumulative index for the first 40 volumes was published under the title *Bibliografie vědecké práce o české minulosti za posledních čtyřicet let; Rejstřík Českého časopisu historického 1895-1934* (Bibliography of scholarly works on the Czech past for the last forty years; an index to "Český časopis historický" 1895-1934), edited by Josef Klik (Praha, Historický klub, 1935, 337 p.).

709. Československý časopis historický (Czechoslovak historical journal). 1953– Praha, Československá akademie věd, Historický ústav.

Continues the role of *Český časopis historický* as the leading historical journal of Czechoslovakia, but with a rigid Marxist orientation, which it shares with all Czechoslovak historical journals started or continued after 1948. Its yearly index is again an important bibliographical tool. A cumulative index for the first 10 volumes was published as number 5/6 of its volume 10, 1962. Because of its emphasis on modern history, another journal was created in the same year to cover older periods. It is cataloged in U.S. libraries as follows:

Československá akademie věd. *Historický ústav*. Sborník historický (Historical review). r. 1– 1953– Praha. Annual. The first volume appeared under the title *Historický sborník*. It should not be confused with *Sborník historický*, which Antonín Rezek published in 1883-1886 in four volumes, or with *Historický sborník* (*see* the two titles listed in the following entry).

710. Historický časopis (Historical journal). 1953– Bratislava, Slovenská akadémia vied. Register 1953-1967 (Index). Bratislava, SAV, 1968.

The leading journal of Slovak history. It superseded *Historický sborník* (Historical review) (r. 1-10, 1940-1952; Bratislava, Slovenská akadémia vied a umení). Volumes 1-7 (1940-1949) of the latter appeared under the title *Historica slovaca*.

To avoid confusion, let us also mention here that another *Historický sborník* was published by Matica slovenská, Historický odbor, in Turčiansky Svätý Martin, 1943-1947, in five volumes.

Volumes 3-4 (1944-1956) of *Historický časopis* had a supplement, *Historické štúdie* (Historical studies), which has been appearing since 1957 as an independent periodical, published also by the Slovak Academy of Sciences.

711. Historica. 1959– Praha, Československá akademie věd.

A representative journal of Czechoslovak historical sciences published for the benefit of foreign readers untrained in the Czech and Slovak languages. It carries articles in English, French, German, or Russian.

A Slovak counterpart is *Studia historica slovaca* (1963–, Bratislava, Slovenská akadémia vied).

712. Acta Universitatis Carolinae. Philosophica et Historica. 1958– Praha, Universita Karlova.

A serial of the Charles University of Prague created by the union of its subseries *Philosophica* and *Historica*, published independently under changing titles since 1954. A great number of historical contributions were carried also in *Acta*'s predecessor, cataloged in U.S. libraries as follows:

Prague. Universita Karlova. *Filosofická fakulta*. Práce z vědeckých ústavů (Contributions from the scientific institutes). v. 1-56, 1922-1949. Praha. Similar series and subseries were published also by other universities:

Brno. Universita. *Filosofická fakulta*. Sborník prací; Řada historická (C) (Review of publications; historical series [C]). 1954–. It supplements its older *Spisy* (Publications) (1923–).

Olomouc, Moravia. Palackého universita. *Filosofická fakulta*. Historica; Sborník prací historických (Historica; review of historical contributions). 1960– Subseries of its *Acta Universitatis Palackianae Olomucensis*, published since 1948, which also carried a number of historical studies.

Olomouc, Moravia. Vysoká škola pedagogická. Sborník; Historie (Review; history). v. 1-6, 1954-1959.

Bratislava. Univerzita. *Filozofická fakulta.* Sborník; Historica (Review; historica). 1958– Superseded in part its *Sborník* (Review) (v. 1-8, 1922-1932).

Pedagogical institutes, such as the Vysoká škola pedagogická in Olomouc mentioned above, have published similar series at one time or another, but they all experienced similar short-lived existence and merger with other series.

713. Prague. Národní museum. Časopis (Journal of the National Museum). roč. 1– 1827–

The oldest Czech scholarly journal still in existence. Title has often varied: *Časopis Společnosti vlastenského museum* (v. 1-4, 1827-1830); *Časopis Českého museum* (v. 5-28, 1831-1954); *Časopis Musea království českého* (v. 29-96, 1855-1922); *Časopis Národního musea* (v. 97–, 1923–). Although it was devoted to all fields of humanities, social and natural sciences, its historical contributions were so numerous that it remains indispensable for the historian. Its index, an important bibliographical tool, was published under the title *Časopis Národního musea, 1827-1956; Rejstřík 125 ročníků muzejního časopisu* (The journal of the National Museum; index to 125 volumes of the museum journal), edited by Pravoslav Kneidl, Mirko Svrček, and Věra Beňová (Praha, Národní muzeum, 1961-1963, 2 v.). Between 1827 and 1831 the museum also published a German journal, first (1827-1829) under the title *Monatsschrift der Gesellschaft des vaterländischen Museums in Böhmen*; and later (1829-1831) as *Jahrbücher des böhmischen Museums für Natur- und Länderkunde, Geschichte, Kunst und Literatur.* Since 1938 the museum has published a purely historical periodical, *Sborník; A. Historický* (Review; A. History). Several other museum journals are important for the historian:

Brno. Moravské museum. Časopis; Acta Musei Moraviae (Journal; Acta Musei Moraviae). 1901– Title varies. Volumes 30-32 (1941-1943) were published under the German title *Zeitschrift des Mährischen Landesmuseums*, Neue Folge, v. 1-3, 1941-1943.

Vlastenecký spolek musejní, *Olomouc.* Časopis (Journal). v. 1-59, 1884-1950. Superseded by *Sborník Vlastivědného muzea v Olomouci* (Review of the Historical and Geographical Museum in Olomouc) (1951–).

Opava, *Czechoslovak Republic.* Slezské museum. Časopis; Vědy společenské (Journal; social sciences). 1951– Volumes 1-4, 1951-1955, published as *Časopis; Serie B. Historia* (Journal; Series B. History).

Turčianský Svätý Martin. Slovenské národné múzeum. Sborník (Review). Volumes 1-45, 1896-1951, appeared as *Sborník Muzeálnej slovenskej spoločnosti* (Review of the Slovak Museum Society). It was published concurrently with its *Časopis*, v. 1-41, 1898-1950.

714. Česká společnost nauk. *Prague. Třída filosoficko-historicko-filologická.* Věstník (Bulletin). 1885-1952.

A periodical of the oldest Czech learned society, devoted to humanities and social sciences with numerous contributions to history. Early volumes appeared also in German, *Sitzungsberichte der Königlichen Böhmischen Gesellschaft der Wissenschaften.* Journals of several other learned societies are of equal importance to the historian:

Společnost přátel starožitností československých v Praze. Časopis (Journal). 1893–

Matice Moravská, Brno. Časopis (Journal). 1869– Beginning with volume 78, 1959, published as *Sborník Matice Moravské* (Review of Matice Moravská).

Slezský sborník; Acta Silesiaca (Silesian review; Acta Silesiaca). 1878– Opava, Matice opavská. Volumes 1-41, 1878-1935, published as *Věstník Matice Opavské* (Bulletin of Matice Opavská).

Matica Slovenská, *Turčiansky Svätý Martin. Sborník* (Review). v. 1-20, 1922-1942.

Učená spoločnosť Šafárikova, *Bratislava.* Časopis Učené spoločnosti Šafárikovej. (Journal of the Šafárik Learned Society). v. 1-11, 1927-1937.

715. Sborník historického kroužku (Review of the historical circle). v. 1-8, 1893-1899; n.s., 1-35, 1900-1934. Praha, Historický kroužek.

A historical journal of a group of Catholic scholars, emphasizing religious, especially Catholic, history.

Protestant history was pursued by *Reformační sborník; Práce z dějin československého života náboženského* (Reformation review; contributions from the history of Czechoslovak religious life) (v. 1-8, 1920-1941, Praha).

For the history of the Jews in Czechoslovakia, the Gesellschaft für Geschichte der Juden in der Čechoslovakischen Republik issued its *Jahrbuch* (v. 1-9, 1929-1938, Prag). Some volumes appeared under a Czech title, *Ročenka Společnosti pro dějiny Židů v Československé republice.*

716. Časopis pro dějiny venkova (Journal for agrarian history). v. 1-28, 1914-1941. Praha.

Important for the economic history of Czechoslovakia. Title varied: *Časopis pro české agrární dějiny* (v. 1, 1914); *Agrární archiv; časopis pro dějiny venkova* (v. 2-6, 1915-1919); *Časopis pro dějiny venkova* (v. 7-28). Beginning with v. 11, 1924, it carried a supplement, *Selský archiv* (Peasant archive), that had appeared independently from 1902 to 1923.

717. Historie a vojenství (History and military affairs). 1953– Praha, Vojenský historický ústav.

A journal of military history, published by the Institute of Military History in Prague. Superseded *Válka a revoluce* (War and revolution) (v. 1-4, 1947-1951). An earlier journal of military history was *Vojensko-historický sborník* (Review of military history) (v. 1-7, 1931-1938; Praha, Vědecký ústav vojenský).

718. Právně-historické studie (Studies in legal history). 1955– Praha. *See also* entry no. 858.

A journal of the Czechoslovak Academy of Sciences specializing in the history of state and law.

719. Verein für Geschichte der Deutschen in den Sudetenländern, *Prague.* Mitteilungen. Bd. 1-78, 1862-1941.

The most important German journal devoted to the study of the history of the Czech lands, with special emphasis on the German minority living there. Volumes 1-76 (1862-1938) were published under the original name of the society, Verein für Geschichte der Deutschen in Böhmen. The society also published a *Jahrbuch* (Bd. 1-3, 1926-1933). Superseded by *Bohemia; Jahrbuch des Collegium Carolinum* (1960–, München), published by German expellees from Czechoslovakia. A similar publication is *Stifter-Jahrbuch* (1949–, Gräfelfing, Adalbert-Stifter-Verein).

Moravian history was emphasized by another German journal, issued by the Deutscher Verein für die Geschichte Mährens und Schlesiens, Brünn: *Zeitschrift für Geschichte und Landeskunde Mährens und Schlesiens* (Bd. 1-46, 1897-1944).

Another German journal published in Moravia was the *Zeitschrift für sudetendeutsche Geschichte* (v. 1-6, 1937-1943); Brünn, R. M. Rohrer). Volume 6, 1943, appeared as *Zeitschrift für Geschichte der Sudetenländer*.

The history of Silesia was pursued by the *Zeitschrift für Geschichte und Kulturgeschichte Schlesiens* (v. 1-20, 1905-1933; Troppau). Volumes 1-17, 1905-1917, appeared under the title *Zeitschrift für Geschichte und Kulturgeschichte Österreich-Schlesiens.*

E. GENERAL SURVEYS

720. Novotný, Václav, *ed.* Dějiny (History). *In*: Dědina, Václav, *ed.* Československá vlastivěda (Czechoslovak encyclopedia). v. 4 and supplement. Praha, Sfinx, 1932-1933. 905 p. Illus.

A balanced survey rendering the history of the whole territory of Czechoslovakia to 1918. Produced as a part of a representative encyclopedia by such leading historians as Václav Novotný, Josef Dobiáš, Otakar Odložilík, Rudolf Urbánek, and Jaroslav Prokeš.

A companion volume of equal strength covering the story to 1945 was published by Kamil Krofta in his *Dějiny československé* (Czechoslovak history) (Praha, Sfinx, 1946, 914 p.).

Shorter one-volume surveys were published between 1918 and 1948 by Josef Pekař, Karel Stloukal, Josef Pešek, Jaroslav Prokeš, Kamil Krofta, Otakar Odložilík, Miloš Kratochvíl, Zdeněk Kalista, Bohdan Chudoba, and František Roubík. Those of Pešek, Prokeš, and Krofta appeared also in several Western languages. Most popular among them was Kamil Krofta's *A Short History of Czechoslovakia* (New York, R. M. McBride, 1934, 198 p., map).

721. Macek, Josef, *ed.* Dějiny (History). *In:* Československá vlastivěda (Czechoslovak encyclopedia). Díl 2, svazek 1. Praha, Orbis, 1963. 647 p. Illus., facsims., maps, plates, ports., bibliographies.

A Marxist pendant to Novotný's survey (*see* entry 720) published as a part of a new version of the national encyclopedia. Part 1, the only one published so far, covers the period to 1781.

A larger and more authoritative product of Marxist scholarship, issued by the Historický ústav of the Czechoslovak Academy of Sciences, is *Přehled československých dějin* (Survey of Czechoslovak history) (Praha, Nakladatelství Československé akademie věd, 1958-1968, 4 v. in 5). It covers the history of the country to 1948, placing emphasis on social and economic developments and the period since 1848.

Shorter surveys reflecting a Marxist interpretation of Czechoslovak history were published by František Kavka, Josef Polišenský, František Kutnar, Arnošt Klíma, Karel Goláň, Václav Husa, Miroslav Kropilák, and others. Kavka's book was published in several languages, including English under the title *An Outline of Czechoslovak History*, 2d rev. ed. (Prague, Orbis, 1963, 164 p.).

A model for these publications was a survey published by a collective of Soviet historians under the title *Istoriia Chekhoslovakii* (History of Czechoslovakia) (Moskva, Izdatel'stvo Akademii nauk SSSR, 1956-1960, 3 v., illus., ports., maps, bibliographies).

Dějiny Československa v datech (Czechoslovakia's history in dates) (Praha, Svoboda, 1968, 557 p.) is a chronology from the beginnings through 1966.

722. Seton-Watson, Robert William. A History of the Czechs and Slovaks. London, Hutchinson, 1943. 413 p. Map., geneal. tables. Bibliography: p. 395-399.

The best available survey of Czechoslovak history in the English language.

Similar to it, though more loosely organized and stressing the place of the Czechs and Slovaks within the orbit of Western civilization, is the book by S. Harrison Thomson, *Czechoslovakia in European History*, 2d enl. ed. (Princeton, Princeton University Press, 1953, 485 p.), which was first published in 1943.

723. Zap, Karel Vladislav. Česko-moravská kronika (Czech-Moravian chronicle). Praha, I. L. Kober, 1862-1905. 8 v. Illus., facsims., col. maps, plans, ports.

An older survey of the history of the Kingdom of Bohemia to 1815, written successively by Karel V. Zap, Josef J. Kořán, Antonín Rezek, Josef Svátek, and Justin V. Prášek. Popular in presentation, but based on scholarly literature and original research, particularly for the period after 1526, for which it is the only detailed survey available.

For German readers a similar survey, written from the position of a passionate nationalist, was the work of Bertold Bretholz, *Geschichte Böhmens und Mährens* (Reichenberg, P. Sollor's Nachfolger, 1921-1924, 4 v.). It covers the period to 1792. A modern and moderate German view of the history of the Bohemian lands prevails in:

Bosl, Karl, *ed.* Handbuch der Geschichte der böhmischen Länder. Stuttgart, Anton Hiersemann, 1966– Three volumes are planned. Volume 1 covers medieval history to 1471.

Purely Moravian history was surveyed by Rudolf Dvořák in his *Dějiny Moravy od nejstarších dob až do r. 1848* (History of Moravia from ancient times to 1848) (Brno, Musejní spolek, 1899-1905, 5 v. in 1, fold. map, geneal. tables. Vlastivěda moravská. 1. země a lid, díl 3. všeobecné části). Issued as a part of an encyclopedic survey of Moravia, covering its history to 1848. A shorter version of the work was published in 1906.

Other important Czech or German surveys of the history of Bohemia and Moravia rarely reached beyond the Middle Ages and will be listed in the section for that period below.

From among older English surveys most popular was the book of Francis H. Lützow, *Bohemia; an Historical Sketch* (London, J. M. Dent, 1920, 359 p.). It stressed the older period to 1620 and was first published in 1896.

724. Bokes, František. Dejiny Slovenska a Slovákov od najstarších čias po oslobodenie (History of Slovakia and the Slovaks from the earliest times to the liberation). Bratislava, Slovenská akadémie vied a umení, 1946. 441 p. Bibliography: p. 405-441.

A balanced survey of the history of the Slovak people and the territory of Slovakia published as a part of a Slovak national encyclopedia.

An earlier survey written from a strongly nationalistic view was published by František Hrušovský in his *Slovenské dejiny* (Slovak history), 6th ed. (Turčiansky Svätý Martin, Matica slovenská, 1940, 451 p.). It appeared in numerous other editions, including a German abridgement, *Die Geschichte der Slowakei* (Bratislava, Verlag "Die Slowakische Rundschau," 1943, 228 p.).

A Marxist survey, edited by L'udovit Holotík, was published under the title *Dejiny Slovenska* (History of Slovakia), v. 1 (Bratislava, Slovenská akadémia vied, 1961, 578 p., 84 plates). The published volume covers the history of Slovakia to 1848.

F. SPECIAL SURVEYS*

1. Legal History

725. Kapras, Jan. Přehled právních dějin zemí České koruny (A survey of the legal history of the lands of the Bohemian Crown). 5th rev. ed.

* For additional historical surveys of special subjects such as law, religion, literature, music, art, education, sciences, and general culture, *see* the respective sections of this book.

Praha, Nákladem vlastním, 1935. 354 p. Fold. maps. Source references (in Czech, German, Latin): p. 293-354.

The most popular of several surveys of legal and constitutional history of the Czech lands with a rich collection of the most important documents. First published in 1913.

For German readers the same purpose was served by a similar outline by Otto Peterka, *Rechtsgeschichte der böhmischen Länder* (Reichenberg, Gebrüder Stiepel, 1923-1928, 2 v.). It covers the period to the reign of Maria Theresa in the second half of the 18th century.

A great classic in this field, however, was Josef Kalousek's *České státní právo; historický výklad* (Bohemian constitutional law; a historical exposé), 2d enl. and rev. ed. (Praha, Bursík a Kohout, 1892, 653 p.). First published in 1871. Written in defense of the rights of the Bohemian Crown vis-à-vis the Habsburg dynasty, it played an important role in the struggles for Bohemian statehood before 1918.

An outline of legal and constitutional history covering the whole territory of Czechoslovakia was Václav Vaněček's book *Malé dějiny státu a práva v Československu* (A concise history of state and law in Czechoslovakia) (Praha, Státní nakladatelství, 1947, 210 p.). It was republished in 1955 and 1961 under slightly different titles, but in a rigid Marxist version which it retained also in the greatly enlarged third edition, published under the title *Dějiny státu a práva v Československu do roku 1945* (History of state and law in Czechoslovakia to 1945) (Praha, Orbis, 1964, 617 p., illus., facsims., maps).

2. Economic History

726. Krofta, Kamil. Dějiny selského stavu (History of the peasantry). 2d ed., edited and enlarged by Emanuel Janoušek. Praha, Jan Laichter, 1949. 458 p. Facsims.

A classic outline of the history of the Czech peasantry emphasizing legal aspects of its development. First published in 1919 as a reprint of a series of the author's articles in *Agrární archiv* (Agrarian archive), I-IV (1914-1918).

Economic aspects were emphasized by Alois Míka in a survey of Czech agricultural production to 1848, *Nástin vývoje zemědělské výroby v českých zemích v epoše feudalismu* (An outline of the development of agricultural production in the Czech lands in the epoch of feudalism) (Praha, Státní pedagogické nakladatelství, 1960, 237 p.).

727. Roubík, František. Z českých hospodářských dějin; přehled vývoje českého průmyslu, obchodu, měny a dopravy (From Czech economic history; an outline of the development of Czech industry, commerce, finance, and transportation). Praha, Státní nakladatelství, 1948. 146 p. Bibliography: p. 147-154.

The only available outline of Czech economic history in these fields. For individual fields only two general surveys have been published so far:

Kořan, Jan. Přehledné dějiny československého hornictví (A survey of the history of the Czechoslovak mining industry). Praha, Nakladatelství Československé akademie věd, 1955– The first, and thus far only, volume covers developments to 1848.

Janáček, Josef. Přehled vývoje řemeslné výroby v českých zemích za feudalismu (A survey of the development of handicraft industry in the Czech lands during feudalism). Praha, Státní pedagogické nakl., 1963. 288 p. Illus., facsims., maps. Bibliography: p. 286-288.

3. Ethnic Group Relations

728. Pražák, Albert. Československý národ (The Czechoslovak nation). Bratislava, Nakl. Akademie, 1925. 68 p. (Sbírka přednášek a rozprav Extense University Komenského v Bratislavě, sv. 10)

One of a number of the author's outlines of Czecho-Slovak relations in history, claiming that the linguistic and cultural affinity of the Czechs and Slovaks had been so close that they must be considered as branches of the same nation, the Czechoslovak nation. Similar views were expounded by a number of Czech and Slovak historians, particularly Kamil Krofta and Václav Chaloupecký, while others remained opposed to them. More recently all of them have come to treat the Czechs and Slovaks as separate nations without denying their close affinity. Good evidence for this is provided by the following two collective works:

Slovenská akadémia vied. *Historický ústav.* O vzájomných vztahoch Čechov a Slovákov; sborník materiálov z konferencie Historického ústavu SAV (18.-21. IV. 1956) (About mutual relations between Czechs and Slovaks; a collection of materials from the conference of the Historical Institute of the Slovak Academy of Sciences [18-21 April 1956]). Edited by L'udovít Holotík. Bratislava, Slovenská akadémia vied, 1956. 450 p.

Sjazd slovenských historikov, *5th, Banská Bystrica, Czechoslovak Republic, 1965.* Slováci a ich národný vývin; sborník materiálov z V. sjazdu slovenských historikov (Slovaks and their national evolution; a collection of materials from the Fifth Congress of Slovak Historians). Edited by Alžbeta Ondrušová. Bratislava, Slovenská akadémia vied, 1966. 292 p.

Similar conclusions were drawn also by a Dutch and a Hungarian historian in these books:

Locher, Theodor J. G. Die nationale Differenzierung und Integrierung der Slowaken und Tschechen in ihrem geschichtlichen Verlauf bis 1848. Haarlem, H. D. Tjelenk Willink, 1931. 208 p.

Gogolák, Lajos (Ludwig von). Die Nationswerdung der Slowaken und die Anfänge der tschechoslowakischen Frage, 1526-1790. München, R. Oldenbourg, 1963. 265 p. (Buchreihe der Südostdeutschen Historischen Kommission, Bd. 7) This is volume one of the author's *Beiträge zur Geschichte des slowakischen Volkes.*

729. Krofta, Kamil. Das Deutschtum in der tschechoslowakischen Geschichte; zwei Vorträge gehalten in der Prager Urania am 16. April und 16. Mai 1934. 2d ed. Prag, Orbis, 1936. 146 p.

See also entry no. 653.

A balanced survey of positive and negative factors in the relations of Czechs and Germans. First published in 1934.

A representative work of a number of Sudeten German historians, proudly surveying the fortunes and achievements of the German minority in Bohemia and Moravia, is *Das Sudetendeutschtum; Sein Wesen und Werden im Wandel der Jahrhunderte*, edited by G. Pirchan, W. Weizsäcker, and H. Zatschek (Brünn, R. M. Rohrer, 1937, 595 p.). Marred by a strong bias of some contributions, which was further strengthened in its second revised edition published in 1939 (Brünn, R. M. Rohrer, 1939, 671 p.).

Many correctives of past errors and interpretations in this field are provided in the outstanding work by Ernst Schwarz, *Volkstumsgeschichte der Sudetenländer* (München, Lerche, 1965-1966, 2 v., illus., map).

A similar goal was pursued with success by the collective work of a number of German and Czech historians investigating past contacts and conflicts of Czechs and Germans within and outside the boundaries of the Czech lands, *Aus 500 Jahren deutsch-tschechoslowakischer Geschichte*, edited by Karl Obermann and Josef Polišenský (Berlin, Rütten & Loening, 1958, 432 p.; Schriftenreihe der Kommission der Historiker der DDR und der ČSR, Bd. 1)

730. Florovskii, Anton Vasil'evich. Chekhi i vostochnye Slaviane; ocherki po istorii cheshsko-russkikh otnoshenii (X-XVIII. vv.) (The Czechs and the Eastern Slavs; studies in the history of Czech-Russian relations [10th-18th centuries]). Praha, Orbis, 1935-1947. 2 v. (Práce Slovanského ústavu v Praze, sv. 13, 20)

The best work on the political, economic, and cultural relations of Czechs and Russians to the 18th century by an outstanding expert who also published several other monographs on this subject.

As a sample of a number of works that have been published recently on this subject one can also refer to Ivan Pfaff's *Tradice česko-ruských vztahů v dějinách* (The tradition of Czech-Russian relations in history) (Praha, Svobodné Slovo-Melantrich, 1957, 298 p).

Since 1958 the Československo-sovětsky institut of the Czechoslovak Academy of Sciences has published an irregular review, *Kapitoly z dějin vzájemných vztahů národů ČSR a SSSR* (Chapters from the history of the mutual relations between the nations of the Czechoslovak Republic and the USSR).

731. Československá akademie věd. *Ústav dějin evropských socialistických zemí.* Češi a Poláci v minulosti (Czechs and Poles in the past). Praha, Nakl. Československé akademie věd, 1964-1967. 2 v. Illus., facsims., maps, bibliographies.

See also entry no. 122.

A collection of contributions on the history of Czechs and Poles and their mutual relations. A similar collection published on the occasion of the millennium of the Polish state is *Tisíc let česko-polské vzájemnosti* (One thousand years of Czech-Polish solidarity) (Opava, Slezský ústav ČSAV, 1966-1967, 2 v.).

Slovak historians contributed a volume of their own to this occasion, *Poliaci a my; K tisícročnej tradícii slovensko-polských vzťahov* (The Poles and ourselves; on the millennial tradition of Slovak-Polish relations), edited by V. Borodovčák and others (Bratislava, Osveta, 1964, 199 p., illus., facsims., ports.; bibliography: p. 189-199).

G. PREHISTORY AND EARLY HISTORY

732. Filip, Jan. Pravěké Československo; Úvod do studia dějin pravěku (Prehistoric Czechoslovakia; introduction to the study of prehistory). Praha, Společnost čs. prehistoriků, 1948. 417 p. Illus., maps. (Výhledy do pravěku evropského lidstva, sv. 3-6. Stopami věku, sv. 19-22)

A survey of prehistory and early history of the territory of Czechoslovakia, based mainly on past achievements of Czechoslovak archaeology and written by one of its masters.

A collective work based on more recent achievements and written in Marxist terminology is the book edited by Jiří Neústupný, *Pravěk Československa* (Prehistory of Czechoslovakia) (Praha, Orbis, 1960, 490 p.).Evžen and Jiří Neústupný published in English summary of the same subject under the title *Czechoslovakia before the Slavs* (London, Thames and Hudson, 1961, 255 p. Ancient Peoples and Places, v. 22).

733. Píč, Josef Ladislav. Starožitnosti země české (Antiquities of Bohemia). Praha, Nákladem vlastním, 1899-1909. 3 v. in 6. Illus., plates, maps.

An inventory of the antiquities of Bohemia with a summary of its prehistory and early history to the 11th century, unfortunately too presuming in some of its conclusions. A revision of this work was attemped by Albín Stocký in his *Pravěk země české* (Prehistory of Bohemia) (Praha, Národní museum, 1926, 199 p., 122 pl.), but volume 1, the only one published, covered only the paleolithic period.

A prehistory of Moravia was published by Innocenc Ladislav Červinka in his *Morava za pravěku* (Moravia in prehistoric times) (Brno, Musejní spolek, 1902, 368 p., 52 pl., 4 maps). Unfortunately, his attempt to create a work on Moravian antiquities comparable to that of Píč did not reach beyond a single volume; neither did his intention to write a prehistory of both Bohemia and Moravia. However, the latter task was accomplished by Josef Schranil in a survey written in German, *Die Vorgeschichte Böhmens und Mährens* (Berlin, W. de Gruyter, 1929, 374 p., illus.). A number of Germans wrote on prehistory and early history of Bohemia and Moravia as well, usually emphasizing the extent and duration of Germanic settlements there.

For Slovakia an excellent survey of prehistory was published by Jan Eisner in his *Slovensko v pravěku* (Slovakia in prehistoric times), (Bratislava, Učená společnost Šafaříkova, 1933, 380 p., illus., plates, fold. map. Práce Učené společnosti Šafaříkovy v Bratislave, sv. 13).

734. Dobiáš, Josef. Dějiny československého území před vystoupením Slovanů (History of the Czechoslovak territory before the appearance of the Slavs). Praha, Nakl. Československé akademie věd, 1964. 475 p. Illus., maps. English summary: p. 345-390. Bibliography: p. 391-442.

An excellent survey of early history of the territory of Czechoslovakia and its contacts with the Roman Empire at the time when it was occupied by Celtic and Germanic tribes, by an outstanding expert in ancient history.

Roman influences in Bohemia were studied by another authority in ancient history, Bedřich Svoboda, in his *Čechy a římské Imperium* (Bohemia and the Roman Empire) (Praha, Národní museum, 1948, 252 p., 24 pl. Sborník Národního musea, sv. 2- A. Historie). He continued the story of the country in his *Čechy v době stěhování národů* (Bohemia in the times of the migration of nations) (Praha, Academia, 1965, 375 p., 111 pl., maps. Monumenta Archeologica, t. 13).

735. Filip, Jan. Počátky slovanského osídlení v Československu (The beginnings of Slavic settlement in Czechoslovakia). Praha, Společnost přátel starožitností, 1946. 96 p. Illus., maps. (Knihovna Společnosti přatel starožitností, 1946, c. 5)

An expert tracing of the first Slavic settlements on the territory of Czechoslovakia belonging to the Lusatian culture.

The same subject was covered more extensively by Helmut Preidel in his book *Die Anfänge der slawischen Besiedlung Böhmens und Mährens* (Gräfelfing bei München, E. Gans, 1954-1957, 2 v.).

736. Památky archeologické a místopisné (Archaeological and topographical memorials). 1854– Praha, Národní museum.

The oldest, and still the leading, journal of Czechoslovak archaeology, now published by the Czechoslovak Academy of Sciences. Since volume 25 (1913) appearing as *Památky archeologické.* Since 1949 the Academy has also published a bimonthly periodical *Archeologické rozhledy* (Archaeological observations), more responsive to current developments in the field. On the other hand, *Zprávy Československé společnosti archeologické* (The newsletter of the Czechoslovak Archaeological Society) is more a professional bulletin of Czechoslovak archaeologists.

The National Museum of Prague has published since 1958 *Fontes Archeologici Pragenses*, while *Slovenská archeológia* (Slovak archaeology) has been an official journal of the Slovak Academy of Sciences since 1953.

Large monographs are published in the irregular series *Monumenta Archeologica* by the Czechoslovak Academy of Sciences since 1948; and *Archaeologica Slovaca* by the Slovak Academy since 1957.

Older periodicals in this field that still deserve attention include *Pravěk* (Prehistory) (v. 1-9, 1903-1933); *Sudeta; Zeitschrift für Vor- und Frühgeschichte* (v. 1-14, n.s. 1-2, 1925-1942); *Anthropozoikum* (v. 1-11, 1951-1961); and also *Obzor prehistorický* (Prehistoric review (v. 1-14, 1922-1950), which should not be confused with a bulletin of the same title that was a newsletter of the Society of Friends of Czech Antiquities (Společnost přátel starožitností) and was published as a supplement to the Society's journal *Časopis* between 1910 and 1914.

H. MEDIEVAL HISTORY

1. General Surveys

737. Novotný, Václav, Kamil Krofta, *and* Josef Macek, *eds.* České dějiny (Czech history). Praha, Jan Laichter, and Nakladatelství Československé akademie věd, 1912-1966. 3 v. in 16 pts.

A monumental work of Czech historiography. Planned to be the most comprehensive scholarly survey of the whole of Czech history, it covers almost 12,000 pages, but brings it only to 1462 and most probably will remain torso owing to little sympathy for the project among Marxist directors of Czech historiography today. Individual volumes were written by such outstanding historians as Václav Novotný (to 1271), Josef Šusta (1272-1355), František M. Bartoš (1378-1437), Rudolf Urbánek (1438-1462), and Josef V. Šimák, who completed Václav Novotný's assignment by a special volume on internal colonization of Bohemia. The period 1355-1378 was not completed owing to the death of Josef Šusta.

The greatest classic of Czech historiography, of course, is František Palacký's *Dějiny národu českého v Čechách a v Moravě* (History of the Czech nation in Bohemia and Moravia) (Praha, J. G. Kalve and Bedřich Tempský, 1848-1867, 5 v.). Originally started in German in 1836. The best of several revised editions is the third, edited in 1876-1878 by Josef Kalousek. Covering Czech history only to 1526 and considerably dated today, it played an important role in the Czech national revival by giving the Czech people a historical basis for their claims to statehood. Several attempts to write a German pendant to Palacký's work by such historians as Adolf Bachmann, Beda Dudik, and Bertold Bretholz, though equally dated and loaded with nationalist sentiment, are still worthy of attention.

An attempt to suggest a Marxist interpretation of the Czech history to the high Middle Ages is Zdeněk Nejedlý's *Dějiny národa českého* (History of the Czech nation) (Praha, Svoboda, Státní nakladatelství politické literatury, 1949-1955, 2 v.).

738. Varsík, Branislav, *ed.* Slovenské dejiny (Slovak history). Bratislava, Slovenská akadémia vied a umení, 1947-1951. 2 v. Illus., fold, col. maps. (Vlastivedná knižnica Slovenskej akadémie vied a umení, sv. 3)

A representative survey of Slovak history by prominent Slovak historians. Originally planned for the whole of Slovak history in eight volumes, but covers it only to the tenth century.

A good older, though much debated, work covering Slovak history to the thirteenth century is Václav Chaloupecký's *Staré Slovensko* (Old Slovakia) (Bratislava, Universita Komenského, 1924, 424 p., maps. Universita Komenského v Bratislave. Filosofická fakulta. Spisy. Číslo 3).

2. Studies of Individual Periods or Topics

739. Československá akademie věd. *Archeologický ústav. Pobočka v Brně.* Das Grossmährische Reich; Tagung der wissenschaftlichen Konferenz des Archäologischen Instituts der Tschechoslowakischen Akademie der Wissenschaften, Brno-Nitra, 1.-4. X., 1963. Praha, Akademia, 1966. 444 p., 16 pl.

A collection of papers relating to the history of Great Moravia, the first major statelike formation on the territory of Czechoslovakia, presented in the German, French, and Russian languages at a special conference organized by the Czechoslovak Academy of Sciences in Brno and Nitra. Based on past studies and most recent, often spectacular, archaeological discoveries.

The arrival of Slavic apostles Constantine and Methodius to Moravia in 863, a decisive moment in the cultural history of the Czechs and Slovaks, was commemorated by another collection of papers edited by Josef Macůrek under the title *Magna Moravia; Sborník k 1100. výročí příchodu byzantské mise na Moravu* (Magna Moravia; a memorial on the 1110th anniversary of the arrival of the Byzantine mission to Moravia) (Státní nakladatelství pedagogické, 1965, 639 p., plates. Spisy University J. E. Purkyně v. Brně. Filosofická Fakulta, 102).

The most comprehensive collection of historical sources relating to Great Moravia is being published under the title *Magnae Moraviae Fontes Historici; Prameny k dějinám Velké Moravy* (Brno, 1966– Universita J. E. Purkyně v Brně. Filosofická Fakulta, 104–). Four volumes are planned.

In Bohemia's early history similar attention was paid to Saint Wenceslas, the Duke of Bohemia at the beginning of the tenth century, whose martyr's death in 929 was commemorated by a collective work of prominent Czechoslovak medievalists summarizing results of numerous studies on the saintly duke issued by the Národní výbor pro oslavu svatováclavského tisíciletí under the title *Svatováclavský sborník; na památku 1000. výročí smrti knížete Václava Svatého* (Saint Wenceslas memorial; in commemoration of the 1000th anniversary of the death of Duke Wenceslas the Saint), edited by Jan Kapras, Karel Stloukal, and Antonín Novák (Praha, 1934-1939, 2 v. in 3).

740. Fiala, Zdeněk. Přemyslovské Čechy; Český stát a společnost v letech 995-1310 (Přemyslid Bohemia; Czech state and society in the years 995-1310). Praha, Nakl. politické literatury, 1965. 221 p. Illus., facsims., geneal. table.

A general survey of the history of Czech lands under the Přemyslid dynasty, based on a thorough knowledge of sources and secondary literature and considerably freer from the gross deformations usual in earlier Marxist historiography. Continued in his *Předhusitské Čechy, 1310-1419* (Prehussite Bohemia, 1310-1419) (Praha, Svoboda, 1968, 272 p.).

Economic and religious problems leading to the Hussite revolution were the most frequent subjects of monographs on this period. František Graus applied Marxist yardsticks to class relations in the Czech countryside in his *Dějiny venkovského lidu v Čechách v době předhusitské* (History of the rural people in Bohemia in the prehussite time) (Praha, Státní nakl. politické literatury and Československá akademie věd, 1953-1957, 2 v.). He further wrote a book on class problems in the cities on which we also have an excellent older study by Bedřich Mendl, *Sociální krise a zápasy v městech čtrnáctého věku* (Social crises and struggles in the cities of the 14th century) (Praha, Historický klub, 1926, 203 p.).

Among religious surveys of this period there still stands out Václav Novotný's *Náboženské hnutí české ve XIV. a XV. století; I. Do Husa* (Czech religious movement in the 14th and 15th centuries; I. To Hus) (Praha, J. Otto, 1915, 281 p. Universita Karlova, Sbírka přednášek a rozprav, ser. 6, č. 10).

741. Novotný, Václav, *and* Vlastimil Kybal. M. Jan Hus; Život a učení M. Jan Hus; life and teaching). Praha, Laichter, 1919-1931. 2 v. in 5.

The most extensive treatment of the life and theology of this famous Bohemian reformer of the 14th century, which shows that he was much less a heretic than had been assumed. The work aroused a lively polemic from Catholic writers, but more recently Paul de Vooght, a Belgian Catholic scholar, has come to a similar conclusion in his *L'hérésie de Jean Hus* (Louvain, Bureaux de la Revue, Bibliothèque de l'Université, Publications universitaires de Louvain, 1960, 494 p. Bibliothèque de la Revue d'histoire ecclésiastique, fasc. 34).

Several past attempts to publish all works of Hus will now be superseded by the most comprehensive and critical edition of his works, published under the title *Magistri Ioannis Hus Opera omnia; Spisy Mistra Jana Husa* (Praha, Československá akademie věd, 1959–). Only volumes 7 and 22 out of a total of 25 planned have been published to date.

742. Pekař, Josef. Žižka a jeho doba (Žižka and his time). Praha, Vesmír, 1927-1933. 4 v. Map.

The most extensive and learned, though controversial, work on this military leader of the Hussites and Hussite wars, challenging older interpretations by František Palacký and Vráclav V. Tomek, but subjected to lively dispute by Kamil Krofta, Jan Slavík, František M. Bartoš, and a host of Marxist writers.

A middle road between these interpretations was attempted by Frederick G. Heymann in his *John Žižka and the Hussite Revolution* (Princeton, N.J., Princeton University Press, 1955, 521 p., 4 plates, maps). Howard Kaminsky traced the ideological development of the Hussite movement from the precursors of Hus to the death of Žižka in 1424 in his study, *A History of the Hussite Revolution* (Berkeley, University of California Press, 1967, 580 p., maps).

For a sample of a Marxist interpretation of the Hussite movement *see* Josef Macek's *Husitské revoluční hnutí* (The Hussite revolutionary movement) (Praha, Rovnost, 1952, 203 p., maps). Available also in German, Russian, and Hungarian translations.

The much debated problem of Hussite influences in Slovakia has recently been thoroughly reinvestigated by one of its most active students, Branislav Varsík, in his *Husitské revolučné hnutie a Slovensko* (The Hussite revolutionary movement and Slovakia) (Bratislava, Slovenská akadémia vied, 1965, 374 p., maps; bibliography: p. 344-350. Publikácie Slovenskej historickej spoločnosti pri Slovenskej akadémii vied, 9).

743. Heymann, Frederick G. George of Bohemia; King of Heretics. Princeton, N.J., Princeton University Press, 1965. 671 p. Plates, maps. Bibliography: p. 621-655.

A meticulous, richly documented study of the Hussite king George of Poděbrady. Equally outstanding, though more interpretive in nature and emphasizing international perspectives of the Hussite movement, is Otakar Odložilík's *The Hussite King; Bohemia in European Affairs, 1440-1471* (New Brunswick, N.J., Rutgers University Press, 1965, 337 p., plates, maps).

One of the best histories of the Unity of Czech Brethren, a religious group originated in this period, is Rudolf Říčan's *Dějiny Jednoty bratrské* (History of the Unity of Brethren) (Praha, Kalich, 1957, 518 p.). Available also in a shortened German version.

Political and social doctrines of this church were ably expounded in Peter Brock's *The Political and Social Doctrines of the Unity of Czech Brethren in the Fifteenth and Early Sixteenth Centuries* (The Hague, Mouton, 1957, 302 p. Slavistic Printings and Reprintings, 11).

744. Truhlář, Josef. Počátky humanismu v Čechách (The beginnings of Humanism in Bohemia). Praha, Nákl. České akademie Císaře Františka Josefa pro vědy, slovesnost a umění, 1892. 51 p. (Rozpravy České akademie Císarě Františka Josefa pro vědy, slovesnost a umění v Praze. Roč. 1, třída 3, čís. 3)

Continued in his *Humanismus a humanisté v Čechách za krále Vladislava II* (Humanism and humanists in Bohemia in the time of King Vladislav II) (Praha, Nákl. České akademie císarě Františka Josefa pro vědy, slovesnost a umění, 1894, 208 p. Česká akademie věd a umění, Praha. Třída 3. Rozpravy, roč. 3, čís. 4). The two volumes offer a balanced survey of the development of Bohemian humanism from its beginnings in the second half of the 14th century to the end of the 15th century.

Early humanism in Bohemia was also highly appraised in a recent study by Eduard Winter, *Frühhumanismus; seine Entwicklung in Böhmen und deren europäische Bedeutung für die Kirchenreformbestrebungen im 14. Jahrhundert* (Berlin, Akademie-Verlag, 1964, 236 p. Beiträge zur Geschichte des religiösen und wissenschaftlichen Denkens, Bd. 3).

Academia Istropolitana, a humanistic center of higher studies in Bratislava, was the subject of a collective study of Slovak historians, *Humanizmus a renesancia na Slovensku v 15.-16. storočí* (Humanism and the Renaissance in Slovakia in the 15th and 16th centuries) (Bratislava, Slovenská akadémia vied 1967, 552 p., illus.).

I. MODERN HISTORY, 1471-1750

745. Denis, Ernest. Fin de l'indépendence bohême. Paris, A. Colin, 1890. 2 v.

Continued in his *La Bohême depuis la Montagne Blanche* (Paris, E. Leroux, 1903, 2 v.). The two works represent a fairly detailed survey of modern Czech history from the middle of the 15th century to the closing decades of the 19th century. Based on a thorough knowledge of sources and literature of the time, it is still useful in the absence of other such surveys in Western languages. The Czech editions of these works, *Konec samostatnosti české*, 2d rev. ed. (Praha, F. Simáček, 1909, 469 p.) and *Čechy po Bílé Hoře* (Praha, Bursík a Kohout, 1904-1905, 2 v.), include corrections and notes by the translator and editor, Jindřich Vančura.

Monographic surveys of this period include Otto Placht's *Lidnatost a společenská skladba českého státu v 16.-18. století* (The population and social structure of the Czech state in the 16th-18th centuries) (Praha, Nakl. Československé akademie věd, 1957, 366 p.), and an investigation of agrarian developments from the 15th to the 19th centuries by Václav Černý, based on economic instructions of noble estate owners to their bailiffs.

A survey of Slovak history from 1514 to 1848 emphasizing economic developments is the work of Štefan Janšák, *Slovensko v dobe uhorského feudalizmu* (Slovakia in the time of Hungarian feudalism) (Bratislava, Nakl. Kuratoria Čs. zemedel. muzea, 1932, 298 p., illus.).

746. Macůrek, Josef, and Miloš Rejnuš. České země a Slovensko ve století před Bílou Horou (The Czech Lands and Slovakia in the century before the White Mountain). Praha, Státní pedagogické nakladatelství, 1958. 418 p.

A solid scholarly study of the social, economic, and political development of the Czech lands and Slovakia and their mutual relations from the beginning of the 16th century to the battle on the White Mountain in 1620, which seriously affected the independence of the Czech state. A collection of documents on this subject fills pages 171-392. Most other works on this period were concerned only with the Czech lands.

In the political field these focused on the problem of the accession of the Habsburgs to the throne of Bohemia in 1526 and the gradual extension of their control of the state institutions. They were written by such historians as Antonín Rezek, Karol Tieftrunk, and František Roubík, while the important question of national relations in the state was studied by Josef Klik in his *Národnostní poměry v Čechách od válek husitských do bitvy bělohorské* (National conditions in Bohemia from the Hussite Wars to the Battle of the White Mountain) (Praha, Historický klub, 1922, 176 p.).

In the social and economic field Antonín Gindely, Kamil Krofta, Otto Placht, Václav Pešák, and Miloslav Volf wrote important studies on the financial problems of the state. František Teplý, František Hrubý, Alois Mika, Josef Petráň, and František Matějek studied developments in Czech agriculture, while Zikmund Winter and Josef

Janáček investigated the evolution of trade and industry in this period. A contribution to Slovak history in this field is Peter Ratkoš' *Povstanie baníkov na Slovensku, 1525-1526* (The uprising of the miners in Slovakia, 1525-1526) (Bratislava, Vydavatel'stvo Slovenskej akadémie vied, 1963, 340 p., illus.; bibliography: p. 296-299). Ratkoš also published a volume of documents relating to this event.

In the religious field a general survey for this period is Zikmund Winter's *Život církevní v Čechách; kulturně-historický obraz z XV. a XVI století* (Church life in Bohemia; cultural-historical portrayal from the 15th and 16th centuries) (Praha, Česká akademie císaře Františka Josefa pro vědy, slovesnost a umění, 1895-1896, 2 v.). Historians such as Antonín Gindely, Ferdinand Hrejsa, Jaroslav Bidlo, and Amedeo Molnár followed up the development of the Unity of the Czech Brethren, while František Kryštůfek, František Hrubý, Otakar Odložilík, Václav Husa, and Rudolf Říčan studied introduction of Protestant reformation to Bohemia and Moravia. Ján Kvačala wrote on the Reformation in Slovakia from 1517-1711.

The cultural atmosphere in the Czech lands was described in Zikmund Winter's *Kulturní obraz českých měst; život veřejný v XV. a XVI. věku* (Cultural picture of Czech cities; public life in the 15th and 16th centuries) (Praha, Matice česká, 1890-1892, 2 v.). Winter also published two volumes on secondary education and higher education in Bohemia in this period, while Josef Volf, Zdeněk V. Tobolka, and Čeněk Zíbrt wrote on the beginnings of Czech book printing.

747. Gindely, Antonín. Dějiny českého povstání léta 1618 (History of the Czech Uprising of 1618). Praha, B. Tempský, 1870-1880. 4 v.

A classic work on the Czech revolt against the Habsburgs that was a starting point of the Thirty Years War. Available in German as *Geschichte des dreissigjährigen Krieges* (Prag, F. Tempský, 1869-1880, 4 v. in 2). Gindely also published a more general survey of this war in both languages. Josef Dobiáš investigated treasonable trends in the Czech uprising, while František Hrubý, F. Dostál, and Otakar Odložilík traced its fortunes in Moravia. Other authors studied the attitude of foreign powers to the uprising, Spain (Bohdan Chudoba), England and the Netherlands (Josef Polišenský), and Poland (Josef Macůrek). An attempt to challenge the general view that the debâcle of the White Mountain was the root of everything bad in modern Czech history was made by Josef Pekař in his *Bílá hora; její příčiny a následky* (White Mountain; its causes and consequences) (Praha, "Vesmír," 1921, 159 p.).

Later stages of the war were studied by Antonín Rezek, Josef Pekař, and Otakar Odložilík. Registers of documents relating to the war were published by Václav Líva in a vast collection entitled *Prameny k dějinám třicetileté války; Regesta Fondu Militare Archivu Ministerstva vnitra ČSR v Praze* (Sources on the history of the Thirty Years War; regests of the military fund of the archives of the Ministry of Interior of the Czechoslovak Republic in Prague) (Praha, Naše vojsko, 1951-1957, 6 v.; Prameny k československým dějinám vojenským, sv. 3-8).

748. Pekař, Josef. Valdštejn, 1630-1634; dějiny valdštejnského spiknutí (Wallenstein, 1630-1634; history of the Wallenstein conspiracy). 2d rev. ed. Praha, Melantrich, 1933-1934. 2 v. Illus., ports., maps, facsims.

By far the best work on this military genius of the Thirty Years War. First published in 1895. Also available in a shortened and revised German edition, *Wallenstein 1630-1634; Tragödie einer Verschwörung* (Berlin, A. Metzner, 1937, 2 v.). Important contributions on the activities of Wallenstein as far as they were related to Czech history were also made by Cyrill Straka, František Roubík, Václav Letošník, and R. Maršan.

Other important personalities of the Thirty Years War from the Czech lands — Jindřich Matyáš Thurn, Ladislav Velen of Žerotín, and Karel Starší of Žerotín — found their biographers in P. Chlumecký, František Hrubý, and Otakar Odložilík. The vast correspondence of Karel Starší of Žerotín, an outstanding figure in European politics, was published by Vincenc Brandl and František Dvorský. A biography of a Slovak participant in the Czech uprising was published by Mária Bokesová-Uherová in her *Ján Jessenius, 1566-1621* (Bratislava, Slovenská akadémia vied, 1967, 67 p.).

749. Novák, Jan V., *and* Josef Hendrich. Jan Amos Komenský; jeho život a spisy (Jan Amos Komenský; his life and works). Praha, Dědictví Komenského, 1932. 722 p. (Příležitostné vzdělávací spisy: "Dědictví Komenského," čís. 214)

The best biography of Comenius — the famous bishop of the Czech Brethren, educator, and humanist of the 17th century and subject of a vast number of works by writers of many nations. A complete bibliography of works by and on Comenius fills much of the huge fifth volume of Čeněk Zíbrt's *Bibliografie české historie* (*see* entry 693), and many more works have been published since. In the English language the best survey of his life and work is Matthew Spinka's *John Amos Comenius, That Incomparable Moravian* (Chicago, University of Chicago Press, 1943, 177 p.; bibliography: p. 156-170).

Among the most devoted students of Komenský was Ján Kvačala, a Slovak educator, who after 1922, edited the periodical — published in Brno since 1910 — *Archiv pro bádání o životě a díle J. A. Komenského* (Archives for research on the life and work of J. A. Komenský). In 1957, starting with volume 16, it was converted into an international organ of Comenian studies and has been published since then in Prague under the title *Acta Comeniana; Archiv pro bádání o životě a díle J. A. Komenského.* In Germany a similar purpose was pursued by the Comenius-Gesellschaft in Berlin, which published a periodical from 1893-1934 under the successive titles of *Mitteilungen, Comenius-Blätter, Monatsschriften,* and *Geisteskultur,* with a supplement *Comenius-Schriften zur Geistesgeschichte,* which served also for the purposes of general enlightenment.

Kvačala also, in cooperation with Jan V. Novák, Stanislav Souček, and others, made an attempt to publish the complete works of Comenius under the title *Veškeré spisy Jana Amosa Komenského* (Brno,

Ústřední spolek jednot učitelských na Moravě, 1910-1929, 8 v.). However, only 8 of the 30 volumes planned were published and the project will be superseded by a completely new and critical edition of his works in 43 volumes by the Czechoslovak Academy of Sciences under the title *Johannis Amos Comenii Opera Omnia.* The first volume was scheduled for late 1968.

750. Rezek, Antonín, *and others.* Dějiny Čech a Moravy nové doby (History of Bohemia and Moravia in the new era). Praha, I. L. Kober, 1892-1905. 10 v.

A detailed survey of Czech history from 1648 to 1815. In principle a recast reprint of volumes 6-8 of Karel Zap's *Česko-moravská kronika* (entry no. 723). A Marxist interpretation of the period of "darkness" between the Thirty Years War and the national revival at the end of the 18th century was attempted by Arnošt Klíma in his *Čechy v období temna* (Bohemia in the time of darkness), 2d rev. and enl. ed. (Praha, Státní pedagogické nakl., 1961, 263 p.). Numerous monographs were devoted to individual aspects of this period.

Václav V. Tomek, Antonín Rezek, Jaroslav Prokeš, František Čáda, Jan Muk, and Václav Líva studied the legal and political consequences of the Czech defeat at the White Mountain, especially the assertion of Habsburg power over the Czech state and the influx of foreign nobility and middle class, particularly German, into the country.

The forceful recatholicization of the country was the subject of works by many other authors. Most active among them, perhaps, was Tomáš V. Bílek, who set the basic tone for such studies in his *Reformace katolická; neboli Obnovení náboženství katolického v království českém po bitvě na Bílé hoře* (The Catholic Reformation; or Restoration of the Catholic religion in the Kingdom of Bohemia after the battle of the White Mountain) (Praha, F. Bačkovský, 1892, 336 p.). Hynek Kollmann edited documents of the Sacred Congregation for the Propaganda of the Faith relating to Bohemia, while Josef V. Šimák published confession lists of the archbishopric of Prague. Other important contributions on this subject were published by Antonín Gindely and Josef Hanuš.

In the economic field a number of works were written on the vast confiscations of properties of dead or exiled owners starting with Tomáš V. Bílek's *Dějiny konfiskací v Čechách po roku 1618* (History of the confiscations in Bohemia after 1618) (Praha, F. Řivnáč, 1882-1883, 2 v.). Other authors studied economic exploitation of the Czech lands by heavy taxation based on new cadasters of taxable properties on which Josef Pekař wrote the best study in his *České katastry, 1654-1789* (Czech cadasters, 1654-1789), 2d enl. ed. (Praha, Historický klub, 1932, 363 p.). Some data on these cadasters were published as:

Czechoslovak Republic. *Archív bývalé země české.* Berní rula (Tax register). Praha, 1949-1955. 16 v. These volumes were published before the project was temporarily abandoned.

Otakar Mrázek published a survey of industrial development of the Czech provinces from the manufacture period to 1918, while

Arnošt Klíma focused his attention on the manufacture period itself, which in the Czech lands extended from the middle of the 17th to the beginning of the 19th century. Numerous authors wrote on popular uprisings; most famous of these were the uprising of the Chods in western Bohemia which was studied by František Roubík and František Teplý, and the uprisings connected with so-called crusaders' wars (kurucké války) with the Turks in Slovakia, on which Bedřich Swieteczký wrote a monograph.

751. Kalista, Zdeněk. České baroko; studie, texty, poznámky (Czech Baroque; studies, texts, and comments). Praha, Evropský literární klub, 1941. 351 p. Illus.

A collection of works, mostly literary in nature, edited, commented on, and studied by the author to show that the period after the battle of the White Mountain was far less a period of "darkness" than had been often assumed. Similar works were produced by other authors. Kalista tried to make his point also in several monographs on the Černín (Czernin) family and in a gallery of personalities representative for this period, entitled somewhat boastfully, *Čechové kteří tvořili dějiny světa* (Czechs who made world history) (Praha, Českomoravský kompas, 1939, 236 p.). Bohuslav Balbín, a Jesuit, but an ardent patriot at the same time, was the subject of several studies by Václav Ryneš, Wladyslaw Bobek, and Kamil Krofta.

The Slovak authors Ján Ďurovič, Ján Oberuč, and Anton Baník wrote monographs on Juraj Tranovský, Matej Bel, and Ján Baltazár Magin, important personalities in Slovak national life in this period, while Branislav Varsík studied national conditions at the Jesuit university of Trnava.

J. MODERN HISTORY, 1750-1918*

752. Kárníková, Ludmila. Vývoj obyvatelstva v českých zemích, 1754-1914 (Development of the population in the Czech lands, 1754-1914). Praha, Nakladatelství Československé akademie věd, 1965. 401 p. Illus., map. Bibliography: p. 368-373.

See also entry no. 638.

A reliable survey based on census data and reflecting interaction of various economic, social, and political factors of this new and dynamic period of Czech history. Earlier, similar problems in Slovakia, with emphasis on changing national composition of its population, were studied by Aleksei L. Petrov in his work *Příspěvky k historické demografii Slovenska v 18. a 19. století* (Contributions to the historical demography of Slovakia in the 18th and 19th centuries) (Praha, Česká akademia věd a umění, 1928, 69, 330 p., maps). Branislav Varsík traced the development of the ethnic boundary between Slovaks and Hungarians from the 18th to the 20th century, as it was affected by such changes. Jozef Škultéty chronicled the evolution of the Slovak national life in the 125 years between 1790

* The arrangement in this section is chronological by coverage.

and 1914, while more recently František Červinka outlined the development of Czech nationalism in the 19th century. Ernst Birke and Kurt Oberdorffer edited a collection of mostly polemical papers of several Sudeten German writers on the Bohemian *Staatsrecht* in the Czech-German disputes of the 19th and 20th centuries. Oldřich Říha briefly outlined all these developments in an early Marxist interpretation of the economic, social, and political fortunes of the Czechs and Slovaks from 1790 to 1945.

753. Kerner, Robert J. Bohemia in the Eighteenth Century; a Study in Political, Economic and Social History; With Special Reference to the Reign of Leopold II, 1790-1792. New York, Macmillan, 1932. 412 p. Bibliography: p. 375-406.

The "special reference to the reign of Leopold II" fills most of the work, but the book does provide also an informed survey of, and insight into, the reigns of his predecessors, Maria Theresa and Josef II, whose reform activities contributed to the rise of Czech and Slovak national revival in the following period and attracted attention of numerous writers.

Agrarian reforms of the 18th century were studied by Karl Grünberg, Josef Kazimour, Jan Pocházka, Václav Černý, and Karol Rebro, while Archivní správa ministerstva vnitra published selected data from the Theresian cadasters for Bohemia and Moravia, an extremely important source for social and economic history of the period. Oldřich Janeček published a monograph on the peasant uprising of 1775 in Bohemia, on which we also have a collective work edited by Václav Husa and Josef Petrán. Miloslav Volf compiled an inventory of documents relating to the work of the Patriotic Economic Society (Vlastenecko-hospodářská společnost) for the economic, particularly agrarian, advancement of the country. Josef Kazimour published an excellent work on the state care for the forests in Bohemia from 1754 to the Napoleonic wars, while Ákoš Paulínyi wrote on mining and metallurgy in Slovakia at the turn of the 18th and 19th centuries. Karel Hoch ably surveyed all economic developments from Maria Theresa to 1848 in his *Čechy na prahu moderního hospodářství* (Bohemia at the threshold of modern economy) (Praha, A. Neubert, 1936, 289 p.).

In the religious field Ferdinand Hrejsa, Jan B. Čapek, Josef Lukášek, and Richard Pražák studied the movement for the Protestant emancipation and the Tolerance Patent of Josef II. František Bednář published documents relating to this movement in Moravia, whereas Antonín Rezek, Josef V. Šimák, and Karel Adámek edited several volumes of materials on various popular religious movements in Bohemia. František Roubík and Václav Žáček wrote on the situation of the Jews in Bohemia at the turn of the 18th and 19th centuries.

The cultural atmosphere of the period was captured by Arnošt Kraus in his work on the Theresian schools and by Josef Kalousek and Jaroslav Prokeš in their studies of the history of the Royal Bohemian Society of Sciences founded in 1774. Jiří Klabouch studied enlightened influences and trends in Czech law, Teodor Münz in

Slovak philosophy. František Kutnar and Květa Mejdřická measured the impact of the French revolution in the Czech lands.

Administrative changes effected by Maria Theresa and Josef II were studied by Jaroslav Prokeš and František Roubík. Among several studies of the policy of Germanization and Magyarization of the Czechs and Slovaks in this period, the best is Daniel Rapant's first major work, *K počiatkom maďarizácie* (On the beginnings of Magyarization) (Bratislava, Filosofická fakulta Univerzity Komenského, 1927-1931, 2 v.; Spisy Filozofickej fakulty Univerzity Komenského v Bratislave, čís. 8).

754. Pražák, Albert. České obrození (Czech revival). Praha, E. Beaufort, 1948. 430 p.

A balanced study of the revival of Czech national consciousness and culture at the end of the 18th and the first part of the 19th century by an eminent expert in literary history, who also published several other books on the subject. Marxist interpretations of this development include a study of social thought of this period by František Kutnar and an outline by Josef Kočí, *Naše národní obrození* (Our national revival) (Praha, Státní nakladatelství politické literatury, 1960, 251 p., illus.). Josef Hanuš and František Kop studied the role of the Czech National Museum, founded in 1818, in the advancement of Czech culture, on which we also have a collective work edited by Gustav Skalský. Karel Tieftrunk and Antonín Grund evaluated the role of "Matice česká," founded in 1831 to publish and disseminate works of scholarship and enlightenment. Josef Volf and Vladimír Klimeš wrote on Czech journalism in this period.

The political atmosphere of the period was captured by Josef Heidler in a study of Czech political pamphlets, and by Miloslav Novák in a monograph on Austrian police in Bohemia. Antonín Okáč wrote on the Bohemian diet and government prior to 1848, whereas Rudolf Dvořák published regests from the protocols of the Moravian diet in two volumes covering the years 1792-1848.

The movement for social and economic emancipation of Czech peasants was chronicled by František Kutnar, while Mořic Michálek edited a collection of biographies of "economic awakeners" active in this movement, as well as in general efforts to advance agriculture in the Czech lands. Such efforts were studied in detail by František Lom in a monograph on the organization of large estates. An inventory of documents on this last stage of feudalism in the Czech lands was published recently under the title *Soupis pramenů k dějinám feudálního útisku* (Inventory of documents for the history of feudal oppression) (Praha, Nakladatelství Československé akademie věd, 1954–).

Cooperation of Czechs and Slovaks during their national revival was surveyed by Jan Novotný, whereas Milan Hodža earlier wrote on the linguistic separation of the Slovaks from the Czechs in the 1840's. Contacts of Czechs and Slovaks with other Slavs were outlined by Miloš Weingart in general, while Vladimir A. Frantsev and Josef Jirásek concentrated on their relations with the Russians, and Marjan Szyjkowski and Józef Gołabek on the relations with the Poles. Karel

Paul published correspondence of Czech and Slovak writers with the South Slavs.

Equally important German contacts and influences were investigated by Eugen Lemberg, who focused his attention on the role of Josef Georg Meinert; and Eduard Winter, who wrote on, and published works of, Bernard Bolzano. Josef Pfitzner studied the German national revival in the Czech lands in his controversial work *Das Erwachen der Sudetendeutschen im Spiegel ihres Schrifttums bis zum Jahre 1848* (Augsburg, Stauda, 1926, 409 p.).

755. Československá akademie věd. *Sekce jazyka a literatury.* Josef Dobrovský, 1753-1953; sborník studií k dvoustému výročí narození (Josef Dobrovský, 1753-1953; a collection of studies on the bicentennial anniversary of his birth). Praha, Československá akademie věd, 1953. 592 p. Illus., ports.

Scholarly contributions on the life and work of this great figure of the Czech national revival based on most recent research. A similar collection, edited by Jiří Horák and others, was published in 1929 to commemorate the centennial anniversary of his death. Individual biographies of Dobrovský were published by Vincenc Brandl, Arne Novák and Josef Volf. More specialized monographs by Benjamin Jedlička, Miloš B. Volf and Josef Volf were appearing in an irregular series, *Archiv pro bádání o životě a díle Josefa Dobrovského* (Archives for research on the life and work of Josef Dobrovský) (Praha, Komise pro vydávání spisů Josefa Dobrovského při Královské české společnosti nauk, 1934-1935, 4 v.). Most of Dobrovský's works were published by the same society under the title *Spisy a projevy Josefa Dobrovského* (Works and papers of Josef Dobrovský) (Praha, Nakl. Komise pro vydávání spisů Josefa Dobrovského; v generální komisi nakl. Melantrich, 1936–). Fourteen volumes have appeared so far.

František Palacký, a famous historian and political leader of the Czechs, found his biographers in Václav Řezníček, Václav Chaloupecký, František Kutnar, and Emanuel Chalupný. Zdeněk V. Tobolka studied his political and historical work, Tomáš G. Masaryk his concept of the Czech nation, and Josef Fischer his whole work and thought in his formidable study *Myšlenka a dílo Františka Palackého* (The thought and work of František Palacký) (Praha, Čin, Tiskové a nakl. družstvo československých legionářů, 1926-1927, 3 v. in 2). Masaryk published a substantial study of Palacký's closest collaborator in his *Karel Havlíček; snahy a tužby politického probuzení* (Karel Havlíček; efforts and desires of the political revival), 2d rev. ed. (Praha, Nakl. J. Laichtera, 1904, 522 p.). Biographers and students of Havlíček include Emanuel Chalupný, Karel Kazbunda, Jaromír Bělič, Václav Procházka and Stanislav Budín. Zdeněk V. Tobolka published his political works in five volumes.

Other authors wrote on other important personalities of this period: Josef Dvorský on Count František J. Kinský, Stanislav Dvořák on František M. Pelcl, Jan Novotný on Václav M. Kramerius, Václav Zelený and Julius Dolanský on Josef Jungmann, Vincenc Brandl and Antonín Grund on Karel J. Erben. Václav Černý and Jaroslav Šťastný published correspondence and records of František L. Čelakovský. A collective work edited by František Páta and others was published on Jan. E. Purkyně, whose complete works have thus far appeared in ten volumes.

756. Várossová, Elena. Slovenské obrodenecké myslenie; Jeho zdroje a základné idey (The thought of the Slovak revival; its sources and fundamental ideas). Bratislava, Vydavatel'stvo Slovenskej akadémie vied, 1963. 220 p. Bibliography: p. 211-214. (Filozofická biblioteka, zv. 13)

An informed survey in a Marxist interpretation. The movement for concentration of all Slovak forces between 1780 and 1848 was studied by Jozef Butvín, while Ján Tibenský published a selection from Slovak literature praising or defending the Slovak nation. Persistent efforts to Magyarize the Slovaks in violation of existing laws were studied in another great work of Daniel Rapant, *Ilegálna maďarizácia, 1790-1840* (Illegal Magyarization, 1790-1840) (Turčianky Svätý Martin, Matica slovenská, 1947, 246 p.; Spisy historického odboru Matice slovenskej sv. 9). Rapant also wrote a work on the first major defensive action of the Slovaks, a petition to the imperial throne in 1842, while František Bokes traced the development of concepts of what Slovak territory was in the 19th century.

In the social and economic field, the best work again is a study of Daniel Rapant on the peasant uprising in eastern Slovakia in 1831. Ján Novotný published a survey of industrial development in Slovakia in this period, *Vývoj priemyselnej výroby na Slovensku v prvej polovici 19. storočia* (Development of industrial production in Slovakia in the first half of the 19th century) (Bratislava, Vydavatel'stvo Slovenskej akadémie věd, 1961, 278 p., illus., bibliography; Publikácie Slovenskej historickej spoločnosti pri Slovenskej akadémii vied, 5).

757. Slovenská akadémia vied. *Historický ústáv.* L'udovít Štúr; Život a dielo, 1818-1856; sborník materiálov z konferencie Historického ústavu SAV (L'udovít Štúr; life and work, 1818-1856; a collection of materials from a conference of the Historical Institute of the Slovak Academy of Sciences). Bratislava, Vydavatel'stvo Slovenskej akadémie vied, 1956. 519 p. Illus.

Studies of life and work of this greatest of Slovak "awakeners." Individual biographies or more specific studies of Štúr and his collaborators were written by Andrej Mráz, Vladimír Matula, Karel Goláň, L'udovít Bakoš, Samuel Š. Osuský, and Jozef Paučo. A useful survey in French is Helène Tourtzer's *Louis Štúr et l'idée de l'independance slovaque 1815-1856* (Paris, Cahors & Alençon, Imprimeries typographiques A. Coveslant, 1913, 246 p.). Ján V. Ormis compiled a bibliography of works on Štúr, and Jozef Ambruš published his works in five volumes. There are recent facsimile reprints of the journals issued by Štúr and Jozef Hurban, *Slovenskej národňje novini* (Slovakian people's news) (Prešpork, 1845-1848. Reprinted: Bratislava, Slovenské vydavatel'stvo politickej literatúry, 1956, 3 v.); *Orol tatránski* (The eagle of the Tatras) (Prešpork, 1845-1846. Reprinted: Bratislava, v Slovenskom vydavatel'stve politickej literatúry vydal Novinarský študijný ústav, 1956, 774 p.); *Slovenskje pohl'adi na vedi, umeňje a literatúru* (Slovak review of science, art and literature), originally published from 1846 to 1852 and now available in facsimile. Hurban's thought was studied by Albert Pražák and Samuel Š. Osuský, who also wrote on Michael M. Hodža, another collaborator of Štúr.

Pavel Jozef Šafárik (Šafařík) found his biographers in Josef Hanuš, Jaroslav Vlček, and Karel Paul. A special volume, volume 6 (1963), of *Slovanské štúdie* was devoted to a collective study of his life and work in commemoration of the centennial anniversary of his death in 1861. His works and correspondence were partially published in several volumes. Ján Kollár was the subject of a collective study edited by František Pastrnek and a more recent essay by Jan Jakubec. A bibliography of works on Kollár was compiled by Ján V. Ormis. The work of Anton Bernolák and his circle has recently been re-evaluated in a number of minor studies, and Imrich Kotvan published a bibliography of works on this circle.

Juraj Fándly has been the subject of works by J. G. Žatkuliak and Ján Tibenský, who also wrote a book on Juraj Papánek and Juraj Sklenár. Alexander Hirner wrote on Ján Feješ, Vendelín Jankovič on Ján Čaplovič, and Štefan Adamovič on Ján L. Bartolomeides.

758. Kazbunda, Karel. České hnutí roku 1848 (The Czech movement in 1848). Praha, Historický klub, 1929. 434 p. Illus.

Perhaps the best work, so far published, on the revolution of 1848 in the Czech lands. František Roubík and Arnošt Klíma wrote more recent surveys, but more for the general public. Roubík also wrote on the Czech National Guards, as did Jaroslav Křížek, while Karel Slavíček focused his attention on the secret society *Český Repeal* (Czech repeal). The Slavonic Congress in Prague in 1848 was studied by Zdeněk V. Tobolka and a collective work edited by Václav Čejchan, who also published a monograph on Bakunin's activities in Bohemia. Václav Žáček edited a collection of documents relating to the Congress and published a large study on Czech-Polish relations in 1848. Otakar Odložilík examined the records of the commissions investigating the Prague riots of June 1848, while Hugo Traub studied the so-called May conspiracy of 1849. Josef Kazimour studied the role of students and workers in the revolutionary movement. Peasant involvement was examined by Vladimír Klimeš and, earlier, František Roubík, who also edited and published a collection of documents relating to this subject, *Petice venkovského lidu z Čech k Národnímu výboru z roku 1848* (Petitions of the peasants from Bohemia to the National Committee of 1848) (Praha, Nakl. Československé akademie věd, 1954, 542 p., fold. map, facsims.). Miloslav Novotný edited a collection of leaflets, Jaroslava Václavková a collection of popular songs, and František Hampl a selection of poetry and prose reflecting the atmosphere of the time. Karel J. Beneš collected other manifestations of public opinion.

Developments in Moravia and Silesia were surveyed by Josef Macůrek and Józa Vochala. Rudolf Dvořák studied the activities of the Moravian Diet, while Bedřich Šindelář examined the impact of the Hungarian revolution in Moravia and Silesia. Jiří Radimský and Milada Wurmová edited a collection of petitions of the Moravian people.

The best work on the revolution in Slovakia, perhaps the best work of Slovak historiography in general, is Daniel Rapant's *Slovenské povstanie roku 1848-1849; Dejiny a dokumenty* (The Slovak Uprising of 1848-1849; history and documents) (Turčiansky Svätý Martin, Matica slovenská; Bratislava, Slovenská akadémia vied, 1937-1968, 5 v. in 12). Shorter studies of the uprising were published by Karel Goláň and Ján Holák.

A book on *The Czech Revolution of 1848*, by Stanley Z. Pech, is scheduled for publication in 1969 by the University of North Carolina Press.

759. Tobolka, Zdeněk V. Politické dějiny československého národa od r. 1848 až do dnešní doby (Political history of the Czechoslovak people from 1848 to our times). Praha, Nakl. Československého kompasu, 1932-1937. 4 v. in 5. Ports., facsims.

See also entry no. 785.

A detailed survey of the period 1848-1918 by a prominent historian and politician, somewhat slanted in favor of his party, the Young Czechs. Political developments in the Czech lands only were surveyed in an earlier work edited by the author under the title *Česká politika* (Czech politics) (Praha, J. Laichter, 1906-1913, 5 v. in 6). A similar survey for the period 1861-1918 was published by Adolf Srb, and for the period 1878-1897 by Josef Penížek. Jan M. Černý edited a large collection of documents relating to the period 1848-1860.

Monographic studies, focusing mostly on the relations of the Czechs and Germans or the efforts of the Czechs to obtain restoration of their state's rights, were written by Otakar Zeithammer, Karel Kazbunda, Hugo Traub, Václav Šlesinger and Andělín Grobelný. František Roubík studied administrative developments and compiled a valuable bibliography of periodical literature in Bohemia for this period, in which he was emulated by Milada Wurmová, who compiled a similar bibliography for the periodical literature of Moravia. The movement for the erection of a Czech National Theater in Prague, which was chronicled by several authors, provided an opportunity for a case study in Czech nationalism for Stanley B. Kimball in his *Czech Nationalism; a Study of the National Theater Movement, 1845-1883* (Urbana, University of Illinois Press, 1964, 186 p., illus., ports.; bibliography: p. 164-172. Illinois Studies in the Social Sciences, 54).

In the social and economic field most works dealt with the development of the workers' movements in the Czech lands, from the first outlines of Cyril Horáček, Zdeněk V. Tobolka, František Soukup, and Miloslav Volf, to the more engaged Marxists works by Zdeněk Šolle, Jiří Kořalka, Pavel and Michal Reiman, Arnošt Klíma, Jiří Doležal, and Karel Malý. Several volumes of bibliographies and documentary collections relating to this subject were also published recently. Histories of the most important enterprises, including the

Škoda works in Pilsen (by Václav Jíša), or the Bat'a shoe concern (by Bohumil Lehár), are also becoming available. Josef Pohl wrote a significant demographic study on the depopulation of the Czech countryside from 1850-1930, while Alfred Bohmann studied the shifts in the ratio of the Czechs and Germans in the population of Bohemia from 1847-1947.

Contacts with the Slovaks were recorded in connection with the histories of "Československá jednota" (Czechoslovak union), an organization that fostered such contacts, by Jóža Vochala and Josef Rotnágl. Contacts with other Slavs were followed by Josef Jirásek (relations of Czechs and Slovaks with the Russians), Karel Kazbunda (Czech pilgrimage to Moscow in 1867), Jiří Doležal and J. Beránek (the impact of the Russian revolution of 1905 in the Czech lands), and Václav Žáček (the impact of the Polish uprising of 1863 in Bohemia).

760. Bokes, František. Pokusy o slovensko-mad'arské vyrovnanie r. 1861-1868 (Attempts at a Slovak-Hungarian settlement in 1861-1868). Turčiansky Svätý Martin, Matica slovenská, 1941, 232 p. (Spisy Historického odboru Matice slovenskej, 5)

An impressive study of Slovak efforts to obtain national recognition and self-government in Hungary. The author is also editing an important collection of documents relating to the Slovak national life in this period, *Dokumenty k slovenskému národnému hnutiu v rokoch 1848-1914* (Documents on the Slovak national movement in 1848-1914) (Bratislava, Vydavatel'stvo Slovenskej akadémie vied, 1962–). Two volumes, covering the period to 1884, have been published so far. Other monographic studies focusing on important stages of this development were written by Jaroslav Vlček, Jozef Škultéty, František Hrušovský, Jozef Cieker, and Daniel Rapant. Július Botto and Andrej Mráz wrote on the history of "Matica slovenská," a cultural center of the Slovak people founded in 1863.

In the economic field, Július Mésároš studied the survivals of feudalism in Slovakia in the second half of the 19th century, while Miloš Gosiorovský surveyed the history of the Slovak workers' movement from 1848-1918.

Studies on Slovak contacts with other Slavs in this period include Viktor Borodovčák's examination of the impact of the Polish uprising of 1863 in Slovakia, and Mikuláš Písch's work on Slovak response to the Russian revolution of 1905.

761. Nejedlý, Zdeněk. T. G. Masaryk. Praha, Melantrich, 1930-1935. 4 v. in 5.

The best and largest work on the young Masaryk, covering the first 36 years of his life, 1850-1886, and presenting, at the same time, a broad study of social, cultural, and political life of the Czechs in these years, free from the author's later Marxist bias. Among numerous biographies covering his whole life, the most popular was that of Jan Herben. English biographies of Masaryk include those of Arnold A. Lowrie, Paul Selver, Cecil J. C. Street, Victor Cohen, and Edward

W. P. Newman. All of them are only provisional sketches for the general public. More scholarly contributions were minor studies published in several Festschriften dedicated to Masaryk on various occasions, or in periodicals. A special periodical devoted to the study of the life and work of Masaryk was published between 1924 and 1931 by V. K. Škrach under the title *Masarykův sborník; Časopis pro studium života a díla T. G. Masaryka* (Masaryk review; a journal for the study of the life and work of T. G. Masaryk) (Praha, Čin). Masaryk's own story of his life, published in the form of his conversations with Karel Čapek, appeared also in English in two separate volumes: *President Masaryk Tells His Story* (New York, G. P. Putnam, 1935, 302 p.); and *Masaryk on Thought and Life* (London, G. Allen and Unwin, 1938, 214 p.). Similar works on Masaryk's thought were published by Emil Ludwig and William P. Warren. The best, though incomplete, bibliography of earlier works on Masaryk was published by Boris Jakowenko in 1935.

Marxist works on Masaryk were as hostile to him as many of the earlier works were adulatory. They include studies of Masaryk's role in Czech politics and his attitudes toward the working class by Jurij Křížek, his attitudes toward Russia by Theodor Syllaba, and his "counterrevolutionary" activities in the World War by Václav Král, who, however, repudiated parts of his book in 1968 when Czechosovak historiography abandoned its rigid Marxist line in favor of a more balanced scholarship.

Biographies of other important Czech and Slovak leaders in this period are also rather provisional in nature. Those that rise above this level include Hugo Traub's biography of František L. Rieger, Josef Matoušek's study of Karel Sladkovský, Jaroslav Purš' examination of the controversy over Karel Sabina, Josef Gruber's biography of Albín Bráf, and several more recent studies of Czech radicals represented best in a collective work edited by Václav Žáček and Karel Kosík. Kosík also published a reader from the writings of the radicals and a survey of the whole trend, the latter in his *Česká radikální demokracie* (Czech radical democracy) (Praha, Státní nakladatelství politické literatury, 1958, 482 p.). Still more valuable are editions of works, memoirs, papers and correspondence of some of these important individuals of this period, notably, Rieger, Bráf, Sabina, Emanuel Arnold, Josef V. Frič, Alois Pražák, Josef Kaizl, Karel S. Sokol, Karel Mattuš, Alfons Štastný, and Eduard Gréger. The same could be said about biographies and materials of such Slovak leaders in this period as Štefan M. Daxner, Ján Francisci, G. K. Zechenter-Laskomerský, Pavel Blaho, Vavro Šrobár, and Andrej Hlinka.

762. Sychrava, Lev, *and* Jaroslav Werstadt. Československý odboj (The Czechoslovak revolution). Praha, Státní nakladatelství, 1923. 200 p. (Knihy pro každého; sbírka spisů poučných. Ročník [1] 5)

A survey of the struggle of Czechs and Slovaks for independence during the First World War emphasizing the movement abroad led by Tomáš G. Masaryk, Edvard Beneš, and Milan R. Štefánik. In contrast to that, Zdeněk V. Tobolka emphasized the domestic developments in his version of the story published in the first volume of *Politika,* which he edited in Prague in 1923-1925. A more balanced, richly documented account of the movement was presented by Jan Opočenský in several works on the collapse of Austria-Hungary and the rise of independent states in her place, some of which appeared also in Western languages. Such is also the work of a German author, Emil Strauss, *Die Entstehung der Tschechoslowakischen Republik* (Prag, Orbis, 1934, 356 p., ports.) A collection of documents, *The Birth of Czechoslovakia,* was edited by Cestmir Jesina (Washington, D.C., Czechoslovak National Council of America, 1968, 110 p.).

Among the large number of monographs of more specific nature, special attention is deserved by: Vlastimil Kybal's study of the diplomatic origins of the Czechoslovak state (in several languages); Robert W. Seton-Watson's book on Masaryk's work in England; Madeleine Levée's work on the Czechoslovak movement in Paris (in French); Jaroslav Papoušek's examination of Tsarist Russia's attitude toward the Czechoslovak movement; J. F. N. Bradley's study on the Czechoslovak legions in Russian (in French); Karel Stloukal's essay on Masaryk's concepts of the future Czechoslovak state; Dagmar Perman's study of the shaping of Czechoslovak frontiers; Milada Paulová's works on the underground organization *Maffia* and cooperation of the Czechs with the South Slavs; Václav Chaloupecký's description of the struggle for Slovakia; Karol Sidor's survey of Slovak efforts abroad; Ivan Dérer's and Konštantín Čulen's interpretations of the Pittsburgh Agreement on the future union of the Czechs and Slovaks; and Martin Grečo's essay on the Declaration of Turčiansky Svätý Martin on the same matter. From among numerous memoirs and documentary materials most valuable are memoirs of Masaryk and Beneš (both in several languages, including English), the notebooks of Milan Štefánik, and documents relating to the trials of Karel Kramář and other resistance leaders at home published by Zdeněk V. Tobolka. Between 1924 and 1938 a special periodical was published for the study and collection of materials on the independence movement under the title *Naše revoluce; Čtvrtletní historický sborník* (Our revolution; quarterly historical review) (Praha, Československá obec legionářská, historický odbor, 1924-1938, 14 v.).

Marxist writers tended to minimize positive contributions of the Western powers and the "bourgeois" leaders at home and abroad to the independence movement (Jiří Hájek in a work on the "Wilsonian legend," L'udovít Holotík on the "Štefánik legend," Václav Král and František Nečásek on the "counterrevolutionary" activities of Masaryk and Beneš; Jindřich Veselý, Jiří Muška and Ján Kvasnička in works on the Czechoslovak legions in Russia). At the same time they emphasized the role of the working class supposedly inspired by the October Revolution in Russia (see works by Oldřich Říha, Jurij and Jaroslav Křížek, Mieroslav Hysko, L'udovít Holotík, Michal Dzvoník, Zdeněk Šolle, Karel Pichlík, and others).

Several volumes of documents were published to back up this interpretation under the title *Prameny k ohlasu Velké říjnové social-*

istické revoluce a vzniku ČSR (Documents on the impact of the Great October Socialist Revolution and the foundation of the Czechoslovak Republic) (Praha, Československá akademie věd, 1957–). Also here the most rigid expressions of this interpretation were abandoned in 1968. Dissatifaction with them was cautiously expressed earlier, particularly by Karel Pomaizl in his *Vznik ČSR, 1918; Problém marxistické vědecké interpretace* (The rise of the Czechoslovak Republic, 1918; a problem of Marxist scientific interpretation) (Praha, Československá akademie věd, 1965, 301 p.; bibliography: p. 289-298).

K. MODERN HISTORY, 1918-1968*

763. General surveys and materials on the Czechoslovak Republic, 1918-1938:

For a collection of essays by Czechoslovak and Western scholars surveying the development of Czechoslovakia from 1918 to 1938, *see* Robert J. Kerner's *Czechoslovakia* (entries no. 505, 776, and 873). Shorter surveys were published by Harry Klepetář (1937, in German), and Kamil Krofta (1939). A more recent Marxist textbook by Věra Olivová and Robert Kvaček covers the survey to 1945, a German outline by Jörg K. Hoensch to 1965.

Among books that cover shorter periods and more specific subjects, the best is Ferdinand Peroutka's study on the first three years of the state, 1918-1921, *Budování státu; Československá politika v letech popřevratových* (entry no. 779). An official survey of the first decade of the state, distinguished by a vast amount of data collected by government experts, was published under the title *Deset let Československé republiky* (Ten years of the Czechoslovak Republic) (Praha, Předsednictvo vlády, 1928, 3 v., illus., ports., maps). A companion to it is a similar work on the Czechoslovak National Assembly, *Národní shromáždění republiky Československé v prvém desítiletí* (The National Assembly of the Czechoslovak Republic in the first decade) (Praha, Předsednictvo Poslanecké sněmovny *and* Předsednictvo Senátu, 1928, 1315 p., illus.). In 1938 a second volume and a supplement were added to it to survey the second decade of the state. Josef Borovička outlined the first ten years of the state in a short survey that was published in several languages, including English. Marxist outlines covering the early years of the state were published by Jaroslav Koutek and Jan Křen; Marxist monographs focusing on the National Committees of 1918 and bourgeois politics of 1921-1923 by Václav Peša and Věra Olivová. Books and documentary collections reflecting the impact of the Russian Revolution on Czechoslovakia that were quoted above also relate to these first years of the state.

* For other titles relating to this period *see also* the pertinent sections on Government and Politics, The Economy, The Society, Literatures, History of Thought, Culture and Science, Religion, Education, The Fine arts, and Music. In the interest of space economy, materials of historical relevance for this period appearing also elsewhere in this guide are here only briefly summarized, with cross references to the other locations.

Among institutional studies still the best is Edward Táborský's *Czechoslovak Democracy at Work* (see entry no. 784). A similar English outline was published by Louis Brackett. Czechoslovak political parties were surveyed by Karel Hoch (in French and English) and analyzed by Paul Hartmann (in German). Marxist contributions to this field include a survey of the development of state administration by Miroslav Cihlář and a monograph on the "fascization" of legislation in the "bourgeois" republic by Radim N. Foustka.

For an official history of the Communist Party of Czechoslovakia *see*:

Prague. Ústav dějin Komunistické strany Československa. Dějiny Komunistické strany Československa (History of the Communist Party of Czechoslovakia). Praha, Státní nakladatelství politické literatury, 1961. 710 p. Also available in Russian.

Later modifications resulting from subsequent shifts in Party ideology were included in a shorter survey, *Dějiny KSČ; studijní příručka* (History of the Communist Party of Czechoslovakia; a study guide). 3d rev. ed. (Praha, Svoboda, 1967, 296 p. Also indispensable is *Příruční slovník k dějinám KSČ* (A dictionary for the history of the Communist Party of Czechoslovakia) (Praha, Nakladatelství politické literatury, 1964, 2 v.). Both books were published by the same Institute and are cataloged accordingly. That Institute also publishes a periodical, *Příspěvky k dějinám KSČ* (Contributions to the history of the Communist Party of Czechoslovakia) (Praha, 1957–). A Slovak pendant to it is:

Bratislava. Ústav dejín KSS. Sborník (Miscellany). roč 1– 1959– Bratislava, Slovenské Vydavateľstvo politickej literatúry.

Monographic studies of the history of the Communist Party of Czechoslovakia focus on either the early 1920s, when the party was founded, or the late 1930s, when the party and the state faced the Nazi challenge. An American view of the party's politics is offered by Paul Zinner in his *Communist Strategy and Tactics in Czechoslovakia, 1918-48* (New York, Praeger, 1963, 264 p.; Praeger Publications in Russian History and World Communism, no. 129).

Early surveys of the Czechoslovak economy of this period were published by Alois Rašín and Josef Gruber (in English), and Jaroslav Veselý, Lucien Graux, and André Tibal (in French). The most comprehensive Marxist survey, edited by Rudolf Olšovský is *Přehled hospodářského vývoje Československa v letech 1918-1945* (Survey of the economic development of Czechoslovakia in 1918-1945) (Praha, Státní Nakl. politické literatury, 1961, 718 p.). Olšovský also wrote a survey of Czechoslovak foreign trade between 1918 and 1938, while Milan Otáhal studied Czechoslovak land reform and Antonín Chyba the conditions of the working class in the same period. Josef Faltus focused his attention on the crisis in Czechoslovak industry and finances in the period 1921-1923.

Early surveys of Czechoslovak foreign policy in this period were published by John F. Vondracek (in English) and Emil Strauss (in German); Marxist surveys by Alena Gajanová and a collective headed by Vladimír Soják. Valerii A. Shishkin studied Czechoslovak-Soviet relations in 1918-1925, Igor A. Peters in 1918-1934, while Věra

Olivová published a collection of documents on this subject for the years 1918-1922. Koloman Gajan wrote a monograph on the relations of Germany to Czechoslovakia in 1919-1921 and published a collection of documents on this subject for the period 1918-1939. A small selection of these documents was published also in English by Gajan and Robert Kvaček under the title *Germany and Czechoslovakia, 1918-1945; Documents on German Policies* (Prague, Orbis, 1965, 171 p.).

764. Lettrich, Jozef. A History of Modern Slovakia. New York, F. Praeger, 1955. 329 p.

A survey emphasizing the period 1918-1948. Earlier surveys were published by Josef Jirásek and Ivan Dérer. Robert W. Seton-Watson wrote a critical book on the new Slovakia after 1918 and edited a collection of essays by various Slovak writers contrasting the gains of the Slovaks with their conditions before that date, *Slovakia Then and Now; a Political Survey* (London, G. Allen and Unwin, 1931, 356 p., illus.). A similar book was written by Cecil J. C. Street. The Slovak separatist point of view is represented by several books, such as those by Jozef Mikuš, Jozef Kirschbaum, and Karol Sidor. Sidor's *Slovenská politika na pode pražského snemu (1918-1938)* (Slovak politics on the grounds of the Prague Parliament [1918-1938]) Bratislava, Knihtlačiaren Andreja, 1943, 2 v.) is largely a collection of excerpts from parliamentary debates on the Slovak question.

Marxist works, while critical of the conditions of Slovakia between 1918 and 1938 and hostile to the separatists, commend communist efforts there. Ján Svetoň studied the development of Slovak population under capitalism, Ján Pašiak examined various proposals for the solution of the Slovak question since the 19th century, and Ladislav Lipscher traced the evolution of local government in Slovakia in 1918-1938. Lipscher also wrote on autonomist and separatist movements in Slovakia, as did Imrich Stanek, Andrej Sirácky, and Juraj Kramer, who also published a survey on Slovak industry, while Ján Mlynárik studied unemployment and strike movements in Slovakia in 1918-1938. Communist efforts in Slovakia in this period were described by Viliam Plevza, Lubomír Vébr, Sammel Cambel, Zdenka Holotíková, and Milan Filo. Václav Král wrote on the impact of the Hungarian Soviet Republic in Slovakia and the Czechoslovak war against it in 1919, while Martin Vietor studied the history of the short-lived Slovak Soviet Republic established in eastern Slovakia in the spring of that year.

Separation of Slovakia from the Czech lands in 1939 was studied by Imrich Stanek, Bohuslav Graca, and Jozef Danáš. For the German and Hungarian involvement in this development we now have two excellent studies of Jörg K. Hoensch: *Die Slowakei und Hitlers Ostpolitik; Hlinkas Slowakische Volkspartei zwischen Autonomie und Separation, 1938/1939* (entry no. 889), and *Der ungarische Revisionismus und die Zerschlagung der Tschechoslowakei* (Tübingen, Mohr, 1967, 323 p.; bibliography: p. 296-311. Tübinger Studien zur Geschichte und Politik, nr. 23). Jozef Kirschbaum, in a book on the separatists' struggle for independence, and Miloslav S. Ďurica, in an Italian study on German-Slovak relations in 1938-1939, presented the separatists' interpretation, as did Ferdinand Durčanský in a "White book" on the Slovak right to independence.

765. Czech-German relations and the Munich agreement.

The basic studies on this subject are Elizabeth Wiskemann's *Czechs and Germans* (entries no. 659 and 880) and Johann W. Brügel's *Tschechen und Deutsche, 1918-1938* (entries no. 649 and 789). Many Sudeten German authors tend to exaggerate the grievances and claims of the German minority in Czechoslovakia. German surveys in this trend were published by Josef Pfitzner, Eugen Lemberg, Hermann Raschhofer and Wenzel Jaksch. Monographic studies were devoted to the opposition of the Sudeten Germans to the Czechoslovak Republic in its first years (Paul Molisch and Kurt Rabl) and the resulting problem of state loyalty (Rabl). Early Czech surveys and studies of the German problem in Czechoslovakia were published by Kamil Krofta, Emanuel Rádl, and Josef Chmelař. A more recent Marxist study of the subject was produced by Jaroslav César and Bohumil Černý (*see* entry no. 769). For a collection of documents on the Czechoslovak Germans in this and the following period *see* Václav Král's *Die Deutschen in der Tschechoslowakei, 1933-1947; Dokumentensammlung* (entry no. 652).

The best book on the Munich crisis of 1938 is still Boris Čelovský's *Das Münchener Abkommen von 1938* (entries no. 228 and 885). Helmuth Rönnefahrt's book on Munich is only an unsuccessful attempt to refute Čelovský. Other studies of the Munich crisis include the books of Hubert Ripka, John W. Wheeler-Bennett, R. G. D. Laffan and Veronica M. Toynbee (in the *Survey of International Affairs* for 1938, v. 2-3), Keith Eubank (all these in English), and Henri Noguères (in French and English). Among Marxist surveys of the Munich crisis belong books by Jiří S. Hájek, Miloš Hájek, and a collective work edited by Karl Obermann and Josef Polišenský that was published in 1958 on the occasion of the 20th anniversary of the Munich Agreement in several languages, including English. Another collective work, edited by Gerhard Fuchs, was devoted to the cooperation of Czech and German opponents to Nazism in 1933-1938. Robert Kvaček traced the roots of the crisis in European politics between 1933 and 1937, while Z. S. Belousov, Vladimir G. Poliakov, and M. Baturin (all in Russian) concentrated on the attitudes of France, England, and the United States respectively. Polish-Czechoslovak relations in the late 1930s and Polish involvement in the Munich crisis were examined by Jerzy Kozeński, Stefania Stanislawska, Marian Zagoriak, and Michał Pułaski (all in Polish).

The best collection of Czechoslovak documents relating to the Munich crisis is the volume edited by Václav Král under the title *Das Abkommen von München, 1938; Tschechoslowakische diplomatische Dokumente, 1937-1939* (Praha, Akademia, 1968, 369 p.). Earlier collections of documents on this subject were often selected with the obvious purpose to show that the loyalty of the Western powers and the Czechoslovak bourgeoisie to the Czechoslovak state was as lacking as the loyalty of Czechoslovak communists and the

Soviet Union was unswerving. They include: *Mnichov v dokumentech* (Munich in documents) (Praha, 1958, 2 v.), and *Nové dokumenty k historii Mnichova* (New documents on the history of Munich) (Praha, 1958, 124 p.), as well as *Politické strany a Mnichov; dokumenty* (Political parties and Munich; documents), edited by Václav Král. Praha, Svobodné slovo, 1961. 225 p. Illus.

Prague. Ústav dějin Komunistické strany Československa. Chtěli jsme bojovat; Dokumenty o boji KSČ a lidu na obranu Československa, 1938 (We wanted to fight; documents on the struggle of the Communist Party of Czechoslovakia and the people in defense of Czechoslovakia, 1938). Praha, Nakl. politické literatury, 1963. 2 v. Illus., facsims.

Leták, Miroslav, *ed.* V osidlech zrady; dokumenty 1933-1938 (In the snares of treason; documents, 1933-1938). Praha, Svobodné slovo, 1965. 252 p.

A substantial number of documents relating to the Munich crisis can also be found in the collections on the Germans in Czechoslovakia and the German-Czechoslovak relations quoted above. Several volumes of German, French, British, American, and Hungarian documents published by the respective governments for the years 1937-1939 are also indispensable.

766. Král, Václav, *comp.* Lesson from History; Documents on Nazi Policies for Germanization and Extermination in Czechoslovakia. Praha, Československá akademie věd, 1962.

A selection of documents relating to the German occupation of Czechoslovakia in 1939-1945. Also available in Czech and German. For similar documents *see*:

Czechoslovak Republic. Československo a norimberský proces; Hlavní dokumenty norimberského procesu o zločinech nacistů proti Československu (Czechoslovakia and the Nürnberg trials; main documents of the Nürnberg trials on the Nazi crimes against Czechoslovakia). Praha, Ministerstvo informací, 1946. 405 p.

Libuše Otáhalová edited still another collection of documents from this period, relating more to the policies and operations of the Czech government under German occupation and the Czechoslovak government in exile, under the title *Dokumenty z historie československé politiky, 1939-1943* (entry no. 798). Also indispensable for the study of this subject are memoirs and speeches of Dr. Edvard Beneš, president of the exile government, and Dr. Ladislav K. Feierabend, a member of both governments. An interesting Marxist study of the formation of the exile government was produced by Jan Křen. Václav Král published a three-volume study on German exploitation of the Czech economy in 1938-1945.

Materials on the Slovak government can be found in the partial transcripts of the postwar trials with members of that government, published under the title *Pred súdom národa; proces s Dr. J. Tisom, Dr. F. Durčanským* [*a*] *A. Machom v Bratislave v dňoch 2. dec. 1946-15. apr. 1947* (Facing the court of the people; the trial of Dr. J. Tiso, Dr. F. Durčanský [and] A. Mach in Bratislava between December 2, 1946-April 15, 1947) (Bratislava, Povereníctvo informácií, 1947, 5 v.). Igor Daxner, president of the People's Court of Bratislava, supplemented much of this material in his reminiscences on this and other such trials in 1945-1947. Important supplements are also: the full text of Tiso's defense published by Jozef Paučo; Tiso's biography by Konštantín Čulen; and a collective work on the wartime Slovak Republic edited by Mikuláš Šprinc. Also relevant is the "white book" of Ferdinand Durčanský and other books on Slovakia (*see* entry no. 790). These can be supplemented by a study of economic exploitation of Slovakia by the Germans published by L'ubomier Lipták, studies of Hungarian occupation of southern Slovakia by Martin Vietor and Vladimír Vipler, and Hungarian relations with the rest of Slovakia by Juraj Fabián.

Czechoslovak resistance in the Second World War was the subject of numerous books, from the first outline by Karel Veselý-Štainer to the most recent work by a Marxist collective headed by Gustav Bareš. Jiří Doležal's book was also published in English as *Czechoslovakia's Fight; Documents on the Resistance Movement of the Czechoslovak People, 1938-1945* (Prague, Published by Orbis on behalf of the Publ. House of the Czechoslovak Academy of Sciences, 1964, 156 p., illus., maps). A survey by A. N. Nedorezov and a collective work edited by A. Kh. Klevanskii and I. N. Mel'nikova are available to Russian-reading students. The 20th anniversary of the most celebrated chapter of the Czechoslovak resistance, the Slovak National Uprising in August 1944 and subsequent partisan warfare in Slovakia, was recently commemorated by a collective work of the Slovak Academy of Sciences and a vast collection of documents edited by Vilém Prečan under the title *Slovenské národné povstanie; dokumenty* (Slovak National Uprising; documents) (Bratislava, Vydavatel'stvo politickej literatúry, 1966, 1220 p.). Both are, like so much else, strongly biased in favor of the communist, as opposed to noncommunist, participants. The 20th anniversary of the Czech uprising in Prague in May, 1945, the climax of Czech resistance, was commemorated by a Marxist study of Karel Bartošek and a collective work of noncommunist participants edited by Otakar Machotka.

Organization and exploits of the Czechoslovak army in exile were described by Otakar Španiel, Eduard Čejka, and Oldřich Janeček. A collective headed by Antonín Benčik published a three-volume work on the liberation of Czechoslovakia by the Soviet Army in 1944-1945, while Čestmír Amort wrote a monograph on the help of the Communist Party of the Soviet Union and published a collection of documents on that subject. Also published jointly by the Czechoslovak and Soviet Ministries of Foreign Affairs was a collection of documents on Czechoslovak-Soviet relations under the title *Československo-sovětské vztahy v době Velké vlastenecké války, 1941-1945; dokumenty a materiály* (Czechoslovak-Soviet relations in the time of the Great Patriotic War, 1941-1945; documents and materials) (Praha, Státní nakl. politické literatury, 1960, 267 p.). Supplementary to such publications are memoirs of Zdeněk Fierlinger, erstwhile Czechoslovak minister in Moscow.

767. Korbel, Josef. The Communist Subversion of Czechoslovakia, 1938-1948; The Failure of Coexistence. Princeton, N.J., Princeton University Press, 1959. 258 p.

See also entry no. 793.

Still the best treatment of this subject. Other studies, mostly focused on the communist coup d'état of February, 1948, include books of Hubert Ripka, Vlastimil Chalupa, and Morton A. Kaplan, all in English. Among numerous Marxist books on this subject more recommendable appear to be a study of Jaroslav Opat on the "national-democratic revolution" in Czechoslovakia in 1945-1948, and two collective works of the Historical Institute of the Czechoslovak Academy of Sciences on the Czechoslovak "revolution" of 1944-1948 and the rise and development of "people's democracy" in Czechoslovakia. Jiří S. Hájek wrote on the "pernicious" role played by the noncommunist socialists in Czechoslovakia in this period as well as before. Miloš Klimeš edited a collection of documents relating to the "May revolution" of 1945, when the foundations of the people's democracy were laid, under the title *Cestou ke květnu; vznik lidové demokracie v Československu* (On the way to May; the rise of people's democracy in Czechoslovakia) (Praha, Nakladatelství Československé akademie věd, 1965, 2 v.). Earlier Václav Král edited a collection of documents relating to the "February revolution" of 1948, when the communists took complete control of the country, under the title *Cestou k únoru* (On the way to February) (Praha, Svobodné slovo, 1963, 432 p.).

The expulsion of the Sudeten Germans from Czechoslovakia, which took place in 1945-1947, was studied by Radomír Luža against a wide background of Czech-German relations in his *The Transfer of the Sudeten Germans; A Study of Czech-German Relations, 1933-1962* (entries no. 655 and 900). Linked with the problem of the German question in postwar international politics, this matter also became a subject of a collective Marxist study edited by L'udovít Holotík and others. German authors and books dealing with this subject are mentioned above. To that must be added a collection of documents:

Germany (Federal Republic, 1949–) *Bundesministerium für Vertriebene, Flüchtlinge und Kriegsgeschädigte.* Die Vertreibung der deutschen Bevölkerung aus der Tschechoslowakei. Bonn, 1957. 2 v. Fold. maps. (Dokumentation der Vertreibung der Deutschen aus Ost-Mitteleuropa, Bd. 4, 1-2)

The Soviet takeover of Ruthenia, the easternmost province of Czechoslovakia, in 1945 was described by František Němec and V. Moudrý in a joint book on this subject.

Further development of communism in Czechoslovakia was followed by Edward Táborský in his *Communism in Czechoslovakia, 1948-1960* (entries no. 828 and 1026). Collective surveys of the same development were edited also by Vratislav Bušek and Jan Hajda. Ivan Gadourek centered his attention on the political control of Czechoslovakia by the communists, while Vladimír Reisky-Dubnic wrote on communist propaganda methods in Czechoslovakia, and

Ludvík Němec described the suppression of the Catholic Church in the country. In the economic field Thad Alton and Boris Pešek studied national income and national product of Czechoslovakia under the communists, Jan Michal wrote on communist central planning in the country, and Gregor Lazarčík examined the performance of communist agriculture.

So far the best attempt at a Marxist survey of the developments in Czechoslovakia after 1948 is Karel Kaplan's monograph *Utváření generální linie výstavby socialismu v Československu; od února do IX sjezdu KSČ* (Formation of a general line of building of socialism in Czechoslovakia; from February to the 9th Congress of the Communist Party) (Praha, Academia, 1966, 295 p.). The Central Commission of People's Control and Statistics (Ústřední komise lidové kontroly a statistiky) published a survey of the general development of Czechoslovakia in 1945-1965, and a survey of social development based on the census of 1961. The Ideological Commission of the Central Committee of the Communist Party of Czechoslovakia published a survey of the Czechoslovak economy in the 20 years since 1945. The Central Administration of Geodesy and Cartography (Ústřední správa geodesie a kartografie) published an atlas of the Czechoslovak population, which is also the subject of a monograph by Ján Svetoň. Pavel Machonin edited a collective work on the social structure of the socialist society. Karol Laco wrote a comparative study of the new Constitution of Czechoslovakia and that of pre-Munich Czechoslovakia. Most recently Evžen Löbl published a testimony on the trial of Rudolf Slánský, the deposed Secretary General of the Communist Party of Czechoslovakia, in 1952, while Zdenka Holotíková and Viliam Plevza published a biography of Vladimír Clementis, another victim of the same trial. Both are explicit denunciations of communist justice and, perhaps, harbingers of better times to come. The most recently published inventory of pertinent writings is *Bibliografie k dějinám ČSR a KSČ 1917-1938. Historiografická produkce za léta 1945-1967* (Bibliography of the history of the Czechoslovak Republic and the Communist Party of Czechoslovakia, 1917-1938. The historiographic production for 1945-1967) by Helena Engová and others (Praha, Knihovna Ústavu dějin socialismu, 1968, 4 v.).

18

the state

by Edward Taborsky

A. GOVERNMENT AND POLITICS*

1. Prior to the Second World War

768. Čapek, Karel. President Masaryk Tells His Story. New York, G. P. Putnam's Sons, 1935. 302 p.

Revealing conversations which the well-known Czech writer had with President Thomas Masaryk about the latter's life, work, and philosophy. Translation of Karel Čapek's *Hovory s T. G. Masarykem* (Conversations with T. G. Masaryk) (Prague, Aventinum-Čin, 1931,

* *See also* chapter 17, particularly its section K.

2 v.). *See also* Karel Čapek's *Masaryk on Thought and Life; Conversations with Karel Čapek* (New York, Macmillan, 1938, 214 p.).

769. César, Jaroslav, *and* Bohumil Černý. Politika německých buržoasních stran v Československu v letech 1918-1938 (The policies of the German bourgeois parties in Czechoslovakia between 1918 and 1938). Praha, Nakl. Československé akademie věd, 1962. 2 v. Illus.
See also entry no. 650.

An exhaustive and critical examination of the activities and policies of the German bourgeois parties in prewar Czechoslovakia. See also *Die Deutschen in der Tschechoslowakei, 1933-1947* (Praha, Nakl. Československé akademie věd, 1964, 663 p.), a collection of documents on pro-Nazi activities in Czechoslovakia.

770. Československá vlastivěda (Book of knowledge on Czechoslovakia). Praha, Sfinx, 1929-1936. 10 v. in 12. Illus., ports., maps (part fold. col.), facsims. Includes bibliographies.
See also entries no. 495, 614, *and* 840.

Volume 5, entitled *Stát* (The state), contains many contributions by prominent Czechoslovak scholars on government and politics both prior to and after 1918.

771. Chmelař, Josef. Political Parties in Czechoslovakia. Prague, Orbis, 1926. 102 p.

A good survey of Czechoslovakia's prewar political parties by an official of the Czechoslovak Foreign Ministry. *See also* Karel Hoch's *The Political Parties in Czechoslovakia* (Prague, Orbis, 1936, 70 p., fold. tab.). For a juristic analysis of the Czechoslovak party system prior to the Second World War *see* Paul Hartmann's *Die politische Partei in der Tschechoslowakischen Republik* (Brünn, R. M. Rohrer, 1931, 260 p.).

772. Dějiny Komunistické strany Československa (The history of the Communist Party of Czechoslovakia). Praha, Nakl. politické literatury, 1961. 412 p.

The official history of the Czechoslovak Communist Party issued in commemoration of the party's fortieth anniversary. Considered more complete and less biased than the earlier outlines from the "personality-cult" era. See also *Dejiny KSČ; študijná príručka* (The history of the KSČ; a study manual) (Bratislava, Vydavatel'stvo politickej literatury, 1967, 255 p., illus., bibliography: p. 253-256), and *Príručný slovník k dejinám KSČ* (A dictionary of the history of the KSČ) (Bratislava, Vydavatel'stvo politickej literatury, 1964, 1058 p.).

Other books dealing with various stages of the history of the Czechoslovak Communist party include: *Založení Komunistické strany Československa* (The foundation of the Communist Party of Czechoslovakia) (Praha, Státní nakladatelství politické literatury, 1954, 201 p.); Jindřich Veselý's *Z prvních bojů KSČ (1921-1924)* (From the first struggles of the KSČ [1921-1924]) (Praha, Státní nakladatelství politické literatury, 1958, 180 p.); Vojtěch Mencl's

Na cestě k jednotě; KSČ v letech 1921-1923 (On the way to the unity; the KSČ in the years 1921-1923) (Praha, Státní nakladatelství politické literatury, 1964, 387 p., illus., facsims., ports., bibliography: p. 375-381); *V bojích se zocelila KSČ; sborník dokumentů o bojích a persekuci Komunistické strany Československa v létech 1921-1938* (The KSČ grew stronger in the struggle; a collection of documents on the struggles and the persecution of the Communist Party of Czechoslovakia in the years 1921-1938) (Praha, Státní nakladatelství politické literatury, 1956, 557 p.); *Za svobodu českého a slovenského národa; sborník dokumentů k dějinám KSČ v letech 1938-1945* (For the freedom of the Czech and Slovak peoples; a collection of documents on the history of the KSČ in the years 1938-1945) (Praha, Státní nakladatelství politické literatury, 1956, 374 p.); and Ladislav Kovář's *KSČ v boji za jednotnou frontu proti fašismu (1933-1935)* (KSČ in the struggle for the united front against fascism [1933-1935]) (Praha, Státní nakladatelství politické literatury, 1958, 344 p.).

773. Fuchs, Gerhard. Gegen Hitler und Henlein. Berlin (East), Rütten und Loening, 1961. 334 p. Illus. Includes bibliography. (Schriftenreihe der Kommission der Historiker der DDR und der ČSSR, Bd. 4)

A rather distorted dissertation on the "common struggle of the Czech and German anti-Fascists" against German and Sudeten-German Nazism between 1933 and 1938. The author, an East German communist, views the struggle as a class conflict between the Czech and German working class on one side and the Czech and German bourgeoisie on the other.

774. Giannini, Amedeo, *ed.* La Cecoslovacchia. Roma, Anonima Romana Editoriale, 1925. 477 p.

A collection of essays by Czechoslovak and Italian authors on various aspects of Czechoslovakia during the early twenties. A number of contributions to the volume, prepared under the auspices of the Italian Institute for Eastern Europe, deal with political life and organization. For another Italian volume on Czechoslovakia *see* Umberto Nani's *T. G. Masaryk e l'Unità Cecoslovacca* (Milano, Fratelli Treves, 1931, 246 p.).

775. Hassinger, Hugo. Die Tschechoslowakei; ein geographisches, politisches und wirtschaftliches Handbuch. Wien, Rikola Verlag, 1925. 618 p. Fold. maps. Bibliography: p. 602-618.

See also entry no. 500.

An examination of political, economic, and social developments in the early years of Czechoslovakia by a Swiss professor, with particular attention to nationality problems (interpreted with a slight pro-German bias).

776. Kerner, Robert J., *ed.* Czechoslovakia, Twenty Years of Independence. Berkeley and Los Angeles, University of California Press, 1940. 504 p. Front., illus. (maps), plates, ports., bibliographies.

See also entries no. 505 *and* 873.

This excellent collection of scholarly articles contains six contributions discussing various aspects of Czechoslovakia's political system between the two world wars: "The Historical Roots of Czech Democracy," by Hans Kohn; "Constitutional and Political Structure" and "Parties and Politics," by Malbone W. Graham; "Czechoslovakia and Her Minorities," by Joseph S. Roucek; "The Problems of Sub-Carpathian Ruthenia," by Oszkár Jászi; and "Czechoslovak Democracy: Was It Worth While?", by James T. Shotwell.

777. Kramer, Juraj. Slovenské autonomistické hnutie v rokoch 1918-1929 (The Slovak autonomist movement in the years 1918-1929). Bratislava, Vydavatel'stvo Slovenskej akadémie vied, 1962. 483 p. Includes bibliography.

A Marxist analysis of the emergence and early development of the Slovak autonomist movement.

778. Krebs, Hans. Der Kampf um die sudetendeutsche Autonomie. Aussig, N.S.P. Verlag, 1933. 146 p. Illus.

An advocacy of the Sudeten German case for autonomy by one of the leading Sudeten German politicians. *See also* the same author's *Kampf in Böhmen* (Berlin, Volk und Reich, 1936, 228 p., illus., plates, ports., maps, facsims.). Other publications conveying the Sudeten German viewpoint include *Sudetendeutschtum im Kampf* (Karslbad, Frank, 1936, 186 p.), and Hans Singule's *Der Staat Masaryks* (Berlin, Freiheitsverlag, 1937, 326 p. illus.).

779. Peroutka, Ferdinand. Budování státu (The building of the state). Praha, Borový, 1933-1936. 4 v.

This monumental work, ably written by one of the most prominent political commentators of democratic Czechoslovakia, is the most thorough political study of the early formative years (1918-1921). *See also* the same author's *Boj o dnešek* (The struggle for today) (Praha, Borový, 1925, 282 p.).

780. Rádl, Emanuel. Der Kampf zwischen Tschechen und Deutschen. Reichenberg, Böhmen, Gebrüder Stiepel, 1928. 208 p.

A challenging discussion of Czech-German relations by a prominent Czech philosopher who makes a forceful and persuasive plea for reconciliation and cooperation between the two peoples.

A similar position, from the German point of view, is taken by Gustav Peters in his *Der neue Herr von Böhmen* (Berlin, Deutsche Rundschau, 1927, 134 p., tables, illus.; bibliography: p. 123-134).

781. Selver, Paul. Masaryk. London, Michael Joseph, 1940. 326 p. Front. (port.), illus. (facsims.), plates, ports.

An authorized biography of Czechoslovakia's first president. Some of the many other biographical works on T. G. Masaryk include: Donald A. Lowrie's *Masaryk of Czechoslovakia* (London, New York, Oxford University Press, 1937, 222 p., front., ports., fold. map); Emil Ludwig's *Defender of Democracy; Masaryk of Czechoslovakia* (New York, Robert M. McBride, 1936, 278 p., front.); Emile Fournier-Fabre's *La Vie et l'œuvre politique et sociale de M. Thomas Garrigue*

Masaryk (Paris, G. Ficker, 1927, 345 p., plates, ports., fold. map); Ernst Rychnovsky's *Masaryk* (Prague, Staatliche Verlagsanstalt, 1930, 337 p., ports., bibliography: p. 331-332); Jan Herben's *T. G. Masaryk, život a dílo presidenta-Osvoboditele* (T. G. Masaryk, the life and work of the President-liberator) (Praha, Sfinx, B. Janda, 1946, 475 p., front., plates, ports., facsims.); and Zdeněk Nejedlý's *T. G. Masaryk* (Praha, Melantrich, 1930-37, 4 v. in 5, illus., ports.).

782. Seton-Watson, Robert W., *ed.* Slovakia Then and Now; a Political Survey. London, G. Allen and Unwin; Prague, Orbis, 1931. 356 p. Col. front., plates, ports., fold. map.
See also entry no. 502.
A symposium of scholarly papers on developments in Slovakia before and after 1918.

783. Sobota, Emil, *and others.* Československý President republiky (The Czechoslovak President of the Republic). Prague, Orbis, 1934. 453 p.
A scholarly study of Czechoslovakia's Presidency under the 1920 Constitution, exploring, from the political and juristic viewpoint, the extent and limits of presidential powers and prerogatives.

784. Táborský, Edward. Czechoslovak Democracy at Work. London, G. Allen and Unwin, 1945. 159 p.
Referred to as "a planned and properly articulated account of the structure and operation of Czechoslovak democracy under the constitution of 1920" by Sir Ernest Barker in his preface, this "succinct and yet comprehensive study" constitutes the most complete discussion of Czechoslovakia's prewar political system in the English language. One chapter briefly reviews the Czechoslovak wartime governmental system in exile.

785. Tobolka, Zdeněk V. Politické dějiny československého národa od r. 1848 až do dnešní doby (The political history of the Czechoslovak nation from 1848 until the present time). Praha, Nakl. Československého kompasu, 1932-1937. 4 v. in 5. Ports., facsims.
See also entry no. 759.
A massive scholarly account of political developments under Austria-Hungary.

786. Warren, William Preston. Masaryk's Democracy; a Philosophy of Scientific and Moral Culture. Chapel Hill, University of North Carolina Press, 1941. 254 p. Bibliography: p. 239-243.
See also entry no. 1183.
A valuable analysis of Masaryk's philosophy and practice of democracy.

2. Munich and the Second World War

787. Beneš, Edvard. Democracy Today and Tomorrow. New York, Macmillan, 1939. 244 p.

Based mainly on the author's lectures at the University of Chicago in the spring of 1939, the volume is an ardent exposé of President Beneš's democratic credo. In a substantially expanded two-volume Czech edition, *Demokracie dnes a zítra* (London, Kruh přátel československé knihy, 1941), Dr. Beneš further develops his ideas concerning the reforms needed to improve democracy after the war.

788. Beneš, Edvard. Šest let exilu a druhé světové války (Six years of exile and the Second World War). Praha, Orbis, 1946. 478 p.

A collection of President Benes's wartime speeches and other documents pertaining to the Czechoslovak liberation movement abroad during the Second World War.

789. Brügel, Johann W. Tschechen und Deutsche 1918-1938. München, Nymphenburger Verslagshandlung, 1967. 662 p. Bibliography: p. 637-654.

See also entry no. 649.

A thorough and well-documented study of Czech-German relations from the end of the 19th century to Munich. Written by a former Sudeten German Social Democrat and Secretary to a Sudeten German member of the prewar Czechoslovak cabinet, it analyzes dispassionately the causes of the Czech-German frictions and conflicts. For a discussion of Czech-German relations from a rather nationalistic Sudeten German viewpoint, see *Die Sudetenfrage in europäischer Sicht* (München, Robert Lerche Verlag, 1962, 281 p.), a collection of papers read and discussed at a conference of Sudeten German politicians and scholars in West Germany.

790. Dérer, Ivan. Slovenský vývoj a ľud'ácká zrada (Slovak development and the People's Party's betrayal). Praha, Kvasnička a Hampl, 1946. 364 p. Ports.

A discussion of political developments in prewar Slovakia and the pernicious role played by the separatist Slovak People's Party. The author was a leading Slovak Social Democratic politician, a former cabinet minister, and a consistent supporter of Czech-Slovak unity. For a communist account of Slovak separatist activities, see Immrich Staněk's *Zrada a pád* (The betrayal and the fall) (Praha, Státní nakladatelství politické literatury, 1958, 411 p., illus.) and Anna Kociská's *Robotnická trieda v boji proti fašizmu na Slovensku (1938-1941)* (The working class in the struggle against fascism in Slovakia [1938-1941]) (Bratislava, Vydavateľstvo Slovenské akadémie vied, 1964, 339 p.; bibliography: p. 329-339). The Slovak separatists' viewpoint is presented in *Právo Slovákov na samostatnost vo svetle dokumentov* (The Slovaks' right to independence in the light of documents) (Buenos Aires, Slovenský Oslobodzovací výbor, 1954, 996 p.), edited by Ferdinand Durčanský; and Jozef Mikus's *Slovakia, a Political History: 1918-1950* (Milwaukee, Marquette University Press, 1963, 392 p.).

791. Feierabend, Ladislav K. Ve vládě v exilu (In the government-in-exile). Washington, D.C., 1965-1966. 2 v. Facsims.

Political memoirs of the former member of the Czechoslovak cabinets in the post-Munich Republic, in the Protectorate Bohemia-Moravia, and in exile in London during the Second World War, dealing with the policies and activities of the Czechoslovak liberation movement in London. The two volumes cover the period 1940-1942. A third volume, *Beneš mezi Washingtonem a Moskvou* (Beneš between Washington and Moscow) (Washington, D.C., 1966, 182 p.), and a fourth volume *Soumrak československé demokracie* (The twilight of Czechoslovak democracy) (Washington, D.C., 1967, 183 p.), carry the story to the author's return to Czechoslovakia in June 1945. *See also* Dr. Feierabend's previously published memoirs covering his experience in the cabinets of the post-Munich Republic and the Protectorate Bohemia-Moravia, and his escape to London: *Ve vládách Druhé republiky* (In the governments of the Second Republic) (New York, Universum Press Co., 1961, 202 p., map); and *Ve vládě Protektorátu* (In the government of the Protectorate) (New York, Universum Press Co., 1962, 171 p.).

792. Husák, Gustav. Svedectvo o Slovenskom národnom povstaní (Testimony about the Slovak National Uprising). Bratislava, Vydavatel'stvo politickej literatury, 1964. 617 p. Front. Bibliography: p. 609-611.

An account of the 1944 Slovak uprising against the Nazis, by a participant who was at the time a member of the Central Committee of the illegal Slovak Communist Party. See also *Slovenské národné povstanie roku 1944* (The Slovak National Uprising of the year 1944) (Bratislava, Slovenská akadémie vied, 1965, 744 p.), a collection of papers on the uprising and its antecedents, read at a conference of historians. Other books on the Slovak uprising include: *Slovenské národné povstanie; dokumenty* (The Slovak National Uprising; documents), edited by Vilém Prečan and Miroslav Kropilák (Bratislava, Vydavatel'stvo politickej literatury, 1966, 1220 p.) and J. Jablonický's *Malý slovník Slovenského národního povstania* (A small dictionary of the Slovak National Uprising) (Bratislava, Vydavatel'stvo politickej literatury, 1964, 311 p.).

793. Korbel, Josef. The Communist Subversion of Czechoslovakia, 1938-1948; the Failure of Coexistence. Princeton, Princeton University Press, 1959. 258 p. Includes bibliographies.

See also entry no. 767.

A pithy story of President Beneš's abortive efforts to reach an acceptable *modus vivendi* with the Czechoslovak communists and Soviet Russia. Relying not only on written sources but also on interviews with direct participants and personal knowledge obtained in wartime service with the Czechoslovak government in exile, the author assesses the factors that contributed to Czechoslovakia's "conquest through coexistence."

794. Křen, Jan. Do Emigrace; buržoasní zahraniční odboj, 1938-1939 (Into emigration; the bourgeois resistance abroad, 1938-1939). Praha,

Naše vojsko, 1963. 579 p. Illus., ports., fold. maps, facsims. Bibliography: p. 573-577. (Živá minulost, sv. 51)

Planned as the first volume of a triology designed to give a synthetic picture of the Czechoslovak liberation struggle in the Second World War, this study concerns itself with the activities of the Czechoslovak "bourgeois emigration" at the time of Munich and the German occupation of Czechoslovakia in 1939.

795. Laštovička, Bohuslav. V Londýně za války; zápasy o novou ČSR, 1939-1945 (In London during the war; struggles for a new Czechoslovakia, 1939-1945). Praha, Státní nakladatelství politické literatury, 1960. 611 p. Illus.

A biased account of Czechoslovak politics in exile, by a prominent Czechoslovak communist who spent the war years in London.

796. Lockhart, *Sir* Robert H. B. Jan Masaryk, a Personal Memoir. New York, Philosophical Library, 1951. 80 p. Plate.

An intimate portrait of Thomas Masaryk's son, who was serving as Foreign Minister of Czechoslovakia at the time of the communist coup of 1948. *See also* Jan G. Masaryk's *Volá Londýn* (London calling) (Praha, Práce, 1947, 311 p., a collection of Jan Masaryk's wartime radio talks from London to his countrymen in Czechoslovakia, also published in an abridged version, *Speaking to My Country* (London, Lincolns-Praeger, 1944, 150 p.); and Viktor Fischl's *Hovory s Janem Masarykem* (Conversations with Jan Masaryk (Chicago, Kruh přátel Československé knihy, 1952, 127 p.).

797. Mackenzie, *Sir* Compton. Dr. Beneš. London, Toronto, G. G. Harrap, 1946. 356 p. Col. front., plates (part col.), ports. (part col.). Bibliography: p. 6.

The most recent and probably the best-written of the many biographies of Edvard Beneš. Appended are over 100 pages of conversations which the author had with Dr. Beneš in 1944 when gathering materials for the biography. Other biographies published since the beginning of the Second World War include: Edward B. Hitchcock's *"I Built a Temple for Peace"; the Life of Eduard Beneš* (New York, London, Harper, 1940, 364 p.); Godfrey Lias's *Beneš of Czechoslovakia* (London, G. Allen and Unwin, 1940, 303 p.); František M. Hník's *Edvard Beneš, filosof demokracie* (Edvard Beneš, philosopher of democracy) (Praha, Melantrich, 1946, 205 p.). See also *Edvard Beneš*, edited by Jan Opočenský (London, G. Allen and Unwin, 1945, 191 p.), a collection of appreciative essays in honor of Dr. Beneš's 60th birthday.

798. Otáhalová, Libuše, *and* Milada Červinková, *eds.* Dokumenty z historie československé politiky, 1939-1943 (Documents from the history of Czechoslovak politics, 1939-1943). Praha, Akademia, 1966. 2 v. Facsims. Chronological list of references: p. 755-794.

A very important collection of documents relating to the activities of the wartime Czechoslovak liberation movement in the West and to the inner-political developments in the Protectorate of Bohemia-Moravia. The documents are from the archives of President Edvard Beneš and the Protectorate President Emil Hácha.

799. Táborský, Edward (Eduard). Pravda zvítězila (Truth prevailed). Praha, Družstevní práce, 1947. 460 p.

The first volume of a prize-winning diary kept by President Beneš's personal secretary. Covers events from Munich through 1939.

800. Veselý-Štainer, Karel. Cestou národního odboje (The path of the Czechoslovak resistance). Praha, Sfinx-Janda, 1947. 295 p. Illus., maps.

A discussion of the activities of the resistance movement in Czechoslovakia from 1938 to 1945, written by one of the participants. For another volume on a similar topic *see* Jaroslav Jelínek's *Politické ústředí domácího odboje* (The political center of the resistance at home) (Praha, Kvasnička and Hampl, 1947, 214 p.). For the communist viewpoint on the wartime resistance movement in Czechoslovakia see *KSČ v boji za svobodu* (KSČ in the struggle for freedom), edited by B. Pavlik (Praha, Svoboda, 1949, 280 p.); *Z bojů za svobodu* (From the struggles for freedom) (Praha, Státní nakladatelství politické literatury, 1963, 404 p.); and *Odboj a revoluce, 1938-1945* (The resistance and the revolution, 1938-1945), edited by Oldřich Janeček (Praha, Naše vojsko, 1965, 434 p.).

3. Since 1945

801. Barton, Paul, *pseud.* Prague à l'heure de Moscou: analyse d'une démocratie populaire. Paris, P. Horay, 1954. 355 p.
See also entry no. 954.

A solid analysis of Czechoslovakia's political system in the Stalinist era. Lucidly written by a former Czechoslovak trade union functionary.

802. Bertelmann, Karel. Vývoj národních výborů do ústavy. 9. května, 1945-1948 (The development of the national committees until the Ninth-of-May Constitution, 1945-1948). Praha, Nakl. Československé akademie věd, 1964. 421 p. Bibliography: p. 396-402.

A detailed study of the emergence and the development of national (people's) committees, the postwar organs of local government that became a major locale of communist influence. *See also* the same author's *Vznik národních výborů* (The origin of the national committees) (Praha, Československá akademie věd, 1956, 129 p.).

803. Bolton, Glorney. Czech Tragedy. London, Watts, 1955. 240 p.

A rather nostalgic sketch of Czechoslovakia's political vicissitudes from the First World War to the communist coup of 1948, as reflected in the life and work of Thomas Masaryk, Edvard Beneš, and Jan Masaryk.

804. Bušek, Vratislav, *and* Nicolas Spulber, *eds.* Czechoslovakia. New York, Praeger, 1957. 520 p. Maps, tables. Bibliography: p. 484-499. (Praeger Publications in Russian History and World Communism, no. 19)

See also entries no. 509, 581, *and* 909.

Part 2 of this general reference work contains several articles examining Czechoslovakia's political system under communism; an appendix presents biographical sketches of leading personalities of the communist regime.

805. Bystřina, Ivan. Lidová demokracie (The people's democracy). Praha, Nakl. Československé akademie věd, 1957. 240 p.

People's democracy, specifically the Czechoslovak variety, is discussed as a form of the dictatorship of the proletariat. *See also* the same author's *K teorii socialistické státnosti* (Concerning the theory of socialist statehood) (2d ed., Praha, Nakl. Československé akademie věd, 1964, 308 p., bibliographical footnotes).

806. Chalupa, Vlastislav. Rise and Development of a Totalitarian State. Leiden, H. E. Stenfert Kroese, 1959. 294 p. Diagrs., tables. (Library of the Czechoslovak Foreign Institute in Exile, 2)

The first part (about one-fourth of the book) deals with the rise of the totalitarian state in general, and the second analyzes specific developments in Czechoslovakia from 1944 to 1953. The author's emphasis is on the techniques used in the communist seizure of control and their consolidation through skillful manipulation and "managerization" of the entire society.

807. Czechoslovak Republik. *Československá tisková kancelář.* Organizace Československé socialistické republiky (Organization of the Czechoslovak Socialist Republic). v. 1. Edited by Václav Brož. Praha, 1965– (loose-leaf)

A directory of 400 political, administrative, social, and cultural organizations and of some 4,000 of their principal officers.

808. Diamond, William. Czechoslovakia between East and West. Published under the auspices of the London Institute of World Affairs. London, Stevens, 1947. 258 p. Fold. map. Bibliography: p. 243-249.

An overly optimistic examination of political developments in postwar Czechoslovakia prior to the communist coup of 1948.

809. Eliáš, Zdeněk, *and* Jaromír Netík. Czechoslovakia. *In* Griffith, William E., *ed.* Communism in Europe; Continuity, Change, and the Sino-Soviet Dispute. Cambridge, The MIT Press, 1966. p. 157-276.

A good survey of the developments of the Czechoslovak Communist Party from its beginning to 1963-1964, with emphasis on the post-1948 period.

810. Friedman, Otto. The Break-up of Czech Democracy. London, Gollancz, 1950. 176 p.

A dispassionate study of the events and factors that led to the demise of Czechoslovakia's democracy in 1948.

811. Gadourek, Ivan. The Political Control of Czechoslovakia; a Study in Social Control of a Soviet Communist State. Leiden, Stenfert Kroese, 1953. 285 p. Bibliography: p. 237-238.

See also entry no. 959.

In the first part of the study the author describes how and to what extent the communist rulers control the various spheres of the societal life of Czechoslovakia. In the second part, entitled "Conceptualization," he identifies the principal agencies and mechanisms of control and evaluates their impact.

812. Gottwald, Klement. Spisy (Writings). Praha, Státní nakladatelství politické literatury, 1953-1961. 15 v.

Collected works of the late long-time leader of the Communist Party of Czechoslovakia and the first communist president of Czechoslovakia. *See also* Klement Gottwald's *Vybrané spisy* (Selected writings) (Praha, Státní nakladatelství politické literatury, 1954-55, 2 v., illus.), containing the most important speeches from 1925 to 1953.

813. Grospič, Jiří, Vlastimír Kolomazník, *and* Karol Ondris. Zastupitelská soustava Československé socialistické republiky (The representative system of the Czechoslovak Socialist Republic). Praha, Orbis, 1962. 167 p. Bibliographical footnotes.

An informative study of socialist Czechoslovakia's system of political representation. See also *Zastupitelské orgány, nástroj pracujícího lidu ve výstavbě socialismu* (The representative organs, the instrument of the working people in the construction of socialism), edited by Pavel Peške (Praha, Orbis, 1954, 68 p.), and Bedřich Rattinger's *Nejvyšší státní orgány lidově demokratického Československa; národní shromáždění a president republiky* (The highest state organs of people's democratic Czechoslovakia; the National Assembly and the President of the Republic) (Praha, Státní nakladatelství politické literatury, 1957, 91 p.; bibliography: p. 87-89).

814. Josten, Josef. Oh, My Country. London, Latimer House, 1949. 255 p. Ports., maps (part col.), facsim.

An account of the communist seizure of Czechoslovakia in 1948, written by a Czechoslovak journalist and former Foreign Ministry official.

815. Knapp, Viktor, *and* Zdenek Mlynar. La Tchécoslovaquie. Paris, Librairie génerale de droit et de jurisprudence, 1965. 263 p.

A study of Czechoslovakia's political system by two prominent scholars of Czechoslovakia's present establishment.

816. Komunistická strana Československa. *Sjezd. 13th, Praha, 1966.* XIII. [Trinásty] sjazd Komunistickej strany Československa (13th

Congress of the Communist Party of Czechoslovakia). Bratislava, Vydavatel'stvo politickej literatury, 1966. 514 p.

Official proceedings of the Congress, containing mainly reports presented, discussion, and resolutions. For the proceedings of the sessions of the Party Central Committee see *Usnesení a dokumenty ústředního výboru Komunistické strany Československa* (Resolutions and documents of the Central Committee of the Communist Party of Czechoslovakia) (Praha, Nakladatelství politické literatury, 1965, 424 p.), as well as previous such collections under the same title.

For a collection of official Czechoslovak documents in English translation pertaining to policies during the liberalization period, see *Czechoslovakia's Blueprint for Freedom*, edited by Paul Ello (Washington, D.C., Acropolis, 1968, 304 p.).

817. Kuhn, Heinrich. Der Kommunismus in der Tschechoslowakei. I. Organisationsstatuten und Satzungen. Köln, Verlag Wissenschaft und Politik, 1965. 304 p. Bibliography.

Contains the statutes and other organizational materials of the Czechoslovak Communist Party from 1920 to 1962, with a historical-political introduction. For official presentations of the history of the Communist Party, *see*:

Prague. Ústav dějin Komunistické strany Československa. Příruční slovník k dějinám KSČ (Reference dictionary for the history of the Communist Party of Czechoslovakia). Praha, Nakl. politické literatury, 1964. 2 v.

Prague. Ústav dějin Komunistické strany Československa. Dějiny KSČ (The history of the Communist Party of Czechoslovakia). Praha, Nakl. politické literatury 1963. 4 pts. Illus., facsims., maps. An interesting document reflecting the liberalization process is:

The Action Programme of the Communist Party of Czechoslovakia; Adopted at the Plenary Session of the Central Committee. . . . on April 5th, 1968. Prague, Komunistická strana Československa, Ústřední výbor, 1968. 90 p.

818. Kuhn, Heinrich. Handbuch der Tschechoslowakei. München, Robert Lerche, 1967. 1021 p.

See also entry no. 512.

An encyclopedic study of Czechoslovakia's political system and its development since 1945. Contains also an exhaustive listing of party and government functionaries.

See also Heinrich Kuhn and Otto Böss' *Biographisches Handbuch der Tschechoslowakei* (München, Robert Lerche, 1961, 640 p.), a Who's Who of communist Czechoslovakia's political personalities and a roster of organizations.

819. Laco, Karol. Ústava předmníchovskej ČSR a ústava ČSSR (The Constitution of pre-Munich Czechoslovakia and the Constitution of the Czechoslovak Socialist Republic). Bratislava, Vydavatel'stvo Slovenskej akadémie vied, 1966. 660 p. Bibliography: p. 597-602.

A Marxist-oriented comparative study of the constitutions of precommunist and communist Czechoslovakia, emphasizing the differences between the bourgeois and socialist political system.

820. Novotný, Antonín. Prejavy a state (Speeches and articles). Bratislava, Vydavatel'stvo politickej literatury, 1964. 3 v.

A collection of the most important speeches delivered from 1954 to 1964 by Czechoslovakia's president and first secretary of the Czechoslovak Communist Party.

821. O stanovách Komunistické strany Československa (On the statutes of the Communist Party of Czechoslovakia). Praha, Státní nakladatelství politické literatury, 1965. 232 p.

The latest version of the Statutes adopted by the Party's 12th Congress and their explanation.

822. Opat, Jaroslav. O novou demokracii (For a new democracy). Praha, Academia, 1966. 266 p. Bibliography: p. 259-262.

An examination of the factors, forces, and circumstances which brought about the emergence of the new people's democracy in Czechoslovakia in 1945-1948.

823. Pavlíček, Václav. Politické strany po únoru. (Political parties after February). Praha, Svobodné slovo, 1966-1968. 2 v.

A discussion of the status and development of the Czech noncommunist parties from 1945 to 1948 and after the communist coup of 1948.

824. Ripka, Hubert. Czechoslovakia Enslaved; the Story of the Communist Coup d'État. London, Gollancz, 1950. 339 p.

A detailed account of the communist "prefabricated revolution" of 1948, written by a prominent member of the Czechoslovak Socialist Party who was also a member of the Czechoslovak cabinet at the time of the coup.

825. Schmidt, Dana A. Anatomy of a Satellite. Boston, Little, Brown, 1952. 512 p. Illus.

An absorbing and ably written account of the 1948 communist takeover of Czechoslovakia and the way in which it transformed the country, by the Prague correspondent of the *New York Times*.

826. Smutný, Jaromír. Únorový převrat 1948 (The February coup 1948). London, Ústav Dr. Edvarda Beneše pro politické a sociální studium, 1953. 3 v. in 1.

A day-by-day description of events leading to the seizure of power by the communists in February 1948 and the subsequent resignation of President Beneš in June 1948 as told by the then head of the President's Chancellery.

827. Táborský, Edward (Eduard). Naše nová ústava (Our new constitution). Praha, Čin, 1948. 598 p. Bibliography: p. 573-576.

The author analyzes what he considers to have been the main defects of prewar Czechoslovakia's constitutional and political system. Having explored a number of other political systems, he recommends as most suitable for postwar Czechoslovakia a new system based mainly on a stronger presidency, fewer political parties, broader local self-government, and an economic system based on a mutually competitive public, cooperative, and private enterprise. *See also* the same author's *O novou demokracii* (For a new democracy) (Praha, F. Borový, 1945, 105 p.).

828. Táborský, Edward. Communism in Czechoslovakia, 1948-1960. Princeton, N.J., Princeton University Press, 1961. 628 p. Bibliography: p. 609-620.

See also entry no. 1026.

The most comprehensive English-language treatment of communist rule in Czechoslovakia from the seizure of power in 1948 to 1960. Based mostly on primary sources, the volume is subdivided into four parts dealing in turn with the Communist Party and its National Front partners, the "transmission belts" of formal government, economic developments, culture, education, and indoctrination. For an analysis of events leading up to the Soviet invasion of Czechoslovakia, and of developments since the occupation, *see* Joseph G. Whelan's *Aspects of Intellectual Ferment and Dissent in Czechoslovakia* (Washington, U.S. Govt. Print. Off., 1969, 165 p.).

For further developments since 1960, *see* Táborský's "Czechoslovakia: Out of Stalinism?" in *Problems of Communism* (Washington), v. 13, no. 3, May/June 1964: 5-14; and "Where Is Czechoslovakia Going?" in *East Europe* (New York), v. 16, no. 2, February 1967: 2-12.

The best literature published on the recent liberalization period of Czechoslovakia is exemplified by the following books:

Czechoslovakia 1968. Canadian Slavonic Papers. Revue Canadienne des Slavistes, v. 10, Winter 1968: 409-597.

Československá akademie věd. *Historický ústav*. The Czech Black-Book. Edited by Robert Littell. New York, Praeger, 1969. 303 p.

Tatu, Michel. L'Hérésie impossible, chronique du drame tchécoslovaque. Paris, B. Grasset, 1968. 291 p.

Tchechoslowakei. August 68. Die Tragödie eines tapferen Volkes. Edited by Hans K. Studer. Zűrich, Weltrundschau Verlag A. G., 1968. 207 p.

Wechsberg, Joseph. The Voices. Garden City, New York, Doubleday, 1969. 113 p.

Windsor, Philip, *and* Adam Roberts. Czechoslovakia 1968. Reform, Repression and Resistance. London, Chatto and Windus for the Institute of Strategic Studies, 1969. 199 p.

Zeman, Z. A. B. Prague Spring. New York, Hill and Wang, 1969. 167 p.

829. Veselý, Jindřich. Kronika únorových dnů 1948 (Chronicle of the

February days of 1948). Praha, Státní nakladatelství politické literatury, 1958. 232 p.

A rather one-sided description of the 1948 communist seizure of power in Czechoslovakia, extolling the role and intentions of the Communist Party and placing blame on the bourgeois parties. Other volumes giving the communist view of the communist revolution in Czechoslovakia include: *Únor 1948; sborník dokumentů* (February 1948; a collection of documents) (Praha, Státní nakladatelství politické literatury, 1958, 243 p.); Gríša Spurný's *Únorové dny* (The February days) (Praha, Státní nakladatelství politické literatury, 1958, 81 p.); *Československá revoluce v letech 1944-1948* (The Czechoslovak revolution, 1944-1948) (Praha, Československá akademie věd, 1965, 288 p.); and *Otázky národní a demokratické revoluce v ČSR* (The questions of the national and democratic revolution in ČSR), edited by Miloš Klimeš (Praha, Československá akademie věd, 1955, 344 p.).

830. Zápotocký, Antonín. Nová odborová politika (The new trade union policy). 3d ed. Prague, Práce, 1948. 517 p.

A collection of speeches and pronouncements concerning the trade unions and their role, delivered in 1945 and 1946 by the communist trade union leader who subsequently became the second communist president of Czechoslovakia. *See also* the same author's *Boj o jednotu odborů* (The struggle for the unity of the trade unions) (Praha, Práce, 1950, 382 p.), a collection of Zápotocký's statements on trade unions from 1927 to 1938. For subsequent communist pronouncements on the trade unions see *KSČ o úloze odborů při výstavbě socialismu* (KSČ on the role of trade unions in the construction of socialism) (Praha, Práce, 1962, 782 p.), a collection of the most important partv decisions and directives concerning the trade unions.

831. Zinner, Paul E. Communist Strategy and Tactics in Czechoslovakia, 1918-48. New York, Praeger, 1963. 264 p. Includes bibliography. (Praeger Publications in Russian History and World Communism, no. 129)

A well-documented history of Czechoslovakia's Communist Party in action, from its origins to its seizure of power in Czechoslovakia in 1948. The longest and most important portion of the study is devoted to a searching analysis of the period 1945-1948, when the party's "grand design" for complete domination was brought to successful completion.

4. Periodicals

832. Československý přehled (Czechoslovak survey). 1954-1958. New York, Free Europe Committee. Monthly.

Contains articles, summaries, and excerpts of articles in periodicals pertaining to current political and other developments in Czechoslovakia. Preceded (since 1950) by *Správa o Československu* (Report on Czechoslovakia). Since 1954 the Free Europe Committee has published the bimonthly *News from Czechoslovakia* (*Československý zpravodaj*).

833. Naše doba (Our time). 1945-1947. Praha. Frequency varies.

Earlier series published (since 1893) before both the First and Second World Wars. Edited at one time by Thomas G. Masaryk and Edvard Beneš, this was undoubtedly the best Czech monthly concerned with a broad spectrum of political, economic, and social problems of contemporary importance.

834. Nová mysl (New thought). 1947– Praha. Monthly.

The main theoretical journal of the Czechoslovak Communist Party, published by the Central Committee.

835. Novinářský sborník (The digest of journalism). 1956– Praha. Quarterly.

Official journal of the Union of Czechoslovak Journalists.

836. Život strany (Party life). 1954– Praha. Bimonthly.

The official journal on internal Communist Party affairs, published by the Central Committee.

B. LAW

1. Monographs

837. Adamovich, Ludwig. Der Grundriss des tschechoslowakischen Staatsrechtes. Wien, Druk und Verlag der öterreichischen Staatsdruckerei, 1929. 517 p. Bibliographies.

A thorough study of the constitutional and administrative law of prewar Czechoslovakia, by a former professor of the German University of Prague.

See also František Weyr's *Československé ústavní právo* (Czechoslovak constitutional law) (Praha, Melantrich, 1937, 339 p.); Jiří Hoetzel's *Československé správní právo* (Czechoslovak administrative law) (Praha, Melantrich, 1937, 507 p.); and Fritz Sander's *Grundriss des tschechoslowakischen Verfassungsrechtes* (Reichenberg, Verlag Gebrüder Stiepel, 1938, 504 p.).

838. Bibliography of Czechoslovak Legal Literature, 1945-1958. Prepared by the Institute of Law of the Czechoslovak Academy of Sciences. Prague, Publishing House of the Czechoslovak Academy of Sciences, 1959. 261 p.

A selected English-language bibliography of books, monographs, and articles by Czechoslovak authors on various aspects of law (primarily Czechoslovak law). Each chapter deals with a different branch of law and is preceded by an explanatory article.

839. Bogszak, Jiří. Základy socialistické zákonnosti v ČSSR (The foundations of socialist legality in the Czechoslovak Socialist Republic).

Praha, Nakl. Československé akademie věd, 1963. 217 p. Bibliographical footnotes.

An analysis of socialist legality as a method for carrying out state functions, especially in the creation of law. Includes German and Russian summaries.

840. Československá vlastivěda (Book of knowledge on Czechoslovakia). Praha, Sfinx, 1929-1936. 10 v. in 12. Illus., ports., maps, facsims. Includes bibliographies.

See also entries no. 495, 614, *and* 770.

Volume five of this encyclopedic work on Czechoslovakia contains a number of background articles on law and the courts.

841. The Constitution of the Czechoslovak Socialist Republic. Prague, Orbis, 1960. 105 p.

The official English translation of the present Czechoslovak constitution. An English translation of the Czechoslovak Constitution of 1948 (the so-called Ninth-of-May Constitution) may be found in Amos J. Peaslee's *Constitutions of Nations* (The Hague, Martinus Nijhoff, 1956, p. 689-728). For an English translation of the Czechoslovak Constitution of 1920 see *The Constitution of the Czechoslovak Republic*, with an introduction by Jiří Hoetzel and V. Joachim (Prague, Édition de la Société l'Effort de la Tchécoslovaquie, 1920, 54 p.).

842. Czechoslovak Yearbook of International Law. London, Published under the auspices of the Czechoslovak Branch of the International Law Association, 1942. 236 p.

This collection of scholarly articles by British and Czechoslovak jurists contains a number of contributions relative to Czechoslovakia (on the Munich agreement, the German occupation of Czechoslovakia, the legal position of the Czechoslovak government in exile, etc.). Edited by Václav Beneš, Alfred Drucker, and Edward Táborský.

843. Mid-European Law Project. Legal Sources and Bibliography of Czechoslovakia. New York, Praeger (for the Free Europe Committee), 1959. 180 p.

A systematized bibliography of legal sources, writings, and materials, compiled by Vladimir Gsovski and others. Includes a list of major Czechoslovak laws enacted between April 1945 and March 1957.

844. Gsovski, Vladimir, *and* Kazimierz Grzybowski, *eds.* Government, Law and Courts in the Soviet Union and Eastern Europe. New York, Praeger, 1959, 2 v. (2067 p.). Bibliography: p. 1945-2009.

See also entry no. 2757.

This massive comparative study contains a number of essays on various aspects of the Czechoslovak communist system of law and courts, including the administration of justice, organization and procedure of the courts, the bar, criminal and civil law, and laws relative to labor and peasantry.

845. Hromada, Juraj, *and others.* Právnický slovník (Legal encyclopedia). 2d ed. Praha, Orbis, 1965. 868 p.

Alphabetically arranged, the encyclopedia contains over one thousand entries on public, private, civil, and criminal law, as well as some basic aspects of international law. Other recent texts on various fields of Czechoslovak law include: *Nové občanské právo* (New civil law), by Zdeněk Kratochvíl and others (Praha, Orbis, 1965, 716 p.); *Občanské právo procesní* (Civil procedure), by František Štajgr and others (Praha, Orbis, 1964, 424 p.); Jaroslav Kovařík's *Pracovní právo ČSSR* (The labor law of the Czechoslovak Socialist Republic) (Praha, Svoboda, 1967, 370 p.); *Rodinné právo* (Family law), by Josef Glos and others (Praha, Orbis, 1965, 304 p.); *Trestný zákon; Trestný poriadok a s nimi suvisiace predpisy* (The criminal code; criminal procedure and related provisions), by František Paníček and others (Bratislava, Obzor, 1965, 936 p.); and *Hospodářský zákoník* (The economic legal code), by Karel Svitavský and others (Praha, Orbis, 1966, 994 p.).

846. Lakatoš, Michal. Občan, právo a demokracie (The citizen, the law, and democracy). Praha, Svobodné slovo, 1966. 159 p. (Živé myšlenky, 10)

An interesting monograph on the relationship of lawmaking and democracy in the socialist system, the limits of lawmaking authority, and the citizens' position, written by a liberal Slovak jurist. *See also* the same author's *Formy československého prava* (The forms of Czechoslovak law) (Praha, Československá akademie věd, 1956, 90 p.), and *Otázky lidové demokracie* (The questions of people's democracy) (Praha, Československá akademie věd, 1957, 134 p., bibliography).

847. Raschhofer, Hermann. Die Sudetenfrage. Ihre völkerrechtliche Entwicklung vom Ersten Weltkrieg bis zur Gegenwart. München, Isar Verlag, 1953. 310 p. Bibliographical footnotes.

See also entry no. 661.

A thorough but one-sided examination of the status of the Sudeten German areas from the viewpoint of international law. The author's thesis is that, having been validly ceded to Germany in 1938, the Sudetenland is merely an "interim protective holding" of Czechoslovakia's.

848. Slovník veřejného práva československého (The encyclopedia of Czechoslovak public law). Brno, Nakl. Polygrafia-Rohrer, 1929-1948. 5 v. Bibliographies.

The most comprehensive encyclopedia of Czechoslovakia's public law prior to the communist seizure of power in 1948. Covers the entire period of precommunist Czechoslovakia from 1918 to 1948, and contains entries on all important aspects of public law prepared by specialists in the respective fields.

849. Sobota, Emil. Co to byl protektorát (What the protectorate was). Praha, Kvasnička and Hampl, 1946. 164 p.

A juridical-political study of various aspects of the German protectorate over Bohemia-Moravia, written during the Nazi occupation by a former high-ranking official of the Czechoslovak president's office who was executed by the Nazi regime a few days before the end of the war.

850. Sobota, Emil. Das tschechoslowakische Nationalitätenrecht. Prague, Orbis, 1931. 461 p. (Tschechoslovakische Quellen und Dokumente, Nr. 7)

A useful German translation of documentary materials relative to nationalities laws in precommunist Czechoslovakia. *See also* Leo Epstein's *Das Sprachenrecht in der Tschechoslowakischen Republik* (Reichenberg, Gebrüder Stiepel, 1927, 353 p., tables, "Literatur": p. 4).

851. Štajgr, František, *and* Otakar Plundr. Organizace justice a prokuratury (The organization of justice and the procuracy). Praha, Orbis, 1957. 242 p.

An informative study of the organization of the Czechoslovak system of courts and public prosecution, by two law professors at Charles University in Prague. *See also* Otakar Plundr's updated volume under the same title (Praha, Orbis, 1964, 288 p.). For a non-Marxist view, *see* Edward Táborský's "Socialist Legality" in his *Communism in Czechoslovakia, 1948-1960* (Princeton, Princeton University Press, 1961), p. 268-303.

852. Táborský, Edward. The Czechoslovak Cause. London, H. F. & G. Witherby, 1944. 158 p. Bibliography: p. 1-2.

An examination and evaluation of Czechoslovakia's case during the Second World War from the standpoint of international law. The main thesis is that, the Munich agreement and other acts against Czechoslovakia notwithstanding, the country has never ceased to exist legally as an International Person within its pre-1938 boundaries. A somewhat enlarged Czech edition of the book was subsequently published under the title *Naše věc* (Our cause) (Praha, Melantrich, 1946, 220 p.).

853. Vaněček, V. Dějiny státu a práva v Československu do roku 1945 The history of state and law in Czechoslovakia until the year 1945). Praha, Orbis, 1964. 620 p.

A massive study of the history of the state and the law in the territories now constituting Czechoslovakia. Written by a professor of law at Charles University in Prague, it covers the period from the emergence of the very first state forms until 1945. *See also* Jiří Klabouch's *Osvícenské právní nauky v českých zemích* (Legal science in the Czech lands at the time of the Enlightenment) (Praha, Československá akademie věd, 1958, 356 p., illus.).

2. Periodicals

854. Bulletin de droit tchécoslovaque. 1945– Prague. Quarterly.

Publication of the Union of Czechoslovak Lawyers. Contains informative articles on various aspects and developments of Czechoslovak law. Includes an English résumé. Since 1951, also published in Russian.

855. Časopis pro mezinárodní právo (Journal of international law). 1957– Praha. Quarterly.

Publication of the Law Institute of the Czechoslovak Academy of Sciences.

856. Časopis pro právní a státní vědu (Journal of legal and political science). 1945-1947. Brno. Monthly.

Publication of the Union of Moravian Lawyers. A scholarly journal devoted to questions of law and politics. It was also published before the Second World War. Ceased publication after the communist coup of 1948.

857. Hlídka mezinárodního práva (Review of international law). 1938-1939. Praha. Quarterly.

Publication of the Czechoslovak Association for International Law. A scholarly journal devoted exclusively to problems of international law. Ceased publication with Hitler's dismemberment of Czechoslovakia.

858. Právně-historické studie (Studies in legal history). 1955– Praha. Annual.

See also entry no. 718.

Publication of the Law Institute of the Czechoslovak Academy of Sciences, specializing in matters of Czechoslovak legal history.

859. Právnické štúdie (Juridical studies). 1953– Bratislava. Quarterly.

A journal of legal studies, with a good deal of attention to legal history, published by the Institute for State and Law of the Slovak Academy of Sciences.

860. Právník (The jurist). 1945– Praha. Monthly.

Published by the Union of Czechoslovak Lawyers, the Law Institute of the Ministry of Justice, and the Law Institute of the Czechoslovak Academy of Sciences. A legal journal with a long tradition, devoted to questions of law and state. First published in 1861.

861. Právný obzor (Legal review). 1945– Bratislava. Monthly.

Published by the Slovak Academy of Sciences. The Slovak equivalent of *Právník*.

862. Czechoslovak Republic. *Laws, statutes, etc.* Sbírka zákonů Československé socialistické republiky (Collection of laws of the Czechoslovak Socialist Republic). 1962– Praha, Ministerstvo spravedlnosti. Irregular.

The official register for the promulgation of the laws enacted by the National Assembly and the Slovak National Council; the legal provisions of the Presidium of the National Assembly; international treaties; ordinances issued by the Council of Ministers, various ministries and central government agencies; the resolutions of the Slovak Board of Commissioners; and other official regulations and announcements by the organs of the central and regional government.

Until 1962 the title was *Sbírka zákonů Republiky československé* (Collection of laws of the Czechoslovak Republic), and prior to 1948 *Sbírka zákonů a nařízení Republiky československé* (Collection of laws and ordinances of the Czechoslovak Republic). Until 1962 *Úřední list Republiky československé* (Official gazette of the Czechoslovak Republic) promulgated official announcements other than those included in the Collection of Laws. *Zbierka zákonov Slovenskej národnej rady* (Collection of laws of the Slovak National Council) was published as a separate law gazette for Slovakia from 1944 to 1961 (Bratislava, Povereníctvo vnútra).

863. Sborník věd právních a státních (The digest of legal and political science). 1945-1958. Praha. Semiannual.

A highly reputable journal of long standing which ceased publication after the communist coup of 1948. Carried a wide range of scholarly studies on various aspects of law and politics.

864. Stát a právo (State and law). 1956– Praha. Semiannual.

Publication of the Law Institute of the Czechoslovak Academy of Sciences. Features essays on law and the state.

865. Studie z mezinárodního práva (Studies in international law). 1955– Praha. Annual.

Published by the Law Institute of the Czechoslovak Academy of Sciences. Devoted to problems of international law, public and private.

866. Universitas Carolina-Iuridica. 1955– Prague. Semiannual.

A collection of legal essays published by the Law School of Charles University in Prague.

C. FOREIGN RELATIONS

1. Through the First World War and the Foundation of Czechoslovakia

867. Beneš, Edvard. My War Memoirs. London, G. Allen and Unwin, 1928. 512 p. Front. (port.).

A considerably abridged translation of *Světová válka a naše revoluce* (The World War and our revolution) (Praha, Orbis, 1927-28, 3 v.), the most comprehensive and authoritative account of the work of the Czechoslovak liberation movement abroad during the First World War. Beneš was Thomas Masaryk's main collaborator and subsequently became Czechoslovakia's foreign minister and Masaryk's successor in the presidency.

868. Dějiny československo-sovětských vztahů, nové a nejnovější doby. 1. Dějiny česko-ruských vztahů 1770-1917 (The history of Czechoslovak-Soviet relations in recent and contemporary times. 1. The history of Czech-Russian relations, 1770-1917). Praha, Academia, 1967. 408 p.

A comprehensive examination of Czech-Russian relations from the 18th century to the Bolshevik Revolution in Russia, by a group of specialists. To be followed by other volumes dealing with relations since 1917.

869. Masaryk, Tomáš Garrigue. The Making of a State: Memories and Observations, 1914-1918. New York, Frederick A. Stokes, 1927. 518 p. Front. (port.).

Personal memoirs of the leader of the Czechoslovak liberation movement during the First World War who subsequently became the first president of Czechoslovakia. The author gives an account of his work and traces the stages in the struggle for his country's independence, but also deals with the deeper causes of the war and revolution and intersperses his narrative with many incisive political and philosophical observations. A translation of *Světová revoluce za války a ve válce, 1914-1918* (The world revolution during the war, 1914-1918) (Praha, Čin a Orbis, 1925, 650 p.). For a German reply, *see* Rudolf Nadobny's *Germanisierung oder Slavisierung?* (Berlin, O. Stolberg, 1928, 208 p.

See also *Cesta demokracie* (The Path of Democracy) (Praha, Čin, 1933, 530 p.), a collection of speeches and essays by Masaryk together with other documents pertaining to the years 1918-1920, edited by Vasil Škrach.

870. Perman, D. The shaping of the Czechoslovak State; Diplomatic History of the Boundaries of Czechoslovakia, 1914-1920. Leiden, E. J. Brill, 1962. 339 p. Bibliography: p. 276-313.

A comprehensive examination of the various factors which influenced the determination of Czechoslovakia's boundaries after the First World War. The author views the result largely as a by-product of other settlements and obligations, as well as of accomplished facts, "haphazardness," and lack of planning.

2. 1919-1937

871. Beneš, Edvard. Boj o mír a bezpečnost státu (The struggle for the peace and the security of the state). Praha, Orbis, 1934. 832 p.

A comprehensive collection of speeches and essays on international affairs from 1924 through 1933 by the then foreign minister.

872. Kapitoly z dějin vzájemných vztahů národů ČSR a SSSR (Chapters from the history of mutual relations of the peoples of Czechoslovakia and the Soviet Union). Praha, Nakl. Československé akademie věd, 1958. 310 p.

A symposium of studies dealing with the work of the scientific institutes of the Czechoslovak Academy of Science and the Prague and Brno universities in the field of Soviet-Czechoslovak relations.

873. Kerner, Robert J., *ed.* Czechoslovakia, Twenty Years of Independence. Berkeley and Los Angeles, University of California Press, 1940. 504 p. Front., illus. (maps), plates, ports., bibliographies.

See also entries no. 505 *and* 776.

Several articles in this commemorative volume deal with Czechoslovakia's prewar foreign relations, including: "Diplomatic Origins and Foreign Policy" by Felix John Vondracek; "The Little Entente and the Balkan Entente" by Harry Nicholas Howard; "The Road to Munich and Beyond" by Bernadotte E. Schmitt; "World War, Revolution and Peace Conference" by Robert J. Kerner; and "What Woodrow Wilson and America Meant to Czechoslovakia" by Herbert Adolphus Miller.

874. Kvaček, Robert. Nad Evropou zataženo. Československo a Evropa 1933-1937 (Clouds over Europe. Czechoslovakia and Europe, 1933-1937). Praha, Svoboda, 1967. 456 p.

A detailed analysis of Czechoslovakia's international relations during the period 1933-1937, based on a substantial body of published literature as well as archival sources. A second volume will deal with Munich.

875. Německý imperialismus proti ČSR, 1918-1939 (German imperialism against the Czechoslovak Republic, 1918-1939). Praha, Státní nakladatelství politické literatury, 1962. 605 p.

A massive collection of documents on German intrigues and actions against Czechoslovakia prior to the Second World War.

876. Soják, Vladimír, *ed.* O československé zahraniční politice, 1918-1939; sborník statí (On Czechoslovak foreign policy, 1918-1939; a symposium of articles). Praha, Státní nakladatelství politické literatury, 1956. 439 p. Facsims. Bibliography: p. 430-434.

A collection of studies and documents on Czechoslovakia's foreign policy between the two world wars, with emphasis on Czechoslovak-German relations.

877. Strauss, Emil. Tschechoslowakische Aussenpolitik. Prag, Orbis-Verlag, 1936. 164 p. Port. Bibliographical references: p. 163-164.

An examination of the foreign policy of pre-Munich Czechoslovakia.

878. Studie z dějin československo-sovětských vztahů, 1917-1938 (Studies

from the history of Czechoslovak-Soviet relations, 1917-1938). Praha, Československá akademie věd, 1967. 126 p.

A symposium on Czechoslovak-Soviet relations prepared by members of the Institute of the History of the European Socialist Countries of the Czechoslovak Academy of Science and the Institute of Slavic Studies of the Academy of Sciences of the USSR. See also *Z najnovších dejín československo-sovietských vzťahov po roku 1945* (From the most recent history of Czechoslovak-Soviet relations after the year 1945) (Bratislava, Vydavatel'stvo Slovenskej akadémie vied, 1962, 221 p.), a collection of studies on various aspects of Czechoslovak-Soviet relations since 1945.

879. Vondracek, Felix J. The Foreign Policy of Czechoslovakia, 1918-1935. New York, Columbia University Press, 1937. 451 p. Fold. map. Bibliography: p. 426-444.

A fairly detailed and solid account of the major stages and developments of Czechoslovakia's foreign relations until the resignation of President Masaryk in 1935.

880. Wiskemann, Elizabeth. Czechs and Germans: a Study of the Struggle in the Historic Provinces of Bohemia and Moravia. London, New York, Oxford University Press, 1938. 299 p. Maps.

See also entry no. 659.

A searching study of the perennial Czech-German feuding by a noted British student of Slav-German relations. Having explored the historical background of Czech-German relations, the author concentrates on the developments and conflicts since the First World War. A second edition was recently published by Macmillan (New York, 1967).

3. Munich and the Second World War

881. Beckmann, Rudolf. K diplomatickému pozadí Mnichova (Concerning the diplomatic background of Munich). Praha, Státní nakladatelství politické literatury, 1954. 371 p.

A somewhat slanted study of the developments leading to the Munich settlement. Highly critical not only of the Western appeasement policy, but also of the attitude and role of the Czechoslovak bourgeoisie. See also *Mnichov v dokumentech* (Munich in documents) (Praha, Státní nakladatelství politické literatury, 1958, 2 v., illus., facsims., ports.), and *Nové dokumenty k historii Mnichova* (New documents concerning the history of Munich) (Praha, Státní nakladatelství politické literatury, 1958, 124 p.).

882. Beneš, Edvard. Memoirs: From Munich to New War and New Victory. Boston, Houghton Mifflin, 1954. 346 p.

A most valuable account by Czechoslovakia's late president concerning his actions as the leader of the Czechoslovak liberation movement abroad during the Second World War. After a brief outline of international developments leading to the Munich settlement, Dr. Beneš deals with the major aspects of international as well as internal politics affecting his country, including his negotiations with Churchill, Roosevelt, Stalin, Eden, Sikorski, the Czechoslovak communist leaders, and others. A translation of *Paměti: od Mnichova k nové válce a novému vítězství* (Memoirs: from Munich to new war and new victory) (Praha, Orbis, 1947, 518 p.).

883. Brod, Toman, *and* Eduard Čejka. Na západní frontě (On the western front). 2d ed. Praha, Naše vojsko, 1965. 609 p. Illus., facsims, ports. Bibliography: p. 577-583.

The first book published in communist Czechoslovakia evaluating in a positive fashion the role and activities of the Czechoslovak armed forces that fought against the Germans on the western front during the Second World War. First published in 1963.

884. Buk, Pierre, *pseud.* (Franz C. Weiskopf). La Tragédie Tchécoslovaque de Septembre 1938 à Mars 1939. Paris, Editions du Sagittaire, 1939. 207 p. Fold. map.

An account of the destruction of Czechoslovakia, from Munich to the German occupation of Bohemia-Moravia and the creation of the puppet Slovak state in March 1939. Written by an official of the Czechoslovak government.

885. Čelovský, Boris. Das Münchener Abkommen von 1938. Stuttgart, Deutsche Verlags-Anstalt, 1958. 518 p. Maps. Bibliography: p. 487-504.

See also entry no. 228.

Written by a Czech scholar in exile and richly documented, this is probably the most thorough western-language examination to date of the Munich agreement and the events leading up to it.

886. Eubank, Keith. Munich. Norman, University of Oklahoma Press, 1963. 322 p. Illus., ports., maps. Bibliography: p. 304-312.

A dispassionate, scholarly discussion of the events leading up to Munich and its aftermath.

887. Fierlinger, Zdeněk. Ve službách ČSR (In the service of the Czechoslovak Republic). Praha, Dělnické nakladatelství, 1947-1948. 2 v. 12 facsims.

Wartime memoirs of a former Czechoslovak ambassador to Moscow, subsequently the first premier of postwar Czechoslovakia, who joined the Communist Party after the communist seizure of power in 1948. *See also* the same author's *Od Mnichova po Košice 1939-1945* (From Munich to Košice, 1939-1945) (Praha, Práce, 1946, 427 p., illus.), containing Fierlinger's radio talks from Moscow and Kuybyshev.

888. Grant Duff, Sheila. Europe and the Czechs. Harmondsworth, Middlesex, Eng., Penguin Books, 1938. 217 p. Illus. (maps).

A concise discussion of the Sudeten German problem by a British writer sympathetic to Czechoslovakia's cause. *See also* the same author's *A German Protectorate, the Czechs Under Nazi Rule* (New York, Macmillan, 1942, 295 p.).

889. Hoensch, Jörg K. Die Slowakei und Hitlers Ostpolitik: Hlinkas Slowakische Volkspartei zwischen Autonomie und Separation 1938/1939. Köln, Graz, Böhlau, 1965. 390 p. Bibliography: p. 359-379.

A detailed analysis of the role of the autonomist Slovak People's Party in the liquidation of Czechoslovakia and the establishment of the Slovak State in 1938-1939. Using both Czechoslovak sources and materials from the German archives, the author assesses the parts played by Slovak Premier Tiso, the radical groups within the People's Party, the Nazi regime, Slovakia's Germans, and the Prague government.

890. Jaksch, Wenzel. Europe's Road to Potsdam. New York, Praeger, 1963. 468 p. Ports., maps, facsims. Includes bibliographies.

Much of this volume, written by a former leader of the Sudeten German Social Democratic Party, deals with Czechoslovakia and the Czechoslovak attitude toward and treatment of the Sudeten Germans. The author is highly critical of Czechoslovakia's President Beneš and his associates. A condensed translation (with additions and annotations by the translator) of *Europas Weg nach Potsdam* (Stuttgart, Deutsche Verlags-Anstalt, 1958, 522 p., illus.).

891. Kovacs, Endre, *and* Jan Novotný. Mad'aři a my; z dějin mad'arsko-československých vztahů (The Hungarians and we; the history of Hungarian-Czechoslovak relations). Praha, Státní nakladatelství politické literatury, 1959. 313 p. Illus.

See also entry no. 125.

An investigation of Czechoslovak-Hungarian relations. The recurrent conflicts between the two peoples are blamed on the bourgeoisie of the two countries. *See also* Václav Chaloupecký's *Zápas o Slovensko, 1918* (The struggle for Slovakia, 1918) (Praha, Čin, 1930, 251 p.).

892. Němec, František, *and* Vladimír Moudrý. The Soviet Seizure of Subcarpathian Ruthenia. Toronto, W. B. Anderson, 1955. 375 p. Bibliography: p. 367-369; "Documents": p. 207-361; "Bibliographical note": p. 363-366.

A documented account of the events that led to the Soviet annexation of Subcarpathian Ruthenia, the easternmost province of Czechoslovakia, in 1944-1945. Mr. Němec served as the Czechoslovak government delegate in Ruthenia at the time.

893. Ripka, Hubert. Munich: Before and After. London, V. Gollancz, 1939. 523 p. Illus. (maps). "List of documents": p. 521-522.

The first book-length treatment of Munich and its consequences. Written by a prominent Czechoslovak journalist and close associate of President Beneš who subsequently joined Beneš's government-in-exile in London.

For a selection of personal papers and official dispatches prepared by the author while serving as Secretary of Legation in Prague, *see*:

Kennan, George F. From Prague after Munich. Diplomatic Papers, 1938-1940. Princeton, N.J., Princeton University Press. London, Oxford University Press, 1968, 266 p. Illus., maps.

894. Rönnefarth, Helmuth. K. Die Sudetenkrise in der Internationalen Politik: Entstehung, Verlauf, Auswirkung. Wiesbaden, F. Steiner, 1961. 2 v. 3 fold. maps, ports. (Veröffentlichungen des Instituts für europäische Geschichte, 21) Bibliography: v. 2, p.1-15.

See also entry no. 658.

A thorough German exploration of the Sudeten German problem through the Munich crisis.

895. Svoboda, Ludvík. Z Buzuluku do Prahy (From Buzuluk to Prague). Praha, Naše vojsko, 1961. 405 p. Illus.

An account of the creation and activities of the Czechoslovak Army in Soviet Russia during the Second World War. Written by its commander, who subsequently became defense minister in postwar Czechoslovakia and is currently its President.

896. Wandycz, Piotr S. Czechoslovak-Polish Confederation and the Great Powers, 1940-43. Bloomington, Indiana University, 1956. 152 p. (Indiana University Publications. Slavic and East European Series, v. 3)

A critical study of the abortive attempt to form a confederative union undertaken by the Czechoslovak and Polish governments-in-exile in Britain during the Second World War. *See also* the same author's *France and Her Eastern Allies, 1919-1925: French-Czechoslovak-Polish Relations from the Paris Peace Conference to Locarno* (Minneapolis, University of Minnesota Press, 1962, 454 p., "bibliographical essay": p. 407-425), in which the author criticizes Dr. Edvard Beneš (as well as Lloyd George and the French) for defeating earlier attempts at a Polish-Czechoslovak rapprochement.

897. Wheeler-Bennett, John W. Munich: Prologue to Tragedy. New York, Duell, Sloan and Pearce, 1963. 507 p. Illus., maps. Bibliography: p. 489-493.

See also entry no. 237.

A reissue of a noted British historian's brilliantly written classic on the Munich agreement and its background, first published in 1948 (by Macmillan), with pertinent maps and documentary appendices. For the Czechoslovak Communist view concerning Munich, *see* J. S. Hájek's *Mnichov* (Munich) (Praha, Státní nakladatelství politické literatury, 1958, 162 p., illus.), and Jan Křen's *Mnichovská zrada* (The Munich betrayal) (Praha, Státní nakladatelství politické literatury, 1958, 66 p.).

4. Since 1945

898. Dokumenty československé zahraniční politiky, 1945-1960 (Documents of Czechoslovak foreign policy, 1945-1960). Praha, Státní nakladatelství politické literatury, 1960. 784 p.

A massive collection of various documents relative to Czechoslovakia's foreign relations. Includes a general discussion of the major aspects of the country's foreign policy.

899. Lamberg, Robert F. Prag und die dritte Welt. Hannover, Verlag für Literatur und Zeitgeschehen, 1966. 291 p. Bibliography: p. 286-291; "Anhang" (p. 207-285) includes documents.

An examination of Czechoslovakia's relations with the Third World.

900. Luža, Radomír. The Transfer of the Sudeten Germans; a Study of Czech-German Relations, 1933-1962. New York, New York University Press, 1964. 365 p. Illus., maps. Bibliography: p. 329-356.
See also entry no. 655.

A scholarly study of the massive expulsion of Sudeten Germans from Czechoslovakia following the Second World War. In an effort to explain the reasons for the transfer, the author analyzes the entire background of Czech-German relations since 1918. He views the transfer as "the last act of the long German-Czech dispute" and "a response to circumstances created by the Sudeten Germans themselves and implicit in the Nazi war regime."

901. Nemecká otázka a Československo (1938-1961); sborník statí (The German question and Czechoslovakia [1938-1961]; a collection of articles). Bratislava, Vydavatel'stvo Slovenskej akadémie vied, 1962. 291 p. Bibliographical footnotes.

A collection of papers on Czechoslovak-German relations from 1938 to 1961 presented at a conference of the Historical Institute of the Slovak Academy of Science. Contains studies on such subjects as the transfer of the Germans, German imperialism, and the role of the German minority in Slovakia.

902. Šnejdárek, Antonín. Revanšisté proti Československu (The Revanchists against Czechoslovakia). Praha, Státní nakladatelství politické literatury, 1963. 259 p. Tables.

A critical examination of the various organizations, institutes, press organs, and activities of the Sudeten Germans expelled from Czechoslovakia to Germany after the Second World War. Includes citations from speeches by Sudeten German leaders and recounts their activities in Czechoslovakia prior to and during the Second World War.

903. Wiskemann, Elizabeth. Germany's Eastern Neighbours: Problems Relating to the Oder-Neisse Line and the Czech Frontier Regions. London, New York, Oxford University Press, 1956. 309 p. Maps, tables. Bibliography: p. 297-300.
See also entries no. 132 *and* 2793.

The author, a prominent British specialist in Slav-German relations, examines the Czech-German dispute over the Sudeten areas, with emphasis on postwar developments.

5. Periodicals

904. Mezinárodní otázky (International affairs). 1956– Praha. Quarterly.
Features articles on international questions.

905. Mezinárodní politika (International politics). 1957– Praha. Monthly.
Issued by Československá společnost pro šíření politických a vědeckých znalostí.

906. Mezinárodní vztahy (International relations). Praha. Annual.
Covers various issues in international politics and economics.

907. Zahraniční politika (Foreign policy). 1922– Praha. Semimonthly.
Published under the auspices of the Czechoslovak Ministry of Foreign Affairs.

19

the economy

by George J. Staller

A. SURVEY WORKS AND GENERAL PERIODICALS

908. Blažek, Miroslav. Ekonomická geografia ČSSR (Economic geography of Czechoslovakia). Bratislava, Osveta, 1964. 297 p. Illus., maps. Bibliography: p. 292-297.

An informative text on the country's population and natural resources, and the location of its industries. Descriptions are given of individual economic regions, with special attention to Slovakia. This is a revised, Slovak edition of the author's *Hospodářský zeměpis Československa* (Economic geography of Czechoslovakia), published in 1958 (Praha, Orbis, 407 p.).

909. Bušek, Vratislav, *and* Nicolas Spulber, *eds.* Czechoslovakia. New York, Praeger, 1957. 520 p. Maps, tables. Bibliography: p. 484-499.
See also entries no. 509, 581, *and* 804.

Part 4 contains descriptive material on the economy.

910. Czechoslovak Economic Papers. 1959– Prague. Annual.

Provides translations of original Czech contributions covering a wide range of topics.

For papers dealing with the theoretical and practical problems of individual sectors of the Czechoslovak economy, see the monthly *Plánované hospodářství*, published by the State Planning Commission (1948- Praha).

For an English text and explanatory remarks on the Two-Year

Plan of 1947-1948, see *The First Czechoslovak Economic Plan* (Prague, Orbis, 1948, 122 p.), with an introduction by E. Outrata, Chairman of the State Planning Commission.

911. Czechoslovak Republic. *Ústřední správa geodezie a kartografie.* Atlas Československé socialistické republiky (Atlas of the Czechoslovak Socialist Republic). Praha, 1967. 58 sheets with 433 maps, diagrs., tables.

See also entry no. 569.

Parts 8, 24, and 31-54 present detailed, excellent maps and graphs with general descriptions of the postwar economy and references to the prewar period.

912. Kouba, Karel, *ed.* Politická ekonomie socialismu; sborník (The political economy of socialism). Praha, Nakladatelství politické literatury, 1964. 694 p. Bibliography.

Collection of essays on the theoretical aspects of socialist economics. Includes discussion of the law of value, labor productivity, fixed assets, and the role of money.

913. Machová, Dušana. ČSSR v socialistické mezinárodní dělbě práce (The Czechoslovak Socialist Republic in the international socialist division of labor). Praha, Nakladatelství politické literatury, 1962. 252 p. Diagrs., tables.

A very good analysis of prewar and postwar trade patterns and their influence on the Czechoslovak economy.

914. Mervart, Josef, *and* Čestmír Konečný. Ekonomický rozvoj socialistických zemí (Economic development of the socialist countries). Praha, Nakladatelství politické literatury, 1963. 324 p. Tables, bibliography.

A good survey of the levels of output and economic growth of the socialist countries after the Second World War; includes discussions of individual economic sectors, of investment, and of foreign trade.

915. New Trends in Czechoslovak Economics. 1966– Prague.

A pamphlet series containing texts of important decrees, resolutions, interviews, and popular expositions of the "New System of Planning and Management" (1967).

916. Novinky literatury. Společenské vědy. Řada II: Bibliografie ekonomické literatury (Bibliography of literature on economics). roč. 4– 1964– Praha. 12 no. a year.

Current economic documentation. Prior to 1964 published only under the title *Bibliografie ekonomické literatury*, volume 2 of which presents a cumulative listing of Czechoslovak economic literature for 1948-1961.

For Slovak bibliographies see: *Ekonomické dizertácie a habilitácie v ČSSR. Diplomové práce a záverečné práce postgraduálneho štúdia na Slovensku* (Dissertations and advanced economic research studies in economics in Czechoslovakia. Diploma studies and finals of postgraduate work in Slovakia), issued annually since 1963/1964 under variant titles by the Ústredná ekonomická knižnica in Bratislava; and *Súpis slovenskej a českej ekonomickej literatúry, 1938-1944* (List of Slovak and Czech literature on economics, 1938-1944), prepared by G. Kyselová (Bratislava, Slovenské pedagogické nakl., 1964–).

917. Politická ekonomie (Political economy). 1953– Praha. Monthly.

Published by the Czechoslovak Academy of Sciences. Includes theoretical papers, discussions, reviews, and surveys of current problems.

918. Rozvoj národního hospodářství ČSSR od XI do XII sjezdu KSČ (The development of the national economy of the Czechoslovak Socialist Republic between the 11th and 12th Congresses of the Czechoslovak Communist Party). Praha, Nakladatelství politické literatury, 1962. 206 p. Illus.

Offers a survey of officially claimed achievements up to 1961.

B. ECONOMIC HISTORY

919. Chmela, Leopold. The Economic Aspects of the German Occupation of Czechoslovakia. Prague, Orbis, 1948. 166 p. (Czechoslovak Sources and Documents, no. 30)

An elaboration of Dr. Chmela's testimony against K. H. Frank, the book deals with economic policies in the "historical provinces" of Bohemia and Moravia during the Nazi occupation. It is a translation of *Hospodářská okupace ČSR, její metody a důsledky* (Praha, Orbis, 1946, 179 p.).

920. Dobrý, Anatol. Hospodářská krize československého průmyslu ve vztahu k Mnichovu (Economic crisis of Czechoslovak industry in relation to Munich). Praha, Československá akademie věd, 1959. 197 p. Bibliography.

Current view of the industry of the '20s and '30s.

921. Král, Václav. Otázky hospodářského a sociálního vývoje v českých zemích v létech 1938-1945 (The questions of economic and social development in the Czech lands in the years 1938-1945). Praha, Československá akademie věd, 1957-59. 3 v.

A Marxist view of the changes in the economy of the "historical provinces" of Bohemia and Moravia during the Nazi occupation.

922. Olšovský, Rudolf. Světový obchod a Československo 1918-1938 World trade and Czechoslovakia, 1918-1938). Praha, Státní nakladatelství politické literatury, 1961. 287 p. Bibliography, illus.

Current view of the country's position in the world economy and its commercial and financial policies between the two world wars.

923. Olšovský, Rudolf, *and others*. Přehled hospodářského vývoje Čes-

koslovenska v letech 1918-1945 (Survey of the economic development in Czechoslovakia from 1918 to 1945). 2d rev. ed. Praha, Nakl. politické literatury, 1963. 740 p. Diagrs., tables. Bibliography: p. 727-733.

A Marxist version of Czechoslovakia's economic history through the end of the Second World War.

924. Veselý, Jaroslav, *ed.* Československá vlastivěda. Díl IX. Technika (Book of knowledge on Czechoslovakia. Volume IX. Technology). Praha, Sfinx, 1929. 687 p.

Extensive description of the industrial structure and development during the first ten years of the First Republic.

C. PLANNING

925. Czechoslovak Republic. *Laws, statutes, etc.* The First Czechoslovak Economic Five-Year Plan. Translated from the Czech by O. F. Stein. Prague, Ministry of Information and Public Culture, 1949. 258 p.

The text of the first Czechoslovak long-term plan, with an introduction by Prime Minister A. Zápotocký.

926. Goldmann, Josef. Czechoslovakia, Test Case of Nationalization; a Survey of Postwar Industrial Development and the Two-Year Plan. 3d ed. Prague, Orbis, 1947. 63 p.

A simple exposition of the Czechoslovak two-year plan of reconstruction and development (1947-1948).

927. Kadlec, Vladimír. Některé matematické metody a jejich použití v národním hospodářství (Some mathematical methods and their use in economics). Praha, Státní nakladatelství politické literatury, 1959. 402 p. Bibliography, illus.

One of the first Czech texts on the application of the mathematical approach (primarily input-output analysis) to planning problems.

928. Pokyny a formuláře k sestavení státního plánu rozvoje národního hospodářství ČSR (Directives and forms for drafting the state plan for development of the national economy of the Czechoslovak Republic). Praha, Státní úřad plánovací, 1953–

Issued by the State Planning Office. Contains detailed instructions to all economic sectors as well as goals to be achieved.

929. Prague. Vysoká škola ekonomická. *Katedra národohospodářského plánování* Národohospodářské plánovaní v ČSSR (Planning of the national economy in the Czechoslovak Socialist Republic). Praha, Nakladatelství politické literatury, 1963. 588 p. Tables, diagrs.

A thorough text for graduate students on Soviet-type planning, written by the members of the Department of Planning, University of Prague. For an investigation into the effects of the application of the Soviet development model to a relatively mature industrial economy *see*:

Feiwel, George R. New Economic Patterns in Czechoslovakia. New York, Praeger, 1968. 450 p. Tables, bibliography.

930. Šik, Ota. K problematice socialistických zbožních vztahů (On the problem of commodity relationships in socialism). Praha, Nakladatelství Československé akademie věd, 1964. 400 p. Bibliography: p. 367-374.

Collection of essays on planning, price formation, and the role of money in a socialist country, by the man usually identified as the architect of the current (1967) economic reforms. A second edition was published in 1965. For an English-language presentation of the same author's economic thinking, *see*:

Plan and Market under Socialism. White Plains, N.Y., International Arts and Sciences Press, 1967. 382 p.

931. Typolt, Jiří, Vladimír Janza, *and* Milan Popelka. Plánování cen průmyslových výrobků (Price planning of industrial products). Praha, Orbis, 1959. 331 p. Bibliography.

D. STATISTICS

932. Statistická ročenka Československé socialistické republiky (Statistical yearbook of the Czechoslovak Socialist Republic). 1934– Praha. Annual.

See also entries no. 563 *and* 574.

This work is the most comprehensive source of statistical information on Czechoslovakia. Other important statistical information can be found in the following publications:

Czechoslovak Republic. *Státní úřad statistický*. Zprávy (Reports of the State Statistical Office). 1920– Praha. Irregular. This is an important source of quantitative information on the Czechoslovak economy between the wars and during the immediate postwar years.

Statistika (Statistics), a monthly publication (1964– Praha) containing papers on the theoretical and practical aspects of statistical investigations.

Statistika a demografie, an annual publication (1959– Praha), containing original Czech and foreign contributions with summaries in Russian and English.

Statistický obzor (Statistical review), a publication of the State Statistical Office (1920-1961, Praha), containing papers on prewar and postwar economic and statistical problems.

Statistické přehledy (Statistical surveys), a monthly publication (1964– Praha) containing up-to-date information on all aspects of the economy.

Statistický zpravodaj (Statistical reporter), a monthly publication (1938-1950, Praha), containing short papers and current statistical tables.

E. AGRICULTURE, INDUSTRY, AND FOREIGN TRADE

933. Burger, Miroslav. Directory of the Czechoslovak Manufacturing Industries. London, Flegon, 1967. 390 p.

A convenient reference tool on a variety of industrial enterprises of the Czechoslovak economy.

934. Čvančara, František. Zemědělská výroba v číslech (Agricultural production in figures). Praha, Československá akademie zemědělských věd, 1948-65. 2 v. (741, 1013 p.)

Volume 1 is a technical analysis of crop production. Volume 2 deals with animal husbandry.

935. Czechoslovak Foreign Trade. 1961– Praha. Monthly.

An official journal of the Czechoslovak Chamber of Commerce. An informative source on current Czechoslovak export capabilities. Includes photographs and advertising. Published also in French, German, Russian, and Spanish.

In a similar vein is the annual *Facts on Czechoslovak Foreign Trade* (1962– Praha), which contains graphs and data on postwar foreign trade by countries and by commodities and on treaties and trade agreements. It also contains a list of Czechoslovak foreign trade corporations with addresses.

936. Czechoslovak Republic. *Ústřední úřad státní kontroly a statistiky.* Rozvoj československého průmyslu (Development of Czechoslovak industry). Praha, SEVT, 1962. 346 p. Illus., bibliography.

Detailed discussion of industrial growth and structural changes. Includes a brief historical introduction, discussion of the raw material base, organizational changes, and regional location.

937. Grolig, Alois. Ekonomika socialistického zemědělství (The economics of socialist agriculture). Praha, Státní pedagogické nakl., 1963. 417 p. Diagrs., tables. Bibliography: p. 415-417.

A mimeographed text for graduate students in agricultural economics.

938. Lazarčík, Gregor. The Performance of Socialist Agriculture; a Case Study of Production and Productivity in Czechoslovakia, 1934-1938 and 1946-1961. New York, L. W. International Financial Research, 1963. 121 p. Tables, bibliography.

See also entry no. 597.

Western evaluation of the growth of output and efficiency changes of Czechoslovak agriculture since the '30s.

939. Precioso, Artemio. Proporce mezi průmyslem a zemědělstvím a její vytváření v Československu (The balance between industry and agriculture and its determination in Czechoslovakia). Praha, Státní nakladatelství politické literatury, 1959. 239 p. Bibliography, illus.

A thorough discussion of wholesale and retail price formation in a Soviet-type economy.

A good descriptive account of the relationship between the two sectors and of the ways to reduce their inequality.

940. Šilhán, Věněk, *ed.* Ekonomika průmyslu ČSSR (Economics of industry of the Czechoslovak Socialist Republic). Praha, Nakladatelství politické literatury, 1964. 656 p. Bibliography, illus.

An extensive, informative text for graduate students in economics, written at the end of the Soviet-type planning period.

941. Švantner, Miloš, J. Sláma, *and* M. Borák. Odvětvová struktura československého průmyslu (Structure of Czechoslovak industry). Praha, Státní nakladatelství politické literatury, 1959. 112 p. Bibliography, illus.

A good description of the claimed growth and changes in the structure of industry, from the prewar period to the mid-fifties.

942. Wannenmacher, Walter. Die Umstellung auf sozialistische Ernährungswirtschaft, untersucht an dem Beispiel der Tschechoslowakei. München, Lerche, 1960. 228 p. Bibliography, illus. (Veröffentlichungen des Collegium Carolinum, Bd. 8)

A study of Czechoslovak agriculture and the system of food supply in the framework of central planning and collectivization.

For German-language treatments of Czechoslovak agriculture prior to the Second World War, *see* Vladislav Brdlík's *Die sozialökonomische Struktur der Landwirtschaft in der Tschechoslowakei* (Berlin, F. Vahlen, 1938, 240 p.) and Walter Hildebrandt's *Die Kleine Wirtschaftsentente als agrarpolitisches Problem der Tschecho-Slowakei* (Breslau, Priebatschs Buchhandlung, 1938, 125 p.).

943. Zauberman, Alfred. Industrial Progress in Poland, Czechoslovakia, and East Germany, 1937-1962. London, New York, Oxford University Press, 1964. 338 p. Bibliography.

See also entries no. 270, 602, 1520, *and* 2829.

Decription and comparison of industrial development patterns. Contains the author's own growth indexes, which register substantially lower rates than the official indexes.

944. Zemědělská ekonomika (Agricultural economics). 1955– Praha. Monthly.

Published by the Institute of Scientific and Technical Information, Ministry of Agriculture and Nutrition. Contains papers on various aspects and problems of Czechoslovak agricultural development.

945. Žůrek, Oldřich. Rozmisťování výrobních sil v ČSR (Distribution of the labor force in Czechoslovakia). Praha, Státní nakladatelství technické literatury, 1960. 291 p.

A useful volume on the location of economic activity and distribution of labor force. Maps and tables.

F. NATIONAL INCOME AND FINANCES

946. Alton, Thad Paul, *and others.* Czechoslovak National Income and Product, 1947-1948 and 1955-1956. New York, London, Columbia University Press, 1962. 255 p.

A well-documented cross-sectional study of the structure of the Czech economy, both by sectors of origin and by final use. Western concepts and methodology are applied to Czech data.

For a detailed and current treatment of Czechoslovakia's financial system *see*:

Alton, Thad P., *and others.* Financial and Fiscal Systems of Czechoslovakia. Washington, D.C., United States Arms Control and Disarmament Agency, 1968. 328 p.

947. Finance a úvěr (Finance and credit). 1951– Praha. Monthly.

Contains papers on various aspects of the role of money and credit in the economy.

948. Goldmann, Josef, *and* Karel Kouba. Hospodářský růst v ČSSR (Economic growth in the Czechoslovak Socialist Republic). Praha, Academia, 1967. 142 p.

An interesting analysis of economic growth during the '50s and of the difficulties of the '60s. Kalacki's growth model is applied to the Czech economy. For an English translation see *Economic Growth in Czechoslovakia* (Prague, Academia, 1969, 150 p.).

949. Michal, Jan M. Central Planning in Czechoslovakia: Organization for Growth in a Mature Economy. Stanford, Stanford University Press, 1960. 274 p.

An informative account of changes in the postwar economy; includes chapters on individual sectors of the economy, foreign trade, finance, and living standards.

950. Czechoslovak Republic. *Ministerstvo financí.* Státní hospodaření za války a po revoluci (State economics during the war and after the revolution). Praha, Ministerstvo financí, 1946. 390 p. (Knihovna Ministerstva financí, sv. 3)

A commentary on the first postwar State budget.

951. Pešek, Boris P. Gross National Product of Czechoslovakia in Monetary and Real Terms, 1946-58. Chicago, London, University of Chicago Press, 1965. 60 p.

First Western attempt at an independent measure of the growth of the Czechoslovak Gross National Product and its four major final use components. Estimated current values are deflated by appropriate price indexes. Measured growth rates are significantly lower than those officially claimed.

952. Stádník, Miloš. Národní důchod a jeho rozdělení, se zvláštním zřetelem k Československu (National income and its distribution, with

special reference to Czechoslovakia). Praha, Nakl. Knihovny Sborníku věd právních a státních, 1946. 2 v. 280 p. (Knihovna Sborníku věd právních a státních. Nová řada. B; Obor státovědecký, čís. 23) Bibliography: p. 252-259.

The first serious attempt to apply national income methodology to Czechoslovakia; includes estimates for the years 1929-1937 and 1939-1943.

953. Prague. Vysoká škola ekonomická. *Katedra financí a úvěru.* Československé finance (Czechoslovak finance). Praha, Státní pedagogické nakl., 1956. 553 p.

A graduate text. Includes chapters on financing of industry, local economy, agriculture, and trade and a discussion of the State budget and financial planning.

For a brief account of State finance during the immediate postwar years, *see* Bedřich Spáčil's *Veřejné hospodářství v ČSR v roce 1947* (Public finance in Czechoslovakia in the year 1947) (Praha, Ministerstvo informací, 1947, 43 p.).

20

the society

by Jan Hajda
(except for sections G and H)

A. OVERVIEW OF SOCIETY

954. Barton, Paul, *pseud.* Prague à l'heure de Moscou; analyse d'une démocratie populaire. Paris, P. Horay, 1954. 355 p.
See also entry no. 801.
Summary and analysis of the Slánský trial; typology of the main cliques and description of their struggle for power; insights into the decision-making processes; based on an analysis of trial records, on literature published by leading Czech and Slovak Communists, and on communist press and refugee sources. Some of the generalizations seem to be founded only on speculation.

955. Bauer, Otto. Die Nationalitätenfrage und die Sozialdemokratie. Wien, Brand, 1907. 576 p.
A classic study of the social stratification of Austria-Hungary in the second half of the 19th century. A special emphasis is placed on the process of industrialization and the accompanying change in the relation between Czechs and Germans in Bohemia. Valuable statistical data. Second edition: Wien, Verlag der Wiener Volksbuchhandlung, 1924, 576 p.

956. Bednárik, Rudolf. Duchovná kultúra slovenského l'udu (Spiritual culture of the Slovak people). *In*: Slovenská vlastivěda (Book of knowledge on Slovakia). v. 2. Bratislava, Slovenská akadémia vied a umení, 1944. p. 7-121.

See also entry no. 1146.

An ethnographic study, emphasizing folklore. Covers the *rites de passage* of birth, marriage, and death, and seasonal festivals. Purely descriptive; contains valuable source materials.

957. Bláha, Inocenc Arnošt. Poznámky sociologovy na okraju tragických dnů (A sociologist's notes on the tragic days). Sociologická revue (Brno), v. 9, 1938, no. 3/4: 237-254.

Analysis of the development of relations between Czechs and Germans in the period 1918-1938. Emphasis on the differences in the social structure and political attitudes.

958. Eder, Richard. Some Interesting Happenings in Prague. The New York Times Magazine, November 12, 1967: p. 32, 92-98, 104, 109.

An overview of the conflicts between the intellectuals and the Communist Party in 1963-1967. A discussion of withdrawal patterns among the youth.

959. Gadourek, Ivan. The Political Control of Czechoslovakia; a Study in Social Control of a Soviet Communist State. Leiden, Stenfert Kroese, 1953. 285 p. Bibliography: p. 237-238.

See also entry no. 811.

A sociological analysis of the communist social system, with short passages on the cultural aspects and changes in the structure of social action under communist rule; a concise description of the changes in the Communist Party of Czechoslovakia, in government, economy, education, religion, science and the arts, recreation, and morals. The period covered is 1948-1952. Valuable both for its insights and as a reference book.

960. Hajda, Jan, *ed.* A Study of Contemporary Czechoslovakia. Chicago, University of Chicago for the Human Relations Area Files, 1955. 637 p. Maps, tables.

See also entry no. 508.

A portion of this volume presents an analysis of Czechoslovak society and culture in the period 1930-1955. Of special interest is the chapter on social stratification in 1930 and the analysis of the role of intellectuals since 1945.

961. Hajšman, Jan. Mafie v rozmachu; vzpomínky na odboj doma (The growth of the Mafia; memoirs of the national revolution). 2d ed. Práha, Orbis, 1934. 436 p. Illus., port., map, facsims. (Stopami dějin, řada 2)

Memoirs of a Czech newspaperman covering the years 1914-1918. Many insights into the radicalization of the Czechs. Description of the varying degrees of opposition to and support for the Habsburg monarchy among Czechs and Germans in Bohemia during the First World War.

962. Jászi, Oscar. The Dissolution of the Habsburg Monarchy. Chicago, The University of Chicago Press, 1929. 488 p. Bibliography: p. 461-480.

See also entry no. 1904.

A classic study of the consensual and dissensual forces in the Austria-Hungary of the 19th and 20th centuries. Focus on the mystique of the monarchy, universalistically oriented elites, and national and economic particularism. Phoenix paperback reprint: 1961, 482 p.

963. Kolarz, Walter. Myths and Realities in Eastern Europe. London, Lindsay Drummond, 1946. 273 p. Illus., maps. Bibliography: p. 266-268.

A perceptive and argumentative treatise on ethnic relations, ethnic identity, and the role of the historical myths of national mission in Czechoslovakia and elsewhere in Central-Eastern Europe. Focuses on the period 1918-1938.

964. Machonin, Pavel, *ed.* Sociální struktura socialistické společnosti (sociologické problémy soudobé československé společnosti); sborník (The social structure of socialist society [sociological problems of contemporary Czechoslovak society]; a collections of articles). Praha, Svoboda, 1966, 672 p.

A series of essays on Marxist philosophy and sociological theory, with some observations on recent trends in the social stratification of Czechoslovakia.

Jiří Kolaja's survey of the development of sociology in Czechoslovakia, to be published in 1968 as part of the second volume of *The Czechoslovak Contribution to World Culture*, edited by Miloslav Rechcígl Jr., will provide a broader view of work in this field.

965. Placht, Otto. Lidnatost a společenská skladba českého státu. v 16.-18. století (Population density and social structure of the Czech State in the 16th-18th centuries). Praha, Nakl. Československé akademie věd, 1957. 366 p. Illus., map. (Československá akademie věd. Sekce filosofie a historie. Studie a prameny, sv. 14) Bibliography: p. 330-343.

See also entry no. 630.

The population and its development in the Czech lands from the 16th century to the first census in 1754; population movements during this period; the population of the Czech state in the war with the Habsburg-Roman coalition; consequences of the Thirty Years' War on the population in the Czech lands between 1650 and 1750. Statistical data.

966. Sociologická revue (Sociological review). 1930-1938, 1945-1948. Brno. Quarterly.

The most important sociological periodical published in Czechoslovakia before the Second World War and for a short period thereafter. Organ of the Masarykova sociologická společnost.

967. Sociologický časopis (Sociological chronicle). roč. 1– 1965– Praha, Academia. Bimonthly. Illus.

A Czechoslovak Academy journal containing studies on Czechoslovak society. Universita Palackého, Olomouc, started in 1969 the quarterly *Sociologica*. For an English-language serial with material of sociological interest, see *Social Policy in Czechoslovakia* (1966– Prague, The National Social Security Office).

For a survey study of contemporary sociology in Czechoslovakia *see* the condensed proceedings of the First Conference of Czechoslovak Sociologists (1966), published as *Sociologie* (Praha, 1968, 256 p.). The material is arranged by topics such as sociology of youth, methods and techniques of sociological research, urban, rural, industrial, sociological and other subjects.

See also Pavel Machonin's "Studie o rozvoji československé sociologije do roku 1980" (Study of the development of Czechoslovak sociology through 1980), *Sociologický časopis*, 1967, no. 4: 389-397.

968. Štefánek, Anton. Sociologický výzkum Slovenska (Sociological research on Slovakia). Sociologická revue (Brno), v. 14, 1948, no. 3-4: 152-158.

A survey of the development of Slovak social structure in the years 1945-1948, especially in regard to the leveling tendencies. Insightful, informative.

969. Štefánek, Anton. Základy sociografie Slovenska (Outline of the sociography of Slovakia). *In* Slovenská vlastivěda (Book of knowledge on Slovakia) v. 3. Bratislava, Slovenská akadémia vied a umení, 1944. 339 p.

An extensive sociological study including typology, development, and role of the intelligentsia and other social strata; ideal type patterns of Slovak national expression; economic factors in the formation of Slovak national character; social disorganization; education; cooperative movement; national minorities in Slovakia; relationship between Czechs and Slovaks in Slovakia, 1918-1938. Most valuable are parts dealing with individual social strata and the relationship between the Czechs and Slovaks. The work has an anti-Semitic bias. Only a small section of the treatise is based on field research.

B. NATIONAL CHARACTER

970. Bláha, Inocenc Arnost. Dvě sociologické poznámky (Two sociological notes). Sociologická revue (Brno), v. 11, no. 1-4, 1940: 221-227.

An analysis of the ideal patterns of Czech reaction to the German occupation. A valuable note on behavioral patterns under stress and in crisis.

971. Chalupný, Emanuel. Národní filosofie československá. Díl I. Národní povaha československá (The Czechoslovak national philosophy. Part I. The Czeskoslovak national character). Praha, Nákladem vlastním, 1935. 256 p.

A speculative treatise on the Czech national character, with introductory essays examining the character of other nations, emphasizing in particular that of the Germans.

972. Gašparec, Ignác. Maďarizácia v sociologickom ašpekte (Magyarization in its sociological aspect). Sociologická revue (Brno), v. 13, 1947, no. 4: 247-257.

Magyarization of Slovaks in the 19th and 20th centuries as a function of the semifeudal social order and of geographic and social mobility. Role of the national character in the process of assimilation.

973. Jurovský, Anton. Slovenská národná povaha (Slovak national character). *In*: Slovenská vlastivěda (Book of knowledge on Slovakia). v. 2. Bratislava, Slovenská akadémia vied a umení, 1944. p. 335-398.

Inconclusive and speculative study, possibly applicable to the main body of the Slovak peasant population. Contains good insight into the cultural conditioning of some Slovak social strata in the past two centuries.

974. Kovárna, František. Česká střízlivost a český pathos (Czech sobriety and Czech pathos). Praha, Václav Petr, 1939. 31 p.

A speculative analysis of Czech national character in terms of an interplay between two opposing attributes, sobriety and pathos. Interpretation of the public response to the national crisis of 1938-1939.

975. Obrdlík, Antonín. Gallows Humor — A Sociological Phenomenon. The American Journal of Sociology, v. 47, March 1942: 709-716.

An analysis of the popular satire current in the Czech regions during the German occupation, and of the role of satire in maintaining the morale of the population.

976. Sigl, Franz. Die soziale Struktur des Sudetendeutschtums, ihre Entwicklung und volkspolitische Bedeutung. Leipzig, Selbstverlag, 1938. 202 p. Bibliography: p. 195-202.

The development and political implications of the Sudeten German social structures.

977. Štefánek, Anton. Novoslováci (New Slovaks). Sociologická revue (Brno), v. 4, 1933, no. 3/4: 272-277.

An analysis of the "re-Slovakization" of the Slovak intelligentsia which was Magyarized before 1918. Covers the period 1918-1934.

978. Štefánek, Anton. Syngenza a spoločenské "já" (Synthesis and the social "I"). Sociologická revue (Brno), v. 10, 1939, no. 1: 265-296.

A sociological analysis of the development of the relationship between Czechs and Slovaks in the period of 1918-1939. An interpretation of the failure of the Czech intelligentsia in Slovakia and the causes of Slovak separatism.

C. SOCIAL STRATA AND OCCUPATIONAL GROUPS

979. Bláha, Inocenc Arnošt. Problém lidu (The problem of people). Praha, V. Petr, 1947. 39 p. (Svazky úvah a studií, čís. 98)

A sociological analysis of the various meanings of the concept "people" as it is found in popular usage as well as in scholarly literature in Czechoslovakia. Valuable for the study of social stratification.

980. Bláha, Inocenc Arnošt. Sociologie inteligence (Sociology of the intelligentsia). Praha, Orbis, 1937. 395 p. (Sociologická knihovna. Menší řada, sv. 10)

A mainly theoretical interpretation of the role and function of the intelligentsia, its social origin, style of life, subtypes, and crisis. Numerous observations are based on the data pertaining to Czech intellectuals. Although too speculative in some respects, the work ranks among the most valuable European contributions on the intelligentsia of prewar times.

981. Bláha, Inocenc Arnošt. Sociologie sedláka a dělníka; příspěvek k sociologii společenských vrstev (Sociology of the peasant and worker; a contribution to the sociology of social strata). 2d ed. Praha, Orbis, 1937. 223 p. (Sociologická knihovna. Menší řada. Řídí výbor Masarykovy sociologické společnosti, sv. 1)

A study based on firsthand observation and on analysis of novels from the life of peasants and workers. The section dealing with the peasant population is particularly illuminating.

982. Boček, L. Jsou obchodníci, živnostníci, řemeslníci, nižší úředníci "pány" či "lidem"? (Are the merchants, tradespeople, artisans, and lower white-collar workers to be considered "masters" or "people"?). Sociologická revue (Brno), v. 11, no. 1-2, 1940: 73-82.

A field study attempting to discover the socially recognized boundary between the low strata and the middle class. Based on questionnaires administered in the late '30s.

983. Deutsch, Karl W. Nationalism and Social Communication; an Inquiry into the Foundations of Nationality. Cambridge, Published jointly by the Technology Press of the Massachusetts Institute of Technology and Wiley, New York, 1953. 292 p. Maps, diagrs. Bibliography: p. 251-266.

One chapter and an appendix in this volume contain valuable comparison of the major occupational groupings among Czechs and Germans in the period 1900-1947. The author uses this data for an estimation of trends in the growth of national consciousness and conflict.

984. Hajda, Jan. The Role of the Intelligentsia in the Development of the Czechoslovak Society. *In* Rechcígl, Miloslav Jr., *ed.* The Czechoslovak Contribution to World Culture. The Hague, Mouton, 1964. p. 307-312.

An analysis of the social conditions which enabled the Czech intelligentsia to play the leading role in the formation of the Czech society in the 19th century. Contrasting role of the Slovak intelligentsia.

985. Hanáček, Jaroslav. K otázce dělníkova sociálního sebevědomí (On the question of workers' social self-confidence). Sociologická revue (Brno), v. 12, 1946: no. 1, 41-46; no. 2, 24-35.

Presents a good typology of the industrial workers; a description of the trends in the social mobility of workers and of the lessening of their antagonism to other social strata. Based on field studies in Moravia in the '30s.

986. Hrouda, Miloslav. Vysoké školy a vědeckotechnická revoluce (Universities and the scientific-technical revolution). Sociologický časopis (Praha), v. 2, 1966: 205-212.

A study of the production of university graduates and scientists in comparison with the United States and the Soviet Union.

987. Kotek, Josef. Odborové hnutí zaměstnanců (Trade union movement of the white-collar employees). Praha, A. Němec, 1930. 335 p. (Publikace Sociálního ústavu, číslo 48). Bibliography: p. 333-335.

History and stucture of white-collar trade unionism in the first quarter of this century, with emphasis on the years 1918-1928. Statistical tables.

988. Kraus, Wolfgang. Der fünfte Stand. Bern, München, Wien, Scherz, 1966. 176 p. Bibliography: p. 171-176.

A portion of this general treatise on the role of the intellectuals in the West and East offers good insights into the relationship between the intellectuals and the larger public in Czechoslovakia of the '60s.

989. Kubát, Daniel. Social Mobility in Czechoslovakia. American Sociological Review, v. 28, no. 2, April 1963: 203-212.

The author demonstrates that a command economy both encourages and discourages upward social mobility. His argument is based on the analysis of the career patterns of industrial workers during 1948-1960, leveling off of income differences, labor recruitment and transfer, and official disapproval of mobility ethos.

990. Květ, Karel. Advokacie (Lawyers). Praha, Mazáč, 1938. 165 p.

A speculative sociological study of the role and function of Czechoslovak lawyers.

991. Lowie, Robert H. Imperial Austria. *In his* Social Organization. New York, Rinehart, 1948. p. 380-406.

A descriptive statement on the social strata in the Austrian part of the Habsburg monarchy in the late 19th and the 20th centuries. In contrast to Otto Bauer, Lowie emphasizes the subcultural variations rather than the economic factors.

992. Mertl, Jan. Byrokracie (Bureaucracy). Praha, Orbis, 1937. 265 p. (Politická knihovna . . . řada II, kn. 23) "Literatura": p. 257-265.

An excellent analysis of the role, types, and ideological orientation of the higher bureaucratic stratum under Austria-Hungary and in prewar Czechoslovakia. Especially valuable are observations on the relationship between bureaucracy and political parties and on the relation of both to the social structure of Czechoslovakia.

993. Myška, Milan. Počátky vyváření dělnické třídy v železárnách na Ostravsku (The beginning of the formation of the working class in the iron works in the Ostrava region). Ostrava, Krajské nakl., 1962. 253 p. Illus. (Publikace Slezského ústavu ČSAV v Opavě, sv. 42)

The beginning of the labor movement in Ostrava industry in the first half of the 19th century.

994. Obrdlík, Antonín. Povolání a veřejné blaho (Occupation and public welfare). Praha, Orbis, 1937. 263 p.

A study in the prestige of social utility of different occupations in the light of social attitudes. A good illustration of latent radical populism in central and western Moravia before the war. Conclusions based on an unrespresentative sample.

995. Obrdlík, Antonín. Sociální mobilita jedné z našich venkovských obcí (Social mobility in one of our rural communities). Sociologická revue (Brno), v. 5, 1934, no. 1/3: 25-52.

An outline of the social stratification and the pattern of social mobility in a southern Moravian village.

996. Obrdlík, Juliana. Social Distance in the Village. *In*: International Congress of Sociology. 14th, Rome, 1950. Proceedings. Rome, International Institute of Sociology, 1950. p. 69-83.

An analysis of the changes in the social stratification of rural communities in the period 1945-1948. Based on field studies in central Moravia.

997. Oberschall, Albin. Berufliche Gliederung und soziale Schichtung der Deutschen in der Tschechoslowakei. Teplitz-Schönau, Wia-Verlag, 1936. 59 p.

998. Raupach, Hans. Der tschechische Frühnationalismus, ein Beitrag zur Gesellschaft- und Ideengeschichte des Vormärz in Böhmen. Essen, Essener Verlagsanstalt, 1939. 155 p. (Volkslehre und Nationalitätenrecht in Geschichte und Gegenwart, hrsg. von K. G. Hugelmann, M. H. Boehm und Werner Hasselblatt. 2. Reihe: Geschichte des na-

tionalen Gedankens und des Nationalitätenrechts, Bd. 3) Bibliography included in "Anmerkungen": p. 139-155.

Contains a valuable analysis of social stratification in Bohemia in the first half of the 19th century.

999. Šmejkal, Karel. Sociologie vojáka (Sociology of the soldier). Praha, Orbis, 1931. 169 p. (Sociologická knihovna, menší řada, sv. 8)

A sociological study of the antimilitaristic tradition of Czechs and its underlying causes; also contains a description of the Czech soldier's style of life before the Second World War.

1000. Verunáč, Václav. Technik ve společnosti (Technician and society). Sociologická revue (Brno), v. 7, no. 3/4, 1936:381-394.

Typology, social origins, and role of technicians in the Czech society between the two world wars. Informative.

1001. Viney, D. E. Czech Culture and the "New Spirit," 1948-1952. Slavonic and East European Review (London), June 1953: 466-494.

An insightful analysis of the intellectual life and the role of intellectuals in Czechoslovakia, 1948-1952, and an evaluation of the literary and artistic trends of that period.

1002. Ziegler, Heinz O. Die berufliche und soziale Gliederung der Bevölkerung in der Tschechoslowakei. Brünn, R. M. Rohrer, 1936. 239 p. 43 tables. Bibliographical footnotes. (Rechts- und Staatswissenschaftliche Abhandlungen. Heft 10)

An analysis of the occupational structure of Czechoslovakia, based on 1930 census data. An attempt to isolate homogeneous substrata of the population. Also a thorough critique of the occupational census. This is the best study of its kind related to Czechoslovakia. Many observations and conclusions are very illuminating for even the postwar development.

D. COMMUNITY STRUCTURE

1003. Banícka dedina Žakarovce (The mining village of Žakarovce). Bratislava, Vydavatel'stvo Slovenskej akadémie vied, 1956. 665 p. Illus., music. Bibliography: p. 659-661.

Collection of articles on the life and activities of the inhabitants of Žakarovce in Eastern Slovakia. Treats of historical development, economic activity, folklore, and folk art.

1004. Galla, Karel. Dolní Roveň; sociologický obraz české vesnice (Dolní Roveň; a sociological picture of a Czech village). Praha, Spolek péče o blaho venkova, 1939. 408 p. Illus. (Knihovna Spolku péče o blaho venkova, 24)

A study of the social organization of a rural community in Bohemia in the late '30s.

1005. Galla, Karel. Sociology of the Cooperative Movement in the Czechoslovak Village. Praha, Spolek péče o blaho venkova, 1936. 124 p. Illus., maps. (Library of the Country Life Association in Prague, vol. 8)

A study of the social structure of a progressive rural community in eastern Bohemia. The monagraph is based entirely on field research. An important contribution to the study of the prewar cooperative movement and of the social stratification of the Czech countryside. A translation of *Sány, vzorná družstevní vesnice.*

1006. Hrůza, Jiří. Česká města (Czech cities). Praha, Nakl. československých výtvarných umělců, 1960. 214 p. Illus. (Česká architektura. Velka řada, sv. 5)

The influence of historical events, economic development, social conditions, and architectural traditions on the growth of cities in Bohemia and Moravia since feudal times.

1007. Šmakalová, Iva. Integrálna dedina; studia slovenskej Zemianskej dediny v Turci (The integral village; a study of a Slovakian rural hamlet in Turec). Praha, Sociální ústav, 1936. 111 p. (Publikácia socialného ústavu ČSR, čis. 67)

A descriptive study of the social organization of a village in northern Slovakia. Based on field research.

1008. Srb, Vladimir, *and* Milan Kučera. Struktura obyvatelstva v městech a na vesnici v ČSSR (The population structure in the cities and the countryside of Czechoslovakia). Sociologický časopis (Praha), v. 2, 1966: 405-416.

Occupational and age composition of communities, by size of community in 1961.

1009. Tauber, J. Kdo žije na vesnici; sociologická rozprava (Who lives in the countryside; a sociological study). České Budějovice, Nakl. České Budějovice, 1965. 188 p. Illus., bibliographical footnotes.

A survey of the social and economic conditions of the agricultural population with special emphasis on data from six South Bohemian agricultural cooperatives and 21 villages.

1010. Ullrich, Zdeněk, *ed.* Soziologische Studien zur Verstädterung der Prager Umgebung. Prag, Im Verlag der Revue "Soziologie und soziale Probleme," 1938. 335 p. Illus., maps (part fold. col.). (Bibliothek der sozialen Probleme, Bd. 6)

A collective work of Czech empirical sociologists from Prague. The whole study is based on field research done in suburbs of Prague in the early '30s. Includes the analysis of the movement of population, social stratification, religiosity, family, and political associations. Very valuable for the understanding of the process of urbanization in the Czech countryside.

E. FAMILY ORGANIZATION

1011. Musil, Jiří. Příspěvek k teorii sociální organisace současné rodiny A contribution to the theory of the social organization of the contemporary family). Sociologický časopis (Praha), v. 1, 1965: 524-536.

A study of the social organization of the family based on a survey of 8,000 households. Focuses on the distribution of household work and employment of women.

1012. Slejška, Dragoslav. Problémy aktivity žen při účasti na řízení v průmyslovém závodě (Problems of women's activity in industrial plant management). Sociologický časopis (Praha), v. 1, 1965: 509-523.

A comparison of male and female career lines in a Prague engineering plant and a consideration of the role of the life cycle in women's employment opportunities.

1013. Uher, Jan. Student a rodina (The student and the family). Sociologická revue (Brno), v. 5, 1934, no. 1/3: 93-111.

A note on the relation of children to parents, based on questionnaires. Points out the significant dimensions of the Czech family configuration.

F. MEDICINE, HEALTH, WELFARE

1014. Czechoslovak Republic. *Ministerstvo zdravotnictví.* ČSSR zdravotnictví 1965 (Czechoslovak health services, 1965). Praha, Duben, 1966. 302 p.

Includes English summary. For an earlier book in English, *see:* Štich, Zdeněk. Czechoslovak Health Service. Prague, Ministry of Health, Czechoslovak Socialist Republic, 1962. 103, 47 p. Illus., plates.

1015. Machotka, Otakar. Sociálně potřebné rodiny v hlavním městě Praze (Socially needy families in the capital city of Prague). Praha, Vyd. Státní úřad statistický, 1936. 302 p. Tables, diagrs. (Knihovna statistického obzoru, sv. 36)

A survey of 11,982 low income families in Prague. Descriptive; tables.

1016. Prokůpek, J. Problems and Research in Czechoslovakia. *In* Williams, Richard H., *and* Lucy D. Ozarin. Community Mental Health: An International Perspective. San Francisco, Jossey-Bass, 1968. 529 p.

A survey of present-day public health and psychiatric care, postgraduate medical education and research. Information on statistical reporting, disability statistics, outpatient clinics, inpatient data, readmissions, and suicides.

1017. Urban, Rudolf. Das Gesundheitswesen der Tschechoslowakei. Marburg/Lahn, Johann Gottfried Herder-Institut, 1959. 179 p. Wissenschaftliche Beiträge zur Geschichte und Landeskunde Ost-Mitteleuropas, 45)

G. MASS MEDIA AND PUBLIC OPINION

by Edward Táborský

1018. Adamec, Čeněk. Počátky výzkumu veřejného mínění u nás (The beginning of our public opinion research). Sociologický časopis (Praha), v. 2, 1966: 383-399.

A survey of the public opinion polls in Czechoslovakia in 1946-1947 and a description of their organization. For earlier descriptions, *see*:

Adamec, Čeněk, *and* T. Víden. Polls Come to Czechoslovakia. Public Opinion Quarterly, v. 11, 1947: 548-552.

Adamec, Čeněk, Bohuš Pospíšil *and* Milan Tesař, *comps.* What's Your Opinion? A Year's Survey of Public Opinion in Czechoslovakia. Prague, Orbis, 1947. 41 p.

1019. Československý svaz mládeže. Příručka propagandisty Československého svazu mládeže (Handbook for the propagandist of the Czechoslovak Youth League). Praha, Oddělení agitace a propagandy ÚVČSM v nakl. Mladá fronta, 1957. 83 p.

Several new editions were published subsequently.

1020. Darmo, Jozef. Slovenská žurnalistika, 1918-1938 (Slovak journalism, 1918-1938). Bratislava, Matica slovenská, 1967. 580 p.

A Marxist-oriented examination of prewar Slovak journalism, written by a member of the Institute for the Study of Journalism. Part of a planned four-volume study of Slovak journalism, to be completed by 1975.

1021. Ehrlich, Josef, *ed.* Jak se poslouchá rozhlas (On the preferences of radio listeners). Praha, Orbis, 1947. 69 p.

Summary and plans of the radio audience research in 1946-1947.

1022. Kracauer, Siegfried, *and* Paul L. Berkman. Satellite Mentality: Political Attitudes and Propaganda Susceptibilities of Non-Communists in Hungary, Poland and Czechoslovakia. New York, Praeger, 1956. 194 p. Bibliographical footnotes.

A study of modes of thought, preferences, hatreds, and fears of noncommunists under communist rule, based on interviews with several hundred refugees from Czechoslovakia, Poland, and Hungary in 1951-1952.

1023. Reisky-Dubnic, Vladimir. Communist Propaganda Methods; a

Case Study on Czechoslovakia. New York, Praeger, 1960. 287 p. Includes bibliography.

An examination of indoctrination carried out by the Communist Party of Czechoslovakia and its agitation and propaganda vehicles, among both party members and nonmembers. In evaluating the effectiveness of communist propaganda for home consumption, the author concludes that it tends to lead more to apathy and opportunism than to genuine conviction.

1024. Selective Bibliography of Publications on Journalism Published in Czechoslovakia Since 1945. Prague, Novinářský studijní ústav, 1957. 12 p.

A useful bibliography, prepared by the Czechoslovak Institute for the Study of Journalism.

1025. Sturm, Rudolf. Propaganda. *In* Bušek, Vratislav, and Nicolas Spulber, *eds.* Czechoslovakia. New York, Praeger, 1957. p. 101-127.

A brief survey of communist uses of such media as radio, television, and books for purposes of propaganda.

1026. Táborský, Edward. Communism in Czechoslovakia, 1948-1960. Princeton, N.J., Princeton University Press, 1961. 628 p. Bibliography: p. 609-620.

See also entry no. 828.

Part 4 of the book, "The Making of the New Communistic Man" (p. 471-594), deals with communist internal propaganda and indoctrination media and their use in an effort to convert the Czechoslovak people to communism.

H. PSYCHOLOGY

by Josef Brožek

1027. Activitas nervosa superior. v. 1– May 1959– Praha, Státní zdravotnické nakl. Quarterly.

Journal of Společnost pro studium vyšší nervové činnosti. Addressed to an international audience; some articles are in English, German, Russian, or French, while summaries and tables of contents are given in Czech, English, and Russian. Includes news, reports, and book reviews.

1028. Bažány, Miroslav, *and* Karol Adamovič, *eds.* Problémy psychológie diet'at'a a mládeže (Problems of the psychology of the child and the adolescent). Bratislava, Slovenské psychologické nakl., 1964. 257 p. Illus. Includes bibliographies.

The proceedings of the first Slovak Psychological Congress, held April 8-10, 1963. The papers are grouped into three sections, dealing with developmental, educational, and clinical psychology, respectively.

1029. Bratislava. Psychologická výchovna klinika. Určovanie duševného vývinu diet'at'a (Characterization of the mental development of the child). Edited by Miroslav Bažány and Karol Adamovič. Bratislava, Slovenské pedagogické nakl., 1965. 212 p. Illus. Includes bibliographies. (*Its* Práce, 2)

Contains papers contributed by the staff of the clinic. Dr. Bažány wrote the opening article concerned with the methodological problems of measuring abilities and personality characteristics. Table of contents also in Russian and English; summaries in the same languages.

1030. Bratislava. Univerzita. *Filozofická fakulta.* Sborník: Psychologica (Collected papers: psychologica). v. 1– 1961– Bratislava, Slovenské pedagogické nakl. Illus., diagrs., tables. Irregular.

This is one of a series of collected papers issued by the Philosophical Faculty of the Comenius University in Bratislava, where a Psychological Institute was established in 1957 and a Department of Psychology, in 1959. Tables of contents also in Russian, English, German, and French; summaries in some of the same languages.

1031. Brichcín, Milan. Teoretické a metodologické problémy výzkumu průběhu volních pohybů (Theoretical and methodological problems of research concerning the time course of voluntary movements). Praha, Universita Karlova, 1966. 170 p. (Acta Universitatis Carolinae. Philosophica et historica. 1966. Monographia, 12)

Deals with a topic to which much attention was devoted at the Institute of Psychology of Charles University. Extensive summaries in English and Russian.

1032. Brno. Universita. *Filosofická fakulta.* Sborník prací. Řada filosofická (B) (Collected papers. Philosophical series [B]). no. 1– 1953– Brno, Státní pedagogické nakl. Illus., facsims. Annual.

Psychological papers were included in this series (cf. no. 9, published in 1962, which was dedicated to the 70th anniversary of Vilém Chmelař). More recently, a new subseries has been started, *Řada pedagogicko-psychologická (I)* (Educational-psychological series [I]). Some papers are in English or Russian; there are summaries in Russian, English, French, or German.

1033. Brožek, Josef, *and* Jiří Hoskovec. Contemporary Psychology in Czechoslovakia: The General Setting. Psychologia, an International Journal of Psychology in the Orient, v. 9, Mar. 1966: 53-59.

Lists papers available in English on currents in experimental and clinical psychology, book reviews published in *Contemporary Psychology*, professional associations, periodicals, educational institutions, and research centers.

1034. Celoštátna konferencia československých psychológov. *1st, Smolenice, 1957.* Využitie psychológie v socialistickej spoločenskej praxi (Utilization of psychology in socialist social practice). Bratislava, Vydavatel'stvo Slovenskej akadémie vied, 1959. 403 p. Illus. Bibliographical footnotes.

The conference aimed to explore the possibilities of a more extensive application of psychology in the realms of production, education, and health care. Presentations by participants from Bulgaria, Hungary, and Romania are followed by reports of the committees for industrial, educational, and clinical psychology. Summaries in Russian.

1035. Československá akademie věd. *Sekce historická.* Sborník psychologických prací (Collection of psychological studies). Scientific editor: Jan Doležal. Praha, 1957. 300 p. Illus. Includes bibliographies.

The editor notes that these papers represent the work of a transitional era characterized by a search for a new orientation in regard to methodology and the beginnings of independent research. Summaries in English and Russian.

1036. Československá psychologie; časopis pro psychologickou teorii i praxi. (Czechoslovak psychology; journal for psychological theory and practice). v. 1– 1957– Praha. Illus., ports. Quarterly.

See also entry no. 1222.

Issued by Československá akademie věd. Contains original articles, brief notes (especially on methods), news and commentary on psychology at home and abroad, and book reviews. Table of contents also in Russian and English; summaries in the same languages.

1037. Jurovský, Anton. Kultúrny vývin mládeže (The cultural development of adolescents). Bratislava, Slovenské pedagogické nakl., 1965. 324 p. Illus. (Práce Psychologickej výchovnej kliniky v Bratislave) Bibliography: p. 305-308.

Centered on a study of the frequency of cultural activities among young people. Summaries in Russian and English.

1038. Linhart, Josef. Psychologické problémy teorie učení (Psychological problems of the theory of learning). Praha, Nakl. Československé akademie věd, 1965. 351 p. Illus. Bibliography: p. 316-329.

An attempt to synthesize both the literature on the subject and the results of experimental studies carried out over a period of years by the author and his collaborators. Summary in English (p. 330-336); table of contents also in English.

1039. Matoušek, Oldřich, *and* Jiří Růžička. Psychologie práce; základní otázky (Psychology of work; basic problems). Praha, Nakl. politické literatury, 1965. 286 p. Illus. Bibliography: p. 284-285.

The first systematic presentation of the subject to appear in Czech since the publication of *Encyklopedie výkonnosti* (Encyclopedia of efficiency) (Praha, Sfinx, 1934, 626 p.).

1040. Olomouc, Moravia. Palackého universita. *Filosofická fakulta.* Paedagogica-psychologica. 1– 1960– Praha, Státní pedagogické nakl.

Subseries of its *Acta.* Text in Czech; summaries in Russian and German. Supersedes *Pedagogika-Psychologie,* issued by Vysoká škola pedagogická. The second and fourth numbers, published in 1962 and 1963 and edited by E. Holas, are subtitled *Sborník prací o zobecňování* (Collection of studies in generalization).

1041. Petráň, Václav. Psychiatrická péče o pracující, zvláště v průmyslových závodech (The psychiatric care of workers, especially in industrial enterprises). Praha, Státní zdravotnické nakl., 1963. 237 p. Illus. Bibliography: p. 221-225.

Considers the relations between industrial psychiatry and industrial psychology, and discusses various topics of importance to psychologists, such as motivation, fatigue, changing shifts, automation, and determinants of personality. Summaries in Russian (p. 200-210) and English (p. 211-220).

1042. Psychológia a patopsychológia diet'at'a (Psychology and psychopathology of the child). v. 1– 1966– Bratislava, Slovenské pedagogické nakl. 2 no. a year.

Issued by the Research Institute on Child Psychology and Psychopathology in Bratislava. Publishes articles, case studies, notes on instrumentation, and book reviews. Summaries in Russian and English.

1043. Slovenská akadémia vied. *Ústav experimentálnej psychológie.* Studia psychologica. 1– 1956– Bratislava, Vydavatel'stvo Slovenskej akadémie vied.

Title varies: 1956-64, *Psychologické štúdie SAV* (Psychological studies of the Slovak Academy of Sciences). Frequency varies. Publishes theoretical and experimental papers in various areas of psychology. In addition to articles in Slovak and Czech, contributions in English, German, French, and Russian are now published. The same institute also issues a series of psychological monographs, the first of which appeared in 1964.

Institute of Experimental Psychology (Bratislava, Slovak Academy of Sciences, 1963, 9 p.) is a pamphlet in English sketching the history of the institute, founded in 1952 as the Psychological Laboratory; the present name was taken in 1962. Research activity was at first directed to the study of conditioned reflexes; in 1957 its scope was enlarged to include psychophysiology, sensory psychology, and the psychology of work.

1044. Votava, Zdeněk, Milan Horváth, *and* Oldřich Vinař, *eds.* Psychopharmacological Methods; Proceedings of a Symposium on the Effects of Psychotropic Drugs on Higher Nervous Activity, Held in Prague From 30 October to 2 November 1961, under the Auspices of the Society for the Study of Higher Nervous Activity, Section of

Czechoslovak Medical Society. New York, Macmillan, 1963. 360 p. Illus., diagrs. Includes bibliographies.

Of particular relevance are the contributions by M. Horváth, E. Frantík, and J. Formánek on methodology (p. 131-150) and by O. Vinař on the study of conditioned reflexes in patients as indicators of drug-induced changes (p. 259-267).

1045. Záplata, Zdeněk, *comp.* Bibliografický soupis české a slovenské psychologické literatury, 1961-1965 (Bibliography of the Czech and Slovak literature on psychology, 1961-1965). Praha, Státní knihovna ČSSR, 1967. 192 p. (Novinky literatury. Společenské vědy. Řada 9. Roč. 1967, čís. 1-2)

21

Intellectual and Cultural Life

A. LANGUAGES

by Ladislav Matejka

1. Czech Language

a. Bibliographies and Periodicals

1046. Bibliographie linguistique. 1939/1947– Utrecht, Spectrum. Annual.

A general bibliography including selective references to the studies of Czech, published since 1939. The earlier period of research is basically covered in the bibliographic surveys of *Archiv für slavische Philologie* (Bd. 1-42, 1875-1929, Berlin, Wiedmann), *Indogerman-*

isches Jahrbuch (1914-1955), *Revue des études slaves* (1921–, Paris, Impr. Nationale), and *Zeitschrift für slavische Philologie* (1925–, Leipzig, Markert und Peters). A concise critical bibliography appears in K. Horálek's *Úvod do studia slovanských jazyků* (Praha, 1962, Práce Československé akademie věd, sv. 4), p. 490-494.

1047. Naše řeč (Our language). 1917– Praha, Československá akademie věd.

The linguistic journal primarily concerned with normativeness of contemporary standard Czech.

1048. Slovo a slovesnost (Word and literature). 1935– Praha, Melantrich. Quarterly.

Originally the organ of the Prague Linguistic Circle; still a prominent linguistic periodical.

1049. Travaux linguistiques de Prague. 1– 1964– Prague, Éditions de l'Academie tchécoslovaque des sciences. Annual.

See also entry no. 428.

This series attempts to continue in the tradition of the *Travaux du Cercle linguistique de Prague* (Prague, 1929-1939).

1050. Tyl, Zdeněk, *ed.* Bibliografie české lingvistiky. 1945/1950– Praha, Nakl. Československé akademie věd, 1955–

An annotated bibliography of works on Czech and of the Czech contributions to general, Indo-European, and Slavic linguistics. Three volumes published in 1955, 1957, and 1963 cover 1945-1950, 1951-1955, and 1956-1960 respectively.

The following recently published bibliographies should also be consulted:

Prague. Universita Karlova. Bibliografický soupis publikační činnosti členů slavistických kateder Filosofické fakulty University Karlovy v Praze za léta 1958-1962 (Bibliographic list of publications by members of the Slavistic chairs of Charles University in Prague, 1958-1962). 2d ed. Praha, Státní pedagogické nakladatelství, 1968. 124 p.

Tylová, Milena. České a slovenské jazykovedné bibliografie 1867-1967. Materiály (Czech and Slovak linguistic bibliographies, 1867-1967). Praha, Státní knihovna ČSSR, 1968. 44 p.

b. Sound and grammar

1051. Daneš, František. Intonace a věta ve spisovné češtině (Sentence intonation in contemporary standard Czech). Praha, Československá akademie věd, 1957. 161 p. (Studie a práce lingvistické, 2)

A functional inquiry into the general principles governing the intonational characteristics of utterances in modern Czech. English and Russian summaries.

1052. Frinta, Antonín. A Czech Phonetic Reader. London, University of London Press, 1925. 107 p.

The author's research contributed prominently to the phonological investigation of Czech; his *Novočeská výslovnost* (Pronunciation of modern Czech) (Prague, 1909) still belongs to the basic works on the Czech sound system.

1053. Gebauer, Jan. Historická mluvnice jazyka českého (Czech historical grammar). 2d ed. Praha, Československá akademie věd, 1958-1963. 4 v. Bibliographies.

The fundamental work on the history of the Czech language. More recent diachronic observations are available in M. Komárek's *Hláskosloví* (The sound system) (Praha, Státní pedagogické nakl., 1958, 178 p.) and A. Lamprecht's *Vývoj fonologického systému českého jazyka* (The development of the Czech phonological system) (Brno, Universita J. E. Purkyně, 1966, 108 p.). The Czech historical syntax is outlined in F. Trávníček's *Skladba* (Syntax) (Praha, Státní pedagogické nakl., 1956, 200 p.). A substantial contribution to the development of the Czech sentence structure appears in J. Bauer's *Vývoj českého souvětí* (The development of Czech sentence structure) (Praha, 1960, 402 p.).

1054. Havránek, Bohuslav. Vývoj spisovného jazyka českého (The development of standard Czech). *In* Spisovný jazyk. Československá vlastivěda, series 2, v. 1. Praha, Sfinx, 1936. p. 1-126.

A brilliant work on the history of literary Czech. Unfortunately, not readily accessible. B. Havránek's studies of contemporary standard Czech appear in his *Studie o spisovném jazyce* (Praha, Nakl. Československé akademie věd, 1963, 371 p.).

1055. Havránek, Bohuslav, *ed.* Tvoření slov v češtině (Lexical derivation in Czech). Praha, Československá akademie věd, 1962–

A distinguished project of leading grammarians investigating derivational devices of Czech. In the first volume, M. Dokulil discusses theory of lexical derivation, *Teorie odvozování slov* (Praha, 1962, 264 p.). The second volume, edited by F. Daneš and others, contains several studies on substantial derivation, *Odvozování podstatných jmen v češtině* (Praha, 1967, 780 p.). English and Russian summaries.

1056. Hujer, Oldřich, *ed.* Jazyk (Language). *In* Československá vlastivěda. Series I, v. 3. Praha, Sfinx, 1934.
See also entry no. 1101.

The volume includes B. Havránek's survey of Czech dialects (p. 84-218) as well as O. Hujer's historical outline of Czech (p. 1-83). His introduction to the history of the Czech language is available in Russian translation by A. G. Shirokova, *Vvedenie v istoriiu cheshskogo iazyka* (Moskva, Izd. inostrannoi literatury, 1953, 130 p.).

1057. Jakobson, Roman. Phonological Studies. 's-Gravenhage, Mouton, 1962. 678 p. Illus. (*His* Selected Writings, v. 1)
See also entry no. 1078.

The volume comprises several remarkable studies of the Czech sound system. R. Jakobson's discussion of various aspects of the Czech phonology also appears in *Fundamentals of Language* ('s-Gravenhage, Mouton, 1956, 87 p.; Janua linguarum, nr. 1) and in *Preliminaries to Speech Analysis; The Distinctive Features and Their Correlates* (Cambridge, Mass., M.I.T. Press, 1967, 64 p., illus.; bibliography: p. 53-55) by Roman Jakobson, C. Gunnar Fant, and Morris Halle.

1058. Kučera, Henry. The Phonology of Czech. 's-Gravenhage, Mouton, 1961. 112 p. Illus.

An intelligent inquiry into the various aspects of the Czech sound system with a good selective bibliography.

1059. Mann, Stuart E. Czech Historical Grammar. London, University of London, 1957. 183 p.

A general introduction.

1060. Mathesius, Vilém. Čeština a obecný jazykozpyt (The Czech language and general linguistics). Praha, Melantrich, 1947. 463 p.

A compendium of several stimulating studies by the founder of the Prague Linguistic Circle.

1061. Mazon, André. Grammaire de la langue tchèque. 2d ed. Paris, H. Champion, 1931. 292 p. (Collection de grammaire de l'Institut d'études slaves, II)

A thorough synchronic grammar of Czech.

1062. Sgall, Petr. Generativní popis jazyka a česká deklinace (Generative description of language and the Czech declension). Praha, Academia, 1967. 240 p.

An experimental description of the Czech declension. English and Russian summaries.

1063. Trávníček, František. Grammatika cheshskogo literaturnogo iazyka (Grammar of standard Czech). Moskva, Izdatel'stvo inostrannoi literatury, 1950. 466 p.

A standard synchronic grammar.

1064. Vachek, Josef, *ed.* A Prague School Reader in Linguistics. Bloomington, Indiana University Press, 1964. 485 p.

A representative compendium including methodologically advanced works on Czech. *See also* J. Vachek's *The Linguistic School of Prague; an Introduction to Its Theory and Practice* (Bloomington, Indiana University Press, 1966, 184 p., ports.).

c. Monolingual Dictionaries and Textbooks*

1065. Československá akademie věd. *Ústav pro jazyk český.* Příruční slovník jazyka českého (Reference dictionary of the Czech language).

* For multilingual dictionaries see chapter 14, section D.

Chief editors: Bohuslav Havránek and others. Praha, Státní pedagogické nakladatelství, 1937-1959. 9 v.

The most comprehensive lexical source of contemporary Czech. The compilation of an up-to-date lexicographic work, under the same sponsorship and editorship, entitled *Slovník spisovného jazyka českého* (Dictionary of the Czech standard language), has been in progress for several years (Praha, Nakladatelství Československé akademie věd, 1966–). So far two volumes have been published.

1066. Jelínek, Jaroslav, *and others, comps.* Frekvence slov, slovních druhů a tvarů v českém jazyce (The Czech word count). Praha, Státní pedagogické nakladatelství, 1961. 588 p. Bibliography.

A valuable source of data about frequency of Czech words and word classes.

1067. Machek, Václav. Etymologický slovník jazyka českého a slovenského (Czech and Slovak etymological dictionary). Praha, Československá akademie věd, 1957. 627 p. Illus. (Práce Československé akademie věd. Sekce jazyka a literatury, sv. 6)

A very imaginative as well as erudite etymological source which has appeared in a 2d revised and enlarged edition (Praha, Academia, 1968, 866 p.); more reliable than *Etymologický slovník jazyka českého* (Praha, Státní nakl. učebnic, 1952. 575 p.) by Josef Holub and František Kopečný. Earlier editions published under title: *Stručný slovník etymologický jazyka československého. See also*:

Holub, Josef. Stručný etymologický slovník jazyka českého (Brief etymological dictionary of the Czech language). Praha, Státní pedagogické nakl., 1967. 527 p.

1068. Sova, Miloš. A Practical Czech Course for English Speaking Students. 2d ed. Praha, Státní pedagogické nakladatelství, 1962. 521 p. Illus., maps.

A well-planned textbook supplemented by the *Key and Vocabulary* (106 p.). Essentials of the Czech grammar, organized as a textbook, are available in W. E. Harkins' *A Modern Czech Grammar* (New York, King's Crown Press, 1953, 338 p., illus.).

2. Slovak Language

a. Bibliographies and Periodicals

1069. Dvonč, Ladislav. Bibliografia slovenskej jazykovedy za roky 1948-1952 (Bibliography of Slovak linguistics). Martin, Matica slovenská, 1957. 236 p.

The annotated bibliography of works on Slovak and of Slovak contributions to the linguistic field in general. *See also* V. Blanár's *Bibliografia jazykovedy na Slovensku v rokoch 1939-1947* (Linguistic bibliography in Slovakia, 1939-1947) (Bratislava, Slovenská akadémia vied a umení, 1950, 210 p., Knižnica linguistica slovaca, sv. 6), and *Bibliographie linguistique* (entry no. 1046).

1070. Jazykovedný časopis (Linguistic journal). 1946– Bratislava. Illus., maps. Quarterly.

An important source of linguistic works on Slovak. See also *Jazykovedné štúdie* (Linguistic studies) (Bratislava, 1956–) and *Linguistica slovaca* (Bratislava, Slovenská akadémia vied a umení, 1939-1948).

1071. Kuzmík, Josef. Bibliografia kníh v západných rečiach týkajúcich sa slovenských vecí vydaných od XVI. stor. do r. 1955 (Bibliography of books in the Western languages about Slovak affairs published from the 16th century to 1955). Martin, Matica slovenská, 1959. 420 p.

See also entry no. 464.

Covers writings about Slovak matters of the last five centuries. *See also* J. Kuzmík's *Bibliografia slovenských kníh týkajúcich sa slovenských vecí vydaných od XVI. stor. do r. 1955* (Bibliography of Slavic books about Slovak affairs published from the 16th century to 1955) (Martin, Matica slovenská, 1959, 456 p.).

1072. Slovenská reč (Slovak language). 1932– Bratislava.

This periodical chiefly deals with standard Slovak. Its review section provides a good bibliographic source.

b. Sound, Grammar, Monolingual Dictionary

1073. De Bray, R. G. A. Guide to the Slavonic Languages. London, J. M. Dent; New York, Dutton, 1951. 798 p. Bibliography: p. 791-797.

This general introduction to the comparative study of modern Slavic languages contains a short sketch of Slovak, its dialects, and linguistic history. *See also* Charles E. Bidwell's *Slavic Historical Phonology in Tabular Form* (The Hague, Mouton, 1963, 88 p.).

1074. Dvonč, Ladislav. Rytmický zákon v spisovnej slovenčine (The rhythmical law in standard Slovak). Bratislava, Vydavatel'stvo Slovenskej akadémie vied, 1955. 254 p.

Quantity and its restriction in the sound system of contemporary Slovak.

1075. Hála, Bohuslav. Základy spisovné výslovnosti slovenské a srovnání s výslovností českou (Fundamentals of Slovak standard pronunciation compared with the Czech). Praha, Nakl. Filosofické fakulty University Karlovy, 1929. 134 p. Illus. (Práce z vědeckých ústavů, 23)

An instructive phonetic analysis of contemporary standard Slovak with a concise French summary. *See also* "Phonemic Notes on Standard Slovak," by Roman Jakobson, in his *Selected Writings*, v. 1 ('s-Gravenhage, Mouton, 1962).

1076. Horecký, Jan. Morfematická štruktúra slovenčiny (Morphemic structure of Slovak). Bratislava, Vydavatel'stvo Slovenskej akadémia vied, 1964. 194 p.

A synoptic treatment of Slovak morphology. See also *Morfologia slovenského jazyka* (Bratislava, Vydavatel'stvo slovenskej akadémie vied, 1966), a compendium of morphological studies by the leading Slovak grammarians.

1077. Isačenko, A. V. Grammatischeskii stroi russkogo iazyka v sopostavlenii s slovatskim (Grammatical structure of Russian contrasted with Slovak). Bratislava, Slovenská akadémia vied a umení, 1954-1960. 2 v.

A revealing inquiry into the grammatical devices of Russian and Slovak.

1078. Jakobson, Roman. Phonological Studies. 's-Gravenhage, Mouton, 1962. 678 p. Illus. (*His* Selected Writings, v. 1)

See also entry no. 1057.

Slovak is discussed in several studies. A survey of the comments appears in the index on page 669.

1079. Mistrík, Jozef. Slovosled a vetosled v slovenčine (Word order and sentence order in Slovak). Bratislava, Vydavatel'stvo Slovenskej akadémie vied, 1966. 276 p. Illus. Bibliography: p. 251-257.

A valuable contribution to the study of syntax. Russian and English summaries.

1080. Orlovský, Jozef. Slovenská syntax (Slovak syntax). 2d rev. and enl. ed. Bratislava, Obzor, 1965. 362 p. Illus.

A survey of Slovak syntax, chiefly oriented towards pedagogical application.

1081. Pauliny, Eugen. Štruktúra slovenského slovesa (Structure of the Slovak verb). Bratislava, Slovenská akadémia vied a umení, 1943. 112 p. Bibliography: p. 111-112. (Spisy Slovenskej akadémie vied a umení, sv. 2)

A structural study of the lexico-syntactic characteristics appearing in the Slovak verbal system.

1082. Pauliny, Eugen, Jozef Ružička, *and* Jozef Štolc. Slovenská gramatika (Slovak grammar). 5th enl. ed. Bratislava, SNP, 1968. 583 p. Illus., map.

A descriptive and prescriptive grammar of standard Slovak.

1083. Pauliny, Eugen. Fonológia spisovnej slovenčiny (Phonology of standard Slovak). Bratislava, Slovenská akadémia vied, 1963. 122 p.

The sound system of contemporary standard Slovak is described.

1084. Pauliny, Eugen. Fonologický vývin slovenčiny (Phonological development of Slovak). Bratislava, Vydavatel'stvo Slovenskej akadémie vied, 1963. 358 p. Maps.

A modern diachronic study of the Slovak language. Russian and English summaries. *See also* his *Dejiny spisovnej slovenčiny* (History of standard Slovak) (Bratislava, Slovenská akadémia vied a umení, 1948, 104 p.).

1085. Peciar, Štefan, *ed.* Slovník slovenského jazyka (Dictionary of Slovak). Bratislava, Slovenská akadémia vied, 1959-1966. 5 v.

A major lexicographic project well mastered by its erudite editor-in-chief.

1086. Stanislav, Ján. Dejiny slovenského jazyka (History of the Slovak language). New updated ed. Bratislava, Vydavatel'stvo Slovenskej akadémie vied, 1967. 3 v.

An original interpretation.

1087. Vážný, Václav. Nářečí slovenská (Slovak dialects). *In* Československá vlastivěda. Series I, v. 3. Praha, Sfinx, 1934. p. 219-310.

The best available survey of Slovak dialects. At this writing the forthcoming publication in Bratislava of the Slovak-language *Atlas slovenského jazyka*, prepared by Jozef Štolc, is announced.

B. LITERATURES

by Ladislav Matejka

1. Czech Literature

a. Bibliographies and Periodicals

1088. Bibliografický katalog Československé republiky (Bibliographic catalog of the Czechoslovak Republic). 1929– Praha, Nakl. Národní a universitní knihovny. Annual.

See also entry no. 1120.

A complete catalog of published books. A basic survey of specific bibliographies, relevant to the studies of Czech literature, is available in Z. Tyl's *Bibliografie české lingvistiky* (Bibliography of Czech linguistics) (Praha, Nakl. Československé akademie věd, 1955–). Special studies and sources are well covered in the bibliographic apparatus of *Dějiny české literatury* (History of Czech literature), edited by J. Mukařovský (Praha, Nakl. Československé akademie věd, 1959–). *See also* J. Jakubec's *Dějiny literatury české* (History of Czech literature) (Praha, J. Laichter, 1929–, Laichterův výbor nejlepších spisků poučných, kn. 53), J. Vlček's *Dějiny české literatury* (History of Czech literature) (Praha, Československý spisovatel, 1951, 2 v.), and A. Novák's *Přehledné dějiny literatury české* (Survey history of Czech literature) (Olomouc, R. Promberger, 1946).

1089. Čapek, Thomas, *and* Anna V. Čapek. Bohemian (Čech) Bibliography; a Finding List of Writings in English Relating to Bohemia and the Čechs. New York, F. H. Revell, 1918. 256 p. Front., facsims., plates, ports. Bibliography: p. 64-65.

See also entry no. 467.

Contains interesting data about Czech literature published in the United States.

1090. Česká literatura (Czech literature). roč. 1– 1953– Praha. Quarterly. Illus., ports.

The journal of literary scholarship. See also *Časopis pro moderní filologii* (1911–, Praha, Klub Moderních filologů, quarterly).

1091. Halík, Miroslav, *and* Hana Teigeová. Československá kniha v cizině (Czechoslovak books abroad). Praha, Nákladem obce pražské, 1938. 190 p. (Prague. Městská knihovna. Spisy, 28)

See also entry no. 468.

A representative selection of Czech and Slovak literature published outside of Czechoslovakia.

1092. Havel, Rudolf, *and* Jiří Opelík, *eds.* Slovník českých spisovatelů (Dictionary of Czech writers). Praha, Ceskoslovensky spisovatel, 1965. 625 p. Ports.

See also entry no. 532.

A useful reference book. *See also* J. Kunc's *Slovník soudobých českých spisovatelů; krásné písemnictví v letech 1918-45* (Dictionary of contemporary Czech writers; belles lettres, 1918-45) (Praha, 1945-1946, 2 v.) as well as his *Slovník českých spisovatelů beletristů 1945-1956* (Dictionary of Czech writers 1945-1956) (Praha, Státní pedagogické nakl., 1957, 483 p.).

1093. Knihopis československých tisků od doby nejstarši až do konce XVIII století (Bibliography of Czech and Slovak imprints from the earliest time to the end of the 18th century). Praha, V komisi knihkupectví F. Topiče, 1925–

See also entry no. 463.

A monumental bibliographic contribution, originally prepared under the editorship of Zdeněk V. Tobolka, and now under that of František Horák. The eighth part (S-V) appeared in 1965. See also *Soupis československé literatury za léta 1901-1925* (Index of Czechoslovak literature for the years 1901-1925) (Praha, Nakl. Svaz knihupců a nakladatelů Československé republiky, 1931-1938, 2 v.).

1094. Kunc, Jaroslav. Česká literární bibliografie, 1945-1963 (Czech literary bibliography, 1945-1963). Praha, Státní knihovna ČSSR, 1963-1964. 2 v. (Bibliografický katalog ČSSR. České knihy, zvl. sešit 6, 1963; 5, 1964)

———. Dodatky (Supplements). Praha, Státní knihovna ČSSR, 1964– (Bibliografický katalog ČSSR. České knihy, zvl. sešit 7, 1964)

Lists articles, essays, and reviews from books and periodicals about works of contemporary Czech writers. Alphabetic arrangement by authors. Other, though less elaborate, bibliographic sources on the subject are, e.g.:

Prague. Universita Karlova. *Knihovna.* Klasikové české literatury 19. století (Classics of Czech 19th century literature). Compiled by Helena Winklerová, Praha, 1958. 140 p. (Čteme a studujeme, sešit 2)

Prague. Universita Karlova. Základní bibliografia k dějinám české a slovenské literatury (Basic bibliography on the history of Czech and Slovak literature). Praha, SPN, 1960. 68 p.

b. Studies and Sources

1095. Černý, Václav. Staročeská milostná lyrika (Old Czech erotic poetry). Praha, Družstevní práce, 1948. 320 p. Plates.

The essay heavily emphasizes the external impact of Romance culture on early Czech lyric poetry.

1096. Chudoba, František. A short Survey of Czech Literature. New York, E. P. Dutton, 1924. 280 p.

An outline of Czech literature with emphasis on its extrinsic aspects. A short anthology is included.

1097. Chyzhevs'kyi, Dmytro (Dmitry Čiževsky). Outline of Comparative Slavic Literatures. Boston, American Academy of Arts and Sciences, 1952. 143 p. (Survey of Slavic Civilization, v. 1)

See also entry no. 444.

A synopsis of significant trends in the history of Slavic literatures. Czech literary topics are also discussed in Chyzhevs'kyi's *Aus zwei Welten* ('s-Gravenhage, Mouton, 1956, 352 p., Slavistic Printings and Reprintings, 10). The author's interest in Comenius resulted in several excellent studies, e.g., "Comenius' Labyrinth of the World: Its Themes and their Sources," *Harvard Slavic Studies*, I (Cambridge, Mass., Harvard University Press, 1953), p. 83-135. His famous discoveries of Comenius' manuscripts are described in *Rok; Kulturní sborník* (New York, Moravian Library, 1957), p. 14-18.

1098. Doležel, Lubomír. O stylu moderní české prózy (Style of modern Czech prose). Praha, Nakl. Československé akademie věd, 1960. 219 p. Illus. (Československá akademie věd. Sekce jazyka a literatury. Studie a prameny, 15)

An intelligent structural analysis of modern Czech prose art. French and Russian summaries.

1099. Harkins, William E. The Russian Folk Epos in Czech Literature, 1800-1900. New York, King's Crown Press, 1951. 282 p.

A learned monograph on the Czech literary response to the Russian heroic epos with a short foreword by Roman Jakobson.

1100. Harkins, William E. Karel Čapek. New York, Columbia University Press, 1962. 193 p. Illus.

A thorough monographic contribution discussing various aspects of K. Čapek's literary work. See also *Karel Čapek: Man Against Destruction* (London, G. Allen, 1964, 426 p., illus.), an extensive essay by the Slovak writer Alexander Matuška.

1101. Hujer, Oldřich, *ed.* Jazyk. *In* Československá vlastivěda. Series I, v. 3. Praha, Sfinx, 1934.
See also entry no. 1056.

The volume contains R. Jakobson's important study "Verš staročeský" (Old Czech versification), p. 429-459, and J. Mukařovský's "Obecné zásady a vývoj novočeského verše" (General principles and development of modern Czech versification), p. 376-429. *See also* J. Hrabák's *Studie o českém verši* (Studies of Czech versification) (Praha, Státní pedagogické nakl., 1959, 369 p.).

1102. Jakobson, Roman. O cheshskom stikhe preimushchestvenno v sopostavlenii s russkim (On Czech versification primarily contrasted with Russian). Berlin-Moskva, 1923. 120 p.

A pioneering work on Czech poetic usage. Its revised Czech version is called *Základy českého verše* (Fundamentals of Czech versification) (Praha, 1926, 140 p.).

1103. Jakobson, Roman. The Kernel of Comparative Slavic Literature. *In* Harvard Slavic Studies, v. 1, 1953: 1-71.
See also entry no. 446.

A superb outline revealing the inherent relationship of Czech literature to other Slavic literatures. The earliest period of literacy in the Czechoslovak area is discussed by R. Jakobson in his contributions to the compendium *Co daly naše země Evropě a lidstvu* (Praha, 1939) and in his book *Moudrost starých Čechů* (New York, Nakl. Československého kulturního kroužku, 1943, 240 p.). *See also* his study "Some Russian Echoes of Czech Hagiography," *Annuaire de l'Institut de philologie et d'histoire orientales et slaves*, VII (New York, 1944), p. 155-180, and "Řeč a písemnictví českých židů v době přemyslovské" (Language and literature of Czech Jews in the Premyslide period), *Rok* (New York, Moravian Library), 1957, p. 35-46.

1104. Lützow, Francis H., *Count.* A History of Bohemian Literature. New York, D. Appleton, 1900. 425 p.

Early Czech literature traditionally viewed in its historical framework.

1105. Mukařovský, Jan. Kapitoly z české poetiky (Chapters of Czech poetics). 2d expanded ed. Praha, Svoboda, 1948. 3 v.

A collection comprising several rigorous inquiries into the intrinsic problems of Czech literature. *See also* his *Studie z estetiky* (Studies on esthetics) (Praha, Odeon, 1966, 376 p.).

1106. Mukařovský, Jan., *ed.* Dějiny české literatury (History of Czech literature). Praha, Československá akademie věd, 1959–

The work is strangely misconceived but contains a useful bibliographic apparatus. Three volumes published so far.

1107. Novák, Arne. Die tschechische Literatur. Potsdam, Athenaion, 1931-1932. 114 p. Illus., facsims., plates, ports. (Handbuch der Literaturwissenschaft, edited by O. Walzel, Lieferungen 167, 170, 186)

A well-balanced outline of Czech literature from its beginnings to the early twentieth century. A. Novák's *Stručné dějiny literatury české* (Concise history of Czech literature) (4th ed., Olomouc, R. Promberger, 1946, 818 p.) is the most versatile reference source.

1108. Rechcígl, Miloslav Jr., *ed.* The Czechoslovak Contribution to World Culture. The Hague, Mouton, 1964. 682 p. Illus.

See also entries no. 511, 681, *and* 1165.

The collection contains several important studies of contemporary Czech literature and includes a good selective bibliography. Sponsored by the Czechoslovak Society of Arts and Sciences in America.

1109. Smith, Horatio E., *ed.* Columbia Dictionary of Modern European Literature. New York, Columbia University Press, 1947. 899 p.

See also entry no. 1137.

Comprises R. Wellek's sketch of Czech literature and a series of his short monographs characterizing important Czech writers of the 19th and 20th centuries.

1110. Součková, Milada. The Czech Romantics. 's-Gravenhage, Mouton, 1958. 168 p. Bibliography: p. 164-165. (Slavistic Printings and Reprintings, 17)

A well-informed study centered around literary contributions of Karel Hynek Mácha, Karel Jaromír Erben and Božena Němcová. The art of Jaroslav Vrchlický, the most influential poet of the last decades of the 19th century, is skillfully characterized in M. Součková's monograph, *The Parnassian, Jaroslav Vrchlický* (The Hague, Mouton, 1964, 151 p., illus., Slavistic Printings and Reprintings, 40).

1111. Vašica, Josef. České literární baroko (Czech literary baroque). Praha, Vyšehrad, 1938. 352 p.

A valuable monograph on a remarkable period in the history of Czech literature. *See also* V. Bitnar's *Zrození barokového básníka* (The birth of the baroque poet) (Praha, 1940, 624 p.), and D. Chyzhevs'kyi's "Neue Veröffentlichungen über die čechische Barockdichtung," *Zeitschrift für slavische Philologie* (1934, 1935, 1938, 1943, and 1945).

1112. Vilikovský, Jan. Písemnictví českého středověku (Literature of the Czech Middle Ages). Praha, Universum, 1948. 255 p.

A collection of profound studies of Old Czech literature. *See also* J. Hrabák's *Studie ze starší české literatury* (Studies of Old Czech literature) (Praha, Státní pedagogické nakl., 1956, 279 p.).

1113. Vodička, Felix. Počátky krásné prózy novočeské (The beginnings of the prose art in Modern Czech). Praha, Melantrich, 1948. 366 p.

An important structural inquiry into Czech literary problems of the early 19th century. *See also* his *Cesty a cíle obrozenské literatury* (Literature of the Czech revival) (Praha, Československý spisovatel, 1958, 323 p.).

1114. Weingart, Miloš. Československý typ cirkevnej slovančiny (The Czechoslovak type of Church Slavonic). Bratislava, Slovenská akadémia vied a umení, 1949. 133 p. Port. Bibliographies. (Naučná knižnica Slovenskej akadémie vied a umení, sv. 13)

A survey of the records characterizing the usage of Church Slavonic in the Czechoslovak area. See also *Magna Moravia* (Praha, 1935), a compendium of studies in English, Russian, German, and Czech by several specialists studying various aspects of the early Christian culture in Bohemia, Moravia, and Slovakia.

1115. Wellek, René. Essays on Czech Literature. The Hague, Mouton, 1963. 214 p. Port. (Slavistic Printings and Reprintings, 43) Bibliography: p. 11-16.

An exquisite treatment of various representative topics pertinent to the history of Czech literature. The volume includes a bibliography of R. Wellek's writings in Czech on Czech and Slavic literary problems.

c. Anthologies

1116. Eisner, Paul. Die Tschechen. Eine Anthologie aus fünf Jahrhunderten. München, R. Piper, 1928. 442 p.

A selection of texts characterizing five centuries of Czech cultural life.

1117. Garvin, Paul L., *ed. and trans.* A Prague School Reader on Esthetics, Literary Structure, and Style. 3d ed. Washington, D.C., Georgetown University Press, 1964. 163 p.

Originally published in 1955. A collection of samples selected with the intention of presenting certain aspects of the literary scholarship of the Prague Linguistic Circle. It includes a critical bibliography. *See* R. Wellek's review in *Language*, v. 31, 1955: 584-587.

1118. Harkins, William E. Anthology of Czech Literature. New York, King's Crown Press, 1953. 226 p.

A representative selection by a prominent American Bohemist. *See also* F. C. Weiskopf's *Hundred Towers; a Czechoslovak Anthology of Creative Writing* (New York, L. B. Fischer, 1945, 277 p.), and *The Linden Tree; an Anthology of Czech and Slovak Literature* (Prague, Artia, 1962, 403 p., illus.), compiled by Mojmír Otruba and Zdeněk Pešat.

1119. Havránek, Bohuslav, *and* Josef Hrabák. Výbor z české literatury od počátků po dobu Husovu (Readings in Czech literature from its beginning to Hus). Praha, Nakl. Československé akademie věd, 1957. 851 p. Illus.

An annotated reader of the oldest Czech literary period. See also *Výbor z české literatury doby husitské* (Readings in Czech literature of the Hussite period), edited by B. Havránek and others (Praha, Nakl. Československé akademie věd, 1963-1964, 2 v., illus.).

2. Slovak Literature

a. Bibliographies and Periodicals

1120. Bibliografický katalog Československé republiky (Bibliographic catalog of the Czechoslovak Republic). 1929– Praha, Nakl. Národní a universitní knihovny. Annual.

See also entry no. 1088.

See also *Soupis československé literatury za léta 1901-1925* (The index of Czechoslovak literature for the years 1901-1925) (Praha, Svaz knihkupců a nakladatelů Československé republiky, 1931-1938, 2 v.).

1121. Kováč, Michal, *ed.* Poznajme súčasnú slovenskú literatúru (Let us become acquainted with contemporary Slovak literature). Martin, Matica Slovenská, 1961. 745 p.

A popularizing bibliography of Slovak literary production in the years 1945-1960.

1122. Litteraria. Štúdie a dokumenty (Literary studies and documents). v. 1– 1958– Bratislava, Vydavateľstvo slovenskej akadémie vied. Annual.

One of the best serials of literary scholarship published in Czechoslovakia.

1123. Mišianik, Ján. Bibliografia slovenského písomníctva do konca XIX. storočia (A bibliography of Slovak literature up to the end of the 19th century). Bratislava, Slovenská akadémia vied a umení, 1946. 300 p. Facsims. Bibliography: p. 7-8. (Práce z vedeckých ústavov Slovenskej akadémie vied a umení, Rád A., sv. 5)

A useful supplement to L'. V. Rizner's *Bibliografia písomníctva slovenského* (Bibliography of Slovak literature) (Martin, Matica Slovenská, 1929-1934). *See also* Z. V. Tobolka's *Knihopis československých tisků od doby nejstarší až do konce 18. století* (Bibliography of Czech and Slovak imprints from the earliest time to the end of the 18th century) (Praha, V. komisi knihkupectví F. Topiče, 1925–) and A. Apponyi's *Hungarica* (München, J. Rosenthal, 1903-1927).

1124. Potemra, Michal, *comp.* Bibliografia slovenských novín a časopisov do roku 1918 (Bibliography of Slovak newspapers and periodicals

to 1918). Martin, Matica slovenská, 1958. 145 p. (Slovenská národná bibliografia. Séria B. Periodiká, zväzok la)
See also entry no. 483.
A survey of the Slovak periodical press from its beginning to 1918.

1125. Slovenská literatura. Roč. 1– 1954– Bratislava, Slovenská akadémia vied. Quarterly. Illus.
Supersedes the Academy's *Literárnohistorický sborník*. A modern journal of literary scholarship.

b. Studies and Sources

1126. Bakoš, Mikuláš. Problém vývinovej periodizácie slovenskej literatúry (Periodization of the development in Slovak literature). Trnava, F. Urbánek, 1944. 30 p.
An application of a structural method to the stylistic typology of Slovak literature. Includes German summary.

1127. Bakoš, Mikuláš. Vývin slovenského verša od školy Štúrovej (Evolution of Slovak versification since Štúr). 2d ed. Bratislava, Slovenská akadémia vied a umení, 1949. 215 p. (Náučná knižnica Slovenskej akademie vied a umení, sv. 9)
An inquiry into the linguistic foundation of the Slovak rhythmical devices developed in poetry.

1128. Bakoš, Mikuláš. Problémy literárnej vedy včera a dnes (The problems of literary scholarship yesterday and today). Bratislava, Slovenská akadémia vied, 1964. 391 p.
A compendium of studies reflecting methodological struggles in the literary scholarship of Slovakia during the last three decades. A short summary in German. *See also* M. Bakoš's *Literatúra a nadstavba* (Literature and superstructure) (Bratislava, Slovenský spisovatel', 1960, 312 p.).

1129. Béder, Ján. Dejiny slovenskej literatúry (History of Slovak literature). Bratislava, Slovenské pedagogické nakladatel'stvo, 1963. 448 p.
A handy reference book.

1130. Dejiny slovenskej literatúry (History of Slovak literature). Bratislava, Slovenská akadémia vied, 1958– Illus., facsims., ports.
A collective work by Slovak literary historians. Three volumes have been published and others are forthcoming.

1131. Harkins, William E., *and* Klement Šimončič. Czech and Slovak Literature. New York, Columbia University Press, 1950. 50 p.
A bibliographic outline.

1132. Krčméry, Štefan. A survey of Modern Slovak Literature. Slavonic and East European Review, v. 7, 1928: 160-170.
General data about Slovak literature during the first decade of the Czechoslovak republic.

1133. Mistrík, J. Slovenská štylistika (Slovak stylistics). Bratislava, Slovenské pedagogické nakladatel'stvo, 1965. 312 p. Bibliography: p. 311-313.

A useful monograph concerned with stylistic devices in contemporary standard Slovak.

1134. Mráz, Andrej. Die Literatur der Slowaken. Berlin, Volk und Reich Verlag, 1943. 201 p. Illus., ports.

A knowledgeable account of Slovak literature.

1135. Mráz, Andrej. Zo slovenskej literárnej minulosti (The Slovak literary past). Bratislava, Slovenské vydavatel'stvo krásnej literatúry, 1953. 373 p.

Two centuries of Slovak literature surveyed in a selection of characteristic topics.

1136. Pražák, Albert. Dějiny slovenské literatury (History of Slovak literature). Praha, Melantrich, 1950. 378 p. Includes bibliographies.

Written by an erudite Czech literary scholar.

1137. Smith, Horatio E., *ed.* Columbia Dictionary of Modern European Literature. New York, Columbia University Press, 1947. 899 p.

See also entry no. 1109.

The compendium includes several brilliant characterizations of Slovak literary personalities by René Wellek, as well as his concise encyclopedic presentation of Slovak literature.

1138. Vlček, Jaroslav. Dejiny literatúry slovenskj (History of Slovak literature). 4th ed. Bratislava, Slovenské vydavatel'stvo krásnej literatúry, 1953. 417 p. Illus.

A basic work in the history of Slovak literature written by an ardent promoter of the Czech and Slovak cultural symbiosis. *See also* his *Kapitoly zo slovenskej literatúry* (Chapters from Slovak literature) (Bratislava, Slovenské vydavatel'stvo krásnej literatúry, 1954, 445 p., illus.).

3. Anthologies

1139. Mišianik, Ján. Antológia staršej slovenskej literatúry (An anthology of older Slovak literature). Bratislava, Vydavatel'stvo Slovenskej akadémie vied, 1964. 849 p. Illus., facsims., ports., bibliographical footnotes.

A comprehensive reader representatively covering one millennium of literacy in the Czechoslovak area, with emphasis on the documents particularly relevant to the history of Slovak literature. It includes short English and Russian summaries.

1140. Otruba, Mojmír, *and* Zdeněk Pešat, *eds.* The Linden Tree; an Anthology of Czech and Slovak Literature. Prague, Artia, 1962. 403 p. Illus.

See also P. Selver's *A Century of Czech and Slovak Poetry* (London, 1946, 212 p.), his *Anthology of Czechoslovak Literature* (London, 1929, 301 p.), and F. C. Weiskopf's *Hundred Towers: A Czechoslovak Anthology of Creative Writing* (New York, L. B. Fischer, 1945, 278 p.).

C. FOLKLORE

by Barbara Krader

1. Bibliographies

1141. Kunz, Ludvík. Česká ethnografie a folkloristika v letech 1945-1952. České bibliografie národopisné (Czech ethnography and folklore studies in 1945-1952. Czech ethnographic bibliography). Praha, Nakl. Československé akademie věd, 1954. 381 p.

Precise, detailed bibliography of Czech articles and books, arranged alphabetically by author, with subject and geographical indexes. A valuable introductory essay, with summaries in Russian and German, surveys bibliographies before 1945. *See also* the same author's "Eine Übersicht bedeutenderer Arbeiten auf dem Gebiet der tschechischen und slowakischen Volkskunde von 1945 bis 1955," in *Deutsches Jahrbuch für Volkskunde*, v. 2, 1956, p. 359-378. From 1956, see *Internationale volkskundliche Bibliographie*, to which Kunz contributes Czechoslovak entries.

1142. Zíbrt, Čeněk. Bibliografický přehled českých národních písní; seznam studií, starších sbírek rukopisných, sbírek tištěných překladů . . . (Bibliographical survey of Czech folk songs; list of studies, older manuscript collections, collections of printed translations . . .). Praha, Nakl. České akademie císaře Františka Josefa pro vědy, slovesnost a umění, 1895. 326 p. (Sbírka pramenův ku poznání literárního života v Čechách, na Moravě a v Slezku. Skupina 3.: Práce bibliografické, čís. 1)

Includes index of first lines of published Czech and some Slovak folk songs (p. 129-314). A basic reference; a revised edition is being prepared by the Czechoslovak Academy of Sciences.

2. Periodicals

1143. Český lid (The Czech people). v. 1– 1891– Praha. Illus., ports., music. Bimonthly.

See also entry no. 606.

Suspended publication: 1915-1922, 1933-1945. Volumes for 1946-1951 numbered volumes 1-6; beginning in 1951, volumes are numbered in new and old series. Volumes 5-32 edited by Čeněk Zíbrt. Since 1946 it has been the organ of the Institute of Ethnography and Folklore Studies of the Czechoslovak Academy of Sciences. A subject index to volumes 1-32, entitled *Soupis prací Zíbrtova Českého* lidu (Index of articles in Zíbrt's *Česky lid*) (Praha, Vydala Společnost čsl. národopisců při ČSAV, 1960, 229 p.), compiled by Ludvík Kunz, was issued as *Příručky Společnosti československých národopisců*, sv. 1.

Currently contains articles (with German summaries), reviews, news, and annual bibliographies of Czech ethnography and folklore. Tables of contents are also given in Russian, German, and French.

1144. Národopisný věstník československý. Revue d'ethnographie tchécoslave. v. 1-33; Praha, 1906-1956. Quarterly. Illus., plates, ports.

Supersedes *Národopisný sborník československý* (Czechoslovak ethnographic miscellany) (v. 1-11; 1897-1905, Praha). Published by the Národopisná společnost československá; editors have included Jiří Polívka, Jiří Horak, Karel Chotek, and D. Stránská. An index to volumes 1-20 was published in volume 20. Contains outstanding articles on folklore and lengthy reviews of Czech, Slovak, and foreign publications. Resumed publication in 1966 under editorship of Václav Frolec as *Národopisný věstník československý* (Brno, Národopisná společnost československá při ČSAV).

1145. Slovenský národopis (Slovak ethnography). v. 1– 1953– Bratislava. Illus., ports., maps, music.

See also entry no. 610.

Annual, 1953; quarterly, 1954-1955; bimonthly from 1956. Supersedes *Národopisný sborník* (Ethnographic miscellany) (v. 1-11; 1939-1952. Bratislava. Complete index published in *Slovenský národopis*, v. 2, 1954, p. 410-442). Organ of the Ethnographic Institute of the Slovak Academy of Sciences. Articles (with summaries in Russian, German, English, or Hungarian), reviews, and annual bibliographies of Slovak ethnography and folklore. Tables of contents are also given in Russian, German, English, and French. An index to the first 10 volumes has been published.

Foreign journals frequently treating Czech and Slovak folklore include *Demos* (v. 1– 1960– Berlin, Akademie-Verlag), *Deutsches Jahrbuch für Volkskunde* (v. 1– 1955– Berlin, Akademie-Verlag), and *Fabula* (v. 1– 1957– Berlin, W. de Gruyter).

3. Surveys

1146. Bednárik, Rudolf. Duchovná kultúra slovenského l'udu (Spiritual culture of the Slovak people). *In* Slovenská vlastiveda (Book of knowledge on Slovakia). v. 2. Bratislava, Slovenská akadémia vied a umení, 1943. p. 7-121. Illus., 50 plates, music.

See also entry no. 956.

Melicherčík, Andrej. Slovenský folklor (Slovak folklore). *In* Slovenská vlastiveda. v. 2. Bratislava, Slovenská akadémia vied a umení, 1943. p. 259-331. Illus., music.

Bednárik's survey describes customs of birth, marriage, and death, and rites and customs associated with certain times of year. It was published, together with another essay by the same author, in a German translation under the title *Slowakische Volkskultur* (Bratislava-Pressburg, Verlag "Die Slawische Rundschau," 1943, 242 p., illus.).

Melicherčík's article concerns the Slovak folk song, tales, plays, proverbs, and riddles.

1147. Bogatyrev, Petr Grigor'evich. Lidové divadlo české a slovenské (Czech and Slovak folk theater). Praha, F. Borový, 1940. 314 p. Illus., music.

See also entry no. 1306.

Description and functional analysis are followed by the texts of plays, one with melodies of songs. *See also* Jan Malík's *Puppetry in Czechoslovakia* (Prague, Orbis, 1948, 56 p., illus.), and *Cheshskii kukol'nyi i russkii narodnyi teatr* (Czech puppet and Russian folk theater), by Bogatyrev and Roman Jakobson (Berlin, Izd-vo Opoiaz, 1923, 121 p.).

1148. Horák, Jiří. Národopis československý; přehledný nástin (Czechoslovak ethnography; general outline). *In* Československá vlastivěda (Book of knowledge on Czechoslovakia). v. 2. Člověk (Man). Praha, Sfinx, 1933. p. 305-472. Illus., Notes: p. 607-608.

Exhaustive account of theories, organizational activities, and literature in the field of Czech and Slovak ethnography and folklore from the Middle Ages to 1929. An indispensable reference. *See also* the same author's "Les études ethnographiques en Tchéco-Slovaquie," in *Revue des études slaves*, v. 1, 1921, p. 71-97, 228-236.

1149. Jirásek, Alois. Some Aspects of Czech Culture. New Haven, Human Relations Area Files, 1953. 54 p. Illus.

By one of the greatest Czech writers, this essay was first published as "Charakter, Sagen, Trachten, Ortsanlagen und Wohnungen der Slaven," in volume 14, "Böhmen," part 1, of *Die Österreichisch-Ungarische Monarchie in Wort und Bild* (Wien, K. K. Hof- und Staatsdruckerei, 1894), p. 392-437. For an outstanding account of the Slavs in Moravia, *see* "Volksleben der Slaven," by František Bartoš, in the same series, volume 17, "Mähren und Schlesien" (Wien, 1897), p. 177-220. Volumes 14, 15, and 17 contain excellent material on both the Slavic and the German culture of Bohemia and Moravia.

A longer, classic description of folk customs is Čeněk Zíbrt's *Veselé chvíle v životě lidu českého* (Merry times in the life of the Czech people), 2d ed. (Praha, Vyšehrad, 1950, 639 p., illus., bibliographic notes).

4. Collections

1150. Erben, Karel Jaromír, *ed.* Prostonárodní české písně a říkadla (Czech folksongs and nursery rhymes). Praha, Jaroslav Pospíšil, 1862-1864. 2 v. [v. 1, 1864]

Volume 2 has title Nápěvy prostonárodních písní českých (Melodies of Czech folksongs).

Still the definitive edition of this fundamental collection, containing more than 2,200 texts of songs, rhymes, riddles, and children's games. The next edition, undated (new foreword signed 1886) is a poorly edited reprint of the one of 1862-1864, but adds, for the first time, 811 melodies. A later edition, without music edited by Jiří Horák, appeared in 1937 (Praha, Evropský literární klub, 454 p.) and was reprinted in 1939.

Should be paired with František Sušil's *Moravské národní písně s nápěvy do textu vřaděnými* (Moravian folksongs, with melodies inserted into the text), 4th ed. (Praha, Vyšehrad, 1951, 797 p.), illus., ports., facsims., music), an equally fundamental collection of the same period, first published in this form in 1860. It includes 2,361 numbered song texts and about 1,890 melodies. This edition reprints from the 1941 (3d) edition a valuable essay, by Robert Smetana and Bedřich Václavek, appraising Sušil's collection and comparing its music with that collected by Erben.

1151. Horák, Jiří, *comp.* Slovenské ľudové balady (Slovak folk ballads). Bratislava, Slovenské vydavateľstvo krásnej literatúry, 1956. 420 p. Illus.

Contains 127 texts, most of them previously published, with sources identified; includes no music. There is a valuable study by Horák (p. 11-85) on the development of Slovak ballads and their types.

A larger collection devoted to one type of ballad is *Zbojnícke piesne slovenského ľudu* (Outlaw songs of the Slovak people) (Bratislava, Slovenské vydavateľstvo krásnej literatúry, 1965, 698 p., col. illus., maps, bibliographical notes). It includes 689 texts, selected by Jiří Horák and Karel Plicka, mostly from unpublished collections. Sources are given, and there are 289 melodies, collected by Plicka. A cultural historical study by Horák appears on pages 7-129.

1152. Jech, Jaromír, *comp.* Tschechische Volksmärchen. Berlin, Rütten & Loening, 1961. 591 p.

Contains 67 texts from 19th and 20th century collections, with comparative notes. Jech, a leading young tale specialist and collector, contributes a valuable survey of collectors, collections, best tellers of tales, and characteristics of Czech folk prose (p. 481-542).

See also *Hlučínský pohádkář Josef Smolka; pohádky, povídky a vyprávění Josefa Smolky* (Josef Smolka, storyteller from Hlučín; fairy tales, stories, and anecdotes of Josef Smolka) (Ostrava, Krajské nakl., 1958, 263 p., illus.), recorded and annotated by Antonín Satke. This is an outstanding monograph on a Silesian tale-teller, with a study, photographs, and 55 tales. Russian and German summaries.

1153. Melicherčík, Andrej. Slovenský folklór; chrestomatia (Slovak folklore; an anthology). Bratislava, Vydavateľstvo Slovenskej akadémie vied, 1959. 790 p. Illus. (Práce Národopisného ústavu Slovenskej akadémie vied, zv. 11) Bibliography: p. 763-770.

Useful collection of poetry and prose with sources indicated.

The bibliography, however, is marred by errors and misprints, and the introductions to the sections are superficial and doctrinaire. Summaries in Russian, German, and English.

See also Adolf Petr Záturecký's *Slovenská přísloví, pořekadla a úsloví* (Slovak proverbs, sayings, and expressions) (Praha, Nakl. České akademie císaře Františka Josefa, 1896, 389 p.), an outstanding collection of folk material arranged by subject with frequent notes concerning use. The 1965 edition is inferior, omitting religious and some other proverbs.

1154. Polívka, Jiří. Súpis slovenských rozprávok. Collection de contes slovaques populaires. Turčiansky sv. Martin, Matica slovenská, 1923-1931. 5 v. Bibliography: v. 5, p. 422-443.

Basic compendium by a great international tale specialist. An introduction on Slovak tale collectors and collections in volume 1, pages 1-158, is followed by an exhaustive compilation of tales from published and archival sources, grouped by subject and accompanied by comparative notes. Tables of contents in each volume and indexes in the last volume facilitate use, although the arrangement is not that of Aarne-Thompson.

1155. Tille, Václav. Soupis českých pohádek (Inventory of Czech tales). Praha, 1929-37. 2 v. in 3 (619, 451, 663 p.). (Rozpravy České akademie věd a umění. Třída 3, čís. 66, 72, 74) Survey of literature: v. 2, p. 509-641.

Vast compilation of tale summaries from Czech and Moravian collections; difficult to use because of its arrangement. At the end of the final volume there is a brief index of the headings used and a few others. A valuable survey describes and evaluates tale collections. Walter Anderson included a type index, using the Aarne-Thompson classification, of Tille's *Soupis* in his reviews, published in *Zeitschrift für slavische Philologie*, v. 9, 1932, p. 509-516; v. 14, 1937, p. 227-228; and v. 18, 1942, p. 245-249.

5. Studies

1156. Horák, Jiří. Naše lidová píseň (Our folk song). Praha, J. R. Vilímek, 1946. Ports. (Za vzděláním. Řada 2, sv. 1 [139])

The best outline and analysis of Czech folk songs as poetry.

1157. Hořnácko; život a kultura lidu na moravsko-slovenském pomezí v oblasti Bílých Karpat (Horňácko; life and culture of the people in the Moravian-Silesian borderland in the White Carpathian region). Brno, Blok, 1966. 615 p. Illus., music.

Regional monograph including chapters on occupations, social and family life, folk music, dance, and storytelling. *See also* the collective studies issued by the ethnographic institutes of the Slovak and Czechoslovak academies, respectively: *Banícka dedina Žakarovce* (The mining village of Žakarovce) (Bratislava, Vydavateľstvo Slovenskej akadémie vied, 1956, 665 p., illus., music, bibliography, summaries in Russian, German, and English); and *Kladensko; život a kultura lidu v průmyslové oblasti* (In the Kladno area; life and culture of the people in an industrial region), edited by Olga Skalníková (Praha, Nakl. Československé akademie věd, 1959, 591 p., illus., map, music, bibliographies, summaries in Russian and German). The latter, about an industrial region near Prague, includes studies of storytelling, miners' humor, and workers' songs. The former contains an important study of folk music and others on costume, customs, and verbal lore.

1158. Melicherčík, Andrej. Jánošíkovská tradícia na Slovensku (The Jánošík tradition in Slovakia). Bratislava, Nakl. Slovenskej akadémie vied a umění, 1952. 301 p. Illus.

A useful reference, though politically colored; it provides background for the region where Jánošík, a famed outlaw hero, lived (1688-1713), and includes folk texts and documents.

See also Viera Gašparíková's *Zbojník Michal Vdovec v histórii a folklóre gemerského l'udu* (The outlaw Michal Vdovec in the history and folklore of the Gemer people) (Bratislava, Vydavatel'stvo Slovenskej akadémie vied, 1964, 318 p., illus., facsims., music, bibliography, summaries in Russian and German).

D. HISTORY OF THOUGHT, CULTURE, AND SCIENCE

by Miloslav Rechcígl, Jr.

1. Intellectual and Cultural Life in General

1159. Československá vlastivěda. Díl X. Osvěta (Book of knowledge on Czechoslovakia. V. 10, Learning). Edited by Otakar Kádner. Praha, Sfinx-Bohumil Janda, 1931. 650 p. Index, illus.

An authoritative survey of the advances in education, scholarship and science in Czechoslovakia with emphasis on the preceding fifty years. Covers many fields of the natural and social sciences. The book is a sequel to an earlier, equally authoritative, publication, *Památník na oslavu padesátiletého panovnického jubilea jeho veličenstva císaře a krále Františka Josefa I. Vědecký a umělecký rozvoj v národě českém 1848-1898* (A Festschrift commemorating the 50th anniversary of the reign of His Majesty the Emperor and King Franz Josef I. The scientific and artistic advances of the Czech nation 1848-1898) (Praha, Nakl. České akademie císaře Františka Josefa pro vědy, slovesnost a umění, 1898, 1089 p.).

1160. Czechoslovak Society of Arts and Sciences in America, Inc. Directory. Compiled by Eva Rechcígl. New York, Czechoslovak Society of Arts and Sciences in America, 1969. 100 p.

Brief biographies of some 1,000 members of the Czechoslovak Society of Arts and Sciences in America representing prominent Czechoslovaks — in just about every field of cultural endeavor — who live in the United States, Canada, Latin America, Australia, and Western Europe. The members are listed in alphabetical order as well as by geographical location and by field of interest. A report on the activities and publications of the Society for 1956-1966 is appended.

1161. Dolenský, Antonín, *ed.* Kulturní adresář ČSR; biografický slovník žijících kulturních pracovníků a pracovnic (Cultural directory of the Czechoslovak Republic; a biographical dictionary of living cultural workers). Praha, Nakladatelství J. Zeibrdlich, 1934. 586 p. Illus., port., col. plates.

Still the best and, in fact, the only available one-volume reference source, providing 5,500 short biographies of prominent Czechoslovak personalities in various fields of arts, letters, and science — from the era of the First Czechoslovak Republic. Persons entered are also listed according to their field of interest as well as alphabetically. The book includes lists of Czechoslovak cultural and research centers, universities, technical and arts schools, scientific institutions, libraries, museums, archives, societies, academies, and foundations, as well as pseudonyms.

1162. Kultura-dodatky; sborník právních předpisů (Culture-supplements; collection of legal regulations. Compiled by Karel Neumann. Praha, Orbis, 1968. 1306 p.

A compendium updating three similar editions previously published on legal provisions concerning Czechoslovakia's cultural establishment.

1163. Mathesius, Vilém, *ed.* Co daly naše země Evropě a lidstvu (What our country has contributed to Europe and to mankind). 2d ed. Praha, Sfinx-Bohumil Janda, 1940. 430 p.

See also entry no. 504.

An excellent collection of articles and essays written by leading Czech scholars of the prewar era. Probably the best single-volume work in the Czech language dealing with various aspects of Czechoslovak culture and its influences on other civilizations, from the beginnings of the Great Moravian Empire up to the Second World War. May be supplemented by Ferdinand Tadra's *Kulturní styky Čech s cizinou až do válek husitských* (The cultural contacts of Bohemia with other countries up to the Hussite Wars) (Praha, Královská Česká společnost nauk, 1897, 436 p.). The latter publication is a thorough and objective survey, based on primary sources, of the mutual relations of Bohemia and other countries, covering all fields of human endeavor, including scholarship, arts, commerce, etc.

1164. Nosek, Vladimír. The Spirit of Bohemia: A Survey of Czech History, Music and Literature. London, George Allen and Unwin, 1926. 379 p. Bibliography: p. 209-211, 370-372.

Although somewhat out of date, this book provides a good introduction to Czechoslovakia's culture, character, mentality, and spiritual achievements. Despite the title, information on Slovakia is also given; in particular, Slovak literature is covered in fair detail. Among contemporary publications of this type, one may refer to Emil Schieche and Friedrich Repp's *Die Kultur der Tschechen und der Slowaken* (Frankfurt a.M., Athenaion, 1966, 136 p.). Slovak culture is dealt with in Stephen J. Palickar's *Slovakian Culture in the Light of History, Ancient, Medieval and Modern* (Cambridge, Massachusetts, The Hampshire Press, 1954, 283 p.). The book is partisan in approach, being written by a supporter of the Slovak separatist cause.

1165. Rechcigl, Miloslav Jr., *ed.* The Czechoslovak Contribution to World Culture. The Hague, Mouton, 1964. 682 p. Illus. Bibliography: p. 555-634.

See also entries no. 511, 681, *and* 1108.

A collection of 57 papers, most of which were originally presented at the First Congress of the Czechoslovak Society of Arts and Sciences in America. A wide variety of topics is covered under the headings: literature and literary criticism; linguistics; music and fine arts; history; political science and philosophy; sociology; economics; law; science and technology; Czechs and Slovaks abroad; and bibliography. Appendixes include biographies of authors, and a detailed name and subject index. The proceedings of other congresses sponsored by the Czechoslovak Society of Arts and Sciences in America include the forthcoming *Czechoslovakia Past and Present* and *Studies on Czechoslovak Culture and Society*, both to be published by Mouton in The Hague.

1166. Rechcigl, Miloslav Jr. Czechoslovakia and its Arts and Sciences: A Selective Bibliography in the Western European Languages. *In*: The Czechoslovak Contribution to World Culture. The Hague, Mouton, 1964. p. 555-634.

See also entries no. 469 *and* 565.

A comprehensive bibliography of books and important articles concerning Czechoslovakia with emphasis on its cultural accomplishments and influences throughout history. Altogether there are 1,318 entries in classified arrangement, covering the humanities, the arts, the social sciences, the natural sciences, technology, and Czechs and Slovaks in the United States and other countries. On the literary production of general cultural publications concerning contemporary Czechoslovakia, *see* Milan Jakubíček's *15 (i.e. Patnáct) let kultury v lidově demokratickém Československu* (15 years of culture in the Czechoslovak People's Democracy) (Brno, Universitní knihovna, 1960, 64 p.).

1167. Rosenbaum, Karol, *ed.* Slovenská kultúra 1945-1965 (Slovak culture, 1945-1965). Bratislava, Obzor, 1965. 156 p.

Six essays by different authors presenting an official evaluation of the 20 years progress in Slovakia after the Second World War. Significant contemporary achievements in literature and the arts are attributed to the favorable policies of the present socialist government in Czechoslovakia. For a Marxist interpretation of cultural developments in Slovakia from the time of the Great Moravian Empire up to the present, *see* Štefan Pasiar and P. Paška's *Osveta na Slovensku; jej vznik, počiatky a vývoj* (Learning in Slovakia; its origin, beginnings and development) (Bratislava, Osveta, 1964, 352 p.; bibliography, p. 345-347).

2. Academies, Learned Societies, and Institutions

1168. Československá akademie věd. Věstník (Bulletin). v.1– 1891– Praha, Nakladatelství Československé akademie věd. Bimonthly.

The official journal of the Czechoslovak Academy of Sciences, reporting on research and publishing activities, with information on officials and organization changes. Issued October 1891-October 1952 by Česká akademie věd a umění (called through June 1918 Česká akademie císaře Františka Josefa pro vědy, slovesnost a umění). Indexes: v. 1-25, 1891-1916, in v. 25. A recent history of the Czechoslovak and Slovak Academies of Sciences appeared as a special issue of the *Věstník* under the following title: *Československá akademie věd, Slovenská akadémia vied 1952-1966* (The Czechoslovak Academy of Sciences, The Slovak Academy of Sciences, 1952-1966) (Praha, Academia, 1967, 325 p., illus., ports.).

1169. Československá akademie zemědělských věd; organizace a činnost, 1953-1959 (The Czechoslovak Academy of Agricultural Sciences; organization and activities, 1953-1959). Edited by Bohuslav Mařan. Praha, Státní zemědělské nakladatelství, 1960. 220 p.

Furnishes basic data about the Czechoslovak Academy of Agricultural Sciences (including its affiliated branch in Slovakia). Comparable information about the prewar Czechoslovak Academy of Agriculture is given in *The Czechoslovak Academy of Agriculture; Its Foundation, Programme, Organisation and Activities*, compiled by Edward Reich and Bohuš Vláčil (Prague, Czechoslovak Academy of Agriculture, 1931, 53 p., illus.).

1170. 10 (i.e. Deset) let Nakladatelství Československé akademie věd, 1953-1962 (Ten years of the Publishing House of the Czechoslovak Academy of Sciences, 1953-1962). Praha, 1963. 196 p.

A catalog of books (arranged by subject), and periodicals issued by the Academy during its first ten years of existence, with the projected publishing program for 1963. A comparable catalog of the Slovak Academy of Sciences' publications appeared in *Publikationen des Verlages der Slowakischen Akademie der Wissenschaften, 1953-1962*, compiled by Valéria Poničanová and Edita Šutková (Bratislava, Verlag der Slowakischen Akademie der Wissenschaften, 1963, 165 p.). The current publications of the Prague Academy are listed in its annual, *Bibliografický katalog*.

For a list of publications of the Academy's predecessor, the Czech Academy of Sciences and Arts, see *Věstník České akademie věd a umění* (Bulletin of the Czech Academy of Sciences and Arts), supplement to v. 58, 1948, and *Publikace České akademie vydané v létech 1891-1903* (Praha, Česká akademie císaře Františka Josefa pro vědy, slovesnost a umění, 1904, 19 p.).

1171. Hanuš, Josef. Národní museum a naše obrození (The National Museum and our [Czech] renaissance). Praha, Nakl. Národního musea, 1921-23. 2 v. Index, illus., ports., fold. plans, facsims.

Published on the occasion of the one hundredth anniversary of the founding of the National Museum. A monumental work of the Czech national revival, emphasizing the role of the National Museum of Bohemia — the symbol of Czech national traditions. An overall review of the recent organization and activities of the Museum, together with a historical evaluation of the contributions of and the advances made by various departments, and a brief history of the closely related Společnost Národního musea (The Society of the National Museum) and Matice česká (The Czech "Matice") is presented in *Národní museum 1818-1948* (The National Museum 1818-1948) by Gustav Skalský and others (Praha, Národní museum, 1949, 253 p.).

1172. Matica slovenská v našich dejinách; sborník statí (The Slovak "Matica" in our history; a collection of articles). Bratislava, Slovenská akadémia vied, 1963. 431 p. Plates, index.

Based on a series of lectures presented in 1963 at a conference sponsored by the Historical Institute of the Slovak Academy of Sciences on the occasion of the one hundredth anniversary of the founding the Slovak Matica. The papers depict the role the Matica played in the national history of the Slovaks. The founding of the Matica may be viewed as the most important event in the Slovak national development of the whole 19th century; it soon became the symbol of the entire spiritual life of the Slovak people.

For information on the "Učená spoločnosť Šafárikova" (The Learned Šafárik Society), and its role in the development of scientific life in Slovakia as well as on the Society's successors — the Slovak Learned Society, the Slovak Academy of Sciences and Arts, and the present Slovak Academy of Sciences, *see* František Bokes' *Snahy o organizovanie slovenskej vedy od konca 18. storočia do vzniku SAV* (Efforts to organize Slovak science from the end of the 18th century up to the founding of the Slovak Academy of Sciences) (Bratislava, VSAV, 1967, 120 p.).

1173. Prokeš, Jaroslav. Počátky České společnosti nauk do konce 18. století. Díl 1: 1774-1789 (The beginnings of the Bohemian Society of Sciences up to the end of the 18th century. v. 1: 1774-1789). Praha, Královská Česká společnost nauk, 1938. 362 p.

An authoritative treatise rendering a detailed account of the origin and the beginnings of the Society — the starting point and the center of organized scientific and scholarly research in Bohemia. A critical survey of the literary activities and scholarship sponsored by the Society during its first hundred years is presented in Josef Kalousek's *Geschichte der Kön. Böhmischen Gesellschaft der Wissenschaften sammt seiner kritischen Übersicht ihrer Publicationen aus dem Bereiche der Philosophie, Geschichte und Philologie* (Prag, Verlag der Kön. Böhmischen Gesellschaft der Wissenschaften, 1885, 303 p.) and in František Josef Studnička's *Bericht über die mathematischen und naturwissenschaftlichen Publikationen der Königl. Böhmischen Gesellschaft der Wissenschaften während ihres hundertjährigen Bestandes* (Prag, 1885, 351 p.). An index to the publications of this society is provided by:

Obecný rejstřík spisů Královské České společnosti nauk 1905-1935. Operum a Regia Societate Scientiarum Bohemica annis 1905-1935 editorum index generalis. Prague, 1938. 69 p. A general index to the publications issued by the Royal Bohemian Society of Sciences 1905-1935.

For earlier writings sponsored by the Society *see* the following indexes:

Hanuš, I. J. Systematisch und chronologisch geordnetes Verzeichnis sämmtlicher Werke und Abhandlungen der königl. böhmischen Gesellschaft der Wissenschaften. Prag, 1854. 80 p.

Weitenweber, Wilhelm Rudolph. Repertorium sämmtlicher Schriften der königl. böhmischen Gesellschaft der Wissenschaften vom Jahre 1769 bis 1868. Prag, 1869. 120 p.

Wegner, Georg. Generalregister zu den Schriften der königl. böhmischen Gesellschaft der Wissenschaften 1784-1884. Prag, 1884. 160 p.

———. Generalregister der Schriften der königl. böhmischen Gesellschaft der Wissenschaften 1884-1904. Prag, 1905. 106 p.

For a recent English-language treatment *see*:

Zacek, Joseph F. The Virtuosi of Bohemia: The Royal Bohemian Society of Sciences. East European Quarterly, v. 2, June 1968: 147-159.

3. Philosophy

1174. Revue des travaux scientifiques tchécoslovaques. Section première. Philosophie, philologie, histoire, sciences sociales, economie, politique, jurisprudence. v. 1-6; 1919-1924. Praha, 1924-1931. Section deuxième. Mathematiques, physique, chimie, sciences biologiques . . . techniques . . . médicales. v. 1-3; 1919-1924. Praha, 1924-1931.

Published under the joint auspices of the Royal Bohemian Society of Sciences and the Czech Academy of Sciences and Arts. The volumes, containing concise and authoritative French or English summaries of scholarly and scientific works and papers written in Czech or Slovak, provide an excellent view of Czechoslovak scholarship during the First Czechoslovak Republic.

1175. Science in Czechoslovakia and the Czechoslovak Academy of Sciences. Prague, Academia, 1966. 173 p. 19 plates.

A recapitulation of the mission, organization, and activities of the

Czechoslovak Academy of Sciences (including the Slovak Academy of Sciences) — the "supreme working and directing scientific body of the Czechoslovak Socialist Republic." The word science, in this context, should be interpreted in its broadest sense, being equivalent to the German "Wissenschaft," which covers all fields of human endeavor. The useful monograph includes a brief description of each of the Academy's research institutions, a list of learned societies affiliated with the Academy, and a list of journals issued by the Academy. An earlier report on the work of the Academy is contained in:

The Czechoslovak Academy of Sciences. The Slovak Academy of Sciences. 1964. Handbook. Prague, 1964. 246 p. Index. Prepared by the Czechoslovak Academy of Sciences, this handbook provides data concerning the Academy, including the Slovak Academy of Sciences, as of January 1, 1964. Contains information regarding the legal aspects of the establishment of the Academy, its statutes, biographical sketches of the Academy members, executive bodies and organs of the Academy, and lists of its institutes and scientific societies affiliated with the Academy, as well as journals published by the Academy. Progress reports concerning research activities of various institutes and laboratories of the Academy are to be found in "Československá akademie věd. Slovenská akadémia vied. 1952-1965," a special issue of the *Věstník Československé akademie věd* (no. 5, 1965), also published in English as *Czechoslovak Academy of Sciences. Slovak Academy of Sciences 1952-1966* (Prague, Academia, 1967, 371 p.).

1176. Československá akademie věd. *Sekce ekonomie, práva a filosofie. Filosofický ústav.* Filosofie v dějinách českého národa (Philosophy in the history of the Czech nation). Praha, Československá akademie věd, 1958. 321 p.

Transactions of the National Conference on the History of Czech Philosophy held in Liblice during April 14-17, 1958. The papers were intended as a first step toward an authoritative synthesis of Czech philosophy from a Marxist point of view. Includes chapters on Hussite thought, J. A. Komenský, B. Bolzano, Czech Herbartism, Masaryk, Marxist philosophy is Czech Lands, and the history of philosophy viewed as philosophy. German and Russian summaries. For special periods of Czech philosophy, as viewed by the contemporary Marxist historians of philosophy, *see:*

Kosík, Karel. Česká radikální demokracie (Czech radical democracy). Praha, Státní nakladatelství politické literatury, 1958. 482 p.

Kalivoda, Robert. Husitská ideologie (Hussite ideology). Praha, Československá akademie věd, 1961. 560 p.

1177. Comenius, Johann Amos. Johannis Amos Comenii Opera Omnia. Praha, Československá akademie věd, 1967–

This is the first edition of the complete works of Jan Ámos Komenský (Comenius), one of the most eminent figures in Bohemian history, an educator and a scholar of world fame, whose lifelong endeavor centered around pansophy — the principle of unification of all scientific, philosophical, political and religious knowledge into an all-embracing, unified system. Of the numerous books about him, the following are recommended:

Spinka, Matthew. John Amos Comenius; That Incomparable Moravian. Chicago, University of Chicago Press, 1943. 177 p. Bibliography: p. 156-170.

Kopecký, Jaromír, Jan Patočka, *and* Jiří Karásek. Jan Ámos Komenský; nástin života a díla (Jan Ámos Komenský; an outline of his life and work). Praha, Státní pedagogické nakl., 1957. 272 p. Illus., maps, plans.

Bečková, Marta. Komeniana vydaná knižně od roku 1945 (Comeniana issued in book form since 1945). Praha, Státní pedagogická knihovna Komenského, 1967. 56 p.

1178. Kalivoda, Robert, *and* Josef Zumr, *ed.* Antologie z dějin československé filosofie. Díl I (Anthology of the history of Czechoslovak philosophy. v. 1), Praha, Československá akademie věd, 1963. 560 p. Illus., index.

The first of the projected two-volume anthology of the history of Czechoslovak philosophy, prepared by the members of the Institute of Philosophy at the Czechoslovak and the Slovak Academies of Sciences, jointly with members of the philosophical faculties of Charles University (Prague) and of Purkyně University (Brno). An attempt to present a synthetic picture of the history of Czech and Slovak philosophy from the Marxist viewpoint. Starts with the medieval Hussite movement and ends with the epoch of "radical democracy" in the 1850s. The forthcoming second volume will cover the period from 1848 to 1945.

1179. Král, Josef. Československá filosofie; nástin vývoje podle disciplin (Czechoslovak philosophy; a sketch of its development according to disciplines). Praha, Melantrich, 1937. 337 p. (Vysokoškolské rukověti. III Řada spisů duchovědných, sv. 3)

A concise historical survey of the development of the philosophical thought in Czechoslovakia from its beginnings up to the end of 1935. Special chapters are devoted to noetics, logic, ethics, psychology, esthetics, philosophy of religion, pedagogy, sociology, history of philosophy, the spiritual basis of the Czech philosophy, and to German and Slavonic philosophy in Czechoslovakia. The book includes an exhaustive bibliography of original works as well as translations.

Slovak philosophy before the Second World War is treated in:

Osuský, Sam. Št. Prvé slovenské dejiny filozofie (The first Slovak history of philosophy). Liptovský Sv. Mikulaš, Tranoscius, 1939. 426 p.

1180. Pawlow, Andrej, *and* Boris Jakowenko. Kurze Bibliographie der neuen tschechoslowakischen Philosophie. Prague, 1935. 58 p. Index. Internationale Bibliographie für Philosophie, Bd. 1, Nr. 3)

A bibliography of philosophical writings, both books and articles, published in Czechoslovakia. Covers publications in all languages, mostly from the period following the establishment of independent Czechoslovakia in 1918, although important publications of the earlier period are also included. Another excellent bibliography of Czechoslovak philosophy from its beginnings up to the modern times, ending in the era of the First Czechoslovak Republic, is included in Josef Král's *Československá filosofie* (see entry no. 1179). For a philosophy after the Second World War, *see* Dezider Šlesiar's *Bibliografia filozofie; výber základnej knižnej tvorby z oblasti filozofie a metodické pokyny k štúdiu* (A bibliography of philosophy; a selection of basic books in philosophy and in methodological guidance to its study) (Martin, Matica slovenská, 1964, 115 p.), which lists mostly Slovak publications. Information on the current production, especially articles, is available in a monthly index, *Novinky literatury—Společenské vědy. Řada 1. Filosofické vědy* (1962– Praha, Státní knihovna ČSSR and Bibliografické středisko společenských věd).

1181. Preh'lad dejín slovenskej filozofie (A concise history of Slovak philosophy). Edited by Elena Várossová. Bratislava, Vydav. Slovenskej akadémie vied, 1965. 555 p. Illus.

A greatly enlarged and rewritten version of an earlier publication, *Kapitoly z dejín slovenskej filozofie* (Chapters from the history of Slovak philosophy) (Bratislava, Vydav. Slovenskej akadémie vied, 1957, 476 p.). Offers a comprehensive account of the history and development of philosophical and social thought in Slovakia, as viewed by the contemporary Slovak Marxist historiographers. German and Russian summaries. For the Marxist interpretation of specific epochs of Slovak philosophical thinking, *see* Teodor Münz's *Filozofia slovenského osvietenstva* (Philosophy of the Slovak revival period) (Bratislava, Vydavatel'stvo slovenskej akadémie vied, 1961, 257 p., illus.); Elena Várossová's *Slovenské obrodenecke myslenie* (Slovak ideology in the period of the national revival) (Bratislava, Vydavatel'stvo Slovenskej akadémie vied, 1963, 220 p.); Ján Uher's *Filozofia v boji o dnešok. Problémy rozvoja filozofie na Slovensku po roku 1945* (Philosophy in its struggle for the present. Problems of the development of philosophy in Slovakia after 1945) (Bratislava, Slovenská akadémia vied, 1961, 250 p. Filozoficka biblioteka, zv. 10).

1182. Strohs, Slavomil. Marxisticko-leninská filosofie v Československu mezi dvěma světovými válkami (Marxist-Leninist philosophy in Czechoslovakia between the two World Wars). Praha, Nakl. Československé akademie věd, 1962. 223 p.

A history of Marxist-Leninist philosophy in Czechoslovakia before the Second World War, its influence on the philosophical thinking of other countries, and the role it played in the origin and establishment of the socialist system in today's Czechoslovakia. Deals with personalities who can be considered the founders of modern Czechoslovak Marxist-Leninist philosophy. On the origins of Marxism in Czechoslovakia, *see*:

Dubský, I. Pronikání marxismu do českých zemí (Penetration of Marxism into the Czech Lands). Praha, Státní nakladatelství politické literatury, 1963. 493 p.

The growth of Marxist-Leninist philosophy in Czechoslovakia following the Second World War is ably described and evaluated in Nikolaus Lobkowicz' *Marxismus-Leninismus in der ČSR. Die tschechoslowakische Philosophie seit 1945* (Dordrecht, D. Reidel, 1962, 267 p., Sovietica; Abhandlungen des Osteuropa Instituts, Universität Freiburg, Schweiz, 2).

1183. Warren, William Preston. Masaryk's Democracy; a Philosophy of Scientific and Moral Culture. Chapel Hill, University of North Carolina Press, 1941. 254 p. Bibliography: p. 239-243.

See also entry no. 786.

An attempt at synthesis of the philosophy of Tomáš Garrigue Masaryk. His practical philosophy encompassing learning, politics, morality, and religion, which was the foundation of all of his political activities, had a profound influence in molding the mind of his nation. His convictions are clearly reformulated in Karel Čapek's *Hovory s T. G. Masarykem* (Conversations with T. G. Masaryk) (Praha, F. Borový, 1931-1935, 3 v.). English translations by M. and and R. Weatherall appeared as *President Masaryk Tells His Story* (London, G. Allen and Unwin, 1934, 302 p.) and *Masaryk on Thought and Life* (London, G. Allen and Unwin, 1938, 214 p.). For further information on Masaryk as a thinker, *see* the bibliography and articles in *Festschrift Thomas G. Masaryk zum 80. Geburtstag*, edited by Boris J. Jakowenko (Bonn, F. Cohen, 1930, 2 v.).

4. Scientific and Technical Thought

1184. Česká bibliografie dějin přírodních věd, lékařství a techniky (Czech biliography of the history of natural sciences, medicine, and technology). *In* Sborník pro dějiny přírodních věd a techniky. v. 3– 1957– Praha, Nakl. Československé akademie věd. Annual.

A yearly bibliography of books and articles (including book reviews and reports) on history of science, medicine and technology published in the Czech provinces of Czechoslovakia during the course of the year. Classified arrangement. The corresponding Slovak bibliography appears in *Z dejín vied a techniky na Slovensku* (Bratislava), v. 1–, 1962–. Books and articles dealing with the planning of science in Czechoslovakia, as well as in other countries are listed in:

Československá akademie věd. *Ústav plánování vědy*. Bibliografie literatury o organizaci, řízení, plánování a koordinaci vědeckého výzkumu (Bibliography of publications on organization, direction, planning, and coordination of scientific research). Praha, 1964. 194 p.

1185. Málek, Ivan. Otevřené otázky naší vědy (Unresolved problems of our [Czechoslovak] science). Praha, Academia, 1966. 312. p. Illus.

A sequel to Málek's earlier publication, *Boj nového se starým v dnešní naší vědě* (The struggle between the old and the new in our [Czechoslovak] present-day science) (Praha, Nakl. ČSAV, 1955, 170 p., Práce ČSAV, Sv. 7). An interpretative analysis of the Czechoslovak experience with science planning, and of the relation between scientific progress and the building of socialist society. Russian summary.

1186. Nový, Luboš, *ed.* Dějiny exaktních věd v českých zemích (History of the exact sciences in the Czech lands). Praha, Nakl. Československé akademie věd, 1961. 432 p. Illus.

An authoritative history of mathematics, astronomy, physics, and chemistry in the Czechoslovak provinces of Bohemia, Moravia, and Silesia, written by a collective of scientific workers of the Historical Institute of the Czechoslovak Academy of Sciences. Contains a comprehensive biographical index and an adequate summary in English and Russian. A comparable history concerning Czechoslovak technology is currently being prepared by the Czechoslovak Academy of Sciences, under the title *Dějiny československé techniky* (History of Czechoslovak technology).

1187. Polák, Bedřich, *ed.* Na prahu naší techniky (On the threshold of our technology). Praha, Státní nakladatelství technické literatury, 1957. 419 p. Illus., index.

A collection of studies depicting the technological progress and the beginnings of technological education and technical museum science in Czech Lands. Written by a collective of workers of the National Technical Museum in Prague on the occasion of the 250th anniversary of the founding of the Prague Engineering School, the oldest engineering school in Europe. Russian and German summaries. For additional reading, *see* František Kadeřávek and J. Pulkrábek's *250 let technických škol v Praze, 1707-1957* (250 years of the Prague technical schools, 1707-1957) (Praha, Nakl. Československé akademie věd, 1958, 69 p., illus.). From the older literature (the following publication is recommended: *Z vývoje české technické tvorby* (The growth of Czech technological creativity), edited by Josef B. Stránský (Praha, Spolek českých inženýrů, 1940, 402 p., illus.).

1188. Prague. Universita Karlova. *Fakulta všeobecného lékařství.* Dějiny československého lékařství. I. Od pravěku do roku 1740 (The history of Czechoslovak medicine. I. From primitive times up to the year 1740). By E. Chlumská and others. 173 p. II. Od roku 1740-1848 (From the year 1740 to 1848). By L. Sinkulová. Praha, Státní pedagogické nakladatelství, 1965. 209 p.

An outline of the history of Czechoslovak medicine with interpretative analysis of the events and the development of thought based on current Marxist ideology. Primarly intended as a textbook for medical schools. On the history of Czech medicine *see*:

Vinař, Josef. Obrazy z minulosti českého lékařství (Sketches from the past of Czech medicine). Praha, Státní zdravotnické nakladatelství, 1959. 240 p. On the history of Slovak medicine, *see*:

Rippa, B. K. K histórii medicíny na Slovensku (On the history of medicine in Slovakia). Bratislava, Slovenská akadémia vied, 1956. 202 p.

1189. Purkyňova společnost, *Prague*. In Memoriam Joh. Ev. Purkyně, 1787-1937. Pragae, Purkyňova, společnost, 1937. 100 p.

A collection of historical studies and essays in French, German and English, by various authors, concerning the scientific contributions of Jan Evangelista Purkyně, a physiologist of world repute and the most prominent Czech scientist of all times. More recent collections include:

Zaunick, Rudolph, *ed*. Purkyně Symposion der Deutschen Akademie der Naturforscher Leopoldina in Gemeinschaft mit der Tschechoslowakischen Akademie der Wissenschaften am 31. Oktober und 1. November 1959 in Halle/Salle. Nova Acta Leopoldina, n. F., Bd. 24, Nr. 151:1-230.

John, Henry J. Jan Evangelista Purkyně; Czech Scientist and Patriot, 1787-1869. Philadelphia, American Philosophical Society, 1959. 94 p. Bibliography: p. 84-94.

1190. Sborník pro dějiny přírodních věd a techniky. Acta historiae rerum naturalium nec non technicarum. v. 1– 1954– Praha, Nakl. Československé akademie věd. Annual.

An annual of the Historical Institute of the Czechoslovak Academy of Sciences, devoted to the history of science and technology, with emphasis on Czech Lands. The corresponding Slovak serial, *Z dejín vied a techniky na Slovensku* (From the history of science and technology in Slovakia), has been published at irregular intervals since 1962 by the Historical Institute of the Slovak Academy of Sciences. From 1967, Academia, the Publishing House of the Czechoslovak Academy of Sciences has begun publication of a quarterly, *Dějiny věd a techniky* (History of sciences and technology).

1191. Sosna, Milan, *ed*. G. Mendel. Memorial Symposium. 1865-1965. Proceedings of a Symposium held in Brno, August 4-7, 1965. Praha, Academia, 1966. 288 p.

The collection contains papers and summaries of discussions presented at a special symposium commemorating the centenary of the classic scientific discoveries of Gregor J. Mendel, which later became the foundation of the theory of genetics. The revised edition of Mendel's works with a collection of 27 papers published during the rediscovery era has appeared in *Fundamenta Genetica,* selection and commentary by Jaroslav Kříženecký with introduction by Bohumil Němec (Praha, Československá akademie věd, 1966, 400 p.).

The above collections may be supplemented by Jaroslav Kříženecký's *Gregor Johann Mendel 1822-1844. Texte und Quellen zu seinem Wirken und Leben* (Leipzig, Johann Ambrosius Barth, 1965, 198 p.). For a good biography of Mendel, *see*:

Iltis, Hugo. Life of Mendel. London, George Allen and Unwin, 1932. 336 p.

1192. Viniklář, Ladislav, *comp.* Vývoj české přírodovědy (The development of Czech natural science). Praha, Přírodovědecký klub, 1931. 187 + 23 p. Illus., ports.

A memorial volume published on the occasion of the 60th year of the existence of the Natural History Club in Prague. In addition to the personal reminiscences of members pertaining to the history and activities of the club, it contains critical surveys on the development of natural sciences in the Czech Lands, including anthropology, zoology, botany, geology, mineralogy, and petrology. For the role of the Bohemian Society of Sciences in the development of natural sciences, from the point of view of the Marxist historiography, *see* Mikuláš Teich's *Královská česká společnost nauk a počátky vědeckého průzkumu přírody v Čechách* (The Royal Bohemian Society of Sciences and the beginnings of scientific surveys of natural resources in Bohemia) (Praha, Československá akademie věd, 1959, 77 p. Rozpravy Československé akademie věd, Řada společenských věd, v. 69, No. 4), a condensed English version of which appears in *Historica* (Praha) v. 2, 1960: p. 161-181).

E. THE CHRISTIAN RELIGIONS

by Jaroslav J. Pelikan

1. Up to 1918

1193. Borbis, Johannes. Die evangelisch-lutherische Kirche Ungarns in ihrer geschichtlichen Entwicklung. Nördlingen, Beck, 1861. 520 p.

Despite its title the book pays much attention to the Slovaks. It contains much of the ecclesiastical legislation of Hungary during the struggles of the 19th century.

1194. Hrejsa, Ferdinand. Dějiny křesťanství v Československu (History of Christianity in Czechoslovakia). Praha, Husova československá fakulta bohoslovecká, 1947. 6 v. Bibliography.

A detailed narrative of the church history of Czechoslovakia, especially of Bohemia, from its conversion to the Reformation. Unfortunately not completed. Summary in French.

1195. Hromádka, J. L. Masaryk. Praha, Vydavatelské oddělení, 1930. 242 p.

Masaryk's philosophy of religion and his religious interpretation of Czech history are summarized in the light of his idealistic philosophy.

1196. Kvačala, Ján. Dejiny reformácie na Slovensku 1517-1711 (History of the Reformation in Slovakia, from 1517 to 1711). Mikuláš, Tranoscius, 1935. 302 p.

The coming of the German Reformation to the Slovaks and the history of Slovak protestantism until the age of Pietism are outlined.

1197. Macek, Josef. The Hussite Movement in Bohemia. 2d enl. ed. Translated by Vilém and Ian Milner. Prague, Orbis, 1958. 138 p. Illus., maps. Bibliography: p. 137-138.

An interesting example of how present-day historians in Czechoslovakia view the "revolutionary" character of the Hussite Reformation in relation to its more explicitly "religious" message.

1198. Macek, Josef, *and others*. Mezinárodní ohlas husitství (The international echo of Hussitism). Praha, Československá akademie věd, 1958. 329 p. Illus.

Written in connection with Macek's *Hussite Movement* (*see* entry 1197), this work is an examination of the impact of the Hussite "revolution" upon other Slavic lands and upon Germany, as well as of its subsequent mythos.

1199. Naegle, August. Kirchengeschichte Böhmens quellenmässig und kritisch dargestellt. Wien, Leipzig, Braumüller, 1915-1918. 2 v. in 1.

Unfinished. This portion concentrates on the Christianization of the Czechs, summarizing the monographic literature of the 19th and early 20th century in Czech and other languages.

1200. Osuský, Samuel Štefan. Filozofia Štúrovcov (The philosophy of Štúr and his followers). Myjava, Daniela Pazickeho, 1926-1932. 3 v.

Examines the philosophy of Ľudovít Štúr, Jozef Miloslav Hurban, and M. M. Hodža, who developed their philosophical and religious thought under the influence of Herder and Hegel and helped to shape Slovak national and literary history in the 19th century.

1201. Pelikan, Jaroslav. Obedient Rebels; Catholic Substance and Protestant Principle in Luther's Reformation. New York, Harper and Row, 1964. 212 p. Bibliography.

The book contains an account (p. 104-158) of the relations between Luther and the Hussites, culminating in his publication of the *Confessio Bohemica* in 1538.

1202. Ratkoš, Peter, *ed.* Dokumenty k baníckemu povstaniu na Slovensku (1525-1526) (Documents on the uprising of miners in Slovakia [1525-1526]). Bratislava, Vydavatel'stvo Slovenskej akadémie vied, 1957. 560 p. Illus.

A prime illustration of how Marxist theory raises new questions about the interrelation between religious and economic factors in the history of the Reformation. Many of the texts are in Latin and German, as well as the Slavic languages.

1203. Říčan, Rudolf. Die böhmischen Brüder: ihr Ursprung und ihre Geschichte. Berlin, Union Verlag, 1961. 375 p.

By the professor of church history at the Protestant Theological Faculty in Prague, translated by Bohumir Popelář. Summary chapter on Hussite theology by Amedeo Molnár. Less thorough than earlier works by Gindely, Müller, etc., but up-to-date and readable.

1204. Spinka, Matthew. John Amos Comenius; That Incomparable Moravian. Chicago, The University of Chicago Press, 1943. 170 p. Bibliography: p. 156-170.

Has the advantage over most biographies of Komenský in that it stresses his work as a churchman, not merely as an educator, and his pioneering of the ecumenical movement.

1205. Spinka, Matthew, *ed. and tr.* John Hus at the Council of Constance. New York, Columbia University Press, 1965. 303 p.

A very useful collection of documents hitherto available only in Latin and Czech.

1206. Tumpach, Josef, *and* Antonín Podlaha. Bibliografie české katolické literatury náboženské od roku 1828 až do konce roku 1913 (Bibliography of Czech Catholic religious literature from 1828 to the end of 1913). Praha, Cyrillo-Metodějská knihtiskárna, 1912-1923. 5 v.

An exhaustive and indispensable tool for the study of Czech religious history under Austria-Hungary. Its principal drawback is that so little of the literature cited is available in the Western world.

2. 1918-1945

1207. Acta et monumenta primi congressus Catholicorum reipublicae Cecoslovakae. Prague, 1936.

A collection of documents on the adjustments of the Church to the Czechoslovak Republic in the years before Munich.

1208. Cinek, F. K náboženské otázce v prvních letech naší samostatnosti 1918-1925 (On the religious question in the first years of our independence, 1918-1925). Olomouc, 1926.

Helpful especially for the development of the "Los-von-Rom" movement into the "Czechoslovak Church."

For a presentation of the Orthodox Church *see* Vladimír Grigorič's *Pravoslavná církev ve státě Československém* (The Orthodox Church in the Czechoslovak State) (Praha, V. Čerych, 1928, 174 p.).

1209. Hník, František M., Alois Spisar, *and* Frank Kovář. The Czechoslovak Church. Prague, The Central Council of the Czechoslovak Church, 1937. 100 p. Illus.

An interpretation by its spokesmen of the "indigenous" Czechoslovak Church and its relation to Orthodoxy and Unitarianism, as well as to Roman Catholicism.

1210. Die Kirchen der Tschechoslowakei. Ekklesia, v. 5, no. 20, 1937: 1-250.

A handy compendium of facts and figures about the relative strength of the various religious bodies. All the more useful because similar statistics are not now being published.

1211. Spinka, Matthew. The Religious Situation in Czechoslovakia. *In* Kerner, Robert A., *ed.* Czechoslovakia. Twenty Years of Independence. Berkeley, Los Angeles, University of California Press, 1940. p. 284-301.

A brief but helpful summary, written during the Nazi occupation.

1212. Vašečka, Félix. Buržoázny štát a cirkev (The bourgeois state and the Church). Bratislava, Vydavatel'stvo Slovenskej akadémie vied, 1957. 307 p. Bibliography.

A Marxist interpretation of the social and political role of the churches — Roman Catholic, Eastern Orthodox, and Protestant — during the "first" Czechoslovak Republic.

3. Since 1945

1213. César, Jaroslav, *and others.* Církve v našich dějinách (The churches in our history). Praha, Orbis, 1960. 230 p. Bibliography.

A symposium reflecting how present-day historians in Czechoslovakia view the place of the churches in the national and cultural development of the Czech people. Highly critical.

1214. Hromádka, J. L. Theology between Yesterday and Tomorrow. Philadelphia, Westminster Press, 1957. 106 p.

A summary statement, by the leading spokesmen for the new relation of Christianity to the current régime, of a theological stance "beyond ideologies."

1215. Kirchen in der Zange: die Kirchenpolitik der Tschechoslowakei, 1945-1960. München, Wolf, 1960. 92 p.

Volume 4 of "Mitteleuropäische Quellen und Dokumente," this is an objective account of church-state relations in Czechoslovakia since the overthrow of the Nazis.

1216. Kocvara, Stephen, *and* Henry Nosek. Czechoslovakia: Churches and Religion. New York, Mid-European Studies Center, n.d. 54 p.

A digest and summary of the legal situation of the churches under the current régime in Czechoslovakia.

1217. Němec, Ludvík. Church and State in Czechoslovakia, Historically and Theologically Documented. New York, Vantage Press, 1955. 577 p. Bibliography.

The plight of the Roman Catholic Church under the present régime as described by an American Roman Catholic priest.

F. EDUCATION

by Vojtech E. Andic

1. Bibliographies and Reference Works

1218. Apanasewicz, Nellie M., *in collaboration with* Seymour M. Rosen. Selected Bibliography of Materials on Education in Czechoslovakia. Washington, D.C. U.S. Department of Health, Education and Welfare, Office of Education, International Education Division, 1960. 37 p. (U.S. Office of Education. Studies in Comparative Education, OE-14053)

A systematic bibliography, based on the Office of Education and Library of Congress catalogs.

1219. Henek, Tomáš. Soupis českých a slovenských pedagogických časopisů do roku 1965 (List of Czech and Slovak pedagogical periodicals through 1965). Brno, Státní politické nakl., 1967. 177 p. Illus.

An extensive listing of 423 periodicals relating to education. Indexes of names of editors, subjects, and publication dates are included.

1220. Pedagogická encyclopedie (Pedagogical encyclopedia). Edited by O. Chlup, J. Kubálek, and J. Uher. Praha, Novina, 1938-1940. 3 v.

In addition to pertinent information on educational practices, includes biographies of contemporary educators and selections from the writings of Czech and Slovak experts in the field.

1221. Španiel, Blahoslav, *ed.* Soupis pedagogických bibliografií (Collection of bibliographies on education). Praha, Státní knihovna, 1966. 92 p.

Lists 1,033 Czech and Slovak bibliographies, including those of foreign works available in the scientific libraries in Czechoslovakia.

2. Periodicals and Occasional Papers

1222. Československá psychologie; časopis pro psychologickou teorii i praxi (Czechoslovak psychology; journal for psychological theory and practice). v. 1– 1957– Praha. Illus., ports. Quarterly.

See also entry no. 1036.

This journal, published by the Czechoslovak Academy of Sciences, deals with the theoretical and practical problems encountered in the new educational system of Czechoslovakia.

1223. Jednotná škola (Consolidated school). 1946– Bratislava. Bimonthly.

Published by the Slovak Academy of Sciences. Articles on basic educational theories and practices, as well as the philosophy of reforms. Includes summaries with statistical data and tables of contents in Russian and German.

1224. Učitelské noviny (Teachers' news). 1951– Praha. Weekly.

Published by the Ministry of Education and Culture and the Trade Union of its employees. A similar weekly, *Učitelské noviny*, is published in Bratislava by the Office of the Commissioner of Education for Slovakia and its Trade Union.

1225. Vysoká škola (University). Praha. Monthly.

Published by the Ministry of Education and Culture. Includes university regulations and discussions on educational theories.

1226. Kádner, Otakar. Vývoj a dnešní soustava školství (Development of today's educational system). Praha, Sfinx, 1929-1931. 2 v.

A systematic treatment of the development of various types of schools.

3. General Works and Surveys

a. Up to 1945

1227. Narizhnyi, Simon. Ukrains'ka emigratsiia (Ukrainian emigration). v. 1. Praha, 1942. 367 p., 232 p. Illus. (Studii Muzeiu vyzvol'noi borot'by Ukrainy, 1)

A review of Ukrainian and Russian schools in Czechoslovakia between the two world wars. *See also* V. E. Andic's "The Economic Aspects of Aid to Russian and Ukrainian Refugee Scholars in Czechoslovakia," *Journal of Central European Affairs*, v. 21, no. 2, July 1961: 176-187.

1228. Stránský, R. The Educational and Cultural System of the Czechoslovak Republic. Prague, Vladimír Žikeš, 1938. 142 p. Plates.

Historical discussion of regular and specialized schools, including pedagogical institutions.

1229. Štefánek, Anton. Education in Pre-War Hungary and in Slovakia Today. *In* Seton-Watson, Robert W., *ed.* Slovakia Then and Now; a Political Survey. London, Allen and Unwin; Prague, Orbis, 1931. p. 115-138.

An analysis of conditions prior to 1918 and after the establishment of the Republic of Czechoslovakia. The author discusses the Slovak schools under the Slovak State (1939-1945) in his *Sociografia Slovenska* (Sociography of Slovakia) (Bratislava, 1945).

1230. Stuerm, Francis H. Training in Democracy: the New Schools of Czechoslovakia. New York, Inor Publishing Co., 1938. 256 p.

Based on the author's own observations during 1934 and 1935.

A penetrating analysis of curriculum, teacher training, and reforms inspired by educators who studied American educational theories.

b. Since 1945

1231. Andic, Vojtech E. A Comparative Study of Education in Czechoslovakia for the Periods of 1918 to 1938 and 1948-1953. New York, New York University, 1953. 325 p.

A Ph.D. dissertation on changes in the educational system of Czechoslovakia, with special emphasis on the impact of economic planning on school practices.

1232. Education Act of the Czechoslovak Socialist Republic. Prague, State Pedagogical Publishing House, 1961. 64 p.

The text of the Act of December 15, 1960, and its relationship to previous acts. Refer also to *Československé školské zákonodarství 1918-1968* (Czechoslovak school legislation, 1918-1968) by Marta Šolcová (Olomouc, Státní vědecká knihovna, 1968, 94 p.).

1233. Kasková, Alena, *ed.* Education in Czechoslovakia. Prague, State Pedagogical Publishing House, 1958. 127 p. Illus.

A descriptive and historical discussion of all levels of the school system, from preschool to university. Includes charts and statistics.

1234. Korbel, Pavel. Czechoslovak Universities. New York, National Committee for a Free Europe, Inc., 1952. 24 p.

An account of changes in university life after the Second World War. Part 2 of this report (August 1954, 21 p.) covers academies of sciences and military schools and provides university statistics. *See also* Joseph S. Roucek's "Czechoslovakia's Higher Education and Its Changes" (*Journal of Higher Education*, v. 27, January 1956: 21-24).

1235. Prague. Universita Karlova. Stručné dějiny University Karlovy (A brief history of Charles University). Praha, 1964. 345 p. Illus., ports.

An excellent history in English is Otakar Odložilík's *The Caroline University, 1348-1948* (Prague, Orbis, 1948, 95 p.). For other university surveys see *Universitas Brunensis 1919-1969* (Brno, Univ. J. E. Purkyně, 1969, 418 p.); and Andrej Mráz' *Tridsať rokov Slovenskej university* (Thirty years of the Slovak University) (Bratislava, 1950, 37 p.).

1236. Singule, František. Das Schulwesen in der Tschechoslowakischen Sozialistischen Republic. Weinheim, Beltz, 1967. 112 p. (Dokumentationen zum in- und ausländischen Schulwesen, Bd. 9).

An up-to-date survey treatment by a prominent Czechoslovak educator.

1237. Slovakia. *Planovací úrad.* Školstvo na Slovensku (The school system in Slovakia). Bratislava, 1949. 217 p. Maps, diagrs., tables.

Emphasis is on the period from 1918 to 1948.

c. Special Aspects

1238. Buriánek, Bohuslav. Studium na vysokých školách (University study). 9th enl. ed. Praha, Státní pedagogické nakl., 1968. 142 p.

1239. Comenius, Johann A. The Great Didactic of John Amos Comenius. Translated into English and edited with biographical, historical and critical introductions by M. W. Keatinge. New York, Russell and Russell, 1967. 2 v.

A collection of the educational writings of Comenius (Jan Ámos Komenský), the founder of visual education.

1240. Kulich, Jindra. The Role and Training of Adult Educators in Czechoslovakia. Vancouver, Faculty of Education and Department of University Extension, University of British Columbia, 1967. 131 p. Bibliography: p. 117-131.

Reviews various aspects of adult education problems and organization of party education.

1241. Příhoda, Václav, *and* Stanislav Vrána. Deset let pokusné práce na měšťanských školách ve Zlíně, 1929-39 (Ten years' work at the experimental junior high schools in Zlín, 1929-39). Zlín, 1939. 180 p. Illus., tables.

Dr. Příhoda is considered a pioneer of the new education in Czechoslovakia. See also *The Reform Practice of the School* by Příhoda, Nykl, and Hanuš (Prague, The Czechoslovak Graphic Union, 1936).

1242. Czechoslovakia. *In* World Survey of Education. II: Primary Education. Paris, UNESCO, 1958. p. 287-296.

Includes basic information, charts, statistics, and a bibliography.

G. THE FINE ARTS

by Mojmír S. Frinta

1. Reference Works

1243. Bleha, Josef. Bibliografie české výtvarně umělecké literatury, 1918-1958 (Bibliography of Czech literature on the creative arts, 1918-1958). Praha, Státní knihovna ČSSR, 1960, 315 p. (Bibliografický katalog ČSSR. České knihy, 1960. Zvláštní seš. 7, pros. 1960)

Classified listing, with some annotations, of books written by Czech authors or published in Czechoslovakia. More than half the 2,460 numbered entries relate to the arts and artists of Czechoslovakia. Table of contents and summary of the foreword are given in Russian, German, and English. Indexed. For a continuation of this bibliography *see*:

Bleha, Josef. Bibliografie české a slovenské výtvarně umělecké literatury, 1959-1964. Praha, Státní knihovna ČSSR, 1966. 173 p. (Novinky literatury. Společenské vědy. Řada 7)

1244. Soupis památek historických a uměleckých v republice Československé. A. Země Česká (Inventory of historic and artistic monuments in the Czechoslovak Republic. A. Bohemia). v. 1-42, 44-47; 1897-1935. Praha. 46 v. Illus., plans, maps. Includes bibliographies.

Title varies: 1897-1918. *Soupis památek historických a uměleckých v království Českém od pravěku do polovice XIX. století* (Inventory of historic and artistic monuments in the Czech kingdom from earliest times to the middle of the 19th century). Issued by the Archaeologická komise of the Česká akademie věd a umění. A parallel series was published in German under the title *Topographie der historischen und kunstgeschichtlichen Denkmale in der Tschechoslowakischen Republik. A. Land Böhmen* (previously *Topographie der historischen und Kunst-Denkmale im Königreiche Böhmen*). Apparently not all volumes were issued in both series; volumes 43, 50, and 51 seem to have been published only in German, and volumes 8, 11-12, 14, 16-18, 20-21, 23, 25-26, 29, 31-33, 39, 41 and 44-49, only in Czech.

A detailed, richly illustrated catalog. Each volume deals with a separate political district. Volumes for Prague, of which at least four were issued, came in a separately numbered series entitled *Soupis hlavního města Prahy* (at first called *Soupis královského hlavního města Prahy*). Three also appeared in German.

1245. Toman, Prokop. Nový slovník československých výtvarných umělců (New dictionary of Czechoslovak creative artists) 3d. enl. ed. Praha, R. Ryšavý, 1947-1950. 2 v. Ports. Bibliography: v. 1, p. 3-4. *See also* entry no. 543.

———., *and* Prokop H. Toman. Dodatky ke Slovníku československých výtvarných umělců (Supplement to the dictionary of Czechoslovak creative artists). Praha, Státní nakl. krásné literatury, hudby a umění, 1955. 224 p. Port.

The main work contains 10,733 entries, and the supplement gives additional information for 2,963 artists and data for 1,783 who were not previously listed. Entries include bibliographical references.

A reference work on Slovak art is *Slovník súčasného slovenského umenia* (Dictionary of contemporary Slovak art), edited by Marian Váross (Bratislava, Vydavateľstvo Slovenského fondu výtvarných umení, 1967).

2. Periodicals

1246. Architektura ČSSR (Architecture of the Czechoslovak Socialist Republic). v. 1– 1939– Praha. Illus. 10 issues a year.

Suspended publication 1943-1945. Title varies. 1939-1958, *Architektura ČSR* (Architecture of the Czechoslovak Republic).

Journal of Svaz architektů ČSSR. Offers aesthetic and formal consideration of architecture, design, and urban planning. Summaries in English, French, German, and Russian. *Památková péče* (Care of monuments) (v. 1– 1937– Praha, Státní pedagogické nakl., illus., bimonthly, suspended publication 1943-1946; title varies: 1942-

1961, *Zprávy památkové péče*) deals with problems of conservation and restoration of architectural monuments. Summaries in Russian, French, and German.

1247. Památky archeologické (Achaeological monuments). v. 1– 1854– Praha. Illus., plates, facsims.

Frequency varies; since 1958, semiannual. Title varies slightly. Now issued by Archeologický ústav ČSAV. Studies in prehistoric archaeology; earlier volumes also include material on the history of the fine arts in Czechoslovakia. Summaries in French, German, or Russian. Of related interest is *Časopis Národního musea* (Journal of the National Museum) (v. 1– 1827– Praha, illus., ports., maps; frequency and title vary, suspended publication 1941-1945).

1248. Umění (Art). v. 1– 1953– Praha, Nakl. Československé akademie věd. Illus., ports., maps. Quarterly; since 1964 bimonthly.

Journal of Kabinet theorie a dějin umění of the Československá akademie věd. Deals chiefly with indigenous art; major articles have summaries in Russian, English, German, or French. Includes book reviews. Of similar character were two earlier periodicals: *Umění, sborník pro českou výtvarnou práci* (Art, miscellany of Czech creative work) (v. 1-17; 1919/21-1945-49, Praha, J. Štenc, illus., quarterly), and *Volné směry, umělecký měsíčník* (Free trends; artistic monthly) (v. 1-41; 1897-1949, Praha, Spolek výtvarných umělců Mánes, illus., plates, ports., 10 issues a year).

1249. Umění a řemesla (Arts and crafts). v. 1– 1959– Praha, Ústředí lidové umělecké výroby. Illus., samples. Bimonthly.

Devoted to folk arts and handicrafts such as textiles, costume, jewelry, furniture, glass, ceramics, wood carving, musical instruments, etc. Summaries in Russian, English, French, and German. May be supplemented by *Tvar; časopis pro užité umění a průmyslové výtvarnictví* (Form; journal of applied art and industrial design) (v. 1– 1948– Praha, illus., 10 issues a year), issued by Svaz československých výtvarných umělců. This is focused more on design and manufacture in the applied arts. Summaries in Russian, English, French, and other languages.

1250. Výtvarné umění (Creative art). v. 1– 1950– Praha. Illus. (part col.), ports. 10 issues a year.

Issued by Svaz československých výtvarných umělců. Concerned with contemporary art. Summaries in Russian, German, French, and English.

3. History of Art*

a. General

1251. Wirth, Zdeněk, *ed.* Dějepis výtvarných umění v Československu (History of the creative arts in Czechoslovakia). Praha, Sfinx, 1935. 351 p. Illus., 14 col. plates. Includes bibliographies.

* Arrangement is chronological, with comprehensive works listed first.

An offprint, with some additional material, from volume 8, *Umění* (The arts) of *Československá vlastivěda* (Book of knowledge on Czechoslovakia) (Praha, Sfinx, 1935, 758 p., illus., plates, bibliographies). A brief survey in English, with illustrations, is available in Wirth's *Czechoslovak Art From Ancient Times Until the Present Day* (Prague, Orbis, 1926, 36 p., 102 plates). A more recent summary in English, with bibliographies but illustrated only by a few maps, appears in volume 4 of the *Encyclopedia of World Art* (New York, McGraw-Hill Book Co., 1961) p. 198-224. For Slovakia, see *Umění na Slovensku, odkaz země a lidu* (The arts in Slovakia, heritage of the land and the people) (Praha, Melantrich, 1938, 88 p., 1331 illus., map), edited by Karel Šourek.

1252. Poulík, Josef. Prehistoric Art, Including Some Recent Cave-culture Discoveries and Subsequent Developments up to Roman Times. Photographs and graphic arrangements by W. and B. Forman. London, Spring Books, 1956. 47 p. 212 plates (part col.)

Translation of *Pravěké umění* (Praha, Státní nakl. krásné literatury, hudby a umění, 1956, 45 p., 203 plates). Includes photographs of carvings, pottery, glass, metalwork, jewelry, textiles, armor, and other objects.

1253. Böhm, Jaroslav, *and others.* La Grande-Moravie; tradition millénaire de l'État et de la civilisation. The Great Moravian Empire; Thousand Years of Tradition of State and Culture. Prague, Éditions de l'Académie tchécoslovaque des sciences, 1963. 137 p. Illus., facsims., plans, bibliographies.

Translation of *Velká Morava tisíciletá tradice státu a kultury* (Praha, Nakl. Československé akademie věd, 1963, 112 p., illus.). Includes results of excavations of ninth-century sites in South Moravia. Monographs of related interest are Josef Cibulka's *Velkomoravský kostel v Modré u Velehradu* (The Great Moravian church in Modrá near Velehrad) (Praha, Nakl. Československé akademie věd, 1958, 362 p., illus., maps) and Vilém Hrubý's *Staré Město, Velkomoravský Velehrad* (Praha, Nakl. Československé akademie věd, 1965, 467 p., illus., maps). A recent survey edited by Jan Filip, *Investigations archéologiques en Tchécoslovaquie; état actuel des recherches et leur organisation* (Prague, Academia, 1966, 317 p., 40 p. of illus.) is also useful.

1254. Dějepis výtvarného umění v Čechách (History of creative art in Bohemia). v. 1, Středověk (The Middle Ages). Edited by Zdeněk Wirth. Praha, SVU Mánes, 1931. 435 p. Illus. (part col.) Bibliography: p. 418-419.

May be supplemented for the Romanesque period by *Praha románská* (Romanesque Prague) (Praha, V. Poláček, 1948, 233 p., illus., maps, bibliographies), by Václav Chaloupecký, Jan Květ, and Václav Mencl.

1255. Kutal, Albert, Dobroslav Líbal, *and* Antonín Matějček. České umění gotické (Czech Gothic art). v. 1. Stavitelství a sochařství (Architecture and sculpture). Praha, Mánes, 1949. 80 p., 192 p. of plates, 13 p. (Zlatý list, sv. 4)

Regional treatment, covering architecture, sculpture, and painting, is presented by Vladimír Denkstein and František Matouš in *Gothic Art in South Bohemia* (Prague, Artia, 1955, 340 p., illus., plates), translated from their *Jihočeská gotika* (Praha, Státní nakl. krásné literatury, hudby a umění, 1953, 125 p., illus., bibliography).

1256. Lamač, Miroslav. Contemporary Art in Czechoslovakia. Prague, Orbis, 1958. 139 p. Illus. (part col.)

May be supplemented by *Naše současné výtvarné umění* (Our contemporary creative arts) (Praha, Nakl. československých výtvarných umělců, 1955, 84 p., illus.), a collection of articles edited by Vlastimil Fiala and Dušan Šindelář. For Slovakia, *see* Karol Vaculík's *Umenie XIX. storočia na Slovensku* (19th-century art in Slovakia) (Bratislava, Tvar, 1952, 114 p., illus., plates).

b. Architecture

1257. Knox, Brian. Bohemia and Moravia, an Architectural Companion. London, Faber and Faber, 1962. 168, 64 p. Illus., plates, maps, plans.

Based on the author's travels; erudite and well written. See also *Česká architektura* (Czech architecture), by Oldřich Starý and others (Praha, Nakl. Českosl. umělců, 1962). Slovak architecture is discussed in *Architektúra na Slovensku do polovice XIX. storočia* (Architecture in Slovakia to the middle of the 19th century) (Bratislava, Slovenské vydavatel'stvo krásnej literatúry, 1958, 607 p., plates, maps, plans), by Ladislav Foltyn, Alexander Keviczky, and Ivan Kuhn. The unique beauty of Prague has been well displayed in many volumes, particularly those publishing the photographs of Karel Plicka. In addition, the following may be recommended: Zdeněk Wirth's *Prague in Pictures of Five Centuries*, 2d ed. (Prague, J. Štenc, 1938, 68 p., 264 illus.), and Vojtěch Volavka's *Kunstwanderungen durch Prag* (Prague, Artia, 1959, 286 p., illus.).

1258. Mencl, Václav. Czech Architecture of the Luxemburg Period. Prague, Artia, 1955. 61 p., 186 illus.

Translation of *Česká architektura doby lucemburské* (Praha, Sfinx, 1949, 200 p., plates, plans, bibliography). The entire Gothic period is discussed by Dobroslav Líbal in *Gotická architektura v Čechách a na Moravě* (Gothic architecture in Bohemia and Moravia) (Praha, Umělecká beseda, 1948, 290 p., plates, plans). A major 14th century architect is treated in Karl Maria Swoboda's *Peter Parler, der Baukünstler und Bildhauer* (Wien, A. Schroll, 1940, 42 p., illus., plans, 112 plates). For Slovakia, Václav Mencl's *Stredoveká architektúra na Slovensku* (Medieval architecture in Slovakia) may be mentioned. Only one volume was published: *Stavebné umenie na Slovensku od najstarších čias až do konca doby románskej* (The art of building in Slovakia from the earliest times to the end of the Romanesque period) (Praha- Prešov, Nákl. Československej Grafickej Unie, 1937, 478 p., illus., maps, plans, 86 p. of plates).

1259. Šamánková, Eva. Architektura české renesance (The architecture of the Czech Renaissance). Praha, Státní nakl. krásné literatury a umění, 1961. 141 p. 266 illus. Bibliography: p. 113-114.

Surveys chiefly the secular architecture of the 16th century. A single influence is discussed by Olga Vaňková-Frejková in her study, *Palladianismus v české renesanci* (Palladianism in the Czech Renaissance) (Praha, Nakl. České akademie věd a umění, 1941, 263 p., 83 illus., bibliographical references, summaries in German and French). Additional treatment of the period is found in Zdeněk Wirth's "Die böhmische Renaissance," published in *Historica*, v. 3, 1961, p. 87-107, with 22 plates.

1260. Franz, Heinrich Gerhard. Bauten und Baumeister der Barockzeit in Böhmen; Entstehung und Ausstrahlungen der böhmischen Barockbaukunst. Leipzig, E. A. Seemann, 1962. 486 p. Illus., plans. Bibliography: p. 469-477.

Discusses buildings and architects of the 17th and 18th centuries. Less objective is Hans Werner Hegemann's *Die deutsche Barockbaukunst Böhmens* (München, F. Bruckmann, 1943, 120 p. incl. plates, illus., map, plans, bibliography). Of related interest is Franz's *Die deutsche Barockbaukunst Mährens* (München, F. Bruckmann, 1943, 136 p. incl. plates, illus., map, bibliography). For Prague, see *Baroque Architecture of Prague* (Paris, The Sign of the Pegasus, 1927, 31 p., col. front., 151 plates), by Eugen Dostál and Josef Šíma.

1261. Koula, Jan E. Nova česká architektura a její vývoj ve XX. století (New Czech architecture and its development in the 20th century). Praha, Čes. graf. Unie, 1940. 234 p. (Technické příručky, sv. 6)

The preceding period is covered in *Česká architektura, 1800-1920* (Czech architecture, 1800-1920) (Praha, J. Štenc, 1922, 104 p., illus.), by Zdeněk Wirth and Antonín Matějček.

c. Sculpture

1262. Kutal, Albert. České gotické sochařství, 1350-1450 (Czech Gothic sculpture, 1350-1450). Praha, Státní nakl. krásné literatury a umění, 1962. 180 p. 265 plates (9 col.) Bibliography: p. 143-149. (Edice České dějiny, sv. 30)

An authoritative study of the important flowering of sculpture during the Luxemburg period, including the "beautiful style." Summaries in Russian, French, and German. Treating the same period is *Die Plastik in Böhmen zur Zeit der Luxemburger* (Prag, J. Štenc, 1936, 154 p., illus., 100 p. of plates), by Josef Opitz. This is the first of two planned parts; the second was never published. A monograph by Julius Pašteka discusses a work of Pavel z Levoče in *Der spätgotische Altar zu St. Jakob* (Praha, Artia, 1961, 44 p., illus., 147 plates, facsim., plan, summaries in English and French). See also *Majstor Pavol z Levoče* (Master Pavol z Levoče) by Jaromír Homolka and others (Bratislava, 1964, 155 p.).

1263. Štech, Václav Vilém. Baroque Sculpture. London, Spring Books, 1959. 132 p. Illus., 203 plates (part col.)

Treating roughly the same period is Oldřich Jan Blažíček's *Sochařství baroku v Čechách; plastika 17. a 18. věku* (Sculpture of the baroque in Bohemia; plastic art of the 17th and 18th centuries) Praha, Státní nakl. krásné literatury, hudby a umění, 1958, 682 p., illus., bibliography, summaries in German and French). Among the monographs may be mentioned Emanuel Poche's *Matyáš Bernard Braun, sochař českého baroka a jeho dílna* (Matthias Bernard Braun, sculptor of the Bohemian baroque, and his workshop) (Praha, Státní nakl. krásné literatury a umění, 1965, 321 p., 185 illus. incl. ports., bibliography, summaries in Russian, French, and German), on an artist of the early 18th century, originally from the Tyrol; and Zdeňka Skořepová's *O sochařském díle rodiny Platzerů* (On the sculptural works of the Platzer family) (Praha, Státní nakl. krásné literatury, hudby a umění, 1957, 173 p., illus.), on Ignac F. Platzer, a Bohemian sculptor of the latter part of the 18th century, and his family. Good informative essays are in the catalog *L'arte del Barocco in Boemia* (Milano, Palazzo Reale, 1966, 170 p., 113 pl.).

1264. Volavka, Vojtěch. Sochařství devatenáctého století (Sculpture of the 19th century). Praha, Umělecká beseda, 1948. 71 p. Illus., plates (Cesta k umění. Díl 6, sv. 2)

The outstanding sculptor of the late 19th century receives monographic treatment by Václav Vilém Štech and others in *Josef Václav Myslbek* (Praha, Státní nakl. krásné literatury, hudby a umění, 1954, 58 p., 176 illus.).

d. Painting

1265. United Nations Educational, Scientific and Cultural Organization. Czechslovakia: Romanesque and Gothic Illuminated Manuscripts. Pref. by Hanns Swarzenski; introd. by Jan Květ. Greenwich, Conn., New York Graphic Society, 1959. 20 p. 32 plates. Bibliography: p. 21-22. (UNESCO World Art Series, 12)

Concise scholarly text accompanies excellent, full-size reproductions. More detailed studies include the following: *Velislavova bible a její místo ve vývoji knižní ilustrace gotické* (The Velislav Bible and its place in the development of Gothic book illustration) (Praha, J. Štenc, 1926, 139 p., 50 p. of illus.), by Antonín Matějček; *Iluminované rukopisy královny Rejčky* (The illuminated manuscripts of Queen Rejčka) (Praha, Nákl. České akademie věd a umění, 1931, 288 p., illus.), by Jan Květ; and *Das Evangeliar des Johannes von Troppau* (Klagenfurt, J. Leon sen., 1948, 69 p., 18 plates, bibliography), by Ernst Trenkler.

1266. Mašín, Jiří. Romanesque Mural Painting in Bohemia and Moravia. La peinture murale en Bohême et en Moravie à l'époque romane. Praha, Artia, 1954. 33 p. 88 plates (part col.) Bibliography: p. 30-31.

A brief summary of the text of *Románská nástěnná malba v Čechách a na Moravě* (Praha, Nakl. Československé akademie věd, 1954, 89 p., illus.). Treats little-known masterpieces of 12th century painting, beginning with those in the rotunda of Svatá Kateřina at Znojmo, to which is devoted Antonín Friedl's *Přemyslovci ve Znojmě* (Přemyslids in Znojmo) (Praha, Odeon, 1966, 113 p., 112, 16 illus.).

1267. Friedl, Antonín. Magister Theodoricus; das Problem seiner malerischen Form. Prag, Artia, 1956. 338 p. Illus., 196 plates (part col.)

The 14th century murals at Karlštejn castle are the subject of other books by Friedl: *Mistr karlštejnské apokalypsy* (The Master of the Karlštejn Apocalpse) (Praha, Tvar, 1950, 40 p., 63 plates, English summary), and *Mikuláš Wurmser, mistr královských portrétů na Karlštejně* (Nicholas Wurmser, master of the royal portraits at Karlštejn) (Praha, Státní nakl. krásné literatury, hudby a umění, 1956, 70 p., illus.).

1268. Dvořáková, Vlasta, *and others.* Gothic Mural Painting in Bohemia and Moravia, 1300-1378. London, New York, Oxford University Press, 1964. 160 p. Maps, plates (part col.) Bibliography: p. 153-160.

Discusses the outstanding production of the Luxemburg period. The works of the first half of the century are exhaustively treated in the first volume, covering 1300-1350, of *Gotická nástěnná malba v zemích českých* (Gothic mural painting in the Czech Lands) (Praha, Nakl. Československé akademie věd, 1958, 414 p., illus., map, 251 plates, bibliography, summaries in English, German and Russian).

1269. Matějček, Antonín, *and* Jaroslav Pešina. Czech Gothic Painting, 1350-1450. 4th ed. Prague, Artia, 1956. 97 p. 279 plates (part col.)

A revised and abridged translation of *Česká malba gotická; deskové malířství 1350-1450* (Czech Gothic painting; panel painting, 1350-1450) first published in Prague by Melantrich in 1938. It is continued by Pešina's *Painting of the Gothic and Renaissance Periods, 1450-1550* (Prague, Artia, 1958, 98 p., 304 plates, bibliography), a translation of his *Česká malba pozdní gotiky a renesance* (Praha, Orbis, 1950, 144 p., 265 illus., bibliography). Pešina's article, "Nový pokus o revizi dějin českého malířství 15. století" (A new attempt at revising the history of Czech painting of the 15th century), in *Umění*, v. 8, no. 2, 1960, p. 109-134, is relevant. Bohemian production is also treated in volumes 1, 2, and 9 of Alfred Stange's monumental *Deutsche Malerei der Gotik* (Berlin, Deutscher Kunstverlag, 1934-61, 11 v.). Contemporary developments in Slovakia are described by Vladimír Wagner in *Gotické tabuľové maliar-*

stvo na Slovensku (Gothic panel painting in Slovakia) (Turčianský sv. Martin, Matica slovenská, 1942, 37 p., 28 p. of plates).

1270. Neumann, Jaromír. Malířství XVII. století v Čechách. Barokní realismus (17th-century painting in Bohemia. Baroque realism). Praha, Orbis, 1951. 171 p. 198 plates (part col.) Bibliography: p. 143. Edice České dějiny, sv. 3)

Treatment of the revival of painting after the decline at the close of the 16th century. Summaries in Russian, English, and French. Except for short publications, monographs have yet to be written on Karel Škréta, Petr Jan Brandl, Václav Vavřinec Rainer, and František Xaver Palko.

1271. Dvořák, František. Kupecký, the Great Baroque Portrait Painter. Prague, Artia, 1957. 48 p. Illus., 110 plates (part col.) Bibliography: p. 49.

Translation of *Kupecký* (Bratislava, Slovenské vydavatel'stvo krásnej literatúry, 1955, 157 p., illus., plates). Jan Kupecký, originally of Bohemia, was active in Rome, Vienna, and Nuremberg. This study may be supplemented by *Das Barockporträt in Böhmen* (Prag, Artia, 1957, 145 p., plates, ports., bibliography), by Olga Strettiová.

1272. Urzidil, Johannes, *and* Franz Sprinzels. Wenceslaus Hollar, der Kupferstecher des Barock. Wien, Leipzig, Dr. R. Passer, 1936. 160 p. Illus., 47 plates. Bibliography: p. 156-157.

On an internationally renowned Czech artist who was active in Western Europe during the 17th century.

1273. Neumann, Jaromír. Czech Classic Painting of the XIXth Century. Prague, Artia, 1955-58. 2 v. Illus., plates (part col.)

Volume 2 has title: *Modern Czech Painting and the Classical Tradition*. Masters of landscape, portrait, genre, and historical and national themes are treated. Monographs have been devoted to several of these artists, e.g., *Wandmalereien des Biedermeiers; ein Werk Josef Navrátils* (Prag, Artia, 1958, 37, 72 p., illus.), by Václav Vilém Štech and Vladimír Hnízdo; *Adolf Kosárek* (Praha, Státní nakl. krásné literatury, hudby a umění, 1959, 100 p., illus.), by Libuše Halasová and V. V. Štech; *Josef Mánes* (Praha, Nakl. Československých výtvarných umělců, 1956, 237 p., illus., port., plates, bibliography), by Miroslav Lamač; and *Antonín Chittussi* (Praha, Státní nakl. krásné literatury, hudby a umění, 1954, 97 p., illus.), by František Dvořák. The work of Mikuláš Aleš is being published by Státní nakladatelství krásné literatury a umění (earlier volumes were issued by Orbis) in Prague in a multivolume series entitled *Dílo Mikuláše Alše*. As of 1964, volumes 1-5, 7-8, and 11 had appeared. For Slovakia, see Karol Vaculík's *Maliarstvo XIX. storočia na Slovensku* (19th-century painting in Slovakia) (Bratislava, Slovenské vydavatel'stvo krásnej literatúry, 1956, 17 p., 19 col. illus. in portfolio).

1274. Kotalík, Jiří. Moderní československé malířství (Modern Czechoslovak painting). Československo, v. 2, Jan. 1947. 129-207. Illus., part col.

Among the monographs on contemporary painters may be mentioned *The Modern Symbolist: the Painter Jan Zrzavý* (Prague, Artia, 1958, 42 p., illus., 63 plates), by Dalibor Plichta; *Karel Svolinský* (Praha, Nakl. československých výtvarných umělců, 1962, 177 p., 59 illus., 104 plates, bibliography, summaries in Russian, German, French, and English), by Jan Spurný; and *Rudolf Kremlička* (Praha, Státní nakl. krásné literatury, hudby a umění, 1955, 210 p., illus.), by Vítězslav Nezval. Contemporary painting in Slovakia is displayed in *Moderne Maler der Slowakei* (Praha, Artia, 1961, 37 p., illus., 61 col. plates, summaries in English and French), by Marian Váross, and Radislav Matuštík's *Moderné slovenské maliarstvo* (Modern Slovak painting) (Bratislava, Slovenské vydavatel'stvo krásnej literatúry, 1965, 197 p., illus., plates, includes bibliography).

1275. Mucha, Jiří. Alphonse Mucha, the Master of Art Noveau. Prague, Artia, 1966. 291 p. Illus. (part col.), facsims., ports.

Matějček, Antonín. Jan Preisler. Praha, Melantrich, 1950. 118 p., 274 plates (part col.). Bibliography: p. 103.

Richly illustrated studies of a distinguished representative of the art noveau movement who achieved fame in Paris, and of a lyrical symbolist working in Paris and Prague during the early decades of this century.

1276. Siblík, Emanuel. František Kupka. Praha, Aventinum, 1928. 38 p. 32 plates.

Cassou, Jean, *and* Denise Fédit. Kupka, Gouaches and Pastels. New York, H. M. Abrams, 1965. 68 p. Illus. (part col.), port. Bibliography, p. 66-68.

Monographs on one of the pioneers of nonrepresentational painting, working in Paris from 1894 until his death in 1957.

1277. Hlaváček, Luboš. Současná československá grafika (Contemporary Czechoslovak graphic art). Praha. Nakl. Československých výtvarných umělců, 1964. 145 p. 126 illus., 10 col. plates. Bibliography: p. 122-123. (Grafika, sv. 2)

Summaries in Russian, German, French, and English. It continues Jaroslav Pešina's *Česká moderní grafika* (Czech modern graphic art) (Praha, Sdružení českých umělců grafiků Hollar, 1940, 198 p., illus., bibliography). Of related interest is Jan Květ's monograph, *Max Švabinský, der grosse tschechische Maler und Graphiker* (Praha, Artia, 1960, 32 p., illus., 93 plates).

4. Minor Arts and Folk Art

1278. Hasalová, Věra, *and others.* Tvořivost českého lidu v tradiční umělecké výrobě; sborník statí (The creativity of the Czech people in traditional art production; a collection of articles). Praha, Orbis, 1953. 179 p. Illus.

Among the topics treated are domestic architecture and decoration, weaving, lace making, basketry, ceramics, painting on glass, jewelry, paper cutouts, and bread and cake forms. Folk arts in the entire country are treated in *Umění československého lidu* (The arts of the Czechoslovak people) (Praha, Nakl. Vesmíru, 1928, 47 p., 192 illus.), compiled by Zdeněk Wirth, and *Československé lidové výtvarnictví* (Czechoslovak folk creative art) (Praha, Orbis, 1948, 119 p., illus.), by Naděžda Melniková-Papoušková.

1279. Hetteš, Karel. Glass in Czechoslovakia. Prague, SNTL, 1958. 68 p. Illus. (part col.)

Reviews the history of glass production in Czechoslovakia from its earliest known beginnings. Economic, technical, and artistic aspects are touched on. May be supplemented for present-day production by *Modernes böhmisches Glas* (Praha, Artia, 1963, illus.), by Josef Raban and others, which includes a short historical introduction and biographical information on contemporary artists working in glass.

1280. Kalesný, František, L'udové umenie na Slovensku (Folk art in Slovakia). Martin, Osveta, 1956. 274 p. Illus., col. plates. Bibliography: p. 273-275.

Surveys such traditional arts as ceramics, metalwork, basketry, wood carving, weaving, embroidery, costume, domestic architecture, lace, work in leather and straw, and the decoration of Easter eggs. Summaries in German and Russian. A single art is treated by Josef Vydra in *L'udová architektúra na Slovensku* (Folk architecture in Slovakia) (Bratislava, Vydavatel'stvo Slovenskej akadémie vied, 1958, 337 p., illus., summaries in Russian, German, and French), and by Ladislav Foltyn in *Volksbaukunst in der Slowakei* (Praha, Artia, 1960, 233 p., illus., plates, maps, plans, bibliography). The two volumes of *Slovak Folk Art* (Prague, Artia, 1964) are well-produced picture books covering architecture, costume, and embroidery (v. 1) and ceramics, carving, and painting (v. 2).

1281. Poche, Emanuel. Bohemian Porcelain. Photographs by Josef Ehm. Prague, Artia, 1956. 69 p. Illus., 176 plates (part col.) Bibliography: p. 71.

Translation of *Český porcelán* (Praha, Orbis, 1954, 71, 139 p., illus.). Historical survey of Bohemian porcelain manufacture. Folk production is treated by Karel Černohorský in *Moravská lidová keramika* (Moravian folk ceramics) (Praha, J. Otto, 1941, 284 p., illus., plates, bibliography); a related art is discussed in *Painting on Folk Ceramics* (London, Spring Books, 1956, 78 p., illus., 156 plates, bibliography), by Josef Vydra and Ludvík Kunz.

1282. Václavík, Antonín, *and* Jaroslav Orel. Textile Folk Art. London,

Spring Books, 1956. 58 p. Illus., 59 col. plates.

Includes discussion of weaving, embroidery, block-printing, and lace and their use in Czechoslovak folk costume.

H. MUSIC

by Barbara Krader

1. Reference Works

1283. Barvík, Miroslav, Jan Malát, *and* Karel Tauš, *eds.* Stručný hudební slovník (Brief musical dictionary). 5th rev. and enl. ed. Praha, Státní nakladatelství krásné literatury, hudby a umění, 1960. 415 p. Music. Bibliography: p. 396-398.

First edition, edited by Malát (*Malatův hudební slovník*), appeared in 1881. Most recent editions modeled upon the first volume of the next entry. Chiefly definitions of terms.

1284. Černušák, Gracian, *and* Vladimír Helfert, *eds.* Pazdírkův hudební slovník naučný (Pazdírek's scholarly musical dictionary), Brno, Ol. Pazdírek, 1929-1940. 2 v. in 3.

Volume 1: Část věcná (Subject entries); volume 2: Část osobní (Personalia). Of volume 2, only A-M published, the second part of the second volume also edited by Bohumír Štědron. Fascicules 20-25 were published under German occupation; no. 26 was printed but banned by censorship. Still a fundamental Czech musical dictionary. Also important and not entirely superseded is:

Dlabač, Jan B. (Gottfried B. Dlabacž), *comp. and ed.* Allgemeines historisches Künstler-Lexikon für Böhmen und zum Theil auch für Mähren und Schlesien, Prag, gedruckt bei Gottlieb Haase, 1815. 3 v. Provides information about numerous performers and composers.

1285. Černušák, Gracian, Bohumír Štědroň, *and* Zdenko Nováček, *eds.* Československý hudební slovník osob a institucí (Czechoslovak music dictionary of persons and institutions). Praha, Státní hudební vydavatelství, 1963-1965. 2 v. Illus., facsims., ports., bibliographies. *See also* entry no. 533.

Most extensive postwar reference work of its kind, though not entirely satisfactory. *See* the review in *Die Musikforschung*, v. 18, 1965: 347-349. A supplementary volume is planned, to be edited by B. Štědroň and Z. Nováček.

1286. Gardavský, Čeněk, *ed.* Contemporary Czechoslovak Composers. Prague-Bratislava, Panton, 1965. 562 p.

Survey of composers, arranged in alphabetical order. Titles of works in English only. Czech and Slovak music institutions and organizations described on pages 523-538. Contemporary works by Czech and Slovak composers available on Czechoslovak recordings listed on pages 539-562, with titles in English only. Records not identified. French edition published 1966. For performers, *see also*:

Kozák, Jan, *and others*. Českoslovenští koncertní umělci a komorní soubory; sborník s fotografiemi umělců a souborů (Czechoslovak concert artists and chamber groups; with photographs of artists and groups). Praha, Státní hudební vydavatelství, 1964. 482 p. Illus., ports, bibliographies and discographies.

1287. Potúček, Juraj, *comp*. Súpis slovenských hudobnín a literatúry o hudobníkoch (včítane hudobnoteoretických prác) za r. 1953-60 (Bibliography of Slovak music and literature on musicians [including works of music theory] for the years 1953-60). Bratislava, Slovenská akadémia vied, 1963.

A continuation of his bibliographies described below, bringing them to the end of 1960: Súpis slovenských hudobnín a literatúry o hudobníkoch (A bibliography of Slovak music and literature on musicians). Bratislava, Slovenská akadémia vied a umení, 1952. 435 p. Covers the earliest times to 1949.

Súpis slovenských hudobnoteoretických prác (Bibliography of Slovak works on music theory). Bratislava, Slovenská akadémia vied a umení, 1955. 467 p. Books and articles on music, concert life in Slovakia, music education, etc., covering the years 1901-1952; also a supplement to previous bibliography.

Doplnky k hudobnej bibliografii (Supplements to musical bibliography). *Hudobnovedné štúdie* (Musicological studies). Bratislava, v. 3, 1959: 205-275. Supplements to both preceding volumes, containing 1,600 entries, and name index. Imprints only through 1952.

2. Serials

1288. Hudební rozhledy (Musical review). 1948– Praha, Svaz československých skladatelů. Fortnightly.

Basic source for current information on Czech musical scene. Brief accounts of musical activity abroad, often hostile concerning the West. Subjects include jazz. Occasional brief articles by musicologists. Reviews and notices of books, records, music. Organ of the Union of Czechoslovak Composers.

Titles and dates of other 19th and 20th century Czech musical journals are given in entry 1285 under the heading "Časopisy hudební," with additional information furnished under individual title headings.

1289. Hudební věda (Musical scholarship). 1964– Praha, Československá akademie věd, Ústav pro hudební vědu. Quarterly.

Supersedes an irregular publication of the same title, issued from 1961 as Series B of *Knižnice Hudebních rozhledů*.

A new Czech scholarly periodical, concerned with aesthetic problems and the sociology of music perhaps more than with historical research, it contains articles and reviews. German and Russian résumés and table of contents in German, Russian, French, and English.

Also important, particularly for Janáček research is *Musikologie; sborník pro hudební vědu a kritiku* (Musicology; miscellany for musical scholarship and criticism) (Praha, Státní nakl. krásné literatury, hudby a umění, 1938-1958, 5 v.), which was founded by Vladimír Helfert and later edited by Jan Racek.

1290. Hudobnovedné štúdie (Musicological studies). 1– 1955– Bratislava, Slovenská akadémia vied, Ústav hudobnej vedy. Irregular.

Supersedes *Hudobnovedný sborník* (Musicological miscellany) (Bratislava, 1953-1954, 2 v.). This Slovak scholarly publication emphasizes historical research and often contains lengthy bibliographies and surveys, as well as many long reviews. In interrelation, and occasional disagreement, with Hungarian musicologists. Most articles have German résumés.

1291. Slovenská hudba (Slovak music). 1957– Bratislava, Sväz slovenských skladatel'ov. Ten issues yearly.

Articles on Slovak composers, aesthetic problems, historical musicology. Surveys of current concert life throughout Slovakia, with comments on that of Bohemia and Moravia and book reviews. Organ of the Union of Slovak Composers.

3. Surveys and Histories

1292. Burlas, Ladislav, Ján Fišer, *and* Antonín Hořejš. Hudba na Slovensku v XVII. storočí (Music in Slovakia in the 17th century). Bratislava, Vydavatel'stvo Slovenskej akadémie vied, 1954. 422 p Illus., music.

A solid historical work devoted to specific works of one century: the Vietoris Codex, the so-called Cithara Sanctorum and Cantus Catholici, and ten organ or lute tabulatura collections of Levoča. Music transcriptions in modern notation pages 157-418. Index of names.

1293. Dejiny slovenskej hudby (History of Slovak music). Bratislava, Vydavatel'stvo Slovenskej akadémie vied, 1957. 540 p. Music.

A symposium by twelve authors, comprising the first comprehensive history of Slovak music. Less ambitious, but a useful survey, for teachers, is *Dejiny slovenskej hudby* (History of Slovak music) by Ladislav Mokrý and Jozef Tvrdoň (Bratislava, Slovenské pedagogické nakladatel'stvo, 1964, 193 p., music). Historical section reviews concert life, composers and musicologists. Post-1945 section gives information on eight composers born in the 1930's. Extensive bibliography and music examples.

1294. Helfert, Vladimír, *and* Erich Steinhard. Histoire de la musique dans la République Tchécoslovaque. Prague, Orbis, 1936. 301 p. Illus.

Condensed but valuable account of evolution of Czech and Slovak music by Helfert, brief account of German music in Czechoslovakia by Steinhard. List of musical works arranged by genres, titles in French only, by Bohumir Štědroň on pages 193-298. A German edition appeared in 1936, and a second enlarged edition in 1938.

Rosa H. Newmarch's *The Music of Czechoslovakia* (London, New York, Toronto, Oxford University Press, 1942, 244 p., illus., music) is affectionate and knowledgeable but not an expert survey of Czech music. *See also*:

Štěpánek, Vladimír, *and* Bohumil Karásek. An Outline of Czech and Slovak Music. Part 1. Czech Music. Prague, Orbis, 1964. 145 p. Illus., facsims., ports. Over 30 pages on post-1945 period. Yet generally superficial and not comparable to Helfert.

1295. Hrušovský, Ivan. Slovenská hudba v profiloch a rozboroch (Slovak music in profiles and analyses). Bratislava, Štátne hudobné vydavatel'stvo, 1964. 460 p. Music. Bibliography: p. 445-446.

In part, historical surveys of pre-1918, 1918-1945, and post-1945 periods, in part analyses, with musical examples, of works of 18 composers, from Ján Levoslav Bella (1843-1936) to Ján Zimmer, born 1926. Index of names.

1296. Nejedlý, Zdeněk. Dějiny husitského zpěvu (The history of the Hussite chant). 2d ed. Praha, Nakladatelství Československé akademie věd, 1954-1956. 6 v. (Sebrané spisy Zdeňka Nejedlého, sv. 40-45)

Fundamental study of Hussite chant, by a great Czech musicologist, first published in 1904-1913 in three volumes. Second edition unchanged, but has new foreword by author.

1297. Němeček, Jan. Nástin české hudby XVIII. století (Outline of Czech music of the 18th century). Praha, Státní nakladatelství krásné literatury, hudby a umění, 1955. 399 p. Illus. Bibliography. p. 358-378.

Not definitive, but a useful survey of an important period, enhanced by its bibliography and index of names. *See* further:

Schoenbaum, Camillo. Die tschechische musikwissenschaftliche Literatur 1945-1960; Publikationen zur älteren böhmischen Musikgeschichte. In *Musik des Ostens*, v. 1, Kassel, Bärenreiter, 1962, p. 52-62.

1298. Racek, Jan. Česká hudba od nejstarších dob do počátku 19. století (Czech music from oldest times to the beginning of the 19th century). Praha, Státní nakladatelství krásné literatury, hudby a umění, 1958. 333 p. Illus.

Fullest recent account of period before Smetana, by Brno scholar, student of Helfert. German résumé (p. 277-293) by Pavel Eisner. Extensive bibliographies, indexes of proper names and titles of works. Can be paired with Jaroslav Pohanka's *Dějiny české hudby v příkladech* (History of Czech music in examples) (Praha, Státní nakladatelství krásné literatury, hudby a umění, 1958, 402, 58 p., bibliography) which contains music examples from the earliest known to 1848.

A view of Czech music as wholly dependent on or derived from German sources is found in Rudolf Quoika's *Die Musik der Deutschen in Böhmen und Mähren* (Berlin, Merseburger, 1956). *See* C. Schoenbaum's "Zur Problematik der Musikgeschichte Böhmens," *Die Musikforschung*, v. 10, 1957: 520-526, for an objective commentary on the national complications.

1299. Šíp, Ladislav. An Outline of Czech and Slovak Music. Part 2. Slovak Music. Translated from the Czech by Margaret Milner. Prague, Orbis, 1960. 57 p. Illus., facsims., ports.

Time span from earliest known period through postwar operas of Suchoň and Cikker. Good brief survey with appropriate background. Index of composers.

4. Individual Composers*

1300. Smetana, Bedřich.

Budiš, Ratibor, *and* Věra Kafková. Bedřich Smetana; výběrová bibliografie (Bedřich Smetana; a selective bibliography). Praha, Kniha, Národní podnik Hlavního města Prahy, 1964. 205 p. Illus., facsims, map, ports. Annotated bibliography covering biography and compositions. Name and subject indexes. *See also* the extensive bibliography with the article on Smetana by Kurt Honolka in *Die Musik in Geschichte und Gegenwart* (Kassel, Basel, London, Bärenreiter-Verlag), Band 12, 1965, columns 774-789.

Smetana, Bedřich. Bedřich Smetana; Letters and Reminiscences. Edited by František Bartoš. Translated from the Czech by Daphne Rusbridge. Prague, Artia, 1955. 293 p. Illus., ports., facsims. A translation of a Czech original the most recent edition of which is *Smetana ve vzpomínkách a dopisech*, edited and with commentary by František Bartoš, 9th ed. (Praha, Státní nakl. krásné literatury, hudby a umění, 1954, 247 p., illus., ports. Paměti, korespondence, dokumenty, sv. 1).

Nejedlý, Zdeněk. Frederick Smetana. London, G. Bles, 1924. 154 p. Front., facsims., music. An early, brief biography in English.

———. Bedřich Smetana. 2d rev. ed. Praha, Orbis, 1950-1954. 7 v. Illus., ports., maps, facsims., geneal. tables, music. (Sebrané spisy Zdeňka Nejedlého, sv. 21-27) The fullest account by the lead-

* Arrangement is chronological by date of birth, listing first bibliographies, followed by writings of each composer and by works about the composer.

ing Smetana specialist, the first edition of which appeared in four volumes in 1924-1933.

1301. Dvořák, Antonín.

Burghauser, Jarmil. Antonín Dvořák: thematický katalog; bibliografie; přehled života a díla (Antonin Dvorak: thematic catalog; bibliography; survey of life and work). Praha, Státní nakladatelství krásné literatury, hudby a umění, 1960. 735 p. Facsims., music. Entire text in Czech, German, and English. Indispensable reference.

Šourek, Otakar, *ed.* Antonín Dvořák: Letters and Reminiscences. Translated by Roberta Finlayson Samsour. Prague, Artia, 1954. 234 p. Illus., ports., facsims. A translation of *Dvořák ve vzpomínkách a dopisech* (9th ed., Praha, Orbis, 1951, 234 p., illus., ports., facsims.).

Clapham, John. Antonín Dvořák; Musician and Craftsman. London, Faber; New York, St. Martin's Press, 1966. 341 p. Illus., plates, ports., music. Bibliography: p. 326-330. Outstanding study of Dvořák's music. Brief biographical section. Includes a catalog of all completed works, a chronological list of compositions, and a genealogical tree. Foreword by Gerald Abraham.

The basic work in Czech is Otakar Šourek's *Život a dílo Antonína Dvořáka* (The life and work of Antonín Dvořák) (Praha, Státní nakl. krásné literatury, hudby a umění, 1954-1957, 4 v., illus., ports., music).

1302. Janáček, Leoš.

Štědroň, Bohumír, *comp.* Dílo Leoše Janáčka; abecední seznam Janáčkových skladeb a úprav. Bibliografie a diskografie (The work of Janáček: alphabetical list of his compositions and arrangements; bibliography and discography). Praha, 1959. 87 p. Illus., ports. (Knižnice hudebních rozhledů, Ročník V, sv. 9) Published also in Russian, German, and English, the latter under the title *The Work of Leoš Janáček* (Prague, Knižnice hudebních rozhledů, Ročník V, sv. 10, 1959, 116 p.).

Janáček, Leoš. Letters and Reminiscences. Edited by Bohumír Štědroň. Translated from the Czech by Geraldine Thomsen. Prague, Artia, 1955. 233 p. Illus., music, bibliography. The Czech original is *Leoš Janáček ve vzpomínkách a dopisech* (Praha, Topičova edice, 1946, 296 p.). Also available in German.

Janáček, Leoš. O lidové písni a lidové hudbě; dokumenty a studie (On folk song and folk instrumental music; documents and studies). Edited by Jiří Vysloužil and Jan Racek. Praha, Státní nakladatelství krásné literatury, hudby a umění, 1955. 661 p. Illus., ports., fold. map, music, bibliographical footnotes. (Janáčkův archiv, Řada II, Theoretické a literární dílo, sv. 1) Contains almost all Janáček's writings on speech melody as well as on folk music, including the classic study of Moravian folk song contributed to František Bartoš, *Národní písně moravské v nově nasbírané* (Moravian folk songs newly collected) (Praha, Nákladem České akademie císaře Františka Josefa pro vědy, slovesnost a umění, 1901, p. i-cxxxvi).

Hollander, Hans. Leoš Janáček; His Life and Work. Translated by Paul Hamburger. New York, St. Martin's Press, 1963. 222 p. Illus., ports., music. Bibliography: p. 217-218. An original and perceptive appraisal.

Vogel, Jaroslav. Leoš Janáček; His Life and Works. Translated from the Czech by Geraldine Thomsen-Muchová. London, P. Hamlyn, 1963. 425 p. Illus., facsims., music, ports. Bibliography: p. 410. Presents more details than the work by Hollander. The Czech original is *Leoš Janáček; život a dílo* (Praha, Státní hudební vydavatelství, 1963, 385 p.). Also available in a German translation.

5. Folk Song

See also section C, on folklore

1303. Bartók, Béla, *comp.* Slovenské ľudové piesne: zapísal a hudobne zatriedil Béla Bartók. Slovakische Volkslieder; aufgezeichnet und systematisiert von Béla Bartók. v. 1. Bratislava, Vydavateľstvo Slovenskej akadémie vied, 1959. 752 p. Illus., music.

First volume to be published (two more in preparation) of over 3,200 Slovak songs Bartók collected from 1906-1918. Importance lies especially in his classification based on analysis of his own material and of 12,000 other Czech, Moravian, and Slovak tunes. Introduction by Oskár Elschek and Bartók's preface are in Slovak and German. Résumés in Hungarian, Russian, English (poor), and French. Bartók's comments on songs in Slovak and German. *See* Jozef Kresánek's "Bartóks Sammlung slowakischer Volkslieder," in *Studia Memoriae Belae Bartók Sacra*, edited by Benjamin Rajeczky (2d ed., Budapestini, Aedes Academiae Scientiarum Hungaricae, 1957, p. 51-68). For references to other more comprehensive Slovak folk song collections, *see* entries no. 1150 and 1304.

1304. Vetterl, Karel, *and others, eds.* Czech and Slovak Folk Song, Music and Dance. Czech part ellaborated [sic] by K. Vetterl et al. Slovak part contributed by A. Elscheková et al. Praha, Bratislava, 1962. 57 p. Music.

Authoritative survey, although English is imperfect. Extensive bibliographies. Published for the Fifteenth Conference of the International Folk Music Council, by the Ethnographic Institutes of the Czechoslovak Academy in Prague and Brno, and of the Slovak Academy.

See also Juraj Potúček's recent "Slovenská hudobnofolkloristická literatúra (Výberová bibliografia za roky 1823-1961)" (Slovak folk music literature; a selective bibliography for the years 1823-1961), *Hudobnovedné štúdie* (Bratislava), v. 7, 1966: 200-227. Contains 480 entries and author index.

I. THEATER AND CINEMA

by Mojmir Drvota

1. Theater

1305. Buzková, Pavla. České drama (Czech drama). Praha, Melantrich, 1932. 258 p. (Výhledy; knihy zkušeností a úvah, 15)

A critical study of the eight best modern Czech dramatists from the period between the two wars.

1306. Bogatyrev, Petr Grigor'evich. Lidové divadlo české a slovenské (Czech and Slovak folk theater). Praha, F. Borový, 1940. 314 p. Illus., music.

See also entry no. 1147.

A scholarly study of a unique phenomenon: folk theater. It includes five selected plays.

1307. Císař, Jan. Divadla, která našla svou dobu (Theaters which found their times). Praha, Orbis, 1966. 128 p.

Contemporary cultural ferment in the field of the theater as represented by two internationally known stage directors and a few avant-garde "little theaters."

1308. Coleman, Marion Moore. Czech (Bohemian) Drama. *In*: Clark, Barret H., *and* George Freedly, *eds*. A History of Modern Drama. New York, Appleton-Century, 1947. p. 504-512.

A brief survey of Czech dramatic literature.

1309. Dějiny Národního divadla (History of the National Theater). Edited by Jaroslav Jelínek. Praha, Sbor pro zřízení druhého Národního divadla, 1933-36. 6 v. Illus., ports.

A monumental work by a group of prominent scholars and critics on the crucial factor of Czech cultural life: the National Theater in Prague. *See also*:

Doležil, Hubert, *and* A. M. Píša, *comps*. Soupis repertoáru Národního divadla v Praze, 1881-1935 (Repertory of the National Theater in Prague, 1881-1935). Praha, Sbor pro zřížení druhého Národního divadla, 1939. 206 p.

Kniha o Národním divadla, 1883-1963 (A book about the National Theater, 1883-1963). Edited by Pavel Keclík. Praha, Orbis, 1964. 168 p. Illus., ports.

1310. Divadlo (The theater). 1950– Praha. Monthly.

News, reviews, and articles on dramatic arts. *See also*:

Slovenské divadlo (The Slovak theater). 1953– Bratislava. Bimonthly.

1311. Fischer, Otakar. Činohra v pražkých divadlech: Prozatímním, Národním, Městském, 1862-1934 (Drama in Prague theaters; provisional, national, municipal, 1862-1934). *In*: Československá vlastivěda (Book of knowledge on Czechoslovakia). v. 8, Praha, Sfinx, 1935. p. 357-432.

A brief survey of the history of Czech drama in three leading theaters.

1312. Kimball, Stanley Buchholz. Czech Nationalism; a Study of the National Theatre Movement, 1845-1883. Urbana, University of Illinois Press, 1964. 186 p. Illus., ports. Bibliography: p. 164-172. (Illinois Studies in Social Sciences, 54)

A thorough, extremely well-documented work written from a political point of view.

1313. Nettel, Pavel, *and others*. Dějiny operního divadla v Československu (History of the opera in Czechoslovakia). *In*: Československá vlastivěda (Book of knowledge on Czechoslovakia). v. 8, Praha, Sfinx, 1935. p. 667-734.

A concise outline of the opera and its theaters in Czechoslovakia.

1314. Obst, Milan, *and* Adolf Scherl. K dějinám české divadelní avantgardy: Jindřich Honzl, E. F. Burian (A contribution to the avant-garde Czech theater: Jindřich Honzl and E. F. Burian). Praha, Nakl. Československé akademie věd, 1962. 322 p. Illus.

This compilation presents two outstanding Czech stage directors from the period between the two wars.

1315. Rampák, Zoltán. Náčrt dejín slovenského divadla (An outline of the history of the Slovak theater). Bratislava, Slovenská akadémia vied a umení, 1948. 50 p. Illus. Bibliography: p. 49. (Vlastivedná knižnica Slovenskej akadémie vied a umení, sv. 13; Odtlačok zo Slovenskej vlastivedy, diel2).

An introductory work written by a devoted student of Slovak drama and theater. For a recent comprehensive study of the Slovak theater *see*:

Kapitoly z dejín slovenského divadla (Chapters from the history of Slovak theater). Prepared by Milada Cesnaková-Michalcová and others. Bratislava, Vydavatel'stvo Slovenskej akademie vied, 1967– v. 1: Od najstarších čias po realizmus (From the oldest times up to realism).

1316. Šalda, František X. O naší moderní kultuře divadelně dramatické (Our modern dramatic theater culture). Praha, Girgal, 1937. 36 p.

A major evaluation of Czech dramatic art by a great critic.

1317. Šolcová, Marta, *and* Lucy Topolská, *comps.* Literatura o divadle a divadelní hry. Soupis knižních publikací, vydaných v letech 1961-1965 (Literature about the theater and plays. A list of books published from 1961 to 1965). Praha, Státní pedagogické nakl., 1967. 402 p. (Publikace Státní věd. knihovny v Olomouci, čís. 7)

This is the continuation of a bibliography previously published under the same title and covering the period 1945-1960. *See also*:

Laiske, Miroslav. Divadelní periodika v Čechách a na Moravě, 1772-1963. Díl 1. Divadelní časopisy a programy (Theatrical serials in Bohemia and Moravia, 1772-1963. Part 1: Theatrical periodicals and programs). Praha, Divadelní ústav, 1967. 290 p. An alphabetic list of 984 titles, with author, subject, chronological, and geographic indexes.

Zach, Aleš. Publikace Divadelního ústavu 1958-1967 (Publications of the Theater Institute, 1958-1967). Praha, Divadelní institut, 1968. 41 p.

1318. Vodák, Jindřich, *and* Josef Träger. Tváře českých herců; od J. J. Kolára k V. Burianovi (The faces of Czech actors; from J. J. Kolár to V. Burian). Praha, Orbis, 1967. 272 p.

Two well-known critics present profiles of many outstanding Czech actors of the past one hundred years.

1319. Vondráček, Jan. Dějiny českého divadla; doba obrozenská, 1771-1824 (History of the Czech theater; the awakening period, 1771-1824). Praha, Orbis, 1956. 687 p. Illus., ports.

A comprehensive standard work of the highest quality. *See also* his *Dějiny českého divadla; doba předbřeznová, 1824-1846* (History of the Czech theater; the prerevolutionary period, 1824-1846) (Praha, Orbis, 1957, 490 p.).

Černý, František, *ed.* Dějiny českého divadla. Od počátku do sklonku osmnáctého století (History of the Czech theater. From the beginnings to the close of the 18th century). Praha, Academia, 425 p.

1320. Zich, Otakar. Estetika dramatického umění; teoretická dramaturgie (The aesthetics of dramatic art; a theoretical dramatury). Praha, Melantrich, 1931. 408 p. (Výhledy knihy zkušeností a úvah, sv. 11-12)

A basic, outstanding scholarly study of the principles of the dramatic arts.

2. The Cinema

1321. Boček, Jaroslav. Jiří Trnka; historie díla a jeho tvůrce (Jiří Trnka; a history of the art work and its creator). Praha, Státní nakladatelství krásné literatury a umění, 1963. 292 p. Illus. (Edice České dějiny, sv. 33)

A sensitive monograph on the world famous puppet film director and painter.

1322. Brousil, Antonín M. Česká hudba v českém filmu (Czech music in the Czech film). Praha, Petr, 1940. 43 p.

The author of two other minor film studies explores the function of music in the Czech film.

1323. Brož, Jaroslav, *and* Myrtil Frída. Historie československého filmu v obrazech (A history of Czechoslovak film in pictures). Praha, Orbis, 1959-1966. 2 v. Illus.

Volume 1 covers the period from 1898 to 1930; volume 2, the period from 1930 to 1945.

1324. Canadian Film Archives, *Ottawa.* New Face of the Czechoslovak Cinema. Ottawa, Canadian Film Institute, 1966. 20 p.

An introduction to a series of programs presented at Ottawa's National Film Theater in January 1966. Text is in English and French. For a recent English-language survey *see*:

Žalman, Jan. Films and Film-Making in Czechoslovakia. Translated by George Theiner. Prague, Orbis. 99 p. Illus.

1325. Film a doba (Motion picture and time). 1955– Praha. Monthly.

Critical and theoretical articles and discussions on film and film making.

1326. Gürtler, František. Malý filmový slovník (Concise film dictionary). Praha, Československé filmové nakladatelství, 1949. 433 p.

An encyclopedic work which includes outlines of the film history of many countries.

1327. Janoušek, Jiří, *ed.* Tři a půl (Three and a half). Praha, Orbis, 1965. 264 p.

Critical examinations of four young successful Czech film directors of the "new wave." Samples of their film scripts are included.

1328. Janoušek, Jiří, *ed.* Tři a půl podruhé (Three and a half for the second time). Praha, Orbis, 1967. 256 p.

Critical examinations of four more outstanding Czech film directors.

The two books by J. Janoušek give a fine picture of the successful Czech "new wave" movement.

1329. Kučera, Jan. Kniha o filmu (A book about film). Praha, Orbis, 1941. 225 p.

The first Czech film theory. Quite broad in scope, but its level is only elementary.

Boček, Jaroslav. Kapitoly o filmu (Chapters about cinematography). Praha, Orbis, 1968. 238 p.

1330. Ponděliček, Ivo. Film jako svět fantómů a mytů (Film as the world of phantoms and myths). Praha, Orbis, 1964. 208 p. Bibliography: p. 201-203.

A study of the effects of the cinema in its psychological and sociological aspects.

1331. Smrž, Karel. Dějiny filmu (A history of film). Praha, Družstevní práce, 1933. 781 p. Illus. (Orbis pictus, řídí Václav Poláček. Nová řada V) Bibliography: p. 14-16.

An extensive work covering Czech and international film production from both the technical and artistic viewpoints.

1332. Šteinerová, Svatava. Bibliografie dějin čs. fotografie a kinematografie (Bibliography of the history of Czechoslovak photography and cinematography). Praha, Nár. techn. muzeum, 1967. 259 p.

For a recent catalog of Czechoslovak films, *see*:

Bartosková, Šárka. Československý film, 1960-1965 (Czechoslovak films, 1960-1965). Praha, Filmový ústav, 1966. 2 v.

1333. Wolf, Steffen, *ed.* Der tschechoslowakische Film; eine Dokumentation. Mannheim, Verband der deutschen Filmclubs e. V., 1965. 156 p. Illus.

A brief outline of the history of the Czechoslovak cinema with emphasis on contemporary achievements.

PART THREE

EAST GERMANY

22

General Reference Aids and Bibliographies

by Arnold H. Price

A. BIBLIOGRAPHY

1. Bibliographies of Bibliographies

1334. Bibliographie der deutschen Bibliographien. v. 1– 1966– Leipzig, Verlag für Buch- und Bibliothekswesen. Monthly.

Prepared by the Deutsche Bücherei in Leipzig in continuation of its irregular serial with the same title (8 v., 1954-1964) and its *Bibliographie der versteckten Bibliographien* (1956, 371 p.), which covers the years 1930 to 1953. A useful guide to bibliographies appearing currently in German-language monographs and serials, often as parts of larger studies or articles. Entries are arranged by subject.

1335. Totok, Wilhelm, Rolf Weitzel, *and* Karl Heinz Weimann. Handbuch der bibliographischen Nachschlagewerke. 3d enl. and rev. ed. Frankfurt a. M., Klostermann, 1966. 362 p.

An annotated West German guide to bibliographical reference works, covering also non-German countries and providing information on all disciplines. An excellent introduction to German bibliographical reference works.

2. Bibliographies of Books

1336. Deutsche Nationalbibliographie. 1931– Leipzig, Verlag für Buch- und Bibliothekswesen.

Prepared by the Deutsche Bücherei in Leipzig as accession catalogs in two series: Reihe A, Neuerscheinungen des Buchhandels, issued weekly; Reihe B, Neuerscheinungen ausserhalb des Buchhandels, issued semimonthly. Each issue is indexed, and each series has quarterly cumulated indexes. Many of these entries are included in the *Jahresverzeichnis des deutschen Schrifttums* (1945/46– Leipzig, 1948–), an annual with an edition for each imprint year. These are cumulated quinquennially in the *Deutsches Bücherverzeichnis* (Leipzig, 1916–). Both are equipped with separate subject indexes.

A national bibliography, prepared by the East German depository library, it attempts to list all books and maps issued in Germany or in German. It also notes serials. Dissertations are included but are cumulated in the annual *Jahresverzeichnis der deutschen Hochschulschriften* (1885/86– Leipzig, Verlag für Buch- und Bibliothekswesen). Also issued by the Deutsche Bücherei are the specialized music and art bibliographies, the *Deutsche Musikbibliographie* (entry no. 1560), and *Bibliographie der Kunstblätter* (1907– Leipzig. Quarterly).

The East German national bibliography corresponds to the West German *Deutsche Bibliographie*, which is issued by the Deutsche Bibliothek in Frankfurt am Main and also covers both West and East German publications. Its organization is quite similar, except that it has semiannual cumulations.

1337. Leipziger Bücherkatalog. 1956/57– Leipzig, Deutscher Buch-Export und -Import. Annual.

A catalog of books in print, which limits itself to East German publications. A subject index is provided in a separate volume. For current reports on new books see *Vorankündigungsdienst der Verlage der Deutschen Demokratischen Republik*.

3. Bibliographies of Periodicals and Government Publications

1338. Childs, James B. German Democratic Republic Official Publications, With Those of the Preceding Zonal Period, 1945-1958; a Survey. Washington, D.C., Library of Congress, 1960-1961. 4 v.

"An operational document for limited distribution issued in an edition of 50 copies." A specialized guide to both monographs and serials but excluding local government publications. Entries are arranged by issuing agency.

1339. Deutsche Bibliographie; Zeitschriften-Verzeichnis. 1945/52– Frankfurt a. M., Buchhändler-Vereinigung, 1954– Quinquennial.

A West German bibliography of West and East German periodicals, prepared by the Deutsche Bibliothek in Frankfurt am Main as part of the national bibliography. Issued in two parts: Teil 1, Systematisches Titelverzeichnis; Teil 2, Register. Lists periodicals by subject and is particularly useful because of the detailed bibliographical descriptions it furnishes and because of its many, carefully prepared indexes.

1340. Internationale Bibliographie der Zeitschriftenliteratur aus allen Gebieten des Wissens. v. 1– 1965– Osnabrück, F. Dietrich. Semiannual.

Supersedes *Bibliographie der deutschen Zeitschriftenliteratur* (1896-1964) and *Bibliographie der fremdsprachigen Zeitschriftenliteratur* (1911-1964). The great, general German periodical index, analyzing well over 12,000 German and non-German serials and symposia. Entries are arranged by subject. Each volume includes a list of the serials analyzed and an author index.

1341. Postzeitungsliste für die Deutsche Demokratische Republik. 1949– Berlin, Ministerium für Post- und Fernmeldewesen. Annual.

Issued in two parts: Teil 1, Presseerzeugnisse der Deutschen Demokratischen Republik; Teil 2, Ausland. A list of newspapers and periodicals currently available for subscription in East Germany through the East German postal system.

4. Bibliographies on East Germany

1342. Novaia literatura po Germanskoi Demokraticheskoi Respublike (New literature on the German Democratic Republic) 1– 1962– Moskva. Monthly.

Prepared by the Fundamental Library on the Social Sciences of the Soviet Academy of Sciences, this useful bibliography contains references to books and articles, listed by subject, in West as well as in East European languages. Supersedes *Germanskaia Demokraticheskaia Respublika; bibliograficheskii ukazatel'* (German Democratic Republic, a bibliographical index) (Moskva, 1949-1961), issued annually by the All-Union State Library of Foreign Literature.

1343. U.S. *Library of Congress. Slavic and Central European Division.* East Germany: a Selected Bibliography. Compiled by Arnold H. Price. Washington, U.S. Govt. Print. Off., 1967, 133 p.

Lists books, articles, and journals dealing with East Germany, emphasizing publications since 1959. Designed as a convenient guide to serve American research and reference needs, it is in a way a sequel to Fritz T. Epstein's bibliography, which was published under the same auspices and with the same title in 1959 and on which it relies for earlier publications. For another useful bibliography see *Studien und Materialien zur Soziologie der DDR* (Köln, Westdeutscher Verlag, 1964), edited by Peter Christian Ludz as Sonderheft 8 of *Kölner Zeitschrift für Soziologie und Sozialpsychologie.*

B. REFERENCE AIDS

1. Handbooks, Encyclopedias, Statistical Reference Works

1344. American University, *Washington, D.C. Foreign Areas Studies Division.* Area Handbook for Germany. 2d ed. Washington, Headquarters, Dept. of the Army, 1964. 955 p. Illus., maps. (U.S. Dept. of the Army Pamphlet no. 550-29)

Organized by subject, this compendium deals with all of Germany but has special sections on East Germany in every chapter. It stresses subjects of current interest but also provides a wide, factual coverage supplemented by maps, charts, tables, and bibliographies. Directed toward the general reader rather than the scholar. There is no index.

1345. Berlin (*West Berlin*) *Büro für Gesamtberliner Fragen.* Berlin, Sowjetsektor; die politische, rechtliche, wirtschaftliche, soziale und kulturelle Entwicklung in acht Berliner Verwaltungsbezirken. Edited by Lieselotte Berger. Berlin, Colloquium Verlag, 1965. 227 p. Illus., maps, bibliographies.

A symposium covering various aspects of East Berlin, with contributions by well-known authorities. The factual presentation is supplemented by statistics, maps, and graphs. Of particular importance because of the special status of East Berlin. For additional information see Walter Krumholz' *Berlin-ABC* (1965, 586 p.), which offers wide coverage on both West and East Berlin in its alphabetically arranged topics.

1346. Deutsches Institut für Zeitgeschichte. Handbuch der Deutschen Demokratischen Republik. Berlin, Staatsverlag der Deutschen Demokratischen Republik, 1964. 910 p. Illus., maps, music, ports.

A broadly conceived handbook, designed largely to serve as a record of East German achievements. It is informative, however, providing many factual data as well as East German interpretations.

A similar work designed more for popular consumption is *DDR: 300 Fragen, 300 Antworten,* 6th rev. ed. (Berlin, Verlag Die Wirtschaft, 1965, 320 p.), issued by the official Ausschuss für Deutsche Einheit. This is also available in an English-language edition, *German Democratic Republic: 300 Questions, 300 Answers,* 5th ed. (Leipzig, Edition Leipzig, 1962, 193 p.).

No longer current but still useful among East German official handbooks is the *Jahrbuch der Deutschen Demokratischen Republik* (Berlin, Verlag Die Wirtschaft, 1956-1961), an annual report on East German developments which includes statistics, illustrations, maps, and lists of organizations.

1347. Germany (*Democratic Republic, 1949–*) *Staatliche Zentralverwaltung für Statistik.* Statistisches Jahrbuch der Deutschen Demokratischen Republik. v. 1– 1955– Berlin, Deutscher Zentralverlag. Annual.

Basic official East German statistical yearbook, with maps, graphs, and a subject index. A convenient English-language abridgment is the *Statistical Pocket Book of the German Democratic Republic* (Berlin, Deutscher Zentralverlag), issued annually by the same office since 1959.

1348. Herz, John H. Berlin and the Soviet Zone. *In* Carter, Gwendolen M., *and* John H. Herz. Major Foreign Powers. 4th ed. New York, Harcourt, Brace & World, 1962. p. 459-473.

A readable and knowledgeable survey of East Germany with special emphasis on the political and social forces. Well organized and equipped with a bibliography (p. 661).

1349. Meyers neues Lexikon. Leipzig, Bibliographisches Institut, 1961-1964. 8 v. Illus., maps, ports.

The leading East German encyclopedia, in design similar to earlier German reference works of this kind but reflecting East German ideological concepts. Useful as a compilation of data on East Germany but lacks bibliographical references.

The same publisher also issues an abridged version, the one-volume encyclopedia *A-Z* (also known as *Meyers Taschenlexikon A-Z*), the sixth edition of which was published in 1966 (1062 p.).

1350. SBZ von A bis Z. Bonn, Deutscher Bundesverlag, 1953– Irregular.

A basic and convenient reference work prepared by the West German Ministerium für Gesamtdeutsche Fragen. It has been issued almost annually, the 10th edition (1966) being the latest. The articles, which are alphabetically arranged, include bibliographical references; there is also an extensive bibliography. The work covers all aspects of East German developments and is indispensable for reference or research work on East Germany.

2. Periodicals

1351. Deutsche Fragen; Beiträge zur Situation im geteilten Deutschland zur Wiedervereinigung. Ausg. A. Published by the Untersuchungsausschuss Freiheitlicher Juristen. 1955– Berlin. Monthly.

An informative journal, published earlier under the title *Aus der Zone der Unrechts; Berichte aus Mitteldeutschland*, reporting on current East German developments. Contains signed articles, book reviews, chronology, and illustrations.

1352. SBZ-Archiv. 1950–68 Köln, Verlag für Politik und Wirtschaft. Semimonthly.

Started as *PZ-Archiv* and includes a supplement entitled *Sammlung von Gesetzen und Verordnungen aus der sowjetischen Besatzungszone Deutschlands.*

The leading journal on East German developments. Discusses current affairs and provides documented and signed articles, book reviews, and regular bibliographical surveys. Indexed annually. Superseded in 1968 by the monthly *Deutschland-Archiv* (Köln, Kiepenheuer & Witsch).

3. Biographies

1353. Directory of East German Officials. Washington, D.C., 1964. 221 p. (Biographic Reference Aid, BA64-3)

East German officials are listed by organization, including government agencies, political parties, mass organizations, and public media. Indexes of organizations and persons.

1354. Wer ist wer? 14th ed. Berlin, Arani, 1962-1965. 2 v.

The second volume of this traditional German reference work deals with East German personalities, listing almost 5,000 names. Provides brief, factual biographies which include publications.

Still useful is the *SBZ-Biographie*, a new edition of which (406 p.) was issued by the West German Bundesministerium für Gesamtdeutsche Fragen in Bonn in 1964.

C. GENERAL AND DESCRIPTIVE WORKS

1355. Dönhoff, Marion, *Gräfin*, Rudolf W. Leonhardt, *and* Theo Sommer. Reise in ein fernes Land. Bericht über Kultur, Wirtschaft und Politik in der DDR. Hamburg, Nannen-Verlag, 1964. 143 p.

See also entry no. 1532.

A sensitive assessment of East German life as seen through the eyes of three leading West German journalists on a 1964 trip.

1356. Hangen, Welles. The Muted Revolution; East Germany's Challenge to Russia and the West. New York, Knopf, 1966. 231 p. Illus., map, ports.

See also entry no. 1460.

A critical reappraisal of East Germany's changing role. Based largely on personal impressions and informal in organization, the work nevertheless tries to arrive at a new synthesis in interpreting the forces that determine the direction of East German developments.

1357. Koenigswald, Harald von. The Soviet Zone of Germany: Pictures of Everyday Life. Esslingen, Bechtle, 1959. 1 v. (chiefly illus.)

A pictorial account of various aspects of East German developments, including views not publicized by the communist press.

1358. Newman, Bernard. Behind the Berlin Wall. London, R. Hale, 1964. 187 p. Illus., maps.

A popular account of the East German scene, based largely on the author's travels. Provides background and basic data. For more recent accounts *see* Arthur M. Hanhardt's *The German Democratic Republic* (Baltimore, Johns Hopkins Press, 1968, 126 p.) and Jean Edward Smith's *Germany beyond the Wall* (Boston, Little, Brown, 1969, 338 p.).

1359. Richert, Ernst. Das zweite Deutschland; ein Staat der nicht sein darf. Gütersloh, S. Mohn, 1964. 341 p. Bibliographies.

See also entry no. 1473.

A popularized version of the author's scholarly studies on the East German regime. Addressed to the general reader but provides a solid and systematic survey of the communist system of government and its effects.

1360. Rühmland, Ullrich. Mitteldeutschland, "Moskaus westliche Provinz"; fünfzehn Jahre Sowjetzonenstaat. 2d ed. Bonn-Röttgen, Bonner Druck- und Verlagsgesellchaft, 1963. 328 p.

An informative and useful survey of all aspects of East German life, organized by subject. Provides a mass of data, but lacks both index and bibliography.

1361. Wechsberg, Joseph. Journey Through the Land of Eloquent Silence. Boston, Little, Brown, 1964. 146 p.

A readable and informative account of East Germany as seen through the eyes of a widely traveled observer.

For a more recent and challenging analysis of changing East German attitudes by another American traveler *see* Hans Apel's *DDR 1962, 1964, 1966* (Berlin, Voltaire Verlag, 1967, 412 p.).

D. LIBRARIES

1362. Berlin. Deutsche Staatsbibliothek. Deutsche Staatsbibliothek, 1661-1961. Leipzig, Verlag für Buch- und Bibliothekswesen, 1961. 2 v. Illus., ports., diagrs., facsims., tables.

A well-documented account of the leading German resarch library, providing a historical survey as well as insight into its current operations. The second volume is a bibliography of 2,038 items.

1363. Leipzig. Deutsche Bücherei. Deutsche Bücherei, 1912-1962. Festschrift zum fünfzigjährigen Bestehen der Deutschen Nationalbibliothek. Edited by Helmut Rötzsch, Gerhard Hesse, and Hans-Martin Plesske. Leipzig, Verlag für Buch- und Bibliothekswesen, 1962. 400 p. Illus., ports., facsims.

A carefully prepared survey of the history and present role of the East German depository library, which also serves as the country's bibliographical center. Contains a bibliography of 1,180 items.

1364. Thilo, Martin. Das Bibliothekswesen in der sowjetischen Besatzungszone Deutschlands. 2d rev. and enl. ed. Bonn, Bundesministerium für Gesamtdeutsche Fragen, 1965. 243 p.

A thorough and balanced account of the fate of East German libraries under communist rule, providing both facts and interpretation. Includes official regulations, a bibliography, and indexes.

For a directory of East German libraries, see *Jahrbuch der Bibliotheken, Archive und Dokumentationsstellen der Deutschen Demo-*

kratischen Republik, issued irregularly since 1959 by the Deutsche Staatsbibliothek, Berlin.

1365. Zentralblatt für Bibliothekswesen. v. 1– 1884– Leipzig, Bibliographisches Institut. Monthly.

Well-known German library journal of long standing, now the leading East German periodical for research libraries. Contains articles, book reviews, bibliographies, and news of current library developments. In recent years it has offered an annual supplement with details of the bibliographical works planned and in progress in East German libraries and documentation centers.

E. PRESS AND PUBLISHING

1366. Börsenblatt für den deutschen Buchhandel; Fachzeitschrift für Buchwesen und Buchhandel. 1834– Leipzig, Fachbuch Verlag. Weekly.

The chief German publishers' journal of long standing, now the main periodical of its kind in East Germany. Not to be confused with the West German serial of similar scope and title. Contains general articles and advertisements of current publications.

Its supplement entitled *Vorankündigungsdienst der Verlage der Deutschen Demokratischen Republik* announces forthcoming East German books.

1367. Herrmann, Elisabeth M. Zur Theorie und Praxis der Presse in der sowjetischen Besatzungszone Deutschlands; Berichte und Dokumente. Berlin, Colloquium Verlag, 1963. 158 p. Bibliographical notes: p. 145-157. (Abhandlungen und Materialien zur Publizistik, Bd. 2)

A penetrating analysis of the role of the East German press. This work and her earlier *Die Presse in der sowjetischen Besatzungszone Deschlands* (Bonn, Bundesministerium für Gesamtdeutsche Fragen, 1957, 163 p.), which is more factual in approach, constitute the best studies on the East German press, including the periodical press.

1368. Verband der Deutschen Journalisten. Journalistisches Handbuch der Deutschen Demokratischen Republik. Leipzig, Verlag für Buch- und Bibliothekswesen, 1960. 488 p. Illus.

A descriptive and factual account of the East German press. Designed as a reference work for the East German journalist. Lists newspapers and periodicals and includes an extensive bibliography (p. 308-369).

23

the land

by Chauncy D. Harris

A. PHYSICAL OR REGIONAL GEOGRAPHY OF GERMANY AS A WHOLE

1369. Braun, Gustav. Deutschland, dargestellt auf Grund eigener Beobachtung, der Karten und der Literatur. 2d rev. ed. Berlin, Gebrüder Borntraeger, 1936. 926 p. Plate, maps (part fold.). Bibliographies.

Detailed regional geography with descriptions of *Landschaften*. Good bibliographies. Numerous detailed maps.

1370. Deutschland: die natürlichen Grundlagen seiner Kultur. Herausgegeben von der Kaiserlich Leopold. Deutschen Akademie der Naturforscher zu Halle. Leipzig, Quelle & Meyer, 1928. 361 p., Illus., maps, profiles, diagrs. Bibliographies.

Systematic examination of the geology, climate, waters, minerals, vegetation, and settlement of Germany, by specialists in each field.

1371. Dickinson, Robert E. Germany: a General and Regional Geography. 2d ed. London, Methuen, 1964. 716 p. Illus., maps. Bibliography: p. 682-702.

The most detailed geographical treatment of Germany in English. Includes both topical material on the lands, peoples, habitat, economy, and historical-political structure on one hand and detailed regional analyses and descriptions on the other.

1372. Elkins, Thomas Henry. Germany. London, Christophers, 1960. 272 p. Illus.

Best brief introduction in English to the geography of Germany.

1373. Gellert, Johannes Fürchtegott. Grundzüge der physischen Geographie von Deutschland. v. 1. Geologische Struktur und Oberflächengestaltung. Berlin, VEB Deutscher Verlag der Wissenschaften, 1958. 492 p. Illus., maps (part fold.), facsims. Bibliography: p. 439-453.

Detailed examination of geology and surface configuration.

1374. Germany (*Federal Republic, 1949–*) *Bundesanstalt für Landeskunde.* Handbuch der naturräumlichen Gliederung Deutschlands. Remagen, 1953-1962. 2 v. Maps (part fold., 1 col. in pocket). Bibliography.

Thorough original descriptions of the areal structure of Germany by natural regions, produced through the collaboration of nearly a hundred geographers from both the Federal Republic of Germany and the German Democratic Republic and edited by Emil Meynen and J. Schmithüsen. Includes an index.

1375. Haefke, Fritz. Physische Geographie Deutschlands; eine Einführung mit Betonung der Geomorphologie. Berlin, VEB Deutscher Verlag der Wissenschaften, 1959. 357 p. Illus., maps (part col.). Bibliography: p. 348-357.

A regional physical geography. The section on northern Germany is by Margot Sander and Hella-Maria Kinzel.

1376. Handbuch der geographischen Wissenschaft. . . *Edited* by Fritz Klute. Potsdam, Akademische Verlagsgesellschaft Athenaion, 1940-1950. Illus., plates, maps.

For a well-illustrated regional geography, *see* volume 4:

Brandt, Bernhard. Das Deutsche Reich in Natur, Kultur und Wirtschaft. 2 pts. (698 p.).

1377. Krebs, Norbert, *ed.* Landeskunde von Deutschland. Leipzig und Berlin, B. G. Teubner, 1931-1935. 3 v. Illus., maps, plates.

Band 1, Der Nordwesten, by Hans Schrepfer. 1935, 279 p. Band 2, Der Nordosten, by Bernhard Brandt. 1931, 148 p. Band 3, Der Südwesten, by Norbert Krebs. 2d ed. 1931, 219 p. Detailed regional geography.

1378. Maull, Otto. Deutschland. Leipzig, Bibliographisches Institut, 1933. 542 p. Plates, maps (part fold.). (Allgemeine Länderkunde)

A balanced regional geography.

B. PHYSICAL GEOGRAPHY OF THE GERMAN DEMOCRATIC REPUBLIC

1379. Germany (*Democratic Republic, 1949–*) *Meteorologischer und Hydrologischer Dienst.* Klima-Atlas für das Gebiet der Deutschen

Demokratischen Republik. Berlin, Akademie-Verlag, 1953. 75 leaves, 64 col. maps, diagrs. "Erläuterungen" in pocket, 19 p.

1380. Matz, Rudolf. Agraratlas über das Gebiet der Deutschen Demokratischen Republik. 1. Bodenarten und bodenartliche Ertragsbedingungen nach den Ergebnissen der Bodenschätzung. Gotha, Hermann Haack, 1956. 4 p. 67 maps (col.)

See also entry no. 1513.

Published under the auspices of Deutsche Akademie der Landwirtschaftswissenschaften zu Berlin, Institut für Agrarökonomik, and based on a detailed 1948-1954 field survey, this atlas presents six different aspects of soil types and utilization in ten sheets on a scale of 1:250,000. Supplemented by a volume entitled *Erläuterungen und Ortsverzeichnis* and by six survey maps on a scale of 1:750,000 summarizing the basic presentations. Limited to agricultural land.

1381. Schultze, Joachim Heinrich, *and others.* Die naturbedingten Landschaften der Deutschen Demokratischen Republik. Gotha, Geographisch-Kartographische Anstalt, 1955. 329 p. (Petermanns geographische Mitteilungen, Ergänzunsheft 257)

The natural regions (physical geographic landscapes) and their soils, hydrology, climate, and vegetation.

1382. Stremme, Hermann. Die Böden der Deutschen Demokratischen Republik; Einführung in die biogenetische Bodenkunde und ihre Nutzanwendung. Berlin, Deutscher Zentralverlag, 1950. 175 p. Illus., maps (1 fold. col. in pocket). Bibliography: p. 173-175.

The characteristics of the 13 major soil types with maps of distribution, discussions of productivity, and practical utilization.

C. ECONOMIC GEOGRAPHY OF THE GERMAN DEMOCRATIC REPUBLIC

1383. Mukhin, Aleksandr Ivanovich. Germanskaia Demokraticheskaia Respublika; ekonomicheskaia geografiia (German Democratic Republic; economic geography). 2d ed. Moskva, Institut mezhdunarodnykh otnoshenii, 1962. 225 p.

Discussion of the economy as a whole by branches and of economic regions, with a statistical supplement. First published in 1957.

1384. Schmidt-Renner, Gerhard, *ed.* Wirtschaftsterritorium Deutsche Demokratische Republik; ökonomisch-geographische Einführung und Übersicht. 3d ed. Berlin, Verlag die Wirtschaft, 1962. 483 p. Illus., maps. Bibliography: p. 459-470.

See also entry no. 1499.

Detailed study of the principal branches of industry and of the economic regions (*Bezirke*) by a group of authors from the Institut für

Ökonomische Geographie und Regionalplanung of the Hochschule für Ökonomie in Berlin. First published in 1959.

1385. Zhirmunskii, Mikhail Matveevich, *and others.* Germaniia: ekonomicheskaia geografiia Germanskoi Demokraticheskoi Respubliki i Federativnoi Respubliki Germanii (Germany: economic geography of the German Democratic Republic and the Federal Republic of Germany). Moskva, Izdatel'stvo Akademii nauk SSSR, 1959. 708 p.

Published under the auspices of Akademiia Nauk SSSR, Institut Geografii. The economic geography of the German Democratic Republic is treated on pages 289-452. Systematic examination of the population, manufacturing, agriculture, transport, and foreign economic relations. Produced by a group of specialists at the Institute of Geography of the Academy of Sciences of the USSR.

D. GAZETTEERS

1386. Krupkat, Werner G., *ed.* Ortslexikon der Deutschen Demokratischen Republik. 2d ed. Berlin, Deutscher Zentralverlag, 1958. 384 p. Map.

The official gazetteer.

1387. U.S. *Office of Geography.* Germany: Soviet Zone and East Berlin; Official Standard Names Approved by the United States Board on Geographic Names. Washington, D.C., U.S. Govt. Print. Off., 1959. 487 p. (U.S. Board on Geographic Names Gazetteer no. 43)

40,000 names with latitude, longitude, political unit in which located, and type of feature (such as populated place, forest, or hill).

E. SERIALS

1388. Geographische Berichte. 1– 1956– Gotha, VEB Hermann Haack. Quarterly. (Geographische Gesellschaft der Deutschen Demokratischen Republik. Mitteilungen)

The official organ of the Geographical Society of the German Democratic Republic. Articles range from physical geography to economic geography. Geographical notes.

1389. Geographisches Taschenbuch und Jahrweiser für Landeskunde. 1949– Wiesbaden. Biennial.

Rich source of bibliographies, lists of geographical and related institutes with personnel, biographical information on German geographers, and short articles.

1390. Leipzig. Deutsches Institut für Länderkunde. Wissenschaftliche Veröffentlichungen. Heft 1-13 (1896-1914). Neue Folge, 1–, 1932– Irregular.

Title of publisher varies. Formerly Abteilung für (vergleichende)

Länderkunde of the Museum für Völkerkunde and later Museum für Länderkunde. 1-13 issued as *Veröffentlichungen*. Scholarly monographs and articles. *See* especially n. F. 21/22, 1964, 73 p., devoted mainly to the Leipzig region.

1391. Petermanns geographische Mitteilungen. 1– 1855– Gotha, VEB Hermann Haack. Quarterly.

One of the oldest and most respected international scholarly geographical periodicals. Long and short articles. News. Reviews. Statistics. Cartography. Many issues include a pocket with separate plates and maps, often folded and in color.

1392. Zeitschrift für den Erdkundeunterricht. 1– 1949– Berlin, Volk und Wissen Volkseigener Verlag. Monthly.

Devoted mainly to the problems of teaching geography in the schools of the German Democratic Republic. Contains useful short articles on contemporary policies and geography of the country.

F. BIBLIOGRAPHY

1393. Berichte zur Deutschen Landeskunde. 1– 1941– Bad Godesberg, Bundesanstalt für Landeskunde und Raumforschung. 2 v. per annum, each of 2 nos.

The "Neues Schriftum" and "Kartenneuerscheinungen," which are separately paged appendixes to each issue, provide detailed bibliographies of new publications each six months region by region for all parts of Germany.

24

the people

by Arnold H. Price

A. DEMOGRAPHIC ASPECTS

1394. Berlin. *Statistisches Amt.* Die Ergebnisse der Volkszählung vom 29. Oktober 1946 für Gross-Berlin. Berlin, Verlag Das Neue Berlin, 1948. 64 p. (Berliner Statistik, Sonderheft 6)

Provides extensive and detailed demographic data from the 1946 German census on East Berlin. Supplemented by *Die Ergebnisse der Berufszählung vom 29. Oktober 1946 für Gross-Berlin* (Berlin, Verlag Das Neue Berlin, 1949, 79 p. [Berliner Statistik, Sonderheft 7]), which gives the manpower statistics of the same census for Berlin, but only general data on East Berlin. For East Berlin data from the 1945 census see *Ergebnisse der Volks- und Berufszählung in Berlin am 12. August 1945* (Berlin, Verlag Das Neue Berlin, 1948, 72 p. [Berliner Statistik, Sonderheft 5]).

1395. Die Bevölkerungsbilanz der sowjetischen Besatzungszone, 1939 bis 1954. Bonn, Bundesministerium für Gesamtdeutsche Fragen, 1954. 51 p.

A brief analysis of the East German population development, supplemented by 22 statistical tables.

1396. Germany (*Territory under Allied Occupation, 1945-1955. Russian Zone*) *Statistisches Zentralamt.* Volks- und Berufszählung vom 29.

Oktober 1946 in der sowjetischen Besatzungszone Deutschlands. Berlin, Deutsche Zentralverlag, 1948-49. 4 v.

V. 1: Amtliches Gemeindeverzeichnis; v. 2: Gemeindestatistik; v. 3: Landes- und Kreisstatistik; v. 4: Sowjetische Besatzungszone. This census published by the statistical office of the Deutsche Wirtschaftskommission of the Soviet zone is the broadest recent survey available for this area. The data, which include statistics on age, sex, 1939 residence, nationality, mother tongue, country of birth, family status, religious affiliation, social position, and type of employment, are broken down by state (*Land*) and some even by county (*Kreis*). For the first postwar census see *Die Volkszählung vom. 1. Dezember 1945 in der sowjetischen Besatzungszone Deutschlands* (Berlin, Deutscher Zentralverlag, 1946, 46 p.). For the corresponding data on East Berlin *see* entry no. 1394 above.

1397. Germany (*Democratic Republic, 1949–*) *Staatliche Zentralverwaltung für Statistik.* Wohnbevölkerung nach Geschlecht, Alter und Gebiet am 31. Dezember 1964. Berlin, 1965. 305 p.

Contains some of the data from the 1964 census.

1398. Germany. (*Democratic Republic, 1949–*) *Staatliche Zentralverwaltung für Statistik. Abteilung Bevölkerung und Kulturell-Soziale Bereiche der Volkswirtschaft.* Bevölkerungsstatistisches Jahrbuch der Deutschen Demokratischen Republik. 1965– Berlin. Annual.

Contains a systematic statistical survey of the East German population structure and of the demographic trends of the postwar period. Volume 1 uses 1964 census as well as earlier data.

1399. Germany (*Federal Republic, 1949–*) *Bundesministerium für Gesamtdeutsche Fragen.* Die Flucht aus der Sowjetzone und die Sperrmassnahmen des kommunistischen Regimes vom 13. August 1961 in Berlin. 2d rev. ed. Bonn, 1961. 159 p.

A West German official account of the flight of millions of East Germans to the West between 1949 and 1961. This work is also available in an English-language version, entitled *The Flights from the Soviet Zone and the Sealing-off Measures of the Communist Regime of 13th August 1961 in Berlin* (Bonn, 1961, 77 p.).

1400. Kabermann, Heinz. Die Bevölkerung des sowjetischen Besatzungsgebietes; Bestands- und Strukturveränderungen, 1950-1957. Published by the Bundesministerium für Gesamtdeutsche Fragen. Bonn, 1961. 143 p.

A basic and comprehensive study undertaken under the auspices of the West German government.

B. MANPOWER

1401. Baum, Samuel, *and* Jerry W. Combs. The Labor Force of the Soviet Zone of Germany and the Soviet Sector of Berlin. Washington, D.C.,

U.S. Govt. Print. Off., 1959. 30 p. (U.S. Bureau of the Census. International Population Statistics Reports. Series P-90, no. 11)

A thorough and competent analysis, replete with statistical tables and a discussion of future trends.

1402. Die Entwicklung der Beschäftigung in Mitteldeutschland seit 1960. *In* Berlin. Deutsches Institut für Wirtschaftsforschung. Wochenbericht, v. 33, Nov. 4, 1966: 207-210.

Brings the report contained in the next entry up to date on the basis of the 1964 census data.

1403. Mitzscherling, Peter. Zur Entwicklung der sozialen Struktur der mitteldeutschen Bevölkerung. Vierteljahrshefte zur Wirtschaftsforschung, v. 31, no. 3, 1964: 281-295.

A competent analysis of East German demographic trends with particular emphasis on manpower problems. Statistical tables are provided. Continued by preceding entry.

1404. Rexin, Manfred. Veränderungen der Berufs- und Beschäftigtenstruktur und Probleme der Arbeitskräftelenkung in der DDR. *In* Studien und Materialien zur Soziologie der DDR. Edited by Peter Christian Ludz. Köln, Westdeutscher Verlag, 1964. p. 59-85. (Kölner Zeitschrift für Soziologie und Sozialpsychologie, Sonderheft 8)

A competent analysis.

1405. Stolper, Wolfgang F. The Labor Force and Industrial Development in Soviet Germany. Quarterly Journal of Economics, v. 71, November 1957: 518-545.

A well-reasoned analysis by a leading American expert in the field of East German economic studies.

1406. Storbeck, Dietrich. Arbeitskraft und Beschäftigung in Mitteldeutschland; eine Untersuchung des Arbeiterkräftepotentials und der Beschäftigung von 1950 bis 1965. Köln, Westdeutscher Verlag, 1961. 104 p. Statistical tables: p. 89-101. (Dortmunder Schriften zur Sozialforschung, Bd. 18)

This statistical analysis stresses the regional development and points to the continuing problems of mobilizing manpower resources in spite of a greater utilization than in the prewar period.

C. ETHNOLOGICAL ASPECTS

1407. Deutsches Jahrbuch für Volkskunde. 1– 1955– Berlin, Akademie-Verlag. Semiannual.

This journal published by the Institute für Deutsche Volkskunde of the Deutsche Akademie der Wissenschaften in Berlin does not limit itself to East German phenomena, but also reports on meetings and reviews current publications. Emphasis is on folklore.

1408. Seraphim, Peter Heinz. Die Heimatvertriebenen in der Sowjetzone. Berlin, Duncker & Humblot, 1954. 202 p. (Schriften des Vereins für Sozialpolitik, Gesellschaft für Wirtschafts- und Sozialwissenschaften, n.F., Bd. 7/I)

Replete with maps and graphs, this work is mostly a statistical analysis, but it does provide a demographic and social profile of the expellees in East Germany, who as a group constitute a large and more or less ethnologically differentiated segment of the population.

25

history

by Lyman H. Legters

A. GENERAL

1409. Albrecht, Günter, *ed.* Dokumente zur Staatsordnung der Deutschen Demokratischen Republik. Introduction by Herbert Kröger. Berlin, Deutscher Zentralverlag, 1959. 2 v.

A compendious East German collection of documentation on both the Soviet occupation and the East German regime up to 1958.

1410. Berlin. Institut für Marxismus-Leninismus. Wir sind die Kraft; der Weg zur Deutschen Demokratischen Republik; Erinnerungen. v. 1. Berlin, Dietz, 1959. Illus.

A symposium by various East German leaders relating their impressions of the 1945-49 period.

1411. Doernberg, Stefan. Kurze Geschichte der DDR. 3d rev. ed. Berlin, Dietz, 1968. 736 p. Illus., ports. Bibliography: p. 697-702.

Written by an East German historian, this work is designed for the general public.

1412. Duhnke, Horst. Stalinismus in Deutschland; die Geschichte der sowjetischen Besatzungszone. Köln, Verlag für Politik und Wirtschaft, 1955. 375 p.

See also entry no. 1458.

A West German account in considerable detail of the Soviet occupation and the early years of the East German Republic. For a French interpretation *see*:

Castellan, Georges. La République Démocratique Allemande (R.D.A.). Paris, Presses Universitaires de France, 1961. 126 p.

1413. Frank, Henning. 20 Jahre Zone; kleine Geschichte der "DDR."

München, Wilhelm Goldmann Verlag, 1965. 208 p. Maps. Bibliography: p. 196-198.

Although cursory in treatment, this is the only up-to-date history of East Germany written from a Western viewpoint. A corresponding treatment from an East German point of view may be found in the book by Stefan Doernberg (*see* entry 1411).

1414. Germany (*Federal Republic, 1949–*) *Bundesministerium für Gesamtdeutsche Fragen.* SBZ von 1945 bis 1954. Die sowjetische Besatzungszone Deutschlands in den Jahren 1945-1954. Bonn, Deutscher Bundes-Verlag, 1956. 361 p. Maps, diagrs.

A chronological survey of all events in East Germany, each item presented in capsule summary. Further volumes have been issued for the following periods: 1955-1956 (1958, 255 p.), 1957-1958 (1960, 370 p.), and 1959-1960 (1964, 317 p.). The same office has published *SBZ von A bis Z; ein Taschen- und Nachschlagebuch über die sowjetische Besatzungszone Deutschlands* (10th ed., Bonn, Deutscher Bundes-Verlag, 1966, 605 p.).

1415. Hartmann, Frederick. Germany between East and West; the Reunification Problem. Englewood Cliffs, N.J., Prentice-Hall, 1965. 181 p. Bibliography: p. 175-176.

A recent study of the diplomatic problem posed by the confrontation of East and West Germany, with a useful recapitulation of the diplomatic background. A more specialized study of the background is:

Snell, John L. Wartime Origins of the East-West Dilemma over Germany. New Orleans, Hauser Press, 1959. 268 p.

1416. Hubatsch, Walther. Die deutsche Frage. 2d enl. ed. Würzburg, Ploetz, 1964. 348 p. Maps. Bibliography: p. 305-326.

A convenient reference work.

1417. Lukas, Richard. Zehn Jahre sowjetische Besatzungszone; Politik, Wirtschaft, Kultur, Rechtswesen. Mainz-Gonsenheim, Deutscher Fachschriften-Verlag, 1955. 215 p. Illus., map. Bibliography: p. 211-212.

See also entry no. 1468.

A useful and factual survey of East German developments up to 1954. The work has a general section, as well as chapters dealing with political parties, the economy, education, and so forth.

1418. Nettl, J. P. The Eastern Zone and Soviet Policy in Germany, 1945-50. London, New York, Oxford University Press, 1951. 324 p. Maps, diagrs., bibliographical footnotes.

See also entry no. 1470.

The fullest account in English of the Soviet occupation in East Germany, giving particular attention to the restoration of administration and the economy. Broader coverage for a longer period but without comparable depth may be found in the work by Richard Lukas (*see* entry no. 1417).

1419. Stulz, Percy, *ed.* Die Deutsche Demokratische Republik auf dem Wege zum Sozialismus. Berlin, Volk und Wissen, 1959-61. 2 v. Illus.

An East German selection of documents illustrating the history of the Soviet zone since 1945.

1420. Zeitschrift für Geschichtswissenschaft. 1– Jahrg.; 1953– Berlin, Rütten und Loening. Monthly.

The principal journal of the historical profession in East Germany; it has had a high frequency of contributions dealing with recent German history and with modern Europe generally in the framework of the prevailing ideology.

B. HISTORIOGRAPHY

1421. Fischer, Alexander. Der Weg zur Gleichschaltung der sowjetzonalen Geschichtswissenschaft, 1945-1949. Vierteljahrshefte für Zeitgeschichte, 10. Jahrg., April 1962: 149-177.

1422. Hamburg. Universität. *Collegium Politicum.* Geschichtswissenschaftler in Mitteldeutschland. Bonn, F. Dümmler, 1964. 100 p.

A biographical reference book.

1423. Kopp, Fritz. Die Wendung zur "nationalen" Geschichtsbetrachtung in der Sowjetzone. 2d ed. München, G. Olzog, n.d. 120 p. "Verzeichnis der wichtigsten Schriften der SBZ zur 'nationalen Geschichtsbetrachtung' ": p. 119-120.

A study of the introduction of an ostensibly national viewpoint into the reinterpretation of German history by East German scholarship. *See also*:

Timm, Albrecht. Das Fach Geschichte in Forschung und Lehre in der sowjetischen Besatzungszone seit 1945. 4th enl. ed. Bonn, Deutscher Bundesverlag, 1965. 195 p.

Rauch, G. v. Das Geschichtsbild der Sowjetzone. Jahrbuch der Ranke-Gesellschaft, 1954: p. 101-119.

1424. Lücke, Peter R. Sowjetzonale Hochschulschriften aus dem Gebiet der Geschichte, 1946-1963. Bonn, 1965, 98 p.

A bibliography of 726 doctoral dissertations and habilitation works in history prepared in East Germany during the period.

1425. Riese, Werner. Geschichtswissenschaft und Parteiauftrag; zur Situation der Geschichtswissenschaft in der "DDR." Bremen, C. Schünemann, 1966. 200 p.

Assesses the impact of the SED party line on the discipline of history and the importance of historical scholarship to the regime.

C. SPECIAL ASPECTS

1426. Baring, Arnulf. Der 17. Juni 1953. 2d ed. Foreword by Richard Lowenthal. Köln, Berlin, Kiepenheuer und Witsch, 1965. 184 p.

See also entry no. 1452.

The most critical available treatment of the East German rising. Useful supplements include:

Leithäuser, Joachim G., *ed.* Der Aufstand im Juni; ein dokumentarischer Bericht. Berlin, Grunewald Verlag, 1954. 55 p.

Brant, Stefan, *pseud.* (Klaus Harpprecht). Der Aufstand; Vorgeschichte, Geschichte und Deutung des 17. Juni 1953. Stuttgart, Steingrüben, 1954. 324 p.

The latter also appeared in an English translation, *The East German Rising* (New York, Praeger, 1957, 202 p.).

1427. Clay, Lucius D. Decision in Germany. New York, Doubleday, 1950. 522 p. Illus., ports., maps.

A memoir account of the confrontation between the Western and the Soviet occupations, culminating in the Berlin blockade. *See also*:

Howley, Frank L. Berlin Command. New York, Putnam, 1950. 276 p.

Davison, Walter Phillips. The Berlin Blockade: a Study in Cold War Politics. Princeton, N. J., Princeton University Press, 1958. 423 p. Illus., ports., maps. Bibliographical notes: p. 393-415.

1428. Bohn, Helmut, *ed.* Ideologie und Aufrüstung in der Sowjetzone; Dokumente und Materialien. Köln, Markus Verlag, 1956. 241 p.

This collection of official documents and utterances forms an account of remilitarization in East Germany, including the justifications drawn by East German officials from German history as well as from the revolutionary tradition.

1429. Finn, Gerhard. Die politischen Häftlinge der Sowjetzone, 1945-1959. Pfaffenhofen, Ilmgauverlag, 1960. 243 p. Illus.

A factual account of Soviet and East German concentration camps and political prisons in the Soviet zone up to 1958.

1430. Fricke, Karl Wilhelm. Selbstbehauptung und Widerstand in der sowjetischen Besatzungszone Deutschlands. Bonn, 1964. 191 p. Bibliography: p. 186-[192].

See also entry no. 1554.

Reviews the several phases of opposition encountered by the Ulbricht regime since its inception within East Germany.

1431. Galante, Pierre. The Berlin Wall. Garden City, N.Y., Doubleday, 1965. 277 p.

See also the earlier works:

Heaps, Willard A. The Wall of Shame. New York, Duell, Sloan and Pearce, 1964. 175 p.

Heller, Deane, *and* David Heller. The Berlin Wall. New York, Walker, 1962. 242 p. Illus.

1432. Germany (*Federal Republic, 1949–*) *Bundesministerium für Gesamtdeutsche Fragen.* The Compulsory Collectivization of Independent Farms in the Soviet Zone of Occupation in Germany. Bonn, 1960. 121 p. Illus., facsims.

This account, which is based on a larger German study, describes the socialization of the last major group of entrepreneurs in East Germany. For the earlier fate of craft shops *see* Bartho Plönies and Otto Schönwalder's *Die Sowjetisierung des mitteldeutschen Handwerks* (Bonn, Bundesministerium für Gesamtdeutsche Fragen, 1953, 134 p.), and for that of commercial enterprises *see* Felix Pöhler's *Der Untergang des privaten Einzelhandels in der sowjetischen Besatzungszone* (Bonn, 1952, 63 p.), as well as his *Die Vernichtung des privaten Grosshandels in der sowjetischen Besatzungszone* (Bonn, Bundesministerium für Gesamtdeutsche Fragen, 1952, 88 p.).

1433. Klimov, Gregory. Terror Machine; the Inside Story of the Soviet Administration in Germany. New York, Praeger, 1953. 400 p.

One of the rare items of memoir literature on the inner workings of the Soviet occupation. Some insights are added by the recollections of a German refugee, Lali Horstman, *We Chose To Stay* (New York, Houghton, 1954, 206 p.), and Fritz Löwenthal's *News from Soviet Germany* (London, Gollancz, 1950, 343 p.).

1434. Koenen, Wilhelm. Das ganze Deutschland soll es sein; zur Geschichte der patriotischen Bewegung in Deutschland. Berlin, Kongress-Verlag, 1958. 430 p. Illus.

A survey of the background and history of the "national" movement in East Germany.

1435. Kraus, Herbert. Die Oder-Neisse-Linie; eine völkerrechtliche Studie. Köln-Braunsfeld, R. Müller, 1954. 47 p. (Osteuropa und der deutsche Osten, Beiträge aus Forschungsarbeiten und Vorträgen der Hochschulen des Landes Nordrhein-Westfalen. Reihe 1: Rheinische Friedrich-Wilhelms-Universität Bonn)

A review of the international legal background surrounding the boundary between East Germany and Poland. *See also*:

Rhode, Gotthold *and* Wolfgang Wagner, *eds.* Quellen zur Entstehung der Oder-Neisse-Linie. 2d enl. ed. Stuttgart, Brentano-Verlag, 1959. 331 p. (Die deutschen Ostgebiete, ein Handbuch, Bd. 3)

1436. Krieg, Harald. LDP und NDP in der "DDR" 1949-1958. Ein Beitrag zur Geschichte der nichtsozialistischen Parteien und ihrer Gleichschaltung mit der SED. Köln und Opladen, Westdeutscher Verlag, 1965. 77 p. Bibliography: p. 62-64. "Anmerkungen" (bibliographical): p. 65-77.

A brief account of two nonsocialist parties, partly tolerated and partly exploited by the regime, with emphasis on the role they came to play after the East German government was established.

1437. Krippendorff, Ekkehart. Die Liberal-Demokratische Partei Deutschlands in der sowjetischen Besatzungszone, 1945/48; Entstehung, Struktur, Politik. Düsseldorf, Droste, 1961. 178 p. (Beiträge zur Geschichte des Parlamentarismus und der politischen Parteien, Bd. 21)

See also entry no. 1467.

A monograph on the founding and early years of the Liberal Party before it was completely subjected to the manipulation of the regime.

1438. Richert, Ernst. Aus der Praxis totalitärer Lenkung; die politische Entwicklung im Kreis Schmalkalden, 1945-1949. *In* Gurland, Arcadius R. L., *ed.* Faktoren der Machtbildung. Berlin, Duncker und Humblot, 1952. p. 162-187. (Schriften des Instituts für Politische Wissenschaft, Bd. 2)

An illuminating case study of communist political manipulation of a small district during the early years of occupation.

1439. Rosenthal, Walther, *and others.* Die Justiz in der sowjetischen Besatzungszone Deutschlands. 4th enl. ed. Bonn, Deutscher Bundes-Verlag, 1959. 205 p.

Relates the development of a new legal system in East Germany, Rosenthal dealing with its organization, Lange with criminal law, and Blomeyer with civil law.

1440. Scheurig, Bodo, *ed.* Verrat hinter Stacheldraht? Das Nationalkomitee "Freies Deutschland" und der Bund Deutscher Offiziere in der Sowjetunion, 1943-1945. München, Deutscher Taschenbuch Verlag, 1965. 285 p.

A collection of documents important for the "prehistory" of the German Democratic Republic, with an interpretive introduction based on the author's earlier monograph, *Freies Deutschland; das Nationalkomitee und der Bund Deutscher Offiziere in der Sowjetunion 1943-1945* (München, Nymphenburger Verlagshandlung, 1960, 268 p.).

1441. Siegler, Heinrich, *Freiherr* von. Wiedervereinigung und Sicherheit Deutschlands; eine dokumentarische Diskussionsgrundlage. 5th rev. ed. Bonn, Siegler, 1964. 381 p. Maps.

Covers the diplomatic history of postwar Germany with emphasis on the problem of reunification, presenting extensive quotations from official documents. The same author's collection of documents, *Dokumentation zur Deutschlandfrage; von der Atlantik-Charta, 1941 bis zur Berlin-Sperre 1961* (2d rev. and enl. ed. Bonn, Siegler, 1961, 3 v.) affords valuable amplification.

1442. Stern, Carola, *pseud.* Ulbricht; eine politische Biographie. Köln, Kiepenheuer und Witsch, 1963. 356 p. Illus., ports. Bibliography: p. 347-350.

See also entry no. 1483.

A study of the career of Walter Ulbricht covering his activity before and during the Second World War, as well as his role in postwar East Germany. The most instructive comparisons are with some of Ulbricht's own writings, notably *Die Entwicklung des deutschen volksdemokratischen Staates, 1945-1958* (Berlin, Dietz, 1958, 691 p.), and *Zur sozialistischen Entwicklung der Volkswirtschaft seit 1945* (Berlin, Dietz, 1959, 796 p.).

26

the state

by Melvin Croan

A. GOVERNMENT AND POLITICS

1. Sources

1443. Germany (*Democratic Republic, 1949–) Constitution.* Die Verfassung der sowjetischen Besatzungszone Deutschlands. Edited and with commentary by Siegfried Mampel. Frankfurt am Main, A. Metzner, 1962. 452 p.

The text of East Germany's Constitution (1949) with extensive commentary on each and every article of that constitution. Often legalistic in tone but nonetheless valuable for an appreciation of the gap between constitutional doctrinal and political practice in the German Democratic Republic.

1444. Germany (*Democratic Republic, 1949–) Volkskammer.* Handbuch. 1957– Berlin, Kongress-Verlag.

Contains the text of laws pertaining to the Volkskammer and biographic data on members of that body as well as other related material. Latest edition bears the title *Die Volkskammer der Deutschen Demokratischen Republik: 4. Wahlperiode* (Berlin, Staatsverlag der Deutschen Demokratischen Republik, 1964, 1007 p.).

1445. Germany (*Federal Republic, 1949–) Bundesministerium für Gesamtdeutsche Fragen.* Die Wahlen in der Sowjetzone; Dokumente und Materialien. 6th enl. ed. Bonn, Deutscher Bundes-Verlag, 1964. 218 p.

Chronological coverage of the major elections in East Germany, together with selections from relevant documents, all designed to show how East German elections have violated democratic norms.

1446. Riklin, Alois. Selbstzeugnisse des SED-Regimes. Köln, Verlag Wissenschaft und Politik, 1963. 211 p.

Contains the texts of three major SED documents: The "National Document," of 1962, the 1963 SED Party Program, and the 1963 SED Party Statutes, together with detailed critical commentaries by the two editors.

1447. Sozialistische Einheitspartei Deutschlands. Dokumente; Beschlüsse und Erklärungen des ZK sowie seines Politbüros und seines Sekretariats. v. 1– 1951– Berlin, Dietz.

An indispensable primary source. Unfortunately, volumes 1 through 3 are extremely difficult to obtain nowadays.

1448. Sozialistische Einheitspartei Deutschlands. *Parteikonferenz.* Protokoll der Verhandlungen. Jan. 1949-Juli 1952-März 1956. Berlin, Dietz, 1949-1956. 3 v.

1449. Sozialistische Einheitspartei Deutschlands. *Parteitag.* Protokoll der Verhandlungen. 2.-6. Parteitag; 1947-1963. Berlin, Dietz, 1947-1963. 11 v.

Proceedings of the party congresses of the SED. For the minutes of the founding congress of this party, *see* entry no. 1450.

1450. Vereinigungsparteitag der Sozialdemokratischen Partei Deutschlands und der Kommunistischen Partei Deutschlands, *Berlin, 1946.* Protokoll des Vereinigungsparteitages der Sozialdemokratischen Partei Deutschlands (SPD) und der Kommunistischen Partei Deutschlands (KPD) am 21. und 22. April 1946 . . . in Berlin. Berlin, J. H. W. Dietz Nachf., 1946. 215 p.

Minutes of the founding congress of the Sozialistische Einheitspartei Deutschlands.

1451. Weber, Hermann, *ed.* Der deutsche Kommunismus: Dokumente. Köln, Kiepenheuer & Witsch, 1963. 679 p.

A useful compilation of basic documents. Only about a third of the collection is devoted to party documents since 1945.

2. Reference Materials, Studies, Surveys

1452. Baring, Arnulf. Der 17. Juni 1953. Foreword by Richard Lowenthal. 2d ed. Köln, Berlin, Kiepenheuer & Witsch, 1965. 184 p.
See also entry no. 1426.

A study of the background, actual course, and consequences of the East German uprising of 1953. An excellent case study in the political sociology of revolution.

1453. Brant, Stefan, *pseud.* (Klaus Harpprecht). Der Aufstand; Vorgeschichte, Geschichte und Deutung des 17. Juni 1953. Stuttgart, Steingrüben, 1954. 324 p. Illus.

A thorough study of the June 1953 uprising. More detailed than Baring's *Der 17. Juni*, although the latter may be analytically more insightful. Appeared in English as *The East German Rising, 17th June 1953* (London, Thames and Hudson, 1955; New York, Praeger, 1957, 202 p.).

1454. Castellan, Georges, *and others.* D.D.R., Allemagne de l'Est. Preface by Edmond Vermeil. Paris, Éditions du Seuil, 1955. 412 p. Maps. Bibliography: p. 393-412.

A comprehensive approach to political institutions, economic practices and social arrangements in East Germany as of the mid-fifties. Beginning with a geographic and demographic survey, separate chapters deal with Soviet policy, Marxist ideology and German national tradition, the state structure, political life and parties, the economic apparatus, the working class, the middle class, the peasantry, the churches, justice and law, education and indoctrination, and "progressive" German culture. The study plays down political repressiveness and the role of coercion more generally. Moreover, it is now substantially out of date.

1455. Castellan, Georges. La République Démocratique Allemande (R.D.A.). Paris, Presses Universitaires de France, 1961. 121 p. Illus.

A superficial coverage whose favorable bias is recorded in the author's unfounded conclusion that the German Democratic Republic constitutes "the Switzerland of the socialist camp."

1456. Croan, Melvin. East Germany. *In* Bromke, Adam, *ed.* The Communist States at the Crossroads between Moscow and Peking. New York, Praeger, 1965. p. 126-139. (Praeger Publications in Russian History and World Communism, no. 154)

A general political assessment as of 1964.

1457. Drath, Martin. Verfassungsrecht und Verfassungswirklichkeit in der sowjetischen Besatzungszone; Untersuchungen über Legalität, Loyalität und Legitimität. 2d rev. and enl. ed. Bonn, Deutscher Bundes-Verlag, 1954. 91 p.

A thoughtful essay focusing on problems of loyalty, legitimacy, and legality in the theory and practice of East German constitutional law.

1458. Duhnke, Horst. Stalinismus in Deutschland; die Geschichte der sowjetischen Besatzungszone. Köln, Verlag für Politik und Wirtschaft, 1955. 375 p.

See also entry no. 1412.

An early attempt to write a comprehensive political history of East Germany. Organized in seven parts: "The Political and Diplomatic Background," "Sovietization of the Economy, 1945-1954," "Administration and Politics, 1945-1954," "The 'Construction of Socialism' and German Unity," "Mass Organizations," "Berlin," and "The Sovietization of Society." Although now obviously dated, it still offers much valuable basic information on the earlier period.

1459. Germany (*Federal Republic, 1949–*) *Bundesministerium für Gesamtdeutsche Fragen.* SBZ-Biographie; ein biographisches Nachschlagebuch über die sowjetische Besatzungszone Deutschlands. Compiled by the Untersuchungsausschuss Freiheitlicher Juristen, Berlin. 3d ed. Bonn, 1964. 406 p.

A useful biographic register.

1460. Hangen, Wells. The Muted Revolution; East Germany's Challenge to Russia and the West. New York, Knopf, 1966. 231 p. Illus., map, ports.

See also entry no. 1356.

A lively journalistic account, designed to describe "East Germany as it actually is." Full of interesting vignettes and provocative observations based on the author's visits, but falls short of providing either a complete picture of East Germany's political, economic, or social life or an incisive analysis of "East Germany's challenge to Russia and the West."

1461. Harvard University. The Soviet Zone of Germany. Edited by Carl J. Friedrich. New Haven, Conn., Human Relations Area Files, 1956. 646 p. Maps, diagrs., tables.

A survey of society, politics, and economics as they had developed by the mid-fifties.

1462. Heidenheimer, Arnold J. The Governments of Germany. 2d ed. New York, Crowell, 1966. 254 p. Map.

Perhaps the only textbook that attempts to deal with government and politics in both West Germany and East Germany and to compare and contrast their social structures. The two chapters devoted specifically to East Germany, "One-Party Rule and Its Instruments" and "The Institutions for Implementing Policy," provide reliable treatment of the East German governmental system.

1463. Hildebrandt, Rainer. The Explosion; the Uprising behind the Iron Curtain. Translated by E. B. Ashton. Introduction by Norbert Muhlen. New York, Duell, Sloan and Pearce, 1955. 198 p. Illus.

Another treatment of the June 1953 uprising, less satisfactory although more dramatically written than that of either Brant or Baring.

1464. Informationsbüro West. Chronologische Materialien zur Geschichte der SED. Berlin-Schlachtensee, 1956. 637 p.

1465. Jänicke, Martin. Der dritte Weg; die antistalinistische Opposition gegen Ulbricht seit 1953. Köln, Neuer Deutscher Verlag, 1964. 267 p. Bibliographical references included in "Anmerkungen": p. 225-262.

A detailed recapitulation of all manifestations of resistance to or deviation from official SED policies between 1953 and 1963. Altogether undiscriminating in its treatment, it conveys the dubious impression of a powerful "third force" within East Germany, opposed both to the Ulbricht regime and to the West. Despite the author's highly questionable analysis, still of value for the wealth of factual information it contains.

1466. Knop, Werner Gustav John. Prowling Russia's Forbidden Zone; a Secret Journey into Soviet Germany. New York, A. A. Knopf, 1949. 200 p. Map.

An impressionistic and, as the title itself suggests, sometimes overdramatic account in the journalistic vein.

1467. Krippendorff, Ekkehart. Die Liberal-Demokratische Partei in der sowjetischen Bezatzungszone, 1945/48; Entstehung, Struktur, Politik. Published by the Kommission für die Geschichte des Parlamentarismus und der politischen Parteien. Düsseldorf, Droste, 1961. 178 p. (Beiträge zur Geschichte des Parlamentarismus und der politischen Parteien, Bd. 21)

See also entry no. 1437.

A scholarly monograph dealing with the reduction to political impotence of the Liberal Democratic Party in East Germany.

1468. Lukas, Richard. Zehn Jahre sowjetische Besatzungszone; Politik, Wirtschaft, Kultur, Rechtswesen. Mainz-Gonsenheim, Deutscher Fachschriften-Verlag, 1955. 215 p. Illus., map. Bibliography: p. 211-212.

See also entry no. 1417.

Treats social conditions and economic policies as well as political developments.

1469. Mampel, Siegfried. Die Entwicklung der Verfassungsordnung in der Sowjetzone Deutschlands von 1945 bis 1963. Tübingen, Mohr, 1964. 125 p.

A learned discussion of the Marxist-Leninist theory of the state and its application in East Germany. Reprinted from *Jahrbuch des öffentlichen Rechts*, Band 13, p. 455-579.

For an analysis of the 1968 constitution *see* Dietrich Müller-Römer's *Ulbrichts Grundgesetz* (Köln, Verlag Wissenschaft und Politik, 1968).

1470. Nettl, J. P. The Eastern Zone and Soviet Policy in Germany, 1945-50. London, New York, Oxford University Press, 1951. 324 p. Maps, diagrs. Bibliographical footnotes.

See also entry no. 1418.

An early detailed study of Soviet policies in East Germany, still useful, especially for its treatment of economic affairs, including reparations, the postwar economic revival, and the introduction of planning.

1471. Norden, Albert. Ein freies Deutschland entsteht; die ersten Schritte der neuen deutschen Demokratie. Berlin, Staatsverlag der DDR, 1963. 118 p. Illus., facsims., ports.

Official treatment of the early years of communist power in East Germany with heavy emphasis on measures against fascism and militarism.

1472. Pritzel, Konstantin. Die wirtschaftliche Integration der sowjetischen Besatzungszone Deutschlands in den Ostblock und ihre politischen Aspekte. 2d rev. and enl. ed. Bonn, Deutscher Bundes-Verlag, 1965. 294 p.

A useful survey of the stages of East Germany's economic integration with the Eastern bloc, together with a discussion of its effects upon specific branches and sectors of the East German economy.

1473. Richert, Ernst. Das zweite Deutschland; ein Staat, der nicht sein darf. Gütersloh, S. Mohn, 1964. 341 p. Bibliographies.

See also entry no. 1359.

A comprehensive, if sometimes uneven, survey of the "second Germany," this study touches briefly on the Cold War origins of the German Democratic Republic and its historical evolution, but devotes more attention to political institutions and economic and social arrangements in the '60s. Most interesting and controversial is its assessment of the emerging relationship between the communist regime and the East German population. The author has also written *Macht ohne Mandat* (2d ed., Köln, Opladen, Westdeutscher Verlag, 1963, 305 p.), a detailed study of East German governmental institutions and processes, and *Die Sowjetzone in der Phase der Koexistenzpolitik* (Hannover, Niedersächsiche Landeszentrale für Politische Bildung, 1961, 66 p.).

1474. Schultz, Joachim. Der Funktionär in der Einheitspartei. Kaderpolitik und Bürokratisierung in der SED. Introduction by Otto Stammer. Stuttgart, Ring-Verlag, 1956. 285 p. Bibliography: p. 277-285. (Schriften des Instituts für Politische Wissenschaft, Bd. 8)

A careful study of the SED's policies in regard to the selection, training, and assignment of cadres up to the mid-fifties.

1475. Stern, Carola, *pseud.* East Germany. *In* Griffith, William E., *ed.* Communism in Europe. v. 2. Cambridge, Mass., M.I.T. Press, 1966. p. 41-154.

An informed discussion of the SED's attitudes toward the Sino-Soviet conflict, showing that, although necessarily loyal to the Soviet Union, the SED leadership has not favored a final Sino-Soviet split.

1476. Stern, Carola, *pseud.* Porträt einer bolschewistischen Partei. Entwicklung, Funktion und Situation der SED. Köln, Verlag für Politik und Wirtschaft, 1957, 367 p. Illus. Bibliography: p. 358-362.

See also the author's *Die SED; ein Handbuch über Aufbau, Organisation und Funktion des Parteiapparates* (Köln, Rote Weissbücher, 1954, 256 p., chart), which includes thumbnail sketches of leading party personages of the early '50s. For a recent study of the SED *see* Peter Christian Ludz' *Parteielite im Wandel* (Köln, Westdeutscher Verlag, 1968, 438 p.).

3. Biographies, Memoirs

1477. Becher, Johannes R. Walter Ulbricht; ein deutscher Arbeitersohn. 9th ed. Berlin, Dietz, 1964. 224 p. Illus., ports.

More or less the official biography of Ulbricht, Becher's treatment is, as might be expected, adulatory in tone.

1478. Brandt, Heinz. Ein Traum, der nicht entführbar ist. Mein Weg zwischen Ost und West. Foreword by Erich Fromm. München, Paul List Verlag, 1967. 376 p.

Memoirs of a former German communist functionary who fled to the West in 1958 only to be kidnapped in 1961 and imprisoned by the East Germans for three years. Contains political reflections going back to the '30s but especially valuable for information about the period just before and during the 1953 uprising in East Germany.

1479. Gniffke, Erich W. Jahre mit Ulbricht. Foreword by Herbert Wehner. Köln, Verlag Wissenschaft und Politik, 1966. 376 p.

The posthumously published memoirs of a former Social Democratic (SPD) politician in East Germany who held a high position in the dominant Socialist Unity Party (SED) until his flight to the West in 1948. Contains much valuable information about political developments and personal relationships in the initial period of Soviet occupation.

1480. Krüger, Horst, *ed.* Das Ende einer Utopie; Hingabe and Selbstbefreiung früherer Kommunisten (Eine Dokumentation im zweigeteilten Deutschland). Olten, Walter-Verlag, 1963. 234 p.

Reflective essays by a number of former German communists who broke with the party. Although uneven, does convey a sense of the political atmosphere within German communism at various stages of its evolution, including the period of its rule in East Germany.

1481. Leonhard, Wolfgang. Die Revolution entlässt ihre Kinder. Köln, Kiepenheuer & Witsch, 1955. 557 p.

The memoirs of a former German communist functionary who fled East Germany in 1948. Contains some valuable information on the preparations for and the early days of the Soviet occupation. Appeared in English as *A Child of the Revolution* (Chicago, Regnery, 1958, 447 p.).

1482. Schenk, Fritz. Im Vorzimmer der Diktatur; 12 Jahre Pankow. Köln, Kiepenheuer & Witsch, 1962. 412 p.

Memoirs of a former ranking official in the East German planning apparatus who fled to the West. Interesting for its treatment of the atmosphere of economic and political decision-making, especially during the crisis years 1953-1956.

1483. Stern, Carola, *pseud.* Ulbricht; eine politische Biographie. Köln, Kiepenheuer und Witsch, 1963. 356 p. Illus., ports. Bibliography: p. 347-350.

See also entry no. 1442.

An excellent critical political biography of the East German leader, covering his career from earliest youth until old age. The only biography of Ulbricht to appear so far in the West. Invaluable for an understanding of the man's narrow mental outlook and his extraordinary political survival over the years. Unfortunately, the English edition, *Ulbricht: A Political Biography* (New York, Praeger, 1965, 231 p.), has been adapted in such a way as to omit some significant portions of the original.

1484. Thoms, Lieselotte *and others.* Walter Ulbricht. Arbeiter, Revolutionär, Staatsmann. Eine biographische Skizze. Berlin, Staatsverlag der Deutschen Demokratischen Republik, 1968. 338 p. Illus.

A series of uncritical biographic sketches, officially published.

B. FOREIGN AFFAIRS, MILITARY AFFAIRS

1485. Deutsches Institut für Zeitgeschichte. Dokumente zur Aussenpolitik der Regierung der Deutschen Demokratischen Republik. Bd. 1– 1954– Berlin, Rütten und Loening.

1486. Forster, Thomas M. NVA, die Armee der Sowjetzone. 2d rev. ed. Köln, Markus-Verlag, 1966. 287 p. Illus., map, ports.

Analyzes the role of the National People's Army within the Warsaw Treaty Organization and attempts to assess the army's reliability as a fighting force. Emphasizes Soviet checks on East Germany's armed forces. Also available in translation as *The East German Army* (London, Allen & Unwin, 1967, 255 p.).

1487. Kabel, Rudolf. Die Militarisierung der sowjetischen Besatzungszone Deutschlands. Bonn, Deutscher Bundes-Verlag, 1966. 316 p. Illus.

A brief survey of the East German armed forces and paramilitary organizations, followed by a useful collection of documents pertaining to various aspects of the military since 1960. Published by the Bundesministerium für Gesamtdeutsche Fragen.

1488. Kopp, Fritz. Kurs auf ganz Deutschland? Die Deutschlandpolitik der SED. Stuttgart, Seewald, 1965. 345 p. Bibliography: p. 329-339.

A survey of the role of nationalism in German communist strategy and tactics, taking the account back to the founding of the KPD after the First World War but concentrating on the period 1945-1965. The book is rich in quotations but short on analysis and does not really do justice to the many complexities of the important theme with which it deals.

1489. Kopp, Fritz. Chronik der Wiederbewaffnung in Deutschland; Daten über Polizei und Bewaffnung, 1945-1958, Rüstung der Sowjetzone — Abwehr des Westens. Köln, Markus Verlag, 1958. 160 p.

A chronological survey of rearmament; contains data on police, quasi-military, and military forces in East Germany.

27

the economy

by Hans J. Torke

A. ECONOMIC HISTORY

1490. Die sowjetische Hand in der deutschen Wirtschaft; Organisation und Geschäftsgebaren der sowjetischen Unternehmen. Bonn, Bundesministerium für Gesamtdeutsche Fragen, 1952. 100 p.

Summarizes the early period of East German economic development when enterprises operated directly by the Soviet Union in their occupation zone still played a leading role in the economy.

1491. Münke, Stephanie, *comp.* Symptomatische Aussagen über wirtschaftliche und soziale Verhältnisse in der Sowjetzone 1952 (Ergebnisse von Flüchtlingsbefragungen). Berlin, Duncker und Humblot, 1952. 54 p. 29 tables. (Deutsches Institut für Wirtschaftsforschung. Sonderhefte. N.F., nr. 19. Reihe C: Quellen)

The reports by refugees on their economic situations back home have to be taken with a grain of salt. The reports are analyzed according to age, social structure, income, home towns, etc. See also *Einkommensstruktur und Lebenshaltung in der sowjetischen Besat-*

zungszone by Dorothea Faber (Bonn, Bundesministerium für Gesamtdeutsche Fragen, 1953, 96 p.).

1492. Mussler, Werner. Die volkseigenen Betriebe. Entstehung, Organisation, Aufgaben. Berlin, Freie Gewerkschaft, 1948. 128 p. Illus.

An early study summarizing all previous publications on the subject. A guide for union functionaries and workers' representatives. Several orders of the Soviet military administration in the appendix.

1493. Oelssner, Fred. Die Übergangsperiode vom Kapitalismus zum Sozialismus in der Deutschen Demokratischen Republik. Berlin, Akademie-Verlag, 1955. 91 p. (Deutsche Akademie der Wissenschaften zu Berlin. Vorträge und Schriften, Heft 56)

This speech by a then still powerful party functionary deserves special interest because of the conclusions the author reaches: Ideology has not caught up with economic development; theoreticians have failed to take practice into consideration; and Marxism-Leninism is no dogma, but a guide for action.

1494. Slusser, Robert, *ed.* Soviet Economic Policy in Postwar Germany. New York, Research Program on the U.S.S.R., 1953. 184 p.

A useful account of Soviet objectives and conduct in the postwar occupation of East Germany. For a broader consideration of Soviet policies, *see* Werner Erfurt's *Die sowjetrussische Deutschland-Politik; eine Studie zur Zeitgeschichte* (6th ed. München, Bechtle, 1962, 274 p.).

1495. Ulbricht, Walter. Zur sozialistischen Entwicklung der Volkswirtschaft seit 1945. Berlin, Dietz, 1959. 796 p.

Contains a collection of speeches and articles by the East German party chief on the different stages of the East German economic development: the period of overcoming war damages (1945-1948), the two-year plan (1949-1950), the first five-year plan (1951-1955), and the second five-year plan (1956-1960). It is interesting to compare the author's views with a speech he made on July 14, 1946, in Jena: *Demokratischer Wirtschaftsaufbau* (Berlin, Dietz, 1946, 48 p.).

B. GENERAL ECONOMIC STUDIES

1496. Knauthe, Erhart. Verzeichnis ausgewählter laufender Literatur über die Volkswirtschaft der Deutschen Demokratischen Republik. Edited by Karl W. Roskamp. Detroit, Wayne State University, 1967. 13 leaves.

A useful bibliography of East German monographs, articles, and legislative acts pertaining to the organization and development of the East German economy.

1497. Materialien zur Wirtschaftslage in der sowjetischen Zone. Bonn, Berlin, Bundesministerium für Gesamtdeutsche Fragen, 1951–

A series of monographs and source material on various economic fields, published irregularly since 1951 by the West German government. Sometimes not free from polemical overtones.

1498. Samson, Benvenuto. Grundzüge des mitteldeutschen Wirtschaftsrechts. Frankfurt am Main, Metzner, 1960. 146 p.

A highly useful completely revised edition of an earlier (1953) book called *Planungsrecht und Recht der volkseigenen Betriebe in der sowjetischen Besatzungszone.* The first study on the East German nationalization from the juridical standpoint was done by Eckart Krömer in his *Die Sozialisierung in der sowjetischen Besatzungszone Deutschlands als Rechtsproblem* (Göttingen, Otto Schwartz, 1952, 184 p. Göttinger rechtswissenschaftliche Studien, Heft 4).

1499. Schmidt-Renner, Gerhard, *ed.* Wirtschaftsterritorium Deutsche Demokratische Republik; ökonomisch-geographische Einführung und Übersicht. 3d ed. Berlin, Die Wirtschaft, 1962. 483 p. Illus., maps. Bibliography: p. 459-470.

See also entry no. 1384.

A detailed economic-geographic survey prepared by a team of associates of the Institut für Ökonomische Geographie und Regionalplanung der Hochschule für Ökonomie, Berlin.

1500. Stolper, Wolfgang F. The Structure of the East German Economy. Cambridge, Harvard University Press, 1960. 478 p. Tables. Bibliography: p. 445-455.

A pioneering work by an American economist. For a French-language study *see* Guy Roustang's *Développement économique de l'Allemagne orientale* (Paris, Société d'édition d'enseignement supérieur, 1963, 236 p., illus. École pratique des Hautes Études. Développement économique, 6).

1501. Thalheim, Karl C. Die Wirtschaft der Sowjetzone in Krise und Umbau. Berlin, Duncker und Humblot, 1964. 190 p. Bibliography: p. 184-190. (Wirtschaft und Gesellschaft in Mitteldeutschland, Bd. 1)

A convincing analysis of the nature of the failures of the East German economic system, covering also the latest experiment, i.e., the "New Economic System." There is a comparison with the Federal Republic, as well as an index, and about 60 pages of documents.

1502. Die Volkswirtschaft der Deutschen Demokratischen Republik. Berlin, Die Wirtschaft, 1960. 395 p. Plates, maps, diagrs. Bibliography: p. 355-395.

This rather propagandistic symposium edited by Kurt Depolt and others was published on the occasion of the 15th anniversary of the liberation of Germany from fascism. The authors try to prove that the development of the East German economy is superior to that of West Germany. Chapters are on transition from capitalism to socialism, planning, industry, agriculture, traffic, internal and foreign trade, finances, and the distribution of the national income. The most valuable part of the book is a bibliography of 571 titles.

1503. Wilmut, Adolf. Analyse der betriebswirtschaftlichen Struktur der volkseigenen Betriebe als Voraussetzung für eine richtige Beurteilung östlicher Tatsachen- und Zahlenberichte. Berlin, Duncker und Humblot, 1958. 158 p. Illus. (Osteuropa-Institut an der Freien Universität Berlin. Wirtschaftswissenschaftliche Veröffentlichungen, Bd. 7)

The internal organization of a nationalized industrial plant is, according to the author, the key to understanding the East German economy as a whole. Section B gives a critical analysis of the real value of East German facts and figures. There are also some theses about what should be done in case of a German reunification. Preface by Karl C. Thalheim. *See also* Hellmut Heuer's *Zur Organisation der Betriebsplanung in der volkseigenen Industrie des sowjetischen Besatzungsgebietes* (Berlin, Duncker und Humblot, 1958, 130 p. Wirtschaftswissenschaftliche Abhandlungen, Heft 10).

C. ECONOMIC THEORY AND PLANNING SYSTEM

1504. Germany (*Federal Republic 1949–*) *Bundesministerium für Gesamtdeutsche Fragen.* Die Enteignungen in der sowjetischen Besatzungszone und die Verwaltung des Vermögens von nicht in der Sowjetzone ansässigen Personen. 3d rev. ed. Bonn, Deutscher Bundes-Verlag, 1962. 360 p.

Chiefly a collection of laws and statutes intended to serve as an informational guide for persons in the West who own property in East Germany. The book even goes back to the orders of the Soviet military administration. For the concept of property in East Germany see *Das Eigentum und das Eigentumsrecht in der sowjetischen Besatzungszone Deutschlands* by Joachim Grünewald (Bonn, Röhrscheid, 1961, 144 p. Bonner rechtswissenschaftliche Abhandlungen, Bd. 49).

1505. Propp, Dietrich P. Zur Transformation einer Zentralverwaltungswirtschaft sowjetischen Typs in eine Marktwirtschaft. Berlin, Duncker und Humblot, 1964. 300 p. Bibliography: p. 290-300. (Osteuropa Institut an der Freien Universität Berlin. Wirtschaftswissenschaftliche Veröffentlichungen, Bd. 20)

An incisive analysis of the transformations of the economy of the DDR. For a recent thesis-based study of economic policy see *Das sowjetische Herrschaftsprinzip des demokratischen Zentralismus in der Wirtschaftsordnung Mitteldeutschlands* by Hannelore Hamel (Berlin, Duncker und Humblot, 1966, 210 p., bibliography: p. 197-205).

1506. Rudolph, Johannes, *and* G. Friedrich, *eds.* Grundriss der Volkswirtschaftsplanung. Berlin, Die Wirtschaft, 1957. 603 p. Illus. Bibliography: p. 595-604.

A handbook for students and functionaries published by the Hochschule für Ökonomie und Planung. Ideologically the state of affairs before the third party conference is reflected. Summary at the end of each chapter.

1507. Schenk, Fritz. Magie der Planwirtschaft. Köln, Kiepenheuer und Witsch 1960. 286 p. Illus. Bibliography.

The author, a former high functionary in the East German economic hierarchy, covers two important stages in the economic development: the Sovietization (until 1955) and the integration in the Eastern bloc (since 1954-55). Statutes of COMECON are contained in the appendix. *Verwaltung, Lenkung und Planung der Wirtschaft in der sowjetischen Besatzungszone* by Otto Walther (Bonn, Bundesministerium für Gesamtdeutsche Fragen, 1953, 59 p.) is now outdated, but has a valuable appendix on laws and institutions.

1508. Spitzner, Osmar. Wirtschaftsverträge, sozialistische Wirtschaftsleitung. Rolle und Bedeutung der Wirtschaftsverträge im neuen ökonomischen System der Planung und Leitung der Volkswirtschaft. Berlin, Staatsverlag der Deutschen Demokratischen Republik, 1965. 633 p. Bibliographies.

The book should be viewed in connection with the law of February 25, 1965, according to which the old administrative form of economic direction is to be replaced by the system of socialist contracts as it had been introduced first in 1951. The author, who also helped to prepare the law, is an expert on cooperation between enterprises. Very good index. See also *Die sozialistische Leitung der Industrie in der Deutschen Demokratischen Republik* by Johannes Thamm (Berlin, Die Wirtschaft, 1961, 207 p.).

1509. Ulbricht, Walter. Zum neuen ökonomischen System der Planung und Leitung. Berlin, Dietz, 1966. 763 p. Bibliographies.

A collection of speeches, articles, and letters by the East German party chief on the "new economic system."

1510. Wolf, Herbert, *ed.* Der sozialistische Arbeitsstil und die Tätigkeit der Wirtschaftsräte. Berlin, Die Wirtschaft, 1959. 80 p. (Volkswirtschaftsplanung, Heft 1)

Written in connection with the seven-year plan, this symposium deals mainly with "democratic centralism" and the "councils on the economy." In the preface the authors chose to voice self-criticism, admitting that they have failed to emphasize the role of the state as the essential instrument for the victory of socialism.

D. STATISTICS

1511. Kalus, Hellmuth. Wirtschaftszahlen aus der SBZ. 4th ed. Bonn, Deutscher Bundes-Verlag, 1964. 194 p.

A publication of Bundesministerium für Gesamtdeutsche Fragen, giving statistical data on all economic fields, including East Berlin, partly in comparison with the Federal Republic. Based on the best available figures.

E. AGRICULTURE

1512. Germany (*Federal Republic, 1949–*) *Bundesministerium für Gesamtdeutsche Fragen.* Die Zwangskollektivierung des selbständigen Bauernstandes in Mitteldeutschland. Bonn, 1960. 142 p. Illus., facsims.

A selection of documents containing reports by refugees, official documents, and newspaper articles.

1513. Matz, Rudolf. Agraratlas über das Gebiet der Deutschen Demokratischen Republik. 1. Bodenarten und bodenartliche Ertragsbedingungen nach den Ergebnissen der Bodenschätzung. Gotha, Hermann Haack, 1956. 4 p. 67 maps (col.)

See also entry no. 1380.

The only work of its kind, with index of locations.

1514. Merkel, Konrad, *and* E. Schuhans. Die Agrarwirtschaft in Mitteldeutschland; "Sozialisierung" und Produktionsergebnisse. 2d enl. ed. Bonn, Bundesministerium für Gesamtdeutsche Fragen, 1963. 200 p. Tables. Bibliography: p. 181-183.

This book (with 253 tables) represents a continuation of Matthias Kramer's *Die Bolschewisierung der Landwirtschaft in Sowjetrussland, in den Satellitenstaaten und in der Sowjetzone* (Köln, Kiepenheuer und Witsch, 1951, 144 p.).

1515. Schmidt, Walter. Die Grundzüge der Entwicklung der Landwirtschaft in der DDR von 1945 bis zur Gegenwart. Berlin, Deutscher Landwirtschaftsverlag, 1960-1961. 2 v. (Vorlesungen zur Agrarökonomik, Heft 2/1, 2/2)

The first volume of this university textbook covers the period of the land reform (1945-1952) while the second bears the subtitle "The Socialist Reshaping of Agriculture." There is also a comparison with West German forms of farming. See also *Die Stellung der Landwirtschaft in der Volkswirtschaft der DDR* by Gerhard Seidel (Berlin, Deutscher Landwirtschaftsverlag, 1960, 60 p. Vorlesungen zur Agrarökonomik, Heft 4).

F. INDUSTRY AND TRANSPORT

1516. Berlin. Hochschule für Ökonomie. *Institut für Materialwirtschaft.* Die Materialwirtschaft der DDR. Berlin, Wirtschaft, 1964. 443 p. Illus., forms. Bibliography: p. 436-443.

A presentation of interindustry economics.

1517. Demmler, Horst. Verkehrspolitik in der Sowjetzone Deutschlands. Heidelberg, Quelle und Meyer, 1967. 255 p. Illus., maps. Bibliography: p. 237-245. (Veröffentlichungen des Forschungsinstituts für Wirtschaftspolitik an der Universität Mainz, Bd. 21)

The author points to the difficulties of traffic planning in East Germany, such as coordinating local plans and selecting the most rational solutions. The study reaches until late 1965.

1518. Horn, Werner. Die Errichtung der Grundlagen des Sozialismus in der Industrie der DDR, 1951-1955. Berlin, Dietz, 1963. 369 p.

A communist view of the first five-year plan in East Germany. For a later period (seven-year plan) and, at the same time, for a Western viewpoint, see *Die Industrie der Sowjetzone unter dem gescheiterten Siebenjahrplan* by Bruno Gleitze (Berlin, Duncker und Humblot, 1964, 375 p. Wirtschaft und Gesellschaft in Mitteldeutschland, Bd. 2).

1519. Knop, Hans. Die Energiewirtschaft der DDR und die Planung ihrer künftigen Entwicklung. Berlin, Die Wirtschaft, 1960. 239 p. (Volkswirtschaftsplanung, Heft 2)

On the planning of the power industry.

1520. Zauberman, Alfred. Industrial Progress in Poland, Czechoslovakia, and East Germany, 1937-1962. London, New York, Toronto, Oxford University Press, 1964. 338 p. Bibliography.

See also entries no. 270, 602, 943, *and* 2829.

An important study on the subject, issued under the auspices of the Royal Institute of International Affairs.

G. LABOR

1521. Haas, Gerhard, *and* Julian Lehnecke. Der Gewerkschaftsapparat der SED. Organisation, Hauptaufgaben und politische Entwicklung der kommunistischen Pseudo-Gewerkschaft in der Sowjetzone. Bonn, Bundesministerium für Gesamtdeutsche Fragen, 1963. 40 p.

This publication should be read in conjunction with *Industriearbeiterschaft in der Sowjetzone. Eine Untersuchung der Arbeiterschaft in der volkseigenen Industrie der SBZ* by Graf Viggo Blücher (Stuttgart, F. Enke, 1959, 103 p.), which focuses on the position of the workers, and is based on interviews with refugees.

H. MONEY, FINANCE, COMMERCE

1522. Bader, Heinrich, *and others*. Das Finanzsystem der DDR. Berlin, Die Wirtschaft, 1962. 655 p. Tables. Bibliographies.

A university textbook on the East German finance system, containing chapters on the state budget, finances in the socialist economy, banks, and insurance.

The Western viewpoint is represented in a booklet by Eberhard Sawitzki, *Das Geld- und Kreditwesen in Mitteldeutschland* (Frankfurt am Main, Fritz Knapp, 1964, 83 p.). The author describes the difficulties of adjusting the finance system to the continuing nationalization. The Deutsche Notenbank as the central financial institution is taken as a case study.

1523. Holbik, Karel, *and* H. Meyers. Postwar Trade in Divided Germany: The Internal and International Issues. Baltimore, Johns Hopkins, 1964. 138 p. Tables. Bibliography: p. 127-132.

This is the first book on the development of trade relations between East and West Germany from 1946 to 1962. The authors state that there is no precedent for this kind of bilateral trade, which, oddly enough, is regarded as internal by the West Germans and as international by the East Germans. The interest of the book is more in political issues than in economic problems. Index.

1524. Piltz, Rosemarie. Die Konsumgenossenschaften in der Sowjetzone. Bonn, Bundesministerium für Gesamtdeutsche Fragen, 1960. 63 p. Illus.

The author points out that cooperatives in East Germany are state-controlled organizations which, as "mass organizations," fulfill political functions. The statute of 1955 is quoted in the appendix.

1525. Schlenk, Hans. Der Binnenhandel in der sowjetischen Besatzungszone Deutschlands. Bonn, Bundesministerium für Gesamtdeutsche Fragen, 1960. 207 p. Illus.

The author suggests that domestic trade is one of the weakest points within the East German economic system. He gives a survey of the theory, function, and structure as well as of the history of his subject. The organization of domestic trade is also covered. Documents and tables make up one fourth of the book and there is an index. See also *Privater Einzelhandel und sozialistische Entwicklung* by Hans Rössler and others (Berlin, Die Wirtschaft, 1960, 108 p.).

I. FOREIGN ECONOMIC RELATIONS

1526. Klinkmüller, Erich. Die gegenwärtige Aussenhandelsverflechtung der sowjetischen Besatzungszone Deutschlands. Berlin, Duncker und Humblot, 1959. 196 p. Tables. (Wirtschaftswissenschaftliche Veröffentlichungen des Osteuropa-Instituts an der Freien Universität Berlin, Bd. 8)

Four-fifths of East Germany's foreign trade was concentrated in the Soviet bloc when this book was written. Its presentation along with extensive source materials, statistical data, 23 tables, and a bibliography, is still useful today. See also *Das Aussenhandelssystem der sowjetischen Besatzungszone Deutschlands. Die Entwicklung der Organisation und Technik des sowjetzonalen Aussenhandels* by Wolfgang Förster (3d rev. ed., Bonn, Bundesministerium für Gesamtdeutsche Fragen, 1957, 137 p.). For a communist view one may consult *Aussenhandel und Nationaleinkommen im Sozialismus* by Heinz Brass (Berlin, Die Wirtschaft, 1961, 148 p.).

1527. Kohler, Heinz. Economic Integration in the Soviet Bloc; with an East German Case Study. New York, Washington, London, Praeger, 1965. 402 p. Tables. Bibliography: p. 396-402.

Based on a doctoral thesis, this book emphasizes East Germany, though the entire Eastern bloc is covered. May be supplemented by *Die wirtschaftliche Integration der SBZ in den Ostblock und ihre politischen Aspekte* by Konstantin Pritzel (2d enl. ed., Bonn, Bundesministerium für Gesamtdeutsche Fragen, 1965, 296 p.).

1528. Spröte, Wolfgang, *and* G. Hahn. DDR-Wirtschaftshilfe contra Bonner Neokolonialismus. Studie über die wirtschaftliche und wissenschaftlich-technische Unterstützung der Nationalstaaten durch die DDR und die staatsmonopolistische Förderung der neokolonialistischen Expansion des westdeutschen Monopolkapitals. Berlin, Staatsverlag der Deutschen Demokratischen Republik, 1965. 256 p. Tables.

The aim of this book is to prove that East Germany helps the underdeveloped countries to become economically independent from neocolonialism.

J. SERIALS

1529. Akademie der Wissenschaften, *Berlin. Institut für Wirtschaftswissenschaften.* Jahrbuch. 1957–

The leading East German journal on the basic problems of the political economy.

28

the society

by Melvin Croan

A. GENERAL

1530. Bosch, Werner. Die Sozialstruktur in West- und Mitteldeutschland. Published by Bundesministerium für Gesamtdeutsche Fragen. Bonn, 1958. 239 p. Bibliography.

A study sponsored by the West German Research Council for Reunification.

1531. Dahrendorf, Ralf. Gesellschaft und Demokratie in Deutschland. München, R. Piper, 1965. 516 p. Bibliography: p. 483-492.

Broad-gauged and altogether first-rate discussion of major themes in Germany's social and political development. Contains perceptive treatment of the major divergences between East German and West German societies in the post-World War II period. An English edition entitled *Society and Democracy in Germany* was published in 1967 (Garden City, N.Y., Doubleday; 482 p.).

1532. Dönhoff, Marion, *Gräfin*, Rudolf W. Leonhardt, *and* Theo Sommer. Reise in ein fernes Land; Bericht über Kultur, Wirtschaft und Politik in der DDR. Hamburg, Nannen-Verlag, 1964. 143 p.

See also entry no. 1355.

A series of intelligent and sensitive reports covering cultural, economic, and political life in East Germany, based on the authors' travels there in 1964. First appeared in the Hamburg newspaper, *Die Zeit*, to whose staff the authors belong.

1533. Ludz, Peter Christian, *ed.* Studien und Materialien zur Soziologie der DDR. Köln, Opladen, Westdeutscher Verlag, 1964. 540 p. (Köl-

ner Zeitschrift für Soziologie und Sozialpsychologie. Sonderheft, 8)
See also entry no. 1622.

A collection of scholarly papers, some extremely informative, on various aspects of East German society, e.g., occupational structure, the family, industrial organization, educational practices, basic research, the role of ideology, sociology, and philosophy. The editor has contributed a searching, if not wholly satisfactory theoretical essay which attempts to delineate the major characteristics of the political society as a whole. The book also contains a highly useful bibliographical list of over 1,500 citations, both East and West, on East German society.

1534. Lungwitz, Kurt. Über die Klassenstruktur in der Deutschen Demokratischen Republik; eine sozial-ökonomische statistische Untersuchung. Berlin, Verlag Die Wirtschaft, 1962. 190 p. Bibliography.

An East German statistical analysis of the social structure.

1535. Storbeck, Dietrich. Soziale Strukturen in Mitteldeutschland; eine sozial-statistische Bevölkerungsanalyse im gesamtdeutschen Vergleich. Berlin, Duncker & Humblot, 1964. 323 p. Illus. (Wirtschaft und Gesellschaft in Mitteldeutschland, Bd. 4)

A detailed analysis of East Germany's demographic and social structure, replete with important data on all sectors of society.

B. INTELLECTUAL, RELIGIOUS, AND EDUCATIONAL SITUATION

1536. Croan, Melvin. East German Revisionism: The Spectre and the Reality. *In* Labedz, Leopold, *ed.* Revisionism; Essays on the History of Marxist Ideas. New York, Praeger, 1962. p. 239-256.

A discussion of revisionist intellectuals in East Germany in the mid-fifties and their fate.

1537. Friedrich, Gerd. Der Kulturbund zur Demokratischen Erneuerung Deutschlands: Geschichte und Funktion. Köln, Rote Weissbücher, 1952. 143 p.
See also entry no. 1614.

A monograph on the organization and policies of the SED's mass organization for intellectuals. Contains some useful information on the organization's early years.

1538. Havemann, Robert. Dialektik ohne Dogma? Naturwissenschaft und Weltanschauung. Reinbeck bei Hamburg, Rowohlt, 1964. 168 p.
See also entry no. 1628.

Critical lectures, delivered during 1963-1964 at the Humboldt University by an East German professor of physical chemistry and veteran German communist, which were enormously popular with the East German audience that heard them but which were severely castigated by the SED for their ostensible revisionism and led to punitive measures against Havemann.

1539. Kersten, Heinz. Gärung in Mitteldeutschland. *In his* Aufstand der Intellektuellen. Wandlungen in der kommunistischen Welt; ein dokumentarischer Bericht. Stuttgart, H. Seewald, 1957. p. 139-182.

A survey of the intellectual unrest which accompanied the de-Stalinization of the mid-fifties in East Central Europe and East Germany.

1540. Kantorowicz, Alfred. Deutsches Tagebuch. München, Kindler, 1959-1961. 2 v.

The memoirs of an East German scholar and sometime professor of German literature at the Humboldt University in Berlin who fled to the West in 1957. The first volume covers the years up to 1949, while the second carries the author's reminiscences up to his decision to flee in 1957. Much of the contents of both volumes is highly personal, but there are many pertinent observations throughout on the relationship between the sensitive, critical, intellectual spirit and the typical German communist party functionary.

1541. Koch, Hans Gerhard. Neue Erde ohne Himmel; der Kampf des Atheismus gegen das Christentum in der "DDR," Modell einer weltweiten Auseinandersetzung. Stuttgart, Quell-Verlag, 1963. 592 p. Illus. Bibliography: p. 551-575.

A discussion of the SED policies toward organized religion, stressing the party's offensive against the churches and its efforts to inculcate society with the atheistic world view.

1542. Köhler, Hans. Zur geistigen und seelischen Situation der Menschen in der Sowjetzone. 2d rev. and enl. ed. Bonn, 1954. 46 p.

An essay on the impact of communist rule, written from the vantage point of the Stalinist period, on various sectors of society ein East Germany. Issued under the sponsorship of the Bundesministerium für Gesamtdeutsche Fragen.

1543. Matthias, Erich, *and* Hansjürgen Schierbaum. Errungenschaften; zur Geschichte eines Schlagwortes unserer Zeit. Pfaffenhofen/Ilm, Ilmgauverlag, 1961. 307 p. Bibliographical footnotes.

A critical examination of a central concept in SED progaganda.

1544. Müller, Marianne. ". . . stürmt die Festung Wissenschaft!" Die Sowjetisierung der mitteldeutschen Universitäten seit 1945. Berlin-Dahlem, Colloquium-Verlag, 1953. 415 p. Illus., ports. Bibliography: p. 388.

See also entry no. 1600.

A detailed account of the Sovietization of East Germany's universities during the late '40s and early '50s.

1545. Richert, Ernst. Sozialistische Universität. Die Hochschulpolitik der

SED. Berlin, Colloquium Verlag, 1967. 279 p. Bibliographical references included in "Anmerkungen": p. 260-270.
See also entry no. 1603.

Comprehensive treatment of higher education in East Germany, stressing changing SED objectives in this realm. Updates and is more analytical than ". . . *stürmt die Festung Wissenschaft*!" (entry no. 1544).

1546. Riemschneider, Ernst G. Veränderungen der deutschen Sprache in der sowjetisch besetzten Zone Deutschlands seit 1945. Düsseldorf, Pädagogischer Verlag Schwann, 1963. 102 p. Bibliography: p. 95-102. (Beihefte zur Zeitschrift "Wirkendes Wort," 4)

Deals objectively with a problem of increasing concern to many West Germans.

1547. Solberg, Richard W. God and Caesar in East Germany; the Conflicts of Church and State in East Germany since 1945. Foreword by Bishop Otto Dibelius. New York, Macmillan, 1961. 294 p. Illus.
See also entry no. 1645.

The author, an American churchman, presents a sensitive account of the religious dilemma in East Germany which has resulted from the various forms of pressure exerted by the communist regime against the churches and the faithful.

C. SOCIAL, OCCUPATIONAL, AND AGE GROUPS

1548. Friedrich, Gerd. Die Freie Deutsche Jugend; Auftrag und Entwicklung. Köln, Rote Weissbücher, 1953. 201 p.

A monograph surveying the origins and functions of the SED's mass organization for youth.

1549. Haas, Gerhard, *and* Alfred Leutwein, *pseud.* (Siegfried Mampel). Die rechtliche und soziale Lage der Arbeitnehmer in der sowjetischen Besatzungszone. 5th, enl. & rev. ed. Bonn, Bundesministerium für Gesamtdeutsche Fragen, 1959. 2 v.

Inquiry into the legal and social aspects of labor relations.

1550. Müller, Karl Valentin. Die Manager in der Sowjetzone; eine empirische Untersuchung zur Soziologie der wirtschaftlichen und militärischen Führungsschicht in Mitteldeutschland. Köln, Opladen, Westdeutscher Verlag, 1962. 200 p. (Schriftenreihe des Instituts für Empirische Soziologie, Bd. 2)

Most of the data are from the '50s.

1551. Sarel, Benno. La Classe ouvrière d'Allemagne orientale; essai de chronique. Foreword by Pierre Naville. Paris, Éditions Ouvrières, 1958. 268 p.

A discussion of the working class in East Germany, from a critical

Marxist point of view. Contains perceptive observations on labor's role in the 1953 uprising.

1552. Stolz, Helmut. Über das Kind und seine sozialen Beziehungen in der DDR. München, Basel, E. Reinhardt, 1966. 119 p. Bibliography: p. 119-120.

A thorough treatment of the subject.

1553. Zapf, Wolfgang, *ed.* Beiträge zur Analyse der deutschen Oberschicht. 2d rev. ed. München, R. Piper, 1965. 166 p. (Studien zur Soziologie, Bd. 3)

Contains several excellent sociological studies comparing and contrasting leadership groups in West and East Germany, the social profile of parliamentary representatives, and the top military echelons in the Federal Republic and the DDR.

D. MASS MEDIA AND PUBLIC OPINION

1554. Fricke, Karl Wilhelm. Selbstbehauptung und Widerstand in der sowjetischen Besatzungszone Deutschlands. Bonn, 1964. 191 p. Bibliography: p. 186-[192].

See also entry no. 1430.

A survey of resistance and opposition to the East German regime, touching briefly and often superficially on each of the social forces that have shown themselves inimical to communist rule.

1555. Grothe, Peter. To Win the Minds of Men; the Story of the Communist Propaganda War in East Germany. Palo Alto, California, Pacific Books, 1958. 241 p.

A reliable but scarcely comprehensive account of communist propaganda techniques in East Germany, based on personal observation as well as on documentary materials.

1556. Richert, Ernst. Agitation und Propaganda; das System der publizistischen Massenführung in der Sowjetzone. Introduction by Otto Stammer. Berlin, F. Vahlen, 1958. 331 p. (Schriften des Instituts für Politische Wissenschaft, Bd. 10)

A thorough study of the manipulation of public opinion in East Germany, treating the institutions for molding public opinion and the content of agitation and propaganda through the mid-fifties, and containing some general observations on the Soviet theory behind the SED's efforts. Written in collaboration with Carola Stern and Peter Dietrich.

1557. Schimanski, Hans. Leitgedanken und Methoden der kommunistischen Indoktrination; Parteischulung, Agitation und Propaganda in der sowjetischen Besatzungszone Deutschlands. Bonn, Deutscher Bundes-Verlag, 1965. 163 p. Bibliography: p. 153-159.

A knowledgeable discussion of the theory and practice of party schooling, agitation, and propaganda in East Germany.

29

intellectual and cultural life

by Robert M. Slusser
(except for section C)

A. BIBLIOGRAPHIES AND REFERENCE WORKS

1558. Albrecht, Günter, *and others.* Deutsches Schriftstellerlexikon von den Anfängen bis zur Gegenwart. 4th rev. and enl. ed. Weimar, Volksverlag, 1963. 732 p. Ports.

Compact, exhaustive, indispensable. Covers all of German literature. For bibliographies limited to DDR authors, *see*:

Germany (*Democratic Republic, 1949–) Zentralinstitut für Bibliothekswesen.* Schriftsteller der Deutschen Demokratischen Republik und ihre Werke; biographisch-bibliographischer Nachweis. Leipzig, Verlag für Buch- und Bibliothekswesen, 1955. 249 p.

Schriftsteller der Deutschen Demokratischen Republik. Leipzig, Verlag für Buch- und Bibliothekswesen, 1961. 196 p.

1559. Bütow, Hellmuth G. Die Entwicklung des dialektischen und historischen Materialismus in der Sowjetzone. Berlin, in Kommission bei O. Harrassowitz, Wiesbaden, 1960-1963. 3 v. (Bibliographische Mitteilungen des Osteuropa-Instituts an der Freien Universität Berlin, Heft 4)

A systematic and thorough listing of writings on all major aspects of Marxism-Leninism (including Stalinism) in the DDR. Indispensable.

1560. Deutsche Musikbibliographie. 1829– Leipzig, F. Hofmeister. Monthly.

Title varies. Now issued by Deutsche Bücherei in Leipzig as part of the national bibliography. Cumulated in *Jahresverzeichnis der deutschen Musikalien und Musikschriften* (Leipzig, 1853–). Another bibliographical work on music is *Komponisten und Musikwissenschaftler der Deutschen Demokratischen Republik; Kurzbiographien und Werkverzeichnisse*, issued by Verband Deutscher Komponisten und Musikwissenschaftler (Berlin, Verlag Neue Musik, 1959, 198 p.).

1561. Fleischer, Wolfgang, *and* Ernst Eichler, *comps.* Bibliographie der germanistischen Sprachwissenschaft in der Sowjetunion 1950-1960. Leipzig, 1963. 191 p.

1562. Handbuch für den Kulturfunktionär. 2d rev. ed. Berlin, Verlag Tribüne, 1965. 685 p. Bibliography: p. 666-676.

See also entry no. 1616.

Updated edition of a convenient compendium of materials in the cultural field prepared by Herbert Bischoff *et al.* for officials of the DDR labor unions; first published 1961. Includes texts of speeches by Ulbricht and others, discussion from the second "Bitterfeld Conference," and materials on cultural policy in the FDGB (trade union organization). Texts of important cultural laws given; list of FDGB literary and art prize winners, 1955-1963.

For current developments *see* the FDGB organ, *Kulturelles Leben, Zeitschrift für die Kulturarbeit der Gewerkschaften* (Berlin, 1953–).

1563. Lasch, Hanna. Architekten-Bibliographie; deutsch-sprachige Veröffentlichungen, 1920-1960. Leipzig, Seemann, 1962. 215 p.

A valuable reference work. Gives biographical data and references to literature; not limited to Germany or the 20th century.

1564. Rost, Gottfried, *and* Annemarie Halm. Kunst und Leben; eine bibliographische Information über die theoretischen Grundlagen der sozialistischen Kulturrevolution in der Deutschen Demokratischen Republik und ihre Verwirklichung in Kunst und Literatur. Leipzig, Deutsche Bücherei, 1963. 30 p. (Bibliographischer Informationsdienst der Deutschen Bücherei, Nr. 2)

Valuable guide to the theoretical literature on the "cultural revolution," especially useful for its reference to unpublished scholarly studies and to newspaper articles.

B. CULTURAL POLICIES AND TRENDS

1565. Abusch, Alexander. Kulturelle Probleme des sozialistischen Humanismus; Beiträge zur deutschen Kulturpolitik, 1946-1961. Berlin, Aufbau-Verlag, 1962. 547 p. (*His* Schriften, Bd. 3)

Valuable both as a chronicle of cultural developments in the DDR and as the viewpoint of one of the most articulate and talented East German communist intellectuals. *See also* his *Im ideologischen Kampf für eine sozialistische Kultur. Rede auf der Kulturkonferenz der SED am 23. Oktober 1957 in Berlin* (Berlin, Dietz, 1957) and "Die nationale Aufgabe der sozialistischen Kultur in der DDR. Rede auf dem VI. Bundeskongress des Deutschen Kulturbundes am 8. Juni 1963 in Berlin" in *Sonntag* (Berlin), v. 18, no. 24, June 16, 1963, supplement.

1566. Aufbau; kulturpolitische Monatsschrift. 1945– Berlin.

Organ of the Kulturbund zur Demokratischen Erneuerung Deutschlands and a faithful mirror of official policy shifts in the cultural field.

1567. Balluseck, Lothar von. Kultura; Kunst und Literatur in der sowjetischen Besatzungszone. Köln, Rote Weissbücher, 1952. 132 p.

A critical but well-informed survey of DDR cultural policy.

1568. Berlin. Institut für Gesellschaftswissenschaften. *Lehrstuhl für Theorie und Geschichte der Literatur und Kunst.* Kultur in unserer Zeit; zur Theorie und Praxis der sozialistischen Kulturrevolution in der DDR. Berlin, Dietz, 1965. 447 p. Bibliographies.

Essays on various aspects of the "cultural revolution" in DDR policy, compiled under the direction of Horst Kessler and Fred Staufenbiel. Includes a useful appendix, "Chronology of cultural policy events 1945-1964."

1569. Berlin. Institut für Gesellschaftswissenschaften. *Lehrstuhl für Theorie und Geschichte der Literatur und Kunst.* Kultur und Arbeiterklasse; fünf Aufsätze. Berlin, Dietz, 1959. 230 p. Bibliographies.

Essays by five cultural functionaries designed to carry out the task set by the Fifth Congress of the SED, "to complete the building (Aufbau) of socialism in the DDR."

1570. Deutscher Kulturbund. *6th Congress, June 8-9, 1963.* VI. Bundeskongress des Deutschen Kulturbundes, 8.-9. Juni 1963 in Berlin. Berlin, Deutscher Kulturbund, 1963. 164 p.

1571. Deutscher Kulturkongress. *1st, Leipzig, 1951.* Deutsche sprechen mit Deutschen. Aus dem Protokoll vom Ersten Deutschen Kulturkongress in Leipzig, vom 16. bis 18. Mai 1951. (n.p.), 1952. 139 p.

Documentary record of an early effort to employ culture in the drive to reunify Germany on communist terms.

1572. Germany (*Democratic Republic, 1949–*) *Laws, statutes, etc.* Kulturrecht; eine Sammlung kulturrechtlicher Bestimmungen für Kulturfunktionäre und Kulturschaffende. 2d rev. ed. Berlin, Staatsverlag der Deutschen Demokratischen Republik, 1963. 992 p.

An indispensable compilation of basic legislation in the cultural field. Compiled by Georg Münzer for the Ministerium für Kultur. First edition published in Berlin (Deutscher Zentralverlag, 1959, 1004 p.).

1573. Germany (*Democratic Republic, 1949–*) *Ministerium für Kultur.* Theorie und Praxis der kulturellen Massenarbeit. Meissen, Siebeneichen, 1961–

Correspondence course for cultural functionaries, prepared by the "Martin Andersen Nexö School" of the Ministry of Culture.

1574. Germany (*Democratic Republic, 1949–*) *Ministerium für Kultur.* Über die weitere Verbesserung der Kulturarbeit auf dem Lande; Referat, Diskussion und Dokumente der Kollegiumssitzung des Ministeriums für Kultur in Seelow am 29. November 1960 zur Vorbereitung des V. Deutschen Bauernkongresses. Berlin, Deutscher Zentralverlag, 1961. 111 p.

Records of an attempt to upgrade DDR cultural policies for the peasantry.

1575. Germany (*Democratic Republic, 1949–*) *Ministerium für Kultur.* Zur Verteidigung der Einheit der deutschen Kultur; Programmerklärung, März 1954. Berlin, 1954. 80 p.

Culture as a weapon in the reunification campaign. Includes the text of the decree establishing the DDR Ministry of Culture, p. 71-80.

1576. John, Erhard. Probleme der Kultur und der Kulturarbeit. 2d rev. ed. Berlin, Henschel, 1965. 339 p.

Updated edition of a work first published in 1957 by one of the most prolific and influential party theorists in the field of culture. *See also* his *Das Leben wird schöner; Betrachtungen zur sozialistischen Kulturrevolution* (Leipzig, Urania-Verlag, 1961, 94 p.); *Propädeutik zur einer Theorie der Kultur und der Kulturrevolution*, doctoral dissertation (Berlin, Humboldt University, 1956); *Die sozialistische Kulturrevolution in der Deutschen Demokratischen Republik* (Berlin, Dietz, 1960, 32 p.); and *Technische Revolution und kulturelle Massenarbeit* (Berlin, Dietz, 1965, 188 p.).

1577. Koch, Hans. Kultur in den Kämpfen unserer Tage; theoretische Probleme der sozialistischen Kulturrevolution in der Deutschen Demokratischen Republik. Berlin, Dietz, 1959. 223 p. Bibliography.

A product of the Institut für Gesellschaftswissenschaften under the Central Committee of the SED. Contrasts the "cultural revolution" in the DDR with the "militarization of culture" in Western Germany and sets forth a program of "socialist national culture."

1578. Kurella, Alfred. Erfahrungen und Probleme der sozialistischen Kulturarbeit; Referat auf der Kulturkonferenz in Berlin. Berlin, Aufbau, 1960. 71 p.

Report by an influential communist literary politician.

1579. Lange, Marianne, *ed.* Zur sozialistischen Kulturrevolution: Dokumente, 1957-1959. Berlin, Aufbau-Verlag, 1960. 2 v.

Documents on SED cultural policy during the early Khrushchev era, with some Soviet texts as guidelines.

1580. Sozialistische Einheitspartei Deutschlands. *5. Parteitag, Berlin, 1958.* Für den Sieg der sozialistischen Revolution auf dem Gebiet der Ideologie und der Kultur. Aus dem Referat und dem Schlusswort des Genossen Walter Ulbricht, aus den Diskussionsreden und dem Beschluss des V. Parteitages der Sozialistischen Einheitspartei Deutschlands, Berlin, 10. bis 16. Juli 1958. Berlin, Dietz, 1958. 304 p.

Basic texts on a turning point in communist cultural policy in East Germany.

1581. Sozialistische Einheitspartei Deutschlands. *Ideologische Kommission.* Zweite Bitterfelder Konferenz 1964; Protokoll der von der Ideologischen Kommission beim Politbüro des ZK der SED und dem Ministerium für Kultur am 24. und 25. April im Kulturpalast des Elektrochemischen Kombinats Bitterfeld abgehaltenen Konferenz. Berlin, Dietz, 1964. 527 p.

Documentary record of the attempt to maintain the spirit of the first "Bitterfeld Conference" in DDR cultural policy. For an informed Western commentary, *see* "Die Revolution von Bitterfeld. Von der ersten zur zweiten SED-Kulturkonferenz," by Heinz Kersten, *Der Monat* (Berlin), v. 12, no. 141, 1964: 87-92.

1582. Sozialistische Einheitspartei Deutschlands. *Kulturkonferenz, Berlin, 1957.* Für eine sozialistische deutsche Kultur; die Entwicklung der sozialistischen Kultur in der Zeit des zweiten Fünfjahrplanes. Thesen der Kulturkonferenz der Sozialistischen Einheitspartei Deutschlands 23. und 24. Oktober 1957 in Berlin. Berlin, Dietz, 1957. 77 p.

Record of an early stage in the effort to evolve a viable cultural policy within the framework of the DDR's economic plans.

1583. Sozialistische Einheitspartei Deutschlands. *Kulturkonferenz, Berlin, 1960.* Protokoll der vom Zentralkomitee der SED, dem Ministerium für Kultur und dem Deutschen Kulturbund vom 27. bis 29. April 1960 im VEB Elektrokohle, Berlin, abgehaltenen Konferenz. Berlin, Dietz, 1960. 460 p.

Documentary record of a major landmark in the development of communist cultural policy in East Germany.

1584. Sozialistische Einheitspartei Deutschlands. *Zentralkomitee.* Der Kampf gegen den Formalismus in Kunst und Literatur, für eine fortschrittliche deutsche Kultur. Einheit (Berlin), v. 6, 1951: 579-592.

Text of the resolution adopted at a plenum March 15-17, 1951, which marked the beginning of the imposition of socialist realism as the obligatory style in the arts and literature in the DDR.

1585. Staufenbiel, Fred. Wesen und nationale Bedeutung der sozialistischen Kulturrevolution in der Deutschen Demokratischen Republik. Berlin, Institut für Gesellschaftswissenschaften, 1962. 2 v. (typescript).

This dissertation, published under the auspices of the Central Committee of the SED, is both a theoretical analysis of the concept of culture and a practical consideration of the problems involved in the use of cultural nationalism in DDR policy. *See also* the author's article, "Grundfragen der Leninschen Theorie von der sozialistischen Kulturrevolution und die kulturelle Entwicklung in der DDR," in *Deutsche Zeitschrift für Philosophie* (Berlin), v. 8, no. 8, 1960: 901-917.

1586. Ulbricht, Walter. Referat: Das Programm des Sozialismus und die geschichtliche Aufgabe der Sozialistischen Einheitspartei Deutschlands. Schlusswort des Genossen Walter Ulbricht zur Diskussion über die schriftlich vorgelegten Berichte, über das Programm und über das Referat. Programm der SED. Berlin, Dietz, 1963. 394 p.

Authoritative pronouncements on party cultural policy by the SED First Secretary. For a volume of tributes to Ulbricht, see *Walter Ulbricht: Schriftsteller, Künstler, Wissenschaftler und Pädagogen zu seinem siebzigsten Geburtstag,* edited by Alexander Abusch and others (Berlin, Aufbau-Verlag, 1963, 283 p., ports.).

1587. Ulbricht, Walter, *and* Kurt Hager. Parteilichkeit und Volksverbundenheit unserer Literatur und Kunst. Reden auf der Beratung des Politbüros des Zentralkomitees und des Präsidiums des Ministerrats mit Schriftstellern und Künstlern am 25. und 26. März 1963. Berlin, Dietz, 1963. 103 p.

Speeches on cultural policy emphasizing party controls and anathematizing Western influences at the conference called by the SED in faithful imitation of the Soviet conference held in the Kremlin March 7-8, 1963.

1588. Wagner, Helmut R. The Cultural Sovietization of East Germany. Social Research (New York), v. 24, Winter 1957: 395-426.

Report by an American sociologist, based on a longer study.

1589. Wandel, Paul. Reden zur Kulturpolitik. Berlin, 1955. 98 p. Port.

C. EDUCATION AND LEARNING

by Lyman H. Legters

1. Education

1590. Baske, Siegfried, *ed.* Zwei Jahrzehnte Bildungspolitik in der Sowjetzone Deutschlands. Dokumente. Heidelberg, Quelle & Meyer, 1966. 2 v. Bibliography: v. 2, p. 470-473. (Osteuropa-Institut an der Freien Universität Berlin. Erziehungswissenschaftliche Veröffentlichungen, Bd. 2)

A full and judicious selection of documents covering educational developments from 1945 through 1965. René Frenzel has also edited for the East German Ministerium für Volksbildung a documentary collection entitled *Sozialistische Schule; eine Zusammenstellung der wichtigsten gesetzlichen Bestimmungen und Dokumente* (Berlin, Staatsverlag der Deutschen Demokratischen Republik, 1963, 544 p.).

1591. Bodenman, Paul S. Education in the Soviet Zone of Germany. Washington, D.C., U.S. Dept. of Health, Education, and Welfare, Office of Education, 1959. 162 p. Illus., maps, tables. Bibliography: p. 141-155. (U.S. Office of Education Bulletin, 1959, no. 26)

Surveys the East German school system and its role in society, giving particular attention to the organization of education, with substantial statistical data for the period covered. More recent treatment is found in:

Froese, Leonhard. Sowjetisierung der deutschen Schule; Entwicklung und Struktur des mitteldeutschen Bildungswesens. Freiburg, Herder, 1962. 83 p. Illus.

1592. Education in the German Democratic Republic. Leipzig, VEB Edition, 1962. 182 p. Bibliography: p. 177-182.

This translation of a German work is a convenient and official exposition of the East German school system.

1593. Germany (*Federal Republic, 1949–*) *Bundesministerium für Gesamtdeutsche Fragen.* Universitäten und Hochschulen in der Sowjetzone. 4th ed. Bonn, Bundesministerium für Gesamtdeutsche Fragen, 1964. 69 p.

A convenient list of institutions of higher education with basic information about them and the system to which they belong.

1594. Gutsche, Heinz. Die Erwachsenenbildung in der sowjetischen Besatzungszone Deutschlands. Bonn, Bundesministerium für Gesamtdeutsche Fragen, 1958. 2 v.

A study of adult education in the first volume with a documentary collection in the second. See also *Erwachsenenbildung, Erwachsenenqualifizierung* (Heidelberg, Quelle & Meyer, 1968, 216 p.), a study with documentation by Joachim H. Knoll and Horst Siebert.

1595. Das Hochschulwesen. 1– Jahrg.; Aug. 1953– Berlin, Deutscher Verlag der Wissenschaften. Monthly.

This journal, issued by the Staatssekretariat für Hoch- und Fachschulwesen, emphasizes problems of academic administration.

1596. Kaltenbach, Bernd. Die Fachrichtung Philosophie an den Universitäten der Sowjetzone 1945 bis 1958. Bonn, Deutscher Bundesverlag, 1959. 117 p.

An account of philosophy as an academic discipline at East German universities and the effects that official ideology had on it.

1597. Lange, Max Gustav. Totalitäre Erziehung; das Erziehungssystem der Sowjetzone Deutschlands. Frankfurt am Main, Verlag der Frankfurter Hefte, 1954. 432 p. (Schriften des Instituts für Politische Wissenschaft, Bd. 3)

An analysis of educational policy and its implementation with particular reference to the doctrinal aims of the regime.

1598. Lücke, Peter R. Das Schulbuch in der Sowjetzone; Lehrbücher im Dienst totalitärer Propaganda. 11th rev. and enl. ed. Bonn, Bundesministerium für Gesamtdeutsche Fragen, 1966. 143 p.

A compilation of excerpts from East German textbooks in history, government, geography, German, and mathematics illustrating the style of indoctrination used in the schools.

1599. Möbus, Gerhard. Unterwerfung durch Erziehung; zur politischen Pädagogik im sowjetisch besetzten Deutschland. Mainz, Hase und Koehler, 1965. 434 p. Bibliography.

Details the use of pedagogy for the political ends of the regime. *See also* Erwin Säuberlich's *Vom Humanismus zum demokratischen Patriotismus; Schule und Jugenderziehung in der sowjetischen Besatzungszone* (Köln, Verlag für Politik und Wirtschaft, 1954, 169 p.).

1600. Müller, Marianne. ". . . stürmt die Festung Wissenschaft!" Die Sowjetisierung der mitteldeutschen Universitäten seit 1945. Berlin-Dahlem, Colloquium Verlag, 1953. 415 p. Illus., ports. Bibliography: p. 388.

See also entry no. 1544.

A detailed account of the subjugation of higher education in East Germany, paying particular attention to the position of faculty and students in the process. A compact supplement on conditions leading to the splitting off of a Free University in Berlin is found in Georg Kotowski's "Der Kampf um Berlins Universität" in *Veritas, Iustitia, Libertas; Festschrift zur 200-Jahrfeier der Columbia University, New York, . . .* (Berlin, Colloquium-Verlag, 1954, p. 7-31).

1601. Pädagogik; Zeitschrift für Theorie und Praxis der sozialistischen Erziehung. 1. Jahrg.– Aug. 1946– Berlin, Volk und Wissen. Monthly.

This journal, issued by the Deutsches Pädagogisches Zentralinstitut, aims at supplying East German teachers with up-to-date educational insights.

1602. Pädagogische Enzyklopädie. Edited by Heinz Frankiewicz and others. Berlin, Deutscher Verlag der Wissenschaften, 1963. 2 v. (1078 p.) Bibliographies.

This comprehensive reference work consists of signed articles with individual bibliographies and covers various aspects of the East German school system, as well as other subjects of interest to educators.

1603. Richert, Ernst. Sozialistische Universität. Die Hochschulpolitik der SED. Berlin, Colloquium Verlag, 1967. 279 p. Bibliographical references included in "Anmerkungen": p. 260-270.

See also entry no. 1545.

Reviews the development of East German universities since 1945, relating the several distinct phases of higher educational policy to the stages of development through which the East German regime has passed.

1604. Studien- und Hochschulführer der Deutschen Demokratischen Republik. Berlin, Deutscher Verlag der Wissenschaften. Annual.

A guide to the curricula offered at East German universities and colleges.

1605. Wendt, Emil. Die Entwicklung der Lehrerbildung in der sowjetischen Besatzungszone seit 1945. 2d rev. & enl. ed. Bonn, Bundesministerium für Gesamtdeutsche Fragen, 1959. 131 p.

Provides a background of East German teacher training.

1606. Wittig, Horst E. Pläne und Praktiken der polytechnischen Erziehung in Mitteldeutschland. Harzburg, Verlag für Wissenschaft, Wirtschaft und Technik, 1962. 135 p. Illus. Bibliography. (Wirtschaft und Schule, Bd. 3)

A compact review of the implementation of educational policy followed by a selection of pertinent documents. The same author has provided a selected bibliography, *Das Bildungswesen der "DDR"; Literatur zur Einführung in die ideologischen, historischen, politischen Grundlagen und pädagogischen Probleme des mitteldeutschen Bildungswesens* (Frankfurt am Main, Hochschule für Internationale Pädagogische Forschung, 1960, 172 p.).

2. Cultural Institutions*

1607. Akademie der Wissenschaften, *Berlin.* Deutsche Akademie der Wissenschaften zu Berlin, 1946-1956. Edited by Johannes Irmscher and Werner Radig. Berlin, Akademie-Verlag, 1956. 447 p. Illus., ports., maps. Bibliographies.

**See also* chapter 22, section D.

A symposium providing a broad panorama of the academy's organization and work.

1608. Archivmitteilungen; Zeitschrift für Theorie und Praxis des Archivwesens. 1– 1951– Berlin, Staatsverlag der Deutschen Demokratischen Republik. Bimonthly.

A journal devoted to East German archival practice and to the description of East German archives.

1609. Art Treasures of the Berlin State Museums. Introduction by John Russell. New York, H. N. Abrams, 1965. 269 p. Illus., plates.

This well-illustrated work is the American edition of a survey of East Berlin art collections.

1610. Dunken, Gerhard. Die Deutsche Akademie der Wissenschaften zu Berlin in Vergangenheit und Gegenwart. 2d enl. ed. Berlin, Akademie-Verlag, 1960. 235 p. Illus., ports., facsims. Bibliography: p. 209-220.

A detailed survey describing the development of the Berlin Academy of Sciences since its foundation in 1700.

1611. Germany (*Democratic Republic, 1949–*) *Staatliche Archivverwaltung*. Aufbau und Entwicklung des Archivwesens der Deutschen Demokratischen Republik. Berlin-Wilhelmsruh, Verlag des Ministeriums des Innern, 1959. 80 p. Illus.

A brief and informative account of the development and structure of the East German archival system.

1612. Knorr, Heinz Arno. Handbuch der Museen und wissenschaftlichen Sammlungen in der Deutschen Demokratischen Republik. Halle/Saale, Fachstelle für Heimatmuseen beim Ministerium für Kultur, 1963. 520 p.

A well-indexed and useful reference work on East German museums and scientific collections by district.

1613. Menz, Henner. The Dresden Gallery. Translated from the German by Daphne Woodward. New York, Abrams, 1962. 320 p.

A profusely illustrated guide to one of the great art collections. A translation of *Die Dresdener Gemäldegalerie* (München, Droemer, 1962, 319 p.).

3. The Impact of Ideology

1614. Friedrich, Gerd. Der Kulturbund zur demokratischen Erneuerung Deutschlands: Geschichte und Funktion. Köln, Rote Weissbücher, 1952. 143 p.

See also entry no. 1537.

Reviews the history and function of the East German agency founded to gear cultural and intellectual activity to the purposes of the regime.

1615. Germany (*Federal Republic, 1949–*) *Bundesministerium für Gesamtdeutsche Fragen.* Polit-Kunst in der sowjetischen Besatzungszone Deutschlands. Die Deutschen Kunstausstellungen in Dresden. 4th rev. and enl. ed. Bonn, 1965. 64 p. Illus.

Sketches the history of the East German party line concerning art and shows its consequences in the painting and sculpture exhibited in the Dresden art shows.

1616. Handbuch für den Kulturfunktionär. 2d rev. ed. Berlin, Verlag Tribüne, 1965. 685 p. Bibliography: p. 666-676.
See also entry no. 1562.

This handbook, primarily designed for the use by East German trade union functionaries, provides useful insights into cultural policies and programs.

1617. Hiob, Frank. Aspekte der Wissenschaftspolitik in der SBZ. Bonn, Bundesministerium für Gesamtdeutsche Fragen, 1962. 26 p.

Reflections on the official guidance and control of science and scholarship.

1618. Kersten, Heinz. Repercussions in East Germany. Survey, No. 48, July 1963: 36-46.

An informative survey of the impact of Soviet cultural policies on the East German scene.

1619. Krebs, Herbert. Ein kulturvolles Leben entwickeln; die Leitung der kulturellen Massenarbeit in den städtischen Wohnbezirken und Dörfern. Berlin, Staatsverlag der Deutschen Demokratischen Republik, 1963. 250 p.

An East German publication on the extension of cultural activities on the local level.

1620. Lange, Max Gustav. Wissenschaft im totalitären Staat; die Wissenschaft der sowjetischen Besatzungszone auf dem Weg zum Stalinismus. Stuttgart, Ring-Verlag, 1955. 295 p. (Schriften des Instituts für Politische Wissenschaft, Bd. 5)

The experience of scholarship under the East German regime is shown as an instance of totalitarian subjugation to ideological control.

1621. Leutwein, Alfred, *pseud.* (Siegfried Mampel). Die technische Intelligenz in der sowjetischen Besatzungszone. Bonn, Deutscher Bundes-Verlag, 1953. 56 p.

A review of the state of technically trained manpower and of the regime's concern with this segment of the East German population.

1622. Ludz, Peter Christian, *ed.* Studien und Materialien zur Soziologie der DDR. Köln, Opladen, Westdeutscher Verlag, 1964. 540 p. (Kölner Zeitschrift für Soziologie und Sozialpsychologie. Sonderheft Nr. 8)

See also entry no. 1533.

Contains substantial chapters on the Academy of Sciences, the organization of research, the state of sociology and social research, cybernetics, and the history of philosophy and philosophy of history, as well as a detailed bibliography.

D. PHILOSOPHY AND AESTHETICS

1623. Bloch, Ernst. Das Prinzip Hoffnung. Berlin, Aufbau-Verlag, 1954-59. 3 v.

The magnum opus of one of the leading neo-Marxist philosophers of postwar Germany. *See also* "Werkausgabe in fünfzehn Bänden Plan," as published on p. 417 of *Ernst Bloch zu Ehren*, edited by S. Unseld (Frankfurt am Main, Suhrkamp, 1965): I. Spuren. II. Thomas Münzer als Theologe der Revolution. III. Geist der Utopie. IV. Erbschaft dieser Zeit. V. Das Prinzip Hoffnung. VI. Naturrecht und menschliche Würde. VII. Geschichte und Gehalt des Begriffs Materie. VIII. Subjekt-Objekt. Erläuterungen zu Hegel. IX. Literarische Aufsätze. X. Philosophische Aufsätze. XI. Politische Aufsätze. XII. Leipziger Vorlesungen zur Geschichte der Philosophie. XIII. Tübinger Einleitung in die Philosophie. XIV. Experimentum Mundi, Religion des Exodus und des Reichs. Zentren der Logik und Metaphysik. XV. Geist der Utopie (Erste Fassung 1918).

For critical and polemical studies of Bloch's philosophy, *see* entry no. 1634.

1624. Bütow, Hellmuth G. Geschichte der Philosophie und Philosophie der Geschichte in der DDR. Eine ideologiekritische Analyse. *In* Ludz, Peter C., *ed.* Studien und Materialen zur Soziologie der DDR. Köln, Opladen, 1964. p. 442-463. Bibliography: p. 535-540.

A systematic, chronological survey of the literature on philosophy, history of philosophy, and philosophy of history in the DDR, with extensive bibliographical references.

1625. Die deutsche Philosophie von 1895-1917. Berlin, Deutscher Verlag der Wissenschaften, 1962. 112 p.

One of a series of popularized surveys of the development of modern German philosophy in Marxist reinterpretation. For other volumes in the series see: *Die deutsche Philosophie von 1917-1945* (Berlin, Deutscher Verlag der Wissenschaften, 1961, 160 p., Taschenbuchreihe "Unser Weltbild," Bd. 18) and *Die deutsche Philosophie nach 1945* (Berlin, Deutscher Verlag der Wissenschaften, 1961, 111 p., Taschenbuchreihe "Unser Weltbild," Bd. 19).

1626. Deutsche Zeitschrift für Philosophie. Oktoberrevolution und Philosophie. Beiträge der Deutschen Zeitschrift für Philosophie zum 40. Jahrestag der Grossen Sozialistischen Oktoberrevolution. Berlin,

Deutscher Verlag der Wissenschaften, 1958. 263 p. (Taschenbuchreihe "Unser Weltbild," Bd. 2)

Takes in not only questions of philosophy but also national and international politics — German reunification and "peaceful coexistence" as interpreted at the November 1957 Moscow conference of communist parties.

The sponsoring journal, *Deutsche Zeitschrift für Philosophie* (Berlin, 1952–) is the official DDR philosophy organ.

1627. Gropp, Rugard Otto. Der dialektische Materialismus; kurzer Abriss. 2d ed. Leipzig, Verlag Enzyklopädie, 1961. 163 p.

Revised edition of a popularized account first published in 1958, reprinted in West Germany (Munich) 1960. The author, a favored spokesman for the political line in philosophy, has also written *Das nationale philosophische Erbe; über die progressive Grundlinie in der deutschen Philosophiegeschichte* (Berlin, Deutscher Verlag der Wissenschaften, 1960, 140 p., bibliographies).

1628. Havemann, Robert. Dialektik ohne Dogma? Naturwissenschaft und Weltanschauung. Reinbeck bei Hamburg, Rowohlt, 1964. 168 p. *See also* entry no. 1538.

The basic text of one of the leading intellectual *causes célèbres* in the DDR. Havemann, a prominent scientist and theorist (author of a textbook on thermodynamics and over 100 scientific papers), delivered a series of lectures and seminar presentations from October 18, 1963, to January 31, 1964, at Humboldt University in East Berlin. The lectures were taped and mimeographed, and the published text is a corrected version checked by the author. Its publication, unauthorized and by a leading West German publisher, ended the author's career as a philosopher of science, a member of the SED, and a professor. According to the *Times Literary Supplement* (London), August 24, 1967, page 755, "[the book] contains a frank discussion of the political and scientific discussions which took place under Stalin and it makes a strong plea for greater freedom and honesty in all fields of academic inquiry and for a more flexible approach to moral values under socialism." *See also* "Freiheitsphilosophie oder aufgeklärter Dogmatismus? Zum Denken Robert Havemanns" by Peter Christian Ludz, *SBZ-Archiv* (Köln), v. 15, 1964, nos. 12, 13.

For an orthodox treatment of the same subject, *see* H. Hörz' *Natur und Erkenntnis: philosophisch-methodologische Fragen der modernen Naturwissenschaft* (Berlin, Deutscher Verlag der Wissenschaften, 1964, 292 p., bibliographies).

For an earlier Marxist discussion of some of the same problems see *Naturwissenschaft und Philosophie; Beiträge zum Internationalen Symposium über Naturwissenschaft und Philosophie anlässlich der 550-Jahr-Feier der Karl-Marx-Universität Leipzig*, edited by Gerhard Harig and Josef Schleifstein (Berlin, Akademie-Verlag, 1960, 436 p.). See also *Moderne Naturwissenschaft und Atheismus*, edited by Olof Klohr (Berlin, Deutscher Verlag der Wissenschaften, 1964,

312 p.); *Streitgespräche über Grundfragen der Naturwissenschaft und Philosophie* by Alfred Pfeiffer, foreword by Robert Havemann (Berlin, Deutscher Verlag der Wissenschaften, 1961, 149 p.); and *Naturforschung und Weltbild; eine Einführung in Probleme der marxistischen Naturphilosophie*, edited by Martin Guntau and Helge Wendt (Berlin, Deutscher Verlag der Wissenschaften, 1964, 286 p.).

1629. John, Erhard. Untersuchungen über die Bedeutung der Widerspiegelungstheorie für die Ästhetik. Leipzig, 1961. 2 parts in 3 v. (typescript).

Author's doctoral dissertation, on the "reflection theory" of art and its practical application to the problems posed by the "socialist cultural revolution." For other writings by the prolific and influential author, *see* his *Gegenstand und Aufgaben der Marxistisch-Leninistischen Ästhetik. Methodische Anleitung, Thesen und Literatur* (Leipzig, Karl-Marx-Universität, Fakultät für Journalistik, 1959, 121 p.), *Zum Problem der Beziehungen zwischen Kunst und Wirklichkeit; Vortrag gehalten auf der Literaturwissenschaftlichen Tagung des Slawischen Instituts am 24. Juni 1960* (Leipzig, Verlag Enzyklopädie, 1961, 19 p.), and "Ästhetik und sozialistische Praxis," *Deutsche Zeitschrift für Philosophie* (Berlin), v. 11, no. 1, 1963: 80-93. *See also* his writings listed above under Section B.

1630. Klaus, Georg. Moderne Logik; Abriss der formalen Logik. Berlin, Deutscher Verlag der Wissenschaften, 1964. 452 p.

A textbook by a leading Marxist philosopher in the DDR. *See also* his *Kybernetik in philosophischer Sicht* (3d rev. ed., Berlin, Dietz, 1963, 543 p.), *Die Macht des Wortes; ein erkenntnistheoretisch-pragmatisches Traktat* (Berlin, Deutscher Verlag der Wissenschaften, 1964, 198 p.), and *Semiotik und Erkenntnistheorie* (Berlin, Deutscher Verlag der Wissenschaften, 1963, 164 p.).

1631. Klaus, Georg, *and* Manfred Buhr, *eds.* Philosophisches Wörterbuch. Leipzig, Bibliographisches Institut, 1964. 634 p.

Defines nearly 1,000 terms, in accordance with the works of Marx, Engels, and Lenin, and the "basic documents of the SED and the CPSU, as well as the programs of both parties." Covers dialectical and historical materialism; history of philosophy; modern logic; theory of science and methodology; aspects of natural science and cybernetics relevant to philosophy. Prepared with the aid of the Institute for Philosophy and the Institute for the History of the Natural Sciences and Technology of the Soviet Academy of Sciences and the editorial board of the Philosophical Encyclopedia, Moscow.

1632. Klaus, Georg, A. Kosing, *and* G. Redlow. Dialektischer Materialismus. Berlin, Dietz, 1959. 5 v.

1633. Koch, Hans. Marxismus und Ästhetik; zur ästhetischen Theorie von Karl Marx, Friedrich Engels und Wladimir Iljitsch Lenin. Berlin, Dietz, 1961. 627 p.

A publication of the Institut für Gesellschaftswissenschaften attached to the Central Committee of the SED.

1634. Unseld, Siegfried, *ed.* Ernst Bloch zu Ehren; Beiträge zu seinem Werke. Frankfurt am Main, Suhrkamp, 1965. 413 p. Bibliography: p. 395-413.

A collection of critical essays by a number of writers on Bloch's philosophy. The work of Bloch has attracted widespread interest in postwar Germany. The following should be consulted:

Bütow, Hellmuth G. Philosophie und Gesellschaft im Denken Ernst Blochs. Wiesbaden, Harrassowitz, 1963. 159 p. (Philosophische und soziologische Veröffentlichungen des Osteuropa-Instituts an der Freien Universität Berlin, v. 3)

Ernst Blochs Revision des Marxismus. Kritische Auseinandersetzungen Marxistischer Wissenschaftler mit der Blochschen Philosophie. Berlin, Deutscher Verlag der Wissenschaften, 1957. 352 p. Contributions by a number of DDR scholars, including R. O. Gropp, originally presented at a "Conference on Questions of Bloch's Philosophy" held April 4-5, 1957, at the Institute for Philosophy of the Karl-Marx-Universität, Leipzig, on the initiative of the SED Politburo, aimed at overcoming the "harmful influence" exerted by Bloch's philosophy on "certain circles of the intelligentsia and students." The symposium reached the conclusion that Bloch's philosophy could not be reconciled with the principles of the writings of Marx, Engels, and Lenin.

Gropp, Rugard O., *ed.* Festschrift. Ernst Bloch zum 70. Geburtstag. Berlin, Deutscher Verlag der Wissenschaften, 1955. 305 p. Bloch's DDR scholarly colleagues salute him as a humanist socialist whose work "has been devoted to the struggle against imperialist, militarist, and antidemocratic forces." Includes a brief biographical sketch of Bloch, culminating in his election, in March 1955, as a regular member of the German Academy of Sciences, Berlin. Bibliography of Bloch's writings, p. 13-15.

Gropp, Rugard O. Mystische Hoffnungsphilosophie ist unvereinbar mit dem Marxismus. *In*: Forum (Berlin), 1957, no. 6.

E. RELIGION

1635. Arnold, Heinz, *ed.* Die Jugendweihe in der Deutschen Demokratischen Republik; Materialsammlung. Zusammengestellt für die Mitarbeiter und Helfer der Jugendweihe, die Elternbeiräte und Klassenelternaktivs, die Lehrer und Erzieher. Berlin, Deutscher Zentralverlag, 1961. 96 p. (Sozialistische Erziehung und Bildung der Kinder und Jugendlichen, 5)

Basic documentary materials on the youth ceremony, designed to replace religious (Jewish or Christian) induction rites for young people. For other DDR materials on the youth ceremony, see *Gewerkschaften und Jugendweihe*, by Gerhard Allendorf (Berlin, Verlag Tribüne, 1960, 50 p.), and *Mein Kind und unsere Welt;*

über den Sinn der Jugendweihe in der DDR, by Herbert Steininger (Berlin, Dietz, 1961, 89 p.).

For critical West German studies of the youth ceremony, see *Die Jugendweihe in der Sowjetzone*, by U. Jeremias (2d enl. ed., Bonn, Bundesministerium für Gesamtdeutsche Fragen, 1958, 120 p.; 1st ed., 1956, 78 p.), and *Pseudo-sakrale Staatsakte in Mitteldeutschland*, by Hans Köhler (Witten, Luther-Verlag, 1962, 71 p.).

1636. Bessert, Lieselotte. Getrennte, die zusammengehören; Bericht aus dem Leben der Evangelischen Kirche in Berlin-Brandenburg. Stuttgart, Kreuz-Verlag, 1963. 93 p. Illus., ports.

A West German report on the Evangelical Church in the DDR. For first-hand reports issued under the auspices of the church itself, *see*:

Evangelische-Lutherische Kirche in Thüringen. In disciplina Domini; In der Schule des Herrn. Berlin, Evangelische Verlagsanstalt, 1963. 310 p.

Friedrich, Karl J. Christliche Zeugen. Berlin, Evangelische Verlagsanstalt, 1963. 207 p.

Fritzsche, Hans G. Evangelische Ethik; die Gebote Gottes als Grundprinzipien christlichen Handelns. Berlin, Evangelische Verlagsanstalt, 1961. 299 p.

Wachler, Günter. Das Geheimnis der Frömmigkeit; ein Jahrgang Predigten. Berlin, Evangelische Verlagsanstalt, 1964. 506 p.

For a hostile critique of the church's activities see *Der Kreuzzug der evangelischen Akademien gegen den Marxismus*, by Dieter Bergner (Berlin, Dietz, 1960).

1637. Dohmann, Albrecht, *and others, comps.* Der Wiederaufbau der Kirchen in der Deutschen Demokratischen Republik. Berlin, Union Verlag, 1964. 242 p. Illus. Bibliography.

On postwar reconstruction. For an illustrated survey, see *Kirchen in Mitteldeutschland; Bestand, Vernichtung, Erhaltung*, by Horst Hempert (Frankfurt am Main, Weidlich, 1962, 112 p., illus., Deutschland im Bild, Sonderheft 2).

1638. Fischer, Gerhard, *and others.* Fruchtbares Gespräch. Der Christ und die moderne Wissenschaft. Essays. Berlin, Union Verlag, 1962. 185 p.

Essays selected to demonstrate the compatibility of Christian belief with science. See also *Vom Jenseits zum Diesseits. Wegweiser zum Atheismus*, edited by G. Heyden and others (Leipzig-Jena, 1959-62, 3 v., Wegweiser zum Atheismus, Bd. 1-3); *Wissenschaft, Weltanschauung und religiöser Glaube* by R. Kirchoff (Berlin, 1959, 97 p.); *Naturwissenschaft, Religion und Kirche* by O. Klohr (Berlin, 1959, 139 p.); *Naturerkenntnis oder Gottesglaube; über Wesen und Funktion der naturwissenschaftlich-atheistischen Aufklärung* by Horst Mädicke (Leipzig, Urania-Verlag, 1961, 238 p.); and *Gottbekenntnisse moderner Naturforscher* by Hubert Muschalek (3d rev. and enl. ed., Berlin, Morus-Verlag, 1960, 296 p.).

1639. Germany (*Democratic Republic, 1949–*) *Staatsrat.* Marxisten und Christen wirken gemeinsam für Frieden und Humanismus. Mit einer ausführlichen Fassung des Gesprächs des Vorsitzenden des Staatsrates der DDR, Walter Ulbricht, mit Landesbischof D. Moritz Mitzenheim auf der Wartburg bei Eisenach am 18. August 1964 und weiteren wichtigen Dokumenten und Materialien. Berlin, Staatsverlag der Deutschen Demokratischen Republik, 1964. 88 p. (Schriftenreihe des Staatsrates der Deutschen Demokratischen Republik, Nr. 5)

Documentation on one of the more important efforts in the continuing campaign by DDR political leaders to enlist the support of the churches in their policies. For other materials on this subject *see:*

Germany (*Democratic Republic, 1949–*) *Staatsrat.* Sozialisten und Christen verbinden gemeinsame Ideale und Ziele. Berlin, Deutscher Zentralverlag, 1961. 31 p.

Krüger, Ulrich. Das Prinzip der Trennung von Staat und Kirche in Deutschland. Berlin, 1958. 27 p.

Meinecke, Werner. Die Kirche in der volksdemokratischen Ordnung der Deutschen Demokratischen Republik; ein Beitrag zur Klärung einiger Grundfragen des Verhältnisses von Staat und Kirche in der DDR. Berlin, Union Verlag, 1962. 176 p. Bibliography: p. 171-177.

Zu den Beziehungen zwischen Kirche und Staat in der DDR. Eine Dokumentation mit Äusserungen führender Persönlichkeiten des staatlichen und kirchlichen Lebens. Berlin, Union-Verlag, 1956. 74 p. Materials collected by the Parteileitung of the CDU.

1640. Götting, Gerald. Entscheidung des Christen für die Sache der Nation. Berlin, Union-Verlag, 1962. 35 p.

Published by the Zentrale Schulungsstätte "Otto Nuschke" in cooperation with the Parteileitung of the CDU. For other writings by the same author, who is Deputy Chairman of the State Council, see *Der Christ sagt ja zum Sozialismus* (Berlin, Union-Verlag, 1960, 247 p.) and *Der Christ beim Aufbau des Sozialismus* (Berlin, Union-Verlag, 1963, 165 p., illus., ports., bibliography).

For other CDU publications on cooperation between Christians and the socialist state, see *Emil Fuchs und die Anfänge des Christlichen Arbeitskreises im Friedensrat der Deutschen Demokratischen Republik*, by Walter Bredendieck (Berlin, 1964, 79 p.); *Politische Diakonie im Sozialismus*, by Hans H. Jenssen (Berlin, 1964, 31 p.); *Christliche Existenz in der sozialistischen Ordnung*, by Gerhard Kehnscherper (Berlin, 1962, 51 p.); and *Suchet der Stadt Bestes; aus dem Leben der evangelischen Kirchen in der Deutschen Demokratischen Republik*, edited by Carl Ordnung (Berlin, 1961, 79 p., illus., ports.).

1641. Mitzenheim, Moritz, *Bishop.* Politische Diakonie; Reden, Erklärungen, Aufsätze, 1946 bis 1964. Berlin, Union Verlag, 1964. 122 p.

1642. Orthodox Eastern Church, Russian. *Patriarch.* Eine kurze Erklärung der göttlichen Liturgie der Orthodoxen Kirche. Berlin, 1960. 22 p.

Prepared by the Central European Exarchate of the Moscow Patriarch. There appears otherwise to be almost no published evidence of the activity of the Russian Orthodox Church in Germany since 1945.

1643. Rittenbach, Willi, *ed.* Verzeichnis der katholischen Pfarreien, Vikarien, Kuratien und sonstiger Seelsorgestellen in der Deutschen Demokratischen Republik und dem demokratischen Berlin, nebst einem Ortsverzeichnis mit Angabe des Kreises und der zuständigen Seelsorgestelle. Leipzig, St. Benno-Verlag, 1962. 326 p.

An official guide to the territorial and administrative structure of the Catholic Church in the DDR. See also *Die Katholische Kirche in Berlin und Mitteldeutschland* (4th rev. ed., Berlin, Morus-Verlag, 1962, 80 p., illus.). There is an English translation of an earlier edition: *The Roman Catholic Church in Berlin and in the Soviet Zone of Germany* (Berlin, Morus-Verlag, 1959, 63 p.).

1644. Schüffler, Joachim, *ed.* Bild und Verkündigung; Festgabe für Hanna Jursch zum 60. Geburtstag. Berlin, Evangelische Verlagsanstalt, 1962. 182 p.

An important vehicle for religious scholarship in the DDR is the festschrift for leading scholars, theologians, and ecclesiastics. Other publications in this form include: *Bekenntnis zur Kirche; Festgabe für Ernst Sommerlath zum 70. Geburtstag* (Berlin, Evangelische Verlagsanstalt, 1960, 403 p.); *Gemeinde Gottes in dieser Welt; Festgabe für Friedrich-Wilhelm Krummacher zum sechzigsten Geburtstag* (Berlin, Evangelische Verlagsanstalt, 1961, 345 p.); *Reich Gottes und Wirklichkeit; Festgabe für Alfred Dedo Müller zum 60. Geburtstag* (Berlin, Evangelische Verlagsanstalt, 1961, 417 p.); *Ruf und Antwort; Festgabe für Emil Fuchs zum 90. Geburtstag* (Leipzig, Koehler und Amelang, 1964, 575 p.); *". . . und fragten nach Jesus." Beiträge aus Theologie, Kirche und Geschichte. Festschrift für Ernst Barnikol zum 70. Geburtstag* (Berlin, Evangelische Verlagsanstalt, 1964, 448 p.); and *Verantwortung; Untersuchungen über Fragen aus Theologie und Geschichte; zum sechzigsten Geburtstag von Landesbischof D. Gottfried Noth D.D.* (Berlin, Evangelische Verlagsanstalt, 1964, 307 p.).

1645. Solberg, Richard W. God and Caesar in East Germany; the Conflicts of Church and State in East Germany Since 1945. Foreword by Bishop Otto Dibelius. New York, Macmillan, 1961. 294 p. Illus.

See also entry no. 1547.

Based on field research carried out in 1959 while the author was on leave from Augustana College and on a "12-year personal acquaintance with the Churches of Germany, dating from 1949 and including almost five years of residence and work in their midst."

According to Bishop Dibelius, "he has presented the course of events with astonishing accuracy and insight." Looks forward to the survival of Christianity in East Germany as a persecuted but militant minority. German translation: *Kirche in der Anfechtung. Die Konflikte zwischen Staat und Kirche in Mitteldeutschland seit 1945* (Berlin and Hamburg, Lutherisches Verlagshaus, 1962, 276 p.). For works of related interest, *see*:

Dibelius, Otto, *Bishop*. Hier spricht Dibelius; eine Dokumentation. Berlin, Rütten und Loening, 1960. 135 p. Illus., ports., maps, facsims.

Duquaire, Henri. Les Chrétiens en Allemagne de l'Est. Paris, Guy Victor, 1960. 182 p. Illus.

Hamel, Johannes. A Christian in East Germany; Writings Gathered from Several Sources. Translation by Ruth and Charles C. West. New York, Association Press, 1960. 126 p.

Heidtmann, Günter, *ed.* Kirche im Kampfe der Zeit; die Botschaften, Worte und Erklärungen der Evangelischen Kirche in Deutschland und ihrer östlichen Gliedkirchen. Berlin, Lettner-Verlag, 1954. 448 p.

Hutten, Kurt. Christen hinter dem Eisernen Vorhang; die christliche Gemeinde in der kommunistischen Welt. Stuttgart, Quell-Verlag, 1962-63. 2 v. The DDR is covered in volume 2.

Klausener, Erich. Sie hassen Gott nach Plan; zur Methodik der kommunistischen Propaganda gegen Religion und Kirche in Mitteldeutschland. Berlin, Morus-Verlag, 1962. 308 p. Illus., bibliography.

Koch, Hans Gerhard. Neue Erde ohne Himmel; der Kampf des Atheismus gegen das Christentum in der "DDR," Modell einer weltweiten Auseinandersetzung. Stuttgart, Quell-Verlag, 1963. 591 p.

Zimmermann, Wolf Dieter. Die Welt soll unser Himmel sein; atheistische Propaganda in der DDR. Stuttgart, Kreuz-Verlag, 1963. 74 p.

Hermann, Friedrich-Georg. Der Kampf gegen Religion und Kirche in der sowjetischen Besatzungszone. Stuttgart, Quell, 1966. 139 p. Bibliography.

F. LANGUAGE

1646. Bartholmes, Herbert. Das Wort Volk im Sprachgebrauch der SED; wortgeschichtliche Beiträge zur Verwendung des Wortes Volk als Bestimmungswort und als Genitivattribut. Düsseldorf, Pädagogischer Verlag Schwann, 1964. 242 p. Bibliography: p. 231-242. (Die Sprache im geteilten Deutschland, Bd. 2)

A careful study of a significant linguistic process in the DDR, of wider political-linguistic implications. *See also* by the same author: *Tausend Worte Sowjetdeutsch. Beitrag zu einer sprachlichen Analyse der Wörter und Ausdrücke der Funktionärsprache in der sowjetischen Besatzungszone, 1945-1956* (2d ed., Vänersborg, Selbstverlag, 1961,

59 sheets). For other West German studies of linguistic developments in the DDR, *see*:

Geck, Ludwig H. A. Über das Eindringen des Wortes "sozial" in die deutsche Sprache. Göttingen, Schwartz, 1963. 48 p.

Hecht, Gerd. Sprachregelung in der sowjetischen Besatzungszone; Technik, Voraussetzungen und Auswirkungen der Lenkung der Tagespresse und des Rundfunks in der SBZ. Starnberg, published by the author, 1961. 115 p. (Dissertation, Freie Universität, Berlin)

Matthias, Erich, *and* Hansjürgen Schierbaum. Errungenschaften; zur Geschichte eines Schlagwortes unserer Zeit. Pfaffenhofen/Ilm, Ilmgauverlag, 1961. 307 p.

Riemschneider, Ernst G. Veränderungen der deutschen Sprache in der sowjetisch besetzten Zone Deutschlands seit 1945. Düsseldorf, Pädagogischer Verlag Schwann, 1963. 102 p. Bibliography: p. 95-102. Supplement to the journal *Wirkendes Wort*, no. 4. Based on the author's M.A. thesis, University of Kentucky, 1960.

Rühmland, Ullrich, *comp.* Short Dictionary of Terms Used in the Soviet Zone of Occupation of Germany. Bonn-Röttgen, Bonner Druck- und Verlagsgesellschaft Rühmland, 1962. 23 p.

1647. Baumgärtner, Klaus. Zur Syntax der Umgangssprache in Leipzig. Berlin, Akademie-Verlag, 1959. 131 p. Diagrs. (Deutsche Akademie der Wissenschaften zu Berlin. Veröffentlichungen des Instituts für Deutsche Sprache und Literatur, 14)

A study based on the author's doctoral dissertation, Karl-Marx-Universität, Leipzig, 1957. For other East German studies of DDR linguistics, *see*:

Gernentz, Hans Joachim. Niederdeutsch, gestern und heute; Beiträge zur Sprachsituation in den nördlichen Bezirken der Deutschen Demokratischen Republik in Geschichte und Gegenwart. Berlin, Akademie-Verlag, 1964. 202 p.

Hucke, Herman. Thüringischer Dialektatlas, begründet und bearbeitet von Herman Hucke auf Grund des von Thüringer Dialektologen unter Mitwirkung der Lehrerschaft gesammelten Sprachguts. Berlin, Akademie-Verlag, 1961– (Deutsche Akademie der Wissenschaften zu Berlin. Veröffentlichungen des Instituts für Deutsche Sprache und Literatur, Bd. 7–)

Kettmann, Gerhard. Die Sprache der Elbschiffer. Halle (Saale), Niemeyer, 1959-1961. 2 v. (555 p.) Illus., map. (Mitteldeutsche Studien, 22, 23) Bibliography: p. 507-525.

Rosenkranz, H. Der thüringische Sprachraum. Untersuchungen zur dialektgeographischen Struktur und zur Sprachgeschichte Thüringens. Halle (Saale), Niemeyer, 1964. 298 p. (Mitteldeutsche Studien, 26)

Teuchert, Hermann. Die Mundarten der brandenburgischen Mittelmark und ihres südlichen Vorlandes. Berlin, Akademie-Verlag, 1964. 190 p. Maps. Bibliography: p. 175-182. (Deutsche Akademie der Wissenschaften zu Berlin. Veröffentlichungen des Instituts für Deutsche Sprache und Literatur, 30)

G. LITERATURE

1648. Abusch, Alexander. Literatur und Wirklichkeit. Beiträge zu einer neuen deutschen Literaturgeschichte. Berlin, Aufbau-Verlag, 1952. 348 p.

Revised essays on German and non-German literatures from Goethe to the present, designed to contribute to "our fight for a great realistic literature, for a German national literature of the present time, linked with the people." Discussion includes both Soviet and U.S. writers (e.g., Norman Mailer). For political-cultural works by Abusch, *see* entry no. 1565.

1649. Balluseck, Lothar von. Dichter im Dienst; der sozialistische Realismus in der deutschen Literatur. 2d rev. and enl. ed. Wiesbaden, Limes Verlag, 1963. 286 p.

Analysis by an unsympathetic but well-informed West German writer. *See also* his *Literatur und Ideologie 1963; zu den literaturpolitischen Auseinandersetzungen seit dem VI. Parteitag der SED* (Bad Godesberg, Hohwacht, 1963, 48 p., bibliography: p. 43-45).

For other Western studies of literature in the DDR, *see* "Literature in Ulbricht's Germany," by Peter Demetz in *Problems of Communism* (Washington, D.C.), v. 11, July-August 1962: 15-21, and *Die Schriftsteller und der Kommunismus in Deutschland*, by Jürgen Rühle (Köln, Kiepenheuer und Witsch, 1960, 272 p.). Combines materials from two earlier books, *Literatur und Revolution* (Köln, Kiepenheuer und Witsch, 1960, 610 p., ports., bibliography, p. 571-599) and *Das gefesselte Theater*, *see* entry no. 1678.

1650. Becher, Johannes R. Auswahl. Berlin, Aufbau Verlag, 1952. 6 v. Port.

Both as the semiofficial first poet laureate of the DDR and as a leading German poet whose life and writings span the years from the socialism of the First World War, through the period of exile in Moscow during the Hitler regime, to the establishment of a Soviet-dominated communist state in East Germany, Becher (1891-1958) is a pivotal figure in modern German cultural history, notwithstanding the fact that he has found virtually no readers or critical attention in the West. For a collection of his writings *see*:

Gesammelte Werke. Prepared by the Johannes-R.-Becher-Archiv of the Deutsche Akademie der Künste zu Berlin. Berlin and Weimar, Aufbau-Verlag, 1966– Contents of the published volumes: 1, Ausgewählte Gedichte, 1911-1918; 2, Ausgewählte Gedichte, 1919-1925; 3, Gedichte, 1926-1935; 4, Gedichte, 1936-1941. For critical writings on Becher *see*:

Abusch, Alexander. Johannes R. Becher, Dichter der Nation und des Friedens. Enl. ed. Berlin, Aufbau-Verlag, 1953. 58 p. (Schriftenreihe der Deutschen Akademie der Künste, 4).

Birkan, Pavel R. Oruzhiem slova; estetischeskie vzgliady i tvorchestvo I. Bekhera (Armed with words; the esthetic views and work of J. Becher). Leningrad, Sovetskii pisatel', 1959. 284 p.

Greiner, Martin. Literatur ohne Leser; Johannes R. Becher als Repräsentant der sowjetzonalen Literatur. *In* Giessener Abhandlungen zur Agrar- und Wirtschaftsforschung des europäischen Ostens, v. 3, 1957. p. 168-182.

Haase, Horst. Dichten und Denken. Einblicke in das Tagebuch eines Poeten. Halle (Saale), Mitteldeutscher Verlag, 1966. 99 p.

Haase, Horst. Johannes R. Bechers Deutschland-Dichtung; zu dem Gedichtband "Der Glücksucher und die sieben Lasten" (1938). Berlin, Rütten und Loening, 1964. 399 p.

Hinckel, Ericka. Gegenwart und Tradition; Renaissance und Klassik im Weltbild Johannes R. Bechers. Berlin, Dietz, 1964. 323 p. Bibliography: p. 297-315.

Lange, M. Johannes R. Bechers poetische Konzeption — Konzeption einer sozialistisch-realistischen deutschen Dichtung und Literatur. Berlin, Parteihochschule "Karl Marx" beim ZK der SED, 1962. 362 sheets (typescript). A dissertation.

Znamenskaia, G. N. Iogannes Bekher. Moskva, Znanie, 1955. 31 p. (Vsesoiuznoe obshchestvo po rasprostraneniiu politicheskikh i nauchnykh znanii. Seriia 6, no. 17)

For a biography *see*:

Becher, Lilly, *and* Gert Prokop. Johannes R. Becher; Bildchronik seines Lebens. With an essay by Bodo Uhse. Berlin, Aufbau-Verlag, 1963. 303 p. Illus., ports., maps, facsims.

1651. Bobrowski, Johannes. Levins Mühle, 34 Sätze über meinen Grossvater; Roman. Frankfurt am Main, S. Fischer, 1964. 294 p.

Little known in the West, Bobrowski (1917-1965) combined a richly evocative memory of his East German-Baltic childhood with a sophisticated poetic technique in prose and verse. His other writings include: *Litauische Claviere* (Berlin, Wagenbach, 1967, 170 p.), a novel; *Sarmatische Zeit* (Stuttgart, Deutsche Verlags-Anstalt, 1960, 99 p.), a long poem; *Shadow Land; Selected Poems*, translated by Ruth and Matthew Mead (London, D. Carroll, 1966, 59 p.).

1652. Bredel, Willi. Gesammelte Werke in Einzelausgaben. Berlin, Aufbau Verlag, 1962–

Bredel (born in 1901), a German communist of working-class origin, is the author of a number of fictional epics of Teutonic length and density. For a biography see *Willi Bredel, Dokumente seines Lebens* (Berlin, Aufbau-Verlag, 1961, 268 p., illus.). For a bibliography *see*:

Moscow. Vsesoiuznaia gosudarstvennaia biblioteka inostrannoi literatury. Villi Bredel; bio-bibliograficheskii ukazatel' (Willi Bredel; biographic-bibliographic guide). Compiled by V. S. Troianker. Moscow, 1954. 25 p. Illus.

1653. Deutsche Akademie der Künste, *Berlin. Sektion Dichtkunst und Sprachpflege.* Zur Tradition der sozialistischen Literatur in Deutschland; eine Auswahl von Dokumenten. Berlin, Aufbau-Verlag, 1962. 529 p. Bibliography: p. 498-525.

An attempt to anchor Soviet-style socialist realism in literature into the German literary tradition.

1654. Deutscher Schriftsteller-Verband. Deutscher Schriftstellerkongress, vom 25. bis 27. Mai 1961. Referate und Diskussionsbeiträge. Berlin, Aufbau-Verlag, 1962. 330 p. (Beiträge zur Gegenwartsliteratur, Heft 5)

Documentary record of an important landmark in the evolution of the relations between writers and the SED. *See also*:

Koch, Hans. Unsere Literaturgesellschaft; Kritik und Polemik. Berlin, Dietz, 1965. 635 p. Bibliography: p. 609-631.

Paulick, Wolfgang, *ed.* Junge Schriftsteller. Leipzig, Bibliographisches Institut, 1965. 196 p. Autobiographical sketches of young DDR writers born around 1925.

For current developments in DDR literature, the following journals are valuable: *Neue Deutsche Literatur* (Berlin, Aufbau-Verlag, 1953–), monthly, issued by the Deutscher Schriftstellerverband; *Sinn und Form; Beiträge zur Literatur* (Berlin, Rütten und Loening, 1949–), bimonthly, issued by the Deutsche Akademie der Künste, Berlin; *Weimarer Beiträge. Zeitschrift für Literaturwissenschaft* (Berlin and Weimar, Aufbau-Verlag), 8 times a year.

1655. Fradkin, Il'ia M. Literatura novoi Germanii; stat'i i orcherki (Literature of the New Germany; articles and sketches). 2d rev. and enl. ed. Moskva, Sovetskii pisatel', 1961. 507 p.

Studies by a leading Soviet authority on literature in the DDR. See also: *Literatur Germanskoi Demokraticheskoi Respubliki; sbornik statei* (Literature of the DDR; a collection of essays) (Moskva, Akademiia nauk SSSR, 1958, 574 p., bibliography: p. 481-574.

1656. Mitteldeutscher Verlag, *Halle*. Greif zur Feder, Kumpel; Protokoll der Autorenkonferenz des Mitteldeutschen Verlags Halle (Saale) am 24. April 1959 im Kulturpalast des Elektrochemischen Kombinates Bitterfeld. Halle (Saale), Mitteldeutscher Verlag, 1959. 129 p.

Documentary record of a conference at which an effort was made to bridge the gap between intellectuals and workers in the DDR. See also: *Unsere sozialistische Literatur und die Arbeiterklasse*, a dissertation by M. Draeger (Potsdam, Pädagogische Hochschule, 1961, 141, 91 leaves); and "Das Verhältnis zur Arbeiterklasse — das Grundproblem der sozialistischen Literatur," by Marianne Lange, *Einheit* (Berlin), v. 13, 1958, no. 9: 1276-1294.

1657. Radványi, Netty (Anna Seghers, *pseud.*). Gesammelte Werke in Einzelausgaben. Berlin, Aufbau-Verlag, 1960–

One of the few German communist writers to win an audience in the West, "Anna Seghers" (1900–) spent the Hitler years not in Moscow, like J. R. Becher and the older political leadership group in the DDR, but in the West, and it is probably not mere coincidence that she has defended the individual's right to expression against excessive interference by the Communist Party or its literary spokesmen, both in her creative writing and in political-critical statements. Her acceptance of party discipline in the last analysis, however, has enabled her to retain her position as an established figure in the DDR literary pantheon. For critical studies *see*:

Albrecht, Friedrich. Die Erzählerin Anna Seghers 1926-1932. Berlin, Rütten und Loening, 1965. 287 p. (Neue Beiträge zur Literaturwissenschaft, v. 25)

Diersen, Inge. Seghers-Studien; Interpretationen von Werken aus den Jahren 1926-1935; ein Beitrag; zu Entwicklungsproblemen der modernen deutschen Epik. Berlin, Rütten und Loening, 1965. 367 p.

Krohn, Paul Günter, *ed.* Anna Seghers. Berlin, Volk und Wissen, 1962. 138 p. Bibliography. (Schriftsteller der Gegenwart, 4)

Znamenskaia, G. N. Anna Zegers. Moskva, Znanie, 1953. 39 p. (Vsesoiuznoe obshchestvo po rasprostraneniu politicheskikh i nauchnykh znanii, seriia 2, no. 50)

On Anna Seghers' works, *see*:

Germany (*Democratic Republic, 1949–*) *Zentralinstitut für Bibliothekswesen.* Anna Seghers Leben und Werk; ein Literaturverzeichnis. Prepared by Joachim Scholz. Leipzig, Verlag für Buch- und Bibliothekswesen, 1960. 40 p. Published in honor of the author's sixtieth birthday.

Moscow. Vsesoiuznaia gosudarstvennaia biblioteka inostrannoi literatury. Anna Zegers; biobibliograficheskii uzakatel' (Anna Seghers; a biobibliographical index). Compiled by A. A. Volgina. Moskva, Kniga, 1964. 86 p. Port.

For a biography see *Anna Seghers; Briefe ihrer Freunde* (Berlin, Aufbau-Verlag, 1960, 106 p.).

1658. Reich-Ranicki, Marcel, *comp.* Deutsche Literatur in West und Ost; Prosa seit 1945. München, Piper, 1963. 497 p. Bibliographies.

A useful anthology for comparative purposes, incorporating material on DDR writers from an earlier compilation by the same editor: *Auch dort erzählt Deutschland; Prosa von "drüben"* (München, List, 1960, 163 p.). For other anthologies of DDR literature, *see*:

Deutscher Schriftsteller-Verband. Menschen und Werke; vom Wachsen und Werden des neuen Lebens in der Deutschen Demokratischen Republik. Edited by Günter Caspar. Berlin, Aufbau-Verlag, 1952. 382 p. Includes personal narrative, poetry, and drama.

Besten, Ad den, *ed.* Deutsche Lyrik auf der anderen Seite; Gedichte aus Ost- und Mitteldeutschland. München, Hanser, 1960. 139 p.

Pfeffer, Ernst, *ed.* Deutsche Lyrik unter dem Sowjetstern. Eine Anthologie von Gedichten aus der sowjetischen Besatzungszone Deutschlands, für den Schulgebrauch zusammengestellt. 2d enl. ed. Frankfurt am Main, Diesterweg, 1964. 120 p.

1659. Zweig, Arnold. Ausgewählte Werke in Einzelausgaben. Berlin, Aufbau-Verlag, 1957–

Of the older generation of German writers who settled in the Soviet Zone of Occupation after 1945, Arnold Zweig (born in 1887) is perhaps the best known in the West. Between the wars, his antiwar novel, *Der Streit um den Sergeanten Grischa*, achieved wide popularity in English translation. Since 1945 he has resided in East Germany, but has been content to serve as a figurehead of DDR literature, contributing little to its actual development. For a bibliography *see*:

Moscow. Vsesoiuznaia gosudarstvennaia biblioteka inostrannoi literatury. Arnol'd Tsveig; biobibliograficheskii uzakatel' (Arnold Zweig; biographical-bibliographical guide). Introduction by E. M. Zaks. Moskva, Izdatel'stvo Vsesoiuznoi knizhnoi palaty, 1961. 111 p.

See also *Arnold Zweig*, edited by Johannes Rudolph (Berlin, Deutscher Kulturbund, 1962, 119 p., bibliography: p. 110-111).

H. PAINTING, GRAPHIC MEDIA, SCULPTURE

1660. Balluseck, Lothar von. Zur Lage der bildenden Kunst in der sowjetischen Besatzungszone. 3d ed. Bonn, Bundesministerium für Gesamtdeutsche Fragen, 1953. 130 p.

A characteristic study by the omnicompetent West German art critic. Includes a historical summary, a documentary appendix of official texts on art policy in the DDR, and illustrations chosen to confirm the worst fears of opponents of socialist realism. For another West German survey of DDR art, *see*:

Germany (*Federal Republic, 1949–*) *Bundesministerium für Gesamtdeutsche Fragen*. Polit-Kunst in der sowjetischen Besatzungszone Deutschlands; die Deutsche Kunstausstellung 1962 in Dresden und ihre Vorgänger. 3d rev. and enl. ed. Edited by K. P. Werth. Bonn, 1965. 64 p. Illus. *See also*:

Lehmann-Haupt, Hellmut. Art under a Dictatorship. New York, Oxford University Press, 1954. 277 p. Illus., ports. Primarily concerned with art in Hitler's Germany, but includes a chapter on "German Art behind the Iron Curtain," p. 200-215.

1661. Beyer, Ingrid. Die Künstler und der Sozialismus. Published by the Institut für Gesellschaftswissenschaften beim ZK der SED. Berlin, Dietz, 1963. 229 p. Plates.

Contrasts the "gulf between the artist and the people, between art and reality, under capitalism" with the "new social relations" in the DDR. Sets as its goal the establishment of relations between the artist and society in the DDR similar to those believed to exist in the USSR, where "communist society" will become a reality "in the foreseeable future." For other DDR political theorizing on art, *see*:

Korn, Rudolf. Kandinsky und die Theorie der abstrakten Malerei. Berlin, Henschelverlag, 1960. 211 p. Illus., bibliography. An attempt to undermine the theoretical basis of modern abstract art, seen as a "spiritual reflex" satisfying "an ideological need of the parasitic-exploiter class" under capitalism. The author unwittingly undermines his own thesis by demonstrating through comparative illustrations the lifelessness of socialist realism in painting and the unquenchable vitality of even tendentiously chosen examples of modern Western experimental art. *See also* "Modern ist nur der sozialistische Realismus. Bildende Künstler diskutieren Probleme ihrer Arbeit," in *Neues Deutschland* (Berlin), v. 18, no. 81, March 22, 1963, p. 4, a discussion from the party-artist conference held in imitation of the similar meeting in the Kremlin, March 7-8, 1963.

1662. Deutsche Akademie der Künste, *Berlin.* Die nationale Aufgabe der Deutschen Akademie der Künste zu Berlin. Berlin, 1962. 92 p. Illus., port.

Formulation of tasks set by the SED for organized art in the GDR. For a West German commentary, *see* "Die sozialisierte Akademie. Zur Gleichschaltung der Ostberliner Akademie der Künste und ihre Vorgeschichte" by Heinz Kersten, *SBZ-Archiv*, v. 13, 1962, no. 14, p. 210-213.

1663. Feist, Peter H. Plastik in der Deutschen Demokratischen Republik. Dresden, Verlag der Kunst, 1965. 158 p. Illus.

A well-presented and intelligently chosen survey of work in a wide variety of media, avoiding the clichés of socialist realism and emphasizing monumentality and expressiveness. Includes biographical and bibliographical notes on the artists (p. 143-153), bibliography of critical articles (p. 154), and a list of exhibitions (p. 154-156).

1664. Henschel, Walter. Bibliographie zur sächsischen Kunstgeschichte. Berlin, Akademie-Verlag, 1960. 273 p. (Deutsche Akademie der Wissenschaften zu Berlin. Arbeitsstelle für Kunstgeschichte. Schriften zur Kunstgeschichte, Heft 4)

One of a series of basic art bibliographies on the Länder of East Germany prepared under the auspices of the DDR Academy of Sciences. Others in the series are *Bibliographie zur brandenburgischen Kunstgeschichte* by Edith Neubauer and Gerda Schlegemilch (Berlin, Akademie-Verlag, 1961, 231 p., Schriften zur Kunstgeschichte, Heft 7); and *Bibliographie zur Kunstgeschichte von Mecklenburg und Vorpommern* by Edith Fründt (Berlin, Akademie-Verlag, 1962, 123 p., Schriften zur Kunstgeschichte, Heft 8).

1665. Kunst in der Deutschen Demokratischen Republik; Plastik, Malerei, Grafik, 1949-1959. Dresden, Verlag der Kunst, 1959. 311 p.

An official survey, well presented and cumulatively impressive. For other volumes on DDR painting, *see*:

Hütt, Wolfgang. Junge bildende Künstler der DDR. Skizzen zur Situation der Kunst in unserer Zeit. Leipzig, Bibliographisches Institut, 1965. 211 p. Illus., ports., plates. Works and biographies of 25 contemporary DDR artists.

Verlag der Kunst, VEB, *Dresden.* Dezennium 1; zehn Jahre

VEB Verlag der Kunst. Dresden, 1962. 353 p. Illus., ports. Bibliography: p. 340-350.

For current art developments in the DDR, *see*:

Bildende Kunst. Zeitschrift für Malerei, Plastik, Grafik, Formgestaltung und Gebrauchsgrafik. Dresden, VEB Verlag der Kunst, 1954-56. Published in Dresden by the Verband Bildender Künstler Deutschlands, Berlin.

I. ARCHITECTURE

1666. Deutsche Bauakademie. Plenartagung. New series. 2d meeting. 1962– Berlin. Irregular.

Number 1 of this series was never published; preceded by earlier series with same title. Official records of party controls over architecture. *See also*:

Städtebau und Siedlungswesen. Kurzberichte über Forschungsarbeiten und Mitteilungen aus dem Forschungsinstitut für Städtebau und Siedlungswesen. 1955– Berlin. Semiannual. (Deutsche Bauakademie, Schriften des Forschungsinstituts für Städtebau und Siedlungswesen)

Jahrbuch Deutsche Bauakademie 1961, mit Anlagen: Radikale Standardisierung als Hauptkettenglied des industriellen Bauens, Beschleunigung des industriellen Bauens im Industriebau (28. Plenartagung der Deutschen Bauakademie von 5. bis 7. Dezember in Berlin). Berlin, 1961.

1667. Magritz, Kurt, *ed.* Architektur und Städtebau in der Deutschen Demokratischen Republik. Berlin, Henschelverlag, 1959. 254 p. Illus.

A survey prepared for the tenth anniversary of the DDR, edited by the chief editor of the journal *Deutsche Architektur*, and including brief essays by leading architects and civic officials. The extensive illustrations provide a handsome survey of postwar building in the DDR.

For current developments, *see* the official journal, *Deutsche Architektur*, published jointly by the Deutsche Bauakademie and the Bund Deutscher Architekten, Berlin.

1668. Ullmann, Ernst. Baudenkmäler in der Deutschen Demokratischen Republik. Leipzig, Edition Leipzig, 1961. 151 p. (p. 37-151, plates). Bibliographies.

A photographic survey of major architectural monuments in the DDR. Primary emphasis is on historical sites, but a small group of contemporary buildings are included, among them the national memorial at Buchenwald. Includes plans, descriptions, and references to critical literature.

J. FOLK ART, BOOK DESIGN

1669. Akademie der Wissenschaften, *Berlin. Institut für Deutsche Volkskunde.* Zwischen Kunstgeschichte und Volkskunde; Festschrift für

Wilhelm Fränger. Berlin, Akademie-Verlag, 1960. 238 p. (*Its* Veröffentlichungen, Bd. 27)

A volume of scholarly essays in honor of one of the most original and stimulating art historians of the present time, also published in volume 6, number 1 of *Deutsches Jahrbuch für Volkskunde.* Includes a bibliography of Fränger's contributions to art history and German folk art, p. 239-241. The work by which Fränger is best known in the West is:

Fränger, Wilhelm. Hieronymus Bosch: Das Tausendjährige Reich. Grundzüge einer Auslegung. Coburg, Winkler-Verlag, 1947. 142 p. English translation: The Millennium of Hieronymus Bosch. Outlines of a New Interpretation. Translated by Eithne Wilkins and Ernst Kaiser. London, Faber and Faber, 1950. 164 p. *See also*:

Akademie der Wissenschaften, *Berlin. Institut für Deutsche Volkskunde.* Jacob Grimm; zur 100. Wiederkehr seines Todestages. Festschrift des Instituts für Deutsche Volkskunde. Edited by Wilhelm Fränger and Wolfgang Steinitz. Berlin, Akademie-Verlag, 1863. 290 p. (*Its* Veröffentlichungen, Bd. 32)

1670. Germany (*Democratic Republic, 1949–*) *Ministerium für Kultur.* Volkskunstschaffende, schmückt die Republik. Referat, Diskussion, Schlusswort und Entschliessung der Volkskunstkonferenz am 4. und 5. Juli 1963 in Leipzig. Berlin, 1963. 221 p.

Official record of one of the recurring efforts to inject new life into German folk art and enlist it in the political service of the DDR.

For current developments, see *Volkskunst. Monatsschrift für das künstlerische Volksschaffen* (Leipzig, Zentralhaus für Kulturarbeit).

1671. Kapr, Albert. Buchgestaltung. Dresden, Verlag der Kunst, 1963. 354 p. Illus., col. samples. Bibliography: p. 343-345.

The national centers of the German book trade, one of Europe's most vital before 1933, lay to a considerable extent in what became the Soviet zone of occupation after 1945, the present DDR. Under communist rule the book industry has been able to maintain something of its old élan, though it has had to reorient its interests and markets and face the competition of its powerful and well organized West German counterpart. Book design and typography, which reached a high degree of excellence in pre-Hitler Germany, have made at least a partial comeback in recent years in the DDR. The emphasis is now on publishing and printing in the socialist states of Eastern Europe and the USSR; influences from the West, though strong, are not explicitly acknowledged. Evidence of recent trends in DDR book production can be found in the book cited, as well as in the following:

Germany (*Democratic Republic, 1949–*) *Staatliche Kommission für Kunstangelegenheiten.* Deutsche Buchkunst-Ausstellung. Foreword by Helmut Holtzhauer. Leipzig, 1952. 70 p. Illus. A brief illustrated history of German book art, from a manuscript of the early 14th century to an inscribed scroll presented by the University of Leipzig to Generalissimus Stalin.

Buchkunst. Dresden, Verlag der Kunst, 1963. 235 p. (Internationale Beiträge zur Buchgestaltung, Bd. 4)

Leipzig. Deutsche Bücherei. Neue deutsche Buchkunst; Beispiele aus der Sammlung Künstlerische Drucke in der Deutschen Bücherei. Chosen and with an introduction by Prof. Dr. Julius Rodenburg. Leipzig, Deutsche Bücherei, 1960. 37 p. Illus. Includes examples of post-1945 West German typography.

K. MUSIC

1672. Beiträge zur Musikwissenschaft. 1959– Berlin. 4 no. a year.

See also:

Musik und Gesellschaft. 1951– Berlin. Monthly.

Blum, Fred. East German Music Journals, a Checklist. Music Library Association Notes, 2d series, v. 19, June 1962: 399-410.

1673. Brüder am Werk. Chorliederbuch. Leipzig, Verlag Friedrich Hofmeister, 1955. 494 p.

Politically inspired songs represent one of the most direct means of using music for the purposes of the party. One of a series of song books, this one is prepared by an editorial board of the FDGB (DDR trade unions). *See also*:

Lammel, Inge, *and* Günter Hofmeyer, *comps.* Lieder der Partei. Leipzig, Verlag Friedrich Hofmeister, 1961. 213 p. Illus.

1674. Dessau, Paul. Der kaukasische Kreidekreis. Berlin, Henschelverlag, 1961. 142 p.

Score of the incidental music to Brecht's play, for solo voices and instrumental ensemble, by the composer most closely associated with Brecht. For a comprehensive study of Dessau's scores to Brecht, *see*:

Henneberg, Fritz. Dessau-Brecht musikalische Arbeiten. Published for the Deutsche Akademie der Künste. Berlin, Henschelverlag, 1963. 551 p.

1675. Eisler, Hanns. Hanns Eisler; eine Auswahl von Reden und Aufsätzen. Edited by Winfried Höntsch. Leipzig, Reclam, 1961. 222 p.

Writings by the DDR composer perhaps best known in the U.S. through his work for the film industry. Includes lists of compositions and bibliography. *See also*:

Brockhaus, Heinz Alfred. Hanns Eisler. Leipzig, Breitkopf und Härtel, 1961. 209 p.

1676. Germany (*Federal Republic, 1949–*) *Bundesministerium für Gesamtdeutsche Fragen.* Beethoven, verdienter Aktivist der Musik. Aus dem Instrumentarium totalitärer Kulturpolitik in der Sowjetzone. Berlin, 1952. 19 p.

Derisive West German comments on DDR use of music for political purposes. *See also*:

Rudorf, Reginald. Jazz in der Zone. Köln, Kiepenheuer und Witsch, 1964. 133 p.

Wagner, Hermann. Ratgeber für ost- und mitteldeutsche Musik der Gegenwart. Kiel, 1961. 63 p. (Schriftenreihe zur Förderung der ostdeutscher Kulturarbeit, Heft Nr. 2)

1677. Laux, Karl. Das Musikleben in der Deutschen Demokratischen Republik, 1945-1959. Leipzig, Deutscher Verlag für Musik, 1963. 527 p. Illus.

A valuable survey of developments. For a documentary record of political direction of DDR musical activities, *see*:

"Für eine sozialistische Musikkultur. Stellungnahme des Verbandes Deutscher Komponisten und Musikwissenschaftler zu Stand und Aufgaben des musikalischen Schaffens in der DDR." *Sonntag*, v. 18, no. 22, June 2, 1963, Supplement.

L. THEATER, CINEMA, DANCE

1678. Balluseck, Lothar von. Volks- und Laienkunst in der sowjetischen Besatzungszone. Introduction by Hans Köhler. Bonn, Bundesministerium für Gesamtdeutsche Fragen, 1953. 92 p.

Studies of theater art in the DDR by a semiofficial West German specialist on East German cultural affairs. For other West German studies of DDR theater, *see*:

Germany (*Federal Republic, 1949–*) *Bundesministerium für Gesamtdeutsche Fragen*. Volkskunst im politischen Dienst. 2d rev. and enl. ed. Bonn, 1961. 70 p. Illus.

Haese, Jürgen. Das Gegenwartshörspiel in der sowjetischen Besatzungszone Deutschlands; ein Beitrag zur Erforschung künstlerischer Formen in der sowjetisch-totalitären Publizistik. Berlin, Colloquium Verlag, 1963. 218 p. (Abhandlungen und Materialien zur Publizistik, Bd. 3)

Hain, Sybille. Vom Volkstheater zur politischen Massenveranstaltung. Eine Studie über die theoretischen Wirkungselemente in der sowjetisch-kommunistischen Publizistik. München, Verlag Pohl, 1958. 119 p.

Rühle, Jürgen. Das gefesselte Theater; vom Revolutionstheater zum sozialistischen Realismus. Köln, Kiepenheuer und Witsch, 1957. 456 p. Illus., ports. Bibliography: p. 443-448. Revised edition under title, *Theater und Revolution* (München, Deutsche Taschenbuch Verlag, 1963, 207 p.). A study of the communist theater, with special reference to the DDR. Includes a section on "Brecht and the Dialectics of the Epic Theater."

Theater hinter dem Eisernen Vorhang. Basel, Basilius Press, 1964. 160 p. Includes material on the DDR theater.

Tobias, Josef. Die neuere Entwicklung des Theaters in der sowjetischen Besatzungszone, mit einer Übersicht über die Ur- und Erstaufführungen der Spielzeit 1955-56. Bonn, Bundesministerium für Gesamtdeutsche Fragen, 1957. 34 p. Sober, factual, useful.

Includes brief extracts from reviews in the DDR press. Issued as a supplement to the following item.

Weber, Jochen. Das Theater in der sowjetischen Besatzungszone. Bonn, Bundesministerium für Gesamtdeutsche Fragen, 1955. 143 p. Includes children's theater, puppet theater, cabaret, variété, circus. Provides a section (p. 63-109) of official documents and statements on DDR theater policy.

1679. Berliner Ensemble. Chronik der Aufführungen und Gastspiele 1949 bis 1961. Berlin, Henschelverlag Kunst und Gesellschaft, 1961. 34 p. Illus.

Basic documentation on the most famous postwar theater in Germany, the East Berlin Berliner Ensemble, with which Bertolt Brecht (q.v.) worked closely, and which presented a number of his plays in their first performance. For other studies of the Berliner Ensemble, *see*:

Berliner Ensemble. Theaterarbeit; 6 Aufführungen des Berliner Ensembles. 2d rev. ed. Berlin, Henschelverlag Kunst und Gesellschaft, 1961. 462 p. Richly illustrated studies of six characteristic presentations, including three plays by Brecht. Includes as an appendix (p. 425-451), the chronology 1949-1961 listed above.

Brecht, Bertolt. Helene Weigel, Actress; a Book of Photographs. Text by Bertolt Brecht. Translated by John Berger and Anna Bostock. Leipzig, VED Edition, 1961. 94 p. Helene Weigel, Brecht's wife, was the most prominent actress in the Berliner Ensemble.

Wekwerth, Manfred. Theater in Veränderung. 15 Aufsätze aus der Praxis des Berliner Ensembles. Berlin, Aufbau-Verlag, 1960. 175 p.

1680. Brecht, Bertolt. Gesammelte Werke. London, Malik Verlag, 1938 (printed in Czechoslovakia). 2 vols. were issued.

One of the acknowledged masters of the modern theater, Bertolt Brecht (1898-1956) has had a wider and more profound influence in the noncommunist experimental theater of the West than in the DDR, which he adopted as his homeland after the years of exile during the Hitler period. His work for the theater exemplifies in graphic form the attractions and dangers which communism presents to a creative intellectual. Other collected editions of his writings are:

Plays. London, Methuen, 1960–.

Prosa. Frankfurt am Main, Suhrkamp, 1965. 5 v.

Schriften zur Literatur und Kunst. Edited by Werner Hecht. Frankfurt am Main, Suhrkamp, 1967. 3 v.

Stücke aus dem Exil. Berlin, Suhrkamp, 1957. 5 v.

Stücke für das Theater am Schiffbauerdamm. Berlin, Suhrkamp, 1955-57. 3 v.

Schriften zum Theater. Edited by Werner Hecht. Frankfurt am Main, Suhrkamp, 1963-64. 7 v. A partial English translation exists: *Brecht on Theater; the Development of an Aesthetic*, translated and edited by John Willett (New York, Hill and Wang, 1964; London, Methuen, 1964, 294 p., illus., ports., bibliography: p. 284-285).

Gesammelte Werke in 8 Bänden. Frankfurt am Main, Suhrkamp, 1967. 8 v.

For critical studies, *see*:

Demetz, Peter, *ed.* Brecht; a Collection of Critical Essays. Englewood Cliffs, N.J., Prentice-Hall, 1962. 186 p. Bibliography.

Esslin, Martin. Brecht: a Choice of Evils. A Critical Study of the Man, His Work, and His Opinions. London, Eyre and Spottiswoode, 1959. 305 p. Illus. German translation: Brecht: das Paradox des politischen Dichters. Frankfurt am Main, Athenäum Verlag, 1962. 420 p.

Ewen, Frederic. Bertolt Brecht: His Life, His Art and His Times. New York, Citadel, 1967.

Szczecny, Gerhard. Das Leben des Galilei und der Fall Bertolt Brecht. Frankfurt am Main, Ullstein, 1967. 211 p. Based on an analysis of Brecht's successive revisions of his play, "The Life of Galileo"; attacks Brecht as a "cynical, opportunistic jailer of mankind."

For a bibliography *see*:

Moscow. Vsesoiuznaia gosudarstvennaia biblioteka inostrannoi literatury. Bertol'd Brekht; bio-bibliograficheskii ukazatel' (Bertolt Brecht; a biobibliographic guide). Compiled by V. S. Troianker. Moskva, 1955. 28 p.

1681. Germany (*Federal Republic, 1949–*) *Bundesministerium für Gesamtdeutsche Fragen.* Die Spielfilmproduktion in der Sowjetzone. Berlin, 1964. 87 p.

Describes briefly all feature films produced in the DDR between 1946 and 1963. Supersedes earlier publications by the same agency with similar titles. *See also*:

Kersten, Heinz. Das Filmwesen in der sowjetischen Besatzungszone Deutschlands. 2d rev. and enl. ed. Bonn-Berlin, Bundesministerium für Gesamtdeutsche Fragen, 1963. 2 v. Illus.

Jahrbuch des Films. 1958– Berlin, Henschelverlag. Annual.

Deutsche Filmkunst. 1953-1962. Berlin. Monthly. No longer published.

1682. Rebling, Eberhard. Ballett, gestern und heute. 3d ed. Berlin, Henschelverlag, 1961. 420 p. Illus.

A history of dancing in the past 30 years, West as well as East, and an attempt to "help the German ballet creators of today to avoid errors and to find the road to a new realistic ballet." Although the emphasis is on the "struggle for realism" in choreography, both text and illustrations include extensive material on dance in the nonsocialist countries. A special section of the illustrations (p. 374-398) shows dance groups in the DDR, revealing their close dependence on Soviet models, especially for folk dance ensembles.

1683. Stahnke, G. Gute Absicht und falsche Konzeption. Sonntag (Berlin), v. 18, no. 15, 1963. Supplement.

Self-criticism of the DEFA director concerning his films "Fetzers Flucht" and "Monolog für einen Taxifahrer."

1684. Theater der Zeit; Blätter für Bühne, Film und Musik. 1946– Berlin, Henschelverlag. Semimonthly.

For other DDR periodicals on the theater, *see*:

Dramatiker und Komponisten auf den Bühnen der Deutschen Demokratischen Republik. Berlin, Deutsche Akademie der Künste. Annual.

Theater und Film in der Deutschen Demokratischen Republik. Published by the Büro für Theaterfragen. Berlin, Henschel. Annual.

part four

hungary

30

General Reference Aids and Bibliographies

by Elemer Bako

A. BIBLIOGRAPHIES

1. Bibliographies of Bibliographies and Reference Books

1685. A magyar bibliográfiák bibliográfiája. Bibliographia bibliographiarum Hungaricarum. 1956/1957– Budapest, Országos Széchényi Könyvtár, 1960–

The three volumes so far issued list bibliographies published in Hungary during 1956-1957 (1960, 223 p), 1958-1960 (1963, 420 p.), and 1961-1964 (1966, 431 p.). Bibliographies appearing in journals or as parts of books are included. Arrangement is by subject (UDC); there is a separate section for bibliographical periodicals, also arranged by UDC. The 1956-1957 volume has a list of publishers and book distributors; all volumes are indexed.

1686. Szentmihályi, János, *and* Miklós Vértesy. Útmutató a tudományos munka magyar és nemzetközi irodalmához. A Guide to Hungarian and Foreign Reference Books. Budapest, Gondolat, 1963. 730 p.

The Hungarian equivalent of such guides to reference works as those compiled by Winchell, Walford, Malclès, Totok and Weitzel, and Kirpicheva. Although Hungarian sources are emphasized, the major current foreign works are included. Arranged by subject. A general section — listing encyclopedias, biographical dictionaries, national bibliographies, bibliographies of periodicals, and works on library science — is followed by sections on the individual social sciences, humanities and natural sciences. Brief annotations and a subject index are furnished, but there is no author-title index.

2. National Bibliographies

a. Current

1687. Magyar nemzeti bibliográfia. Bibliographia Hungarica. 1946– Budapest, Országos Széchényi Könyvtár. Monthly, 1946-1960; semimonthly, 1961–

A current bibliography of books, maps, records, and music published in Hungary, arranged by subject (UDC). Contents of collections are given. Each issue is indexed, and an annual author index (including titles of anonymous works) and an index of series are provided.

Magyar folyóiratok repertóriuma (*see* entry no. 1702) is issued as a supplement to *Magyar nemzeti bibliográfia.*

b. Retrospective

1688. Magyar könyvészet (Hungarian bibliography). 1712/1860-1911/1920. Budapest, 1882-1942. 6 v. in 12.

Title varies: 1712-1860, *Magyarország bibliografiája.* Details of scope and arrangement vary among the volumes of this series, but in general each includes an alphabetical listing of books in Hungarian, published in Hungary during the period covered.

The volumes for 1712-1860, 1860-1875, and 1901-1910 list periodical titles in the main alphabetical sequence and thereunder show the contents of the issues published during the period covered. A separate list of periodicals, without contents, is given in the volume for 1876-1885. Only the volumes for 1712-1860 include material published in Hungary in languages other than Hungarian, and works relating to Hungary published elsewhere. Subject indexes or classified lists of publications are provided for the periods 1860-1875, 1876-1885, and 1886-1900. Géza Petrik's *Kalaúz az újabb magyar irodalomban* (Guide to recent Hungarian literature) (Budapest, Magyar Könyvkereskedők Egylete, 1894, 288 p.) is a subject bibliography of books published in Hungary during the years 1860-1893, excluding textbooks.

1689. Magyar könyvészet; a Magyarországon nyomtatott könyvek szakosított jegyzéke. Bibliographia Hungarica; catalogus systematicus librorum in Hungaria editorum. 1920/1944-1945/1960. Budapest, Országos Széchényi Könyvtár, 1964–

The National Széchényi Library has begun publication of retrospective national bibliographies for the period 1920-1960, beginning with the past 16 years. Arrangement is by subject. Four volumes in the 1945/1960 series have been published: v. 1, *Opera universalia, philosophia, theologia, sociologia, linguistica* (1965, 719 p.); v. 2, *Scientiae naturales, medicina, agronomia* (1966, 382 p.); v. 3, *Scientiae technicae, technologia* (1967, 608 p.); and v. 4, *Artes, litteratura, geographia, historia* (1964, 616 p.). The fifth volume, an alphabetical index of authors, collaborators, titles, and personal and geographical names mentioned in titles, is to appear later. Upon completion of these volumes, the publication will begin of the volumes for 1920-1944. Meanwhile, the following works are available for parts of the earlier period:

1921-1923: *Magyar könyvészet, 1921-1923; az 1921-23. években megjelent magyar könyvek betűrendes jegyzéke és tárgymutatója* (Hungarian bibliography, 1921-1923; alphabetical list and subject index of Hungarian books published in the years 1921-23), edited by Blanka Pikler (Budapest, Magyar Könyvkiadók és Könyvkereskedők Országos Egyesülete, 1924-1926, 491 p.). Author and title entries, and name and subject cross-references, are arranged in a single alphabet.

1924-1929: For this period there are only the announcements of new publications in *Corvina*, the weekly bulletin of the Hungarian publishers and booksellers.

1930: *Magyar könyvészet*, edited by Pál Gulyás (Budapest, Magyar Könyvkiadók és Könyvkereskedők Országos Egyesülete, 1932, 208 p.)

1931-1935: From 1931 through June 1934, *Magyar könyvészet* was published, in quarterly cumulations, as a supplement to *Corvina*; for the remainder of 1934 and for 1935, the regular announcements of new publications in *Corvina* are the only source.

1936-1941: *Magyar könyvészet*, edited by Ella Szollás, Olga Droszt, and Júlia Mokcsay (Budapest, Országos Széchényi Könyvtár, 1939-1944, 6 v.). Each volume contains lists of printing and duplicating establishments, an alphabetically arranged list of books followed by an index of names of editors and names mentioned in titles, a list of newspapers and periodicals, and analyses, with statistics, of the year's book and serial publishing. The sixth volume, for 1941, also has a list of atlases and maps, with place-name index, and a list of music publications.

1690. Magyar könyvészet (Hungarian Bibliography). 1961/1962– Budapest, Országos Széchényi Könyvtár, 1963–

The three volumes already published, covering 1961-1962 (1963, 1138 p.), 1963 (1964, 736 p.), and 1964 (1965, 826 p.), list books, music, and maps in a subject arrangement like that of *Magyar nemzeti bibliográfia*, and each contains an explanatory preface in French, an alphabetical index, and an index of series. Beginning with the 1963 volume, phonograph records are included, and there is also an index of conference and congress publications.

1691. Szabó, Károly. Régi magyar könyvtár (Old Hungarian library). Budapest, Magyar Tudományos Akadémia, 1879-1898. 3 v. in 4.

Chronologically arranged catalog. The first volume lists 1,793 Hungarian works published during the period 1531-1711; the second, 2,452 works in languages other than Hungarian, published in Hungary during the period 1473-1711; the third, in two parts, prepared with the assistance of Árpád Hellebrant, lists 4,831 works by Hungarian authors published abroad in languages other than Hungarian, for the years 1480-1711. Indexed.

Addenda compiled by György Ráth were published at intervals in *Magyar könyvszemle* during the years 1880-1889. A further supplement by Hiádor Sztripszky, *Adalékok Szabó Károly Régi magyar könyvtár című munkájának I., II. kötetéhez; pótlások és igazítások, 1472-1711* (Addenda to v. 1-2 of Károly Szabó's Old Hungarian library; supplements and corrections, 1472-1711) was issued in 1912 (Budapest, Lantos, 710 p.). It lists 451 Hungarian and 281 foreign-language works, and contains a combined author index which includes references to Szabó's original compilation.

A revision to encompass all items listed in *Régi magyar könyvtár* and published supplements, as well as additional items found subsequently, is currently in preparation at the National Széchényi Library.

3. Other General Bibliographies

1692. Állami Könyvterjesztő Vállalat. Általános könyvjegyzék (General booklist). 1950/1951– Budapest, 1952– Annual.

A list of books published in Hungary for the book trade; excludes textbooks and music. Arranged by subject heading, with name and title indexes. Entries include price. Intended for booksellers and librarians.

1693. Apponyi, Sándor, *gróf*. Hungarica. Ungarn betreffende im Auslande gedruckte Bücher und Flugschriften. München, J. Rosenthal, 1903-1927. 4 v.

An annotated, chronologically arranged catalog of 2,509 foreign books and pamphlets relating to Hungary published from 1470 through 1795. Each volume includes an alphabetical index of authors and titles of anonymous works and an index of personal and place names. Lajos Dézsi assisted in the preparation of v. 3-4. Issued also in a parallel Hungarian edition.

1694. Bibliographia Hungariae. Verzeichnis der 1861-1921 erschienenen,

Ungarn betreffenden Schriften in nicht ungarischer Sprache. Zusammengestellt vom Ungarischen Institut an der Universität Berlin. Berlin und Leipzig, W. de Gruyter, 1923-1929. 4 v. in 1. (Ungarische Bibliothek, 3. Reihe, 1.-4. Bd.)

Edited by Robert Gragger and Gyula Farkas. Contents: 1. Historica. 2. Geographica. Politico-oeconomica. 3. Philologica. Periodica. 4. Register. Classified arrangement with index.

1695. Kertbeny, Károly M. Bibliografie der ungarischen nationalen und internationalen Literatur. v. 1. Ungarn betreffende deutsche Erstlings-Drucke, 1454-1600. Budapest, Königl. ungarische Univ.-Buchdr., 1880. 760, 14 p.

No more published. A chronologically arranged catalog of 1,427 German books relating to Hungary, with extensive annotations and a detailed name and subject index. The introduction, in Hungarian and German, contains a lengthy essay on the history and development of Hungarian bibliography.

1696. Kertbeny, Károly, *and* Géza Petrik. Ungarns deutsche Bibliographie, 1801-1860. Verzeichnis der in Ungarn und Ungarn betreffend im Auslande erschienenen deutschen Drucke. Budapest, Kön. ung. Univ.-Buchdr., 1886. 2 v.

Contents: Pt. 1. Enthaltend die Literatur der Jahre 1801-1830, nebst wissenschaftlicher Übersicht zum ganzen Werke. Pt. 2. Enthaltend die Literatur der Jahre 1831-1860. The first part is arranged chronologically and the second by author and title in a single alphabet. A subject index precedes the main bibliography, and there is an alphabetical author index.

1697. Kont, Ignác. Bibliographie française de la Hongrie, 1521-1910, avec un inventaire sommaire des documents manuscrits. Paris, E. Leroux, 1913. 323 p.

The first part is a chronological catalog of French publications concerning Hungary; the second lists manuscripts. Partly annotated; gives location of copies in France; indexed.

Béla Zsolnay, in his review in *Magyar könyvszemle*, v. 22, April/June 1914, gives a list of additional items (p. 175-176). Other supplements are as follows:

Leval, André. Supplément à la Bibliographie française de I. Kont. Budapest, G. Ranschburg, 1914. 50 p. Lists 347 titles.

Baranyai, Zoltán. Újabb adalékok Kont Ignác "Bibliographie française de la Hongrie"-jához (New addenda to Ignác Kont's "Bibliographie française de la Hongrie"). Magyar könyvszemle, v. 26, January/June 1918: 68-77.

Baranyai, Zoltán. Pótlások a "Bibliographie française de la Hongrie"-hoz (Supplements to the "Bibliographie française de la Hongrie"). Magyar könyvszemle, v. 29, January/December 1922: 168-170.

1698. Magyar Tudományos Akadémia, *Budapest*. A Magyar Tud.

Akadémia kiadásában megjelent munkák és folyóiratok betűrendes czím- és tartalomjegyzéke, 1830-1899. junius hó végéig (Alphabetical title and contents list of books and periodicals published by the Hungarian Academy of Sciences, 1830 to the end of June 1889). Budapest, 1890. 502 p.

———. A Magyar Tud. Akadémia kiadásában megjelent munkáknak és folyóiratok tartalmának betűrendes czímjegyzéke, 1889-1910 (Alphabetical title list of works and contents of periodicals issued by the Hungarian Academy of Sciences, 1889-1910). Budapest, 1911. 1188 p.

Both bibliographies are alphabetically arranged. The earlier volume lists periodical articles separately in the main alphabet and also in the display of contents given under the entries for periodical titles. There is a separate subject index. The second volume does not show contents of periodicals and lacks a subject index, but books and periodical articles are listed both under author and under title keywords.

A subsequent catalog, *A Magyar Tudományos Akadémia kiadványainak jegyzéke* (List of publications of the Hungarian Academy of Sciences) (Budapest, 1934, 135 p.), is an alphabetical listing of separate publications, with contents given for some serials. The Academy's more recent publications are included in *Kiadványaink jegyzéke, 1964* (List of our publications, 1964), issued by Akadémiai Kiadó (1964, 258 p.). This catalog is arranged by subject and indexed.

4. Bibliographies and Indexes of Periodicals and Newspapers

1699. Dezsényi, Béla, Zoltán Falvy, *and* Judit Fejér, *comps.* A magyar sajtó bibliográfiája, 1945-1954 (Bibliography of the Hungarian press, 1945-1954). Budapest, "Művelt Nép" Tudományos és Ismeretterjesztő Kiadó, 1956. 159 p. (Az Országos Széchényi Könyvtár kiadványai, 36)

Alphabetically arranged bibliography of serials regularly published at least twice a year. There are separate sections for serials published in cyrillic characters and publications of which only one issue appeared. Details given include title, subtitle, place and inclusive dates of publication, inclusive dates of any periods of suspension, frequency, editor, publisher, press, and size. There are lists of foreign-language periodicals arranged by language and selected professional and literary journals arranged by UDC, and geographical and name indexes. Additional volumes, to cover the periods 1705-1919 and 1920-1944, are planned.

Specialized bibliographies of the provincial press are being issued by county libraries; five have so far been published, covering the following counties: Borsod-Abaúj-Zemplén, Komárom, Somogy, Vas, and Veszprém.

1700. Kemény, György. Magyarország időszaki sajtója 1911-től 1920-ig

(The periodical press of Hungary from 1911 to 1920). Budapest, A Magyar Nemzeti Múzeum Országos Széchényi Könyvtára, 1942. 474 p. Tables. (Magyarország időszaki sajtójának könyvészete, 4)

An introductory analysis precedes the alphabetically arranged bibliography. Entries give title, frequency, place and inclusive dates of publication, editor, publisher, press, and format. There are lists of titles arranged by place of publication and by subject, a name index, and a summary in German.

1701. Kereszty, István. A magyar és magyarországi időszaki sajtó időrendi áttekintése, 1705-1867 (Chronological survey of the periodical press in Hungarian and in Hungary, 1705-1867). Budapest, 1916. 98 p. (A Magyar Nemzeti Múzeum Könyvtárának címjegyzéke, 5. Hírlapok és folyóiratok 1867-ig)

The chronological listings, in two sections (1705-1849 and 1850-1867), are accompanied by alphabetical lists, grouped by language of publication. The brief entries give place and inclusive dates of publication; for the serials in the second section, a subject key is provided.

1702. Magyar folyóiratok repertóriuma. Repertorium bibliographicum periodicorum Hungaricorum. 1946– Budapest, Országos Széchényi Könyvtár. Quarterly (irregular), 1946-1949; monthly, 1950-1964; semimonthly, 1965–

Indexes the most important Hungarian periodicals. Entries for articles are arranged by UDC. Each issue is indexed, and an annual cumulated index is provided.

Issued as a supplement to *Magyar nemzeti bibliográfia* (see entry no. 1687).

B. GENERAL PERIODICALS

1703. Budapesti szemle (Budapest review). 1857-1943. Budapest, Magyar Tudományos Akadémia. Frequency varies.

See also entry no. 2184.

Includes articles and book reviews relating to various fields of Hungarian culture.

1704. The Hungarian Quarterly. v. 1-8; Spring 1936-1942. Budapest, New York. Plates.

Hungary's foremost general journal in English during the period between the world wars. Contains articles on various aspects of the country and its people, such as history, economy, legislation, literature, arts, language, etc. Includes book reviews, news, and translations of poetry and short stories.

A Companion to Hungarian Studies (Budapest, Society of the Hungarian Quarterly, 1943, 532 p., illus., ports., maps) constituted the 1942 issues of *The Hungarian Quarterly*.

1705. The Hungarian Quarterly. v. 1– 1961– New York. Illus.

Published by a group of exiles, this general political, cultural, and literary journal contains articles by Hungarian emigrés, book reviews, texts of significant documents, and translations of Hungarian short stories and poetry.

1706. Magyar szemle (Hungarian review). v. 1-46; 1927-1944. Budapest, Magyar Szemle Társaság. Monthly.

See also entry no. 2277.

Includes scholarly articles on political, social, cultural, and economic problems in Hungary and elsewhere, shorter commentaries, and book reviews.

1707. Magyar tudomány (Hungarian science). v. 1– 1890– Budapest, Magyar Tudományos Akadémia. Illus.

See also entry no. 2278.

Frequency varies. Publication suspended 1944-1945. Supersedes the Academy's *A Magyar Tudományos Akadémia értesítője* (Journal of the Hungarian Academy of Sciences), published 1867-1889. Title varies. 1890-1955, *Akadémiai értesítő* (Academy journal).

The Academy began publishing *Magyar académiai értesítő* in 1840. In 1860 the journal was subdivided into three series, published respectively by the linguistic and humanistic sciences section; the philosophical, legal, and historical sciences section; and the mathematical and natural sciences section. These three were merged in 1867 to form the journal which was superseded in 1890 by the publication listed above. Contains papers, reports, and news items relating to policy, administration, membership, and scientific activities of the Academy and its section and offices.

An index covering the period 1840-1960, compiled by Pál Gergely and Zoltán Molnár, has been published: *Az Akadémiai Értesítő és a Magyar Tudomány repertóriuma, 1840-1960* (Budapest, 1962, 377 p.). It contains references only to scholarly articles, about 4,000 in number, which are arranged chronologically under each of 36 subject groupings.

1708. The New Hungarian Quarterly. v. 1– Sept. 1960– Budapest, Corvina Press. Illus.

English-language cultural journal intended for circulation abroad. Carries articles and news on various aspects of Hungarian history, culture, current affairs, and relations with the English-speaking world; translations of short stories and poetry by Hungarian writers; book reviews, and occasional bibliographies.

1709. Nouvelle revue de Hongrie. v. 1-70; March 1908-1944. Budapest. Illus. Monthly, March 1908-July 1914; semimonthly, September 1914-August 1916; monthly, September 1916-1944.

Publication suspended November 1918-June 1920, inclusive. Organ of the Société littéraire française de Budapest, 1908-1915. Title varies: March 1908-December 1931, *Revue de Hongrie*. Contains scholarly articles on various aspects of Hungarian history and culture, emphasizing Franco-Hungarian relations. Includes book reviews and some bibliographies.

1710. Ural-altaische Jahrbücher. v. 1– 1952– Wiesbaden. Frequency varies. Illus.

See also entry no. 2256.

Each volume issued in parts. Publication suspended 1944-1951. Supersedes *Ungarische Jahrbücher*, 1921-1943. Carries scholarly articles, news, book reviews, and occasional bibliographies on Hungarian and, more recently, the larger field of Ural-Altaic studies. The earlier volumes included special articles on Hungarian-German contacts throughout history. Current emphasis is on linguistic studies.

C. ENCYCLOPEDIAS

1711. A Pallas nagy lexikona (The great encyclopedia of Pallas). Budapest, Pallas, 1893-1904. 18 v. Illus., plates, maps.

A general encyclopedia of high quality; edited by József Bokor, founder and first president of the Hungarian Philosophical Society. Largely outdated although still useful as a source on topics relating to Hungary at the time of publication. The bibliographies are still useful. Volumes 17-18 contain addenda.

1712. Révai nagy lexikona (The great encyclopedia of Révai). Budapest, Révai Testvérek, 1911-1935. 21 v. Illus., plates, maps.

A more recent general encyclopedia, similar in quality to *Pallas*, and still in general use today. Includes bibliographies. Volume 19, pages 769-863, and volumes 20-21 are supplements. Edited by Mór János Révai, with the assistance of Zoltán Kovács and János Sziklay; volume 21 was edited by Elemér Varjú.

Two other Hungarian general encyclopedias published before the end of the Second World War are still of value: *Tolnai új világlexikona* (Tolnai's new world encyclopedia) (Budapest, Tolnai, 1926-1933, 20 v., illus., ports., maps), and *Új Idők lexikona* (Encyclopedia of the "New Times") (Budapest, Singer és Wolfner, 1936-1942, 24 v., illus., ports., maps).

1713. Új magyar lexikon (New Hungarian encyclopedia). Budapest, Akadémiai Kiadó, 1959-1962. 6 v. Illus., plates, maps.

The most recent multivolume general Hungarian encyclopedia, it fully reflects communist viewpoints and interpretations. Bibliographies accompany the articles; volume 6 includes supplements to volumes 1-5.

The first general encyclopedia published in Hungary after the Second World War, *Révai kétkötetes lexikona* (The two-volume encyclopedia of Révai), edited by Vilmos Juhász (Budapest, Révai Irodalmi Intézet, 1947-1948, 2 v., illus., maps), includes no bibliographies. The second volume shows the effects of communist ideology.

D. HANDBOOKS

1714. Erdey, Ferenc, *ed.* Information Hungary. Budapest, Akadémiai Kiadó, Publ. House of the Hungarian Academy of Sciences, 1968. 1144 p. Illus. (Information Series: Countries of the World, v. 2)

An officially prepared handbook of contemporary Hungary in English, written by prominent subject specialists. The English version was edited by the staff of the Pergamon Press. According to the foreword, the "period covered . . . extends, in general, up to the end of 1963." Subject chapters include a general description of the state and affairs of the Hungarian People's Republic, and others entitled "Land and People," "History," "State and Society," "Economy," "Health," "Education," "Scientific Life," "Literature," Theatre, Cinema and Music," "Arts," "International Relations." Name and subject indexes, lists of general and historical maps, and colored illustrations are also included. A useful supplement is:

Erdey-Grúz, Tibor, *and* Imre Trencsényi-Waldapfel, *eds.* Science in Hungary. Budapest, Corvina Press, 1965. 316 p. Bibliography. illus. An introductory chapter, "Principal Features of the Organization of Scientific Research in Hungary," is followed by essays, contributed by leading authorities, describing activities in Hungary in the major fields of the physical, biological, and social sciences and the humanities. Not indexed.

1715. Az ezeréves Magyarország (Millennial Hungary). Budapest, Pesti Hírlap, 1939. 1200 p. Illus., ports., maps, facsims.

A general reference guide to the history, culture, geography, economy, and other aspects of the country; articles were prepared with reference to pre-1920 boundaries. Indexed. "Magyarország vármegyéi" (Counties of Hungary): pages 1031-1160. Includes maps and coats of arms. "Az ezeréves Magyarország számokban" (Millennial Hungary in figures): pages 1161-1176.

1716. Helmreich, Ernst C., *ed.* Hungary. New York, Published for the Mid-European Studies Center of the Free Europe Committee by Praeger, 1957. 466 p. Maps, tables. Bibliography: p. 423-499. (Praeger Publications in Russian History and World Communism, no. 49)

See also entry no. 1923.

A general handbook, with emphasis on recent political, economic, and social developments. Indexed.

1717. Jekelfalussy, József, *ed.* The Millenium of Hungary and Its People. Budapest, Pesti Könyvnyomda, 1897. 672 p. Illus., maps.

The first modern handbook on Hungary in English, with chapters on various aspects of the country, its people, history, and culture, contributed by leading specialists. Published also in Hungarian, Croatian, French, and German.

1718. Lóczy, Lajos, *ed.* A magyar szent korona országainak földrajzi, társadalomtudományi, közművelődési és közgazdasági leírása (A geographical, sociological, cultural, and economic description of the lands of the Holy Crown of Hungary). Budapest, Kilián F., 1918. 528 p. Maps.

Issued by the Magyar Földrajzi Társaság (Hungarian Geographical Society) and prepared with the cooperation of experts in Hungary, Croatia-Slavonia, and Bosnia-Hercegovina.

An extract was published in English under the title *A Geographical, Economic and Social Survey of Hungary* (Budapest, "Pátria" Press, 1919. 121 p., maps).

1719. Magyar Államvasutak. Hungary, by Stephen Bársony and others. Edited for The Royal Hungarian State Railways by Albert Kain. Budapest, Erdélyi, 1910. 400 p. Illus., ports., maps.

Handbook on the history, economy, administration, and culture of Hungary, with chapters by subject specialists. Published also in French and German.

1720. Magyar Bizottság. Facts about Hungary. Compiled by Imre Kovács. New York, Hungarian Committee, 1958. 280 p. Map.

An introductory chapter, "History of the Hungarians," is followed by a selection of articles on postwar Hungary, the 1956 revolution, United Nations handling of the Hungarian problem, the Nagy case, and related topics. An appendix offers ethnic and social data and a chronology from Mar. 19, 1944, to Sept. 8, 1958. A second, revised edition entitled *The Fight for Freedom* (1966, 382 p.) extends the chronology of the Hungarian question on the agenda of the United Nations, adds a selection of world opinion on Hungary's internal strifes, includes new chapters on Hungarian minority groups in neighboring countries, and expands the bibliographical coverage.

1721. Magyar föld, magyar faj (Hungarian land, Hungarian race). By Gyula Prinz and others. Budapest, Királyi Magyar Egyetemi Nyomda, 1936-1938. 4 v. Illus., ports., maps.

Bibliographies included in "Jegyzetek" (notes) in each volume. A background manual for the research. Contents. V. 1-3. Magyar földrajz (Hungarian geography). Pt. 1. Magyarország tájrajza (Regional description of Hungary), by Gyula Prinz. A magyar éghajlat és a folyók vízjárása (The Hungarian climate and the streamflow of rivers), by Jenő Cholnoky. Pt. 2. A magyar munka földrajza (Geography of Hungarian labor), by Gyula Prinz and Count Pál Teleki. V. 4. A magyar ember (The Hungarian man), by Lajos Bartucz.

1722. Magyar tájékoztató zsebkönyv (Hungarian reference pocket-book). 2d ed. With a preface by Baron Zsigmond Perényi. Budapest, Magyar Nemzeti Szövetség, 1943. 1200 p. Maps.

Chapters deal with Hungary in general, its history, economy, social and political developments, culture, nationality problems, foreign relations, and press. There are chronologies of the nation's history (from 200 B.C.) and of the Second World War and the events leading to it (from January 1938 through November 1942). Also included are a selective bibliography of foreign-language books on Hungary and a name and subject index.

1723. Magyarország vármegyéi és városai. Magyarország monográfiája (The counties and cities of Hungary. Monograph on Hungary). Budapest, Apollo, 1896-1911. 22 v. in 23. Illus., ports., maps, bibliographies.

Each volume is a comprehensive handbook on the history, demography, geography, and other aspects of an administrative unit (county or self-governing municipality) of Hungary as it existed before the First World War, and of the Kingdom of Crotia and Slavonia.

This is an extensive revision of the relevant parts of *Az Osztrák-Magyar Monarchia írásban és képben* (Budapest, Magyar Királyi Államnyomda, 1887-1901, 21 v.), Hungarian edition of *Die Österreichisch-Ungarische Monarchie in Wort und Bild* (Wien, K. K. Hof- und Staatsdruckerei, 1886-1902, 24 v.).

E. BIOGRAPHICAL DICTIONARIES

1724. Gulyás, Pál. Magyar írói álnév lexikon; a magyarországi írók álnevei és egyéb jegyei. Függelék: Néhány száz névtelen munka jegyzéke. Lexicon pseudonymorum Hungaricum; pseudonyma et alia signa scriptorum Regni Hungariae. Appendix: Elenchus aliquot centum operum anonymorum. Budapest, Akadémiai Kiadó, 1956. 706 p.

See also entry no. 2172.

The main list of pseudonyms is followed by sections on pseudonyms using Greek letters, numerals, and other symbols. There is also a list of writers, showing the pseudonyms they used. An appendix identifies the authors of anonymous works arranged alphabetically by title.

1725. Magyar életrajzi lexikon (Hungarian biographical encyclopedia). Editor-in-chief: Ágnes Kenyeres. Budapest, Akadémiai Kiadó, 1967-1968. 2 v.

A comprehensive reference work containing circa 11,000 biographies of prominent personalities in Hungarian public life, particularly in the past 30 years.

1726. Szinnyei, József. Magyar írók élete és munkái (The lives and works of Hungarian writers). Budapest, Hornyánszky, 1891-1914. 14 v.

See also entry no. 2180.

A bio-bibliographical handbook of the cultural history of Hungary. Entries for nearly 30,000 writers are arranged alphabetically. The bibliographies include references to periodical and newspaper articles as well as to books, and citations to book reviews are also given. A reprint edition (totaling 10,512 pages) has been announced by the Zentralantiquariat der Deutschen Demokratischen Republik, Leipzig.

Magyar írók élete és munkái, by Pál Gulyás (Budapest, Magyar Kónyvtárosok és Levéltárosok Egyesülete, 1939-1944, 6 v.), intended as a continuation and extension of Szinnyei's work, was never completed; the volumes published cover A through D only.

F. GAZETTEERS, LISTS OF ABBREVIATIONS, STATISTICAL WORKS

1727. Elekes, Dezső. Hazánk, népünk, szomszédaink (Our Fatherland, our people, our neighbors). 2d ed. Budapest, A Magyar Statisztikai Társaság és Kir. Pázmány Péter Tudományegyetem Kisebbségjogi Intézete, 1941. 133 p. Col. map. Bibliography: p. 132-133. (A Magyar Statisztikai Társaság kiadványai, no. 13)

———, *ed.* A mai Magyarország; a második világháború és a párizsi békeszerződés következményei (Present-day Hungary; the consequences of the Second World War and the Paris Peace Treaty). Budapest, Hungária Lloyd, 1946. 314 p.

Semiofficial statistical surveys of Hungary. The editor was president of the Hungarian Central Statistical Office.

1728. Hungary. *Központi Statisztikai Hivatal.* Figures about Hungary. Budapest, Statisztikai Kiadó, 1964. 136 p. Illus.

A general statistical survey of the country.

1729. Hungary. *Központi Statisztikai Hivatal.* Magyarország helységnévtára 1962 (Gazetteer of localities in Hungary, 1962). Budapest, Statisztikai Kiadó, 1963. 1044 p. Maps in pocket.

Reflects the country's administrative structure and population data as of July 1, 1962. Cultural and educational data represent the situation as of December, 1960; population statistics are based on the 1960 census. Part 4 contains a master index of names.

1730. Hungary. *Központi Statisztikai Hivatal.* Statistical Yearbook, 1957– Budapest, 1959–

English-language version of the official *Statisztikai évkönyv* (1949/1955–; Budapest, 1957–), which superseded *Magyar statisztikai évkönyv* (1872-1946; Budapest, Athenaeum, 1872-1948).

Also available in English is *Statistical Yearbook of Hungary, 1949-1955, compiled by Central Bureau of Statistics; from Statisztikai évkönyv, Budapest, 1957* (New York, U.S. Joint Publications Research Service, 1958, 443 p.). The Joint Publications Research Service also issued a *Monthly Digest of Hungarian Statistical Periodicals* in 1958.

1731. Magyarország címtára (Directory of Hungary). Edited by István Pálos. Budapest, Közgazdasági és Jogi Könyvkiadó, 1961. 632 p.

The standard directory of official, party, and public agencies in

Hungary. Arranged under 17 headings, covering government organizations, foreign diplomatic representatives in Hungary, Communist Party and mass organizations, and economic, social, and cultural agencies. Information is based on data collected in the Central Statistical Office as of June 30, 1960.

1732. U.S. *Library of Congress. Slavic and Central European Division.* Hungarian Abbreviations, a Selective List. Compiled by Elemer Bako. Washington, D.C., 1961. 146 p.

Alphabetical list of abbreviations in current usage, covering names of government agencies, public institutions, societies, industrial and trade enterprises, and other organizations. Many general abbreviations frequently used in Hungarian publications are also included. Abbreviations are followed by their expansions and by English translations.

1733. U.S. *Office of Geography.* Hungary; Official Standard Names Approved by the United States Board on Geographic Names. Washington, D.C., U.S. Govt. Print. Off., 1961, 301 p. (U.S. Board on Geographic Names. Gazetteer no. 52)

Contains about 25,000 entries for places and features in Hungary.

G. LIBRARIANSHIP AND PUBLISHING

1734. Bak, János. A magyar könyvkiadás, 1945-1959 (Hungarian book publishing, 1945-1959). Budapest, Zeneműnyomda, 1960. 381 p. Illus.

Covers all aspects of Hungarian book publishing during the period indicated. Indexed. It extends the author's *Az új magyar könyvkiadás tíz éve, 1945-1955* (Budapest, Kiadói Főigazgatóság, 1956, 128 p.), also issued in English as *Ten Years of the New Hungarian Book Publishing* (Budapest, 1956).

1735. Fitz, József. A magyar nyomdászat, könyvkiadás és könyvkereskedelem története (The history of Hungarian printing, book publishing and book trade). Budapest, Akadémiai Kiadó, 1957-1967. 2 v. Illus.

Volume 1, *A mohácsi vész előtt* (Before the Mohács disaster), 258 p. Volume 2, *A reformáció korában* (In the age of Reformation), 295 p. Deals with the beginnings of publishing in Hungary. Volume 2 was issued under slightly changed main title: *A magyarországi nyomdászat, könyvkiadás és könyvkereskedelem története.* (The history of printing, book publishing and book trade in Hungary).

1736. Books from Hungary. v. 1– Sept. 1959– Budapest. Quarterly. Illus.

Issued by the Book Publishers' and Booksellers' Information Center, this journal carries feature articles on recent publications in various fields, profiles of prominent writers, artists, and other personalities in connection with current publications, Hungarian and foreign book news, and a classified bibliography of books recently published in Hungary (English translations are supplied for Hungarian titles). Published also in French and German.

1737. Corvina; a Magyar Könyvkiadók és Könyvkereskedők Országos Egyesületének közlönye (Corvina; Bulletin of the National Association of Hungarian Publishers and Bookdealers). Budapest, September 5, 1878-March 2, 1951. Weekly.

Publication suspended: October 8, 1944-August 26, 1945; February 24-March 24, 1950. Contains news, articles, and advertisements of interest to the book trade, and lists of newly published books and musical works.

Tájékoztató a megjelenő könyvekről (Guide to newly published books), a monthly periodical of a somewhat similar nature, with illustrated articles, news, and bibliographies, has been published since 1957 by Állami Könyvterjesztő Vállalat (State Book Distribution Enterprise).

1738. Hungarian Library Directory. Budapest, Országos Széchenyi Könyvtár, Könyvtártudományi és Módszertani Központ, 1965. 2 v.

The first volume reprints the Hungarian text of the directory information in *Könyvtári Minerva*, adding table of contents, foreword, and introductory essay on the Hungarian library system, in English. The directory contains entries for nearly 2,000 libraries. The second volume contains indexes of institutions in Hungarian, English, and Russian; a name index; an index of subject specializations; and other useful data on libraries, librarianship, and publishing.

1739. Magyar Könyvszemle (Hungarian book review). v. 1– 1876– Budapest, Akadémiai Kiadó. Quarterly. Illus., facsims., ports.

See also entry no. 2296.

Publication suspended, 1947-1954. Organ of Section 1 (Linguistics and Literary Sciences) of the Hungarian Academy of Sciences. A scholarly journal of librarianship, with emphasis on Hungary. Includes articles on publishing, printing, and library history, topics in library science, library legislation, news in the library world, and reviews of books and bibliographies. Major articles are accompanied by summaries in English, French, German, Italian, or Russian.

1740. Sallai, István, *and* Géza Sebestyén. A könyvtáros kézikönyve (The librarian's handbook). 2d rev. and enl. ed. Budapest, Gondolat, 1965. 831 p. Illus., facsims., maps.

Fully illustrated survey of the field of librarianship, reflecting conditions and practices in Hungary. Ten separate sections, each with its own extensive bibliography (including citations to non-Hungarian sources), cover the following topics: books, libraries, and library science; library architecture and furnishings; development of collections; catalogs, shelving and preservation; readers' services; bibliography and documentation, including machine applications; special collections, such as children's books, local history, rare books, serials, and music; library administration; and the library system and legislation in Hungary. Indexed.

Librarians with a limited knowledge of Hungarian who must make use of Hungarian bibliographical and book-trade publications will find assistance in Endre Moravek's *Verzeichnis ungarischer Fachausdrücke und Abkürzungen aus dem Buch- und Bibliothekswesen* (Wien, Österreischische Nationalbibliothek, 1958, 61 p.). Translations are given in German, French, and English.

1741. Zala, Imre, *ed.* A könyvterjesztés alapismeretei (Fundamentals of book distribution). Budapest, Tankönyvkiadó, 1959. 424 p. Illus. Bibliography: p. 406-408.

A useful summary, including historical background, of information on publishing, bookselling, and libraries, intended primarily to help young persons beginning work in the book trade in Hungary.

H. GUIDE BOOKS AND TRAVEL AIDS

1742. Hungary; a Comprehensive Guidebook for Visitors and Armchair Travellers, with Many Colored Illustrations and Maps. Edited by Iván Boldizsár. 5th ed. New York, Hastings House, 1967. 401 p. Illus., maps.

See also:

Ryalls, Alan. Your Guide to Hungary. London, Alvin Redman, 1967. 239 p. Illus., maps.

1743. Hungary 66. Edited by Miklós Gárdos. Budapest, Pannonia Press, 1966. 403 p. Illus., ports., map.

First in a series of yearbooks on Hungary. Covers, in several chapters, current development in the country. Includes also biographical articles on leading government and party officials. Issued also in French, German, Hungarian, Russian, and Spanish.

1744. Kartográfiai Vállalat, *Budapest.* Magyarország autóatlasza. Road atlas of Hungary. 2d ed. Budapest, 1963. 7 p., 96 p. of maps, 39 p.

Twenty-two sectional maps (1 : 360,000) alternate with plans of the capital and 79 of the larger provincial towns. Each town plan is marked with agencies of importance to travelers, such as hotels, restaurants, post offices, pharmacies, hospitals, travel agents, government offices, and police. Endpapers give a key to the sectional maps and a table of distances. Map symbols and road signs are illustrated and explained, and there is a place-name index to the maps. Explanatory notes are given in Hungarian, German, English, French, and Russian.

1745. Pap, Miklós, László Székely, *and* András Vitéz, *eds.* Budapest; a

Guide to the Capital of Hungary. Budapest, Corvina Press, 1964. 330 p. Illus., maps.

1746. Radisics, Elemér, *ed.* Hungary; Pictorial Record of a Thousand Years. Budapest, Athenaeum, 1944. 190 p. Illus., ports., maps, facsims.

Published also in French.

31

the land

by George W. Hoffman

A. BIBLIOGRAPHIES AND SURVEY STUDIES

1747. Blanc, André. Hungary. *In* Deffontaines, Pierre, *ed.* Larousse Encyclopedia of Geography. 1. Europe. New York, Prometheus Press, 1961. p. 263-270.

Survey of regional geography of Hungary.

1748. Bodor, Antal, *ed.* Magyarország helyismereti könyvészete, 1527-1940. Bibliographia locorum Hungariae, MDXXVII-MCMXL. Budapest, 1944. 424 col.

A historical bibliography of books, pamphlets, and periodical articles relating to the cultural and physical geography, geology, economy, and history of localities in Hungary. Localities are listed in alphabetical order.

1749. Bulla, Béla, *and* Tibor Mendöl. A Kárpát-medence földrajza (Geography of the Carpathian Basin). Budapest, Egyetemi Nyomda, 1947. 611 p. Maps, plates. Bibliography: p. 589-590. (Nevelők könyvtára, 2)

The best known geography, but available only in Hungarian.

1750. Cartographia, *Budapest.* National Atlas of Hungary. Prepared with the cooperation of the Geographical Committee of the Hungarian Academy of Sciences. Editor-in-chief: Sándor Radó. Budapest, 1967. 112 p. of col. maps (one in pocket)

Translation of 1967 original edition in Hungarian, entitled *Magyarország nemzeti atlasza.* Most recent comprehensive atlas of Hungary. Maps are grouped as follows: physical conditions; population and settlement; agriculture; industry; transport and communication;

retail trade, tourism, foreign trade and international relations; cultural and social conditions. To be supplemented for earlier periods by:

Kogutowicz, Manó. Teljes földrajzi és történelmi atlasz. (Complete geographical and historical atlas.) 5th enl. and rev. ed. Budapest, Magyar Földrajzi Intézet, 1911. 104 l. (chiefly col. maps, part fold.)

1751. Havass, Rezső. Magyar földrajzi könyvtár. Bibliotheca geographica Hungarica. Budapest, F. Pál, 1893. 532 p.

A comprehensive bibliography of geographical publications pertaining to the territory of pre-World War I Hungary. Hungarian and foreign-language publications are listed. Includes an introductory study on the history of Hungarian geography research. Arrangement by subject. *See also*:

Dubovitz, István, *comp.* A magyar földrajzi irodalom, 1937-1940 (Hungarian geographical literature, 1937-1940). Budapest, Magyar Földrajzi Társaság, 1939-1942. 240 p.

Reprinted from the journal *Földrajzi közlemények* (Geographical review) published in Budapest since 1873. A continuation for the years 1946-1955 is reportedly in preparation.

1752. Martonne, Emmanuel de. La Hongrie. *In* Martonne, Emmanuel de, *ed.* Géographie universelle. v. 4. Paris, Armand Colin, 1931. p. 505-532.

Survey of regional geography of Hungary.

1753. Pécsi, Márton, *and others.* Applied Geography in Hungary. Translated by Béla Kecskés. Budapest, Akadémiai Kiadó, 1964. 211 p. Illus., maps (part fold.), bibliographies. (Studies in Geography, no. 2)

See also Béla Sárfalvi's *Research Problems in Hungarian Applied Geography* (Budapest, Akadémiai Kiadó, 1969, 203 p., illus.).

1754. Pécsi, Márton, *and* Béla Sárfalvi. The Geography of Hungary. London, Collet's, in cooperation with Corvina Press, Budapest, 1964. 299 p. Illus., maps.

Detailed physical and economic geography of Hungary, well illustrated. Originally published in Hungarian as *Magyarország földrajza* (Budapest, 1960). Also available in a German translation. *See also* Márton Pécsi's *Ten Years of Physiogeographic Research in Hungary* (Budapest, Publishing House of the Hungarian Academy of Sciences, 1964, 132 p., illus. maps., bibliog.).

1755. Radó, Sándor, *ed.* Magyarország gazdasági földrajza (Economic geography of Hungary). Budapest, Gondolat Kiadó, 1963. 366 p. Illus., charts, maps (part fold., part in pocket). Bibliography: p. 361-363.

Also contains data on the population and the major branches of the economy.

German edition: *Ökonomische Geographie der Ungarischen Volksrepublik* (Berlin, Verlag Die Wirtschaft, 1963, 225 p.).

1756. Teleki, Pál, *gróf*. The Evolution of Hungary and Its Place in European History. New York, Macmillan, 1923. 312 p. Front., maps, diagrs. Bibliography: p. 245-312.

See also entries no. 1841 *and* 1915.

A political geography by the well-known Hungarian geographer and statesman, analyzing the historical evolution of Hungary, the economic situation after the First World War, and the nationality problem.

B. SERIALS

1757. Acta Geographica. 1955– Szeged. Irregular.

Contributions in various languages focus on contemporary issues and developments, published by the University of Szeged.

1758. Földrajzi értesítő (Journal of geography). 1952– Budapest. Quarterly.

Organ of the Research Institute of Geography of the Hungarian Academy of Sciences. Articles, discussions, and reviews, with emphasis on Hungary. Summaries in English, Russian or German.

1759. Studies in Geography. 1964– Budapest. Irregular.

Important series of monographs in English, presenting results of geographical research at the Institute of Georgraphy of the Hungarian Academy of Sciences.

1760. Magyar Földrajzi Társaság. Földrajzi közlemények (Geographical review). v. 1-76, 1873-1948; new series, v. 1(77)- 1953– Budapest. Frequency varies.

One of the oldest geographical journals in the world, with emphasis on Hungary. In Hungarian, with summaries in English, French German, or Russian.

C. REGIONAL STUDIES AND SPECIAL ASPECTS

1761. Beynon, Erdmann D. Budapest: an Ecological Study. Geographical Review (New York), v. 33, April 1943: 256-275.

Detailed study stressing the historical geography of Budapest, growth and distribution of population, distribution of functional areas, impact on the country, and possible future development.

1762. Den Hollander, A. N. J. The Great Hungarian Plain: a European Frontier Area. Comparative Studies in Society and History (The Hague), v. 3, 1960/1961: 74-88, 155-169.

Discussion of the characteristics of the region and the traditions of its people.

1763. Enyedi, György. A Délkelet-Alföld mezőgazdasági földrajza (Agrogeography of the Southeastern Great Plain). Budapest, Akadémiai Kiadó, 1964. 314 p. Maps. Bibliography: p. 307-312. (Földrajzi monográfiák, 6)

Abstract in English published by the Institute of Geography, Hungarian Academy of Sciences (Budapest, 1964, 26 p.).

1764. Lettrich, Edit. Urbanizálódás Magyarországon (Urbanization in Hungary). Budapest, Akadémiai Kiadó, 1965. 83 p. Illus., maps. (Földrajzi tanulmányok, no. 5)

Study of the effects of urbanization on the way of life. Emphasis on changes in the occupational structure. Abstract in English published by the Institute of Geography, Hungarian Academy of Sciences (Budapest, 1965, 10 p.).

1765. Pounds, Norman J. G. Land Use on the Hungarian Plains. *In* Pounds, Norman J. G., *ed.* Geographical Essays on Eastern Europe. Bloomington, Indiana University, 1961. p. 54-74.

Historical analysis of the functions of the Hungarian plain.

1766. Simon, László. A belterjes mezőgazdaság területi kérdései Magyarországon (Regional problems of intensive agriculture in Hungary). Budapest, Akadémiai Kiadó, 1964. 127 p. (Földrajzi tanulmányok, no. 1)

Study of the regional structure of Hungarian agriculture. Abstract in English published by the Institute of Geography, Hungarian Academy of Sciences (Budapest, 1965, 5 p.).

32

the people

by Elemer Bako

A. ARCHAEOLOGY

1767. Acta archaeologica. 1951– Budapest, Magyar Tudományos Akadémia. Quarterly.

See also entry no. 1832.

Published by the Magyar Tudományos Akadémia. Contains scholarly articles, bibliographies, biographies, etc., related to archaeological research, with emphasis on Hungary. Communications in English, French, German, and Russian. Earlier activities of the Academy's Committee for Archaeology are covered in *Archaeologiai Közlemények* (Publications on archaeology) (Pest, 1863-1868; Budapest, 1873-1897).

1768. Archaeologia Hungarica. A Magyar Nemzeti Múzeum Régészeti Osztályának kiadványai. Acta archaeologica Musei Nationalis Hungarici. v. 1-28, 1926-1944; v. 29– 1946– Budapest.

Monographic series, published by the Archaeological Department of the Hungarian National Museum. Contains mainly reports and descriptions of excavation activities conducted by the professional staff of the National Museum. Texts in Hungarian and German in parallel columns. Volumes issued since 1946 are called "Series nova." See also *Folia archaeologica. A Magyar Nemzeti Múzeum évkönyve* (Yearbook of the Hungarian National Museum) (v. 1–, 1941–, Budapest, annual), published by the Hungarian National Museum, which includes articles, progress reports on excavations, and personnel news, with summaries in English, French, and German.

1769. Archaeologiai értesítő (Journal of archaeology). v. 1– 1869– Budapest. Semiannual.

Published by the Magyar Régészeti, Művészettörténeti és Éremtani Társulat. Contains studies on archaeology, art history, and numismatics, excellent book reviews, and reports on events in these fields of research. Includes summaries in English, French, German, or Russian.

1770. Banner, János, *comp.* Bibliographia archaeologica Hungarica, 1793-1943. Szeged, Institutum Archaeologicum Universitatis Szegediensis, 1944. 588 p. (Fontes rerum archaeologicarum Hungaricarum, tomus 1)

A classified, historical bibliography of archaeological literature issued in Hungary. See also János Banner and Imre Jakabffy's *A Közép-Dunamedence régészeti bibliográfiája, a legrégibb időktől a XI. századig* (Archaeological bibliography of the Central Danube Basin, from the earliest times to the 11th century) (Budapest, Akadémiai Kiadó, 1954, 581 p.), which includes titles and introduction in Russian, German, and French. This work was continued by Imre Jakabffy in his *A Közép-Dunamedence régészeti bibliográfiája, 1954-1959; Archäologische Bibliographie des Mittel-Donau-Beckens, 1954-1959* (Budapest, Akadémiai Kiadó, 1961, 250 p.), which also gives titles, introduction, and table of contents in French, German, and Russian. These bibliographies cover significant periods of Hungarian archaeological research as well as a large volume of materials published by foreign authors on the archaeology of Hungary and adjoining areas.

1771. Budapest. Tudományegyetem. *Régészeti Intézet.* Régészeti dolgozatok az Eötvös Loránd Tudományegyetem Régészeti Intézetéből. Dissertationes archaeologicae ex Instituto Archaeologico Universitatis de Rolando Eötvös nominatae. v. 1– 1958– Irregular.

Includes articles, doctoral dissertations, abstracts of state examination theses, and selective bibliographies in the field of archaeology, as well as reports on research conducted at the institute.

1772. Thomas, Edit (Baja), *ed.* Archäologische Funde in Ungarn. Compiled by László Vértes and others. Translated by Jenő Kende. Budapest, Corvina, 1956. 425 p. Illus., charts, map.

A classified guide to archaeological sitings in the country; includes extensive bibliographical notes.

B. ANTHROPOLOGY AND ETHNOLOGY

1773. Allodiatoris, Irma. A Kárpátmedence antropológiai bibliográfiája. Bibliographie der Anthropologie des Karpatenbeckens. Budapest, Akadémiai Kiadó, 1958. 183 p.

Classified bibliography listing 450 publications. Titles also in German.

Special aspects of anthropology in its relation to historical research are covered in "La bibliographie de l'anthropologie historique en Hongrie, 1945-1955," compiled by Pál Lipták and János Nemeskéri, *Crania Hungarica* (Budapest), v. 1, no. 1, 1956, p. 33-36.

1774. Anthropológiai közlemények (Communications in anthropology). v. 1– 1953– Budapest. Quarterly.

Issued also as: *Biológiai közlemények* (Communications in biology), *Pars anthropologica*; *Anthropológiai közlemények*. Journal of the Anthropological Section of the Hungarian Biological Society. Chiefly in Hungarian, with summaries in English, French, German, or Russian; occasional articles in German or French, with summaries in Hungarian. See also *Crania Hungarica* (v. 1– 1956–, Budapest, irregular), published in French and German by the Anthropological Section of the Hungarian National Museum.

1775. Bartucz, Lajos. Fajkérdés, fajkutatás (Race question, race research). Budapest, Királyi Magyar Egyetemi Nyomda, 1941. 322 p. Illus., plates.

A study refuting by implication various tenets of Nazi race theories. Professor Bartucz's materials on the physical anthropology of the Hungarians, originally published in volume 19 of the *Ungarische Jahrbücher*, Berlin, are also available in the following reprint:

Balogh, Béla, *and* Ludwigh Bartucz. Ungarische Rassenkunde. Berlin, W. de Gruyter, 1940. p. 141-320. Plates, bibliography. (Ungarische Bibliothek, 1. Reihe, 27)

1776. Ethnologische Mitteilungen aus Ungarn. v. 1-9; 1885-1905. Budapest. Irregular.

See also entry no. 2253.

Published by the Hungarian Academy of Sciences. The first scholarly journal of general ethnology published in Hungary in a foreign language. Some volumes published in parts. Emphasis on issues related to Hungarian ethnological research.

1777. Ferenczy, Endre. A magyar föld népeinek története a honfoglalásig (History of the peoples of the Hungarian land prior to the Conquest). Budapest, Gondolat Kiadó, 1958. 191 p. Bibliographical references included in "Jegyzetek": p. 141-178. (Studium könyvek, 3)

A thorough account, with numerous references to historical source materials, of all peoples whose presence in the territory of Hungary has been traced.

1778. Flachbart, Ernst. A History of Hungary's Nationalities. Budapest, Society of the Hungarian Quarterly, 1944. 133 p. Bibliographical notes.

A political history, with emphasis on legislation related to various ethnic groups in Hungary prior to the First World War.

1779. Hajdú, Péter. A magyarság kialakulásának előzményei (Antecedents of the ethnogenesis of the Hungarians). Budapest, Akadémiai

Kiadó, 1953. 92 p. Maps (part fold.) Bibliographical references in "Jegyzetek" (Notes): p. 66-84. (Nyelvtudományi értekezések, 2)

A critical survey of research related to the prehistory of the Hungarian people, based upon ethnolinguistic, archaeological, and cultural-geographic studies. Includes the first public rejection of the then officially propagated ideas concerning the "Asian origin" of the Hungarians and Finno-Ugrians.

The same issues are discussed by Tamás Bogyay in an extensive survey article entitled "Research into the Origin and Ancient History of the Hungarian Nation after the Second World War" (*The Hungarian Quarterly*, New York, v. 3, no. 1-2, April 1962: 52-68; no. 3-4, October/December 1962: 65-98), which includes a review of publications issued outside Hungary.

1780. Kniezsa, István. Ungarns Völkerschaften im XI. Jahrhundert. Budapest, Danubia Verlag, 1938. 172 p. Map. (Ostmitteleuropäische Bibliothek, 16)

An ethnolinguistic study, based on onomatological documentation of the presence of various ethnic elements in the new kingdom of Hungary during the first century of its existence.

1781. László, Gyula. A honfoglaló magyar nép élete (The life of the Hungarians at the time of the Conquest). Budapest, Magyar Élet Kiadó, 1944. 512 p. Illus., charts, 45 tables, 46 plates. Bibliography: p. 499-509. (Népkönyvtár, 4)

A new evaluation of combined results of research in the fields of archaeology, anthropology, linguistics, and folklore.

1782. Lipták, Pál. An Anthropological Survey of Magyar Prehistory. Acta Linguistica (Budapest), v. 4, 1954, no. 1/2: 133-170.

A comprehensive survey of the results of anthropological research conducted both in Hungary and abroad with regard to the anthropological characteristics of ancient Hungarians. Anthropological links between the Hungarians and other members of the Finno-Ugrian group are described by Lajos Bartucz in a paper entitled "Die finnisch-ugrischen Beziehungen der ungarischen Anthropologie," presented at the First Congress of Finno-Ugrists (Congressus Internationalis Fenno-Ugristarum, *1st, Budapest, 1960*), and published in its *Vorträge*, p. 432-440.

1783. Műveltség és hagyomány (Culture and tradition). Studia ethnologica Hungariae et Centralis ac Orientalis Europae. v. 1– 1960– Budapest. Annual.

Also carries the title *A Debreceni Kossuth Lajos Tudományegyetem Néprajzi Intézetének évkönyve* (Yearbook of the Ethnographical Institute of the Louis Kossuth University of Debrecen). Articles, research reports, and book reviews covering all aspects of ethnological research, with emphasis on Hungarian and Finno-Ugrian ethnology.

1784. Ortutay, Gyula. Kleine ungarische Volkskunde. Budapest, Corvina Verlag, 1963. 231 p. 24 plates. Bibliographical notes.

Systematic discussion of issues related to Hungarian ethnological research, with a contemporary presentation of Hungarian folklore. A shorter Hungarian version was published as *Magyar népismeret* (Hungarian ethnology) (Budapest, Magyar Szemle Társaság, 1937, 80 p.).

1785. Szabó, István. Ungarisches Volk, Geschichte und Wandlungen. Published by the Ungarisches Institut für Geschichtsforschung. Budapest, Verlagsanstalt Danubia, 1944. 328 p. 5 col. maps (in pocket). Bibliography: p. 256-322.

An ethnohistorical study of the Hungarian people, based largely on the author's *A magyarság életrajza* (An ethnic biography of the Hungarians) (Budapest, Magyar Történelmi Társulat, 1941, 276 p.). *See also* Elemér Mályusz's *Geschichte des ungarischen Volkstums von der Landnahme bis zum Ausgang des Mittelalters* (Budapest, Pannonia Verlag, 1940, 120 p., fold. map).

1786. Teleki, Pál, *gróf*. Ethnographical Map of Hungary, Based upon the Density of Population. The Hague, W. P. van Stockum and Son, 1920. 4 p., fold. map. (Editions in varying sizes)

The actual volume of ethnic settlement areas is mapped by expanding units of higher population density (such as city populations) into adjoining regions of lesser density (such as thinly populated mountainous areas). Also issued in French. *See also* Károly Kogutowicz's *Ethnographical Map of Hungary; Majorities and Minorities of Nationalities; Density of Population* (Budapest, Hungarian Geographical Institute, 1919, 5 p., 2 fold. col. maps; scale of main map: 1 : 1,000,000). Both maps are based on the census of 1910.

1787. Viski, Károly. Etnikai csoportok, vidékek (Ethnic groupings, regions). Budapest, Magyar Tudományos Akadémia, 1938. 25 p. Bibliographical references. (A magyar nyelvtudomány kézikönyve, 1. kötet, 8. füzet)

A discussion of Hungary's regional settlement units and regional subdivisions of the Hungarian people.

1788. Vuorela, Toivo. The Finno-Ugric Peoples. Translated by John Atkinson. Bloomington, Ind., Indiana University Press; The Hague, Mouton, 1964. 392 p. Illus., charts, maps, plans, port. Bibliography: p. 372-392. (Indiana University Publications. Uralic and Altaic Series, v. 39)

Prepared in connection with the "Research and Studies in Uralic and Altaic Languages" program of the American Council of Learned Societies. Includes chapters on each of the peoples of the Finno-Ugrian group and a statistical table of Finno-Ugrians in the USSR. *See also* Péter Hajdú's *Finnugor népek és nyelvek* (Finno-Ugrian peoples and languages) (Budapest, Gondolat Kiadó, 1962, 425 p., illus., plates (part col.), fold. maps, diagrs., facsims.; bibliography: p. 404-423), which contains chapters on the prehistory and ancient history of the Finno-Ugrians (including the Hungarians), with examples from the fields of ethnolinguistics, comparative folklore, cultural geography, physical anthropology, and archaeology. Recent research is discussed in Bertalan Korompay's article entitled "Die finnisch-ugrische Ethnologie," *Acta Linguistica* (Budapest), v. 10, 1960, no. 1/2, p. 131-180, which approaches Finno-Ugrian ethnology as a separate field of study and includes a selective bibliography. The causes and factors which create communication barriers between American and Hungarian anthropologists are analyzed by Bela C. Maday in "Hungarian Anthropology: The Problem of Communication," *Current Anthropology*, v. 9, no. 1, April/June, 1968, p. 61-65. Includes an annotated list of "Organizations of Anthropologically Related Activities" in Hungary.

C. DEMOGRAPHY

1789. Demográfia (Demography). v. 1– 1958– Budapest. Quarterly.

Published by Központi Statisztikai Hivatal. Includes articles on the demography of Hungary and neighboring countries and on research problems related to the field of demography. Summaries and tables of contents in English and Russian.

1790. Hungary. *Központi Statisztikai Hivatal.* Az 1960. évi népszámlálás (The population census of 1960). Budapest, 1960-1964. 21 v. Col. maps (part fold.), diagrs. (part col.), tables.

Volume 1 lists "preliminary data"; volumes 2-21 (19 for the counties and one volume for Budapest) contain data of the 1960 census and related literature. Also issued as part of the 1960 census series was a historically significant work entitled *Az első magyarországi népszámlálás, 1784-1787* (The first census held in Hungary, 1784-1787), edited by Dezső Danyi and Zoltán Dávid (Budapest, 1960, 389 p., maps, tables). *See also* András Klinger and Egon Szabady's "Az 1960. évi népszámlálás előkészítése, adatgyüjtési és feldolgozási programja" (Preparations for the 1960 population census; program of collecting and processing of the data) in *Statisztikai Szemle* (Statistical review) (Budapest, v. 37, 1959: 795-839). Population trends and procedural changes are covered in Lajos Thirring's *Népszámlálási kérdések; az 1949 évi népszámlólás tapasztalatai* (Population census problems; experiences gained by the population census of 1949) (Budapest, Központi Statisztikai Hivatal, 1957, 95 p.), which should be supplemented by the Hungarian Central Statistical Office's official publication, *Az 1949. évi népszámlálás.* (The population census of 1949) (Budapest, 1949-1951, 12 v.), and by its *Az 1941. évi népszámlás; demográfiai adatok községek szerint* (The population census of 1941; demographical data according to communities) (Budapest, Stephaneum Nyomda, 1947, 21, 697 p., tables). Interim census data are contained in the Statistical Office's *Mikrocenzus; 1963. évi személyi és családi adatai* (Micro-census; its individual and family census data for the year of 1963) (Budapest, Statisztikai Kiadó, 1964, 214 p.).

1791. Hungary. *Központi Statisztikai Hivatal.* Budapest népmozgalma (Population changes in Budapest). 1964– Budapest.

Monographic series. First volume contains data for 1961 and 1962. Complete statistical coverage of all reportable changes related to the population of the capital city. The Settlement Statistical Working Group (Településstatisztikai Munkaközösség) of the Central Statistical Office has also issued a volume entitled *Magyar városok és községek; statisztikai adatgyüjtemény* (Hungarian cities and villages; a collection of statistical data) (Budapest, Közgazdasági és Jogi Kiadó, 1958, 811 p.), which includes materials on demography, habitation, professional and economic standards, and local transportation. Special problems of the population of Budapest are treated statistically in Dezső Laky's *Budapest székesfőváros népességének fejlődése 1900-tól 1920-ig, különös tekintettel a fejlődés gazdasági rugóira* (Development of the population of the capital and residence city of Budapest from 1900 to 1920, with special reference to the economical incentives of the development) (Budapest, Statisztikai Hivatal, 1927-1929, 2 v.).

1792. Hungary. *Központi Statisztikai Hivatal.* A magyar korona országaiban az 1870. év elején végrehajtott népszámlálás eredményei a hasznos házi állatok kimutatásával együtt (Results of the population census conducted at the beginning of the year 1870 in the lands of the Hungarian Crown, with a survey of the domestic animal stock). Pest, Athenaeum, 1871. 615 p. Tables.

Texts in Hungarian and German, with an added title page in German. The first of the decennial census reports of the Hungarian Statistical Office. Special studies on census problems related to various historical periods are discussed in György Györffy's *Einwohnerzahl und Bevölkerungsdichte in Ungarn bis zum Anfang des XIV. Jahrhunderts* (Budapest, Akadémiai Kiadó, 1960, 31 p.), and in Alajos Kovács' *The Development of the Population of Hungary Since the Cessation of the Turkish Rule* (London, Low, W. Dawson and Sons; New York, Steiger, 1921, 32 p.).

1793. Hungary. *Központi Statisztikai Hivatal.* A termékenységi, családtervezési és születésszabályozási vizsgálat fontosabb adatai (Main results of research related to fertility, planned parenthood, and birth control). Budapest, 1964. 115 p.

Statistical information on an issue which provoked worldwide criticism of official Hungarian policy and practices. A survey of these complex problems is given by Zoltán Sztáray in his *Birth Control in Hungary Since 1956* (Brussels, The Imre Nagy Institute, 1961, 22 p.). The different attitude which characterized the period prior to the Second World War is expressed in Dezső Laky's *Népesedéspolitika* (Population Policy) (Budapest, Magyar Szemle Társaság, 1933, 80 p.).

1794. Hungary. *Központi Statisztikai Hivatal. Népességtudományi Kutatócsoport.* A Központi Statisztikai Hivatal Népességtudományi Kutatócsoportjának és a Magyar Tudományos Akadémia Demográfiai Elnökségi Bizottságának kiadványai (Publications of the Research Group for Demographic Science of the Central Statistical Office and of the Presidial Committee on Demography of the Hungarian Academy of Sciences). v. 1– 1963– Budapest.

Monographic series. Includes studies on topics related to demographic research, with emphasis on Hungary. *See also* the same group's *Magyarország népességének demográfiai jellemzői régiónként* (Demographic characteristics of the population of Hungary according to regions) (Budapest, 1964–).

1795. Kovacsics, József. Magyarország történeti demográfiája. Magyarország népesedése a honfoglalástól 1949-ig. (Historical demography of Hungary. The population changes in Hungary from the Conquest of the land to 1949). Budapest, Közgazdasági és Jogi Kiadó, 1963. 441 p. Maps, charts, indexes, tables (4 fold. leaves) in pocket.

Systematic discussion of population development and related research. Includes a "selective bibliography of historical demography" (p. 389-406), a set of "historical demographic charts" (p. 407-412), and summaries in English and Russian.

1796. Kovacsics, József, *ed.* A történeti statisztika forrásai (Sources of historical statistics). Budapest, Közgazdasági és Jogi Könyvkiadó, 1957. 460 p. Maps, facsims., tables. Bibliography: p. 339-367.

See also entry no. 2003.

A collection of articles on research problems arising in the area of historical statistical studies. The Library of the Central Statistical Office of Hungary publishes current statistical literature in *Történeti statisztikai évkönyv* (Historical statistical yearbook) (Budapest, 1960– and *Történeti statisztikai közlemények* (Historical statistical publications) (Budapest, 1963–, quarterly); the former is issued jointly with the Department of Archives of the Ministry of Cultural Affairs, and the latter with the National Center of Archives. *See also* Gusztáv Bokor's *Geschichte und Organisation der amtlichen Statistik in Ungarn* (Budapest, Pester Buchdruckerei Actien-Gesellschaft, 1896, 291 p.), a comprehensive survey which covers the history of legislation on official statistical services and the organization of population censuses and special population studies, as well as a bibliography of statistical publications (p. 279-291).

1797. Siegel, Jacob S. The Population of Hungary. Washington, D.C., U.S. Govt. Print. Off., 1958. 186 p. Illus., maps, diagrs. (U.S. Bureau of the Census. International Population Statistics Reports, Series P-90, no. 9)

See also entry no. 2073.

A study of Hungary's postwar population, with detailed analyses of earlier population transfers, migrations, and emigrations. Supplementary data for the years since 1956 are available in *Magyarország népesedése* (Population changes in Hungary) (Budapest, 1958–, annual), issued by the Hungarian Central Statistical Office. A League of Nations publication entitled *The Official Vital Statistics of the Kingdom of Hungary* (Geneva, Imprimérie Sonor, 1927, 78 p., illus. [maps], forms) provides information on the period after the First World War.

1798. Szabady, Egon, *ed.* Bevezetés a demográfiába (Introduction to demography). Budapest, Közgazdasági és Jogi Kiadó, 1964. 609 p. Illus., maps. Bibliography: p. 584-600.

An account of issues, methods, and results of current demographic research. The same author describes current Hungarian demographic programs in an article entitled "A Magyar Tudományos Akadémia Demográfiai Bizottságának feladatai" (Tasks of the Demographic Commission of the Hungarian Academy of Sciences), *Magyar Tudomány*, (Budapest), 1961, p. 175-180.

1799. Zala, György. Magyarország ipari dolgozóinak inga-vándorlása (The "pendulum migration" of industrial workers of Hungary). Földrajzi Közlemények (Budapest), v. 82, 1964: 265-285.

An analysis of the effects of the two-way migration of a large contingent of the Hungarian industrial working force between home village (usually for food and to visit the family) and industrial city (for better employment conditions). The costs of this weekend migration are great both for the individual and for the state.

D. HUNGARIANS ABROAD

1. General

1800. Borsody-Bevilaqua, Béla. Régi magyar világjárók (Hungarian world travelers of old). Edited and with an introduction by Ferenc Agárdi. Maps by Gábor Bodnár. Illustrated by Róbert Muray. Budapest, Művelt Nép Kiadó, 1954. 341 p. Maps.

Selections of texts (from diaries, memoirs and travelogs) by early Hungarian travelers, scholars, emigrés (of the 17th through the 19th centuries) which reflect their experiences in distant parts of the world.

Other works include Gyula Halász' *Öt világrész magyar vándorai; magyar fölfedezők Benyovszkytól napjainkig* (Hungarian travelers across five continents; Hungarian explorers from Benyovszky to our days) (Budapest, Grill K., 1936, 191 p., illus.), and László Vajda's *Nagy magyar útazók; 19. század* (Great Hungarian travelers; 19th century) (Budapest, Művelt Nép Kiadó, 1951, 219 p., illus.)

1801. Hungary. *Statisztikai Hivatal.* A Magyar Szent Korona országainak kivándorlása és visszavándorlása, 1899-1913 (Emigration and remigration in the lands of the Holy Crown of Hungary, 1899-1913). Budapest, Hornyánszky, 1924. 106, 120 p.

A penetrating statistical analysis of the emigration (mostly to the

United States) of all nationality groups (including Hungarians) from pre-World War I Hungary. Important for the study of the history of Hungarian settlements in the United States.

From the political and economic point of view, Imre Kovács' *A kivándorlás* (The emigration) (Budapest, Cserépfalvi, 1938, 196 p., bibliography) offers a critical retrospective evaluation of the prewar emigration policy.

1802. Krisztics, Sándor, *ed.* A Magyarok Világkongresszusának tárgyalásai. 1-2; 1929-1938 (Proceedings of the World Congress of Hungarians. 1-2; 1929-1938). Budapest, "A Magyarok Világszövetsége Központi Irodájának kiadása," 1930-1939. 2 v. Illus.

Speeches, reports, statistical and cultural surveys made among Hungarian groups abroad, and other publications which reflect upon the activities of Hungarians all over the world are included.

1803. Nagy, Iván. Öt világrész magyarsága (Hungarians on five continents). Budapest, Magyar Szemle Társaság, 1935. 80 p. Bibliographical notes.

A survey, with emphasis on statistics.

2. Hungarians in the United States and Canada

1804. Fishman, Joshua A. Hungarian Language Maintenance in the United States. Bloomington, Ind., Indiana University, 1966. 68 p. Indiana University Publications. Uralic and Altaic Series, v. 62)

Summary of a survey of trends, channels, forms, and degrees of the usage of Hungarian as a second language both in speech and writing in the United States.

Main aspects of a dialectological collection and research program related to the American versions of Hungarian dialects were first discussed by Elemer Bako in his "The Goals and Methods of Hungarian Dialectology in the United States," *Communications et rapports du Premier congrès international de dialectologie générale* Louvain, Centre international de dialectologie générale, 1965, p. 23-29). A comprehensive report by John Lotz entitled "Magyar nyelvészeti kutatások az Amerikai Egyesült Államokban" (Studies in Hungarian linguistics in the United States of America) in *A magyar nyelv története és rendszere* (History and system of the Hungarian language) (Budapest, Akadémiai Kiadó, 1967, p. 32-37), contains numerous references to research on American Hungarians and to study and area centers of American universities where educational and research programs related to Hungarian are in progress.

1805. Hírünk a világban. Our Reputation in the World. v. 1– 1951– Washington, D.C., Occidental Press. Irregular.

A cultural survey of Hungarian cultural issues, events, and personalities abroad, with occasional references to Hungary. Includes *Bibliográfia*, a special supplement to list Hungarian publications issued abroad, both in Hungarian and other languages. Occasional illustrated supplements.

For the period of 1951-1956, to be supplemented by *Új magyar út. New Hungarian Way*, published by the Hungarian Cultural Fellowship (first in Munich, Germany, in 1950-1952, then in Washington, D.C.).

1806. Hungary. *Országos Levéltár*. I. Országos Levéltár. 10. Gyüjtemények (I. National Archives. 10. Collections). Compiled by Zoltán Dávid, Emma Iványi, and Miklós Komjáthy. Budapest, Levéltárak Országos Központja, 1956. 249 p.

Index no. 10 of the holdings of the Hungarian National Archives which describes special collections, among them those containing unpublished and formerly unreported materials (correspondence, diaries, personal documents, and other items such as decorations, weapons, etc.) related to Hungarian immigrants of the 1850's, among them General Alexander Asboth (later U.S. Minister to Argentina and Uruguay), Medal of Honor winner Julius Stahel, and many others.

1807. Kende, Géza. Magyarok Amerikában. Az amerikai magyarság története (Hungarians in America. History of the American Hungarians). Cleveland, Szabadság, 1927-1928. 2 v. Illus.

The first introduction to the history of the Hungarians in the United States, intended for popular consumption. It should be used together with Emil Lengyel's *Americans from Hungary* (Philadelphia, Lippincott, 1948, 319 p.), which also includes numerous biobibliographical references to notable Americans of Hungarian extraction.

1808. Ruzsa, Jenő. A kanadai magyarság története (History of the Hungarians in Canada). Toronto, 1940. 510 p. Illus., ports.

A first attempt, by a Hungarian Protestant minister, to provide a comprehensive history of the rapidly growing Hungarian ethnic group in Canada. Useful for information on church and social history of the Canadian Hungarians. It should be consulted in conjunction with John Kosa's *Land of Choice, the Hungarians in Canada* (Toronto, University of Toronto Press, 1957, 104 p.), a sociological study which outlines trends toward assimilation as well as retention of various traditional values by Canadian Hungarians. For the position of Hungarians among other immigrant groups see *Immigrants in Canada* (Montreal, 1955, 63 p.), edited by John Kosa and written by Imre Bernolák and others.

1809. Sebestyén, Endre. Kossuth, a Magyar Apostle of World Democracy. Pittsburgh, Expert Printing Co., 1950. 218 p. Illus., map.

The work, dedicated to the centenary of Louis Kossuth's celebrated visit to the United States in 1851-1852, contains the first comprehensive story of the United States' contacts with the Hungarian government of 1848-1849 and of the subsequent efforts of the

American government to free Kossuth from his exile in Turkey, together with selections of statements made by him during his tour of the United States and of poems by prominent contemporary American poets.

More details on United States involvement in the affairs of 1848-1849 are provided in Sándor Szilassy's article, "America and the Hungarian Revolution of 1848-49," *The Slavonic and East European Review*, v. 44, no. 102, Jan. 1966: 180-196.

1810. Szy, Tibor, *ed.* Hungarians in America; a Biographical Directory of Professionals of Hungarian Origin in the Americas. New York, Hungarian University Association, 1963. 606 p.

The first edition, issued with an introduction by Nobel Prize winner Albert Szent-Györgyi, contains about 7,000 bio-bibliographical articles, supplemented by professional directories, lists of Hungarian newspapers, periodicals issued in the Americas (listed by country), lists of churches and churchmen, associations, U.S. libraries with Hungarian holdings, etc. The second, revised edition was published by The Kossuth Foundation, Inc. (New York, 1966, 487 p.). It includes only bio-bibliographical articles, mostly updated versions of the first edition.

1811. Testvériség. Fraternity. v. 1– 1923– Washington, D.C., Hungarian Reformed Federation of America. Monthly.

Title varies: *Református újság* (Reformed journal), 1923-1940. Organ of a fraternal order which also carries articles, short stories, poetry, and cultural news items related to the life of Hungarians in America. In Hungarian and English.

1812. Vasvary, Edmund. Lincoln's Hungarian Heroes; the Participation of Hungarians in the Civil War, 1861-1865. Washington, D.C., The Hungarian Reformed Federation of America, 1939. 171 p. Illus., ports., facsims.

The first extensive work which describes the roles played in the Civil War by numerous representatives of the first important group of Hungarian emigrés in the United States, the so-called "Kossuth emigration." It includes separate listings of "Hungarians in the Union Armies" (p. 43-89) and of "Hungarians in the Confederate Army" (p. 91-94), and a bibliography (p. 95-101). In English and Hungarian, with added title-page in Hungarian.

To be supplemented by the following works by Tivadar Ács: *Magyar úttörők az Újvilágban* (Hungarian pioneers in the New World) (Budapest, 1942, 199 p.), which contains the diary of Louis Kossuth's former secretary for the years 1850-1867; *New-Buda* (Budapest, 1941, 322 p.), the story of the first Hungarian settlement in the United States founded in Decatur County, Iowa, in 1850, and *Magyarok az északamerikai polgárháborúban, 1861-1865* (Hungarians in the American Civil War, 1861-1865) (Budapest, Pannonia, 1964, 150 p., illus., ports.; bibliography: p. 146-149), which in several respects supplements the work by Vasvary.

1813. The Young Magyar-American. v. 1-v. 4, no. 1; March 1936-March 1939. New York, Lulu Putnik Payerle. Monthly.

Illustrated cultural magazine issued for second-generation American Hungarians. Contains numerous translations of Hungarian prose and poetry, with emphasis on conservative authors, and news of Hungarian cultural life in America.

3. Hungarians in Europe Outside Hungary

1814. Budapest. Magyar Statisztikai Társaság. *Államtudományi Intézet.* A felvidéki magyarság 20 éve, 1918-1938 (Twenty years of the Hungarians of the Upper-Land, 1918-1938). Budapest, 1938. 139 p.

Studies on the political, economic, cultural, and other conditions of the Hungarians in Slovakia during the first two decades of their separation from Hungary. *See also*:

Research Institute for Minority Studies on Hungarians Attached to Czechoslovakia and Carpatho-Ukrania, Inc., New York. Hungarians in Czechoslovakia. By Dr. Francis S. Wagner, Dr. John Holota, Charles J. Hokky, Stephen Revay, and Coloman Brogyányi. New York, 1959. 166 p. Maps, charts. Contains studies, texts of documents, chronologies, bibliographical references illustrative of changes which affected the life of Hungarians in Czechoslovakia after the Second World War.

1815. Mildschütz, Kálmán, *comp.* A magyar nyelvű emigrációs sajtó bibliográfiája (Bibliography of the Hungarian language press of the emigration). München, 1963. 23 p.

Lists newspapers and periodicals issued by Hungarian emigrés in the Federal Republic of Germany from 1945 through 1962. Changes of titles, editors, and publishers are indicated.

1816. Révay, Stephen. Hungarian Minorities Under Communist Rule. The Hungarian Quarterly (New York), v. 1, no. 4, October 1961: 42-47.

The author analyzes the components in the struggle for national existence of the Hungarian minority groups in Romania, Yugoslavia, Czechoslovakia, and the USSR, i.e., the Carpatho-Ukraine.

1817. U.S. *Library of Congress.* Hungarians in Rumania and Transylvania. A Bibliographical List of Publications in Hungarian and West European Languages Compiled from the Holdings of the Library of Congress, by Elemer Bako and William Sólyom-Fekete. Washington, D.C., 1966, 193 p.

Contains 1,730 bibliographical entries in 13 subject chapters. Titles in Hungarian and Latin are translated into English. In each chapter, separate subchapters list special reference works, periodicals and serials, monographs, and minor publications. Works by Romanian authors are not included.

33

history

by Francis S. Wagner

A. REFERENCE AIDS

1. Sources

1818. Bartoniek, Emma, *comp.* Magyar történeti forráskiadványok (Hungarian historical source publications). Budapest, Magyar Történelmi Társulat, 1939. 203 p. (A magyar történettudomány kézikönyve, köt. 1, füzet 3/b)

Contains 3,109 entries, partly annotated, covering historical Hungary, Transylvania inclusive, from the Conquest up to the Compromise of 1867. Also, lists guides to domestic (Hungarian) and foreign archives storing documents relating to the country's history.

1819. Marczali, Henrik, *ed.* A magyar történet kútfőinek kézikönyve (Handbook of sources relating to Hungarian history). Budapest, Athenaeum, 1901. 967 p.

Collection of most important sources from the pre-Conquest times up to the third quarter of the 19th century, including Law no. XXX of 1868. Greek and Latin sources are published also in Hungarian translation. Name and subject index, as well as bibliographical notes.

1820. Pauler, Gyula, *and* Sándor Szilágyi, *eds.* A magyar honfoglalás kútfői (Sources relating to the Hungarian conquest). Budapest, Magyar Tudományos Akadémia, 1900. 877 p. Illus.

Publishes most important Western as well as Oriental sources in the original language and in Hungarian translation with commentaries and bibliography.

2. Bibliography, Historiography, Cartography

1821. Banner, János, *and* Imre Jakabffy, *comps.* A Közép-Dunamedence régészeti bibliográfiája a legrégibb időktől a XI. századig. Archäologische Bibliographie des Mittel-Donau-Beckens von den frühesten Zeiten an bis zum XI. Jahrhundert. Budapest, Akadémiai Kiadó, 1954. 581 p.

With emphasis on historical Hungary and its neighboring countries, lists monographs, periodical articles, and book reviews. Contains 17,590 entries.

1822. Bibliographia Hungariae. I. Historica. Verzeichnis der 1861-1921 erschienenen Ungarn betreffenden Schriften in nichtungarischer Sprache. Zusammengestellt vom Ungarischen Institut an der Universität Berlin. Berlin und Leipzig, Walter de Gruyter, 1923. 318 p. (Ungarische Bibliothek für das Ungarische Institut an der Universität Berlin, herausgegeben von Robert Gragger. Dritte Reihe, I)

Chronological and subject arrangement covering the ancient times up to the peace treaties concluded after the First World War. Besides Hungary, the entire Habsburg Empire is covered. National minorities, foreign relations, military history, auxiliary sciences of history, etc., are among subject groups.

1823. Eperjessy, Kálmán, *comp.* A bécsi hadilevéltár magyar vonatkozású térképeinek jegyzéke (List of maps relative to Hungary housed in the Vienna Kriegsarchiv). Szeged, Szeged Városi Nyomda és Könyvkiadó Rt, 1929. 172 p. (A Szegedi Alföldkutató Bizottság Könyvtára, 3. Szakosztály közleményei, 6 sz.)

Contains 2,676 items with index of place names. Material grouped as follows: political maps; physical maps; special maps; city plans; military history maps, etc.

1824. Halasz de Beky, I. L., *comp.* A Bibliography of the Hungarian Revolution 1956. Published under the auspices of the Canadian Institute of International Affairs. Toronto, University of Toronto Press, 1963. 179 p.

Contains 2,136 entries, of which 428 are books and pamphlets, 12 motion pictures, 88 monitored broadcasts, and 1,608 periodical articles, covering the period from October 1956 to December 1960. The entries are arranged by language (15 languages) and into books and articles. Hungarian and Slavic book entries are provided with English translations. The index lists authors and titles of books and authors of articles, but titles of articles are omitted.

1825. Hóman, Bálint, *ed.* A magyar történetírás új útjai (New ways of Hungarian historiography). Budapest, Magyar Szemle Társaság, 1931. 464 p. (A Magyar Szemle könyvei, 3)

Surveys past and present of most important branches of Hungarian as well as universal historiography such as literary history by Tivadar

Thienemann; art history by Tibor Gerevich; church history by Imre Révész; economic and social history by István Dékány; political historiography by Gyula Szekfű, etc.

1826. Kogutowicz, Károly, *comp.* Atlasz a világtörténelem tanításához (Atlas for teaching world history). Budapest, Magyar Földrajzi Intézet, 1913. 58 p.

Colored maps covering the world, with emphasis on Hungary, and the Habsburg Monarchy. Thirteen pages (maps) show Hungary in the Roman times; during the periods of the Árpáds, the Anjou dynasty and Sigismund; under the Hunyadis and Jagiellos; during Turkish rule; and during the periods 1718-1848, 1848-1849, and 1849-1860.

1827. Kosáry, Domokos G. Bevezetés a magyar történelem forrásaiba és irodalmába (Introduction to the sources and literature of Hungarian history). Budapest, Közoktatásügyi Kiadóvállalat, 1951-1954. 3 v.

A detailed description, together with sometimes critical analysis of sources and their literature. Volume 1 covers period of greater Hungary up to 1711; volume 2 was issued by Művelt Nép Könyvkiadó and deals with the period 1711-1825. Volume 3 contains name index.

1828. Magyar Történész Kongresszus, *Budapest, 1953.* Magyar Történész Kongresszus 1953 június 6-13 (Congress of Hungarian historians, June 6-13, 1953). Budapest, Akadémiai Kiadó, 1954. 688 p.

Contains lectures and proceedings of the first Congress held in Budapest with Hungarian and other Marxist-Leninist historians attending. Attention concentrated on the independence movements of Hungary and its neighboring countries, progressive traditions of the people's democracies and the Soviet Union, correlations among the historical sciences in the USSR and in the people's democracies, etc.

1829. Magyar Tudományos Akadémia, *Budapest. Történettudományi Intézet.* Bibliographie d'œuvres choisies de la science historique hongroise 1945-1959. Bibliografiia izbrannykh sochinenii vengerskoi istoricheskoi nauki 1945-1959 gg. Budapest, Akadémiai Kiadó, 1960. 279 p.

Contains 2,059 entries of monographs and periodical articles on Hungarian and universal history, with French and Russian title translations and French-language abstracts. This is a selective list representing post-1945 Marxist-Leninist historiography.

1830. Magyar Tudományos Akadémia, *Budapest. Történettudományi Intézet.* Magyar történeti bibliográfia 1825-1867 (Hungarian historical bibliography, 1825-1867). Budapest, Akadémiai Kiadó, 1950-1959. 4 v.

See also entry no. 169.

Contents: Volume 1, General Part, 5,654 entries; volume 2, Economy, 15,855 entries; volume 3, Politics, Law, Education, Science and Humanities, Press, Religion, 24,698 entries; volume 4, Non-Hungarian Peoples, 29,682 entries. Volume 1-3 compiled under the general editorship of Zoltán I. Tóth, volume 4 under that of G. G. Kemény and L. Katus.

1831. Wagner, Ferenc (Francis S.). A magyar történetírás új útjai 1945-1955 (New ways of Hungarian historiography, 1945-1955). Washington, D.C., 1956. 28 p.

Surveys — within the framework of the country's political development — monographic as well as periodical literature and the role of the Academy of Sciences, and reviews the June 1954 Budapest Congress of Historians, the first post-1945 international meeting of Marxist-Leninist historians. Russian, Polish, Czech, and Slovak language works are also analyzed.

3. Serials

1832. Acta archaeologica. 1951– Budapest, Magyar Tudományos Akadémia. Quarterly.

See also entry no. 1767.

Articles on archaeology, with emphasis on Hungary and neighboring countries, including the Soviet Union. Articles in English, French, German, and Russian, with summaries in a language other than that used in the article.

1833. Budapest. Legújabbkori Történeti Múzeum. Legújabbkori Történeti Múzeum Évkönyve (Yearbook of the Museum of Contemporary History). 1959– Budapest. Annual. Illus., ports., facsims.

Lists materials housed in the Museum and publishes sources and articles relating to the labor movement, party history (social democratic and communist), the Hungarian Soviet Republic of 1919, as well as post-1945 events.

1834. Századok (Centuries). 1867– Budapest. Bimonthly.

Issued by the Hungarian Historical Association. Articles on Hungarian history, mostly modern, and on European history, with emphasis on the Habsburg Monarchy. French and Russian summaries, table of contents in English, French, German, and Russian.

1835. Történelmi Szemle (Historical review). 1958– Budapest. Quarterly.

Issued by the Institute of Historical Research, Hungarian Academy of Sciences. Articles on history, mostly modern, from Marxist-Leninist viewpoint, with emphasis on Hungary and its neighboring countries, including the USSR. Supersedes *A Magyar Tudományos Akadémia Történettudományi Intézetének Értesítője*.

1836. Történeti statisztikai közlemények (Historical statistical communications). 1957– Budapest. Quarterly.

Issued by the Library of the Central Statistical Office and the National Center of Archives. Articles on statistics pertaining to the history of the Habsburg Empire, with special emphasis on Hungary, based mainly on unpublished sources.

B. GENERAL WORKS

1837. Brabourne, Cecil Marcus Knatchbull-Hugessen, *4th baron.* The Political Evolution of the Hungarian Nation. London, National Review Office, 1908. 2 v.

From the beginnings up to the 1867 Compromise. Well footnoted. Index.

1838. Hóman, Bálint, *and* Gyula Szekfű. Magyar történet (History of Hungary). 7th ed. Budapest, Királyi Magyar Egyetemi Nyomda, 1941-1943. 5 v. Illus., maps.

The most detailed survey of historical development from ancient times up to the end of the First World War, based on archival documents, with source criticism, annotated, critical bibliographies, and a chronology.

1839. Kosáry, Domokos G. A History of Hungary. Cleveland, New York, Benjamin Franklin Bibliophile Society, 1941. 482 p. Illus., maps. Bibliography: p. 439-455.

See also entry no. 1908.

Relates events up to the Second World War with special regard to Hungarian populated territories of the neighboring countries. The bibliography emphasizes Western-language publications. Includes chronological and statistical tables.

1840. Szekfű, Gyula. Der Staat Ungarn; eine Geschichtsstudie. Stuttgart und Berlin, Deutsche Verlags-Anstalt, 1918. 224 p.

Discusses the development of Hungarian statehood and national politics since the Conquest up to the end of the First World War. Special chapter is devoted to the role of Transylvania. Relevant sources and literature extensively surveyed. It has been translated into Hungarian as *A magyar állam életrajza; történelmi tanulmány* (2d ed., Budapest, Dick Manó, 1923, 238 p.).

1841. Teleki, Pál, *gróf.* The Evolution of Hungary and Its Place in European History. New York, Macmillan, 1923. 312 p. Front., maps, diagrs. Bibliography: p. 245-312.

See also entries no. 1756 *and* 1915.

Summarizes events, especially those connected with the making of the state (King Stephen I), the Turkish invasion, the Age of Dualism (1867-1918), as well as the nationality question. Its bibliography lists monographs written in Western languages.

1842. Yolland, Arthur B. Hungary. London, T. C. & E. C. Jack; New York, Frederick A. Stokes, 1917. 336 p. Front., illus., plates. Bibliography: p. 304-305.

Describes development up to the First World War. Lists monographic and periodical literature mostly in Western languages. Statistical appendix prepared by Olga Epstein.

C. WORKS ON SPECIFIC PERIODS

1. Up to 1526

1843. Elekes, Lajos. A középkori magyar állam története megalapításától mohácsi bukásáig (History of the medieval Hungarian state from its founding up to its collapse at Mohács). Budapest, Kossuth Könyvkiadó, 1964. 327 p.

Deals chiefly with feudal characteristics and attempts at centralization. Includes source criticism (p. 300-308), and a literature survey (p. 308-314).

1844. Hóman, Bálint. König Stefan I, der Heilige; die Gründung des ungarischen Staates. Breslau, Wilh. Gottl. Korn, 1941. 281 p. Illus., maps.

Represents a lifetime of intensive research. The title of the original Hungarian-language work is *Szent István*.

1845. Hóman, Bálint. A magyar királyság pénzügyei és gazdaságpolitikája Károly Róbert korában (Financial matters and economic policy of the Hungarian Kingdom in the age of Charles Robert). Budapest, Budavári Tudományos Társaság, 1921. 306 p. Fold. map, tables.

Summarizes economic and financial development of medieval Hungary between 1000 A.D. and the first decade of the 14th century, focusing on the reign of Charles Robert. Commercial policy, monetary reforms, financial administration, and the material foundations of the medieval kingdom are also analyzed, the analysis based heavily upon unpublished sources.

1846. Hóman, Bálint. Magyar középkor (The Hungarian Middle Ages). Budapest, Magyar Történelmi Társulat, 1938. 675 p.

Collection of articles, essays, treatises covering many aspects of medieval Hungary.

1847. Lukinich, Imre, *ed.* Mátyás király; emlékkönyv születésének ötszázéves fordulójára 1440-1940 (King Matthias; memorial volume commemorating the 500th anniversary of his birth, 1440-1940). Budapest, Franklin Társulat, 1940. 2 v.

A many-sided description of 15th century Hungary based on primary sources and select literature, including material on the so-called Hunyadi question, and the Hungarian-Romanian relationship. Contains pictures and coins bearing the king's image.

2. 1526-1848/49

1848. Gracza, György. Az 1848-49-iki magyar szabadságharc története

(History of the fight for freedom in 1848-1849). Budapest, Lampel Róbert (Wodianer F. és Fiai) 1894-1898. 5 v. Illus., facsims.

Reviews military as well as political developments by using contemporary correspondence and personal and official papers stored in the National Archives of Budapest and other repositories.

1849. Hengelmüller von Hengervár, Ladislas. Hungary's Fight for National Existence; or, the History of the Great Uprising Led by Francis Rákóczi II, 1703-1711. London, Macmillan, 1913. 342 p. Fold. map.

Introduction (p. 1-79) reviews Austro-Hungarian political relationship between 1526-1700; Chapter 1 is Rákóczi's biography (p. 79-106).

1850. Horváth, Mihály. Huszonöt év Magyarország történelméből 1823-tól 1848-ig (Twenty-five years of Hungary's history from 1823 to 1848). 2d rev. and enl. ed. Pest, Ráth Mór, 1868-1886. 3 v.

Describes the work of the national assembly, political trends, the Hungarian-Croatian relationship, the nationality question in general, intellectual life, etc. The author was himself an active statesman during that period.

1851. Kosáry, Domokos G. A Görgey-kérdés és története (History of the Görgey question). Budapest, Királyi Magyar Egyetemi Nyomda, 1936. 328 p.

Analyzes the role that Arthur Görgey (1818-1916) played in the 1848-1849 events, including his conflicts with Lajos Kossuth. Also surveys relevant literature.

1852. Lukinich, Imre. Erdély területi változásai a török hódítás korában 1541-1711 (Territorial changes of Transylvania during the age of the Turkish yoke, 1541-1711). Budapest, Magyar Tudományos Akadémia, 1918. 646 p.

Based chiefly on unpublished documents. Equipped with maps and place-name and subject indexes.

1853. Lukinich, Imre. A szatmári béke története és okirattára (History of the Treaty of Szatmár and the collection of its documents). Budapest, Magyar Történelmi Társulat, 1925. 633 p.

The Treaty of Szatmár of 1711 is described entirely on the basis of archival (Budapest and Vienna) sources.

1854. Marczali, Henrik. Hungary in the Eighteenth Century; With an Introductory Essay on the Earlier History of Hungary by Harold W. V. Temperley. Cambridge, University Press, 1910. 377 p. Fold. map, fold. tab.

A detailed survey of economic conditions, social system, nationality problem, church life, and politics. Statistical tables, glossary, and subject index.

1855. Salamon, Ferenc. Magyarország a török hódítás korában (Hungary in the age of the Turkish yoke). 2d rev. ed. Budapest, Franklin Társulat, 1886. 472 p.

Based mainly on archival documents.

1856. Stephen Széchenyi, 1860-1960. Journal of Central European Affairs, v. 20, no. 3, October 1960: 251-313.

This special issue was devoted to István Széchenyi (1791-1860), commemorating the 100th anniversary of his death. Contents: "The Széchenyi Problem," by George Barany (p. 251-269); "From Feudalism to Capitalism: The Economic Background to Széchenyi's Reform in Hungary," by B. G. Iványi (p. 270-288); "Széchenyi and the Nationality Problem in the Habsburg Empire," by Francis S. Wagner (p. 289-311). As the manuscript of the present bibliographic guide went to press, an excellent English-language work on Széchenyi became available:

Barany, George. Stephen Széchenyi and the Awakening of Hungarian Nationalism, 1791-1841. Princeton, N.J., Princeton University Press, 1968. 487 p. Illus., facsims., ports., bibliographical footnotes.

1857. Széchenyi, István, *gróf.* A mai Széchenyi; eredeti szövegek Széchenyi munkáiból (Széchenyi of today; original texts from István Széchenyi's works). Compiled with an introduction and notes by Gyula Szekfű. Budapest, Magyar Kulturális Egyesületek Szövetsége, 1935. 488 p.

1858. Széchenyi, István, *gróf.* Széchenyi István válogatott írásai (Selected writings of István Széchenyi). Edited with explanatory notes and an introductory essay by István Barta. Budapest, Gondolat, 1959. 469 p.

One of the most recent and authoritative annotated Széchenyi editions which has been widely accepted by the historical profession.

1859. Szekfű, Gyula. Bethlen Gábor (Gábor Bethlen). Budapest, Magyar Szemle Társaság, 1929. 314 p. (A Magyar Szemle Könyvei, 1)

Reviews within the framework of 17th century European politics the life and work of Gábor Bethlen (1580-1629), Prince of Transylvania, with emphasis on the Czech alliance and his Polish plans. Surveys literature on Bethlen as well as on Transylvania.

1860. Szekfű, Gyula, *ed.* Iratok a magyar államnyelv kérdésének történetéhez 1790-1848 (Documents relating to the history of the problem of the Hungarian state language, 1790-1848). Budapest, Magyar Történelmi Társulat, 1926. 664 p.

Introduction (p. 7-208) relates changing political situations in the Habsburg Empire, focusing on the Hungarian Diets and the language question. Significant documents housed in Vienna archives (Latin, German, and Hungarian sources) are published with comments. Name and subject index.

1861. Takáts, Sándor. Művelődéstörténeti tanulmányok a XVI-XVII. századból (Studies in the cultural history of the 16th-17th centuries). Edited by Kálmán Benda. Budapest, Gondolat Kiadó, 1961. 419 p. Illus.

Describes social life and customs.

1862. Tóth, Zoltán I., *ed.* Emlékkönyv Kossuth Lajos születésének 150. évfordulójára 1802-1952 (Memorial volume commemorating the 150th anniversary of the birth of Lajos Kossuth, 1802-1952). Budapest, Akadémiai Kiadó, 1952. 2 v. Ports., illus., bibliographical footnotes.

Articles by Domokos Kosáry, István Sinkovics, Győző Ember, Gyula Szekfű, Lajos Vayer, Zoltán I. Tóth, and others on Lajos Kossuth's life (1802-1894) and political activities including his years in exile.

1863. Waldapfel, Eszter V. A független magyar külpolitika, 1848-1849 (The independent Hungarian foreign policy, 1848-1849). Budapest, Akadémiai Kiadó, 1962. 379 p. Illus., fold. map, ports. Bibliography: p. 339-352.

Reviews the foreign relations of the Hungarian government during the uprising of 1848-1849.

3. 1849-1918

1864. Andrássy, Gyula. Ungarns Ausgleich mit Österreich vom Jahre 1867. Leipzig, Duncker & Humblot, 1897. 422 p.

By the son of one of the architects of the Austro-Hungarian Compromise of 1867.

1865. Berzeviczy, Albert. Az abszolutizmus kora Magyarországon, 1849-1865 (The age of absolutism in Hungary, 1849-1865). Budapest, Franklin Társulat, 1922-1937. 4 v.

Deals with the laws of 1848, the development of the Bach system, first years of the Kossuth emigration, financial situation, socioeconomic conditions, foreign policy constellation, literature, art, and the position of Transylvania. Based almost entirely on unpublished sources housed in the Budapest National Archives and in the Archives of the National Museum. Budapest-Vienna relations are discussed in detail.

1866. Dolmányos, István. A magyar parlamenti ellenzék történetéből 1901-1904 (Data on the history of the Hungarian parliamentary opposition, 1901-1904). Budapest, Akadémiai Kiadó, 1963. 435 p. Illus., ports.

Discusses the role of the Independence Parties, the Social Democratic Party, and the parties of national minorities. Policies of István Tisza are also reviewed. The study is based on unpublished documents.

1867. Ferenczi, Zoltán. Deák élete (Life of Deák). Budapest, Magyar Tudományos Akadémia, 1904. 3 v.

A biography of Ferenc Deák (1803-1876), utilizing unpublished sources, with emphasis on his activities leading toward the Austro-Hungarian Compromise in 1867.

1868. Horváth, Jenő. Felelősség a világháborúért és a békeszerződésért (Responsibility for the World War and the peace treaty). Budapest, Magyar Tudományos Akadémia, 1939. 453 p. (A magyar kérdés a XX. században, 1)

Diplomatic history of the First World War and its peace treaties with emphasis on Hungary's role. A well-documented polemic study.

1869. Mérei, Gyula. Magyar politikai pártprogrammok 1867-1914 (Hungarian political party platforms, 1867-1914). Budapest, 1934.

Collection of all party programs with a short history of the country's political parties.

1870. Pethő, Sándor. Világostól Trianonig; a mai Magyarország kialakulásának története (From Világos to Trianon; a history of the development of today's Hungary). 5th ed. Budapest, Enciklopédia, 1926. 324 p. Ports., maps, diagrs.

Reviews occurrences from 1849 up to the collapse of the Austro-Hungarian Empire in 1918. The last chapter (p. 249-324) by Ferenc Fodor is entitled "A magyar állam földje és népe Trianon után" (Hungary and its people after the Treaty of Trianon).

1871. Pölöskei, Ferenc. A koalíció felbomlása és a Nemzeti Munkapárt megalakulása 1909-1910 (Dissolution of the coalition and the founding of the National Labor Party, 1909-1910). Budapest, Akadémiai Kiadó, 1963. 201 p.

A Marxist-Leninist analysis of the work of the Khuen-Héderváry Cabinet, the 1910 general election, and its consequences, with special regard to the role of the National Labor Party. Describes activities of István Tisza, Gyula Andrássy, Albert Apponyi, and Sándor Wekerle.

1872. Szekfű, Gyula. Három nemzedék és ami utána következik (Three generations and the sequel). 5th ed. Budapest, Királyi Magyar Egyetemi Nyomda, 1938. 514 p. Bibliographical footnotes.

See also entry no. 1914.

Summarizes and elucidates Hungary's political as well as economic development between the Reform Age of the first half of the 19th century and the '30s of this century. Based entirely on Gyula Szekfű's research conducted in the archives of Vienna and Budapest.

1873. Velikaia Oktiabr'skaia Sotsialisticheskaia Revoliutsiia i Vengriia; sbornik statei (The Great October Socialist Revolution and Hungary; a collection of articles). Budapest, Akadémiai Kiadó, 1959. 183 p. (Studia Historica Academiae Scientiarum Hungaricae, 17)

Nine articles by leading Hungarian Marxist-Leninist historians (Erik Molnár, László Réti, and others) on the effect of the Russian Revolution on political developments in the Habsburg Empire, especially Hungary.

1874. Wertheimer, Eduard, *von.* Graf Julius Andrássy; sein Leben und seine Zeit, nach ungedruckten Quellen. Stuttgart, Deutsche Verlags-Anstalt, 1910-1913. 3 v. Bibliographical footnotes.

Reviews the statesman's life (1823-1890) with special emphasis on his role in preparing the Austro-Hungarian Compromise of 1867 and his activities as prime minister of Hungary and as the minister of foreign affairs of the Dual Monarchy. Based largely on unpublished documents.

4. 1918–

1875. Bandholtz, Harry H. An Undiplomatic Diary, by the American Member of the Inter-allied Military Mission to Hungary, 1919-1920. New York, Columbia University Press, 1933. 394 p. Illus., map, ports., facsims.

A well-informed, detailed account of Hungarian domestic and foreign policy situations.

1876. Buchinger, Manó. Küzdelem a szocializmusért; emlékek és élmények (Struggle for socialism; reminiscences and experiences). Budapest, Népszava Könyvkiadó, 1946-1947. 2 v.

Political memoirs by a noted Social Democrat covering the period from 1905, focusing on the fight for a democratic election law prior to 1914 and the October 1918 revolution, after which he went into exile until November 1929. Describes also the work of the Socialist International in which he was active. Contains important data on the country's socialist movement.

1877. Garami, Ernő. Forrongó Magyarország; emlékezések és tanulságok (Turbulent Hungary; recollections and lessons). Leipzig, Vienna, Pegazus, 1922. 243 p.

By a socialist leader in exile. Personal reminiscences of the October 1918 revolution and the 133-day Hungarian Soviet Republic of 1919. It is stated that the Entente note delivered by Col. Vyx to the Károlyi Government was directly responsible for proclaiming the Soviet system on March 21, 1919. A strong criticism of the proletarian dictatorship and counterrevolutionary regimes alike.

1878. Gratz, Gusztáv, *ed.* A bolsevizmus Magyarországon (Bolshevism in Hungary). Budapest, Franklin, 1921. 861 p. Maps, bibliographical notes.

A detailed, documentary analysis of the politics, economy, public administration, culture, and the terror in the 1919 Hungarian Soviet Republic, with a description of Russia's influence.

1879. Gratz, Gusztáv. A forradalmak kora; Magyarország története 1918-1920 (The age of the revolutions; a history of Hungary, 1918-1920). Budapest, Magyar Szemle Társaság, 1935. 354 p. (A Magyar Szemle könyvei, 10)

Relates the October 1918 revolution and the 1919 proletarian dictatorship, as well as the counterrevolutionary "White Terror." Based heavily on unpublished documents and the best literature. Has annotated bibliography and detailed chronology of events.

1880. Hajdú, Tibor. Az őszirózsás forradalom (The October revolution). Budapest, Kossuth Könyvkiadó, 1963. 217 p. Illus., ports., bibliographical notes.

Relates political history from the outbreak of the First World War up to March 1919 with emphasis on the founding of the Nemzeti Tanács (National Council) and the October 1918 revolution under the leadership of Mihály Károlyi.

1881. Hetés, Tibor, *ed.* A magyar Vörös Hadsereg 1919; válogatott dokumentumok (The Hungarian Red Army of 1919; selected documents). Budapest, Kossuth Könyvkiadó, 1959. 530 p. Maps, diagrs., facsims.

This is much more than a military history of the period of March-August 1919. Significant data on political, economic and foreign policy situations are included. The overwhelming majority of these documents are housed in the Hadtörténelmi Levéltár és Múzeum (Archives and Museum of Military History). Place-name index.

1882. Horthy, Miklós, *nagybányai.* Memoirs. New York, Robert Speller, 1957. 268 p.

See also entry no. 1903.

Autobiography of Admiral Horthy (1868-1957) who was regent of Hungary (1920-October 15, 1944) until Ferenc Szálasi's Arrow-Cross Movement came to power with the aid of Germany. Events of the '30s and those of the Second World War are stressed. Originally published under the title *Ein Leben für Ungarn* (Bonn, Athenaeum, 1953, 327 p.). Published also in Hungarian as *Emlékirataim* (Memoirs) (Buenos Aires, 1953, 314 p.), and in French as *Mémoires de l'Admiral Horthy, Régent de Hongrie* (Paris, Hachette, 1954, 287 p.).

1883. Horthy, Miklós, *nagybányai.* Confidential Papers. Budapest, Corvina Press, 1965. 439 p. Facsims.

The material of the Budapest National Archives was used for this volume which covers the reign of Regent Horthy, with heavy emphasis on the '30s and the period of the Second World War. Translation of original Hungarian entitled *Horthy Miklós titkos iratai* (Budapest, Kossuth Könyvkiadó, 1963, 533 p.). With explanatory notes, list of right-wing political parties.

1884. Horváth, Jenő. Az országgyarapítás története 1920-1941 (History of the territorial growth, 1920-1941). Budapest, Magyar Külügyi Társaság, 1941. 160 p.

Describes the country's foreign policy situation between 1918 and 1941.

1885. Jászi, Oszkár. Revolution and Counter-revolution in Hungary. New York, H. Fertig. 1969. 239 p.

See also entry no. 1905.

Deals with the collapse of the Austro-Hungarian Monarchy, the October 1918 revolution, the personality of Count Mihály Károlyi, the Hungarian Soviet Republic of 1919, and the counterrevolution ("White Terror"). Undocumented. Introduction by R. W. Seton-Watson. Reprint of 1924 edition.

1886. Juhász, Gyula. A Teleki-kormány külpolitikája 1939-1941 (The foreign policy of the Teleki Government, 1939-1941). Budapest, Akadémiai Kiadó, 1964. 368 p. Bibliography: p. 358-360.

Based entirely on archival documents. Index.

1887. Kállai, Gyula. A magyar függetlenségi mozgalom, 1936-45 (The Hungarian independence movement, 1936-1945). 5th rev. ed. Budapest, Kossuth Könyvkiadó, 1965. 330 p. Illus., ports.

See also entry no. 1906.

Deals chiefly with the period of the Second World War including the country's occupation by German troops. Activities of the Hungarian Communist Party are widely reviewed. Index. Undocumented.

1888. Károlyi, Mihály, *gróf*. Memoirs; Faith without Illusion. London, Cape, 1956. 392 p. Illus., ports., col. map.

By a politician-author who from 1919 to 1946 lived in exile. Though an autobiography written in self-defense, it contains much of historical value regarding the country's history in the 20th century. Includes interesting notes and an index. Undocumented.

1889. Kertesz, Stephen D. Diplomacy in a Whirlpool; Hungary between Nazi Germany and Soviet Russia. Notre Dame, Ind., University of Notre Dame Press, 1953. 273 p. Maps. Bibliographical references included in "Notes" (p. 189-229).

See also entry no. 1978.

1890. Lackó, Miklós, *ed.* Tanulmányok a magyar népi demokrácia történetéből (Studies on the history of the Hungarian People's Democracy). Budapest, Akadémiai Kiadó, 1955. 685 p.

Collection of articles by leading Marxist-Leninist historians grouped under different subject headings. Copious footnotes.

1891. Macartney, C. A. October Fifteenth; a History of Modern Hungary, 1929-1945. Edinburgh, University Press, 1956-1957. 2 v. Maps. (Edinburgh University Publications; History, Philosophy and Economics, no. 6)

Focused on Hungarian-German relationships, role of Ferenc Szálasi, etc. Equipped with index, bibliography, and explanatory notes.

1892. Mályusz, Elemér. The Fugitive Bolsheviks. London, G. Richards, 1931. 441 p.

A critical approach to the history of the Hungarian Soviet Republic of 1919 based partly on unpublished documents. English translation of *Sturm auf Ungarn* (München, A. Dresler, 1931, 295 p.).

1893. Montgomery, John F. Hungary: The Unwilling Satellite. New York, Devin-Adair Co., 1947. 281 p. Ports., maps, facsim. Bibliography: p. 272-275.

See also entry no. 1928.

The author served as United States Minister to Hungary during the critical years from 1933 to 1941. Reviews extensively Germany's gradually mounting pressure on the country. Publishes treaties and agreements affecting Hungary between 1933 and 1945.

1894. Nagy, Ferenc. The Struggle behind the Iron Curtain. Translated from the Hungarian by Stephen K. Swift. New York, Macmillan, 1948. 471 p. Map.

See also entry no. 1929.

Personal reminiscences by the former prime minister (1946-1947) of the events of the Second World War with heavy emphasis on post-1945 developments in Hungary. Undocumented.

1895. Paál, Jób, *and* Antal Radó, *eds.* A debreceni feltámadás (The revival in Debrecen). Debrecen, 1947. 384 p.

A collection of indispensable on-the-spot reports by 16 well-informed authors on 1944-1946 Hungarian-Soviet relations, including the Moscow intergovernmental negotiations (1944) and the very beginnings of the communist-dominated postwar administration.

1896. Szekfű, Gyula. Forradalom után (After the Revolution). Budapest, Cserépfalvi, 1947. 207 p.

See also entry no. 1934.

Reviews Hungary's post-1945 political development and the new foreign policy constellation with special emphasis on the role of the Soviet Union and the fate of the middle classes. By the most outstanding Hungarian historian of the century. Undocumented.

1897. Váli, Ferenc A. Rift and Revolt in Hungary; Nationalism versus Communism. Cambridge, Harvard University Press, 1961. 590 p. Fold. map, diagrs. Bibliography: p. 515-520.

See also entry no. 1940.

A scholarly account of the October 1956 revolution, using maps and charts, by an eyewitness.

1898. Wagner, Francis S., *ed.* The Hungarian Revolution in Perspective. Washington, D.C., F.F. Memorial Foundation, 1967. 350 p.

Articles by a number of authors on subjects such as John F. Dulles' relation to the Hungarian revolution of 1956, the role of communist China, and the economic and social causes and results. Includes bibliography.

D. LOCAL HISTORY

1899. Budapest történetének bibliográfiája (Bibliography of the history of Budapest). Editor-in-Chief: József Zoltán; Editor: László Berza. Budapest, Fővárosi Szabó Ervin Könyvtár, 1963–

Covers Greater Budapest. To be completed in seven volumes: Volume 1: History; volume 2: Description, City Planning, Hygiene, etc.; volume 3: Economy; volume 4: Society; volume 5: Politics and Administration; volume 6: Culture; volume 7: Indexes. Volumes 2, 4, and 5 have already been published.

1900. Eperjessy, Kálmán. A magyar falu története (History of the Hungarian village). Budapest, Gondolat Kiadó, 1966. 299 p. (Stúdium könyvek, 58) Bibliography: p. 284-298.

From the earliest times up to the present; based on unpublished sources and best available literature. It is arranged within the framework of the national history. Includes a multilingual, annotated bibliography (p. 284-298).

1901. Salamon, Ferenc. Budapest története (A history of Budapest). Budapest, Athenaeum, 1878-1885. 3 v.

Based on unpublished sources.

34

the state

by Ferenc A. Váli

A. POLITICS AND GOVERNMENT

1. Before 1945

1902. Eckhart, Ferenc. Magyarország története (The history of Hungary). 2d enl. ed. Budapest, Renaissance, 1940. 340 p.

A standard, concisely written history of Hungary by a distinguished professor of the history of law at the University of Budapest. Useful bibliography of earlier historical works.

1903. Horthy, Miklós, *nagybányai.* Memoirs. New York, Robert Speller, 1957. 268 p. Illus.

See also entry no. 1882.

Personal reminiscences of the last admiral of the Austro-Hungarian Navy who was Regent of Hungary from 1920 until his removal by the Germans in 1944. Originally published in German as *Ein Leben für Ungarn* (Bonn, Athenaeum, 1953, 327 p., illus.); available also in French as *Mémoires* (Paris, Hachette, 1954, 287 p.).

1904. Jászi, Oszkár. The Dissolution of the Habsburg Monarchy. Chicago, The University of Chicago Press, 1929. 488 p. Bibliography: p. 461-480.

See also entry no. 962.

A classic in the field of Central European history, with particular emphasis on the nationality problems of Austria and Hungary. Analyzes the evolution of nation states in Danubian Europe, and the social and political conditions which led to the dissolution of the Habsburg monarchy.

1905. Jászi, Oszkár. Revolution and Counter-Revolution in Hungary. New York, H. Fertig, 1969. 239 p.

See also entry no. 1885.

An analysis of political developments in Hungary following the defeat of the Central Powers in the First World War, including the Károlyi government, the short-lived communist regime under Béla Kun, and the establishment of the regency under Admiral Horthy. Introduction by R. W. Seton-Watson. Reprint of 1924 edition.

1906. Kállai, Gyula. A magyar függetlenségi mozgalom, 1936-45 (The Hungarian independence movement, 1936-1945). 5th rev. ed. Budapest, Kossuth Könyvkiadó, 1965. 330 p. Illus., ports.

See also entry no. 1887.

The chairman of the Council of Ministers analyzes the main trends of Hungarian political developments during the period covered. Written from the communist viewpoint, the book tends to exaggerate the role of the communists and to belittle other important factors.

1907. Kállay, Miklós. Hungarian Premier; a Personal Account of a Nation's Struggle in the Second World War. New York, Columbia University Press, 1954. 518 p.

The political memoirs of the wartime prime minister who tried to detach Hungary from her German ally and was imprisoned by the Germans in 1944.

1908. Kosáry, Domokos G. A History of Hungary. Cleveland, New York, Benjamin Franklin Bibliophile Society, 1941. 482 p. Illus., maps. Bibliography: p. 439-455.

See also entry no. 1839.

Written by a leading contemporary Hungarian historian, this useful and concise study reviews Hungarian history from its origins all the way to the outbreak of the Second World War.

1909. Macartney, C. A. Hungary and Her Successors; the Treaty of Trianon and Its Consequences, 1919-1937. London, New York, Oxford University Press, 1937. 504 p. Maps. Bibliographical note: p. xii-xxi.

See also entry no. 234.

Discusses the political consequences of the Treaty of Trianon, the situation of the Hungarian minorities in the successor states, and the entire border question between Hungary and her neighbors.

1910. Mende, Tibor. Hungary. London, Macdonald, 1944. 175 p. Map.

A good political survey of Hungarian history with special emphasis on the interwar period and on the wartime developments of the years 1939-1943.

1911. Nemes, Dezső, *ed.* A magyar forradalmi munkásmozgalom története (The history of the Hungarian revolutionary workers' movement). Budapest, Kossuth Kőnyvkiadó, 1966. 278 p. Illus.

A fascinating account of the Hungarian labor movement from its 1848-1849 antecedents to the 1918-1919 period. Essential background material for a fuller understanding of the strengths and weaknesses of the Hungarian communist movement.

1912. Pálóczy-Horváth, György. In Darkest Hungary. London, V. Gollancz, 1944. 158 p.

This concise and well-written survey reviews the recent political evolution of Hungary from three different perspectives. It studies the country's peasant problem, its "civilization," and the highlights of its history since the First World War.

1913. Radisics, Elemér, *ed.* Hungary, Yesterday and Today. London, Richards, 1932. 233 p. Illus., maps. Bibliography: p. 220-225.

This volume is a useful collection of the writings of several authors. Individual sections deal with the history of Hungarian art, the biographies of its political leaders, etc. It also contains a special bibliography containing "a hundred works about Hungary."

1914. Szekfű, Gyula. Három nemzedék és ami utána következik (Three generations and the sequel). 5th ed. Budapest, Királyi Magyar Egyetemi Nyomda, 1938. 514 p. Bibliographical footnotes.

See also entry no. 1872.

This standard work on the history and political evolution of modern Hungary was written by probably the most prominent Hungarian historian of this century, long-time professor at the University of Budapest and director of the prestigious Eötvös Lóránd Kollégium.

1915. Teleki, Pál, *gróf.* The Evolution of Hungary and Its Place in European History. New York, Macmillan, 1923. 312 p. Front., maps, diagrs. Bibliography: p. 245-312.

See also entries no. 1756 *and* 1841.

The eminent political geographer and former prime minister of Hungary traces the course of Hungarian history. Excellent section of Hungarian nationality problems. Useful historical and geopolitical bibliography.

1916. Tőkés, Rudolf L. Béla Kun and the Hungarian Soviet Republic; the Origins and Role of the Communist Party of Hungary in the Revolutions of 1918-1919. New York, Published for the Hoover

Institution on War, Revolution and Peace, Stanford University, Stanford, Calif., by F. A. Praeger, 1967. 292 p. Bibliography: p. 262-277.

Based on source material which has become available in recent years since the communist rehabilitation of Béla Kun. Includes translations of some documents and a biographical directory of leading figures of the Hungarian Soviet Republic of 1919.

2. Since 1945

1917. Aczél, Tamás, *ed.* Ten Years After; the Hungarian Revolution in the Perspective of History. New York, Holt, Rinehart and Winston, 1967. 253 p. Bibliography: p. 209-232.

Contributors of Hungarian and foreign origin explore the meaning and significance of the Hungarian Revolution in the light of subsequent events. There is a chronology of events in Hungary, 1953-1965, on pages 233-253.

1918. Aczél, Tamás, *and* Tibor Méray. The Revolt of the Mind; a Case History of Intellectual Resistance Behind the Iron Curtain. New York, Praeger, 1960. 449 p. (Praeger Publications in Russian History and World Communism, no. 73)

The writers' role in the events leading to the 1956 revolution is narrated by two participants. Intellectual trends in Hungary during and after the Stalinist period which preceded the revolution are analyzed by István Mészáros in *La Rivoltà degli intelettuali in Ungheria* (Torino, G. Einaudi, 1958, 213 p.).

1919. Bibó, István. Harmadik út; politikai és történeti tanulmányok (The third road; political and historical studies). London, Magyar Könyves Céh, 1960. 380 p.

Analysis of the situation in Hungary following the Second World War and proposals for dealing with the postrevolutionary problems of the country, by a professor who represented the Petőfi Party in Imre Nagy's coalition government during the uprising.

1920. Dobi, István. Vallomás és történelem (Confession and history). Budapest, Kossuth Könyvkiadó, 1962. 2 v.

The autobiography of the chairman of the Presidential Council and former chairman of the Council of Ministers, in which he describes his peasant origin and his political career. Though essentially self-exculpatory and propagandistic, it contributes to an understanding of the period and the circumstances of the author's life.

1921. Fejtő, François. Behind the Rape of Hungary. New York, D. McKay, 1957. 335 p.

Analysis of the 1956 revolution and the events leading to it. Originally published in French as *La tragédie hongroise; ou, Une révolution socialiste anti-soviétique* (Paris, P. Horay, 1956, 314 p., map).

1922. Fejtő, François. Hungarian Communism. *In* Griffith, William E., *ed.* Communism in Europe; Continuity, Change, and the Sino-Soviet Dispute. v. 1. Cambridge, Mass., M.I.T. Press, p. 177-300.

Many details on internal developments in the Hungarian Party. *Issues of World Communism* (Princeton, N.J., Van Nostrand, 1966, 264 p., illus.), edited by Andrew Gyorgy, contains a chapter (p. 86-107) by Ferenc A. Váli entitled "Hungary Since 1956: the Hungarian Road to Communism." The collapse of the Hungarian Communist Party during the 1956 revolution, and its subsequent restoration, are described by George Ginsburg in "Demise and Revival of a Communist Party: an Autopsy of the Hungarian Revolution," published in *Western Political Quarterly*, v. 13, September 1960, p. 780-802.

1923. Helmreich, Ernst C., *ed.* Hungary. New York, Published for the Mid-European Studies Center of the Free Europe Committee by Praeger, 1957. 466 p. Maps, tables. Bibliography: p. 423-449. (Praeger Publications in Russian History and World Communism, no. 49)

See also entry no. 1716.

Various contributors discuss different aspects of Hungary under the communist regime from 1945 to 1956.

1924. Kádár, János. Socialist Construction in Hungary; Selected Speeches and Articles, 1957-1961. Budapest, Corvina Press, 1962. 358 p. Illus.

Partly based on *Szilárd népi hatalom: független Magyarország* (The power of a strong people: independent Hungary) (Budapest, Kossuth Könyvkiadó, 1959, 429 p.). There is a German translation of the latter, *Eine starke Volksmacht bedeutet ein unabhängiges Ungarn; Reden und Artikel, Auswahl aus den Jahren 1957-1959* (Berlin, Dietz, 1961, 250 p., illus.). Kádár's more recent addresses, reflecting his new policy ("Who is not against us, is with us") are made available in *On the Road to Socialism; Selected Speeches and Interviews, 1960-1964* (Budapest, Corvina Press, 1965, 283 p., port.).

1925. Kecskemeti, Paul. The Unexpected Revolution; Social Forces in the Hungarian Uprising. Stanford, Calif., Stanford University Press, 1961. 178 p.

Analyzes the factors leading to the revolutionary events of 1956. Of related interest is the author's "Limits and Problems of Decompression: the Case of Hungary," published in the *Annals* of the American Academy of Political and Social Science, v. 317, May 1958, p. 97-106, discussing the policy of relaxation which preceded the revolution.

1926. Király, Ernő. Die Arbeiterselbstverwaltung in Ungarn. Aufstieg und Niedergang 1956-1958. Ein Dokumentarbericht. München, Oldenbourg, 1961. 111 p. (Untersuchungen zur Gegenwartskunde Südosteuropas, 3)

The story of the workers' councils created during the revolution of 1956.

1927. Méray, Tibor. Thirteen Days That Shook the Kremlin. New York, Praeger, 1959. 290 p. (Praeger Publications in Russian History and World Communism, no. 77)

A detailed, closely observed account of the 1956 revolution by a Communist Party member who subsequently left the country in disillusion.

1928. Montgomery, John F. Hungary: The Unwilling Satellite. New York, Devin-Adair Co., 1947. 281 p. Maps, ports., facsims. Bibliography: p. 272-275.

See also entry no. 1893.

After a brief tracing of Hungary's politics and government since 1918, this work offers a detailed portrayal of the country's "take-over" by the communists during the crucial years of 1944-1947. Important American viewpoint since the author was then U.S. Minister to Hungary.

1929. Nagy, Ferenc. The Struggle behind the Iron Curtain. Translated from the Hungarian by Stephen K. Swift. New York, Macmillan, 1948. 471 p. Map.

See also entry no. 1894.

A former prime minister of Hungary describes the communist takeover of his country during the period 1945-1947.

1930. Nagy, Imre. On Communism; in Defense of the New Course. New York, F. A. Praeger, 1957. 306 p.

The former prime minister's justification of his policy of liberalization.

1931. Orbán, Sándor. Egyház és állam; a katolikus egyház és az állam viszonyának rendezése, 1945-1950 (Church and state; normalization of the relationship between the Catholic Church and the State, 1945-1950). Budapest, Kossuth Könyvkiadó, 1962. 232 p. Bibliographical footnotes.

Published under the auspices of the Institute of Historical Science of the Hungarian Academy of Sciences.

1932. Savarius, Vincent, *pseud.* (Béla Sándor Szász). Freiwillig für den Galgen. Translated from the Hungarian by Rudolf Schröder. Köln, Verlag Wissenschaft und Politik, 1963. 251 p.

The László Rajk trial, 1949.

1933. Sulyok, Dezső. Zwei Nächte ohne Tag. Translated from the Hungarian by Hugo Wyss. Zürich, Thomas-Verlag, 1948. 464 p.

This work first traces the major events in Hungarian domestic and foreign policies since 1945, and then gives a step-by-step analysis of the communist take-over of Hungary. The author was the parliamentary leader of one of the small opposition parties. Forced into exile in 1947, he wrote this book in Switzerland.

1934. Szekfű, Gyula. Forradalom után (After the Revolution). Budapest, Cserépfalvi, 1947. 207 p.
See also entry no. 1896.
An appraisal by a leading Hungarian historian of the Second World War and immediate postwar involvement of Hungary in the broader "revolution" of East Central Europe.

1935. Szentpéteri, István. A közvetlen demokrácia fejlődési irányai (Trends of development of direct democracy). Budapest, Akadémiai Kiadó, 1965. 481 p.
A theoretical monograph explaining "direct democracy," practiced in Hungary and other People's Democracies, as distinguished from "bourgeois democracy."

1936. Társadalmi Szemle (Social review). 1946– Budapest. Monthly.
Theoretical journal of the Hungarian Communist Party.

1937. The Truth About the Nagy Affair: Facts, Documents, Comments. With a Preface by Albert Camus. London, Published for the Congress for Cultural Freedom by Secker & Warburg; New York, Praeger, 1959. 215 p. Illus.
A heavily documented presentation of the trial of Imre Nagy, Hungarian prime minister during the 1956 revolution. Originally published in French as *La vérité sur l'affaire Nagy; les faits, les documents, les témoignages internationaux* (Paris, Plon, 1958, 256 p., illus.).

1938. United Nations. *General Assembly. Special Committee on the Problem of Hungary.* Report. New York, 1957. 148 p. Map, facsim. (United Nations. Document A/3592)
A thorough description and analysis of the 1956 revolution. There is a condensation of the report, by Marshall Andrews, entitled *Anatomy of Revolution* (Washington, Public Affairs Press, 1957, 65 p., illus.). The Association of Hungarian Jurists (Magyar Jogász Szövetség) published its views on the report as *Some Comments on the Juristic Aspects of the "Hungarian Question"* (Budapest, 1957, 28 p.), edited by Jenő Benedek.

1939. Váli, Ferenc A. Hungary. In Bromke, Adam, *ed.* The Communist States at the Crossroads between Moscow and Peking. New York, Praeger, 1965. p. 71-86.
East Central Europe and the World: Developments in the Post-Stalin Era (Notre Dame, Ind., University of Notre Dame Press, 1962, 386 p., map, tables, bibliographical footnotes), edited by Stephen D. Kertesz, also contains a chapter on Hungary (p. 120-155), written by the editor.

1940. Váli, Ferenc A. Rift and Revolt in Hungary; Nationalism versus Communism. Cambridge, Harvard University Press, 1961. 590 p. Fold. map, diagrs. Bibliography: p. 515-520.

See also entry no. 1897.

A detailed presentation of the events leading to the 1956 revolution and a political analysis of the revolution and its aftermath. The author has also contributed a chapter (p. 66-80) entitled "The Hungarian Revolution" to *Problems in International Relations*, 2d ed. (Englewood Cliffs, N. J., Prentice-Hall, 1962), edited by Andrew Gyorgy and Hubert S. Gibbs.

1941. Zinner, Paul E. Revolution in Hungary. New York, Columbia University Press, 1962. 380 p. Bibliographical footnotes. "Bibliographical note": p. 365-370.

An analytical discussion of the communist take-over in Hungary after the Second World War, the Stalinist Rákosi regime, and the 1956 revolution. The author examines the causes of the revolution in an article, "Revolution in Hungary; Reflections on the Vicissitudes of a Totalitarian System," published in the *Journal of Politics*, v. 21, February 1959, p. 3-36.

B. LAW

1. Bibliographies

1942. Magyar Tudományos Akadémia, *Budapest. Állam- és Jogtudományi Intézet.* Állam- és jugtudományi bibliográfia (Bibliography of administrative and legal sciences). 1945/51– Budapest, Közgazdasági és Jogi Könyvkiadó, 1954– Biennial.

Eight volumes have been published so far: 1945-1951 (1957, 243 p.); 1952 (1954, 154 p.); 1953 (1955, 151 p.); 1954-1955 (1956, 163 p.); 1956-1957 (1959, 185 p.); 1958-1959 (1961, 278 p.); 1960-1961 (1962, 251 p.); 1962-1963 (1965, 248 p.). The volumes for 1952 and 1953 were entitled *Jogi és államigazgatási bibliográfia* (Bibliography of law and administration). The volume covering 1958-1959 includes a cumulative author index for the first six volumes.

1943. Mid-European Law Project. Legal Sources and Bibliography of Hungary, by Alexander Kálnoki Bedő and George Torzsay-Biber; Vladimir Gsovski, general editor. New York, Published for Free Europe Committee by F. A. Praeger, 1956. 157 p. Facsim. (Praeger Publications in Russian History and World Communism, no. 20)

1944. Nagy, Lajos, *ed.* Bibliography of Hungarian Legal Literature, 1945-1965. Budapest, Akadémiai Kiadó, 1966. 315 p.

Published by the Institute for Legal and Administrative Sciences of the Hungarian Academy of Sciences under the auspices of the International Association of Legal Science and the International Committee for Science Documentation. Covers works of reference, theory of state and law, constitutional law, administrative law, financial law, civil law, labor law, land law, family law, criminal law and its auxiliary sciences, judicial organization, the law of civil and criminal procedure, public and private international law, and the history of state and law. Author and subject indexes.

2. Periodicals

1945. Acta juridica. v. 1– 1959– Budapest, Akadémiai Kiadó. Quarterly.

Legal journal of the Hungarian Academy of Sciences. Studies are published in English, French, German, or Russian, with summaries in two other languages.

1946. Hungarian Law Review. v. 1– 1960– Budapest. Semiannual.

Published by Magyar Jogász Szövetség (Association of Hungarian Jurists).

1947. Hungary. Magyar közlöny; a Magyar Népköztársaság hivatalos lapja (Hungarian gazette; official bulletin of the Hungarian People's Republic). Budapest. Daily (irregular)

Title varies: 1867-March 21, 1919, *Budapesti közlöny*; March 21-August 2, 1919, *Tanácsköztársaság*; August 2-7 1919, *Hivatalos közlöny*; August 8, 1919-1944, *Budapesti közlöny*. The official gazette of Hungary, in which all legislation must be published.

1948. Jogtudományi közlöny (Legal science bulletin). Budapest. Monthly.

Began publication in 1860. It is now the journal of the Institute for Legal and Administrative Sciences of the Hungarian Academy of Sciences.

1949. Magyar jog (Hungarian law). v. 1– October 1954– Budapest, Közgazdasági és Jogi Könyvkiadó. Monthly.

Journal of Magyar Jogász Szövetség (Association of Hungarian Jurists). An index to volumes 1-3, October 1954-1956, was issued with volume 3.

3. Before 1945

1950. Andrássy, Gyula, *gróf*. A magyar állam fönnmaradásának és alkotmányos szabadságának okai (Causes of the survival and constitutional freedom of the Hungarian state). Budapest, Franklin-társulat, 1901-1911. 3 v.

The author, son of a former prime minister of Hungary and foreign minister of Austria-Hungary, analyzes the character of the Hungarian Constitution, its customary legal basis, and the history of its defense against encroachments by the court of Vienna.

There is a partial English translation, covering the period from 896 to 1619 A.D., entitled *The Development of Hungarian Constitutional Liberty* (London, K. Paul, Trench, Trubner, 1908, 465 p.).

1951. Bernatzik, Edmund. Das staatsrechtliche Verhältnis zu Ungarn. Wien, Manz, 1911. 1114 p.

Basic edition of the Austrian and Hungarian constitutional laws of the Dual Monarchy.

1952. Deák, Ferencz. Adalék a magyar közjoghoz (A contribution to Hungarian public law). Pest, Pfeifer, 1865. 188 p.

A presentation of the Hungarian constitutional viewpoint regarding the situation resulting from Austrian absolutism after the 1848-1849 War of Independence, written by the father of the Austro-Hungarian Compromise of 1867. Originally published in *Budapesti szemle* for February 1865; a German translation was published as *Ein Beitrag zum ungarischen Staatsrecht* (Pest, G. Emich, 1865, 234 p.).

1953. Eckhart, Ferenc. Magyar alkotmány- és jogtörténet (The history of the Hungarian constitution and law). Budapest, Politzer, 1946. 468 p. Bibliographical footnotes.

The standard textbook on these subjects prior to 1945, by the leading scholar of his time.

1954. Hungary. *Laws, statutes, etc.* (*Indexes*). Magyar törvények és egyéb jogszabályok mutatója (Index to Hungarian laws and other statutory provisions). Szombathely, Martineum, 1939. 1100 p.

———. 1.-5. Pótfüzet (Supplementary issues 1-5). Budapest, 1940-1944.

The main volume covers legislation from 1000 to March 31, 1939; the supplements cover material for the years 1939-1943. To be supplemented by *Hatályos jogszabályok mutatója, 1945-1957* (Index to statutory provisions in force, 1945-1957) (Budapest, Közgazdasági és Jogi Könyvkiadó, 1958, 208 p.).

1955. Marczali, Henrik (Heinrich). Ungarische Verfassungsgeschichte. Tübingen, Mohr, 1910. 179 p.

A history of the Hungarian traditional constitution presented by a professor of history of the University of Budapest. For a concise presentation of Hungarian constitutional law prior to the First World War, see *Ungarisches Verfassungsrecht* (Tübingen, Mohr, 1911, 234 p.) by the same author.

1956. Mayer, Sal. Das ungarische Strafgesetzbuch über Verbrechen und Vergehen. Wien, Manz, 1878. 313 p.

The Hungarian Criminal Code of 1878.

1957. Timon, Ákos von. Die Entwicklung und Bedeutung des öffentlichrechtlichen Begriffs der Heiligen Krone in der ungarischen Verfassung. München, Duncker und Humblot, 1914. 554 p.

A historical analysis of the constitutional-legal doctrine of the Holy Hungarian Crown of St. Stephen by a professor of legal history.

1958. Timon, Ákos von. Ungarische Verfassungs- und Rechtsgeschichte.

Mit Bezug auf die Rechtsentwicklung der westlichen Staaten. 2d enl. ed. Berlin, Puttkammer u. Mühlbrecht, 1909. 835 p.

A comparative history of Hungarian law and constitution by a prominent professor of legal history. First edition, 1904, reviewed in *Zeitschrift für Rechtsgeschichte*, Germanische Abt (Weimar), v. 26, 1905: 326-340.

4. After 1945

1959. Antalffy, György. L'État socialiste et la théorie marxiste de l'état et du droit. Szeged, 1965. 93 p. (Acta Universitatis Szegediensis. Acta juridica et politica. t. 12, fasc. 3)

A professor of Szeged University analyzes theoretically the concept of the socialist state with emphasis on the Hungarian experience.

1960. Bihari, Ottó. Államjog (Constitutional and administrative law). Budapest, Tankönyvkiadó, 1964. 296 p.

University textbook of the constitutional and administrative law of the Hungarian People's Republic, written by a professor of the Budapest University. Another current textbook on the same subject is *Magyar államjog*, 2d ed. (Budapest, Tankönyvkiadó, 1964, 555 p.), by János Beér, István Kovács, and Lajos Szamel.

1961. Hungary. *Constitution.* Constitution of the Hungarian People's Republic. Budapest, Hungarian Review, 1959. 87 p. Illus.

With introduction and concluding remarks by János Beér. The most recent Hungarian edition is *A Magyar Népköztársaság alkotmánya* (Budapest, Közgazdasági és Jogi Könyvkiadó, 1965, 46 p., col. illus.).

For a German translation of the constitution of August 20, 1949, see: *Verfassung der Ungarischen Volksrepublik. Stand vom 31. März 1960* (Berlin, VEB Deutscher Zentralverlag, 1960, 48 p.).

1962. Hungary. *Laws, statutes, etc.* A büntető eljárás (Criminal procedure). Budapest, Közgazdasági és Jogi Könyvkiadó, 1962. 268 p.

Text of law-decree No. 8 of 1962 and its supplementary rules. A university textbook on the subject is *A magyar büntető eljárási jog* (Hungarian law of criminal procedure) (Budapest, Tankönyvkiadó, 1961, 689 p.), by Mihály Móra and Mihály Kocsis. For a German text *see*:

Mezőfy, Ladislaus. Das ungarische Strafverfahren. Gesetzkräftige Verordnung Nr. 8 von 1962. Berlin, de Gruyter, 1966. 140 p.

1963. Hungary. *Laws, statutes, etc.* Civil Code of the Hungarian People's Republic. Budapest, Corvina, 1960. 200 p.

English translation of the Hungarian civil code of 1959 and of the report by the minister of justice to parliament recommending approval.

The Hungarian original, *A Magyar Népköztársaság polgári törvénykönyve* (Budapest, Közgazdasági és Jogi Könyvkiadó, 1963,

862 p.), includes the ministerial justifications. There is also a German translation of the code, *Zivilgesetzbuch der Ungarischen Volksrepublik* (Budapest, Corvina, 1960, 147 p.).

1964. Hungary. *Laws, statutes, etc.* Corpus juris hungarici. Magyar törvénytár. Millenniumi emlékkiadás (Collection of Hungarian laws. Millennial commemorative edition). 1000/1526-1904, 1906-1918, 1920-1948. Budapest, Franklin Társulat, 1899-1949. 71 v. Annual.

The most comprehensive compilation of laws promulgated since A.D. 1000. It includes the first Hungarian law collection, István Werbőczy's *Tripartitum Opus Juris* (first published in 1517) and the law collections of Transylvania for the period 1540-1848. To be supplemented by *Törvények és rendeletek hivatalos gyűjteménye* (Official collection of laws and decrees) (1949– Budapest, 1950– annual) and *Hatályos jogszabályok gyűjteménye, 1945-1858* (Collection of statutory provisions in force, 1945-1958) (Budapest, Közgazdasági és Jogi Könyvkiadó, 1960, 4 v.).

1965. Hungary. *Laws, statutes, etc.* Criminal Code of the Hungarian People's Republic. Budapest, Corvina Press, 1962. 133 p.

English translation of the Hungarian criminal code of 1961 and of the report by the minister of justice to parliament recommending its approval.

The Hungarian original, *A Magyar Népköztársaság büntető törvénykönyve* (Budapest, Közgazdasági és Jogi Könyvkiadó, 1962, 632 p.), includes the ministerial justifications. There is also a German translation of the code, *Strafgesetzbuch der Ungarischen Volksrepublik* (Budapest, Corvina, 1963, 143 p.). See also *Strafkodex der Ungarischen Volksrepublik. 5. Gesetz vom Jahre 1961 über das Strafgesetzbuch und die wichtigsten Vorschriften der Einführungsgesetze und der Durchführungsverordnungen* (Berlin, de Gruyter, 1964, 135 p.).

1966. Hungary. *Laws, statutes, etc.* A családjogi törvény; a módosított és egységes szerkezetbe foglalt 1952. évi IV. tv. és a családjogra vonatkozó jogszabályok (Family law; the amended and consolidated Act No. IV of 1952 and statutory provisions relating to family law). Budapest, Közgazdasági és Jogi Könyvkiadó, 1964. 86 p.

The most recent official collection of all laws and regulations concerning marriage, divorce, the status of children, guardianship, etc.

1967. Hungary. *Laws, statutes, etc.* A polgári eljárás (Civil procedure). Budapest, Közgazdasági és Jogi Könyvkiadó, 1964. 371 p.

Gives the texts of statutes and commentaries. A university textbook on the subject is *Magyar polgári eljárásjog* (Hungarian law of civil procedure), 2d ed. (Budapest, Tankönyvkiadó, 1962, 558 p.), by Ferenc Bacsó and others. For the role of the public prosecutor in civil actions, see *Az ügyész a polgári eljárásban* (The procurator in civil procedure) (Budapest, Közgazdasági és Jogi Könyvkiadó, 1961, 224 p.), by Jenő Szilbereky.

1968. Hungary. *Laws, statutes, etc.* A tanácsok szervezetére és működésére vonatkozó jogszabályok (Statutory provisions relating to the organization and operation of councils). Budapest, Közgazdasági és Jogi Könyvkiadó, 1963. 1023 p.

A collection of statutes and ordinances concerning the municipal and regional councils (soviets) in Hungary. The historical development of these councils is discussed by János Beér in *A helyi tanácsok kialakulása és fejlődése Magyarországon, 1945-1960* (The formation and development of local councils in Hungary, 1945-1960) (Budapest, Közgazdasági és Könyvkiadó, 1962, 646 p.). Of related interest is *Államigazgatási kézikönyv* (Administrative handbook) (Budapest, Közgazdasági és Jogi Könyvkiadó, 1966, 546 p.), by Károly Besnyő.

1969. International Commission of Jurists (*Founded 1952*). The Hungarian Situation and the Rule of Law. The Hague, 1957. 144 p. Bibliographical footnotes.

———. The Continuing Challenge of the Hungarian Situation to the Rule of Law; Supplement to the Report. The Hague, 1957. 33 p.

A legal appraisal, by an independent international body, of the 1956 Hungarian Revolution and the Soviet intervention and occupation, and an analysis of the violation of human rights in Hungary following the suppression of the revolution. *The Legal Aspects of the Hungarian Question* (Geneva, 1963, 219 p.), by Joseph A. Szikszoy, is a thesis by an American lawyer offering a detailed analysis of the legal problems, both international and Hungarian constitutional, following in the wake of the revolution. A briefer treatment is offered by Ferenc A. Váli in an article entitled "The Hungarian Revolution and International Law," published in *The Fletcher Review*, v. 2, 1959, no. 1, p. 9-25.

1970. Meznerics, Iván, Gyula Simon, *and* János Hidas. Devizajog (Foreign exchange law). Budapest, Közgazdasági és Jogi Könyvkiadó, 1959. 339 p. Bibliography: p. 277-287.

Commentaries on Hungary's foreign currency law, with the texts of the relevant statutes and decrees.

1971. Mezőfy, Ladislaus. Der strafrechtliche Staatsschutz in Ungarn. *In*: Der strafrechtliche Staatsschutz in der Sowjetunion, der Tschechoslowakei, Ungarn und Polen. Herrnalb/Schwarzwald, Verlag für internationalen Kulturaustausch, 1963. p. 149-247.

Survey of the historical development of the criminal law for the defense of the state since 1945, and analysis of the law in force.

1972. Névai, László. Magyar törvénykezési szervezeti jog (Hungarian law on judicial organization). Budapest, Tankönyvkiadó, 1961. 325 p. Includes bibliographies.

A university textbook on the organization of the courts.

1973. Réczei, László. Internationales Privatrecht. Translated by Alexander Karcsay. Budapest, Akadémiai Kiadó, 1960. 478 p.

Private international law as applied in contemporary Hungary.

1974. Szlezak, Ludwig. Das Staatsangehörigkeitsrecht von Ungarn. Frankfurt am Main, Berlin, Metzner, 1959. 211 p.

The law of citizenship presently in force. For the nationality law till 1918 *see*:

Milner, Emanuel. Die österreichische Staatsbürgerschaft und der Gesetzartikel L:1879 über der Erwerb und Verlust der ungarischen Staatsbürgerschaft. Tübingen, Fues, 1880. 105 p. (Studien zum österreichischen Staatsrecht, 1)

1975. Weltner, Andor. A magyar munkajog (Hungarian labor law). 2d rev. ed. Budapest, Tankönyvkiadó, 1960-1962. 2 v. Bibliography: v. 2, p. 289-294.

A university textbook reviewing the development and present provisions of labor law in Hungary.

C. FOREIGN RELATIONS

1976. Deák, Francis. Hungary at the Paris Peace Conference; the Diplomatic History of the Treaty of Trianon. New York, Columbia University Press, 1942. 594 p. Maps. Bibliography: p. 563-567.

The story of the negotiations leading to the Treaty of Trianon between the Allies and the Central Powers after the First World War, by which Hungary lost 71 percent of her prewar territory and about two-thirds of her population.

1977. Kállai, Gyula. A nemzetközi kommunista mozgalom és a nemzetközi politika kérdéseiről (On the problems of the international communist movement and international politics). Budapest, Kossuth Könyvkiadó, 1966. 54 p.

The chairman of the Hungarian Council of Ministers analyzes international political questions and Hungarian foreign policy.

1978. Kertesz, Stephen D. Diplomacy in a Whirlpool; Hungary between Nazi Germany and Soviet Russia. Notre Dame, Ind., University of Notre Dame Press, 1953. 273 p. Maps. Bibliographical references included in "Notes" (p. 189-229).

See also entry no. 1889.

Treats Hungary's involvement in the Second World War, her attempts to extricate herself from the German alliance, the consequences of Soviet occupation, and the problems of negotiating peace under communist pressures.

1979. Kertesz, Stephen D., *ed.* The Fate of East Central Europe: Hopes and Failures of American Foreign Policy. Notre Dame, Ind., University of Notre Dame Press, 1956. 463 p. Map. Bibliographical footnotes.

Contains many references to Hungary's situation since the Second World War, and a chapter on Hungary (p. 219-248) written by the editor.

1980. Magyar Tudományos Akadémia, *Budapest. Történettudományi Intézet.* Allianz Hitler-Horthy-Mussolini, Dokumente zur ungarischen Aussenpolitik, 1933-1944. Introductory study and preparation of documents for printing by Magda Ádám, Gyula Juhász, and Lajos Kerekes. Edited by Lajos Kerekes. Budapest, Akadémiai Kiadó, 1966. 409 p.

1981. Magyar Tudományos Akadémia, *Budapest. Történettudományi Intézet.* Diplomáciai iratok Magyarország külpolitikájához, 1936-1945 (Diplomatic documents concerning Hungary's foreign policy, 1936-1945). Edited by László Zsigmond. Budapest, Akadémiai Kiadó, 1962–

To be completed in six volumes, of which volumes 1, 2, and 4 have so far been published: *A Berlin-Róma tengely kialakulása és Ausztria annexiója, 1936-1938* (The formation of the Berlin-Rome axis and the annexation of Austria, 1936-1938), edited by Lajos Kerekes (Budapest, 1962, 823 p.); *A müncheni egyezmény létrejötte és Magyarország külpolitikája, 1936-1938* (The signing of the Munich Agreement and Hungary's foreign policy, 1936-1938), edited by Magda Ádám (Budapest, 1965), 1029 p.); and *Magyarország külpolitikája a II. világháború kitörésének időszakában, 1939-1940* (Hungary's foreign policy at the time of the outbreak of the Second World War, 1939-1940), edited by Gyula Juhász (Budapest, 1962, 904 p.). Tables of contents and summaries of documents are also given in German.The volumes still to be published will cover Hungary's participation in the complete partition of Czechoslovakia, 1938-1939 (v. 3), Hungary and the preparations for a war against the Soviet Union, 1940-1941 (v. 5), and the participation of Hungary in the Second World War, 1941-1945 (v. 6).

1982. Ránki, György. Emlékiratok és valóság Magyarország második világháborús szerepéről; horthysta politika a második világháborúban. (Memoirs and reality about Hungary's role in the Second World War; Horthyite policy during the Second World War). Budapest, Kossuth Könyvkiadó, 1964. 302 p. Bibliographical footnotes.

Analyzes memoirs written by émigré statesmen in the light of material found in Hungarian archives (documents of the Ministry of Foreign Affairs) and captured German papers.

1983. Sík, Endre. Egy diplomata feljegyzései (Notes of a diplomat). Budapest, Kossuth Könyvkiadó, 1966. 343 p.

The author of these memoirs is a Moscow-trained scholar of Hungarian origin who, after his return to Hungary in 1945, entered the diplomatic service. He served as Hungarian envoy to the United States and was for some time minister of foreign affairs.

35

the economy

by Laszlo Zsoldos

A. BIBLIOGRAPHIES, GENERAL REFERENCE AIDS, AND STATISTICAL HANDBOOKS

1. Bibliographies

1984. The American Bibliography of Russian and East European Studies. 1956– Bloomington. (Indiana University Publications. Russian and East European series)

See also entry no. 6.

The best single source for articles in English on Hungarian economics.

1985. Balázsy, Sándor. Economics. *In* Erdey-Grúz, Tibor, *and* Imre Trencsény-Waldapfel, *eds.* Science in Hungary. Budapest, Corvina Press, 1965. p. 124-148.

A comprehensive bibliographical essay on the economic literature of Hungary, emphasizing the period since 1945.

1986. Hungary. *Központi Statisztikai Hivatal.* A kiadványok bibliográfiája, 1949-1961 (Bibliography of publications, 1949-1961). Budapest, 1962. 87 p.

A complete listing of the official publications issued by the Central Statistical Office during the period covered; includes some 1,700 items.

1987. Közgazdasági bibliográfia (Economic bibliography). 1945/1953– Budapest, Közgazdasági és Jogi Könyvkiadó, 1955–

Arrangement is by subject under six major headings. Entries for periodical articles and books are intermingled; some entries are annotated. There are author and subject indexes, and a list of periodicals surveyed. The first three volumes were issued under the title *Tervgazdasági, statisztikai és számviteli bibliográfia* (A bibliography of economic planning, statistics, and accountancy).

1988. Magyar közgazdasági és statisztikai művek; bibliográfia (Hungarian economic and statistical writings; bibliography). 1957/59– Budapest, Magyar Tudományos Akadémia Közgazdaságtudományi Intézetének Könyvtára és a Marx Károly Közgazdaságtudományi Egyetem Központi Könyvtára, 1960–

Classified arrangement; titles are also given in Russian and English. The first volume was issued under the title *Magyar közgazdasági művek* (Hungarian economic writings).

2. General Reference Aids

1989. Faragó, Lászlóné. Tájékoztató a magyar tudományos és szakkönyvtárakról és szolgáltatásaikról (A guide to Hungarian scientific and special libraries and their services). 2d rev. and corr. ed. Budapest, 1962. 147 p.

1990. Közgazdasági enciklopédia (Encyclopedia of economics). Budapest, Athenaeum, 1929-1931. 4 v. Illus., maps.

1991. Lukács, László, *ed.* Üzemszervezés, üzemgazdaság (Business organization, business economics). Budapest, Terra, 1966. 212 p. (Műszaki értelmező szótár, 27)

A dictionary of basic economic, business, and management terms. Definitions of entries are given in Hungarian followed by the German, Russian, and English equivalents. Useful research aid for those with a basic knowledge of Hungarian.

1992. Rózsa, György. A közgazdasági kutatás forrásai és segédletei; tájékoztatási-bibliográfiai kézikönyv (Sources and aids for economic research; reference-bibliographical handbook). Budapest, Közgazdasági és Jogi Könyvkiadó, 1959. 283 p. Tables, bibliographies.

A thesaurus and annotated bibliography of major research aids for students of economics. Hungarian items constitute a minor part of the annotated material, but appendix 2 is entirely devoted to a bibliographic essay on the most important Hungarian source materials in economics for the period 1919-1959. Summary and two tables in German.

1993. Simalcsik, Miklós, *and* László Soós. A vállalati és szövetkezeti gazdálkodás szabályai (Regulations for enterprise and cooperative management). Budapest, Közgazdasági és Jogi Könyvkiadó, 1966. 446 p.

3. Statistical Publications

1994. Baum, Samuel. The Labor Force of Hungary. Washington, U.S. Dept. of Commerce, Bureau of the Census, 1962. 34 p. Diagrs., tables, bibliographies. (International Population Statistics Reports, ser. P-90, no. 18)

See also entry no. 2062.

1995. Gazdaságstatisztikai tájékoztató. Economic Statistical Bulletin. v. 1-3; Dec. 1946-July 1949. Budapest. Monthly.

Edited by the Secretary of the Supreme Economic Council and the Central Statistical Office, this report fills the gap in the series of statistical yearbooks (see entry no. 1999). It also contains detailed figures on Hungary's reparations after the Second World War, although the reliability of these figures cannot be established. Table of contents and headings in statistical tables are also in English, French, and Russian.

1996. Hungary. *Központi Statisztikai Hivatal.* Adatok és adalékok a népgazdaság fejlődésének tanulmányozásához, 1949-1955 (Data and contributions for the study of the development of the national economy, 1949-1955). Budapest, 1957. 460 p.

A compendium of statistical reports previously published by the Central Statistical Office, devoted chiefly to economic activity. It complements the *Statisztikai évkönyv, 1949-1955* (entry no. 1999), for a period during which the reporting of data was not systematically organized. Some information in this volume cannot be found elsewhere. Selected portions are available in English, translated and published by the U.S. Joint Publications Research Service as *Statistics and Data for a Study of the Development of the People's Economy, 1949-1955, Hungary* (Washington, D.C., 1961, 327 p., JPRS 7784).

1997. Hungary. *Központi Statisztikai Hivatal.* Magyar statisztikai közlemények (Hungarian statistical bulletin). New series. no. 1-117; 1902-1947. Budapest. Irregular.

Statistics of economic, demographic, and economic-geographic conditions and activity, and the census of Hungary, published by the Central Statistical Office. The census information and economic statistics in physical terms are particularly detailed, and elaborately presented and cross-classified. This continues a Central Statistical Office publication with the same title issued during the period 1893-1901, and with the title *Hivatalos statistikai közlemények* (Official statistical bulletin) during the period 1868-1875. Table headings, explanatory notes, and connecting text are given in German, French, or English.

1998. Hungary. *Központi Statisztikai Hivatal.* Megyei és városi statisztikai értesítő (County and city statistical journal). v. 1– Oct. 1949– Budapest, Statisztikai Kiadó Vállalat. Illus. Monthly.

Regional breakdown of major economic and demographic information. Until 1957 it was published under the title *Statisztikai értesítő.*

1999. Hungary. *Központi Statisztikai Hivatal.* Statisztikai évkönyv (Statistical yearbook). 1949/1955– Budapest, 1957–

Official yearbook issued by the Central Statistical Office, presenting tabulated summaries of economic, demographic, and miscellaneous conditions and activities. The first volume summarizes the years 1949-1955; subsequent volumes cover the record for single years. Most of the data in the several volumes are standardized and may be linked together to form time series. The 1957 and 1963 volumes are also available in English and contain, in addition to the regularly published information, input-output tables for the Hungarian economy (also table of coefficients and the inverted matrix of coefficients). This serial succeeds *Magyar statisztikai évkönyv*, published 1872-1946 and available also in German (*Ungarisches statistisches Jahrbuch*) and in French (*Annuaire statistique hongrois*).

Among other titles, the Central Statistical Office also has published in English, annually since 1958, the *Statistical Pocket Book of Hungary*, an abbreviated, general-purpose statistical guide. The volumes for the 1960 census (*1960. évi népszámlálás*) are noteworthy for their detail and scope. A complete listing of publications issued by the Central Statistical Office during the period 1949-1961 is given in entry no. 1986.

2000. Hungary. *Központi Statisztikai Hivatal.* Statisztikai havi közlemények (Monthly bulletin of statistics). New series. 1957– Budapest. Monthly.

Presents regular series of major economic information in tabular form, as well as some demographic and meteorological data. Many of the monthly series which cover an 18-month period can be reconciled with the annual information published in entry no. 1999. In 1961 a supplement entitled *A fogalmak magyarázata* (80 p.) was issued also in English as *Explanation of Terms and Expressions* (75 p.). Beginning in 1963 an annual supplement giving English translations of table headings has been provided. This serial succeeds one with the same title and issuing body, covering the period 1897-1944, with table headings in French and/or German. During 1937-

1944, it appeared quarterly under the title *Statisztikai negyedévi közlemények* (Quarterly bulletin of statistics).

2001. Hungary. *Központi Statisztikai Hivatal.* Statisztikai időszaki közlemények (Occasional statistical bulletin). no. 1– 1957– Budapest, Statisztikai Kiadó.

Irregularly published special reports usually concentrating on a single economic sector, condition, or activity, with tables, textual material, and methodological notes. The following issues are particularly useful because of the time periods covered: no. 11, *Az ipar termelési indexe 1949-1957* (The index of industrial production, 1949-1957) (1958, 81 p.); no. 17, *A munka termelékenysége a magyar iparban, 1949-1957* (Labor productivity in Hungarian industry, 1949-1957 (1958, 90 p.); no. 25, *Építőipari adatok, 1949-1957* (Construction data, 1949-1957) (1959, 292 p.); no. 37, *Az ipar termelése és szerkezete, 1949-1959* (Industrial production and structure, 1949-1959) (1960, 124 p.); and no. 44, *A magyar magánkisipar statisztikai adatgyűjteménye, 1938-1960* (Statistical data for Hungarian private craft industry, 1938-1960) (1961, 190 p.). All issues have English or Russian summaries. Some have been translated and published by the U.S. Joint Publications Research Service, e.g., no. 30, *Income and Consumption of Blue- and White-Collar Workers' and Peasants' Households in 1958* (1961, 350 p., JPRS 8972); no. 37, *The Production and Structure of Industry, 1949-1959* (1961, 340 p., JPRS 8877); no. 53, *The Fixed Assets of the Hungarian National Economy* (1964, 70 p., JPRS 26215); and no. 56, *Hungarian National Income and the Living Condition of the Population, 1962* (1964, 185 p., JPRS 26538). The translations are accurate but stylistically deficient, and the professional reader may find the translation of technical terms often crude and confusing.

2002. Hungary. *Központi Statisztikai Hivatal.* Statisztikai szótár; 1700 statisztikai kifejezés hét nyelven (Statistical dictionary; 1700 statistical terms in seven languages). 3d ed. Budapest, Statisztikai Kiadó Vállalat, 1962. 171 p.

The seven languages are Russian, Hungarian, Bulgarian, Czech, Polish, German, and English.

2003. Kovacsics, József, *ed.* A történeti statisztika forrásai (The sources of historical statistics). Budapest, Közgazdasági és Jogi Könyvkiadó, 1957. 460 p. Maps, facsims., tables. Bibliography: p. 339-367.
See also entry no. 1796.

A complete survey of the history of statistical activity in Hungary, including fragments from the 13th through 16th centuries, as well as of such early works in the field as Matthias Bél's *Hungariae antiquae et novae prodromus* (Norimbergae, 1723, 204 p.) and his *Notitia Hungariae novae* (Viennae Austriae, 1735-1742, 5 v.). Rich in facsimiles, maps, and tables, it is particularly valuable for its comprehensive bibliography and appendix of historical data. There are summaries in Russian and English.

B. GENERAL ECONOMIC QUESTIONS

2004. Bognár, József. Planned Economy in Hungary; Achievements and Problems. Budapest, Pannonia Press, 1959. 99 p.

A quasi-official survey briefly explaining the rationale, tasks, and processes of planning, and some of its achievements, weaknesses, and limitations. It is comparable in its approach to Imre Vajda's *The Second Five-Year Plan in Hungary* (see entry no. 2025).

2005. Csikós Nagy, Béla. Árpolitika az átmeneti gazdaságban (Price policy in the transitional economy). Budapest, Közgazdasági és Jogi Könyvkiadó, 1958. 455 p.

Fundamental study of the role of price and cost-profit relations in the "transitional state" of the economy. The exploration of the various roles of prices, rules of price formation, and the systematization of individual prices is followed by a description of prices and pricing in the several major economic sectors, including the consumer sector.

2006. Ecker-Rácz, L. László. The Hungarian Economy, 1920-1954. Washington, D.C., 1954. 114 l. Tables. (Council for Economic and Industry Research. Report no. A-21) Bibliography: leaves 87-92.

General statistical survey of the economy with a good bibliography of statistical sources.

2007. The Economy of Hungary, 1950 to 1954. Economic Bulletin for Europe, v. 7, August 1955: 85-110.

This summary of major economic developments during the period of the first five-year plan provides an easy overview of objectives and attainments under planning. The appendixes on statistical methods and sources used and the extensive explanatory notes to the statistical tables are helpful.

2008. Erdős, Sándor, *and others*. Élelmiszertermelés és fogyasztás (The production and consumption of food). Budapest, Közgazdasági és Jogi Könyvkiadó, 1961. 411 p.

A survey of the structure of production and the composition of consumption by socioeconomic groups.

2009. Kiss, Pál, *and* U. Pál Kralovánszky. A hústermelés és húsellátás kérdései hazánkban (Problems of domestic production and supply of meat). Budapest, Közgazdasági és Jogi Könyvkiadó, 1962. 363 p. Bibliography: p. 353-359.

Deals with questions similar to the ones raised in the Erdős book (see entry no. 2009). Extensive bibliography of sources.

2010. Kornai, János. Overcentralization in Economic Administration; a Critical Analysis Based on Experience in Hungarian Light Industry. Translated by John Knapp. London, Oxford University Press, 1959. 236 p.

A compact, scholarly assessment of the nature and sources of the failures of central direction in the light industrial sector. Systematically analyzes the planning process and the role of industry management in this process; the consequences of excessive centralization and possible remedies are given detailed treatment. There are 35 tables.

2011. Kovács, Dénes. Élelmiszer-fogyasztásunk távlatai (Prospects for our food consumption). Budapest, Közgazdasági és Jogi Könyvkiadó, 1965. 281 p.

A review of consumption patterns and aggregates is followed by estimates of the consumption trends for major food staples.

2012. Markos, György. Magyarország gazdasági földrajza (An economic geography of Hungary). Budapest, Közgazdasági és Jogi Könyvkiadó, 1962. 581 p. Maps, diagrs., tables. Bibliography: p. 563-567.

An up-to-date survey of resource endowment in general terms, by industrial sector and by economic region. Running commentary on the prospective development of resources in terms of technological rather than economic feasibility is one of its chief strengths. There is an extensive bibliography and a subject index.

2013. Schmidt, Ádám. A személyi jövedelemeloszlás a szocializmusban (The distribution of personal income under socialism). Budapest, Közgazdasági és Jogi Könyvkiadó, 1964. 361 p. Illus. Bibliography: p. 333-343.

A complete analysis of the chief characteristics of personal income and its distribution, with an emphasis on economic consequences. The role of planning in the personal income sector is a useful contribution to the understanding of the entire planning process. Tables, graphs, and English table of contents.

2014. Surányi-Unger, Theo. Studien zum Wirtschaftswachstum Südosteuropas. Stuttgart, G. Fischer, 1964. 216 p. Bibliographical footnotes.

An objective assessment of the goals and prospects of economic growth in Albania, Bulgaria, Romania, and Hungary. Richly documented, particularly with regard to Hungarian source materials. The three-part monograph on growth objectives, underlying fiscal resources, and the problems of growth and development constitutes a well-integrated analysis of the economies of Southeastern Europe. Author and subject indexes.

C. PLANNING

2015. Balassa, Béla A. The Hungarian Experience in Economic Planning, a Theoretical and Empirical Study. New Haven, Yale University Press, 1959. 285 p. Tables. Bibliography: p. 277-279; bibliographical footnotes. (Yale Studies in Economics, 11)

A comprehensive and critical analysis of the nature, scope, operation, and achievements of economic planning, this is the best work of its kind in English. In addition to its theoretical merits, the richly documented descriptive material makes it a good source on the organization of the firm and the planning process in a centrally directed system.

2016. Bródy, András. Az ágazati kapcsolatok modellje (The model of interbranch relations). Budapest, Akadémiai Kiadó, 1964. 217 p. Bibliography: p. 207-211.

A critical analysis of the limitations of input-output methods in economic planning. It also summarizes mathematical investigations with a relevance to economics. Complements the Kornai work (entry no. 2018). Good bibliography.

2017. Kemény, György. Economic Planning in Hungary, 1947-9. London, New York, Royal Institute of International Affairs, 1952. 146 p. Tables.

A critical analysis of the background, evolution, establishment, and implementation of the first Hungarian economic plan, which was to become a schema for the central direction of the economic process. The fundamentals of policy-making and some of the planning techniques of this period are also described. There is a subject index.

2018. Kornai, János. A beruházások matematikai programozása (Mathematical programming of investments). Budapest, Közgazdasági és Jogi Könyvkiadó, 1962. 323 p. Bibliography: p. 313-321.

Applications of linear programming methods and other apparatus to the measurement of investment profitability. The formal exposition of the elements in a program is followed by a consideration of other models and techniques, with illustrations drawn from industry and the foreign trade sector. Some of the problems and the choice of methods for decision-making under uncertainty are then considered. The exercise is designed to show the applicability of mathematical methods to the preparation of perspective plans. Very good bibliography of Hungarian and foreign sources.

2019. Kőszegi, László. A területi tervezés főbb elvi és módszertani kérdései (Major theoretical and methodological problems of regional planning). Budapest, Közgazdasági és Jogi Könyvkiadó, 1964. 399 p. Illus., maps. Bibliography: p. 397-399.

Historical and analytical review with special reference to Hungarian planning.

2020. László, Imre, *ed.* Népgazdasági tervezés (National economic planning). Budapest, Közgazdasági és Jogi Könyvkiadó, 1962-64. 2 v. Bibliographical footnotes.

A detailed description of the principles, organization, functions, and activities in central planning. Chapter 2 is useful in spelling out the major considerations of the entire planning process; it identifies the types of plans and their structures and deals with the details of implementation and control of plans.

2021. Linder, Willy. Die kommunistische Planwirtschaft am Beispiel Ungarns. Zürich, Buchverlag d. Neuen Zürcher Zeitung, 1964. 143 p.

A well-written and lucid commentary on Hungarian economic planning, originally serialized in the *Neue Zürcher Zeitung.*

2022. Molnár, László, *ed.* Beruházások-felújítások tervezése és megvalósítása (The planning and realization of investments-renewals). Budapest, Közgazdasági és Jogi Könyvkiadó, 1963. 345 p.

A general survey of the evolution and current status of investment concepts, plans, (micro) practices and implementation of macroeconomic plans in the short- and long-run context. There are comprehensive references to laws and regulations that guide and coordinate investment processes at the enterprise level. Subject index.

2023. Schweng, Lóránd D. Economic Planning in Hungary Since 1938. New York, Mid-European Studies Center of the National Committee for a Free Europe, 1951. 80 p. (National Committee for a Free Europe. Mid-European Studies Center. Publication no. 1)

Describes and compares four different plans (between 1938 and 1950) from the point of view of their content and intent. Briefly explains differences in the mechanisms of the plans. Offers an appendix of statistical tables and a short bibliography.

2024. The Three-Year Plan of Hungary's National Economy, 1958-1960. Budapest, Hungarian Review, 1958. 79 p. Illus.

Contains the legislation of the three-year plan with commentary and ten tables summarizing the plan targets by economic sector.

2025. Vajda, Imre. The Second Five-Year Plan in Hungary; Problems and Perspectives. Budapest, Pannonia Press, 1962. 118 p. Illus., map, bibliographical footnotes.

The origins and objectives of this plan are described and analyzed within a modified Marxist frame of reference. Apart from its ideological commitment it is a good general commentary on the lessons learned (and not learned) from previous plans, as well as on the scope and structure of this plan.

D. AGRICULTURE

2026. Csáki, Norbert, *and* Balázs Szitó. Magyarország mezőgazdasági kivitele (Hungary's agricultural exports). Budapest, Közgazdasági és Jogi Könyvkiadó, 1963. 259 p. Bibliography: p. 253-256.

Detailed analysis of the conditions, trends, and problems of agricultural exports to the communist bloc and to Western Europe.

2027. Erdei, Ferenc, László Csete, *and* József Márton. A mezőgazdaság belterjessége (The intensification of agriculture). Budapest, Közgazdasági és Jogi Könyvkiadó, 1963. 383 p. Tables, maps, bibliographies.

Some theoretical and practical considerations of agricultural production and productivity under the constraining influence of the land factor. Individual essays deal with problems of measuring productivity and related topics. Table of contents also in Russian, German, and English.

2028. Erdei, Ferenc, *ed.* A termelőszövetkezeti üzemszervezés gyakorlati kézikönyve (Practical handbook on business organization for agricultural cooperatives). 2d rev. and enl. ed. Budapest, Akadémiai Kiadó, 1962. 848 p.

2029. Halász, Aladár, *ed.* Erdőgazdaságunk, faiparunk és faellátásunk helyzete és fejlődése, 1920-1958-ig (The condition and development of our forestry, wood-products industry, and wood-products supply from 1920 to 1958). Budapest, Közgazdasági és Jogi Könyvkiadó, 1960. 333 p.

A resource inventory in tabulated form with virtually no textual material.

2030. Nyers, Rezső. The Cooperative Movement in Hungary. Translated by Gyula Gulyás. Budapest, Pannonia Press, 1963. 259 p. Bibliography: p. 251-252.

Reflections by a leading Communist Party member on the achievements, objectives, organization, and issues of cooperative organizations in agricultural and nonagricultural production.

2031. Sanders, Irwin T., *ed.* Collectivization of Agriculture in Eastern Europe. Lexington, University of Kentucky Press, 1958. 214 p. Maps, tables. Includes bibliographical references.

See also entry no. 259.

Well-documented commentary and analysis of the background and development of collectivization in agriculture. The sixth essay, by Nicolas Spulber, deals with Hungary and Rumania.

2032. Sebestyén, József. Matematikai módszerek alkalmazása a mezőgazdasági termelés vizsgálatában (The application of mathematical methods to research on agricultural production). Budapest, Akadémiai Kiadó, 1962. 134 p. Diagrs., tables. Bibliography: p. 133-134.

A handbook on the concept, construction, and use of mathematical models and methods in agricultural production. The role of simple cost and demand functions and applications of the differential calculus, optimality, and linear programming are explained with examples drawn from agriculture and agricultural sciences.

2033. Szabó, István, *ed.* A parasztság Magyarországon a kapitalizmus korában, 1848-1914 (The peasantry in Hungary during the capitalist period, 1848-1914). Budapest, Akadémiai Kiadó, 1965. 2 v. Bibliography: v. 2, p. 695-724.

Well-documented, comprehensive social and economic history with commentary on parallel developments elsewhere in Europe. Very good footnotes and bibliography.

E. INDUSTRY

2034. Bródy, András, *and* Jenő Rácz. A termelés tőkeigényessége a kapitalizmusban (Capital output under capitalism), by András Bródy. Az állóalapok és a termelés összefüggése a magyar iparban (The relation between fixed capital and output in Hungarian industry), by Jenő Rácz. Budapest, Akadémiai Kiadó, 1966. 331 p. Illus.

The second and major part of the book (p. 75-331), by Jenő Rácz, analyzes capital growth in Hungarian industry during the period 1950-1963 with special reference to capital-labor productivity and capital-output relations and their contribution to the construction of long-run economic plans.

2035. Fáth, János. Nagyvállalatok korszerű vezetése (Modern management of large-scale enterprises). Budapest, Közgazdasági és Jogi Könyvkiadó, 1966. 203 p. Illus., bibliographical footnotes.

Analysis of the functions of management and their effectiveness under alternative organizational rules. It evaluates the reciprocal influences between structure and management function as they relate to the short-run objectives of the enterprise and to the task of long-range planning. In conclusion, the problems of organizing management activity and some aspects of the production process in a large-scale enterprise are considered.

2036. Hungary. *Központi Statisztikai Hivatal.* A magyar ipar; statisztikai adatgyűjtemény (Hungarian industry; a statistical compendium). Budapest, 1961. 775 p. (chiefly tables)

Comprehensive statistical information on the structure and performance of industry. Time series extend as far back as availability of data and rules of comparability permit. Appendix reconciles the Hungarian industrial classification with those of the Council of Mutual Economic Aid and the United Nations.

2037. Ipari és építőipari statisztikai értesítő (Journal of industrial and construction statistics). 1949– Budapest, Központi Statisztikai Hivatal. Illus. Monthly.

2038. Lukács, Ottó, *and* Lajos Ollé. Iparstatisztika (Industrial statistics). 2d ed. Budapest, Közgazdasági és Jogi Könyvkiadó, 1965. 369 p.

Textbook on statistical methods applicable to industry. Introductory part describes reporting rules and practices, information flows, classificatory systems, and the work of information processing agencies in the industrial sector of the economy. The balance of the book presents measurement and processing methods for the principal activity variables of the system.

2039. Szakasits, D. György. Ipari kutatás és fejlesztés (Industrial research and development). Budapest, Közgazdasági és Jogi Könyvkiadó, 1962. 339 p. Bibliography: p. 307-311.

A survey of the methods, costs, and applications of industrial research in development planning. With regard to efficiency of research and development activity and its measurement, a work by János Klár, *A kutatásgazdaságosság és mérési módszerei* (The efficiency of research and methods of measuring it) (Budapest, Közgazdasági és Jogi Könyvkiadó, 1966, 127 p., illus., bibliographical footnotes) is a good complementary volume.

F. LABOR

2040. Jászai, Samu. A magyar szakszervezetek története (History of the Hungarian trade unions). Budapest, Magyarországi Szakszervezeti Tanács, 1925. 332 p.

A retrospective, at times idealized, personal account of the "classical" period in the Hungarian labor movement, narrated by a leader of the social democratic party of Hungary. Statistical tables on membership, unemployment relief payments to members, and a compendium of brief histories of 55 craft unions are valuable complements to the text.

2041. Kocsis. Ferenc, *and others, ed.* A munkás és a munkatermelékenység az építőiparban (Labor and labor productivity in the construction industry). Budapest, Közgazdasági és Jogi Könyvkiadó, 1963. 286 p. Bibliographical footnotes.

Essays on the sources, planning, innovation, resource management, norms, wages, and employee welfare in the construction industry, and their relevance to labor productivity.

2042. Ozsvald, László. A műszaki dolgozók anyagi ösztönzési rendszere (The pecuniary incentive system for technical workers). Budapest, Közgazdasági és Jogi Könyvkiadó, 1963. 185 p. Bibliography: p. 183-184.

Detailed exploration of incentive systems and their characteristics and objectives, from 1950 on. Summary in English and Russian; good bibliography.

G. NATIONAL INCOME, DOMESTIC TRADE, AND FINANCE

2043. Alton, Thad P., *and others.* Hungarian National Income and Product in 1955. New York, Columbia University Press, 1963. 254 p. Bibliography: p. 239-243.

An attempt to reconstruct Hungarian national income in terms of Western income concepts. Most of the work involves an adjustment of official statistical information to the methodology adopted by the authors, and only to a lesser extent does it use estimates based on indirect, esoteric sources or informed guesses. Detailed methodological appendices, numerous tables, and a subject index are provided.

2044. Eckstein, Alexander. National Income and Capital Formation in Hungary, 1900-1950. *In* International Association for Research in Income and Wealth. Income and Wealth. Series 5. London, Bowes & Bowes, 1955. p. 152-223.

A study in depth about national income in Hungary, with the weight of the analysis on the causes and manifestations of economic change during the first half of this century. Footnotes provide a good listing of works that matter in the history of national income accounting in Hungary.

2045. Kovács, Dénes, *and others.* A belkereskedelem fejlődése a számok tükrében, 1960-1963 (The development of domestic trade as reflected in statistics, 1960-1963). Budapest, Közgazdasági és Jogi Könyvkiadó, 1964. 375 p. Illus.

Statistical enumeration and commentary on domestic commercial activity, the size and composition of consumption, and related magnitudes. The first part (188 pages) contains a complete description of the organization and scope of retail trade (state and private networks) relative to other activities. The remainder of the book consists of statistical tables.

2046. Lehr, György, *ed.* A pénzintézetek működése és kapcsolatuk a gazdálkodó szervekkel és a lakossággal (The functioning of financial institutions and their relation to economic organs and to the population). Budapest, Közgazdasági és Jogi Könyvkiadó, 1960. 611 p.

Comprehensive textbook and handbook on the organization and functions of banking in the planned economy. Detailed description is also given of financial accounting methods and forms, credit instruments, financial institutions other than banks (e.g., savings institutions, the state lottery, insurance), central banking, note issue, and foreign exchange. There are organization tables, charts, forms, and other exhibits. For a recent English-language treatment *see*:

Czirjak, Laszlo. Financial and Fiscal Systems of Hungary. Edited by Thad P. Alton and Elizabeth Bass. Washington, D.C., United States Arms Control and Disarmament Agency, 1968, 578 p.

2047. Matolcsy, Mátyás, *and* István Varga. The National Income of Hungary, 1924/25-1936/37. London, P. S. King, 1938. 116 p. Diagrs.

A pioneering study of national income and product covering a period which includes the worldwide depression of 1929-1935. The methodology is dated, but the information given is perhaps the best for that period.

2048. Varga, István. Az újabb magyar pénztörténet és egyes elméleti tanulságai (Recent Hungarian monetary history and some of its theoretical lessons). Budapest, Közgazdasági és Jogi Könyvkiadó, 1964. 217 p. Bibliography: p. 211-216.

Posthumously published, excellent short history of monetary developments in Hungary. A brief review of the monetary system of the Austro-Hungarian monarchy is followed by a detailed account of monetary problems and management after the First and Second World Wars. The bibliography contains a fair sampling of Professor Varga's more significant articles on money, foreign exchange, and monetary policy, appearing in such publications as *Weltwirtschaftliches Archiv*, *International Economic Papers*, *Osteuropa*, and *Finanzarchiv*.

H. FOREIGN TRADE

2049. Obláth, György. A külkereskedelem technikája (Techniques of foreign trade). 3d, rev. ed. Budapest, Közgazdasági és Jogi Könyvkiadó, 1958. 521 p.

Handbook and textbook on the organization, functions, and practices of the foreign trade sector. The part dealing with the organization of foreign trade (p. 409-517) has been translated and published by the U.S. Joint Publications Research Service as *The Techniques of Hungarian Foreign Trade* (New York, 1959, 141 p., JPRS 832-D).

2050. Szányi, Jenő, József Gulyás, *and* Endre Antal. A külkereskedelem technikája és szervezése (The techniques and organization of foreign trade). Budapest, Tankönyvkiadó, 1963. 389 p. 27 forms in pocket.

Standard text with numerous exhibits; intended for the student and the practitioner. Similar to entry no. 2049.

2051. Vajda, Imre. Külkereskedelmünk a második hároméves terv időszakában, 1958-1960 (Our foreign trade during the period of the second three-year plan, 1958-1960). Budapest, Kossuth, Könyvkiadó, 1961. 71 p.

An explanation of foreign trade developments in textual and tabulated form, including the geographic and commodity composition of trade and the reasons for shifts in these patterns.

2052. Vajda, Imre. The Role of Foreign Trade in a Socialist Economy; New Essays in Persuasion. Budapest, Corvina Press, 1965. 336 p. Illus.

Comments by a leading economist on Hungary's accomplishments and policies in the foreign trade sector. Emphasis is given to the role of foreign trade in the Council of Mutual Economic Aid and in the economic development of Hungary, and to the structure and terms of trade in recent years, as well as to special problems.

2053. Zsoldos, Laszlo. The Economic Integration of Hungary into the Soviet Bloc; Foreign Trade Experience. Columbus, Bureau of Business Research, College of Commerce and Administration, Ohio State University, 1963. 149 p. Illus. Bibliography: p. 137-149. (Ohio State University. Bureau of Business Research Monograph no. 109)

An exploration of activity in the foreign trade sector for the period 1950-1960, with an emphasis on changing patterns of trade and the terms of trade, and their relevance to domestic planning. Provides a large number of tables and extensive bibliography of Hungarian writings in this field.

I. SERIALS

2054. Acta oeconomica. v. 1– January 1967– Budapest, Magyar Tudományos Akadémia. Quarterly.

Official publication of the Hungarian Academy of Sciences. Articles by leading Hungarian economists in English, French, German (with summaries in Russian) or Russian (with summaries in English). Reviews are also included.

2055. Budapest. Magyar Gazdaságkutató Intézet. A Magyar Gazdaságkutató Intézet gazdasági helyzetjelentése. Bulletin of the Hungarian Institute for Economic Research. v. 1-54; January/March 1929-1945/1947. Budapest, 1929-1948. Illus., tables. Irregular.

Standard statistical survey of current developments in the economy, with occasional English and German table headings and notes.

2056. Hungary. *Központi Statisztikai Hivatal.* Statisztikai szemle (Statistical review). v. 1– January 1923– Budapest. Illus. Monthly (irregular).

Publication suspended September 1944-June 1945. Official publication of the Central Statistical Office, devoted to professional papers and articles. It also publishes book reviews, the current acquisitions list of the Central Statistical Office Library, historical-statistical notes, and a review of foreign periodicals. Abstracts in English, German, and Russian.

2057. Közgazdasági szemle (Economic review). v. 1– October 1954– Budapest. Monthly.

The official periodical of the Economic Institute of the Hungarian Academy of Sciences, and the chief forum for the theoretical and nontheoretical economist. Beginning with the March/April 1955 issue, summaries in English and Russian are provided. This periodical continues the work of the Academy previously published in *Nemzetgazdasági szemle* (1877-1892), *Közgazdasági és közigazgatási szemle* (1893-1894), and *Közgazdasági szemle* (1895-1949).

2058. Külkereskedelem (Foreign trade). v. 1– 1957– Budapest, Magyar Kereskedelmi Kamara Sajtó és Tájékoztatási Főosztálya. Illus. Monthly.

Published by the Hungarian Chamber of Commerce chiefly for

those engaged in foreign trade, although from time to time it also reports on plan fulfillment, current economic developments, and related topics in the foreign trade sector. Summaries in Russian and English or German.

2059. Magyar Nemzeti Bank. Monthly Bulletin.

Report issued in English by the Hungarian National Bank on monetary and banking developments.

2060. Pénzügy és számvitel (Finance and accountancy). v. 1– October 1957– Budapest. Illus. Monthly.

Sponsored by the Hungarian Ministry of Finance. It succeeds the monthly periodicals *Számvitel* (November 1950-September 1956) and *Pénzügyi szemle* (May 1954-September 1956), and it is the source for major articles on financial topics, including budgetary matters, taxation, and public finance in general.

36

the society

by John Kosa
(with the exception of section on psychology)

A. OVERVIEW OF SOCIETY, POPULATION, NATIONAL CHARACTER, SOCIAL TYPES

2061. Balogh, Béla, *and* Lajos Bartucz. Ungarische Rassenkunde. Berlin, W. de Gruyter, 1940. 141-320 p. Plates, bibliography. (Ungarische Bibliothek, 1. Reihe, 27)

Reprinted from *Ungarische Jahrbücher*, v. 19, Dec. 1939. A careful analysis of the racial composition of the Hungarians in terms of physical anthropology. An abbreviated version by Bartucz, "La composition raciale du peuple hongrois," appears in the *Journal de la Société hongroise de statistique*, v. 17, 1939, no. 1/2: p. 32-55.

2062. Baum, Samuel. The Labor Force of Hungary. Washington, U.S. Dept. of Commerce, Bureau of the Census, 1962. 34 p. Diagrs., tables, bibliographies. (International Population Statistics Reports. Series P-90, no. 18)

See also entry no. 1994.

2063. Csizmadia, Andor. Feudális jogintézmények továbbélése a Horthy-korszakban; a kegyúri jog történetéhez (The survival of feudal legal institutions during the Horthy period; toward the history of the ecclesiastical patronage right). Budapest, Tankönyvkiadó, 1961. 55 p. (Studia juridica auctoritate Universitatis Pécs publicata, 19)

2064. Eckhardt, Sándor, *ed.* Úr és paraszt a magyar élet egységében (Lord and peasant in the unity of Hungarian life). Budapest, Magyarságtudományi Intézet, 1941. 224 p.

A collection of scholarly studies on the two basic social types of old Hungary.

2065. Hanák, Péter. Skizzen über die ungarische Gesellschaft am Anfang des 20. Jahrhunderts. Acta Historica (Budapest), v. 10, 1963, no. 1/2: 1-47.

2066. Herman, Ottó. A magyar nép arcza és jelleme (The face and character of the Hungarian people). Budapest, K. M. Természettudományi Társulat, 1902. 212 p. Illus., plates.

A classic study written by a pioneer of Hungarian anthropology.

2067. Illyés, Gyula. Magyarok; naplójegyzetek (Hungarians; notes for a diary). Budapest, Nyugat, 1938. 2 v. in 1 (468 p.)

Written by the poet, this is an impressionistic interpretation of the national character from the viewpoint of the "populist" movement. See also *People of the Puszta* (Budapest, Corvina Press, 1967, 308 p.), an English translation of the original *Pusztâk népe* (1936) by the same author. German and French translations of this work are also available.

2068. Kiss, Lajos. A szegény ember élete (The life of the poor man). Budapest, Athenaeum, 1939. 283 p.

A socioanthropological study of the "poor peasant."

2069. Kosa, John. A Century of Hungarian Emigration, 1850-1950. American Slavic and East European Review, v. 16, December 1957: 501-514.

2070. Kosa, John. Hungarian Society in the Time of the Regency, 1920-1944. Journal of Central European Affairs, v. 16, October 1956: 253-265.

2071. A magyar nacionalizmus kialakulása és története (The emergence and history of Hungarian nationalism). Budapest, Kossuth Könyvkiadó, 1964. 463 p.

A collection of essays written by historians, with a foreword by Erzsébet Andics, a leading party theoretician.

2072. Márai, Sándor. Egy polgár vallomásai (Confessions of a bourgeois). Budapest, Pantheon, 1934. 315 p.

A novelist's autobiography, giving a description of upper-middle-class life at the beginning of this century.

2073. Siegel, Jacob S. The Population of Hungary. Washington, D.C., U.S. Govt. Print. Off., 1958. 186 p. Illus., maps (U.S. Bureau of the Census. International Population Statistics Reports. Series P-90, no. 9)

See also entry no. 1797.

A summary of the size, growth, composition, and distribution of the Hungarian population. It should be supplemented by the results of the 1960 census of Hungary, published by the Central Statistical Office under the title *1960. évi népszámlálás.*

2074. Sipos, János. A népi demokratikus forradalom magyarországi sajátosságaihoz (On the Hungarian characteristics of the people's democratic revolution). Magyar filozófiai szemle, v. 8, 1964, no. 1: 16-74.

Discusses national characteristics from the communist viewpoint.

2075. Szabó, Imre. A burzsoá állam- és jogbölcselet Magyarországon (The bourgeois philosophy of state and law in Hungary). Budapest, Akadémiai Kiadó, 1955. 533 p.

2076. Szekfű, Gyula, *ed.* Mi a magyar? (What is the Hungarian?) Budapest, Magyar Szemle Társaság, 1939. 558 p. Plates. (A Magyar Szemle könyvei, 15)

A collection of scholarly articles illuminating the national character from the points of view of different disciplines.

2077. Weis, István. A mai magyar társadalom (Contemporary Hungarian society). Budapest, Magyar Szemle Társaság, 1930. 239 p. (A Magyar Szemle könyvei, 2)

Bibliographical references included in "Jegyzetek" (notes), p. 232-237. An impressionistic description of Hungarian society by a political supporter of the *ancien régime.*

B. SOCIAL AND OCCUPATIONAL STRATA, OLD AND NEW

2078. Balázs, Béla. A középrétegek szerepe társadalmunk fejlődésében; egy évszázad magyar történelmének néhány sajátosságáról, 1849-1945 (The place of the middle classes in the development of our society; on some characteristics of a century of Hungarian history, 1849-1945). Budapest, Kossuth Könyvkiadó, 1958. 234 p.

2079. Budapest. *Statisztikai Hivatal.* A munkások szociális és gazdasági viszonyai Budapesten. Die sozialen und wirtschaftlichen Verhältnisse der Arbeiter in Budapest. By Lajos I. Illyefalvi. Budapest, Székesfőváros Statisztikai Hivatalának kiadása, 1930. 38, 1143 p. Tables.

One of the best-known volumes in the series of monographs published by the Statistical Office of Budapest. Text and table headings in Hungarian and German.

2080. Coulter, Harris L. The Hungarian Peasantry, 1948-1956. American Slavic and East European Review, v. 18, December 1959: 539-555.

2081. Illyés, Gyula, *and* Flóra Kozmutza. Lélek és kenyér (Spirit and bread). Budapest, Nyugat, 1939. 262 p. Illus., tables.

Interprets the psychology of peasant children, making use of the results of Rorschach tests.

2082. Kádár, Iván. A munkásosztály helyzete a Horthy-rendszer idején; adalékok (The situation of the working class in the time of the Horthy regime; contributions). Budapest, Szikra, 1956. 334 p. Tables.

2083. Karsai, Elek, *and* István Pintér. Darutollasok; Szegedtől a Királyi Várig (The crane-feathered ones; from Szeged to the Royal Castle). Budapest, Zrinyi Kiadó, 1960. 255 p. Illus. Bibliography: p. 249.

The title refers to the feathers worn by the military force, under Admiral Horthy's command, of the Anti-Bolshevist Committee which established itself first at Szeged in May 1919 and eventually took control of the government the following year. These events are narrated from the communist viewpoint, and the group which was in power during the period 1920-1944 is portrayed.

2084. Kerék, Mihály. A magyar földkérdés (The Hungarian land problem). Budapest, MEFHOSZ Könyvkiadó, 1939. 514 p. Bibliography: p. 494-505.

The best study of land tenure and peasant economy in old Hungary.

2085. Korolovszky, Lajos. Hungarian Workers in a New Society. New Hungarian Quarterly, 1. 2, January 1961: 74-93.

Report on a survey carried out in 1958 by 2,000 party workers, who interviewed 45,00 workers in important factories in Hungary. A similar survey made in 1962 is reported by Zoltán Halász in "Sociographic Survey in a Workers' District of Budapest," published in *The New Hungarian Quarterly*, v. 4, July/September 1963, p. 63-72.

2086. Rézler, Gyula, *ed.* Magyar gyári munkásság; szociális helyzetkép (Hungarian factory workers; social survey). Budapest, Magyar Közigazgatási Társaság, 1940. 242 p.

Describes the working class by branches of industry.

2087. Sinkovics, Julianna K. Rákoskeresztúr. Budapest, Bibliotheca Kiadó, 1958. 122 p. Plates (Tanulmányok Budapest néprajzából, 1)

A socioanthropological study of Rákoskeresztúr, a working-class suburb of Budapest.

2088. Social Stratification in Hungary. Budapest, Hungarian Central Statistical Office, 1967. 217 p. Tables.

This survey of 15,000 households, carried out in 1963, describes occupational, educational, and income-related stratification. Translation of the Hungarian original: *Társadalmi rétegződés Magyarországon* (Budapest, Központi Statisztikai Hivatal, 1967, 255 p. Statisztikai időszaki közlemények, v. 90). For additional data *see*: Központi Statisztikai Hivatal. A munkások és alkalmazottak száma, keresete a munkajellegek szerint (Number and income of workers and employees by types of work). Budapest, Központi Statisztikai Hivatal, 1966. 180 p. (Statisztikai időszaki közlemények, v. 85)

2089. Tanner, József. A Cooperative Village. New Hungarian Quarterly, v. 1, September 1960: 89-107.

As a supplement, see "Tévedések és tanulságok: a Hortobágyi Állami Gazdaság tizenöt évéből" (Mistakes and lessons; from fifteen years of the Hortobágy State Farm), by Tibor Zám, published in *Valóság*, v. 7, 1964, no. 5: 59-69.

2090. Varga, Gyula. Changes in the Peasant Living Standard. New Hungarian Quarterly, v. 7, 1966, no. 21: 86-101.

For additional data *see* "The Household Plot" by the same author in the *New Hungarian Quarterly*, v. 7, 1966, no. 23: 7-23.

C. SOCIAL CHANGE, SOCIAL MOBILITY

2091. Kosa, John. Two Generations of Soviet Man; a Study in the Psychology of Communism. Chapel Hill, University of North Carolina Press, 1962. 214 p. Includes bibliography.

A study of the changes in political attitudes, social relationships, and social stratification, mainly between 1949 and 1960.

2092. Kulcsár, Kálmán. A vándorlás és a társadalmi átrétegeződés szociológiai jelentősége (The sociological significance of migration and change of social status). Valóság, v. 4, 1961, no. 4: 23-31.

For a case study of the same problem *see* "A társadalmi átrétegeződés és a vándorlás összefüggésének néhány kérdése Bélapátfalván" (Some questions on the relationship between change of social status and migration in Bélapátfalva), by Kálmán Kulcsár and (Miklósné) Nozdroviczky, published in *Demográfia*, v. 1, 1958, no. 2: 281-288.

2093. Sós, Aladár, *and others, eds.* Sztálinváros, Miskolc, Tatabánya: városépítésünk fejlődése (Sztálinváros, Miskolc, Tatabánya; our urban development). Budapest, Műszaki Könyvkiadó, 1959. 191 p. Illus., maps, plans.

Three case studies in urbanization, city planning, and housing needs.

2094. Szabady, Egon, *ed.* Studies on Fertility and Social Mobility. Budapest, Akadémiai Kiadó, 1964. 331 p.
Seven papers, written by demographers, dealing with social mobility and its relations to fertility and domestic migration.

2095. Szakács, Sándor. Földosztás és agrárfejlődés a magyar népi demokráciában, 1945-1948 (Land reform and agriculture development in the Hungarian People's Democracy, 1945-1948). Budapest, Közgazdasági és Jogi Könyvkiadó, 1964. 175 p. Bibliographical footnotes. Marx Károly Közgazdaságtudományi Egyetem közleményei, no. 5)

2096. Szamos, Rudolf. Barakkváros (Shantytown). Budapest, Kossuth Könyvkiadó, 1960. 187 p. Illus.
An impressionistic description of a notorious slum in Budapest, cleared in the 1950s.

D. PUBLIC HEALTH, FERTILITY, MORTALITY

2097. Acsádi, György. A termékenység néhány tényezője Magyarországon (Some factors affecting fertility in Hungary). Demográfia, v. 4, 1961, no. 4: 407-420. Tables.
Summaries in Russian and English.

2098. Fülöp, Tamás. A magyar egészségügy szervezete és működése (The organization and activity of Hungarian public health). Budapest, Medicina, 1959. 239 p.
A description of the public health administration and the state health insurance system.

2099. Fülöp, Tamás. Über die Rolle sozialer und kultureller Faktoren in der Säuglingssterblichkeit. Acta Paediatrica Academiae Scientiarum Hungaricae, v. 6, 1965, no. 3/4: 375-387.
For information on public health programs concerned with this question, *see* Jenő Sárkány's article, "A csecsemőhalálozás elleni küzdelem eredményei Magyarországon" (The results of the fight against infant mortality in Hungary), published in *Népegészségügy*, v. 43, December 1962: 353-362.

2100. Hahn, Géza, *ed.* Az egészségügyi ellátás alakulása a 20 év folyamán (The development of health services during the past 20 years). Népegészségügy, v. 46, April 1965: 105-124.

2101. Mányi, Géza, *and* János Kerekes. Orvoshoz nem fordult lakosság egészségi állapota egy községben (The health situation of people not using medical services in a community). Népegészségügy, v. 46, February 1965: 42-45. Diagrs., tables.
An epidemiological description of the village of Tetétlen.

2102. Marton, Zoltán. A halálokok szerkezeti összetéle; a vezető halálokok (The structural composition of the causes of death; leading causes of death). Demográfia, v. 4, 1961, no. 2: 171-210. Diagrs., tables, bibliography.

Summaries in Russian and English.

2103. Ozsváth, Imre, *and* Sándor Radó. Tapasztalataink terhességmegszakításokkal kapcsolatban (Our experiences with induced abortions). Népegészségügy, v. 42, April 1961: 121-125.

Barsy, Gyula, *and* Jenő Sárkány. A művi vetélések hatása a születési mozgalomra és a csecsemőhalandóságra (The impact of induced abortions on the birth rate and on infant mortality). Demográfia, v. 6, 1963, no. 4: 427-467. Diagrs., tables, bibliography.

Two studies analyzing the medical and social aspects of legalized abortions. The second article has summaries in Russian and English.

2104. Szabady, Egon, *ed.* A születésszabályozás (Birth control). Budapest, Közgazdasági és Jogi Könyvkiadó, 1958. 205 p.

Contributors representing various disciplines discuss the problem.

E. FAMILY, CHILDREN, YOUTH, SPORT

2105. Csirszka, János. Budapesti tanulók pályaválasztási indítékai (Motives in the choice of career among schoolchildren in Budapest). Budapest, Tankönyvkiadó, 1961. 199 p.

Supplemented by the author's article, "Legnépszerűbb pályák és leggyakoribb pályaválasztási indítékok" (The most popular careers and the most frequent motives in the choice of career), published in *Pszichológiai tanulmányok* (Studies in psychology), v. 8, 1965, p. 341-357.

2106. Lantosyné Dabas, Erzsébet. A felbomló család gyermeke (Children of dissolved families). Budapest, Akadémiai Kiadó, 1965. 138 p.

A psychological study of the children of divorced parents.

2107. Mező, Ferenc. Golden Book of Hungarian Olympic Champions. Translated by István Farkas. Livre d'or des champions olympiques hongrois. Translated by János Hajdú. Budapest, Sport Lap-és Könyvkiadó, 1955. 131 p. Illus., tables.

See also the following books by the same author: *Negyven év a magyar sport múltjából* (Forty years of Hungarian sport) (Budapest, 1935) and *A magyar sport múltja és jelene* (Past and present of Hungarian sport) (Budapest, 1931). Both publications contain bibliographies.

2108. Tamásy, József. Magyarország népességének család-összetétele (The family composition of Hungary's population). Demográfia, v. 4, 1961, no. 2: 135-170. Diagrs., tables.

Summaries in Russian and English.

F. SOCIAL PROBLEMS

2109. Cseh-Szombathy, László. A nyugdíjasok helyzete és problémái (The position and problems of old-age pensioners). Demográfia, v. 7, 1964, no. 1: 88-103. Tables, bibliography.

Russian and English summaries.

2110. Cseh-Szombathy, László. Az öngyilkosság társadalmi jellege (The social character of suicides). Demográfia, v. 6, 1963, no. 2: 186-216. Diagrs., tables, bibliography.

Summaries in Russian and English.

2111. Huszár, Tibor. Fiatalkorú bűnözők; adalékok a fiatalkori bűnözés problematikájához az 1950-1959. évek felmérései alapján (Juvenile delinquents; contributions to the question of juvenile delinquency on the basis of investigations during the years 1950-1959). Budapest, Tankönyvkiadó, 1964. 238 p.

2112. Marton, Zoltán, *and* Emilné Szabó. Az elme- és idegbetegségek Magyarországon (Mental and nervous diseases in Hungary). Demográfia, v. 2, 1959, no. 2/3: 329-339. Diagrs., tables, bibliography.

Summaries in Russian and English.

2113. Salamon, Lajos. A házasságon kívüli születések (Births out of wedlock). Demográfia, v. 7, 1964, no. 2: 285-302. Diagrs., tables, bibliography.

Summaries in Russian and English.

2114. Vukovich, György. Az alkoholizmus egyes demográfiai és szociális jellemzői (Some demographic and social characteristics of alcoholism). Demográfia, v. 4, 1961, no. 2: 211-244. Diagrs., tables, bibliography.

Summaries in Russian and English.

G. MASS MEDIA AND PUBLIC OPINION

2115. Horváth, Lajos. A televízió technikája (The technology of television). Budapest, Műszaki Könyvkiadó, 1963. 354 p. Illus.

Describes the most important components of the television system and lists the internationally recognized television channels. *A televízió otthonunkban* (Television in our homes), 2d enl. ed. (Budapest, Műszaki Könyvkiadó, 1963, 139 p., illus.), by László Nozdroviczky, offers practical guidance with technical instructions.

2116. Lengyel, Géza. Magyar újságmágnások (Hungarian newspaper magnates). Budapest, Akadémiai Kiadó, 1963. 193 p. (Irodalomtörténeti füzetek, 41)

Biographical essays on leading Hungarian newspaper publishers prior to the Second World War.

2117. Magay, András. Hírközlés földrészek között (Intercontinental telecommunication). Budapest, Táncsics Kiadó, 1965. 257 p. Illus.

Surveys the history of the subject from the first submarine cables to contemporary methods of global communication.

2118. Magyar hírek (Hungarian news). v. 1– 1948– Budapest, Magyarok Világszövetsége. Weekly.

Illustrated official organ of the World Federation of Hungarians, addressing its message to persons of Hungarian extraction.

2119. Magyar sajtó (The Hungarian press). 1939-1944, 1951– Budapest, Országos Magyar Sajtókamara. Monthly.

Journal of the National Chamber of the Hungarian Press containing articles, news items, book reviews and other information in the press, publishing, and journalism in Hungary and abroad.

2120. Magyar Szocialista Munkáspárt. *Központi Bizottság.* Az agitátor kézikönyve. Tények és adatok (Agitator's handbook. Facts and data). 1958– Budapest, Kossuth Könyvkiadó. Illus., charts.

Irregularly issued propaganda for Party workers, compiled by the Department of Agitation and Propaganda of the Central Committee of the Hungarian Socialist (Communist) Workers' Party, and other governmental and cultural propaganda agencies.

2121. Molnár, Edit S. A tömegközlés mikrostruktúrájáról (On the microstructure of mass communication). Magyar filozófiai szemle, v. 9, 1965, no. 1: 101-104.

———, *and* Bálint Surányi. Az adatgyűjtők befolyásoló szerepének vizsgálata közvéleménykutatásban (The influencing role of interviewers in a public opinion survey). Pszichológiai tanulmányok, v. 8, 1965: 71-82.

Two interesting empirical studies on the reliability and operation of public-opinion surveys in Hungary.

2122. Pál, Ottó. Írók és olvasók; író-olvasó találkozók rendezésének módszertana (Writers and readers; how to organize meetings between writers and readers). Budapest, A Tudományos Ismeretterjesztő Társulat Könyvkiadója, 1964. 102 p.

Contains an introductory essay and, on pages 33-102, short biographical articles on numerous contemporary Hungarian writers not listed in recently published Hungarian encyclopedias.

2123. Rádió és televízió újság (Radio and television journal). v. 1– 1956– Budapest, Magyar Rádió és Televízió. Weekly.

Supersedes *Magyar rádió* (1945-1946), issued by Magyar Rádió, Budapest. Title varies: *Rádió-újság* (1956– October 1957). Illustrated journal of the Hungarian radio and television networks. Carries feature articles on current issues of general and professional interest, interviews with prominent personalities of the public life, and weekly programs.

2124. Sajtóalmanach (Press almanac). 1927– Debrecen, F. Csáthy. Annual.

Title varies: *Csonkamagyarország sajtója* (The press of truncated Hungary). Includes articles, biographic essays, and studies on the history, organization, and professional problems of the press in Hungary; contains cumulative listings of publishers, newspapermen, and other writers. Should be supplemented by: *A magyar sajtó évkönyve* (Yearbook of the Hungarian press), 1938-1944, published by Hungária Lloyd Lapkiadó Vállalat, Budapest.

2125. Szántó, Miklós. Egy kisérleti felmérés módszertani tapasztalatai (The methodological experiences gained in a pilot survey). Magyar filozófiai szemle, v. 5, 1961, no. 3: 355-378.

Report on a small-scale public opinion survey in Sztálinváros. Summaries in Russian and English.

2126. Szirmai, István. A kommunista eszmék győzelméért (For the victory of communist ideology). Budapest, Kossuth Könyvkiadó, 1963. 260 p.

Propagandistic treatise explaining the essence of communist doctrine, written by a Politburo member and leading party theoretician.

2127. Tardos, András. Nyugati rádiók a lélektani hadviselés szolgálatában (Western radio stations in the service of psychological warfare). Budapest, M. Rádió és Televízió, 1966. 110 p. (Rádió szakkönyvtár, 8)

Examines the role of Hungarian-language broadcasts from foreign stations and their influence on listeners.

Among public opinion studies conducted by the Free Europe Committee are *Inquiry into Political and Social Attitudes in Hungary of the Free Europe Press* (New York, 1957, 157 p., Technical Report no. 1) and *The Attitudes of Czechoslovak, Hungarian and Polish Respondents Toward Cooperation with the Government* (Munich, Radio Free Europe, Audience Research Department, 1966, 11 p.).

H. PSYCHOLOGY

by Josef Brozek

2128. Adam, G. Interception and Behaviour; an Experimental Study. Translated by R. de Chatel. Translation rev. by H. Slucki. Budapest, Akadémiai Kiadó, 1967. 151 p. Illus. Bibliography: p. 141-149.

A summary of 12 years of experimental work on the interaction between the peripheral (visceral) mechanisms and the central nervous system.

2129. Kardos, Lajos. Grundfragen der Psychologie und die Forschungen Pawlows. Translated from the Hungarian by Sophie and Robert

Boháti. Budapest, Verlag der Ungarischen Akademie der Wissenschaften, 1962. 400 p.

The author, professor of psychology at the Budapest University, reviews Pavlov's concepts and findings on conditioned reflexes and brings out their significance for psychology. Special attention is given to Pavlov's "second signal system," a system of conditioned reflexes to symbols, especially to verbal stimuli.

2130. Magyar pszichológiai szemle (Hungarian review of psychology). v. 1– 1928– Budapest, Akadémiai Kiadó. Quarterly.

Issued since 1960 by the Magyar Tudományos Akadémia Pszichológiai Bizottsága (Committee on Psychology of the Hungarian Academy of Sciences) with Magyar Pszichológiai Tudományos Társaság (Hungarian Society of the Science of Psychology), under the editorship of Professor Gegesi Kiss. Covers all areas of scientific psychology. Summaries in Russian and French.

2131. Pszichológiai tanulmányok (Studies in psychology). 1– 1958– Budapest, Akadémiai Kiadó. Annual.

Issued since 1958 by Magyar Tudományos Akadémia Pszichológiai Bizottsága (Committee on Psychology of the Hungarian Academy of Science). Covers a broad spectrum of psychology research, with emphasis on the applied areas and activities of Hungarian institutions concerned. Provides also a bibliography of recent publications by Hungarian psychologists. The fourth volume (1962, 800 p.) was edited by Professor Gegesi Kiss. Summaries in Russian and English.

37

Intellectual and Cultural Life

A. LANGUAGE

by Albert Tezla

1. Bibliography

2132. Halasz de Beky, I. L., *comp.* Bibliography of Hungarian Dictionaries, 1410-1963. Toronto, University of Toronto Press, 1966. 148 p. Bibliography: p. xi-xiv.

Contains 1,025 entries: 505 language and 520 subject dictionaries. Only the latest editions recorded. English translations of Hungarian titles. Language and subject indexes. For an earlier bibliography of dictionaries and of Hungarian grammars, *see*:

Sági, István, *comp.* A magyar szótárak és nyelvtanok könyvészete (Bibliography of Hungarian dictionaries and grammars). *In*: Magyar

Könyvszemle, v. 28, 1920-1921: 96-116; and v. 29, 1922: 72-156. A chronological catalogue of 666 Hungarian dictionaries and grammars. Also books on Hungarian orthography and handbooks on Hungarian style and philology. Also published separately: Budapest, 1922, 105 p.

2133. Hídvégi, Andrea P., *and* László Papp, *comps.* Magyar nyelvjárási tanulmányaink 1945-től 1958-ig (Our studies on Hungarian dialectology from 1945 to 1958). Magyar Nyelv, v. 55, 1959: 288-302, 434-441, 551-559; Supplement, v. 57, 1961: 386.

A nearly exhaustive survey of articles and monographs on all aspects of Hungarian dialectology for the period. Critical comments and often extensive descriptions of content. An effort is made to indicate the strengths and weaknesses in the various fields. A bibliography for an earlier period is provided by:

Benkő, Loránd, *and* Lajos Lőrincze, *comps.* Magyar nyelvjárási bibliográfia, 1817-1949 (Hungarian dialect bibliography, 1817-1949). Budapest, Akadémiai Könyvkiadó, Vállalat, 1951. 259 p. A selective enumerative bibliography of articles and monographs on Hungarian dialects. Organized alphabetically by counties with the section for each divided into general works, regions, and localities. Name index.

2134. Magyar Tudományos Akadémia. A magyarországi nyelvtudomány bibliográfiája. Bibliographie linguistique de la Hongrie. 1961– Budapest, Magyar Tudományos Akadémia Nyelvtudományi Intézete, 1963– (A Nyelvtudományi Intézet közleményei; új folyam, I)

A series reporting on linguistic works published in Hungary during the year, including those on the Hungarian language. The second and third issues, for the years 1962 and 1963 respectively, were published in 1965. For coverage of an earlier period, *see*:

Nyelvészeti munkák bibliográfiája (Bibliography of linguistic works). Budapest, Magyar Tudományos Akadémia Nyelvtudományi Intézete, 1951-1954. 3 fascicles. A record of scholarly articles and monographs published on Hungarian linguistics and language during the years 1950-1952.

2135. Sebestyén, Árpád, *comp.* Nyelvművelő irodalmunk 1945-től 1960-ig (Our puristic literature from 1945 to 1960). Magyar Nyelv, v. 57, 1961: 108-119, 250-257.

A record of articles and monographs on the cultivation of the Hungarian language and its correct use, published in Hungary from 1945 to 1960.

2136. Szabó, Dénes. A magyar nyelvemlékek (Hungarian linguistic monuments). 2d enl. ed. Budapest, Tankönyvkiadó, 1959. 80 p. Facsims., bibliographies.

A handbook providing a detailed description, a record of available editions, and a bibliography for each entry. Closes with a discussion of the most important editions and the dictionaries most helpful with the text. A university handbook.

2137. Tompa, József, *comp.* Az 1945-től 1960-ig megjelent magyar leíró nyelvtani közlemények (Publications on Hungarian descriptive grammar appearing from 1945 to 1960). Magyar Nyelv, v. 58, 1962: 115-125, 243-255, 387-395.

A detailed and critical survey of articles and monographs on all aspects of Hungarian descriptive grammar published from 1945 to 1960. In the manner of the Hídvégi and Papp survey of dialectology.

2. Periodicals

2138. Magyar Nyelv (Hungarian language). v. 1– 1905– Budapest. Quarterly.

Its articles report the most important findings on the Hungarian language by members of the Society of Hungarian Linguistics. Contains historical studies and treatises on grammar, phonetics, morphology, methodology, etymology, dialects, orthography, and correct usage. Since 1954 has contained a critical survey of language studies classified by subjects. *See* entry no. 2174 for the Hellebrant bibliography. Two indexes, both compiled by Jenő Juhász, have been published. The first is *A Magyar Nyelv I-XXV. évfolyamának mutatója* (Index to volumes 1-25 of *Magyar Nyelv)* (Budapest, Magyar Nyelvtudományi Társaság, 1931, 347 p.). It contains name, subject, word, and dialect indexes. The second is *A Magyar Nyelv mutatója a XXVI-L. kötetéhez* (Index to volumes 26-50 of *Magyar Nyelv)* (Budapest, Akadémiai Kiadó, 1957, 480 p.). It contains a table of contents and subject and word indexes.

2139. Magyar Nyelvjárások (Hungarian dialects). v. 1– 1951– Debrecen. Annual.

Scholarly articles on all aspects of Hungarian dialectology. Also contains studies on neighboring countries. English, French, German, or Russian summaries in its later numbers. Superseded *Magyar Népnyelv* (Hungarian folk speech), published annually during 1939-1949 in Debrecen and Kolozsvár, the early numbers containing summaries in German.

2140. Magyar Nyelvőr (Hungarian purist). v. 1– 1872– Budapest. Monthly.

Its purpose is to advance the development of the Hungarian language and the correctness of its use. Also scholarly articles on problems in Hungarian linguistics, reviews, and reports on the resolutions of the Academy of Sciences. Suspended 1941-1945. Published at present by the Linguistic Committee of the Academy of Sciences. A published index: *Nyelvőrkalauz; tartalomjegyzék, szó- és tárgymutató a Magyar Nyelvőr 1-69. kötetéhez* (Index to *Magyar Nyelvőr*; table of contents, word, and subject index in volumes 1-69 of *Magyar Nyelvőr)* (Budapest, Magyar Nyelvőr és Országos Néptanulmányi társaság, 1898-1941, 3 v.). It omits materials on dialects.

2141. Magyarosan (In true Hungarian style). v.1-17; 1932-1948. Budapest. Frequency varies.

Aimed exclusively at the cultivation of the Hungarian language through articles on correct usage. Reviews and announcements of publications.

2142. Nyelvtudományi Közlemények (Linguistic studies). v. 1– 1862– Budapest. Quarterly.

Mainly scholarly studies on historical and Finno-Ugrian comparative philology but also frequent articles on the Hungarian language and reviews. Suspended 1944-1947. Published by the Society of Hungarian Linguistics and the Academy of Sciences. Index to the first 25 volumes in volume 25. A separate index, compiled by Jenő Juhász, is *Mutató a Nyelvtudományi Közlemények 1-50. kötetéhez* (Index to volumes 1-50 of *Nyelvtudományi Közlemények*) (Budapest, Akadémiai Kiadó, 1950, 670 p.). In three parts: articles by name of contributors, subject index, and word index arranged by Uralic and Altaic languages and by individual languages.

Acta Linguistica. 1951– Budapest, Akadémiai Kiadó. 4 issues a year. "Papers on the subjects of Finno-Ugrian (including Hungarian), Slavonic, Germanic, Oriental, and Romance linguistics as well as general linguistics," in English, French, German, and Russian.

Computational Linguistics. v. 1– 1963– Budapest, Akadémiai Kiadó. 4 numbers a year. Illus. Issued by the Computing Centre of the Hungarian Academy of Sciences.

3. General description and grammar

2143. Balassa, József. A magyar nyelv könyve; a magyar nyelv múltja és jelene; helyes magyarság (Book of the Hungarian language; the past and present of the Hungarian language; correct Hungarian). Budapest, Dante, 1943. 469 p.

The structure and proper use of the language. The present-day language linked with its past to show the forces that affected its historical development. For the educated reader. Word and subject index. Russian translation published in 1951.

2144. Bárczi, Géza. A magyar nyelv életrajza (Biography of the Hungarian language). Budapest, Gondolat, 1963. 462 p. Facsims., port. Bibliography: p. 389-402.

A very authoritative and highly readable account of the entire history of the language. Shows the links between the language and the condition of the people during various periods. Facsimiles from important codexes. Word and name index.

2145. Bárczi, Géza, Loránd Benkő, *and* Jolán Berrár. A magyar nyelv története (History of the Hungarian language). Budapest, Tankönyvkiadó, 1967. 599 p.

A comprehensive and systematic history of the Hungarian language from the earliest days to the mid-twentieth century. For university students. Brief bibliographies at the ends of sections.

2146. Berrár, Jolán. Magyar történeti mondattan (Hungarian historical syntax). Budapest, Tankönyvkiadó, 1957. 191 p. Bibliographies.

A university textbook examining the flow and mode of changes in the Hungarian sentence and explaining the causes of the changes as today's sentences developed from old forms.

Zsilka, János. The System of Hungarian Sentence Patterns. Bloomington, Indiana University, 1967. 167 p. Illus. (Indiana University Publications. Uralic and Altaic Series, v. 67) Translation of *A magyar mondatformák rendszere és az esetrendszer.*

2147. Hall, Robert A., Jr. Hungarian Grammar. Baltimore, Linguistic Society of America, 1944. 91 p. Bibliography: p. 91. (Linguistic Society of America. Language Monograph no. 21)

Still the only such work seeking to meet the need for a descriptive, learned grammar in English. A revision of his first grammar, with the analysis now based on phonemes, *An Analytical Grammar of the Hungarian Language* (Baltimore, Linguistic Society of America, 1938, 113 p.; bibliography: p. 112-113; Linguistic Society of America, Language Monograph no. 18).

For up-to-date teaching aids *see* the following publications, the first two of which were sponsored by the U.S. Foreign Service Institute.

Koski, August A., *and* Ilona Mihályfy. Hungarian Basic Course, Units 1-24. Washington, D.C., U.S. Govt. Printing Office, 1963-1964. 2 v. Illus., map.

Mihályfy, Ilona, *and* August A. Koski. Hungarian Graded Reader. Washington, D.C., U.S. Govt. Printing Office, 1968. 592 p. Illus.

Bánhídi, Zoltán, *and others.* Learn Hungarian. Budapest, Tankönyvkiadó, 1965. 530 p. Illus.

2148. Lotz, János. Das ungarische Sprachsystem. Stockholm, Ungarisches Institut, 1939. 295 p.

Designed to provide a basic understanding of the Hungarian language for foreigners. Describes the contemporary literary language, and remains one of the clearest and most informative works on its characteristics and structure. Rich apparatus.

2149. Simonyi, Zsigmond (Siegmund). Die ungarische Sprache; Geschichte und Charakteristik. Strassburg, Karl J. Trübner, 1907. 443 p. Front., bibliographies.

A sound history and characterization of the structure of the language with very valuable apparatus. Chapter bibliographies include Hungarian titles translated into German, brief annotations, and frequent critical comments. A revision of his *A magyar nyelv* (The Hungarian language) (2d ed., Budapest, Athenaeum, 1905, 485 p.).

2150. Simonyi, Zsigmond. Tüzetes magyar nyelvtan, történeti alapon;

első kötet, magyar hangtan és alaktan (Complete Hungarian grammar, on a historical basis. Volume 1: Hungarian phonology and morphology). Prepared with the assistance of József Balassa. Budapest, Magyar Tudományos Akadémia, 1895. 734 p.

This historical treatment is out of date in methodology, but its rich materials are still very useful. Word index. The second volume was never published.

2151. Tolnai, Vilmos. A nyelvújítás; a nyelvújítás elmélete és története (The language reform; the theory and history of [Hungarian] language reform). Budapest, Magyar Tudományos Akadémia, 1929. 240 p. Bibliographical footnotes. (A Magyar nyelvtudomány kézikönyve, 2. köt., 12. füzet)

A comprehensive study of language reform in Hungary devoting most of its attention to the critical period from around the middle of the 18th century to the end of the 19th. Bibliographies at the ends of sections.

2152. Tompa, József, *ed.* A mai magyar nyelv rendszere; leíró nyelvtan (The system of today's Hungarian language; descriptive grammar). Budapest, Akadémiai Kiadó, 1961-1962. 2 v. Illus.

The most thorough exploration of the characteristics of present-day Hungarian. Bibliographies of the most important studies at the ends of chapters. Volume 1 treats phonetics and morphology; volume 2, syntax. Subject index in volume 2. See also *Ungarische Grammatik* by the same author (Budapest, Akadémiai Kiadó, 1968, 426 p.).

4. Pronunciation and Orthography

2153. Bárczi, Géza. Magyar hangtörténet (Hungarian phonological developments). 2d enl. ed. Budapest, Tankönyvkiadó, 1958. 196 p.

Phonological developments in the Hungarian language to the end of the Middle Ages. Thoroughly documented analyses of the changes. A university textbook. Bibliographies at the ends of sections. Word index. Another important work on phonology:

Papp, István. Leíró magyar hangtan (Descriptive Hungarian phonology). Budapest, Tankönyvkiadó, 1966. 191 p. Illus. Bibliography: p. 187-190.

2154. Kniezsa, István. Helyesírásunk története a könyvnyomtatás koráig (History of our orthography to the age of printing). Budapest, Akadémiai Kiadó, 1952. 204 p. (Nyelvészeti tanulmányok II)

The first methodical effort to deal with the history of Hungarian orthography. Covers the 11th to the 15th centuries, and uses the best editions of chancellery documents, monuments, and codexes. Indexes: sound values of the signs; transcriptions of sounds; codexes; and name and subject. Bibliographical footnotes.

2155. Kniezsa, István. A magyar helyesírás története (History of Hungarian orthography). 2d rev. ed. Budapest, Tankönyvkiadó, 1959. 35 p.

A clear discussion of the changes in Hungarian orthography from the Middle Ages to the present. For university students. Bibliographies at the ends of sections.

2156. Magyar Tudományos Akadémia, *Budapest.* A magyar helyesírás szabályai (Rules of Hungarian orthography). 10th rev. and enl. ed., 6th imp. Budapest, Akadémiai Kiadó, 1966. 272 p.

This standard guide to present-day Hungarian orthography consists of an explanation of the basic spelling rules, a subject index to the dictionary, and the dictionary, in which the word entries are generally followed by the forms causing the greatest difficulty.

5. Dictionaries and Studies of Vocabulary

2157. Bárczi, Géza. A magyar szókincs eredete (Origins of the Hungarian vocabulary). 2d enl. ed. Budapest, Tankönyvkiadó, 1958. 187 p.

A very detailed discussion of the origins of the vocabulary: the native vocabulary and that derived from other languages. Also treats personal and geographic names. A university textbook. Bibliographies at the ends of sections. Word index.

2158. Magyar nyelvtörténeti-etimológiai szótár (Historical and etymological dictionary of the Hungarian language). Chief editor, Loránd Benkő. Editors, Lajos Kiss and László Papp. v. 1– Budapest, Akadémiai Kiadó, 1967–

The best and most extensive etymological dictionary of the Hungarian language. When completed, it will contain about 12,000 entries chosen from everyday spoken language including words considered to be foreign but common in international and foreign usage as well as the most important dialect words and specimens of obsolete words. Omits proper nouns, which will be reported in a separate publication. Each main entry followed by its first occurrence with its date and original spelling, the first case of common usage in a quotation, its explanation, and its main bibliographical data. Introduction also in German. Volume 1, A-Gy. Previous etymological dictionaries include:

Bárczi, Géza. Magyar szófejtő szótár (Hungarian etymological dictionary). Budapest, Királyi Magyar Egyetemi Nyomda, 1941. 348 p. Bibliography: p. xix-xxiii. The only comprehensive Hungarian etymological dictionary so far. Very concise treatment of about 6,000 words, with useful bibliographies under each word entry. Omits obsolete, dialect or rare words, and, for the most part, lay words derived from foreign languages.

Budenz, József. A Comparative Dictionary of the Finno-Ugric Elements in the Hungarian Vocabulary. Bloomington, Indiana University, 1966. 986 p. (Indiana University Publications. Uralic and Altaic Series, v. 78) A reprint edition of the original published between 1873 and 1881. Text in Hungarian, with English-language introduction by Gyula Décsy.

Gombocz, Zoltán. Magyar etymologiai szótár (Hungarian etymological dictionary). Budapest, Magyar Tudományos Akadémia, 1914-1944. 2 v. By far the largest work of its kind, with very useful documentation and entries under each word-entry. Volume one, A-Érdem, runs to 1600 columns; volume two was left uncompleted with "geburnus." János Melich, coauthor of the work, directed its continuation after Gombocz's death in 1935.

2159. A magyar nyelv értelmező szótára (Explanatory dictionary of the Hungarian language). Chief editors, Géza Bárczi and László Országh. Budapest, Akadémiai Kiadó, 1959-1962. 7 v. Tables.

The best and most authoritative dictionary of the Hungarian language. Definitions of some 60,000 learned and everyday words. Entries also concerned with collocations of words, current usage, idiomatic expressions, synonyms, and phrases. Meanings presented in well-chosen examples. Words formed from the root at the end of entry.

2160. Póra, Ferenc. A magyar rokonértelmű szók és szólások kézikönyve (Handbook of Hungarian synonymous words and expressions). Budapest, Athenaeum, 1907. 523 p.

A mere enumeration, but the only collection of Hungarian synonyms.

2161. Szarvas, Gábor, *ed.* Magyar nyelvtörténeti szótár (Historical dictionary of the Hungarian language). Budapest, Viktor Hornyánszky, 1890-1893. 3 v.

A fully documented historical dictionary from the earliest sources to about 1780. Word equivalents also in German and Latin. Index of 290 pages in volume 3.

2162. Szily, Kálmán. A magyar nyelvújítás szótára a kedveltebb képzők és képzésmódok jegyzékével (Dictionary of Hungarian neologisms with a list of the most popular endings and methods of formation). Budapest, Viktor Hornyánszky, 1902-1908. 1 v. in 2.

The development of neologisms from the last quarter of the 18th century through the first half of the 19th. Word index.

2163. Szinnyei, József, *ed.* Magyar tájszótár (Hungarian dialect dictionary). Budapest, Viktor Hornyánszky, 1893-1901. 2 v.

The most comprehensive dictionary of Hungarian dialect words. Contains more than 80,000 entries. The main entry is given in its standard form and followed by dialect forms in alphabetical order with the place of use and the source from which the word was taken.

6. Stylistics and Versification

2164. Fábián, Pál, István Szathmári, *and* Ferenc Terestyéni. A magyar stilisztika vázlata (Outline of Hungarian stylistics). Budapest, Tankönyvkiadó, 1958. 297 p.

A comprehensive introduction to Hungarian stylistics: style and stylistics, principles of vocabulary and phraseology, word meanings, emotional elements in words, principles and categories of morphology, and sentence categories and forms. A university textbook. Bibliographies at the ends of sections.

2165. A magyar stilisztika útja (The path of Hungarian stylistics). Edited, the lexicon written, and the bibliography compiled by István Szathmári. Budapest, Gondolat, 1961. 699 p. Bibliographies.

Contains works by János Sylvester, István Geleji Katona, and Ferenc Verseghy, and several studies on Hungarian style by Endre Kulcsár, Gyula Kulcsár, and Aladár Zlinszky, with notes to the texts. Very valuable materials in the appendixes: an extensive lexicon of stylistic terms, a bibliography of articles and studies in Hungarian on concepts of stylistics, and a bibliography of articles and studies dealing with the style of Hungarian authors.

2166. Vargyas, Lajos. A magyar vers ritmusa (Rhythms of Hungarian verse). Budapest, Akadémiai Kiadó, 1952. 263 p. Bibliography: p. 255-258.

The application of phonetics, the relations between language and rhythms, and the connections between the rhythms of texts and melodies in folk songs to the verse rhythms in the major periods of Hungarian poetry.

Rákos, Petr. Rhythm and Metre in Hungarian Verse. Praha, Universita Karlova, 1966. 102 p. Illus. (Acta Universitatis Carolinae. Philologica. Monographia, 11, 1966) Bibliography: p. 99-102.

7. Dialectology

2167. Balassa, József. A magyar nyelvjárások osztályozása és jellemzése; melléklet: a magyar nyelvjárások térképe (Classification and characterization of Hungarian dialects; supplement: Map of Hungarian dialects). Budapest, Magyar Tudományos Akadémia, 1891. 150 p. Fold. col. map.

Remains an authoritative classification and characterization of Hungarian dialects. Useful map.

2168. Horger, Antal. A magyar nyelvjárások (Hungarian dialects). Budapest, Kókai, 1934. 172 p. Map, bibliographical footnotes.

Descriptions of Hungarian dialects and their subregions.

2169. Kálmán, Béla. Nyelvjárásaink (Our dialects). Budapest, Tankönyvkiadó, 1966. 149 p.

A concise study for the use of university students. Brief bibliographies at ends of sections. Fourteen maps.

A magyar nyelvjárások atlasza (Atlas of the Hungarian dialects). Collected by Benkő Loránd and others. Budapest, Akadémiai Kiadó,

1968– Maps, notes, bibliographies. Sponsored by the Institute of Linguistics of the Hungarian Academy of Sciences.

2170. Laziczius, Gyula. A magyar nyelvjárások (Hungarian dialects). Budapest, Magyar Tudományos Akadémia, 1936. 58 p. (A magyar nyelvtudomány kézikönyve, 1. köt., 2 füzet)

The first structural systematization of Hungarian dialects. Characterizations of Hungarian studies on the subject and of individual dialects, and division of the dialects into classes.

B. LITERATURE

by Albert Tezla

No translations of belles-lettres are listed. Two sources may be used for such information. The first was compiled by Pál Gulyás: *Magyar szépirodalom idegen nyelven a Magyar Nemzeti Múzeum könyvtárában* (Hungarian literature in foreign languages in the Library of the Hungarian National Museum) (Budapest, Magyar Nemzeti Múzeum Könyvtára, 1915-1919, 2 v.). The title of the second part of this compilation is: *Magyar szépirodalom idegen nyelven a Magyar Nemzeti Múzeum naptárgyűjteményében* (Hungarian literature in foreign languages in the almanac collection of the Hungarian National Museum). The second bibliography is more recent and was compiled by Tibor Demeter: *Magyar szépirodalom idegen nyelven* (Hungarian literature in foreign languages) (Budapest, Demeter Tibor, 1957-1958, 11 v.). This mimeographed compilation is not widely available. The University of Minnesota Library, Minneapolis, owns a copy and will reply to inquiries about its contents.

1. Reference Works

2171. Benedek, Marcell, *ed.* Magyar irodalmi lexikon (Hungarian literary lexicon). Budapest, Akadémiai Kiadó, 1963-1965. 3 v. Illus., facsims., ports.

Major source for information about authors whose reputations developed after the First World War. In addition to a record of the published writings and a selected bibliography for each author, provides information about the languages into which his works have been translated. The articles reflect the Marxist-Leninist viewpoint prevailing in present-day Hungary. The first volume is marred by omissions and errors of fact. A supplement is under preparation.

2172. Gulyás, Pál. Magyar írói álnév lexikon; a magyarországi írók álnevei és egyéb jegyei. Függelék: Néhány száz névtelen munka jegyzéke. Lexicon pseudonymorum hungaricum; pseudonyma et alia signa scriptorum Regni Hungariae. Appendix: Elenchus aliquot centum operum anonymorum. Budapest, Akadémiai Kiadó, 1956. 706 p.

See also entry no. 1724.

Selections on pseudonyms with Greek letters, number pseudonyms, and various other kinds of signatures. The appendix provides the names of authors or translators of anonymous works and translations. Name index.

2173. Gulyás, Pál. Magyar írók élete és munkái (The lives and works of Hungarian writers). New series. Budapest, Magyar Könyvtárosok és Levéltárosok Egyesülete, 1939-1944. 6 v. Bibliographies.

A continuation and enlargement of the Szinnyei entry. Equally important, though not as readable. Updates the lives and bibliographies of authors in the Szinnyei work. Reports on 2,939 writers, 480 of whom are also covered by Szinnyei. Most of the writers are from the 19th and 20th centuries, with 393 from the 20th. Never completed, ending with the entry for László Dzurányi, but Gulyás continued to collect data until his death in 1963. This unpublished material is in the National Széchényi Library, Budapest.

2174. Hellebrant, Árpád, *comp.* A magyar philológiai irodalom, 1855-1918. években (Hungarian philological literature in the years 1885-1918). *In*: Egyetemes Philologiai Közlöny (Journal of universal philology), v. 10-43, 1886-1919.

A current bibliography of monographs, articles, and reviews on philological subjects, including Hungarian language, literature, and folklore published in Hungary.

2175. Az Irodalomtörténet folyóiratszemléje (*Irodalomtörténet* review of periodicals). *In: Irodalomtörténet* (Literary history), v. 1-36, 1912-1947.

A current bibliography of articles on Hungarian literary history appearing in the most important Hungarian learned journals and newspapers from 1912 to 1947. Brief annotations of the entries.

2176. Irodalomtörténeti repertórium (Repertorium of literary history). *In*: Irodalomtörténeti Közlemények (Communications in literary history), v. 28-41, 1918-1931.

A current bibliography of monographs, editions of belles-lettres, and articles on Hungarian literature serving as a continuation of the Hellebrant bibliography (entry no. 2174). In two parts: general studies and individual authors. Compilers: Árpád Hellebrant, 1918-1924; Alice Goriupp, 1925-1927; Sándor Kozocsa, 1927-1931.

2177. Kozocsa, Sándor, *comp.* Az 1932-1944. év (magyar) irodalomtörténeti munkássága (Publications in [Hungarian] literary history for the years 1932-1944). Budapest, Pallas, 1933-1940; Országos Széchényi Könyvtár Bibliográfiai Osztálya, 1941-1946. 13 fascicles.

An annual bibliography of monographs, author editions, articles, and reviews in two sections: general studies and individual authors. Continued as:

Kozocsa, Sándor, *comp.* A magyar irodalom bibliográfiája, 1945– (Bibliography of Hungarian literature, 1945). Budapest, Közoktatasügyi Kiadóvállalat, 1950– As of 1965, volumes had been published covering the period to 1958.

2178. Pintér Jenő magyar irodalomtörténete; tudományos rendszerezés (Jenő Pintér's Hungarian literary history; a systematic arrangement). Budapest, Stephaneum, 1930-1941. 8 v.

See also entry no. 2203.

A literary history with a vast bibliographical apparatus which can also serve as a bibliography for Hungarian literature to the publication date of each volume until a retrospective bibliography is published. Its nearly exhaustive record of author editions and monographs and articles on each of the authors, periods, and literary movements makes it an indispensable research aid.

2179. Szinnyei, József, *comp.* Irodalomtörténeti repertórium (Repertorium of literary history). *In*: Figyelő (Observer), v. 1-26, 1876-1889.

The first and still an important bibliography of monographs, articles, and reviews concerned with Hungarian literary history published from 1875 to 1889.

2180. Szinnyei, József. Magyar írók élete és munkái (The lives and works of Hungarian writers). Budapest, Hornyánszky, 1891-1914. 14 v.

See also entry no. 1726.

A remarkably accurate and readable bio-bibliography of nearly 30,000 Hungarian literary and learned writers. The sketches report on the major phases of each writer's life. The bibliographies are an invaluable research aid. They provide a chronological record of each author's writings and of monographs and articles dealing with his life and works. For a German biographical dictionary of Hungarians who have contributed to learning, *see*:

Krücken, Oszkár, *and* Imre Parlagi. Das geistige Ungarn; biographisches Lexikon. Wien und Leipzig, Wilhelm Braumüller, 1918. 2 v.

2181. Tezla, Albert. An Introductory Bibliography to the Study of Hungarian Literature. Cambridge, Harvard University Press, 1964. 290 p.

A classified bibliography of 1,295 numbered items with annotations, evaluations of author editions, and locations of titles in a limited number of American and European libraries. Its usefulness lies more in the coverage of reference works, general works on literary history and fields related to its study, and surveys and studies of literary periods and types than in the reportage of a few biographies and selected editions for a limited number of authors.

Tezla's *Hungarian Authors: a Bibliographical Handbook* will be published in 1970 by Harvard University Press. Focused almost exclusively on writers of belles-lettres, it provides data on 162 authors from all periods of the literature under the following headings: biographical sketch, first editions, later editions, bibliography, biography, and criticism.

2182. Ványi, Ferenc, *ed.* Magyar irodalmi lexikon (Hungarian literary lexicon). Budapest, Studium, 1926. 880 p.

A reliable handbook for data on the lives and works of Hungarian authors. Critical comments on their writings, a record of their most important works, and a selective bibliography of studies about their lives and writings.

A lexicon of world literature containing very authoritative articles on Hungarian language, literature, and authors is *Irodalmi lexikon* (Literary lexicon), compiled by Marcell Benedek (Budapest, Győző Andor, 1926, 1224 p.).

2. Periodicals

2183. Acta Litteraria Academiae Scientiarum Hungaricae. 1957– Budapest, Akadémiai Kiadó. Annual.

An excellent source for studies on all aspects of literature in English, French, German, and Russian.

2184. Budapesti Szemle (Budapest review). 1857-1943. Budapest, Magyar Tudományos Akadémia. Frequency varies.

See also entry no. 1703.

Scholarly articles on learned subjects, including literary history. Important to literary research because the major literary historians, critics, and authors were among its contributors throughout its history, especially from 1873 to 1909, when it was edited by Pál Gyulai, the noted writer and influential critic. Publication was suspended from 1869 to January 1873. An index for the years 1873-1893 appeared in volume 33, 1883: 1-22, and volume 76, 1893: 473-504.

2185. Csillag (Star). 1947-1956. Budapest. Monthly. Illus., ports.

A literary journal fostering the development of socialistic literature in keeping with the views of the Hungarian Communist Party. Articles on all aspects of cultural life. Original literary works and reviews. Became an organ of the Hungarian Writers' Federation in August 1950.

2186. Egyetemes Philologiai Közlöny (Journal of universal philology). 1877-1948. Budapest. Quarterly.

Important scholarly articles on Hungarian language and literature as well as Greek, Latin, Teutonic, Classical, and Oriental philology. Good source for studies on the relations between Hungarian literature and foreign literatures. Reviews. An occasional article in English, French, German, or Italian. See entry no. 2174 for its current bibliography. A valuable index, compiled by János Pruzsinszky: *Az Egyetemes Philologiai Közlöny I-XX. kötetének név- és tárgymutatója; a 20 kötet teljes tartalomjegyzékével* (Name and subject index to volumes 1-20 of *Egyetemes Philologiai Közlöny*; with the complete table of contents for the 20 volumes) (Budapest, Budapesti Philologiai Társaság, 1898, 346 p.).

Superseded by *Filológiai Közlöny* (Philological journal) (March 1955– Budapest, Akadémiai Kiadó, quarterly). It is concerned mainly with world literature, Hungarian philological questions, and the relations between Hungarian and world literature. Contains summaries of articles in English, French, German, or Russian, and reports regularly on the activities of philological circles in Hungary.

2187. Figyelő (Observer). 1876-1889. Pest. Monthly.

The first journal of Hungarian literary history. Remains a very important source because its contributors were among the most important scholars of the time. *See* entry no. 2179 for its current bibliography.

2188. Irodalomtörténet (Literary history). 1912-1962. Budapest, Magyar Irodalomtörténeti Társaság. Monthly.

Scholarly and critical studies of Hungarian literature in the latter part of the 19th century and in the 20th century. Encouraged the publication of research by young scholars. Reviews. After 1949 it published articles with a Marxist viewpoint, when György Lukács became president of the Society of Hungarian Literary History, its publisher. Summaries in English, French, German, or Russian during its last years. *See* entry no. 2176 for its annotated current bibliography.

Superseded by *Kritika* (Criticism) (September 1963– Budapest, monthly). It originally contained articles on sociology and music but is now concerned with Hungarian literature and theater and publishes original literary works. Published by the Institute of Literary History, the Society of Hungarian Literary History, and the Hungarian Writers' Federation.

2189. Irodalomtörténeti Közlemények (Studies in literary history). 1891– Budapest. Quarterly.

Its major interest is in older Hungarian literature, especially unknown works, but it gives attention to the newer literature in recent numbers. An excellent source for previously unpublished manuscripts and letters. Reviews. Since 1958 the only Hungarian journal reviewing all scholarly monographs on Hungarian literary history. A current bibliography of publications in Hungarian literary history, compiled by Sándor V. Kovács, has appeared since 1962. Summaries and titles in French, German, and Russian, as well as summaries in English, in recent years. Publication suspended 1946-1947, 1948 (only one number), and 1949-1952. *See* entry no. 2174 for the Hellebrant bibliography.

2190. Kortárs (Contemporary). 1957– Budapest. Monthly. Illus.

Original Hungarian literary works and studies and criticisms of living Hungarian poets and writers of prose fiction. Very little attention to earlier authors. Publishes the works of those authors, scholars, and critics who view literature as a way of building Hungarian socialism.

2191. Magyar Tudományos Akadémia Nyelv- és Irodalomtudományi Osztályának Közleményei (Communications of the section on language and literary scholarship of the Hungarian Academy of Sciences). 1951– Budapest. Quarterly.

Publishes the best lectures and discussions of the section as well as the research of its members dealing with questions of Hungarian and foreign languages and literatures. Occasional articles in English, French, or German.

2192. Nyugat (West). 1908-1941. Budapest. Semimonthly (monthly, 1935-1941). Illus.

The most important literary and critical periodical seeking to develop new trends in 20th century Hungarian literature, especially the cultivation of the impressionistic-symbolist forms of modern West European literature. The most significant writers and scholars of the time were among its contributors. Original literary works, translations, and reviews as well as articles. Its editorial policy was continued by its successor: *Magyar Csillag* (Hungarian star) (1941-1944, Budapest, monthly). Important predecessors:

A Hét (The week). 1890-1924. Budapest.
Magyar Géniusz (Hungarian spirit). 1892-1903. Budapest.
Szerda (Wednesday). 1906-1907. Budapest.
Figyelő (Observer). January 1905-December 1905. Budapest.

Indexes to *Nyugat*, *Magyar Csillag*, *Magyar Géniusz*, *Szerda*, and *Figyelő* were compiled by Ferenc Galambos in his *Nyugat repertórium* (Budapest, Magyar Tudományos Akadémia Irodalomtörténeti Intézete, 1959, 571 p.).

2193. Új Hang (New voice). 1952-1956. Budapest. Monthly.

A critical journal of contemporary Hungarian and foreign literatures. Important mainly as the organ of the young generation of writers. Original literary works and reviews. Published jointly by the Federation of Working Youths and the Hungarian Writers' Federation.

2194. Új Írás (New writing). 1961– Budapest. Monthly.

Its studies and critiques aim at the consolidation of literary creativity in Hungary. Reports and discussions of important contemporary questions about literature. Excellent source for new belles-lettres. Also concerned with problems in the arts and society.

3. General History and Theory

2195. Benedek, Marcell. A magyar irodalom története (History of Hungarian literature). Budapest, Singer és Wolfner, 1938. 255 p. Illus., ports.

An effort to show the emergence and development of the Hungarian national spirit through an examination of the literature to the end of the 19th century. Also analyzes the literary artistry of the authors. For the general reader.

2196. Beöthy, Zsolt. A magyar nemzeti irodalom történeti ismertetése (Historical survey of Hungarian national literature). 14th ed. Budapest, Athenaeum, 1920-1922. 2 v.

Generations of Hungarians studied their country's literature to 1867 in this work which places emphasis on biography and cultural backgrounds. First published in 1877-1879; last edition appeared in 1928, edited and supplemented by Lajos Kéky. First part of each volume is a history, the second, an anthology. The first volume extends to Károly Kisfaludy; the second, to the era 1820-1867.

2197. Horváth, János. Rendszeres magyar verstan (Systematic Hungarian prosody). Budapest, Akadémiai Kiadó, 1951. 210 p. Bibliography: p. 5-14.

The most authoritative treatment of the elements of Hungarian verse forms, rhythms, and rhymes. Examines the questions from the viewpoint of natural Hungarian rhythms. Analyzes prosodic practices from Gedeon Ráday to Sándor Petőfi and the search for new forms after Petőfi and János Arany to its own time, but considering only those poets who are no longer living.

2198. Klaniczay, Tibor, József Szauder, *and* Miklós Szabolcsi. History of Hungarian Literature. London, Collet's, 1964. 361 p. Ports., bibliographies.

The first survey in English in over 50 years. Most attention is given to 20th century literature. Reflects present-day viewpoints of the literature. Valuable bibliography for each period as well as important collections of texts, author editions, and literary journals, compiled by György Szabó (p. 319-348). Bibliography of selected English translations, compiled by Tibor Demeter (p. 349). Also available in Hungarian, French, and German editions.

2199. Kont, Ignác. Histoire de la littérature hongroise. Paris, Félix Alcan, 1900. 420 p.

An adaptation of several learned histories of the literature from the Middle Ages to 1867. Especially informative about the literature of the 19th century, for which Kont provides biographical sketches, analyses of works, and translations from the best collections of Hungarian poetry. Bibliography of French studies and translations (p. 411-413).

A work in German by the same author is *Geschichte der ungarischen Literatur* (Leipzig, C. F. Amelang, 1906, 272 p.; bibliography: p. 262-265).

2200. A magyar irodalom története (History of Hungarian literature). General editors, István Sőtér, Pál Pándi, and Miklós Szabolcsi. Budapest, Akadémiai Kiadó, 1964-1966. 6 v. Bibliographies.

A Marxist synthesis of the development of the literature prepared under the auspices of the Institute of Literary History, the Academy of Sciences. A substantial recent history, indispensable to an understanding of present-day evaluations of authors from the beginnings to the generation after the Second World War. Its selected bibliographies are an especially valuable source for data on editions and studies published since the Pintér history.

Two volumes of another series also using the Marxist approach: *A magyar irodalom története 1849-ig* (History of Hungarian literature to 1849) (Budapest, Bibliotheca, 1957, 489 p.); *A magyar irodalom története; 1849-1905* (History of Hungarian literature, 1849-1905) (Budapest, Gondolat, 1963, 492 p.). The first was edited by László Bóka and Pál Pándi; the second by István Király, Pál Pándi, and István Sőtér. Both volumes contain bibliographical apparatus. The third volume, dealing with the literature from 1905 to the present, is under preparation.

2201. A magyar írók első kongresszusa (First congress of Hungarian writers). Budapest, Művelt Nép Könyvkiadó, 1951. 310 p.

The reports made during the Congress held April 27-April 30, 1951, dealing with the problem of the means by which Hungarian literature can build socialism. An expansion of the reports published in *Csillag*, v. 5, 1951: 515-601.

2202. Menczer, Béla. A Commentary on Hungarian Literature. Castrop-Rauxel, Amerikai Magyar Kiadó, 1956. 147 p.

Not a scholarly work but informative and useful for its discussion of the literature of each period as a part of European trends and currents.

2203. Pintér Jenő magyar irodalomtörténete; tudományos rendszerezés (Jenő Pintér's Hungarian literary history; a systematic arrangement). Budapest, Stephaneum, 1930-1941. 8 v.

See also entry no. 2178.

Often justifiably criticized for its political conservatism and facile critical commentary, but almost encyclopedic in character, it remains the best source for information about the literature. Also extensive data about all forces related to the development of Hungarian literature. *See* entry no. 2178 for its bibliographical apparatus.

2204. Reich, Emil. Hungarian Literature: an Historical and Critical Survey. London, Jerrold and Sons, 1898. 272 p. Fold. map. Bibliography: p. 257-258.

The main literary movements and authors from the beginnings through most of the 19th century. Uses the comparative method of historical investigation and analysis.

2205. Reményi, Joseph. Hungarian Writers and Literature; Modern Novelists, Critics, and Poets. Edited and with an introduction by August J. Molnar. New Brunswick, N.J., Rutgers University Press, 1964. 512 p. Bibliography: p. 472-489.

This collection of previously published studies will serve as the best survey of the literature in English until a scholarly history is written. Consists of critically sensitive studies of the lives and writings of the most important authors from the 19th century to the Second World War. An overview of the literature is provided by a short survey and another on the decades 1925-1955. Bibliography of basic reference works, studies of Hungarian literary history and criticism, and translations.

Sőtér, István. Aspects et parallélismes de la littérature hongroise. Budapest, Akadémiai Kiadó, 1966. 291 p.

2206. Riedl, Frigyes. A History of Hungarian Literature. London, William Heinemann, 1906; Detroit, Gale Research Co., 1968. 293 p. Bibliography: p. 287.

A survey from the beginnings through the 19th century.

2207. Schwicker, Johann Heinrich. Geschichte der ungarischen Literatur. Leipzig, Wilhelm Friedrich, 1889. 944 p.

Concentrates on important literary figures to the 1880's and gives major attention to poets of more recent times. Stresses the subject matter of the writings and the effect of European trends upon them, the influence the writers exerted upon their time, the reception given to their works, and critical evaluations.

2208. Szerb, Antal. Magyar irodalomtörténet (Hungarian literary history). Introduction by István Sőtér. Budapest, Magvető Könyvkiadó, 1958. 538 p.

Applies the history-of-ideas approach to literature. First published in 1934, it has exerted a strong influence on subsequent literary thought.

2209. Toldy, Ferenc. Geschichte der ungarischen Literatur im Mittelalter. Translated by Moritz Kolbenheyer. Pest, Gusztav Heckenast, 1865. 292 p.

Written by the influential founder of Hungarian literary history. A translation of the third Hungarian edition.

4. Histories and Studies of Separate Periods*

2210. Toldy, Ferenc. A magyar nemzeti irodalom története a legrégibb időktől a jelenkorig rövid előadásban (History of Hungarian national literature from the most ancient times to the present day in a short version). 4th ed. Pest, 1878. 404 p.

Influenced the outlook on the literature to 1867 and the approach to Hungarian literary history for decades. Though intended for high school students, it is written in a scholarly manner by one considered to be the father of Hungarian literary history.

2211. Horváth, János. A magyar irodalmi műveltség kezdetei Szent Istvántól Mohácsig (The beginnings of Hungarian literary culture; from Saint Stephen to Mohács). Budapest, Magyar Szemle Társaság, 1931. 312 p.

* Entries are listed chronologically by era covered.

Develops the thesis that a literature in the Hungarian language emerged from that written in Latin. From King Stephen (997-1038) to the Disaster at Mohács (1526).

2212. Horváth, János. Az irodalmi műveltség megoszlása; magyar humanizmus (The pattern of literary culture; Hungarian humanism). 2d ed. Budapest, Magyar Szemle Társaság, 1944. 318 p.

A study of the expressions of humanism in the literature and of the first experimentations of the Hungarian Reformation.

Continued by his *A reformáció jegyében; a Mohács utáni félszázad magyar irodalomtörténete* (In the spirit of the reformation; 50 years of Hungarian literary history after Mohács) (Budapest, Akadémiai Kiadó, 1953, 544 p.; 2d ed., 1957).

2213. Alszeghy, Zolt. A tizenhetedik század (The 17th century). Budapest, Szent István-Társulat, 1935. 292 p.

A discussion of the literature of the century from a Catholic point of view. Also valuable is his *A XIX. század magyar irodalma* (Hungarian literature of the nineteenth century) (Budapest, Szent István-Társulat, 1923, 285 p.). Both contain fresh and basic views of the literature.

2214. Jones, David M. Five Hungarian Writers. Oxford, Clarendon Press, 1966. 307 p.

Separate studies of Miklós Zrínyi, Kelemen Mikes, Mihály Vörösmarty, József Eötvös, and Sándor Petőfi. Informative and scholarly discussions of their lives and works with English translations of passages substantial enough to place comment about their writings in context.

2215. Horváth, János. A magyar irodalmi népiesség Faluditól Petőfi-ig (Popular trends in Hungarian literature from Faludi to Petőfi). Budapest, Magyar Tudományos Akadémia, 1927. 390 p.

An authoritative and readable discussion of the indebtedness of the literature to folk songs and folk poetry from the latter part of the 18th to the second quarter of the 19th century.

2216. Waldapfel, József. Ötven év Buda és Pest irodalmi életéből, 1780-1830 (Fifty years from the literary life of Buda and Pest, 1780-1830). Budapest, Magyar Tudományos Akadémia, 1935. 368 p.

A study of the forces affecting the development of literary activities in Buda and Pest and leading to the establishment of a center for the creation of a national literature: publishing, printing, newspapers and periodicals, literary and learned societies, theaters, original literary works, etc.

2217. Rónay, György. Petőfi és Ady között; az újabb magyar irodalom életrajza, 1849-1899 (Between Petőfi and Ady; a biography of the newer literature, 1849-1899). Budapest, Magvető Könyvkiadó, 1958. 249 p. Bibliography: p. 245-247.

A critical examination of the development of the literature during an important period of transition. Most attention to poetry.

2218. Komlós, Aladár. Irodalmi ellenzéki mozgalmak a XIX. század második felében (Opposing literary movements in the second half of the 19th century). Budapest, Akadémiai Kiadó, 1956. 115 p. (Irodalomtörténeti füzetek, 7 sz.)

An illuminating exploration of the bases on which literary cliques, periodicals, literary and learned societies, scholars, and authors judged the new developments in the literature of the time.

2219. Várkonyi, Nándor. Az újabb magyar irodalom, 1880-1940 (The newer Hungarian literature, 1880-1940). Budapest, Szukits, 1942. 579 p.

Characterizations of the writers and their contributions to the literature. The discussion of each author concludes with a brief biographical sketch followed by a chronological list of his independently published works and studies of his life and writings.

2220. Schöpflin, Aladár. A magyar irodalom története a XX. században (History of Hungarian literature in the 20th century). Budapest, Károly Grill, 1937. 311 p.

A critical survey beginning with the end of the 19th century and closing with the important writers after the First World War. Very helpful to an understanding of the overlapping and stratification of the various literary currents.

2221. Szabolcsi, Miklós, *and* László Illés, *ed.* Tanulmányok a magyar szocialista irodalom történetéből (Studies from the history of Hungarian socialist literature). Budapest, Akadémiai Kiadó, 1962. 676 p.

Individual studies of the development of a socialist literature. Bibliographies and sketches of the writers.

2222. Sivirsky, Antal. Die ungarische Literatur der Gegenwart. Bern und München, Francke, 1962. 109 p.

Discussion of the literature from 1900 to 1945 by types or authors. Main attention is given to the literary character of the writings. Concluding chapter is concerned with Hungarian literature written in foreign countries. Somewhat cursory.

2223. Gömöri, George. Polish and Hungarian Poetry, 1945-1956. Oxford, Clarendon Press, 1966. 266 p. Bibliographical footnotes.
See also entry no. 3008.

Traces the disenchantment of Hungarian poets of the new generation with their social order by examining their writings. In three stages: 1945-1948, 1948-1953, 1953-1956.

2224. Tóth, Dezső. A felszabadulás utáni magyar irodalom története (History of post-liberation Hungarian literature). Budapest, Magyar Tudományos Akadémia Irodalomtörténeti Intézete, 1963. 146 p.

The only substantial survey of the literature after 1945 published separately to date. Views the developments in four periods: 1945-1948, 1948-1953, 1953-1956, 1956-1963. Characterizes the literature of each period and then discusses the genres. Mimeographed.

5. Anthologies and Chrestomathies

2225. Magyar irodalmi szöveggyűjtemény (Hungarian literary chrestomathy). Edited by József Waldapfel and László Bóka. Budapest, Tankönyvkiadó, 1951-

A scholarly series of period editions. Seven volumes to 1963: the old literature, the Literary Revival, the Reform Period, the Revolution and the War for Freedom, the second half of the 19th century, the *Nyugat* (West), and the time of Endre Ady.

2226. A magyar próza könyve (Book of Hungarian prose). Edited by Gyula Bisztray and Dezső Kerecsényi. Budapest, Magyar Szemle Társaság, 1942-1948. 2 v.

A collection of artistic prose with an introduction and annotated dictionary for each volume. The third volume, which was to contain contemporary prose, was never published.

2227. Magyar versek könyve (Book of Hungarian verses). Edited and with an introduction and annotated dictionary by János Horváth. 2d enl. ed. Budapest, Magyar Szemle Társaság, 1942. 724 p.

Still the best one-volume collection. Selections from the 16th century to the 1930s.

Hét évszázad magyar versei (Hungarian poetry of seven centuries). Compiled by István Király and others. 3d rev. and enl. ed. Budapest, Szépirodalmi Kiadó, 1966. 3 v. With notes and short biographies of the writers included. Previous editions prepared by Tibor Klaniczay.

Hungarian Anthology; a Collection of Poems. Translated by Joseph Grosz and W. Arthur Boggs. Munich, Griff, 1963. 251 p.

Leader, Ninon A. M. Hungarian Classical Ballads and Their Folklore. Cambridge, Engl., Cambridge University Press, 1967. 367 p. Maps. Bibliography: p. 350-352.

6. Editions and Monographs*

2228. Ady, Endre.

Ady Endre összes versei (Endre Ady's complete poems). Edited by Gyula Földessy. Budapest, Szépirodalmi Könyvkiadó, 1955. 2 v. The fullest and best edition of this outstanding and most influential poet of the twentieth century.

* The authors selected are those who, in the judgment of the compiler, stand out in the literature. *See* entry no. 2181 for other important authors. Writings by or relative to the same author are consolidated in one entry in the following sequence: (1) "first choice" edition of collected or selected works; (2) alternate edition of collected or selected works; (3) separate works or monographs about the author such as studies, biographies, dictionaries, bibliographies, etc.

Ady Endre összes prózai művei (Endre Ady's complete prose works). General editor, Gyula Földessy. Budapest, Akadémiai Kiadó, 1955– The first complete and critical edition. Five volumes to 1966: newspaper articles, studies.

Ady Endre válogatott versei (Endre Ady's selected poems). Edited by György Bölöni, László Bóka, and Kálmán Vargha. Budapest, Szépirodalmi Könyvkiadó, 1952. 339 p. Poems in order of composition.

Ady Endre válogatott cikkei és tanulmányai (Endre Ady's selected articles and studies). Edited by Gyula Földessy. Budapest, Szépirodalmi Könyvkiadó, 1954. 503 p.

Ady Endre az irodalomról (Endre Ady on literature). Edited by József Varga and Erzsébet Vezér, with an introductory study by József Varga. Budapest, Magvető, 1961. 450 p. A critical edition with extensive bibliographical notes.

Kovalovszky, Miklós, *ed.* Emlékezések Ady Endréről (Recollections about Endre Ady). Budapest, Akadémiai Kiadó, 1961– Plates, ports., fold. map, facsims., geneal. table. Bibliography: v. 1, p. 628-629. The first volume of recollections by many individuals. An introduction to each section and connecting commentary within sections. Closes with his student days in Zilah. Contains a chronological table of his family history, a genealogical table, and a map of Hungary showing the most important places connected with him in the text.

Bóka, László. Ady Endre élete és művei. v. 1. Ady Endre pályakezdése (Endre Ady's life and works. v. 1. The beginning of Endre Ady's career). Budapest, Akadémiai Kiadó, 1955. 319 p. The first of a two-volume biographical and critical study. Covers the years 1877-1905. A survey of previous scholarship in the introduction. The second volume will contain the index and bibliography to the entire work.

Földessy, Gyula. Ady, az ember és költő (Ady, the man and the poet). Budapest, Exodus, 1943, 192 p. Fourteen previously published studies of his life and writings by an authority.

Hatvany, Lajos. Ady; cikkek, emlékezések, levelek (Ady; articles, recollections, letters). Budapest, Szépirodalmi Könyvkiadó, 1959. 2 v. A defense against his detractors and expositions of his poems.

Révai, József. Ady. 3d ed. Budapest, Szikra, 1952. 129 p. Its emphasis on his revolutionary and political viewpoints, and its examination of the social and political symbolism in his poetry reflect the character of present-day approaches to his writings.

Schöpflin, Aladár. Ady Endre. 2d ed. Budapest, Nyugat, 1945. 188 p. Valuable for its attempt to view Ady's character as a man and poet through his poetry.

Varga, József. Ady Endre; pályakép-vázlat (Endre Ady; a career-outline). Budapest, Magvető, 1966. 633 p. Both a biographical and literary study tracing the attitudes toward Ady and his writings through succeeding generations and critical evaluations. Extensive bibliographical footnotes.

2229. Arany, János.

Arany János összes művei (János Arany's complete works). Edited by Géza Voinovich. Budapest, Akadémiai Kiadó, 1951– The fullest and best critical edition of a Hungarian 19th century narrative poet, critic, and literary historian. Twelve volumes to 1965: lyric and narrative poems, translations of dramas, prose works, official writings as general secretary of the Hungarian Academy of Sciences.

Arany János összes művei (János Arany's complete works). Edited by Géza Voinovich. Budapest, Franklin-Társulat, 1924. 5 v.

Hermann, István. Arany János esztétikája; az Elveszett alkotmánytól a Buda haláláig (János Arany's aesthetics; from *The Lost Constitution* to the *Death of Buda*). Budapest, Kossuth, 1956. 285 p. A Marxist study of his aesthetics, mainly from 1849 to 1863, and its effects on his own creative writings.

Riedl, Frigyes. Arany János. 7th ed. Edited, annotated, and with an introduction by László Balassa. Budapest, Gondolat Kiadó, 1957. 335 p. Valuable for its examination of his writings and their connection with his life, personality, and environment. First published in 1877, and frequently revised. Very useful bibliographical apparatus.

Voinovich, Géza. Arany János életrajza (János Arany's biography). Budapest, Magyar Tudományos Akadémia, 1929-1938. 3 v. The most comprehensive study of his life and works.

2230. Babits, Mihály.

Babits Mihály művei (Mihály Babits's works). Budapest, Európa, 1957-1964. 7 v. The best edition of an important poet, essayist, and translator of the 20th century. Does not contain his translation of Dante's *Divine Comedy*.

Babits Mihály válogatott művei (Mihály Babits's selected works). Selected and with an introduction by Dezső Keresztury. Budapest, Szépirodalmi Könyvkiadó, 1959. 2 v.

Illyés, Gyula, *ed.* Babits emlékkönyv (Babits memorial volume). Budapest, Nyugat, 1941. 311 p. Illus., plates, ports. "Babits-bibliográfia": p. 287-308. A collection of individual studies of his works, thought, artistry, personality, and last days. Edited by a distinguished poet.

Soltész, Katalin J. Babits Mihály költői nyelve (Mihály Babits's poetic language). Budapest, Akadémiai Kiadó, 1965. 387 p. Bibliography: p. 382-384. (Nyelvészeti tanulmányok, 8) An analysis of his language leading to characterizations of his style: phonetics, morphology, syntax, and means of poetic expression. A registry of his poems according to verse forms.

2231. Balassi, Bálint.

Balassa Bálint összes művei (Bálint Balassi's complete works).

Collected by Sándor Eckhardt. Budapest, Akadémiai Kiadó, 1951-1955. 2 v. Port., facsims. The fullest and best critical edition of the first true lyric poet in 16th century Hungary.

Balassa Bálint minden munkái (Bálint Balassi's complete works). Edited and with a biographical introduction and notes by Lajos Dézsi. Budapest, Genius, 1923. 2 v. A reliable edition containing a bibliography of the individual poems and the original sources in which they are found (v. 2, p. 665-779).

Eckhardt, Sándor. Az ismeretlen Balassi Bálint (The unknown Bálint Balassi). Budapest, Magyar Szemle Társaság, 1943. 313 p. Illus. Bibliographical notes: p. 221-304.

A biography based on new primary sources. Additional materials on his life are to be found in a later work by Eckhardt: *Új fejezetek Balassi Bálint viharos életéből* (New chapters from the stormy life of Bálint Balassi) (Budapest, Akadémiai Kiadó, 1957, 104 p.; Magyar Tudományos Akadémia. Irodalomtörténeti füzetek, 10. sz.).

Erdélyi, Pál. Balassi Bálint, 1551 (1554)-1594. Budapest, Magyar Történelmi Társulat, 1899. 251 p. Illus., facsims. A biographical and critical study relating the poet and his works to his time.

2232. Déry, Tibor.

Déry, Tibor. A befejezetlen mondat (The unfinished sentence). Budapest, Szépirodalmi Könyvkiadó, 1963. 3 v. An important novel by a significant contemporary writer of prose fiction.

———. Felelet (Reply). Budapest, Szépirodalmi Könyvkiadó, 1954. 2 v. A novel that created much controversy.

———. A ló meg az öregasszony (The horse and the old woman). Edited by József Füsi and with an introduction by György Lukács. Budapest, Magvető, 1955. 515 p. A selection of his short stories.

———. Útkaparó (Road-mender). Budapest, Magvető Könyvkiadó, 1956. 393 p. A collection of his studies.

———. A kiközösítő (The outlaw). Budapest, Szépirodalmi Könyvkiadó, 1966. 379 p. A historical novel.

2233. Illyés, Gyula.

Illyés Gyula összes versei (Gyula Illyés's complete poems). Budapest, Nyugat és Révai, 1947. 3 v. The poetry of one of the most important contemporary poets. His poems to 1947. No later edition of his collected poems has been published.

Illyés Gyula válogatott versei (Gyula Illyés's selected poems). Budapest, Szépirodalmi Könyvkiadó, 1952. 422 p. Contains some new poems.

Illyés, Gyula. Nem volt elég . . . (It was not enough . . .). Budapest, Szépirodalmi Könyvkiadó, 1962. 691 p. Port. A selection of new poems.

———. Három dráma (Three dramas). Budapest, Szépirodalmi

Könyvkiadó, 1957. 257 p. *Dózsa György* (György Dózsa), *Fáklyaláng* (Torch-flame), and *Ozorai példa* (Ozora example).

———. Ingyen lakoma (Free feast). Budapest, Szépirodalmi Könyvkiadó, 1964. 2 v. Facsim. Studies and confessions from 1927 to 1964.

Gara, László. Az ismeretlen Illyés (The unknown Illyés). Washington, D.C., Occidental Press, 1965. 178 p. Bibliography. The only monograph. A biographical and critical study centering its attention on his artistic career. Contains some previously unpublished poems.

2234. Jókai, Mór.

Jókai Mór összes művei (Mór Jókai's complete works). Edited by Miklós Nagy. v. 1– Budapest, Akadémiai Kiadó, 1962– When completed it will be the fullest and best critical edition of this important 19th century novelist. Thirty-one volumes to 1965.

Jókai Mór összes művei (Mór Jókai's complete works). Budapest, Révai Testvérek, 1896-1906. 100 v. The reliable national edition published on the 50th anniversary of his literary career. Supplemented by *Jókai Mór hátrahagyott művei* (Mór Jókai's works omitted from the national edition) (Budapest, Révai Testvérek, 1912, 9 v.).

Jókai Mór válogatott művei (Mór Jókai's selected works). Budapest, Szépirodalmi Könyvkiadó, 1954-1962. 41 v. A good popular edition with many editors.

Gál, János. Jókai Mór élete és írói jelleme (Mór Jókai's life and literary character). Berlin, Ludwig Voggenreiter, 1925. 303 p. Biographical, but mainly concerned with establishing the characteristics of his writings by types. Contains a list of his translated works.

Mikszáth, Kálmán. Jókai Mór élete és kora (Mór Jókai's life and times). Budapest, Művelt Nép, 1954. 398 p. His life and relations with his time by an important writer of prose fiction. Attention to his writings. Contains a glossary of foreign words appearing in his works. First published in 1907.

Sőtér, István. Jókai Mór. Budapest, Franklin-Társulat, 1941. 173 p. Bibliography: p. 170-173. An important effort to appraise his creativity and to determine the distinctive form of his artistic expression.

Zsigmond, Ferenc. Jókai. Budapest, Magyar Tudományos Akadémia, 1924. 415 p. Bibliography. A penetrating study of Jókai and his works.

2235. József, Attila.

József Attila összes művei (Attila József's complete works). Edited by József Waldapfel and Miklós Szabolcsi. 2d rev. and enl. ed. Budapest, Akadémiai Kiadó, 1955– When completed it will be the best and fullest critical edition of this important and tragic poet of the period between the two World Wars.

József Attila összes versei és műfordításai (Attila József's complete poems and translations). Edited by Miklós Szabolcsi. Budapest, Magyar Helikon, 1963. 973 p.

József Attila válogatott művei (Attila József's selected works). Edited by Miklós Szabolcsi. Budapest, Szépirodalmi Könyvkiadó, 1952. 462 p. Illus.

Forgács, László. József Attila esztétikája; tanulmánygyűjtemény (Attila József's aesthetics; collection of studies). Budapest, Magvető, 1965. 658 p. Takes issue with Marxist and bourgeois interpretations of his poetic art.

Gyertyán, Ervin. Költőnk és kora; József Attila költészete és esztétikája (Our poet and his times; Attila József's poetry and his aesthetics). Budapest, Szépirodalmi Knyvkiadó, 1963. 305 p. An analysis of his poetry, aesthetics, and theories of creativity seeking to determine his place in the vanguard of 20th century revolutionary poetry in Hungary.

József, Jolán. József Attila élete (The life of Attila József). 4th ed. Budapest, Szépirodalmi Könyvkiadó, 1955. 327 p. A biography by his sister, based on recollections.

Németh, Andor. József Attila. Budapest, Cserépfalvi, 1944. 219 p. A biographical and critical study. By one who knew him.

Rousselot, Jean. Attila József (1905-1937). Sa vie, son œuvre avec une suite de poèmes du hongrois par Jean Rousselot d'après les traductions de Ladislas Gara. Paris, Les Nouveaux Cahiers de Jeunesse, 1958. 119 p. Mainly concerned with the characteristics of his poetry and the development of his views of literature and his relation with his times.

Szabolcsi, Miklós, *ed.* József Attila emlékkönyv (Attila József memorial volume). Budapest, Szépirodalmi Könyvkiadó, 1957. 496 p. Illus. Seventy-one studies dealing with various aspects of his life, character, and writings. By periods of his life.

2236. Juhász, Ferenc.

Juhász, Ferenc. A tenyészet országa; összegyűjtött versek, 1946-1956 (The land of vegetation; collected poems, 1946-1956). Budapest, Szépirodalmi Könyvkiadó, 1956. 719 p. The works of one of the most original poets of the new generation.

———. Virágzó világfa; válogatott versek (Blossoming world-tree; selected poems). Budapest, Szépirodalmi Könyvkiadó, 1965. 416 p. Contains new poems.

———. Harc a fehér báránnyal (War with the white lamb). Budapest, Szépirodalmi Könyvkiadó, 1965. 146 p. New poems.

2237. Kassák, Lajos.

Kassák Lajos összegyűjtött versei (Lajos Kassák's collected poems). Budapest, Singer és Wolfner, 1946. 470 p. The best collection, to 1946, of a writer whose poetry and prose fiction have made important contributions to avant-garde and socialist literature.

Kassák Lajos válogatott versei, 1914-1949 (Lajos Kassák's selected poems, 1914-1949). With an introduction by Albert Gyergyai. Budapest, Magvető Könyvkiadó, 1956. 514 p. Contains some new poems.

Kassák, Lajos. Költemények, rajzok, 1952-1958 (Poems, sketches, 1952-1958). Budapest, Szépirodalmi Könyvkiadó, 1958. 358 p.

———. Vagyonom és fegyvertárom (My property and arsenal). Budapest, Magvető, 1963. 361 p. New poems.

———. A tölgyfa levelei (Leaves of the oak tree). Budapest, Magvető, 1964. 166 p. New poems.

———. Egy lélek keresi magát (A soul searches for itself). Budapest, Új Idők, 1948. 203 p. One of his most important novels.

———. Válogatott elbeszélések (Selected short stories). Budapest, Szépirodalmi Könyvkiadó, 1957. 358 p.

———. Egy ember élete (A man's life). Budapest, Dante és Pantheon, 1928-1939. 8 v. The only complete edition of his autobiography. To the time of the Hungarian Commune.

2238. Kosztolányi, Dezső.

Kosztolányi Dezső összegyűjtött munkái (Dezső Kosztolányi's collected works). Budapest, Révai, 1936-1940. 13 v. The poems, novels, short stories, and translations of one of the most important members of the *Nyugat* (West) generation.

Kosztolányi Dezső hátrahagyott művei (Dezső Kosztolányi's posthumous works). Budapest, Nyugat, 1940-1948. 11 v. Studies, critical writings, sketches, and travel journal. All but one volume edited by Gyula Illyés, an important poet of Kosztolányi's generation.

Baráth, Ferenc. Kosztolányi Dezső. Zalaegerszeg, Pannonia, 1938. 130 p. Bibliography: p. 128-130. A critical study of his literary development and the connection between his lyric poetry and prose writings. Also discussion of his contributions as a reporter, linguist, stylist, and translator.

Heller, Ágnes. Az erkölcsi normák felbomlása; etikai kérdések Kosztolányi Dezső munkásságában (The disintegration of ethical norms; ethical questions in the lifeworks of Dezső Kosztolányi). Budapest, Kossuth Könyvkiadó, 1957. 142 p. From a socialist point of view as a guide to writers in present-day Hungary.

Kosztolányi, *Mrs.* Dezső. Kosztolányi Dezső. Budapest, Révai, 1938. 366 p. Illus., facsims. A biography by his wife. Contains parts of his journal and some of his letters.

2239. Madách, Imre.

Madách Imre összes művei (Imre Madách's complete works). Edited and with an introduction and notes by Gábor Halász. Budapest, Révai, 1942. 2 v. The best edition of a 19th century poet whose dramatic poem, *The Tragedy of Man*, is a landmark in Hungarian literature.

Madách, Imre. Az ember tragédiája (The tragedy of man). Edited by Vilmos Tolnai. 2d rev. and enl. ed. Budapest, Magyar Tudományos Társaság, 1923. 256 p. The best critical edition of his most important work.

Madách Imre válogatott művei (Imre Madách's selected works). Edited and with an introduction and notes by István Sőtér. Published by the Society of Hungarian Literary History. Budapest, Szépirodalmi Könyvkiadó, 1958. 647 p. A reliable edition.

Morvay, Győző. Magyarázó tanulmány "Az ember tragédiájá"-hoz. (Explanatory Study of *The Tragedy of Man*). Nagybánya, Molnár Mihály, 1897. 527 p. Indispensable to an understanding of its background, form, and meaning.

Palágyi, Menyhért. Madách Imre élete és költészete (Imre Madách's life and poetry). Budapest, Athenaeum, 1900. 441 p. Illus. Views Madách through his writings. Extensive analysis and discussion of *The Tragedy of Man.*

Sőtér, István. Álom a történelemről; Madách Imre és Az ember tragédiája (A dream about history; Imre Madách and *The Tragedy of Man*). Budapest, Akadémiai Kiadó, 1965. 101 p. Bibliography: p. 99-101. For another recent study *see* Lajos Kántor's *Százéves harc "Az ember tragédiájáért"* (A century of struggle for "The Tragedy of Man"). (Budapest, Akadémiai Kiadó, 1966, 143 p.)

Voinovich, Géza. Madách Imre és Az ember tragédiája (Imre Madách and *The Tragedy of Man*). 2d ed. Budapest, Franklin-Társulat, 1922. 596 p. Bibliography: p. 569-596. An authoritative biography and critical study of his works, especially *The Tragedy of Man.*

2240. Mikszáth, Kálmán.

Mikszáth Kálmán összes művei (Kálmán Mikszáth's complete works). Edited by Gyula Bisztray and István Király. Budapest, Akadémiai Kiadó, 1956– This will be the first complete and critical edition of one of the most important figures in 19th century prose fiction. Thirty-two volumes to 1964: novels, short stories, letters, newspaper articles, sketches.

Király, István. Mikszáth Kálmán. Budapest, Szépirodalmi Könyvkiadó, 1960. 487 p. A biographical and critical study. Its tracing of the development of realism in his style reflects present-day concern with his works.

Rubinyi, Mózes. Mikszáth Kálmán élete és művei; az összes művek bibliográfiájával (Kálmán Mikszáth's life and works; with a bibliography of his complete works). Budapest, Révai Testvérek, 1917. 129 p. Bibliography: p. 95-130. A brief biographical section followed by a critical analysis of his literary works. Some attention to his predecessors and followers.

———. Mikszáth Kálmán stílusa és nyelve (Kálmán Mikszáth's style and language). Budapest, Révai Testvérek, 1910. 246 p. A thorough and sound analysis. Last part consists of an extensive dictionary of words and phrases frequently appearing in his literary works.

Schöpflin, Aladár. Mikszáth Kálmán. Budapest, Franklin-Társulat, 1941. 156 p. Very helpful to an understanding of the substance and form of his writings and his literary development.

2241. Móricz, Zsigmond.

Móricz Zsigmond összegyűjtött művei (Zsigmond Móricz's collected works). Editorial Board: Tibor Barabás, József Darvas, Miklós Gimes, Endre Illés, and Péter Nagy. Budapest, Szépirodalmi Könyvkiado, 1952– When completed it will be the fullest and most reliable, though not critical, edition of an important 20th century realistic novelist and short-story writer. Forty-two volumes to 1959: novels, short stories, dramas, reports, criticism, and studies.

Móricz Zsigmond levelei (Zsigmond Móricz's letters). Edited and with notes by Dóra Csanak and with an introduction by Kálmán Vargha. Budapest, Akadémiai Kiadó, 1963. 2 v. Illus., ports. A critical edition.

Kozocsa, Sándor, *comp.* Móricz Zsigmond irodalmi munkássága; bibliográfia (Zsigmond Móricz's literary activities; bibliography). Budapest, Művelt Nép, 1952. 263 p. Illus., facsims. In three parts: works published as editions, those published in periodicals, and biographical and critical studies.

Nagy, Péter. Móricz Zsigmond. 2d rev. and enl. ed. Budapest, Szépirodalmi Könyvkiadó, 1962. 518 p. Port. A biographical and critical study. Its bibliography supplements the Kozocsa compilation.

Vargha, Kálmán, *ed.* Kortársak Móricz Zsigmondról; tanulmányok és kritikák, 1900-1919 (Contemporaries on Zsigmond Móricz; studies and critiques, 1900-1919). Budapest, Magyar Tudományos Akadémia Irodalomtörténeti Intézete, 1958. 500 p. A collection of 135 studies arranged by years.

Vargha, Kálmán. Móricz Zsigmond és az irodalom (Zsigmond Móricz and literature). Budapest, Akadémiai Kiadó, 1962. 402 p. Bibliographical footnotes. (Irodalomtörténeti könyvtár, 8) A study of his aesthetic principles based on his writings dealing with literary questions, on the effects of the philosophical and aesthetic views of his times, on his views of literary realism, and other related subjects.

2242. Németh, László.

Németh, László. Bűn (Sin). With a postscript by Péter Nagy. Budapest, Szépirodalmi Könyvkiadó, 1961. 2 v. One of the most important novels of a major contemporary critic, novelist, and playwright. First published in 1937. A widely translated writer.

———. Égető Eszter (Esther Égető). 4th ed. Budapest, Magvető, 1963. 821 p. One of his most important novels. First published in 1956.

———. A minőség forradalma (The revolt of quality). Budapest, Magyar Élet, 1940-1943. 6 v. in 3. Mainly social and political studies.

———. Kisebbségben (In the minority). Budapest, Magyar Élet, 1942. 4 v. Mainly social and political studies.

———. A kísérletező ember (The experimenting man). Budapest, Magvető, 1963. 558 p. Illus. His most recent studies.

———. Történeti drámák (Historical dramas). Budapest, Szépirodalmi Könyvkiadó, 1958. 2 v. Eight of his dramas.

———. Társadalmi drámák (Social dramas). 2d enl. ed. Budapest, Szépirodalmi Könyvkiadó, 1964. 2 v. Ten of his dramas.

2243. Petőfi, Sándor.

Petőfi Sándor összes művei (Sándor Petőfi's complete works). Budapest, Akadémiai Kiadó, 1951– This will be the fullest critical edition of one of the most important lyric poets in the literature. Seven volumes to 1964: poems, dramas, prose translations, letters.

Petőfi Sándor összes művei (Sándor Petőfi's complete works). Edited by Adolf Havas. Budapest, Athenaeum, 1892-1896. 6 v. The best of the older critical editions.

Ferenczi, Zoltán. Petőfi Sándor életrajza (Sándor Petőfi's biography). Budapest, Franklin-Társulat, 1896. 3 v. The thoroughness of its basic research makes it the best biography.

Hatvany, Lajos. Így élt Petőfi (This is how Petőfi lived). Budapest, Akadémiai Kiadó, 1955-1957. 5 v. A valuable collection of previously published studies of his life arranged by chronological periods with comment pertinent to the material covered.

Horváth, János. Petőfi Sándor. 2d ed. Budapest, Pallas, 1926. 597 p. An illuminating tracing of the development of his lyric poetry. An index of the poems mentioned in the text, listing poems by other writers as possible influences on each.

Illyés, Gyula. Petőfi Sándor. Rev. ed. Budapest, Szépirodalmi Könyvkiadó, 1963. 681 p. Port. A biography by an important contemporary poet giving considerable attention to Petőfi's relations with his times and to his viewpoints and attitudes. This edition contains about a third more material than the several earlier editions. First published in 1936. Translated into several languages, including French: *Vie de Petőfi*, translated by Jean Rousselot (Paris, Gallimard, 1962, 335 p.).

Oláh, Gábor. Petőfi képzelete (Petőfi's imagination). Budapest, Franklin-Társulat, 1909. 295 p. The characteristics of his poetic imagination and the images it used for its expression. Also attention to literary influences.

2244. Sánta, Ferenc.

Sánta, Ferenc. Az ötödik pecsét (The fifth seal). Budapest, Szépirodalmi Könyvkiadó, 1963. 299 p. The best novel to date of a significant novelist and short-story writer of the new generation.

———. Farkasok a küszöbön (Wolves on the threshold). Budapest, Szépirodalmi Könyvkiadó, 1961. 236 p. A collection of his more recent short stories.

2245. Sarkadi, Imre. A szökevény (The fugitive). Collected, edited and with a postscript by László B. Nagy. Budapest, Szépirodalmi Könyvkiadó, 1962. 2 v. Illus., ports.

The only substantial edition of an important member of the new generation, no longer living. Selected: dramas, novelettes, short stories, sketches.

2246. Simon, István.

Simon, István. Gyümölcsoltó; versek, 1949-1963 (Fruit grafter; poems, 1949-1963). Budapest, Magvető, 1964. 398 p. The poems of an important poet of the new generation who writes in the tradition of folk poetry and realism.

———. A virágfa árnyékában; tanulmányok, kritikák, cikkek, 1953-1963 (In the shade of the flowering tree; studies, criticisms, newspaper articles, 1953-1963). Budapest, Szépirodalmi Könyvkiadó, 1964. 297 p.

2247. Tóth, Árpád.

Tóth Árpád összes művei (Árpád Tóth's complete works). Edited by László Kardos. Budapest, Akadémiai Kiadó, 1964– The first complete critical edition of one of the most important lyric poets and translators of the first quarter of the 20th century. Two volumes to 1964; poems, translations.

Tóth Árpád összes versei, versfordításai és novellái (Árpád Tóth's complete poems, verse translations, and short stories). Edited by László Kardos with the assistance of Gizella Kocztur. Budapest, Szépirodalmi Könyvkiadó, 1962. 906 p. A reliable edition.

Kardos, László. Tóth Árpád. 2d rev. ed. Budapest, Akadémiai Kiadó, 1965. 491 p. Illus., ports. Bibliographical notes: p. 435-482. A biographical and critical study. Uses materials unearthed after the publication of the first edition in 1955.

2248. Vörösmarty, Mihály.

Vörösmarty Mihály összes művei (Mihály Vörösmarty's complete works). Edited by Károly Horváth and Dezső Tóth. Budapest, Akadémiai Kiadó, 1960– This will be the fullest critical edition of one of the most romantic poets. Nine volumes to 1965: poems, epics, dramas, letters.

Vörösmarty Mihály válogatott művei (Mihály Vörösmarty's selected works). Edited by József Waldapfel. Budapest, Szépirodalmi Könyvkiadó, 1950. 2 v. A reliable edition of his poems, epics, dramas, and prose writings.

Gellért, Jenő. Vörösmarty élete és költészete (Vörösmarty's life and poetry). Budapest, Lampel Róbert, 1901. 193 p. Illus., ports. Bibliography: p. 178-193. Some discussion of his life, but mainly a critical analysis of his epics, dramas, and lyric poetry.

Gyulai, Pál. Vörösmarty életrajza (Vörösmarty's biography). Budapest, Franklin-Társulat, 1942. 233 p. By one of Hungary's most influential critics. Much attention to the subject matter and form of his writings. First published in 1866, and frequently revised.

Tóth, Dezső. Vörösmarty Mihály. Budapest, Akadémiai Kiadó, 1957. 631 p. (Irodalomtörténeti Könyvtár, 1) A biography giving major consideration to the qualities of his romanticism and the stylistic character of his epics and lyric poems. Summary in German, p. 599-614.

C. FOLKLORE

by Albert Tezla

1. Bibliographies

2249. Néprajzi könyvészet (Ethnographical bibliography). Ethnographia, v. 1-37, 1890-1926.

A current bibliography of scholarly articles and monographs on ethnography appearing every year or two years. The section was entitled "Néprajzi könyvtár" (Ethnographical library) from 1890 to 1896. Compiled by Árpád Hellebrant to 1924 and by Alice Goriupp in 1925.

2250. Sándor, István, *comp.* A magyar néprajztudomány bibliográfiája; 1945-1954 (Bibliography of Hungarian ethnographical research; 1945-1954). Budapest, Akadémiai Kiadó, 1965. 453 p.

A classified bibliography of scholarly articles and monographs on Hungarian ethnography in 60 sections, including bibliography and the various areas of folklore. Introduction and table of contents also in English, German, and Russian.

An earlier bibliography of 600 entries for the use of university students, also compiled by Sándor: *Magyar néprajztudomány, 1945-1955; válogatott bibliográfia* (Hungarian ethnographical research, 1945-1955; selected bibliography) (Budapest, Tankönyvkiadó, 1956, 68 p.; Bibliográfiák az egyetemi oktatás számára, 8).

2. Serials

2251. Acta Ethnographica. v. 1– 1950– Budapest. Quarterly.

Scholarly articles on ethnographical subjects in English, French, German, and Russian. Published by the Hungarian Academy of Sciences.

2252. Ethnographia. v. 1– 1890– Budapest. Frequency varies.

The basic journal on the subject. Scholarly articles on theoretical problems of ethnography and on research relating to the ethnography of the Hungarian, related, and neighboring peoples, including all aspects of their material and spiritual culture. Recently its table of contents has also been given in English, French, German, and Russian. Illustrations.

Title varies. Index to volumes 1-10 in volume 10 (1899), p. 427-492. Separately published index compiled by Zsigmond Szendrey: *Mutató az Ethnographia Népélet I-L. évfolyamához* (Index to volumes 1-50 of Ethnographia-Népélet) (Budapest, Kertész Nyomda, 1942, 72 p.).

Also had an important supplement containing mostly short, detailed articles on all aspects of ethnology and numerous illustrations: *A Magyar Nemzeti Múzeum Néprajzi Osztályának Értesítője* (Bulletin of the Ethnographical Section of the Hungarian National Museum) (v. 1-26, 1900-1916, 1926-1934, Budapest).

2253. Ethnologische Mitteilungen aus Ungarn. v. 1-9; 1885-1905. Budapest. Irregular.

See also entry no. 1776.

Articles on ethnology in German, including Hungarian folklore. Published by the Hungarian Academy of Sciences.

2254. Index Ethnographicus. v. 1– 1956– Budapest. Semiannual.

The library bulletin of the Ethnographical Museum of the Hungarian National Museum. Contains a current bibliography of publications in Hungarian ethnography, compiled by István Sándor, Ilona Dobos, and Magda S. Gémes. Reviews. Published in mimeographed form.

2255. Néprajzi Közlemények (Ethnographical studies). v. 1– 1956– Budapest. Quarterly.

Main purpose is to publish primary materials on ethnographical subjects, including folklore, as a basis for later analysis and evaluation. Published by the Hungarian National Museum and the Ethnographical Museum. In manuscript form.

2256. Ural-altaische Jahrbücher. v. 1– 1952– Wiesbaden. Illus. Frequency varies.

See also entry no. 1710.

Scholarly studies on Uralic and Altaic linguistics, folklore, and general comparative philology. Reviews. Supersedes *Ungarische Jahrbücher*, 1921-1943.

3. Surveys and Studies

2257. Györffy, György, *ed.* A magyar néptudomány kézikönyve (Handbook of Hungarian folklore research). Budapest, Magyar Néprajzi Múzeum, 1947-1949. 24 pamphlets.

A series of short monographs on various special areas of research in Hungarian folklore containing valuable bibliographies and references to the history of the research in each subject.

2258. Kandra, Kabos. Magyar mythologia (Hungarian mythology). Eger, Beznák Gyula, 1897. 532 p. Bibliographical notes: p. 461-522.

A study of the myths and legends of Hungary from ancient times to the Middle Ages, with many quotations from sources. Materials on gods, good and evil spirits, origin of the earth, concepts of the after-life, etc. Name and subject index.

2259. A magyarság néprajza (Ethnography of the Hungarian people). Written by Zsigmond Bátky, István Györffy, and Károly Viski. Edited by Elemér Czakó. 3d unrev. ed. Budapest, Királyi Magyar Egyetemi Nyomda, 1943-1944. 4 v.

Articles by subjects on all aspects of Hungarian folklore and folk customs. Bibliographies at ends of sections, including extensive ones, in volume 4, on the dance, folk customs, superstitions, creeds of pagan times, and games. Volume 3 is devoted entirely to poetry, style, and language.

2260. Ortutay, Gyula. Kis magyar néprajz (Short Hungarian ethnography). 3d rev. and enl. ed. Budapest, Bibliotheca, 1958. 174 p. Bibliographies.

Prepared for high school students but valuable for others, including specialists in some areas, as a survey and description of the major principles and findings of Hungarian ethnography. Chapters on its various areas, including the folk song, folk ballad, folk tale, and folk play. Selected bibliographies for each chapter. For a German edition, *see*:

Ortutay, Gyula. Kleine ungarische Volkskunde. Translated by Géza Engl and István Frommer. Weimar, Böhlau, 1963. 229 p.

2261. Ortutay, Gyula. Magyar népismeret (Hungarian ethnology). Budapest, Magyar Szemle Társaság, 1937. 80 p. (Kincsestár, 9)

A concise survey of contemporary Hungarian research in ethnology with source references.

2262. Ortutay, Gyula. The Science of Folklore in Hungary between the Two World Wars and during the Period Subsequent to the Liberation. Acta Ethnographica, v. 4, 1955: 5-89. Bibliography: p. 81-88.

A discussion of the principles and problems in folklore research and their manifestation in the work of Hungarian researchers. A good introduction to the subject and source of knowledge about major Hungarian folklorists and their principles and methodology.

4. Collections

2263. Berze Nagy, János. Magyar népmesetípusok (Types of Hungarian folktales). Edited and with an introductory study by István Banó. Pécs, Baranya Megye Tanácsa, 1957. 2 v. Bibliography: v. 2, p. 726-732.

An important collection and classification of Hungarian folktales by a major Hungarian researcher in ethnography.

2264. Magyar népmesék (Hungarian folktales). Edited and with an introduction by Gyula Ortutay. Selected and annotated by Linda Dégh and Ágnes Kovács. Budapest, Szépirodalmi Könyvkiadó, 1960. 3 v.

A good representative collection of various types of tales to be found in volume 3. Volumes 1 and 2 are entirely fairy tales.

2265. Ortutay, Gyula, *ed.* Hungarian Folk Tales. Selected and with an introduction and annotations by the editor. Budapest, Corvina, 1962. 544 p. Illus.

A good illustrated modern selection. The long introduction provides a concise survey of the history of and research on the Hungarian folktale and an analysis of its stylistic characteristics. Contains a bibliography of important collections of Hungarian folktales and legends published in foreign languages. Almost the same materials in the German edition: *Ungarische Volksmärchen* (2d ed., Budapest, Corvina, 1961, 561 p.).

2266. Régi magyar népmesék Berze Nagy János hagyatékából (Old Hungarian folktales from János Berze Nagy's literary remains). Edited by István Banó and Sándor Dömötör. Pécs, Tudományos Ismeretterjesztő Társulat Baranya Megyei Szervezete, 1960. 271 p.

Previously unpublished tales translated into English, German, and Russian.

2267. Új magyar népköltési gyűjtemény (New anthology of folk poetry). Edited by Gyula Ortutay. Budapest, Akadémiai Kiadó, 1953–

A scholarly series with introductions and annotations. Eleven volumes to 1963: mostly folktales by regions. An important earlier collection:

Magyar népköltési gyűjtemény (Anthology of Hungarian folk poetry). Edited by László Arany, Pál Gyulai, Gyula Vargha, and Gyula Sebestyén under the auspices of the Kisfaludy Society. Budapest, Athenaeum, 1872-1924. 14 v.

5. Studies and Materials on Individual Genres

2268. Dégh, Linda. Märchen, Erzähler und Erzählgemeinschaft; dargestellt an der ungarischen Volksüberlieferung. Translated from the Hungarian by Johanna Till. Tales in the appendix translated by Henriette and Géza Engl. Berlin, Akademie-Verlag, 1962. 435 p. Bibliography: p. 419-435. (Deutsche Akademie der Wissenschaften zu Berlin. Veröffentlichungen des Instituts für Deutsche Volkskunde, Bd. 23)

An analytical and well-documented study of the folktales of the Szekler families transferred to the Tolna region. Shows the function of storytelling in the community through the storytellers. Relates the history of the community members and their social organization to show their influence on the function of storytelling and the outlook in the stories. The third part consists of more than 200 tales, each preceded by bibliographical and historical data.

2269. Honti, Hans. Verzeichnis der publizierten ungarischen Volksmärchen, auf Grund von Antti Aarnes Typenverzeichnis zusammengestellt. Helsinki, Suomalainen Tiedeakatemia, 1928. 42 p. (Folklore Fellows Communications, 81)

A landmark in the application of the classification to Hungarian folk tales.

2270. Imre, Sándor. A néphumor a magyar irodalomban (Folk humor in Hungarian literature). Budapest, Franklin-Társulat, 1890. 166 p.

The history of Hungarian folk humor to the early decades of the 19th century, characterizing its nature and discussing works containing examples. Attention to translations of humorous writings from foreign languages.

2271. Kovács, Ágnes. Magyar állatmesék típusmutatója (Index of the types of Hungarian animal stories). Néprajzi Közlemények, v. 3, no. 3, 1958: 1-125.

A classification providing summaries of the contents of 295 tales, the locality in which they appear, and their published source. Geographical index. Introduction and summary of each tale in German.

2272. Ortutay, Gyula. Das ungarische Volksmärchen. Acta Litteraria (Budapest), v. 2, 1959: 113-156.

A survey of the history and structure of the Hungarian folktale. Discussion of its characteristics, sources, and major contributors and their theories.

2273. Sebestyén, Gyula. A magyar honfoglalás mondái (Legends of the original settlement of Hungary). Budapest, Franklin-Társulat, 1904-1905. 2 v.

A history and critical study of the origins of Hungarian legends, sagas, and myths and of their use by Hungarian poets from the beginnings to the period of János Arany.

2274. Vargyas, Lajos. Researches into the Mediaeval History of Folk Ballad. Budapest, Akadémiai Kiadó, 1967. 303 p. Bibliography: p. 287-303.

A comparative study of the Hungarian folk ballad dealing primarily with the originally French stratum in the ballad, the heroic epic elements surviving in them, providing an extensive documentation of "Walled-up Wife," and summarizing conclusions about the genre and its history. Bibliographies for each of the ballads by countries. Numerous comparative tables.

2275. Vezényi, P. Die Geschichte der ungarischen Märchen- und Aberglaubenforschung im 20. Jahrhundert. Freiburg (Germany), Paulus Druckerei, 1960. 104 p.

A doctoral dissertation criticizing contemporary Hungarian research mainly for its political attitudes.

D. HISTORY OF THOUGHT, CULTURE, AND SCHOLARSHIP

by Francis S. Wagner

1. Intellectual and Cultural Life

a. Bibliography and Periodicals

2276. Hungary. *Népművelési Minisztérium. Népművelési Főosztály.* A magyar népművelés tíz éve, 1945-1954; válogatott bibliográfia (Ten years of Hungarian adult education, 1945-1954; a selected bibliography). Budapest, Fővárosi Szabó Ervin Könyvtár, 1956-1957. 3 v.
See also entry no. 2333.

Lists the most important publications on cultural activities and intellectual life. The third volume was issued by Népművelési Intézet (Institute of Public Instruction). Classified arrangement; indexed.

2277. Magyar Szemle (Hungarian review). v. 1-46; 1927-1944. Budapest, Magyar Szemle Társaság. Monthly.
See also entry no. 1706.

Surveys Hungarian cultural activities, past and present. Edited by Gyula Szekfű.

2278. Magyar Tudomány (Hungarian science). v. 1– 1890– Budapest, Magyar Tudományos Akadémia. Illus.
See also entry no. 1707.

Frequency varies; publication suspended 1944-1945. Supersedes the Academy's *A Magyar Tudományos Akadémia értesítője* (Journal of the Hungarian Academy of Sciences), published 1867-1889. Title varies. 1890-1955, *Akadémiai értesítő* (Academy journal). Reviews the history and present state of the sciences, technology, and humanities, with emphasis on Hungary. Includes a news section and book reviews.

2279. Minerva. v. 1– 1922– Budapest. 10 no. a year.

Issued by the Minerva Society of the Faculty of Philosophy at the Péter Pázmány University, Budapest; ceased publication during the Second World War. Its proclaimed purpose was to promote the humanities; it deals with Hungarian art, philosophy, and cultural and intellectual life, and has an extensive book-review section.

b. Books

2280. Andritsch, Johann, *ed.* Ungarische Geisteswelt, von der Landnahme bis Babits. Gütersloh, Bertelsmann Lesering, 1960. 324 p. Bibliography; p. 312-314.

Describes Hungary's cultural and intellectual development from the conquest up to the Second World War. Excerpts characteristic of such leading figures as Péter Pázmány, Ferenc Kazinczy, Ferenc Kölcsey, István Széchenyi, Lajos Kossuth, József Eötvös, Imre Madách, Pál Gyulai, Ottokár Prohászka, Gyula Kornis, Béla Bartók, and Mihály Babits illustrate the main features of the country's culture and civilization in historical perspective.

2281. Domanovszky, Sándor, *ed.* Magyar művelődéstörténet (Hungarian cultural history). Budapest, Magyar Történelmi Társulat, 1939-1942. 5 v. Illus., maps, facsims.

Contents: v. 1. Ancient and medieval culture; v. 2. The Hungarian renaissance; v. 3. The bastion of Christianity; v. 4. The baroque period and the enlightenment; v. 5. The new Hungary. Based on primary sources and prepared with the assistance of leading scholars.

2282. Eckhardt, Sándor. A francia forradalom eszméi Magyarországon (Ideas of the French Revolution in Hungary). Budapest, Franklin Társulat, 1924. 222 p. Includes bibliographical references. (Ember és természet, 7)

Describes French influence on Hungarian intellectual life in the 18th and 19th centuries, and provides a documented study of the Enlightenment in Hungary.

2283. Farkas, Julius von, *ed.* Ungarns Geschichte und Kultur in Dokumenten. Wiesbaden, O. Harrassowitz, 1955. 234 p. Bibliography included in "Anmerkungen," p. 215-234.

A collection of documents by 40 authors chiefly in Hungarian and Latin from the Renaissance to modern times, illustrating the country's cultural life and civilization. Name index.

2284. Halász, Zoltán. Cultural Life in Hungary. Budapest, Pannonia Press, 1966. 319 p. Illus., ports.

A factual analysis of contemporary cultural activities including public education, science, literature, theater, motion pictures, music, the arts, press, radio, and television. The organization and activities of the Hungarian Academy of Sciences are described in detail. Published also in German.

2285. Hankiss, János. A magyar géniusz (The Hungarian genius). Budapest, Székesfőváros kiad., 1941. 275 p. Illus., ports., facsims.

Analyzes the foundations and development of Hungarian civilization, describes its characteristics, especially in the fields of literature and the fine arts, and discusses Italian, German, and French influences.

2286. Hencz, Aurél. A művelődési intézmények és a művelődésigazgatás fejlődése, 1945-1961 (The development of cultural institutions and cultural administration, 1945-1961). Budapest, Közgazdasági és Jogi Könyvkiadó, 1962. 515 p. Bibliography: p. 403-484.

See also entry no. 2346.

A detailed survey and analysis of cultural life. Chapters deal with the administration of scientific creativity, publishing and the book trade, and international cultural affairs. The structure and function of the Hungarian Academy of Sciences are described in detail, as is the post-1945 legislation on cultural and scientific activities. Table of contents also in English, French, German, and Russian.

See also Kornél Révy's *Policy of Hungarian Public Culture* (Budapest, Edition "Athenaeum," 1946, 38 p.), a comparative study of Hungarian culture with those of neighboring countries, as well as a summary of facts and figures, with emphasis on the 20th century.

2287. Horváth, Zoltán. Die Jahrhundertwende in Ungarn; Geschichte der zweiten Reformgeneration, 1896-1914. Neuwied am Rhein, Luchterhand, 1966. 547 p.

See also entry no. 230.

Translation of *Magyar századforduló; a második reformnemzedék története, 1896-1914* (Budapest, Gondolat, 1961, 647 p.). Describes the country's intellectual life, with emphasis on literature, law, philosophy, sociology, science, education, painting, music, and the press. The influence of Endre Ady (1887-1919) upon cultural movements is discussed. Includes chronology of events, name index, bibliographical footnotes, and a list of Hungarian newspapers and periodicals of the time.

2288. Hungary. *Központi Statisztikai Hivatal.* Magyarország művelődési viszonyai, 1945-1958 (Cultural relations of Hungary, 1945-1958). Budapest, Közgazdasági és Jogi Könyvkiadó, 1960. 342 p. Col. illus., maps, diagrs., tables.

Compiled by the Department of Cultural Statistics of the Hungarian Central Statistical Office under the editorship of Mrs. Tibor Erdész.

Additional statistics on cultural matters are given in two issues (no. 49 and 55, respectively) of the *Statisztikai időszaki közlemények* (Statistical periodical communications) series, also published by the Central Statistical Office. These are: *Magyarország kulturális helyzete (tájegységek és megyék szerint), 1961* (The cultural situation of Hungary [according to areas and counties], 1961) (Budapest, Statisztikai Kiadó Vállalat, 1962, 145 p.), and *Kultúrstatisztikai adattár, 1962* Compendium of cultural-statistical data) (Budapest, Statisztikai Kiadó Vállalat, 1963, 176 p.), both with English summaries.

2289. Klebelsberg, Kunó, *gróf.* Ungarische Kulturpolitik nach dem Kriege; Rede, gehalten in der Aula der Berliner Friedrich Wilhelms-Universität am 21. Oktober 1925. Berlin, W. de Gruyter, 1925. 23 p. (Ungarische Bibliothek, für das Ungarische Institut an der Universität Berlin. 2. Reihe, 5)

Describes also the role of learned societies. For more detailed analysis, see the author's *Beszédei, cikkei és törvényjavaslatai, 1916-1926* (Speeches, articles, and legislative bills, 1916-1926) (Budapest, Athenaeum, 1927, 687 p.).

2290. Kornis, Gyula. Hungary and European Civilization. Budapest, Royal Hungarian University Press, 1938. 37 p.

The topic is analyzed from earliest times to the mid-nineteenth century. The author concludes: "From Asia the Hungarian culture brought an aboriginal substratum onto which Slav, German and Italian cultural strata were grafted after the Conquest, the whole being glazed over with a veneer of Christianity." An abridgment was published in German: *Die Entwicklung der ungarischen Kultur* (Berlin, W. de Gruyter, 1933, 24 p.).

2291. Ligeti, Lajos, *ed.* A magyar tudomány tíz éve, 1945-1955 (Ten years of Hungarian science, 1945-1955). Budapest, Akadémiai Kiadó, 1955. 431 p.

Prepared by leading specialists on the development of the sciences and the humanities. It is also an account of the effects of dialectical materialism on intellectual life.

2292. Magyary, Zoltán, *ed.* Die Entstehung einer internationalen Wissenschaftspolitik; die Grundlagen der ungarischen Wissenschaftspolitik, im Auftrage des Landesverbandes der ungarischen wissenschaftlichen Gesellschaften und Einrichtungen. Leipzig, F. Meiner, 1932. 683 p. Tables, map. Includes bibliography.

A collection of well-documented studies by experts on the past and present state of civilization, cultural policy, the sciences, the humanities, and the creative arts in Hungary; includes descriptions of scientific research, artistic, and educational institutions. Name index.

2293. Rácz, Endre. Az újabbkori magyar művelődés szelleme (The spirit of Hungarian culture in the modern age). Budapest, 1946. 51 p.

After a short historical analysis of Hungarian culture between the 10th and 20th centuries, the author investigates the social background, contemporary creative arts, literature, music, and foreign influences. Statistics on the foreign orientation of the reading public, based chiefly on the work of Mihály Babits, are included and analyzed. See also Lajos Nékám's *The Cultural Aspirations of Hungary from 896 to 1935* (Budapest, Central Committee of the Budapest Thermal Baths and Health Resorts, 1935, 319 p., illus.), which describes the development of culture, printing, scientific societies, and the fine arts. Richly illustrated.

2294. Szigeti, József. A magyar szellemtörténet bírálatához (On the criticism of Hungarian humanities). Budapest, Kossuth Könyvkiadó, 1964. 273 p. Includes bibliographical references.

Embraces a much wider subject field than indicated by the title. It is a Marxist-Leninist-Stalinist review of the humanities in Hungary between the wars. The views and methodology of Gyula Szekfű, one of the central figures in the intellectual life of the period, come under particular scrutiny.

2. History of the Book and Printing

2295. Fitz, József, *and* Béla Kéki. A magyar könyv története. I. A magyar könyv története 1711-ig (History of the Hungarian book. v. 1. History of the Hungarian book to 1711). Budapest, Magyar Helikon, 1959. 201 p. Illus., maps, facsims. Bibliographical references included in "Jegyzetek" (notes), p. 177-181.

The completed work will cover the subject through modern times. Dr. Fitz, formerly director of the National Széchényi Library, has prepared another comprehensive study: *A magyar nyomdászat, könyvkiadás és könyvkereskedelem története* (History of Hungarian printing, book publishing, and the book trade) (Budapest, Akadémiai Kiadó, 1959-67, 2 v., illus., facsims., bibliographies). The two volumes which have so far appeared are subtitled *A mohácsi vész előtt* (Before the Mohács disaster) and *A reformáció korában* (In the age of the Reformation). A more limited period is dealt with by the same author in *A magyar nyomdászat, 1848-49* (Hungarian printing, 1848-49) (Budapest, Hungária Hírlapnyomda, 1948, 213 p., illus., ports., facsims., bibliography), which describes the printers' trade union movement and gives statistical information on printing houses, publishers, writers, readers, books, and periodicals in Budapest and the provinces. Dr. Fitz's briefer, more general *A könyv története* (History of the book) (Budapest, Magyar Szemle Társaság, 79 p., bibliography), includes material on the Hungarian book. For contemporary data, see *A magyar könyvkiadás, 1945-1959* (Hungarian book publishing, 1945-1959), by János Bak (Budapest, Zeneműnyomda, 1960, 381 p., illus.).

2296. Magyar könyvszemle (Hungarian book review). v. 1– 1876– Budapest, Akadémiai Kiadó. Quarterly. Illus., facsims., ports.
See also entry no. 1739.

Publication suspended 1947-1954. Organ of Section I (Linguistics and Literary Sciences) of the Hungarian Academy of Sciences. Contains scholarly studies on the history of Hungarian books, printing, and publishing; news and book reviews; and bibliographies.

3. Academies, Learned Societies, and Institutions

2297. Kont, Ignác. La Hongrie littéraire et scientifique. Paris, E. Leroux, 1896. 459 p.

Deals with scientific, scholarly, and literary societies and institutions.

2298. Magyar Tudományos Akadémia, *Budapest.* Hungarian Academy of Sciences. Editor: Helen Antal. Budapest, 1964. 127 p.

Presents the history and structure of the national scientific organization. Periodicals issued by the Academy are listed on p. 101-110.

2299. Staub, Móricz. Társadalmunknak a nemzeti kultúra érdekében kifejtett tevékenysége a jelen században (Activities of our society in promoting the national culture in the present century). Budapest, Pesti Könyvnyomda, 1898. 183 p. Map.

Reprinted from the ninth volume of Matlekovits' *Magyarország az ezredik évben* (Hungary in the millennial year).

2300. Tudományos Társulatok és Intézmények Országos Szövetsége, *Budapest.* Ungarische Kulturstätten. Foyers intellectuels en Hongrie. Hungarian Education Institutions. Centri di cultura in Ungheria. Budapest, Typographia Regiae Universitatis Hungaricae, 1931. 192 p. incl. 152 plates. Bibliography: p. 191-192.

Text in German, French, English, and Italian.

4. Philosophy

a. Bibliography and Periodicals

2301. Athenaeum. v. 1-19; 1892-1910. New series, v. 1-34, 1915-48. Budapest. Four no. a year, 1892-1910; new series, 6 no. a year.

Issued by the Magyar Tudományos Akadémia (new series was jointly issued with the Magyar Filozófiai Társaság). Analyzes all fields of philosophy with regard to domestic developments; excellent book-review section. Its annual bibliographies, compiled by Ilona Gáspár, were also issued as offprints with the title *A magyar filozófiai irodalom bibliográfiája* (Bibliography of Hungarian philosophical literature), covering the years 1930-1943 (Budapest, Királyi Magyar Egyetemi Nyomda, 1932-44).

2302. Filozófiai Évkönyv (Philosophical yearbook). 1952– Budapest, Akadémiai Kiadó.

Reviews problems of dialectical and historical materialism, with emphasis on Hungary and the Soviet bloc; includes book reviews. A summary is published in German as *Philosophisches Jahrbuch; Zusammenfassung* (Budapest, Akadémiai Kiadó).

2303. Magyar Filozófiai Szemle (Hungarian philosophical review). v. 1– 1957– Budapest, Akadémiai Kiadó. Four no. a year, 1957-1960; 6 no. a year, 1961 onward.

Organ of the Philosophical Institute of the Hungarian Academy of Sciences. Discusses chiefly contemporary problems of Hungarian philosophy within a universal framework. Has a well-developed book-review section. Summaries of articles in Russian, English, and German.

2304. Magyar Tudományos Akadémia, *Budapest.* Studia philosophica. 1– 1961– Budapest, Akadémiai Kiadó.

Irregularly issued; articles in English, German, French, and Russian.

b. Books

2305. Ballagi, Géza. A politikai irodalom Magyarországon 1825-ig (Political literature in Hungary to 1825). Budapest, Franklin Társulat, 1888. 847 p.

A well-documented description of political thinking and philosophy since the founding of the kingdom, based on the essential writings.

2306. Kornis, Gyula. A magyar philosophia fejlődése és az Akadémia

(The development of Hungarian philosophy and the Academy). Budapest, Magyar Tudományos Akadémia, 1926. 48 p. Bibliographical footnotes.

A lecture delivered at the February 22, 1926, session of the Hungarian Academy of Sciences in Budapest. Concentrates on the period 1831-1840 when the Magyar Tudós Társaság (Hungarian Learned Society) published several books on philosophy, including a philosophical dictionary. Philosophical trends during the first half of the 19th century are described on the basis of contemporary sources. Hungarian books and periodicals published between 1830 and 1890 in the field of philosophy are reviewed.

2307. Magyar Filozófiai Társaság, *Budapest.* Gedenkschrift für Ákos von Pauler; mit Unterstützung der Ungarischen Wissenschaftlichen Akademie und der P. Pázmány-Universität Budapest, hrsg. von der Ungarischen Philosophischen Gesellschaft. Compiled by Ludwig Prohászka, with the assistance of Julius Kornis. Berlin, W. de Gruyter, 1936. 249 p. Port.

A collection of studies devoted to the life and philosophy of Ákos Pauler (1876-1933), one-time professor of philosophy at the Pázmány University and the greatest philosopher of Hungary. Among the many contributors are Gyula Kornis, Béla Brandenstein, József Halasy-Nagy, Pál Kecskés, Gyula Moór, and Lajos Prohászka.

2308. Philosophiai pályamunkák (Prizewinning philosophical works). Pesten, Eggenberger, 1835-1845. 3 v.

Essays which were awarded prizes in competitions sponsored by the Hungarian Academy of Sciences (then Magyar Tudós Társaság). All are concerned with the historical development and contemporary situation of philosophy, including psychology and educational theory, in Hungary. Significant older Hungarian philosophical writings are collected in *Régi magyar filozófusok, XV.-XVII. század* (Old Hungarian philosophers, 15th-17th centuries), edited by László Mátrai (Budapest, Gondolat, 1961, 239 p., illus.), and *A magyar felvilágosodás breviáriuma* (Breviary of the Hungarian enlightenment), edited by Miklós Koroda (Budapest, Anonymus-kiad., 194–?, 189 p.), which contains writings from the 18th century. Concerning the present, the following collection of essays is noteworthy: *Problemy marksistsko-leninskoi filosofii; stat'i vengerskikh avtorov* (Problems of Marxist-Leninist philosophy; articles by Hungarian authors), edited by M. T. Ivochuk (Moskva, Progress, 1965, 443 p., bibliographical footnotes).

2309. Sándor, Pál. A filozófia története (History of philosophy). Budapest, Akadémiai Kiadó, 1965. 3 v. Includes bibliographies.

Offers extensive treatment of Hungarian philosophical movements and philosophers of the 17th through 20th centuries. Name index. Hungarian philosophical thought from the European point of view is analyzed in the following: "Hungarian Philosophy," by Béla Tankó, in *Acta Litterarum ac Scientiarum Regiae Universitatis Hungaricae*

Francisco-Josephinae; Section Philosophica, t. 5, 1934/35, p. 119-136; "Die ungarische Philosophie," by Lajos Rácz, in Friedrich Ueberweg's *Grundriss der Geschichte der Philosophie*, 12th ed., v. 5 (Berlin, E. S. Mittler, 1928), p. 348-359; "A magyar bölcseleti irodalom vázlata," by Gyula Mitrovics, on p. 447-544 of *A bölcselet története* (Budapest, Franklin Társulat, 1904), the Hungarian translation of the 15th edition of Albert Schwegler's *Geschichte der Philosophie im Umriss*; and *Grundlagen der Philosophie*, by Ákos Pauler (Berlin, W. de Gruyter, 1925. 348 p. A short article on Hungarian philosophy by Julius Kövesi is included in the fourth volume (p. 93-95) of *The Encyclopedia of Philosophy* (New York, Macmillan, 1967).

E. RELIGION

by István Csicsery-Rónay

1. Histories, Surveys, and Reference Works

2310. Bedő, Alexander, *and others*. Church and State in Hungary. *In* Mid-European Law Project. Church and State Behind the Iron Curtain: Czechoslovakia, Hungary, Poland, Rumania. New York, Praeger, 1955. p. 69-157 (Praeger Publications in Russian History and World Communism, no. 17)

A survey of changes in the status of churches after the Second World War, the trials of Cardinal Mindszenty and Archbishop Grősz, texts of the laws concerning the churches, etc. It brings up to date the Mid-European Law Project's *Hungary, Churches and Religion* (Washington, D.C., Library of Congress, 1951, 74 p.).

Bedő's work may be supplemented by William Sólyom-Fekete's "Church and State in Hungary" in the Library of Congress's (Law Library) *The Church and State Under Communism; a Special Study* (Washington, U.S. Govt. Print. Off., 1965) p. 1-11.

2311. Bucsay, Mihály. Geschichte des Protestantismus in Ungarn. Stuttgart, Evangelisches Verlagswerk, 1959. 226 p. Illus., bibliography.

A concise standard work. May be supplemented by George A. Knight's *History of the Hungarian Reformed Church* (Washington, D.C., Hungarian Reformed Federation of America, 1956, 163 p.). This is a translation and abridgement of *A Magyar Református Egyház története*, edited by Imre Révész.

2312. Diószegi, Vilmos. A sámánhit emlékei a magyar népi műveltségben (Remnants of shamanistic beliefs in Hungarian folk culture). Budapest, Akadémiai Kiadó, 1958. 472 p. Illus.

A scholarly work on ancient Hungarian religion. Summaries in German and Russian. May be supplemented by Arnold Ipolyi's *Magyar mythologia* (Hungarian mythology) (Budapest, Zajti F., 1929, 2 v.) and by Uno Harva's *Finno-Ugric, Siberian* [*Mythology*] (New York, Cooper Square Publishers, 1964, 587 p. The Mythology of All Races, v. 4).

2313. Fraknói, Vilmos. Magyarország egyházi és politikai összeköttetései a Római Szentszékkel (The ecclesiastical and political relations of Hungary with the Holy See in Rome). Budapest, Szent István Társulat, 1902-1903. 3 v. Bibliography.

Covers the period 1000-1689. May be supplemented by his *A magyar királyi kegyúri jog, Szent Istvántól Mária Teréziáig; történelmi tanulmány* (The Hungarian King's right of advowson from St. Stephen to Maria Teresa; a historical study) (Budapest, Magyar Tudományos Akadémia, 1895, 559 p.).

2314. Hungary. *Laws, statutes, etc.* A hatályos anyakönyvi, házassági és vallásügyi jogszabályok, az idevonatkozó összes törvények, rendeletek, valamint az érdekelt minisztériumok fontosabb elvi jelentőségű határozatai (Legal provisions in force in regard to birth registration, marriage, and religious affairs; all relevant laws and decrees as well as the more significant decisions of fundamental importance by the ministries concerned). Budapest, Hernádi Á., 1948. 760 p.

A comprehensive work, assimilating the post-1945 radical changes. May be supplemented by Zoltán Kérészy's *Katholikus egyházi jog a Codex Iuris Canonici alapján* (Canon law based upon the Codex Iuris Canonici) (Pécs, Danubia, 1927, 336 p.); and by Béla Szentpéteri Kún's *A magyarországi református egyház külső rendje* (The external order of the Reformed Church of Hungary) (Budapest, Magyar Református Egyház, 1948, 562 p.).

2315. Katholikus lexikon (Catholic encyclopedia). Edited by Béla Bangha. Budapest, Magyar Kultúra, 1931-1933. 4 vl. Illus.

Standard Catholic reference work. May be supplemented by Jenő Zoványi's *Cikkei a Theológiai Lexikon részére a magyar protestantizmus történetéből* (Articles for the theological encyclopedia on the history of Hungarian Protestantism) (Budapest, Sylvester Nyomda, 1940, 549 p.).

2316. Kiss, János. A katholikus Magyarország; a magyarok megtérésének és a magyar királyság megalapításának kilencszázados évfordulója alkalmából (Catholic Hungary; on the occasion of the 900th anniversary of the conversion of the Hungarians and of the founding of the Hungarian Kingdom). Budapest, Stephaneum, 1902. 2 v. Illus.

History and organization of Hungarian Catholicism. May be supplemented by Lajos Balics' *A római katholikus egyház története Magyarországban* (History of the Roman Catholic Church in Hungary) (Budapest, Szent István Társulat, 1885-1890, 2 v.).

2317. Révész, Imre. Magyar református egyháztörténet (Hungarian Reformed Church history). v. 1. Debrecen, Debrecen Sz. Kir. Város és a Tiszántúli Református Egyházkerület Könyvnyomda-Vállalata, 1938. 408 p. Bibliography. (Református Egyházi Könyvtár, 20)

Comprehensive account of how protestantism was gradually — if not permanently — embraced by almost the entire population of Hungary. Only one volume was published. May be supplemented by Alexander St.-Ivanyi's *A magyar vallásszabadság* (Hungarian religious liberty) (New York, American Hungarian Library and Historical Society, 1964, 194 p.).

2318. Serédi, Jusztinián György, *Cardinal, comp.* Emlékkönyv Szent István király halálának kilencszázadik évfordulóján (Memorial volume for the 900th anniversary of the death of King Stephen the Saint). Budapest, Magyar Tudományos Akadémia, 1938. 3 v. Illus., bibliography.

2. The Situation since 1945

2319. Barth, Karl. Christliche Gemeinde im Wechsel der Staatsordnungen; Dokumente einer Ungarnreise, 1948. Zollikon-Zürich, Evangelischer Verlag, 1948. 76 p.

Thoughts and advice conveyed to Hungarian church leaders by the great German theologian.

2320. Bereczky, Albert. A keskeny út; igehirdetések, előadások, cikkek (The narrow way; sermons, lectures, articles). Budapest, Református Egyetemes Konvent Sajtóosztálya, 1953. 427 p.

Theoretical and practical guide for the compromise between church and communism as professed by the leader of the Reformed Church.

2321. Budapest. Tudományegyetem. *Könyvtár.* Az ateizmus kérdésének újabb irodalma (Recent literature on the problem of atheism). Budapest, Tankönyvkiadó, 1961. 84 p. (Bibliográfiák az egyetemi oktatás számára, 13)

A short bibliography with annotations.

2322. Gombos, Gyula. The Lean Years; a Study of Hungarian Calvinism in Crisis. New York, Kossuth Foundation, 1960. 130 p.

Basic analysis of the history of the Hungarian Reformed Church after the Second World War. For a fiercely partisan and opposing view *see* Imre Kádár's *The Church in the Storm of the Time; the History of the Hungarian Reformed Church During the Two World Wars, Revolutions and Counter-Revolutions* (Budapest, Bibliotheca, 1958, 175 p.).

2323. Hutten, Kurt. Iron Curtain Christians; the Church in Communist Countries Today. Minneapolis, Augsburg Publishing House, 1967. 495 p.

Contains an up-to-date survey of postwar developments in Hungarian churches.

2324. Mindszenty, József, *Cardinal.* Cardinal Mindszenty Speaks; Authorized White Book. Introduction by Ákos Zombory. New York, Longmans, Green, 1949. 234 p.

Documents sent abroad by the cardinal to be published in event of his arrest. For the communist point of view *see* Sándor Orbán's *Egyház és állam; a katolikus egyház és az állam viszonyának rendezése, 1945-1950* (Church and state; normalization of the relationship between the Catholic Church and the state, 1945-1950) (Budapest, Kossuth Könyvkiadó, 1962, 232 p.).

2325. Mindszenty, József, *Cardinal.* Mindszenty-Dokumentation. Edited and translated by Josef Vecsey and Johann Schwendemann. St. Pölten, Verlag der Pressevereindruckerei, 1956-1959. 3 v. Illus.

The story of the Cardinal's resistance, trial, and liberation in documents, 1944-1956.

2326. Scheiber, Thomas. Le christianisme en Europe orientale. Paris, Spes, 1961. 222 p. Bibliography.

Concise survey of the postwar situation of Hungarian churches.

2327. Tobias, Robert. Communist-Christian Encounter in East Europe. Indianapolis, School of Religion Press, 1956. 567 p. Bibliography: p. 560-561.

Contains a short survey of postwar events, as well as statistics, chronology, and documents (p. 426-487).

3. Periodicals

2328. Evangélikus Élet (Lutheran life). 1935– Budapest. Weekly.

National Lutheran journal.

2329. Hungarian Church Press. 1949– Budapest. Semimonthly.

Journal published by the Reformed Church, the Lutheran Church, and the Federation of Free Churches: Baptists, Methodists, etc. Issued also in French and German.

2330. Katolikus Szemle (Catholic review). 1887-1944. Budapest. Monthly. 1946– Rome. Monthly.

Religious and literary periodical closely watching developments in Hungary. To be supplemented by *Vigilia* (1935–, Budapest, monthly.)

2331. Református Egyház (Reformed Church). 1949– Budapest. Monthly.

Official paper of the Reformed Church. Occasionally carries book reviews. May be supplemented by *Reformátusok Lapja* (Journal of the Reformed) (1957–, Budapest, weekly).

2332. Új Ember (New man). 1945– Budapest. Weekly.

Independent Catholic paper. May be supplemented by *Katolikus Szó* (Catholic word) (1957–, Budapest, weekly), published by the Catholic Committee of the National Peace Council.

F. EDUCATION

by István Csicsery-Rónay

1. Bibliographies

2333. Hungary. *Népművelési Minisztérium. Népművelési Főosztály.* A magyar népművelés tíz éve, 1945-1954; válogatott bibliográfia (Ten years of Hungarian adult education, 1945-1954; a selected bibliography). Budapest, Fővárosi Szabó Ervin Könyvtár, 1956-1957. 3 v.

See also entry no. 2276.

List of publications (books and articles) on all aspects of extracurricular (cultural and ideological) mass education. The third volume consists of an index.

2334. Jáki, László. Pedagógiai szakbibliográfiák száz éve (One hundred years of pedagogical bibliographies). Pedagógiai Szemle (Pedagogical review) (Budapest), v. 9, 1959, nos. 1/6: 203-210.

Bibliographical data on more than one hundred bibliographies. Should be supplemented by Mária Baranyai and Adolf Keleti, *comps.*, *A magyar nevelésügyi folyóiratok bibliográfiája, 1841-1936* (Bibliography of Hungarian educational periodicals, 1841-1936) (Budapest, Budapest Székesfőváros Házinyomdája, 1937, 148 p.; A Fővárosi Pedagógiai Könyvtár kiadványai, 3 sz.).

2335. Magyar pedagógiai irodalom (Hungarian pedagogical literature). 1959– Budapest. Quarterly.

Lists monographs, articles, etc. Also contains book reviews. Published by Országos Pedagógiai Könyvtár (National Library of Education).

2. Periodicals

2336. East Europe. 1952– New York, National Committee for a Free Europe. Monthly.

Close observer of political and cultural affairs in the communist countries of Europe, including education in Hungary. It was preceded by *News from Behind the Iron Curtain* (1950-1952), also published by the National Committee for a Free Europe.

2337. Hungary. *Művelődésügyi Minisztérium.* Művelődésügyi Közlöny (Gazette of cultural affairs). 1957– Budapest. Semimonthly.

Official gazette, published by the Ministry of Cultural Affairs. Contains pertinent laws, directives, instructions, professional news items, etc.

2338. Köznevelés (Public education). 1945– Budapest. Semimonthly.

Professional journal for primary and secondary school teachers, published by the Ministry of Cultural Affairs. Table of contents also in English. For university and college teaching personnel, the professional periodical is *Felsőoktatási Szemle* (Review of higher education) (1952–, Budapest, monthly).

2339. Magyar Pedagógia (Hungarian pedagogy). 1892– Budapest, Akadémiai kiadó. Quarterly.

A basic tool discussing all aspects of education. Reviews of Hungarian and foreign books. Summaries and tables of contents also in English. A similar journal, *Pedagógiai Szemle* (Pedagogical review) (Budapest, 1951–, quarterly), contains, in addition, bibliographies. Tables of contents in Russian, German and French.

3. History of Education

2340. Budapest. Tudományegyetem. A Királyi Magyar Pázmány Péter Tudományegyetem története (History of the Hungarian Royal Péter Pázmány University). Budapest, Királyi Magyar Egyetemi Nyomda, 1935-1938. 4 v. Illus.

A comprehensive history of Hungary's principal university. For a popular, foreign-language survey in French and German, *see*:

Hekler, Antal. L'université de Budapest. Die Universität Budapest. Basel, F. Lindner, 1935. 152 p. Illus. Concerning the 600-year old Pécs University, *see*:

Csizmadia, Andor, *ed.* A Pécsi Egyetem történetéből (From the history of the Pécs University). Pécs, Tudományegyetem, 1967. 285 p. Illus. Russian, French and German summaries.

2341. Hungary. *Vallás- és Közoktatásügyi Minisztérium.* Mai magyar művelődéspolitika (Hungarian educational policy of today). Budapest, 1946. 142 p.

The principles, plans, and results of educational policy during the postwar democratic period. Should be complemented by contemporary issues of *Köznevelés* (*see* entry no. 2338).

2342. Kemény, Ferenc, *ed.* Magyar pedagógiai lexikon (Hungarian pedagogical encyclopedia). Budapest, Révai, 1933-1936. 2 v.

The standard encyclopedia on education. Consult also the numerous writings of Ernő Fináczy on the history of Hungarian education.

2343. Kornis, Gyula. Education in Hungary. New York, Teachers College, Columbia University, 1932. 289 p. Illus. Plates, facsims., diagrs. (Studies of the International Institute of Teachers College, Columbia University, no. 13)

A comprehensive survey of the Hungarian educational system between the two World Wars. May be supplemented by the same author's *Ungarische Kulturideale, 1777-1848* (Leipzig, Quelle & Meyer, 1930, 608 p., illus.), and by Mór Kármán's *Ungarisches Bildungswesen; geschichtlicher Rückblick bis zum Jahre 1848* (Budapest, Kön. Ung. Universitätsdruckerei, 1915, 212 p.).

2344. Kubinszky, Lajos. Magyar közoktatásügyi politika a két háború között (Hungarian educational policy between the two wars). New

York, A Magyar Nemzeti Bizottmány, 1953. 126 p. (Kis magyar könyvtár, 2. sz.)

A thorough and enlightened study of the prewar Hungarian educational system, and of the interwar reforms. Includes educational statistics, curricula, organization charts, etc.

4. Recent and Current Developments

2345. Héberger, K. The Hungarian Higher Education. Budapest, Tankönyvkiado, 1966. 92 p. Illus.

A short official survey of the history, present status, statistics, etc. of Hungarian universities and colleges. For a college handbook in Hungarian with all necessary data about admission, curricula, degree requirements, etc., *see*:

Hungary. *Művelődésügyi Minisztérium.* Tájékoztató a felsőoktatási intézményekről; nappali, esti, levelező tagozatok, 1964 (A guide to institutions of higher education; day, night and correspondence branches, 1964). Budapest, 1964. 135 p. Illus.

2346. Hencz, Aurél. A művelődési intézmények és a művelődésigazgatás fejlődése, 1945-1961 (The development of cultural institutions and cultural administration, 1945-1961). Budapest, Közgazdasági és Jogi Könyvkiadó, 1962. 515 p. Bibliography: p. 403-484.

See also entry no. 2286.

A basic survey of the postwar developments in all cultural areas, including the educational system. Table of contents also in English, French, German, and Russian.

2347. Hungary. *Művelődésügyi Minisztérium.* Tanterv és utasítás az általános iskolák számára (Curriculum and directives for the general schools). Budapest, Tankönyvkiadó, 1963. 670 p.

A comprehensive sourcebook about the material and the point of views to be used in teaching in the elementary schools.

2348. Juhász, William (Vilmos). Blueprint for a Red Generation. New York, Mid-European Studies Center, 1952. 101 p. (National Committee for a Free Europe. Mid-European Studies Center. Publication no. 7)

An analysis in perspective of Stalinist education in Hungary. Its scope best indicated by its subtitle: "The Philosophy, Method, and Practices of Communist Education as Imposed on Captive Hungary." Includes bibliography. May be supplemented by:

Sager, Peter, *ed.* Die Schul- und Wissenschaftspolitik der ungarischen Volksrepublik, 1945-1958. Bern, Osteuropa Bibliothek, 1958. 59 p. (Schriftenreihe der Osteuropa-Bibliothek. Reihe Materialien, Heft 1)

2349. Sándor, Frigyes, *ed.* Musical Education in Hungary. Translated by Barna Balogh and others. London, Barrie and Rockliff, 1966. 253 p. Illus., music, ports., facsims, tables, diagrs.

A thorough treatment of all aspects of musical education from nursery schools to institutions of higher education, written by the foremost experts in the field. Includes musical examples, tables, statistics, diagrams. No index.

2350. Simon, Gyula. Nevelésügyünk húsz éve, 1945-1964; tanulmányok a magyar népi demokrácia neveléstörténetéből (Twenty years of our educational affairs, 1945-1964; studies in the educational history of the Hungarian People's Democracy). Budapest, Tankönyvkiadó, 1965. 601 p.

Essays on the history of education in the Hungarian People's Republic. Summaries also in English and Russian.

2351. Sólyom-Fekete, William. Laws on Public Education in Hungary after World War II. Washington, U.S. Library of Congress, European Law Division, 1959. 133 p.

An annotated list of all pertinent laws and directives, including digests of the more important ones. May be supplemented by Lajos Kubinszky's *A vallás- és közoktatásügyi igazgatási jog vázlata* (A survey of administrative law concerning religious and educational affairs) (Budapest, Egyetemi Nyomda, 1947, 291 p.), and by *Művelődésügyi Közlöny* (*see* entry no. 2337).

G. FINE ARTS

by Francis S. Wagner

1. Bibliography and Periodicals

2352. Bíró, Béla, *ed.* A magyar művészettörténeti irodalom bibliográfiája. Bibliographie der ungarischen kunstgeschichtlichen Literatur. Budapest, Képzőművészeti Alap Kiadóvóllalata, 1955. 611 p.

Comprehensive bibliography of books and articles published from the 18th century to the end of 1954; arranged in nine topical sections, with an index of authors' and artists' names. Can be supplemented by the bibliographies appearing annually in *Művészettörténeti Értesítő*.

2353. Magyar Építőművészet (Hungarian architecture). 1– 1952– Budapest, Magyar Építőművészek Szövetsége. 6 no. a year. Illus., ports., plans.

2354. Művészettörténeti Értesítő. (Bulletin of art history). 1– 1952– Budapest, Akadémiai Kiadó. Two no. a year through 1955; four no. a year since then.

As of 1954, journal of the Magyar Régészeti, Művészettörténeti és Éremtani Társulat (Hungarian Society of Archaeology, Art History, and Numismatics). Concentrates on the fine arts with emphasis on historic Hungary. Includes book reviews and an annual bibliography of Hungarian writings on art history.

2. Art History and Surveys

2355. Boskovits, Miklós, Miklós Mojzer, *and* András Mucsi. Das christliche Museum von Esztergom (Gran). Budapest, Verlag der ungarischen Akademie der Wissenschaften, 1964. 197 p. Plates.

Translation of *Az Esztergomi Keresztény Múzeum Képtára.*

2356. Gerevich, Tibor. Magyarország románkori emlékei (Monuments of the romanesque era in Hungary). Budapest, Műemlékek Országos Bizottsága, 1938. 842 p. Illus., map, plans. Bibliography: p. 273-276. (Magyarország művészeti emlékei, 1)

A well-illustrated survey of Hungarian and Christian art, including architecture.

2357. Kampis, Antal. The History of Art in Hungary. Budapest, Corvina Press, 1966. 399 p. Illus.

Translation of *A Magyar művészet története* (Budapest, Corvina, 1966). Covers the subject in seven chapters from the conquest up to the present, and includes treatment of socioeconomic and political background.

2358. Lyka, Károly. Nagy magyar művészek (Great Hungarian artists). Budapest, Gondolat Kiadó, 1957. 186 p. Plates. (Élet és tudomány kiskönyvtár, 1)

A collection of scholarly articles and addresses by the greatest art historian and critic. Ten painters and four sculptors, all of the nineteenth and twentieth centuries, are included.

Biographies, portraits, and evaluations of living artists are presented by Lajos Czeizing and Zsuzsa D. Fehér in *Művészek* (Artists) (Budapest, Gondolat, 1963, 208 p., illus., ports.).

2359. Lyka, Károly. Nemzeti romantika; magyar művészet, 1850-1867 (National romanticism; Hungarian art, 1850-1867). Budapest, Singer és Wolfner, 1942. 348 p.

Investigates the birth of modern Hungarian art within the framework of political and literary romanticism, with emphasis on the fine arts. The same author analyzes the effect of the Munich School on Hungarian artists in *Magyar művészélet Münchenben, 1867-1896* (Hungarian artist life in Munich, 1867-1896) (Budapest, Művelt Nép Könyvkiadó, 1951, 86 p.).

2360. A magyarországi művészet története (The history of art in Hungary). 3d corr. ed. Budapest, Képzőművészeti Alap Kiadóvállalata, 1964– Illus., plates, ports. Includes bibliographies.

Two volumes have been issued so far. The first, *Magyarországi művészet a honfoglalástól a XIX. századig* (Art in Hungary from the conquest to the 19th century), edited by Dezső Dercsényi, treats various art forms during the chronological periods (Romanesque, Gothic, Renaissance, Baroque); the second, *Magyar művészet, 1800-1945* (Hungarian art, 1800-1945), edited by Anna Zádor, describes the beginning of a national art and traces artistic developments during the historical periods of the 19th and 20th centuries. There is a glossary and personal and place name indexes.

An earlier work of general coverage is András Péter's *A magyar művészet története* (The history of Hungarian art) (Budapest, Lampel, 1930, 2 v., illus., ports., facsims., bibliography). For a comparative study, *see* Tibor Gerevich's article, "A régi magyar művészet európai helyzete," published in *Minerva*, v. 3, 1924, no. 1/5: 98-122. There are numerous entries relating to aspects of Hungarian art in *Művészeti lexikon* (Art encyclopedia), under the general editorship of Anna Zádor and István Genthon (Budapest, Akadémiai Kiadó, 1965- illus., ports.); three of the projected four volumes have so far appeared.

3. Painting, Drawing, Sculpture

2361. Aggházy, Mária. Early Wood Carvings in Hungary. Budapest, Akadémiai Kiadó, Pub. House of the Hungarian Academy of Sciences, 1965. 38 p. 88 plates (part col.) Bibliography: p. 33.

The representative selection of carvings described and shown here, all with religious themes, dating to about 1770, are largely from the collections of the Budapest Museum of Fine Arts and the Christian Museum at Esztergom. An introductory chapter reviews the history of the art from the Gothic period onward.

2362. Gádor, Endre, *and* Ödön Gábor Pogány. Hungarian Sculpture. Budapest, Corvina, 1955. 138 p. (chiefly plates)

History and evaluation. Interesting personal reminiscences are included in Károly Lyka's *Szobrászatunk a századfordulón, 1896-1914* (Our sculpture at the turn of the century, 1896-1914) (Budapest, Képzőművészeti Alap Kiadóvállalata, 1954, 92 p.).

2363. Genthon, István. A régi magyar festőművészet (Old Hungarian painting). Vác, Pestvidéki Nyomda, 1932. 127 p. Illus.

One of the country's leading art historians describes medieval and early modern development of painting. See also his *La peinture médiévale hongroise* (Paris, A la Croisée des chemins, 1948, 16 p., 32 plates), a translation of *Középkori magyar festészet*; his *Az új magyar festőművészet története 1800-tól napjainkig* (History of the new Hungarian painting from 1800 to the present) (Budapest, Magyar Szemle Társaság, 1935, 294 p.); and Károly Lyka's *Festészetünk a két világháború között, 1920-1940; visszaemlékezések* (Our painting between the two world wars, 1920-1940; reminiscences) (Budapest, Képzőművészeti Alap Kiadóvállalata, 1956, 105 p.).

2364. Pataky, Dénes. Hungarian Drawings and Water-Colours. Budapest, Corvina, 1961. 66 p. 191 plates. Bibliographical references.

Translation of *A magyar rajzművészet* (Budapest, Képzőművészeti Alap Kiadóvállalata, 1960, 61, 191 p.). Acknowledged as standard works for their selection are two volumes on painting by Ödön Gábor Pogány: *19th Century Hungarian Painting*, 2d ed. (Budapest, Corvina, 1956, 13 p., 36 col. plates), a translation of *Magyar festészet a XIX. században*, which has also been issued in a German translation; and *Hungarian Painting in the Twentieth Century* (Budapest, Corvina, 1960, 41 p., 48 col. plates, bibliography), a translation of *Magyar festészet a XX. században.*

2365. Radocsay, Dénes. A középkori Magyarország falképei (Mural paintings of medieval Hungary). Budapest, Akadémiai Kiadó, 1954. 254 p. 132 plates, col. map. Includes bibliographies.

See also the author's *Gothic Panel Painting in Hungary* (Budapest, Corvina Press, 1963, 64 p., 48 mounted col. illus., facsims.), dealing with medieval paintings now in the Budapest Museum of Fine Arts and the Christian Museum at Esztergom; translated from his *Gótikus festmények Magyarországon (*Budapest, Képzőművészeti Alap Kiadóvállalata, 1963, 54 p., 48 mounted col. plates, bibliography).

4. Architecture

2366. Genthon, István, *ed.* Magyarország művészeti emlékei (Art monuments of Hungary). Budapest, Képzőművészeti Alap Kiadóvállalata, 1959-1961. 3 v. Plates. Includes bibliographies.

Describes Hungarian art and architecture by region. The first volume covers Dunántúl; the second, Duna-Tisza köze, Tiszántúl, and Felsővidék; the third, Budapest.

2367. Gerő, László. Hungarian Architecture through the Ages. New Hungarian Quarterly, v. 4, April/June 1963: 158-169.

2368. Major, Máté. Geschichte der Architektur. Berlin, Henschelverlag, 1957-1960. 3 v. Illus. Includes bibliographies.

Contents: v. 1. Die Architektur der Urgemeinschaften und Sklavenhaltergesellschaften; v. 2. Architektur des Feudalismus; v. 3. Die Entwicklung der Architektur von der französischen Revolution bis zur Gegenwart. Translation of *Építészettörténet.* Includes some information on architecture in Hungary.

5. Folk and Decorative Art

2369. Boncz, Klára, *and* Károly Gink. Herend China. Budapest, Pannonia Press, 1962. 81 p. (chiefly illus.)

Presents the eventful history of the Herend factory and its most characteristic porcelain designs and products.

2370. Fél, Edit, *and* Tamás Hofer. Saints, Soldiers, Shepherds; the Human Figure in Hungarian Folk Art. Budapest, Corvina Press, 1966. 65, 48 p. Illus. Bibliography: p. 51-52.

Includes embroidery, wood carving, pottery, and other folk arts to the middle of the 19th century.

2371. Malonyay, Dezső. A magyar nép művészete (Hungarian folk art). Budapest, Franklin-Társulat, 1907-1922. 5 v. Illus., maps, plates.

Contents: v. 1. Hungarian folk art of Kalotaszeg; v. 2. Hungarian folk art in Transylvania; v. 3. Folk art of Hungarian shepherds in the Balaton region; v. 4. Folk art of the Dunántúl (Veszprém, Zala, Somogy, Tolna); v. 5. Folk art of the Palóc (Hont, Nógrád, Heves, Gömör, Borsod).

Other general works on the subject are: Gyula Ortutay's *A magyar népművészet* (Hungarian folk art) (Budapest, Franklin-Társulat, 1941, 2 v., illus.); *Hungarian Decorative Folk Art*, compiled by experts of the Hungarian Ethnographical Museum (Néprajzi Múzeum) (Budapest, Corvina, 1954, 36 p., 208 illus.); and *Hungarian Peasant Art*, by Edit Fél, Tamás Hofer, and Klára K. Csilléry (Budapest, Corvina, 1958, 82 p., plates, maps), which was also published in German.

László Madarassy deals with the popular folk art of wood carving in *Művészkedő magyar pásztorok* (Hungarian shepherd artists) (Budapest, Magyar Könyvbarátok, 193–?, 164 p., illus., bibliography). Another form is treated by Edit Fél in *Hungarian Peasant Embroidery* (London, B. T. Batsford, 1961, 138 p., illus., plates), also issued in German as *Ungarische Volksstickerei*; and by Mária Varjú-Ember in *Hungarian Domestic Embroidery* (Budapest, Corvina Press, 1963, 61, 48 p., illus., bibliography).

H. MUSIC

by Halsey Stevens

2372. Bartók, Béla. Összegyűjtött írásai (Collected writings). Edited by András Szőllősy. v. 1. Budapest, Zeneműkiadó, 1966. 943 p. Illus., music.

Contains all of Bartók's known articles from periodicals and encyclopedias, as well as two books, *A magyar népdal* (1924) and *Népzenénk és a szomszéd népek népzenéje* (1934). Of these, the former was also published in English as *Hungarian Folk Music*, translated by M. D. Calvocoressi (London, Oxford University Press, 1931, 218, 87 p.), and the latter in German as *Die Volksmusik der Magyaren und der benachbarten Völker* (Berlin, Walter de Gruyter, 1935, 64 p., transcriptions of the music [principally unacc. melodies]: p. 33-64).

2373. Bartók, Béla, *and* Zoltán Kodály, *eds.* A magyar népzene tára (Thesaurus of Hungarian folk music). Budapest, Akadémiai Kiadó, 1951– Illus.

I. Gyermekjátékok (Children's games), 934 p.; II. Jeles napok (Special days, 1245 p.; IIIA/B. Lakodalom (Weddings), 1089, 704 p.; IV. Párosítók (Pairing songs), 905 p.; V. Siratók (Laments), 1139 p. The definitive publication on Hungarian folk music, from the collection of the Hungarian Academy of Sciences. Later volumes will include the main body of folksongs associated with no special occasion. Beginning with volume 5, the text and notes are in both Hungarian and English.

2374. Böhm, László. Zenei műszótár; magyarázatokkal, kottapéldákkal, táblázatokkal és hangjegyírás-útmutatóval (A special music dictionary with notes, samples of music scores, charts, and a guide to writing musical notation). Rev. and enl. ed. Budapest, Zeneműkiadó Vállalat, 1961. 347 p. Music, bibliography.

First published in 1952.

2375. Eösze, László. Zoltán Kodály: His Life and Work. Translated by István Farkas and Gyula Gulyás. London, Collet's, 1962. 183 p. Illus., ports.

Concise study of Kodály's career as ethnomusicologist, teacher, and composer. Originally published as *Kodály Zoltán élete és munkássága* (Budapest, Zeneműkiadó Vállalat, 1956, 227 p., ports., facsims.). *See also* Percy M. Young's *Zoltán Kodály, a Hungarian Musician* (London, Ernest Benn, 1964, 231 p., music, plates, [incl. facsims.]).

2376. Gombosi, Ottó. Bakfark Bálint élete és művei, 1507-1576 (Life and music of Valentin Bakfark, 1507-1576). Budapest, Az Országos Széchenyi Könyvtár Kiadása, 1935. 166, 32 p. (music). Illus. (music).

Comprehensive study of the life and work of the 16th century lutanist; appendix includes scores of ten Fantasies for lute. Text in Hungarian and German. A new edition was recently published in German: *Der Lautenist Valentin Bakfark, Leben und Werke, 1507-1576*, edited by Zoltán Falvy (Budapest, Akadémiai Kiadó, 1966, 140 p.).

2377. Kárpáti, János. Bartók vonósnégyesei (Bartok's string quartets). Budapest, Zeneműkiadó Vállalat, 1967. 252 p.

Analytical and stylistic study.

2378. Kodály, Zoltán. Visszatekintés (Retrospect). Edited by Ferenc Bónis. Budapest, Zeneműkiadó, 1964. 2 v. Illus., facsims., music, ports. (Magyar zenetudomány, 5-6)

Collected writings on music; does not include Kodály's important book *A magyar népzene* (Hungarian folk music) (3rd ed., Budapest, Zeneműkiadó Vállalat, 1952, 307 p., illus., ports., music). The German translation of this work, *Die ungarische Volksmusik* (Budapest, Corvina, 1956, 183 p., plates, ports., music), omits many of the folk tunes.

2379. Lendvai, Ernő. Bartók dramaturgiája (Bartók's dramaturgy). Budapest, Zeneműkiadó, 1964. 285 p. Diagrs., music.

Analytical study of Bartók's three stage works and the *Cantata profana*; continues the author's analysis of Bartók's style begun in *Bartók stílusa* (The style of Bartók) (Budapest, Zeneműkiadó, 1955, 155 p., illus., music), based upon the Sonata for Two Pianos and

Percussion and the Music for String Instruments, Percussion, and Celesta. *See also* György Kroó's *Bartók Béla színpadi művei* (Béla Bartók's stage works) (Budapest, Zeneműkiadó Vállalat, 1962, 294 p., illus.).

2380. Liszt, Franz. The Gipsy in Music. London, William Reeves, 1926. 2 v. Fronts., ports.

Discursive and romantic, but of historical importance. Many of Liszt's conclusions have been refuted by later evidence. A translation by Edwin Evans of *Die Zigeuner und ihre Musik in Ungarn* (Pressburg, Heckenast, 1861).

2381. Prahács, Margit, *ed.* Franz Liszt: Briefe aus ungarischen Sammlungen, 1835-1886. Budapest, Akadémiai Kiadó, 1966. 484 p. Music, 24 plates (incl. facsims., ports.) Bibliography: p. 453-456.

More than 600 letters from Hungarian collections, with historico-biographical commentary (including extended biographical summaries of many recipients).

2382. Prahács, Margit. Magyar témák a külföldi zenében. Éléments hongrois dans la musique européenne; essai bibliographique. Preface by Zoltán Kodály. Budapest, Királyi Magyar Pázmány Péter Tudományegyetem Magyarságtudományi Intézete, 1943. 88 p. Plates. (A Magyarságtudományi Intézet kiadványai, 39)

2383. Stevens, Halsey. The Life and Music of Béla Bartók. New York, Oxford University Press, 1964. 364 p. Illus., facsim., music, ports.

A biographical study and critical examination of all published works. First published in 1953. *See also* Halsey Stevens' "Some 'Unknown' Works of Bartók," in *Musical Quarterly* (New York), v. 52, no. 1, Jan. 1966: 37-58, and Bence Szabolcsi's "La vie de Béla Bartók," in *Bartók, sa vie et son oeuvre*, edited by Bence Szabolcsi (Budapest, Corvina, 1956, p. 9-42).

2384. Studia Musicologica. 1961– Budapest. Biannual.

Musicological studies, chiefly by Hungarian writers, in English, French, German or Russian. Principal concerns are the history of Hungarian music and universal music history from a Hungarian standpoint. Includes extensive coverage of ethnomusicology. Volume 3 (1962) is a *Festschrift* marking Kodály's 80th birthday; volume 5 (1963) is devoted to Liszt and Bartók.

Other scholarly monographic series and current serials include *Magyar Zene* (Hungarian music, 1960–, bimonthly) and *Magyar Zenetudomány* (Hungarian musicology, 1959–, annual), both issued by Zeneműkiadó Vállalat, Budapest; *Zenetudományi tanulmányok* (Studies in musicology) (1953–, annual); the monographic series *Monumenta Hungariae musica* (1963–); and *Régi magyar dallamok tára* (Thesaurus of ancient Hungarian melodies) (1958–). The three last-mentioned publications are sponsored by the Hungarian Academy of Sciences.

2385. Szabolcsi, Bence. A Concise History of Hungarian Music. Translated from the Hungarian by Sára Karig. London, Barrie and Rockliff, 1964. 239 p. Facsims. (incl. music), ports.

Text (94 p.) supplemented with examples of Hungarian music from the time of the great migrations to the 20th century. Originally published as *A magyar zenetörténet kézikönyve* (Budapest, Corvina, 1964, 245 p.). *See also* Bence Szabolcsi's *A magyar zene évszázadai* (The centuries of Hungarian music) (Budapest, Zeneműkiadó Vállalat, 1959-1961, 2 v.), and Dezső Legány's *A magyar zene krónikája* (History of Hungarian music) (Budapest, Zeneműkiadó Vállalat, 1962, 535 p., illus.).

2386. Szabolcsi, Bence. Tinódi zenéje (The music of Tinódi). Budapest, Magyar Zenei Dolgozatok, 1929. 20, 35 p.

The historical songs of Sebestyén Tinódi's *Cronica* (1554) in facsimile and transcription, with a critical commentary.

2387. Szabolcsi, Bence, *and* Dénes Bartha, *eds.* Erkel Ferenc és Bartók Béla emlékére (In memory of Ferenc Erkel and Béla Bartók). Budapest, Akadémiai Kiadó, 1954. 558 p. Illus., ports., facsims., music. Zenetudományi tanulmányok, 2)

A collection of essays dealing mainly with the works of Ferenc Erkel (1810-1893), originator of the Hungarian opera and composer of the music of the Hungarian national anthem, and of Béla Bartók (1881-1945). Summaries in English and Russian.

2388. Szabolcsi, Bence, *and* Dénes Bartha, *eds.* Zenetudományi tanulmányok (Studies in musicology). Budapest, Akadémiai Kiadó, 1953-62. 10 v.

Concerned chiefly with Hungarian music from its origins to the twentieth century. Volumes 1 and 6 are *Festschriften* honoring Kodály; volume 5 is dedicated to Mozart, and volume 8 to Haydn. Volume 9 is concerned with the history of opera in Hungary. Volumes 2, 3, 7, and 10 include an extensive documentary biography of Béla Bartók, compiled by János Demény. Text in Hungarian with summaries in English, French, or German. Can be supplemented by:

Keresztúry, Dezső, Jenő Vécsey, *and* Zoltán Falvy. A magyar zenetörténet képeskönyve (A pictorial book of Hungarian music history). Budapest, Magvető Könyvkiadó, 1960. 335 p. Illus., col. plates, ports., facsims.

2389. Zenei lexikon (Encyclopedia of music). By Bence Szabolcsi and Aladár Tóth. Rev. ed. Editor-in-chief: Dénes Bartha. Budapest, Zeneműkiadó, 1965-1967. 3 v. Illus., plates, ports., facsims.

First edition: 1930-1931.

I. THEATER, DRAMA, DANCE, CINEMA

by Albert Tezla

1. Theater

2390. Bayer, József. A nemzeti játékszín története (History of national theater). Budapest, Hornyánszky Viktor, 1887. 2 v.

An authoritative history of Hungarian theatrical activity mainly from 1790 to the opening of the National Theater in 1837. Its appendixes provide data on performances in theaters in Pest, Székesfehérvár, and Kassa, and the names of persons connected with the theater in Pest from 1790 to 1795 and 1807 to 1814.

2391. Dömötör, Tekla. Naptári ünnepek — népi színjátszás (Calendar holidays — folk drama). Budapest, Akadémiai Kiadó, 1964. 271 p.

An interesting and informative discussion of Hungarian folk theater customs attending calendar holidays. Arranged by holiday periods, beginning with Lent, and based on sources preceding the 19th century. Contains chapters on the historical sources of the customs and on the aesthetic character of the Hungarian folk theater. Bibliography of sources in Hungarian and other languages (p. 253-265). Summary in German.

2392. Gyárfás, Miklós, *and* Ferenc Hont, *eds.* Nagy magyar színészek (Great Hungarian actors). Budapest, Bibliotheca, 1957. 489 p.

Individual portraits of 23 Hungarian actors and actresses, mainly concerned with establishing the theatrical individuality of each. Selected from a span of 170 years.

2393. A hetvenötéves magyar Állami Operaház; 1884-1959 (The 75-years-old Hungarian National Opera House; 1884-1959). Budapest, Révai-nyomda, 1959. 251 p. Illus. (part col.), ports., facsims., tables.

Individual essays on the history, performers, and programs of the National Opera House. Tables of performances.

2394. Hont, Ferenc, *ed.* Magyar színháztörténet (Hungarian theatrical history). Written by the panel of theater history of the Institute of Theater Research: Mihály Cenner and others. Budapest, Gondolat, 1962. 331 p. Illus., ports., facsims. Bibliography: p. 293-301.

The first survey of the Hungarian theater since the 19th century. Marxist-Leninist approach. The theater viewed as a part of the history of Hungarian society. Provides the results of research in the 1930's. Valuable selective and critical bibliography of both European and Hungarian sources for each chapter.

2395. Pukánszky, Jolán Kádár. A Nemzeti Színház százéves története (Hundred-year history of the National Theater). Budapest, Magyar Történelmi Társulat, 1938-1940. 2 v. Bibliographical notes: v. 1, p. 521-545.

The most authoritative and comprehensive history of the Hungarian National Theater, from its founding in 1837 to 1937. The first volume focuses on the fulfillment of its purposes and the development of its traditions, and its contributions to the cultural and intellectual development of Hungary. The second volume provides previously unpublished letters, records, and documents dealing with the National Theater in chronological sequence. Other histories of the National Theater include:

Rédey, Tivadar. A Nemzeti Színház története; az első félszázad (History of the National Theater; the first 50 years). Budapest, Királyi Magyar Egyetemi Nyomda, 1937. 405 p. Illus. From 1837 to 1887. Information on actors, singers, plays, operas, etc.

Székely, György, *ed.* A Nemzeti Színház (The National Theater). Written by Mihály Cenner and others. Budapest, Gondolat, 1965. 269 p. Illus., ports. An illustrated history of the Hungarian National Theater from 1837 to 1964. Contains its programs for the 127 years, compiled by Géza Staud (p. 153-239).

2396. Schöpflin, Aladár, *ed.* Magyar színművészeti lexikon; a magyar színjátszás és drámairodalom enciklopédiája (Lexicon of Hungarian theater arts; encyclopedia of Hungarian theater arts and dramatic literature). Budapest, Országos Színészegyesület és Nyugdíjintézete, 1929-1931. 4 v. Illus. (part col.), ports. (part col.).

An encyclopedia of the theater and dramatic literature of Hungary to the 1920's. Cultural, literary, technical, and biographical information. The only such encyclopedia.

2397. Staud, Géza. Magyar színészeti bibliográfia. Bibliographia theatralis hungarica. Budapest, Magyar Színháztudományi és Színpadművészeti Társaság, 1938. 351 p.

An alphabetical catalog, by author, of 1,506 monographs and reprints of articles on the Hungarian theater published to the 1930s. Frequently provides details on contents and reviews. A record of previously published bibliographies on the subject in the introduction. Indexes: works in foreign languages by countries, titles of cited works alphabetically, and name and subject.

2398. Staud, Géza, *ed.* Magyar színházművészet; 1949-1959 (Hungarian theater arts; 1949-1959). Budapest, Színháztudományi Intézet, 1960. 219 p.

A history of the first ten years of Hungarian theaters after their nationalization in 1949. Consists mainly of individual studies on specific theaters arranged under two main divisions: Budapest and provincial theaters. Much statistical information about performances.

2399. Staud, Géza. A magyar színháztörténet forrásai (Sources of Hungarian theater history). Budapest, Színháztudományi Intézet, 1962-1963. 3 v. Facsims. Bibliography: v. 3, p. 52-118. (Színháztörténeti Könyvtár, 6., 8.-9. sz.)

An indispensable tool for research on the Hungarian theater. Highly informative and critical discussions of both primary and secondary sources. Its extensive critical bibliography is arranged by subjects: published sources, bibliographies, lexicons, history of the drama, theater history, individual theaters, and individual actors and actresses.

2400. Váli, Béla. A magyar színészet története (History of Hungarian performing arts). Budapest, Aigner Lajos, 1887. 464 p. Bibliography: p. 460-464.

Hungarian theater and acting from the 15th century to the founding of the National Theater in 1837.

2401. Vogl, Ferenc. Theater in Ungarn 1945 bis 1965. With the assistance of Peter Bochow. Köln, Verlag Wissenschaft und Politik, 1966. 198 p. Plates. Bibliography: p. 193-199.

2. Drama

2402. Bayer, József. A magyar drámairodalom története (History of Hungarian dramatic literature). Budapest, Magyar Tudományos Akadémia, 1897. 2 v.

Hungarian dramatic literature from the Middle Ages to 1867. Parallels the subject with the history of the theater to show the effect of one upon the other, and discusses the historical and political events of each period. Very valuable appendixes providing data on plays and performances. Name and title indexes in each volume.

2403. Dombi, Béla. A drámaírás kísérletei Magyarországon a XVI-XVII. században (Efforts at writing drama in Hungary during the 16th and 17th centuries). Pécs, "Dunántúl" Pécsi Egyetemi Könyvkiadó és Nyomda, 1932. 196 p.

Th development of Hungarian poetic drama during the 16th and 17th centuries. Separate discussion of church and secular drama and 17th century school dramas and morality plays that developed from them. Links the drama with the theatrical stage.

2404. Galamb, Sándor. A magyar dráma története, 1867-1896 (History of Hungarian drama, 1867-1896). Budapest, Magyar Tudományos Akadémia, 1937-1944. 2 v.

The development of Hungarian drama viewed chronologically by literary movements and types. Examination of subject matter, form, and techniques.

2405. Kardos, Tibor. Régi magyar drámai emlékek (Monuments of old Hungarian drama). Budapest, Akadémiai Kiadó, 1960. 2 v.

An anthology containing an extensive literary and historical treatment of Hungarian drama from the 11th century to the end of the 17th. Bibliographical notes at ends of chapters and after each dramatic text.

2406. Vértessy, Jenő. A magyar romantikus dráma (Hungarian romantic drama). Budapest, Magyar Tudományos Akadémia, 1913. 348 p.

A very detailed study of the forces, foreign influences, and playwrights that helped to create Hungary's first real dramatic literature, from 1837 to 1850. Separate name and title indexes.

3. Dance

2407. Rearick, Elizabeth C. Dances of the Hungarians. New York, Teachers College, Columbia University, 1939. 151 p. Illus., map. Bibliography: p. 150-151.

After an introductory ethnological study of rural life, traditional festivals, and the general history of Hungarian dancing, the author presents detailed descriptions of individual dances, with music and with translations of the verses of singing games.

2408. Varjasi, Rezső, *and* Vince Horváth. Hungarian Rhapsody; the Hungarian State Folk Ensemble. Translation of folk songs by Ferenc Kemény. Budapest, Corvina, 1956. 175 p. Illus., music.

Describes the country's leading folk ensemble (Magyar Állami Népi Együttes), which consists of a dance group, an orchestra, and a chorus. Deals also with some basic elements of folk dancing. Published also in German as *Ungarische Rhapsodie; das Ungarische Staatliche Volksensemble.* The group's work is also displayed in *The Hungarian State Folk Ensemble*, edited by János Gerő (Budapest, Institute for Cultural Relations, 1953, 1 v., chiefly illus.). Alexander F. Károlyi depicts the leading pre-1945 folk-dance group, "Gyöngyösbokréta," in *Hungarian Pageant; Life, Customs and Art of the Hungarian Peasantry* (Budapest, G. Vajna, 1939, 113 p., plates, port., music).

2409. Viski, Károly. Hungarian Dances. London, Simpkin, Marshall, 1937. 192 p. Illus., music, plates, group port. Bibliography and notices: p. 193.

Describes the most popular folk dances, among them the recruiting dances, the csárdás, the Kállai Kettős, and craftsmen's dances. Dances of the Hungarians of Transylvania have been described by Mária Bándy and Géza Vámszer in *Székely táncok* (Székler dances) (Cluj, 1937). Also of interest is *Dances of Hungary*, by György Buday (New York, Chanticleer Press, 1950, 40 p., illus., map, music, bibliography). The most comprehensive work, especially from the historical viewpoint, is Marián Réthei Prikkel's *A magyarság táncai* (Dances of the Hungarians) (Budapest, "Studium," 1924, 311 p., illus., music). "Symbolic Dances in Hungarian Folklore," by Ákos Szendrey, appears in the *Hungarian Quarterly*, v. 1, Spring 1936: 124-135. An illustrative description with music is *Vengerskie narodnye tantsy* (Hungarian folk dances (Moskva, Iskusstvo, 1960, 77 p., illus.). A practical aid is offered by Edith W. Elekes in *Hungarian Dances; Guide Book for Teachers of Hungarian Dances* (Budapest, 1936, 69 p.).

4. Cinema

2410. Balázs, Béla. Theory of the Film; Character and Growth of a New Art. Translated by Edith Bone. London, Dennis Dobson, 1952. 291 p. Illus.

A summary of the work and thought of a pioneer in film theory and aesthetics who influenced the development of the cinematic arts in Europe and the Soviet Union. Translation of his *Filmkultúra; a film művészetfilozófiája* (Budapest, Szikra, 1948, 255 p.).

2411. Film kislexikon (Short lexicon of the film). Edited by Péter Ábel. Major collaborators, István Nemeskürty and Gábor Pozsonyi. Budapest, Akadémiai Kiadó, 1964. 981 p. Illus., ports.

Contains detailed articles on the cinema in Hungary.

2412. A magyar film húsz éve; 1945-1965 (Twenty years of the Hungarian film; 1945-1965). Edited by József Homoródy. Budapest, Magvető, 1965. 235 p. Illus.

Mainly illustrations from films of the period but also a number of short studies: a survey of the period, the Béla Balázs Studio, cartoons, documentaries, educational and art films, and newsreels.

2413. Nemeskürty, István. A magyar film története; 1912-1963 (History of the Hungarian film, 1912-1963). Budapest, Gondolat Kiadó, 1965. 333 p. Illus., ports. Bibliographical notes: p. 319-331.

The only comprehensive survey. The appendix is a chronological record of feature-length films listing their titles and the names of three or four major actors for each film.

Part Five

Poland

38

General Reference Aids and Bibliographies

by Janina W. Hoskins

A. BIBLIOGRAPHIES

1. Bibliographies of Bibliographies

2414. Bibliografia bibliografii i nauki o książce. Bibliographia Poloniae bibliographica (Bibliography of bibliographies and library science literature) 1947– Warszawa, Biblioteka Narodowa. Annual.

Each issue lists approximately 2,500 books and articles, the majority of which are published in Poland. Included are bibliographies of writings pertaining to Poland, studies on documentation, the theory and history of bibliography, book publishing, and library science. Author, title, and subject index, and a list of periodicals containing bibliographical sections. Issued by the Bibliographic Institute of the National Library of Poland. This supersedes an earlier annual *Bibliografia bibliografii, bibliotekarstwa i bibliofilstwa* (Bibliography of bibliographies, library science and bibliophily), v. 1-7, 1928-1936 (Kraków, 1929-1938) which was published in Kraków, as a supplement to *Przegląd biblioteczny* (Library review). The period between 1937 and 1946 has been covered in two extra volumes, 1945/46, published in 1955, and 1937/44, issued in 1965.

2415. Chojnacki, Władysław, *and* Jan Kowalik. Bibliografia niemieckich bibliografii dotyczących Polski, 1900-1958 (Bibliography of German bibliographies concerning Poland, 1900-1958). Poznań, Instytut Zachodni, 1960. 252 p.

About 1,300 entries for German bibliographic compilations concerning Poland, both monographs and lists appearing in books and periodicals. Subject classification.

2416. Hahn, Wiktor. Bibliografia bibliografij polskich (Bibliography of Polish bibliographies). 3d ed., rev. and enl. by Henryk Sawoniak. Wrocław, Zakład Narodowy im. Ossolińskich, 1966. 586 p.

Selective bibliography of over 7,500 bibliographies published prior to 1951, mainly in Poland. Entries are arranged in 25 broad classes, and include separate bibliographies and bibliographical compilations in books and periodicals. Author and subject indexes. The first edition appeared in 1921, and the second, much extended, in 1956. The 1966 edition adds about 1,000 titles. A continuation covering the years 1951-1960 is provided by:

Sawoniak, Henryk. Bibliografia bibliografii polskich, 1951-1960. Wrocław, Zakład Narodowy im. Ossolińskich, 1967. 483 p. Lists 5,795 briefly annotated numbered entries. Alphabetical and subject indexes.

For lists of unpublished Polish bibliographies on file at the Bibliographic Institute of the National Library of Poland, consult *Wykaz polskich bibliografii nie opublikowanych (planowanych, opracowanych i ukończonych)* compiled by Elżbieta Słodkowska, 4th ed. (Warszawa, 1967, 218 p.; Biblioteka Narodowa. Prace Instytutu Bibliograficznego, nr. 7).

2417. Korpała, Józef. Zarys dziejów bibliografii w Polsce (Outline of the history of Polish bibliography). Wrocław, Zakład Narodowy im. Ossolińskich, 1953. 231 p. Ports., facsims. (Książka w dawnej kulturze polskiej, 5)

An informative history of Polish bibliographic achievement from the 12th century through 1952, discussing in an essay form basic general and specialized bibliographies. This basic work also is available in a German translation: *Abriss der Geschichte der Bibliographie in Polen* (Leipzig, O. Harrassowitz, 1957. 258 p., ports., facsims.).

A more popular presentation is Korpała's *O bibliografiach dla wszystkich; poradnik, informator* (Bibliographies for all; a guide) issued by the Stowarzyszenie Bibliotekarzy Polskich (Warszawa, 1964. 184 p.).

Maria Dembowska's article "Polen" in *Die Bibliographie in den europäischen Ländern der Volksdemokratie* (Leipzig, Verlag für Buch- und Bibliothekswesen, 1960), p. 47-67, is a brief historical sketch of bibliographic work in Poland.

Bibliographic activities in the postwar times are described by Maria M. Biernacka in "Dwadzieścia lat polskiej bibliografii, 1944-1964" (Twenty years of Polish bibliography, 1944-1964), *Przegląd biblioteczny* (Library review), v. 33, 1965, p. 143-157, and by Marta Burbianka in "Dorobek bibliografii w Polsce Ludowej" (Bibliographic achievements in People's Poland), *Roczniki biblioteczne* (Library annals), v. 10, 1966, no. 3/4, p. 411-461.

2418. Kowalik, Jan. Bibliografia bibliografij polskich, wydanych poza Polską po r. 1939. Bibliography of Polish Bibliographies Published Outside Poland Since 1939. London, B. Świderski, 1965. 35 p.

Includes 626 entries in three main groups: general bibliographies of bibliographies, regional (country) bibliographies of bibliographies, and special bibliographies of bibliographies. Reprint from *Literatura polska na obczyźnie, 1940-1960,* v. 2 (London, B. Świderski, 1965) p. 645-680.

2. General Bibliographies

2419. Estreicher, Karol Józef T. Bibliografia polska (Polish bibliography). Kraków, Wydawn. Towarzystwa Naukowego Krakowskiego. v. 1– 1872–

The most comprehensive and important retrospective bibliography of writings in Poland and about Poland issued in or outside the country from 1455 to 1900. This is a huge compilation in three parts: Part 1. Bibliografia polska XIX. stólecia (Polish bibliography of the 19th century). Kraków, 1872-1882. 7 v. Lists in alphabetical order books published between 1800 and 1880. Supplement: Bibliografia polska XIX. stulecia; lata 1881-1900 (Polish bibliography of the 19th century; years 1881-1900). Kraków, Nakł. Spółki Księgarzy Polskich, 1906-1916. 4 v. Continuation of Part I of the original work covering the last 20 years of the nineteenth century. Titles listed alphabetically. Part 2. Bibliografia polska. Chronologicznie (Polish bibliography. Chronological). Kraków, Akademia Umiejętności, 1882-1890. 4 v. (i.e., v. 8-11, called also v. 1-3 of part 2). In chronological order lists books published between 1455 and 1889. Part 3. Bibliografia polska. Stólecie XV-XVIII w układzie abecadłowym (Polish bibliography. 15-18th centuries; in alphabetical order). Kraków, Akademia Umiejętności, 1891-1951. 23 v. (i.e., v. 12-34, called also v. 1-22 of part 3). Volume 33, ending with the letter Y, was published in 1939; volume 34, fascicle 1, Z-Załuski; remaining unfinished, appeared in 1951. Volumes 23-33 were edited by the author's son Stanisław Estreicher, and volume 34 by his grandson Karol Estreicher. Entries often have brief annotations.

Second revised edition, now in progress, of the *Bibliografia polska XIX stulecia* (Polish bibliography of the 19th century) (Kraków, Państwowe Wydawn. Naukowe, 1959–), prepared under the auspices of the Polish Academy of Sciences, will include the original Part 1, supplements, and many works subsequently located. There were six volumes issued during 1959-1967 covering the letters A-E.

For early Polish imprints these works should be used in conjunction with:

Wierzbowski, Teodor. Bibliographia Polonica XV ac XVI ss. Varsoviae, in Officina Typ. C. Kowalewsky, 1889-1894. 3 v. Reprinted in Nieuwkoop (Netherlands) by B. De Graaf, 1961.

Budzyk, Kazimierz. Bibliografia konstytucyj sejmowych XVII wieku w Polsce (Bibliography of 17th century Polish laws). Wrocław, Wydawn. Zakładu Narodowego im. Ossolińskich, 1952. 191 p. Illus. (Książka w dawnej kulturze polskiej, 3).

Triller, Eugenia. Bibliografia konstytucji sejmowych XVII wieku w Polsce w świetle badań archiwalnych (Bibliography of 17th century Polish laws as compared with the archival materials). Wrocław, Zakład Narodowy im. Ossolińskich, 1963. 122 p. Facsims. (Wrocławskie Towarzystwo Naukowe. Śląskie prace bibliograficzne i bibliotekoznawcze, t. 7).

2420. Katalog rozpraw doktorskich i habilitacyjnych (Catalog of doctoral dissertations and Habilitationsschriften). 1959/61– Warszawa, Państwowe Wydawn. Naukowe, 1962– Annual.

The first issue lists dissertations accepted for the doctoral degree and to qualify as "Dozent" during 1959-1961. Subsequent volumes have been published annually. The volume published in 1965 lists 2,504 dissertations accepted in 1964. The more recent editions include abstracts of dissertations. The publication is sponsored by the Ministry of Higher Education.

2421. Klanowski, Tadeusz, Stanisław Kubiak, *and* Mirosława Stempniewicz. Bibliografia publikacji pracowników Uniwersytetu im. Adama Mickiewicza w Poznaniu, 1945-1964 (Bibliography of publications of the staff of the Adam Mickiewicz University in Poznań, 1945-1964). Poznań, 1965. 970 p.

Titles of books, articles, collections and book reviews, 13,415 in all, arranged by the departments sponsoring them, and within each department — alphabetically by authors.

2422. Korbut, Gabrjel. Literatura polska od początków do wojny światowej; książka podręczna informacyjna dla studjujących naukowo dzieje rozwoju piśmiennictwa polskiego (Polish literature from the beginning to the outbreak of the World War; a reference book for students of the historical development of Polish literary production) 2d ed. enl. Warszawa, Kasa im. Mianowskiego, 1929-1931. 4 v.

An important bibliography of works of Polish writers, mainly in humanities, from the 10th century to 1914, with short biographies and lists of critical studies. A revised, updated, and augmented edition, projected in 20 volumes, has been in progress since 1963 under the auspices of the Literary Institute of the Polish Academy of Sciences. By 1965 three volumes had appeared, edited by Roman Pollak, which provide bio-bibliographies of writers of the 10th through the 17th centuries: *Piśmiennictwo staropolskie; hasła ogólne i anonimowe* (Old Polish literature; general and anonymous writings) (Warszawa, Państwowy Instytut Wydawniczy, 1963, 390 p.) and *Piśmiennictwo staropolskie; hasła osobowe* (Old Polish literature; production of individual writers) (Warszawa, Państwowy Instytut Wydawniczy, 1964-1965, 2 v.). The first part of volume 4, prepared by Elżbieta Aleksandrowska and others, appeared in 1966 as *Oświecenie: hasła ogólne, rzeczowe i osobowe* (Enlightenment: writings on general and specialized subjects, and by individual writers) (Warszawa, Państwowy Instytut Wydawniczy, 547 p.).

2423. Krzyżanowski, Ludwik, *and others.* Bibliography; Materials Written in English on Poland and Items by Polish Authors. The Polish Review (New York, 1956–).

Useful selective compilation of books, pamphlets, and articles, published in Poland and abroad, printed at least twice a year in issues of *The Polish Review* (see entry no. 2438), of which Dr. Krzyżanowski is editor.

2424. New Polish Publications; A Monthly Review of Polish Books. 1953– Warsaw, Ars Polona. Illus.

A bulletin issued by Ars Polona, Poland's central agency for export of books, announcing new publications. Includes review articles. Supplement (annotated in English) in every issue for books "Soon to appear." Prices given in American dollars.

Another useful tool for trade book selection is *Nowe książki; przegląd literacki i naukowy* (New books; literary and scholarly review) (v. 1– October 1949– biweekly), containing long signed reviews, literary articles, and silhouettes of Polish writers and also a chronicle of literary activities. Destined primarily for the Polish domestic market. *See also*:

Zapowiedzi wydawnicze (Books to appear). 1952– Warszawa, Państwowe Przedsiebiorstwo Składnica Księgarska. Weekly. An annotated list of forthcoming books prepared on the basis of information supplied by the publishers and issued by Poland's center for domestic book trade. It includes about 6,000 titles annually.

2425. Polonica zagraniczne; bibliografia (Polonica abroad; a bibliography). 1960– Warszawa, Biblioteka Narodowa. Annual.

A record of books, articles, and periodicals issued abroad in Polish and in other languages relating to Poland. Volume 1 treats publications issued during 1956. It is compiled by the Bibliographic Institute of the National Library of Poland as a part of Poland's national bibliography. By 1968, the volumes covering the years 1956-1963 had appeared.

An inventory of foreign Polonica prior to World War II was maintained by *Wykaz druków polskich lub Polski dotyczących, wydanych zagranicą. Bulletin bibliographique des imprimés polonais ou concernant la Pologne édités à l'étranger* issued monthly by the National Library of Poland (Warszawa, 1928-1938). This also was a supplement to the national bibliography of Poland.

Robert J. Kerner's *Slavic Europe* (see entry no. 18) offers a general guide to Polonica. In his bibliography (chapter 3, p. 149-188), Kerner includes 550 books on Polish history, literature, and language. The compilation consists mostly of Polish books, and is largely limited to holdings of the Harvard University Library. Polish titles are preceded by English translations. Still valuable, especially as a guide to older reference books in humanities. For a recent survey *see* Kazimierz Grzybowski's *Poland in the Collections of the Library of Congress; an Overview* (Washington, D.C., Library of Congress, 1969, 26 p., illus.).

Another source is the *Bibliography of Works by Polish Scholars and Scientists Published Outside Poland in Languages Other Than Polish*, compiled by Maria Danilewicz and Jadwiga Nowak (London, Polish Society of Arts and Sciences Abroad, 1964–).Volume 1 covers the years 1939-1962. It may be supplemented by the *Bibliography of Books in Polish or Relating to Poland, Published Outside Poland since September 1st, 1939*, compiled by Janina Zabielska (London, 1953– v. 1: 1939-1951; v. 2: 1952-1957).

For Polonica by individual languages see:

The American Bibliography of Russian and East European Studies (see entry no. 6) which lists in each volume titles dealing with Poland under various subject classifications. For a detailed listing of U.S. Government publications in English on Poland consult the *Monthly Catalog of U. S. Government Publications*, issued by the Superintendent of Documents, U.S. Government Printing Office. The December number of each year includes a cumulative annual subject index. Robert F. Byrnes' *Bibliography of American Publications on East Central Europe, 1945-1957* (Bloomington, Ind., 1958) lists over 500 titles of books and articles dealing with Poland and published in the United States. Material covering a preceding period may be found in Alphonse S. Wolanin's *Polonica in English. Annotated Catalogue* (Chicago, 1945, 186 p.) which is a guide to books and pamphlets in English concerning Poland to be found in the Archives and Museum of the Polish Roman Catholic Union in Chicago.

Lorentowicz, Jan, *and* A. M. Chmurski. La Pologne en France; essai d'une bibliographie raisonnée. Paris, H. Champion, 1935-1941. 3 v. (Institut d'études slaves de l'Université de Paris. Bibliothéque polonaise, 4) One of the best bibliographies of foreign Polonica. Endeavors to include all books and articles on Poland published in France prior to the Second World War. Volume 1 surveys Polish literature, drama, and the arts; volume 2, geography, the natural sciences, and law. Supplement to all three volumes in volume 3.

Bersano Begey, Maria. La Polonia in Italia; saggio bibliografico, 1799-1948. Torino, R. E. Sellier, 1949. 295 p. (Pubblicazioni dell'Istituto di cultura polacca Attilio Begey, Università di Torino, n. 2) Lists 3,375 titles of Italian Polonica, including periodical articles.

Akademiia nauk SSSR. *Fundamental'naia biblioteka obshchestvennykh nauk.* Sovetskoe slavianovedenie; literatura o zarubezhnykh slavianskikh stranakh na russkom iazyke, 1918-1960 (Soviet Slavic studies; writings on Slavic countries in the Russian language, 1918-1960). Compiled by I. A. Kaloeva. Moscow, Izd-vo Akademii nauk SSSR, 1963. 401 p. Pages 151-256 of a survey of Russian literature on Slavic countries comprise writings on Polish history, folklore, literature, archaeology, and linguistics, with almost 2,900 entries in all.

Current acquisitions concerning Poland of three major Soviet libraries, The Fundamental Library of Social Sciences of the Academy of Sciences of the USSR, the All-Union State Library of Foreign Literature, and the Gor'kii Library of Moscow State University, are recorded in the monthly index, *Novaiia literatura po Pol'she* (New literature about Poland) (1960– Moskva. Title varies: 1960-1961, *Novaiia literatura po evropeiskim stranam . . . Pol'sha*). The first issue, published in 1960, includes titles published in 1959. About 7,500 titles in Russian, Polish, and other languages are recorded per years. Entries are arranged by subject.

Trypućko, Józef. Bibliografi over svenska Polonica, 1918-1939. Uppsala, Slaviska institutionen vid Uppsala universitet, 1955. 2 v. Mimeographed list continuing the bibliography by Stanisław Wędkiewicz: *La Suède et la Pologne. Essai d'une bibliographie des publications suèdoises concernant la Pologne* (Stockholm, 1918). The 3,443 Swedish writings listed by Trypućko include translations from the Polish. Grouped under subject headings.

2426. Polska Akademia Nauk. *Ośrodek Rozpowszechniania Wydawnictw Naukowych.* Katalog wydawnictw (Catalog of publications) 1956– Wrocław, Zakład Narodowy im. Ossolińskich. Annual.

Catalog of monographs and periodicals issued by the Polish Academy of Sciences in Warsaw and its affiliated learned societies, prepared by the Academy's Center of Distribution of Scholarly Works. Volume one covers 1952-1955. Entries, some of which are annotated, are grouped under subject headings. Author index and list of titles in each issue.

See also the Polish Academy of Sciences' *Publications in Foreign Languages, 1951-1965* (Warszawa, 1966, 116 p.) listing 461 entries grouped in four categories, including publications in social sciences, biological, and pure and technical sciences.

Publications of the Academy's predecessor, the Polish Academy of Sciences and Letters in Kraków, whose activities were discontinued in 1951, were recorded in Polska Akademia Umiejętności. *Katalog wydawnictw, 1873-1947* (Kraków, 1948, 2 v.). Volume 1 lists works in humanities and social sciences; volume 2 includes publications of the Academy's departments of medicine, and of mathematics and natural sciences.

Significant lists of publications of other learned societies of Poland include:

Bielińska, Stanisława, *and* Michał Witkowski. Bibliografia wydawnictw Poznańskiego Towarzystwa Przyjaciół Nauk, 1856-1956 (Bibliography of publications of the Poznań Society of Friends of Learning, 1856-1956) *Roczniki historyczne* (Poznań), v. 23, 1957. 134 p. (Supplement to volume commemorating the centennial of the Society).

Towarzystwo Naukowe w Toruniu. Bibliografia prac Towarzystwa Naukowego w Toruniu, 1875-1960 (Bibliography of works of the Learned Society in Toruń, 1875-1960). Toruń, 1961. 142 p.

Towarzystwo Naukowe Warszawskie. Katalog wydawnictw, 1907-1932 (Catalog of publications of the Warsaw Learned Society, 1907-1932). Compiled by Henryka Szellerowa and Wanda Konarska. Warszawa, 1933. 261 p.

2427. Przewodnik bibliograficzny; urzędowy wykaz druków wydanych w Polskiej Rzeczypospolitej Ludowej (Bibliographic guide; the official list of printed matter in the Polish People's Republic) 1946– Warszawa, Biblioteka Narodowa. Weekly.

Official national bibliography of Poland, issued by the Bibliographic Institute of the National Library, superseding and continuing the volume numbering of the *Urzędowy wykaz druków wydanych w Rzeczypospolitej Polskiej. Bulletin bibliographique officiel des imprimés édités dans la République Polonaise* (v. 1-12, 1928-August 26, 1939). Publication was begun with volume 2 (14) in 1946. Volume one, listing titles issued during 1944-1945, came out in 1955. It also registers publications for 1946 and 1947 that were omitted in the issues for these years. The bibliography is an inventory of material currently published in Poland — books, pamphlets, albums, maps, music scores, and first and last issues of periodicals begun or discontinued. About 9,000 items are entered each year. Arrangement by 26 major classes. An author and title index is supplied monthly, and there are annual indexes of authors and subjects.

2428. Rister, Herbert. Schrifttum über Polen mit besonderer Berücksichtigung des Posener Landes, 1945-60. Marburg/Lahn, 1953– (Wissenschaftliche Beiträge zur Geschichte und Landeskunde Ost-Mitteleuropas, no. 10, 20, 33, 47, 49, and 75. In Progress. Mimeographed.

A general bibliography of books and articles in several languages on Poland with a separate section for Greater Poland issued under the auspices of the Johan Gottfried Herder-Institut. The first volume covers the years 1943-1951. Author and title indexes.

2429. Stowarzyszenie Bibliotekarzy Polskich. *Commission nationale de bibliographie.* Bibliographie sur la Pologne; pays, histoire, civilisation. 2d ed., with a supplement for 1960-1963. Edited by Helena Hleb-Koszańska and others. Warszawa, PWN — Éditions scientifiques de Pologne, 1964. 300 p.

A selective annotated bibliography of 1,574 books and periodicals on the humanities and social sciences published prior to 1964 in Polish and in Western European languages. The second edition is a reprint of the first edition (published 1963 under the auspices of the Polish Commission for UNESCO) with the same title, plus a supplement listing 365 works issued during 1960-1963. Materials in both parts grouped under 13 main headings. Polish titles followed by French translations and usually by annotations in French. Compiled with the cooperation of 19 subject specialists.

3. Regional Bibliographies

2430. Czarnecki, Feliks. Bibliografia Ziem Zachodnich, 1945-1958 (Bibliography of works on the Western Territories, 1945-1958). Poznań, Instytut Zachodni, 1962. 545 p.

Through 4,753 selected works this bibliography attempts to illustrate developments in Silesia, Western Pomerania, Masurenland, Ermland, and the Danzig area. Fifty-page author and title index. Other regional bibliographies are:

Bibliografia Śląska (Bibliography of Silesia). Katowice, Państwowe Wydawn. Naukowe. Oddział w Krakowie, 1963– Supersedes *Wykaz literatury o Śląsku* (List of writings on Silesia), edited by Jacek Koraszewski (Katowice, Instytut Śląski, 1935-1939).

Bibliografia Warszawy (Bibliography of Warsaw). Wrocław, Zakład Narodowy im. Ossolińskich, 1958-1964. 2 v.

Rister, Herbert. Schlesische Bibliographie. Marburg/L., 1953– (Wissenschaftliche Beiträge zur Geschichte und Landeskunde Ost-Mitteleuropas, no. 5, 18, 24, 56, 60, 65) In progress. Mimeographed. Covers 1928-1934; 1942-1957.

Wadowski, Jerzy. Morze i Pomorze; książki, czasopisma, filmy (The [Baltic] Sea and Pomerania; books, serials, and films). Warszawa, Stowarzyszenie Bibliotekarzy Polskich, 1964. 448 p.

For writings on Greater Poland, especially on Poznań province, *see* H. Rister (entry no. 2428).

A comprehensive coverage of regional bibliographies is provided by Wiktor Hahn (see entry no. 2416), p. 458-475 and Henryk Sawoniak (entry no. 2416a), p. 258-284.

4. Bibliographies of Serials

2431. Bibliografia czasopism i wydawnictw zbiorowych (Bibliography of periodicals and monograph series) 1958– Warszawa. Annual.

This annual list of current serials is a part of the Polish national bibliography. The titles, listed alphabetically, range from daily newspapers to yearbooks. There are separate lists of publishing institutions and editors. Issued by the Instytut Bibliograficzny of the Biblioteka Narodowa (Bibliographical Institute of the National Library). Volumes to cover 1944-1957 are in preparation.

For the earlier period consult *Bibliografia prasy polskiej, 1944-48. Prasa krajowa* (Bibliography of Polish press of 1944-48. The domestic press) (Warszawa, Państwowe Wydawn. Naukowe, 1966. 324 p.) issued by the Pracownia Historii Czasopiśmiennictwa Polskiego XIX i XX wieków of the Polska Akademia Nauk. This bibliography registers 1,771 new periodicals, newspapers, and government serials, listed chronologically by date of initial appearance. Indexes to titles, places of publication, and names of editors.

For a general guide to periodicals and newspapers available on subscription see *Katalog prasy polskiej* (Catalog of the Polish press) (Warszawa, Biuro Wydawnicze "Ruch," 1957– irregular) which is a commercial catalog issued by "Ruch," the central export agency for Polish periodicals. Annotated list of newspapers and periodicals issued in Poland, giving complete bibliographical data, addresses of editorial offices, and prices. Some government serials are also included. "Ruch" also publishes each year in English the *Price List of Polish Scientific Periodicals* (the most recent for 1966/67 lists alphabetically 273 scholarly journals, the Polish titles of which are followed by English translation) and *Price List of Polish Dailies and Popular Periodicals* (over 350 titles in each annual issue).

A prewar press guide, *Spis gazet i czasopism Rzeczypospolitej Polskiej* (List of newspapers and periodicals of the Polish Republic) was published in Warsaw by Biuro Ogłoszeń Teofil Pietraszek with eight editions between 1921 and 1939.

2432. Gutry, Czesław. Bibliografia scalonych spisów zawartości czasopism (Bibliography of indexes to serials). Wrocław, Zakład im. Ossolińskich, 1953. 174 p.

A useful bibliographic guide to the contents of Polish periodicals and periodicals relating to Poland. Two supplements appeared in *Roczniki biblioteczne. Organ naukowy bibliotek szkół wyższych* (Warszawa), 1962: 217-306; 1965: 387-420.

2433. U.S. *Bureau of the Census.* Bibliography of Social Science Periodicals and Monograph Series: Poland, 1945-1962. Washington, D.C., 1964. 312 p. (Foreign Social Science Bibliographies. Series P-92, no. 16)

See also entry no. 21.

Inventory of serials in the Library of Congress collections, consisting of 346 periodical titles and 1,434 monograph series, published in Poland between 1945 and 1962. Arrangement is by subject. Indexes of subjects, titles, authors, and issuing agencies. Library of Congress call numbers are given.

2434. Wepsiec, Jan. Polish Serial Publications 1953-1962; an Annotated Bibliography. Chicago, Ill., The Author, 1964. 506 p.

A useful catalog of 4,345 serials issued in Poland during 1953-1962, including journals, newspapers, and publications of government agencies and learned societies. Polish titles accompanied by English translations. *See also* the same author's *Polish American Serial Publications, 1842-1966. An Annotated Bibliography* (Cchiago, Ill., 1968, 191 p.).

2435. Zieliński, Stanisław. Bibliografja czasopism polskich zagranicą, 1830-1934 (Bibliography of Polish periodicals published outside of

Poland between 1830 and 1934). Warszawa, Światowy Związek Polaków z Zagranicy, 1935. 308 p. Fold. map.

Entries are listed alphabetically, chronologically, and by place of publication.

B. GENERAL PERIODICALS

2436. Poland. no. 1– 1954– Warsaw, Polonia. Monthly. Illus. (part col.)

Lavishly illustrated magazine for foreign circulation, covering a broad range of subjects, published also in French, German, Russian, Spanish, and Swedish. Some articles are by prominent Polish scholars.

2437. Polish Perspectives. v. 1– May 1958– Warsaw. Monthly.

See also entry no. 2795.

Illustrated journal for foreign circulation containing articles on the cultural, scientific, economic, and artistic life in Poland, and short reviews of new books. Also appears in French.

2438. The Polish Review. v. 1– Winter 1956– New York, Polish Institute of Arts and Sciences in America. Quarterly.

See also entries no. 2591 *and* 2752.

Devoted to scholarly articles dealing with Poland's past and present, mainly cultural history. Carries reviews of books, chronicle of events taking place in Poland, and, at least twice a year, a bibliography of articles, pamphlets, and books in English published in Poland and abroad and concerning Poland (*see* entry no. 2423).

2439. Polska Akademia Nauk. The Review. 1964– Warsaw. Quarterly.

Published by the Polish Academy of Sciences in Warsaw, providing information on activities and publications of the Academy and other learned societies.

C. ENCYCLOPEDIAS

2440. Polska Ludowa; słownik encyklopedyczny (People's Poland; encyclopedic dictionary) Józef Gutt, chief editor. Warszawa, Wiedza Powszechna, 1965. 482 p.

Encyclopedic handbook with brief articles, arranged in dictionary style, covering many aspects of contemporary Poland. Numerous illustrations, maps, and charts — some in color — enhance the usefulness of this compact work.

2441. Wielka encyklopedia powszechna PWN (The great universal encyclopedia PWN). Warszawa, Państwowe Wydawn. Naukowe, 1962– Illus., col. plates, ports., maps.

The latest important undertaking of Polish encyclopedists, scheduled for completion in 13 volumes. Volume 11 (published in 1968) carries the contents through the letter U. Like the *Mała encyklopedia powszechna PWN* (see below) it is being produced under state auspices, with Bogdan Suchodolski as chief editor. In its Marxist orientation and its increased attention to science it differs from the earlier *Wielka ilustrowana encyklopedja powszechna*, which was published in Kraków by Wydawnictwo "Gutenberga." That work, originally issued in parts, appeared in 20 volumes between 1929 and 1933, with two supplementary volumes in 1937-1938. Volume 13 (1932) was devoted exclusively to Poland ("Polska," 334 p.). A part of volume 9 of *Wielka encyklopedia powszechna PWN* which deals exclusively with Poland also appeared separately as *Polska* (Warszawa, Państwowe Wydawn. Naukowe, 1967, 230 p., illus., maps).

The first encyclopedia that was brought out in Poland after the war was *Mała encyklopedia powszechna PWN* (The short universal encyclopedia PWN) (Warszawa, Państwowe Wydawn. Naukowe, 1959, 1124 p., illus., plates, ports., maps). A selection of its articles relating to Poland, with some additional material, was published in five languages — English, German, Russian, Spanish, and Esperanto — "for the convenience of foreigners who would like to know more about Poland." The English edition is entitled *Poland; Land, History, Culture; An Outline* (Warsaw, Państwowe Wydawn. Naukowe, 1959, 156 p.).

A more popular encyclopedia, issued for broader circulation, is *A-Z: Encyklopedia popularna PWN*, 3d rev. ed. (Warszawa, Państwowe Wydawn. Naukowe, 1965, 1292 p., illus., map).

Other notable encyclopedias are: *Ilustrowana encyklopedia Trzaski, Everta i Michalskiego*, edited by Stanisław Lam (Warszawa, 1927-1938) of international scope with attention centered on Poland. The supplementary volume 6 (1938), which deals exclusively with the 20th century, includes a chronology of important events in Polish history from 1928 to 1937; and *Encyklopedja powszechna Ultima Thule*, edited by Stanisław Michalski (Warszawa, 1927-1938, 10 v., illus., maps, plans) was left unfinished at the opening of the Second World War (up to Szymonowicz). Samuel Orgelbrand's *Encyklopedja powszechna* (Warszawa, 1859-1868, 28 v.; 2d ed., 1883-1884, 14 v.; rev. ed. 1898-1912, 18 v.) is still valuable as a source for study of 19th century Polish culture and intellectual trends.

D. HANDBOOKS, SURVEYS, GUIDEBOOKS

2442. Barnett, Clifford R. *and others*. Poland, Its People, Its Society, Its Culture. New Haven, HRAF Press, 1958. 470 p. Illus. (Survey of World Cultures, 1)

See also entry no. 2706.

Study of the country as seen through the eyes of social scientists. This is one of a series based on the extensive collection of materials relating to Poland in the interdisciplinary Human Relations Area Files.

Another handbook, surveying in 21 chapters the situation in Poland during 1943-1955 was edited by Oskar Halecki, *Poland* (New

York, F. A. Praeger, for the Free Europe Committee, 1957, 601 p.). It also provides a chronology of events in Poland during that period.

Encompassing a wide spectrum of knowledge is a survey edited by Bernadotte E. Schmitt, *Poland* (Berkeley and Los Angeles, University of California Press, 1945. 500 p. illus., tables, ports.; bibliography: p. 465-476). This work consists of eight parts written by leading scholars in America, some of them Polish expatriates. Coverage includes anthropology, history, political developments to 1939, economic and social conditions, cultural life, Polish-American relations, and foreign policy.

2443. Markert, Werner, *ed.* Polen. Köln, Böhlau Verlag, 1959. 829 p. Maps, diagrs., tables. Bibliography: p. 743-781. (Osteuropa-Handbuch, Bd. 2)

See also entry no. 3137.

Handbook containing concise, well documented articles by German scholars on recent Polish politics and government, economy, and culture. The chronological table covers events from 1914 to 1956, though emphasis is on the post-1945 period. Includes biographical sketches of about 200 prominent Poles, some now living in Poland and abroad. Extensive bibliography by chapters, author and subject index. A more recent publication emphasizing cultural developments in Poland is:

Hartmann, Karl. Polen. Zürich, Christiana Verlag, 1966. xii, 498 p. Plates. Bibliography: p. 475-482. (Kultur der Nationen, 17)

2444. Poland. Prepared by a group of Polish university teachers, under the general supervision of Paul Wagret. English version by Helga S. B. Harrison. New York, McGraw-Hill, 1964. 383 p. Col. maps, plans.

One of the best short guides in English. Summary of Polish history and contemporary conditions, followed by travel notes on Warsaw and the rest of the country and by practical information on hotels, resorts, and other items of tourist concern. Also worth noting is Edward T. Appleton's *Your Guide to Poland* (London, Redman, 1966, 271 p., 17 plates, maps, tables).

Poland, Travel Guide, edited by Zofia Uszyńska (Warszawa, AGPOL, Foreign Trade Advertising & Publishing Agency, 1960) is a set of seven booklets, describing separate tourist regions. The first and sixth parts contain general information.

Noteworthy also are Adam Bajcar's *Poland; a Guidebook for Tourists*, 2d enl. ed. (Warsaw, Polonia Publishing House, 1966, 200 p.), and *Pologne*, by Jean-Jacques Fauvel, new edition (Paris, Hachette, 1967, 735 p., illus., col. maps; Les Guides bleus. First edition 1939, by Annie and Henri de Montfort.

The U. S. Embassy in Poland provides *Information for American Visitors to Poland* (Warsaw, 1967, 15 p.).

One of the most informative Polish language guides is *Przewodnik po Polsce* (Guide to Poland), 2d ed. (Warszawa, Sport i Turystyka, 1965, 779 p., maps, plans), which provides plans of numerous towns, itineraries, road maps, and other pratical information for motorists. First edition, 1963.

Useful information for commercial travelers as well as for anyone interested in Poland's economy and its trade relations with other countries is provided in *Information for Businessmen Trading with Poland* (Warszawa, Polish Chamber of Foreign Trade, 1965, 135 p., illus., maps) sponsored by the Polska Izba Handlu Zagranicznego. This guide gives addresses and descriptions of the most important export firms in Poland.

2445. Pologne, 1919-1939. Neuchâtel, La Baconnière, 1946-1947. 3 v. Illus., maps, diagrs., bibliographies.

See also entry no. 2680.

An encyclopedic survey prepared by émigré Polish scholars, and translated from the Polish by H. Epstein and J. Kassianof, containing about 140 articles on Polish life during the interwar period. The three volumes treat (1) political and social life; (2) economic life; (3) intellectual and artistic life. For pre-World War II handbooks *see*:

Olszewicz, Bolesław. Obraz Polski dzisiejszej; fakty, cyfry, tablice (Poland of today ;facts, numbers, tables). Warszawa, M. Arct, 1938. 255 p. Maps, tables.

Piltz, Erasmus, *ed.* Poland, Her People, History, Industries, Finance, Science, Literature, Art, and Social Development. London, H. Jenkins, 1918. 416 p. Illus., maps. This is an authorized version of *Petite encyclopédie polonaise* (Lausanne-Paris, Payot, 1916, 478 p.).

Retinger, Joseph H., *ed.* All About Poland; Facts, Figures, Documents. 2d rev. ed. London, Minerva Publishing Co., 1941. 292 p. Map.

Wunderlich, Erich, *ed.* Handbuch von Polen. Beiträge zu einer allgemeinen Landeskunde. Auf Grund der Studienergebnisse der Mitglieder der Landeskundlichen Kommission beim Generalgouvernement Warschau. Berlin, Reimer, 1917. 466 p. Tables, maps. 2d ed., 1918. 511 p.

2446. Polska, jej dzieje i kultura od czasów najdawniejszych do chwili obecnej (Poland, her history and culture from the oldest times to the present). Warszawa, Nakł. Trzaski, Everta i Michalskiego, 1927-1932. 3 v. Illus., ports., maps, music.

See also entry no. 2626.

Notable prewar survey covering the whole course of Polish history and culture. The three volumes are chronological: volume 1, to 1572; volume 2, 1572 to 1795; volume 3, 1796 to 1930. Richly illustrated. Bibliography with each chapter.

Informative also is *Wiedza o Polsce* (Knowledge about Poland) (Warszawa, Wydawn. "Wiedza o Polsce," 1931-1933 [?], 3 v. in 4; illus., ports., maps, music).

2447. Rocznik polityczny i gospodarczy (Political and economic yearbook) 1948– Warszawa, Państwowe Wydawn. Annual. Ekonomiczne.

See also entry no. 2718.

This annual handbook provides a wealth of information and statistics on Polish government, economy, social welfare, education, culture, etc. Supersedes a prewar publication of the same title published from 1932 to 1938. The first volume of the new series appeared in 1948, and was then suspended until 1958, since which time there have been annual volumes. Some of these carry lists of Polish towns with data on population, industry, and culture.

A survey of the governmental structure of People's Poland by a professor of state law at Warsaw University is Stefan Rozmaryn's *La Pologne* (Paris, Librarie générale de droit et de jurisprudence, 1963, 363 p.; Comment ils sont gouvernés, t. 8).

For a concise and up-to-date survey *see* James F. Morrison's *The Polish People's Republic* (Baltimore, Johns Hopkins Press, 1968, 160 p. Integration and Community Building in Eastern Europe, JH-EE2).

E. BIOGRAPHIC AND GENEALOGICAL MATERIAL

2448. Bar, Adam, Władysław T. Wisłocki, *and* Tadeusz Godłowski. Słownik pseudonimów i kryptonimów pisarzy polskich oraz Polski dotyczących (Dictionary of pseudonyms and cryptonyms of Polish writers or of those whose works deal with Poland) Kraków, Krakowskie Koło Związku Bibliotekarzy Polskich, 1936-1938. 3 v.

Volumes 1 and 2 give pseudonyms and cryptonyms (initials only, used as pen names), followed by full names of the authors. Volume 3 is an alphabetical listing of authors, followed by pseudonyms.

2449. Czy wiesz kto to jest? (Who's who?) Edited by Stanisław Łoza. Warszawa, Wydawn. Głównej Księg. Wojskowej, 1938. 858 p. Ports.

Useful reference tool presenting short biographies of men and women prominent in Poland in the 1920s and 1930s. Some entries include portraits.

Another "who's who" of contemporary figures in Polish cultural life was edited by Antoni Peretiatkowicz and Michał Sobeski: *Współczesna kultura polska: nauka, literatura, sztuka: życiorysy uczonych, literatów i artystów z wyszczególnieniem ich prac* (Contemporary Polish culture; science, literature, art: biographies of scholars, men of letters and artists, with lists of their works) (Poznań, 1932, 319 p.).

Short biographies (and bibliographies) of prominent Polish personalities in the 1930s can also be found in *Who's Who in Central & East Europe, 1933/34-1935/36*, edited by Stephen Taylor (Zurich, Central European Times Publishing Co., 1935-1937, 2 v.).

Biographies of over 7,000 Polish participants in the October Revolution and civil war in Russia, 1917-1920, are provided in *Księga Polaków uczestników rewolucij październikowej 1917-1920, Biografie* (Warszawa, Książka i Wiedza, 1967, 992 p.), prepared by Lidia Kalestyńska, Aleksander Kochański, and Wiesław Toporowicz and sponsored by the Historical Institute of the Central Committee of the Polish Communist Party. Photographs and bibliographic materials are included.

2450. Directory of Polish Officials. n. p., 1966. 233 p.

The various sections of this directory list officials in Polish central and local governments, political parties, mass organizations, educational, cultural, economic, and social organizations by names, positions held, and dates of tenure without further biographical information and based on the situation of mid-December 1965.

2451. Mizwa, Stephen, *ed.* Great Men and Women of Poland. New York, Macmillan, 1941. 397 p. Ports.

This volume of narrative biographies, edited by the director of the Kościuszko Foundation, was announced as the "Polish Plutarch." It contains 30 short biographies by various writers of the most famous Polish men and women from the tenth century to the present.

Scheduled for publication in 1968 by Ludowa Spółdzielnia Wydawnicza in Warsaw is *Wybitni Polacy XIX i XX wieku* (Prominent Poles of the 19th and 20th centuries).

A collection of 14 biographies is provided by Witold Jakóbczyk in *Wybitni Wielkopolanie XIX wieku* (Prominent men of the 19th century in Wielkopolska) (Poznań, Wydawnictwo Poznańskie, 1959, 463 p., ports.).

2452. Niesiecki, Kasper. Herbarz polski (Polish amorial) Lipsk, Breitkopf i Haertel, 1839-1846. 10 v. Illus.

First published in parts before the death of the author in 1744. The present impressive compilation was assembled with additional materials by Jan N. Bobrowicz. Volume 1 is devoted to descriptions and illustrations of coats of arms of the Kingdom of Poland and the Grand Duchy of Lithuania, the Polish Commonwealth bishoprics, and high secular and church officials. Volumes 2 to 10 give coats of arms and genealogical and biographical information on noble families of Poland and Lithuania. Bibliographical data in text.

A more scholarly modern work is Adam Boniecki's *Herbarz polski; wiadomości historyczno-genealogiczne o rodach szlacheckich* (Polish amorial; historical and genealogical information on noble families) Warszawa, 1899-1913; 16 v. plus supplement). Never finished, it covers the letters A-M.

A modern work on titled families of Poland published abroad is Szymon Konarski's *Armorial de la noblesse polonaise titrée* (Paris, 1958, illus., ports., coats of arms; bibliography: p. 433-457).

2453. Polska Akademia Umiejętności, *Kraków.* Polski słownik biograficzny (Polish biographical dictionary) v. 1– Kraków, Gebethner i Wolff, 1935– In progress.

A compilation of biographical sketches of prominent deceased Poles. Most articles are followed by bibliographies. Begun under the auspices of the Polish Academy of Science and Letters in Kraków, it has appeared in parts since 1935. Publication was suspended with volume 5, part 24, 1939, resumed in 1946, and again suspended from 1949 to 1958. Since 1958 it has been published by the Historical Institute of the Polish Academy of Sciences in Warsaw.

An attempt to cover biographies of prominent Poles omitted from the volumes of *Altpreussische Biographie*, edited by Ch. Krollmann (Königsberg, 1934-1944) was made by Tadeusz Oracki in his *Słownik biograficzny Warmii, Mazur i Powiśla od połowy XV w. do 1945 roku* (Biographical dictionary of Poles active in the territories of Ermland, Masuria, and lower part of the Vistula river, between the 15th century and 1945) (Warszawa, Instytut Wydawn. Pax, 1963, 328 p.). In this volume Poles active in art, literature, journalism, politics, and religious life in Danzig and Eastern Pomerania from the mid-fifteenth to mid-twentieth centuries are represented.

See also *Słownik współczesnych pisarzy polskich* (Dictionary of contemporary Polish writers), edited by Ewa Korzeniewska (Warszawa, Państwowe Wydawn. Naukowe, 1963-1964, 3 v. Supplement and indexes in v. 4, 1966). For silhouettes of members of the Polish Academy of sciences, see issues of *Nauka polska*, the bimonthly organ of the Polish Academy of Sciences.

2454. Who's Who in Polish America; a Biographical Directory of Polish-American Leaders and Distinguished Poles Resident in the Americas. 3d ed. Edited by Francis Bolek. New York, Harbinger House, 1943. 581 p.

See also entry no. 2584.

An expansion of previous editions, containing about 5,000 biographies of prominent living and deceased persons of Polish descent residing in the United States, Canada, and South America. Indexes by places of residence and by occupation. The first edition of 100 brief biographies was published in 1938; the second, enlarged to 1,000 biographies, appeared in 1940.

Other Poles active outside Poland are described in Stanisław Zieliński's *Mały słownik pionierów polskich kolonjalnych i morskich; podrożnicy, odkrywcy, zdobywcy, badacze, eksploratorzy, emigranci-pamiętnikarze, działacze i pisarze migracyjni* (A dictionary of Polish pioneers, colonists and seafarers, travelers, scholar-investigators, discoverers, explorers, emigrant-diarists, civic-political leaders, and writers, all active abroad) (Warszawa, 1932, 680 p.). Alphabetical listing of about 2,000 short life stories.

F. INDEXES, ABSTRACTS, AND TRANSLATIONS

2455. Bibliografia zawartości czasopism (Bibliography of periodical articles) v. 1– July 1947– Warszawa, Biblioteka Narodowa. Semiannual, July 1947-June 1951; monthly, July 1951–

An index to post-1947 Polish periodical literature, issued by the Bibliographic Institute of the National Library of Poland. This pioneering work contains an annual average of about 80,000 articles, selected from some 70 journals and major newspapers. Entries follow the subject classification of the Polish national bibliography *Przewodnik bibliograficzny*. Each monthly issue contains a subject index. An annual index includes lists of authors, books reviewers, translators, composers, illustrators, subject index, and a list of periodicals indexed during the year. This cumulation of indexes appears with considerable delay.

2456. Polish News Bulletin. 1950– Warsaw. Daily.
See also entry no. 52.

Published jointly by the American and British Embassies in Warsaw, containing translated news items from the Polish press.

Summary of the Polish Provincial Press has been provided weekly by the U.S. Joint Publications Research Service since 1958.

The Research Departments of Radio Free Europe publish a daily *Polish Press Survey* and, irregularly, a *Situation Report*, summarizing or translating and commenting on the Polish press.

2457. Polska Akademia Nauk. *Ośrodek rozpowszechniania wydawnictw naukowych.* Quarterly Review of Scientific Publications. 1962– Warszawa, Ossolineum.

Contains reviews of currently published books by the Polish Academy of Sciences, universities, and learned societies, in three branches — the social sciences, biological sciences, and pure and technical sciences. Published between 1958 and 1961 as three separate series, and consolidated into one publication in 1962. Polish titles are followed by English translations and annotations are in English. Issued by the Distribution Center for Scientific Publications of the Polish Academy of Sciences in Warsaw.

The publication may be supplemented by a serial index, *Polish Scientific Periodicals: Current Contents with Author Directory* (10 issues a year) issued by the same center. This also was begun as three separate series in 1958, and brought into one publication with no. 11, 1964. It gives English translations of tables of contents (titles of articles and book reviews) of regular and irregular scholarly journals in the fields of social sciences, biological sciences, and pure and technical sciences. During the year some 500 periodicals are covered.

G. DICTIONARIES

2458. Grzegorczyk, Piotr. Index Lexicorum Poloniae. Bibliografia słowników polskich. Warszawa, Państwowe Wydawn. Naukowe, 1967. 286 p.

Historical survey of Polish dictionaries — monolingual bilingual, general, and specialized — from the earliest times to the present. Alphabetical and subject indexes.

2459. The Kościuszko Foundation Dictionary: English-Polish, Polish-English. New York, 1960-1962. 2 v.

Stanisławski, Jan. Wielki słownik angielsko-polski. The Great English-Polish Dictionary. Warszawa, Państwowe Wydawn. "Wiedza Powszechna," 1964. 1175 p.

Two excellent, up-to-date lexicographic works.

2460. Lewanski, Richard C. A Bibliography of Polish Dictionaries, with a Supplement of Lusatian and Polabian Dictionaries. New York, New York Public Library, 1959. 63 p. Facsim. (*His* Bibliography of Slavic Dictionaries, v. 1)

The most complete bibliography of Polish dictionaries available, though by now a little outdated. Contains titles of 457 works, monolingual, bilingual, and polyglot, including dictionaries of special terms.

2461. U.S. *Library of Congress. Slavic and Central Division.* Polish Abbreviations; a Selective List. Compiled by Janina Wojcicka. 2d rev. and enl. ed. Washington, D.C., 1957. 164 p.

List of Polish abbreviations, giving the words for which they stand together with English translations. Contains about 2,600 abbreviations, most of them terms which have gained currency in Poland since the Second World War, particularly names of government agencies, societies, institutions, etc. First edition: 1955, 122 p.

H. LIBRARIES AND PUBLISHING

2462. Łuczyńska, Alfreda, *and* Helena Wiącek. Informator o bibliotekach w Polskiej Rzeczypospolitej Ludowej (Guide to libraries in the Polish People's Republic). Warszawa, Stowarzyszenie Bibliotekarzy Polskich, 1961. 552 p.

Directory published by the Association of Polish Librarians. The 3,600-odd libraries described are classed by subdivisions for university and college libraries, libraries of the Polish Academy of Sciences and other learned societies, special libraries, and public libraries, and by administrative subdivision under each such heading. This is the most comprehensive guide to Polish libraries at present available, although many small special libraries and school libraries are omitted. Information for each library includes full library name, address, date of establishment, and extent of holdings. For the larger libraries there are additional data relating to their history, special collections, and publications.

A shorter version in English translation, *Libraries in Poland; Information Guide*, by Alfreda Łuczyńska and Krystyna Remerowa, was published by Polonia Publishing House (Warszawa, 1961, 108 p.).

For currently published information about research libraries and their collections *see* the following periodicals:

Przegląd biblioteczny; organ naukowy Stowarzyszenia Bibliotekarzy Polskich (Library review; scholarly publication of the Association of Polish Librarians). v. 1– 1908– Warszawa. Quarterly.

Roczniki biblioteczne; organ naukowy bibliotek szkół wyższych

(Library annals; scholarly publication of college and university libraries). v. 1– 1957– Wrocław-Warszawa, Państwowe Wydawn. Naukowe. Annual.

Warsaw. Biblioteka Narodowa. Rocznik Biblioteki Narodowej (Yearbook of the National Library). 1– 1965– Warszawa.

2463. Warsaw. Biblioteka Narodowa. *Instytut Bibliograficzny.* Ruch wydawniczy w liczbach. Polish Publishing in Figures. 1955– Warszawa. Tables. Annual.

See also entries no. 55 *and* 2936.

Prepared by the Bibliographic Institute of the National Library of Poland to provide official statistical data about book, magazine, and newspaper publishing in Poland each year. Categories of material published, languages used, and number of copies printed are indicated. Statistical information concerning translations into Polish is also included. The English subtitle, "Publishers' Activities in Figures" (during the years 1959-1962), was changed with volume 9, 1963, to the present form. A descriptive study of publishing in Poland is to be found in:

Bromberg, Adam. Książki i wydawcy. Ruch wydawniczy w Polsce Ludowej w latach 1944-1964 (Books and publishers. Publishing in the People's Republic of Poland during 1944-1964). Warszawa, Państwowy Instytut Wydawniczy, 1966. 287 p. Tables. After a background historical outline of publishing in Poland the author discusses the last 20 years' developments in various fields of publishing — sociopolitical writings, belles lettres, children's literature, technology, and agriculture. Abundant statistical data.

Czarnowska, Maria. Ilościowy rozwój polskiego ruchu wydawniczego, 1501-1965 (Quantitative development of Polish publishing). Warszawa, 1967. 201 p. Illus. (Biblioteka Narodowa. Prace Instytutu Bibliograficznego, nr. 6)

2464. Więckowska, Helena, *and* Hanna Pliszczyńska. Podręczny słownik bibliotekarza (Librarian's reference dictionary). Warszawa, Państwowe Wydawn. Naukowe, 1955. 309 p.

A glossary of about 3,000 terms relevant to library work. In two parts; the first, terms and definitions in Polish with equivalents in English, French, German, and Russian; the second, lists of the terms in these languages, with their Polish equivalents.

I. MISCELLANEOUS REFERENCE AIDS

2465. Informator nauki polskiej (Guide to Polish scholarly activity) 1958– Warszawa, Państwowe Wydawn. Naukowe, 1962– Annual.

Handbook of the Polish learned world, giving information about all institutions and organizations concerned with scholarship. It begins with the Polish Academy of Sciences, listing its departments, with names of chairmen and important members of each, also regular and corresponding members. Comparable data are given for universities and other academic schools, museums, archives, and learned societies, after the pattern of *The World of Learning*. There is an alphabetical index of the institutions listed, and a roster of individuals mentioned in the volume. Names of scholars pursuing independent research are not included.

An English translation of the 1964 edition, entitled *Polish Research Guide*, was published by the National Science Foundation in Washington, D.C.

Also useful is Jan Wepsiec's *Polish Institutions of Higher Learning* (New York, Polish Institute of Arts and Sciences in America, 1959, 110 p.) providing information on learned societies, institutes, universities, observatories and botanical gardens, art galleries, libraries, and bibliographical centers in Poland and Polish institutions outside of Poland. Also lists periodicals issued by these institutions.

Information about the activities of the Polish learned world is currently provided by *Nauka polska* (Polish science and learning) (1953– Warszawa, Polska Akademia Nauk; bimonthly).

2466. Lorentz, Stanisław. Museums and Collections in Poland, 1945-1955. Warsaw Polonia Publishing House, 1956. 132 p. Illus.
See also entry no. 3214.

An English translation of *Muzea i zbiory w Polsce, 1945-1955* (Warszawa, Wydawn. "Polonia," 1956, 134 p.; bibliography: p. 109-115) prepared by the director of the National Museum in Warsaw.

Now dated but still a source of useful information, especially about Polish collections outside of Poland, is:

Chwalewik, Edward. Zbiory polskie; archiwa, biblioteki, gabinety, galerie, musea i inne zbiory pamitek przeszłości w ojczyźnie i na obczyźnie (Polish collections; archives, libraries, private collections, galleries, museums and other collections relating to Poland's past in that country and abroad). Warszawa, J. Mortkowicz, 1926-1927. 2 v. Bibliography: p. 109-115. Also useful are:

Brzostowski, Stanisław. Muzea w Polsce; przewodnik-informator (Museums in Poland; a reference book). Warszawa, Wydawn. Związkowe CRZZ, 1968. 338 p. Illus., maps.

Warsaw. Muzeum Narodowe. The National Museum in Warsaw. Warsaw, 1963. 181 p. Illus.

2467. Podział administracyjny Polskiej Rzeczypospolitej Ludowej (Administrative division of the Polish People's Republic). 3d ed. Warszawa, Urząd Rady Ministrów, Biuro do Spraw Prezydiów Rad Narodowych, 1965.

Official directory published by the Office for Local Government Affairs of the Council of Ministers, listing administrative divisions of Poland by provinces, counties, city, and urban settlements. First edition: 1956.

2468. Poland. *Główny Urząd Statystyczny.* Rocznik statystyczny (Statistical yearbook). 1930– Warszawa. Maps, tables, diagrs. Annual.

Basic official Polish statistical yearbook, published by the Central

Statistical Office of the Polish People's Republic. Publication suspended 1934-1944, 1948-1955. Resumed in 1956 with annual volume covering 1955. Volumes for 1961-1963 augmented by statistical data on the 1960 population census in Poland. Each new issue brings additional information not previously included. Alphabetical index.

For statistical estimates consult *Mały rocznik statystyczny* (Pocket statistical yearbook) (v. 1– 1958–) and its English counterpart, *Concise Statistical Yearbook of Poland* (Warsaw, 1930–; publication suspended 1942-1946), issued by the same office.

Currently released statistical data appear in the monthly *Biuletyn statystyczny* (Statistical bulletin) also issued by the Central Statistical Office.

Yearbooks of statistics are also published under official auspices for the larger cities and provinces of Poland.

Publications issued in the last 50 years by the Central Statistical Office are recorded in *Bibliografia wydawnictw Głównego Urzędu Statystycznego, 1918-1968* (Warszawa, 1968, 466 p.).

2469. Poland. *Naczelna Dyrekcja Archiwów Państwowych.* Les archives de la République Populaire de Pologne. Varsovie, 1956. 30 p. Illus.

Historical background, activities, and publications of the archives in People's Poland.

The losses suffered by the Polish archival collections are described by Adam Stebelski in *The Fate of Polish Archives During World War II* (Warszawa, Państwowe Wydawn. Naukowe, 1964, 59 p., bibliographical footnotes).

For bibliographical information concerning archival literature, *see* Regina Piechota's "Polska bibliografia archiwalna za lata 1945-1965" (Polish bibliography of archival materials, 1945-1965), published as supplements to *Archeion; czasopismo naukowe poświęcone sprawom archiwalnym* (Acheion; a scholarly periodical devoted to archival matters) (Warszawa, Państwowe Wydawn. Naukowe) v. 39, 1963, 15 p.; v. 40, 1964, 23 p.; and v. 45, 1966, 42 p.; a total of 1,121 entries.

2470. Rospond, Stanisław. Słownik nazw geograficznych Polski zachodniej i północnej; według uchwał Komisji Ustalania Nazw Miejscowych (Dictionary of geographic names of the Western and Northern territories of Poland; as approved by the Board of Geographic Names). Wrocław, Polskie Towarzystwo Geograficzne, 1951. 793 p. Fold. maps.

This gazetteer of place names in Poland is limited to the provinces of Lower Silesia, part of Upper Silesia, the Opole region, the Lubus province, Western Pomerania, the area of the former Free City of Danzig, and former Western Prussia, all of which are now included in the Polish state. Volume 1 is Polish-German; volume 2, German-Polish.

The following work is also worth mentioning: *Słownik geografii turystycznej Polski* (Dictionary of tourist geography of Poland), edited by Maria I. Mileska (Warszawa, Komitet do Spraw Turystyki,

1956-1959, 2 v.), which is a quite adequate dictionary listing alphabetically descriptions of places of interest in Poland, especially those of interest to tourists. Much outdated but still useful, especially for places which are no longer within the Polish borders, is *Słownik geograficzny Królestwa Polskiego i innych krajów słowiańskich* (Geographical dictionary of the Polish Kingdom and other Slavic lands), edited by Filip Sulimierski and others (Warszawa, 1880-1914, 16 v.).

2471. Spis miejscowości Polskiej Rzeczypospolitej Ludowej (A list of place names in the People's Republic of Poland). Warszawa, Wydawnictwa Komunikacji i Łączności, 1967. 1381 p. Fold. map.

A gazetteer covering the entire country, the first publication of this magnitude issued in People's Poland. The names are approved by the Board of the Establishment of Geographic and Physiographic Names. Lists alphabetically all the place names and provides information as to the administrative and territorial units, such as provinces, counties, settlements, post offices, railroad stations, and registry offices, to which they are subordinated.

39

the land

by Bogdan Zaborski

A. BIBLIOGRAPHIES AND GENERAL PUBLICATIONS

2472. Bibliografia geografii polskiej (Bibliography of Polish geography). 1936/44– Warszawa, Państwowe Wydawn. Naukowe, 1956– Irregular.

Issued by Instytut Geografii of the Polska Akademia Nauk. Continues the bibliography published through 1935 as a supplement to *Wiadomości geograficzne* (Geographical news). Compiled by Stanisław Leszczycki and others. Covers the period 1936-1960 in five volumes published between 1956 and 1966.

See also the American Geographic Society of New York's *Research Catalogue* (Boston, G. K. Hall), v. 10, 1962, p. 6819-6919, which lists over 2,000 entries relating to Poland.

2473. Czasopismo geograficzne. Geographical Journal. v. 1– 1923– Quarterly. Wrocław.

Organ of the Polish Geographical Society.

2474. Geografia powszechna (General geography). Edited by August Zierhoffer. v. 3. Warszawa, Państwowe Wydawn. Naukowe, 1965. p. 533-605.

Two articles on Polish geography. The first, by Józef Szaflarski, is a general description of the country. The second, by Stanisław Leszczycki, relates to the regional structure of economic life.

2475. Kondracki, Jerzy. Geografia fizyczna Polski (Physical geography of Poland). Warszawa, Państwowe Wydawn. Naukowe, 1965. 575 p. Illus., maps.

The first part deals with aspects of the physical geography of Poland, including the transformation of the land by human activity. The second part is concerned with a description of the various regions. The work grows out of a standard prewar textbook:

Lencewicz, Stanisław. Polska (Poland). Warszawa, Nakł. Trzaski, Everta i Michalskiego, 1937. 446 p. Illus. Lencewicz' first edition appeared in 1922, and editions signed jointly by Lencewicz and Kondracki were published in 1955, 1959, and 1962.

2476. Kostrowicki, Jerzy. Środowisko geograficzne Polski, warunki przyrodnicze rozwoju gospodarki narodowej (The geographical environment of Poland; natural conditions of the development of the nation's economy). Warszawa, Państwowe Wydawn. Naukowe, 1957. 542 p. Illus., maps (part fold.)

A description of the physico-geographical conditions and natural resources as the bases of the economic life of Poland.

2477. Leszczycki, Stanisław. The Geographical Bases of Contemporary Poland. Journal of Central European Affairs, v. 7, January 1948: 357-373.

2478. Martonne, Emmanuel de. La Pologne. *In*: Vidal de la Blache, Paul M. J. Géographie universelle. t. 4: Europe Centrale. Pt. 2. Paris, A. Colin, 1931. p. 521-598.

A geographical description of Poland between the two wars.

2479. Paszkiewicz, Henryk, *ed*. Polska i jej dorobek dziejowy w ciągu tysiąca lat istnienia; zarys i encyklopedia spraw polskich (Poland and her achievements in history during a thousand years of existence; an outline and encyclopedia of Polish affairs). v. 1. Londyn, Księgarnia Polska Orbis, 1956. 208 p. Illus., maps.

Relevant sections are:

Hołub-Pacewiczowa, Zofia. Oblicze ziemi polskiej (The face of the land of Poland), p. 7-26;

———. Krainy Polski (Polish regions), p. 27-34.

Zaborski, Bogdan. Położenie geograficzno-polityczne ziem Polski (Politico-geographic situation of Polish lands), p. 35-40.

2480. Przegląd geograficzny. Polish Geographical Review. v. 1– 1918/19– Warszawa, Państwowe Wydawn. Naukowe. Quarterly.

Organ of the Institute of Geography of the Polish Academy of Sciences.

2481. Zaleska, Maria (Kiełczewska). O podstawy geograficzne Polski (The geographical bases of Poland). Poznań, Wydawn. Instytutu Zachodniego, 1946. 146 p. Maps. (Prace Instytut Zachodniego, nr. 10)

An analysis of the principal geographical elements in Poland's situation. The author also contributed an article on this subject to:

Wojciechowski, Zygmunt, *ed.* Poland's Place in Europe. Poznań, Instytut Zachodni, 1947. p. 9-60.

B. HANDBOOKS AND TRAVEL GUIDES

2482. International Association for Quaternary Research. *6th Congress. Warsaw, 1961.* Guide-Book of Excursions. Warsaw, 1961. 9 v.

Each volume is devoted to a single region of Poland, describing pleistocene geological features.

2483. International Geographical Congress. *14th, Warsaw, 1934.* Excursions. Varsovie, 1934. 12 v.

Each volume is devoted to a single region of Poland.

2484. Poland. *Komitet dla Spraw Turystyki.* Słownik geografii turystycznej Polski (A dictionary of the touristic geography of Poland). Edited by Maria I. Mileska and others. Warszawa, Komitet dla Spraw Turystyki, 1956-1959. 2 v.

Contains articles describing settlements, rivers, forests, geographical regions.

2485. Przewodnik po Polsce (A guide to Poland). Edited by Justyn Wojsznis. Warszawa, Sport i Turystyka, 1963. 752 p. Illus., maps.

A tourist guide to Poland.

2486. Słownik geograficzny Królestwa Polskiego i innych krajów słowiańskich (A geographical dictionary of the Kingdom of Poland and of other Slavic lands). Edited by Filip Sulimierski and others. Warszawa, F. Sulimierski; skł. gł. w red. Wędrowca, 1880-1914. 16 v.

A fundamental work.

C. WORKS ON SPECIFIC TOPICS OR PROBLEMS

2487. Arnold, Stanisław. Geografia historyczna Polski (Historical geography of Poland). Warszawa, Państwowe Wydawn. Naukowe, 1951. 112 p. Illus., maps.

A systematic analysis of the historico-geographical territorial development of Poland.

2488. Berezowski, Stanisław, *ed.* Geografia gospodarcza Polski (Economic geography of Poland). Łódź, Państwowe Wydawn. Naukowe, 1959. 454 p. Maps, plans, tables.

Includes chapters on the physical geography and population of Poland as well as detailed descriptions of economic geography. Economic geography of the pre-World War II Poland is treated in:

Srokowski, Stanisław. Geografia gospodarcza Polski (Economic geography of Poland). New rev. ed. Warszawa, Nakł. Instytutu Społecznego, 1939. 588 p. Illus., maps. Bibliography: p. 537-557.

2489. Dobrowolska, Maria. Dynamika krajobrazu kulturalnego (The dynamism of the cultural landscape). Kraków, Biblioteka Wyższej Szkoły Nauk Społecznych w Krakowie, 1948. 53 p.

A survey through time of the shrinking of the forest and expansion of farmland, largely based on Polish examples.

2490. Fisher, Jack C., *ed.* City and Regional Planning in Poland. Ithaca, N.Y., Cornell University Press, 1966. 491 p. Illus. maps (part fold.), plans.

See also entries no. 2814 *and* 2913.

2491. Jarosz, Stefan. Krajobrazy Polski i ich pierwotne fragmenty (The Polish landscapes and their original fragments). 2d rev. and enl. ed. Warszawa, Budownictwo i Architektura, 1956. 443 p. Illus., fold. col. map.

Contains 375 excellent illustrations of landscape, vegetation, and animals with text explanations. The best existing album of this type.

2492. Książkiewicz, Marian. Zarys geologii Polski (An outline of the geology of Poland). Warszawa, Wydawn. Geologiczne, 1965. 379 p. Maps.

Standard textbook of geology for Polish universities.

2493. Miasta polskie w tysiącleciu (Polish cities during the millennium). Edited by Mateusz Siuchniński. Wrocław, Zakład Narodowy im. Ossolińskich, 1965-1967. 2 v. Illus., facsims., maps, ports.

2494. Mikulski, Zdzisław. Zarys hydrografii Polski (An outline of Polish hydrography). Warszawa, Państwowe Wydawn. Naukowe, 1963. 286 p. Illus., maps.

A university textbook.

2495. Natanson-Leski, Jan. Rozwój terytorialny Polski; od czasów najdawniejszych do okresu przebudowy państwa w latach 1569-1572. (The territorial development of Poland; from ancient times to the transformation of the state in 1569-1572). Warszawa, Państwowe Wydawn. Naukowe, 1964. 167 p. Fold. col. maps.

2496. Szafer, Władysław, *ed.* Szata roślinna Polski. Opracowanie zbiorowe. (Flora of Poland; a collective work). Warszawa, Państwowe Wydawn. Naukowe, 1959. 2 v. Illus., tables, maps, bibliography.

2497. Zaborski, Bogdan. O kształtach wsi w Polsce i ich rozmieszczeniu. (On village forms in Poland and their distribution). Kraków, 1926. 122 p. Illus., map. (Prace Komisji Etnograficznej Polskiej Akademii Umiejętności, nr. 1)

This includes a French summary. A German translation appeared as *Über Dorfformen in Polen und ihre Verbreitung* (Breslau, Priebatsch's Buchhandlung, 1930, 112 p. Osteuropa-Institut. Bibliothek geschichtlicher Werke aus den Literaturen Osteuropas, Nr. 3).

D. THE REGIONS OF POLAND

2498. Deresiewicz, Janusz, *ed.* Pomorze Zachodnie (Pomerania). 2d ed. Poznań Instytut Zachodni, 1949. 2 v. Illus., ports., maps. (Ziemie Staropolski, t. 2, cz. 1-2)

2499. Dolny Śląsk (Lower Silesia). Edited by Ewa Maleczyńska and others. Wrocław, Książnica-Atlas, 1948. 2 v. Illus., ports., maps.
A detailed geographical description of the Northwestern part of Silesia. Also to be noted is:
Sosnowski, Kirył, *ed.* Dolny Śląsk (Lower Silesia). Poznań, Instytut Zachodni, 1948. 2 v. Illus., maps. (Ziemie Staropolski, t. 1).

2500. Górny Śląsk (Upper Silesia). Edited by Kazimierz Popiołek and others. Poznań, Instytut Zachodni, 1959. 2 v. Illus. (Ziemie Staropolski, t. 5)
A detailed geographical description of Upper Silesia. An earlier work is:
Wrzosek, Antoni, *ed.* Górny Śląsk; prace i materiały geograficzne (Upper Silesia; geographical papers and materials). Kraków, Wydawn. Literackie, 1955. 680 p. Illus., maps. Scholarly articles by a number of eminent specialists, describing the physical, human, economic, and historical geography of the region.

2501. Grodek, Andrzej, *ed.* Monografia Odry; studium zbiorowe (A monograph on the Oder River; collective study). Poznań, Instytut Zachodni, 1948. 591, 25 p. Illus., maps.

2502. Jahn, Alfred. Wyżyna lubelska; rzeźba i czwartorzęd (The Lublin highland; relief and Quaternary features). Warszawa, Państwowe Wydawn. Naukowe, 1956. 453 p. Illus., maps. (Polska Akademia Nauk. Instytut Geografii. Prace geograficzne, nr. 7)
A detailed physico-geographical and regional description.

2503. Jordan, Zbigniew A. Oder-Neisse Line; a Study of the Political, Economic and European Significance of Poland's Western Frontier. London, Polish Freedom Movement "Independence and Democracy," 1952. 133 p. Illus.

2504. Lencewicz, Stanisław. Morfologia i dyluwium Środkowego Powiśla (Geomorphology and Pleistocene of the middle Vistula basin). Warszawa, Państwowy Instytut Geologiczny, 1927.

2505. Lutman, Roman, *ed.* Śląsk, ziemia i ludzie (Silesia, land and people). Katowice, Drukarnia Cieszyńska, 1948. 283 p. Illus., fold. maps. (Pamiętnik Instytutu Śląskiego, seria II, 10)

2506. Morcinek, Gustaw. Ziemia Cieszyńska (The land of Cieszyn). Katowice, Śląsk, 1962. 174 p. Illus.

2507. Polish Western Territories. Authors: Bohdan Gruchman and others. Poznań, Instytut Zachodni, 1959. 267 p. Maps, bibliographical footnotes.

See also entry no. 2784.

2508. Straszewicz, Ludwik. Opole Silesia; Outline of Economic Geography. Warsaw, Published for the Department of Commerce, Washington, by the Scientific Publications Foreign Cooperation Center, Central Institute for Scientific, Technical and Economic Information, 1965. 251 p. Illus., maps.

2509. Szafer, Władysław, *ed.* Tatrzański Park Narodowy (The Tatra Mountains National Park). 2d rev. and enl. ed. Kraków, 1962. 675 p. Illus., ports., maps. (Polska Akademia Nauk. Zakład Ochrony Przyrody. Wydawnictwa popularno-naukowe, nr. 21)

Articles by several authors on geographical subjects as well as on nature protection.

2510. Wasylewski, Stanisław. Na Śląsku Opolskim (In Opole Silesia). Katowice, Warszawa, Nasza Księgarnia, 1937. 286 p. Illus.

A historico-geographical description of Opole Silesia (the Western part of Upper Silesia which in the interwar years remained under German administration).

2511. Zaborski, Bogdan. Studia nad morfologią dyluwium Podlasia i terenów sąsiednich (Studies of the morphology of the Pleistocene in Podlasia and neighboring regions). Warszawa, 1927. 52 p. Map.

Résumé in French.

2512. Zajchowska, Stanisława. Nad środkową Odrą i dolną Wartą (On the middle Oder and lower Warthe Rivers). Warszawa, Wiedza Powszechna, 1959. 189 p. Illus.

A physical, economic, historical, and human geography of the region.

2513. Zajchowska, Stanisława, *ed.* Warmia i Mazury (Warmia and Masuria). Poznań, Instytut Zachodni, 1953. 2 v. Illus., ports., maps (part fold.), facsims., plans. (Ziemie Staropolski, t. 4)

A full geographical description of the northeastern Polish lake regions.

E. ATLASES AND MAPS

2514. Buczek, Karol. The History of Polish Cartography from the 15th to the 18th Century. Translated by Andrzej Potocki. Wrocław, Zakład Narodowy im. Ossolińskich, Wydawn. Polskiej Akademii

Nauk, 1966. 135 p. Maps. (Monografie z dziejów nauki i techniki, t. 24)

The Polish edition appeared as *Dzieje kartografii polskiej od XV do XVIII wieku* (Wrocław, Zakład Narodowy im. Ossolińskich, 1963, 119 p., 48 maps).

2515. Jażdżewski, Konrad. Atlas to the Prehistory of the Slavs. Łódź, 1948-1949. 2 v. (20 col. maps, 143 p. text). Bibliography: v. 2, p. 19-25. (Acta Praehistorica Universitatis Lodziensis, 1-2).

See also entry no. 333.

A unique series of historico-ethnic maps to illustrate gradual changes which occurred between 1300 B.C. and the eleventh century A.D. in the Polish lands and adjacent territories.

2516. Kraus, Theodor, *and others, eds.* Atlas östliches Mitteleuropa. Bielefeld, Velhagen und Klasing, 1959. 289, 19 p. Illus., maps (part fold.).

See also entries no. 65 *and* 145.

A rich series of maps dealing with an area which includes prewar Poland and adjacent lands. There are physical, historical, economic, and population maps, but maps of the postwar distribution of languages and religion are lacking.

2517. Poland. *Centralny Urząd Geodezji i Kartografii.* Atlas Polski (Atlas of Poland). Warszawa, Państw. Przeds. Wydawn. Kartogrficznych, 1953-1956. 1 v. 24 fold. col. maps.

Contains maps illustrating the position of Poland in Europe, and the geophysical, geological, morphological, climatological, hydrographic, and bio-geographic description of the country.

2518. Polska. Atlas geograficzny (Poland. Geographic atlas). Edited by Henryk Górski. Warszawa, Państwowe Przedsiębiorstwo Wydawn. Kartograficznych, 1966. 37 p.

An atlas for use in the schools, containing 114 very useful maps.

2519. Polska Akademia Nauk. *Instytut Geografii.* National Atlases, Sources, Bibliography, Articles. Compiled by J. Drecka and H. Tuszyńska-Rękawek, under the direction of Stanisław Leszczycki. Warsaw, 1960. 56 p. (Dokumentacja geograficzna, zesz. 4)

2520. Romer, Eugeniusz, *and* Józef Wąsowicz. Atlas Polski współczesnej (Atlas of contemporary Poland). 5th ed. Wrocław, Książnica Atlas, 1950. 16 p. of col. maps.

2521. Warsaw. Instytut Geodezji i Kartografii. Atlas kartowania form terenu Polski (Atlas of mapping of the forms of relief of Poland). Warszawa, Państwowe Przedsiębiorstwo Wydawn. Kartograficznych, 1961, 74, 2 p. Illus., col. maps.

Shows, by means of colored maps and transparent overlays, forms of presentation of relief. Composed of well selected examples of large scale maps which are not otherwise available. One map on the scale 1:1,500,000, compiled by Jan Rokicki, is an attempt to construct a morphometric map of the types of landscape. The first work in this field was Bogdan Zaborski's *Carte des types des paysages de la Pologne du Nord, Lithuanie et Allemagne de l'est*, published in 1928 on the scale 1 : 1,000,000 in Warsaw.

2522. Warsaw. Instytut Geologiczny. Atlas geologiczny; zagadnienia stratygraficzno-facjalne. Geological atlas of Poland; stratigraphic and facial problems. Warszawa, 1957-1964. 13 pts. Col. maps.

Title, text, and legends in Polish, Russian, and English.

2523. Zaborski, Bogdan, *ed.* Antropogeograficzny atlas Polski. Atlas de géographie humaine de Pologne. Warszawa, Libraria Nova, 1934. 3 col. maps with index. Scale 1:300,000.

Only one set of maps of a projected series of 16 was issued. This is devoted to the Bydogoszcz-Gdynia area and provides data derived from the census of 1931 and other sources for the tax structure, density of population, and nationality of the inhabitants. Reprinted on a scale of 1:500,000 in London in 1944.

2524. Zaborski, Bogdan. Map of Poland and Adjacent Countries. London, The Association of Polish University Professors and Lecturers in Great Britain, 1948. Col. map. Scale 1:1,100,000.

A map showing the forms of terrain, the rivers, railroads, forests, and prewar and postwar boundaries of Poland.

There were prewar editions of maps of Poland on the scales 1:25,000, 1:100,000, 1:300,000, 1:500,000 and 1:1,000,000 and there also survive maps made before 1918 by Russia, Germany, and Austria-Hungary, among whom Poland was then divided.

2525. Zaremba, Józef. Atlas ziem odzyskanych (Atlas of the recovered territories of Poland). 2d ed. Warszawa, Główny Urząd Planowania Przestrzennego, 1947. 25 p. 43 col. maps.

Maps, on the scale 1:2,000,000, of the physical, human, and economic geography of western and northern Poland.

40

the people

A. ANTHROPOLOGY AND ARCHAEOLOGY

by Imre Boba

1. Bibliographies

2526. Archeologia i prehistoria (Archaeology and prehistory). *In* Hahn, Wiktor. Bibliografia bibliografij polskich do 1950 roku (A bibliography of Polish bibliographies up to 1950). Wrocław, Zakład Narodowy im. Ossolińskich, 1966. p. 129-132.

General and specialized bibliographies, bibliographic essays, journals with bibliographic sections, monographs with documentation. Hahn's bibliography lists works published up to and including 1950. For bibliographies published in the next decade, *see*:

Sawoniak, Henryk. Bibliografia bibliografii polskich, 1951-1960. Wrocław, Zakład Narodowy im. Ossolińskich, 1967. p. 22-25.

2527. Polska Akademia Nauk. *Komitet Słowianoznawstwa.* Słownik starożytności słowiańskich (A dictionary of Slavic antiquities). Edited by Władysław Kowalenko and others. Wrocław, Zakład Narodowy im. Ossolińskich, 1961– Illus., maps.

See also entries no. 104 *and* 327.

A compendium of early Slavic history and civilization. Supplies in alphabetic arrangement the essential information on archeology, anthropology, civilization of the Slavs from earliest times to the late 12th century. Each entry is concluded with a bibliography of sources and basic literature. Prepared by the Polish Academy of Sciences with the cooperation of many scholars from other countries. Estimated date of completion: 1969.

2528. Wrzosek, Adam. Bibliografia antropologii polskiej do roku 1955 włącznie (Bibliography of Polish anthropology to and including 1955). Wrocław, 1959-1960. 2 v. (Materiały i prace antropologiczne, nr. 41, 42)

The most comprehensive systematic bibliography listing books, journals, articles, reviews, biographies of anthropologists etc.

2. Serials

2529. Archeologia Polona. 1– 1958– Warszawa, Zakład Narodowy im. Ossolińskich. Annual.

Published by the Institute of the History of Material Culture of the Polish Academy of Sciences and provides in English, French, German, or Russian the results of current archaeological research carried out by the Institute. Lists other archaeological publications of the Institute and includes book reviews. A similar publication for Polish archeologists appears semiannually: *Archeologia Polski* (Polish archaeology) (t. 1–, 1957–, Warszawa). The Polish language articles have English, French, or German summaries. There is also a popular bimonthly published by the Polish Archeological Society: *Z Otchłani wieków* (From the Abyss of Centuries) (1926–, Wrocław-Poznań). In the years 1953-1956 this publication appeared under the changed title: *Dawna kultura* (Old culture). Contains survey articles and notes.

2530. Przegląd antropologiczny (Anthropological review). t. 1– 1926– Wrocław, Państwowe Wydawn. Naukowe. Irregular.

Published by the Polish Anthropological Society, with articles and reports on physical anthropology and related topics. Summaries in Czech, English, French, or German.

2531. Przegląd archeologiczny; czasopismo poświęcone archeologii (Archaeological review; a journal devoted to archaeology). 1919– Poznań, Zakład Narodowy im. Ossolińskich. Irregular.

Published by the Polish Archaeological Society. Contains larger monographic studies, reports on excavations, systematization of archeological finds. Tables of contents and summaries in French. Indispensable for the research scholar. Of similar value is *Archeologia* (1–, 1947– Warszawa, Zakład Narodowy im. Ossolińskich, annual), published by the Polish Academy of Sciences. This publication covers all areas of archaeological research with special interest in Slavic and Polish territory. It contains a bibliographic section with brief summaries of works by Poles or on Poland. Summaries in French and Russian.

3. Monographs and Articles

2532. Czekanowski, Jan. Carte anthropologique de la Pologne et des pays limitrophes. *In* Bulletin de l'Académie Polonaise des Sciences et Lettres (Warsaw), Cl. III, Ser. B., 1950: 381-396.

2533. Czekanowski, Jan. Polska-Słowiańszczyzna; perspektywy antropologiczne (Poland and the Slavic world; anthropological perspectives). Warszawa, S. Arct, 1948. 389 p. Tables, maps. (Biblioteka wiedzy o Polsce, t. 3)

Problems of physical and cultural anthropology of the Polish nation presented against the background of East Central Europe in a historical perspective. A basic study in comparative research relating physical anthropology to cultural. A selective bibliography (p. 358-370) facilitates further readings in the field.

2534. Czekanowski, Jan. Zarys antropologii Polski (Survey of Poland's anthropology). Lwów, K. S. Jakubowski, 1930. 592 p. Illus., maps. Bibliography: p. 559-577. (Lwowska biblioteka slawistyczna, t. 11)

A classic presentation of problems, research, and achievements of anthropological science in Poland before 1930 by the founder of modern Polish anthropology. This study is supplemented by the same author in *Antropologia polska w międzywojennym dwudziestoleciu, 1919-1939* (Polish anthropology during the 20 years between the wars, 1919-39) (Warszawa, Nakł. Tow. Naukowego Warszawskiego, 1948, 221 p.).

2535. Hensel, Witold. Polska przed tysiącem lat (Poland a thousand years ago). 3d rev. ed. Wrocław, Zakład Narodowy im. Ossolińskich, 1967. 287 p. Illus., facsims.

A popular presentation of the archaeological material on the territory of present-day Poland, and a discussion of the civilization and early history of the population of that area. A bibliographic essay concludes the work. There is a French translation of the second edition, *La naissance de la Pologne* (Wrocław, Zakład Narodowy im. Ossolińskich, 1966, 253 p.). A shorter English version of this work is also available, *The Beginnings of the Polish State* (Warsaw, Polonia Publishing House, 1960, 178 p.).

2536. Hensel, Witold, *and* Aleksander Gieysztor. Archeological Research in Poland. Warsaw, Polonia Publishing House, 1958. 74 p. Illus., maps. Bibliography: p. 71-75.

Serves as a convenient brief introduction to the study of archaeology in Poland.

2537. Kostrzewski, Józef, W. Chmielewski, *and* Jażdżewski. Pradzieje Polski (Poland's prehistory). 2d rev. and enl. ed. Wrocław, Zakład Narodowy im. Ossolińskich, 1965. 428 p. Illus., maps, plates.

Deals basically with archaeological problems of Poland's early history. There is an extensive French summary of conclusions.

B. ETHNOGRAPHY

by Imre Boba

1. Bibliography

2538. Etnografia i etnologia (Ethnography and ethnology). *In* Hahn,

Wiktor. Bibliografia bibliografij polskich (A bibliography of Polish bibliographies). 3d ed. Wrocław, Warszawa, Kraków, Zakład Narodowy im. Ossolińskich, 1966. p. 154-160.

A guide to printed bibliographies, monographs with bibliographies, and journals with regular bibliographic surveys. All entries published before 1950. For more recent bibliographic information, see Henryk Sawoniak's *Bibliografia bibliografii polskich, 1951-1960* (Wrocław, Zakład Narodowy im. Ossolińskich, 1967, p. 66-68). Additional bibliographic material may be found in:

Etnografia (Ethnography). *In*: Polska Akademia Nauk. *Instytut Historii.* Bibliografia historii Polski (Bibliography of Polish history). v. 1, pt. 1. Warszawa, Państwowe Wydawn. Naukowe, 1965. p. 318-345. Over 300 basic bibliographies, journals, serials, and monographs relevant to the study of Polish ethnography.

2539. Jackowski, Aleksander. Das volkskundliche Schrifttum Polens seit 1945. *In* Deutsches Jahrbuch für Volkskunde (Berlin), v. 3, 1957, pt. 1: 227-257.

An annotated, selective bibliography of basic Polish contributions to the study of ethnography.

2540. Zambrzycka-Kuchanowicz, Anna. Przegląd bibliografii etnograficznych (Survey of bibliographies on ethnography). Warszawa, Polska Akademia Nauk, 1958. 42 p. (multigraphed)

A guide to bibliographies on Polish ethnography published in book form, contained in journals or appended to monographs etc.

2. Serials and Monographs

2541. Bystroń, Jan Stanisław. Etnografia Polski (Poland's ethnography). Warszawa, Czytelnik, 1947. 232 p.

A lucid introduction to the study of the ethnography of Poland by the prominent teacher of generations of Polish ethnographers. The closing chapter lists the most important journals and monographs in the field (as of 1947).

2542. Etnografia Polska (Polish ethnography). 1958– Warszawa. Annual.

Published by the Ethnography Division of the Polish Academy of Sciences. Reports on the Division's own research, mainly in the field of material culture. Book reviews. Table of contents and summaries in English and Russian.

2543. Polska Akademia Nauk. *Instytut Historii Kultury Materialnej.* Polski atlas etnograficzny (Polish ethnographic atlas). Warszawa, 1964–

The atlas, prepared by the Department of the Polish Ethnographical Atlas of the Polish Academy of Sciences, contains the results of research on a wide range of phenomena of Polish folk culture. The complete work will consist of 12 fascicles, about 60 maps each. Text also in English.

C. DEMOGRAPHY

by Andrew Elias

1. Population Theory

2544. Holzer, Jerzy. Podstawy analizy demograficznej (The principles of demographic analysis). Warszawa, Państwowe Wydawn. Ekonomiczne, 1963. 400 p. Map, bibliography.

A comprehensive presentation of demographic theory, frequently illustrated by tables and graphs based on Polish statistics. It is supplemented by official Polish forms on vital statistics.

2545. Studia demograficzne (Demographic studies). 1963– Warszawa, Państwowe Wydawn. Naukowe. Published twice or three times annually.

Organ of Komitet Nauk Demograficznych of Polska Akademia Nauk, this journal publishes valuable analytical and informative contributions by top Polish and other demographers. The topics relate mostly to the current population of Poland, with an occasional article going back to the pre-World War I period.

2546. Szturm de Sztrem, Edward. Elementy demografii (Elements of demography). Warszawa, Polskie Wydawn. Gospodarcze, 1955. 236 p. Illus.

A broad, but not very deep, analytical presentation of all aspects of demography, published during and reflecting the influence of the "cult of the personality."

2547. Vielrose, Egon. Elementy ruchu naturalnego ludności (Factors in the natural change of the population). Warszawa, Państwowe Wydawn. Ekonomiczne, 1961. 365 p. Illus., bibliography.

An extensive study of the factors causing changes in the population structure, illustrated by the structural changes in the Polish population.

2. Size, Composition, and Distribution of the Population

2548. Holzer, Jerzy. Prognoza demograficzna Polski na lata 1960-1975 według województw (Demographic projections of Poland for 1960-1975 by regions). Warszawa, Polskie Wydawn. Gospowarcze, 1959. 192 p. Bibliography.

The first attempt at population projections for Poland by age, sex, and region.

2549. Mauldin, Wayman P., *and* Donald S. Akers. The Population of Poland. Washington, D.C., U.S. Govt. Print. Off., 1954. 198 p. Illus., maps. (U.S. Bureau of the Census. International Population Statistics Reports. Series P-90, no. 4)

A comprehensive, though somewhat outdated, analytical discussion of the recent trends in the population structure of Poland as well as in its ethnic, educational, and employment composition.

2550. Pohoski, Michał. Migracje ze wsi do miast (Rural-urban migrations). Warszawa, Państwowe Wydawn. Ekonomiczne, 1963. 241 p. Maps. Bibliography: p. 224-232.

A study of the social and occupational mobility of the rural youth. It is based on a survey of 47 villages located in three different socioeconomic areas of the Old Territories. The time period covered is 1945 to 1957.

2551. Poland. *Główny Urząd Statystyczny*. Ludność Polski w latach 1945-1965 (The population of Poland from 1945 to 1965). Warszawa, 1966. 210 p.

An analytical account of the growth of Poland's population and of its urban-rural and regional segments during the last two decades. It is supplemented by two appendixes containing some of the most detailed tables available on Polish population and projections of reproduction coefficients up to 1981.

Poland's Central Statistical Office also sponsored the following recent serial publication:

Rocznik demograficzny (Demographic yearbook). 1968– Warszawa, Główny Urząd Statystyczny. Annual. The first volume of 643 pages covers the period 1945-1966.

2552. Poland. *Główny Urząd Statystyczny*. Ludność według płci i wieku (Population by sex and age). Warszawa, 1959. 72 p.

Population statistics by provinces and districts as of December 31, 1955. It is based on a single survey.

2553. Rosset, Edward. Oblicze demograficzne Polski Ludowej (A demographic picture of People's Poland). Warszawa, Państwowe Wydawn. Ekonomiczne, 1965. 416 p. Illus. Bibliography: p. 394-402.

An exhaustive account of the demographic and employment changes in the Polish population based essentially on the results of the 1950 and 1960 censuses.

2554. Rosset, Edward. Perspektywy demograficzne Polski (Demographic perspectives of Poland. (Warszawa, Państwowe Wydawn. Ekonomiczne, 1962. 592 p. Illus., bibliography.

A comprehensive historical analysis, by a foremost Polish demographer, of the past growth of the Polish population and its projected growth to the year 2000. Includes separate analyses of the productive segment of the population and of the urban-rural differences in demographic characteristics of the population.

2555. Sobański, Wacław, *ed.* Polskie ziemie zachodnie i północne — Zagadnienia demograficzne (Polish western and northern territories—demographic problems). Poznań, Wydawn. Zachodnie, 1959. 2 v.

A discussion by several Polish demographers of the population structure and development in the areas formerly belonging to Germany.

2556. Wakar, Włodzimierz. Rozwój terytoryalny narodowości Polskiej (The territorial development of the Polish nation). Kielce, Kasa im. J. Mianowskiego, 1917-1918. 3 v. Maps, bibliography.

Essentially an account of the ethnic and religious composition of the population in the territory under Russian administration, toward the end of the last and beginning of the present century.

3. Sources of Population Data

2557. Ładogórski, Tadeusz. Studia nad zaludnieniem Polski XIV wieku (Studies on the population of Poland in the 14th century). Wrocław, Zakład Narodowy im. Ossolińskich, 1958. 231 p. Illus., bibliography.

Population estimates of the then dioceses of the Catholic Church based on the church records.

2558. Ladenberger, Tadeusz. Zaludnienie Polski na początku panowania Kazimierza Wielkiego (Population of Poland at the beginning of the reign of Casimir the Great). Lwów, 1930. 95 p.

An attempt at population estimates of Poland for that period, based on church records.

2559. Poland. *Główny Urząd Statystyczny.* Rocznik statystyczny 1968 (Statistical yearbook, 1968). Warszawa, 1968. 722 p.

The latest of the Polish statistical annuals. Contains the most recent official data on the population and labor force as well as a brief summary of all five censuses taken in 1921, 1931, 1946, 1950, and 1960. More data from the 1931 census were published in 1937 and 1938 in various volumes of *Statystyka Polski* (Statistics of Poland). Incomplete results of the 1946 census were published in 1947 under the title *Powszechny sumaryczny spis ludności z dn. 14. II. 1946 R.* (General summary census of the population of February 14, 1946). Various selections from the 1950 census were published in 1955 under the title of *Narodowy spis powszechny* (General national census). Selected data from the 1950 and 1960 censuses appeared also in various yearbooks, and, in addition, extensive summaries of the population statistics based on the last census were published in *Biuletyn statystyczny* (Statistical bulletin), Series L, nos. 1 to 23.

2560. Poland. *Główny Urząd Statystyczny.* Małżeństwa, urodzenia i zgony 1931, 1932 (Marriages, births, and deaths in 1931 and 1932). Warszawa, 1939. 288 p.

A collection of detailed statistical tables on the vital statistics of Poland for 1931 and 1932. Also published for other prewar years.

D. NATIONALITIES

by Imre Boba

1. Bibliographies

2561. Gunzenhäuser, Max. Bibliographie zur Nationalitätenfrage und zur Judenfrage der Republik Polen 1919-1939. 2d ed. Stuttgart, 1943. 76 p.

2562. Kwestia mniejszości narodowych . . . (Problem of nationalities . . .). *In* Hahn, Wiktor. Bibliografia bibliografij polskich (A bibliography of Polish bibliographies). 3d ed. Wrocław, Warszawa, Kraków, Zakład Narodowy im. Ossolińskich, 1966. p. 162 (entry 2152a), 446-447 (entries 6034-6038).

A short but important bibliography of bibliographies in Polish and German. Details on bibliographies contained in *Sprawy narodowościowe* (see entry 2570). Hahn's work lists bibliographies printed up to and including 1950.

2563. Symmons-Symonolewicz, Konstantin (Konstanty). Studies in Nationality and Nationalism in Poland between the Two Wars (1918-1939): a Bibliographic Survey. New York. Polish Institute of Arts and Sciences in America, 1944. 73 p.

Also appeared in:

Polish Institute of Arts and Sciences in America. Bulletin (New York), v. 2, 1943/44: 57-125.

2. Serials and Monographs

2564. Brozek, A. Zur Statistik der deutschen Bevölkerung in Polen seit 1930. *In* Jahrbuch für Geschichte der UdSSR und der volksdemokratischen Länder Europas (Berlin), v. 7, 1963: 473-494.

2565. Czech, Joseph. Die Bevölkerung Polens, Zahl und völkische Zusammensetzung. Breslau, M. und H. Marcus, 1932. 232 p. Bibliographie: p. 216-229. (Veröffentlichungen der Schlesischen Gesellschaft für Erdkunde e. V. und des Geographischen Instituts der Universität Breslau, 16. Heft)

2566. Horak, Stephen. Poland and Her National Minorities 1919-1939; a Case Study. New York, Washington, D.C., Hollywood, Vantage Press, 1961. 259 p. Illus. Bibliography: p. 232-254.

A sensitive problem presented by a Ukrainian scholar. Includes excerpts from treaties and laws governing issues of nationalities in Poland. For a review of this book by William J. Rose, see *Slavic Review* (Seattle, Wash.), v. 21, June 1962: 357-358, and a reply by S. Horak, *ibid.*, Dec. 1962: 789.

2567. Les minorités nationales. *In* Pologne 1919-1939. v. 1. Neuchâtel, La Baconnière, 1946. p. 393-446.

A collection of brief but informative surveys of minority groups; Ukrainians, Belo-Russians, Jews, and Germans. Very useful bibliographies.

The same volume contains a chapter on Poles in foreign countries (before 1939), "Les Polonais à l'étranger" (p. 447-508).

2568. Mussakovska, Olha. Ukrainians in Present-day Poland. Ukrainian Review (London), v. 6, 1959, no. 4: 72-79.

2569. Minority Affairs and Poland; an Informatory Outline. Edited by S. J. Paprocki. Warsaw, Nationality Research Institut [sic], 1935. 184 p.

A brief presentation of a complex problem by the director of the Institute for the Study of Nationality Problems (of Poland). The same publication available also in German, *Polen und das Minderheitenproblem* (Warschau, 1935, 173 p.).

2570. Sprawy narodowościowe; czasopismo poświęcone badaniu spraw narodowościowych (Problems of nationalities, a journal devoted to the study of nationality problems). 1927-1939. Warszawa.

Published by the (Polish) Institute for the study of Nationality Problems (Instytut Badań Spraw Narodowościowych). There are indexes to volumes 1-5 (1927-1931) and volumes 6-10 (1932-1936). French summaries of the articles were published separately as *Questions minoritaires* (1927-1937). The research work and publications of the Institute were summarized in separate publications, e.g., *Dziesięciolecie działalności Instytutu Badań Narodowościowych* (Ten years of activity of the Institute for the Study of Nationality Problems) (Warszawa, 1932, 45 p.); *Działalność Instytutu Badań Spraw Narodowościowych 1921-1936* (Activities of the Institute for the Study of Nationality Problems, 1921-1936) (Warszawa, 1936, 49 p.). A similar survey of activities of the Institute was published by Józef Skrzypek in *Niepodległość* (Warszawa), v. 15, 1937: 137-146.

The volumes of *Sprawy narodowościowe* contain numerous bibliographies of books and articles published in Poland and abroad.

E. POLES ABROAD

by Konstantin Symmons-Symonolewicz

1. General Materials and Historical Surveys

2571. Gadon, Lubomir. Wielka emigracja w perwszych latach po powstaniu listopadowym (The great emigration in the first years after the uprising of November 1830). 2d ed. Paryż, Księg. Polska, 1960. 576 p. Illus., ports., facsims.

First edition appeared as *Emigracya polska; pierwsze lata po upadku powstania listopadowego* (The Polish emigration; the first years after the failure of the November uprising) (Kraków, Spółka Wydawn. Polska, 1901-1902, 3 v. in 1).

2572. Janik, Michał. Dzieje Polaków na Syberii (A history of the Poles in Siberia). Kraków, Nakł. Krakowskiej Spółki Wydawn., 1928. 472 p. Illus., ports, map, bibliographies. (Z historji i literatury, 35)

2573. Lewak, Adam. Dzieje emigracji polskiej w Turcji, 1831-1878 (A history of the Polish emigration in Turkey, 1831-1878). Warszawa, Nakł. Instytutu Wschodniego, 1935. 280 p. Illus.

This book and those cited in entries 2571 and 2572 deal with three important areas where the 19th century Polish political emigrants or exiles found themselves in relatively large numbers.

2574. Okołowicz, Józef. Wychodźtwo i osadnictwo polskie przed wojną światową (Polish emigration and settlement before the World War). Warszawa, Nakł. Urzędu Emigracyjnego, 1920. 412 p.

An important account of the emigration from Poland up to the time of the First World War.

2575. Retinger, Joseph H. Polacy w cywilizacjach świata do końca wieku XIX-go (Poles in the civilizations of the world to the end of the 19th century) Warszawa, Światowy Związek Polaków z Zagranicy, 1937. 224 p. Illus., ports.

A historical account of the contributions of individual Poles to the cultures of other nations.

2576. Rocznik Polonii. Poles Abroad; Yearbook and Directory. London, Taurus, 1958. 462 p.

A statistical handbook of the Polish population outside the boundaries of Poland, compiled by the Union of Poles Abroad.

2577. Zieliński, Stanisław. Mały słownik pionerów polskich kolonjalnych i morskich, podróżnicy, odkrywcy, zdobywcy, badacze, eksploratorzy, emigranci-pamiętnikarze, działacze i pisarze emigracyjni (A concise dictionary of Polish pioneers in colonial and overseas countries, of travelers, discoverers, conquerors, scholars, explorers, diarists, and of emigrant leaders and writers). Warszawa 1932. 680 p.

A useful collection of brief biographies of Polish travelers, explorers, and scientists as well as the more prominent leaders and writers of the Polish emigration overseas. Was published serially. Includes bibliographies.

2. Europe

2578. Czaykowski, Bogdan, *and* Bolesław Sulik. Polacy w Wielkiej Brytanii (Poles in Great Britain). Paryż, Instytut Literacki, 1961. 586 p. (Biblioteka "Kultury," t. 63)

An informative account of Polish organizations and life in Great Britain, in part descriptive and in part analytical. A portion of this book, dealing with the Poles in Scotland, was also published in *Kultura* (Paris), no. 9 (131), September 1958: 105-123; no. 10 (132),

October 1958: 107-124. For a discussion of the post-war Polish communities in other countries of Western Europe, *see*:

Czechanowski, Stanisław. Polacy w Niemczech (Poles in Germany). *In* Kultura (Paris), no. 11 (97). November 1955: 134-142.

Malanowski, Jan. Adaptacja Polaków w Danii (Adjustment of the Poles in Denmark). *In* Problemy Polonii Zagranicznej, I, Warszawa, 1960: 124-154.

2579. Zubrzycki, Jerzy. Polish Immigrants in Britain; a Study of Adjustment. Preface by René Clemens. The Hague, M. Nijhoff, 1956. 219 p. Bibliography: p. 216-219. (Studies in Social Life, 3)

A systematic historical and sociological analysis of the present Polish community in Great Britain and its problems of adjustment, with some information about the Polish immigration in the United States, France, and Brazil. A portion of this book was published also in *Kultura* (Paris), no. 9 (83), September, 1954: 77-93.

3. United States, Canada, and Australia

2580. Haiman, Miecislaus. Polish Past in America, 1608-1865. Chicago, The Polish Roman Catholic Union Archives and Museum, 1939. 178 p. Illus., ports., maps, facsims. Bibliography: p. 163-164.

A general outline history of the Poles in the United States, written by their foremost historian. The book covers the first two and a half centuries of Polish colonization in America and summarizes the author's considerable achievements in tracing the little known history of a handful of early settlers and somewhat more numerous groups of political immigrants up to 1865.

2581. Szawleski, Mieczysław. Wychodźtwo polskie w Stanach Zjednoczonych Ameryki (Polish immigration in the United States of America). Lwów, Wydawn. Zakładu Narodowego im. Ossolińskich, 1924. 472 p. Illus., fold. map. Bibliography: p. 468.

An early, but still useful, discussion of Polish-American society by an objective and scholarly observer from Poland.

2582. Thomas, William I., *and* Florian Znaniecki. The Polish Peasant in Europe and America. 2d rev. ed. New York, Dover Publications, 1958. 2 v.

See also entry no. 2917.

A classic sociological study of the transplanted peasant community, its disorganization and reorganization. A mine of information about the culture of rural Poland, and a model of theoretical *Problemstellung*, this monograph has been a required reading in the field of social science for almost half a century. For an appreciation of its continuing influence in the field of studies of the Polish-American community, *see* the study by Helena Z. Lopata, "The Function of Voluntary Associations in an Ethnic Community: 'Polonia' " in *Contributions to Urban Sociology*, edited by Ernest W. Burgess (Chicago, University of Chicago Press, 1964), p. 203-223; and the article by Konstanty Symonolewicz (Symmons), "Polonia Amerykańska" (Poles in America) published in *Kultura* (Paris), no. 7/8 (225-226), July-August, 1966: 105-135. One may also consult the latter author's "The Polish-American Community — Half a Century After 'The Polish Peasant'" in *The Polish Review*, v. 11, 1956: 67-73.

Previous editions of *The Polish Peasant . . .* appeared in 1918-1920 (Chicago, University of Chicago Press, 1918-1920, 5 v.) and in 1927 (New York, A. A. Knopf, 1927, 2 v.).

2583. Wachtl, Charles Henry. Polonia w Ameryce; dzieje i dorobek (Poles in America; history and achievements). Filadelfia, Nakł. autora, 1944. 466 p. Bibliography: p. 465-466.

An interesting account of the evolution of "Polonia" as seen by one of its distinguished leaders and educators. The book is poorly organized and is highly personal in its point of view, but it contains much valuable information and is honest and straightforward in the handling of facts.

2584. Who's Who in Polish America; A Biographical Directory of Polish-American Leaders and Distinguished Poles Resident in the Americas. 3d ed. Edited by Francis Bolek. New York, Harbinger House, 1943. 581 p.

See also entry no. 2454.

A useful compilation, even though somewhat lacking in discrimination and not without an occasional error. For an informative survey of Polish and Polish-American contributions to science and learning in the United States *see* two articles by Miecislaus Haiman: "Nauka Polska w Stanach Zjednoczonych Ameryki Północnej" (Polish scholarship in the United States), *Nauka Polska* (Warszawa), v. 21, 1936: 203-234; and "Polish Scholarship in the United States, 1939-1946," *Polish-American Studies*, v. 4, no. 3/4, July-Dec., 1947: 65-87.

2585. Wood, Arthur. Hamtramck, Then and Now; A Sociological Study of a Polish-American Community. New York, Bookman Associates, 1955. 253 p. Illus.

An interesting analysis of a small Polish-American political community surrounded completely by the metropolitan city of Detroit.

2586. Wytrwal, Joseph Anthony. America's Polish Heritage; A Social History of the Poles in America. Detroit, Mich., Endurance Press, 1961. 350 p. Illus.

The only attempt in English to present a complete history of the Polish Americans from the beginnings of immigration to the 1950s. Informative and useful, but lacking in clear focus and uneven. For a critical evaluation, see the review by Konstantin Symmons (Konstanty Symmons-Symonolewicz) in *Slavic Review* (Seattle), v. 21, 1962: 362-363.

2587. Mazurkiewicz, Roman. Polskie wychodźtwo i osadnictwo w Kanadzie (Polish immigration and settlement in Canada). Warszawa, Nakł. Naukowego Instytutu Emigracyjnego, 1929. 146 p. Illus., maps.

An early, but still valuable, account of the Polish immigration in Canada, written by a member of the Polish consular service. For a more recent discussion of the Canadian Poles and their problems, see the following:

Turek, Wiktor. Emigracja polska w Kanadzie (The Polish immigration in Canada). *In* Problemy Poloni Zagranicznej, v. 1. Warszawa, 1960. p. 51-94.

Jaworski, Adam. Wynaradawianie się Polaków w Kanadzie (Denationalization of the Poles in Canada). *In Kultura* (Paris) no. 6 (116), June 1957: 66-89.

Jaworski, Adam. Polonia kanadyjska w gąszczu statystyki (The Canadian Poles in the thicket of statistics). *In* Kultura (Paris) no. 5 (127), May 1958: 89-96.

Heydenkorn, Benedykt. Polonia kanadyjska (The Canadian Poles). *In* Kultura (Paris) no. 10 (144), October 1959: 85-107.

2588. Zubrzycki, Jerzy. Immigrants in Australia; a Demographic Survey Based upon the 1954 Census. Parkville, Melbourne University Press, 1960. 118 p. Diagrs., tables. (Australian National University [Canberra], Social Science Monograph, 17)

This excellently executed demographic survey contains the data on geographic distribution, sex, and occupational status of immigrants from Poland. For a discussion of their organizational life and problems one may consult:

Chciuk, Andrzej. Najnowsza emigracja w Australii (The most recent emigration to Australia). *In* Kultura (Paris) no. 6 (140), June 1959: 77-99.

4. Latin America

2589. Włodek, Józef. Argentyna i emigracja; ze szczególnem uwzględnieniem emigracji polskiej (Argentina and emigration; with particular attention to Polish emigration). Warszawa, Wydaw. M. Arcta, 1923. 513 p. Illus., tables, diagrs., maps. Bibliography: p. 503-506.

A dated, but still useful, book on early Polish immigration into Argentina. For a more recent view *see*:

Kuss, Witold. Polacy w Argentynie (The Poles in Argentina). *In* Kultura (Paris) no. 12 (206), December 1964: 116-128; no. 1-2 (207-208), January 1965: 197-204; no. 3 (209), March 1965: 108-122; no. 5 (211), May 1965: 99-105.

2590. Żabko-Potopowicz, Antoni. Osadnictwo polskie w Brazylji (Polish settlement in Brazil). Warszawa, Autor. Skł. Syndykat Emigracyjny, 1936. 228 p. Illus.

An older study of the Polish immigration in Brazil, reflecting the situation before the Second World War. For a more recent account, focusing on the southernmost section of the country, *see*:

Gardoliński, Edmund. Pionierzy polscy w Stanie Rio Grande

do Sul (Polish pioneers in the State of Rio Grande do Sul). *In* Problemy Polonii Zagranicznej, v. 1. Warszawa, 1960. 95-123.

5. The Polish Press outside Poland

a. The Polish-American Press

2591. The following newspapers and journals may be considered the most representative organs of the Polish-American press:

Ameryka-Echo. Chicago, Ill. 1886– An old weekly which seems to have taken a new hold on life in recent years and to have become an important organ of Polish-American public opinion.

Dziennik Chicagoski (The Polish Chicago daily news). Chicago, Ill. 1890– Published by the Resurrectionist Fathers, it represents points of view of the Polish-American Roman Catholic hierarchy.

Dziennik Polski (The Polish daily news). Detroit, Mich. 1904– A privately owned, influential daily.

Dziennik Związkowy. The Polish Daily Zgoda. Chicago, Ill. 1908– Represents the Polish National Alliance, the largest of the Polish-American fraternal organizations and is the only daily published by such an organization.

Nowy Świat (The new world). New York. 1896– Probably the most broadly oriented and ambitious daily of Polonia.

The Polish-American Journal. Scranton, Penn. 1911– An English-language continuation of two local Polish weeklies which ably represents the point of view of the younger generation.

Polish-American Studies. v. 1– New York. 1944– This journal, which is published irregularly, contains much valuable material on the history and development of the Polish community in America. The first five volumes were published by the Polish-American Historical Commission of the Polish Institute of Arts and Sciences in America. With volume six, the journal became an official organ of an independent organization, the Polish American Historical Association.

The Polish Review. 1956– New York, Polish Institute of Arts and Sciences in America, Inc. Quarterly. This publication is devoted to Poland, past and present, and includes contributions both of Polish scholars in exile and of writers of other nationalities.

b. The Polish Press in Other Countries

2592. Dziennik Polski (The Polish daily). 1940– Londyn.

This daily paper was founded as the official organ of the Polish government in exile and since 1945 has appeared as a private, self-supporting publication. It is easily the most important newspaper of the recent political emigration from Poland. It reports on both events in Poland and on developments in the Polish diaspora.

2593. Kultura; szkice, opowiadania, sprawozdania (Culture; essays, stories, reports). 1947– Paryż, Instytut Literacki. Monthly.

See also entry no. 2981.

A literary and socio-cultural monthly published since 1948 in Paris and representing a strong liberal and democratic tradition among the Poles abroad. It has gained a large following and may be considered the most important ideological and cultural organ of Polish intelligentsia in exile.

2594. Teki historyczne (Historical papers). 1947– Londyn. Irregular. *See also* entry no. 2614.

This valuable publication of the Polish Historical Society in London is easily the most notable of several learned periodicals published by the recent emigration from Poland.

2595. Wiadomości (The news). 1947– Londyn. Weekly.

A literary weekly continuing the tradition of the well-known interwar Warsaw journal *Wiadomości Literackie.* It publishes essays in literary criticism, short stories and poems by Polish writers in exile, and much historical and biographical material.

41

history

by Piotr S. Wandycz

A. BIBLIOGRAPHIES

2596. Bibliografia historii Polski (A bibliography of Polish history). Edited by Helena Madurowicz-Urbańska. Warszawa, Państwowe Wydawn. Naukowe, 1965–

New standard bibliography, published under the auspices of the Institute of History of the Polish Academy of Sciences. Volume 1 (in three parts) covers the period up to 1795. Volume 2, parts 1 and 2, covers the period 1795-1918.

2597. Bibliografia historii Polski XIX wieku (A bibliography of Polish history in the 19th century). v. 1, 1815-1831. Edited by Stanisław Płoski. Wrocław-Warszawa, Ossolineum, 1958. 662 p.

Published under the auspices of the Institute of History of the Polish Academy of Sciences. Designed as a continuation of Finkel's bibliography. Only one volume appeared.

2598. Bibliografia historii polskiej . . . (Bibliography of Polish history . . .). Kraków, Nakł. Polskiego Towarzystwa Historycznego. 1952–

Published under the auspices of the Institute of History of the Polish Academy of Sciences. Edited by Jan Baumgart and Stanisław Głuszek for the years 1944-1947, by Jan Baumgart for the years 1948-1955, and by Jan Baumgart and Anna Malcówna for the years 1956-1965. Generally a yearly publication continuing the bibliographies which appeared in *Kwartalnik historyczny* (Historical quarterly) before the Second World War. Complete coverage of all historical publications.

2599. Finkel, Ludwik. Bibliografia historyi polskiej (A bibliography of Polish history). Warszawa, Państwowe Wydawn. Naukowe, 1955. 3 v. Facsim.

A photo-offset reprint of the 1891-1914 edition of the standard bibliography covering the period up to 1815.

2600. Gunzenhäuser, Max. *comp.* Bibliographie zur Geschichte der polnischen Frage bis 1919. Stuttgart, Institut für Weltpolitik, 1940. 160 p. (Bibliographien der Weltkriegsbücherei, Nr. 26/27/28).

A useful selection.

2601. Manteufflowa, Maria. Histoire. *In* Commission nationale de bibliographie. Bibliographie sur la Pologne: pays, histoire, civilisation. 2d ed. Warszawa, Państwowe Wydawn. Naukowe, 1964. p. 73-117.

A short bibliography prepared for UNESCO. Useful.

B. HISTORIOGRAPHY

2602. Dembiński, Bronisław, Oskar Halecki, *and* Marceli Handelsman. L'Historiographie polonaise du XIXème et du XXème siècle. Varsovie, Société polonaise d'histoire, 1933. 37 p.

Papers presented at the Seventh International Congress of Historians in Warsaw. Provides a useful summary.

2603. Rose, William J. Polish Historical Writing. Journal of Modern History (Chicago), v. 2, December 1930: 569-585.

A brief and useful introduction by a prominent specialist.

2604. Smoleński, Władysław. Szkoły historyczne w Polsce (Historical schools in Poland). Warszawa, 1890. 160 p.

A classic survey. Recently reprinted with an introduction by the leading Polish historiographer Marjan H. Serejski (Wrocław, Ossolineum, 1952, 155 p., bibliographies [Biblioteka narodowa, ser. 1, nr. 142]).

2605. Valkenier, Elizabeth. Soviet Impact on Polish Post-War Historiography, 1946-1950. Journal of Central European Affairs (Boulder, Colo.), v. 11, January 1952: 372-396.

A useful analysis of problems confronting Polish historians after the Second World War.

2606. Ziffer, Bernard. Poland: History and Historians. Three Bibliographical Essays. New York, Mid-European Studies Center, 1952. 107 p. Bibliographies.

A good introduction to problems of Polish historiography, with useful bibliographical indications.

C. SERIALS: JOURNALS AND SOURCES

2607. Acta Poloniae historica. 1958– Wrocław, Zakład Narodowy im. Ossolińskich. Annual.

Issued by the Institute of History of the Polish Academy of Sciences. An important historical publication in foreign languages.

2608. Antemurale. 1954– Romae. Annual. Illus.

See also entry no. 3151.

A review in language other than Polish published by the Institutum Historicum Polonicum Romae, whose membership includes historians living outside of Poland. Collections of sources bearing on Polish history in Western archives appear in the serial *Elementa ad Fontium Editiones* (1960–, Romae), which the Institute publishes in the original languages.

2609. Kwartalnik historyczny (Historical quarterly). 1887– Warszawa.

The principal and oldest historical journal, at present published by the Institute of History of the Polish Academy of Sciences. Previously published in Lwów and Kraków.

2610. Najnowsze dzieje Polski: materiały i studia z okresu 1914-1939 (Contemporary Polish history: materials and studies for the period 1914-1939). 1958– Warszawa, Państwowe Wydawn. Naukowe.

Published by the Institute of History of the Polish Academy of Sciences. This and its parallel publication covering the Second World War should be complemented by *Niepodległość*, published by the Józef Piłsudski Historical Institute (1929-1939, Warszawa; new series, 1948–, London), and by *Bellona* (1929-1939, Warszawa; new series, 1940–, London), published by the General Sikorski Historical Institute.

2611. Odrodzenie i Reformacja w Polsce (Renaissance and Reformation in Poland). 1956– Warszawa. Annual.

Published by the Institute of History of the Polish Academy of Sciences. Should be compared to *Reformacja w Polsce* (Reformation in Poland), a quarterly edited by Stanisław Kot (1921-1939, Warszawa).

2612. Pomniki dziejowe Polski, Monumenta Poloniae historica. v. 1-6, 1864-1893. Lwów, Kraków; new series: 1946– Kraków, Warszawa.

Published since 1962 under the auspices of the Institute of History of the Polish Academy of Sciences in Warsaw. Basic chronicles and sources for early Polish history.

2613. Studia i materiały z dziejów Polski w okresie Oświecenia (Studies and materials for Polish history during the Enlightenment). v. 1– 1957– Warszawa.

Title varies: *Studia z dziejów Polski w okresie Oświecenia.* Published by the Institute of History of the Polish Academy of Sciences.

2614. Teki historyczne (Historical papers). 1947– Londyn. Irregular.
See also entry no. 2594.

Published by the Polish Historical Society in Great Britain.

2615. Volumina Legum. v. 1-10, 1733-1952; new series, 1952–

Basic collection of laws, statutes and constitutions of Poland and the Grand Duchy of Lithuania. Separate volumes under different titles, printed in Warsaw, St. Petersburg, Kraków, and Poznań.

2616. Zeszyty historyczne (Historical notes). 1962– Paryż. Biannual.

Published by the Instytut Literacki. Concentrates on 20th century Polish history.

D. SURVEY HISTORIES

2617. Bobrzyński, Michał. Dzieje Polski w zarysie (An outline of Polish history). 4th ed. Warszawa, Gebethner i Wolff, 1927-1931. 3 v. Fold. maps, geneal. tables, bibliographies.

A very important and stimulating interpretation of Polish history by a prominent historian of the Kraków school and an enlightened conservative. Created a great impression when published.

2618. The Cambridge History of Poland. Edited by William F. Reddaway and others. Cambridge, England, The University Press, 1941-1950. 2 v. Plates, fold. maps.
See also entry no. 3122.

The most extensive history of Poland in English, written by Polish and Western specialists. Valuable though uneven. Lacks a bibliography.

2619. Dyboski, Roman. Poland in World Civilization. Edited by Ludwik Krzyżanowski. New York, J. M. Barrett, 1950. 285 p. Port., map. Bibliography: p. 259-263.
See also entry no. 3066.

A posthumous edition of a major survey of history and civilization by a leading Polish scholar. Roughly similar in scope to two other surveys by prominent historians, William J. Rose's *Poland Old and New* (London, G. Bell & Sons, 1948, 354 p., plates, ports., fold. maps), and *Poland's Place in Europe* (Poznań, Instytut Zachodni, 1947, 460 p., maps), edited by Zygmunt Wojciechowski.

2620. Gieysztor, Aleksander, *and others.* History of Poland. Translation from the Polish manuscript by Krystyna Cękalska and others. Warszawa, PWN, Polish Scientific Publishers, 1968. 783 p. Illus., maps, ports. Bibliography: p. 727-740.

Contents: "Introduction," by S. Kieniewicz; "Medieval Poland," by A. Gieysztor; "The Commonwealth of the Gentry," by J. Tazbir and E. Rostworowski; "Poland under Foreign Rule 1795-1918," by

S. Kieniewicz and H. Wereszycki; "Poland 1918-1939," by H. Wereszycki; and "Conclusion," by S. Kieniewicz.

A short, beautifully illustrated, popular survey reflecting present-day tendencies in Polish historiography is *Millennium: A Thousand Years of the Polish State*, by Aleksander Gieysztor, Stanisław Herbst, and Bogusław Leśnodorski (Warsaw, Polonia, 1961, 208 p., illus., plates, ports., maps).

2621. Halecki, Oskar (Oscar). A History of Poland. New York, Roy Publishers, 1956. 359 p.

Survey by a leading political historian of conservative leanings.

2622. Kridl, Manfred, Władysław Malinowski, *and* Józef Wittlin, *eds.* For Your Freedom and Ours: Polish Progressive Spirit Through the Centuries. Translated by Ludwik Krzyżanowski. New York, Frederic Ungar, 1943. 359 p.

See also entry no. 3100.

A useful anthology of well selected documents.

2623. Kukiel, Marian. Dzieje Polski porozbiorowe, 1795-1921 (A history of post-partition Poland, 1795-1921). London, B. Świderski, 1961. 663 p.

An important synthesis, intended as a university textbook and a sequel to Roman Grodecki, Stanisław Zachorowski, and Jan Dąbrowski's *Dzieje Polski średniowiecznej* (A history of medieval Poland) (Kraków, Krak. spółka wydawn, 1926, 2 v.), and Władysław Konopczyński's *Dzieje Polski nowożytnej* (A history of modern Poland) (London, reprint by B. Świderski, 1959, 2 v., bibliographies).

2624. Kutrzeba, Stanisław. Grundriss der polnischen Verfassungsgeschichte. Berlin, Puttkamer und Mühlbrecht, 1912. 261 p.

A translation of the third edition of a Polish classic. The most extensive Polish edition is *Historia ustroju Polski w zarysie* (An outline of Polish constitutional history) (Warszawa, Lwów, 1920-1949, 4 v.).

2625. Polska Akademia Nauk. *Instytut Historii.* Historia Polski (A history of Poland). Tadeusz Manteuffel, general editor. Warszawa, Państwowe Wydawn. Naukowe, 1958–

A huge undertaking, intended as the first Marxist synthesis of Polish history. The first volume (in two parts) covers the period to 1764, the second (in four parts) the period 1764-1864. Third and fourth volumes not yet completed. Rich in material for social and economic history, but uneven. Alterations introduced in various editions.

2626. Polska, jej dzieje i kultura od czasów najdawniejszych do chwili obecnej (Poland, her history and culture from the oldest times to the present). Warszawa, Nakł. Trzaski, Ewerta i Michalskiego, 1927-1932. 3 v. Illus., ports., maps, music, bibliographies.

See also entry no. 2446.

The major synthesis of Polish history up to 1914, by leading historians of interwar Poland. A somewhat comparable though much shorter history published abroad is *Polska i jej dorobek dziejowy w ciągu tysiąca lat istnienia* (Poland and her historical achievements), edited by Henryk Paszkiewicz (London, Orbis-Polonia, 1956, 582 p., illus., ports., maps).

2627. Rhode, Gotthold. Geschichte Polens: ein Überblick. Darmstadt, Wissenschaftliche Buchgesellschaft, 1966. 543 p.

Written by a leading specialist among German historians. A useful survey.

2628. Żółtowski, Adam. Border of Europe; a Study of the Polish Eastern Provinces. London, Hollis and Carter, 1950. 348 p. Fold. col. map. Bibliography: p. 329-333.

A stimulating treatment of Polish eastern problems. A valuable monograph on an important aspect of the question is Antoine Martel's *La langue polonaise dans les pays ruthènes, Ukraine et Russie blanche, 1569-1667* (Lille, Travaux et mémoires de l'Université de Lille, 1935, 318 p., map, bibliographical footnotes [Droit et lettres, no. 20]).

E. HISTORY TO 1795

2629. Askenazy, Szymon. Danzig and Poland. London, G. Allen and Unwin, 1921. 132 p.

A classic by a great historian, now a little outdated. For a synthetic treatment of Polish Baltic problems *see* Wacław Sobieski's *Der Kampf um die Ostsee von den ältesten Zeiten bis zur Gegenwart* (Toruń, Baltic Institute, 1933, 286 p.).

For an important, though in the opinion of some Polish historians controversial, history of Poland's eastern boundaries in the Middle Ages *see* Gotthold Rhode's *Die Ostgrenze Polens . . . im Mittelalter bis zum Jahr 1401* (Köln, Böhlau Verlag, 1955, 457 p., maps, geneal. tables. Bibliography: p. 383-435).

2630. Berga, Auguste. Un prédicateur de la cour de Pologne sous Sigismond III: Pierre Skarga (1536-1612). Paris, Société française d'imprimeries et de librairies, 1916. 376 p. Bibliography: p. vii-xiv.

See also entry no. 3021.

A serious study of an important political preacher by a French expert.

2631. Etienne Batory, roi de Pologne, prince de Transylvanie. Edited by Jan Dąbrowski. Cracovie, Impr. de l'Univ. des Jagellons, 1935. 591 p. Illus., ports., fold. maps.

Published under the auspices of the Polish Academy of Arts and Sciences and the Hungarian Academy of Sciences. A joint Polish-

Hungarian study of an outstanding Polish 16th century ruler. Chapters written by specialists.

2632. Fabre, Jean. Stanislas-Auguste Poniatowski et l'Europe des lumières. Paris, Institut d'études slaves, 1952. 746 p. Bibliographical references included in "Notes": p. 685-695. (Collection historique de l'Institut d'études slaves, 16)

See also entry no. 3073.

An important study of the last king of Poland in a broad intellectual context of the Enlightenment. The author is a well-known French specialist. Among the other Western-language studies of the king, the most important is probably Otto Forst-Battaglia's *Stanislaw August Poniatowski und der Ausgang des alten Polenstaates* (Berlin, P. Franke, 1927, 393 p., plates, ports.; bibliography: p. 391-394.).

2633. Forst-Battaglia, Otto. Jan Sobieski, König von Polen. Zűrich, Benziger, 1946. 378 p. Ports. Bibliography: p. 379.

Probably the best biography in a Western language. John B. Morton's *John Sobieski: King of Poland* (London, Eyre & Spottiswoode, 1932, 286 p., front., plates, maps) is a more popular though still useful study.

2634. Fox, Paul. The Reformation in Poland: Some Social and Economic Aspects. Baltimore, The Johns Hopkins Press, 1924. 153 p. Bibliography: p. 149-150 (John Hopkins University Studies in Historical and Political Science, ser. 42, no. 4).

See also entry no. 3126.

Practically the only book in English on the Polish Reformation. Is neither very original nor profound, but given the subject may be profitably consulted.

2635. Haiman, Miecislaus. Kosciuszko, Leader and Exile. New York, Polish Institute of Arts and Sciences in America, 1946. 183 p. Plates, ports., facsims. (Polish Institute Series, no. 9)

The author is Polish-American and the book is a sequel to his *Kosciuszko in the American Revolution* (New York, Polish Institute of Arts and Sciences in America, 1943, 198 p., ports., plans, facsims. Bibliography: p. 168-179 [Polish Institute Series, no. 4]).

2636. Halecki, Oskar. Dzieje unii Jagiellońskiej (A history of the Jagiellonian Union). Kraków, Akademia Umiejętności, 1919-1920. 2 v. Bibliographical footnotes.

See also entry no. 3127.

A monumental history of the Polish-Lithuanian union by an authority who considers it the greatest achievement of Polish history. May be used jointly with another important study by Ludwik Kolankowski, *Polska Jagiellonów: dzieje polityczne* (Poland of the Jagiellonians: political history) (Lwów, Gubrynowicz, 1936, 374 p., illus., ports., map. Bibliography: p. 337-348).

The same historical period is recently discussed in a popular but beautifully written essay by Paweł Jasienica, *Polska Jagiellonów*. (Warszawa, Państwowy Instytut Wydawniczy, 1965, 439 p., illus.).

2637. Halecki, Oskar (Oscar). From Florence to Brest (1439-1596). Rome, Sacrum Poloniae Millennium, 1958. 444 p. Bibliographical footnotes.

See also entry no. 3128.

A study, by a great expert, of the religious unions affecting the Polish-Lithuanian Commonwealth. Includes much new material. May be used jointly with Kazimierz Chodynicki's *Kościół Prawosławny a Rzeczpospolita Polska, zarys historyczny 1370-1632* (The Orthodox Church and the Polish Commonwealth 1370-1632) (Warszawa, Kasa Mianowskiego, 1934, 632 p.), a major synthesis.

2638. Hensel, Witold. La naissance de la Pologne. Wrocław, Zakład Narodowy im. Ossolińskich, 1966. 253 p. Illus., maps, plans.

A useful study of the origins of Poland. Translation of *Polska przed tysiącem lat* (Latest, 3d, edition: 1967).

2639. Jobert, Ambroise. La Commission d'éducation nationale en Pologne, 1773-1794. Paris, Droz, 1941. 500 p. Ports., fold. map. Bibliography: p. 1-24. (Collection historique de l'Institut d'études slaves, 9)

See also entry no. 3111.

Pioneering work based on documents no longer in existence. Complemented by the author's short study, *Magnats polonais et physiocrates français 1767-1774* (Paris, Belles Lettres, 1941, 92 p. Bibliography: p. 7-11 [Collection historique de l'Institut d'études slaves, 10]).

2640. Kalinka, Walerian. Der vierjährige polnische Reichstag, 1788 bis 1791. Berlin, E. S. Mittler und Sohn, 1896-1898. 2 v. Bibliography: v. 2, p. ix-xii.

A great classic of the "pessimistic" Kraków school, translated from the Polish. It was answered by the monumental work of the Warsaw school, Tadeusz Korzon's *Wewnętrzne dzieje Polski za Stanisława Augusta, 1764-1794* (Domestic history of Poland under Stanisław August, 1764-1794 (Warszawa, T. Paprocki, 1897-1898, 6 v., illus., ports., fold. maps). An important recent study is Bogusław Leśnodorski's *Dzieło Sejmu Czteroletniego, 1788-1792* (The work of the Four-Year Diet, 1788-1792) (Wrocław, Ossolineum, 1951, 473 p., illus., ports.).

2641. Kaplan, Herbert H. The First Partition of Poland. New York, Columbia University Press, 1962. 215 p. Illus.

The first study in English of a topic which had not been treated in monograph form for nearly a century.

2642. Konopczyński, Władysław. Le Liberum veto: étude sur le développement du principe majoritaire. Paris, Champion, 1930. 297 p.

Diagr. (Institut d'études slaves de l'Université de Paris. Bibliothèque polonaise, II)

A very important comparative study of the unanimity rule in the old Polish Diet and outside Poland by a prominent historian. Translated from the Polish *Liberum veto* (Kraków, Kasa im. Mianowskiego, 1918, 468 p.).

2643. Kostrzewski, Józef. Les origines de la civilisation polonaise; préhistoire- protohistoire. Paris, Presses Universitaires de France, 1949. 671 p. Illus., bibliographical references. (Publications de l'Institut occidental, no. 1)

Translation of *Kultura prapolska* (Poznań, Instytut Zachodni, 1949, 615 p., illus., maps). The author is one of the greatest authorities on the origins of Polish and Slav civilization. His work may be complemented by Kazimierz Tymieniecki's *Ziemie polskie w starożytności; ludy i kultury najdawniejsze* (Polish lands in antiquity; the oldest peoples and cultures) (Poznań, Nakł. Poznańskiego Tow. Przyjaciół Nauk, 1951, 834 p.), viewed as the first synthesis of this kind, and also by Konrad Jażdżewski's *Poland* (New York, Praeger, 1965, 240 p., illus., maps; bibliography: p. 178-190 [Ancient Peoples and Places, 45]), an archaeological study going back to the paleolithic period.

2644. Kutrzeba, Stanisław, *and* Władysław Semkowicz, *eds.* Akta unji Polski z Litwą, 1385-1791 (Acts of union between Poland and Lithuania, 1385-1791). Kraków, Polska Akad. Umiejętności, 1932. 570 p. Bibliography: p. xxxix-xli.

Basic collection of documents, edited by two great Polish constitutional historians.

2645. Lord, Robert H. The Second Partition of Poland: a Study in Diplomatic History. Cambridge, Mass., Harvard University Press, 1915. 586 p. Bibliography: p. 557-572. (Harvard Historical Studies, v. 23)

A classic on a subject which has received no additional monographic treatment.

2646. Lord, Robert H. The Third Partition of Poland. The Slavonic and East European Review (London), v. 3, March 1925: 481-498.

An introductory account of a subject not yet treated in a monograph.

2647. Rose, William J. Stanislaw Konarski, Reformer of Education in Eighteenth Century Poland. London, J. Cape, 1929. 288 p. Bibliography: p. 279-283.

An early work of a great British specialist.

2648. Rutkowski, Jan. Histoire économique de la Pologne avant les partages. Translated by Maria Rakowska. Paris, Champion, 1927. 268 p. (Institut d'études slaves de l'Université de Paris. Bibliothèque polonaise, I)

A basic and pioneering economic history. The latest Polish edition, *Historia gospodarcza Polski* (Poznań, Księgarnia Akademicka, 1947-1950, 2 v. Bibliography: v. 1, p. 363-412; v. 2, p. 453-512), covers the post-partitions period up to 1918. For town history *see* the unique study by Jan Ptaśnik, *Miasta i mieszczaństwo w dawnej Polsce* (Towns and burghers in old Poland) (2d ed., Warszawa, Państwowy Instytut Wydawniczy, 1949, 438 p.). The most recent survey is *Dzieje gospodarcze Polski do 1939 r.* (Economic history of Poland till 1939) by Benedykt Zientara and others (Warszawa, Wiedza Powszechna, 1965, 539 p., illus., facsims., maps, plan; bibliography: p. 524-537).

2649. Smoleński, Władysław. Przewrót umysłowy w Polsce wieku XVIII; studja historyczne (The intellectual upheaval in 18th century Poland; historical studies). 2d enl. ed. Warszawa, Ministerstwo Wyznań Religijnych i Oświecenia Publicznego, 1923. 448 p. Illus., ports.
See also entry no. 3071.

A very important collection of studies on the intellectual revolution produced by the Enlightenment. Other editions: 1891, 382 p.; 1949, 424 p.

2650. Warnke, Charlotte. Die Anfäge des Fernhandels in Polen. Würzburg, Holzner, 1964. 275 p. Maps. (Marburger Ostforschungen, Bd. 22) Bibliography: p. 258-275.

Well-documented and important analysis of Poland's part in early medieval European and Oriental trade.

2651. Wojciechowski, Zygmunt. L'État polonais au moyen âge: histoire des institutions. Paris, Recueil Sirey, 1949. 365 p. Fold. maps. Bibliography: p. 321-351. (Bibliothèque d'histoire du droit, no. 7)

Translation of *Państwo Polskie w wiekach średnich: dzieje ustroju* (The Polish state in the Middle Ages: constitutional history) (2d ed., Poznań, 1948, 405 p.). *See also*:

Gieysztor, Aleksander. La Pologne et l'Europe au Moyen Âge. Warszawa, Państwowe Wydawn. Naukowe, 1963. 14 p. (Académie polonaise des sciences. Centre scientifique à Paris. Conférences, fasc. 44) A lecture given in 1962 at the Sorbonne.

2652. Wojciechowski, Zygmunt. Mieszko I and the Rise of the Polish State. Toruń-Gdynia, The Baltic Institute, 1936. 233 p. Illus., fold. maps, bibliographical references.

An important contribution by a well-known Polish medievalist.

2653. Wotschke, Theodor. Geschichte der Reformation in Polen. Leipzig, R. Haupt, 1911. 316 p.
See also entry no. 3149.

The author is an authority on Polish protestantism and, together with Karl Völker, belongs to the group of German ecclesiastical historians who greatly advanced the study of Polish religious history. The most recent contribution coming from Germany is Gottfried

Schramm's *Der polnische Adel und die Reformation 1548-1607* (Wiesbaden, F. Steiner, 1965, 380 p. Bibliography: p. 330-358).

F. HISTORY 1795-1918

2654. Askenazy, Szymon. Napoléon et la Pologne. Paris, E. Leroux, 1925. 404 p.

Incomplete translation of *Napoleon a Polska* (Napoleon and Poland) (Warszawa, Towarz. Wydawn., 1918-1919, 3 v.), which treats the early years of Napoleon. For a later period see Marceli Handelsman's *Napoléon et la Pologne 1806-1807* (Paris, F. Alcan, 1909, 280 p.).

2655. Askenazy, Szymon. Poland and the Polish Revolution. *In* The Cambridge Modern History. v. 10. Cambridge, The University Press, 1907. p. 445-474.

A treatment of the same subject in Polish is the author's important synthesis, *Rosya-Polska, 1815-1830* (Russia and Poland, 1815-1830) (Lwów, H. Altenberg, 1907, 206 p.).

2656. Askenazy, Szymon. Le prince Joseph Poniatowski, maréchal de France (1763-1813). Paris, Plon-Nourrit, 1921. 334 p.

A classic biography, renowned for its style.

2657. Chodźko, Leonard. Recueil des traités, conventions et actes diplomatiques concernant la Pologne, 1762-1862, par le Comte d'Angeberg. Edited by Jakób Borejko. Paris, Amyot, 1862. 1171 p.

Though undoubtedly dated, this remains a most useful collection of diplomatic papers concerning Poland from the late 18th to late 19th centuries.

2658. Dmowski, Roman. La question polonaise. Paris, Armand Colin, 1909. 336 p. Fold. map.

A very important political book originally published in Polish in 1908. The author, one of the most influential Polish political figures, expounded in it his beliefs on the Polish question vis-à-vis Germany and Russia. The original book, *Niemcy, Rosja i kwestja Polska* (Germany, Russia, and the Polish question) (Lwów, 1908, 271 p.), was reprinted as volume 2 of Dmowski's *Pisma* (Writings) (Częstochowa, A. Gmachowski, 1937-1938, 5 v.).

2659. Feldman, Wilhelm. Geschichte der politischen Ideen in Polen seit dessen Teilungen (1795-1914). München, Berlin, R. Oldenbourg, 1917. 448 p.

See also entry no. 3105.

A shorter version of *Dzieje polskiej myśli politycznej w okresie porozbiorowym* (A history of Polish political thought in the post-partition period) (Kraków, Warsaw, F. Hoesick, 1913-1920, 3 v.). Still indispensable. May be complemented by Marceli Handelsman's

Les idées françaises et la mentalité politique en Pologne au XIXe siècle (Paris, F. Alcan, 1927, 213 p.).

2660. Komarnicki, Titus. Rebirth of the Polish Republic. A Study in the Diplomatic History of Europe, 1914-1920. Melbourne, London, Toronto, William Heinemann, 1957. 776 p.

A basic work on the subject. For a still very useful collection of documents on the Polish question during the First World War *see* Stanislas Filasiewicz's *La question polonaise pendant la guerre mondiale* (Paris, Comité National Polonais, 1920, 520 p. Recueil des actes diplomatiques, traités et documents concernant la Pologne, t. 2).

2661. Kukiel, Marian. Czartoryski and European Unity, 1770-1861. Princeton, Princeton University Press, 1955. 354 p. Illus.

A very valuable work. The fundamental study on the subject in Polish is Marceli Handelsman's *Adam Czartoryski* (Warszawa, Tow. Nauk. Warszawskie, 1948-1950, 3 v., illus., ports., bibliography [Rozprawy historyczne, t. 23-25]).

2662. Leslie, Robert F. Polish Politics and the Revolution of November 1830. London, University of London, Athlone Press, 1956. 307 p. Maps. (University of London Historical Studies, 3)

Contains valuable material but is marred by half-truths and biased interpretations.

2663. Leslie, Robert F. Reform and Insurrection in Russian Poland, 1856-1865. London, University of London, Athlone Press, 1963. 272 p. (University of London Historical Studies, 13)

An important study, although marred by somewhat extreme interpretations. The 1863 insurrection is still a very controversial topic. It received the most detailed treatment in Walery Przyborowski's *Dzieje 1863 roku* (A history of the year 1863) (Kraków, Anczyc, Gebethner i Wolff, 1897-1919, 5 v., bibliographical footnotes), followed and preceded by three other multivolume publications.

2664. Piłsudski, Józef. Joseph Pilsudski: The Memories of a Polish Revolutionary and Soldier. Translated and edited by D. R. Gillie. London, Faber and Faber, 1931. 377 p. Front., plates, ports., fold. maps.

A useful selection of Piłsudski's writings prior to 1923. The collected writings in Polish appeared as *Pisma zbiorowe* (Collected writings) by Józef Piłsudski (Warszawa, Instytut Józefa Piłsudskiego, 1937-1938, 10 v., fronts. [ports., v. 1-9], fold. maps, facsims., diagrs.).

2665. Rose, William J. The Rise of Polish Democracy. London, G. Bell & Sons, 1944. 253 p. Illus., map.

See also entry no. 3103.

A valuable discussion of 19th and 20th century political and social trends and institutions. A similar topic is brilliantly treated by a veteran Polish socialist, Bolesław Limanowski, in his *Historia demo-*

kracji polskiej w epoce porozbiorowej (A history of Polish democracy during the postpartition era) (Warszawa, Kraków, J. Mortkowicz, 1922-1923, 3 v., bibliographical footnotes). The 1946 edition of this work is incomplete.

2666. Skarbek, Fryderyk F. Dzieje Xięstwa Warszawskiego (A history of the Duchy of Warsaw). 2d ed. Poznań, J. K. Żupański, 1876.

An old and detailed monograph, still not superseded.

2667. Sokolnicki, Michał (Michel). Les origines de l'émigration polonaise en France, 1831-1832. Paris, F. Alcan, 1910. 239 p.

A good analysis of the early stages of the Great Emigration. For an almost contemporary Polish treatment, *see* the new edition of Ludomir Gadon's *Wielka emigracja w pierwszych latach po powstaniu listopadowym* (The Great emigration in the first years after the uprising of November 1830) (Paris, Księgarnia Polska, 1960, 576 p., illus., ports., facsims.). The original edition was entitled *Emigracja polska; pierwsze lata po upadku powstania listopadowego* (The Polish emigration; the first years after the failure of the November uprising) (Kraków, Spółka Wydawn. Polska, 1901-1902, 3 v., illus., ports.).

2668. Tims, Richard W. Germanizing Prussian Poland: the H-K-T Society and the Struggle for the Eastern Marches in the German Empire, 1894-1919. New York, Columbia University Press, 1941. 312 p. Front. (port.), illus. (map). Bibliography: p. 289-308.

A useful study of an important topic.

2669. Wereszycki, Henryk. Historia polityczna Polski w dobie popowstaniowej: 1864-1918 (A political history of Poland during the post-Insurrection period: 1864-1918). Warszawa, Instytut Pamięci Narodowej, 1948. 374 p. Bibliography: p. 365-368.

An important monograph which does not employ a Marxist interpretation.

2670. Winiarski, Bohdan. Les institutions politiques en Pologne au XIXe siècle. Paris, Picart, 1924. 271 p.

A very useful survey of political institutions in the various parts of partitioned Poland. The original is entitled *Ustrój polityczny ziem polskich w XIX wieku* (Political institutions in Polish lands in the nineteenth century) (Poznań, Fiszer, Majewski, 1923, 286 p. Bibliography: p. 281-282).

G. HISTORY 1918-1945

2671. Anders, Władysław. An Army in Exile; the Story of the Second Polish Corps. London, Macmillan, 1949. 319 p. Plates, ports., maps.

An important account by a leading Polish general during the Second World War.

2672. Beck. Józef. Final Report: Diplomatic Memoirs of Colonel Józef Beck. New York, R. Speller & Sons, 1957. 278 p. Illus., ports.

An important account, written in exile by the controversial erstwhile Polish Minister of Foreign Affairs. It appeared first as *Dernier rapport: politique polonaise 1926-1939* (Neuchâtel, La Baconnière, 1951, 352 p., port., map, facsims.). Should be complemented by the diary of Beck's Undersecretary of State, *Diariusz i teki Jana Szembeka* (The diary and papers of Jan Szembek), edited by Tytus Komarnicki (London, Polish Research Centre, 1964-1965, 2 v.), and Jozef Lipski's *Diplomat in Berlin, 1933-1939*. edited by Wacław Jędrzejewicz (New York, Columbia University Press, 1968, 679 p.), the papers and memoirs of the Polish Minister in Berlin, including 163 documents.

2673. Cyprian, Tadeusz, *and* Jerzy Sawicki. Nazi Rule in Poland, 1939-1945. Warsaw, Polonia Publishing House, 1961. 261 p. Illus.

2674. Debicki, Roman. Foreign Policy of Poland, 1919-1939. New York, Praeger, 1962. 192 p.

Concise survey, useful mainly as a factual guide. Should be complemented by Bordan B. Budurowycz's *Polish-Soviet Relations. 1932-1939* (New York, Columbia University Press, 1962, 229 p.), Aleksander Bregman's *La Politique de la Pologne dans la Société des Nations* (Paris, F. Alcan, 1932, 329 p. Bibliography: p. 330-333), and the recent studies in diplomatic history in Polish by Jerzy Krasuski, Marian Wojciechowski, Tadeusz Kuźmiński, and Jerzy Kozeński.

2675. Fisher, Harold H. America and the New Poland. New York, Macmillan, 1928. 403 p. Plates, maps, diagrs.

A study particularly useful for Polish-American relations after the First World War.

2676. Kokot, Józef. The Logic of the Oder-Neisse Frontier. Poznań, Wydawn. Zachodnie, 1959. 289 p. Bibliography: p. 269-280.

See also entry no. 2787.

An analysis of Polish western borders from the point of view of international law and economic and demographic implications. The best German analysis of the diplomatic background is Wolfgang Wagner's *Die Entstehung der Oder-Neisse-Linie in den diplomatischen Verhandlungen während des Zweiten Weltkrieges* (2d rev. and enl. ed., Stuttgart, Brentano-Verlag, 1959, 164 p., Die deutschen Ostgebiete, Bd. 2). English translation: *The Genesis of the Oder-Neisse Line* (2d rev. and enl. ed., Stuttgart, Brentano-Verlag, 1964, 192 p., 3 maps, bibliography).

2677. Komorowski, Tadeusz (Bór-). The Secret Army. New York, Macmillan, 1950. 407 p. Ports., maps.

An important account of the activities of the Polish underground army during the Second World War by the commander-in-chief.

2678. Malinowski, Władysław. Najnowsza historia polityczna Polski, 1864-1945 (A contemporary political history of Poland 1864-1945). Paris, London, Imprimerie de la S.N.I.E., and Gryf Printers, 1953-1960. 3 v.

See also entry no. 3117.

A monumental synthesis, still unrivaled. A mine of information, even though uneven in parts and marred by partisan interpretation.

2679. Piłsudski, Józef. L'année 1920. Paris, La Renaissance du Livre, 1929. 335 p. Maps.

A translation of *Rok 1920* (The year 1920), the final edition of which appears as volume seven of *Pisma zbiorowe* (Warszawa, 1937-1938). Written as a polemic of the account of the 1920 campaign by the Soviet commander Mikhail Tukhachevskii (which is included in the volume). Very important, although controversial.

2680. Pologne, 1919-1939. Nêuchatel, La Baconnière, 1946-1947. 3 v. Illus., maps, diagrs.

See also entry no. 2445.

A very informative survey dealing with political, social, economic, and intellectual developments. May be supplemented by *Problèmes politiques de la Pologne contemporaine* (Paris, Gebethner i Wolff, 1931-1933, 4 v., plates, maps; bibliography: v. 2, p. 449-452), and the stimulating study by Andrzej Micewski, *Z geografii politycznej II Rzeczpospolitej* (On the political geography of the Second Polish Republic) (Warszawa, Znak, 1964, 406 p.).

2681. Próchnik, Adam (Henryk Swoboda). Pierwsze piętnastolecie Polski niepodległej, 1918-1933: Zarys dziejów politycznych (The first 15 years of independent Poland, 1918-1933: an outline of political history). Warszawa, Książka i Wiedza, 1957. 493 p. Port.

A stimulating study, by a socialist. There exists an unauthorized German version, *Die ersten fünfzehn Jahre des unabhängiges Polens, 1918-1933: Abriss der politischen Geschichte.* (Vertrauliche Übersetzung der Publikationsstelle des Preuss. Geheim. Staatsarchivs im Berlin-Dahlem, Berlin, 1935, 328 p.). For the early years of the Republic, this book may be profitably compared with Kazimierz (Casimir) Smogorzewski's *La Pologne restaurée* (Paris, Gebethner & Wolff, 1927, 360 p., illus.).

2682. Przybylski, Adam. La Pologne en lutte pour ses frontières, 1918-1920. Paris, Gebethner & Wolff, 1929. 172 p. Illus. (maps), fold. maps.

A brief and useful survey. Translated from the Polish original, *Wojna polska, 1918-1920* (The Polish War, 1918-1920) (2d ed., Warszawa, 1930, 239 p., port., 32 plans).

2683. Roos, Hans. Polen und Europa; Studien zur polnischen Aussenpolitik, 1931-1939. Tübingen, J. C. B. Mohr, 1957. 421 p. Bibliography: p. 401-412.

Surveys Poland's foreign policy during an important period of its recent history.

2684. Roos, Hans. A History of Modern Poland, From the Foundation of the State in the First World War to the Present Day. New York, Knopf, 1966. 303 p. Maps. Bibliography: p. 293-295.

The most up-to-date presentation, by a noted German specialist. Translated from *Geschichte der polnischen Nation, 1916-1960* (Stuttgart, Kohlhammer, 1961, 263 p.). May be compared with a somewhat dated work by Robert Machray, *The Poland of Pilsudski* (London, G. Allen and Unwin, 1936, 508 p., front., ports., fold. map. Bibliography: p. 487-489), which is far more detailed. A series of short volumes published in Poland will eventually cover the interwar period. The two already published are by Henryk Jabłoński and Andrzej Ajnenkiel and cover the period to 1926.

2685. Rosé, Adam Charles. La politique polonaise entre les deux guerres. Nêuchatel, La Baconnière, 1944? 207 p.

A concise and well organized essay, very informative. The author was Poland's undersecretary for industry and commerce.

2686. Rothschild, Joseph. Pilsudski's Coup d'État. New York, Columbia University Press, 1966. 435 p. Maps, bibliographical references.

A valuable analysis of a crucial event in the history of interwar Poland.

2687. Rozek, Edward J. Allied Wartime Diplomacy: A Pattern in Poland. New York, J. Wiley, 1958. 481 p. Maps. Bibliography: p. 465-470.
See also entry no. 235.

An important study of Poland's place in the diplomacy of the Second World War. For a dispassionate and scholarly treatment of one of the most dramatic events of the period, *see* J. K. Zawodny's *Death in the Forest: The Story of the Katyn Forest Massacre* (Notre Dame, University of Notre Dame Press, 1962, 235 p., illus.).

2688. Schmitt, Bernadotte, E., *ed.* Poland. Berkeley, University of California Press, 1945. 500 p. Illus. (maps), tables, front., plates, ports.

A useful general treatment of interwar Poland, with some historical background.

2689. Zweig, Ferdynand. Poland between Two Wars; a Critical Study of Social and Economic Changes. London, Secker and Warburg, 1944. 176 p. Bibliography: p. 163-170.
See also entry no. 2830.

A useful study by a Polish economist.

42

the state

A. POLITICS AND GOVERNMENT

by Adam Bromke

To compile a systematic bibliography on contemporary Polish politics is not easy. The selection and classification of the relevant materials is complicated by the unique character of Poland's traditions as well as the peculiar nature of the postwar developments in that country. In particular, three difficulties should be mentioned.

First, the addiction of the Poles to historicism (even when used only as a means to defeat censorship) obscures the boundary between political and historical works. As a result the section on political programs includes a few books historical in form, but political in substance. The special reasons for their inclusion are explained in the annotations.

Second, the predilection of the Poles for legalism, aggravated in the postwar years by communist formalism, is responsible for the fact that virtually all books on Poland's political system, published at home, are confined to the analysis of political institutions. To balance this, a special section on political dynamics, composed mostly of books published abroad, is added.

Last but not least, the traditional interdependence between the external and internal aspects of Polish politics, manifested in the postwar years by repeated Soviet interference in Poland, makes it difficult to draw a distinction between the books on domestic and foreign affairs. Consequently, the works on Poland's relations with the USSR. are listed together with those on internal politics, while the books included in the section on foreign relations are limited almost exclusively to Poland's relations with the West.

These sections cover works published after 1945. Writings on political and diplomatic history issued prior to this year are treated in the preceding chapter, "History."

1. Political Programs

2690. Bierut, Bolesław. O partii (On the Party). 2d rev. ed. Warszawa, Książka i Wiedza, 1952. 341 p.

A selection of the most important speeches and articles by the First Secretary of the Polish United Workers' Party in the years 1948-1952. The book comes closest to an official exposition of the communist program during the Stalinist years. Additional materials on the same period may be found in *Podstawy ideologiczne PZPR* (The ideological basis of the Polish United Workers' Party), by Bolesław Bierut and Józef Cyrankiewicz (Warszawa, Książka i Wiedza, 1952, 143 p.).

2691. Gomułka, Władysław. Przemówienia (Speeches). 1956– Warszawa, Książka i Wiedza. Annual.

A virtually complete collection of the official speeches of the First Secretary of the Polish United Workers' Party expounding its official program in the years following the changes in 1956.

2692. Gomułka, Władysław. W walce o demokrację ludową; artykuły i przemówienia (In the struggle for the People's Democracy; articles and speeches). Warszawa, Książka i Wiedza, 1947. 2 v.

Articles and speeches by the Secretary General of the Polish Workers' Party expounding its program in the years 1943-1947. A more complete collection of Gomułka's writings from the period 1943-1945 may be found in his *Artykuły i przemówienia* (Articles and speeches) (Warszawa, Książka i Wiedza, 1962, v. 1, 590 p.).

2693. Kołakowski, Leszek. What is Socialism? *In* Stillman, Edmund, *ed.* Bitter Harvest; the Intellectual Revolt Behind the Iron Curtain. New York, Praeger, 1959. p. 47-50. (Praeger Publications in Russian History and World Communism, no. 78)

A biting denunciation of the socialist system in Poland by a young philosopher and a leading exponent of the so-called "revisionist" program in the Polish United Workers' Party. The article was to appear in the confiscated issue of *Po prostu* in the fall of 1957, but it was widely circulated in Poland in manuscript. The volume also contains Kołakowski's critical essay on Marxism-Leninism: "Responsibility and History"; and pieces by other writers denouncing the reality of life in Poland, notably, Adam Ważyk's "Poem for Adults." Additional contemporary writings, literary in form but political in contents, by Kołakowski, Woroszylski, Strzelecki and others are included in *The Broken Mirror; a Collection of Writings from Contemporary Poland*, edited by Paweł Mayewski (New York, Random House, 1958, 209 p.).

2694. Kuroń, Jacek, *and* Modzelewski. List otwarty do Partii (An open letter to the Party). Paryż, Instytut Literacki, 1966. 95 p.

Criticism of the communist leadership, especially for tolerating bureaucracy and suppressing democracy, by two members of the Communist Party cell of the University of Warsaw. The book reflects the dissatisfaction among some segments of the communist youth somewhat in the tradition of *Po prostu.* In 1964 the authors were expelled from the Communist Party and in the following year imprisoned for spreading anti-state propaganda.

2695. Kurowski, Stefan. Apatia — czyli poszukiwanie celu (Apathy — or the search for an aim). *In* Mond, Jerzy, *ed.* 6 lat temu; kulisy polskiego października (Six years ago; behind the scenes of the Polish October). Paryż, Instytut Literacki, 1962.

An article by a well known noncommunist economist in which he strove to formulate the program of the "Polish October." The piece was to appear in the fall 1957 issue of *Po prostu* which was confiscated, but it was widely circulated in Poland in manuscript form.

2696. Mieroszewski, Juliusz. Ewolucjonizm (Evolutionism). Paryż, Instytut Literacki, 1964. 69 p. (Biblioteka "Kultury," t. 106)

A collection of articles by a leading émigré political writer. The author advocates a program of gradual change in the communist political system in the direction of democracy. Mr. Mieroszewski's book has been strongly denounced in the Polish communist press.

2697. Piasecki, Bolesław. Zagadnienia istotne. Artykuły z lat 1945-1954 (The essential problems. Articles from the years 1945-1954). Warszawa Pax, 1954. 207 p.

Articles by the Pax leader expounding the program of the "progressive Catholic" movement in the first eight years of its existence. In 1955 the book was formally condemned by the Holy Office of the Catholic Church. A collection of Piasecki's articles in the years 1955-1959 was published under the title *Patriotyzm polski* (Polish patriotism), 2d ed. (Warszawa, Pax, 1960, 205 p.).

2698. Pruszyński, Ksawery. Margrabia Wielopolski (Margrave Wielopolski). 2d ed. Warszawa, Pax, 1957. 160 p.

A plea for Polish-Russian cooperation in the name of political realism by a prominent noncommunist writer. The book, written in London towards the end of the Second World War, was deliberately disguised as a biography of the leading exponent of political realism in the mid-nineteenth century. The second edition produced a lively political debate in the Pax organ *Kierunki.*

2699. Schaff, Adam. Marksizm a jednostka ludzka (Marxism and an individual). Warszawa, Państwowe Wydawn. Naukowe, 1965. 186 p. (Współczesna biblioteka naukowa Omega, 37)

An attempt at a revision of some aspects of the official communist doctrine by the senior Polish Marxist philosopher and hitherto leading Party ideologist. Inspired by the early writings of Marx, the author emphasized the need to pay more attention to the role of the individual in a socialist society. The book was submitted to open criticism by the leadership of the Polish United Workers' Party.

2700. Schizmy (The schisms). Paryż, Instytut Literacki, 1966. 77 p.

The volume is composed of two parts. The first contains the confidential ideological guide of the Pax group issued in 1966. The second contains the manifesto of the unrepentant Stalinist elements in the ranks of the Polish United Workers' Party. It was issued by Kazimierz Mijał, who in 1956 was one of the leaders of the "Natolin" faction, and who in subsequent years has steadfastly opposed Gomułka. In 1966 Mijał secretly escaped from Poland to Albania, where he now poses as the leader of the pro-Chinese Communist Party of Poland and claims many supporters among the communists at home.

2701. Stomma, Stanisław. Myśli o polityce i kulturze (Thoughts on politics and culture). Kraków, Znak, 1960. 191 p.

A collection of articles from the years 1957-1960 by a prominent leader of the Znak Catholic political group. The book comes closest to the formulation of the Znak program.

2702. Wyszyński, Stefan Cardinal. The Deeds of Faith. New York, Harper and Row, 1966. 187 p. Illus., port.

Excerpts from the sermons and official letters of the Primate of Poland. Many of these deal with the issue of religious freedom in the late 1950s and the early 1960s. Part 1 on "The Rights of Man" is particularly relevant to this section of bibliography.

2703. Załuski, Zbigniew. Siedem polskich grzechów głównych (The Polish seven deadly sins). Warszawa, Czytelnik, 1962. 242 p.

An attempt to overcome the political apathy in the country by reviving the romantic tradition of heroism and sacrifice by a writer closely linked with the "Partisans" faction in the Polish United Workers' Party. Załuski's program, expounded in the form of historical essays, provoked a lively and prolonged debate in the press. The official Party stand on the issues under discussion were presented in a pamphlet: *Spór o ideały wychowawcze socjalizmu* (The dispute over the educational models of socialism) (Warszawa, Książka i Wiedza, 1963, 44 p.).

2704. Periodicals

Dziś i jutro (Today and tomorrow). 1945-1956. Warszawa. Weekly. Organ of Pax. Superseded by *Kierunki.*

Głos ludu (The voice of the people). Daily. Organ of the Polish Workers' Party. Discontinued in 1948.

Kierunki (The directions). v. 1– 1956– Warszawa. Weekly. Organ of Pax. Replaced *Dziś i jutro.*

Kultura (Culture). 1963– Warszawa. Weekly. Replaced *Nowa kultura* and *Przegląd kulturalny*. Committed to the rigid ideological line in the cultural sphere adopted by the Communist Party in 1963.

Nowa kultura (The new culture). 1950-June 1963. Warszawa. Weekly. Played an important role in the intellectual ferment in 1955-1957 and again in 1961-1962.

Nowe drogi (The new roads). 1947– Warszawa. Monthly. Theoretical organ of the Polish United Workers' Party.

Polityka (Politics). 1957– Warszawa. Weekly. A popular journal whose views are close to those of Gomułka.

Po prostu (Speaking frankly). 1947-1957. Warszawa. Weekly. For students and the young intelligentsia. In 1956-1957 openly expounded what was labeled the "revisionist program."

Przegląd kulturalny (The cultural review). 1952-June 1963. Warszawa. Weekly. Like *Nowa kultura*, played an important part in the intellectual ferment in 1955-1957 and 1961-1962. Superseded by *Kultura*.

Trybuna ludu (The people's tribune). Daily organ of the Polish Workers' Party.

Tygodnik demokratyczny (The democratic weekly). 1953– Warszawa. Weekly. Organ of the Democratic Party.

Tygodnik powszechny (Popular weekly). 1945– Kraków. Weekly. An organ of the Catholic group Znak. In the years 1953-1955 temporarily taken over by Pax.

Wieś współczesna (Contemporary village). 1957– Warszawa. Monthly. Theoretical organ of the United Peasant Party.

Zielony sztandar (The green flag). 1949– Warszawa. Weekly. Organ of the United Peasant Party.

Znak (Sign). 1949– Kraków. Monthly. Organ of the Catholic group Znak.

Z pola walki (From the battlefield). 1958– Warszawa. Quarterly. Published by the Party Institute of History; concerned with history of the Polish Workers' movement. Many articles, through the mirror of the past, throw valuable light on the contemporary communist political program.

2. Political Institutions

2705. Balicki, Stanisław W., *and others.* Twenty Years of the Polish People's Republic. Warszawa, Państwowe Wydawn. Ekonomiczne, 1964. 219 p.

The book contains several chapters on the various aspects of the political system as well as political parties in postwar Poland. Parts 3 and 4 are pertinent to this section of bibliography.

2706. Barnett, Clifford R., *and others.* Poland, Its People, Its Society, Its

Culture. New Haven, HRAF Press, 1958. 470 p. Illus. (Survey of World Cultures, 1)

See also entry no. 2442.

The book contains a concise analysis of the legal foundations and governmental structure in postwar Poland. Chapters 6-9 are of special interest to this section of bibliography.

2707. Beneš, Václav. Poland. *In* Beneš, Václav, *and others*. Eastern European Government and Politics. New York, Harper and Row, 1966. p. 23-62.

A concise analysis of the governmental structure in Poland presented against a broad background of political developments. Special emphasis is given to the post-1956 period. For a penetrating analysis of the government structure and process in Poland viewed in a broad context of the developments in Eastern Europe *see* H. Gordon Skilling's *The Governments of Communist Eastern Europe* (New York, Thomas Y. Crowell, 1966, 256 p. Bibliography: p. 235-240).

2708. Bierut, Bolesław. O Konstytucji Polskiej Rzeczypospolitej Ludowej (On the constitution of the Polish People's Republic). Warszawa, Książka i Wiedza, 1952. 88 p. Illus., port.

A speech delivered by the communist leader on July 18, 1952, on the occasion of the adoption by the Polish parliament of the new constitution patterned after that of the USSR.

2709. Burda, Andrzej, *and* Romuald Klimowiecki. Prawo państwowe (The constititutional law). Warszawa, Państwowe Wydawn. Naukowe, 1959. 643 p.

A comprehensive review of the origin and nature of the postwar political system and the detailed analysis of the functioning of the government in Poland by two prominent constitutional lawyers.

2710. Brussels. Université libre. *Centre d'étude des pays de l'Est, Institut de Sociologie Solvay*. Le régime et les institutions de la République Populaire de Pologne. Bruxelles, 1959. 139 p.

A collection of eight papers delivered by Polish, Belgian, and French scholars at a conference held in 1959 in Brussels. Particularly relevant to this section of bibliography are the papers by Maurycy Jaroszyński on political institutions, Stefan Rozmaryn on parliamentary control of the executive, and Jules Wolf on the judicial system.

2711. Gryziewicz, Stanisław, *and others*, *eds*. Ramy życia w Polsce (The framework of life in Poland). Paryż, Instytut Literacki, 1952. 3 v. Bibliographies.

A collection of well-documented papers on various aspects of life in Poland in 1945-1951 by leading émigré specialists. Volume 1 includes papers on political institutions and the administration of justice; volume 2 contains papers on the constitution of 1952, the role of the political parties and the army.

2712. Grzybowski, Kazimierz, *and others.* Studies in Polish Law. Leyden, A. W. Sythoff, 1962. 167 p.
See also entry no. 2756.

The book consists of four scholarly papers on the Polish legal system in the late 1950s. From the political point of view, the parts by B. Hełczyński on administrative procedures and by Zygmunt Nagórski, Sr. on the legislation of 1958-1959 are especially relevant.

2713. Gwiżdż, Andrzej. Le régime politique de la République Populaire de Pologne. Varsovie, Polonia, 1966. 87 p.

A popular but fairly complete exposition of the origin and nature of the political and social system, and the main policies followed by the Polish communist government in the postwar years. The author is director of the Parliamentary Office in Warsaw.

2714. Gwiżdż, Andrzej, *and* Janina Zakrzewska, *comps.* Konstytucja i podstawowe akty ustawodawcze Polskiej Rzeczypospolitej Ludowej (The constitution and the fundamental acts of the Polish People's Republic). 3d rev. ed. Warszawa, Wydawn. Prawnicze, 1958. 438 p. Illus.

A collection of all the main documents pertaining to the political system in Poland enacted in the years 1944-1957.

2715. Halecki, Oskar, *ed.* Poland. New York, Praeger, 1957. 601 p. Bibliography: p. 572-586. (Praeger Publications in Russian History and World Communism, v. 50)

The book contains a special part with a fairly detailed analysis of the constitutional system and political developments in Poland in the years 1945-1956. Special attention is given to the propaganda and security apparatuses.

2716. Jaroszyński, Maurycy, *and others.* Polskie prawo administracyjne (Polish administrative law). Warszawa, Państwowe Wydawn. Naukowe, 1956. 511 p.

A comprehensive review of the organization and functioning of the public administration in Poland by a prominent constitutional lawyer.

2717. Lange, Oskar, *and others.* Węzłowe zagadnienia budownictwa socjalizmu w Polsce (The crucial problems of socialist construction in Poland). Warszawa, Książka i Wiedza, 1960. 608 p.

A collection of general papers on the various political problems in contemporary Poland. Particularly relevant to this section of bibliography are the chapters by Professor Sylwester Zawadzki on the nature of the people's democracy, and by Ludwik Krasucki and Andrzej Kurz on the role of the Polish United Workers' Party.

2718. Rocznik polityczny i gospodarczy (Political and economic yearbook). 1932– Warszawa, Państwowe Wydawn. Ekonomiczne. Annual.
See also entry no. 2447.

Each volume contains exhaustive information on the political system and the political parties, with special emphasis on the developments in the year immediately past.

2719. Rozmaryn, Stefan. Konstytucja jako ustawa zasadnicza Polskiej Rzeczypospolitej Ludowej (The constitution as the fundamental law of the Polish People's Republic). Warszawa, Państwowe Wydawn. Naukowe, 1961. 325 p. Bibliographical footnotes.

A detailed analysis of the Polish constitution by a leading specialist in the field who is Professor of constitutional law at the University of Warsaw and director of the Office of the Council of Ministers. The role of parliament, the People's Councils, and the electoral procedure in the Polish political system are discussed in greater detail in his *La Diète et les Conseils du peuple dans la République Populaire de Pologne* (Varsovie, Polonia, 1958, 186 p.).

2720. Sharp, Samuel L. New Constitutions in the Soviet Sphere. Washington, D.C., Foundation for Foreign Affairs, 1950. 114 p. Bibliographical footnotes.

The book includes a comprehensive analysis of the constitutional developments in Poland in the early stages of communist rule. Chapter 3 is particularly relevant.

2721. Starościak, Jerzy. Decentralizacja administracji (The decentralization of administration). Warszawa, Państwowe Wydawn. Naukowe, 1960. 287 p. Bibliographical footnotes.

Analysis of the reforms in the administrative structure and especially the decentralization of public administration in mid-1950 by a well-known Polish specialist in the field.

2722. Periodicals

Dziennik ustaw (Journal of laws). 1918– Warszawa. Annual. 1950– The official publication containing all the legislative acts and executive decrees.

Państwo i prawo (The state and law). 1946– Warszawa. Monthly. Published by the Institute of Law, Polish Academy of Sciences. Contains articles on contemporary legal as well as political problems. Prawo i życie (Law and life). 1956– Warszawa. Weekly. Organ of the Association of Polish Lawyers. Contains articles on the judicial and political system.

Zycie gospodarcze (Economic life). 1946– Warszawa. Weekly. Frequently has articles pertaining to political and especially administrative problems.

3. Political Dynamics

2723. Blit, Lucjan. The Eastern Pretender: Boleslaw Piasecki, His Life and Times. London, Hutchinson, 1965. 223 p.

A journalistic but well-researched account of the political career of Piasecki and the growth and activities of the Pax movement. Part 3 and the Epilogue bear specially on this section of bibliography.

2724. Bromke, Adam. Poland's Politics: Idealism vs. Realism. Cambridge, Mass., Harvard University Press, 1967. 316 p. Bibliography: p. 293-304. (Russian Research Center Studies, 51)

An attempt at a systematic inquiry into the nature of Poland's politics viewed as a conflict between idealism and realism. The historical background is sketched but most of the volume is devoted to developments in the postwar period. For an examination of the impact of the Polish political experiences upon other communist countries in Eastern Europe by the same author, *see*: "Poland's Role in the Loosening of the Communist Bloc," *Eastern Europe in Transition*, edited by Kurt London (Baltimore, The John Hopkins Press, 1966, 364 p.).

2725. Brzezinski, Zbigniew K. The Soviet Bloc: Unity and Conflict. Cambridge, Mass., Harvard University Press, 1960. 470 p. Bibliography: p. 443-457. (Russian Research Center Study no. 37. Center for International Affairs Study no. 1)

See also entry no. 153.

The book contains two penetrating chapters specifically concerned with developments in Poland: one on the upheaval of 1956, and the other on Gomułka's policies in the late 50s. A revised edition was published in 1961, and another in 1967.

2726. Dallin, Alexander, *ed.* Diversity in International Communism; a Documentary Record, 1961-1963. New York, Columbia University Press, 1963. 867 p.

The book contains the major statements made by the Polish communist leaders in 1961-1963 on the Sino-Soviet dispute and the unity of the international communist movement.

2727. Dziewanowski, M. K. The Communist Party of Poland; an Outline of History. Cambridge, Mass., Harvard University Press, 1959. 369 p. Bibliography: p. 293-314. (Russian Research Center Studies, 32)

See also entry no. 3124.

Parts 3 and 4 of the book contain a systematic and extremely well documented history of the Polish Communist Party from the World War II until the late 1950s. For the author's analysis of the political developments in Poland in the early 1960s *see* the article "Poland" in *The Communist States at the Crossroads Between Moscow and Peking*, edited by Adam Bromke (New York, Praeger, 1965), p. 56-70. [Praeger Publications in Russian History and World Communism, no. 154]).

2728. Flemming, George J. *pseud.* Polska mało znana (Poland little known). Paryż, Instytut Literacki, 1966. 163 p. (Biblioteka "Kultury," 131)

A highly critical, almost satirical, yet extremely informative report on the political climate prevailing in Poland in the early 1960s by an author who left the country in 1965. The topic was subsequently expanded in another similar volume: *Czym to się je? Czyli dobre rady dla emigrantów i turystów* (Who are you? Good advice for emigrants and tourists) (Paryż, Instytut Literacki, 1966, 131 p.).

2729. Gibney, Frank. The Frozen Revolution; Poland: a Study in Communist Decay. New York, Farrar, Straus and Cudahy, 1959. 269 p. Illus.

An impressionistic but informative and essentially objective review of the political developments in Poland in 1956 and in the first few years after Gomułka's return to power, by an American journalist. For a similar picture of the country as seen by a popular British writer, *see* Bernard Newman's *Portrait of Poland* (London, Robert Hale, 1959, 221 p., illus.).

2730. Hiscocks, Richard. Poland, Bridge for the Abyss? An Interpretation of Developments in Post-war Poland. London, Oxford University Press, 1963. 359 p. Fold. map. Bibliography: p. 335-344.

A systematic and fairly well documented analysis of the political developments in Poland in the postwar period, with major emphasis on the years after 1956. The book advances the thesis that due to its special geographical as well as political position, Poland could perform the role of a bridge between the East and the West.

2731. Jedlicki, Witold. Klub Krzywego Koła (The club of the crooked circle). Paryż, Instytut Literacki, 1963. 168 p. (Dokumenty, 12; Biblioteka "Kultury," t. 89)

A first-hand account of the activities and the suppression of the Club of the Crooked Circle in Warsaw, which played a very important role in promoting intellectual ferment in Poland in the mid-1950s and again in the early 1960s. The book also contains an interesting, although controversial, analysis of the struggle in the Polish United Workers' Party. The author, who now lives in the West, was an active member of the club. (The club's name was derived from the street called Krzywe Koło [The Crooked Circle] in Warsaw's old city, where the Club was located. It fitted very well, however, the extremely complex and suspect position of the Club in the communist political system.)

2732. Jelenski, K. A. Poland. *In* Laqueur, Walter, *and* Leopold Labedz, *eds.* Polycentrism, The New Factor in International Communism. New York, Praeger, 1962. p. 59-71. (Praeger Publications in Russian History and World Communism, no. 116)

(Note: The expression "who are you?" has a double meaning in Polish. In the grammatically proper language it means: "What do you eat it with?" It seems, however, that the author's intention was to follow the meaning used in the peasant dialect: "Who are you?" One way or the other it is a deliberate quip at the lack of culture of the present ruling elite in Poland.)

A review of the political situation in Poland in late 1961 and early 1962 by a well informed outside observer. Special attention is given to Gomułka's stand in the Sino-Soviet dispute and the ferment among the Polish intellectuals. For a penetrating analysis of the developments in Poland in the late 1950s and the early 1960s viewed in a broad context of the changes in Eastern Europe *see* James F. Brown's *The New Eastern Europe; the Khrushchev Era and After* (New York, Frederick A. Praeger, 1966, 306 p.; bibliography: p. 297-299. [Praeger Publications in Russian History and World Communism, no. 169]).

2733. Karol, K.S. Visa for Poland. London, MacGibbon and Kee, 1959. 259 p.

A popular treatment of the history of communism in Poland and especially the developments in the mid-1950s, by an author who himself had been linked with the movement until he chose to live in the West in the late 1940s. As such, the book provides a good deal of interesting although at times one-sided information.

2734. Korbonski, Andrzej. Politics of Socialist Agriculture in Poland: 1945-1960. New York, Columbia University Press, 1965. 330 p. Bibliography: p. 317-322. (East Central European Studies of Columbia University)

See also entry no. 2862.

A systematic and extremely well-documented analysis of the communist policies in agriculture, and the response to them on the part of the Polish peasants. The book includes valuable information on the peasants' political movements.

2735. Korowicz, Marek S. W Polsce pod sowieckim jarzmem (In Poland under the Soviet yoke). Londyn, Veritas, 1955. 360 p. (Seria czerwona Biblioteki polskiej, 19)

Personal observations of the developments in Poland by a well-known professor of international law who left the country for the West in 1954. The book is particularly informative on the subject of Communist controls over higher education in the Stalinist period.

2736. Kwiatkowski, Jan K., *pseud.* Komuniści w Polsce; rodowód, taktyka, ludzie (The communists in Poland; origin, tactics, personalities). Bruksela, Polski Instytut Wydawniczy, 1946. 123 p.

An analysis of the origin and program of the Polish Workers' Party and its bonds with Moscow, by a strongly anticommunist émigré writer who covers his identity with a pseudonym. The book presents rich, if one-sided, information, especially on the personal background of some of the communist leaders.

2737. Lane, Arthur Bliss. I Saw Poland Betrayed. Indianapolis, Bobbs-Merrill, 1948. 344 p. Illus., ports., maps.

The memoirs of the American Ambassador in Poland in 1945-1947. The book presents a detailed and well-documented record of the suppression of the opposition and the consolidation of power by the communists with the assistance of the Soviets.

2738. Lewis, Flora. A Case History of Hope; the Story of Poland's Peaceful Revolutions. Garden City, N.Y., Doubleday, 1958. 267 p.

An informative and basically objective report on political developments in Poland from the death of Stalin until Gomułka's return to power, by a well-known American newswoman who visited the country frequently during those years.

2729. Mikołajczyk, Stanisław. The Pattern of Soviet Domination. London, Sampson Low, Marston, 1948. 353 p. Port.

The memoirs of the leader of the Polish Peasant Party covering the periods from 1943 to 1944, when he was premier of the Polish Government-in-Exile in London, and from 1945 to 1947, when he led the official opposition against the establishment of the communist régime in Poland. Valuable additional information on the suppression of the opposition by the communists is included in the memoirs of another Polish Peasant Party leader, Stefan Korboński: *W imieniu Kremla* (In the name of the Kremlin) (Paryż, Instytut Literacki, 1956, 381 p. [Biblioteka "Kultury," t. 13]). For a scholarly analysis of the communists' seizure of power in Poland treated in a broad context of the developments in Eastern Europe *see* Hugh Seton-Watson's *The East European Revolution* (New York, Praeger, 1956, 435 p., illus.).

2740. Miłosz, Czesław. Zniewolony umysł (The captive mind). Paryż, Instytut Literacki, 1953. 236 p. (Biblioteka "Kultury," t. 3)

A first-hand account of the communist cultural policies and especially the methods used in regimenting writers in the late 1940s. Although the study is literary in its form, by the author's own admission, it is also "something of a political treatise." An English translation by Jane Zielonko is available as *The Captive Mind* (New York, Alfred A. Knopf, 1953, 251 p.).

2741. Rocznik spraw krajowych (Annals of homeland affairs). Edited by Stefan Mękarski. Londyn, Instytut Badania Zagadnień Krajowych, 1958/59-1960. 2 v.

A collection of papers on various aspects of life in Poland in the late fifties by émigré specialists cooperating with the Research Institute for the Homeland's Affairs in London. Particularly relevant to this section of bibliography is the paper by Adam Ciołkosz on the Communist Party and the government. For an analysis of the situation in Poland in 1957 by another prominent émigré leader *see* Zbigniew Stypułkowski's *Polska na progu 1958 r.* (Poland at the beginning of 1958) (Londyn, Gryf, 1958, 91 p.).

2742. Shneiderman, Samuel L. The Warsaw Heresy. New York, Horizon Press, 1959. 253 p. Illus.

A picture of Poland in the mid-1950s with some penetrating

glimpses into the complex political situation, as seen by an American newsman of Polish background.

2743. Skilling, H. Gordon. Communism, National and International; Eastern Europe after Stalin. Toronto, University of Toronto Press, 1964. 168 p. Bibliographical footnotes.

In the chapter "The Two Unorthodox Satellites," the author analyzes political developments in Poland since 1956 and compares them with those in Hungary. For the author's more informal view of Poland *see*: "Communism in Eastern Europe; Personal Impressions, 1961-62" in *Canadian Slavonic Papers*, v. 6, edited by A. Bromke (Toronto, University of Toronto Press, 1964), p. 18-37.

2744. Staar, Richard F. Poland, 1944-1962; the Sovietization of a Captive People. New Orleans, Louisiana State University Press, 1962. 300 p. Illus., maps. Bibliography: p. 277-290.

An attempt at a comprehensive political analysis of the developments in Poland in the postwar period. The book, even if fairly well-researched and systematically planned, is marred by the author's apparent desire to prove the thesis defined in its subtitle; this at times adversely affects his objectivity. For a more concise treatment from a similar position *see* Oscar Halecki's article "Poland" in Stephen D. Kertesz's *East Central Europe and the World; Developments in the Post-Stalinist Era* (Notre Dame, Indiana, University of Notre Dame Press, 1962), p. 45-63.

2745. Staliński, Tomasz, *pseud.* Widziane z góry (Seeing from above). Paryż, Instytut Literacki, 1967. 319 p. (Biblioteka "Kultury," 148)

A brilliant satire on the communist ruling elite in the 1960s. Although the plot of the book is fictitious, various political events described in it are closely based on reality.

2746. Stehle, Hansjakob. Nachbar Polen. Frankfurt am Main, S. Fischer, 1963. 416 p. Illus., ports., map. Bibliography: p. 406-408.

An extremely informative and, as a whole, well-balanced presentation of the political situation in Poland by a West German journalist who stayed in the country from 1957 to 1962. For a more systematic analysis of the situation in Poland by the same author *see* "Polish Communism," in *Communism in Europe*, v. 1, edited by William E. Griffith (Cambridge, Mass., The M.I.T. Press, 1964), p. 85-176.

2747. Stypułkowski, Zbigniew. W zawierusze dziejowej; wspomnienia, 1939-1945 (In the storm of history; memoirs, 1939-1945). London, Gryf, 1951. 496 p.

The memoirs of one of the leaders of the non-Communist wartime underground. The part of the book especially relevant to this section of bibliography describes the arrest of the 16 Polish underground leaders and their trial in Moscow by the Soviet military authorities in the spring of 1945. For information on the remnants of the underground even beyond that time *see* the memoirs of another of its leaders, Zygmunt Zarema: *Wojna i konspiracja* (The war and the underground) (Londyn, Veritas, 1957, 347 p. illus.).

2748. Światło, Józef. Za kulisami bezpieki i partii (Behind the scenes of the security apparatus and the party). New York, Free Europe Press, 1955. 39 p.

The most detailed report on the political realities prevailing in Poland at the climax of the Stalinist period. The author, who had been one of the key officials in the communist security apparatus, defected to the West in 1953. The Światło revelations, which were conveyed to Poland through Free Europe broadcasts and leaflets, led to the undermining of the position of the security apparatus which, in turn, paved the way for the intellectual "thaw" of 1955-1956. For information on the political and economic situation in Poland in the same period, and, especially, repeated Soviet interference in Polish affairs, *see* the testimony of Seweryn Bialer, a high-ranking Communist Party member who defected to the West in 1956: *Wybrałem prawdę* (I chose the truth) (New York, Free Europe Press, 1956).

2749. Syrop, Konrad. Spring in October; the Story of the Polish Revolution, 1956. London, Weidenfeld and Nicolson, 1957. 207 p. Illus.

A well organized and researched, though essentially journalistic, account of the upheaval in 1956, by a writer of Polish background who made his home in Britain after the war. An interesting account of the events in Poland in 1956 by an outside observer is also included in Hubert Ripka's *Eastern Europe in the Post-War World* (London, Methuen, 1961, 266 p.).

2750. Ulam, Adam B. Titoism and the Cominform. Cambridge, Mass., Harvard University Press, 1952. 243 p. Bibliographical note: p. 235-236. (Russian Research Center Studies, 5)

See also entry no. 166.

The book contains a penetrating section on "The Crisis in the Polish Communist Party," discussing the expulsion of Gomułka and his followers from the Polish Workers' Party for the "rightist-nationalist deviation" in 1948-1949.

2751. Zinner, Paul E., *ed.* National Communism and Popular Revolt in Eastern Europe. A Selection of Documents on Events in Poland and Hungary, February-November, 1956. New York, Columbia University Press, 1956. 563 p.

The book contains virtually all the most important official statements by the Polish communists and the reaction thereto among foreign communists during the period of crucial changes in Poland in 1956. Brief but penetrating editorial comments are included.

2752. Periodicals

Dziennik polski i dziennik żołnierza (Polish daily and soldier's daily). London. Daily.

Horyzonty (The horizons). 1956– Paryż. Monthly.

Kultura (Culture). 1953– Paryż. Monthly.

Myśl polska (Polish thought). 1941– London. Biweekly.

Nowy świat (The new world). New York. Daily.

Polemiki (Polemics). 1963– London. Quarterly.

Polish Affairs. 1952– London, Council of National Unity. Monthly.

The Polish Review. 1956– New York, Polish Institute of Arts and Sciences in America. Quarterly.

Wiadomości o życiu w Polsce (The news from Poland). 1954– New York, Free Europe Committee. Weekly.

Związkowiec (The alliance member). 1933– Toronto. Semiweekly.

A. LAW

by Alexander Uschakow

1. Texts and Surveys

2753. Burda, Andrzej. Polskie prawo państwowe (Polish constitutional law). 2d ed. Warszawa, Państwowe Wydawn. Naukowe, 1965. 357 p.

This is a textbook on Polish constitutional law for university students. The first edition appeared in 1962. An earlier and more extensive work on the same subject is *Prawo państwowe* (Constitutional law), by Burda and Romuald Klimowiecki (Warszawa, Państwowe Wydawn. Naukowe, 1959. 643 p.).

2754. Comité des Sciences Juridiques de l'Académie polonaise des sciences. Rapports polonais présentés au Sixième Congrès International de Droit Comparé. Varsovie, Polska Akademia Nauk, Komitet Nauk Prawnych, 1962. 234 p.

This volume is a collection of 16 papers on general and Polish legal problems presented by leading Polish legal scholars at the Sixth International Congress on Comparative Law. The papers are in French and English. The 28 papers on the same subject presented at the Seventh International Congress (also in French and English) are presented in *Rapports polonais présentés au Septième Congrès International de Droit Comparé* (Varsovie, Polska Akademie Nauk, Komitet Nauk Prawnych, 1966, 496 p.).

2755. Geilke, Georg. Die polnische Strafgesetzgebung seit 1944. Berlin, der Gruyter, 1955. 143 p. Bibliography: p. 12-18. (Sammlung Ausserdeutscher Strafgesetzbücher in deutscher Übersetzung, 70)

A selection of the most important Polish criminal laws in German translation. The appendix contains a complete table of Polish legislation in the field of criminal law, 1944-1953. Parallels in part Curt Poralla's *Justizgesetze der Volksrepublik Polen im Wortlaut* (Berlin, 1954, Berichte des Osteuropa-Instituts an der Freien Universität

Berlin, 14; Rechtswissenschaftliche Folge, 6), which contains the four most important laws on judicial institutions and court procedures issued since 1950.

2756. Grzybowski, Kazimierz, *and others.* Studies in Polish Law. Leyden, A. W. Sythoff, 1962. 167 p.
See also entry no. 2712.

This collection contains contributions by Kazimierz Grzybowski on "The Draft of the Civil Code for Poland"; by B. Hełczyński, on "The Polish Code of Administrative Procedure"; by Zygmunt Nagórski, Sr., on "Legislation of the Polish People's Republic, 1958-1959"; and by D. Lasok, on "Polish Private International Law". Because of recent Polish legislation, some of the papers are of primarily historical interest.

2757. Gsovski, Vladimir, *and* Kazimierz Grzybowski, *eds.* Government, Law, and Courts in the Soviet Union and Eastern Europe. New York, Praeger, 1959. 2 v. (2067 p.). Bibliography: p. 1945-2009.
See also entry no. 844.

Individual contributions in this collective effort are of varying quality. The first volume contains contributions by Grzybowski and Gwóźdź on Polish constitutional law (p. 320-367) and by Siekanowicz on administrative law (p. 728-787). The second volume has articles by Grzybowski on criminal law (p. 1048-1079) and labor and economic law (p. 1534-1557) and by Siekanowicz on civil law (p. 1307-1344) and agricultural law (p. 1809-1851).

2758. Iserzon, Emanuel, *and* Jerzy Starościak. Prawo administracyjne (Administrative law). 4th ed. Warszawa, Państwowe Wydawn. Naukowe, 1966. 582 p. Bibliography, illus.

This is a textbook of Polish administrative law depicting the current state of scholarship and legislation in the field. The first edition was published in 1963.

2759. Klafkowski, Alfons. Prawo międzynarodowe publiczne (International public law). 2d ed. Warszawa, Państwowe Wydawn. Naukowe, 1966. 372 p.

A college-level textbook (first edition, 1964). Two other recent textbooks are *Prawo międzynarodowe publiczne, Część I* (International public law, Part I), by Cezary Berezowski (Warszawa, Państwowe Wydawn. Naukowe, 1966, 268 p.) and *Zarys prawa międzynarodowego* (Survey of international law), by Ludwik Gelberg (Warszawa, Państwowe Wydawn. Naukowe, 1967, 259 p.).

2760. Korkisch, Friedrich. Staatsaufbau und Gesetzgebung der Volksrepublik Polen. *In* Markert, Werner, *ed.* Polen. Köln, Böhlau Verlag, 1959. p. 327-355 (Osteuropa-Handbuch, Bd. 2)

2761. Kraus, Herbert. Der völkerrechtliche Status der deutschen Ostgebiete innerhalb der Reichsgrenzen nach dem Stande vom 31. Dezember 1937. Göttingen, Otto Schwartz, 1964. 155 p.

This work represents the German point of view on the status of the German-Polish boundary. Polish studies on the same subject are Manfred Lachs' *The Polish-German Frontier* (Warsaw, Polish Scientific Publishers, 1964, 80 p.) and Alfons Klafkowski's *Umowa Poczdamska z dnia 2. VIII. 1945 r.* (The Potsdam Agreement of August 2, 1945) (Warszawa, Instytut Wydawniczy Pax, 1960, 630 p.). The latter is also available in an English translation, *The Potsdam Agreement* (Warsaw, 1963, 340 p.), as well as in a French one *L'accord de Potsdam du 2 août 1945* (Varsovie, 1964, 374 p.).

2762. Nagórski, Zygmunt, *ed.* Legal Problems under Soviet Domination; Studies of the Association of Polish Lawyers in Exile. New York, 1956. 132 p.

2763. Rozmaryn, Stefan. La Pologne. Paris, Librairie Générale de Droit et de Jurisprudence, 1963. 363 p. (Comment ils sont gouvernés). Bibliography: p. 359-363.

A textbook of Polish constitutional law by the well-known Warsaw university professor and member of the Polish Academy of Sciences. He has also published a parallel comprehensive exposition of the Polish constitution entitled *Konstytucja jako ustawa zasadnicza Polskiej Rzeczypospolitej Ludowej* (The Constitution as the basic law of the People's Republic of Poland), 2d ed. (Warszawa, Państwowe Wydawn. Naukowe, 1967, 372 p.).

2764. Rozmaryn, Stefan. The Seym and People's Council in Poland. Warsaw, Polonia Pub. House, 1958. 153 p.

Translated into English from the author's manuscript. The German edition is entitled *Sejm und Volksräte in der Volksrepublik Polen* (Warszawa, 1958, 153 p.). French, Spanish, and Russian translations were also published in the same year.

2765. Rozmaryn, Stefan, *comp.* Introduction à l'étude du droit polonais. Warszawa, Państwowe Wydawn. Naukowe, 1967. 588 p. Bibliography: p. 583-588.

A symposium of 16 papers in which the main aspects of Polish law, the organization of the courts, and the administration of justice are treated by leading Polish specialists under the direction of Professor Rozmaryn. Sponsored by the Comité des sciences juridiques de l'Académie polonaise des sciences.

2766. Wolter, Aleksander. Prawo cywilne: Zarys części ogólnej (Civil law: outlines to general part). 3d ed. Warszawa, Państwowe Wydawn. Naukowe, 1967. 331 p.

First published in 1955, this text in its new edition reflects the status of Polish civil law as it was in force on December 31, 1966, including family, guardianship, and procedural law. For the special parts of the Civil Code, see *Zobowiązania* (Obligations), by Alfred

Ohanowicz and Józef Górski (Warszawa, 1966, 487 p.) and for the law of inheritance, *see* Jan Gwiazdomorski's *Prawo spadkowe w zarysie* (Outline of inheritance law) (Warszawa, 1967, 367 p.).

2. Documentation

2767. Documents on Polish-Soviet Relations, 1939-1945. v. 1. London, General Sikorski Institute. 1961-1968. 2 v.

Contains international agreements and diplomatic notes on Polish-Soviet relations. Its Polish counterpart is *Dokumenty i materiały do historii stosunków polsko-radzieckich* (Documents and materials on the history of Polish-Soviet relations) (v. 1, Warszawa, Polska Akademia Nauk, Książka i Wiedza, 1962–). This collection, which will have ten volumes when completed, begins with Polish-Soviet relations in 1917-1918 and will cover the whole period between 1917 and 1960. To date, six volumes, covering the period up to 1938, have been published.

2768. Gwiżdż, Andrzej, *and* Janina Zakrzewska. Konstytucja i podstawowe akty ustawodawcze Polskiej Rzeczypospolitej Ludowej (The constitution and basic legislation of the People's Republic of Poland). 5th ed. Warszawa, Wydawn. Prawnicze, 1966. 350 p.

Contains the texts of the basic legislative enactments affecting Polish constitutional law, as of February 15, 1966.

2769. Zbiór umów międzynarodowych Polskiej Rzeczypospolitej Ludowej (Collection of international agreements of the People's Republic of Poland). Warszawa, Polski Instytut Spraw Międzynarodowych, 1960–

To date eleven volumes have been published, covering the years 1954-1964. It is intended to be a yearly compilation. Since the Polish government does not publish an official edition of its international treaties, this collection represents the only source for the body of treaties entered into by the People's Republic of Poland. It is of particular value because it also contains agreements that have not been published in the *Dziennik ustaw* (Journal of laws) or in any other official journal.

3. Periodicals

2770. Jahrbuch für Ostrecht. v. 1– 1960– Semiannual.

This publication is issued by the Institut für Ostrecht in Munich and contains articles, analyses, and German translations of legislation and court decisions.

2771. Law in Eastern Europe; a Series of Publications Issued by the Documentation Office for East European Law, University of Leyden. no. 1– 1958– Leyden.

This series, edited by Zsolt Szirmai, contains monographs and English translations of East European legislation.

2772. Osteuropa-Recht. v. 1– 1955– Stuttgart. v. 1-5, semiannual; v. 6–, quarterly.

Issued by the Deutsche Gesellschaft für Osteuropakunde under the editorship of Dietrich A. Loeber (1955-1960), Horst Bahro (1961-1966), and Dietrich Frenzke and Alexander Uschakow (both since 1967), this journal appears in German, but carries contributions in English, Russian, and Polish. It contains articles, bibliographies, and documentation on the law of the East European countries.

2773. Państwo i prawo (State and law). Polska Akademia Nauk, Instytut Nauk Prawnych. 1946– Warszawa. Monthly.

This is the leading Polish law journal. It contains contributions from all fields of law in the form of surveys, reports, court decisions, bibliographies, and book reviews. English, French, and Russian summaries are provided for basic articles.

2774. Wiener Quellenhefte zur Ostkunde, Reihe Recht. 1958-1968. Wien. Looseleaf.

Originally issued by the Arbeitsgemeinschaft Ost, and until 1968 by Österreichisches Ost- und Südesteuropa-Institut in Vienna under the editorship of Helmut Slapnicka. This serial provides German translations and surveys on East European law and also includes book reviews, reports, and bibliographies.

4. Bibliographies

2775. Bibliographie für Staats- und Rechtsfragen. v. 1-8; 1955-1962. Potsdam-Babelsberg. Bimonthly.

Contains an index of publications that appear in Eastern Europe and in East Germany. It was combined in 1963 with the *Referatezeitschrift für die Staats- und Rechtswissenschaft* (v. 1–, 1962–). References to East German translations can be found in the *Bibliographie deutscher Übersetzungen aus den Sprachen der Völker der Sowjetunion und der Länder der Volksdemokratie* (Leipzig, 1952–). Moreover, the Potsdam Academy, through its Institute for International Relations, issues a special bibliography in its journal *Völkerrecht und Internationale Beziehungen* (1965–) and also a *Referatekartei* (1965–).

2776. Polska Akademia Nauk. *Instytut Nauk Prawnych.* Polska bibliografia prawnicza (Polish bibliography of legal publications). Edited by Karol Koranyi. Warszawa, Państwowe Wydawn. Naukowe, 1962-1967. 6 v.

The bibliography covers legal publications issued in Poland during the years 1944-1964. The initiative of this work came from UNESCO, and it was prepared in the Polish language with a French translation. It is paralleled by a special bibliography of civil law prepared by Zbigniew Trybulski entitled *Bibliografia prawa i postępowania cywilnego, 1945-1964* (Bibliography of civil law and procedure, 1945- 1964) (Warszawa, Wydawn. Prawnicze, 1962-1966, 2 v.). Corresponding earlier works are Adolf Suligowski's *Bibliografia prawnicza polska XIX i XX w.* (Polish bibliography of legal publications of the 19th and 20th centuries) (Warszawa, Nakładem i Drukiem Michała Arcta, 1911, 536 p.), and the *Bibliographie juridique polonaise, 1944-1956*, edited by Witold Czachórski (Varsovie, Państwowe Wydawn. Naukowe, 1958, 136 p.).

2777. Siekanowicz, Peter, *and* Vladimir Gsovski, *eds.* Legal Sources and Bibliography of Poland. New York, Praeger, 1964. 311 p. (Praeger Publications in Russian History and World Communism, no. 22)

This selective bibliography lists monographs, handbooks, dictionaries, journal articles, and journals on Polish law in Polish and other languages. It covers the period from before the Partition to 1961.

C. DIPLOMACY AND FOREIGN RELATIONS

by Adam Bromke

2778. Braun, Joachim Freiherr von, *ed.* German Eastern Territories; a Manual and Book of Reference Dealing with the Regions East of the Oder and Neisse. Wuerzburg, Holzner, 1957. 196 p.

A comprehensive statement of German claims to the territories east of the Oder-Neisse. The specialists for the Göttingen Research Committee expound historical, legal and political arguments in favor of the revision of the present German-Polish border.

2779. Bregman, Aleksander. Polska i nowa Europa (Poland and the new Europe). Londyn, Polonia Book Fund, 1963. 86 p.

A stimulating discussion of Western European integration by a leading émigré political writer, who hopes that this process will ultimately overcome the division of Europe and restore Poland's bonds with the West. The author believes that the prospects of such a development will be enhanced if the integration were not restricted to the EEC, but would include the entire Atlantic area. Mr. Bregman's views are further elaborated in a book advocating Polish-German reconciliation: *Jak świat światem. Stosunki polsko-niemieckie wczoraj, dziś i jutro* (As long as the world remains the same. Polish-German relations: yesterday, today and tomorrow) (Londyn, Polska Fundacja Kulturalna, 1964, 274 p., bibliographical footnotes). Both books were strongly denounced by the Polish Communist press and also stirred up a good deal of controversy in the émigré periodicals. (Note: The title of Mr. Bregman's book is an abbreviation of the Polish proverb: "As long as the world remains the same, the Pole and the German will never be brothers." The author is using the phrase as a starting point to argue in favor of the new start in Polish-German relations.)

2780. Campbell, John C. American Policy toward Communist Eastern Europe: The Choices Ahead. Minneapolis, The University of Minnesota Press, 1965. 136 p. Map.

This book, by a leading American specialist on Eastern Europe, devotes a good deal of attention to U.S. policies toward Poland. A special chapter provides a penetrating analysis of Poland's position in the international sphere.

2781. Drachkovitch, Milorad M. United States Aid to Yugoslavia and Poland: Analysis of a Controversy. Washington, D.C., American Enterprise Institute for Public Policy Research, 1963. 124 p. Bibliography.

An argument against U.S. economic aid to Poland by a fervent opponent of such aid.

2782. Drzewieniecki, W. M. The German-Polish Frontier. Chicago, Polish Western Association of America, 1959. 166 p. Illus., bibliographies.

A systematic analysis of the origin and nature of the Polish-German territorial dispute by an American scholar of Polish origin. The author, although he is strongly in favor of upholding Poland's present western border, strives hard to preserve scholarly objectivity.

2783. Feis, Herbert. Between War and Peace; the Potsdam Conference. Princeton, N.J., Princeton University Press, 1960. 367 p. Maps. Bibliography: p. 355-357.

This book, by a prominent American diplomatic historian, contains several sections on the role which the Polish issue played in the Allied councils toward the end of the Second World War. Especially relevant to this section of bibliography are chapters 27-29 dealing with the determination at the Potsdam Conference of Poland's frontiers and the country's political system.

2784. Gruchman, Bohdan, *and others*. Polish Western Territories. Poznań, Instytut Zachodni, 1959. 267 p. Maps, bibliographical footnotes. *See also* entry no. 2507.

A comprehensive statement of Poland's claim to the western territories. Leading Polish specialists from the Western Institute expound historical, demographic, legal, and political arguments in favor of retaining Poland's boundary with Germany along the Oder-Neisse line. For a more recent and similar statement of the Polish case see *Polska zachodnia i północna* (Western and northern Poland), edited by Joanna Kruczyńska (Poznań, Wydawn. Zachodnie, 1961, 542 p., illus.).

2785. Hauptman, Jerzy. Hopes and Fears of German Reunification: a Polish View. *In* Collier, David S., *and* Kurt Glaser, *eds.* Western Policy and Eastern Europe. Chicago, Regnery, 1966. p. 141-154. (Foundation for Foreign Affairs Series, no. 10)

A review of the present state of Polish-German relations by an American scholar of Polish origin. The author advocates Polish-German cooperation, aimed at changing the existing status quo in Central Europe, although he admits that such a program is not at present popular among the Poles, at home or abroad. For a somewhat similar view expounded by a fervently anticommunist émigré writer *see* Józef Mackiewicz's *Zwycięstwo prowokacji* (The victory of provocation) (Monachium, 1962, 222 p.).

2786. Heydenkorn, Benedykt. Poland in 1965: Personal Impressions. *In* Bromke, Adam, *ed.* Canadian Slavonic Papers. v. 8. Toronto, University of Toronto Press, 1966. p. 132-142.

A well known Polish-Canadian journalist reports on the attitudes of the Poles toward Germany and Russia, as he found them during his visit to Poland in 1965. The author's conclusion is that the revival of the Polish-German territorial dispute has contributed to the widespread approval among the Poles of a continuing alliance with the USSR. For an earlier, somewhat similar view *see* Adam Bromke's *A Visit to Poland: Impressions of a Political Scientist* (Cambridge, Mass., Russian Research Center, Harvard University, 1961, 37 p., mimeographed).

2787. Kokot, Józef. The Logic of the Oder-Neisse Frontier. Poznań, Wydawn. Zachodnie, 1957. 289 p. Bibliography: p. 269-280.

See also entry no. 2676.

A systematic exposition of the Polish claims to the western territories essentially argued in terms of international law. For further legal arguments supporting the Polish view *see* Bolesław Wewióra's *Granica polsko-niemiecka w świetle prawa międzynarodowego* (Polish-German frontier from the standpoint of international law) (Poznań, Instytut Zachodni, 1957, 230 p.), and also Alfons Klafkowski's *Umowa Poczdamska z dnia 2. VIII. 1945 r.; podstawy prawne likwidacji skutków wojny polsko-niemieckiej z lat 1939-1945* (The Potsdam Agreement of August 2, 1945; the legal basis for the liquidation of the consequences of the Polish-German War of 1939-1945) (Warszawa, Pax, 1960, 629 p., facsims. Bibliography: p. 15-34).

2788. Kurth, Karl Otto, *ed.* Die deutschen Ostgebiete jenseits von Oder und Neisse im Spiegel der polnischen Presse. Würzburg, Holzner, 1958. 192 p.

A collection in German translation of some 150 excerpts from Polish newspapers, 1956-1957, relating to the situation in the former eastern provinces of Germany. Sponsored by the Göttinger Arbeitskreis. Continued by the same sponsoring institution as *Ostdeutschland 1958-59 in der polnischen Presse* (Würzburg, Holzner, 1959, 303 p.). The selections suffer from the obvious tendency to point out only the failures of the Polish administration.

2789. Maass, Johannes, *ed.* Dokumentation der deutsch-polnischen Beziehungen, 1945-1959. Bonn, Wien, Zürich, Siegler, 1960. 263 p.

A compilation of published official documents and press publications on German-Polish relations 1945-1959, partly of German origin, partly translated into German from English, French, Polish, and Russian.

2790. Małcużyński, Karol. The Gomułka Plan for a Nuclear Armaments Freeze in Central Europe. Warszawa, Zachodnia Agencja Prasowa, 1964. 103 p.

A discussion of the origin and nature of the Gomułka Plan of 1963 viewed in the broad context of European politics by a Polish specialist in international affairs. For a similar review of Rapacki's proposals *see* Andrzej Albrecht's *The Rapacki Plan — New Aspects* (Warszawa, Zachodnia Agencja Prasowa, 1963, 130 p.).

2791. Sharp, Samuel L. Poland, White Eagle on a Red Field. Cambridge, Harvard University Press, 1953. 338 p. Maps, bibliographical footnotes.

A thoroughly realistic evaluation (though occasionally pushing the argument to its extreme) of Poland's position in the international sphere by an American scholar of Polish background. Two chapters on Polish-American relations are particularly thought-provoking. The author's conclusion that, in view of its location, Poland must remain tied to Russia stirred up a good deal of controversy in the Polish émigré press in the mid-1950s.

2792. Wagner, Wolfgang. The Genesis of the Oder-Neisse Line; a Study in the Diplomatic Negotiations During World War II. Stuttgart, Brentano, 1957. 168 p. Maps. Bibliography: p. 156-159.

The final part of the book presents the German interpretation of the provisions of the Potsdam agreement concerning the Polish-German frontier. A second edition, revised and enlarged, was published in 1964. The book is supplemented by another volume, *The Genesis of the Oder-Neisse Line in the Diplomatic Negotiations during World War II: Sources and Documents,* edited by Gotthold Rhode and Wolfgang Wagner (Stuttgart, Brentano, 1959, 287 p., fold. maps).

2793. Wiskemann, Elizabeth. Germany's Eastern Neighbours; Problems Relating to the Oder-Neisse Line and the Czech Frontier Regions. London, New York, Oxford University Press, 1964. 309 p. Maps, tables. Bibliography: p. 297-300.

See also entries no. 132 *and* 903.

A penetrating study of Polish-German conflict by a detached British scholar. The major part of the book is devoted to a well-documented and systematic analysis of the origin and nature of the Polish-German territorial dispute. First published in 1956.

2794. Zdziechowski, Jerzy. Le problème clef de la construction européenne: La Pologne sur l'Oder. Paris, Editions A. Pedone, 1965. 231 p. Maps, bibliographical footnotes.

An eloquent defense on historical and political grounds of Poland's present border with Germany. The author, a well-known prewar economist and politician, played a prominent role among the political exiles until he returned to Poland in the late 1950s.

2795. Periodicals

Cahiers Pologne-Allemagne. 1959-1964. Paris. Quarterly.

The Central European Federalist. 1953– New York. Semiannual. Published by the émigré Czechoslovak, Hungarian, and Polish Committee in New York.

Poland and Germany. 1957– London. Quarterly. Published by the émigré Centre on Polish-German Affairs.

Polish Perspectives. 1958– Warsaw. Monthly.

Polish Western Affairs. 1960– Poznań. Quarterly. Published by the Western Institute.

Sprawy międzynarodowe (International affairs). 1948– Warszawa. Monthly. Published by the Polish Institute of International Affairs.

Świat i Polska (The world and Poland). 1949– Warszawa. Weekly. Merged with *Polityka* in 1958.

D. MILITARY AFFAIRS

by M. Kamil Dziewanowski

1. Books

2796. Bibliografia wojskowa II wojny światowej; materiały za lata 1939-1958. Część polska (Military bibliography of the Second World War; materials for the years 1939-1958. Polish materials). Warszawa, Wojskowy Instytut Historyczny, 1960. 433 p.

Relatively weak in materials concerning Polish military activity outside of Poland, especially in France, but strong on Polish forces in the Soviet Union. For events in Poland, *see*:

Czaplicka, Felicja, *ed.* Bibliografia walki wyzwoleńczej narodu polskiego przeciw hitlerowskiemu okupantowi, 1939-1945; materiały z lat 1945-1960 (A bibliography of the liberation struggle of the Polish nation against the Hitlerite occupation, 1939-1945; materials from the years 1945-1960). Warszawa, Wojskowy Instytut Historyczny, 1961. 102 p. Emphasis on communist participation.

2797. Dziewanowski, Władysław, *and others*, *eds.* Księga jazdy polskiej (A book of the Polish cavalry). Warsawa, Biblioteka Polska, 1938. 430 p. Illus.

A history of the Polish cavalry and horse artillery. Polish artillery from the 14th century to the Partitions is the subject of Konstanty Górski, *Historia artylerii polskiej* (History of the Polish artillery) (Warszawa, Wende, 1902, 280 p., illus.). Kazimierz Lepszy's *Dzieje floty polskiej* (History of the Polish navy) (Gdańsk-Toruń, Instytut Bałtycki, 1947, 350 p., bibliography: p. 333-339), is a useful outline by a specialist.

2798. Komornicki, Stanisław, *ed.* Regularne jednostki ludowego wojska polskiego. Formowanie, działania bojowe, organizacja, uzbrojenie, metryki jednostek piechoty (Regular units of the Polish People's Army. Formation, military activities, organization, armament and genealogies of the infantry units). Warszawa, Wydawn. Ministerstwa Obrony Narodowej, 1965. Illus., maps.

2799. Korzon, Tadeusz. Dzieje wojen i wojskowości w Polsce (A history of wars and military affairs in Poland). Kraków, Akademja Umiejętności, 1912. 3 v. 2d ed. Lwów, Wydawn. Zakładu Narodowego im. Ossolińskich, 1923. 3 v. Illus., maps.

The only comprehensive treatment of Polish military history up to the First World War, presented by a political historian against a broad background. Much bibliographic material is included. A more recent work is:

Sikorski, Janusz, *ed.* Zarys dziejów wojskowości polskiej do roku 1864 (An outline of Polish military history up to 1864). Warszawa, Wydawn. Ministerstwa Obrony Narodowej, 1965-1966. 2 v. Illus., facsims., maps, plans, ports. Bibliography: v. 2, p. 519-564. A symposium by a group of 11 Polish military historians. Volume 1 covers the period up to 1648.

2800. Kozłowski, Eugeniusz. Wojsko Polskie, 1936-1939; próby modernizacji i rozbudowy (The Polish army, 1936-1939; attempts at modernization and expansion). Warszawa, Wydawn. Ministerstwa Obrony Narodowej, 1964. 343 p. Illus., facsims., ports. Bibliography: p. 325-331.

A fairly balanced presentation of a controversial subject.

2801. Kukiel, Marian. Zarys historii wojskowości w Polsce (An outline of Polish military history). 5th ed. Londyn, Orbis, 1949. 242 p. Maps. Bibliographical notes: p. x-xvi.

First published in Warsaw in 1921. A short standard work by a leading military historian. The same author has also written a more detailed study of a single period in his *Dzieje wojska polskiego w dobie napoleońskiej, 1795-1815* (A history of the Polish army during the Napoleonic period, 1795-1815) (Warszawa, E. Wende i spółka, 1918-1920, 3 v., maps).

2802. Kutrzeba, Stanisław, *ed.* Polskie ustawy i artykuły wojskowe od XV do XVIII wieku (Polish military legislation and regulations from the 15th to the 18th centuries). Kraków, Nakł. Polskiej Akademji Umiejętności, 1937. 371 p.

A scholarly analysis by a leading expert.

2803. Piłsudski, Józef. Pisma zbiorowe. Wydanie prac dotychczas drukiem ogłoszonych (Collected works. An edition of hitherto published works). Warszawa, Instytut Józefa Piłsudskiego, 1937-1938. 10 v. Fronts., fold. maps, facsims., diagrs.

Volume 8 includes Piłsudski's work *Rok 1920* (The year 1920). An index is to be found in the tenth volume.

2804. Polskie siły zbrojne w drugiej wojnie światowej (The Polish armed forces in the Second World War). Londyn, Instytut Historyczny im. Gen. Sikorskiego, 1951– Maps, tables, diagrs.

A collective work, still in progress, compiled by the Komisja Historyczna Polskiego Sztabu Głównego (Historic Commission of the Polish General Staff) in London, analyzing Polish military participation in the Second World War. Parts 1-3 of volume 1 are devoted to the campaign of September 1939, and part 5, to the Polish Navy. The Polish Army abroad is the subject of volume 2, and the Home Army of volume 3. On the subject of the Polish People's army, *see*:

Anusiewicz, Marian, *ed.* Organizacja i działania bojowe Ludowego Wojska Polskiego w latach 1943-1945; wybór materiałów źródłowych (Organization and military actions of the Polish People's Army in the years 1943-1945; a selection of source material). Warszawa, Wydawn. Ministerstwa Obrony Narodowej, 1958. 4 v. Illus., bibliography. A heavily documented official study of the origins, development, and early activities of the present-day armed forces of the Polish People's Republic.

2805. Stefańska, Z., *ed.* Żołnierz polski; ubiór, uzbrojenie i oporządzenie od wieku XI do roku 1960 (The Polish soldier; uniforms, weapons and equipment from the 11th century to the year 1960). Warszawa, Wydawn. Ministerstwa Obrony Narodowej, 1960-1966. 5 v. Illus.

A richly illustrated official publication issued to commemorate the millennium of the Polish armed forces. A concise and copiously illustrated history of Polish weapons is Władysław Dziewanowski's *Zarys dziejów uzbrojenia w Polsce* (Outline of the history of weaponry in Poland) (Warszawa, Gł. Księg. Wojsk, 1935, 224 p., illus.).

2806. Wypisy źródłowe do historii polskiej sztuki wojennej (Selected sources for the history of Polish military art). Edited by J. Wimmer. Warszawa, Ministerstwo Obrony Narodowej, Komisja Wojskowo-historyczna, 1953–

An anthology of sources pertaining to Polish military history. Numerous maps and sketches. Bibliographies in each volume.

2. Serials

2807. Bellona; kwartalnik wojskowo-historyczny (Bellona; a military-historical quarterly). 1918– Londyn, Instytut Historyczny im. Gen. Sikorskiego.

Volumes for 1918-1939 issued by Wojskowy Instytut Naukowo-Oświatowy in Warsaw. Publication suspended August 1939-November 1940. Resumed in London. In 1945-1947 a serial of this title was also issued in Poland under the auspices of the Ministry of National Defense.

2808. Broń i barwa (Armor and insignia). 1934-1939. Warszawa. Irregular.

Organ of Stowarzyszenie Przyjaciół Muzeum Wojska. A publication with the same title was issued in London in 1948-1954 by the Sekcja Muzealna Polskiego Towarzystwa Historycznego w Wielkiej Brytanii, and is being continued in Poland.

2809. Przegląd wojsk lądowych (Review of the land forces). 1– 1959– Warszawa. Monthly.

Issued by the Ministry of National Defense as a major military technical review.

2810. Wojsko ludowe (People's army). 1– 1950– Warszawa. Monthly.

A publication of the Political Section of the Polish Army, devoted to military political affairs and indoctrination.

2811. Wojskowy przegląd historyczny (Military-historical review). 1956– Warszawa. Quarterly.

Issued under the auspices of the Ministry of National Defense.

43

the economy

by Alfred Zauberman

A. ECONOMIC HISTORY, GENERAL DATA ON THE ECONOMY, SURVEY STUDIES

2812. Alton, Thad P., *and others.* Polish National Income and Product in 1954-1955, 1956. New York, Columbia University Press, 1965. 252 p. Bibliography: p. 235-242.

This is a recalculation of Polish national income, by statistical methods and conventions generally accepted in the West for the three specific postwar years: all components of national income are revalued at what the authors describe as real factor cost.

For a study by the same author of the Polish economy focusing on developments after the Second World War, through 1953 and economic plans through 1955 (the end of the Polish Six-Year Plan — the basic plan for the restructuring of the economy), see *Polish Postwar Economy* (New York, Columbia University Press, 1955, 330 p., tables; bibliography: p. 307-315).

2813. Dylematy gospodarki polskiej (Dilemmas of the Polish economy). Londyn, Polska Fundacja Kulturalna, 1965. 270 p.

This is a discussion of various aspects of the Polish economy by a group of Polish students living in Britain and the United States.

2814. Fisher, Jack C., *ed.* City and Regional Planning in Poland. Ithaca, N. Y., Cornell University Press, 1966. 491 p. Illus., maps, plans. *See also* entries no. 2490 *and* 2913.

This book deals with matters at the frontier of economic and spatial planning. Contains contributions by planners and administrators.

2815. France. *Institut national de la statistique et des études économiques.* La Pologne — memento économique. Paris, Presses Universitaires de France, 1954. 258 p. Maps, diagrs., tables.

This is a noteworthy description and appraisal of the state of the Polish economy in the early 1950s and of its historical background. There is a wealth of statistical data and estimates. The study was produced under the auspices of the French Ministry of Finance.

2816. Karpiński, Andrzej. Twenty Years of Poland's Economic Development, 1944-64. Warsaw, Polonia Publishing House, 1964. 155 p.

An outline of Polish economic history over the first two postwar decades.

2817. Karpiński, Andrzej. Gospodarka Polski na tle gospodarki świata (The Polish economy in the light of world economy). 3d ed. Warszawa, Książka i Wiedza, 1964. 359 p.

A very useful attempt to present the Polish economy on a comparative basis against the background of the world economy. The first edition appeared in 1957 (149 p.).

2818. König, Kurt. Die Wandlung der inneren Wirtschaftsstruktur in Polen seit 1945. Würzburg, Holzner Verlag, 1963. 212 p. (Marburger Ostforschungen, Bd. 21)

The monograph analyzes the changes in the structure of the Polish economy after the Second World War. Special consideration is given to the degree of economic self-sufficiency.

2819. Mała encyklopedia ekonomiczna (Small economic encyclopedia). Warszawa, Państwowe Wydawn. Ekonomiczne, 1962. 851 p. Diagrs., tables.

A useful economic encyclopedia.

2820. Marczewski, Jan. Planification et croissance économique des démocraties populaires. Paris, Presses Universitaires de France, 1956. 2 v. Bibliography: v. 2, p. 551-560.

See also entry no. 251.

A valuable analysis of problems of planning and growth of seven Central and East European socialist economies with special consideration of the Polish economy. The first volume contains a historical and the second volume an economic analysis. The analytical arguments are supplemented by substantial factual material.

2821. Montias, John M. Central Planning in Poland. New Haven, Yale University Press, 1962. 410 p. Illus. Bibliography: p. 375-392. (Yale Studies in Economics, 13)

A very important study of Polish experience within the frame of the centralist command system. The book describes the development of the economy under the six-year plan and methods of planning and management; separate chapters are devoted to planning of "material balances," with a valuable discussion of basic mathematical instruments of planning, of the programming of investments and long-range plans, and of fiscal and financial policy.

2822. Plan 5-letni na lata 1961-65; dyskusja w Sejmie (The five-year plan for the years 1961-65; the discussion in the Sejm). Warszawa, Książka i Wiedza, 1961. 514 p.

The Polish parliamentary debate on the economic plan for the first half of the 1960s.

2823. Polish National Economic Plan. Warsaw, Central Board of Planning, 1946. 108 p. Tables.

Presentation of the first postwar economic plan. Important source of information on the state of the economy on the threshold of postwar development.

2824. Przegląd bieżącej sytuacji gospodarczej kraju i zadania stojące przed polityką gospodarczą (Review of the current economic situation of the country and of the problems confronting economic policy). Warszawa, Polskie Wydawn. Gospodarcze, 1957. 75 p.

An important analysis of Poland's economic situation at a critical point, in 1957, with an appraisal of tasks confronting the economy and with a number of policy recommendations. The document was produced by the then recently created Economic Council consisting of leading economists of the country.

2825. Rakowski, Mieczyław F., *and others*. Polityka gospodarcza Polski Ludowej (The economic policy of People's Poland). Warszawa, Książki i Wiedza, 1960-1961. 2 v. Illus.

This book, written by a team of well-known economists, deals with principles of economic policy as pursued by the Polish government. Problems discussed are, in particular, the creation and distribution of national income, rational employment and labor productivity, prices and living standards, price policy, and trade.

2826. Wellisz, Stanisław. The Economies of the Soviet Bloc; a Study of Decision Making and Resource Allocation. New York, McGraw-Hill, 1964. 245 p. Bibliographical footnotes.

See also entry no. 267.

The valuable book is conceived by its author as a "primer of Soviet-type economics for the Western reader" and shows in a broad and general way how the system works, largely illustrated by examples from Poland's experience. The cooperation of the Polish Central Planning Commission is acknowledged.

2827. Wyrobisz, Stanisław. Studia i rozważania o rozwoju gospodarczym Polski, 1959-65 (Studies and considerations on the development of the Polish economy, 1959-65). Warszawa, Książka i Wiedza, 1959. 162 p.

Discussion of problems of Polish economy in the post-1956 decade.

2828. Zauberman, Alfred. Industrial Development in Czechoslovakia, East Germany and Poland, 1937-1956. Oxford, Distributed for the Royal Institute of International Affairs by Oxford University Press, 1958. 70 p. Tables.

Recomputation of official post-1937 index series for the three countries with a discussion of theoretical problems. A Polish translation was published in 1960 by the Polish Institute of International Affairs in Warsaw.

2829. Zauberman, Alfred. Industrial Progress in Poland, Czechoslovakia and East Germany, 1937-1962. London, New York, Oxford University Press, 1964. 338 p. Bibliography.

See also entries no. 270, 602, 943, *and* 1520.

A study discussing certain theoretical problems of growth as well as providing descriptive and statistical material.

2830. Zweig, Ferdynand. Poland between Two Wars; a Critical Study of Social and Economic Changes. London, Secker and Warburg, 1944. 176 p. Bibliography: p. 163-170.

See also entry no. 2689.

A very good outline of the interwar economic history of Poland. For an outline of Poland's economic history in this era as viewed in postwar Poland, *see*:

Landau, Zbigniew, *and* Jerzy Tomaszewski. Zarys historii gospodarczej Polski, 1918-1939 (An outline of Polish economic history, 1918-1939). 2d rev. and enl. ed. Warszawa, Książka i Wiedza, 1962. 295 p. illus.

B. ECONOMIC THEORY

2831. Baran, Paul A., *and others*. On Political Economy and Econometrics; Essays in Honour of Oskar Lange. Warsaw, Polish Scientific Publishers, 1964. 661 p. Oxford, New York, Pergamon Press, 1965. 661 p. "Bibliography of Lange's works, 1925-1963": p. 651-661.

Collection of essays by several economists both from the West and East, some of them recognized authorities in the field.

2832. Baran, Paul A., *and others*. Problems of Economic Dynamics and Planning; Essays in Honour of Michał Kalecki. Warsaw, PWN — Polish Scientific Publishers, 1964. 494 p. Port. "Bibliography of Kalecki's works, 1927-1963": p. 481-494.

Collection of essays on various matters of economic dynamics and planning by authors from countries both East and West. Some of the contributions are of considerable significance.

2833. Bauer, R., *and others.* Zarys teorii gospodarki socjalistycznej (An outline of the theory of socialist economy). Warszawa, Państwowe Wydawn. Naukowe, 1965. 490 p.

This is a noteworthy contribution to the theory of socialist economy by a team of seven economists belonging to what can be denoted as the "Wakar school." It has its roots in the post-1956 discussions on the "Polish model." The claim is put forward that it moved away from a priori postulates towards an empirically justified system.

2834. Brus, Włodzimierz. Ogólne problemy funkcjonowania gospodarki socjalistycznej (General problems of the functioning of socialist economy). Warszawa, Państwowe Wydawn. Naukowe, 1964.

One of the best works produced in Poland on the operation of a socialist economy. Discusses in particular the alternative mechanisms which may be employable.

2835. Fedorowicz, Zdzisław. Pieniądz w gospodarce socjalistycznej (Money in a socialist economy). Warszawa, Państwowe Wydawn. Naukowe, 1962. 334 p. Illus.

2836. Feiwel, George R. The Economics of a Socialist Enterprise; a Case Study of the Polish Firm. New York, Praeger, 1965. 398 p. Illus.

A pioneering attempt to explore the economics and the modus operandi of a socialist enterprise within the institutional framework of a centrally planned economy.

2837. Fiszel, Henryk. Efektywność inwestycji i optimum produkcji w gospodarce socjalistycznej (The effectiveness of investment and the optimum of production in a socialist economy). Warszawa, Książka i Wiedza, 1963. 210 p. Diagrs., tables. Bibliography: p. 199-201.

This monograph on the problem of investment efficiency in a socialist system is expanded to deal with the problem of life spans of fixed capital assets and their obsolescence, methods of determination of the rate of interest (in the absence of a capital market), and the link-up of efficiency of investment with that of foreign trade.

2838. Fiszel, Henryk. Szkice z teorii gospodarowania (Essays on the theory of economic policy). Warszawa, Państwowe Wydawn. Ekonomiczne, 1965. 212 p. Illus., Bibliography: p. 205-206.

A collection of *varia* in economics. Includes essays on the criterion of optimality for a socialist system and on economic calculus in investment and foreign trade for a centrally planned economy.

2839. Holtzman, Władysław. Produkcjny majątek trwały przemysłu w rachunku ekonomicznym (Productive durable assets of industry in economic calculations). Warszawa, Państwowe Wydawn. Ekonomiczne, 1963. 192 p. Diagrs., tables. Bibliography: p. 189-191.

This study is an inquiry into the impact of changes in the stock of fixed capital assets on the results of economic calculation. It is richly documented with data taken from the Polish economy.

2840. Kalecki, Michał. Zarys teorii wzrostu gospodarki socjalistycznej (An outline of the theory of socialist economic growth). Warszawa, Państwowe Wydawn. Naukowe, 1963. 118 p. Illus.

One of the most important contributions to the discipline. The central issue discussed is determination of the growth rate with special consideration of the impact on consumption, balancing of foreign trade and technological structure. For further writings by Kalecki, *see*:

Kalecki, Michał. Z zagadnień gospodarczo-społecznych Polski Ludowej (Economic and social affairs of People's Poland). Warszawa, Państwowe Wydawn. Naukowe, 1964. 100 p. An important discussion of certain key problems of economic strategy in Poland.

———. Prace z teorii koniunktury, 1933-1939 (Works in the theory of trade cycles, 1933-1939). Warszawa, Państwowe Wydawn. Naukowe, 1962. 103 p. Illus. Includes the famous paper which, as is generally agreed, anticipated Keynes's theory of multiplier and accelerator.

2841. Kotarbiński, Tadeusz. Traktat o dobrej robocie (A treatise about good work). Warszawa, Państwowe Wydawn. Naukowe, 1955. 210 p.

Although this treatise by the noted philosopher does not formally belong to the corpus of economic writing, it is included here because of its powerful intellectual impact on the leading school in Polish economics (the Lange school). It is devoted to problems of efficient action integrated as a system of "praxiology." A more direct link with economics will be found in the last chapter dealing with the dynamics of progress in technical improvements. An English translation by O. Wojtasiewicz appeared as *Praxiology* (Oxford, Pergamon Press, New York, Macmillan, 1964).

2842. Kurowski, Stefan. Historyczny proces wzrostu gospodarczego (The historical process of economic growth). Warszawa, Państwowe Wydawn. Naukowe, 1963. 432 p. Illus.

An analysis of secular trends of economic development as related to output of iron and steel, with patent implications for the strategy of growth of socialist countries, Poland in particular.

2843. Lange, Oskar. Ekonomia polityczna (Political economy). Warszawa, Państwowe Wydawn. Naukowe, 1959-1966. 2 v.

A system of political economy by one of the leading Polish economists with a great international name. It is written essentially from the Marxian angle but with a conceptual link-up with post-Marxian Western economic thought. The second volume, published posthumously, forms a rather loose collection of essays. An English translation of the first volume by A. H. Walker appeared under the title *Political Economy* (Oxford, Pergamon Press, 1963). Other significant works by Lange include:

Lange, Oskar. Człowiek i technika w produkcji (Man and technology in production). Warszawa, Państwowe Wydawn. Naukowe, 1965. 157 p. Illus. (Współczesna biblioteka naukowa Omega, 29) Bibliography: p. 118-151. A discussion of some principal problems of production specifically of the "man-nature cooperation," of quantification of the processes of production, of renovation of capital assets.

———. Optymalne decyzje; zasady programowania (Optimal decisions; the principles of programming). Warszawa, Państwowe Wydawn. Naukowe, 1964. 311 p. Illus. Bibliography: p. 295-297. Systematized lectures given at the University of Warsaw on the theory of economic decision-making treated as a part of praxiology; almost half of the work deals with decision-making under uncertainty. Restates basic propositions of the theory in the field with some original contributions to it by the author.

———. Teoria reprodukcji i akumulacji (The theory of reproduction and accumulation). Warszawa, Państwowe Wydawn. Naukowe, 1961. 216 p. An important book dealing with mathematical elaboration of the theory of capital formation and growth. Attempts to reconcile Marx's "theory of reproduction" with contemporary trends in the theory of growth. Discusses in particular intesectoral relations ("departments" I and II in the Marxian system) and more generally the input-output system, also proolems of theory of amortization and replacement.

———. Wstęp do cybernetyki ekonomicznej (An introduction to economic cybernetics). Warszawa, Państwowe Wydawn. Naukowe, 1965. 177 p. Illus. Bibliography: p. 167-168. This is one of the few attempts to build a system of economic cybernetics (a rather vague name in the terminology accepted in socialist countries). Discusses general principles of control and regulation, some growth models. the dynamics of control processes, and problems of stability of controlled systems.

———. Wstęp do ekonometrii (An introduction to econometrics). 2d rev. and enl. ed. Warszawa, Państwowe Wydawn. Naukowe, 1961. 415 p. Illus. Deals with some fundamental problems of econometrics, i.e., trade cycle research, forecasting, market research and theory of programming — with a relatively modest mathematical apparatus. First systematic treatise on econometrics after the ban of mathematical argument in economics was lifted in socialist countries. (The author actively contributed to the lifting of this ban.) An English translation appeared under the title *Introduction to Econometrics* (Oxford, New York, Pergamon Press, 1962, 433 p., illus.).

2844. Łaski, Kazimierz. Zarys teorii reprodukcji socjalistycznej (An outline of the theory of socialist reproduction). Warszawa, Książka i Wiedza, 1965. 574 p. Illus. Bibliography: p. 551-555.

This is an outline of the theory of growth under socialism. In substance it is an expansion of the Kalecki model (see entry 2840).

2845. Lisowski, Witold. Zastosowanie relacji majątek-praca-produkcja w programowaniu rozwoju produkcji (The application of the relationship of capital assets-work-production in programming the development of production). Warszawa, Państwowe Wydawn. Ekonomiczne, 1962. 286 p.

A discussion of factor-intensity ratios in the planning of output.

2846. Minc, Bronisław. Zarys teorii kosztów produkcji i cen (An outline of the theory of production costs and prices). Warszawa, Państwowe Wydawn. Naukowe, 1958. 333 p. Illus.

On the whole, representative of the traditionalist Marxian school, and interesting from this angle.

2847. Nove, Alec, *and* Alfred Zauberman, *eds.* Studies on the Theory of Reproduction and Prices. Warsaw, PWN — Polish Scientific Publishers, 1964. 437 p. Illus. Bibliography: p. 415-434. (Problems of Economic Theory and Practice in Poland, 1)

A collection of papers by Polish economists on problems of theory of growth and prices. The volume contains a critical introduction by the editors, written in London.

2848. Pajestka, Józef. Zatrudnienie i inwestycje a wzrost gospodarczy (Employment, investment, and economic growth). Warszawa, Państwowe Wydawn. Naukowe, 1961. 148 p. Illus.

This is a noteworthy analysis of problems of employment and capital formation as related to economic growth. It is supported by statistical data for Poland.

2849. Pohorille, Maksymilian. Wstęp do teorii regulowania cen rolnych w okresie przejściowym do socjalizmu (An introduction to the theory of regulation of agricultural prices in the period of transition to socialism). Warszawa, Państwowe Wydawn. Naukowe, 1960. 583 p. Illus.

2850. Porwit, Krzysztof. Zagadnienia rachunku ekonomicznego w planie centralnym (Problems of economic calculation in central planning). Warszawa, Państwowe Wydawn. Ekonomiczne, 1964. 280 p. Bibliography: p. 265-271.

A valuable work on methods and techniques of planning. Discusses the iterative methods of formulation of a macro-plan and criteria to be adopted. Links up with the problem of pricing.

2851. Rakowski, Mieczysław F., *ed.* Efektywność inwestycji (The effectiveness of investment). Warszawa, Państwowe Wydawn. Naukowe, 1963. 555 p. Illus.

This is a work of a team of economists (who in this field form what can be broadly described as the Kalecki school) on the subject of measurement of investment efficiency on both macro and micro levels. The theoretical part is supplemented by a large collection of applicational examples derived from various branches of the economy.

An English translation by E. Lepa was published as *Efficiency of Investment in a Socialist Economy* (Oxford, New York, Pergamon Press, 1966, 528 p., illus., bibliography: p. 337-339).

2852. Sadowski, Wiesław. Teoria podejmowania decyzji (The theory of decision making). Warszawa, Polskie Wydawn. Gospodarcze, 1960. 314 p.

An exposition of theory and techniques of operational research. Discusses principles of differential calculus, linear programming, probabilistic methods, theory of games, statistical methods, and dynamic programming.

2853. Secomski, Kazimierz. Podstawy planowania perspektywicznego (The principles of long-term planning). Warszawa, Państwowe Wydawn. Ekonomiczne, 1966. 386 p. Map. Bibliography: p. 372-378.

Methodology of plan construction, models, conceptions, and assumptions are discussed with reference to the experience of socialist economies. Some parts of the work are addressed to the nonspecialist.

2854. Strzeszewski, Czesław. Problem czasu w ekonomice (The time factor in economics). Lublin, Towarzystwo Naukowe Katolickiego Uniwersytetu Lubelskiego, 1959. 127 p. (TNKUL. Rozprawy Wydziału Nauk Społecznych, t. 2)

A theoretical discussion of the problem of the time factor in economics and the dynamic approach in macro-economic analysis.

2855. Sulmicki, Paweł. Proporcje gospodarcze (Economic proportions). Warszawa, Państwowe Wydawn. Naukowe, 1962. 204 p. Illus.

A discussion of the problems of balanced growth.

2856. Wakar, Aleksy. Morfologia bodźców ekonomicznych (The morphology of economic incentives). Warszawa, Państwowe Wydawn. Naukowe, 1963. 157 p.

A contribution to the theory of incentives. The problem of incentives is treated as a part of the wider one of the management of the national economy.

2857. Welfe, Władysław. Indeksy produkcji (Production indices). Warszawa, Państwowe Wydawn. Naukowe, 1966. 427 p.

A contribution to the theory of indices. Deals in particular with problems of measuring production in a planned economy. Discusses, among other subjects, questions of concepts, of aggregation, of pricing, and of computation for such an economy.

2858. Zieliński, Janusz G. Rachunek ekonomiczny w socjalizmie (Economic calculation under socialism). Warszawa, Państwowe Wydawn. Naukowe, 1961. 225 p. Diagrs. Bibliography: p. 209-214.

A noteworthy contribution to the analysis of the problem of economic calculation under socialism. It discusses, among other subjects, the methods of calculation, the functions of the market, and the plan.

C. SPECIAL ASPECTS AND BRANCHES OF THE ECONOMY; VARIA

2859. Brus, Włodzimierz, *ed.* Materiały do studiowania ekonomii politycznej socjalizmu; wybór tekstów (Materials for the study of the political economy of socialism; a selection of texts). Warszawa, Książka i Wiedza, 1964. 1180 p. Illus.

This large volume is a collection of papers by many writers apparently treated as basic materials for the study of economics. In fact, they vary in importance and value. They deal with both macro and micro economics and are ordered under headings such as: transition from capitalism to socialism; national income; economic growth; law of value; choice of techniques; market equilibrium; foreign trade; etc.

2860. Drewnowski, Jan, *ed.* Problemy optymalizacji handlu zagranicznego Problems of optimizing foreign trade). Warszawa, Polska Akademia Nauk, 1961. 300 p.

Contains a collection of papers on the subject by several economists and a report from a conference at which the contributions were discussed.

For a mathematical approach to foreign trade efficiency problems *see* the following noteworthy contributions, which are representative of what can be termed the formalized ("Trzeciakowski") approach to the problem.

Głowacki, Jerzy, *and* Bronisław Wojciechowski. Rachunek efektywności handlu zagranicznego na nowym etapie (Efficiency computation of foreign trade in the new stage). Warszawa, 1965, 15 p.

Głowacki, Jerzy. Optymalizacja produkeji i handlu zagranicznego w przedsieborstwie i zjednoczeniu (Optimization of production and foreign trade in enterprise and economic trust). Warszawa, 1968. 148 p. Bibliography.

2861. Dyskusja o cenach rolnych (A discussion of agricultural prices). Warszawa, Książka i Wiedza, 1959. 2 v.

Part 1 gives an analysis of the price system and policies in agriculture; part 2 discusses pricing from the angle of a policy for intensification of agriculture.

2862. Korbonski, Andrzej. Politics of Socialist Agriculture in Poland, 1945-1960. New York, Columbia University Press, 1965. 330 p. Bibliography: p. 317-322 (East Central European Studies of Columbia University)

See also entry no. 2734.

A discussion of the development of Polish agriculture and policies in the first decade and a half after the war. The general political background is analyzed.

2863. Kucharski, Mieczysław. Pieniądz, dochód, proporcje wzrostu (Money, income, structural proportions in growth). Warszawa, Pańtwowe Wydawn. Ekonomiczne 1964. 390 p. Bibliography: p. 382-385.

Analysis of the financial system as related to national income and growth.

Holešovský, Václav, *and* Claus Wittich. Financial and Fiscal Systems of Poland. Washington, D.C., United States Arms Control and Disarmament Agency, 1968. 812 p. Tables. Bibliography: p. 806-812.

2864. Machowski, Heinrich. Staatliche Preispolitik auf dem Steinkohlenmarkt in Polen nach 1945. Berlin, 1967. 238 p. (Osteuropa-Institut an der Freien Universität Berlin. Wirtschaftswissenschaftliche Veröffentlichungen, 28)

The author uses the case of Polish coal mining as a example for an outline of principles of price policy and of the role of prices in centralized economy.

2865. Mrzygłód, Tadeusz. Polityka rozmieszczenia przemysłu w Polsce, 1946-1980 (The policy of industrial location in Poland, 1946-1980). Warszawa, Książka i Wiedza, 1962. 278 p. Maps, diagrs., tables. Bibliography: p. 276-279.

Discussion of problems of location of Polish industry since the last war with an attempt at very long-run planning for the future.

2866. Polaczek, Johannes. Die Entwicklung der oberschlesischen Montanindustrie in den Jahren, 1945-1955. Marburg/L., Johann-Gottfried-Herder-Institut, 1958. 180 p. (Wissenschaftliche Beiträge zur Geschichte und Landeskunde Ostmitteleuropas, no. 35)

An investigation of economic policy, investment, production, and infra structure of the mining industry in Upper Silesia and its branches.

2867. Poralla, Curt. Die nachkriegszeitliche Wasserwirtschaft Polens. Unter Einbeziehung der Wasserbauprojekte in den Randgebieten. Berlin, Duncker und Humblot, 1954. VIII. 132 p. Bibliography: p. 129-132. (Osteuropa-Institut an der Freien Universität Berlin. Wirtschaftswissenschaftliche Verffentlichungen, Bd. 1)

Analytical description of waterways, hydroelectric power, irrigation, water supply, and fresh water fishing. Emphasis is placed on the Vistula basin.

2868. Prochazka, Zora, *and* Jerry W. Combs. The Labor Force of Poland. Washington, D.C., Bureau of the Census, 1964. 46 p. (International Population Statistics Reports, Ser. P-90, no. 20)

D. SERIALS

2869. Ekonomista; kwartalnik poświęcony nauce i potrzebom życia (The economist; a quarterly devoted to theory and practice). 1– 1901– Warszawa.

Issued under the joint auspices of the Polish Academy of Sciences and the Polish Society of Economists. This is the principal Polish theoretical journal in economics, with a long established reputation. Problems in theory, to which most attention is devoted, are in particular those of growth and of planning. The journal also publishes important surveys, book reviews, and bibliographical notes. Short resumés in English.

2870. Prace i materialy Zakładu Badań Ekonomicznych (Papers and materials of the Institute of Economic Research). Warszawa, Zakład Badań Ekonomicznych.

A serial issued under the auspices of the Planning Commission of the Council of Ministers and often dealing with significant problems of theory. In particular, *see* no. 7, edited by Józef Pajestka and others (Warszawa, 1957, 167 p.) for a discussion of matters of foreign trade, and no. 11, edited by Krzysztof Porwit and others (Warszawa, 1958, 226 p.) for papers on the use of input-output techniques in central planning.

2871. Przegląd statystyczny; kwartalnik poświęcony nauce i potrzebom życia (Statistical review; a quarterly devoted to theory and practice). Warszawa, Państwowe Wydawn. Naukowe, 1954–

Published under the auspices of the Statistical Section of the Polish Society of Economists in Warsaw. Major emphasis is given to economic statistics but there is also concern with related problems in other fields and disciplines such as demography.

2872. Życie gospodarcze (Economic life). 1946– Warszawa. Weekly.

This journal is addressed to a wide reading public with interest in economic affairs. It deals essentially with matters of practice but it also popularizes some theoretical issues by means of contributions from academic economists, kept at appropriate levels.

44

the society

by Imre Boba
(except for sections E and F)

A. OVERVIEW

1. Bibliographies and Serials

2873. Nauka o społeczeństwie (socjologia) (The study of society [sociology]). Emigracja (Emigration). Praca i opieka społeczna (Labor and social welfare). Samorząd (Self-government). *In*: Hahn, Wiktor. Bibliografia bibliografij polskich (A bibliography of Polish bibliographies). 3d ed. Wrocław, Warszawa, Kraków, Zakład Narodowy im. Ossolińskich, 1966. p. 161-162, 167-168, 168-169, 191-192.

A guide to bibliographies published up to 1950. More recent bibliographic references are included in Henryk Sawoniak's *Bibliografia bibliografii polskich* (Wrocław, Zakład Narodowy im. Ossolińskich, 1967), in the following sections: "Socjologia" (Sociology) entries 3133-3143; "Polacy za granicą" (Poles abroad) entries 2638-2650; "Praca" (Labor) entries 2688-2709, and 'Opieka społeczna" (Social welfare) entries 2382-2388. *See also*:

Socjologia (Sociology). *In*: Polska Akademia Nauk. *Instytut Historii.* Bibliografia historii Polski (Bibliography of Polish history). v. 1, part 1. Warszawa, Państwowe Wydawn. Naukowe, 1965. p. 345-361. A selective bibliography of bibliographies, journals and serials, works on methodology, social classes, and on social aspects of literature, press, and the arts. For annual bibliographies of works on Polish sociology see the current volumes of *Przegląd sociologiczny* (entry no. 2875).

2874. The Polish Sociological Bulletin. 1961– Warsaw, Ossolineum, The Polish Academy of Sciences Press. Semiannual.

The English language organ of the Polish Sociological Association. Publishes studies by Polish sociologists, reviews books by Western and Polish authors. The first issue (no. 1-2, 1961) describes in length the Polish centers for sociological research, giving details on current research interests, publishing outlets, and names of staff members. Subsequent issues report on changes and provide tables of contents of current issues of Polish sociological journals. The main papers presented to the Third All-Polish Congress of Sociologists are summarized in no. 2 (12), 1965: 71-124. Parts of the proceedings are being published in book form.

2875. Przegląd socjologiczny (Sociological review). 1930– Łódź. Quarterly.

Published by several sociological institutes as the leading journal in the field of sociology. Current volumes include the annual bibliographies of Polish sociological books and articles. Summaries in English. The journal was suspended during the years 1932-1933, 1940-1945, and 1949-1956.

2876. Rudzińska, Regina. Bibljografja pracy społecznej, 1900-1928 (Bibliography of social work, 1900-1928). Warszawa, 1929. 285 p. (Prace Seminarjum Bibliograficznego, nr. 2)

An excellent guide to the study of social problems in Poland before and after the First World War.

2. Monographs and Articles

2877. Chałasiński, Józef. Vergangenheit und Zukunft der polnischen Intelligenz. Marburg/Lahn, Herder-Institut, 1965. 270 p. (Wissenschaftliche Übersetzungen, 41)

German translation of an important sociological analysis of the Polish "inteligencja" by the leading Polish sociologists. Translation based on the 1958 Polish edition: *Przeszłość i przyszłość inteligencji polskiej. See also* the more recent and broader study by the same author, *Kultura i naród* (Culture and the nation) (Warszawa, Ksiażka i Wiedza, 1968, 616 p.).

2878. Ehrlich, Stanisław, *ed.* Social and Political Transformations in Poland. Warszawa, Państwowe Wydawn. Naukowe, 1964. 329 p. Table. (Polish Association of Political Sciences. Publication, 1)

Presents the results of extensive research conducted by Polish scholars on effects of industrialization upon the countryside and urban settlements. A bibliographic chapter by Władysław Markiewicz surveys "Sociological Research in People's Poland." Supplementing this collection is a volume edited by Adam Sarapata, *Przemiany społeczne w Polsce Ludowej* (Social changes in the Polish People's Republic) (Warszawa, Państwowe Wydawn. Naukowe, 1965, 649 p., illus., maps), a collection of studies with footnotes.

2879. Gross, Feliks. Sociology in Poland. East Europe (New York), v. 11, May 1962: 55-57.

———. Some Trends in Polish Sociology. East Europe (New York), v. 12, February 1963: 54-56.

Review articles.

2880. Markiewicz, Władysław. Sociological Problems in the Western Territories. Polish Western Affairs (Poznań), v. 6, 1965, no. 2: 266-289.

The Polish western territories, repopulated since 1945, offer unique opportunities for sociological investigations. The study presents problems of organization of research, topics of research, and achievements. Numerous bibliographic references, and a list of sociological studies published by the Instytut Zachodni (Institute for Western Affairs), Poznań. The same study appeared in French in *La Pologne et les affaires occidentales* (Poznań), v. 1, 1965, no. 1-2: 291-310.

2881. Studies in Polish Political System. Chief editor: Jerzy J. Wiatr. Warsaw, Ossolineum, 1967. 242 p.

An up-to-date broad survey of the sociopolitical structure of contemporary Poland undertaken by leading Polish specialists under the sponsorship of the Institute of Philosophy and Sociology, Polish Academy of Sciences. Among subjects covered are: social change and social structure; economic growth and social structure; changes in the class structure; political parties and interest groups; the hegemonic party system in Poland; control without opposition; and other related topics.

2882. Szczepański, Jan. Les classes sociales de la société polanaise contemporaine. Cahiers internationaux de sociologie, v. 18, 1965, no. 39: 197-216.

Survey article on the social stratification in present-day Poland.

2883. Szczepański, Jan, *ed.* Empirical Sociology in Poland. Warsaw, Polish Scientific Publications, 1966. 150 p.

A compact survey of some empirical studies by Polish sociologists; "Social Stratification and Mobility in Poland," "Changes in the Class Structure," "Changes in Poland's Rural Areas," etc.

2884. Third All-Polish Congress of Sociologists (Warsaw, 2-6 February, 1965). Polish Sociological Bulletin (Warsaw), 1965, no. 2 (12): 71-124.

Summary of main papers, discussions, and a complete listing of supplementary papers. Topics of seminars: 1. Social aspects of industrialization in Poland; 2. Social aspects of urbanization in Poland; 3. Social transformations in rural areas; 4. Mass culture in Poland; 5. Socialist model of the industrial enterprise in Poland; 6. Political institutions in People's Poland. Parts of the proceedings are being published in Polish in book form, including *Socjologiczne problemy industrializacji w Polsce Ludowej* (Sociological problems of industrialization in People's Poland), edited by Jan Szczepański (Warszawa, 1967, 186 p.), and *Procesy urbanizacyjne w powojennej Polsce* (Trends in urbanization in postwar Poland), edited by Stefan Nowakowski (Warszawa, Państwowe Wydawn. Naukowe, 1967, 272 p.).

2885. Zaremba, Zygmunt. Transformation in Contemporary Polish Society. Journal of Central European Affairs (Boulder, Colo.), v. 12, 1952/53: 140-153.

———. Social Transformation in Poland. *Ibid.*: p. 276-289.

A survey of social trends in Poland during the "Stalinist" period of industrialization and collectivization.

B. WOMEN, FAMILY, AND YOUTH

2886. Winiarz, J. Ochrona praw matki, dziecka i rodziny (Protection of the rights of mother, child, and family). Warszawa, Wydawn. Prawnicze, 1954. 57 p. (Biblioteka popularyzacji prawa, nr. 21)

Laws governing family relations; marriage, divorce, paternity, maintenance payments. Comparison of socialist and capitalist legal theory. An extensive English-language treatment has now become available in:

Losok, Dominik. Polish Family Law. Leiden, A. W. Sijthoff, 1968. 304 p.

2887. Centralna Rada Związków Zawodowych w Polsce. The Situation of the Working Woman in People's Poland. Warsaw, Trade Union Publishing House, 1963. 67 p.

An official presentation, available also in French and German. Originally published under the title *Sytuacja kobiety pracującej w Polsce Ludowej.*

2888. Cyprian, Tadeusz. Chuligaństwo wśród młodzieży; problem społeczny i prawny (Juvenile delinquency; a social and legal problem). Poznań, Państwowe Wydawn. Naukowe, 1956. 69 p. (Poznańskie Towarzystwo Przyjaciół Nauk. Wydawnictwa popularnonaukowe Komisji Nauk Społecznych, nr. 1)

A brief but important presentation of a side effect of the social transformations in postwar Poland.

2889. Nagórski, Zygmunt Sr. (The Law of Inheritance in) Poland. *In*: The Law of Inheritance in Eastern Europe and in the People's Republic of China. Leyden, A. W. Sythoff, 1961. p. 183-224. (Law in Eastern Europe, v. 5)

A legal analysis of changes in Polish inheritance law. A bibliography of over 100 titles, unfortunately in English translation only.

2890. Piotrowski, Jerzy. Praca zawodowa kobiety a rodzina (Professional occupation of women and the family). Warszawa, Książka i Wiedza, 1963. 365 p. Diagrs., tables. Bibliography: p. 347-351.

Based on statistical data and interviews conducted by the author. Conditions of the working woman in Poland compared to those in other countries. Includes statistical tables.

2891. Sokołowska, Magdalena, *ed.* Kobiet współczesna (The contemporary woman). Warszawa, Książka i Wiedza, 1966. 378 p.

A collection of studies by sociologists, physicians, economists, psychologists, and educators. Thirteen papers deal with the social position of the working woman. Discussed are problems of occupational preferences, wages, expenditures, etc. Summaries in English and Russian.

C. LABOR RELATIONS AND SOCIAL WELFARE

1. Serials

2892. Centralna Rada Związków Zawodowych. Biuletyn (Bulletin of the Central Council of the Polish Trade Unions). 1954– Warszawa. Irregular.

Informs about current labor laws and regulations. Instructions to local trade union organizations.

2893. Poland. *Ministerstwo Pracy i Opieki Społecznej.* Dziennik Urzędowy (Official gazette). 1946– Warszawa. Irregular.

Official journal of the (Polish) Ministry of Labor and Social Welfare.

2894. Polish Trade Union News. 1958– Warsaw. Bimonthly.

Reports on social, cultural, economic, and political activities of Polish trade unions. Entirely in English.

2895. Praca i zabezpieczenie społeczne (Labor and social security). 1959– Warszawa, Państwowe Wydawn. Ekonomiczne. Monthly.

Articles have English or French summaries. Articles and reports on labor legislation, wages, living standard, prevention of accidents at work, fight against alcoholism, disability and retirement pensions, etc. This monthly supersedes the earlier *Praca i opieka społeczna,* 1929– (with change of title in 1951 to *Przegląd zagadnień socjalnych*) and *Przegląd ubezpieczeń społecznych,* 1926–

2896. Samorząd robotniczy (Workers' self-government). 1957– Warszawa. Monthly.

A journal directed to workers' councils by the trade union and the United Polish Workers' Party of the Warsaw District. Reports on regulations affiecting workers' councils and on achievements of workers' self-government.

2. Labor Laws and Regulations

2897. Krąkowski, Ludwik. Prawo pracy w praktyce przedsiębiorstwa. Według stanu prawnego na dzień 15. Maja 1963 roku (Labor law as applied in an industrial enterprise. Based on the laws in force as of May 15, 1963). Warszawa, Wydawn. Związkowe, 1963. 554 p.

2898. Poland. *Laws, statutes, etc.* Prawo pracy; przepisy, orzecznictwo i wyjaśnienia (The labor code; laws, decisions, and comments). Edited by Józef Zieliński. Warszawa, Wydawn. Prawnicze, 1963. 1411 p.

A commentary on the text of the Labor Code in force on March 15, 1963. Updated editions appear from time to time. An earlier edition by the same author was published in 1959 in two volumes.

2899. Samorząd robotniczy (Workers' self-government). Warszawa, Centralna Rada Związków Zawodowych, 1959. 76 p.

The parliamentary discussion preceding and the text of the law regulating workers' self-government.

2900. Święcicki, Maciej. Instytucje polskiego prawa pracy w latach 1918-1939 (Laws of the Polish labor code between the years 1918 and 1939). Warszawa, Państwowe, Wydawn. Naukowe, 1960. 358 p.

3. Monographs on Labor Relations

2901. Gross, Feliks. The Polish Worker; a Study of a Social Stratum. New York, Roy Publishers, 1945. 274 p. Bibliography: p. 269-274.

An analysis of the social position of the Polish worker at a new turning point in Poland's history. An excellent introduction to the study of changes in Polish society since the war.

2902. Grzybowski, Kazimierz. Workers' Self-Government in Poland—New Style. The Polish Review (New York), v. 4, 1960, no. 4: 57-65.

For an earlier article on this subject, *see*:

Grzybowski, Kazimierz. Workers' Self-Government in Poland a Year After. The Polish Review (New York), v. 3, 1958, no. 1/2: 129-146.

2903. Jarosz, Maria. Samorząd robotniczy w przedsiębiorstwie przemysłowym (Workers' self-government in an industrial plant). Warszawa, Państwowe Wydawn. Ekonomiczne, 1967. 290 p.

2904. Kolaja, Jiri Thomas. A Polish Factory: A Case Study of Workers' Participation in Decisions in Industry. Ann Arbor, University Microfilms, 1960. 308 leaves.

Based on printed sources and interviews with workers of a textile factory in Poland.

2905. Rusiński, Władysław. Położenie robotników polskich w czasie wojny 1939-1945 na terenie Rzeszy i "obszarów wcielonych" (The situation of Polish workers during the war of 1939-1945 in Germany and in "incorporated territories"). Poznań, Instytut Zachodni, 1949. 360 p. (Instytut Zachodni. Badania nad okupacją niemiecką w Polsce, t. 3. Studia nad dziejami gospodarczymi okupacji niemieckiej, zesz. 2)

4. Monographs on Social Welfare

2906. Kąkol, Kazimierz. The Social Security System in Poland. Warsaw, Polonia, 1967. 59 p. Illus., tables.

Survey of Polish laws in force which regulate medical care, sick leave, retirement, social security, and other institutionalized benefits. An earlier survey by the same author appeared in 1959, *Social Rights and Facilities in Poland, According to the Laws in Force on December 31, 1958* (Warsaw, Polonia Pub. House, 1959, 91 p., illus.).

2907. Kasprzak, Marcin, *and* Bogusław Kożusznik. Gesundheitswesen in Polen. Warschau, Polonia, 1963. 147 p.

A popular presentation of Polish medical care for German readers.

2908. Niementowski, Konstanty, *ed.* Zaopatrzenie emerytalne; poradnik szczegółowy. Według stanu prawnego na dzień 1 kwietnia 1966 r. (Retirement benefits; a detailed guidebook. Based on the laws in force as of April 1, 1966). Warszawa, Wydawn. Prawnicze, 1966. 583 p.

D. URBAN AND RURAL CONDITIONS

1. Serials

2909. Miasto (The town). 1950– Warszawa, Polskie Wydawn. Gospodarcze. Monthly.

Journal of the Association of Polish Urbanists. Studies, notes, reviews of books on municipal problems, urban development, housing, city transportation, municipal economy and administration. Supplements (issued separately) include abstracts of Polish and foreign articles and books devoted to housing problems. The supplement appears under the title: *Przegląd dokumentacyjny zagadnień mieszkaniowych* (Documentary survey of housing problems).

2910. Roczniki socjologii wsi; studia i materiały (Annals of rural sociology; studies and materials). 1963– Warszawa, Instytut Socjologii Wsi.

Published by the Institute of Rural Sociology of the Polish Academy of Sciences. Contains studies on economic, cultural, and social changes in traditional village communities. A publication with the same title was issued during 1936-1938.

2911. Wieś współczesna (The contemporary village). 1957– Warszawa, Nakł. Wydawn. Prasa ZSL. Monthly.

A monthly publication of the United Polish Peasant Party directed to party activists in the countryside and community leaders. Reports on cultural and social developments, studies advocating economic changes in agriculture. This monthly supersedes the earlier *Wieś* (Village), a social and literary weekly published between 1944 and 1954.

2. Monographs

2912. Andrzejewski, Adam. Polityka mieszkaniowa; zagadnienia ekonomiczne i socjalne (Housing policy; economic and social problems). Warszawa, Arkady, 1959. 371 p. Tables. Bibliography: p. 359-369.

An introduction to the problems of urbanization and housing in Poland of the postwar period.

2913. Fisher, Jack C., *ed.* City and Regional Planning in Poland. Ithaca, N.Y., Cornell University Press, 1966. 491 p. Illus., maps, plans.
See also entries no. 2490 *and* 2814.

A detailed analysis of urban, regional and national planning prepared by Polish specialists, edited and introduced by Jack C. Fisher. Some of the contributions discuss the sociological implications of urban planning, e.g., the changes in social structure resulting from economic transformation of Poland.

2914. Gałęski, Bogusław. Socjologia wsi; pojęcia podstawowe (Sociology of the village; basic concepts). Warszawa, Państwowe Wydawn. Naukowe, 1966. 118 p. Bibliography: p. 113-118. (Współczesna biblioteka naukowa Omega, 63)

The author analyzes rural life in Poland as a social system. He surveys the social functions of the family, of the homestead, of various occupations, and of the village community.

2915. Nowakowski, Stefan. Narodziny miasta (Birth of a city). Warszawa, Państwowe Wydawn. Naukowe, 1967. 434 p.

A sociological monograph of a town of some 30,000 inhabitants on Poland's western territories. English summary. This thoroughly documented scholarly study is illustrative of the social transformation affecting the Polish society. Further readings on the subject may include:

Ziółkowski, Janusz. Urbanizacja, miasto, osiedle; studia socjologiczne (Urbanization, town, settlement; sociological studies). Warszawa, Państwowe Wydawn. Naukowe, 1965. 279 p. Bibliography: p. 253-271.

2916. Nowakowski, Stefan, *ed.* Socjologiczne problemy miasta polskiego: studia (Sociological problems of the Polish towns; studies). Warszawa, Państwowe Wydawn. Naukowe, 1964. 418 p. Maps. Bibliography: p. 379-405.

Collection of studies on social transformations in Polish society resulting from industrialization and urbanization. Summaries in English and Russian.

2917. Thomas, William I., *and* Florian Znaniecki. The Polish Peasant in Europe and America. 2d rev. ed. New York, Dover Publications, 1958. 2 v.

See also entry no. 2582.

This classic study on Polish peasantry describes the social institutions of the Polish countryside as of the turn of the century and the social transformation in the communities of Polish emigrants in America. The study, which was first published in 1918, had a profound impact upon sociological research in America, Poland, Japan, and China. The (American) Social Science Research Council organized a discussion of the work in 1938 in which the authors participated. The contributions to the discussion were subsequently published by Herbert Blumer; *An Appraisal of Thomas and Znaniecki's "The Polish Peasant in Europe and America"* (New York, Social Science Research Council, 1939, 210 p.; Social Science Research Council, Bulletin 44, 1939).

E. PSYCHOLOGY

by Josef Brozek

2918. Kreutz, Mieczsław. Metody współczesnej psychologii; studium krytyczne (Methods of contemporary psychology; a critical study). Warszawa, Państwowe Zakłady Wydawn. Szkolnych, 1962. 451 p. Illus.

Five chapters are devoted to introspection and ten to objective methods, with special emphasis on mental tests.

2919. Pieter, Józef. Spór a przedmiot psychologii; od ontologicznej do realistycznej koncepcji psychiki (The dispute about the subject of psychology; from an ontological to a realistic conception of the mind). Katowice, 1960. 51 p.

Reprinted from *Chowanny*, no. 1/2, 1960. A chapter from a larger work on the method and aims of psychology; includes detailed summary in English.

2920. Przegląd psychologiczny (Psychological review). v. 1– 1952– Wrocław, Zakład Narodowy im. Ossolińskich. Illus., diagrs., tables. 2 no. a year.

Frequency varies: 1958-1963, annual. Publication suspended 1953-1957. Issued by Polskie Towarzystwo Psychologiczne (Polish Psychological Society). Contains articles, news, and book reviews. Some papers have summaries in Russian and/or English; table of contents is also in English. Recently some papers in French and English have been published.

2921. Psychologia wychowawcza; kwartalnik Związku Nauczycielstwa Polskiego (Educational psychology; quarterly of the Polish Teachers Association). v. 1– July 1958– Warszawa. Illus., tables.

Volumes 1-3 called also volumes 15-17, continuing the numbering of an earlier publication of the same title (v. 1-14; 1926-1949); suspended publication, Sept. 1939-Nov. 1946).

Journal of the Educational Division of the Polish Teachers Association, publishing articles, book and periodical reviews, notes and news, and bibliography. Tables of contents and summaries in Russian and English.

2922. Studia psychologiczne (Psychological studies). v. 1– 1956– Wrocław, Zakład Narodowy im. Ossolińskich. Illus. Annual (irregular).

Issued by Komitet Nauk Pedagogicznych i Psychologicznych (Educational and Psychological Sciences Committee) of the Polish Academy of Sciences to publish research on the themes of activity, speech, and thought, and on personality. Professor Tadeusz Tomaszewski has served as scientific editor since its inception. Summaries in Russian and English.

2923. Szewczuk, Włodzimierz. Psychologia; zarys podręcznikowy (Psychology; outline for a textbook). v. 1. Warszawa, Państwowe Zakłady Wydawn. Szkolnych, 1962. 323 p. Illus. Bibliography: p. 302-308.

The first of two planned volumes, this deals with psychology as a science; its subject, methods, and specialties; the biological basis of the mind, and sensory functions.

2924. Tomaszewski, Tadeusz. Wstęp do psychologii (Introduction to psychology). Warszawa, Państwowe Wydawn. Naukowe, 1963. 294 p. Illus., Bibliography: p. 267-275.

Presents the general characteristics of scientific psychology and the principal systems of psychology, and discusses activity and mechanisms for its regulation as the focal concern of psychology. Concludes with an examination of the applications of psychology. The bibliography includes references to Polish, Western, and Soviet sources.

2925. Żebrowska, Maria, *ed.* Psychologia rozwojowa dzieci i młodzieży (Developmental psychology of children and youth). Warszawa, Państwowe Wydawn. Naukowe, 1965. 515 p. Illus.

A thorough presentation of the subject, introduced by the editor's chapters on the history of developmental psychology and the theories of psychological development. Valuable bibliographies.

F. MASS MEDIA AND PUBLIC OPINION

by M. Kamil Dziewanowski

1. Mass Media

2926. Czasopiśmiennictwo. Wydawnictwa periodyczne (Periodicals. Serials). *In* Hahn, Wiktor. Bibliografia bibliografij polskich do 1950 roku (Bibliography of Polish bibliographies up to 1950). Wrocław, 1966. p. 425-446.

The most complete list available of bibliographies of Polish serials, including also literature on the history of the newspaper and periodical press. Continued in "Prasoznawstwo," in Henryk Sawoniak's *Bibliografia bibliografii polskich, 1951-1960* (Wrocław, 1967), p. 195-196.

See also *Materiały do bibliografii dziennikarstwa i prasy w Polsce w latach 1944-1954; wybor* (A selection of materials for a bibliography of journalism and the press in Poland, 1944-1954), edited by Jan Halpern and others (Warszawa, Państwowe Wydawn. Naukowe, 1957, 788 p.).

2927. Dobroszycki, Lucjan. Centralny katalog polskiej prasy konspiracyjnej, 1939-1945 (Central catalog of the Polish underground press, 1939-1945). Warszawa, Wydawn. Ministerstwa Obrony Narodowej, 1962. 302 p. Facsims.

2928. Introduction. Katalog prasy polskiej, 1960 (Catalog of the Polish press, 1960). Warszawa, 1960. p. iii-xxiii.

This English-language introduction to a catalog of Polish newspapers and periodicals includes data on the organization of the press, statistics, and statements on the function of the press in a people's republic. The catalog also contains a 19-page bibliography on the press during the years 1944-1959, on pages 273-291.

Recent, up-to-date information on the press, radio, and television can be found in the current issues of *Rocznik polityczny i gospodarczy* (Political and economic annual).

2929. Kafel, Mieczysław. Wstęp do prasoznawstwa (An introduction to journalism). Warszawa, Uniwersytet Warszawski, 1959. 143 p.

An introduction to press, radio, and television journalism for students of the Faculty of Journalism, University of Warsaw. The bibliography lists over 300 Polish and foreign sources.

2930. Kel'nik, Vladimir V. Pechat' Pol'shi (The Polish press). Moskva, Izd-vo Moskovskogo universiteta, 1964. 98 p.

A history of the Polish press from the earliest times, with about one-third of the material devoted to the post-World War II period and emphasizing the role of the press in a communist society. Includes a short bibliography of materials in Russian and Polish.

Dobrosław Kobielski's *Trzysta lat prasy polskiej, 1661-1961* (Three hundred years of the Polish press, 1661-1961), published in Warsaw in 1961, includes a 31-page sketch in Polish and a 15-page essay in English on the history of the Polish press. A more comprehensive history of the press up to 1918 is *Zarys historii prasy polskiej* (Warszawa, Państwowe Wydawn. Naukowe, 1956-1959, 2 v.).

2931. Kucharzewski, Jan. Czasopiśmiennictwo polskie wieku XIX w Królestwie, na Litwie i Rusi oraz na emigracji; zarys bibliograficzno-historyczny (Polish periodicals of the 19th century in the Kingdom, Lithuania and Belorussia, and among the émigrés; a bibliographical-historical outline). Warszawa, Gebethner i Wolff, 1911. 121 p.

A classic study which may be supplemented by the following treatments, also limited in scope or chronologically:

Lankau, Jan. Prasa staropolska na tle rozwoju prasy w Europie, 1513-1729 (The old Polish press within the scope of the development of the press in Europe, 1513-1729). Kraków, Państwowe Wydawn. Naukowe, 1960. 264 p. Illus., ports., facsims.

Giełżyński, Witold. Prasa warszawska, 1661-1914 (The Warsaw press, 1661-1914). Warszawa, Państwowe Wydawn. Naukowe, 1962. 525 p.

Młynarski, Zygmunt. Szkice z dziejów rewolucyjnej prasy w Polsce, 1866-1938 (Sketches from the history of the revolutionary press in Poland, 1866-1938). Warszawa, Wydawn. Uniwersytetu Warszawskiego, 1963. 195 p. Bibliography.

Kowalik, Jan. Polskie czasopiśmiennictwo emigracyjne po roku 1939; zarys historyczno-bibliograficzny (Polish émigré periodicals after 1939; a historical-bibliographical outline). London, B. Świderski, 1965. 373-548 p.

2932. Kupis, Tadeusz. Zawód dziennikarza w Polsce Ludowej (The journalist's profession in People's Poland). Warszawa, Książka i Wiedza, 1966. 384 p. Bibliography: p. 325-330.

Based on a poll of over 2,000 persons and the files of 4,000 Polish journalists, this book surveys social, professional, organizational, and political aspects of professional journalists. Summaries in English and Russian.

2933. Kwartalnik prasoznawczy (Journalism quarterly). r. 1-3; 1957-1959. Warszawa, Zakład Badań Prasoznawczych. Quarterly (irregular).

Scholarly journal of the Polish Institute for Press Research, treating problems of the organization and methodology of journalism and the history of the press. Other periodicals dealing with the history and organization of the Polish press and broadcasting are:

Prasa współczesna i dawna (The contemporary and ancient press). r. 1-2; 1958-1959. Kraków. Quarterly.

Zeszyty prasoznawcze (Exercises in journalism). 1960– Kraków. Bimonthly. Successor to *Prasa współczesna i dawna.*

Rocznik historii czasopiśmiennictwa polskiego (Annual of the history of the Polish press). 1962– Wrocław. Annual.

Prasa polska (The Polish press). 1947– Warszawa. Monthly. Organ of the Society of Polish Journalists.

Radio i telewizja (Radio and television). 1945– Warszawa. Weekly. Includes news from radio and television broadcasting as well as the week's programs on Polish stations.

2934. Poland. *Główny Urząd Statystyczny.* Statystyka kultury (Statistics on cultural activities). 1956– Warszawa. Irregular.

Provides information on number, size, patronage, etc. of Polish libraries, theaters, cinemas as well as on the press, radio and TV.

2935. Sokorski, Włodzimierz. Radio i telewizja (Radio and television).

In Kultura Polski Ludowej (The culture of People's Poland). Warszawa, 1966. p. 125-128.

2936. Warsaw. Biblioteka Narodowa. *Instytut Bibliograficzny.* Ruch wydawniczy w liczbach. Polish Publishing in Figures. 1955– Warszawa. Tables. Annual.

See also entries no. 55 *and* 2463.

Annual statistical survey of published works. Compiled by the National Library in Warsaw. Covers newspapers, periodicals, and handbook has appeared so far.

2. Sociopolitical Aspects of Communication

2937. Bureau of Social Science Research, Inc. Mass Communications in Eastern Europe. v. 6: Poland. Washington, D.C., The American University, Special Operations Research Office, 1958. 104 p.

While directed primarily to the study of "communications factors contributing to gaining the attention, understanding, and credibility of the people [of Poland]," this study also contains information on the size and composition of reading and listening audiences, characterizations of leading newspapers and journals, and social factors involved in communication. *See also* the following articles:

Sicinski, A. L'étude des opinions en Pologne. Revue internationale des sciences sociales (Paris), v. 15, no. 1, 1963: 94-112.

Duma, Andrzej. Research on TV Viewers in Poland. A Programme Research Study of "Polskie Radio i Telewizja." Gazette, v. 11, no. 4, 1965: 261-273.

2938. Diffusion and Control of Information. *In* Barnett, Clifford R., *and others.* Poland; Its People, Its Society, Its Culture. New Haven, HRAF Press, 1958. p. 141-161.

Together with the section "Propaganda" in *Poland*, edited by Oskar Halecki (New York, Praeger, 1957, p. 127-148), one of the few studies of censorship, propaganda activities, and control over news media available in English.

See also Wiktor Troscianko, "Polish Journalists and the Censor," *East Europe*, v. 14, November 1965, p. 9-15, describing the methodology of censorship and the manner in which journalists fight back.

2939. Szulczewski, Michał. Prasa i społeczeństwo; o roli i funkcjach prasy w państwie socjalistycznym (The press and society; on the role and functions of the press in a socialist state). Warszawa, Książka i Wiedza, 1964. 301 p.

A communist view of the didactic role of the press. For a popular view of the part played by the press in "agitational" work, *see* A. Radziszewski's *Prasa w pracy agitacyjnej* (The press in propaganda activities) (Warszawa, Wydawn. Ministerstwa Obrony Narodowej, 1954, 31 p.).

45

Intellectual and Cultural Life

A. LANGUAGE

by Edward Stankiewicz

1. Bibliography and General Studies

2940. Schenker, Alexander M. Beginning Polish. New Haven, Yale University Press, 1966-1967. 2 v.

This is the best English textbook of modern Polish. It contains many tables and excellent exercises. Only the first volume of this handbook has appeared so far.

2941. Stankiewicz, Edward, *and* Dean S. Worth. A Selected Bibliography of Slavic Linguistics. The Hague, Mouton, 1966-1969. 2 v. (Slavistic Printings and Reprintings, 49)

See also entry no. 372.

The first volume deals with general Slavic linguistics and with the South Slavic languages. The second contains an analytical bibliography of writings on the Polish language, emphasizing contemporary linguistic research. *See also* the pertinent sections in the third edition of Wiktor Hahn's *Bibliografiia bibliografij polskich* (*entries* 4202a- 4208b, 4273-4295a) and its continuation with the same title by Henryk Sawoniak (entries 1617-1647). Both works are described in entry no. 2416 of the present Guide.

2942. Szober, Sanisław. Gramatyka języka polskiego (Grammar of the Polish language). 5th ed. Warszawa, Państwowe Wydawn. Naukowe, 1959. 389 p. Illus.

Though written in the 20s, this is still the best descriptive grammar of Polish. It suffers from many historical digressions, and lacks a clear analysis of the grammatical categories.

Another useful, though less complete treatment (without the syntax) along similar lines is Witold Doroszewski's *Podstawy gramatyki polskiej* (The bases of Polish grammar), v. 1 (Warszawa, Państwowe Wydawn. Naukowe, 1952, 320 p., illus., bibliography).

2. Serials

2943. The principal serials in the field of Polish linguistics include:

Język polski (The Polish language). 1916– Kraków, Towarzystwo Miłośników Języka Polskiego. Bimonthly.

Polskie Towarzystwo Językoznawcze. Biuletyn. Bulletin. Wrocław, Zakład Narodowy im. Ossolińskich, 1927– Irregular.

Rocznik slawistyczny. Revue slavistique. t. 1– 1908– Kraków, Nakł Studium Słowiańskiego Uniwersytetu Jagiellońskiego, 1908– Semiannual. (Suspended 1923-1930, 1940-1947).

Studia z filologii polskiej i słowiańskiej (Studies in Polish and Slavic philology). 1– Warszawa, Państwowe Wydawn. Naukowe, 1955– Irregular.

Slavia occidentalis. 1– 1921– Poznań, Państwowe Wydawn. Naukowe. Irregular. Sponsored by the Instytut Zachodnio-Słowiański of Poznań University.

3. History of the Language

2944. Brückner, Alexander. Dzieje języka polskiego (History of the Polish language). 4th ed. Wrocław, Zakład Narodowy im. Ossolińskich, 1960. 204 p.

This short outline of the cultural history of Polish, first published in 1906, is extremely useful for the study of loanwords and the formation of the literary language. A modern work along the same lines is:

Klemensiewicz, Zenon. Historia języka polskiego (History of the Polish language). Warszawa, Państwowe Wydawnictwo Naukowe, 1961-1965. 2 v. This work must be used with caution. It contains a very valuable bibliography.

2945. Grappin, Henri. Histoire de la flexion du nom en polonais. Wrocław, Zakład im. Ossolińskich, 1956. 312 p. Bibliography: p. 291-298. (Polska Akademia Nauk. Komitet Językoznawczy. Prace językoznawcze, 7)

This book is the only extensive study of a general problem in Polish historical morphology. Valuable factually, but antiquated methodologically.

2946. Klemensiewicz, Zenon. Gramatyka historyczna języka polskiego (Historical grammar of the Polish language). Warszawa, Państwowe Wydawn. Naukowe, 1955. 596 p. Bibliography: p. 511-512.

This book, written with the cooperation of T. Lehr-Spławiński and S. Urbańczyk, represents a thorough and ambitious effort devoted to the history of the Polish language. Methodologically it is no longer adequate.

In wealth of information and documentation the book is surpassed by Jan Łoś' monumental work, *Gramatyka polska* (Polish grammar) (Lwów, Inst. Ossolinskich, 1922-1927, 3 v.). The three volumes deal with phonetics, derivation, and flexion. The method is piecemeal and antiquated.

An entirely different approach to the history of the Polish language is followed in the lucid and inspiring booklet by J. N. Baudouin de Courtenay, *Zarys historii języka polskiego* (Sketch of the history of the Polish language) (Warszawa, Składnica Pomocy Szkolnych, 1964, 164 p., Biblioteka Składnicy, 10).

2947. Lehr-Spławiński, Tadeusz. Język polski; pochodzenie, powstanie, rozwój (The Polish language; origin and development). 2d ed. Warszawa, S. Arct, 1951. 513 p. Bibliography: p. 500-506. (Biblioteka wiedzy o Polsce, t. 2)

This book places the history of Polish within the framework of other Slavic languages and in a broad anthropological and cultural setting.

2948. Stieber, Zdzisław. Rozwój fonologiczny języka polskiego (Phonological development of Polish). 2d ed. Warszawa, Państwowe Wydawn. Naukowe, 1958. 90 p.

The only comprehensive study of the history of the Polish sound-system, with rich factual documentation.

For the older period of Polish, Stieber's book can be supplemented by the excellent and in many ways pioneering study of Jan Rozwadowski, "Historia języka polskiego" (History of the Polish language), contained in *Gramatyka języka polskiego* (Grammar of the Polish language) (Kraków, Nakł. Polskiej Akademji Umietjętności, 1923, p. 73-206). Reprinted in his *Wybór pism* (Selected works), v. 1 (Warszawa, Państwowe Wydawn. Naukowe, 1959), p. 39-224.

A structual interpretation of Polish historical phonology containing some new insights is also given by Antoni Furdal in *O przyczynach zmian głosowych w języku polskim* (On the causes of sound change in Polish) (Wrocław, Zakł. Narodowy im Ossolińskich, 1964, 145 p., Prace Wrocławskiego Towarzystwa Naukowego, Seria A, nr. 94).

2949. Stieber, Zdzisław. Zarys dialektologii języków zachodnio-słowiańskich; z wyborem tekstów gwarowych (An outline of the dialects of the West Slavic languages; with excerpts of dialect texts). Warszawa, Państwowe Wydawn. Naukowe, 1956. 132 p. Maps. Bibliography: p. 131-132.

Se also entry no. 375.

The best modern survey of the relationship of Polish to the West Slavic languages. Particularly useful are the sections of Lekhitic, and on Polish and Kashubian.

4. Old Polish Texts

2950. Łoś, Jan. Początki piśmiennictwa polskiego; przegląd zabytków językowych (The beginnings of Polish literature; survey of literary monuments). 2d rev. ed. Lwów, Wydawn. Zakładu Narodowego im. Ossolińskich, 1922. 527 p.

This is the best survey of Old Polish literary monuments.

2951. Taszycki, Witold. Najdawniejsze zabytki języka polskiego (The oldest monuments of the Polish language). 2d rev. ed. Wrocław, Wydawn. Zakładu Narodowego im. Ossolińskich, 1950. 210 p. (Biblioteka narodowa, Seria 1, nr. 104)

A concise popular edition of Old Polish texts.

2952. Vrtel-Wierczyński, S. Wybór tekstów staropolskich. Czasy najdawniejsze do r. 1543 (Selection of Old Polish texts; from ancient times to 1543). 2d ed. Warszawa, Państwowe Zakłady Wydawn. Szkolnych, 1950. 368 p. Bibliography.

Taszycki, Witold. Wybór tekstów staropolskich XVI-XVIII wieku (Selection of Old Polish texts of the 16th-18th centuries). 2d ed.

Warszawa, Państwowe Wydawn. Naukowe, 1955. 276 p. Bibliography.

The two volumes provide the best selection of Polish texts with philological annotations and glossaries. More popular editions are S. Vrtel-Wierczyński's *Średniowieczna proza polska* (Medieval Polish prose) (2d rev. ed., Wrocław, Zakład Narodowy im. Ossolińskich, 1959, 365 p.) and *Średniowieczna poezja polska świecka* (Medieval Polish secular poetry) (3d rev. and enl. ed., Wrocław, Zakład Narodowy im. Ossolińskich, 1952, 111 p. Biblioteka narodowa, Seria 1, nr. 60).

5. Phonology, Morphology, and Syntax

2953. Benni, Tytus. Fonetyka opisowa języka polskiego (Descriptive phonetics of Polish). Wrocław, Zakład Narodowy im. Ossolińskich, 1959. 92 p. Illus. Bibliography: p. 60-61.

Reprinted from the collective volume *Gramatyka języka polskiego* (Grammar of the Polish language) (Kraków, Nakł. Polskiej Akademji Umiejętności, 1923), this is a comprehensive, but by now antiquated description of the sounds of standard Polish.

The following studies complement the work of Benni, either providing a different interpretation or dealing in detail with various phonetic problems:

Bargiełówna, M. Grupy fonemów społgłoskowych współczesnej polszczyzny kulturalnej (Groups of consonantal phonemes in contemporary Polish). Biuletyn Polskiego Towarzystwa Językoznawczego, v. 10, 1950: p. 1-25.

Dłuska, Maria. Fonetyka polska, 1. Artykulacja głosek polskich (Polish phonetics, 1. The articulation of Polish sounds). Kraków, 1950. 144 p.

Ułaszyn, Henryk. Ze studiów nad grupami spółgłoskowymi w języku polskim (Remarks on the consonantal groups in Polish). Wrocław, Zakład im. Ossolinskich, 1956. 74 p. (Polska Akademia Nauk. Komitet Językoznawczy. Prace językoznawcze, 8)

2954. Fokker, A. A. Nouns from Verbs; a Contribution to the Study of Present-day Polish Word-Formation. Amsterdam, Noord-Hollandsche U. M., 1966. 122 p.

There is no full treatment of Polish derivation. This study partially fills the gap.

An equally good study devoted to compound formation is Irena Klemensiewiczówna's *Wyrazy złożone nowszej polszczyzny kulturalnej. Próba systematyki* (Compounds of modern standard Polish) (Kraków, 1951, 141 p.).

2955. Heinz, Adam. System przypadkowy języka polskiego (Case system of the Polish language). Kraków, 1965. 111 p. (Zeszyty naukowe Uniwersytetu Jagiellońskiego, 101. Prace językoznawcze, zesz. 13)

This is the best treatment of the Polish case-system from a syntactic point of view. The exposition is somewhat schematic.

2956. Klemensiewicz, Zenon. Składnia opisowa współczesnej polszczyzny kulturalnej (Syntax of modern standard Polish). Kraków, Nakł. Polskiej Akademii Umiejętności, 1937. 302 p.

Though surpassed methodologically, this work remains the only basic study of Polish syntax. Thematically more restricted, but methodologically similar is:

Klemensiewicz, Zenon. Skupienia, czyli syntaktyczne grupy wyrazowe (Syntactic word groups). Kraków, Nakł. Polskiej Akademii Umiejętności, 1948. 96 p. (Polska Akademia Umiejętności. Prace Komisji Językowej, nr. 34).

A valuable structural analysis of a particular syntactic problem (types of predicates and co-predicates) is the study by Krystyna Pisarkowa's *Predykatywność określeń w polskim zdaniu* (Predicativity of modifiers in the Polish sentence) (Wrocław, Zakład Narodowy im. Ossolińskich, 1965, 130 p., Polska Akademia Nauk. Oddział w Krakowie; Prace Komisji Językoznawstwa, nr. 6).

2957. Koneczna, H. Przekroje rentgenograficzne głosek polskich (Roentgenographic profiles of Polish sounds). Warszawa, Państwowe Wydawn. Naukowe, 1951. 16 p. 146 plates.

An up-to-date acoustic analysis of the sounds of standard Polish. Zdzisław Stieber's "Zarys fonologii współczesnej polszczyzny kulturalnej" (Outline of the phonology of contemporary standard Polish) in *Rozwój fonologiczny języka polskiego* (The phonological development of the Polish language), 2d ed., pt. 2 (Warszawa, Państwowe Wydawn. Naukowe, 1958), p. 91-127, contains a lucid survey of the modern Polish phonemes, including a discussion of their distribution and their variants.

2958. Schenker, Alexander. Polish Declension; a Descriptive Analysis. The Hague, Mouton, 1964. 105 p. Bibliography: p. 95-96. (Slavistic Printings and Reprintings, 39)

This book provides an overall description of the Polish noun in terms of its morphemes and their distribution.

The functional and hierarchical patterning of Polish substantives is considered in Edward Stankiewicz's "The Distribution of Morphemic Variants in the Declension of Polish Substantives," *Slavic Word*, v. 11, 1955, no. 4: 554-574.

2959. Tokarski, Jan. Czasowniki polskie; formy, typy, wyjątki, słownik (Polish verbs; forms, types, exceptions, dictionary). Warszawa, S. Arct, 1951. 288 p.

This book is more a pedagogical tool than a scholarly study. It includes a large selection of examples.

6. Lexicography and Orthography

2960. Doroszewski, Witold. Z zagadnień leksykografii polskiej (On problems of Polish lexicography). Warszawa, Państwowy Instytut Wydawniczy, 1954. 147 p.

A good survey of Polish lexicography dealing mostly with methodological problems. It contains a rich bibliography.

A collection of interesting articles devoted to the history of various words is that by Kazimierz Nitsch, *Studia z historii polskiego słownictwa* (Studies in the history of Polish vocabulary) (Kraków, 1948, 193 p., Polska Akademia Umiejętności, Rozprawy, t. 67 nr. 6).

2961. Szober, Stanisław. Słownik poprawnej polszczyzny (Dictionary of correct Polish). 4th enl. ed. Warszawa, Państwowy Instytut Wydawniczy, 1963. 857 p. Bibliography: p. 32-52.

This book defines the norm of the standard language, with its orthoepic and orthographical rules. It is the fourth revised edition of the older work, *Słownik ortoepiczny; jak mówić i pisać po polsku* (Orthoepic dictionary; how to speak and write in Polish) (Warszawa, M. Arct, 1937, 662 p.). A more popular orthographical dictionary is that by Stanisław Jodłowski and Witold Taszycki, *Słownik ortograficzny i prawidła pisowni polskiej* (Orthographic dictionary and rules of Polish spelling) (5th ed., Wrocław, Zakład Narodowy im. Ossolińskich, 728 p.).

2962. Taszycki, Witold. Rozprawy i studia polonistyczne. v. 1. Onomastyka (Polonistic essays and studies. v. 1 Onomastics). Wrocław, Zakład Narodowy im. Ossolińskich, 1958. 345 p.

The most comprehensive study devoted to the history of Polish proper names.

7. Dictionaries

2963. Brückner, Alexander. Słownik etymologiczny języka polskiego (Etymological dictionary of the Polish language). Kraków, Krakowska Spółka Wydawnicza, 1927. 805 p. 2d ed. Warszawa, Wiedza Powszechna, 1957. 805 p.

Despite a lack of rigor and documentation, this remains one of the best Slavic etymological dictionaries. It is now being superseded by Franciszek Sławski's *Słownik etymologiczny języka polskiego* (Etymological dictionary of the Polish language) (Kraków, Nakł. Tow. Miłośników Języka Polskiego, 1952–), which gives a better treatment of the other Slavic languages and a valuable bibliography.

2964. Polska Akademia Nauk. Słownik języka polskiego (Dictionary of the Polish language). Edited by Witold Doroszewski. Warszawa, Wiedza Powszechna, 1958–

The largest up-to-date dictionary of the Polish literary language.

2965. Polska Akademia Nauk. Słownik staropolski (Old Polish dictionary). Edited by Kazimierz Nitsch, Zenon Klemensiewicz, and others. Warszawa, 1953–

This dictionary is the fundamental work of Polish lexicography, providing the fullest coverage of Old Polish texts.

2966. Słownik języka polskiego (Dictionary of the Polish language). Prepared by Jan Karłowicz, A. Kryński, and W. Niedźwiedzki. Warszawa, w drukarni E. Lubowskiego i s-ki, 1900-1927. 8 v.

Reprint edition: 1952-1953 (Warszawa, Państwowy Instytut Wydawniczy, 8 v.; bibliography: v. 8, p. vii-xvii).

This "Warsaw" dictionary may be surpassed in scope and scholarship by the work now being readied by the Polish Academy of Sciences (*see* entry 2964).

8. Polish Dialects

2967. Karłowicz, Jan. Słownik gwar polskich (Dictionary of Polish dialect). Kraków, Nakł. Akademii Umiejętności, 1900-1911. 6 v.

Monumental dictionary of the Polish dialects. It also contains phonetic and grammatical information.

2968. Konferencja pomorska, 1954. Prace językoznawcze (Linguistic studies). Warszawa, Państwowe Wydawn. Naukowe, 1956. 220 p. Map.

This collective volume introduces the reader into the field of Kashubian, which occupies a special position among the Polish dialects. The most informative article in this volume (p. 37-48) in defining the relationship of Kashubian to Polish is that by Zdzisław Stieber, "Stosunek Kaszubszczyzny do dialektów Polski lądowej" (The relation of Kashubian to the continental Polish dialects).

2969. Lorentz, Friedrich. Gramatyka pomorska (Kashubian grammar). Wrocław, Zakład Narodowy im. Ossolińskich, 1958-1962. 3 v. Bibliography: v. 1, p. 1-70.

This work remains the fundamental compendium of Kashubian. It is complemented by Lorentz's Kashubian dictionary, *Pomoranisches Wörterbuch* (Berlin, Akademie Verlag, 1958–), and by his grammar and dictionary of Slovincian, which represents the most archaic dialect of Pomerania, *Slovinzische Grammatik* (St. Petersburg, 1903, 392 p.), and *Slovinzisches Wörterbuch* (St. Petersburg, Buchdr. der Kaiserlichen Akademie der Wissenschaften, 1908-1912, 2 v.).

The most recent dictionary of Kashubian is Bernard Sychta's *Słownik gwar kaszubskich na tle kultury ludowej* (Wrocław, Zakład Narodowy im. Ossolińskich, 1967–).

2970. Nitsch, Kazimierz. Dialekty języka polskiego (Dialects of the Polish language). Wrocław, Zakład Narodowy im. Ossolińskich, 1957. 122 p.

This is a reprint of Nitsch's article in *Encyklopedia polska* of 1923 and the best historical survey of the Polish dialects.

For a fuller description of the Polish dialects consult all the studies of this founder of Polish dialectology, in particular his *Wybór pism polonistycznych* (Selected Polonistic Writings) Wrocław, Zakład im. Ossolińskich, 1954-1958, 4 v.). A bibliography of Nitsch's writings is to be found in volume 1, p. viii-xxxix, of this edition.

A useful pedagogical outline of Polish dialectology is Stanisław Urbańczyk, *Zarys dialektologii polskiej* (Outline of Polish dialectology) (2d ed., Warszawa, Państwowe Wydawn. Naukowe, 1962, 98 p.).

A structural description of the Polish dialectal phonemic systems is Edward Stankiewicz, "The Phonemic Patterns of the Polish Dialects," contributed to *For Roman Jakobson, Essays on the Occasion of his Sixtieth Birthday* (The Hague, Mouton, 1956), p. 513–530.

Dialect texts are contained in Kazimierz Nitsch, *Wybór polskich tekstów gwarowych* (Selection of Polish dialect texts) (2d rev. ed., Warszawa, Państwowe Wydawn. Naukowe, 1960, 379 p., illus.).

2971. Polska Akademii Nauk. *Zakład Słowianoznawstwa.* Atlas językowy kaszubszczyzny i dialektów sąsiednich (Atlas of the Kashubian language and of neighboring dialects). Edited by Zdzisław Stieber. Wrocław, Zakład Narodowy im. Ossolińskich, 1964. 246 p. Fold. maps. Bibliography: p. 241-243.

This atlas is a synthesis of Polish dialectological work on Kashubian during the last decade.

B. LITERATURE

by Czesław Miłosz

1. Bibliographies, Reference Books, Histories of Literature

2972. Coleman, Marion Moore, *comp.* Polish Literature in English Translation: a Bibliography. Cheshire, Conn., Cherry Hill Books, 1963. 180 p.

A thorough bibliographical survey listing books, single poems, articles and short stories in periodicals, items translated from Polish in collections. Valuable data on rare prints of the 17th and 18th centuries.

2973. Jakubowski, Jan Zygmunt, *ed.* Polska krytyka literacka 1800-1918 (Polish literary criticism, 1800-1918). Warszawa, Państwowe Wydawn. Naukowe, 1959. 4 v.

An anthology of literary criticism with biographical and bibliographical data. Coverage of the following period is provided by the same editor's *Polska krytyka literacka, 1919-1939* (Polish literary criticism, 1919-1939) (Warszawa, Państwowe Wydawn. Naukowe, 1966, 655 p.).

2974. Korzeniewska, Ewa, *ed.* Słownik współczesnych pisarzy polskich (A dictionary of modern Polish writers). Warszawa, Państwowe Wydawn. Naukowe, 1963-1966. 4 v.

A very useful tool. It lists living writers or those who have died since 1939. Those, however, who made their debuts in the decade 1956-1966 are not represented. Bibliographies of works by, and of literary criticism about, individual writers.

2975. Kridl, Manfred. A Survey of Polish Literature and Culture. Translated by Olga Scherer-Virski. New York, Columbia University Press, 1956. 525 p. Bibliography: p. 515-517.

Polish literature from its beginnings until the Second World War.

2976. Krzyżanowski, Julian. Historia literatury polskiej; alegoryzm– preromantyzm (A history of Polish literature; allegorism–preromanticism). 3d ed. Warszawa, Państwowy Instytut Wydawniczy, 1966. 654 p. Illus., facsims., ports. Bibliography: p. 549-601.

The most thorough university textbook by an eminent scholar, covering the time from the Middle Ages to the beginning of the 19th century.

2977. Miłosz, Czesław. The History of Polish Literature. New York, Macmillan Co., 1969. 570 p.

See also Wacław Lednicki's *Life and Culture of Poland as Reflected in Polish Literature* (New York, Ray Publishers, 1944, 328 p. Bibliography: p. 317-319). Its emphasis is on the 19th century.

2978. Polska Akademia Nauk. *Instytut Badań Literackich.* Bibliografia literatury polskiej, "Nowy Korbut" (A bibliography of Polish literature, "The New Korbut"). Edited by Kazimierz Budzyk and others. Warszawa, Państwowy Instytut Wydawniczy, 1963–

This is a complete scholarly revision and continuation of Gabrjel Korbut's *Literatura polska od początków do wojny światowej* (Polish literature from its beginnings to the World War) (2d ed., Warszawa, Skład główny w Kasie im. Mianowskiego, 1929-31, 4 v.). A necessary tool. Before the revised sequence appears, the third and fourth volumes of the previous edition should be consulted for bibliography of the 19th century.

2979. Taborski, Bolesław. Polish Plays in English Translation: a Bibliography. The Polish Review, v. 9, 1964, no. 3: 63-101.

———. Polish Plays in English Translation: a Bibliography. Addenda and Corrigenda. The Polish Review, v. 12, 1967, no. 1: 59-82.

The bibliography covers, besides printed texts, also those available in typescript.

2. Serials

2980. Dialog. Miesięcznik poświęcony dramaturgii współczesnej teatralnej, filmowej, radiowej (Dialogue. A monthly dedicated to the contemporary theatrical, film and radio drama). r. 1– 1956– Warszawa, Wydawn. RSW "Prasa." Monthly.

Publishes new Polish plays, film scripts, etc., as well as translations of the most interesting foreign plays.

2981. Kultura; szkice, opowiadania, sprawozdania (Culture; essays, stories, reports). 1947– Paryż, Instytut Literacki. Monthly.
See also entry no. 2593.

An émigré monthly, publishing, besides political articles, literary works of eminent Polish writers, both living abroad and (occasionally) living in Poland.

2982. Pamiętnik literacki; czasopismo kwartalne poświęcone historii i krytyce literatury polskiej (Literary memorial; a quarterly dedicated to history and criticism of Polish literature). 1902– Warszawa, Zakład im. Ossolińskich.

The basic scholarly periodical publication in the field.

2983. Pamiętnik teatralny; czasopismo kwartalne poświęcone historii i krytyce teatru (Theater memorial; a quarterly dedicated to the history of the theater and to theatrical criticism). r. 1– 1952– Warszawa.

A scholarly periodical publication concentrating upon the past of the theater in Poland.

2984. Twórczość; miesięcznik Związku Literatów Polskich (Creativity; monthly of the Union of Polish Writers). r. 1– 1945– Warszawa, Czytelnik.

The most respected literary magazine in Poland that has maintained its position since 1945.

3. Anthologies

2985. Dedecius, Karl, comp. Polnische Poesie des 20. Jahrhunderts. München, C. Hanser, 1964. 236 p. Bio-bibliographical notes: p. 159-205.

The anthology includes poets from the beginning of the century ("Young Poland") as well as those who are now in their 30s. Dedecius is renowned as the best translator of Polish poetry into German.

2986. Dedecius, Karl, *ed. and trans.* Polnische Pointen; Satiren und kleine Prosa des 20. Jahrhunderts. 2d ed. München, C. Hanser, 1962. 154 p.

An anthology of Polish humorous verse and prose of the 20th century; a good translation.

2987. Dedecius, Karl, *ed.* Polnische Prosa des 20. Jahrhunderts. München, Hanser, 1966–

An anthology of Polish fiction from the beginning of the century (Przybyszewski, Żeromski) until today.

2988. Gillon, Adam, *ed.* Introduction to Modern Polish Literature; an Anthology of Fiction and Poetry. New York, Twayne Publishers, 1964. 480 p.

An ambitious attempt to present Polish literature of our century.

The volume may lead to misunderstandings because of the adjective "modern" in its title. Neither Prus or Sienkiewicz in prose nor Konopnicka or Kasprowicz in poetry — to give a few examples — are "modern" writers. The overall impression is that too much was squeezed into the book; thus the prose has a fragmentary character. A certain lack of discrimination leads to an overemphasis upon second-rate authors. Translations by various hands, ranging, especially in poetry, from fair to inadequate.

2989. Hagenau, Gerda, *ed.* Polen Erzählt. Frankfurt, Bücherei, 1962. 188 p.

Twenty-one stories by Polish authors born between 1885 and 1934. Translated by the editor and others.

2990. Jelenski, Constantin, *ed.* Anthologie de la poésie polonaise. Paris, Éditions du Seuil, 1965. 453 p.

The most extensive anthology of Polish poetry in any Western language, it covers the time from the 15th century to 1965. Translations by a team of known French poets, from good to masterpieces of the craft.

2991. Kridl, Manfred, *ed.* An Anthology of Polish Literature. New York, Columbia University Press, 1957. 625 p.

A selection of poetry and prose from the Middle Ages to the Second World War, in Polish, with English annotations; for students of the Polish language.

2992. Kuncewiczowa, Maria, *ed.* The Modern Polish Mind; an Anthology of Stories and Essays. Boston, Little, Brown, 1962. 440 p.

A cross-section of attitudes and beliefs, from orthodox Marxist to Roman Catholic. A good introduction to the Polish literary scene after the Second World War though authors living abroad and exerting great influence in Poland — for instance, Witold Gombrowicz — are not included. Translations by various hands.

2993. Lewański, Julian, *ed.* Dramaty staropolskie (Old Polish dramas). Warszawa, Państwowy Instytut Wydawniczy, 1959-1963. 6 v. Illus., facsims.

An anthology of Polish 16th and 17th century drama, edited by an eminent scholar in the field with an introduction which amounts to a survey of the history of old Polish theater.

2994. Matuszewski, Ryszard, *ed.* Poezja polska 1914-1939 (Polish poetry 1914-1939). Warszawa, Czytelnik, 1962. 898 p.

Though the criteria of selection are open to question and poets are not always represented by their best work, this is a useful book, recommendable also because of biographical and bibliographical data.

2995. Mayewski, Paweł, *ed.* The Broken Mirror; a Collection of Writings from Contemporary Poland. Introduction by Lionel Trilling. New York, Random House, 1958. 209 p.

An anthology of essays and short stories, including also one play, centered upon the intellectual breakthrough of 1956.

2996. Miłosz, Czesław, *ed. and tr.* Postwar Polish Poetry; an Anthology. Garden City, N.Y., Doubleday, 1965. 149 p.

The editor explains in his preface his criteria for selection as dictated by the very possibility or impossibility of rendering given poets in English. Much space is given to younger poets who made their débuts in the last decade.

2997. Ordon, Edmund, *ed.* Ten Contemporary Polish Stories. Translated by various hands, with an introduction by Olga Scherer-Virski. Detroit, Wayne State University Press, 1958. 252 p.

The volume contains some first-rate stories by authors active in the last decades (Dąbrowska, Schulz, Gombrowicz), with an unavoidable portion of less talented writers. A good level of translation.

2998. Pankowski, Marian, *tr.* Anthologie de la poésie polonaise du quinzième au vingtième siècle. Aalter, A. de Rache, 1961. 140 p.

Very competent, often brilliant translations by a bilingual poet and professor at the Free University of Brussels.

2999. Peterkiewicz (Pietrkiewicz), Jerzy, *and* Burns Singer, *eds. and trs.* Five Centuries of Polish Poetry: 1450-1950; an Anthology with Introduction and Notes. London, Secker and Warburg, 1960; Philadelphia, Dufour Editions, 1962. 154 p.

Limited in scope, the anthology is uneven. Best in its presentation of some old Polish poets.

3000. Sokołowska, Jadwiga, *ed.* Poeci polskiego baroku (Poets of the Polish Baroque). Warszawa, Państwowy Instytut Wydawniczy, 1965. 2 v.

The most complete anthology of Polish baroque poets with valuable biographical notes.

3001. Sokołowska, Jadwiga, *and* Kazimiera Żukowska, *eds.* Poeci Renesansu; antologia (Poets of the Renaissance; an anthology). Warszawa, Państwowy Instytut Wydawniczy, 1959. 522 p.

An anthology of minor Polish poets of the 16th century, with biographical notes. The major poet of the period, Jan Kochanowski, is purposely excluded.

3002. Tuwim, Julian, *comp.* Księga wierszy polskich XIX wieku (A book of Polish poems of the 19th century). Edited by Juliusz Wiktor Gomulicki. 2d ed. Warszawa, Państwowy Instytut Wydawniczy, 1956. 3 v. Illus.

An anthology with biographical data, mostly of less known poets. Even richer in forgotten names is another anthology:

Hertz, Paweł, *comp.* Zbiór poetów polskich XIX w. (A collection of Polish poets of the 19th century). Warszawa, Państwowy Instytut Wydawniczy, 1959-1967. 5 v.

3003. Wirth, Andrzej, *ed.* Modernes polnisches Theater. Neuwied und Berlin, Luchterhand, 1967. 2 v.

An anthology of plays, translated by various hands, from the '30s until today, including such masters of vanguard drama as Stanisław Ignacy Witkiewicz and Witold Gombrowicz.

3004. Żabicki, Zbigniew, *comp.* Polish Short Stories. Warsaw, Polonia Publishing House, 1960. 323 p.

A fair selection, covering the second half of the 19th and the first decades of the 20th centuries, from Norwid to Strug. Short biographical notes. Popular level, rather careless editing.

3005. Zhivov, M., *and* B. Stakheev, *eds.* Pol'skaia poeziia (Polish poetry). Moskva, Goslitizdat, 1963. 2 v.

Translations by various poets, including Akhmatova, Pasternak, S. Marshak, Aseev. Poetry from before the 19th century not well represented. The stress is upon the 19th century. In the selection of 20th century poets a strong bias is evident.

4. Studies on Separate Periods or Problems

3006. Dyboski, Roman. Periods of Polish Literary History, Being the Ilchester Lectures for the Year 1923. London, H. Milford, Oxford University Press, 1923. 163 p.

A general survey, perhaps lacking clarity of exposition, by a well-known scholar who was a professor of English literature at the Jagellonian University in Kraków.

3007. Erlich, Victor. The Double Image; Concepts of the Poet in Slavic Literatures. Baltimore, Johns Hopkins Press, 1964. 160 p. Bibliographical footnotes.

Six essays dealing mostly with Russian poetry with the exception of one, on Zygmunt Krasiński. The problem discussed is however of importance to students of Polish poetry, especially of Polish romanticism.

3008. Gömöri, George G. Polish and Hungarian Poetry, 1945-1956. Oxford, Clarendon Press, 1966. 266 p. Bibliographical footnotes.
See also entry no. 2223.

A comparative study on the impact of politics upon poetry in two countries by a Hungarian scholar who is also at home in the Polish language and literature.

3009. Herman, Maxime. Stanislas Przybyszewski (de 1868 à 1900) . . . . Lille, Imprimerie G. Sautai, 1939. 462 p.

For the literary history of that period, the basic Polish work is: Wyka, Kazimierz. Modernizm polski (Polish modernism). Kraków, Wydawn. Literackie, 1959. 338 p.

3010. Ingarden, Roman. Das literarische Kunstwerk. Mit einem Anhang von den Funktionen der Sprache in Theaterschauspiel. 3d rev. ed. Tübingen, Niemeyer, 1965. 430 p. Bibliographical footnotes.

This is the third edition of a book which has acquired the position of a classic since its first appearance in German in 1931. Professor Ingarden, one of the leading European exponents of phenomenology, has written some of his works in German, some in Polish.

3011. Lednicki, Wacław. Bits of Table Talk on Pushkin, Mickiewicz, Goethe, Turgenev and Sienkiewicz. The Hague, M. Nijhoff, 1956. 263 p. Bibliographical footnotes. (International Scholar's Forum; a Series of Books by American Scholars, 5)

A collection of essays. Some deal with Russian, some with Polish literature, but the unifying theme may be defined as Polish-Russian literary relations.

3012. Lednicki, Wacław. Russia, Poland and the West; Essays in Literary and Cultural History. New York, Roy Publishers, 1954. 419 p.

A book centered on Polish-Russian literary relations in the 19th century, packed with data and full of interesting insights by the late professor of the University of California at Berkeley. Chaadaev, Mickiewicz, Pushkin, Dostoevsky, and Blok are the main protagonists.

3013. Scherer-Virski, Olga. The Modern Polish Short Story. s'-Gravenhage, Mouton, 1955. 266 p. Bibliography: p. 249-254. (Slavistic Printings and Reprintings, 5)

An analysis of structures of the genre. The material ranges from romantic prose to literature between the First and Second World Wars. Included are translations on four entire stories. For an important reference work on the subject *see*:

Maciuszko, Jerzy J. The Polish Short Story in English. A Guide and Critical Bibliography. Detroit, Wayne State University Press, 1968. 473 p.

3014. Terlecki, Tymon, *ed.* Literatura polska na obczyźnie, 1940-1960 (Polish literature abroad, 1940-1960). Londyn, B. Świderski, 1964-1965. 2 v. Bibliographies.

A collective work sponsored by the Polish Writers' Union in London. A mine of information on books and periodicals published in exile, beginning with the Nazi occupation of Poland in 1939.

5. Literature before the 19th Century: Texts and Studies*

3015. Bogurodzica. Edited by Jerzy Woronczak. Wrocław, Zakład Na-

* Works in this section have been listed in the following order under each writer's entry: collected or selected works in the original language, individual works in the original language or in translation, and works about the author. Not always are all three categories included.

rodowy im. Ossolińskich, 1962. 416 p. Facsims., music. (Biblioteka Pisarzów Polskich, Seria A. Liryka średniowieczna, t. 1)

The oldest Polish Christian song. Photographic reproduction of extant manuscripts, a modern transcription, a linguistic and musicological commentary.

3016. Frycz Modrzewski, Andrzej.

Frycz Modrzewski, Andrzej. Opera omnia. Edited by Kazimierz Kumaniecki. Warszawa, Państwowy Instytut Wydawniczy, 1953-1960. 5 v. A Latin edition, based upon the original Kraków and Basle editions. There is a Polish translation, *Dzieła wszystkie* (Complete works) (Warszawa, Państwowy Instytut Wydawniczy, 1953-1959, 5 v.).

Kot, Stanisław. Andrzej Frycz Modrzewski; studium z dziejów kultury polskiej w. XVI (Andrzej Frycz Modrzewski; a study in the history of Polish culture in the 16th century). Kraków, Nakł. Krakowskiej Spółki Wydawniczej, 1923. 320 p. The author of this study is a specialist in the history of the Reformation and deals with religious as well as literary quarrels of the period.

3017. Kochanowski, Jan.

Kochanowski, Jan. Dzieła polskie (Polish works). Edited by Julian Krzyżanowski. 5th ed. Warszawa, Panstwowy Instytut Wydawniczy, 1967. 2 v.

———. Chants. Translated from Polish with an introduction and commentary by Jacques Langlade. Paris, Societé d'édition "Les Belles Lettres," 1932. 147 p. A literal, line-by-line translation of *Songs.*

———. Izbrannye proizvedeniia (Selected works). Edited by S. S. Sovetov. Leningrad, Izdatel'stvo Akademii Nauk SSSR, 1960. 370 p. Illus. Verse translations by various hands, from fair to good.

———. Poems. Translated by Dorothea Prall Radin and others. Berkeley, University of California Press, 1928. 156 p. This is a translation of *Laments, St. John's Eve, The Dismissal of the Grecian Envoys.* A meticulous, careful work, not brilliant artistically with the exception of some passages.

Langlade, Jacques. Jean Kochanowski, l'homme, le penseur, le poéte lyrique. Paris, Les Belles Lettres, 1932. 415 p. This is still the basic study in any Western language of the major Polish Renaissance poet.

3018. Krasicki, Ignacy.

Krasicki, Ignacy. Pisma wybrane (Selected works). Edited by Tadeusz Mikulski. Warszawa, Państwowy Instytut Wydawniczy, 1954. 4 v. Illus., facsims., ports.

Cazin, Paul. Le prince-évêque de Varmie, Ignace Krasicki, 1735-1801. Paris, Bibliothèque polonaise, 1940. 316 p. Bibliography: p. 295-304. The author of this monograph, a French writer of renown, was a connoisseur and excellent translator of Polish literature.

3019. Niemcewicz, Julian Ursyn. Under Their Vine and Fig Tree; Travels Through America in 1797-1799; 1805. Edited and translated by Metchie J. E. Budka. Elizabeth, N.J., Grassman Pub. Co., 1965. 398 p. Illus., facsims., maps, ports. (Collections of the New Jersey Historical Society at Newark, v. 14)

This is a translation of a work published in Polish as *Podróże po Ameryce, 1797-1807* (Travels in America, 1797-1807) (Wrocław, Zakład Narodowy im. Ossolińskich, 1959, 459 p.). One of the most colorful figures in Polish literary life of the 18th and the early 19th centuries, a playwright, a poet, and a translator of English poets, Niemcewicz exemplifies attitudes of Polish literati toward the young republic.

3020. Pasek, Jan Chryzostom. Pamiętniki (Memoirs). 2d ed. Edited by Roman Pollak. Warszawa, Państwowy Instytut Wydawniczy, 1963. 485 p. Illus.

———. Les Mémoires de Jean-Chrysostome Pasek, gentilhomme polonais, 1656-1688. Translated and with commentary by Paul Cazin. Paris, Les Belles Lettres, 1929. 350 p.

The Polish text is very carefully and competently edited and misreadings not uncommon in numerous previous editions eliminated. The French version, by an excellent translator, is slightly abridged.

3021. Skarga, Piotr.

Skarga, Piotr. Les sermons politiques (sermons de diète, 1597) du prédicateur du roi de Pologne Sigismond III. Edited and translated by A. Berga. Paris, Société française d'imprimeries et de librairies, 1916. 188 p.

Berga, Auguste. Un prédicateur de la cour de Pologne sous Sigismond III, Pierre Skarga (1536-1612). Paris, Société française d'imprimeries et de librairies, 1916. 376 p. Bibliography: p. vii-xiv. *See also entry* no. 2630. The only monograph on Skarga in any foreign language by a specialist in the history of the Jesuit order. The Polish text of *Sermons* can be found in:

Skarga, Piotr. Kazania sejmowe. Edited by Stanisław Kot. Kraków, Nakł. Krakowskiej Spółki Wydawniczej, 1925. 190 p. (Biblioteka narodowa. Ser. 1, nr. 70) A valuable introduction by the editor, a specialist in the history of the Reformation. For a complete edition *see* Piotr Skarga, *Pisma wszystkie* (Complete works), edited by Stanisław Franciszek Michalski-Iwieński (Warszawa, Wyd. Ultima Thule, 1923-1930, 5 v.).

3022. Trembecki, Stanisław.

Trembecki, Stanisław. Wiersze wybrane (Selected poems). Edited by Juliusz W. Gomulicki. Warszawa, Państwowy Instytut Wydawniczy, 1965. 201 p.

Backvis, Claude. Un grand poète polonais du XVIIIe siècle, Stanislas Trembecki, l'étrange carrière de sa vie et sa grandeur. Paris,

Bibliotèque polonaise, 1937. 281 p. A study on a turbulent figure of the Enlightenment by a well-known Belgian Slavicist.

6. Literature of the 19th and 20th Centuries: Works by and about Individual Authors*

3023. Brzozowski, Stanisław. Dębina. Sam wśród ludzi (Oakwood. Alone among men). Kraków, Wydawn. Literackie, 1957. 484 p.

A key fiction work by a major literary critic and philosopher (1878-1911). His main book of literary criticism is *Legenda Młodej Polski. Studya o strukturze duszy kulturalnej* (The legend of young Poland. Studies on the structure of a cultural phase) (2d ed., Lwów, Połoniecki, 1910, 594 p.). A study on him in English is Czesław Miłosz's "A Controversial Polish Writer: Stanislaw Brzozowski," *California Slavic Studies* (Berkeley and Los Angeles, University of California Press) v. 2, 1963: 53-95).

3024. Dąbrowska, Maria.

Dąbrowska, Maria. Pisma wybrane (Selected works). Warszawa, Czytelnik, 1956. 3 v. Port., facsims.

———. Nächte und Tage. Translated by Leo Lasinski. Berlin, Rütten und Loening, 1955-1957. 3 v. A "roman fleuve" considered a classic of Polish prose, first published in Warsaw in 1932-1934.

Folejewski, Zbigniew. Maria Dąbrowska. New York, Twayne Publishers, 1967. 123 p. Bibliography: p. 109-117. (Twayne's World Authors Series, 16) A presentation of a major Polish novelist of our century (1899-1966) by an American scholar.

3025. Fredro, Aleksander. Pisma wszystkie (Complete works). Edited by Stanisław Pigoń and Kazimierz Wyka. Warszawa, Państwowy Instytut Wydawniczy, 1955-1957. 10 v. Illus.

Though there are some English translations of Fredro's comedies in verse, they cannot be recommended to students or scholars. This is an author whose *vis comica* resides in the language. However, a new book of translation, by Professor Harold B. Segel, is announced for 1968 by Princeton University Press.

3026. Krasiński, Zygmunt.

Krasiński, Zygmunt. Iridion. Translated by Florence Noyes and edited by George Rapall Noyes. London, Oxford University Press, H. Milford, 1927. 281 p.

———. The Un-Divine Comedy. Translated by Harriette E. Kennedy and Zofia Umińska. London, G. G. Harrap; Warszawa, Książnica Polska, 1924. 111 p.

* Works in this section have been listed in the following order under each writer's entry: collected or selected works in the original language, individual works in the original language or in translation, and works about the author. Not always are all three categories included.

English translations are often misleading. The most complete edition in Polish is:

Krasiński, Zygmunt. Pisma (Works). Jubilee ed. Kraków, G. Gebethner i spółka, 1912. 8 v. in 9. Port.

———. Die Ungöttliche Komödie. Translated by Franz Theodor Csokor. Berlin, Wien, Zsolnay, 1936. 142 p. A new edition of a version which has been used for theatrical performances.

Lednicki, Wacław, *ed.* Zygmunt Krasiński, Romantic Universalist; An International Tribute. New York, Polish Institute of Arts and Sciences in America, 1964. 228 p. Bibliographical footnotes. A symposium. Studies and essays by Polish, Belgian, French, and German scholars. This is superior to a rather lyrical work of vulgarization:

Gardner, Monica Mary. The Anonymous Poet of Poland, Zygmunt Krasinski. Cambridge, University Press, 1919. 320 p. Front. Bibliographical note: p. 315-316.

3027. Mickiewicz, Adam.

Mickiewicz, Adam. Dzieła (Works). Edited by Julian Krzyżanowski. Warszawa, Czytelnik, 1955. 16 v. Illus., bibliographies.

———. Cours de littérature slave, professé au College de France, Paris. Paris, L. Martínet, 1860. 5 v. This is the original text of lectures on Slavic literatures read in the years 1840-1844. Polish editions of Mickiewicz's work use a translation into Polish.

———. New Selected Poems. Translated by W. H. Auden and others. Edited by Clark Mills. New York, Voyages Press, 1957. 84 p. A few outstanding versions, many mediocre, some misleading.

———. Pan Tadeusz. Translated by Paul Cazin. Paris, F. Alcan, 1934. 398 p. Illus. A prose version by a most skillful translator from the Polish who renounced the idea of applying the French alexandrine.

———. Pan Tadeusz oder der letzte Einritt in Litauen. Translated by Walter Panitz. Berlin, Aufbau-Verlag, 1956. 602 p. Illus. A translation in verse.

———. Pan Tadeusz oder die letze Fehde in Litauen. Translated by Herman Buddensieg. München, Fink Verlag, 1963. 386 p. Illus. A translation in verse. Both German versions have their admirers.

———. Pan Tadeusz; or the Last Foray in Lithuania; a Story of Life Among Polish Gentlefolk in the Years 1811 and 1812. Translated by George Rapall Noyes. London and Toronto, J. M. Dent; New York, E. P. Dutton, 1930. 354 p. A prose translation, in a way superior to attempts at finding an equivalent of Mickiewicz's verse in the English couplet.

———. Pan Tadeusz; or The Last Foray in Lithuania. Translated by Watson Kirkconnell, with an introductory essay by William J. Rose, and notes by Harold B. Segel. New York, Polish Institute of Arts and Sciences in America, 1962. 388 p. A translation in verse. Rhymed couplets.

———. Pan Tadeusz; or the Last Foray in Lithuania. Translated and with an introduction by Kenneth Mackenzie. London, Dent; New York, Dutton, 1966. 291 p. Illus. (Everyman's Library, no. 842) A translation in verse.

———. Poems. Edited by George Rapall Noyes and translated by various hands. New York, Herald Square Press, 1944. 486 p. Inadequate translations with a Victorian ring inexistent in Mickiewicz's poetry.

———. Sobranie sochinenii (Collected works). Edited by D. D. Blagoi, M. Ryls'kyi, and others. Moscow, Gos. izd.-vo khudzoh. lit-ry, 1948-1954. 5 v. Illus. The most complete edition of Mickiewicz's works in Russian. Translation in verse by various hands, superior to English versions. M. Ryls'kyi was one of the best equipped Soviet writers to edit Mickiewicz and is the author of an excellent translation of *Pan Tadeusz* into Ukrainian.

———. La Tribune des Peuples. Paris, E. Flammarion, 1907. 413 p. The original text of political articles written in French at the time Mickiewicz was in Paris as the editor of an international revolutionary paper (1849).

Adam Mickiewicz 1798-1855. In Commemoration of the Centenary of his Death. Paris, UNESCO, 1955. 277 p. Of particular interest are essays by French scholars (Jean Fabre, Maxime Leroy) on Mickiewicz and ideologies of his time.

Buffalo University. Mickiewicz and the West; a Symposium. Edited by B. R. Bugelski. Buffalo, 1956. 75 p. (University of Buffalo Studies, v. 23, no. 1) A few articles which are in fact commemorative speeches and one longer paper, "Mickiewicz and Emerson" by E. Ordon; the first essay in English on the subject appeared in *Adam Mickiewicz: Poet of Poland*, edited by Manfred Kridl, author anonymous (not Krzyżanowski as Ordon states).

Davie, Donald. The Forests of Lithuania; a Poem. Hessle, Yorkshire, Marvell Press, 1959. 62 p. A free adaptation of some passages from *Pan Tadeusz* by a British poet; in fact, a new poem playing with borrowed images.

Kridl, Manfred, *ed.* Adam Mickiewicz, Poet of Poland; a Symposium. New York, Columbia University Press, 1951. 292 p. Essays by several authors arranged in such a way that the book may serve as an introduction to various aspects of Mickiewicz's work.

Lednicki, Wacław, *ed.* Adam Mickiewicz in World Literature; a Symposium. Berkeley, University of California Press, 1956. 626 p. Illus. Contributors to this volume, scholars of various nationalities discuss the reception of Mickiewicz's work in their respective languages. Particularly rich material on Russia contributed by Lednicki and Gleb Struve.

Lednicki, Wacław. Pushkin's Bronze Horseman; the Story of a Masterpiece. With an appendix including, in English, Mickiewicz's "Digression," Pushkin's "Bronze Horseman" and other poems.

Berkeley, University of California Press, 1955. 163 p. (University of California Publications. Slavic Studies, 1) A study on Mickiewicz-Pushkin relations and polemics through poetry.

Levkovich, Ia. L., *and others, eds.* Adam Mitskevich v. russkoi pechati, 1825-1955; bibliograficheskie materialy (Adam Mickiewicz in the Russian press, 1825-1955; bibliographical materials). Moskva, Akademiia nauk, 1957. 599 p. Ports. A bibliography of translations, press articles, etc., which appeared in Russia.

Scheps, Samuel. Adam Mickiewicz, ses affinités juives. Paris, Nagel, 1964. 103 p. Illus. Bibliography: p. 97-100. The treatise deals with Mickiewicz's known pro-Jewish position and his fascination with Jewish mysticism. Useful bibliographical data.

Weintraub, Wiktor. Literature as Prophecy; Scholarship and Martinist Poetics in Mickiewicz's Parisian Lectures. 's-Gravenhage, Mouton, 1959. 78 p. (Musagetes; Contributions to the History of Slavic Literature and Culture, 10) A study on Mickiewicz as a member of a mystical sect in Paris.

———. The Poetry of Adam Mickiewicz. 's-Gravenhage, Mouton, 1954. 302 p. (Slavistic Printings and Reprintings, 2) A fundamental work on the subject in English.

3028. Norwid, Cyprian.

Norwid, Cypria. Dzieła zebrane (Collected works). Edited by Juliusz W. Gomulicki. Warszawa, Państwowy Instytut Wydawniczy, 1966. 2 v. (v. I: Poems; v. II: Commentary) The first monumental edition of collected works, which will probably embrace eight volumes. Other editions, starting with the one of Leipzig, 1863, are selections. The editor's introduction and a chronicle of Norwid's life amount to a long study in its own right, not to mention the voluminous commentary on poems.

———. Letters. Translated by Jerzy Peterkiewicz. Twelve Poems. Translated by Christine Brooke-Rose. Botteghe oscure (Roma), no. 22, 1958: 178-199. A few letters introducing Norwid's views on poetry. Translations of poems are a rare achievement and probably the only English versions of artistic value.

———. Le Stigmate. Translated by Paul Cazin. Paris, Gallimard, 1932. 222 p. (Collection polonaise, 6) A translation of Norwid's narratives in prose.

Folejewski, Zbigniew. C. K. Norwid's Prose and the Poetics of the Short Story. American Contributions to the Fifth International Congress of Slavists. Volume 2, Literary Contributions. The Hague, Mouton, 1963. p. 115-128.

Kliger, George, *and* Robert C. Albrecht. A Polish Poet on John Brown. The Polish Review, v. 8, 1963, no. 3: 80-85. An article on Norwid's sympathies for the abolitionist movement during his stay in America during 1852-1854, including his two poems on John Brown in a literal translation.

3029. Potocki, Jan.

Potocki, Jan. The Saragossa Manuscript, a Collection of Weird Tales. Edited and with a preface by Roger Callois. Translated by Elisabeth Abbott. New York, Orion Press, 1960. 233 p. This is a translation from a French orginal, based upon *Manuscrit trouvé à Saragosse*, edited by Roger Callois (Paris, Gallimard, 1958, 290 p.). Both French and English editions do not give the text of the novel in its entirety.

———. The New Decameron; Further Tales from the Saragossa Manuscript. Translated by Elisabeth Abbot. New York, Orion Press, 1967. 433 p. Sequel to the preceding, based probably upon an extant Polish translation from French.

3030. Prus, Bolesław.

Prus, Bolesław, *pseud.* (Aleksander Głowacki). Pisma (Works). Edited by Zygmunt Szweykowski. Warszawa, Książka i Wiedza, 1948-1952. 29 v.

———. L'Avant-poste. Translated by Maria Rakowska. 5th ed. Paris, Gallimard, 1930. 301 p. (Collection polonaise, 1)

———. Pharao. Translated by Kurt Harrer. 8th ed. Berlin, Aufbau-Verlag, 1959. 723 p.

———. Der Pharao. Translated by Alfred Loepfe. Olten, Walter Verlag, 1956. 651 p. The first edition by a Swiss, the second by an East-German translator. The success of the novel in Eastern Germany may be ascribed to its subject: a struggle for power in Ancient Egypt.

———. The Pharaoh and the Priest; an Historical Novel of Ancient Egypt. From the original Polish of Alexander Glovatzki by Jeremiah Curtin. Boston, Little, Brown, 1910. 696 p. Front., plates. The English version is hard to read because of the translator's old-fashioned, heavy style.

———. La Poupée. Translated by Simone Deligne, Wenceslas Godlewski, and Michel Marcq. Paris, Del Duca, 1962-1964. 3 v.

———. Die Puppe. Translated by Kurt Harrer. 2d ed. Berlin, Aufbau-Verlag, 1954. 874 p.

———. Sochineniia. Moskva, Gos. izd.-vo khud. lit-ry, 1961– Translation by various hands, which can be recommended to Slavic scholars knowing Russian but not Polish.

3031. Reymont, Władysław Stanisław. The Peasants: Autumn, Winter, Spring, Summer; a Tale of Our Own Times. Translated by Michael H. Dziewicki. New York, A. A. Knopf, 1937. 4 v.

A novel for which the author received a Nobel Prize, though the decision of the Swedish Academy was critiziced in Poland.

3032. Sienkiewicz, Henryk.

Sienkiewicz, Henryk. Dzieła (Works). Edited by Julian Krzyża-

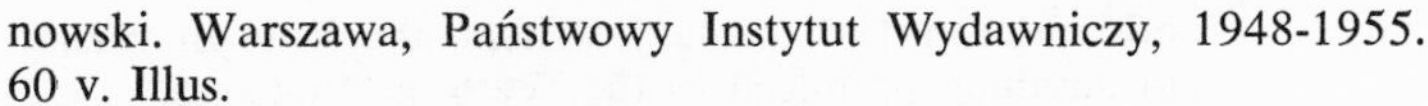

nowski. Warszawa, Państwowy Instytut Wydawniczy, 1948-1955. 60 v. Illus.

———. Quo Vadis? Translated by C. J. Hogarth. London, Dent; New York, Dutton, 1941. 448 p.

———. Tales. Edited by Monica Mary Gardner. London, J. M. Dent, 1946. 332 p.

———. The Teutonic Knights; an Historical Novel. Edinburgh, T. Nelson and Sons, 1943. 728 p.

———. With Fire and Sword. An Historical Novel of Poland and Russia. Translated by Jeremiah Curtin. Boston, Little, Brown, 1898. 779 p. Front., plates, ports.

———. The Deluge. An Historical Novel of Poland, Sweden and Russia. A sequel to "With Fire and Sword." Translated by Jeremiah Curtin. Boston, Little, Brown, 1928. 2 v.

———. Pan Michael. An Historical Novel of Poland, The Ukraine and Turkey. A sequel to "With Fire and Sword" and "The Deluge." Translated by Jeremiah Curtin. London, Dent, 1901. 527 p.

———. Portrait of America; Letters. Edited and translated by Charles Morley. New York, Columbia University Press, 1959. 300 p. Illus. Written in the '70s of the last century during Sienkiewicz's stay in America, mostly in California, these are correspondences sent by him to a Warsaw paper. One of the most balanced and intelligent foreign reports on American mores of the period.

Sienkiewicz's works, particularly *Quo Vadis?*, exist in several German, French, Italian versions. For a general appraisal of Sienkiewicz in English *see*:

Lednicki, Wacław. Henryk Sienkiewicz, a Retrospective Synthesis. 's-Gravenhage, Mouton, 1960. 81 p. Illus. (Slavistic Printings and Reprintings, 28)

The sales of *Quo Vadis?* in France are the subject of Maria Kosko's *Un "Best-Seller" 1900: Quo Vadis?* (Paris, Corti, 1960, 185 p.; bibliography: p. 151-185).

3033. Słowacki, Juliusz.

Słowacki, Juliusz. Dzieła wszystkie (Complete works). Edited by Juliusz Kleiner. Wrocław, Zakład Narodowy im. Ossolińskich, 1952-1960. 14 v.

———. Anhelli. Translated by Dorothea Prall Radin. Edited by George Papall Noyes. London, Allen & Unwin, 1930. 118 p.

———. Le genèse par l'esprit. Translated by St. Dunin Karwicki. Varsovie, J. Mortkowicz, 1926. 55 p. Plates.

———. Izbrannye sochineniia (Selected works). Edited by M. Ryls'kyi. Moskva, Gos. izd.-vo khudozh. lit-ry, 1960. 2 v. Translations by a team of well-known Russian poets, including A. Akhmatova, I. Selvinskii, B. Slutskii, and L. Martynov. As in the case of other Polish 19th century writers, the Russian version is superior to anything produced in the Western languages.

———. Juliusz Słowacki's Mazeppa; a Tragedy. Translated by Cecilia Dolenga Wells and Carlton F. Wells. Ann Harbor, The Alumni Press, 1929. 73 p. Front., port. A prose translation.

———. Mary Stuart; a Romantic Drama. Translated by Arthur Prudden Coleman and Marion Moore Coleman. Schenectady, N.Y., Electric City Press, 1937. 106 p. Translation in verse. Neither *Mazeppa* nor *Mary Stuart* belongs to Słowacki's major works.

Bourilly, Jean. La jeunesse de Jules Słowacki, 1808-1833; la vie et les œuvres. Paris, A. G. Nizet, 1960. 502 p. Plates, ports., facsims. Bibliography: p. 485-497. A thorough scholarly study on Słowacki's intellectual and artistic development. Rich bibliography.

Jules Słowacki (1809-1849). Revue des sciences humaines (Lille), no. 102, Apr./June 1961. A symposium. Studies on Słowacki by French and Polish scholars.

Juliusz Słowacki, 1809-1849; Księga zbiorowa w Stulecie zgonu (Juliusz Słowacki, 1809-1849; a symposium on the centenary of his death). London, The Polish Research Centre, 1951. 448 p. A symposium. Essays mostly in Polish but also in other languages. A valuable publication. Of particular interest is a long study by Claude Backvis, "Słowacki et l'heritage baroque" (p. 27-94), and a pioneering essay by Maryla Falk: "Indian Elements in Słowacki's Thought" (p. 190-231).

Kridl, Manfred, The Lyric Poems of Julius Słowacki. 's-Gravenhage, Mouton, 1958. 77 p. (Musagetes: Contributions to the History of Slavic Literature and Culture, 6) A study on Słowacki's shorter poems by a competent scholar.

3034. Witkiewicz, Stanisław Ignacy. Unersättlichkeit. Roman. Translated by Walter Tiel. München, Piper, 1966. 595 p.

Some data on this playwright, novelist and philosopher (1885-1939) in:

Grabowski, Zbigniew A. S. I. Witkiewicz: a Polish Prophet of Doom. The Polish Review, v. 12, 1967, no. 1: 39-49. A more detailed exposition of Witkiewicz's views and literary techniques can be found in:

Miłosz, Czesław. Stanisław Ignacy Witkiewicz, a Polish Writer for Today. Tri-Quarterly, v. 9, 1967: 143-154.

Witkiewicz's plays are scheduled to be published by the University of Washington Press in 1968.

3035. Wyspiański, Stanisław.

Wyspiański, Stanisław. Dzieła zebrane (Collected works). Edited by Leon Płoszewski. Kraków, Wydawn. Literackie, 1958-1966. 14 v. Plates, ports., facsims.

Backvis, Claude. Le Dramaturge Stanislas Wyspianski, 1869-1907. Paris, Presses universitaires de France, 1952. 387 p. Illus. (Université libre de Bruxelles. Travaux de la Faculté de philosophie et lettres, 14) An excellent study on the initiator of modern Polish theater by a Belgian specialist in the field.

3036. Żeromski, Stefan. Ashes. Translated by Helen Stankiewicz Zand. New York, A. A. Knopf, 1928. 2 v.

One of the author's most significant novels with a setting of the Napoleonic era.

7. Works by Contemporary Authors

3037. Andrzejewski, Jerzy.

Andrzejewski, Jerzy (George Andrzeyevski). Ashes and Diamonds. Translated by D. F. Welsh. London, Weidenfeld and Nicholson, 1962. 238 p. A novel. The Polish original, considered a classic in Poland and running through several editions, was first published in 1948 as *Popiół i diament.*

———. The Gates of Paradise. Translated by James Kirkup. London, Weidenfeld and Nicolson, 1963. 157 p. A short novel on the Children's Crusade in the Middle Ages, a parable on mass movements.

———. The Inquisitors. Translated by Konrad Syrop. New York, Knopf, 1960. 158 p. A short novel on the Spanish Inquisition, in fact a parable on totalitarian terror; the Polish title: *Ciemności kryją ziemię.*

3038. Bochenski, Jacek. Göttlicher Julius. Aufzeichnungen eines Antiquars. Translated by Walter Tiel. München, Ehrenwirth, 1961. 253 p.

Fiction. A ferocious debunking of Julius Caesar, not without allusions to a modern conflict between intellectuals and the Party Establishment.

3039. Borowski, Tadeusz.

Borowski. Tadeusz. This Way for the Gas, Ladies and Gentlemen and Other Stories. Selected and translated by Barbara Vedder. New York, The Viking Press, 1968. 159 p.

———. Le Monde de Pierre. Translated by Erik Veaux. Paris, Calmann-Levy, 1964. 322 p.

———. Die steinerne Welt. Translated by Vera Cerny. München, Piper Verlag, 1959. 277 p. Short stories of a writer whose life was short (1922-1951) but who left one of the most valid testimonies on the inhuman Europe of the Second World War and Nazi concentration camps.

3040. Brandys, Kazimierz. Sons and Comrades. Translated by D. J. Welsh. New York, Grove Press, 1961. 127 p.

Translation of a short novel on the "errors and deviations" of the Stalinist era, first published in 1957. The Polish title: *Matka Królów.*

3041. Breza, Tadeusz. Das eherne Tor; römische Aufzeichnungen. Translated by Peter Lachmann. Berlin, Luchterhand, 196—. 610 p.

A much-discussed book on the structure and policy of the Vatican, combining essay, diary, and fictionalized scenes by a sophisticated writer who served for a few years on the diplomatic staff of the Polish Embassy in Rome.

3042. Gombrowicz, Witold.

Gombrowicz, Witold. Ferdydurke. Translated by Eric Mosbacher. New York, Harcourt, Brace & World, 1961. 272 p. 2d ed., New York, Grove Press, 1967. 272 p.

———. Indizien. Translated by Walter Tiel. Pfullingen, Neske, 1966. 186 p.

———. Pornographia. Translated by Alastair Hamilton. New York, Grove Press, 1967. 191 p.

———. Trans-Atlantic. Translated by Walter Tiel. Pfullingen, Neske, 1964. 158 p.

Philosophical novels of an internationally famous Polish writer, laureate of the "Prix Fomentor," 1967.

3043. Herbert, Zbigniew. Selected Poems. Translated by Czesław Miłosz and Peter Dale Scott. London, Penguin Books, 1968. 139 p.

Issued as one of the series "Penguin Modern European Poets," with an introduction by A. Alvarez, this is a translation of one of the leading Polish postwar poets. For a good German translation, see *Gedichte aus zehn Jahren 1956-1966*, translated by Karl Dedecius (Frankfurt am Main, Suhrkamp Verlag, 1967, 194 p.

3044. Herling, Gustaw. The Island; Three Tales. Translated by Ronald Strom. Cleveland, World Publishing Co., 1967. 151 p.

"The Island," "The Tower," "The Second Coming"—stories by an émigré fiction writer and literary critic, author of a high level report on his stay in a forced labor camp in the Soviet Union, *A World Apart*, translated by Joseph Marek (New York, Roy Publishers, 1951, 262 p., illus.).

3045. Hłasko, Marek.

Hłasko, Marek. The Eighth Day of the Week. Translated by Norbert Guterman. New York, Dutton, 1958. 128 p.

———. The Graveyard. Translated by Norbert Guterman. New York, Dutton, 1959. 126 p.

———. Next Stop—Paradise. Translated by Norbert Guterman. New York, Dutton, 1960. 250 p.

Works by an author who, in 1956-1958, personified the revolt of the young generation in Poland against official literature.

3046. Iwaszkiewicz, Jarosław.

Iwaszkiewicz, Jarosław. Der Höhenflug. Translated by Kurt Harrer. Frankfurt am Main, Suhrkamp Verlag, 1964. 109 p.

———. Der Kongress in Florenz; Die Mädchen vom Wilkohof. 2 Erzählungen. Translated by Kurt Harrer. Leipzig, Ph. Reclam, 1959. 213 p. The author (b. 1894) is valued primarily as a poet of the "Skamander" group but his narratives in prose are highly regarded as well and these two are among his best.

———. Die Liebenden von Marona. Translated by Klaus Dietrich Staemmler. München, Langen/Müller, 1962. 336 p. A collection of stories.

———. Mère Jeanne des Anges. Roman. Translated by Georges Lisowski. Paris, R. Laffont, 1959. 207 p. The subject of this short novel is taken from chronicles of the 17th century, those that inspired Aldous Huxley's *Devils of Loudun.*

3047. Konwicki, Tadeusz. Modernes Traumbuch. Roman. Translated by Peter Lachmann. München, Biederstein, 1964. 364 p.

One of the most sensational postwar Polish novels, because of its technique and its political key, translated by a bilingual, Polish-German poet.

3048. Kott, Jan. Shakespeare, Our Contemporary. Translated by Bolesław Taborski. Garden City, New York, Doubleday, 1964. 241 p.

A book of essays by a Polish theater critic and professor which in fact survey the theatrical interpretation of Shakespeare plays in Poland in the late '50s and early '60s.

3049. Kuncewiczowa, Maria.

Kuncewiczowa, Maria. The Forester. Translated by H. C. Stevens. London, Hutchinson, 1954. 207 p.

———. The Stranger. Translated by Bernard W. A. Massey. London, Hutchinson International Authors, 1945. 172 p.

Novels by a writer considered a representative of "psychological fiction."

3050. Lec, Stanisław J. Unkempt Thoughts. Translated by Jacek Galazka. Introduction by Clifton Fadiman. New York, St. Martin's Press, 1962. 160 p. Illus.

Aphorisms by one of the leading Polish satirical writers, who reached his peak of creativity in the decade 1956-1966.

3051. Mackiewicz, Józef. Road to Nowhere. Translated by Lew Sapieha. London, Collins and Harvill Press, 1963; Chicago, H. Regnery, 1964. 381 p.

A realistic novel on 1940 in Lithuania by a noted émigré author.

3052. Miłosz, Czesław.

Miłosz, Czesław. Lied vom Weltende. Gedichte. Translated and edited by Karl Dedecius. Köln, Kiepenheuer und Witsch, 1966. 80 p.

———. Native Realm; a Search for Self-Definition. Garden City, N. Y., Doubleday, 1968. 300 p.

———. Une autre Europe. Translated by Georges Sédir. Paris, Gallimard, 1964. An autobiographical essay, first published in Polish as *Rodzinna Europa* (Paryż, Instytut Literacki, 1959, 246 p.).

———. Sur les bords de l'Issa, roman. Translated by Jeanne Hersch. Paris, Gallimard, 1956. 330 p. A version of a novel published in Polish as *Dolina Issy* (Paryż, Instytut Literacki, 1955, 196 p.; 2d ed., Londyn, Oficyna Poetów i Malarzy, 1967, 263 p., illus.).

3053. Mrożek, Sławomir.

Mrożek, Sławomir. The Elephant. Translated by Konrad Syrop. New York, Grove Press, 1965. 176 p. Short stories by a popular Polish satirical writer.

———. Six plays. Translated by Nicholas Bethell. New York, Grove Press, 1967. 190 p. Six short plays in the vein of the theater of the absurd.

3054. Różewicz, Tadeusz. Formen der Unruhe, Gedichte. Translated and edited by Karl Dedecius. München, Hanser, 1965. 110 p.

Selected poems of a "poet of inhumanity" (b. 1921) in a very good translation.

3055. Rudnicki, Adolf.

Rudnicki, Adolf. Ascent to Heaven. Translated by H. C. Stevens. London, D. Dobson, 1951. 204 p. Illus.

———. The Dead and the Living Sea and Other Stories. Translated by Jadwiga Zwolska. Warsaw, Polonia Pub. House, 1957. 419 p.

Narratives of a noted prose writer whose work is centered on the tragedy of the Polish Jews during the period 1939-1945.

3056. Schulz, Bruno. The Street of Crocodiles. Translated by Celina Wieniewska. New York, Walker, 1963. 159 p.

Stories of an important prose writer (1892-1942). There are several editions in German.

3057. Wieniewska, Celina, *ed.* Polish Writing Today. London, Penguin Books, 1967. 208 p.

An anthology of prose and poetry. Translations by various hands. Authors who do not live in Poland are excluded.

3058. Wierzyński, Kazimierz. Selected Poems. Edited by Clark Mills and Ludwik Krzyżanowski. New York, Voyages Press, 1959. 45 p. Port.

Translations by various hands, on a good level, from the work of an eminent poet of the "Skamander" group.

3059. Wittlin, Józef. Salt of the Earth. Translated by Pauline de Chary. London, Methuen, 1940. 271 p.

A pacifist novel about a soldier in the First World War, originally intended as the first part of a cycle: *The Patient Infantryman.*

8. Folklore

3060. Glinkin, P., *comp.* Pol'skie narodnye legendy i skazki (Polish folk legends and tales). Leningrad, Khudozhestvennaia literatura, 1965. 381 p. Bibliography: p. 376.

A collection of fairy tales, popular edition without any scholarly notes.

3061. Hernas, Czesław. W kalinowym lesie (Title untranslatable). Warszawa, Państwowy Instytut Wydawniczy, 1965. 2 v. Illus.

The first volume consists of a study on sources for investigation of Polish folklore; the second is an anthology of songs taken from collections of the 17th century.

3062. Kolberg, Oskar. Dzieła wszystkie (Complete works). Edited by Julian Krzyżanowski. Kraków, Polskie Wydawn. Muzyczne, 1961–

This is a new edition of a monumental collection of Polish folklore first published as:

Kolberg, Oskar. Lud, jego zwyczaje, sposób życia, mowa, podania, przysłowia, obrzędy, gusła, zabawy, pieśni, muzyka i tańce (The people, their customs, style of life, speech, legends, proverbs, rites, witchcraft, games, songs, music and dances). Warszawa, W druk. Jana Jaworskiego, 1867-1890. 30 v.

In songs, both music and words are given. The work has remained unsurpassed, as the collector had an access to oral tradition which exists no more. The volumes of the new edition do not appear in numerical order.

3063. Krzyżanowski, Julian, *ed.* Polska bajka ludowa w układzie systematycznym (Polish folk tales in a systematic arrangement). Warszawa, Nakł. Tow. Naukowego Warszawskiego. 1947. 2 v. Bibliographies.

Tales about animals, fairy tales, an index of motifs, applying the Aarne-Thompson system; Polish and foreign variants.

3064. Krzyżanowski, Julian, *ea.* Słownik folkloru polskiego (A dictionary of Polish folklore). Warszawa, Wiedza Powszechna, 1965. 487 p. Illus., facsims., ports., bibliographies.

A work by a team of Polish scholars, directed by Professor Krzyżanowski. Rich information on wandering literary motifs and writers who belong to folklore rather than to literature.

C. HISTORY OF THOUGHT, CULTURE, AND SCHOLARSHIP

by George Krzywicki-Herburt

1. General History of Culture and Scholarship

3065. Brückner. Aleksander. Tysiąc lat kultury polskiej (A thousand years of Polish culture). 3d ed. Paryż, Księgarnia Polska, 1955. 2 v. Illus.

The Paris edition of this classic work contains additional bibliographies and chronological tables forthe period 1914-1939. There is another recent edition, also described as the third one, which retains the original title but does not include the last volume of the second edition: *Dzieje kultury polskiej* (History of Polish culture) (Warszawa, Książka i Wiedza, 1957-1958, 3 v.).

No more recent synthesis of comparable scope is available. For a survey of the field from a Marxist methodological perspective *see* the relevant chapters in *Historia Polski* (History of Poland), published under the auspices of the Polish Academy of Science and the General editorship of T. Manteuffel (Warszawa, Państwowe Wydawn. Naukowe, 1957-1963. Illus., ports., maps, tables, bibliographies). A general survey of the history of various aspects of Polish culture can also be found in *Polska* (Poland), which is a separately published part of the ninth volume of *Wielka encyklopedia powszechna* PWN (Warszawa, Państwowe Wydawn. Naukowe, 1967, illus., maps, tables).

3066. Dyboski, Roman. Poland in World Civilization. Edited by Ludwik Krzyżanowski. New York, J. M. Barrett, 1950. 285 p. Port., map. Bibliography: p. 259-263.

See also entry no. 2619.

A useful, topically arranged survey.

3067. Lednicki, Wacław. Life and Culture of Poland as Reflected in Polish Literature. New York, Roy Publishers, 1944. 328 p. Bibliography: p. 317-319.

See also entry no. 2977.

Lectures given at the Lowell Institute in 1943 by a prominent scholar in the field of Slavonic studies.

3068. Zjazd Naukowy imienia Jana Kochanowskiego, *Kraków, 1930*. Kultura staropolska (Culture of the Old Poland). Kraków. Skł. gł. w Księg Gebethnera i Wolffa, 1932. 752 p. Bibliographies.

A collection of learned studies of all aspects of the Polish culture in the 16th century by a group of the most prominent Polish scholars of the interwar period, published under the auspices of Polska Akademia Umiejętności. May be usefully supplemented by *Renesans i humanizm w Polsce* (Renaissance and humanism in Poland) by

* The arrangement within the following sections combines topical and chronological criteria, general treatments and works on all or several periods preceding those which deal with more specific topics. Because of unavoidable overlapping all three sections should be consulted.

Stanisław Łempicki 2d ed. with an introduction by Kazimierz Budzyk; Warszawa, Czytelnik, 1952, 474 p.).

3069. Polska Akadamia Nauk. Odrodzenie w Polsce. Materiały Sesji Naukowej PAN 25-30 paźdz. 1953 (Renaissance in Poland. Materials of the scholarly session of the Polish Academy of Sciences, October 25-30, 1953). Warszawa, Państwowy Instytut Wydawniczy, 1955-1958. 5 v.

A collection of studies on various aspects of the Polish Renaissance, and a revision of earlier interpretations in the light of Marxist methodology. For information about numerous other new studies of the period see *Bibliografia literatury polskiej. Piśmiennictwo staropolskie* (Old Polish literature) by Roman Pollak (Warszawa, Państwowy Instytut Wydawn., 1963-1965, 3 v.; Instytut Badań Literackich Polskiej Akademii Nauk. Bibliografia literatury polskiej "Nowy Korbut" 1-3). *See also* the annual published by the Institute of History of the Polish Academy of Sciences: *Odrodzenie i Reformacja w Polsce* (Renaissance and Reformation in Poland) (Warszawa, 1956–).

3070. Morawski, Kazimierz. Histoire de l'Université de Cracovie; Moyen âge et renaissance. Paris, A. Picard et fils, 1900-1905. 3 v.

French translation (by P. Rongier) of the same author's *Historia Uniwersytetu Jagiellońskiego* (History of the Jagellonian University) (Kraków, Uniwersytet Jagielloński, 1900, 2 v.). A rich source of information about the early history of the oldest Polish university. *See also* Henryk Barycz's *Alma Mater Jagellonica* (Kraków, Wydawn. Literackie, 1958. 411 p., illus., facsims., ports.) and Kazimierz Lepszy's *Jagiellonian University of Cracow; Past, Present and Future* (Kraków, Jagiellonian University Press, 1964, 63 p., illus., facsims., ports.).

3071. Smoleński, Władysław. Przewrót umysłowy w Polsce wieku XVIII; studja historyczne (The intellectual upheaval in eighteenth-century Poland; historical studies). 2d enl. ed. Warszawa, Ministerstwo Wyznań Religijnych i Oświecenia Publicznego, 1923. 448 p. Illus., ports.

See also entry no. 2649.

Although published for the first time in 1891 (424 p.), this is still one of the best studies of the Polish Enlightenment. Another edition: 1949, 382 p. A general view of the period is provided in Bogdan Suchodolski's *Les conditions sociales du progrès scientifique en Pologne au XVIIIe siècle* (Paris, Éditions du Palais de la découverte, 1960, 26 p. Les Conférences du Palais de la découverte. Ser. D: Histoire des sciences, no. 73).

3072. Kongres Nauki Polskiej. *1st, Warsaw, 1951.* Kołłataj i Wiek Oświecenia (Kołłątaj and the age of enlightenment). Warszawa, Czytelnik, 1951. 291 p. Illus.. ports.

Proceedings of a scholarly meeting devoted to a Marxist reappraisal of the Polish Enlightenment. Six papers and discussion.

3073. Fabre, Jean. Stanislas-Auguste Poniatowski et l'Europe des lumières. Paris, Institut d'études slaves, 1952. 746 p. (Collection historique de l'Institut d'études slaves, 16) Bibliographic references included in "Notes": p. 685-695.

See also entry no. 2632.

Although primarily concerned with the person of the last king of Poland, the book provides a very good picture of the intellectual and artistic currents in 18th century Poland. May be supplemented by the same author's "La propagande des idées philosophiques en Pologne sous Stanislas-Auguste et l'école Varsovienne des Cadets," *Revue de litterature comparée*, v. 15, 1935, p. 643-693.

3074. Wiek XIX. Sto lat myśli polskiej (The 19th century. A hundred years of Polish thought). Edited by Ignacy Chrzanowski and others. Warszawa, Nakł. Gebethnera i Wolffa, 1906-1918. 9 v. Bibliographies.

A monumental anthology presenting biographies and studies of the most important 19th century writers, philosophers and social thinkers, as well as substantial selections from their works.

3075. Kott, Jan. *ed.* Kultura okresu pozytywizmu (Culture of the period of Positivism). Warszawa, Książka i Wiedza, 1949-1950. 3 v.

A topically arranged collection of texts and analytic commentaries dealing with the so-called "positivist" period, i.e., after 1863. Sponsored by Polska Akademia Nauk, Instytut Badań Literackich.

Two earlier general studies of the period are still useful: *Pozytywizm polski* (Polish Positivism) by Aureli Drogoszewski, 2d ed. (Lwów, Zakład Narodowy im. Ossolińskich, 1934, 68 p.) and *Przewrót w umysłowości i literaturze polskiej po roku 1863* (Transformation in Polish thought and literature after 1863) by Konstanty Wojciechowski (Lwów, Książnica-Atlas, 1928, 294 p.).

3076. Pologne 1919-1939. v. 3: Vie intellectuelle et artistique. Neuchâtel, Éditions de la Baconnière, 1947. 784 p.

The third volume of this encyclopedic publication, edited by a committee under the chairmanship of Jan Modzelewski, contains articles on literature, sciences, humanities, arts, and other aspects of cultural life during the interwar period. Of particular interest is the article "La Philosophie" (p. 229-260) by I. M. Bocheński.

3077. Polska Akademia Umiejętności, *Kraków*. Historia nauki polskiej w monografiach (History of Polish scholarship in a series of monographs). Kraków, 1948-1952. 34 v.

This series of slim volumes, written by a group of prominent scholars, covers almost all aspects of scholarship: mathematics, natural sciences, social sciences, and humanities. May be supplemented by *Histoire sommaire des sciences en Pologne* (Cracovie, Druk.

Narodowa, 1933, 154 p. and by a brief general survey provided by Stanisław Kot in his *Five Centuries of Polish Learning* (2d ed., Oxford, The Shakespeare Head Press, 1944, 48 p.).

3078. Studia i materiały z dziejów nauki polskiej (Studies and materials on the history of Polish science). Warszawa, Państwowe Wydawn. Naukowe, 1953– Ports.

An important serial publication sponsored by Zakład Historii Nauki, Polska Akademia Nauk. Tables of contents and summaries also in English and in Russian. Appears in series A-E: A, History of the social sciences; B, History of the biological and medical sciences; C, History of mathematical, physicochemical and geological sciences; D, History of technology and technological sciences; E, General problems.

3079. Hartmann, Karl. Hochschulwesen und Wissenschaft in Polen. Entwicklung, Organisation und Stand 1918-1960. Frankfurt am Main, Metzner, 1962. 606 p. Maps. Bibliography: p. 544-561.

See also entry no. 3194.

A useful compilation of information on the organization of science, institutions of higher learning, libraries, and scholarly societies. Includes a historical introduction and Polish legislation. For information about the activities of the Polish Academy of Sciences, the central scholarly and research institution, see *The Review of the Polish Academy of Sciences* (Warsaw, 1956–), a quarterly which is the English version of *Nauka polska* (Polish science), and *Bulletin de l'Académie polonaise des sciences*, which appears in four series: biological sciences; mathematical, physical and astronomical sciences; chemical, geological, and geographical sciences; and technical sciences.

3080. Galiński, Tadeusz, *ed.* Kultura Polski Ludowej (The culture of People's Poland). Warszawa, Państwowe Wydawn. Ekonomiczne, 1966. 441 p. Illus., facsims.. fold. col. map.

See also entry no. 3193.

A symposium by 23 authors dealing with all major aspects of culture in contemporary Poland.

2. Philosophy

3081. Polska Akademia Nauk. *Komitet Filozoficzny.* Bibliografia filozofii polskiej (Bibliography of Polish philosophy). Edited by Alicja Kadler and others. Warszawa, Państwowe Wydawn. Naukowe, 1955–

A planned bibliography of the entire history of Polish philosophy. Published to date: volume 1, 1750-1830; volume 2, 1831-1864. An indispensable research tool. Publications on the borderlines of philosophy are also recorded, and so the work may be of interest not only to philosophers. For the interwar period *see* Kazimierz Orthwein and Maria Różycka's "Bibliograficzny obraz polskich publikacji filozoficznych w latach międzywojennych" (A bibliography of the Polish philosophical publications between the Wars) in *Kultura i Społeczeństwo* (Culture and society), v. 1, 1957: 192-204. Current bibliographies appear in the quarterly *Ruch filozoficzny* (Philosophical movement) (1911-1914; 1918-1939; 1948-1950; 1958–).

3082. Tatarkiewicz, Władysław. Zarys dziejów filozofii w Polsce (An outline of the history of philosophy in Poland). Kraków, Polska Akademia Umiejętności; skł. gł. w księgarniach Gebethnera i Wolffa, 1948. 36 p. (Polska Akademia Umiejętności. Historia nauki polskiej w monografiach, 32)

A concise account from the beginnings until the Second World War, written by the most eminent living Polish historian of philosophy. The same author's *Historia filozofii* (History of philosophy) (5th ed., Warszawa, Państwowe Wydawn. Naukowe, 1958, 3 v., ports.) covers in respective chapters the same material but provides also rich bibliographies.

3083. Krzywicki-Herburt, George. Polish Philosophy. *In*: Edwards, Paul, *ed.* The Encyclopedia of Philosophy. v. 6. New York, Macmillan, 1967. p. 363-370.

A survey of the history of philosophy in Poland from the 13th century till 1965. The same encyclopedia contains also the following articles on Polish thinkers: "Copernicus," by Norwood R. Hanson (v. 2, p. 219-222); "Leon Chwistek," by Henry Hiż (v. 2, p. 112-113); "Kazimierz Ajdukiewicz," by Zbigniew A. Jordan (v. 1, p. 62-63); "Tadeusz Kotarbiński," by Zbigniew A. Jordan (v. 4, p. 361-363); "Kazimierz Twardowski," by George Krzywicki-Herburt (v. 8, p. 166-167); "Stanisław Leśniewski," by Czesław Lejewski (v. 4, p. 441-443); "Jan Łukasiewicz," by Czesław Lejewski (v. 5, p. 104-107); "Alfred Tarski," by Andrzej Mostowski (v. 8, p. 77-81); "Polish Logicians," by Arthur N. Prior (v. 4, p. 566-568); and "Roman Ingarden," by Henryk Skolimowski (v. 4, p. 193-195).

3084. Filozofia polska (Polish philosophy). Warszawa, Wiedza Powszechna, 1967. 474 p.

A collection of 20 studies, by various authors, on the most important thinkers and trends in the history of Polish philosophy from the second half of the 14th century until the second half of the 19th.

3085. Wąsik, Wiktor. Historia filozofii polskiej (History of Polish philosophy). Warszawa, Pax, 1958-1966. 2 v. Bibliographies.

The first volume covers Scholasticism, Renaissance and Enlightenment, the second — philosophy of the romantic period, ending with Cieszkowski. Although unfinished and in part made obsolete by newer historical research (especially on the medieval period), this is still the only recent attempt to provide a book-length picture of the several centuries of development of Polish philosophy.

3086. Kotarbiński, Tadeusz. La logique en Pologne; son originalité et les influences étrangères. Roma, A. Signorelli, 1959. 24 p. (Accademia polacca di scienze e lettere. Biblioteca di Roma. Conferenze, fascicolo 7)

A brief history of logic in Poland with emphasis on more recent periods. May be supplemented by the same author's "La logique en Pologne" in *Philosophy in the Mid-Century*, edited by Raymond Klibansky for the International Institute of Philosophy, v. 1 (Firenze, Nuova Italia, 1958) p. 45-52. *See also* the chapter "Logika w Polsce" (Logic in Poland) in *Elementy logiki formalnej* (Elements of formal logic) by Henryk Greniewski (Warszawa. Państwowe Wydawn. Naukowe, 1955), p. 432-449.

3087. Polska Akademia Umiejętności. *Komisja do Badania Historii Filozofii w Polsce.* Archiwum (Archives of the Committee for Research on the History of Philosophy in Poland). Kraków, Polska Akademia Umiejętności, skł. gł. w księg. Gebethnera i Wolffa, 1917-1937. 6 v.

Materials, texts, and several important historical studies.

3088. Archiwum historii filozofii i myśli społecznej (Archives of the history of philosophy and social thought). Warszawa, Państwowe Wydawn. Naukowe, 1957– Irregular.

Sponsored by the Institute of Philosophy and Sociology of the Polish Academy of Sciences. Texts, materials, historical studies. Although not limited to the history of Polish philosophy, most of the published volumes contain works devoted to that subject, e.g., in volume 2: Tadeusz Kroński's "Koncepcje filozoficzne Mesjanistów polskich" (Philosophical conceptions of Polish Messianists).

3089. Polska Akademia Nauk. *Instytut Filozofii i Socjologii.* Mediaevalia Philosophica Polonorum. Bulletin d'information concernant les recherches sur la philosophie médiévale en Pologne. Editor-in-chief: Władysław Seńko. 1958– Warszawa.

Multilingual. Other important sources of information about the research on the history of medieval philosophy in Poland include: *Studia i Materiały Zakładu Historii Filozofii Starożytnej i Średniowiecznej* (Studies and materials of the Institute for the History of Ancient and Medieval Philosophy) and *Studia Mediewistyczne* (Mediaeval studies). Both periodicals are sponsored by the Polish Academy of Sciences. See also *Z dziejów filozofii na Uniwersytecie Krakowskim w XV wieku* (From the history of philosophy at the University of Cracow in the 15th century), edited by Z. Kuksewicz (Warszawa, Zakład Narodowy im. Ossolińskich, 1965; 205 p.).

3090. Suchodolski, Bogdan. Studia z dziejów polskiej myśli filozoficznej i naukowej (Studies in the history of Polish philosophical and scientific thought). Wrocław, Zakład Narodowy im. Ossolińskich, 1958. 492 p. Illus. Bibliography. (Monografie z dziejów nauki i techniki, 8)

Essays on Polish philosophy (mostly social philosophy) from the renaissance to the beginning of the 19th century.

3091. Hinz, Henryk, and Adam Sikora, *eds.* Polska myśl filozoficzna. Oświecenie. Romantyzm (Polish philosophical thought. Enlightenment. Romanticism). Warszawa, Państwowe Wydawn. Naukowe, 1964. 497 p. Illus., facsims., ports.

An anthology of writings of major philosophers of the late 18th century and the first half of the 19th century, preceded by introductory essays. The period up to 1831 may be supplemented by an earlier but still useful work: *Dzieje filozoficznej myśli polskiej w okresie porozbiorowym* (History of Polish philosophical thought in the postpartition period) by Maurycy Straszewski (Kraków, Wydawn. koła filozoficznego uczniów Uniwersytetu Jagiellońskiego, 1912, 511 p.). See also Anna Śladkowska's *Poglądy filozoficzne i społeczne Edwarda Dembowskiego* (Philosophical and social views of Edward Dembowski) (Warszawa, Książka i Wiedza, 1955, 295 p.), and "Polish Theories of Art between 1830 and 1850" by Stefan Morawski, in *Journal of Aesthetics and Art Criticism*, v. 16, 1952: 217-236.

3092. Straszewski, Maurycy, *ed.* Polska filozofia narodowa (Polish national philosophy). Kraków, Gebethner, 1921. 502 p.

Essays by various authors on most major philosophers of the first half of the 19th century. There are monographic works devoted to some of the thinkers considered in this volume, e.g.: *Graf A. Cieszkowski's Philosophie der Tat. Die Grundzüge seiner Lehre und der Aufbau seines Systems* by Adam Zółtowski (Posen, Leitgeber, 1904, 203 p.). This is still one of the best general works on Cieszkowski. *See also* Walter Kuehne's *Graf A. Cieszkowski, ein Schueler Hegels und des deutschen Geistes* (Berlin-Liepzig, O. Harrassowitz, 1938, 454 p.).

For literature concerning Hoene Wroński, see *Wroński i o Wrońskim* (Wroński and on Wroński) by Bolesław J. Gawecki (Warszawa, Państwowe Wydawn. Naukowe, 1958, 161 p.).

3093. Kuehne, Walter. Die Polen und die Philosophie Hegels. *In* Tschiževskij, Dmitrij, *ed.* Hegel bei den Slaven. Bad Homburg, Gentner, 1961. 2d ed. p. 7-143.

A survey of most Polish Hegelians. May be supplemented by "Die ersten Einflüsse Hegels in der polnischen Zeitschriftenliteratur" by Henryk Bar, *Germanoslavica* (Prag), no. 1, 1931: 76-82); and "La gauche et la droite hégeliennes en Pologne dans la première moitié du XIX siècle" by Bronisław Baczko, *Annali dell'Istituto Giangiacomo Feltrinelli*, v. 6, 1963: 147-149.

3094. Tatarkiewicz, Władysław, *ed.* Pięćdziesiąt lat filozofii w Polsce (Fifty years of philosophy in Poland). Warszawa, 1948. A special issue of *Przegląd filozoficzny*, v. 44, no. 1/3.

A series of articles on the development of philosophy in Poland, in various centers, between 1898 and 1948. May be supplemented by descriptions of the state of Polish philosophy during the interwar period by two of its most prominent representatives: "Der logistische Anti-Irrationalismus in Polen," by Kazimierz Ajdukiewicz, *Erkennt-*

nis, v. 5, 1955: 151-161; and "Grundlinien und Tendenzen der Philosophie in Polen," by Tadeusz Kotarbiński, *Slavische Rundschau*, v. 5, 1933: 218-229.

3095. Jordan, Zbigniew A. Philosophy and Ideology; the Development of Philosophy and Marxism-Leninism in Poland since the Second World War. Dordrecht, Holland, D. Reidel, 1963. 600 p. Bibliography: p. 538-590.

A detailed and thorough examination of the main developments in Polish philosophy up to 1958, preceded by a concise but highly informative history of Polish philosophy since the beginning of the twentieth century. The problems discussed range from logic and epistemology to the basic theoretical and methodological issues in the social sciences. May be supplemented by "The Philosophical Background of Revisionism in Poland," by the same author, *East Europe*, v. 11, no. 6, June 1962: 11-17, 26-29; v. 11, no. 7, July 1962: 14-23. It is also reprinted in *Political Thought since World War II*, edited by Władysław Stankiewicz (New York, Free Press-Collier- Macmillan, 1964), p. 250-288.

3096. Kotarbiński, Tadeusz. La philosophie dans la Pologne contemporaine. *In* International Institute of Philosophy. Philosophy in the Mid-Century. Edited by Raymond Klibansky. Firenze, 1959. v. 4, p. 224-235.

An outline of the development of Polish philosophy after the Second World War by the most influential Polish thinker of the period. A concise account of the postwar period in English is provided by J. H., "Philosophy in Poland," *East Europe*, v. 9, no. 6, June 1960: 14-16, 49; v. 9, no. 7, July 1960: 29-35. A series of articles under the general title "Filozofia polska w dwudziestoleciu" (Polish philosophy during the past 20 years) appeared in *Studia filozoficzne* Philosophical studies, 1964, no. 3 (38), p. 3-39.

3097. McCall, Storrs. *ed.* Polish Logic, 1920-1939; Papers by Ajdukiewicz and Others. Oxford, Clarendon Press, 1967. 406 p. Bibliography: p. 398-406.

Selections from works of the most outstanding Polish logicians of this century. Introduction by Tadeusz Kotarbiński. Includes a history of mathematical logic in Poland between the two wars by Zbigniew A. Jordan, reprinted from his earlier book, *The Development of Mathematical Logic and of Logical Positivism in Poland between the Two Wars* (London-New York-Toronto, Oxford University Press, 1945, 47 p.; Polish Science and Learning, no. 6).

3098. Skolimowski, Henryk. Polish Analytical Philosophy; a Survey and a Comparison with British Analytical Philosophy. London, Routledge & Kegan Paul; New York, Humanities Press, 1967. 275 p. Tables, diagrs. Bibliography: p. 262-265.

A comparison of contemporary Polish philosophy, including some recent forms of Marxism, with the analytic tradition in British philosophy.

3099. Studia filozoficzne (Philosophical studies). Warszawa, Państwowe Wydawn. Naukowe. Bimonthly, 1957-1962; Quarterly, 1962–

The most important contemporary philosophical periodical in Poland. Historical and systematic contributions, reviews, chronicles. Summaries in English and in Russian. Some other important periodicals; *Przegląd filozoficzny* (Philosophical review) (Warszawa, 1897-1939, 1946-1949); *Kwartalnik filozoficzny* (Philosophical quarterly) (Kraków, 1922-1939, 1946-1950); *Studia philosophica* (Leopoli, 4 v.: 1935-1937, 1948, 1949-1950); *Studia logica* (Warszawa, 1953–). The last two are multilingual.

3. Social and Political Thought*

3100. Kridl, Manfred, Władysław Malinowski, *and* Józef Wittlin, *eds.* For Your Freedom and Ours: Polish Progressive Spirit through the Centuries. Translated by Ludwik Krzyżanowski. New York, Frederic Ungar, 1943. 359 p.

See also entry no. 2622.

An anthology of Polish democratic thought with short biographies of the most important writers. The Polish version of the same work contains somewhat more material: *Polska myśl demokratyczna w ciągu wieków* (Polish democratic thought through the centuries) (New York, Polish "Labor Group," 1945, 423 p.).

3101. Suchodolski, Bogdan. Polskie tradycje demokratyczne . . . (Polish democratic traditions . . .). Wrocław, M. Arct, 1946. 181 p. (Książki dla wszystkich, seria humanistyczna: Naczelne idee Polski, c. 7)

A series of profiles of social and political thinkers from the 18th to the 20th centuries. Two older anthologies, edited by the same author, provide much illustrative material, particularly for more recent periods: *Ideały kultury a prądy społeczne* (Cultural ideals and social movements) (Warszawa, Nasza Księgarnia, 1933, 519 p., ports.), and *Kultura i osobowość* (Culture and personality) (Warszawa, Nasza Księgarnia, 1935).

3102. Z dziejów polskiej myśli filozoficznej i społecznej (From the history of Polish philosophical and social thought). Warszawa, Książka i Wiedza, 1956-1957. 3 v. Illus., ports.

Volume 1, edited by Leszek Kołakowski, covers the 15th to the 17th centuries; volume 2, edited by Bogdan Suchodolski, the 18th century; and volume 3, edited by Bronisław Baczko and Nina Assorodobraj, the 19th century. Each volume contains several studies

* With a few exceptions this section is limited to general survey works. For the recent period, which would require a separate bibliography of its own, the reader should consult also the sections on History and Politics.

on the periods indicated. The work reflects the Marxist methodological outlook of around 1955.

3103. Rose, William J. The Rise of Polish Democracy. London, G. Bell & Sons, 1944. 253 p. Illus., map.

See also entry no. 2665.

A popular, and sometimes incomplete and rather superficial survey of the history of political thought with emphasis on the 19th and 20th centuries up to the outbreak of the Second World War.

3104. Jabłoński, Henryk. U źródeł teraźniejszości (At the sources of the contemporary world). Warszawa, Wiedza, 1947. 158 p.

Essays on various aspects of Polish political thought from the end of the 18th to the 20th centuries.

3105. Feldman, Wilhelm. Geschichte der politischen Ideen in Polen seit dessen Teilungen (1795-1914). München, Berlin, R. Oldenbourg, 1917. 448 p.

See also entry no. 2659.

An earlier but still useful account. The Polish version is *Dzieje polskiej myśli politycznej w okresie porozbiorowym* (Kraków, "Książka," 1913-1920, 3 v.) and the second edition, *Dzieje polskiej myśli politycznej, 1864-1914* (History of Polish political thought, 1864-1914) (Warszawa, Instytut Badania Najnowszej Historji Polski, 1933, 387 p.).

3106. Lipiński, Edward. Studia nad historią polskiej myśli ekonomicznej (Studies in the history of Polish economic thought). Warszawa, Państwowe Wydawn. Naukowe, 1956. 536 p. Bibliography: p. 517-528.

See also *De Copernic à Stanislas Leszczynski. La pensée économique et démographique en Pologne* (Paris, Presses universitaires de France, 1961, 342 p.; bibliography: p. 317-337).

3107. Belch, Stanislaus F. Paulus Vladimiri and His Doctrine Concerning International Law and Politics. The Hague, Mouton, 1965. 2 v. Illus. Bibliography: v. 2, p. 1203-1237.

See also entry no. 3119.

A monumental monography on the thought of an important early political thinker. The second part of the work contains a critical, scholarly edition of his most important works. Another recent publication devoted to Paulus Vladimiri is *Paweł Włodkowic i Stanisław ze Skarbimierza*, by Ludwik Ehrlich (Warszawa, Państwowe Wydawn. Naukowe, 1954, 237 p., illus., bibliography).

3108. Tarnowski, Stanisław. Pisarze polityczni XVI wieku (Political writers of the 16th century). Kraków, 1886. 2 v.

Although old, this is still the only extensive study of this entire period in the history of Polish political thought. There are many recent studies devoted to particular writers, especially to Andrzej Frycz Modrzewski, e.g.: *Frycza Modrzewskiego nauka o państwie i prawie* (Frycz Modrzewski's theory of state and law) by Waldemar Voisé (Warszawa, Książka i Wiedza, 1956, 365 p., plates; Polska Akademia Nauk. Komitet Nauk Prawnych. Studia nad historią państwa i prawa. Seria 2, tom 3). *See also* Pierre Mesnard's *L'essor de la philosophie politique au XVIe siècle* (Paris, Boivin, 1936, 711 p.).

3109. Kot, Stanisław. Socinianism in Poland; the Social and Political Ideas of the Polish Antitrinitarians in the XVIth and XVIIth Centuries. Translated from the Polish by Earl M. Wilbur. Boston, Starr King Press, 1957. 226 p.

English translation of *Ideologia polityczna i społeczna Braci Polskich zwanych Arjanami* (Warszawa, Wydawn. Kasy im. Mianowskiego, 1932, 160 p.). General information on the Polish Brethren is also provided in *A History of Unitarianism, Socinianism and Its Antecedents* by Earl M. Wilbur (3d ed., Cambridge, Harvard University Press, 1947), and in *Toleration and the Reformation* by Joseph Lecler, translated from the French by T. I. Westow (New York, Association Press, 1960, 2 v.). There are numerous recent studies in Polish devoted to the views and influence of Polish antitrinitarians. See *Bibliografia Reformacji, 1945-1960* (Bibliography of the Reformation, 1945-1960) (Warszawa, PAN, 1961).

3110. Czarnowski, Stefan. Filozofia społeczna w Polsce w końcu XVIII i początku XIX wieku (Social philosophy in Poland at the end of the 18th and the beginning of the 19th century). Bibljoteka Warszawska (Warszawa), v. 4, 1904: 209-243.

A general account by one of the most prominent Polish sociologists of this century. Reprinted also in Stefan Czarnowski's *Społeczeństwo. Kultura* (Society. Culture) (Warszawa, 1946).

May be supplemented by *Idee społeczne doby stanisławowskiej* (Social ideas of the King Stanislas era), edited by Bogdan Suchodolski (Warszawa, Trzaska, Evert i Michalski, 1948, 224 p., bibliography; Biblioteka autorów polskich, nr. 2) and some of the available monographic works, such as: *Teoria i utopia Stanisława Staszica* (Theory and utopia of Stanisław Staszic) by Barbara Szacka (Warszawa, Państwowe Wydawn. Naukowe, 1965, 267 p.); and *Les Jacobins polonais* by Bogusław Leśnodorski (Paris, Société des Études Robespierristes, 1965, 367 p.; Bibliothèque d'histoire revolutionnaire, 3 sér., no. 4).

3111. Jobert, Ambroise. La Commission d'éducation nationale en Pologne, 1773-1794. Paris, Droz, 1941. 500 p. Ports., fold. map. Bibliography: p. 1-24. (Collection historique de l'Institut d'études slaves, 9)

See also entry no. 2639.

Provides much information about some aspects of social thought in 18th century Poland. May be supplemented by the same author's *Magnats polonais et physiocrates français 1767-1774* (Paris, Belles Lettres, 1941, 92 p.; bibliography: p. 7-11. Collection historique de l'Institut d'études slaves, 10)

3112. Handelsman, Marceli. Les idées françaises et la mentalité politique en Pologne au XIXe siècle. Paris, F. Alcan, 1927. 213 p.

Studies on the origin and evolution of political ideas in the first half of the 19th century by a noted Polish historian of the interwar period.

3113. Limanowski, Bolesław. Historia demokracji polskiej w epoce porozbiorowej (History of Polish democracy during the postpartition period) 3d ed. Warszawa, Wiedza, 1946. 2 v. Bibliographical footnotes.

Although originally published in 1901, this is still a valuable study of the period from the end of the 18th century to the 1860s.

3114. Tyrowicz, Marian. Z dziejów polskich ruchów społecznych w XIX wieku (From the history of Polish social movements in the 19th century). Warszawa, Ludowa Spółdzielnia Wydawnicza, 1965. 250 p.

Essays on various aspects of social thought in the 19th century. On Mickiewicz *see also* "Adam Mickiewicz. The Mystic-Politician," by Wiktor Weintraub, *Harvard Slavic Studies*, v. 1, 1953: 137-178.

3115. Ciołkoszowa, Lidia, *and* Adam Ciołkosz. Zarys dziejów socjalizmu polskiego (An outline of the history of Polish socialism). Londyn, Gryf, 1966. 520 p. Plates, map. Bibliography: p. 498-504.

Volume 1 of a planned multivolume history of Polish socialism, written by two prominent members of the Polish Socialist Party. This very thorough and detailed "outline" covers the history of Polish social thought in the 19th century until about 1860. The bibliography provides information on most of the numerous recent studies of the period published both in Poland and abroad.

3116. Rudzki, Jerzy. Świętochowski. Warszawa, Wiedza Powszechna, 1963. 255 p.

A study of the ideas of the most distinguished representative of the so-called "Polish positivism." Some selections from Świętochowski's writings are included. May be supplemented by Teofil Wojeński's *Publicystyka okresu pozytywizmu* (Political writings of the period of positivism) (Wrocław, 1953, 198 p., bibliography).

3117. Malinowski, Władysław. Najnowsza historia polityczna Polski. 2d ed. v. 1: 1864-1914 (Recent political history of Poland. v. 1: 1864-1914). London, B. Świderski, 1963. 671 p. Illus.

See also entry no. 2678.

First chapters of this longer work may serve as a useful, although not fully adequate, introduction to the complicated history of political and ideological trends at the turn of the century. *See also* the previously mentioned books by Suchodolski and Jabłoński. For the origins of Marxism, *see* Alina Molska's *Pierwsze pokolenie marksistów polskich* (The first generation of Polish Marxists) (Warszawa, Książka i Wiedza, 1962, 2 v.); and the same author's *Model ustroju socjalistycznego w polskiej myśli marksistowskiej lat 1878-1886* (The model of the socialist social system in Polish Marxist thought, 1878-1886) (Warszawa, Książka i Wiedza, 1965, 292 p.).

D. CHRISTIANITY IN POLAND

by M. Kamil Dziewanowski

Perhaps more than in the case of other nations, Polish history is intertwined with that of the church. Hence many general collections of sources for secular history, such as the *Codex Diplomaticus Polonaie*, the *Acta Tomiciana*, or the *Pomniki dziejowe Polski* also reflect religious problems. Thus the present bibliography is largely limited to basic materials dealing specifically with the history of Christianity in Poland.

1. Monographs

3118. Ammann, Albert Maria, S.J. Abriss der ostlawischen Kirchengeschichte. Wien, Thomas Morus Presse, 1950. 748 p. Bibliographies.

Contains numerous chapters and passages concerning ecclesiastic history of the lands which belonged to Poland, or to the Polish-Lithuanian Commonwealth. Covers the period from the middle of the tenth century to 1945.

3119. Belch, Stanislaus F. Paulus Vladimiri and His Doctrine Concerning International Law and Politics. The Hague, Mouton, 1965. 2 v. Illus. Bibliography: v. 2, p. 1203-1237.

See also entry no. 3107.

The first complete edition of works by a leading Polish churchman, lawyer, and philosopher, accompanied by a well-documented study of his theories. Large bibliography.

3120. Brückner, Aleksander. Dzieje kultury polskiej (A history of Polish culture). 3d ed. Warszawa, Książka i Wiedza. 1957-1958. 3 v.

Volume 1 of this monumental work is largely devoted to religious issues of pagan and early Christian Poland. Bibliographies included in each chapter.

3121. Brückner, Alexander. Różnowiercy polscy; szkice obyczajowe i literackie (Dissidents in Poland; social and literary essays). Warszawa, Państwowy Instytut Wydawniczy, 1962. 214 p. Illus., facsims., ports. Bibliography: p. 206.

Reprint of a work which first appeared in 1905 containing a number of historical essays focusing on the Antitrinitarians.

3122. The Cambridge History of Poland. Edited by William F. Reddaway and others. Cambridge, England, The University Press, 1941-1950. 2 v. Plates, fold. maps.

See also entry no. 2618.

Volume 2 (1951), covering the period 1697-1935, devotes less space to religious matters than volume 1 (1950), which treats history to 1696.

3123. Chodynicki, Kazimierz. Kościół Prawosławny a Rzeczpospolita Polska; zarys historyczny, 1370-1632 (The Orthodox Church and Poland; a historical outline, 1370-1632). Warszawa, Skład główny Kasa im. Mianowskiego-Instytut popierania nauki, 1934. 632 p. Bibliography: p. 604-618.

The first volume of a planned larger project. Scholarly.

3124. Dziewanowski, M. K. The Communist Party of Poland; an Outline of History. Cambridge, Mass., Harvard University Press, 1959. 369 p. Bibliography: p. 293-314. (Russian Research Center Studies, 32)

See also entry no. 2727.

Contains a short, basic chapter on the church-state relationship, 1944-1958.

3125. Elementa ad Fontum Editiones. Edited by Karolina Lanckorońska and Walerian Meysztowicz. Roma, Institutum Historicum Polonicum Romae, 1960–

A series of volumes devoted to publication of documents and inventories of documents pertaining to Poland to be found in various European archives. Focuses on ecclesiastic history.

3126. Fox, Paul. The Reformation in Poland. Some Social and Economic Aspects. Baltimore, The Johns Hopkins Press, 1924. 153 p. (Johns Hopkins University Studies in Historical and Political Science, ser. 42, no. 4) Bibliography: p. 149-150.

See also entry no. 2634.

The author suggests that the causes of the Reformation in Poland were mainly social and economic and not religious. Limited bibliography.

3127. Halecki, Oscar. Dzieje unii Jagiellońskiej (A history of the Jagiellonian Union). Kraków, Akademia Umiejętności, 1919-1920. 2 v. Bibliographical footnotes.

See also entry no. 2636.

A thorough and fundamental study of the Polish-Lithuanian Union up to 1569; a great deal of attention paid to the crucial religious aspects. A bibliographic essay at the end.

3128. Halecki, Oskar. From Florence to Brest (1439-1596). Rome, Sacrum Poloniae Millennium, 1958. 444 p. Bibliographical footnotes.

See also entry no. 2637.

This well-documented study of the road from the Union of Florence to the Union of Brest also appears in *Sacrum Poloniae Millennium; rozprawy, szkice, materiały historyczne* (Sacrum Poloniae

Millenium; articles, essays, historical materials) (Rzym, 1958), p. 13-444.

3129. Halecki, Oskar. Tysiąclecie Polski katolickiej (The millennium of Catholic Poland). Rzym, 1966. 614 p. (Sacrum Poloniae Millennium, 13)

Emphasizes the vital link between Poland and Catholicism.

3130. Jablonowski, Aleksander. Akademia Kijowsko-Mohilanska; zarys historyczny na tle rozwoju ogólnego cywilizacji zachodniej na Rusi (The Kiev-Mohilev Academy; a historic outline against the background of Western civilization in Ruthenia). Kraków, Druk W. L. Anczyca, 1900. 318 p. Illus., ports. Bibliography: p. 7-12. (Materialy i opracowania, dotyczące historyi wyższych zakładów naukowych w Polsce, 5)

A scholarly study of a major religious and secular educational institution.

3131. Kot, Stanisław. Ideologja polityczna i społeczna Braci Polskich zwanych Arjanami (Political and social ideology of the Polish Brethren called Arians). Warszawa, Wydawn. Kasy im Mianowskiego, 1932. 160 p.

Scholarly and well documented. French summary on pages 148-152.

3132. Kot, Stanisław, La réforme dans le Grand-Duché de Luithuanie, facteur d' occidentalisation culturelle. Bruxelles, 1953. 65 p. Map. (Extrait de l'Annuaire de l'Institut de philologie et d'histoire orientales et slaves, tome XII, 2952. Mélanges Henri Grégoire, 4)

A penetrating large essay by a leading historian of the Protestant Reformation in Poland. An English adaptation appeared as *Socinianism in Poland; the Social and Political Ideas of the Polish Antitrinitarians in the XVIth and XVIIth Centuries* (Boston, Starr King Press, 1957, 226 p., bibliographical footnotes).

3133. Książka Katolicka w Polsce, 1945-1965; spis bibliograficzny (The Catholic book in Poland, 1945-1965; a bibliographical list). Compiled by Maria Pszczółkowska. Warszawa, Ars Christiana, 1966. 463 p.

3134. Lanckorońska, Karolina. Studies on the Roman-Slavonic Rite in Poland. Roma, Pont. Institutum Orientalium Studiorum, 1961. 194 p. Illus., fold map. Bibliography: p. 173-183 (Orientalia Christiana analecta, 161)

Erudite and well documented study on the existence of the Christian Slavic rite in early medieval Poland.

3135. Lescœur, Louis Zozime, Élie. L'Église catholique en Pologne sous le gouvernement russe, depuis le premier partage jusqu'à nos jours,

1772-1875. 2d ed., entièrement refondue. Paris, E. Plon, 1876. 2 v. Bibliographical footnotes.

3136. Manthey, Franz. Polnische Kirchengeschichte. Hildesheim, Bernward Verlag, 1965. 335 p. Bibliographical references included in "Anmerkungen": p. 319-324.

A recent, popular but readable survey of Polish church history, informative but not overloaded, written from a Catholic point of view, but with some detachment.

3137. Markert, Werner, *ed.* Polen. Köln, Böhlau Verlag, 1959. 829 p. Maps, diagrs., tables. Bibliography: p. 743–781. (Osteuropa-Handbuch, Bd. 2)

See also entry no. 2443.

Includes five chapters on Polish religious history since 1918 (p. 103-137).

3138. Meysztowicz, Walerian. La Pologne dans la chrétienté; coup d'œil sur mille ans d'histoire (966-1966). Paris, Nouvelles Editions Latines, 1966. 189 p.

Brief popular outline of Polish ecclesiastic history in 13 sketches by a noted historian of the Catholic Church in Poland.

3139. Monumenta Poloniae Vaticana. Cracoviae, Sumptibus Academiae Polonae Litterarum et Scientiarum, 1913-1950. 7 v. (Editionum Collegii Historici Academiae Polonae Litterarum et Scíentarum, nr. 71-74, 82-83)

A selection of vital documents from the Vatican archives pertaining to Poland.

3140. Morawski, Kazimierz Marjan. Źródło rozbioru Polski; studja i szkice z ery Sasów i Stanisławów (The sources of Poland's partition; studies and sketches from the Saxon and Stanislaus era). Poznań, Księgarnia Św. Wojciecha, 1935. 369 p. Illus.

A series of essays analyzing the role of Masonic lodges in the partitions of the Polish-Lithuanian Commonwealth. Bibliography in footnotes.

3141. Naurois, Claude. Dieu contre Dieu; drame des catholiques progressistes dans une église du silence. Fribourg, Éditions Saint-Paul, 1956, 297 p.

A critical appraisal of Bolesław Piasecki's *Pax* movement, which is denounced as an instrument of communism; written by a French Catholic using a pseudonym.

3142. Pius XII a Polska. 1939-1949; przemówienia, listy, komentarze (Pope Pius XII and Poland, 1939-1949; speeches, letters, comments). Edited by Kazimierz Papée. Rzym, Studium, 1954. 178 p. Illus.

Edited and provided with an introduction by the last Polish Ambassador to the Vatican.

3143. Sarrach, Alfons. Das polnische Experiment; im Land der schwarzen Königin. Augsburg, Verlag Winifried/Werk, 1964. 260 p.

Written by a German Catholic from Poland. Although essentially devoted to the coexistence of Roman Catholicism and communism in Poland, the book also contains a lengthy historical essay.

3144. Smend, Gottfried, *ed.* Die Synoden der Kirche Augsburgischer Konfession in Grosspolen im 16., 17., und 18. Jahrhundert. Posen, Luther-Verlag, 1930. 607 p. (Jahrbuch des Theologischen Seminars der Unierten Evangelischen Kirche in Polen, nr. 2)

A publication of reports on the negotiations and conclusions of the Lutheran Church Union in Great Poland as well as of reports of the general synods attended by the Augsburg Confessional Church in Poland.

3145. Stasiewski, Bernhard. Reformation und Gegenreformation in Polen; neue Forschungsergebnisse. Muenster in Westfalen, Aschendorff, 1960. 99 p. (Katholisches Leben und Kämpfen im Zeitalter der Glaubensspaltung, 18)

A critical bibliographic essay written by a leading Catholic Church historian, professor of East European church history at the University of Bonn.

3146. Tazbir, Janusz. Historia kościoła katolickiego w Polsce, 1460-1795 (A history of the Catholic Church in Poland, 1460-1795). Warszawa, Wiedza Powszechna, 1966. 212 p. Maps, illus., bibliography.

One of a series of books published under the auspices of the government to counterbalance the ecclesiastically sponsored publications on church history in Poland.

3147. Völker, Karl. Kirchengeschichte Polens. Berlin und Leipzig, W. de Gruyter, 1930. 337 p. (Grundriss der slavischen Philologie und Kulturgeschichte, hrsg. von Reinhold Trautmann und Max Vasmer. Bd. 7)

A basic handbook on Polish church history up to 1918, not yet superseded by a more up-to-date book. Written from a Protestant point of view, it puts emphasis in modern history on the relationship between Protestantism and Catholicism, but there are also chapters on the Orthdox and the Unitarian Churches.

3148. Völker, Karl. Der Protestantismus in Polen auf Grund der einheimischen Geschichtsschreibung dargestellt. Leipzig, J. C. Hinrichs'sche Buchhandlung, 1910. 238 p.

Written by a Protestant historian who used both Catholic and Protestant sources.

3149. Wotschke, Theodor. Geschichte der Reformation in Polen. Leipzig, R. Haupt, 1911. 316 p.

See also entry no. 2653.

A detailed narrative of the Reformation in Poland, written from a Protestant and German-nationalist point of view. Obsolete in details, but still valuable as source information and as a point of departure for further research.

3150. Załęski, Stanisław, S.J. Jezuici w Polsce (The Jesuits in Poland). Lwów, Nakładem drukarni ludowej, 1900-1906. 5 v. Maps.

From 1555 till 1905; bibliography in the footnotes. Somewhat outdated in detail and approach but a valuable point of departure for further research.

2. Serials

3151. Antemurale. 1954– Romae. Annual. Illus.
See also entry no. 2608.

An irregular serial published by the Polish Historical Institute in Rome; devoted largely to subjects connected with religious history.

3152. Archiwa, biblioteki i muzea kościelne (Church archives, libraries, and museums). 1959– Lublin, Katolicki Uniwersytet Lubelski, Ośrodek Archiwów, Bibliotek i Muzeów Kościenlnych. Annual. Illus.

Publication of the Research Institute of the Catholic University of Lublin, dealing with church archives, libraries, and museums.

3153. Ateneum kapłańskie (Priestly Atheneum). 1909– Włocławek. Bimonthly.

A periodical published by the High Seminary of Włocławek, devoted to Catholic theology and related religious problems.

3154. Nasza przeszłość; studia z dziejów kościoła i kultury katolickiej w Polsce (Our past; studies in the history of the Catholic Church and culture in Poland). t. 1– 1946– Kraków.

An irregular serial devoted to the history of religion and culture in Poland. Issued by the Instytut Teologiczny Księży Misjonarzy w Krakowie (Theological Institute of Missionary Priests in Kraków).

3155. Reformacja w Polsce. La Réforme en Pologne. rocz. 1– 1921– Warszawa. Quarterly.

Organ of Towarzystwo do Badania Dziejów Reformacji w Polsce (Society for Research in the History of the Reformation in Poland). Edited 1921-1928 by Stanisław Kot.

3156. Tygodnik powszechny; katolickie pismo społeczno-kulturalne (General weekly; a Catholic social and cultural journal). 1945– Kraków, Kuria Xiążęco Metropolitalna Krakowska. Weekly.

Suspended by the Government in the period 1953-1956. Each issue contains articles on religious issues.

3157. Znak. (The sign). 1946– Kraków. Monthly. (irregular).

Devoted mainly to philosophical and theological questions; allots, however, a generous amount of space to social and cultural issues connected with religious problems; reviews Polish as well as foreign press; occasional bibliographical notes.

E. EDUCATION

*by George Z. F. Bereday and others**

1. Bibliography and Survey Studies

3158. Apanasewicz, Nellie M. Eastern European Education; a Bibliography of English Language Materials. Washington, D.C., U.S. Department of Health, Education and Welfare, 1966. 35 p. (U.S. Office of Education, Bulletin 1966, no. 15)

Books and articles on Eastern European education, grouped by topics and subdivided by country. For an earlier bibliography, devoted specifically to Poland, *see*:

Apanasewicz, Nellie M. Selected Bibliography of Materials on Education in Poland. Washington, D.C., U.S. Department of Health, Education and Welfare, Office of Education, International Education Division, 1960. 64 p. An annotated bibliography of Polish, English, and non-English materials covering the periods prior to the Second World War, the interwar years and the postwar years up to 1960. The materials are organized into subject categories with cross reference to articles covering one or more specific types of education.

3159. Bibliografia zagadnień polityki kulturalnej (Bibliography of the problems of cultural policy). 1960– Warszawa, Państwowe Wydawn. Naukowe, 1963–

Published as an annual supplement to the journal *Kultura i społeczeństwo* (*see* entry no. 3200).

3160. Dobrowolski, Stanisław, *and* Tadeusz Nowacki. Szkoły eksperymentalne w Polsce 1900-1964 (Experimental schools in Poland in the years 1900-1964). Warszawa, Nasza Księgarnia, 1966. 289 p.

This work is in two parts and presents a broad survey of Polish experimental schools, both primary and secondary. Part 1 treats the years 1900-1939; part 2 the years 1944-1964.

3161. XX lat Polski Ludowej (20 years of People's Poland). Warszawa, Państwowe Wydawn. Ekonomiczne, 1964. 997 p. Illus., facsims., maps (part col.).

A richly-illustrated survey of the political, social and cultural life of the period 1944-1964. Chapter 10, "Education and Science," presents the basic developments in these fields.

* The Polish items of this bibliography were prepared by Mrs. Jadwiga Markert-Depta under the direction of Tadeusz J. Wiloch at the Institute of Pedagogy, Warsaw. Other items were compiled and manuscript was edited by George Z. F. Bereday at Teachers College, Columbia University, and Miss Barbara Symmes.

3162. Dzierzbicka, Wanda, *ed.* Eksperymenty pedagogiczne w Polsce w latach 1900-1939 (Pedagogical experiments in Poland in the years 1900-1939). Warszawa, Zakład Narodowy im. Ossolińskich, 1961. 428 p. Illus. (Źródła do dziejów myśli pedagogicznej. t. 7)

The first part of this work characterizes the outstanding Polish experimental schools and compares them with similar schools in other European countries. The second part discusses various kinds of teaching methods and attempts which have been made to implement them in Poland.

3163. International Bureau of Education, *Geneva.* L'Education en Pologne. Genève, Bureau international d'éducation, 1931. 263 p. (Publications du Bureau international d'éducation, 13. Série de monographies nationales)

Articles by Polish authors on several aspects of Polish education.

3164. Kurdybacha, Łukasz. Dzieje oświaty kościelnej do końca XVIII wieku (The history of ecclesiastical education until the end of the 18th century). Warszawa, Czytelnik, 1949. 201 p. Bibliography: p. 197-198.

An important work in the field of educational history which attempts objectively to present the development of ecclesiastical education from the beginning of Christianity to the end of the 18th century. The last two chapters discuss the history of ecclesiastical education in Poland with special reference to efforts made to break the monopoly of the church in the field of education.

3165. Nawroczyński, Bogdan. Polska myśl pedagogiczna, jej główne linie rozwojowe, stan współczesny i cechy charakterystyczne (Polish pedagogical thought; its main lines of development, present state and characteristic features). Lwów, Książnica-Atlas, 1938. 295 p. Illus. (Biblioteka pedagogiczno-dydaktyczna, nr. 16)

A survey of Polish education, educational sociology, and psychology in the period 1863-1938.

3166. Selected Bibliography of Polish Educational Materials. 1961– Published in Warsaw by the Polish Scientific Publishers for the U.S. Office of Education. Quarterly .

Compiled under the editorship of Kazimierz Dąbrowski. Lists books and articles, historical and contemporary, on several aspects of education and the sociology of education.

3167. Suchodolski, Bogdan, *ed.* Osiągnięcia i problemy rozwoju oświaty w XX-leciu Polski Ludowej (Achievements and problems in the development of education in the first two decades of People's Poland). Warszawa, Państwowe Wydawn. Naukowe, 1966. 601 p.

A history of educational developments in the first 20 years of People's Poland (1944-1964). The new tasks for education which must be realized in the future are also discussed. *See also*:

Suchodolski, Bogdan, *ed.* Rozwój pedagogiki w Polskiej Rzeczypospolitej Ludowej (The development of pedagogics in the Polish People's Republic). Wrocław, Zakład Narodowy im. Ossolińskich, 1965. 439 p. (Monografie pedagogiczne, t. 14) A presentation of the theoretical and practical achievements of Polish pedagogics from 1944 to 1964, in which the development of the science of pedagogy, educational research, and pedagogical research institutes are discussed.

3168. Warsaw. Instytut Pedagogiki. Polska bibliografia pedagogiczna, 1944-1951 (Polish pedagogical bibliography, 1944-1951). Edited by Feliks Korniszewski. Wrocław, Zakład im. Ossolińskich, 1955-1957. 1 v. in 3.

Issued under the sponsorship of the Committee on Pedagogical Sciences of the Polish Academy of Sciences, this lists books and articles on general education at all levels.

3169. Wołoszyn, Stefan. Dzieje wychowania i myśli pedagogicznej w zarysie (The history of education and pedagogical thought in outline). Warszawa, Państwowe Wydawn. Naukowe, 1964. 820 p. Illus., facsims., fold. map.

An important volume dealing with the history of education and pedagogy from ancient times to the period of People's Poland. The descriptive material is supplemented with original source documents on the history of education which are correlated with the chronological arrangement of the book.

3170. Z dziejów podziemnego Uniwersytetu Warszawskiego (From the history of the underground Warsaw University). Warszawa, Iskry, 1961. 315 p.

A collection of writings by such scholars as Cz. Wycech, T. Kotarbiński, J. Krzyżanowski, and T. Manteuffel which tells of the research activities at the University of Warsaw during the Second World War when higher education was prohibited in Poland.

2. Educational Theory and Research

3171. Czerniewski, Wiktor. Rozwój dydaktyki polskiej w latach 1918-1954 (The development of Polish didactics in the years 1918-1954). Warszawa, Państwowe Zakłady Wydawn. Szkolnych, 1963. 487 p.

A thorough survey of literature in the field of Polish didactics during the period 1918-1954. The three sections deal with the developments in the interwar years, in the immediate postwar period (1945-1948), and the period of the Six-Year Plan (1948-1954).

3172. Dawid, Jan Władysław. Pisma pedagogiczne (Pedagogical writings). Edited and with an introduction by Ryszard Wroczyński. Wrocław, Zakład Narodowy im. Ossolińskich, 1961. 191 p. Illus.

A selection of essays by one of the most prominent Polish pedagogues. Deals with such subjects as the mental development of the child, activities and interests of students in school, extracurricular activities, and the teaching profession.

3173. Dobrowolski, Antoni Bolesław. Pisma pedagogiczne (Pedagogical writings). Warszawa, Państwowe Zakłady Wydawnictw Szkolnych, 1958-1964. 3 v.

A three-volume source collection containing the basic works of the distinguished Polish pedagogue, Antoni Bolesław Dobrowolski. The first volume treats problems of educational organization and structure, the second, the author's philosophy of teaching, and the third deals with ways of thinking.

3174. Dyoniziak, Ryszard, *ed.* Młodzież epoki przemian (The youth of the period of transformation). Warszawa, Nasza Księgarnia, 1965. 499 p. (Biblioteka wychowania moralnego, t. 9)

A presentation of some of the important results of research work on youth carried out in recent years. This work focuses on such topics as the basic values held by youth, the problems of social progress, extracurricular and free-time activities, and the difficulties which youth experience in adapting to conventional norms and values.

3175. Hessen, Sergei I. Struktura i treść szkoły współczesnej; zarys dydaktyki ogólnej (The structure and meaning of the contemporary school; the outlines of general didactics). 2d ed. Wrocław, Zakład Narodowy im. Ossolińskich, 1959. 288 p. Illus.

A presentation of the author's ideas about a uniform school system and his proposals for a functional division of the levels of formal education into three units (4 + 4 + 4). The second unit of this system, which is to direct the pupil to studies according to his abilities and interests, is of special importance.

3176. Goldszmit, Henryk (Janusz Korczak, *pseud.*) Wybór pism (A selection of writings). Warszawa, Nasza Księgarnia, 1957- 1958. 4 v.

A broad selection of pedagogical writings by one of the most renowned Polish pedagogues. This collection contains, among others, his famous works, "How to Love the Child" and "The Child's Right to be Esteemed." A preface on Korczak's life and works written by Igor Newerly is included.

3177. Korniszewski, Feliks, *ed.* Pedagogika na usługach szkoły (Pedagogy helps the school). Warszawa, Państwowe Zakłady Wydawnictw Szkolnych, 1964. 355 p.

Deals with the basic problems of the usefulness of pedagogy and related sciences such as logic, psychology, and sociology. Included in this collection are works by such prominent Polish scientists as T. Kotarbiński, J. Nawroczyński, and B. Suchodolski.

3178. Kupisiewicz, Czesław. Niepowodzenia dydaktyczne; przyczyny i niektóre środki zaradcze (Didactic failures; causes and some remedies). Warszawa, Państwowe Wydawn. Naukowe, 1964. 246 p.

A presentation of the results of research on the causes of school failures connected with the didactic actiivties of the teacher. Methods of preventing these failures are also discussed.

3179. Mysłakowski, Zygmunt. Wychowanic człowieka w zmiennej społeczności; studia z filozofii wychowania (Education of man in a changing community; studies on philosophy of education). Warszawa, Książka i Wiedza, 1964. 469 p. Bibliography: p. 461-463.

The author pictures the new function that education must assume in the changing social and political system of contemporary Poland, particularly in developing new values through the process of child rearing, through school textbooks, and by a reorientation of the role of the teacher.

3180. Nowacki, Tadeusz. Wychowanie a cywilizacja techniczna; szkice o wychowaniu politechnicznym (Education and the technical civilization; sketchs on polytechnical education). Warszawa, Książka i Wiedza, 1964. 330 p.

A critique of the existing curricula in Polish schools in which the author urges the necessity of polytechnical education to prepare youth for the newly emerging industrial society.

3181. Okoń, Wincenty. Proces nauczania (The process of teaching). 4th ed. Warszawa, Państwowe Zakłady Wydawnictw Szkolnych, 1966. 307 p.

A discussion of teaching methods. Deals specifically with the organization of the lesson, ways of presenting new material and forming good work habits, and evaluation techniques. For other discussions of teaching methods, *see also*:

Lech, Konstanty. System nauczania (The system of teaching). Warszawa, Państwowe Wydawn. Naukowe, 1964. 272 p.

Nawroczyński, Bogdan. Zasady nauczania (The principles of teaching). 3d ed. Wrocław, Zakład Narodowy im. Ossolińskich, 1961. 376 p.

3182. Okoń, Wincenty. U podstaw problemowego uczenia się (The principles of complex learning). Warszawa, Państwowe Zakłady Wydawnictw Szkolnych, 1964. 220 p. Illus. Bibliography: p. 215-220. (Biblioteka nauczyciela. B. Treść i metody nauczania, 1)

This book deals with the process of learning based on observations of pupils' activities in individual and group learning situations. The author's theoretical considerations are based on his research work carried out at the University of Warsaw and the Institute of Pedagogy.

3183. Okoń, Wincenty, *ed.* Szkoły eksperymentalne i wiodące (Experimental and leading schools). Warszawa, Państwowe Zakłady Wydawnictw Szkolnych, 1966. 312 p.

A source book of 15 essays presenting the foremost experimental research work in various areas of Polish education, such as curriculum, methods, and organization. For research on higher education, *see*:

Szczepański, Jan. Socjologiczne zagadnienia wyższego wykształcenia (Sociological problems of higher education). Warszawa, Państwowe Wydawn. Naukowe, 1963. 373 p. The author discusses the initial results of research on higher education in Poland and suggests perspectives for future research. He deals with such matters as the social functions of higher education, the process of recruitment and selection, the general type of students admitted to higher education, and the influence of college on students and on their lives after graduation.

3184. Polska Zjednoczona Partia Robotnicza. *Komitet Centralny. Plenum* XI (i.e., Jedenaste) Plenum KC PZPR. Węzłowe zadania w dziedzinie szkolnictwa wyższego i badań naukowych (The key tasks in the field of higher education and scientific research). Warszawa, Książka i Wiedza, 1963. 518 p.

An official collection of papers and speeches urging reform of the secondary schools in order to make education more responsive to the needs of the national economy. An earlier statement of the Party's position is to be found in:

Polska Zjednoczona Partia Robotnicza. *Komitet Centralny. Plenum.* VII (i.e. Siódme) plenum KC PZPR o reformie szkolnictwa podstawowego i średniego (The 7th Plenum of the Central Committee of the Polish United Worker's Party on the reform of primary and secondary schools). Warszawa, Książka i Wiedza, 1961. 429 p. An official publication proposing reforms in primary and secondary education; specifically by lengthening the primary level from seven to eight years, by introducing vocational education, and by curriculum changes.

3185. Suchodolski, Bogdan. Aktualne zagadnienia oświaty i wychowania (Present problems of education and upbringing). Warszawa, Nasza Księgarnia, 1959. 509 p.

A discussion of contemporary educational problems in which the author indicates the new substance and function of general education and the necessity of further reforms. Separate chapters deal with higher education and the difficulty of combining theory with practice.

3186. Suchodolski, Bogdan. Nauki filozoficzne współdziałające z pedagogiką (Philosophical sciences cooperating with pedagogy). Warszawa, Nasza Księgarnia, 1966. 409 p.

A discussion of the connection between education and other branches of science such as logic, cybernetics, ethics, esthetics, and anthropology. *See also*:

Suchodolski, Bogdan. Nauki przyrodnicze i społeczne współdziałające z pedagogiką (Branches of natural and social science cooperating with pedagogy). Warszawa, Nasza Księgarnia, 1966. 423 p. A collection of essays dealing with the association of pedagogy and physiology, hygiene, psychology, sociology, and economics. Stresses the necessity of consulting these fields for the solution of theoretical as well as practical pedagogical problems.

3187. Suchodolski, Bogdan. Wychowanie dla przyszłości (Education for posterity). Warszawa, Państwowe Wydawn. Naukowe, 1959. 436 p.

This work has five parts which deal with the principles of contemporary education, the perspectives of modern civilization and the tasks of education, personality development, the organization of education, and theory and practice in education. *See also*:

Suchodolski, Bogdan, *ed.* Szkoła podstawowa w społeczeństwie socjalistycznym (The primary school in the socialist community). Wrocław, Zakład Narodowy im. Ossolińskich, 1963. 238 p. (Monografie pedagogiczne, t. 11) A theoretical presentation of the ideal school and curriculum for a socialist state.

———, *ed.* Zarys pedagogiki. Tom 1. Wprowadzenie; Tom 2. System (The outlines of pedagogy, v. 1, Introduction; v. 2, The system). Warszawa, Państwowe Wydawn. Naukowe, 1964. 2 v. Illus. A large two-volume collection of materials on the historical and contemporary state of Polish education. Includes philosophical, psychological, and organizational aspects.

3188. Wiatr., Jerzy. Ideologia i wychowanie (Ideology and education). Warszawa, Książka i Wiedza, 1965. 132 p.

A work dealing with the influence of ideology on education in which the author analyzes the essence of ideology in general and the historical importance of ideology in particular. Discusses also its connection with politics, morality, and education.

3189. Wiloch, Tadeusz, J. O powszechności kształcenia na poziomie średnim (On the universality of education at the secondary level). Warszawa, Państwowe Wydawn. Naukowe, 1965. 176 p.

Materials on the expansion of opportunity for secondary school education are presented in comparative perspective against the background of similar problems in Polish education. Italy, France, England, Sweden, Germany, and the socialist countries are the primary objects of the discussion.

3190. Wroczyński, Ryszard. Wprowadzenie do pedagogicki społecznej (An introduction to social pedagogy). Warszawa, Państwowe Wydawn. Naukowe, 1966. 250 p. Illus. Bibliography: p. 234-239.

A discussion of the role and importance of environmental factors in the process of education. Focuses particularly on the environment as a stimulant in planned education.

3. The Organization and Practice of Education

3191. Bereday, George Z. F. Indoctrination in Schools in One Country:

Poland. *In his*: Comparative Method in Education. New York, Holt, Rinehart and Winston, 1964. p. 55-69.

A study of the effectiveness of political education in the Polish schools in the '50s. Conflicts between communism and Polish nationalism are the main theme.

3192. Falski, Marian. Problematyka organizacyjna szkolnictwa średnich szczebli (Organizational problems of secondary education). Warszawa, Zakład Narodowy im. Ossolińskich, 1966. 158 p. (Monografie pedagogiczne, t. 15).

An examination of the conditions necessary for the expansion of secondary education and the future development of specialized schools in Poland up to the year 1980. This book deals particularly with the problem of the structural division of the schools into primary and secondary levels. A detailed explanation of the 8 + 4 system is presented. An earlier statement on this subject is:

Falski, Marian. Aktualne zagadnienia ustrojowo-organizacyjne szkolnictwa polskiego (Present problems of structure and organization of Polish education). Warszawa, Zakład Narodowy im. Ossolińskich, 1957. 67 p. Illus.

3193. Galiński, Tadeusz, *ed.* Kultura Polski Ludowej (The culture of People's Poland). Warszawa, Państwowe Wydawn. Ekonomiczne, 1966. 441 p. Illus., facsims., fold. col. map.

See also entry no. 3080.

A broad survey of cultural activities in the period of People's Poland (1944-1965). Several chapters discuss science and education in this period and the last chapter is a detailed chronicle of Polish culture during these years. English, French, and Russian editions also available.

3194. Hartmann, Karl. Hochschulwesen und Wissenschaft in Polen. Entwicklung, Organisation und Stand, 1918-1960. Frankfurt am Main, Metzner, 1962. 606 p. Maps. Bibliography: p. 544-561.

See also entry no. 3079.

A handbook in German on higher education and scientific research in Poland presenting an overview of its developments between the war years and a thorough study of the postwar period to 1960. Treatment includes statistics, a collection of official documents on the universities, and a bibliography. In addition to institutions of higher education, the Polish Academy of Sciences and other learned societies, library collections of sources and publishing enterprises are also described.

3195. Paschalska, Maria. Education in Poland. Warsaw, Polonia Publishing House, 1962. 102 p.

A concise account of the expression, reform and reorganization of 16 years of postwar Polish education documented with statistics. All levels of the educational system, in historical context and in light of future changes, are critically evaluated. This work has also been published in French, German, and Spanish. Previous books of this type in English or French include:

Parnowski, Zygmunt. Education in Poland. Warsaw, Polonia Publishing House, 1958. 79 p. Illus.

Dobosiewicz, Stanisław. Our Progress in Education. Warsaw, Polonia Publishing House, 1955. 46 p.

Simon, Brian. Education in the New Poland. London, Lawrence and Wishart, 1964. 63 p. Illus.

L'éducation en Pologne Populaire. Warszawa, Książka i Wiedza, 1952. 65 p. Illus.

3196. Rosen, Seymour M. Higher Education in Poland, Part 1: Organization and Administration; Part 2: Rules of Admissions, Student Activities and Curriculum. Washington, D.C., U.S. Department of Health, Education and Welfare, Office of Education, 1963-1964. 2 v. Illus., map.

A detailed report on higher education in Poland. Deals with organization and administration, admission procedures, student activities, and curriculum. A particularly valuable source for statistics and tables concerning all aspects of higher education.

3197. Wojciechowski, Kazimierz. Wychowanie dorosłych; zagadnienia andragogiki (Education of adults; problems of adult training). Wrocław, Zakład Narodowy im. Ossolińskich, 1966. 593 p. Illus., ports., bibliography.

A descriptive work which deals with various methods and types of adult education. Both formal, in-school activities and leisure-time activities are presented.

3198. Żółkiewski, Stefan. O kulturze Polski Ludowej (On the culture of People's Poland). Warszawa, Państwowe Wydawn. Naukowe, 1964. 245 p. Bibliography: p. 181-200.

An attempt to characterize the cultural life in People's Poland by tracing the origin of Polish culture. A discussion also of the value and substance of the mass culture now being created in modern Poland.

4. Serials

3199. Kwartalnik pedagogiczny (Pedagogical quarterly). 1956– Warszawa, Państwowe Wydawn. Naukowe.

A leading journal published by the State Publishing House in Warsaw. Contains articles on pedagogy, sociological problems of youth, and cultural and esthetic problems in Poland, the socialist countries, and the West. Summaries in English and in Russian.

3200. Kultura i społeczeństwo (Culture and Society). t. 1– 1957– Warszawa, Państwowe Wydawn. Naukowe. Quarterly.

Published by the Committee for Research on Contemporary Culture of the Polish Academy of Sciences. Articles and reviews on sociology, political science, anthropology, and education in Poland, the socialist countries, and the West.

3201. Ruch pedagogiczny (Pedagogical movement). r. 1– 1959– Warszawa, Nasza Księgarnia. Bimonthly.

A publication of the Polish Teachers' Union. Contains articles on pedagogy and the social aspects of education and book reviews of Polish and foreign publications. Table of contents and summaries in Russian and English.

F. THE FINE ARTS

by B. Philip Lozinski

1. Serials and Bibliographical Sources

3202. Biuletyn historii sztuki (Bulletin of the history of art). 1932/33-1939, 1946– Warszawa. Quarterly.

Issued by the Instytut Sztuki Polskiej Akademii Nauk together with the Stowarzyszenie Historyków Sztuki. A basic periodical in the field, including articles, summaries, reviews. Primarily concerned wth Polish art and architecture. Some special numbers have been devoted to topics such as the city of Warsaw, Polish-French artistic relationships, etc. Since 1956 there have been French résumés. Title varies: *Biuletyn naukowy, Biuletyn historii sztuki i kultury.*

3203. Lipska, Helena. Bibliografia historii sztuki polskiej za czas od 1919 do 1924 r.; . . . za czas od 1925 do 1930 r. (Bibliography of the history of Polish art from 1919 to 1924; . . . from 1925 to 1930). *In*: Przegląd historji sztuki (Review of the history of art) (Warszawa), 1929: 132-156; 1932/33: 39-84.

A bibliography of Polish publications on art and of foreign publications pertaining to Polish art for these periods. May be supplemented by the same author's *Bibliografia historii sztuki polskiej za rok 1938* (Bibliography of the history of Polish art for 1938) (Warszawa, Zakład Architektury Polskiej i Historii Sztuki Politechniki Warszawskiej, 1939, 42 p.).

3204. Polska Akademia Umiejętności, *Kraków. Komisja da Badania Historii Sztuki w Polsce.* Sprawozdania (Transactions). Kraków, Nakł. Akademii Umiejętności, 1879-1913. 11 v.

Reports and notes concerning Polish art, primarily that of the Middle Ages and Renaissance. Papers also deal with works of art connected with Poland iconographically or historically, as well as with foreign works in Polish collections.

3205. Polska Akademia Umiejętności, *Kraków. Komisja Historii Sztuki.* Prace (Memoirs). Kraków, Nakł. Polskiej Akademii Umiejętności. 1917-1952. 10 v.

A richly illustrated continuation of the *Sprawozdania* (See entry no. 3204). A greater emphasis on foreign arts related to Poland. Includes monographic investigations of artists or works of art.

3206. Rocznik historii sztuki (Yearbook of the history of art). t. 1– 1956– Wrocław, Zakład im Ossolińskich. Illus., ports., facsims.

Contains extensive articles on art and its theory, with summaries in other languages. Sponsored by the Komitet Nauk o Sztuce of the Polska Akademia Nauk. The fourth volume contains a bibliography of writings on Polish art history in the years 1945-1963, compiled by A. Ryszkiewicz and J. Wierciński.

3207. Rocznik Krakowski (Kraków yearbook). 1898– Kraków, Tow. Miłośników Historii i Zabytków Krakowa.

A serial published by the Society of Friends of Kraków History and Monuments, including papers or monographs devoted to history, monuments, and artistic problems of Kraków City and region in all periods of its history.

3208. Sztuka i krytyka (Art and critique). r. 1– 1950– Warszawa, Państwowy Instytut Sztuki. Quarterly.

Title varies: v. 1-6, *Materiały do studiów i dyskusji z zakresu teorii i historii sztuki, krytyki artystycznej oraz metodologii badań nad sztuką* (Materials for the study and discussion of the theory and history of art, artistic criticism and methodology of research in art).

Especially valuable for the history of Polish art criticism and esthetics. Since 1954 contains French and Russian résumés.

3209. Sztuki piękne. Miesięcznik poświęcony architekturze, rzeźbie, malarstwu, grafice i zdobnictwu (Fine arts. A monthly devoted to architecture, sculpture, painting, graphic, and decorative arts). v. 1-10, 1924-1934, Kraków. Illus., plates, ports.

Important periodical issued by the Polish Institute of Fine Arts in the interwar period. It chronicled contemporary arts and provided well illustrated articles on outstanding artists.

2. Art Histories, Surveys, and Handbooks

3210. Dobrowolski Tadeusz, *ed.* Historia sztuki polskiej w zarysie (A history of Polish art in outline). Kraków, Wydawn. Literackie, 1962. 3 v. Illus., col. plates, plans.

History of Polish architecture and city planning, sculpture, painting, graphic arts, folk art, etc. from prehistory to the present. Written by a group of authors, chiefly professors of the history of art in Polish universities.

3211. Dobrowolski, Tadeusz. Sztuka Krakowa (The art of Kraków). 2d rev. and enl. ed. Kraków, Wydawn. Literackie, 1959. 580 p. Illus., col. plates, ports., fold. map. Bibliography: p. 532-542.

Survey of architecture, sculpture, and painting in Kraków, arranged chronologically from the Middle Ages to the 20th century.

3212. Dobrowolski, Tadeusz. Sztuka Młodej Polski (The art of "Young Poland"). Warszawa, Państwowe Wydawn. Naukowe, 1963. 453 p. 295 illus., 1 col. plate. Bibliography: p. 428-436.

Development of the arts, primarily in Kraków, in the period from about 1890 to 1914, parallel to the Art Nouveau, including architecture, sculpture, painting, graphic, and decorative arts.

3213. Kozakiewicz, Stefan. Polish Art. *In*: New Catholic Encyclopedia, v. 11. New York, McGraw-Hill, 1967. p. 490-497.

A clear outline of Polish history of art with a bibliography including publications in Western languages.

3214. Lorentz, Stanisław. Museums and Collections in Poland, 1945-1955. Warsaw, Polonia Publishing House, 1956. 132 p. Illus.
See also entry no. 2466.

An outline of the history of Polish art collections, of war losses and contemporary museums with their characteristics and activities. Translation of *Muzea i zbiory w Polsce, 1945-1955* (Warszawa Wydawn. "Polonia," 1956, 134 p.; bibliography: p. 109-115).

3215. Ptaśnik, Jan, *ed.* Cracovia artificum, 1300-1550. Kraków, Nakł. Akademii Umiejętności, 1917-1948. 2 v. (Zródła do historyi sztuki i cywilizacyi w Polsce, t. 4-5)

Extracts from the church and city archives of Kraków relating to art, artists, and artisans for the years 1300-1550.

3216. Swieykowski, Emmanuel. Pamiętnik Towarzystwa Przyjaciół Sztuk Pięknych w Krakowie, 1854-1904 . . . (Memoir of the Society of Friends of Fine Arts in Kraków, 1854-1904 . . .). Kraków,Towarzystwo Przyjaciół Sztuk Pięknych, 1905. 592 p. Illus.

History of the society, biographies of all the Polish artists who exhibited in the society (the majority of Polish artists of the period), and a list of works exhibited.

3217. Tatarkiewicz, Władysław. O sztuce polskiej XVII i XVIII wieku: architektura, rzeźba (On Polish art of the 17th and 18th centuries; architekture and sculpture). Warszawa, Państwowe Wydawn. Naukowe, 1966. 537 p. Illus., facsims., ports. "Nota bibliograficzna:" p. 499-500.

3218. Walicki, Michał, *and* J. Starzyński. . . . Dzieje sztuki polskiej (History of Polish art). Warszawa, M. Arct, 1936. 299 p. Illus., plate, ports. Bibliography: p. 280-289.

Architecture, sculpture, painting, and graphic arts from the Middle Ages to the 20th century.

3219. Warsaw. Muzeum Narodowe. Sztuka Warszawska od średniowiecza do połowy XX wieku; katalog wystawy jubileuszowej zorganizowanej w stulecie powstania muzeum, 1862-1962 (Warsaw's art from the Middle Ages to the mid-twentieth century; catalog of the jubilee exhibit organized on the centenary of the foundation of the museum, 1862-1962). Warszawa, 1962. 2 v. in 1. Plates.

An outline of the historical development of the artistic center of Warsaw, and a catalogue raisonné of painting, drawing, and sculpture of Warsaw and its region, with 2,000 biographical entries of artists.

3220. Warsaw. Państwowy Instytut Sztuki. Katalog zabytków sztuki w Polsce (Catalog of art monuments in Poland). Warszawa, Państwowy Instytut Sztuki, Dział Inwentaryzacji Zabytków, 1953– Illus., ports., maps, plans.

Intended to be completed in 11 volumes, five of which had appeared as of 1967. A topographical catalog of all works of art created in Poland before 1850, but including also more important works of significant artists after this date which are not in museums of private collections.

3221. Wojciechowski, Aleksander, *ed.* Polskie życie artystyczne w latach 1890-1914 (Polish art life in the years 1890-1914). Wrocław, Zakład Narodowy im. Ossolińskich, 1967. 270 p. Illus.

Well-documented collective work containing a chronological survey of events and discussions of architectural problems, artistic schools and organizations, societies and groups of artists, institutions concerned with the arts, collections, and art-trade and artistic periodicals.

3222. Żródła do dziejów sztuki polskiej (Sources for the history of Polish art). Wrocław, Zakład im. Ossolińskich, 1951– Illus., ports.

A collection of documents, correspondence, extracts and reprints of manuscripts and published texts. Pertains chiefly to art of the 19th and 20th centuries.

3. Painting and Graphic Arts

3223. Białostocki, Jan. The Graphic Arts in Poland, 1945-1955. Warsaw, Polonia Publishing House, 1956. 37 p. Illus.

Applied graphics — poster and illustration.

3224. Czarnocka, Krystyna. Półtora wieku grafiki polskiej (One and a half centuries of Polish graphics). Warszawa, Wiedza Powszechna, 1962. 378 p. Illus.

A well-illustrated survey from the end of the 18th century to the present. The only synthesis in this field.

3225. Dobrowolski, Taduesz. Nowoczesne malarstwo polskie (Modern Polish painting). Wrocław, Zakład Narodowy im. Ossolińskich, 1957-1964. 3 v. Illus. Bibliography: v. 3, p. 449-474.

Covers the period 1764-1939, discussing artists, artistic centers, schools, movements, groups, and critics.

3226. Dobrowolski, Tadeusz. Polskie malarstwo portretowe; ze studiów nad sztuką epoki sarmatyzmu (Polish portrait painting; studies on the art of the "Sarmatian" period). Kraków, 1948. 239 p. 26 illus., 187 plates. Bibliographical footnotes.

An attempt to define the specifically Polish ("Sarmatian") portrait as independent from the international court art, from the 16th century to the beginning of the 19th. This portrait type was created primarily for the small nobility and includes portraits for caskets and fantasy cycles of ancestral portraits. Attention is given to social background and customs. French résumé.

3227. Dobrzeniecki, Tadeusz. Sztuka sakralna w Polsce malarstwo (Religious art in Poland: painting). Warszawa, Ars Christiana, 1958. 366 p. (p. 43-334 illus., part mounted col.).

Written with the collaboration of Janina Ruszczycówna and Zofia Niesiołowska-Rothertowa. Historical outline of religious painting in Poland, catalogue raisonné of 303 works of art, all illustrated. Extends from the Romanesque painters to the moderns, including only deceased artists. The catalogue notes contain important iconographic themes in Poland.

3228. Kopera, Feliks. Dzieje malarstwa w Polsce (History of painting in Poland). Kraków, Nakł. Druk. Narodowej, 1925-1929. 3 v. Illus.

An extensive, informative, and well-illustrated history of painting in Poland from the Middle Ages to the 20th century.

3229. Kraków. Uniwersytet Jagielloński. *Biblioteka.* Rękopisy i pierwodruki iluminowane Biblioteki Jagiellońskiej (Illuminated manuscripts and early printed books in the library of the Jagiellonian University). Wrocław, Zakład Narodowy im. Ossolińskich, 1958. 233 p. 154 p. of facsims. Illus. Bibliography: p. 228-231.

Catalogue raisonné of the rich medieval and Renaissance collection of Polish and foreign items, heavy in material of the 15th and early 16th centuries. The principal source of information on Polish illumination.

3230. Michałowski, Piotr. Piotr Michałowski (Piotr Michałowski). Introduction by Jerzy Sienkiewicz. Warszawa, Auriga, 1959. 67 p. 324 illus.

A monography by this important Polish painter and, at the same time, an album of his reproductions. A German version appeared as *Piotr Michałowski* (Warschau, Auriga Verlag, 1960, 78 p., 316 plates).

3231. Mycielski, Jerzy. Sto lat dziejów malarstwa w Polsce, 1760-1860 (A hundred years of the history of Polish painting, 1760-1860). Kraków, w drukarni "Czasu" F. Kluczyckiego i spółki, 1897. 737 p.

An extensive work on Polish painting and its relationship with Western Europe. Contains information on the works in private collections, and biographies including data known from artists' family traditions only.

3232. Rastawiecki, Edward, *Baron.* Słownik malarzów polskich, tudzież obcych w Polsce osiadłych lub czasowo niej przebywających (A dictionary of Polish painters and of foreigners settled in Poland or working there temporarily). Warszawa, Nakł. autora, 1850-1857. 3 v. Ports.

Includes archival data, catalogs of works, and documents pertaining to the organization of painters' guilds.

3233. Rastawiecki, Edward, *Baron.* Słownik rytowników polskich, tudzież obcych w Polsce osiadłych lub czasowo w niej pracujących (Dictionary of Polish engravers and of foreign engravers settled in Poland or working there temporarily). Poznań, Z druk. J. I. Kraszewskiego, 1886. 316 p. Port.

A dictionary giving biographies of graphic artists with lists of all their known works. A handbook of Polish graphic arts.

3234. Tarnowski, Stanisław. Matejko (Matejko). Kraków, Księgarnia Spółki Wydawniczej Polskiej, 197. 562 p. Illus.

Somewhat dated and conservative but still the basic monograph on the important historical painter of Poland, Jan Matejko.

3235. Walicki, Michał. Malarstwo polskie: gotyk, renesans, wczesny manieryzm (Polish painting: Gothic, Renaissance, Early Mannerism). Warszawa, Auriga, 1961. 349 p. (p. 57-286 illus., part mounted, part col., 12 col. plates). Bibliography: p. 52-56.

Includes only easel paintings from Romanesque and Gothic eras of the second half of the 13th century to the end of the 16th century. Outlines the history of development of painting in that period, providing a catalogue raisonné and extensive documentation. Includes many hitherto unknown works.

4. Architecture

3236. Ciołek, Gerard. Ogrody polskie (Polish gardens). Warszawa, Budownictwo i Architektura, 1954. 312 p. Illus., plans. Bibliography: p. 298-301.

Outline of the history of gardens.

3237. Dmochowski, Zbigniew. The Architecture of Poland; an Historical Survey. London, Polish Research Centre, 1956. 429 p. Illus., bibliography.

An extensive history of Polish architecture, especially valuable for its plans, etc., made in Poland before 1940.

3238. Łoza, Stanisław. Architekci i budowniczowie w Polsce (Architects and builders in Poland). Warszawa, Budownictwo i Architektura, 1954. 424 p. Plates, bibliography.

Biographical dictionary of Polish architects and builders, including foreigners working in Poland, from the Middle Ages until the present. Includes lists of works executed or projected, of writings, and of archival materials.

3239. Miłobędzki, Adam. Zarys dziejów architektury w Polsce (An outline of the history of architecture in Poland). Warszawa, Wiedza Powszechna, 1963. 281 p. Illus., maps, plans. Bibliography: p. 251-252.

Excellent handbook of Polish architecture and city planning from the eighth century to 1914.

3240. Świechowski, Zygmunt. Budownictwo romańskie w Polsce; katalog zabytków (Romanesque architecture in Poland; a catalog of the monuments). Wrocław, Zakład Narodowy im. Ossolińskich, 1963. 428 p. 919 illus., fold. map, bibliographies.

The corpus of Romanesque architecture in Poland. Descriptions, sources, technological analyses. Sponsored by the Institute of the History of Material Culture of the Polish Academy of Sciences.

3241. Warsaw. Politechnika. *Zakład Architektury Polskiej.* Architektura polska do połowy XIX wieku (Polish architecture up to the mid-nineteenth century). 2d ed. Warszawa, Budownictwo i Architektura, 1956. 40 p. 499 p. of illus.

Album of photographs including modern architecture and wooden architecture.

5. Sculpture and Minor Arts

3242. Buczkowski, Kazimierz. Dawne szkła artystyczne w Polsce (Old artistic glass in Poland). Kraków, Muzeum Narodowe, 1958. 198 p. Illus.

Extensively illustrated survey of Polish glass. French résumé.

3243. Dettloff, Szczęsny. Wit Stwosz (Veit Stoss). Wrocław, Zakład Narodowy im. Ossolińskich, 1961. 2 v. Illus. Bibliography: v. 1, p. 268-276.

Monograph on this late medieval sculpture, treating both his German and Polish periods. Based on documents. Summaries and lists of illustrations and plates in French and German.

3244. Dutkiewicz, Józef Edward. Małopolska rzeźba średniowieczna, 1300-1450 (Medieval sculpture of Little Poland, 1300-1450). Kraków, Nakł. Polskiej Akademii Umiejętności, 1949. 355 p. (p. 173-316 plates). Fold map, bibliographical footnotes.

Catalogue raisonné of the Gothic wooden sculpture in the Kraków region. An outline of the problems involved. French résumé.

3245. Jarnuszkiewicz, Jadwiga. Modern Sculpture in Poland. Warsaw, Polonia, 1958. 55 p. 40 plates.

A survey of the problems, artistic centers, schools, artists, and monuments.

3246. Kopydłowski, Bogusław. Polskie kowalstwo architektoniczne (Polish architectural forging). Warszawa, Arkady, 1958. 19 p. 262 illus.

Fences, window grills, locks, iron doors, etc. from the 12th to the 20th centuries.

3247. Lepszy, Leonard. Przemysł złotniczy w Polsce (Goldsmithing in Poland). Kraków, Nakł. Miejskiego Muzeum Premysłowego im. Adrjana Baranickiego, 1933. 358 p. Illus.

Well-documented history of Polish goldsmiths. Reproduction of counterstamps of goldsmiths, workshops, guilds, and cities.

3248. Mańkowski, Tadeusz. Lwowska rzeźba rokokowa (Rococo sculpture in Lwów). Lwów, Nakł. Towarzystwa Miłośników Przeszłości Lwowa, 1937. 191 p. 94 plates.

Well-documented monograph on the sculpture of the second half of the 18th century in Lwów, which constituted one of the most interesting groups in Poland, on its relations with the art of Dresden and Saxony, and on its influence on other regions in Poland.

3249. Mańkowski, Tadeusz. Polskie tkaniny i hafty XVI-XVIII wieku Polish tapestry, rugs and embroidery, 16th to 18th centuries). Wrocław, Zakład im. Ossolińskich, 1954. 180 p. Illus. (Studia z dziejów polskiego rzemiosła artystycznego, t. 2)

Basic work on artistic weaving and embroidery, well documented and including material now lost. Captions in English, French, German, and Russian.

3250. Maszkowska, Bożenna. Z dziejów polskiego meblarstwa okresu Oświecenia (History of Polish furniture of the Enlightenment). Wrocław, Zakład Narodowy im. Ossolińskich, 1956. 109 p. 122 illus. (Państwowy Instytut Sztuki. Studia z dziejów polskiego rzemiosła artystycznego, t. 1)

Polish and imported furniture of the second half of the 18th and first half of the 19th centuries. Problems of interior decoration. Catalogue raisonné of 109 pieces. Captions in English and Russian.

3251. Walicki, Michał, *ed.* Drzwi gnieźnieńskie (The doors of Gniezno cathedral). Wrocław, Zakład im. Ossolińskich, 1956-1959. 2 v. Illus. and atlas (8 p., 153 plates).

Collective work illuminating all the problems of the Romanesque bronze doors in Gniezno. Studies discussing the monument's artistic, historical, iconographical and ideological content as well as technological and palaeographical points of view. French and Russian résumés.

G. MUSIC

by Alexander Janta

1. Reference Aids

3252. Błaszczyk, Leon Tadeusz. Dyrygenci polscy i obcy w Polsce działający w XIX i XX wieku (Polish and foreign conductors active in Poland in the XIXth and XXth centuries). Kraków, Polskie Wydawn. Muzyczne, 1964. 358 p. Ports.

Contains over 1,100 biographical notes and an extensive bibliography.

3253. Goldschmidt, Harry, *and others, comps.* Beiträge zur Musikwissenschaft. Sonderreihe Bibliographien: Musikwissenschaftliche Literatur sozialistischer Länder II. VR Polen 1945-1965. Berlin, Verlag Neue Musik, 1966. 192 p.

A very complete and well-organized bibliographical listing of 1,519 Polish publications, essays and articles dealing with music which appeared in postwar Poland.

3254. Michałowski, Kornel. Bibliografia polskiego piśmiennictwa muzycznego (Bibliography of Polish musical literature). Kraków, Polskie Wydawn. Muzyczne, 1955. 280 p.

Suplement za lata 1955-1963 i uzupełnienie za lata poprzednie (Supplement for the years 1955-1963 and additional entries for the previous years): Kraków, Polskie Wydawn. Muzyczne, 1964, 203 p. (Materiały do bibliografii muzyki polskiej, t. 3-4).

A complete bibliography of publications on music in Polish or by Polish authors from the 16th century to 1963, including dissertations from the years 1917-1963. For Polish musical periodicals, *see*:

Bibliografia polskich czasopism muzycznych (A bibliography of Polish musical periodicals). Kraków, Polskie Wydawn. Muzyczne, 1955-1966. 13 v. Each volume provides a bibliographical listing of the contents of one or more Polish music periodicals with indexes of authors and titles.

3255. Michałowski, Kornel. Opery polskie; katalog (Polish operas; a catalog). Kraków, Polskie Wydawn. Muzyczne, 1954. 277 p. Illus., ports. (Materiały do bibliografii muzyki polskiej, t. 1)

See also entry no. 3274.

A catalog of over 600 operas and operettas by Polish composers of the 18th to 20th centuries, or on Polish themes.

3256. Schäfer, Bogusław. Almanach polskich kompozytorów współczesnych (Almanac of Polish contemporary composers). 2d ed. Kraków, Polskie Wydawn. Muzyczne, 1966. 163 p.

A new edition of the popular biographic dictionary of living composers. For an earlier period, *see*:

Chybiński, Adolf. Słownik muzyków dawnej Polski do roku 1800 (Dictionary of the musicians of ancient Poland up to 1800).

Kraków, Polskie Wydawn. Muzyczne, 1949. 163 p. Despite recent discoveries, still a basic biographical guide of composers and performers of Polish music in the old times.

2. History

3257. Gliński, Mateusz, *ed.* Muzyka polska; monografia zbiorowa (Polish music; a collective monograph). Warszawa, Nakładem miesięcznika "Muzyka," 1927. 151 p. plates, illus.

Essays by various authorities, including "Polski styl muzyczny" (Polish musical style) by H. Opieński, "Polska pieśń artystyczna" (The Polish art song) by S. Barbag, "Dzieje symfonii w Polsce" (History of the symphony in Poland) by I. Reiss, and "Muzykologja polska" (Polish musicology) by St. Łobaczewska.

3258. Jarociński, Stefan, *comp.* Antologia polskiej krytyki muzycznej XIX i XX wieku, do roku 1939 (Anthology of Polish musical criticism of the 19th and 20th centuries). Kraków, Polskie Wydawn. Muzyczne, 1955. 523 p. Bibliography: p. 513-514.

Short history, with annotated excerpts, of critical writings on music, ending with 1939. For works relating to specific periods, *see* the following:

Antiquitates Musicae in Polonia. Warszawa, PWN Polish Scientific Publishers; Graz, Austria, Akademische Druck- u. Verlagsanstalt, 1963– To be completed in 14 volumes, this series is to contain original works and documents fromthe history of Polish music.

Feicht, Hieronim, *ed.* Muzyka Staropolska; wybór nie publikowanych utworów z XII-XVIII wieku. (Old Polish music; a selection of hitherto unpublished works from the 11th to 18th centuries). Kraków, Polskie Wydawn. Muzyczne, 1966. xix p., score (404 p.). 48 plates.

Chomiński, Józef M., *and* Zofia Lissa, *eds.* Music of the Polish Renaissance; a Selection of Works from the XVIth and the Beginning of the XVIIth century. Translated from the Polish by Claire Grece Dąbrowska; English translation of the Polish songs by Przemysław Mroczkowski. Kraków, Polskie Wydawn. Muzyczne, 1955. Score (370 p.). Facsims. A selection of recently discovered compositions, with a comprehensive introduction illuminating the musical life of the "Golden Century" of Polish culture.

Wydawnictwo dawnej muzyki polskiej (Publication of ancient Polish music). Parts 1-61. Warszawa, Kraków, 1928-1966. A basic serial publication of compositions from the 16th and 17th centuries, annotated and with critical commentaries by the successive editors, Adolf Chybiński, Hieronim Feicht, and Zygmunt Szweykowski.

Z dziejów polskiej kultury muzycznej (From the history of Polish musical culture). Edited by Stefania Łobaczewska, Tadeusz Strumiłło and Zygmunt Szweykowski. Kraków, Polskie Wydawn. Muzyczne, 1958-1966. 2 v. Bibliography: v. 1, p. 314-312. A monograph on the history of music in Poland up to the epoch of the Polish Baroque.

Strumiłło, Tadeusz. Źródła i początki romantyzmu w muzyce polskiej; studia i materialy (Sources and origins of romanticism in Polish music; studies and materials). Kraków, Polskie Wydawn. Muzyczne, 1956. 207 p. Port., music. Bibliography: p. 201-202. (Studia i materiały do dziejów muzyki polskiej, t. 3 A basic study of the history of Polish music in the period of the Enlightenment and Pre-romanticism.

Janta, Alexander. Early Nineteenth Century American-Polish Music. The Polish Review, v. 6, 1961, no. 1-2: 73-105; v. 9, 1965, no. 2: 59-96. Contains a bibliography of early 19th century sheet music by Poles and on Polish themes.

Other American studies on Polish music have appeared in *Polish Review* (see Subject Index for 1956-1966, Music and Musicology, in v. 12, no. 3, p. 96).

Belza, Igor' F. Istoriia pol'skie muzykal'noi kultury (The history of Polish musical culture). Moskva, Gos. muzykal'noe izd-vo, 1954-1957. 2 v. Plates, ports., music. Bibliographical references: v. 1, p. 297-324. This broad panorama of Polish musical development ends with the year 1830 and does not include Chopin. A continuation is expected. Volume 2 appeared in Polish translation as *Między Oświeceniem i Romantyzmem* (Between Enlightenment and Romanticism) (Kraków, Polskie Wydawn. Muzyczne, 1961, 316 p.).

3259. Jarociński, Stefan, *ed.* Polish Music. Warszawa, Państwowe Wydawn. Naukowe, 1965. 327 p. 40 plates.

Articles on the history of Polish music from the Middle Ages, including folk music, the organization of musical life in Poland, and a number of short biographic notes on composers after Szymanowski. Other surveys of Polish musical history include:

Lissa, Zofia. La musique en Pologne. *In*: La Musique, les hommes, les instruments, les œuvres. Paris, 1965. v. 1: p. 198-204; 267-270; 329, 332; v. 2: p. 241-258.

Źródła do historii muzyki polskiej (Sources for the history of Polish music). Fsc. 1-10. Kraków, Państwowe Wydawn. Muzyczne, 1960-1966. A summary history of Polish music for foreign readers, the first edition of which appeared in 1918, is Henryk Opieński's *La musique Polonaise*, 2d ed. (Paris, Gebethner and Wolff, 1929, 120 p.).

3260. Strumiłło, Tadeusz. Szkice z polskiego życia muzycznego XIX w. (Sketches from Polish musical life in the nineteenth century) Kraków, Polskie Wydawn. Muzyczne, 1954. 242 p. (Małe monografie muzyczne, t. 5)

A popular study of the history of music and musical culture in 19th century Poland.

3. Serials

3261. Muzyka; kwartalnik poświęcony historii i teorii muzyki oraz krytyce naukowej i artystycznej (Music; a quarterly devoted to the history and theory of music and to scholarly and artistic criticism). 1956– Warszawa.

Preceded by *Muzyka; miesięcznik poświęcony zagadnieniom życia muzycznego w Polsce* (Music; a monthly devoted to contemporary music in Poland). 1950-1956. Warszawa, Państwowy Instytut Sztuki. For the pre-1939 period, *see*:

Muzyka; miesięcznik ilustrowany (Music; illustrated monthly). 1924-1938. Warszawa. Edited by Mateusz Gliński, this was Poland's most important musical periodical of the time. Contents are listed in volume 9 of *Bibliografia polskich czasopism muzycznych* (A bibliography of Polish music periodicals) (Kraków, 1955-1966, 13 v.).

3262. Ruch muzyczny (The musical movement). Warszawa, Wydawn. Artystyczne i Filmowe, 1960– Biweekly.

A lively current musical periodical, treating all aspects of musical life in contemporary Poland and abroad. From 1945 to 1949 and 1957 to 1959, published by Polskie Wydawn. Muzyczne, Kraków, under the editorship of B. Rutkowski and Stefan Kisielewski, later, in Warsaw, of Zygmunt Mycielski (up to 1968).

4. Individual Composers

3263. Chopin, Fryderyk Franciszek.

Chopin, Fryderyk Franciszek. Korespondencja. Compiled and edited by Bronisław Edward Sydow. Warszawa, Państwowy Instytut Wydawniczy, 1955. 2 v. Illus., ports.

Although in part already overtaken by new discoveries, this collection, part of which is in French, represents the most thorough presentation of Chopin's annotated and indexed correspondence. Also in French translation as *Correspondance*, compiled, reviewed, annotated, and translated by Bronisław Edward Sydow in collaboration with Suzanne and Denise Chainaye (Paris, Richard-Masse-Ed., 1953-1960, 3 v., illus., ports., facsims.).

Hoesick, Ferynand. Chopin; życie i twórczość (Chopin; life and work). 2d ed. Kraków, Polskie Wydawn. Muzyczne, 1962-1966. 3 v. (Biblioteka Chopinowska, 5).

A new edition of a basic biography, with addition of further critical comments.

International Musicological Congress Devoted to the Works of Frederick Chopin. *1st., Warsaw, 1960*. The Book of the First International Musicological Congress Devoted to the Works of Frederick Chopin. Warszawa, 16th to 22nd February, 1960. Edited by Zofia Lissa. Warszawa, Polish Scientific Publishers, 1963. 755 p. Illus., facsims, music.

Contains the program of the congress and the 136 papers read there on the subject of Chopin's music, Polish music and its relation to other countries. Text in Polish, French, German, and Russian.

Kobylańska, Krystyna. Chopin w kraju; dokumenty i pamiątki

(Chopin in his native land; documents and memoirs). Preface by Jarosław Iwaszkiewicz. Kraków, Polskie Wydawn. Muzyczne, 1955. 296 p. Illus., ports., maps, facsims., music.

An album on Chopin in Poland, profusely documented with many illustrations. An English translation appeared as *Chopin in His Own Land* (Warsaw, Polskie Wydawn. Muzyczne, 1955).

Smoter, Jerzy Maria. Spór o "listy" Chopina do Delfiny Potockiej (The dispute over Chopin's "letters" to Delfina Potocka). Kraków, 1967. 236 p. (Biblioteka Chopinowska, t. XI).

A broadly documented presentation of the controversy about important Chopin letters, the authenticity of which has been questioned. The case remains open.

Sydow, Bronisław Edward. Bibliografia F. F. Chopina (Bibliography of F. F. Chopin). Warszawa, Nakł. Tow Naukowego Warszawskiego, 1949. 586 p. Suplement (Supplement): Warszawa, Państwowe Wydawn. Naukowe, 1954. 178 p.

The largest and most comprehensive Chopin bibliography thus far. Since it is not sufficiently selective, it tends to be confusing and overcrowded. A new, more selective bibliography is in preparation by Kornel Michałowski.

Weinstock, Herbert. Chopin, the Man and His Music. New York, Alfred A. Knopf, 1949. 336 p. Illus., ports., musical notations, bibliography.

A well informed study, useful also for its extensive bibliography and careful index, although the anglicizing of Polish names tends to confuse.

Wierzyński, Kazimierz. The Life and Death of Chopin. Translated by Norbert Guterman with a foreword by Artur Rubinstein. New York, Simon & Shuster, 1949. 444 p. Illus., ports., facsims. "Sources": p. 425-429.

Probably the finest among the books on Chopin in English. Contains an extensive bibliography. Published in Polish under the title: *Życie Chopina* (New York, Roy Publishers, 1953, 384 p.).

3264. Karłowicz, Mieczysław.

Chybiński, Adolf. Mieczysław Karłowicz, 1876-1909; kronika życia artysty i taternika (Mieczysław Karłowicz, 1876-1909. Chronicle of the life of the artist and mountaineer). Kraków, Polskie Wydawn. Muzyczne, 1949. 552 p. Plates, ports., facsims. Bibliography: p. 515-525.

A basic biographical study of an uncommonly gifted composer, killed by an avalanche in the Tatra Mountains at the peak of his creative career.

3265. Moniuszko, Stanisław.

Rudziński, Witold. Stanisław Moniuszko. Kraków, Polskie Wydawn. Muzyczne 1955-1961. 2 v. Illus., ports., bibliographies.

(Studia i materiały do dziejów muzyki polskiej, v. 1)
A basic biography of Stanisław Moniuszko, the creator of the national repertory of operas, set against a broad background of 19th century Wilno and Warsaw.

3266. Paderewski, Ignacy Jan.

Opieński, Henryk. I. J. Paderewski; esquisse de sa vie et de son œuvre. Preface by Gabriel Hanotaux, Gustave Doret and Alfred Cortot. Lausanne, Edition Spes, 1948. 148 p. Illus., ports., facsims.
A popular monograph on the life and work of Paderewski. Also pubilshed in Polish as *Ignacy Jan Paderewski*, new, revised and enlarged edition (Kraków, Polskie Wydawn. Muzyczne, 1960, 165 p., illus., ports.).

Paderewski, Ignacy Jan, *and* Mary Lawton. The Paderewski Memoirs. New York, C. Scribner's Sons, 1938. 404 p. Front., plates, ports., facsim.

To August 1, 1914. "Later memoirs in preparation."

3267. Szymanowski, Karol.

Chomiński, J. M., *ed.* Z życia i twórczości Karola Szymanowskiego; studia i materiały (From the life and works of Karol Szymanowski; studies and materials). Kraków, Polskie Wydawn. Muzyczne, 1960. 404 p. Ports. "Bibliografia Szymanowskiego, 1906-1958": p. 319-382. A collection of studies and materials relating to Szymanowski's life and works.

Łobaczewska, Stanisława. Karol Szymanowski; życie i twórczość, 1882-1927 (Karol Szymanowski; life and works, 1882-1927). Kraków, Polskie Wydawn. Muzyczne, 1950. 667, 30 p. Illus., ports., facsims., geneal. tables. The most important biographical study yet of the great composer and his work. Not free from certain omissions and distortions to conform to the trend prevailing at the time of publication.

Maciejewski, B. M. Karol Szymanowski. His life and Music. Foreword by Felix Aprahamian. London, Poets and Painters Press, 1967. 148 p. Illus., music notations. A biographical essay, the first in English. Includes an extensive catalog of Szymanowski's works and an index.

Michałowski, Kornel. Karol Szymanowski. Katalog tematyczny dzieł i bibliografia (Subject catalogue of works and bibliography). Kraków, PWM, 1967. 348 p. Illus., music.

Sesja Naukowa poświęcona twórczości Karola Szymanowskiego, *Warsaw, 1962*. Karol Szymanowski; księga sesji naukowej, poświęconej twórczości Karola Szymanowskiego. Warszawa, 23-28 marca 1962 (Karol Szymanowski; book of the scholarly session devoted to the work of Karol Szymanowski. Warszawa, March 23-28, 1962). Warszawa, 1964. 382 p. Illus., facsims., music.

H. THEATER AND CINEMA

by Tymon Terlecki

1. Theater

a. Bibliographies, Reference Books, Serials

3268. Estreicher, Karol. Teatra w Polsce (Theaters in Poland). 2nd ed. Warszawa, Państwowy Instytut Wydawniczy, 1953. 4 v.

The first edition appeared in 1873-1879. The creator of the monumental "Polish Bibliography" collected in this work a great deal of primary source material. It is arranged in alphabetical order by names of towns. Although it has not been finished (it stops on the entry "Lwów"), and although it has in part been supplanted by newer research, especially in the field of the old Polish theater, Estreicher's book still retains its value and remains "the breviary of historians of the Polish theater," as one of them put it. The three indexes (of maps, plays and localities) added to the reedition greatly facilitate its use. It may be used jointly with:

Estreicher, Karol. Bibliografia polska XIX stulecia (A Polish bibliography of the 19th century). 2d ed. v. 4-5. Kraków, Uniwersytet Jagielloński — Państwowe Wydawn. Naukowe, 1966-1968. Volume four contains an entry on Polish drama and volume five, on foreign drama in translation, providing an inventory of several thousand original Polish plays and plays translated into Polish from 1750-1900. Apart from printed works, plays in manuscript have also been noted.

Equally helpful may be a large collective undertaking under the auspices of the Institute for Literary Research: *Bibliografia literatury polskiej, "Nowy Korbut"* (A bibliography of Polish literature, the "New Korbut") after Gabriel Korbut, the initiator and individual author of the first, now outdated edition of the work (Warszawa, Państwowy Instytut Wydawniczy, 1963–). This is a basic compendium dealing extensively with, beside the history of literature, the history of the theater. For instance, volume 1 (p. 204-221) contains a bibliography of early dramatic texts, printed and in manuscript and (p. 266-271) of the "dramat sowizdrzalski" (lower middle class drama), while volume 4 lists (p. 85-89, 152-189) works on the theater of the Enlightenment.

3269. Hahn, Wiktor. Shakespeare w Polsce; bibliografia (Shakespeare in Poland; a bibliography). Wrocław, Zakład Narodowy im. Ossolińskich, 1958. 381 p.

A complete coverage by an expert historian of literature and bibliographer. He gives, among other things, a full list of Shakespeare productions in Poland. There is a summary and table of contents in English. *See also*:

Calina, Josephine (Mrs. Allardyce Nicoll). Shakespeare in Poland. London, Pub. for the Shakespeare Association by H. Milford, Oxford University Press, 1923. 76 p. An old, detailed study, not yet superseded by any other monograph on the subject.

3270. Korotaj, Władysław, *ed.* Dramat staropolski od początków do powstania sceny narodowej; bibliografia. Tom I: Teksty dramatyczne drukiem wydane do r. 1765 (Old Polish drama, from the beginnings until the foundation of the National Theater; bibliography. v. I: Dramatic texts printed before 1765). Wrocław, Zakład Narodowy im. Ossolińskich, 1965. 540 p. (Książka w dawnej kulturze polskiej, 14)

A great collective undertaking; it lists more than 600 plays printed before 1765, with detailed bibliographical descriptions of every item as well as of works dealing with them and information concerning their stage productions (the latter incomplete).

3271. Łaska, Maria. Bibliografia ruchu teatrów ludowych w Polsce, 1901-1935 (A bibliography of the popular theaters movement in Poland, 1901-1935). Warszawa, Instytut Teatrów Ludowych, 1936. 92 p.

The first attempt of this kind with 773 entries. It should be supplemented by Piotr Grzegorczyk's *Teatr ochotniczy i tańce polskie; bibliografia informacyjna* (The nonprofessional theater and Polish dances; an informative bibliography) (Warszawa, Centralny Instytut Kultury, 1948, 61 p.), a very careful, well-arranged survey, listing more than 300 bibliographical items dealing with general and theoretical problems, the training of the amateur actor and the preparations for the performance, the popular theater, workers' theater, school theater, puppet theater, rites and songs, the history of the nonprofessional theater, etc.

3272. Maciejewska, Maria Krystyna. Teatralia w książkach. Zestawienie bibliograficzne (Materials on theater in books. A bibliographical register). *In*: Pamiętnik teatralny (Warszawa), 1958, p. 590-594; 1959, p. 602-606; 1961, p. 105-117, 468-477; 1962, p. 295-308; 1964, p. 353-382; 1965, p. 425-438; 1967, p. 134-150.

This is supplemented by Jan Wiśniewski's "Historia teatru polskiego w czasopismach" (History of the Polish theater in periodicals) in the same review, 1958, p. 151-164, 569-590; 1959, p. 591-602; 1961, p. 93-105, 454-467; 1962, p. 287-295.

3273. Maciejewska, Maria Krystyna, *and* Anna Polakowska. Czasopisma teatralne dziesięciolecia 1944-1953. Bibliografia zawartości (Theatrical periodicals of the 1944-1953 decade. A bibliography of contents). Wrocław, Zakład Narodowy im. Ossolińskich, 1956 659 p. (Materiały do dziejów teatru w Polsce t. 3)

A bibliographical monograph in five parts: organization of the knowledge on the theater; history and theory of the theater; the life of the contemporary theater; plays and their authors; and literary texts concerning the theater. Precise and instructive, conveniently provided with three indexes.

3274. Michałowski, Kornel. Opery polskie; katalog (Polish operas; a catalog). Kraków, Polskie Wydawn. Muzyczne, 1954. 277 p. Illus., ports. (Materiały do bibliografii muzyki polskiej, t. 1)

See also entry no. 3255.

An alphabetical and chronological list of Polish operas (or operas concerning Poland), containing also information on their first theatrical productions. A rich bibliography on the Polish opera (p. 15-30). A very carefully prepared compendium.

3275. Misiołek, Edmund. Bibliographie théâtrale polonaise 1944-1964. Varsovie, Ed. "Le Théâtre en Pologne," 1965. 80 p.

A bibliographic survey of separate prints (also offprints from periodicals). Incomplete. Titles translated into French. A very clear arrangement and a detailed table of contents.

3276. Misiorny, Michał. Teatry dramatyczne Ziem Zachodnich 1945-1960 (Playhouses on Poland's western territories, 1945-1960). Poznań, 1963. 220 p. Illus.

A book about theatrical activity in Great Poland, Lower and Upper Silesia, Pomerania, Varmia, and Masuria. With a list of companies, detailed repertoires, and indexes. For the older history of these regions of Poland *see* Zbigniew Raszewski's *Z tradycji teatralnych Pomorza, Wielkopolski i Śląska* (From the theatrical traditions of Pomerania, Great Poland and Silesia) (Wrocław, Zakład Narodowy im. Ossolińskich, 1955, 276 p.).

3277. Polonia. *In*: Enciclopedia dello spettacolo. v. 8. Roma, Casa Editrice le Maschere, 1966. Cols. 292-312.

A concise and up-to-date survey of the Polish theater. One may also consult the article on the Polish theater in *Teatral'naia entsiklopediia* (Theatrical encyclopedia), v. 4 (Moskva, Gosudarstvennoe izdatel'stvo "Sovetskaiia entsiklopediia," 1967), p. 410-423.

3278. Raszewski, Zbigniew, *and* Eugeniusz Szwankowski, *eds.* Materiały do dziejów teatrów w Polsce (Materials on the history of the theatre in Poland). Warszawa, Zakład im. Ossolińskich, 1954-1967. 7 v.

A series of large volumes, some over 600 pages, with new source materials and preparatory compilations.

3279. Simon, Ludwik. Dykcjonarz teatrów polskich czynnych od czasów najdawniejszych do roku 1863 (A dictionary of Polish theaters from the earliest times until 1863). Warszawa, Skład główny w księgarniach s.a. Książnica Atlas, 1935. 147 p.

An encyclopedic work, continuing Estreicher's fragmentary attempt on a much bigger scale and in a more modern way (in comparison with the 34 localities in the latter's book, Simon deals with more than 250 of them). The "Dictionary" is preceded by a concise sketch of the history of the theater in Poland and followed by addenda on such subjects as school theaters in Poland, the theater at the royal courts, etc.

3280. Sivert, Tadeusz, *ed.* Studia z dziejów teatru w Polsce (Studies concerning the history of the theater in Poland). Wrocław, Zakład Narodowy im. Ossolińskich, 1955–

Each of the volumes published so far in this series sponsored by the State Institute of Art is different in character. The first: *Teatr warszawski drugiej połowy XIX w.* (The Warsaw theater in the second half of the 19th century) is a collective work by six contributors, dealing with such topics as the social and economic determinants of the theater, the public, actors, critics, etc. The same subject is treated more freely in Józef Szczublewski's *Wielki i smutny Teatr Warszawski 1868-1880* (The great and sad Warsaw theater) (Warszawa, 1963), a work at once scholarly and interesting as reading matter. The other volumes deal with topics such as the part played by the "moral" periodical "The Monitor" in the shaping of the National Theater in the 1765-1785 period (Stanisław Ozimek); the theatrical traditions of Pomerania, Great Poland, and Silesia (Zbigniew Raszewski); and the theater in Warsaw under the Saxon kings (Karyna Wierzbicka-Michalska). The latest volume is, like the first, a collection of essays by five authors concerned with the history of Adam Mickiewicz's dramas on the stage. In this respect *see also* two books:

Sivert, Tadeusz. Mickiewicz na scenie (Mickiewicz on the stage). Warszawa, Państwowy Instytut Wydawniczy, 1957. 143 p.

Pacewicz, Tadeusz. Mickiewicz na scenach polskich (Mickiewicz on Polish stages). Wrocław, Zakład Narodowy im. Ossolińskich, 1959. 86 p.

Both volumes are lavishly illustrated.

3281. Strauss, Stefan. Bibliografia tytułów czasopism teatralnych (A bibliography of titles of theatrical periodicals). Wrocław, Zakład Narodowy im. Ossolińskich, 1953. 156 p.

A primary compendium in alphabetical order, based on pioneering research in 20 public libraries in six cities. Annotations deal with the characteristics of periodicals, their more eminent collaborators, and titles of the more important contributions, and give a general appraisal.

3282. Strauss, Stefan. Bibliografia źródeł do historii teatru w Polsce (A bibliography of sources on the history of the theater in Poland). Wrocław, Zakład im. Ossolińskich, 1957. 495 p.

A basic and most comprehensive guide. It contains more than 3,000 entries, arranged in 18 parts, richly and precisely annotated. It lists not only books but also ephemeral prints such as leaflets, broadsides, programs, etc. It gives information on Polish as well as foreign language theaters in Poland and on universal theater, from the Chinese to the theater in the U.S.A. There are four indexes.

3283. Szletyński, Henryk, *ed.* Z dziejów inscenizacji w Polsce (From the history of theater productions in Poland). Wrocław, Zakład Narodowy im. Ossolińskich, 1959-1963. 2 v.

The series deals with the theater history of the two greatest romantic poets: Adam Mickiewicz and Juliusz Słowacki. Both volumes are lavishly illustrated and carefully annotated. In addition to this series, there are two works similar in character, but different in method:

Skwarczyńska, Stefania. Leona Schillera trzy opracowania teatralne "Nieboskiej komedii" w dziejach jej inscenizacji w Polsce (Leon Schiller's three scenic interpretations of [Zygmunt Krasiński's] "Undivine Comedy," seen against the background of the history of its production in Poland). Warszawa, Instytut Wydawniczy Pax, 1959. 620 p.

Dąbrowski, Stanisław, *and* Ryszard Górski. Fredro na scenie (Aleksander Fredro on the stage). Warszawa, Wydawnictwa Literackie i Filmowe, 1963. 244 p. 80 plates.

3284. Scena polska; czasopismo Związku Artystów Scen Polskich (The Polish stage; a periodical of the Union of the Polish Stage Artists). 1919-1938. Warszawa. Irregular.

A professional review which passed through various phases, including suspension and resumption of publication. Twice in its career, during 1924-1926 under the editorship of Władysław Zawistowski, and during 1936-1938, as edited by Tymon Terlecki, it had the character of a scholarly quarterly, devoted to the history and theory of the theater as well as to documentation on contemporary theatrical activity. The new incarnation of this review is:

Pamiętnik teatralny, kwartalnik poświęcony historii i krytyce teatralnej (Theater record, a quarterly devoted to history and criticism of the theater). r. 1– 1952– Warszawa. A periodical, published by the Institute of Art at the Polish Academy of Arts and Sciences, founded and edited by Leon Schiller, the preeminent producer, now edited by Bohdan Korzeniewski, a historian, critic and producer, and by the leading historian of the theater, Zbigniew Raszewski. A very serious and at the same time, lively, inventively edited periodical. Absolutely imperative for any student of the Polish theater.

3285. Le Théâtre en Pologne; bulletin mensuel du Centre Polonais de l'Institut International du Théâtre. 1959– Varsovie. Monthly.

Edited by Edward Csató and Andrzej Hausbrandt. Lavishly illustrated review, concerned with contemporary Polish theater, press, and special publications. Carries the regular appendix "Premières théâtrales — First nights." All articles published in both French and English. The content of this periodical is readily accessible through a well-arranged index to its 100 issues edited by Joanna Strzelecka, *Le Théâtre en Pologne. Index 1958-1966* (Varsovie, 1967, 181 p.).

b. Histories and Surveys

3286. Almanach sceny polskiej (Almanac of the Polish stage). 1959/60– Warszawa, Wydawn. Artystyczne i Filmowe.

A compendium of contemporary stage activity in Poland. Seven volumes so far, covering the season through 1965/1966. Each volume is in two parts: the first containing synthetic survey articles, the second is strictly documentary in character. The publication is constantly improved upon, and represents an excellent primary source. Richly illustrated.

It may be completed by "Mały słownik teatru polskiego 1944-1963" (A short dictionary of the Polish theater, 1944-1963) in *Pamiętnik teatralny* (Warszawa), 1965, fascicle 3/4: 222-281. Several scores of entries list basic information about repertoire and organization.

3287. Csató, Edward. The Polish Theatre. Warsaw, Polonia Publishing House, 1963. 172 p. Illus.

An informative survey of the contemporary theater in Poland with an outline of its older history. May be supplemented by:

Grodzicki, August, Roman Szydłowski, *and* Konstanty Puzyna. Theatre in Modern Poland. Warsaw, Wydawnictwa Artystyczne i Filmowe, 1963. 174 p. Illus., facsims., map, ports. An album of 259 annotated photographs. Identical French versions of both books are available. For a comprehensive and impartial survey, followed by a chronicle of events in Polish theaters, indexes, and a useful bibliography, *see*:

Marczak-Oborski, Stanisław. Zycie teatralne w latach 1944-1964. Kierunki rozwojowe (Theatrical life in the years 1944-1964. Trends of development). Warszawa, Państwowe Wydawn. Naukowe, 1968. 308 p. Illus. Bibliography: p. 253-268.

3288. Hartmann, Karl. Das polnische Theater nach dem zweiten Weltkrieg. Marburg, N. G. Elwert Verlag, 1964. 126 p. Illus.

A concise, well organized, and very informative book.

3289. Jurkowski, Henryk, Henryk Ryl, *and* Jan Sztaudynger. Od szopki do teatru lalek (From the Christmas crèche to the puppet theater). Łódź, Wydawn. Łódzkie, 1961. 142 p. Illus.

A survey of the contemporary puppet theater in Poland, with a historical introduction. English, French, and Russian summaries.

3290. Lorentowicz, Jan. Dzieje teatru w Polsce od czasów najdawniejszych do chwili obecnej (History of the theater in Poland from the oldest times to the present day). *In*: Wiedza o Polsce. v. 4, pt. 2. Warszawa, Wydawn. "Wiedza o Polsce," 1933. p. 447-490.

Popular survey, written by an outstanding critic of the theater. It may be used jointly with two newer ones by Eugeniusz Szwankowski, *Teatr Rzeczypospolitej szlacheckiej* (The theater of the Republic of the gentry) (Warszawa, CPARA, 1962, 72 p.), and *Teatr polski w XIX i XX wieku, lata 1799-1939* (Polish theater in the 19th and 20th centuries, the years 1799-1939) (Warszawa, CPARA, 1963, 82 p.).

3291. Poplatek, Jan. Studia z dziejów jezuickiego teatru szkolnego w Polsce (Studies on the history of the Jesuit school theater in Poland).

Wrocław, Zakład Narodowy im. Ossolińskich, 1957. 225 p. Bibliography: p. 211-216.

Two studies based mainly on manuscript sources relating to the Jesuit school theater in Poland and against a European background. French summary.

3292. Raszewski, Zbigniew. Pologne. *In*: Histoire des spectacles. Edited by Guy Dumur. Paris, Gallimard, 1965. p. 1105-1117. (Encyclopédie de la Pléiade, 19)

The most up-to-date outline of the development of the Polish theater from the 13th century up to 1939.

3293. Strzelecki, Zenobiusz. Polska plastyka teatralna (Polish stage design). Warszawa, Państwowy Instytut Wydawniczy, 1963. 3 v. Illus.

A basic survey, written by an active stage designer. It may be completed by a book discussing the great progenitor of modern Polish theater, Alicja Okońska's *Scenografia Stanisława Wyspiańskiego* (Stanisław Wyspiański's scenography) (Wrocław, Zakład im. Ossolińskich, 1961, 323 p., illus.). *See also* Jan Nowacki's "Plastyka teatralna Wyspiańskiego" (Wyspiański's theatrical art) in *Pamiętnik teatralny* (Warszawa), 1957, fascicle 3/4 (23/24): 558-605, entirely devoted to this artist of the theater. *See* the same source, 1958, fascicle 3/4 (27/28): 505-544, for additional information.

Very instructive, though different in character, are the following publications concerning two other eminent stage designers: Karol Frycz's *O teatrze i sztuce* (About theater and art), edited by Alfred Wóycicki (Warszawa, Wydawn. Artystyczne i Filmowe, 1967, 300 p.), a selection of writings with an introductory essay, biographical notes, a list of Frycz's main works, bibliography and index, as well as a special issue dedicated to Andrzej Pronaszko of *Pamiętnik teatralny* (Warszawa), 1964, fascicle 1/2.

3294. Le Théâtre en Pologne. Numéro spécial de la Revue Le Théâtre dans le Monde. Elsevier, 1957. 56 p. Illus.

An introduction to the problems of the contemporary Polish theater. The entire text is printed in both French and English.

3295. Trezzini, Lamberto. Teatro in Polonia. Bologna, Cappelli ed., 1962. 199 p. Illus. Bibliography: p. 201 (Documenti di teatro, 24)

An informative survey of the history of the theater in Poland, not always systematic; best in the parts referring to newer Polish publications. Detailed chapters dedicated to the contemporary Polish theater. An annex gives, among other things, a list of Polish playwrights and the first performances of their works in the years 1945-1959, as well as the repertoire of all the drama playhouses in Poland for the 1960-1961 season. A special issue of *Sipario* (Bologna) 1963, no. 208-209 ("numero doppio dedicato al teatro polacco"), completes the book.

3296. Witczak, Tadeusz. Historia dramatu i teatru do r. 1750 w publikacjach powojennych (The history of drama and theater until 1750 in postwar publications). Pamiętnik teatralny (Warszawa), 1954, fasc. 2 (10): 92-119; 1955, fasc. 2 (14) 199-207.

Also by the same author: "Teatr i dramat staropolski w publikacjach z lat 1955-1960" (Old Polish theater and drama in publications from 1955 to 1960) in *Pamiętnik teatralny*, 1960, fascicle 3-4 (35-36): 561-588.

c. Periods and Personalities

3297. Bernacki, Ludwik. Teatr, dramat i muzyka za Stanisława Augusta (Theater, drama, and music under King Stanisław August Poniatowski). Warszawa, 1925. 2 v. Plates, ports., facsims.

This remains an important bibliographical guide and collection of source material concerning the last, memorable period of prepartition Poland. *See also* Julian Lewański's "Teatr, dramat i muzyka za Stanisława Augusta w świetle nowych źródeł" (Theater, drama, and music in the era of Stanisław August in the light of new sources), in *Pamiętnik teatralny* (Warszawa), 1960, fascicle 1 (33): 115-143, and three collective works: a special issue of *Pamiętnik teatralny* (Warszawa), 1966, fascicle 1/4 (57-60), entirely dedicated to the Polish theater of the second part of the 18th century; the proceedings of a conference *Teatr Narodowy w dobie Oświecenia* (The National Theater in the era of the Enlightenment) (Wrocław, Zakład Narodowy im. Ossolińskich, 1967, 268 p.), and finally a huge, collective volume, rich in source material, intended as a supplement to Bernacki's work, *Teatr Narodowy 1765-1794* (The National Theater 1765-1794), edited by Jan Kott (Warszawa, Państwowy Instytut Wydawniczy, 1967, 934 p., illus.).

3298. Got, I. Jerzy, *and* Józef Szczublewski. Helena Modrzejewska. Warszawa, Państwowy Instytut Wydawniczy, 1958. 258 p.

Szczublewski, Józef *and* Eugeniusz Szwankowski. Alojzy Żółkowski-syn. Warszawa, Państwowy Instytut Wydawn., 1959. 252 p.

Two parts of a series ((Almanachy poświęcone najwybitniejszym artystom sceny polskiej, 1, 2) containing biographical data, repertoire in chronological and alphabetical order, selected notices and criticism, personal statements and correspondence.

As Helena Modrzejewska was also an English-speaking actress (appearing as Helena Modjeska), the work devoted to her also retraces for the first time her American and British tours. *See also*:

Szczublewski, Józef. Helena Modrzejewska. Warszawa, Państwowy Instytut Wydawniczy, 1959. 149 p. Illus.

Terlecki, Tymon. Pani Helena; opowieść biograficzna o Modrzejewskiej (Madame Helena; a biographical account of Modrzejewska). Londyn, "Veritas," 1962. 281 p. (tom 41 serii czerwonej "Biblioteki polskiej")

Correspondence between Modrzejewska and her husband is contained in:

Korespondencja Heleny Modrzejewskiej i Karola Chłapowskiego.

Edited by Jerzy Got and Józef Szczublewski. Warszawa, Państwowy Instytut Wydawniczy, 1966. 2 v.

3299. Monografie czołowych artystów sceny polskiej (Monographs of leading artists of the Polish stage). Warszawa, Państwowy Instytut Wydawniczy, 1954–

A series of concise, popular books, based on original research, concerning actors, producers, directors from the 18th to the 20th centuries. Each volume illustrated often with rare prints and photographs.

3300. Raszewski, Zbigniew. Staroświecczyzna i postęp czasu (Bygone fashions and the progress of time). Warszawa, Państwowy Instytut Wydawniczy, 1963. 450 p. Illus., facsims., ports.

A collection of essays on the Polish theater, covering a period from 1765 to 1865, revealing new facts and interpreting them in a new way.

3301. Schiller, Leon. Teatr ogromny (The immense theater). Edited by Zbigniew Raszewski and Jerzy Timoszewicz. Warszawa, Czytelnik, 1961. 549 p.

A large, carefully annotated selection of the theoretical, historical, critical writings of the greatest modern Polish producer (1887-1954), the creator of the so-called "monumental theater" in Poland. It should be completed by an important English essay by Schiller, "The New Theater in Poland — Stanisław Wyspiański," *The Mask* (Florence), v. 2, 1909/10: 11-27, 57-71. The bibliography concerning Schiller may be supplemented by the monographic issue of *Pamiętnik teatralny* (Warszawa), 1955, fascicle 3/4 (15/16), entirely devoted to him, as well as by:

Csató, Edward. Leon Schiller twórca monumentalnego teatru polskiego (Leon Schiller, the creator of the Polish monumental theater). Warszawa, Centralna Poradnia Amatorskiego Ruchu Artystycznego, 1966. 201 p. A popular treatment of the subject.

Szczublewski, Józef. Artyści i urzędnicy czyli szaleństwa Leona Schillera (Artists and bureaucrats, or the follies of Leon Schiller). Warszawa, Państwowy Instytut Wydawniczy, 1961. 290 p. An almost novelistic presentation of an episode in Schiller's artistic career, but based on serious research.

The following work also deserves special attention:

Timoszewicz, Jerzy. "Dziady" w inscenizacji Leona Schillera (Leon Schiller's production of "Forefathers' Eve" [by Adam Mickiewicz]). Warszawa, Pańnstwowy Instytut Wydawniczny, 1969. 180 p. Illus. This is a monograph on Schiller's most outstanding work (Lwów, 1932; Wilno, 1933; Warszawa, 1934; Sofia, 1937) and contains a reconstruction of the producer's lost scenario.

3302. Sławińska, Irena, Stefan Kruk, *and* Bożena Frankowska. Myśl teatralna Młodej Polski (The concept of the theater in the Young

Poland period). Warszawa, Wydawn. Artystyczne i Filmowe, 1966. 475 p.

An anthology of writings from the period corresponding to European and American symbolism. There is a further discussion of this period, with bibliography, in:

Frankowska, Bożena. Teatr Młodej Polski a literatura (The theater of Young Poland and literature). *In* Literatura Młodej Polski, v. 2. Obraz literatury polskiej XIX i XX wieku, seria piąta (Literature of the Young Poland Period, v. 2. A picture of Polish literature in the 19th and 20th centuries, 5th series). Warszawa, Państwowe Wydawn. Naukowe, 1967. p. 7-53.

3303. Szwankowski, Eugeniusz. Teatr Wojciecha Bogusławskiego w latach 1799-1814. Wrocław, Zakład Narodowy im. Ossolińskich, 1954. 384 p. Illus. (Materiały do dziejów teatru w Polsce, t. 1)

The book deals with the major figure of Wojciech Bogusławski, an important creative personality at the turn of the 18th and 19th centuries (1757-1829), often called "the father of the Polish theater." In 1965 there appeared a photo-offset reedition of his *Dzieje Teatru Narodowego . . . oraz wiadomość o życiu sławnych artystów* (History of the National Theater and information on the life of famous artists) (Warszawa, 1820), with a postscript by S. W. Balicki.

3304. Targosz-Kretowa, Karolina. Teatr dworski Władysława IV, 1635-1648 (The court theater of King Władysław IV, 1635-1648). Kraków, Wydawn. Literackie, 1965. 341 p. Illus., facsims., plans, ports.

A comprehensive monograph with excerpts from source materials and a repertoire. Summaries in English and Italian. *See also* the same author's "Le théâtre d'opéra à la cour de Ladislas IV, roi de Pologne (1635-1648)," *Revue d'histoire du théâtre* (Paris), 1967, no. 1: 33-56.

3305. Terlecki, Tymon. Le théâtre polonais 1919-1939. *In* Pologne 1919-1939. Edited by Józef Modzelewski. Neuchâtel, La Baconnière, 1947. p. 713-735.

With a bibliography in English, French and German. *See also* an earlier and longer but somewhat muddled study about this period:

Orlicz, Michał. Polski teatr współczesny. Próba syntezy (Polish contemporary theater. A tentative synthesis). Warszawa, Drukarnia współczesna, 1935. 470 p. Illus. With summaries in French, English, German, and Czech.

3306. Wierzbicka, Karyna. Źródła do historii teatru warszawskiego od roku 1762 do roku 1833 (Sources for the history of the theater in Warsaw, 1762-1833). Wrocław, Wydawn. Zakładu Narodowego im. Ossolińskich, 1951-1955. 2 v.

Based on archival material, this book provides a fresh interpretation and explanation of the genesis of the National Theater in Warsaw, which in 1965 celebrated the bicentenary of its existence. The early years of the theater in the era of King Stanisław August are surveyed in:

Klimowicz, Mieczysław. Początki teatru stanisławowskiego, 1765-1773 (The origins of the theater of the era of King Stanisław August, 1765-1773). Warszawa, Państwowy Instytut Wydawniczy, 1965. 486 p.

d. Special Aspects

3307. Csató, Edward. Les metteurs en scène polonais. Varsovie, Centre polonais de l'Institut international du théâtre, 1963. 53 p. 63 illus.

An informative essay.

3308. Nowicki, Roman. Theatre Schools in Poland. Warsaw, Polish Centre of the International Theatre Institute, 1963. 43 p.

An informative pamphlet with an introductory historical outline. The period between the two world wars is analyzed in:

Terlecki, Tymon. Theatrical Training in Poland. *In*: Polish Science and Learning, no. 5. London, Oxford University Press, 1944. p. 100-103.

3309. Osiński, Zbigniew. Przekład tekstu literackiego na język teatru. Zarys problematyki (The translation of a literary text into the language of the theater. Outline of the problem). *In*: Trzynadlowski, Jan, *ed.* Dramat i teatr. Konferencja teoretyczno-literacka w Świętej Katarzyne (Drama and the theater. A conference in Święta Katarzyna, devoted to the theory of literature). Wrocław, Zakład Narodowy im. Ossolińskich, 1967. p. 119-156.

A stimulating study based on the principles of semiotics.

3310. Schiller, Irena. Polscy. aktorzy o swoich przeżyciach podczas gry. Materiały z badań (Polish actors about their experiences during acting. Research materials). Pamiętnik teatralny (Warszawa), v. 16, 1967, fasc. 1 (61): 3-21.

The text of 21 of the original questionnaires saved from the disasters of the Second World War with the answers of a number of eminent actors. This is the final chapter of a pioneering work in the field of the psychology of acting. It provides some bibliographical references to works in Polish, French, and German. One may also consult:

Villiers, André, *pseud.* (André Bonnichon). La psychologie du comédien. 4th ed. Paris, Mercure de France, 1942. 326 p. Bibliography: p. 305-317.

3311. Schiller, Irena. Stanisławski a teatr polski (Stanislavskii and the Polish theater). Warszawa, Państwowy Instytut Wydawniczy, 1965. 393 p. Illus., facsims., ports.

A study of the mutual relations between Stanislavskii and the Polish theater. Summaries in Russian and French.

3312. Terlecki, Tymon. Polish Drama and the European Theater. Drama Critique (Detroit), v. 10, Winter 1967: 30-38.

A sketch of the links between the two from the end of the 18th century to the Second World War, emphasizing the interdependence of Stanisław Wyspiański, Edward Gordon Craig, and Leon Schiller.

2. Cinema

a. Theoretical Publications

3313. Dreyer, Regina, *ed.* Zagadnienia estetyki filmowej (The problems of film aesthetics). Państwowy Instytut Sztuki, 1955. 406 p.

A collection of nine theoretical studies, discussing such problems as the structure, the "organization of time and space," the composition, the character, speech, sound, and color in the film.

3314. Ingarden, Roman. Kilka uwag o sztuce filmowej (Some remarks about the art of the film). *In*: Studia z estetyki (Studies in aesthetics). v. 3. Warszawa, Państwowe Wydawn. Naukowe, 1958. p. 299-316.

The author, a preeminent Polish Husserlist, gives in a succinct form a very precise and penetrating introduction to the theory of film.

3315. Irzykowski, Karol. Dziesiąta Muza; zagadnienia estetyczne kina (The Tenth Muse; aesthetic problems of the cinema). 2d ed. Warszawa, Filmowa Agencja Wydawnicza, 1957. 231 p.

A work written by a great critic and original thinker from the period before the Second World War (1873-1944), first published in 1934. At this early stage Irzykowski had already embarked on the task of defining the new art, its individuality, and its artistic potentialities. This is the first philosophy of the cinema; a treatise, unique perhaps not only in Polish literature. Krzysztof Teodor Toeplitz, himself a remarkable film theoretician, says in his long preface to this new edition that *The Tenth Muse* is "the most fascinating work on the film written in Polish" and states that "this book helped to bring up the best cadre of Polish film producers and people interested in film." *See also* Aleksander Kumor's *Karol Irzykowski, teoretyk filmu* (Karol Irzykowski, theoretician of the film) (Warszawa, Wydawn. Artystyczne i Filmowe, 1965, 259 p.).

3316. Jackiewicz, Aleksander, *ed.* Wstęp do badania dzieła filmowego (An introduction to the examination of film work). Warszawa, Wydawn. Artystyczne i Filmowe, 1966. 285 p.

A collection of studies from the workshop of film theory in the Institute of Art of the Polish Academy of Arts and Sciences, developing the theoretical tenets of Siegfried Kracauer's *Theory of Film; The Redemption of Physical Reality* (New York, Oxford University Press, 1960, 364 p.) and André Bazin's *Qu'est-ce que le cinéma?* (Paris, Éditions du Cerf, 1958-1962, 4 v., Collection "7e art," 29, 33). A rich bibliography. *See also* Jackiewicz's "Proces literacki a film" (The literary process and film), in *Proces historyczny w literaturze i sztuce* (The historical process in literature and art), edited by Maria Janion (Warszawa, Państwowy Instytut Wydawn., 1967, 400 p.;

Instytut Badań Literackich Polskiej Akademii Nauk, Historia i teoria literartury; Studia. Historia literatury, 18).

3317. Kwartalnik filmowy (Motion picture quarterly). 1951– Warszawa. Quarterly.

A scholarly publication devoted to theoretical and practical problems of Polish and foreign cinematography. Includes bibliographies and survey of films shown.

3318. Lewicki, Bolesław. Wprowadzenie do wiedzy o filmie (An introduction to knowledge of the film). Wrocław, Zakład im. Ossolińskich, 1964. 198 p.

A theory of film, following the tracks of Roman Ingarden's book, *Das literarische Kunstwerk; eine Untersuchung aus dem Grenzgebiet der Ontologie, Logik und Literaturwissenschaft* (Halle [Saale], M. Niemeyer, 1931, 339 p.). *See also*:

Lewicki, Bolesław. Funkcje informacyjne struktury dzieła filmowego (The informative functions of film structure). *In*: Łódź. Uniwersytet. Zeszyty naukowe, ser. 1, 1963, nr. 29.

———. Formuła struktury estetycznej filmu (The formula of the aesthetic structure of film). *In*: Łódź. Uniwersytet. Zeszyty naukowe, ser. 1, 1966, nr. 43.

———. Zagadnienia semiotyczne w filmie (Semiotic problems in film). Ibid., 1967, nr. 50.

3319. Lissa, Zofia. Estetyka muzyki filmowej (Aesthetics of film music). Kraków, Polskie Wydawn. Muzyczne, 1964. 488 p.

Appeared in German translation as *Ästhetic der Filmmusik* (Berlin, Henschelverlag, 1965, 453 p.; "Literaturverzeichnis": p. 409-424). *See also* the earlier discussion by the same author, *Muzyka i film. Studium z pogranicza ontologii, estetyki i psychologii muzyki filmowej* (Music and film. A study from the borderland of the ontology, aesthetics, and psychology of film music) (Lwów, Księgarnia Lwowska, 1937, 135 p.).

3320. Płażewski, Jerzy. Język filmu (Film language). Warszawa, Wydawnictwa Artystyczne i Filmowe, 1961. 522 p.

A basic work, tracing the changing means of expression in the history of film. An exhaustive bibliography in many languages.

3321. Wert, Pola. Analiza dzieła filmowego (An analysis of film work). *In*: Łódź. Uniwersytet. Zeszyty naukowe. Ser. 1. 1962, nr. 25: 117-130.

A demonstration of the analytical method applied in the famous State Academy of Theater and Film in Łódź and in the Institute of Film Knowledge at the University of the same town.

b. Histories of the Cinema

3322. Andrzej Munk. Warszawa, Wydawnictwa Filmowe i Artystyczne, 1964. 116 p.

A collective work dedicated to one of the greatest Polish film producers, prematurely dead in 1961. Reminiscences of friends and collaborators, personal statements of Munk. His full filmography and an equally exhaustive bibliography.

3323. Banaszkiewicz, Władysław, *and* Witold Witczak. Historia filmu polskiego 1895-1929 (History of the Polish film, 1895-1929). Warszawa, Państwowy Instytut Sztuki, 1967. 331 p.

The first of a planned three-volume scholarly work. It presents the birth of the Polish cinematography against the cultural, political, social and economic background. When finished, this book will supersede the slightly earlier works:

Jewsiewicki, Władysław. Polska kinematografia w okresie filmu niemego w latach 1845-1929 (Polish film production at the time of the silent films). Wrocław, Zakład Narodowy im. Ossolińskich, 1967. 190 p.

Polska kinematografia w okresie filmu dźwiękowego w latach 1929-1939 (Polish film production at the time of sound films, 1929-1939). Wrocław, Zakład Narodowy im. Ossolińskich, 1967. 191 p.

3324. Jewsiewicki, Władysław. Kazimierz Prószyński. Warszawa, Filmowa Agencja Wydawnicza, 1954. 87 p. Illus.

A monograph of a Polish inventor in the field of film projection (the "pleograph," 1894-1895). A larger, more general treatment of the problem can be found in another valuable book by the same author: *Prehistoria filmu* (Prehistory of the film) (Warszawa, Filmowa Agencja Wydawnicza, 1953, 212 p.).

3325. Michałek, Bolesław. Film się zmienia (The film changes). Warszawa, Wydawnictwa Filmowe i Artystyczne, 1967. 131 p.

A collection of essays on the latest evolution in the art of the cinema, including a tentative critical appraisal of film making and its generic, aesthetic, and ideological aspects.

3326. Toeplitz, Jerzy. Dwadzieścia pięć lat filmu Polski Ludowej (Twenty-five years of film making in People's Poland). Warszawa, Polskie Wydawn. Naukowe, 1968. 150 p. Illus.

An outline of the main phases of development of the Polish film after the Second World War. Indexes of names and of titles. Calendar of events.

3327. Toeplitz, Jerzy. Historia sztuki filmowej (History of film art). Warszawa, Filmowa Agencja Wydawnictwa, 1955-1959. 3 v.

A fundamental, most scholarly, and well-documented study, written in an accessible fashion.

PART SIX

SORBIANS (LUSATIANS) AND POLABIANS

46

SORBIANS (LUSATIANS)

by James A. Sehnert

A. BIBLIOGRAPHY

3328. Młyńk, Jurij. Serbska bibliografija 1945-1957 z dodawkami do 1945. Sorbische Bibliographie 1945-1957 mit Nachträgen bis 1945. Budyšin, Domowina, 1959. 287 p. (Spisy Instituta za serbski ludospyt, 10)

Somewhat overlaps Wjacsławk's bibliography for the period since the war (see entry no. 3330), but gives complete Sorbian bibliographical information from 1945 to 1957. Entries according to subject.

3329. Schuster-Šewc, Heinz. Bibliographie der sorbischen Sprachwissenschaft. Bautzen (Budyšin), Domowina, 1966. 79 p. Němska Akademija Wědomośćow w Berlinje. Spisy Instituta za serbski ludospyt, 27)

A very handy and complete bibliography of the major books and articles dealing with Sorbian language problems. Entries according to subject.

3330. Wjacsławk, Jakub (Jacob Jatzwauk). Serbska bibliografija. Sorbische (Wendische) Bibliographie. 2d rev. and enl. ed. Berlin, Akademie-Verlag, 1952. 500 p. (Berichte über die Verhandlungen der Sächsischen Akademie der Wissenschaften zu Leipzig. Philologisch-historische Klasse, Bd. 98, Heft 3)

The first edition of this Sorbian bibliography appeared as Jacob Jatzwauk's *Wendische (Sorbische) Bibliographie* (Leipzig, 1929, 353 p.). It was expanded and brought up to date to 1952. The period since 1952 has been covered by the bibliographies of Jurij Młyńk (*see entry* no. 3328). Contains a complete bibliography for all aspects of Sorbian life. Entries according to subject.

B. PERIODICALS

3331. Bautzen, Germany. Institut za serbski ludospyt. Lětopis Instituta za serbski ludospyt (Annals of the Institute for Sorbian Studies). Rjad A: rěč a literatura (Series A: Linguistics and literature), č. 1– 1952–; Rjad B: stawizny (Series B: History), č. 1– 1953–; Rjad C: ludowěda (Series C: Ethnography), č. 1– 1953–. Budyšin, Domowina. Annual (in one or two fascicles).

This journal, appearing in three series, contains original articles — mainly in Sorbian — on linguistic, literary, historical, and ethnographic problems. Series A does not include belles-lettres. Also contains an annual bibliography of Sorbian publications from the previous year.

3332. Maćica Serbska, *Bautzen, Germany*. Časopis Maćicy Serbskeje (Journal of the Maćica Serbska). 1848-1937. Budyšin, Maćica Serbska. Annual (in one or two fascicles).

Original belles-lettres and articles on literary and linguistic problems. Contributions from nearly all of the great Sorbian writers and scholars for nearly 90 years. From 1848 to 1872 the journal bore the title *Časopis Towaŕstwa Maćicy Serbskeje*; in 1873 the "Towaŕstwa" was dropped.

3333. Rozhlad. Časopis za serbsku kulturu (Journal for Sorbian culture). 1950– Budyšin, Domowina. Monthly.

Original articles in Upper Sorbian dealing with Sorbian cultural affairs including politics, contacts abroad, recent books, etc.

C. LITERATURE AND GENERAL CULTURE

3334. Frinta, Antonín. Lužičtí Srbové a jejich písemnictví (The Lusatian Sorbs and their literature). Praha, Nakl. Československé akademie věd, 1955. 239 p. Illus., ports., maps. Bibliography: p. 201-222. (Československá akademie věd. Sekce jazyka: literatury. Slovanský ústav. Dějiny slovanských literatur, sv. 1)

An account of the history of the Sorbs, their culture, and their literature.

3335. Gołąbek, Józef. Literatura serbołużycka (Sorbo-Lusatian literature). Katowice, 1938. 269 p. Bibliography: p. 248-249. (Instytut śląski, Katowice, Poland. Pamiętnik, t. 5)

Primarily a history of Sorbian literature, but contains information on the history of the Sorbs, the development of national consciousness, the history of the literary language, etc. Up to its time this was probably the best work on the subject. Résumé in French.

3336. Jenč, Rudolf. Stawizny serbskeho pismowstwa (History of Sorbian literature). Budyšin, Domowina, 1954-1960. 2 v. Ports., facsims. (Spisy Instituta za serbski ludospyt, 1, 12)

The most authoritative history of Sorbian literature from its origins to the end of the First World War. A history of the literature since that time has not yet appeared in this series. Volume one reviewed by Marja Kubašec in *Rozhlad*, no. 6, 1955: 189-192; volume two by Jurij Młyńk in *Nowa doba*, 1961, no. 42.

3337. Kochański, Witold. Dole i niedole Serbołużyczan (The fortunes and misfortunes of the Lusatian Sorbs). Warszawa, Książka i Wiedza, 1962. 316 p. Illus., maps.

A popular introduction to the culture of the Sorbs including discussions of their country, history, literature, cultural contacts abroad, and Germanization. A handy little book for an overall nonscholarly survey of Sorbian life. Another convenient little book of this type is *Die Sorben* by Hans Brüchner and others. (Bautzen [Budyšin], Domowina, 1964, 239 p.). Discusses Sorbian culture and history in question-and-answer fashion. Many photographs.

3338. Mětšk, Frido, *ed.* Chrestomatija dolnoserbskego pismowstwa (Chrestomathy of Lower Sorbian literature). Berlin, Volk und Wissen, 1956-1957. 2 v. Illus.

Anthologies of Lower Sorbian literature. Volume one contains the literature from the beginnings to the end of the 19th century. Volume two contains the literature from the third quarter of the 19th century to the end of the Second World War. These two volumes are supplemented by a Lower Sorbian-German glossary compiled by Frido Mětšk and H. Pětrik: *Zapis słowow ku chrestomatiji dolnoserbskego pismowstwa* (List of words for the chrestomathy of Lower Sorbian literature). Berlin, Volk und Wissen, 1957. 75 p.

3339. Młyńk, Jurij. Skicy k stawiznam serbskeje literatury (Sketches on the history of Sorbian literature). Berlin, Volk und Wissen, 1956. 230 p.

An outline history of the most important events and personages in the development of Upper Sorbian literature from the beginnings to 1956.

3340. Młyńk, Jurij. 100 lět serbskeho dźiwadła: 1862-1962 (100 years of the Sorbian theater: 1862-1962). Budyšin, Dom za serbske ludowe wuměłstwo, 1962. 239 p.

Discusses the development of the Sorbian theater with information on playwrights, actors, repertory, and the general growth of the theater in Lusatia.

3341. Młyńkowa, Marja, *and* Jurij Młyńk. Serbska literatura kónc 50. a spočatk 60. lět (Sorbian literature at the end of the '50s and the beginning of the '60s). Budyšin, Serbski pedagogiski institut, 1963. 182 p.

A discussion of developments in the Sorbian novel, short story, drama, and poetry.

3342. Serbšćina; listowy studij za wučerjow (The Sorbian language; correspondence course for teachers). Mały Wjelkow, Serbski pedagogiski institut, 1955-1959? 2448 p. 20 fascicles.

Although designed for teachers in Sorbian schools, this work is one of the most important to appear since the war. Within the twenty fascicles there appear articles by distinguished Sorbian scholars on the history and structure of the Sorbian languages, the history of the Sorbian literatures, phonology, morphology, syntax, orthography, semantics, dialectology, ethnography, history, and teaching methods — all in convenient survey form for easy reference. A necessity for anyone interested in Sorbian affairs.

D. ETHNOGRAPHY AND FOLKLORE

3343. Magnuszewski, Józef. Ludowe pieśni, bajki i podania Łużyczan (The folksongs, tales, and legends of the Lusatians). Wrocław, Zakład narodowy im. Ossolińskich, 1965. 256 p. Illus. (Biblioteka narodowa, ser. 2, 147)

The introduction to this work discusses the state of research and the form and history of the tales, songs, and legends. Most of the Sorbian texts have been translated into Polish. See also *Sorbische Volkserzählungen. Podania łużyckie* by Jerzy Sliziński (Berlin, Akademie, 1964, 93 p., map, photos). (Veröffentlichungen des Instituts für Slawistik, herausgegeben von H. H. Bielfeldt, Nr. 31.)

3344. Nedo, Pawoł. Sorbische Volksmärchen; systematische Quellenausgabe mit Einführung und Anmerkungen. Bautzen (Budyšin), Domowina-Verlag, 1956. 447 p. (Spisy Instituta za serbski ludospyt, 4)

A scholarly study of the Sorbian folktale in which the author discusses the state of research on the Sorbian folktale, the narrators, and the sources and provides notes on each tale. The texts are given in Sorbian with German translations or versions. Arranged according to type: animal tales, tales of magic, etc.

3345. Rawp, Jan. Serbska hudźba. Wobrys wo wuwiću serbskeho hudźbneho tworjenja (Sorbian music. Survey of the development of Sorbian musical creation). Budyšin, Domowina, 1966. 77 p. Photos.

A short survey of Sorbian music, both folk and created.

3346. Schneeweis, Edmund. Feste und Volksbräuche der Sorben vergleichend dargestellt. 2d ed. Berlin, Akademie-Verlag, 1953. 186

p. Plates (part col.). Bibliography: p. 177-183. (Veröffentlichungen des Instituts für Slawistik, Nr. 3)

A scholarly presentation of various Sorbian customs pertaining to marriage, birth, death, holidays, animals, spinning, etc.

3347. Serbske narodne drasty. Sorbische Volkstrachten. Bautzen (Budyšin), Domowina, 1954-1964. 4 v.

Richly illustrated, dealing with Sorbian folk costumes. The individual volumes are as follows:

v. 1. Nowak, Měrćin (Martin Nowak-Neumann), *and* P. Nedo. Drasta Slepjanskich Serbow. Die Tracht der Sorben um Schleife. Bautzen (Budyšin), Domowina, 1954. 117 p.

v. 2. Meschgang (Měškank), Jan. Drasta katolskich Serbow. Bautzen (Budyšin), Domowina, 1957. 129 p. Plates (part col.), map.

v. 3. Schneider (Krawc), Erich. Drasta Serbow wokoło Wojerec. Die Tracht der Sorben um Hoyerswerda. Bautzen (Budyšin), Domowina, 1959. 119 p. Plates (part col.), map.

v. 4. Nowak, Měrćin (Martin Nowak-Neumann). Drasta delnjołužiskich Serbow. Die Tracht der Niederlausitzer Sorben. Bautzen (Budyšin), Domowina, 1964. 65 p. Illus.

E. GRAMMAR

3348. De Bray, Reginald G. A. Lusatian (or Wendish). *In his* Guide to the Slavonic Languages. 2d printing. London, Dent; New York, Dutton, 1963. p. 673-791.

The first and so far the only grammar of Upper Sorbian in English. The section opens with a note on the history of the language and follows with a discussion of Upper Sorbian phonology and morphology. Notes on the differences between Upper and Lower Sorbian also included.

3349. Liebsch, Georg. Syntax der wendischen Sprache in der Oberlausitz. Bautzen (Budyšin), M. Hórnik, in Commission bei Schmaler und Pech in Leipzig, 1884. 240 p. Bibliography: p. 239-240.

So far this is the only book devoted entirely to the problem of Upper Sorbian syntax, although numerous articles have appeared in various journals and in *Serbšćina; listowy studij za wučerjow* (see entry no. 3342). Reviewed by J. Polivka in *Časopis Českého muzea*, 1884: 331.

3350. Mucke, Karl Ernst. Historische und vergleichende Laut- und Formenlehre der niedersorbischen (niederlausitzisch-wendischen) Sprache. Mit besonderer Berücksichtigung der Grenzdialekte und des Obersorbischen. Leipzig, Zentral-Antiquariat, 1965. 615 p.

This work is an unaltered reprint of Mucke's work which first appeared in Leipzig in 1891 in the series *Preisschriften gekrönt und herausgegeben von der Fürstlich Jablonowski'schen Gesellschaft zu Leipzig*, v. 28 (Leipzig), 1891, 612 p. It is still the basic work in

Sorbian historical grammar. Reviewed by J. Karásek in *Archiv für slavische Philologie*, v. 16, 1894: 530-549.

3351. Schwela, Gotthold (Bogumił Šwjela). Grammatik der niedersorbischen Sprache. Edited by Frido Mětšk. 2d ed. Bautzen (Budyšin), Domowina-Verlag, 1952. 107 p.

Contains the phonology and morphology of Lower Sorbian. Some discussion of syntax. Primarily a reference grammar.

3352. Wjela, Jurij. Lehrgang der sorbischen Sprache. Kurs serbskeje rěče. 2d rev. ed. Bautzen (Budyšin), Domowina-Verlag, 1956. 136 p.

A manual for learning Upper Sorbian. Suitable either for self-instruction or classroom work. Other textbooks include:

Zur, Jan. Wuknjemy serbski (We learn Sorbian). Budyšin, Domowina, 1958. 127 p.

Nowak-Njechorński, Měrćin. Wuknimy dolnoserbski; Krótki kurs delnjoserbšćiny za hornjołužiskich Serbow (Let's learn Lower Sorbian; a short course of Lower Sorbian for the Upper Lusatian Sorbs). Budyšin, Domowina, 1952. 67 p. An excellent contrastive grammar of the two languages.

3353. Wowčerk, Pawoł. Kurzgefasste obersorbische Grammatik. Krótka hornjoserbska gramatika. 3d ed. Berlin, Volk und Wissen, 1955. 176 p.

A short reference grammar of Upper Sorbian giving the basic principles of the phonology and morphology. Reviewed by M. Nowak-Njechorński in *Rozhlad*, v. 1, 1951: 185-186.

3354. Žur, Jan. Přiručka za serbsku wučbu na hornim schodźenku dźesaćrjadowniskich powšitkownozdźěłowanskich polytechniskich serbskich wyšich šulow a dźesaćrjadowniskich powšitkownozdźěłowanskich polytechniskich wyšich šulow ze serbskej wučbu (A manual for Sorbian instruction at the upper level of the 10-class Sorbian general polytechnic high schools and the 10-class general polytechnic high schools with Sorbian instruction). Budyšin, Domowina, 1962. 327 p.

Written completely in Upper Sorbian, this work is a reference grammar devoted almost entirely to paradigms. Reviewed by H. Faska, *Lětopis Instituta za serbski ludospyt. Rjad A*, v. 10, 1963: 244-246; H. Faska, *Serbska šula*, 1963: 374-379; 445-448.

F. DICTIONARIES AND LEXICOGRAPHY

3355. Bielfeldt, Hans Holm. Die deutschen Lehnwörter im Obersorbischen. Leipzig, Harrassowitz, 1933. 309 p. Bibliography: p. xv-xix. (Berlin. Universität. Slavisches Institut. Veröffentlichungen, 8)

A detailed study of the phonological and semantic adaptation of German words into Upper Sorbian. An etymological glossary forms a major part of the work.

3356. Jakubaš, Filip. Hornjoserbsko–němski słownik. Obersorbisch-deutsches Wörterbuch. Budyšin, Domowina, 1954. 543 p.

The largest and most complete Upper Sorbian-German dictionary published since the Second World War, in which most of the germanisms and archaic words found in Pfuhl (*see* entry no. 3359) are omitted; however, many neologisms and words of international origin have been added. The introduction gives an outline of Upper Sorbian phonology and morphology.

3357. Kral, Georg (Jurij). Serbsko-němski słownik hornjołužiskeje rěče (Sorbian-German dictionary of the Upper Lusatian language). Budyšin, Maćica serbska, 1931. 968 p.

The second (after Pfuhl) of the big Sorbian-German dictionaries. Highly puristic, it contains almost no archaic expressions, germanisms or dialect forms. For reviews, *see*: H. H. Bielfeldt, *Zeitschrift für slavische Philologie*, v. 7, 1930: 273-279; O. Hujer, *Listy filologické*, v. 59, 1932: 313-314; B. Šwjela (Gotthold Schwela), *Serbske nowiny*, 1933: no. 149.

3358. Mucke, Karl Ernst (Arnošt Muka). Słownik dolnoserbskeje rěcy a jeje narěcow. Wörterbuch der nieder-wendischen Sprache und ihrer Dialekte. Praha, Nákl. České akademie věd a uměni, 1926-1928. 3 v.

The most authoritative and complete dictionary published on the Lower Sorbian language. Volumes 1 and 2 contain the Lower Sorbian lexicon with equivalents in German and Russian. Etymological and dialectal information cited. Volume 3 is devoted to family names. This great work has recently been made available again through the Domowina in Budyšin.

3359. Pfuhl, C. T. (Křesćan Bohuwěr, *pseud.*), *ed.* Łužiski serbski słownik. Lausitzisch wendisches Wörterbuch. Compiled by Pfarrer Seiler and Domvicar Hornik. Budissin, Maćica serbska, 1866. 1210 p.

This was the first of the extensive Sorbian-German dictionaries published. It includes much of the lexical material, including germanisms, from the oldest Sorbian literature. Dialectal forms also given with notations. Although this work is of limited value for reading modern newspapers, literature, and scientific material, it is indispensable for the older literature and for studies in the development of the Upper Sorbian lexicon. Meanings in German; contains a German index.

3360. Pomocny terminologiski słownik němsko-dolnoserbski (A handy German–Lower Sorbian terminological dictionary). Budyšyn, Domowina, 1960. 354 l.

A companion volume of Lower Sorbian terms for the work mentioned immediately below.

3361. Pomocny terminologiski słownik němsko-serbski (A handy German-Sorbian terminological dictionary). Berlin, Volk und Wissen, 1957. 352 p.

A German–Upper Sorbian dictionary, compiled by Sorbian textbook editors, of terminology for linguistics, history, geography, botany, zoology, anthropology, mathematics, physics, and chemistry. The lexicon is basically of three types: international terminology of Greek and Latin origin adapted to Sorbian, calques, and native Sorbian words which have been revived or extended in meaning.

3362. Rězak, Filip. Němsko-serbski wšowědny słownik hornjołužiskeje rěče. Deutsch-wendisches encyklopädisches Wörterbuch. Bautzen (Budyšin), 1920. 1150 p.

The most complete German-Upper Sorbian Dictionary. Contains numerous words and phrases made up by the author and not in general use. Review: B. Havránek, *Listy filologické*, 47, 1920: 352.

3363. Schwela, Gotthold (Bogumił Šwjela). Dolnoserbsko-němski słownik (Lower Sorbian-German dictionary). Edited by A. Mitaš. Budyšyn, Domowina, 1963. 628 p.

The companion volume to this work is:

Schwela, Gotthold (Bogumił Šwjela). Deutsch-niedersorbisches Taschenwörterbuch. Edited by A. Mitaš. Bautzen (Budyšin), Domowina, 1953. 371 p.

3364. Zeman, Henryk. Słownik górnołużycko-polski (Upper Sorbian-Polish dictionary). Warszawa, Państwowe Wydawnictwo Naukowe, 1967. 678 p.

The largest and most complete Upper Sorbian dictionary to appear since the war. Concentrates on the literary language of the 19th and 20th centuries, but does contain dialect words and archaisms. Appended is a list of geographical names and a survey of Upper Sorbian phonology and morphology by Kazimierz Polański.

G. DIALECTOLOGY

3365. Bautzen, Germany. Institut za serbski ludospyt. Sorbische Dialekttexte. Bautzen (Budyšin), Domowina, 1963–

A series of works dealing with the Sorbian dialects. The texts are in phonetic transcription together with the normalized spelling, German translation and notes. The following have appeared so far:

v. 1. Fasske, Helmut, *and* S. Michalk. Sophla, Kreis Hoyerswerda. Bautzen (Budyšin), Domowina, 1963. 101 p.

v. 2. Jentsch, Helmut, *and* S. Michalk. Nochten, Kreis Weisswasser. Bautzen (Budyšin), Domowina, 1964. 80 p.

v. 3. Fasske, Helmut, *and* H. Jentsch. Schmogrow, Kreis Cottbus. Bautzen (Budyšin), Domowina, 1965. 97 p.

v. 4. Fasske, Helmut, *and* S. Michalk. Sollschwitz, Kreis Hoyerswerda. Bautzen (Budyšin), Domowina, 1966. 55 p.

v. 5. Fasske, Helmut, *and* S. Michalk. Klix, Kreis Bautzen mit Spreewiese, Salga und Göbeln. Bautzen (Budyšin), Domowina, 1967. 65 p.

3366. Fasske, Helmut. Die Vetschauer Mundart. Bautzen (Budyšin), Domowina, 1964. 473 p. Maps. Bibliography: p. 305-311. (Spisy Instituta za serbski ludospyt, 19)

The phonology and morphology of the Lower Sorbian dialect around Vetschau (Wětošow). Includes texts and glossary and 73 maps.

3367. Fasske, Helmut, H. Jentsche, *and* S. Michalk. Sorbischer Sprachatlas. Feldwirtschaftliche Terminologie. v. 1. Bautzen (Budyšin), Domowina, 1965. 247 p.

This is the first volume of what will comprise a series of Sorbian dialect atlases. Ninety-six maps of the whole Sorbian language area show the lexical, phonological, and derivational variants of characteristic agricultural terminology.

3368. Michalk, Siegfried. Der obersorbische Dialekt von Neustadt. Bautzen (Budyšin), Domowina, 1962. 483 p. Maps. Bibliography: p. 291-295. (Spisy Instituta za serbski ludospyt, 15)

The phonology and morphology of the Upper Sorbian dialect of Neustadt (Nowe Město). Includes texts and glossary and 103 maps under separate cover.

3369. Stieber, Zdzisław. Stosunki pokrewieństwa języków łużyckich (The relationship between the Lusatian languages). Kraków, Gebethner i Wolff, 1934. 98 p. Maps. (Bibljoteka ludu słowiańskiago, Dział A, 1)

An important Sorbian dialect study in which the author investigates the phonological relation of the Sorbian dialects to one another and to other Slavic languages. Reviews: J. Páta, *Slavia*, v. 14, 1935-37: 172-176; P. Wirth, *Zeitschrift für slavische Philologie*, v. 12, 1935: 221-225.

47

POLABIANS

by James A. Sehnert

3370. Jessen, Christian Hennig von. Vocabularium Venedicum. Edited by Reinhold Olesch. Köln, Böhlau, 1959. 412 p.

A photographic reproduction of Christian Hennig von Jessen's Polabian glossary. Hennig's introduction is in printed Gothic letters; otherwise, the work is a photographic copy of Ms. XXIII/842 found in the Landesbibliothek in Hanover, Germany.

3371. Jugler, Johann Heinrich. Lüneburgisch-wendisches Wörterbuch. Edited by Reinhold Olesch. Köln, Böhlau, 1962. 338 p. Fold. map. (Slavistische Forschungen, Bd. 1)

Johann Heinrich Jugler's Polabian dictionary is published here for the first time, although it was completed in 1809. The Olesch work contains Jugler's foreword, his Polabian-German dictionary, a German index, Olesch's studies on the Polabian source material, a bibliography of the Polabian manuscripts, and a map. Jugler's dictionary itself is of limited value for Polabian studies, but Professor Olesch's studies of the Polabian source material and the bibliography are extremely valuable contributions to Polabian scholarship.

3372. Lehr-Spławiński, Tadeusz. Gramatyka połabska (Polabian Grammar) Lwów, 1929. 278 p. (Lwowska biblioteka slawistyczna, 8)

This work is considerably better than Schleicher's Polabian grammar (*see* entry no. 3378) and remains the primary source for Polabian synchrony and diachrony, although it was to some extent superseded by Trubetzkoi's work (*see* entry no. 3380) the same year it was published. It treats Polabian phonology, morphology, and the noninflected parts of speech. Syntax not treated.

3373. Lehr-Spławiński, Tadeucz. Słownik etymologiczny języka Drzewian połabskich (Etymological dictionary of the language of the Draveno-Polabians). Wrocław, Zakład Narodowy im. Ossolińskich, 1962–

So far only the first fascicle of this work has appeared. The Polabian word is given in normalized transcription together with grammatical and etymological information. The original sources, based on

Rost's work (*see entry* no. 3377), are included. Although numerous articles have treated Polabian etymology, this is the first work which attempts to deal with the whole lexicon.

3374. Olesch, Reinhold. Fontes linguae dravaenopolabicae minores et chronica venedica J. P. Schultzii. Köln, Graz, Böhlau, 1967. 353 p. Illus., maps. (Slavistische Forschungen, Bd. 7).

The publication of this work together with the works of Jessen (*see* entry no. 3370) and Jugler (*see* entry no. 3371) — also edited by Olesch — completes the series of works making the primary sources of Polabian easily accessible to scholars and students. These sources provide not only linguistic material, but also general information on the folklore and life of the Draveno-Polabians.

3375. Polański, Kazimierz. Morfologia zapożyczeń niemieckich w języku połabskim (The morphology of German loanwords in the Polabian language). Wrocław, Zakład Narodowy im. Ossolińskich, 1962. 198 p. (Komitet Językoznawstwa Polskiej Akademii Nauk. Prace językoznawcze, 32)

This work shows how Low German loanwords were taken over into Polabian. Part 2 lists, according to morphological category, all of the German loanwords in Polabian together with etymological information and citations from the original sources.

3376. Polański, Kazimierz, *and* J. A. Sehnert. Polabian-English Dictionary. The Hague, Mouton, 1967. 239 p.

The first complete Polabian dictionary. A brief introduction to the texts is followed by a survey of the phonology. The main glossary lists the Polabian word in a normalized transcription together with etymological, grammatical, and semantic information. This section is followed by a list, according to source, of all of the complete utterances and connected texts found in the Polabian language material. The work ends with a reverse dictionary divided according to morphological category.

3377. Rost, Paul. Die Sprachreste der Draväno-Polaben im Hannöverschen. Leipzig, 1907. 445 p.

An extremely valuable work which has served since the time of its publication as the basis for all Polabian studies. It contains an introduction on the texts, the texts themselves (except for the Buchholtz Lord's Prayer), a study of Polabian place names, and a glossary. The main body of the work is generously footnoted with comparisons of editions and etymological information. The glossary is of limited interest.

3378. Schleicher, August. Laut- und Formenlehre der polabischen Sprache. St.-Petersburg, Commissionäre der Kaiserlichen Akademie der Wissenschaften, 1871. 353 p.

The first Polabian grammar ever published — the pioneer work of serious studies of the Polabian language. Although this long remained the only source of information on Polabian grammar, it is of limited value because much has been learned about the language since Schleicher's day. It was superseded by the works of Lehr-Spławiński and Trubetzkoi.

3379. Szydłowska-Ceglowa, Barbara. Materialna kultura ludowa Drzewian połabskich w świetle poszukiwań słownikowych (The material folk culture of the Draveno-Polabians in the light of lexical research). Lud (Wrocław), v. 48, 1963: 19-275.

A very interesting discussion of the material culture of the Polabians, based on the lexical material found in the few texts which have come down to us. Covers food, clothing, agriculture, architecture, transportation, weaving, spinning, household goods, etc. Several new etymologies suggested.

3380. Trubetzkoi, Nikolai S. Polabische Studien. Wien, Hölder-Pichler-Tempsky, 1929. 167 p. (Akademie der Wissenschaften in Wien. Philosophisch-historische Klasse. Sitzungsberichte, 211 Bd., 4. Abhandlung)

A study on Polabian phonology which appeared the same year as Lehr-Spławiński's grammar and to some extent superseded it because of Trubetzkoi's discovery that Polabian had two reduced vowels instead of one, as had been assumed earlier.

INDEX

Includes names of authors, compilers, editors, translators, and sponsoring organizations; titles of publications; and principal subject headings. Titles of books are italicized, and titles of articles and parts of books are in quotation marks. Subject headings are in capital letters. Numbers refer to entries, not pages. The letter *a* following an entry number indicates that the title is to be found in the annotation to that entry.